Transactional Information Systems

Theory, Algorithms, and the Practice of Concurrency Control and Recovery

The Morgan Kaufmann Series in Data Management Systems

Series Editor: Jim Gray, Microsoft Research

Transactional Information Systems

Theory, Algorithms, and the Practice of Concurrency Control and Recovery

Gerhard Weikum
University of the Saarland, Germany

Gottfried Vossen
University of Münster, Germany

MORGAN KAUFMANN PUBLISHERS

An Imprint of Elsevier

SAN FRANCISCO   SAN DIEGO   NEW YORK   BOSTON
LONDON   SYDNEY   TOKYO

Executive Editor	Diane D. Cerra
Publishing Services Manager	Scott Norton
Assistant Publishing Services Manager	Edward Wade
Assistant Editor	Belinda Breyer
Cover Design	Frances Baca Design
Cover Image	© Ralph A. Clevenger/CORBIS
Text Design	Rebecca Evans & Associates
Composition	TechBooks
Technical Illustration	Dartmouth Publishing, Inc.
Copyeditor	Judith Brown
Proofreader	Jennifer McClain
Indexer	Steve Rath
Printer	Courier Corporation

Designations used by companies to distinguish their products are often claimed as trademarks or registered trademarks. In all instances in which Morgan Kaufmann Publishers is aware of a claim, the product names appear in initial capital or all capital letters. Readers, however, should contact the appropriate companies for more complete information regarding trademarks and registration.

Morgan Kaufmann Publishers
An Imprint of Elsevier
340 Pine Street, Sixth Floor, San Francisco, CA 94104-3205, USA
http://www.mkp.com

ACADEMIC PRESS
An Imprint of Elsevier
525 B Street, Suite 1900, San Diego, CA 92101-4495, USA
http://www.academicpress.com

Academic Press
Harcourt Place, 32 Jamestown Road, London, NW1 7BY, United Kingdom
http://www.academicpress.com

Library of Congress Cataloging-in-Publication Data is available for this book.
ISBN-13: 978-1-55860-508-4
ISBN-10: 1-55860-508-8

This book is printed on acid-free paper.

To science
and for Liz, Maria, and Julia, my mother
Anna, and my late father Oskar.

—*Gerhard Weikum*

For Martina, for the first 24 years and for staying by my side
through the completion of many books, for Laura and
Kathrin, my true challenges, for my mother Marianne,
our sponsor, and for my father, Hans, whose life
transaction was serialized by heaven's scheduler before
the transaction of finishing this book, as he had to
leave this world about nine hours before the central
shadow of the 1999 solar eclipse hit Germany
(and I firmly believe it was a Commit).

—*Gottfried Vossen*

Science! True daughter of Old Time thou art!
Who alterest all things with thy peering eyes.

—*Edgar Allan Poe*

Foreword

Jim Gray, Microsoft, Inc.

This book is a major advance for transaction processing. It synthesizes and organizes the last three decades of research into a rigorous and consistent presentation. It unifies concurrency control and recovery for both the page and object models. As the copious references show, this unification has been the labor of many researchers in addition to Weikum and Vossen; but this book organizes that huge research corpus into a consistent whole, with a step-by-step development of the ideas.

The "classic" books on transaction processing have largely either focused on the practical aspects or taken a rigorous approach presenting theorems and proofs. Most have limited themselves to "flat" transactions because the theory of multilevel transactions was so immature. This is the first book to give an in-depth presentation of both the theory and the practical aspects of the field, and the first to present our new understanding of multilevel (object model) transaction processing.

In reading the book, I was impressed at how much our field has advanced, and how once-complex ideas are now simply explained once the terminology is rationalized, and once the proper perspective is set. You will find it possible to read this book at the superficial level: just following the text, the examples, the definitions, and the theorems. You will also be able to dive as deep as you like into the detailed presentation of the results – both the proofs and the programs. In reviewing the book, I took both perspectives: trying to use it as a reference by diving into the middle of some chapter and seeing how quickly I could find the answer to my question. I also took the linear approach of reading the book. In both cases, the book was very informative and very accessible.

This book is likely to become the standard reference in our field for many years to come.

Contents

PART THREE
RECOVERY

Preface

Teamwork is essential. It allows you to blame someone else.
—Anonymous

The Book's Mission

For three decades transaction processing has been a cornerstone of modern information technology: it is an indispensable asset in banking, stock trading, airlines, travel agencies, and so on. With the new millennium's proliferation of e-Commerce applications, business-to-business workflows, and broad forms of Web-based e-Services, transactional information systems are becoming even more important. Fortunately, the success of the transaction concept does not solely rely on clever system implementations, but builds on and leverages scientifically rigorous foundations that have been developed in the research community. This scientific achievement has most prominently been recognized by the 1998 Turing Award to Jim Gray for his outstanding, pioneering work on the transaction concept. It is exactly such a systematic and fundamental understanding that will allow us to generalize and extend transactional information systems toward the evolving new classes of network-centric, functionally rich applications.

For the above reason this book emphasizes scientific fundamentals of long-term validity and value, and does not cover specific system products, which tend to become quickly outdated. The book does, however, put the presented theory, algorithms, and implementation techniques into perspective with practical system architectures. In this sense, the book is complementary to the systems-oriented literature, most notably, the "TP bible" by Jim Gray and Andreas Reuter and the more recent textbook by Phil Bernstein and Eric Newcomer. Our role model instead is the classic book *Concurrency Control and Recovery in Database Systems*, by Phil Bernstein, Vassos Hadzilacos, and Nat Goodman, which is now out of print. However, the field has made much progress since the time that book was written, and the transaction concept has become of much broader relevance beyond the scope of database systems alone. Our book reflects the advances of the past decade and the trends in modern IT architectures.

Organization of the Book

The two key components of a transactional information system are *concurrency control*, to ensure the correctness of data when many clients simultaneously access shared data, and *recovery*, to protect the data against system failures. The book devotes its two major parts, Part II and Part III, to these two components, organized into 15 chapters altogether. For distributed, multi-tier federations of transactional servers, we will show that the concurrency control and recovery components of each server are the major asset toward viable solutions, but in addition, the *coordination of distributed transactions* becomes a vital issue that will be covered in Part IV. These three technically "hard-core" parts are surrounded by Part I, which contains motivation and background material and outlines the "big picture" of transactional technology, and Part V, which gives an outlook on topics that could not be covered (for lack of space and time) and speculates on future trends. Throughout all five parts, each chapter begins with a brief section on the goal and overview of the chapter, and concludes with the sections Lessons Learned, Exercises, and Bibliographic Notes. (Note: Chapter 20 doesn't include Lessons Learned or Exercises.)

Guidelines for Teaching

This book covers advanced material, including intensive use of formal models. So a solid background in computer science in general is assumed, but not necessarily familiarity with database systems. Whatever knowledge from that area is needed will be provided within the book itself. It is, in fact, one of our major points that transactional technology is important for many other areas, such as operating systems, workflow management, electronic commerce, and distributed objects, and should therefore be taught independently of database classes.

The book is primarily intended as a text for advanced undergraduate courses or graduate courses, but we would also encourage industrial researchers as well as system architects and developers who need an in-depth understanding of transactional information systems to work with this book. After all, engineers should not be afraid of (a little bit of) mathematics.

The book has been class tested at both the University of the Saarland in Saarbrücken and the University of Münster, and partly also at the University of Constance, all in Germany, for advanced undergraduate courses. In Saarbrücken the course was organized in 15 teaching weeks, each with four hours lecturing and additional student assignments. A possible, approximate breakdown of the material for this teaching time frame is given below. Since many universities will allow only two hours of weekly lecturing for such an advanced course, the material can be divided into mandatory core subjects and optional "high-end" issues, as suggested in Table P.1 (with the first and last sections of each chapter always being mandatory and thus omitted in the table).

Table P.1 Suggested teaching schedule for 15-week course.

Week	Mandatory sections	Optional sections
1	Chapter 1: *What Is It All About?* Chapter 2: *Computational Models* 1.2–1.5, 2.2–2.5	
2	Chapter 3: *Concurrency Control: Notions of Correctness* *for the Page Model* 3.2–3.5, 3.7–3.8	3.6, 3.9–3.10
3	Chapter 4: *Concurrency Control Algorithms* 4.2, 4.3.1–4.3.4, 4.4–4.5	4.3.5–4.3.8
4	Chapter 5: *Multiversion Concurrency Control* 5.2, 5.3.1–5.3.2, 5.5	5.3.3, 5.4
5	Chapter 6: *Concurrency Control on Objects: Notions* *of Correctness* 6.2–6.5	6.6
6	Chapter 7: *Concurrency Control Algorithms on Objects* Chapter 8: *Concurrency Control on Relational Databases* 7.2–7.5	7.6, 8.2–8.4
7	Chapter 9: *Concurrency Control on Search Structures* Chapter 10: *Implementation and Pragmatic Issues* 9.2–9.3, 9.4.1, 10.2–10.3	9.4.2, 9.4.3, 9.5, 10.4–10.7
8	Chapter 11: *Transaction Recovery* 11.2–11.4, 11.5.1, 11.6–11.7	11.5.2–11.5.3
9	Chapter 12: *Crash Recovery: Notion of Correctness* Chapter 13: *Page Model Crash Recovery Algorithms* 12.2–12.4, 13.2, 13.3.1–13.3.3, 13.4	12.5, 13.3.4
10	Chapter 14: *Object Model Crash Recovery* 14.2–14.4	14.5
11	Chapter 15: *Special Issues of Recovery* Chapter 16: *Media Recovery* 16.2.1–16.2.2, 16.3.1	15.2–15.6, 16.2.3, 16.3.2, 16.4
12	Chapter 17: *Application Recovery* 17.2–17.4	17.5
13	Chapter 18: *Distributed Concurrency Control* 18.2–18.3, 18.4.1–18.4.2, 18.5	18.4.3, 18.6–18.8
14	Chapter 19: *Distributed Transaction Recovery* 19.2–19.3	19.4
15	Chapter 20: *What Is Next?* 20.2–20.5	

Table P.2 Suggested teaching schedule for 10-week course.

Week	Mandatory sections
1	Chapter 1: *What Is It All About?*
	Chapter 2: *Computational Models*
	1.2–1.4, 2.2–2.5
2	Chapter 3: *Concurrency Control: Notions of Correctness for the Page Model*
	3.2–3.5, 3.7–3.8
3	Chapter 4: *Concurrency Control Algorithms*
	4.2, 4.3.1–4.3.4, 4.4–4.5
4	Chapter 5: *Multiversion Concurrency Control*
	5.2, 5.3.1–5.3.2, 5.5
5	Chapter 6: *Concurrency Control on Objects: Notions of Correctness*
	Chapter 7: *Concurrency Control Algorithms on Objects*
	6.2–6.5, 7.2–7.4
6	Chapter 10: *Implementation and Pragmatic Issues*
	Chapter 11: *Transaction Recovery*
	10.2–10.3, 11.2–11.4, 11.5.1, 11.6–11.7
7	Chapter 12: *Crash Recovery: Notion of Correctness*
	Chapter 13: *Page Model Crash Recovery Algorithms*
	12.2–12.4, 13.2, 13.3.1–13.3.3, 13.4
8	Chapter 14: *Object Model Crash Recovery*
	Chapter 16: *Media Recovery*
	14.2–14.4, 16.2.1–16.2.2, 16.3.1
9	Chapter 17: *Application Recovery*
	Chapter 18: *Distributed Concurrency Control*
	17.2–17.3, 18.2.1–18.2.2, 18.4.1–18.4.2, 18.5
10	Chapter 19: *Distributed Transaction Recovery*
	19.2–19.3

It is also feasible to configure a 10-week course from the book's material. Under such time constraints it is obviously necessary to leave out some of the most advanced topics. Our subjective recommendations for a 10-week course, with either four or two hours lecturing per week, are shown in Table P.2.

Additional teaching materials, most notably, slides for lecturers and solutions to selected exercises are available at *www.mkp.com/tis/*. We will also offer errata of the book as we discover our errors. And we'd appreciate comments, suggestions, and criticisms via email at *weikum@cs.uni-sb.de* or *vossen@uni-mvenster.de*.

Acknowledgments

A number of colleagues provided us with very valuable input: encouragement, constructive criticism, proofreading, and class testing, and also simple "bug fixes." We are most grateful to Jim Gray, Elliot Moss, Dennis Shasha, Betty and Pat O'Neil, K. Vidyasankar, Alan Fekete, Dave Lomet, and Marc Scholl. Significant work on the book's exercises was contributed by Ralf Schenkel; Carolin Letz helped in editing and tracing the numerous bibliographic entries. The book has also implicitly benefited from many technical discussions and collaborations with Catriel Beeri, Yuri Breitbart, Theo Härder, Dave Lomet, and, most notably, Hans-Jörg Schek. Needless to say, all biases and possible errors in this book are our own.

Our editor Diane Cerra and her colleague Belinda Breyer were perfect in their balance between keeping us relaxed and creative and occasionally putting some healthy pressure on us, and they were always responsive to our needs. We wish everybody who is writing a book such a great editorial team. We were also lucky to cooperate with an excellent production team headed by Edward Wade, and including our copyeditor Judith Brown, proofreader Jennifer McClain, designers Rebecca Evans and Frances Baca, and indexer Steve Rath. Last but not least we would like to thank our families for being with us while we were mentally somewhere else.

PART ONE

Background and Motivation

CHAPTER ONE

What Is It All About?

If I had had more time, I could have written you a shorter letter.
—*Blaise Pascal*

*There are two mistakes one can make along the road
to truth—not going all the way, and not starting.*
—*Buddha*

1.1 Goal and Overview

Transaction processing is an important topic in database and information systems. Moreover, it is rapidly gaining importance outside the context in which it was originally developed. In this introductory chapter, we discuss why transactions are a good idea, why transactions form a reasonable abstraction concept for certain classes of real-life data management and related problems, as well as what can and what cannot be done with the transaction concept.

The transaction concept was originally developed in the context of database management systems as a paradigm for dealing with concurrent accesses to a shared database and for handling failures. Therefore, we start out (in Section 1.2) by describing typical application scenarios for database and other information systems in which transactions make sense. The original and most canonical application example is funds transfer in banking; very similar applications in terms of functionality and structure have arisen in a number of other service-providing industries, most notably in the travel industry with its flight, car, and hotel bookings. All these classical application examples are commonly referred to as *online transaction processing,* or *OLTP* for short. In addition, we will show that the application area of the transaction concept includes modern business sectors such as electronic commerce and the management of workflows (which are also known as business processes).

In terms of the underlying computer and network infrastructure, we are typically dealing with distributed systems of potentially large scale and with possibly heterogeneous, interoperating components. Most often, one of these components is a database management system or, more specifically, a *database server* that processes requests issued by clients (workstations, personal

Application areas

computers, portable notebooks, PDAs, electronic sensors, and other embedded systems). It turns out that in today's diverse information technology landscapes, mail servers, Web- or intranet-based document servers, and workflow management systems also play an increasingly important role and call for transactional support.

Transaction concept   The key problem that the transaction concept solves in a very elegant way is to cope with the subtle and often difficult issues of keeping data consistent even in the presence of highly concurrent data accesses and despite all sorts of failures. An additional key property of transactions is that this is achieved in a generic way that is essentially invisible to the application logic (and to application development), so that application developers are completely freed from the burden of dealing with such system issues. This is why transactions are an *abstraction concept*, and why this concept is a cornerstone of modern information technology. Section 1.3 will discuss the role of the transaction concept in state-of-the-art information systems from a strategic viewpoint. We will introduce a fairly general reference architecture as a bird's-eye view of the entire infrastructure that is necessary to implement and deploy an information system, and we will discuss several variations of this reference architecture that are commonly used in practice. In particular, we will identify components that are in charge of managing persistent data under a transaction-oriented access regime, and we will concentrate on these *transactional (data) servers*. We will then discuss, in Section 1.4, the abstract properties that constitute the transaction concept and the great benefit that these properties provide in the context of a transactional data server. We will also outline the requirements on the server's algorithms in terms of *correctness* and *performance*, as well as of *reliability* and *availability*.

Computational models   By far the most important concrete instantiation of a transactional data server is a database system. However, this is not a book about database systems. We limit our discussion to topics that are directly and closely related to transactions, and nothing else. We will briefly survey the kind of knowledge we expect our readers to have about database systems in Section 1.5. This will prepare the setting for the introduction of two computational models for transactional servers in the next chapter.

This chapter, like all subsequent chapters, is wrapped up by summarizing, in Section 1.6, the key insights that the reader should have obtained from reading it.

1.2 Application Examples

We begin our exposition with a few examples of applications in which transactional properties can be brought to bear; these scenarios are

- funds transfer in a banking environment, a classical OLTP application,
- Web-based electronic commerce (e-Commerce),
- travel planning as a workflow example.

From OLTP to e-Commerce and workflow

1.2.1 Online Transaction Processing: Debit/Credit Example

Consider the simplified operation of a bank that uses a relational database for keeping track of its account business. The database contains, among others, a table named Account that describes bank accounts in terms of their account ID, associated customer name, identification of the respective bank branch, and balance. Transactions in the bank are either *withdrawals* or *deposits* (which is why the application is often characterized as consisting of debit/credit transactions), and these transactions are often combined in *funds transfers*. The typical structure of a debit/credit program is shown below, using commands of the standardized database query language SQL and embedding these commands in a C program. Note the distinction between local variables of the invoked program and the data in the underlying database that is shared by all programs. Also note that a realistic, full-fledged debit/credit program may include various sanity checks against the account data (e.g., for high amounts of withdrawals) between the SQL Select command and the subsequent Update step.

```
/* debit/credit program */
void main()
{
  EXEC SQL BEGIN DECLARE SECTION;
    int accountid, amount; /* input variables */
    int balance; /* intermediate variable */
  EXEC SQL END DECLARE SECTION;
/* read user input */
  printf("Enter Account ID, Amount
    for deposit (positive) or withdrawal (negative):");
  scanf("%d%d", &accountid, &amount);
/* determine current balance of the account,
    reading it into a local, intermediate, variable of the
    program */
  EXEC SQL Select Account_Balance Into :balance
    From Account
    Where Account_Id = :accountid;
/* add amount (negative for withdrawal) */
balance = balance + amount;
/* update account balance in the database */
```

```
EXEC SQL Update Account
  Set Account_Balance = balance
  Where Account_Id = :accountid;
EXEC SQL Commit Work;
}
```

Assume the bank operates in a traditional way, with various tellers at its local branches executing transactions. However, the role of a teller's terminal could also be replaced by a customer's PC equipped with home banking software, the credit card reader of a merchant, or some other form of smart cybercash carrier. We will generally refer to these as "clients" and will disregard the details of the client software, as these are irrelevant to the server on which the database resides.

Concurrency and parallelism → concurrency control techniques for isolation
With a huge number of clients potentially issuing simultaneous requests to the bank's database server, *concurrent* (i.e., overlapping in time) or even *parallel* (i.e., on multiple processors) execution of multiple debit/credit transactions is mandatory in order to exploit the server's hardware resources. For example, while the server is waiting for the completion of a disk I/O on behalf of one transaction, its CPU should be utilized to process another transaction; similarly, multiple transactions should be processed in parallel on a multiprocessor machine. Thus, the "outside world" of an individual transaction is continuously changing as concurrently executing transactions are modifying the underlying database of the banking application. In order to be able to ignore the potential fallacies of this concurrency, it is therefore desirable that each transaction be executed in an *isolated* manner, that is, as if there were no other transactions and hence no concurrency. We will show that this tension between concurrency for the sake of performance, on the one hand, and potential sequential execution for the sake of simplicity and correctness, on the other, is reconciled by the *concurrency control techniques* of a transactional server.

The following scenario illustrates that concurrency is indeed trickier than it may seem at first glance, and that it may have a disastrous impact on the consistency of the underlying data and thus the quality of the entire information system, even if each individual transaction is perfectly correct and preserves data consistency.

EXAMPLE 1.1

Consider two debit/credit transactions (i.e., invocations of the debit/credit program outlined above) that are concurrently executed by processes P_1 and P_2, respectively, both operating on the same account x (i.e., the value of the program's input variable "accountid"). To distinguish the two different instances of the local program variable "balance" that temporarily holds the value of the account balance, we refer to them as `balance1` for process P_1 and `balance2` for P_2. For simplicity, we ignore some syntactic details of the embedded SQL commands. The first transaction intends to withdraw $30, and the second transaction intends to deposit $20. We assume that the initial account balance is $100. The table below shows those parts of the two transactions that read and modify the account record.

P_1	Time	P_2
/* balance1 = 0, x.Account_Balance = 100, balance2 = 0 */		
Select Account_Balance Into :balance1 From Account Where Account_Id = x	1	
/* balance1 = 100, x.Account_Balance = 100, balance2 = 0 */		
	2	Select Account_Balance Into :balance2 From Account Where Account_Id = x
/* balance1 = 100, x.Account_Balance = 100, balance2 = 100 */		
balance1 = balance1 − 30	3	
/* balance1 = 70, x.Account_Balance = 100, balance2 = 100 */		
	4	balance2 = balance2 + 20
/* balance1 = 70, x.Account_Balance = 100, balance2 = 120 */		
Update Account Set Account_Balance = :balance Where Account_Id = x	5	
/* balance1 = 70, x.Account_Balance = 70, balance2 = 120 */		
	6	Update Account Set Account_Balance = :balance2 Where Account_Id = x
/* balance1 = 70, x.Account_Balance = 120, balance2 = 120 */		

Upon completion of the execution, the balance of account x, as recorded in the persistent database, will be $120, although it should be $90 after execution of the two transactions. Thus, the recorded data no longer reflects reality and should be considered incorrect. Obviously, for such an information system to be meaningful and practically viable, this kind of anomaly must be prevented by all means. Thus, concurrent executions must be treated with extreme care. Similar anomalies could arise from failures of processes or entire computers during the execution of a transaction, and need to be addressed as well.

A second fundamentally important point is that the various accesses that a transaction has to perform need to occur *in conjunction*. In other words,

Failures
→ recovery
techniques for
atomicity and
durability

once a transaction has started, its data accesses should look to the outside world as an atomic operation that is either executed completely or not at all. This property of *atomicity* will turn out to be a crucial requirement on database transactions. Moreover, this conceptual property should be guaranteed to hold even in a failure-prone environment where individual processes or the entire database server may fail at an arbitrarily inconvenient point in time. To this end, a transactional server provides *recovery techniques* to cope with failures. In addition to ensuring transaction atomicity, these techniques serve to ensure the *durability* of a transaction's effects once the transaction is completed.

The following scenario illustrates that atomicity is a crucial requirement for being able to cope with failures.

EXAMPLE 1.2

Consider the following funds transfer program, which transfers a given amount of money between two accounts, by first withdrawing it from a source account and then depositing it in a target account. The program is described in terms of SQL statements embedded into a host program written in C.

```
/* funds transfer program */
void main()
{
  EXEC SQL BEGIN DECLARE SECTION;
    int sourceid, targetid, amount; /* input variables */
  EXEC SQL END DECLARE SECTION;
/* read user input */
  printf("Enter Source ID, Target ID, Amount to be
  transferred:");
  scanf("%d %d %d", &sourceid, &targetid, &amount);
/* subtract desired amount from source */
  EXEC SQL Update Account
    Set Account_Balance = Account_Balance - :amount
    Where Account_Id = :sourceid;
/* add desired amount to target */
  EXEC SQL Update Account
    Set Account_Balance = Account_Balance + :amount
    Where Account_Id = :targetid;
  EXEC SQL Commit Work;
}
```

Now assume that the above funds transfer program has started executing and has already performed its first update statement, withdrawing the specified amount of money from the source. If there is a computer hardware or software failure that interrupts the program's execution at this critical point, the remaining second part will not be performed anymore. Thus, the target account will not receive the money, so that money is effectively lost in transit.

A recovery procedure, to be invoked after the system is restarted, could try to find out which updates were already made by ongoing transaction program executions and which ones were not yet done, and could try to fix the situation in some way. However, implementing such recovery procedures on a per-application-case basis is an extremely difficult task that is itself error prone by its mere complexity, especially because multiple transactions issued by different programs may have accessed the data at the time of the failure. So rather than programming recovery in an ad hoc manner for each application separately, a systematic approach is needed.

System-provided recovery that ensures the atomicity of transactions greatly simplifies the understanding of the postfailure state of the data and the overall failure handling on the application side. In the example scenario, rather than being left with the inconsistent state in the middle of the transaction, the system recovery should restore the state as of before the transaction began. On the other hand, if the transaction had already issued its "commit transaction" call and had received a positive returncode from the system, then the "all" case of the all-or-nothing paradigm would apply, and the system would henceforth guarantee the durability of the transaction's complete funds transfer.

The above conceptual properties of a transaction—namely, atomicity, durability, and isolation—together provide the key abstraction that allows application developers to disregard concurrency and failures, yet the transactional server guarantees the consistency of the underlying data and ultimately the correctness of the application. In the banking example, this means that no money is ever lost in the jungle of electronic funds transfers and customers can perfectly rely on electronic receipts, balance statements, and so on. As we will show in the next two application scenarios, these cornerstones for building highly dependable information systems can be successfully applied outside the scope of OLTP and classical database applications as well.

1.2.2 **Electronic Commerce Example**

In today's information landscape, client requests may span multiple databases and other information sources across enterprise boundaries, yet the mutual consistency of all this data is crucial and thus important to maintain. Then, the resulting transactions operate in a distributed system that consists of multiple servers, often with heterogeneous software. As a concrete example of such a modern setting, consider what happens when a client intends to purchase something from an Internet-based bookstore; such applications are known as *electronic commerce* (e-Commerce).

The purchasing activity proceeds in the following steps:

1. The client connects to the bookstore's server through an appropriate Internet protocol, and starts browsing and querying the store's catalog.

2. The client gradually fills an electronic shopping cart with items that she intends to purchase.

3. When the client is about to check out, she reconsiders the items in her shopping cart and makes a final decision on which items she will purchase.

4. The client provides all the necessary information for placing a definitive (and legally binding) order. This includes her shipping address and information on her credit card or some other valid form of cybercash. The latter information may be encrypted such that the merchant can only verify its authenticity, but possibly without being able to actually decrypt the provided data.

5. The merchant's server forwards the payment information to the customer's bank, credit card company, or some other clearinghouse for cybercash. When the payment is accepted by the clearinghouse, the shipping of the ordered items is initiated by the merchant's server, and the client is notified on the successful completion of the e-Commerce activity.

So why are transactions and their properties relevant for this scenario? It is obviously important to keep certain data consistent, and this data is even distributed across different computers. The consistency requirement is already relevant during the catalog browsing phase when the user fills her shopping cart, as the client's view of the shopping cart should ideally be kept consistent with the shopping cart contents as maintained by the merchant's server. Note that this should be satisfied in the presence of temporary failures at the client or the server side (e.g., a software failure of a client or server process) and also network failures (e.g., undelivered messages due to network congestion). Further note that this seemingly simple requirement may transitively involve additional data, say, on the inventory for the selected items, which could reside on yet another computer.

While it could be argued that data consistency is merely an optional luxury feature for the shopping cart contents and does not necessarily justify the use of advanced technology like transactions in the technical sense of this book, a very similar situation arises in the last step of the entire activity. There, it is absolutely crucial that three parties agree on the data that tracks the overall outcome:

- The merchant's server must have records on both the order and the successfully certified payment.

- At the same time, the clearinghouse must have a record on the payment, as its approval may be requested again later, or the clearinghouse may be responsible for the actual money transfer.

- Finally, the client must have received the notification that the ordered items are being shipped.

When these three effects on three different computers are known to be atomic, confidence in the correct processing of such e-Commerce activities is greatly increased. Conversely, when atomicity is not guaranteed, all sorts of complicated cases arise, such as the merchant shipping the items but the clearinghouse losing all records of its cybercash approval and ultimately not being able to reclaim the money. Similarly, when the customer is never informed about the shipping and the resulting money transfer, she may order the items again from a different merchant, ending up with two copies of the same book. Even worse, the customer may receive the shipped items and keep them, but pretend that she never ordered and never received them. Then, it is obviously important for the entire e-Commerce industry to rely on atomicity guarantees in order to prove a customer's order when it comes to a lawsuit.

Similar, yet more involved arguments can be brought up about isolation properties, but the case for transactions should have been made sufficiently clear at this point. Of course, we could deal with inconsistent data among the three computers of our scenario in many other ways as well. But the decisive point is that by implementing the last step of the activity as a transaction, all the arguments about atomicity in the presence of failures can be factored out, and the entire application is greatly simplified.

So this example has indeed much more in common with the debit/credit scenario than it might have seemed at first glance. There are, however, a number of important differences as well, and these nicely highlight the potential generalization of the transaction concept beyond the classical setting of centralized database applications:

- The entire application is *distributed* across multiple computers, and the software may be *heterogeneous* in that different database systems are used at the various servers. (Of course, the hardware is likely to be heterogeneous, too, but this is mostly masked by the software and thus less relevant.)

- The servers are not necessarily based on database systems; they may as well be some other form of *information repository* or *document management servers* in general.

- The effects of a transaction may even include *messages* between computers, for example, the notification of the customer. So transactions are not limited to what is usually perceived as "stored data."

We will show in this book that transaction technology can cope well with all these additional, challenging aspects of modern applications. It will take us to some of the advanced material, however, to cover all issues.

1.2.3 **Workflow Management: Travel Planning Example**

A final and most challenging application class that we consider is so-called workflows, also known as (the computerized part of) *business processes*. A *workflow* is a set of activities (or steps) that belong together in order to achieve a certain business goal. Typical examples would be the processing of a credit request or insurance claim in a bank or insurance company, respectively; the work of a program committee for a scientific conference (submissions, reviews, notifications, etc.); the administrative procedures for real estate purchase; or the "routing" of a patient in a hospital. To orchestrate such processes, it is crucial to specify (at least a template for) the control flow and the data flow between activities, although it may still be necessary to improvise at run time (e.g., in medical applications). Making the "flow of work" between activities explicit in that it is factored out of the entire application is exactly the key leverage from workflow technology that allows a company or other institution to largely automate the repetitive, stereotypic parts of its processes while retaining flexibility, and to quickly adjust these processes to changing business needs.

Activities can be completely automated or based on interaction with a human user and intellectual decision making. This implies that workflows can be long lived, up to several days or weeks, or even months and years. A typical characteristic of workflows is that the activities are distributed across different responsible persons and different, independent information systems, possibly across different enterprises. In particular, an activity can spawn requests to an arbitrary "invoked application" that is provided by some server independently of the current workflow. Thus, workflow management is essentially an umbrella for the activities and invoked applications that constitute a particular workflow. To this end, a workflow management system provides a specification environment for registering activities and for specifying, in a high-level declarative way, not only the control and data flow within a process, but also a run-time environment that automatically triggers activities according to the specified flow. Workflow management systems with such capabilities are commercially available and are gaining significant industrial relevance.

As a concrete example of a workflow, consider the activities that are necessary in the planning of a business trip, say, a trip to a conference. Suppose your manager (or professor) allows you to choose one scientific or developer's conference that you can attend as part of a continuing-education program. This involves the following activities:

- Select a conference, based on its subject, technical program, time, and place. If no suitable conference is found, the process is terminated.
- Check out the cost of the trip to this conference, typically by delegation to a travel agency.
- Check out the registration fee for the conference, which often depends on your memberships, tutorials that you may wish to attend, and so on.
- Compare the total cost of attending the selected conference to the allowed budget, and decide to attend the conference only if the cost is within the budget.

With the increasing costs of conferences and ever tighter travel budgets (at the time this book was written), it is desirable to allow several trials with different conferences, but the number of trials should be limited, in order to guarantee termination of the entire process. The activities and the control flow between them are graphically depicted in Figure 1.1. This illustration is based on a specification formalism known as *statecharts*, which is one particular kind of formal specification method that might be used by a workflow management system. Each oval denotes a state in which the workflow can exist during its execution. Each state in turn corresponds to one activity; so

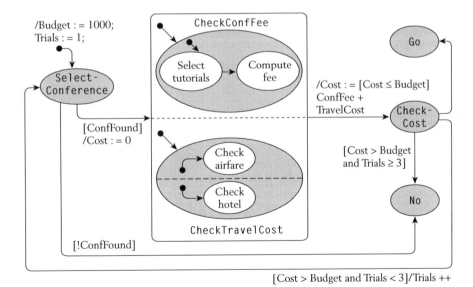

Figure 1.1 Specification of the travel planning workflow.

the activity is spawned when the state is entered. The activity may then invoke further application programs. When the workflow is started, a specified initial state (a state without predecessors) is entered, and the workflow terminates when a final state (a state without successors) is reached. In the example, the initial state is the `SelectConference` state, and the final states are `Go` and `No`.

The transitions between states are governed by event-condition-action rules that are attached to the transition arcs as labels. The meaning of a rule of the form $E[C]/A$ is that the transition fires if event E has occurred and condition C is true in the current state. Then the current state is left and the state where the transition arc points to is entered; during this transition the specified action A is performed. In the example, we only make use of conditions and actions. Both refer to a small set of variables (instantiated for each workflow instance) that are relevant for the control flow. This kind of control flow specification allows conditional execution as well as loops based on high-level predicates. The entire specification can be hierarchical, thus supporting both top-down refinement and bottom-up composition of existing building blocks, by allowing states to be nested. So a state can in turn contain another statechart that is executed when the state is entered. In addition, the specification formalism allows parallel execution, which is graphically indicated by breaking a state down into two or more *orthogonal* statecharts, separated by a dashed line, that are executed in parallel. In the example, the activities that correspond to the two states `CheckConfFee` and `CheckTravelCost` are executed in parallel. These two states are further refined into several steps, where `CheckTravelCost` again leads to two parallel substates.

Although the example scenario is still largely oversimplified, the above discussion already indicates some of the semantically rich process design issues that accompany workflow management. Here we are interested in the connection between workflows and transactions, and how a workflow application could possibly benefit from transaction-supporting services. The answer is threefold and involves different stages of transactional scope:

- The activities themselves can, of course, spawn requests to information systems that lead to transactional executions in these systems. This is almost surely the case with the `CheckTravelCost` activity. The travel agency's invoked application would typically issue transactions against the reservation systems of airlines and hotels. In fact, it seems to make sense that this activity not only figures out the prices, but also makes reservations in the underlying information systems. Obviously, booking a flight to a certain city and a hotel room in that city makes sense only if both reservations are successful. If either of the two is unavailable, the whole trip no longer makes sense. So these two steps need to be tied together in a single transaction. Note that this transaction is a distributed one that involves two autonomous information systems.

- The outcome of the above reservations affects the further processing of the workflow. The requests against the various information systems would return status codes that should be stored in variables of the workflow and would be relevant for the future control flow. For example, not being able to make one of the two necessary reservations in the selected city should trigger going back to the initial SelectConference state for another trial. (To keep the example specification simple, this is not shown in Figure 1.1.) Thus, it is desirable (if not mandatory) that the modification of the workflow's variables be embedded in the same transaction that accesses the airline and hotel databases. In other words, the *state of the workflow application* should be under transactional control as well. This is an entirely new aspect that did not arise in the banking and e-Commerce examples. It is questionable whether today's commercial workflow management systems can cope with this issue in the outlined, transactional way. But as we will show, transactional technology does provide solutions for incorporating application state into atomic processing units as well.

- We could discuss whether the entire travel planning workflow should be a single transaction that incorporates all effects on the underlying information systems as well as the state of the workflow application itself. After all, the entire workflow should have an all-or-nothing, atomic effect. Ideas along these lines have indeed been discussed in the research community for quite a few years; however, no breakthrough is in sight. The difficulty lies in the long-lived nature of workflows and the fact that workflows, like simple transactions, run concurrently. Atomicity is therefore coupled with isolation properties: the atomicity of a workflow would imply that no concurrent workflow could ever "see" any partial effects of it. Regardless of the technical details of how isolation can be implemented at all (to be covered in great depth in this book), maintaining such isolation over a period of hours, days, or weeks raises questions about performance problems with regard to the progress of concurrent workflows. For this reason, the straightforward approach of turning an entire workflow into a single transaction is absolutely infeasible.

The discussion of the third item above does not imply, however, that the one-transaction-per-activity approach is the only kind of transactional support for workflows. Consider the situation when all necessary reservations have been made successfully, but later it is found that the total cost including the conference fees is unacceptable and it is decided not to attend any conference at all. Now you hold reservations that may later result in charges to your credit card, unless you intervene. So you must make sure that these reservations are canceled. One approach could be to extend the workflow specification by additional cancellation activities and the necessary control flow. However, it turns out that cancellation-like activities are fairly common in many business processes, and a lot of time would be spent in specifying these kinds of things over and over again. So a better solution would be to generalize the particular case at hand into a more abstract notion of *compensation activities*. Each compensation activity would be tied to one of the regular activities of the workflow in the sense that their combined effect is a neutral one from the workflow application's viewpoint. Of course, it would still be necessary to provide code (or a high-level declarative specification) for each compensation activity itself, but modifications to the workflow's control flow specification are no longer required. Instead, the appropriate triggering of compensation activities could be delegated to the workflow management system. The transactional technology that we develop in this book does provide the principal means for coping with compensation issues in the outlined, generic way (as opposed to developing specific solutions on a per-application basis over and over again).

At this point in the book, the major insight from this discussion is to realize that the scope of transactions is not a priori fixed and limited to stored data, but can be (carefully) extended to incorporate various aspects of information system applications as well.

1.3 System Paradigms

The three application scenarios of Section 1.2 already provide hints on the various system components that it takes to implement and deploy such applications in their entirety and on putting them together into a complete system architecture. In particular, we have seen that we need to separate *clients*—that is, the computers or terminals from which a human user generates computer work—from the *servers* where data and possibly executable programs reside in various forms. However, this distinction alone is insufficient for characterizing full-fledged modern information systems. We now introduce a more systematic view of these architectural issues in that we set up a *reference architecture* (or framework) to capture the most typical cases that are used in practice.

1.3.1 Three-Tier and Two-Tier Architectures

Reference architecture: three-tier system

Our reference architecture is illustrated in Figure 1.2. It captures what is most frequently referred to by practitioners as a *three-tier architecture*. It consists of a set of clients (PCs, workstations, notebooks, terminals, digital TV set top boxes, "intelligent" sensors, etc.) that interact with an *application server*, which in turn interacts with a *data server*.

Clients send business-oriented (or goal-oriented) requests to the application server. For example, invoking a debit/credit transaction, starting an

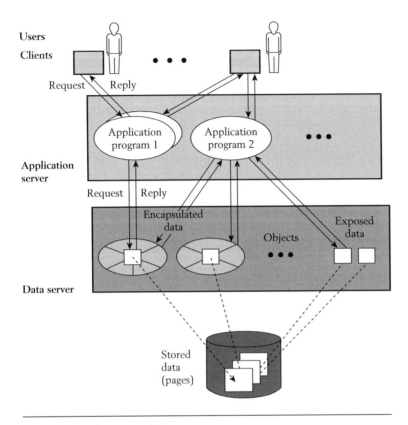

Figure 1.2 Reference architecture.

e-Commerce shopping session, or initiating a travel planning workflow would *Clients:*
be concrete examples for such requests. In modern applications, requests are *presentation*
typically issued from a GUI (Graphical User Interface); likewise, the reply that *processing*
the application server will send back is often presented in a graphical way, using
forms, buttons, charts, or even virtual reality–style animations. All this presentation processing, for both input and output, is done by the client. Therefore,
HTML (Hypertext Markup Language), one of the original cornerstones of the
World Wide Web, is a particularly attractive basis for presentation, because
it merely requires that a Web browser is installed on the client side and thus
applies to a large set of clients.

The application server has a repository of *application programs* in executable *Application*
form, and invokes the proper program that is capable of handling a client *server*
request. Both the application programs and the entire application server can
be organized in a variety of ways. The programs themselves may be anything
from an old-fashioned terminal-oriented COBOL program to a Java applet or
some other program that generates, for example, a dynamic page.

Application programs and business objects

Since the number of such programs that need to be provided for a full-fledged information system application can be very large, a good way of structuring this program repository is to organize the programs according to the object-oriented paradigm. This means that abstract *business objects*, such as accounts, customers, or shopping catalogs, are provided as encapsulated objects, each with an abstract interface that consists of a number of *methods* that can be invoked on such an object. The invokable methods are exactly the application programs that refer to (and are thus centered around) a business object. In programming language terms, a business object would be referred to as an *abstract data type* (ADT). The implementation of these ADTs, as provided by the corresponding application programs, may itself invoke methods on other business objects and issue requests to other servers, particularly, data servers. To give an application example, modern ERP (Enterprise Resource Planning) systems like SAP R/3 largely follow this paradigm.

Request brokering

The application server manages the entirety of application programs or business objects in that it spawns execution threads on behalf of client requests, monitors executions, handles certain generic forms of exceptions, and so on. It thus constitutes the surrounding run-time system of the invoked programs. The functionality of this run-time system also usually includes management of the communication connections between the clients and the application server itself. Often some form of *session* is established between a client and the server, possibly on top of a sessionless protocol such as HTTP (Hypertext Transport Protocol) of the World Wide Web, and the application server is again in charge of creating, monitoring, and terminating these sessions. So, in essence, the application server can be viewed as a *request broker* that establishes and maintains the proper connections between the client requests and the invoked business object methods (or application programs, in more classical terminology). Traditionally, so-called *TP monitors* (Transaction Processing monitors) have been the commercial incarnation of such request brokers, with specific support for OLTP applications. In recent years, so-called *object request brokers* (ORBs) have become popular in this role, based on either the standardized CORBA (Common Object Request Broker Architecture) model of distributed objects or the industry de facto standards DCOM (Distributed Component Object Model) or EJB (Enterprise Java Beans). Yet another category of request brokers includes *Web servers* (occasionally referred to as Internet or intranet information/application servers), which include the functions (and may have grown out) of a simple HTTP server but are significantly enhanced to manage program execution threads, sessions, and so on. As a matter of fact, the boundaries between these three product categories are becoming more and more blurred, with TP monitors becoming object oriented or Web servers being "upgraded" in terms of functionality and scalability. It is not unlikely that in a short time only one blend of request broker will exist and be worth remembering. The proliferation of the XML (Extensible Markup Language) data exchange standard, in particular, will be a major force toward unified and also simpler protocols for network-centric applications. For exactly this reason we refer to a request brokering application server only as an abstract notion throughout this book. This notion would also include a complete workflow management system that has its own integrated request broker or is coupled with an ORB or TP monitor.

As mentioned above, the implementation of a business object method often involves issuing requests to other business objects or other servers. Most importantly, the business objects themselves typically do not contain any persistent state data that would live beyond request/reply boundaries and user sessions for an indefinite time period. Rather, such persistent data is better kept on a *data server* that is specifically geared for the tasks of reliable long-term maintenance of data. *Database systems* are the most prominent type of systems that fall into this category, but for certain types of data, other systems may be even more appropriate. For example, for *semistructured* (text or multimedia) documents and for electronic mail, specific products have a very successful usage record. Thus, *document servers* and *mail servers* are other important types of data servers. All these data servers may also provide some notion of encapsulated objects, as opposed to exposing the raw data at their interface. However, this is an option that does not need to be exercised. For example, the data of a database server may be accessible to the application programs of an application server via the standardized query language SQL (Structured Query Language) in a direct way or via stored procedures, user-defined ADT functions, or other forms of encapsulated interfaces in modern object relational or fully object-oriented database products. In all cases, the actual data items ultimately reside in fixed-size containers commonly known as *database pages* (or *blocks*) on secondary storage, that is, the server's (magnetic) disks.

Data servers: database systems, document servers, mail servers, and others

Most of the elements in the above discussion are illustrated in Figure 1.2. In addition, the figure implicitly includes a number of practically important specializations that are obtained by collapsing two tiers into a single component. There are two major options for such simpler architectures:

Specializations of the reference architecture: two-tier systems

- Combining the client and the application server tiers: This implies that the application programs reside on the clients, leading to an architecture that is often called a client-server system with *fat* clients. Clients then communicate directly with a data server, for example, via SQL, often embedded in a standardized client-server high-level communication protocol such as ODBC (Open Database Connectivity). A possible problem with this approach (and one of the original motivations for the introduction of an explicit middle tier) is that many data server products have traditionally lacked the capabilities for maintaining a very large number of sessions and execution threads, say, 10,000 concurrent sessions, which would not be that unusual for popular information providers on the Web. However, not every application really needs such high degrees of concurrency, and many commercial servers have made tremendous progress in this direction anyway.

■ Combining the application server and the data server tiers: This implies that the application programs reside in the data server, leading to an architecture that is known as a client-server system with *thin* clients. For example, a database system that has rich object encapsulation capabilities could provide business object methods to which the client requests can be directly mapped. The potential drawback of this architectural approach is that the data server may become less scalable and more susceptible to being overloaded. Indeed, if this architecture were the starting point, then outsourcing the application processing load to a separate application server would be another motivation for a three-tier architecture. For example, the SAP R/3 product for comprehensive and integrated business administration originally evolved along this outsourcing path. However, with today's extremely powerful hardware, the specialized two-tier approach using a combined data/application server is a viable option for many low-end and midsized applications.

The bottom line is that specialized two-tier architectures are and will continue to be practically relevant.

To avoid becoming dependent on specific architectures, our approach in this book will be based on computational models (to be introduced in Chapter 2) rather than two- or three-tier system architectures. This will allow us to abstract from the particularities of the specific architecture and derive results that are as general as possible. However, for concrete illustration purposes, it may occasionally be helpful to transfer general results back to a specific system architecture. For this purpose, the two-tier architectures are typically easier to match with the abstract computational models, and we will therefore prefer the two-tier cases over the more general three-tier case whenever we need such an illustration.

1.3.2 **Federations of Servers**

Federated architecture

It would be wishful thinking to assume that the entire information processing of a large enterprise could be concentrated in a single application server and a single data server. Instead, multiple instances of two- and three-tier architectures often exist simultaneously within an enterprise for the different business units and worldwide branches. Adding the various liaisons with external business partners and the general trend to virtual enterprises increases the multitude of information services upon which modern business is based. So we

Distributed, heterogeneous, autonomous servers

really have to cope with a highly distributed architecture consisting of a wide variety of application and data servers. Obviously, these servers can be highly heterogeneous in that they use different products, different interfaces, and even radically different design philosophies (e.g., classically relational versus

Users

Clients

Application
servers

Data servers

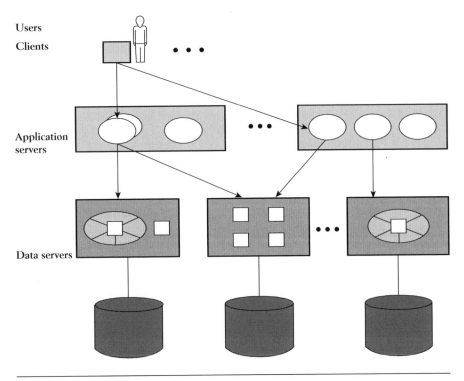

Figure 1.3 Federated system architecture.

object-oriented database systems). In addition, the various servers can differ
widely in terms of their autonomy: some servers may focus explicitly on the
specific workload on behalf of a specific business purpose and specific clients,
whereas less autonomous servers may be more willing and prepared to inter-
operate with other application and/or data servers. So the full spectrum in
this highly diverse information landscape is best characterized as a *federated
system architecture*, with multiple servers working together on a per-business-
case basis. This most general kind of architecture, which is expected to become
ubiquitous in our information society, is illustrated in Figure 1.3.

Federated system architectures require a communication infrastructure   *Middleware*
that can cope well with the heterogeneity and different operation modes of
the underlying application and data servers. This infrastructure is often referred to as *middleware*, as its place is between computer operating systems
and the application programming level, but it may as well be viewed as an
extension of modern operating systems. The key purpose is to provide high-
level communication mechanisms between clients and servers and also between
servers, reconciling programming comfort (e.g., location independence) with
robustness (e.g., reliable sessions). The paradigm that has evolved along these

lines is again an object-oriented one: today's middleware is centered around the concept of *remote method invocation*. That is, methods on remote objects can be invoked as if these were objects in the same local address space; all necessary communication, including the lookup of computer network addresses, is automatically plugged in by the middleware layer. To make this work in a highly heterogeneous software landscape, standardized interfaces are needed. The most prevalent standards to this end are DCOM and CORBA; Java-based services are of increasing importance as well.

As mentioned earlier, both DCOM and CORBA services provide a lot more than bare communication. In particular, both include request brokering facilities, a key feature of an application server. Consequently, it is not possible to tell precisely where the middleware stops and the application server itself begins. But this fuzziness is only an issue in terms of implementation. The overall system architecture can still be viewed as if the application server and the middleware between servers and clients were clearly separated. In fact, it is the intention of this section to condense the often confusing manifold of commercial system components into a sufficiently simple architectural model. From now on, our framework will be set up by the introduced reference model, and we will leave the possible mappings of this model onto commercial software packages to your (past or future) professional experience.

1.4 Virtues of the Transaction Concept

After having set the stage from an architectural point of view, we now turn to the transaction concept itself and discuss its virtues, properties, and programming interface.

1.4.1 Transaction Properties and the Transaction Programming Interface

The three application scenarios of Section 1.2 suggest that the application's view of a transaction is essentially a program execution that reads and modifies one or more data sources, which are managed by database systems or other types of data servers. The key point of a transaction is that it comes with certain system-guaranteed properties that greatly simplify the development of such applications in that the application programs themselves can safely ignore a good portion of the complexity of the overall system. In particular, application programs are completely freed up from taking care of the issues of

- *concurrency*, that is, all effects that may result from concurrent or even parallel program executions and especially data accesses,

- *failures*, that is, all effects that would result from program executions being interrupted (at "inconvenient" points) because of process or computer failures.

So concurrency and failures are, to a large extent, masked to the application programs. Therefore, application programs can be developed as if they were to be executed in a strictly sequential manner in a failure-free system environment. Such simplifications are possible because all the necessary steps to cope with concurrency and failures are factored out from the diversity of applications, and are delegated to the generic run-time system of the underlying transactional servers. This clear separation of responsibilities into application-specific functionality and generic run-time services is indeed the main contribution of transactional information systems and the key to their impressive commercial success: being able to ignore concurrency and computer failures in application development is a tremendous gain in terms of programmer and development productivity, with respect to both time and cost. *Masking concurrency and failures to application development*

All this is based on the simple, yet extremely powerful abstraction concept called *transaction*. Transactions form the "interface contract" between an application program and a transactional server in the following sense:

- The application program simply specifies, during its execution, the boundaries of a transaction, by issuing Begin transaction and Commit transaction calls. In applications that use embedded SQL the former is often implicit, interpreting the start of the program execution or its session with the database server as the transaction begin; whereas the latter is explicit and marked by the Commit work call (see the debit/credit and funds transfer examples in Section 1.2). The end of a transaction may also implicitly mark the begin of a new transaction within the same program invocation.

- The server automatically considers all requests that it receives from the application program within this (dynamic) scope as belonging to the same transaction and, most importantly, guarantees certain properties for this set of requests and their effects on the underlying data.

The properties a server guarantees for a transaction, known as the *ACID properties*, comprise the following four properties: *a*tomicity, *c*onsistency, *i*solation, and *d*urability. *ACID properties*

- *Atomicity:* From the client's and the application program's point of view, a transaction is executed completely or not at all. So the effects of the executing program on the underlying data servers will only become visible (to the outside world or to other program executions) if and when the transaction reaches its "commit" point, that is, the Commit *Atomicity* *Transaction commit* transaction call is successfully returned. This case implies that the transaction could be processed completely, and no errors whatsoever were discovered while it was processed. If, on the other hand, the program is abnormally terminated before reaching its commit point, the data in the underlying data servers will be left in or automatically brought back to the state in which it was before the transaction started. So, in this latter case, the data appears as if the transaction had never been invoked at all. This holds also for system failures that are not related to the executing transaction itself, such as failures of the data server, the operating system that surrounds it, or the computer on which the data server is running.

Consistency preservation

- **Consistency preservation:** Consistency constraints that are defined on the underlying data servers are preserved by a transaction; so a transaction leads from one consistent state to another. For example, the merchant's, the bank's, and the customer's records on an electronic sale should be mutually consistent; or in a hyperlinked document collection, the referential structure should be consistent in that neither dangling references nor unreachable documents exist. Upon the commit of a transaction, constraints like these must be satisfied; however, between the beginning and the end of a transaction, inconsistent intermediate states are tolerated and may even be unavoidable.

Transaction abort (rollback) upon consistency violation

This property of consistency preservation cannot be ensured in a completely automatic manner. Rather, the application must be programmed so that the code between the beginning and the commit of a transaction will eventually reach a consistent state. This can be hidden in the application logic or be done by including corresponding code in the application programs; moreover, the task of checking consistency can be transferred to the database system, by exploiting constraint declaration statements or even triggers. In the latter case, failing to satisfy all specified constraints at the commit point of a transaction results in the data server enforcing an abnormal termination of the transaction. Then, in conjunction with the atomicity property, consistency is preserved. Alternatively, the application program can explicitly notify the data server when it is clear that the application program will no longer be able to reach a consistent state and requests that it be abnormally terminated. In this case, we say that the transaction is deliberately *aborted*, and the application program can achieve this effect by issuing an explicit Rollback transaction call. Again, in conjunction with the atomicity property, data consistency is preserved. The capability to explicitly request such a transaction abort can be a great simplification of the application program's consistency checking and consistency maintenance code.

Isolation

- **Isolation:** A transaction is isolated from other transactions, in the sense that each transaction behaves as if it were operating alone with all resources to itself. In particular, each transaction will "see" only consistent data in the underlying data sources. More specifically, it will see only data modifications that result from committed transactions, and it will see them only in their entirety, and never any effects of an incomplete transaction. This is the decisive property that allows the fallacies and pitfalls of concurrency to be hidden from the application developers. As we will show later, a sufficient condition for isolation is that concurrent executions are equivalent to sequential ones, so that all transactions appear as if they were executed one after the other rather than in an interleaved manner.

■ *Durability:* When the application program is notified that a transaction has been successfully completed (when the Commit transaction call is successfully returned) all updates that the transaction has made in the underlying data servers are guaranteed to survive subsequent software or hardware failures. Thus, updates of committed transactions are durable (until another transaction later modifies the same data items) in that they persist even across failures of the affected data server(s). Hence the name "durability" or "persistence."

Durability (persistence)

In summary, a transaction is a set of operations issued by an application program and executed on one or more data servers, with the ACID properties guaranteed by the run-time system of the involved servers. The ACID contract between the application program and the data servers requires the program to demarcate the boundaries of the transaction as well as the desired outcome—successful or abnormal termination—of the transaction, both in a dynamic manner. To this end, the programming interface of a transactional information system conceptually needs to offer three calls:

Transaction programming interface

■ Begin transaction to specify the beginning of a transaction

■ Commit transaction to specify the successful end of a transaction

■ Rollback transaction to specify the unsuccessful end of a transaction with the request to abort the transaction

Note, once more, that application programs generate the transaction boundaries as well as the operations that constitute a transaction dynamically during program execution (and, as mentioned, often implicitly for beginning transactions and explicitly for committing them). So, in particular, programs can generate sequences of successive transactions, loops of transaction invocations, or even multiple transactions in parallel, provided that the program is itself multi-threaded. Thus, a workflow management system could be viewed as a multi-threaded application program that issues transactions in such a flexible manner. As pointed out earlier, there is a lot more to workflow management, but it is clear at this point that the transaction concept is a great asset for distributed workflows and a wide variety of application classes beyond the traditional OLTP area.

1.4.2 **Requirements on Transactional Servers**

The core requirement on a transactional server is that it provide the ACID guarantees for sets of operations that belong to the same transaction issued by an application program. This requires that the server include at least the following two main components:

Server components: concurrency control and recovery for ACID contract

- *concurrency control* component to guarantee the isolation properties of transactions, for both committed and aborted transactions
- *recovery* component to guarantee the atomicity and durability of transactions

Note that the server may or may not provide explicit support for consistency preservation. One type of server may require the application program to do all consistency checking and maintenance itself with implicit support by means of the rollback option; whereas other servers, especially database systems, could enforce consistency by means of logical rules. Such logical rules are, however, not a specific issue of transactional information systems and will therefore not be considered in this book.

Performance: throughput and response time

In addition to the ACID contract, a transactional server should meet a number of technical requirements: a transactional data server (which could, and most often will, be a database system) must provide *good performance* with a given hardware/software configuration, or more generally, a good cost/performance ratio when the configuration is not yet fixed. Performance typically refers to the following two metrics:

- *high throughput*, which is defined as the number of successfully processed transactions per time unit
- *short response times*, where the response time of a transaction is defined as the time span between issuing the transaction and its successful completion as perceived by the client

It is evident that these performance metrics depend on many issues in the implementation, configuration, and tuning of a server. As far as transactions are concerned, the important requirement is that the concurrency control and recovery components do not become a bottleneck. Therefore, it is desirable that a transactional server be able to execute as many transactions as possible concurrently or in parallel (with the parallel case assuming that the underlying computer is a multiprocessor). Of course, such high degrees of concurrency or parallelism are subject to the condition that the ACID contract is not violated.

In fact, it would be much simpler to provide the ACID properties if performance were not an issue. Real applications, however, dictate that throughput and response time are important yardsticks for assessing the concurrency control and recovery components of a transactional server.

A server must be *reliable*, meaning that it virtually never loses data, unless   *Reliability*
certain forms of catastrophic failures occur, and that it is always able to recover data to a desired consistent state, no matter what complicated forms of one or multiple failures arise. Reliability alone means correct behavior in the presence of failures, but this may incur outages of the server during which client requests are not served. In addition, most applications require high *availability*, which   *Availability*
implies that recovery times after failures are short, and that failures that lead to total outages are infrequent.

Other technical requirements on a data server include security, ease of administration, standards compliance, and so on, but these are not directly related to transactions and will therefore be disregarded in this book.

1.5 Concepts and Architecture of Database Servers

As mentioned earlier, the most important class of data servers is database systems. Throughout this book we assume you are familiar with a number of basics about database systems, and we will discuss and explain in detail only those aspects that refer to transactions, concurrency control, and recovery. In this section, to make the book sufficiently self-contained, we sketch a few principles of database system internals, specifically, the layered architecture of modern database systems, the storage layout of data, the access acceleration provided by index structures, and the basics of query and update processing. For other database issues, particularly the relational, object-oriented, and object relational data models, including the corresponding data definition and manipulation languages such as SQL or OQL, we refer to the relevant literature mentioned in the Bibliographic Notes at the end of this chapter.

1.5.1 Architectural Layers of Database Systems

Virtually all modern database systems have a layered internal architecture on the server side, as illustrated in Figure 1.4. Each layer has an interface that provides services invoked by the layers above it to implement their higher-level services. Note, however, that all layers are within the same server and therefore not visible to application programs. The actual code base of a specific database system may not conform to the simple structure of the figure, but all systems have internal components that can be approximately mapped to the layers shown. When the server is itself a *distributed* database system, all

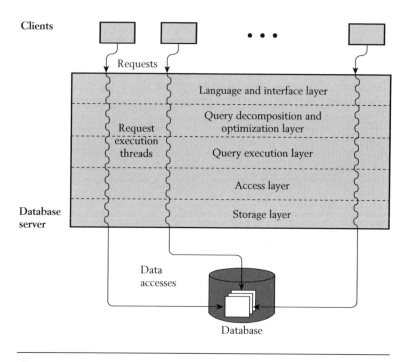

Clients

Requests

Language and interface layer

Query decomposition and optimization layer

Request execution threads

Query execution layer

Access layer

Database server

Storage layer

Data accesses

Database

Figure 1.4 Layered architecture of a database system.

system components and thus all architectural layers are usually installed on all the underlying computers.

Multi-threaded processing of requests

When a client request arrives at the server, the server executes code that transforms the request into one or more operations at each of the underlying layers, ultimately arriving at a sequence of disk accesses (unless caching avoids the disk access). To allow the server to exploit parallelism between the CPU and the disk(s), the server makes use of modern operating system services in that it typically spawns one *thread* (also known as *lightweight process*) per active request, as illustrated by the wavy lines in Figure 1.4. This typically takes place within one (heavyweight) process whose virtual memory address space is shared across all threads. The server may actually keep a pool of preallocated threads that are dynamically assigned to requests rather than creating and destroying a thread for each individual request. This multi-threaded architecture also facilitates disk I/O parallelism between different requests. In addition, by simply assigning more than one thread per request, the architecture is also geared for CPU and I/O parallelism within a single request execution. This is the standard way of implementing a database system on a symmetric (shared memory) multiprocessor (SMP).

Language and interface layer

The *language and interface layer* makes various kinds of interfaces available to the application developer. This layer provides one or more languages for data definition and manipulation, usually in the form of application programming interfaces (APIs). By far the most important language of this kind is SQL; the most important standard for embedding SQL in an API that is usable for a variety of programming languages is ODBC (Open Database Connectivity), but other proprietary or language-specific SQL-based interfaces are widely used as well. In addition to the data manipulation capabilities in the narrow sense, SQL is often combined with or enriched by programming language constructs, so that encapsulated "business objects" can be implemented within the database server and their operations can be provided at the server interface (see the discussion in Section 1.3).

The language and interface layer itself takes care of the client-server communication at the API level and contains initial processing steps such as parsing the SQL command in a request, checking authentication and authorization, and so on. The next lower layer, the *query decomposition and optimization layer*, works on an internal, tree-based representation of a request and is concerned with the further decomposition of the request into smaller units that can be directly executed. In particular, when the request is a full-fledged SQL query with a complex query predicate, this decomposition involves challenging optimization issues. This is the level where the database system makes a choice among different execution plans that are equivalent in that they all implement the same query but can differ widely in terms of their execution efficiency. These optimizations are usually carried out at the application program's compile time, but advanced applications, such as data warehousing systems, and also a fair number of otherwise simple application programs, create the submitted SQL requests dynamically during their run time and thus force the server to decompose and optimize those requests also at run time. *Query decomposition and optimization layer*

The execution plan chosen by the query decomposition and optimization layer is usually represented as a tree (or, more generally, a directed acyclic graph) of operators, where each operator can be directly mapped to a piece of server code. The code for these operators and the code for the control and data flow among operators are provided by the *query execution layer*. For example, this layer includes the code for sorting disk-resident data, for performing a relational join operation based on hash tables, a join algorithm based on sorting and merging, and so on. All these operators consume streams of data records as input and produce such streams as output. In addition to the data records that constitute the primary contents of the database, the query execution layer also depends heavily on index structures to speed up the processing of the records. An index is essentially a search structure, often a specific type of search tree, that helps identify records that match a certain predicate (a search condition). Without indexes, all queries would inevitably end up performing at least one complete scan over a possibly huge collection of data records. Index structures and the capabilities for accessing and manipulating data records are provided by the *access layer* of a database system. Finally, both data records and index structures are ultimately mapped onto pages (fixed-size storage containers for *Query execution layer*

Access layer

Storage layer   the transfer between disk and memory, also known as blocks). The *storage layer* is responsible for managing the pages of a database. This involves disk I/O control and optimization and, especially, caching in memory to exploit locality in the page access patterns. Usually, the most recently or frequently used pages are kept in memory and can be accessed without disk I/O. The area in main memory that serves this caching purpose is known as the *database (page) cache* or *database (page) buffer*.

Note that, a priori, the layered architecture of a database system does not tell us anything about transaction management. The functionality of transactional concurrency control and recovery could indeed be tied to any of the presented five layers. In practice, however, those functions are often integrated into the access and storage layers. We will discuss the embedding of transaction management into a database architecture in more detail when we introduce the book's principal computational models in Chapter 2.

1.5.2 **How Data Is Stored**

Data records   All data objects are kept internally in the form of *data records*. A record consists of a set of *fields*, or *columns*, and is stored on disk as a string of consecutive bytes. The fields correspond to the attributes of a relational schema; so they are of specific data types, but this is not relevant at the storage level other than possibly requiring specific byte encodings.

Pages   Records reside on disk in *pages*. A typical page size is on the order of 16KB; so with typical record sizes of a few hundred bytes, a page usually contains a number of records. Pages are the minimum unit of data transfer between a disk and main memory, and they are the units of caching in memory. A disk I/O can read or write one or more pages, typically pages that are contiguous on disk. Sometimes a fixed number of pages that can be read or written together is called a block, but most often, the notion of a block is merely used as a synonym for a page. In this book we will use pages and blocks as synonyms.

Storage layout
of a page   Each page has a *page header*, typically less than a hundred bytes, that contains administrative information for free space management and similar purposes (e.g., the number of free bytes in the page, the size of the largest free area within the page, etc.). Records that contain variable-length columns such as ones of type `varchar` are themselves variable-length strings within a page; so updates to data records can cause growth and shrinkage of these byte strings and may thus require the movement of records within a page. As the database system usually keeps pointers to records in other places, most notably for indexing purposes, it is important to prevent each and every movement of a record from causing those pointers to change. This is achieved by addressing records indirectly through a *slot array* that resides at the end of the page (also known as a *page trailer*). A pointer to a record, a so-called *RID* (record ID, or row ID),

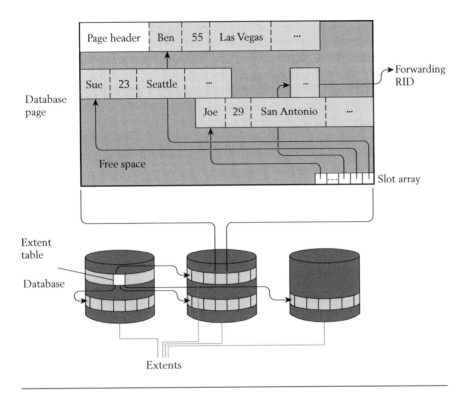

Figure 1.5 Storage layout of database pages.

consists of a page number and a slot number, and it is only this referenced slot inside the page that contains the full byte address of a record. So all record movements are encapsulated within a page, as long as they do not span multiple pages. Sometimes, however, it is unavoidable that a record must move to another page because of lack of space within the original page. In this case, a forwarding pointer, which is itself a RID, is left in the original page. With this technique, all records are reachable through their RID pointers with at most two page accesses, and most records are reachable in one page access. This entire storage layout of a page is illustrated in Figure 1.5, using data records that capture information about persons, customers, or friends, with fields such as Name, Age, City, Zipcode, Street, and so on.

Long fields

A growing number of database applications require support for *long fields*, also known as *BLOBs* (Binary Large OBjects), to capture multimedia data such as images (e.g., a photograph of a person), text, or video data. Such fields are typically much larger than a page and must therefore be decomposed into multiple chunks and spread across multiple pages. A simple implementation technique for long fields would embed a list of page numbers rather than the actual long field in the data record, and those pages would be exclusively reserved for the chunks of a long field. More sophisticated techniques exist for the storage layout of long fields, but the simple approach is sufficient for understanding this book.

Storage layer metadata

In addition to the pages that contain data records, a database system needs to keep a variety of metadata. At the storage level, this mostly refers to the translation of page numbers into physical addresses on disk and to the management of free space within a database. Database systems usually preallocate a certain amount of disk space that consists of one or more *extents*, each of which is a range of pages that are contiguous on disk. A page number is then translated into a disk number and a physical address on the disk by looking up an entry in an *extent table* and adding a relative offset. Extents and the extent table are illustrated in Figure 1.5. When data records are inserted, the database system gradually uses this preallocated space by assigning records to pages and keeping track of the available free space. In particular, all systems maintain some form of *free space management table* from which they can infer which pages are completely empty as well as possibly further free space information.

As mentioned earlier, the access layer of a database system also keeps certain forms of secondary, or derived, data to speed up the searching of records by their contents (as opposed to the access through a given RID). Most notably, this secondary data includes *index structures*, which are the subject of the next subsection. Here we merely point out that those structures are themselves mapped onto pages that are subject to caching, free space management, and other "bookkeeping" at the underlying storage layer. Those pages are referred to as index pages, but the storage layer often treats them in the same way as regular data pages.

1.5.3 **How Data Is Accessed**

Table scan vs. index lookup

Database systems often need to retrieve all data records (of the same table) that have a specified value in a specific field, say, all records with the value "Miami" in their City field. This could be a complete, relatively simple query or merely one step in the processing of a more complex query. The specified value (e.g., "Miami") is referred to as a *search key*; sometimes this term is also used for the name of the field on which the search is performed (i.e., City field in the example). Without any index structures, the only way to retrieve the records with the given search key is through a sequential *table scan* in which all records of the corresponding table are accessed and inspected. The typical implementation of a table scan first looks up, in the free space management table, which (nonempty) pages are assigned to the corresponding data table and then accesses all those pages one by one; the I/O cost of this procedure is linear in the size of the data table. In contrast, a more efficient implementation should retrieve the desired data records with an I/O cost that is at most *logarithmic* in the size of the data table (plus linear in the number of records that satisfy the search condition or, under certain circumstances, the number of pages on which these records reside). This is feasible in conjunction with an index structure that keeps all values of a given field (or combination of fields) that occur in the database, along with pointers to those data records that contain the corresponding value. Using an index structure for resolving a specified search condition is called an *index lookup*.

The index structure itself can be implemented in a variety of ways, most *Search trees* notably as a *search tree* or a *hash table*, both in a page-structured, disk-resident form. Regardless of the implementation, the interface of the index structure provides a function like

$$\text{lookup} \langle \text{index} \rangle \text{ where } \langle \text{indexed field} \rangle = \langle \text{search key} \rangle$$

With a tree-based implementation, which implicitly captures the ordering of search keys, an additional interface function that cannot be easily supported by hash-based implementations would be

$$\text{lookup} \langle \text{index} \rangle \text{ where}$$
$$\langle \text{indexed field} \rangle \text{ between } \langle \text{lower bound} \rangle \text{ and } \langle \text{upper bound} \rangle$$

where one of the two bounds could be omitted and is then implicitly set to the lowest or highest possible value of the field's domain (e.g., zero or infinity in the case of nonnegative integers). For example, we could retrieve all records with values in the Age field that lie between 20 and 30. This type of index lookup is called a *range lookup* (or *range scan*), as opposed to the first type that is known as an *exact match lookup*. Sometimes both types together are referred to as *index scans*. Both return RID lists for the qualifying records.

In the following we restrict ourselves to tree-based implementations as the *B+ trees* more versatile ones. The prevalent data structure in this category is the B^+ *tree*. This is a page-structured search tree whose nodes correspond to pages and where all leaf nodes are at the same tree level (i.e., have the same distance from the root node). An example B^+ tree for an index on the Name field of a Person table is shown in Figure 1.6. This tree has height 2; it consists of a root node and three leaf nodes at the next lower level. The leaf nodes contain all values of the indexed field that exist in the database. Each value is followed by a list of RIDs to the corresponding records. The nonleaf nodes of the index consist of pairs of values and pointers to index nodes of the next lower level. Within a node these entries are sorted by values. These values serve as routers to guide a top-down search for a given key value. To this end, the value associated with a pointer to a subtree must be larger than or equal to the highest existing key in this subtree, and it must be smaller than the lowest existing key in the right neighboring subtree. For example, the entry in the root of Figure 1.6 that points to the leftmost leaf has the value "Carl," which is the (lexicographically) largest

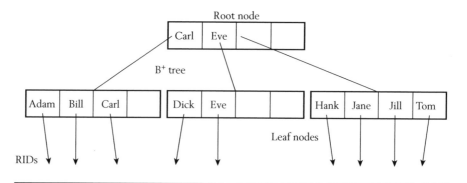

Figure 1.6 Example of a B$^+$ tree.

key value in that subtree. Thus, the values in nonleaf nodes effectively partition the key values into disjoint value ranges.

The rightmost child node of a given nonleaf node is automatically separated from its left neighbor by the router value for this neighbor. Therefore, an entry that points to the rightmost child of a node does not have a value but merely consists of a pointer. In the example of Figure 1.6, the third entry of the root simply points to the rightmost leaf, meaning that all key values in this rightmost subtree are higher than the router value "Eve" in the preceding entry of the root. Note that this technique not only is applicable to the root, but also avoids an explicit router value for the rightmost subtree among the children of the same node at all levels. The highest possible key value within such a rightmost subtree is then determined by the router value for all subtrees with the same parent, which can be found in that parent's parent. As a consequence, each nonleaf node has one more pointer to the next index level than it has router values.

A search for a given key value starts at the root node. It determines within the currently inspected node the smallest value that is larger than or equal to the given search key, and then follows the pointer of this router value. If the search key is higher than all values in the index node, the search follows the pointer to the rightmost child. This step is recursively applied per node until the leaf level is reached. In the example tree, a search for the key "Dick" would follow the "Eve" router in the root and find the key in the middle leaf. In contrast, a search for the key "Joe" would follow the pointer to the rightmost leaf, where it would detect that this key does not exist in the database.

B$^+$ trees are among the most fundamental concepts in database systems. Moreover, they also pose significant challenges for the concurrency control and recovery components of the database system, as an inconsistency of a B$^+$ tree index (e.g., dangling pointers or a violation of the tree invariant) would be disastrous, and it is crucial to preserve consistency with extremely little overhead. Because of the importance of index structures, we will later devote an entire chapter to this issue.

1.5.4 **How Queries and Updates Are Executed**

Now that we have a rough picture of how data records are stored and efficiently accessed, the final issue that we want to consider is the execution of more complex queries and update operations. As an example consider a query that retrieves all persons under 30 years of age who live in Austin, Texas. In the standard query language SQL, this can be phrased as follows:

```
Select Name, City, Zipcode, Street
From Person
Where Age < 30 And City = "Austin"
```

The query decomposition and optimization layer translates this SQL query into an execution plan, taking into account the available indexes and other physical design features that were chosen by the database administrator. This translation involves solving an optimization problem, as its outcome should be the execution plan whose estimated execution cost is minimum or at least close to the minimum. Typically, query optimizers use a variety of sophisticated heuristics for this purpose. The resulting execution plan is usually represented as an operator tree. For our example, the operator tree of a possible execution plan is shown in Figure 1.7. This plan makes use of two indexes (the query optimizer must have determined that they both exist), namely, an index on

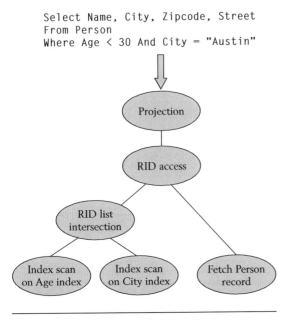

Figure 1.7 Example of a query execution plan.

```
Select Name, City, Zipcode, Street
From Person
Where Age < 30 And City = "Austin"
```

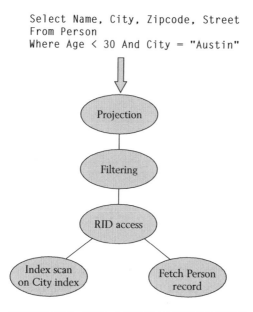

Figure 1.8 Alternative query execution plan for
the query of Figure 1.7.

the Age field and an index on the City field. It performs a range lookup on the
Age index and an exact match lookup on the City field. Both index lookups
return RID lists that are then intersected to determine the RIDs of all qualifying
records. Finally, the last step is to fetch those records based on their RIDs and
perform some output processing such as projecting out the requested fields
(i.e., dropping all other fields of the possibly long records).

   An alternative execution plan is shown in Figure 1.8. In this plan, only one
index is used, namely, the one on the City field. The reason for choosing this
plan (over the previous one) could be that either the Age index does not exist,
or is not very selective for the given range of key values, meaning that the RID
list that would be returned from the range lookup is too large relative to the
total number of records in the Person table.

   The evaluation of such an operator tree proceeds bottom up, from the
leaves to the root. For each operator in the tree, the corresponding code in
the database system fetches the operands and produces its output, which is
then fed into the parent operator. As these operands as well as the intermediate outputs can become fairly large, the evaluation is usually carried out in
a *pipelined* manner. So the output of an operator is not necessarily produced
entirely before the parent operator is invoked. Rather, the parent operator is
invoked as soon as its first input records are available. This evaluation principle
establishes a set of producer-consumer data streams between operators, one

stream for each operand arc in the tree. The benefit of the pipelining is that intermediate results do not have to be "materialized" in their entirety, and this is a significant cost savings, as the materialization would often require writing large intermediate output to disk and reading it again for the subsequently invoked parent operator. In a parallel database system, pipelining leads to true parallelism between operators, and, most importantly, it can be nicely combined with a parallelization of each operator (where the latter is the kind of parallelism that achieves by far the highest speedup).

1.6 **Lessons Learned**

This chapter has introduced transactions as a concept and emphasized their practical importance, from both an application and a system architecture viewpoint. Transactions are essentially a contract between an application program and a collection of transactional servers that allows the program to combine a number of requests to these servers into a logical unit. The decisive part of this contract is that this unit has the ACID properties: atomicity, consistency preservation, isolation, and durability. The benefit that we achieve from the transaction abstraction is twofold:

- Users (i.e., human end users) can rely on the consistency of the data that they see and maintain as part of their day-to-day business. This holds even for distributed, possibly heterogeneous information systems. Furthermore, this quality is not limited to database systems as the underlying data sources, but extends to document servers, mail servers, and other components of modern information systems.

- Application developers greatly benefit from the transaction concept in that the application programming is fundamentally simplified, thus boosting programming productivity and lowering the development and maintenance costs. Thanks to the ACID properties, application developers do not need to care about synchronizing concurrent or parallel data accesses or handling process and computer failures. Rather, programs can be written as if each transaction had all underlying data exclusively for itself and none of the involved system components would ever fail.

These fundamental benefits are achieved by providing each data server, and possibly also other components of the information system, with two key pieces of software:

- a concurrency control component that guarantees the isolation of transactions in the presence of concurrent data accesses,

■ a recovery component that guarantees the atomicity and durability of transactions in the presence of failures.

This book is largely about models and algorithms for these two key building blocks of transactional information systems. The challenge lies in the performance of the concurrency control and recovery components: providing high concurrency, high throughput, and fast response times, and ensuring fast recovery from failures and thus high availability with low overhead during normal operation.

Exercises

1.1 Consider an order entry application, where customers order certain items from a retail seller. Customers place their orders over the phone, and agents enter these orders into a database at the merchant site. An order may consist of multiple order lines, each referring to one product with a specified quantity. Ordered products are shipped to the customer if they are available in sufficient quantity in the retail seller's warehouse. Customers pay by sending a check or transferring funds electronically after receiving the shipped products. Discuss how ACID transactions can help maintain the consistency of the data that underlies this kind of order entry business.

Hint: One possible approach, often used in practice, is to design and implement three basic transaction programs, `NewOrder`, `Shipment`, and `Payment`, for handling new orders, shipping ordered products, and registering payments. The underlying database would need the following tables with appropriate fields: Customers, Products, Orders, OrderLines.

1.2 Discuss further applications of database systems in the context of which the ACID properties of transactions make sense. Contrast these with other applications in which the ACID properties (totally or in part) appear too restrictive.

Bibliographic Notes

Various other textbooks have been published in recent years on the subject of transactions and transaction management; the most important ones of these are Bernstein et al. (1987), Papadimitriou (1986), Bernstein and Newcomer (1997), Cellary et al. (1988), Lynch et al. (1994), and Gray and Reuter (1993). Additional books and original papers on specific subjects will be mentioned later.

Among the above textbooks, Bernstein and Newcomer (1997) as well as Gray and Reuter (1993) provide detailed considerations on the overall architecture and application development aspects of transactional information systems, devoting significant space to TP monitors and other types of request brokers. In this book, we focus instead on the fundamentals of transactional systems and do not further discuss the manifold and continuously evolving issues of programming interfaces and commercial middleware technology. For the latter aspects, refer, for example, to the recent books by Orfali et al. (1999) and Boucher and Katz (1999). We also will not go into more detail on the advanced application scenarios that we used in this chapter, specifically, electronic commerce and workflow management. The interested reader is referred to the survey books by Adam et al. (1998) on e-Commerce and Dogac et al. (1998) or Leymann and Roller (2000) on workflow technology. However, keep in mind that many aspects of these applications are still evolving so that the material in these books may become outdated fairly quickly.

Throughout the rest of this book we assume you are reasonably familiar with the fundamentals of database systems; we refer to Elmasri and Navathe (2000), Garcia-Molina et al. (2000), O'Neil and O'Neil (2000), Özsu and Valduriez (1999), Ramakrishnan and Gehrke (2000), Silberschatz et al. (1997), and Vossen (1991) for introductions to the topic in its full generality. Vossen (1992a, 1996) offer more concise surveys of the field. A good introduction to the specific issues of index structures and query processing in database systems is the book by Yu and Meng (1998). We will also rely on your background in object-oriented programming and systems, in particular as used in the context of database systems; textbooks on this subject include Cattell (1994), Kemper and Moerkotte (1994), and Lausen and Vossen (1998).

CHAPTER TWO

Computational Models

After each symbol conjured up by the director of a Game, each player was required
to perform silent, formal meditation on the content, origin, and meaning of this
symbol, to call to mind intensively and organically its full purport. . . . Beginners
learned how to establish parallels, by means of the Game's symbols, between a
piece of classical music and the formula for some law of nature. Experts and
Masters of the Game freely wove the initial theme into unlimited combinations.

—*Hermann Hesse*

Here I am at a famous school. I'm dressing sharp and I'm acting cool.

—*Frank Zappa*

2.1 Goal and Overview

In the previous chapter, we have made it clear why transactions are important
and what is relevant when we start discussing them from a technical point of
view. In this chapter, we will go even further and introduce two precise computational models for transactional servers around which all our discussions in
subsequent chapters of this book will center. In particular, the theory and algorithms of concurrency control and of recovery that we will present are based
on these two models, from which most of our correctness and efficiency arguments can be carried over to real implementations and applications. Especially
for correctness, it will be necessary to look at transactions even from a formal
point of view, and we will show here to what extent this is possible and what
natural limits exist.

The computational models we will introduce below follow a common
"recipe" for devising transaction models, which we first describe in Section 2.2.
Then we present in detail a simple model—coined the page model—for ease
of concise explanation in Section 2.3, and a more complex one—coined the
object model—to capture advanced issues in Section 2.4. In Parts II and III,
these models form the basis for a wide development of concurrency control
as well as recovery theory and algorithms. Thus, the material in this chapter
together with that of the previous chapter sets the stage for laying out a more
detailed road map of the book's contents and organization, given in Section 2.5,
which ends the introductory part of the text.

2.2 **Ingredients**

Computational models for transactional servers can be made precise in a variety of ways, depending on the level of abstraction chosen, the programming environment, or the application at hand. However, the way in which such a model is devised is not completely arbitrary, but follows a kind of methodology that reflects how to specify the essential and relevant ingredients. The common approach by which our computational models are developed and will later be used is characterized by the following five-step program:

1. First, *elementary operations* on data objects are defined—that is, operations that can be assumed to be indivisible so that each individual operation by itself appears atomic and isolated from other operations. (Note that we are not yet considering the embedding of such operations in the context of a transaction.) This first step leaves some leeway in the definition of what a data object is and what kind of elementary operations we consider, and this will later lead to the distinction between the page model and the object model.

2. Next, *transactions*, as executions of transaction programs, can be modeled as sequences or partial orders of such operations, with the intuitive interpretation that such a collection is to be executed in conjunction in order to guarantee its ACID properties.

3. When several transactions are "shuffled" into a large collection of operations (in such a way that the individual transactions can still be identified), we obtain *schedules* or *histories* as an abstract notion of concurrent (or parallel) executions.

4. From the set of all syntactically correct schedules, we must identify those that can be considered "correct" in the sense of the ACID guarantees.

5. Finally, we need *algorithms* or *protocols* to create correct schedules in an online manner such that operations are scheduled for execution dynamically as they are submitted by the application programs.

These five steps are relevant for virtually every transaction model, in particular when such a model is developed all the way from basic operations to protocols. In the remainder of this chapter we will apply the steps to the two computational models that we want to study in this book. The *page model* (also known as the *read/write model*) is a simple model that can be nicely motivated from looking at the way data pages are accessed (i.e., read or written) at the storage layer of a database system. As will be seen shortly, this model is simple enough to capture the essence of the concurrency control and recovery problem in a concise and elegant way, yet it is general enough to describe many (but not all) important system implementation issues. The major limitation of the page model is that it captures *no* semantics of the data access operations, given the simple low-level nature of page reads and writes.

A richer model would therefore consider higher-level operations, for example, those of the access layer or the query processing layer of a database system. From here it is only a small step to consider even a limited form of application semantics by taking into account an application program's method invocations on business objects, that is, instances of abstract data types (ADTs) that reside in the data server or the application server (see the discussion of system architectures in Section 1.3). All these considerations give rise to our second computational model, the *object model*, in which transactions consist of ADT operations that may themselves invoke operations on other objects, all of which would eventually result in read or write operations on objects of type Page.

In summary, the two computational models we are about to introduce differ in their definitions of data objects. For the page model, these are *pages* with read and write operations; for the object model, these are general *objects* with an encapsulated set of operations applicable to them.

2.3 **The Page Model**

The simple page model to be defined next is motivated by the observation that all higher-level operations on data are eventually mapped into read and write operations on pages. We have shown this in our brief review of database system concepts in the previous chapter, and similar mappings onto pages are used by all other forms of data servers (e.g., mail or document servers). Thus, to study the effects of concurrent executions, in the sense of interleaving the operations of different transactions, it is, in principle, sufficient to inspect the interleavings of the resulting page operations. In doing so, each page read or write is assumed to be an indivisible operation, regardless of whether it takes place in a page cache in memory or on disk. It is clear that we need to revise this assumption once we start discussing recovery issues that arise after server failures, but the "indivisibility axiom" for page operations will take us a fairly long way into recovery considerations as well.

In general, we emphasize once again that the restriction to read/write page operations represents a strong form of abstraction. (This is exactly why we later need the richer object model.) However, as will be seen in the sequel, the abstraction from higher-level data operations, such as SQL commands or method invocations on business objects, down to the view that a resulting transaction consists of reads and writes *only* is an interesting one and suffices for many purposes. In fact, a comprehensive theory of concurrency control and of recovery can be built on it, which is directly applicable to practical systems, albeit with some performance limitations.

We now start going through the five-step procedure discussed in Section 2.2. Formally, a data server is assumed to contain a (finite) set $D = \{x, y, z, \ldots\}$ of (indivisible and disjoint) items with indivisible read and write operations. You may think of these data items as pages, as these are the units onto which all higher-level operations are eventually mapped and for which reads and writes can indeed be regarded as indivisible. As an abstract model, this page model is not necessarily limited to the real notion of pages and rather provides very general insights into concurrency problems and their solutions. Nonetheless, page-oriented concurrency control and recovery at the storage layer of a database system or other type of server is the major application of the page model and the results derived from it. Throughout the book, we will denote data items by small letters (often taken from the end of the alphabet), where indices will be used if necessary (e.g., x_1, y_4).

Before we define transactions in this model in general, let us look at a simplified version first, which we will use to introduce the (somewhat artificial) distinction between the *syntax* and the *semantics* of a transaction. The simplified version considers transactions as *total* orders of steps, while the general model will allow *partial* orders. Since we are not going to make intensive use of transaction semantics in what follows, we briefly explain that issue for total orders here.

"Syntax": totally ordered transaction   Let us consider a *transaction* t (in the page model) to be a (finite) sequence of steps (actions) of the form $r(x)$ or $w(x)$, written

$$t = p_1 \ldots p_n$$

where $n < \infty$, $p_i \in \{r(x), w(x)\}$ for $1 \leq i \leq n$, and $x \in D$. We use r as an abbreviation for "read" and w as an abbreviation for "write." Thus, we abstract from the details of a transaction as a program execution, and concentrate only on the sequence of read and write operations that results from the execution.

Next we look at how we could define some form of semantics for individual transactions. Each step occurring in a transaction can be uniquely identified so that two distinct transactions will not have steps in common. (Of course, the same step *types* can occur in more than one transaction.) Within a single transaction, we often denote steps in the form p_j, that is, with a step number as a subscript. (So p_j is the j-th step of the transaction.) In the presence of multiple transactions, we add a unique transaction number to each transaction, and also use this number as an additional subscript for the steps of the transactions. Then p_{ij} denotes the j-th step of transaction i. Sometimes, a given context does not require an explicit numbering of the steps; in such cases we may simply write p_i for a step of transaction i.

As we have seen, associated with each step is both an action (read or write) and a data item from D. Thus, we use the following terminology when we consider only a single transaction:

$$p_j = r(x) : \text{step } j \text{ reads data item } x$$
$$p_j = w(x) : \text{step } j \text{ writes data item } x$$

In our discussion on semantics that follows, there is always only a single transaction under consideration so that single-level indexing suffices.

According to the above settings, a transaction is a purely syntactic entity whose semantics or interpretation is unknown. If we had more information on the semantics of the program that launches a transaction and the intended state transformation of the underlying data, this knowledge could be used to interpret a transaction and associate a formal semantics with it. In the absence of such information, however, the best that can be done is a syntactic interpretation of the steps of a transaction that is as general as possible:

- In case $p_j = r(x)$, in which the j-th step of a given transaction is a read step, the current value of x is assigned to a local variable v_j:

$$v_j := x$$

- In case $p_j = w(x)$, in which the j-th step of a given transaction is a write step, a possibly new value, computed by the respective program, is written into x. Each value written by a transaction t potentially depends on the values of *all* data items that t has previously read, which is formally expressed as follows:

*"Semantics":
interpretation of
a transaction*

$$x := f_j(v_{j_1}, \ldots, v_{j_k})$$

(x is the return value of an arbitrary but unknown function f_j) such that:

$$\{j_1, \ldots, j_k\} = \{j_r \mid p_{j_r} \text{ is a read step} \wedge j_r < j\}$$

(All values v_{j_r}, $1 \leq r \leq k$, that were read prior to the j-th step of t are used as parameters in function f_j.)

As an example, consider the following transaction:

$$t = r(x)r(y)r(z)w(u)w(x)$$

Here we have $p_1 = r(x)$, $p_2 = r(y)$, $p_3 = r(z)$, $p_4 = w(u)$, and $p_5 = w(x)$. The first three steps assign values (those of data items x, y, and z) to variables v_1, v_2, and v_3, respectively. The values of u and x written by the last two steps depend on these variables, in principle as follows:

$$u = f_4(v_1, v_2, v_3)$$
$$x = f_5(v_1, v_2, v_3)$$

We mention here that the view of a transaction as a *sequence* of steps is a simplification, but not an essential part of the model. Indeed, from a conceptual point of view we do not even have to order *all* steps of a transaction in a straight-line fashion, and it will often be the case that the specific order in which two or more steps are executed does not matter, as long as the ACID principle applies. Also, we should strive to capture a parallelized transaction execution (i.e., on a multiprocessor) as well. Therefore, we can relax the total ordering requirement to the steps of a transaction to a partial ordering and generally modify the previous definition as shown below. For the sake of completeness, we define partial orders first:

Partial order

DEFINITION 2.1   *Partial Order*

Let A be an arbitrary set. A relation $R \subseteq A \times A$ is a *partial order* on A if the following conditions hold for all elements $a, b, c \in A$:

1. $(a, a) \in R$ (reflexivity)
2. $(a, b) \in R \wedge (b, a) \in R \;\Rightarrow\; a = b$ (antisymmetry)
3. $(a, b) \in R \wedge (b, c) \in R \;\Rightarrow\; (a, c) \in R$ (transitivity)

As is well known from mathematics, any relation R over a finite set A (and hence a partial order) can be visualized through a graph in which the elements of A form the nodes, and in which a pair $(a, b) \in R$ is represented by a directed edge of the form $a \to b$. Examples of partial orders appear in Exercises 1 and 2 of this chapter. Note that a total order R of A is a partial order with the additional requirement that for any two distinct $a, b \in A$, either $(a, b) \in R$ or $(b, a) \in R$.

We now exploit the notion of a partial order in the context of transactions.

Page model (read/write) transaction

DEFINITION 2.2   *Page Model Transaction*

A *transaction* t is a partial order of steps (actions) of the form $r(x)$ or $w(x)$, where $x \in D$, and reads and writes as well as multiple writes applied to the same data item are ordered. More formally, a transaction is a pair

$$t = (\text{op}, <)$$

where op is a finite set of steps of the form $r(x)$ or $w(x)$, $x \in D$, and $< \subseteq \text{op} \times \text{op}$ is a partial order on set op for which the following holds: if $\{p, q\} \subseteq \text{op}$ such that p and q both access the same data item and at least one of them is a write step, then $p < q \vee q < p$.

Therefore, in the partial ordering of a transaction's steps, we disallow that a read and write operation on the same data item, or two write operations on the same data item, are unordered. Instead, for each of these two types of action pairs we require an ordering. The reason for this restriction is fairly obvious: with unordered steps of these kinds it would be impossible to tell the exact effect on the respective data item. For example, if we left a read and a write unordered, the value that is read would remain inherently ambiguous; it could be the one before the write or the new value that is written. So the constraints in the above definition serve to ensure an unambiguous interpretation.

In what follows we will generally try to stick to the latter definition (partial orders), and it should be clear that with "conflicting" steps inside a transaction being ordered, the semantics we have introduced for totally ordered transactions carries over to partially ordered ones as well. However, partial orders require considerable effort in some of our formal notation to be introduced in the next chapter (e.g., the so-called shuffle product, which shuffles the steps of multiple transactions into a concurrent execution). Therefore, we will simplify some of the discussion of correctness criteria in Chapter 3 (and elsewhere) by sticking to total orders. Once we have arrived at a standard notion of correctness that we will use for the remaining exposition, we will generalize our notation to partial orders of steps.

Although we will in the sequel consider read/write transactions as syntactic entities only (with the pseudosemantics just sketched), it may be considered as a certain advantage of this model and its theory to be discussed shortly that this theory can be developed in the absence of semantic information and hence can be used for every possible interpretation of the transactions. Thus, the read/write page model is fairly general despite its simple structure.

The page model as described above allows a transaction to read or write the same data item more than once, as is the case in the example

$$t = r(x)w(x)r(y)r(x)w(x)$$

Here t reads and writes x twice, although it is reasonable to assume that the value of x remains available, after having been read the first time, in the local variables of the underlying program for as long as it is needed by t, and that only the last write step determines the final value of x produced by this transaction. To exclude redundancies of this kind, we henceforth make the following assumptions:

- in each transaction each data item is read or written at most once,
- no data item is read (again) after it has been written.

Notice that the latter condition does not exclude the possibility of a *blind write*, which is a write step on a data item that is not preceded by a read of that data item.

2.4 **The Object Model**

This section introduces the *object model* as an alternative to or generalization of the page model. The reason why we explicitly separate this model from the page model, although the latter is implicitly included here, is that many important foundational issues and also basic algorithms and implementation techniques can be more easily understood in the simpler page model first. The object model provides a framework for representing method invocations, or *operations* for short, on arbitrary kinds of objects. This will later allow us to exploit some semantic properties of the invoked operations for the sake of improved performance. In addition, the object model can capture cases where an operation on an object invokes other operations on the same or other objects. Indeed, often the implementation of an object and its operations requires calling operations of some lower-level types of objects.

For example, operations at the access layer of a database system, such as index searches, need to invoke page-oriented operations at the storage layer underneath. Similar invocation hierarchies may exist among a collection of business objects that are made available as abstract data type (ADT) instances within a data server or an application server, for example, a Bank account object type along with operations like Deposit, Withdraw, Get_Balance, Get_History, Compute_Interests, and so on. Figures 2.1 and 2.2 depict two examples of transaction executions against such object model scenarios.

Database system layers example

Figure 2.1 shows a transaction, labeled t_1, which performs, during its execution, (1) an SQL Select command to retrieve, say, all records from a database of persons who live in Austin (i.e., whose City attribute has the value "Austin") and, after inspecting the result set, (2) an SQL command to insert a record for a new person who happens to live in Austin, too. Since SQL commands are already translated into operations at the query processing layer at compile time (see Section 1.5 for a short primer on such database system issues), the operations invoked at run time are those of the query processing layer. Because of the extremely simple nature of the example's SQL commands, the resulting operations are also very simple, and already partly resemble operations at the access layer (i.e., operations of the layer onto which the query processing layer translates its operations). We assume that the Select command is executed by first issuing a Search operation on an index that returns the RIDs (addresses) of the result records. Next, these records, which we refer to as x and y in the figure,

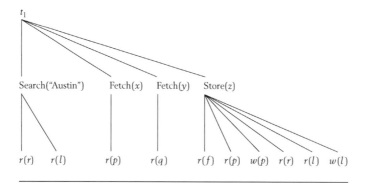

Figure 2.1 Sample scenario for the object model: database system internal layers.

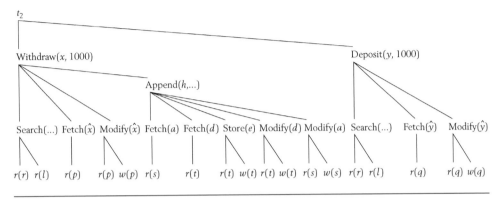

Figure 2.2 Sample scenario for the object model: business objects.

are fetched by dereferencing their RIDs. The Search operation in turn invokes operations at the underlying storage layer, that is, read and write operations on pages. Here we assume that first the root of a B^+ tree is read, labeled as page r in the figure, and then we are pointed to a leaf page, labeled l, that contains the relevant RID list for the search key "Austin." (So, for simplicity, we assume that the B^+ tree has height 2.) The subsequent Fetch operations to access the two result records x and y by their RIDs require only one page access each to pages p and q, respectively. Finally, the SQL Insert command is executed at the query processing layer as a Store operation, storing the new record and also maintaining the index on the City attribute (assuming no other indexes are defined for the underlying table). This involves first reading a storage layer metadata page, labeled f, that holds free space information in order to find a page p with sufficient empty space. Then that page is read and subsequently written after the new record z has been placed in the page. The last thing to do on behalf of the Store operation is to add the RID of the new record z to the RID list of the key "Austin" in the City index; this requires reading the B^+ tree root page r, reading the proper leaf page l, and finally, writing page l after the addition of the new RID.

In Figure 2.1, this entire execution is represented in a graphical, compact form, by connecting the calling operation and the called operation with an edge when operations invoke other operations. As a convention, the caller is always placed closer to the top of the picture than the callee. Furthermore, we represent the order in which operations are invoked by placing them in "chronological" order from left to right. When giving a formal definition shortly, this ordering convention needs to be revised a bit, but the above statement reflects the essence.

The same approach to representing transaction executions in an object model can also be applied to collections of business objects, as shown in the second example in Figure 2.2. The example contains a transaction, labeled t_2, *Business object example* that withdraws money from one bank account x by invoking a Withdraw operation, and subsequently deposits money in another account y by means of the operation Deposit. Here x and y are instances of the object type (or ADT) Account, which provides among its interface operations the mentioned Withdraw and Deposit methods. The implementation of these operations requires calling other operations. Assuming that the implementation is on top of a database system (e.g., inside a database server that supports ADTs), most of it is straightforward and could be directly translated into a sequence of Search, Fetch, and Modify operation invocations at the query processing layer. (The code for the ADT implementation would be precompiled and accessible by the database server, too.) For the underlying storage layer, we assume that the records can be searched by an index on their AccountID attribute and that no other indexes are involved in the example. Thus, the resulting page operations are straightforward and very similar to those of Figure 2.1; to help intuition, we have even kept the labels of the previous example, such as r for a B$^+$ tree root page. To distinguish the account objects x and y from the corresponding stored records on which the Fetch operations are invoked, we label the records as $\hat{x}$ and $\hat{y}$, respectively.

A particularity of the example in Figure 2.2 is that the Withdraw operation also invokes another business object method, labeled Append, in addition to the operations of the database system's query processing layer. This Append operation belongs to an object h of type History, which can be viewed as a specialized way of capturing the recent cash flow history of the bank account. For example, the last 20 cash flows, or all cash flows of the last 30 days, could be kept in a small history queue and this information made accessible by additional Get_History or Browse_History methods. The specific semantics of purging expired entries from the history queue would be built into the object, and this is why it makes sense to encapsulate the history data as an ADT object. In the transaction execution of Figure 2.2, the invoked Append operation is assumed to fetch a header record a (on page s) that contains pointers to the head and tail of the history queue, assuming that the implementation uses a doubly linked list of records. Adding an entry at the tail of the queue would then find the page t with the currently most recent entry, record d. If this page has sufficient empty space for the new record, then this is where the new entry could be placed as record e. Storing the new entry and changing the linked list to connect the previously last entry with the new one results in further write operations on page t. Finally, the queue's header record a in page s needs to be updated to point to the new tail.

Transactions as trees   The two examples and especially their graphical depiction already suggest a definition that essentially views transactions as trees with the invoked operations as tree nodes. However, to ensure that such trees are sufficiently self-contained in that they reflect all relevant aspects of the transaction execution and allow us to reason rigorously about concurrency between transactions, we require that the leaf nodes of a transaction tree be elementary operations in the sense of the page model. So all tree leaves must be read and write operations on pages, or some other notion of abstract operations for which we can safely assume that each operation is indivisible. At this point, we only know about page operations having this property, at least with regard to concurrency effects. Thus, for the time being, you can always associate page operations with the leaves of a transaction tree. If all or some leaf nodes of a given transaction tree do not correspond to page operations, all we have to do is to further expand the operations at these leaves by making their invoked operations explicit at lower implementation levels until we end up with elementary read or write operations on pages. Note that this kind of expansion is always possible, as all forms of data servers eventually store their (permanent) data items in pages (also known as blocks). Further note that the expansion is a dynamic one that tracks all operations invoked during the execution of a higher-level operation, as opposed to a hierarchy derived from the static structure of the operation's code.

Analogously to the introduction of the page model, we still have to make some amendments to the above considerations, to capture the ordering of operations within a transaction. A simple definition would require a sequential ordering of all leaf nodes, matching their left-to-right order in the example figures. However, as in the page model, there are good reasons to require only a partial ordering among the leaf node operations. An additional constraint that arises from the requirement that leaf nodes be elementary page model operations is to enforce the ordering of operation pairs where one or both of the two operations is a write. As in the page model, the argument for this constraint is to ensure an unambiguous interpretation of the transaction.

We are now ready to give the following formal definition of an object model transaction.

DEFINITION 2.3 *Object Model Transaction*

A *transaction t* is a (finite) tree of labeled nodes with

- the transaction identifier as the label of the root node,
- the names and parameters of invoked operations as labels of inner (i.e., nonleaf, nonroot) nodes,
- page model read/write operations as labels of leaf nodes,

along with a partial order "$<$" on the leaf nodes such that for all leaf node operations p and q with p of the form $w(x)$ and q of the form $r(x)$ or $w(x)$ or vice versa, we have $p < q \ \lor \ q < p$.

Object model transaction

Given this tree-based definition, we will from now on use standard terminology for trees to refer to, for example, children, descendants, subtrees, ancestors, siblings, and so on. Note that the definition allows for arbitrary types of operations as inner nodes and that it contains Definition 2.2 as a special case, that is, the object model generalizes the page model. These can be operations on an ADT object or some less stringent, but explicitly specified, form of operational interface (e.g., the interface operations of a database system's query processing layer). Further note that transaction trees do not have to be balanced in the sense that all leaf nodes have the same distance from the root. In Figure 2.2, for example, the leaf node descendants under the Append operation are farther away from the root than those of the Modify operation, although these two inner nodes are at the same tree level as seen from the root. For clarity, however, we will usually attempt to place operations that belong to the same object type(s) or interface within one level of the graphical picture of a transaction tree. This is why we have placed, in Figure 2.2, all operations of the query processing layer adjacently and have decided to let the Append operation stick out. When we later apply the object model to reason about concurrent executions, we will often deal with cases of perfectly balanced transaction trees anyway. The class of transaction trees where all leaf nodes have the same distance from the root is known by the name *layered transactions* or *multilevel transactions*—an important special case of our model.

Inner node ordering
A specific point in our formal definition that could, perhaps, strike you as an accidental omission is that a partial order is defined only for the leaf nodes of the tree. So you may wonder why no ordering has been defined for inner nodes. The answer is that such an ordering is already implicitly defined, and we wanted to keep the definition as concise as possible and avoid producing an overspecification. Namely, for two inner node operations a and b, we say that a precedes b in the execution order if all leaf node descendants of a precede all leaf node descendants of b in the partial order $<$ of the leaf nodes. In other words, we consider a as preceding b only if a terminates its execution before b begins; this is what ensures the required ordering between the two sets of leaf node descendants. Otherwise, we would consider a and b as concurrent operations; and this is a feasible viewpoint as none of them is assumed to be indivisible. If we want to find out their resulting effects on the permanently stored data, we can resort to checking the interleaving of their children and further descendants until we arrive at the leaf nodes whose ordering ensures an unambiguous interpretation.

To conclude this section, we give a brief outlook on how we will later use the introduced object model in laying a foundation for and reasoning about advanced concurrency control algorithms. Once we consider multiple transactions that execute in a concurrent or parallel way, all we have to do is to form the union of the involved transaction trees—that is, a forest of operations—and inspect the partial execution order of leaf node operations (and the implicitly derived order for higher-level operations). The difference from the single transaction case is that the partial order will then be defined on the union of the leaf nodes of all involved trees. Because of the derivation of the inner node ordering from the leaf node order, this approach will allow us to study not only the interleavings at the leaf node level but also concurrency or sequential orderings among higher-level operations. This ability to reason about concurrency at different tree levels is indeed needed to properly exploit the object model for the sake of better performance. The key to such performance enhancements lies in taking into consideration semantic properties of the higher-level, inner node operations.

By far the most important one of such properties is the commutativity or noncommutativity of two operations. For example, two Deposit operations on the same bank account are commutative in that both of the two possible sequential execution orders lead to identical results in terms of the resulting state of the data and the return parameters of the invoked operations, assuming that a Deposit operation does not return the current balance of the account. Two Withdraw operations on the same account, however, do not generally commute because their ordering may be relevant if only the first withdrawal succeeds and the second one is refused due to overdraft protection. In this situation the two possible sequential orderings would result in different return values (i.e., indicators of the withdrawal's success) and could also lead to different final states of the account balance. The point about commutativity or noncommutativity is that these considerations hold for pairs of operations from the same as well as different transactions, so that we can also apply commutativity-based reasoning to concurrent executions of multiple transactions. It will be seen later that commutative operations allow us to tolerate interleaved access patterns that would have to be disallowed if we only knew that the operations read and write the same data item.

2.5 **Road Map of the Book**

In this chapter and the previous one, we have set the stage for a discussion of numerous issues related to transactions, and we are now ready to lay out a road map of this book. Thus, in this section we explain how the book is organized to provide guidance if you are mostly interested in specific topics.

Following this first part on background and motivation, the core of the book is divided into three main parts. As discussed in the previous sections, the two subsystems of a data server that are central to a transactional information system are the concurrency control and the recovery components. The second and third parts of the book are devoted to these two components, mostly from a single server's point of view. The book's fourth part then broadens the view and addresses the additional issues of distributed transaction coordination across multiple servers, based on the foundation laid by the two parts on single server techniques. Together these three main parts provide a comprehensive, in-depth understanding of how transactional information systems work, covering formal models, practical algorithms, and performance considerations for the various components and also the interdependencies among components. After all this technical material, the book concludes with an outlook on future technology and application trends. In the following we briefly outline the contents of the chapters that constitute the three main parts.

Part II: concurrency control

Part II of the book starts out in Chapter 3 with a thorough look at what transactional isolation means. This chapter introduces formal correctness criteria for the concurrent execution of transactions, most importantly the notion of serializability, and thus defines precisely the requirements that we pose on a concurrency control algorithm. It is based on the simplifying assumption that transactions are executed in a failure-free environment, so that there is not (yet) a need to handle transaction aborts. For faster progress on the algorithmic material, this chapter is based on the simpler page model and postpones the analogous discussion on the richer object model until a later chapter. Chapter 4 then presents the most important classes of concurrency control algorithms and shows their correctness in terms of satisfying the serializability criterion of Chapter 3. Chapter 5 extends the algorithmic discussion to a class of algorithms known as multiversion concurrency control, which is more powerful in that it enhances the concurrency among transactions but is also more complex and requires more system resources.

Both Chapters 4 and 5 are based on the page model. The thorough discussion of page-oriented concurrency control sets the stage for the next step, where transactions are reconsidered within the object model. In fact, we will show that many considerations of the page model, both of correctness criteria and algorithms, are extremely useful for object-based concurrency control techniques as well. Chapter 6 is the analog of Chapter 3, discussing formal correctness criteria that can be seen as generalizations of those of the page model. Chapter 7 then presents object-based concurrency control algorithms, largely building on basic techniques already introduced for the page model. Chapter 7 also explains in great detail the major advantage of object-based concurrency control, namely, the enhanced concurrency and resulting performance gains obtained by considering the semantics of the transactions' invoked operations. The presented techniques up to this point are as general as possible and applicable to all kinds of objects and object methods. The next two chapters specialize the object-based approach to two specific settings that are of high practical importance, deriving specific solutions that offer additional performance advantages. Chapter 8 develops techniques for various forms of high-level methods provided by the relational data model, particularly predicate-oriented retrieval and update operations. Chapter 9 is further specialized to the interface and internal operations provided by index structures, most notably, B^+ trees and similar structures. Although these considerations may appear to be of an extremely special nature, they are among the most important ones for the efficiency of a database system. The entire part on concurrency control is concluded in Chapter 10 with a closer look into implementation issues and various pragmatic concerns such as tuning options.

Part III of the book is organized by addressing different classes of failures, mostly in increasing order of potential damage and difficulty to handle. Chapter 11 considers transaction failures, where only a single process or thread behaves abnormally (at the client or server), and thus at most one active transaction is affected by the failure. The major problem to be addressed in this case is that such an abnormal, to-be-aborted transaction does not affect any of the concurrently executing transactions that should make regular progress. Chapter 11 provides the solutions to this problem, in terms of defining correctness criteria and developing practical algorithms, for both the page model and the object model. Chapter 12 then considers a more severe class of failures, namely, crashes of the entire server caused, for example, by failures of the underlying database system or operating system software or by transient hardware failures. This case, which requires crash recovery actions for all in-progress transactions and the server's data, is the most challenging as far as efficient algorithms are concerned. Therefore, after defining the appropriate notion of correctness in Chapter 12, we first limit the discussion to the page model, and develop detailed algorithms for page-oriented crash recovery in Chapter 13. Chapter 14 then extends our algorithmic and performance considerations to the object model. Similar to the concurrency control part, we can reuse many basic techniques from the page model here, but still need a number of additional steps toward a practically viable solution. Also, a number of specific settings, for example, the recovery of index structures, are covered in Chapter 15. At the next stage, Chapter 16 considers failure cases where permanent data becomes corrupted—for example, by a disk failure—and presents media recovery techniques for guarding the data and its consistency against such failures by means of appropriate redundancy. These techniques build directly upon the algorithms for crash recovery, and will also be extended to provide a form of disaster recovery for cases such as fire or flood that may affect entire buildings but leave remote computer sites intact. The focus in Chapters 11 through 16 is to ensure that the server's data remains consistent while disregarding the possible inconvenience of manually restarting the applications after a failure. Chapter 17 addresses this "missing link" toward zero outage, highly available information systems by presenting advanced techniques for application recovery. This final stage of recovery methods aims to mask all sorts of failures from the human users and requires additional considerations to recover the state of application processes and communication sessions.

Part III: recovery

The techniques derived in Parts II and III allow us to build and operate a single server with transactional guarantees. With multiple servers in a distributed or federated system, an obvious thing to do is simply to instantiate the single server concurrency control and recovery components in each of the servers. Indeed, we will see in Part IV that the single server techniques still do most of the job for distributed transactions as well. However, we do need some additional techniques to coordinate and possibly reconcile the effects and outcome of distributed transactions on the involved servers. The theoretical foundation

Part IV: coordination of distributed transactions

and algorithmic solutions for the required kind of coordination are presented in Chapter 18 for the concurrency control aspects, establishing a notion of global serializability based on the local serializability and other properties of the executions in the various servers. In Chapter 19 we will then discuss the extensions needed for the recovery of one or multiple servers after various kinds of failures in a distributed environment. The key addition to the local recovery algorithms is the introduction of a distributed commit protocol to guarantee global atomicity.

2.6 **Lessons Learned**

This book is largely about algorithms for the two key building blocks of transactional information systems—concurrency control and recovery. The challenge lies in the *performance* of concurrency control and recovery components: providing high concurrency, high throughput, and fast response times, and ensuring fast recovery from failures and thus high availability with low overhead during normal operation. To address these issues in a systematic manner that combines algorithms with correctness arguments and efficiency considerations, we have introduced two computational models: the page model as the simplest basis and the richer but also more complex object model. These models allow us to develop a theory and the truly fundamental concepts and techniques of our subject in an abstract and concise manner, without getting lost in the plethora of details of real-life systems. However, following Einstein's quote that "nothing is as practical as a good theory," we will also exploit our abstract basis for deriving concrete algorithms and practically viable, systems-oriented solutions.

Exercises

2.1 Consider a finite alphabet Σ and the set Σ^* of all words over Σ. For $v, w \in \Sigma^*$ define the *prefix order* "$\leq$" by $v \leq w$ if v is a prefix of w. Show that "$\leq$" is a partial order on Σ^*.

2.2 Consider an arbitrary (finite) set M as well as its powerset $\mathcal{P}(M)$, i.e., the set of all subsets of M. Show that $subs \subseteq \mathcal{P}(M) \times \mathcal{P}(M)$, defined by $(M_1, M_2) \in subs$ if $M_1 \subseteq M_2$, is a partial order on $\mathcal{P}(M)$.

2.3 Consider the following read/write page model transaction:

$$t = r(x)r(y)r(z)w(u)w(x)r(v)w(y)w(v)$$

Describe the interpretation of t from an informal as well as from a formal point of view.

2.4 Redo Exercise 2.3 for

$$t = r(x)r(y)r(z)r(u)r(v)$$

2.5 Redo Exercise 2.3 for

$$t = w(x)w(y)w(z)w(u)w(v)$$

2.6 In the literature, the following variations of the read/write page model can be found:

- "No Blind Writes" model: Each transaction writing a data item x must have read x previously.
- "Two-Step" model: All read steps of a transaction occur prior to all write steps.
- "Action" model: Each step of a transaction represents an atomic execution of a read step followed by a write step of the same data item; thus, distinguishing reads from writes is no longer necessary.

Discuss the interpretation of a transaction along the lines of what has been introduced in this chapter for each of these models. What, if any, are the differences in interpretation to the standard read/write model?

Bibliographic Notes

The methodology for devising a transaction model as described in Section 2.2 essentially follows Vossen (1995). The major credit for the (read/write) page model of transactions belongs to the 1998 Turing Award winner Jim Gray; see, especially, Gray (1978, 1981) and Eswaran et al. (1976). Closely related notions of atomic actions have been discussed by other authors at around the same time, including Lampson (1981) and Lomet (1977). The page model transaction concept became the subject of intensive theoretical studies, in particular in the work of Christos Papadimitriou and, independently, Philip Bernstein et al. around 1980; see, for example, Papadimitriou (1979, 1986) as well as Bernstein et al. (1979, 1987). The object model of transactions, on the other hand, has been around for almost two decades, albeit in a rather vague, implicit form, going back to the work of Bjork (1973) and Davies (1973) on "spheres of control," which could be viewed as a form of nested method invocations and thus invocation trees. The first work that made the object model explicit and gave formal definitions is by Beeri et al. (1983, 1989). Parallel work on the special case of multilevel transactions has been done by Moss et al. (1986), Weikum and Schek (1984), and Weikum (1986a, 1986b, 1991).

PART TWO

Concurrency Control

CHAPTER THREE

Concurrency Control: Notions of Correctness for the Page Model

> Nothing is as practical as a good theory.
> —*Albert Einstein*

> If you don't make mistakes, you're not working on hard enough problems. And that's a big mistake.
> —*Frank Wilczek*

3.1 Goal and Overview

In this chapter we concentrate on the page model of transactions and develop notions of correctness for their concurrent execution. This study will reveal a variety of aspects: techniques for proving concurrency control algorithms, syntactic versus semantic notions of correctness, NP completeness results, and hierarchies of classes of correct histories, to mention just a few. Several of the notions presented in this chapter will later be reused in the context of other models; more importantly, the *approach* of developing correctness criteria, which is based on establishing a relationship between concurrent and serial executions, has very few competitors. Indeed, although essentially invented more than 20 years ago, it is even relevant for studies done in recent years, and is often the starting point for novel developments and revisited viewpoints.

We will first model an execution of multiple transactions that is interleaved over time and thus concurrent by the notions of schedules and histories. For these notions two points will be important. First, executing transactions is a highly dynamic situation in reality; therefore, modeling this adequately might not be as easy as it may seem. In fact, the concurrency control component of a data server needs to be ready to decide instantly on the execution of a newly arriving transaction, and needs to synchronize it correctly with already running transactions. The technical tool will be to consider *prefixes* of histories, now called schedules. Second, we need to take into account that some transactions might not terminate successfully, but can be aborted (for reasons to be discussed later). For this purpose, we will follow common practice and introduce termination operations in addition to data operations that serve to terminate a transaction by either a Commit operation or an Abort operation. However, the formal treatment, especially of aborts, can easily become counterintuitive (see the Bibliographic Notes for this chapter), which is why our formal exposition will mostly assume a failure-free environment.

We will take these techniques through a variety of notions of correctness, so you can become familiar with them and study how to apply them in distinct settings. Before doing so, we lay the groundwork for the correctness discussion by covering some prominent synchronization problems.

3.2 Canonical Concurrency Problems

Before we embark on a formal discussion of correctness in the page model of transactions, we will show by way of examples that the model captures a variety of the most important patterns of concurrency problems. To this end, we consider three archetypical "conflicts" that may arise between the read and write operations of distinct transactions in the absence of proper concurrency control measures.

EXAMPLE 3.1

The following problem is known as the *lost-update problem*. Consider two transactions t_1 and t_2, which are concurrently executed as follows:

t_1	Time	t_2
	/* $x = 100$ */	
$r(x)$	1	
	2	$r(x)$
/* update $x := x + 30$ */	3	
	4	/* update $x := x + 20$ */
$w(x)$	5	
	/* $x = 130$ */	
	6	$w(x)$
	/* $x = 120$ */	

↑
update "lost"

Lost-update problem

We suppose that x is a numerical data item having a value of 100 at time 1. Both t_1 and t_2 read this value into local variables and modify the value in their local variables, and then each of the two writes back its local value into the shared data item. For simpler notation, we do not show the local variables of the processes explicitly, and rather refer to them by the name x

in their local assignments. Assume that t_1 adds 20, while t_2 adds 30. So in the end x should have a value of 150. However, since t_2 is the last one to overwrite the original value of x, the final value is 120, which is incorrect. Indeed, because t_1 writes its new value back into the database before t_2 does, the former update is lost.

Notice that it is irrelevant in the previous example what the two processes do with data item x once it has been transferred into their local variables; the important point is the uncontrolled overwriting of the first transaction's result by the second after the concurrent modifications of the local variables. For exactly this reason, we could afford a somewhat loose notation, without explicit names for the local variables. The essence of the problem really is the pattern of interleaved read and write operations:

$$r_1(x)r_2(x)w_1(x)w_2(x)$$

with time proceeding from left to right.

Such problems do not necessarily have to involve two "writers," as the following example with one read-only transaction shows.

EXAMPLE 3.2

This problem is known as the *inconsistent-read problem*. Consider two data items x and y of type Integer, with current values $x = y = 50$; so $x + y = 100$. This could arise in a banking application, where the data items represent account balances. For transfers among the accounts, their sum should obviously remain constant. Transaction t_1, below, computes the current sum, while transaction t_2 transfers a value of 10 from x to y as follows:

Inconsistent-read problem

t_1	Time	t_2
	1	$r(x)$
	2	/* $x := x - 10$ */
	3	$w(x)$
/* sum := 0 */	4	
$r(x)$	5	
$r(y)$	6	
/* sum := sum + x */	7	
/* sum := sum + y */	8	
	9	$r(y)$
	10	/* $y := y + 10$ */
	11	$w(y)$

Clearly, t_1 will return 90 as a result, which is wrong; however, this error cannot be easily recognized by the user who may thus be misguided in some follow-up real-world actions. Again, the essence of the problem is the pattern of interleaved read and write operations:

$$r_2(x)w_2(x)r_1(x)r_1(y)r_2(y)w_2(y)$$

These two simple examples already give rise to two important observations:

- in both cases, the effects are unwanted, although in principle they are not visible to the outside world;
- a *serial* execution of the two transactions, that is, an execution in which one transaction is executed completely before the other (either t_1 before t_2, or vice versa), would have avoided the erroneous effects; this observation will be used later to design a first correctness criterion.

Next we take a look at a problem in which one of the transactions fails, and the transaction-specific rollback option is exerted (e.g., by the data server or by the transaction itself issuing an abort request), thus "erasing" all effects that the process has left on the permanently stored data.

EXAMPLE 3.3

Dirty-read problem

This example is known as the *dirty-read* problem or the problem of *reading uncommitted data*. Its major point is that one transaction fails after having modified some data, which is read by a second transaction between the modification and the failure.

t_1	Time	t_2
$r(x)$	1	
/* $x := x + 100$ */	2	
$w(x)$	3	
	4	$r(x)$
	5	/* $x := x - 100$ */
failure & rollback	6	
	7	$w(x)$

When transaction t_1 fails and is rolled back after the modified value of x has been read by t_2, this puts t_2 in an inconvenient position. Because of the failure, the modified value of x is not a committed one upon which t_2 can rely. Nevertheless, this value is the only one that t_2 has read and will thus use for its own further processing, especially for computing the value that it will subsequently write back into x. For example, if x were a bank account, with an initial balance of 0 and no option for overdrafting the account (i.e., producing a negative balance), and t_1 were to deposit $100, say, in the form of a check, then t_2 would critically rely on the validity of this check and the deposit in its attempt to withdraw \$100 from this no-overdraft account. Obviously, the situation shown, where the withdrawal may eventually succeed but the deposit of the check fails, would severely damage the dependability and reputation of the bank's business. The solution would be that the value read by t_2 is rendered invalid by the rollback of t_1, and appropriate steps should be taken to prevent t_2 from depending on this invalid value.

What can be seen from the above examples is that the data accesses performed by concurrently executing programs have a potential of conflicting with each other. Therefore, some form of concurrency control is necessary, which ultimately even has to take certain failure situations into account, as shown by the dirty-read example. With transactional guarantees, however, all these anomalies should be avoided, and the outside world should always get the impression that the executing transactions are run serially, in some order.

Another important observation from the three examples is that the details of how data is manipulated within the local variables of the executing programs are mostly irrelevant. Rather it is the interleaved patterns of read and write accesses to the permanently stored data (plus the occurrence of rollbacks on the time line) that we should focus on. We will show next that these patterns will indeed guide us to a correctness criterion for concurrent transaction executions, in that we can discriminate the allowable patterns from those that could lead to anomalies.

3.3 Syntax of Histories and Schedules

Following the discussion from the previous section, an immediate requirement for a notion of correctness will be that these situations are captured and even avoided. Obviously, we will also be interested in correctness criteria that can be decided efficiently, since a *scheduler*—the heart of a concurrency control component—will have to apply them online.

As we did for transactions in the previous chapter, we first clarify the syntax of schedules. Here we try to respect the dynamic situation in two ways. First, we assume that schedules contain information on how a transaction ends. Technically, this can be either successfully or unsuccessfully. A successful end is indicated by a *termination operation* called commit (c); that is, the transaction in question ran completely and without an interruption by some failure so that the results it has produced can be made visible to other transactions and made permanent in the database. An unsuccessful end means the transaction has to be terminated prior to reaching its normal end, which will be indicated by another termination operation called abort (a). An aborted transaction should

Termination operation

not have any effect on the underlying database, which will mainly be assured by recovery procedures to be discussed in Part III. Steps of type *c* or *a* will also be called termination operations, in order to distinguish them from *data operations* of type *r* or *w* (in the page model).

Second, we will make a distinction between schedules in which the outcome of every transaction is known and schedules in which this is open for some or even all transactions. Since in reality the outcome of a set of transactions is actually known in retrospect only, we will call schedules of the former type *histories*, and will keep the term *schedule* for transaction interleavings of the second type. In other words, a history will always be complete in the sense that all operations of each transaction appear, including a termination operation for every single transaction. Note that histories in this sense are also called *complete schedules* in the literature. On the other hand, schedules will in general be prefixes of histories, in which data as well as termination operations of transactions may still be missing. We consider this adequate for capturing a dynamic scheduling situation, since a scheduler will generally know a schedule only as the operations of the various transactions arrive step-by-step, and their execution is normally launched before the scheduler has seen the entire transaction. In the ideal situation of continuously error-free operation, a schedule (and hence a history) will even become infinitely long.

Schedules vs. histories
We have mentioned in Chapter 2 that there are two ways of looking at a transaction: either as a total order of steps, in which no parallelism whatsoever occurs, or as a partial order of steps, in which some steps may occur (and hence be executed) in parallel. The same distinction is of course appropriate for schedules and histories, as we will soon discuss (e.g., in Example 3.4). We start by defining the general case (partial order), which puts as few restrictions as possible on the ordering of steps on transactions, schedules, or histories.

DEFINITION 3.1 *Schedules and Histories*

Let $T = \{t_1, \ldots, t_n\}$ be a (finite) set of transactions, where each $t_i \in T$ has the form $t_i = (op_i, <_i)$, with op_i denoting the set of operations of t_i and $<_i$ denoting their ordering, $1 \leq i \leq n$.

1. A history for T is a pair $s = (op(s), <_s)$ such that:

    (a) $op(s) \subseteq \bigcup_{i=1}^{n} op_i \cup \bigcup_{i=1}^{n} \{a_i, c_i\}$ and $\bigcup_{i=1}^{n} op_i \subseteq op(s)$, i.e., s consists of the union of the operations from the given transactions plus a termination operation, which is either a c_i (commit) or an a_i (abort), for each $t_i \in T$;

    (b) $(\forall i, 1 \leq i \leq n)$ $c_i \in op(s) \iff a_i \notin op(s)$, i.e., for each transaction, there is either a commit or an abort in s, but not both;

    (c) $\bigcup_{i=1}^{n} <_i \subseteq <_s$, i.e., all transaction orders are contained in the partial order given by s;

(d) $(\forall\, i, 1 \leq i \leq n)(\forall\, p \in \mathrm{op}_i)\ p <_s a_i$ or $p <_s c_i$, i.e., the Commit or Abort operation always appears as the last step of a transaction;

(e) every pair of operations $p, q \in \mathrm{op}(s)$ from distinct transactions that access the same data item and have at least one write operation among them is ordered in s in such a way that either $p <_s q$ or $q <_s p$.

2. A schedule is a prefix of a history.

Thus, a history (for partially ordered transactions) has to contain all operations from all transactions (a), needs a distinct termination operation for every transaction (b), preserves all orders within the transactions (c), has the termination steps as final steps in each transaction (d), and orders conflicting operations (e). Because of (a) and (b), a history is also called a complete schedule in the literature. The view that two operations that access the same data item and of which at least one is a write operation are in conflict is identical to the notion of conflict that will later be used as the basis for a notion of serializability.

Notice that a prefix of some history can also be the history itself; therefore, histories can be considered a special case of schedules, so that for most considerations that follow, it will suffice to consider some schedule to be given.

DEFINITION 3.2 *Serial History*

Serial history

A history s is *serial* if for any two transactions t_i and t_j in it, where $i \neq j$, all operations from t_i are ordered in s before all operations from t_j, or vice versa.

EXAMPLE 3.4

Consider the three transactions shown in Figure 3.1. For each transaction, shown as a directed acyclic graph (DAG), the edges exhibit the orderings of steps. Figure 3.2 shows two histories (a) and (b) for these transactions, both assuming that each transaction commits. In history (a), the operations are totally ordered as written from left to right. History (b), on the other hand, exhibits a partial order, where the dashed lines are those newly required by condition (e) in Definition 3.1(1).

Note that we often say that a step p in a schedule or history *occurs before* another step q in the same schedule, for which we write "$p < q$"; if the context of a schedule s [transaction t] needs to be expressed, we will analogously write "$p <_s q$" ["$p <_t q$"].

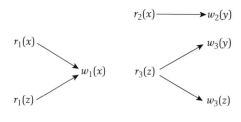

Figure 3.1 Three sample transactions.

We also note that a prefix of a partial order is essentially obtained by omitting pieces from the end of a "reachability chain." More precisely, if $s = (op(s), <_s)$, then a *prefix* of s has the form $s' = (op_{s'}, <_{s'})$ such that:

1. $op_{s'} \subseteq op(s)$
2. $<_{s'} \subseteq <_s$
3. $(\forall\ p \in op_{s'})\ (\forall q \in op(s))\quad q <_s p \Rightarrow q \in op_{s'}$
4. $(\forall\ p, q \in op_{s'})\quad p <_s q \Rightarrow p <_{s'} q$

It is easy to go from a partial order to a total order (by ordering previously unordered steps in an arbitrary way); indeed, partial orders can always be

$$r_1(x)r_2(x)r_1(z)w_1(x)w_2(y)r_3(z)w_3(y)c_1c_2w_3(z)c_3$$

(a)

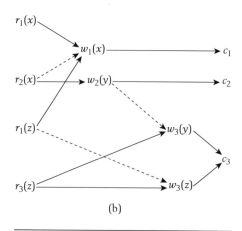

(b)

Figure 3.2 Two histories for the transactions from Figure 3.1: totally ordered (a) and partially ordered (b).

extended to a variety of total orders as special cases. For example, the history shown in Figure 3.2(a) is a totally ordered one obtained from the history shown in Figure 3.2(b) by topologically sorting the given (acyclic!) history graph.

When starting from operation sequences or totally ordered transactions, however, the appropriate technical tool to define histories and schedules is the *shuffle product*: Let $T = \{t_1, \ldots, t_n\}$ be a (finite) set of totally ordered transactions. shuffle(T) denotes the shuffle product of T, that is, the set of all sequences of steps in which each sequence $t_i \in T$ occurs as a subsequence and contains no other steps. Notice that this is the shuffle product in an automata-theoretic sense; it is well defined due to the assumption that distinct transactions do not have steps in common. Formally, the steps of a transaction t_i, $1 \leq i \leq n$, are as before equipped with the index i in an element of a shuffle product.

Shuffle product of transactions

The notion of a shuffle product allows us to derive a definition of totally ordered histories and schedules for transactions in the page model from Definition 3.1 as follows: Let $T = \{t_1, \ldots, t_n\}$ be a (finite) set of totally ordered transactions. A *history* (or complete schedule) s for T is derived from a sequence $s' \in$ shuffle(T) by adding c_i or a_i for each $t_i \in T$ according to rules (b) and (d) of Definition 3.1(1). (For simplification, we will also refer to this augmentation simply as the shuffle product.) A schedule is, as before, a prefix of a history, and a history s is serial if

Totally ordered histories and schedules

$$s = t_{\rho(1)} \ldots t_{\rho(n)}$$

holds for a permutation ρ of $\{1, \ldots, n\}$ (where it is assumed that the termination operations occur last in each transaction).

EXAMPLE 3.5

Consider the set $T = \{t_1, t_2, t_3\}$ of transactions from Example 3.4 again, which are now perceived as total orders as follows:

$$t_1 = r_1(x)r_1(z)w_1(x)$$
$$t_2 = r_2(x)w_2(y)$$
$$t_3 = r_3(z)w_3(y)w_3(z)$$

The history

$$r_1(x)r_2(x)r_1(z)w_1(x)w_2(y)r_3(z)w_3(y)c_1c_2w_3(z)c_3$$

seen earlier is a totally ordered history and has

$$r_1(x)r_2(x)r_1(z)w_1(x)w_2(y)r_3(z)w_3(y),$$
$$r_1(x)r_2(x)r_1(z)w_1(x)w_2(y), \text{ and}$$
$$r_1(x)r_2(x)r_1(z)$$

among its prefixes.

EXAMPLE 3.6

Consider the set $T = \{t_1, t_2, t_3\}$ of transactions, where

$$t_1 = r_1(x)w_1(x)r_1(y)w_1(y),$$
$$t_2 = r_2(z)w_2(x)w_2(z),$$
$$t_3 = r_3(x)r_3(y)w_3(z).$$

Then we have

$s_1 = r_1(x)r_2(z)r_3(x)w_2(x)w_1(x)r_3(y)r_1(y)w_1(y)w_2(z)w_3(z) \in \text{shuffle}(T)$;

$s_2 = s_1c_1c_2a_3$ is a history in the shuffle product of T augmented by termination steps, where s_1 denotes the sequence of page operations;

$s_3 = r_1(x)r_2(z)r_3(x)$ is a schedule;

$s_4 = s_1c_1$ is another schedule;

$s_5 = t_1c_1t_3a_3t_2c_2$ is serial.

It is not difficult to verify that the results obtained in this chapter always hold both for total as well as for partial orders. However, they are mostly easier to state for total orders, which is why we will almost without exception go with total orders, in particular when giving examples. We will point to differences where appropriate.

Instead of studying a static situation first and then transferring the results to the dynamic situation actually given in reality, we will develop the theory of serializability here directly for a dynamic setting. Therefore, we will no longer start from a "given" set T of transactions when considering schedules and histories, but we will "read off" the steps of transactions from a given schedule. To this end, we introduce the following notions, intended to ease the distinction between committed, aborted, and active transactions in a given schedule: let s be a schedule.

Transaction sets of a schedule

1. $\text{trans}(s) := \{t_i \mid s \text{ contains steps from } t_i\}$
   $\text{trans}(s)$ denotes the set of all transactions occurring partially or completely in s.

2. $\text{commit}(s) := \{t_i \in \text{trans}(s) \mid c_i \in s\}$
   $\text{commit}(s)$ denotes the set of all transactions that are committed in s.

3. $\text{abort}(s) := \{t_i \in \text{trans}(s) \mid a_i \in s\}$
   $\text{abort}(s)$ denotes the set of all transactions that are aborted in s.

4. $\text{active}(s) := \text{trans}(s) - (\text{commit}(s) \cup \text{abort}(s))$
   $\text{active}(s)$ denotes the set of all transactions that are still active in s (i.e., for which termination through commit or abort is still open).

These notations will make it easier to argue about schedules. Consider the previous example again; there we have for schedule

$$s_2 = r_1(x)r_2(z)r_3(x)w_2(x)w_1(x)r_3(y)r_1(y)w_1(y)w_2(z)w_3(z)c_1c_2a_3$$

the following transaction sets:

$$\begin{aligned}
\text{trans}(s_2) &= \{t_1, \ t_2, \ t_3\} \\
\text{commit}(s_2) &= \{t_1, \ t_2\} \\
\text{abort}(s_2) &= \{t_3\} \\
\text{active}(s_2) &= \emptyset
\end{aligned}$$

Similarly, we have for schedule

$$s_4 = r_1(x)r_2(z)r_3(x)w_2(x)w_1(x)r_3(y)r_1(y)w_1(y)w_2(z)w_3(z)c_1$$

the following transaction sets:

$$\begin{aligned}
\text{trans}(s_4) &= \{t_1, \ t_2, \ t_3\} \\
\text{commit}(s_4) &= \{t_1\} \\
\text{abort}(s_4) &= \emptyset \\
\text{active}(s_4) &= \{t_2, \ t_3\}
\end{aligned}$$

As a corollary from the definition of these notions, it should be clear that for each history s,

$$\begin{aligned}
\text{trans}(s) &= \text{commit}(s) \cup \text{abort}(s) \\
\text{active}(s) &= \emptyset
\end{aligned}$$

In general, for a schedule s the sets $\text{commit}(s)$, $\text{abort}(s)$, and $\text{active}(s)$ are pairwise disjoint and together constitute $\text{trans}(s)$. As transaction aborts will mostly be ignored in this chapter, we will almost always look at schedules s such that $\text{abort}(s) = \emptyset$.

3.4 **Correctness of Histories and Schedules**

Our next goal is to devise correctness criteria for schedules. If S denotes the set of all schedules, such a criterion can formally be considered as a mapping

$$\sigma : S \rightarrow \{0, \ 1\}$$

associating a Boolean value with each $s \in S$ (where 0 stands for "false" and 1 for "true"). Thus, *correct* schedules will be those $s \in S$ for which $\sigma(s) = 1$ holds:

$$\text{correct}(S) := \{s \in S \mid \sigma(s) = 1\}$$

A concrete criterion σ should at least meet the following requirements:

1. $\text{correct}(S) \neq \emptyset$, that is, there are at least some correct schedules in S;
2. "$s \in \text{correct}(S)$" is efficiently decidable, so it does not take a scheduler forever to determine whether what it has come up with is acceptable;
3. $\text{correct}(S)$ is "sufficiently large," so a scheduler based on the respective criteria intuitively has many possibilities to produce correct schedules for the given set of transactions. The larger the set of allowable schedules, the more concurrency will be possible, and thus better performance can be expected.

Our goal in this chapter is to provide several such criteria, under the prerequisite that the transaction semantics is not known. We will work around this by introducing a "syntactical semantics" for schedules, which will render it possible to state correctness criteria that are intuitively appropriate. However, our initial approaches will not lead to efficiently decidable criteria, so restrictions are needed. An important observation, however, is that the way to obtain another criterion will always be the same.

The fundamental idea of serializability Assuming that schedules should maintain the integrity of the underlying data (i.e., keep it consistent) and assuming that each individual transaction is able to assure this, it is reasonable to conclude (by induction) that serial histories are correct. On the other hand, for performance reasons we are not interested in serial histories, so we will only use them as a correctness measure, via an appropriately chosen *equivalence relation*. In more detail, we will do the following:

1. We define an equivalence relation "$\approx$" on the set S of all schedules. This gives rise to a decomposition of S into equivalence classes [ ] according to $\approx$:

$$[S]_\approx = \{[s]_\approx \mid s \in S\}$$

$[S]_\approx$ denotes the set of all equivalence classes according to $\approx$. Clearly, all schedules in *one* such class are pairwise equivalent, so that any schedule s can be chosen as the representative of that class.

2. According to what we said above, the interest will then be in those classes for which a serial schedule can be chosen as the representative. Elements of such a class will be called *serializable*.

Thus, we will in brief do the following:

1. define a notion of equivalence for schedules,

2. define serializability via equivalence to serial histories.

We will practice this several times in the remainder of this chapter. We will even practice the same, possibly for a different transaction model, in later chapters, the reason being the simple fact that every notion of serializability can indeed be obtained in that way.

Throughout this chapter, and also most of the material in Part II, we will largely disregard transaction aborts. Whenever it is easy to incorporate aborts at the syntactic level, we will do so, but a full account of their subtle semantics is postponed until Part III. Chapter 11 will study the effects that aborts can have on concurrent executions. So for the rest of this chapter you may assume that schedules contain only committed or active transactions. *Aborts disregarded*

3.5 **Herbrand Semantics of Schedules**

We will define equivalence between schedules via a notion of semantics. However, as we have said, this is difficult to make precise in the absence of transaction program or even application semantics. So what we will do is define a syntactical semantics that extends the interpretation of steps of a transaction, introduced in the previous chapter, to the context of a schedule. More precisely, we will first define the semantics of steps occurring in a schedule and then that of the schedule itself. In doing so, we will ignore the fact that transactions may fail, and will hence assume the following for an arbitrary schedule s:

1. a step $r_i(x) \in s$ of a transaction $t_i \in \text{trans}(s)$ reads the value written by the *last* $w_j(x) \in s$, $j \neq i$, that occurs before $r_i(x)$;

2. a step $w_i(x) \in s$ writes a new value that potentially depends on the values of all data items that t_i has read from the database or from other transactions in active$(s) \cup$ commit(s) prior to $w_i(x)$. *Idea of Herbrand semantics*

Notice that the last writer of some data item x is always well defined in a schedule or history, since situations such as

$$w_i(x) \quad \rightarrow \quad r_k(x)$$
$$\nearrow$$
$$w_j(x)$$

are disallowed by the fact that $w_i(x)$ and $w_j(x)$ must be ordered: if $w_i(x) < w_j(x)$, then $r_k(x)$ reads from $w_j(x)$; if $w_j(x) < w_i(x)$, then $r_k(x)$ reads from $w_i(x)$.

In our exposition of this chapter, we avoid problems that may result from taking aborted (or aborting) transactions into account (see Bibliographic Notes) by assuming that transactions are executed in a failure-free environment—in other words, that each and every transaction eventually commits. We will return to this discussion in particular in Part III of the book.

For the first assumption introduced above, a problem could arise from the fact that not every read step is preceded by a write step in a schedule, for example, consider

$$s = r_1(x)r_2(y)w_1(x)r_2(x)\dots$$

In order to make the result of a read operation well defined even in such cases, we will assume in what follows that every schedule has a fictitious initializing transaction t_0 in the beginning, which writes all data items referenced in the schedule (and then commits). For example, the schedule just mentioned thereby becomes

$$s = w_0(x)w_0(y)c_0r_1(x)r_2(y)w_1(x)r_2(x)\dots$$

In words, an initializing transaction defines an initial state to which a given schedule is applied. Clearly, the initializing transaction, which will always be denoted t_0, has to precede all steps from every other transaction occurring in the schedule under consideration. Most of the time, we will not show t_0 explicitly.

The problem with the informal semantics of steps in a schedule given above still is that values read or written, or functions applied, are unknown. One way out of this situation is to use a technique from mathematical logic, namely, to define a Herbrand semantics by using only uninterpreted function symbols, and nothing else.

DEFINITION 3.3 *Herbrand Semantics of Steps*

Let s be a schedule. The *Herbrand semantics* H_s of steps $r_i(x)$, $w_i(x) \in op(s)$ is recursively defined as follows:

1. $H_s(r_i(x)) := H_s(w_j(x))$, where $w_j(x)$, $j \neq i$, is the last write operation on x in s before $r_i(x)$.

2. $H_s(w_i(x)) := f_{ix}(H_s(r_i(y_1)), \dots, H_s(r_i(y_m)))$, where the $r_i(y_j)$, $1 \leq j \leq m$, represent all read operations of t_i that occur in s before $w_i(x)$, and where f_{ix} is an uninterpreted m-ary function symbol.

Note that f_{ix} as used in Definition 3.3(2) is well defined due to our general assumption that there is at most one write step on each data item per transaction. It is then easily verified that $H_s(p)$ is well defined for each data operation $p \in op(s)$. To this end, it is important that s has been extended by t_0; every write step of t_0 writing, say, data item x has not read anything before, and will hence be associated with a 0-ary function $f_{0x}()$ providing a constant (the initial value of x). Informally, the previous definition states that in a schedule a read step returns the value of the last write operation executed on behalf of an unaborted transaction. (Notice that we do not require that only the values produced by committed transactions may be read. This will be the subject of recoverability notions to be introduced in Part III.) The result of a write operation depends—in an unknown way—on the values of those data items previously read by the writing transaction.

As an example, the Herbrand semantics H_s of the steps of the schedule

$$s = w_0(x)w_0(y)c_0r_1(x)r_2(y)w_2(x)w_1(y)c_2c_1$$

is as follows, where $f_{0x}()$ and $f_{0y}()$ are 0-ary functions (constants):

$$H_s(w_0(x)) = f_{0x}()$$
$$H_s(w_0(y)) = f_{0y}()$$
$$H_s(r_1(x)) = H_s(w_0(x)) = f_{0x}()$$
$$H_s(r_2(y)) = H_s(w_0(y)) = f_{0y}()$$
$$H_s(w_2(x)) = f_{2x}(H_s(r_2(y))) = f_{2x}(f_{0y}())$$
$$H_s(w_1(y)) = f_{1y}(H_s(r_1(x))) = f_{1y}(f_{0x}())$$

The example also demonstrates the effect of an initializing transaction, which fixes initial values for all relevant data items.

Next, we will fix a Herbrand universe for transactions and, based on that, the semantics of a schedule.

DEFINITION 3.4   *Herbrand Universe*

Let $D = \{x, y, z, \ldots\}$ be a (finite) set of data items (representing the data of the underlying data server(s)). For a transaction t, let $op(t)$ denote the set of all steps of t. The *Herbrand universe HU* for transactions t_i, $i > 0$, is the smallest set of symbols satisfying the following conditions:

1. $f_{0x}() \in HU$ for each $x \in D$, where f_{0x} is a 0-ary function symbol (i.e., a constant);

2. if $w_i(x) \in op(t_i)$, $|\{r_i(y) \mid (\exists y \in D) r_i(y) <_{t_i} w_i(x)\}| = m$, and if $v_1, \ldots, v_m \in HU$, then $f_{ix}(v_1, \ldots, v_m) \in HU$, where f_{ix} is an m-ary function symbol.

Thus, the semantic domain of data operations in a schedule is a set of values from the Herbrand universe. Notice that a Herbrand universe is a purely syntactical construction that is only about symbols, and that does not say anything about the values actually read or written by the transactions in question. Now we have

Semantics of a schedule

DEFINITION 3.5 *Schedule Semantics*

The *semantics* of a schedule s is the mapping

$$H[s] : D \rightarrow HU$$

defined by

$$H[s](x) := H_s(w_i(x))$$

where $w_i(x)$ is the last operation from s writing x, for each $x \in D$.

In other words, the semantics of a schedule s is the set of values that are written last in s. Since we are considering a failure-free environment, there is no need to state that only unaborted transactions are taken into account.

As an example, let $s = w_0(x)w_0(y)c_0r_1(x)r_2(y)w_2(x)w_1(y)c_2c_1$ be as above. Then we have

$$H[s](x) = H_s(w_2(x)) = f_{2x}(f_{0y}())$$
$$H[s](y) = H_s(w_1(y)) = f_{1y}(f_{0x}())$$

The above definitions, although quite general, have the interesting side effect that they can be adapted to any concrete transaction interpretation (see Exercises 3.2 and 3.3). Clearly, the price to pay for this generality is the fact that Herbrand semantics is intricate to handle.

3.6 **Final State Serializability**

We are now in a position to define a first form of serializability, or equivalence to some serial schedule. Basically, such a notion of equivalence will make sense only for histories (i.e., for complete schedules) since the serial standard of comparison is by definition complete. (All transactions occur completely, one after the other.) We will later have to discuss the question of how to define correctness for (arbitrary) schedules that are not necessarily histories in our sense.

We start with a first notion of equivalence between schedules, which now appears near at hand:

DEFINITION 3.6   *Final State Equivalence*

Let s and s' be schedules. s and s' are called *final state equivalent*, denoted $s \approx_f s'$, if $op(s) = op(s')$ and $H[s] = H[s']$, i.e., s and s' comprise the same set of operations and have the same Herbrand semantics.

Intuitively, two schedules are final state equivalent if they result in the same final state for any given initial state. For example, consider the following pair of schedules:

$$s = r_1(x)r_2(y)w_1(y)r_3(z)w_3(z)r_2(x)w_2(z)w_1(x)$$
$$s' = r_3(z)w_3(z)r_2(y)r_2(x)w_2(z)r_1(x)w_1(y)w_1(x)$$

Notice that both schedules have the same operations and comprise active transactions only; the initializing transaction t_0 is not shown in both cases. Now we have

$$H[s](x) = H_s(w_1(x)) = f_{1x}(f_{0x}()) = H_{s'}(w_1(x)) = H[s'](x)$$
$$H[s](y) = H_s(w_1(y)) = f_{1y}(f_{0x}()) = H_{s'}(w_1(y)) = H[s'](y)$$
$$H[s](z) = H_s(w_2(z)) = f_{2z}(f_{0x}(),\ f_{0y}()) = H_{s'}(w_2(z)) = H[s'](z)$$

Thus, $s \approx_f s'$. Next consider the following two histories:

$$s = r_1(x)r_2(y)w_1(y)w_2(y)c_1c_2$$
$$s' = r_1(x)w_1(y)r_2(y)w_2(y)c_1c_2$$

Now we have

$$H[s](y) = H_s(w_2(y)) = f_{2y}(f_{0y}())$$
$$H[s'](y) = H_{s'}(w_2(y)) = f_{2y}(H_{s'}(r_2(y))) = f_{2y}(H_{s'}(w_1(y)))$$
$$= f_{2y}(f_{1y}(H_{s'}(r_1(x))))$$
$$= f_{2y}(f_{1y}(f_{0x}()))$$

Thus, $s \not\approx_f s'$. This example in particular shows that final state equivalence cannot be decided just by looking at final write operations; whatever has preceded these writes must also be taken into account. In particular, in s only the value of y is newly written (by t_2), and this new value is based on the old value of y previously read by t_2. On the other hand, in s' the value of y already written by t_1 influences the final value of y written by t_2, whereas t_1 is without effect in s.

We next formalize these observations. To this end, it is useful to assume that a history s has not only an initializing transaction t_0 in the beginning but

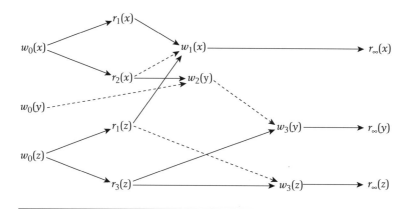

Figure 3.3 A history with an initial and a final transaction.

also a new transaction t_∞ in the end, which reads all data items mentioned in s (and then commits); that is, t_∞ reads the new state produced by s, and all steps of t_∞ occur after all other steps of s. As an example, consider the transactions shown in Figure 3.1 once more. Figure 3.3 shows the history from Figure 3.2 without commits, but completed by initializing and final transactions.

A transaction of type t_∞ does not make sense for a schedule; nevertheless, the following notions can be applied to both histories and schedules, for example, by ignoring t_∞ or by artificially adding it to a given (incomplete) schedule.

Reads-from relation

DEFINITION 3.7 *Reads-From Relation—Useful, Alive, and Dead Steps*

Let s be a schedule.

1. Let $t_j \in \text{trans}(s)$, and let $r_j(x)$ be a read operation of t_j. $r_j(x)$ *reads* x in s *from* $w_i(x)$, $j \neq i$, if $w_i(x)$ is the last write operation on x such that $w_i(x) <_s r_j(x)$.

2. The *reads-from relation* of s is defined by

$$\text{RF}(s) := \{(t_i, x, t_j) \mid \text{an } r_j(x) \text{ reads } x \text{ from a } w_i(x)\}$$

3. A step p is *directly useful* for a step q, denoted $p \to q$, if q reads from p, or if p is a read step and q a subsequent write step from the same transaction.

   Let $\overset{*}{\to}$ (*"useful"*) denote the reflexive and transitive closure of $\to$.

4. A step p is *alive* in s if it is useful for some step from t_∞, i.e.,

$$(\exists q \in t_\infty) \quad p \overset{*}{\to} q$$

and *dead* otherwise.

---

5. The *live reads-from relation* of s is defined by

$$LRF(s) := \{(t_i,\ x,\ t_j)\ | \text{an alive } r_j(x) \text{ reads } x \text{ from a } w_i(x)\}.$$

EXAMPLE 3.7

Consider again the following histories:

$$s = r_1(x)r_2(y)w_1(y)w_2(y)c_1c_2$$
$$s' = r_1(x)w_1(y)r_2(y)w_2(y)c_1c_2$$

Then we have

$$RF(s) = \{(t_0,\ x,\ t_1),\ (t_0,\ y,\ t_2),\ (t_0,\ x,\ t_\infty),\ (t_2,\ y,\ t_\infty)\}$$
$$RF(s') = \{(t_0,\ x,\ t_1),\ (t_1,\ y,\ t_2),\ (t_0,\ x,\ t_\infty),\ (t_2,\ y,\ t_\infty)\}$$

Moreover, in both s and s', $r_2(y) \to w_2(y) \to r_\infty(y)$, i.e., $r_2(y) \overset{*}{\to} r_\infty(y)$, and so $r_2(y)$ is alive.

In s', additionally $r_1(x) \to w_1(y) \to r_2(y)$ holds and hence $r_1(x) \overset{*}{\to} r_\infty(y)$, that is, $r_1(x)$ is alive. (Note that $r_1(x)$ is not alive in s.) This implies

$$LRF(s) = \{(t_0,\ y,\ t_2),\ (t_0,\ x,\ t_\infty),\ (t_2,\ y,\ t_\infty)\}$$
$$LRF(s') = \{(t_0,\ x,\ t_1),\ (t_1,\ y,\ t_2),\ (t_0,\ x,\ t_\infty),\ (t_2,\ y,\ t_\infty)\}$$

After these considerations, it should no longer come as a surprise that final state equivalence can alternatively be characterized as follows, which shows that it is easy to test:

THEOREM 3.1

Let s and s' be histories. Then

$$s \approx_f s' \quad \text{iff} \quad op(s) = op(s') \quad \text{and} \quad LRF(s) = LRF(s')$$

Proof Sketch

For a given schedule s we can construct a "step graph" $D(s) = (V, E)$ as follows:

Step graph of a schedule

$$V := op(s)$$
$$E := \{(p,q) \mid p, q \in V, p \to q\}$$

From a step graph $D(s)$ a *reduced* step graph $D_1(s)$ can be derived by dropping all vertices (and their incident edges) that represent dead steps. Then the following can be proven:

1. $\text{LRF}(s) = \text{LRF}(s')$ iff $D_1(s) = D_1(s')$;
2. $s \approx_f s'$ iff $\text{op}(s) = \text{op}(s')$ and $D_1(s) = D_1(s')$.

Clearly, this shows the theorem.

EXAMPLE 3.8

The histories

$$s = r_1(x)r_2(y)w_1(y)r_3(z)w_3(z)r_2(x)w_2(z)w_1(x)c_1c_2c_3 \quad \text{and}$$
$$s' = r_3(z)w_3(z)r_2(y)r_2(x)w_2(z)r_1(x)w_1(y)w_1(x)c_3c_2c_1$$

considered earlier have the following LRF relations:

$$\text{LRF}(s) = \{(t_0, x, t_1), (t_0, x, t_2), (t_0, y, t_2), (t_1, x, t_\infty), (t_1, y, t_\infty), (t_2, z, t_\infty)\}$$
$$\text{LRF}(s') = \{(t_0, x, t_2), (t_0, x, t_1), (t_0, y, t_2), (t_1, x, t_\infty), (t_1, y, t_\infty), (t_2, z, t_\infty)\}$$

In both histories, read steps $r_1(x)$, $r_2(y)$, and $r_2(x)$ are alive. Their step graphs $D(s)$ and $D(s')$ are shown in Figure 3.4; the corresponding reduced step graphs are obtained by omitting the circled parts. Clearly, $\text{LRF}(s) = \text{LRF}(s')$ implies $D_1(s) = D_1(s')$ and hence $s \approx_f s'$.

EXAMPLE 3.9

For the histories

$$s = r_1(x)r_2(y)w_1(y)w_2(y)c_1c_2 \quad \text{and}$$
$$s' = r_1(x)w_1(y)r_2(y)w_2(y)c_1c_2$$

from Example 3.7, the step graphs $D(s)$ and $D(s')$ are shown in Figure 3.5, where the reductions are again obtained by deleting the circled parts. Notice that in s only $r_2(y)$ is alive $((t_0, y, t_2) \in \text{LRF}(s))$; on the other hand, in s' both $r_1(x)$ and $r_2(y)$ are alive $((t_0, x, t_1), (t_1, y, t_2) \in \text{LRF}(s'))$. Therefore, $D_1(s) \neq D_1(s')$ and hence $s \not\approx_f s'$.

Notice that the step graph of a history is different from the partial order of steps in that history in general. Indeed, in the former, edges are constructed

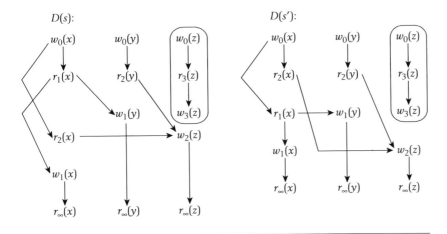

Figure 3.4 (Reduced) step graphs for Example 3.8.

for directly useful steps. For example, if

$$w_i(x) \quad \rightarrow \quad r_k(x)$$
$$\nearrow$$
$$w_j(x)$$

occurs in some given history s, the requirement to order the conflicting writes would yield either $w_i(x) <_s w_j(x)$, or vice versa. Now if $w_i(x) <_s w_j(x)$, there would be no edge from $w_i(x)$ to $r_k(x)$ in $D(s)$, since $r_k(x)$ is forced to read from $w_j(x)$.

The intuition behind a step graph of type $D_1(s)$ for a history s is to restrict the attention to alive steps when testing final state equivalence—that is, steps

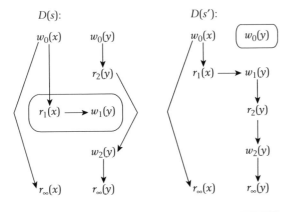

Figure 3.5 (Reduced) step graphs for Example 3.9.

that influence the final state (and hence are on a path to t_∞ in the reduced graph). In light of this interpretation, Theorem 3.1 states that $s \approx_f s'$ holds iff each read step that is alive reads a data item from the same step in both s and s'.

The following is now obvious regarding the complexity of the decision problem asking whether two given schedules are final state equivalent:

COROLLARY 3.1

Final state equivalence of two schedules s and s' can be decided in time polynomial in the length of the two schedules.

Now given a notion of equivalence, we can define our first notion of serializability:

Class FSR   **DEFINITION 3.8** *Final State Serializability*

A history s is *final state serializable* if there exists a serial history s' such that $s \approx_f s'$.

Let FSR denote the class of all final state serializable histories.

EXAMPLE 3.10

Consider $s = r_1(x)r_2(y)w_1(y)r_3(z)w_3(z)r_2(x)w_2(z)w_1(x)c_1c_2c_3$ from above. Then $s \approx_f t_3t_2t_1$, i.e., $s \in$ FSR.

The next question to ask is how membership in class FSR can be tested. Clearly, a "brute force" approach would be to apply Theorem 3.1 to a given history s and—in the worst case—all permutations of its transactions; for each such permutation s' we need to test whether $s \approx_f s'$. As we have observed, a single such test is computationally easy (see Corollary 3.1). Unfortunately, the same may not be expected for the serializability test, since for $|trans(s)| = n$ there are $n!$ permutations of the n transactions—in other words, exponentially many. This is clearly not efficient, and as we will see shortly, there is little hope that a better method exists.

3.7 View Serializability

As we have seen, FSR emphasizes steps that are alive in a schedule. However, since the semantics of a schedule and of the transactions occurring in a schedule are unknown, it is reasonable to require that in two equivalent schedules, *each* transaction reads the same values, independent of its liveliness. In this way, it would be assured that each transaction "does" the same in either schedule, or has the same "view" of the underlying data.

This is particularly important due to the fact that in applications, transactions retrieve information from a database and pass this information to their application programs, which in turn may trigger certain real-world actions such as refilling the stock of a product with low quantity on hand. So the retrieved data values are an integral part of the application programs' semantics, regardless of whether the database itself is updated or not.

The fundamental importance of this observation becomes clear when we reconsider the various types of anomalies that contribute to the need for concurrency control, specifically, the lost-update and inconsistent-read canonical examples. These examples now serve as a sanity check for the applicability of the developed theory. Obviously, the lost-update anomaly is indeed properly classified as a case of inadmissible behavior, for the schedule

Lost-update and inconsistent-read anomalies reconsidered

$$r_1(x)r_2(x)w_1(x)w_2(x)c_1c_2$$

can be shown to violate the FSR criterion. However, the inconsistent-read example reveals that FSR is still insufficient as a correctness criterion, for the schedule

$$r_2(x)w_2(x)r_1(x)r_1(y)r_2(y)w_2(y)c_1c_2$$

would be accepted under the FSR criterion (since the final state is the same as the one produced by t_2t_1) but should actually be disallowed to prevent t_1 from its inconsistent reading. The criterion to be developed next, coined *view serializability*, will prevent such inconsistent-read anomalies.

3.7.1 View Equivalence and the Resulting Correctness Criterion

We make the above intuition precise as follows:

DEFINITION 3.9 *View Equivalence*

Let s and s' be two schedules. s and s' are called *view equivalent*, denoted $s \approx_v s'$ if the following holds:

1. $op(s) = op(s')$,
2. $H[s] = H[s']$,
3. $H_s(p) = H_{s'}(p)$ for all read or write steps p.

View equivalence

Conditions (1) and (2) are just final state equivalents of s and s'. The third condition additionally requires that each data operation has the same semantics *in either schedule*. Thus, view equivalence is more restrictive than final state equivalence. View equivalence can be characterized as follows; again, this notion of equivalence is easy to test.

THEOREM 3.2

Let s and s' be schedules. The following three statements are pairwise equivalent:

1. $s \approx_v s'$
2. $D(s) = D(s')$
3. $RF(s) = RF(s')$

Proof

We here show the equivalence of (1) and (3) and leave the fact that (1) is equivalent to (2) to Exercise 3.5.

"$\Longrightarrow$:" Consider a read step $r_i(x)$ from s. Then

$$H_s(r_i(x)) = H_{s'}(r_i(x))$$

which implies that if $r_i(x)$ reads x from some step $w_j(x)$ in s, the same holds in s', and vice versa. Since $r_i(x)$ was chosen arbitrarily, it follows that $RF(s) = RF(s')$.

"$\Longleftarrow$:" If $RF(s) = RF(s')$, this in particular applies to t_∞; hence $H[s] = H[s']$.

By the same token, for all other reads $r_i(x)$ in s, we have $H_s(r_i(x)) = H_{s'}(r_i(x))$.

Next, suppose that for some $w_i(x)$, $H_s(w_i(x)) \neq H_{s'}(w_i(x))$. Thus, the set of values read by t_i prior to step $w_i(x)$ is different in s and in s', a contradiction to our assumption that $RF(s) = RF(s')$.

COROLLARY 3.2

View equivalence of two schedules can be tested in time polynomial in the number of elements in op(s).

With another notion of equivalence, another notion of serializability is now straightforward:

*View
serializability,
class VSR*

DEFINITION 3.10   *View Serializability*

A history s is *view serializable* if there exists a serial history s' such that $s \approx_v s'$.

Let VSR denote the class of all view-serializable histories.

It follows from Definition 3.9 that VSR $\subseteq$ FSR; our next theorem shows that this inclusion is strict:

THEOREM 3.3

VSR $\subset$ FSR

Proof

It suffices to consider the following history:

$$s = w_1(x)r_2(x)r_2(y)w_1(y)c_1c_2$$

s is final state equivalent to either one of the two possible serial orders, for one transaction is read-only. However, the schedule is clearly not view serializable, for both serial histories differ from s in terms of the reads-from relation.

The following theorem, stated here without proof, shows that the difference between FSR and VSR indeed lies in the treatment of steps that are alive:

THEOREM 3.4

Let s be a history without dead steps. Then $s \in$ VSR iff $s \in$ FSR.

---

*Lost update
and
inconsistent
read revisited*

Before we turn to the question of how to test membership in VSR, let us again consider from an intuitive level whether VSR is appropriate as a correctness criterion for schedules. If VSR was appropriate, it would have to "filter out" the undesirable situations we have identified for concurrently executed transactions, namely, the lost-update and inconsistent-read problems. As we have seen already, a canonical history representing a lost-update situation is

$$L = r_1(x)r_2(x)w_1(x)w_2(x)c_1c_2$$

Correspondingly, one representing an inconsistent read is

$$I = r_2(x)w_2(x)r_1(x)r_1(y)r_2(y)w_2(y)c_1c_2$$

Let us look at these histories in turn. For L, there are two possible serial orderings, $t_1 t_2$ and $t_2 t_1$. So what we have to do is compare their RF relations:

$$RF(L) = \{(t_0, x, t_1), (t_0, x, t_2), (t_2, x, t_\infty)\}$$
$$RF(t_1 t_2) = \{(t_0, x, t_1), (t_1, x, t_2), (t_2, x, t_\infty)\}$$
$$RF(t_2 t_1) = \{(t_0, x, t_2), (t_2, x, t_1), (t_1, x, t_\infty)\}$$

Since all RF relations are pairwise distinct, L does not have a view-equivalent serial history.

Next we look at history I and have the following:

$$RF(I) = \{(t_0, x, t_2), (t_0, y, t_2), (t_2, x, t_1), (t_0, y, t_1),$$
$$(t_2, x, t_\infty), (t_2, y, t_\infty)\}$$
$$RF(t_1 t_2) = \{(t_0, x, t_1), (t_0, y, t_1), (t_0, x, t_2), (t_0, y, t_2),$$
$$(t_2, x, t_\infty), (t_2, y, t_\infty)\}$$
$$RF(t_2 t_1) = \{(t_0, x, t_2), (t_0, y, t_2), (t_2, x, t_1), (t_2, y, t_1),$$
$$(t_2, x, t_\infty), (t_2, y, t_\infty)\}$$

Again, we find that the RF relations are pairwise different; hence $I \notin$ VSR, as expected.

Dirty read revisited   Regarding the third synchronization problem, the dirty-read problem, a canonical history is

$$D = r_1(x) w_1(x) r_2(x) a_1 w_2(x) c_2$$

Since we are ignoring aborted transactions for the time being, there is little we can state about D from the point of view of serializability, since if we omit the aborted t_1, D reduces to $r_2(x) w_2(x) c_2$, for which nothing is wrong so far. We take the fact that D hence seems acceptable under the VSR criterion as an indication that there is something missing in terms of correctness. We will return to this in Part III when we discuss recoverability.

3.7.2 On the Complexity of Testing View Serializability

We now consider the question of how expensive it is to test membership in VSR (and hence in FSR). Of course, the brute force approach described earlier is still applicable: test all possible serial histories for view equivalence to a given history. We will now show that most likely no significantly better approach exists:

THEOREM 3.5

The problem of deciding for a given history s whether $s \in$ VSR holds is NP complete.

In essence, *NP completeness* of a problem means that no deterministic algorithm with polynomial running time can solve the problem, unless the universally accepted, albeit unproven, hypothesis "P $\neq$ NP" were disproven.

We will not give the proof of Theorem 3.5 in full detail, since that would take us way beyond the topic of this book; however, we will give sufficient detail on how the proof proceeds. Two steps are the essence:

NP completeness of VSR testing

1. With a given history, a generalization of directed graphs—a *polygraph*—is associated; for a suitably chosen notion of acyclicity of polygraphs, it can then be shown that a history is in VSR iff its associated polygraph is acyclic. This part of the proof of Theorem 3.5 will be given below.

2. It remains to be shown that testing acyclicity of polygraphs is NP complete. To this end, we refer you to the literature cited in the Bibliographic Notes of this chapter, since this requires a variety of preparations and arguments from complexity theory that would deviate considerably from the subject under discussion here (in particular since, due to this negative complexity result, view serializability will be abandoned as a correctness criterion for transaction histories shortly).

A polygraph is a triple $P = (V, E, C)$, where (V, E) is a directed graph and $C \subseteq V \times V \times V$ is a set of *choices* such that $(u, v, w) \in C$ implies $u \neq v$, $u \neq w$, $v \neq w$, and $(w, u) \in E$. Figure 3.6 shows a sample polygraph P. In this figure, a choice of the form (u, v, w) is shown as two dashed arrows (u, v) and (v, w), which are connected by a partial circle around v. Note that the figure shows four different choices of the form (u, v, w), which we have not distinguished through indexes.

Polygraph

Now let $P = (V, E, C)$ be a polygraph, and let $G = (V, E')$ be a directed graph with the same nodes. G is called *compatible* with P if E' is a minimum set of edges with the following properties (where "minimum" refers to set inclusion):

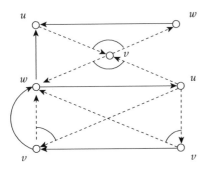

Figure 3.6 A sample polygraph P.

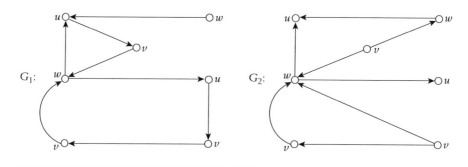

Figure 3.7 Graphs compatible with polygraph P in Figure 3.6.

1. $E \subseteq E'$, that is, the compatible graph G includes all "normal" edges of the polygraph P, and may have (and usually does have) additional edges;

2. $(\forall \ (u, v, w) \in V \times V \times V) \ (((u, v, w) \in C) \Leftrightarrow ((u, v) \in E' \lor (v, w) \in E'))$, that is, each choice of the polygraph is represented by an edge in the compatible graph G;

3. $(\forall \ (u, v, w) \in V \times V \times V) \ (((u, v) \in E' \Leftrightarrow (v, w) \notin E') \land ((u, v) \notin E' \Leftrightarrow (v, w) \in E'))$, that is, each choice is represented by exactly one edge.

In other words, a compatible G "covers" the choices of its underlying polygraph. Now a polygraph P is called *acyclic* if there exists a directed acyclic graph (DAG) G that is compatible with P.

For the sample polygraph from Figure 3.6, Figure 3.7 shows two distinct graphs G_1 and G_2 that are compatible with P (where node labels, as before, may stem from different choices). However, while G_1 is cyclic, only G_2, which is acyclic, can be used to verify that the original P is an acyclic polygraph.

Polygraph associated with a history   Our next goal is to associate a polygraph with a given history. To this end, we will assume for the remainder of this subsection that our history under consideration contains committed transactions only, and is equipped with initializing transaction t_0 and final transaction t_∞. Let s be a history such that $\text{trans}(s) = T \cup \{t_0, t_\infty\}$. The polygraph $P(s) = (V, E, C)$ associated with s is defined as follows:

1. $V = \text{trans}(s)$

2. $E = \{(t_0, t) \mid t \in T\} \cup \{(t, t_\infty) \mid t \in T\} \cup \{(t, t') \mid t'$ reads some data item from $t\}$

3. $C = \{(t', t'', t) \mid (t, t') \in E \land \ t'$ reads x from $t \land$ some $w(x)$ from t'' appears somewhere in $s\}$

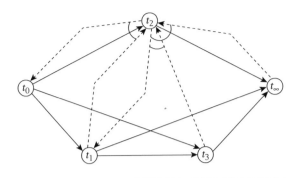

Figure 3.8 A polygraph associated with a history.

Note that condition (3) above implies that the write step of t''—call it $w''(x)$—either precedes the write step of t or follows the read step of t', for t' would not read x from t if $w''(x)$ were between $w(x)$ and $r'(x)$. The two possible orderings, either $w''(x) <_s w(x)$ or $r'(x) <_s w''(x)$, are captured by the two possible compatible edges that are derivable from the corresponding choices. As an example, consider the following history:

$$s = w_0(x)w_0(y)c_0r_1(x)w_2(y)w_1(y)c_1r_3(y)c_3w_2(x)c_2r_\infty(x)r_\infty(y)c_\infty$$

The associated polygraph $P(s)$ is shown in Figure 3.8. Notice in this figure that some of the solid edges (namely, (t_0, t_2), (t_0, t_3), and (t_3, t_∞)) are required only by (part (2) of) the definition, but are not involved in choices. Also notice that not every edge representing a reads-from relationship gives rise to a choice (e.g., (t_2, t_∞)).

LEMMA 3.1

Let s and s' be two histories for the same transactions. If $s \approx_v s'$ then $P(s) = P(s')$.

Proof

From Theorem 3.2, we know that $s \approx_v s'$ iff $D(s) = D(s')$. Now if $D(s)$ is given, the polygraph $P(s)$ can easily be derived:

1. collapse all nodes from $D(s)$ belonging to the same transaction into one node;

2. create a choice for each edge e of $D(s)$ from t to t' and each transaction $t'' \neq t, t'$ that writes the data item that gave rise to edge e.

Since $D(s) = D(s')$, it follows that $P(s) = P(s')$.

LEMMA 3.2

Let s be a history as before. If s is serial, then $P(s)$ is acyclic.

Proof

Let T be the set of transactions in s, and consider the following graph:

$$G = (T \cup \{t_0, t_\infty\}, E)$$

where

$$E = \{(t, t') \mid t, t' \in T \cup \{t_0, t_\infty\} \wedge t <_s t'\}$$

G thus has edges between any pair of nodes, and since s is assumed to be serial, G must be acyclic.

The claim now is that G is compatible with $P(s)$; if this is true, the lemma follows. First consider an edge (t, t') of $P(s)$; this edge must also be in G since it indicates that t writes a data item later read by t'. Second, consider a choice (t, t', t'') of $P(s)$, which indicates that some step p of t' writes a data item that is read by t from t''. Now we need to consider two cases:

1. If p occurs before the write step from t'' on the data item in question, then p must occur in s before all of t'', since s is serial. Thus, t' occurs in s before t'', and hence (t', t'') is an edge in G.

2. p occurs after the read step from t: now all of t' occurs after all of t in s, which means that (t, t') is in G.

The following theorem now completes what we want to show here:

THEOREM 3.6

For each history s, $s \in$ VSR iff $P(s)$ is acyclic.

Proof

(only if) Let $s \in$ VSR. Then there is some serial history s' such that $s \approx_v s'$. By Lemma 3.1, $P(s) = P(s')$; by Lemma 3.2, acyclicity of $P(s')$ implies acyclicity of $P(s)$.

(if) Let $P(s)$ be acyclic, and let G be a DAG compatible with $P(s)$. Note that in G, t_0 is a source node (i.e., a node without incoming edges) and t_∞ is a sink node (i.e., a node without outgoing edges); thus G can be completed to a total ordering G' of the transactions such that t_0 appears in the beginning and t_∞ in the end of G'. This total order can be constructed in ascending order by a procedure known as *topological sorting*. We start out by selecting a node without incoming edges (which is guaranteed to exist in a DAG); if there are several nodes with this property, we can arbitrarily select one of them. Then we remove the selected node and all its outgoing edges from the graph, which renders other nodes to become sources. This simple step is iterated until the graph becomes empty. The order in which the nodes are removed by this procedure is a total order that extends the history's given partial order.

Let s' be a serial history corresponding to G; we will show that $s \approx_v s'$. Suppose, on the contrary, some step $r(x)$ from t reads from a step $w(x)$ from t' in s, but reads from t'' in s'. Then $P(s)$ contains the choice (t, t'', t'), and G, which is compatible with $P(s)$, contains the edge (t', t); thus, $t' <_{s'} t$. On the other hand, since t reads from t'' in s', it must be the case that $t' < t''$ and $t'' < t$ in s'. Thus, G contains neither the edge (t, t'') nor the edge (t'', t'). However, $P(s)$, as we have said, contains the choice (t, t'', t'), a contradiction to compatibility.

We may therefore conclude that $D(s) = D(s')$ and hence $s \in \mathrm{VSR}$.

The crucial part is to prove the following theorem:

THEOREM 3.7

The problem of deciding whether a given polygraph is acyclic is NP complete.

As we said, we are not going to prove this here. As with every NP completeness statement, the proof has two parts: (1) Showing that the problem is in NP is easy: simply guess an "embedded" graph for a given polygraph and verify its compatibility as well as—eventually—its acyclicity. (2) To show completeness, a version of the well-known *satisfiability problem* for Boolean formulas in conjunctive normal form (generally known as SAT) can be reduced to the problem of deciding acyclicity of polygraphs, details of which are beyond the scope of this book.

The bottom line of all this is that, due to the high complexity of its recognition problem, view serializability is inappropriate as a correctness notion for practical scheduling algorithms. However, it turns out that this is not the only reason; to show at least one other, we need the following: Let s be a schedule, $T \subseteq \mathrm{trans}(s)$. $\Pi_T(s)$ denotes the *projection* of s onto T, that is, the schedule s' with operations $\mathrm{op}(s') = \mathrm{op}(s) - \bigcup_{t \notin T} \mathrm{op}(t)$ obtained by erasing from s all steps not from transactions in T. For example, if

Projection operation

$$s = w_1(x)r_2(x)w_2(y)r_1(y)w_1(y)w_3(x)w_3(y)c_1a_2$$

and $T = \{t_1, t_2\}$, then

$$\Pi_T(s) = w_1(x)r_2(x)w_2(y)r_1(y)w_1(y)c_1a_2$$

Monotonicity

DEFINITION 3.11   *Monotone Classes of Histories*

A class E of histories is called *monotone* if the following holds: if s is in E, then $\Pi_T(s)$ is in E for each $T \subseteq \text{trans}(s)$. In other words, E is closed under arbitrary projections.

Monotonicity of a history class E is a desirable property, since it preserves E under arbitrary projections. Taken the other way around, if a projection of some history s does *not* belong to a given class E in a dynamic scheduling situation, then it does not make sense to process s any further (or to extend it with additional operations).

If we now consider the class VSR for E, we can easily verify that VSR is not monotone. Indeed, all we need to exhibit is a counterexample—that is, a history $s \in$ VSR such that for some $T \subseteq \text{trans}(s)$, $\Pi_T(s) \notin$ VSR. To this end, consider

$$s = w_1(x)w_2(x)w_2(y)c_2w_1(y)c_1w_3(x)w_3(y)c_3$$

Then $s \approx_v t_1t_2t_3 \approx_v t_2t_1t_3$. Thus, $s \in$ VSR. However, $\Pi_{\{t_1, t_2\}}(s) \notin$ VSR. Intuitively, in this sample history, the last transaction t_3 "covers" whatever effects have previously been created by the (interleaved) transactions t_1 and t_2; hence, if t_3 disappears by way of a projection, the correction it brings along does not apply anymore.

So in conclusion, VSR as covered here so far is insufficient as a correctness criterion for histories, which is why further restrictions are needed, to be introduced next.

3.8 Conflict Serializability

Our next notion of serializability, *conflict serializability*, is the one that is most important for the practice of transactional information systems, in particular for building schedulers. As will be seen, it is computationally easy to test and thus differs significantly from the notions of serializability discussed so far. In addition, conflict serializability has a number of interesting theoretical properties that can justify an exploitation of this concept in practice in a variety of ways. Finally, it can be generalized to other transaction models and different data settings, as will be demonstrated in subsequent chapters.

3.8.1 **Conflict Relations**

Conflict serializability is based on a simple notion of conflict that was mentioned already in connection with partially ordered histories and is appropriate for the syntactical nature of read/write transactions:

DEFINITION 3.12 *Conflicts and Conflict Relations*   *Conflicts*

Let s be a schedule, $t, t' \in \text{trans}(s)$, $t \neq t'$:

1. Two data operations $p \in t$ and $q \in t'$ are *in conflict* in s if they access the same data item and at least one of them is a write, i.e.,

$$(p = r(x) \wedge q = w(x)) \vee (p = w(x) \wedge q = r(x)) \vee (p = w(x) \wedge q = w(x))$$

2. $\text{conf}(s) := \{(p, q) \mid p, q \text{ are in conflict in } s \text{ and } p <_s q \}$ is called the *conflict relation* of s.

Naturally, only data operations can be in conflict in a schedule; note that the conflict relation of a schedule does not take the termination status of a transaction (i.e., committed or aborted) into account. If aborted transactions were present in a given schedule s, they could, however, simply be ignored, and their conflicts with other transactions omitted from $\text{conf}(s)$. For example, if

$$s = w_1(x)r_2(x)w_2(y)r_1(y)w_1(y)w_3(x)w_3(y)c_1a_2$$

where t_1 is committed, t_2 is aborted, and t_3 is still active, we have

$$\text{conf}(s) = \{(w_1(x), w_3(x)), (r_1(y), w_3(y)), (w_1(y), w_3(y))\}$$

Now we are ready to introduce the following notion of equivalence:

DEFINITION 3.13 *Conflict Equivalence*   *Conflict equivalence*

Let s and s' be two schedules. s and s' are called *conflict equivalent*, denoted $s \approx_c s'$, if they have the same operations and the same conflict relations, i.e., if the following holds:

1. $\text{op}(s) = \text{op}(s')$ and
2. $\text{conf}(s) = \text{conf}(s')$.

Thus, two schedules are conflict equivalent if all conflicting pairs of steps from distinct transactions occur in the same order in both schedules. As an example, let

$$s = r_1(x)r_1(y)w_2(x)w_1(y)r_2(z)w_1(x)w_2(y)$$

and

$$s' = r_1(y)r_1(x)w_1(y)w_2(x)w_1(x)r_2(z)w_2(y)$$

Conflicting-step graph

Then $\mathrm{op}(s) = \mathrm{op}(s')$ and $\mathrm{conf}(s) = \mathrm{conf}(s')$; therefore, $s \approx_c s'$.

Clearly, the notion of conflict equivalence is easy to test: for two given schedules over the same set of operations, derive their conf relations and test them for equality. Similarly, to view equivalence, this can be described in terms of graphs: let s be a schedule, and let a graph $D_2(s) := (V, E)$ be defined by $V = \mathrm{op}(s)$ and $E = \mathrm{conf}(s)$. Graph $D_2(s)$ is called the *conflicting-step graph* of schedule s. Then we can prove that

$$s \approx_c s' \iff D_2(s) = D_2(s')$$

Notice that if s is given as a partially ordered schedule, $D_2(s)$ is essentially derived by considering the edges that represent intertransactional conflicts (the dashed edges in Figure 3.2(b)).

3.8.2 Class CSR

We are now ready to introduce a third notion of serializability:

Conflict serializability, class CSR

DEFINITION 3.14 *Conflict Serializability*

A history s is *conflict serializable* if there exists a serial history s' such that $s \approx_c s'$.

Let CSR denote the class of all conflict-serializable histories.

For a first example, history

$$r_1(x)r_2(x)r_1(z)w_1(x)w_2(y)r_3(z)w_3(y)c_1c_2w_3(z)c_3$$

from Figure 3.2(a) is in CSR. Next, for history $s = r_2(y)w_1(y)w_1(x)c_1w_2(x)c_2$, we have $s \notin \mathrm{CSR}$. For $s' = r_1(x)r_2(x)w_2(y)c_2w_1(x)c_1$ we find $s' \in \mathrm{CSR}$.

Lost update and inconsistent read revisited

Next let us briefly check again on the (undesirable) histories L and I seen in the lost-update and inconsistent-read examples, where

$$L = r_1(x)r_2(x)w_1(x)w_2(x)c_1c_2$$

and

$$I = r_2(x)w_2(x)r_1(x)r_1(y)r_2(y)w_2(y)c_1c_2$$

For L, we have

$$\text{conf}(L) = \{(r_1(x), w_2(x)), (r_2(x), w_1(x)), (w_1(x)w_2(x))\}$$

Now the only possible serial histories are t_1t_2, whose conflict relation would avoid the second pair of conflicting operations, and t_2t_1, whose conflict relation would comprise the second pair only. Thus, L cannot be conflict serializable. Next, for I we find

$$\text{conf}(I) = \{(w_2(x), r_1(x)), (r_1(y), w_2(y))\}$$

which again cannot be obtained from t_1t_2 or from t_2t_1. Thus, $I \notin \text{CSR}$. In other words, conflict serializability avoids lost updates and inconsistent reads.

We next clarify the relationship between class CSR and the classes of serializable histories defined earlier:

THEOREM 3.8

CSR $\subset$ VSR

Proof

The fact that CSR is a subset of VSR follows from the fact that graph $D(s)$ is uniquely determined by $D_2(s)$, provided the set of edges of $D_2(s)$ represents the conflict relation $\text{conf}(s)$ of s (in the sense of Definition 3.12).

Another way to show this is as follows: Consider an $s \in \text{CSR}$. By definition, there is a serial history s' such that $s \approx_c s'$. We show that $\text{RF}(s) = \text{RF}(s')$. Suppose this is not the case, and let (t_i, x, t_j) be in $\text{RF}(s)$, but not in $\text{RF}(s')$. Then an $r_j(x)$ reads x from some $w_i(x)$ in s (and $(w_i(x), r_j(x)) \in \text{conf}(s)$), but $r_j(x)$ reads x from some other $w_k(x)$, $k \neq i$, in s' (and $(w_k(x), r_j(x)) \in \text{conf}(s')$). Clearly, $w_i(x)$ and $w_k(x)$ are also in conflict, and we find $w_i(x) < w_k(x)$ in s', but $w_k(x) < w_i(x)$ in s, a contradiction to the fact that $s \approx_c s'$ (and hence the two histories have the same conflict relations). Therefore, $\text{RF}(s) = \text{RF}(s')$, and $s \approx_v s'$, which implies $s \in \text{VSR}$.

To see that the inclusion is strict, consider the following history:

$$s = w_1(x)w_2(x)w_2(y)c_2w_1(y)c_1w_3(x)w_3(y)c_3$$

Then $s \notin \text{CSR}$, but $s \approx_v t_1t_2t_3$, so $s \in \text{VSR}$.

COROLLARY 3.3

CSR $\subset$ VSR $\subset$ FSR

The following can also be verified:

THEOREM 3.9

1. The class CSR is monotone.

2. $s \in$ CSR $\iff$ ($\forall\, T \subseteq$ trans(s)) $\Pi_T(s) \in$ VSR (i.e., CSR is the largest monotone subset of VSR).

Conflict graph (serialization graph) of a schedule

Clearly, part (1) of this theorem is straightforward, whereas part (2) is not; we leave it to you as an admittedly challenging exercise.

The important difference between CSR and the previously introduced classes FSR and VSR now is that membership in the former can be tested efficiently. To this end, we will characterize conflict serializability in graph-theoretic terms via the *conflict graph* associated with a history; in this graph, nodes represent committed transactions, and an edge from transaction t to transaction t' indicates that there are steps $p \in t$ and $q \in t'$ such that p and q are in conflict.

As a motivation why we can test conflict serializability by using a properly defined graph, consider history

$$s = r_1(y)r_3(w)r_2(y)w_1(y)w_1(x)w_2(x)w_2(z)w_3(x)c_1c_2$$

Intuitively, s cannot be conflict equivalent to a serial history, since "$r_2(y)w_1(y)$" says "$t_2 < t_1$ in an equivalent serial history," while "$w_1(x)w_2(x)$" means "$t_1 < t_2$"; obviously, this is impossible to meet simultaneously. The conflict graph of s would represent each transaction as a node and each conflict as a (directed) edge that respects the ordering of the conflicting steps. The result would be a cycle in the graph, which indicates nonserializability.

DEFINITION 3.15 *Conflict Graph (Serialization Graph)*

Let s be a schedule. The *conflict graph*, also known as the *serialization graph*, $G(s) = (V, E)$ of s, is defined by

$$V = \text{commit}(s),$$
$$(t, t') \in E \iff t \neq t' \wedge (\exists\, p \in t)(\exists\, q \in t')\ (p, q) \in \text{conf}(s)$$

The conflict graph $G(s)$ of a schedule s thus abstracts from individual conflicts between pairs of transactions and represents multiple conflicts between

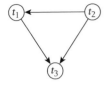

Figure 3.9 Conflict graph $G(s)$
for Example 3.11.

the same (committed) transactions by a single edge. In this sense it contains less information than the graph $D_2(s)$ defined earlier. As will be seen shortly, however, this information suffices for testing membership in CSR.

EXAMPLE 3.11

Consider

$$s = r_1(x)r_2(x)w_1(x)r_3(x)w_3(x)w_2(y)c_3c_2w_1(y)c_1$$

The conflict graph $G(s)$ is shown in Figure 3.9.

The following is widely known as the "(conflict) serializability theorem":

THEOREM 3.10

Let s be a history. Then

$$s \in \text{CSR iff } G(s)$$

is acyclic.

Proof

(only if) Let $s \in$ CSR, then there exists a serial history s' such that $op(s) = op(s')$ and $conf(s) = conf(s')$, i.e., $s \approx_c s'$. Now consider $t, t' \in V$, $t \neq t'$, with $(t, t') \in E$ for $G(s) = (V, E)$. Then we have

$$(\exists\, p \in t)(\exists\, q \in t') \quad p <_s q \quad \text{and} \quad (p, q) \in conf(s)$$

Since the conflict relations of s and s' are equal, $p <_{s'} q$. On the other hand, since s' is serial, all of t must hence occur before all of t' in s'.

Now suppose $G(s)$ were cyclic. Then there must be a cycle of the form, say, $t_1 \rightarrow t_2 \rightarrow \ldots \rightarrow t_k \rightarrow t_1$. The same cycle also exists in $G(s')$, a contradiction to the fact that s' is serial.

(if) Conversely, let $G(s) = (V, E)$, where $V = \{t_1, \ldots, t_n\}$, be acyclic. Then $G(s)$ can be topologically sorted to derive a total order of the nodes that includes partial order E; call the result $t_{\rho(1)} \cdots t_{\rho(n)} = s'$ for some permutation

ρ of $\{1, \ldots, n\}$. Clearly, s' is a serial history. We now show $s \approx_c s'$: if $p \in t$ and $q \in t'$ for $t, t' \in V$ such that $p <_s q$ and $(p, q) \in \text{conf}(s)$, then $(t, t') \in E$. It follows that t is also before t' in the topological sort of s, that is, in s'. Since p and q are still in conflict, we conclude $\text{conf}(s) \subseteq \text{conf}(s')$. Conversely, if $(p, q) \in \text{conf}(s')$ and $p \in t$, $q \in t'$, then $p <_s q$ and hence $(p, q) \in \text{conf}(s)$. Thus, $\text{conf}(s) = \text{conf}(s')$, and the theorem follows.

COROLLARY 3.4

Membership in CSR can be tested in time polynomial in the number of transactions in the given schedule.

By the serializability theorem, the latter is due to the fact that the conflict graph of a given history can be constructed in time linear in the number of operations in the history, and this graph can be tested for cycles in time that is at most quadratic in the number of nodes.

EXAMPLE 3.12

Consider the following histories:

$$s = r_1(y)r_3(w)r_2(y)w_1(y)w_1(x)w_2(x)w_2(z)w_3(x)c_1c_3c_2 \quad \text{and}$$
$$s' = r_1(x)r_2(x)w_2(y)w_1(x)c_2c_1$$

The corresponding conflict graphs $G(s)$ and $G(s')$ are shown in Figure 3.10. Since $G(s)$ contains a cycle, $s \notin \text{CSR}$; since $G(s')$ is acyclic, $s' \in \text{CSR}$.

Let us mention that "serializability theorems" in the style of Theorem 3.10 occur frequently in the literature. Indeed, generalizations of the read/write transaction model, or completely different transaction models, can also give rise to a graph-theoretic characterization of their correctness criterion (or at least of one of their criteria), so that a theorem analogous to the previous one is obtained. We will see several such theorems in the remainder of this book.

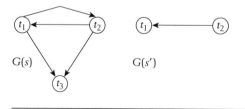

Figure 3.10 Conflict graphs for Example 3.12.

3.8.3 **Conflicts and Commutativity**

We next characterize conflict serializability in a different way. Our presentation initially considers only totally ordered schedules since these are closer to the "algebraic" nature of the following *commutativity rules* for page model data operations. In these rules "$\sim$" means that the ordered pair of actions on the left-hand side can be replaced by the right-hand side, and vice versa.

Rule C1: $r_i(x)r_j(y) \sim r_j(y)r_i(x)$ if $i \neq j$ *Commutativity*
Rule C2: $r_i(x)w_j(y) \sim w_j(y)r_i(x)$ if $i \neq j, x \neq y$ *rules*
Rule C3: $w_i(x)w_j(y) \sim w_j(y)w_i(x)$ if $i \neq j, x \neq y$

Rule C1 says that two read steps $r_i(x)$ and $r_j(y)$, $i \neq j$, which occur in a schedule in this order and are adjacent (with no other operation in between), may be commuted. Similarly, C2 says that a read and write step can be exchanged if the steps are from distinct transactions and access different data items. Finally, C3 says that two write steps can be commuted if they refer to different data items.

The commutativity rules can be applied to a given schedule or history in a stepwise fashion, as in the following example:

$$s = w_1(x)\underbrace{r_2(x)w_1(y)}\,w_1(z)\underbrace{r_3(z)w_2(y)}\,w_3(y)w_3(z)$$
$$\overset{C2}{\Rightarrow} w_1(x)w_1(y)\underbrace{r_2(x)w_1(z)}\,w_2(y)r_3(z)w_3(y)w_3(z)$$
$$\overset{C2}{\Rightarrow} w_1(x)w_1(y)w_1(z)r_2(x)w_2(y)r_3(z)w_3(y)w_3(z)$$
$$\equiv t_1 t_2 t_3$$

The above transformations have implicitly assumed that operations in a schedule are totally ordered. With partial orders, we may need an additional transformation rule as an auxiliary step for applying one of the commutativity rules. This additional rule simply states that two unordered operations can be arbitrarily ordered if they are nonconflicting. We refer to this rule as the *ordering rule*:   *Ordering rule*

Rule C4: $o_i(x),\ p_j(y)$ *unordered*

$$\leadsto o_i(x)p_j(y)\quad \text{if } x \neq y \lor (o = r \land p = r)$$

We next use the commutativity rules for introducing another relation on schedules:

DEFINITION 3.16 *Commutativity Based Equivalence*

Let s and s' be two schedules such that $op(s) = op(s')$. Define $s \sim s'$ if s' can be obtained from s by a single application of C1, C2, C3, or C4 to the steps of the schedule.

Let "$\overset{*}{\sim}$" denote the reflexive and transitive closure of "$\sim$", i.e., $s \overset{*}{\sim} s'$ if s' can be obtained from s by a finite number of applications of C1, C2, C3, and C4.

It is straightforward to verify that "$\overset{*}{\sim}$" is an equivalence relation on the set of all schedules for a given set of transactions.

THEOREM 3.11

Let s and s' be schedules such that $op(s) = op(s')$. Then

$$s \approx_c s' \text{ iff } s \overset{*}{\sim} s'$$

We leave the proof of this theorem as an exercise. A first exploitation of these commutativity rules now is that finitely many applications of the rules may transform a given history into a serial one, as in the example we have seen.

DEFINITION 3.17 *Commutativity Based Reducibility*

A history s is *commutativity based reducible* if there is a serial history s' such that $s \overset{*}{\sim} s'$, i.e., s can be transformed into s' through a finite number of allowed transformation steps according to rules C1, C2, C3, and C4.

COROLLARY 3.5

A history s is commutativity based reducible iff $s \in \text{CSR}$.

An important application of the alternative characterization of conflict equivalence given above is that it can immediately be generalized. Indeed, it is completely irrelevant to know of a schedule whether a step reads or writes or which data item it accesses, as long as we know which steps of the schedule are in conflict. The latter suffices for deciding about the correctness of the schedules, even without any knowledge about the meaning of the operations.

To see this, consider the following schedule, whose steps are not specified any further:

$$s = p_1 q_1 p_2 o_1 p_3 q_2 o_2 o_3 p_4 o_4 q_3$$

Suppose s is a schedule for transactions t_1, t_2, and t_3, and assume we know that the following pairs of steps are in conflict:

1. (q_1, p_2),
2. (p_2, o_1),
3. (q_1, o_2),
4. (o_4, q_3).

As before, we can now establish a conflict graph for this schedule (assuming that all transactions are unaborted) and then see that s is *not* conflict serializable, since that graph has a cycle involving transactions t_2 and t_3.

The important point here is that the steps of a schedule or history to which an argument like the above is applied may be of a completely different type, such as *increment* and *decrement* on a counter object, *push* and *pop* on a stack object, or *enqueue* and *dequeue* on a queue object. We will later show how to exploit this observation for coming up with notions of serializability that are based on semantic information. In essence it suffices to state a conflict or commutativity table for "new" operations and derive conflict serializability from that table.

3.8.4 Restrictions of Conflict Serializability

We next look into several restrictions of conflict serializability that are important in practical applications.

Order-Preserving Conflict Serializability

We first discuss a restriction of conflict serializability, *order-preserving* conflict serializability, which requires that transactions that do not overlap in time (i.e., that occur strictly sequentially in a given schedule) appear in the same order in a conflict-equivalent schedule.

Order preservation

EXAMPLE 3.13

Consider $s = w_1(x)r_2(x)c_2w_3(y)c_3w_1(y)c_1$. Figure 3.11 shows the conflict graph of s; since it is acyclic, it follows that $s \in$ CSR. Now observe that the equivalent serial history is $t_3t_1t_2$. However, t_2 is already committed in s before t_3 starts. This contrast between the serialization order and the actual execution order could be undesirable; for example, if a user wants transactions executed in the order they are submitted to the system, he or

Figure 3.11 Conflict graph for
Example 3.13.

she may be waiting for transactions to complete before submitting the next
one.

A situation like the one just described is avoided by the following criterion:

Order-preserving conflict serializability

DEFINITION 3.18   *Order Preservation*

A history s is called *order-preserving conflict serializable*, if it is conflict
serializable; i.e., there exists a serial history s' such that $op(s) = op(s')$ and
$s \approx_c s'$, and if the following holds for all $t, t' \in trans(s)$: if t occurs completely
before t' in s, then the same holds in s'.

Let OCSR denote the class of all order-preserving conflict serializable
histories.

The following is straightforward:

THEOREM 3.12

OCSR $\subset$ CSR

Indeed, OCSR $\subseteq$ CSR follows from the previous definition, and the sample history s from the previous example shows that the inclusion is strict:
$s \in$ CSR $-$ OCSR.

Commitment Ordering

We next present another restriction of class CSR, which will turn out to be
useful for distributed, possibly heterogeneous, environments as well. It is based
on the observation that for transactions in conflict, an ordering of their commits
in "conflict order" is sufficient for conflict serializability.

Commit order-preserving conflict serializability

DEFINITION 3.19   *Commit Order Preservation*

Let s be a history. s is *commit order-preserving conflict serializable* (or has
the property of *commit order preservation*), if the following holds: for all
transactions $t_i, t_j \in commit(s)$, $i \neq j$, if $(p, q) \in conf(s)$ for $p \in t_i, q \in t_j$,

then $c_i <_s c_j$ in s; i.e., for committed transactions, the ordering of operations in conflict determines the ordering of their Commit operations.

Let COCSR denote the class of all histories that are Commit order-preserving conflict serializable.

The following result is a consequence of the serializability theorem:

THEOREM 3.13

COCSR $\subset$ CSR

Proof

Let $s \in$ COCSR and (t_i, t_j) be an edge in the conflict graph $G(s)$. By the definition of COCSR, we may then conclude that $c_i <_s c_j$ (due to the conflict between the two transactions). By induction, we can generalize this statement from edges to paths in $G(s)$ (details are omitted); that is, if $(t_1, \ldots, t_n)$ is a path in $G(s)$ from t_1 to t_n, then $c_1 <_s c_2, c_2 <_s c_3, \ldots, c_{n-1} <_s c_n$.

Now suppose $s \notin$ CSR. Then, by the serializability theorem, $G(s)$ has a cycle. Without loss of generality, let that cycle have the form $(t_1, \ldots, t_n, t_1)$. By the above, we may then conclude that $c_1 <_s c_1$, a contradiction.

To see that the inclusion is strict, consider the history $s = r_1(x)w_2(x)c_2c_1$, for which $s \in$ CSR $-$ COCSR holds.

Our next theorem essentially states that a history is commit order preserving iff the ordering of the commits corresponds to some serialization order:

THEOREM 3.14

Let s be a history. $s \in$ COCSR iff

1. $s \in$ CSR and
2. there exists a serial s' such that $s' \approx_c s$ and for all $t, t' \in \text{trans}(s)$,
   $$t <_{s'} t' \quad \Rightarrow \quad c_t <_s c_{t'}.$$

Proof

"$\Longrightarrow$:" Let $s \in$ COCSR. By Theorem 3.13, $s \in$ CSR. Thus, there is a serial history s' such that $s' \approx_c s$. Now consider transactions $t, t' \in \text{trans}(s) = \text{trans}(s')$ such that $t <_{s'} t'$. Since s and s' are conflict equivalent, it follows that if operations from t and t', say, p and q, are in conflict in s, then $p <_s q$. Due to the COCSR property, this implies $c_t <_s c_{t'}$.

"$\Longleftarrow$:" Assume that $s \notin$ COCSR. Thus, for two transactions $t_i, t_j \in$ commit(s) there are operations $p \in t_i$ and $q \in t_j$ such that $(p, q) \in$ conf(s), but $c_j < c_i$. Since $s \in$ CSR, let s' be the conflict-equivalent serial schedule, due to the conflict between t_i and t_j, $t_i <_{s'} t_j$. However, by our assumption this implies $c_i <_s c_j$, a contradiction.

We next investigate the relationship between OCSR and COCSR; to this end it turns out that COCSR is even more restrictive than OCSR:

THEOREM 3.15

COCSR $\subset$ OCSR

Proof

Let $s \in$ COCSR, and suppose $s \notin$ OCSR. Then there exists a serial history s' such that $s \approx_c s'$, but for two transactions $t_i, t_j \in$ trans(s), $i \neq j$, we have that $t_i <_s t_j$, while $t_i \not<_{s'} t_j$. From the assumption that s is in COCSR we know that $t_i <_s t_j$ implies $c_i <_s c_j$. Now we need to consider two cases:

1. t_i and t_j are in conflict, that is, there are two data operations p from t_i and q from t_j such that $(p, q) \in$ conf(s). Since $s \approx_c s'$, it follows that $(p, q) \in$ conf(s'), which implies $t_i <_{s'} t_j$, since s' is serial, but this contradicts our finding above.

2. If t_i and t_j are not in conflict, then our assumption that t_i and t_j are reordered in s' must be due to a third transaction t_k, $k \neq i, j$, such that:

   (a) t_k is in conflict with t_i, implying $c_k <_s c_i$, and

   (b) t_j is in conflict with t_k, implying $c_j <_s c_k$,

   both by the COCSR property. Thus, $c_j <_s c_k <_s c_i$, again a contradiction.

The fact that the inclusion is strict is implied by Figure 3.12, which shows the relationship between classes CSR, OCSR, and COCSR, and in which the histories mentioned are as follows:

$$s_1 = w_1(x)r_2(x)c_2w_3(y)c_3w_1(y)c_1 \in \text{CSR} - \text{OCSR}$$
$$s_2 = w_3(y)c_3w_1(x)r_2(x)c_2w_1(y)c_1 \in \text{OCSR} - \text{COCSR}$$
$$s_3 = w_3(y)c_3w_1(x)r_2(x)w_1(y)c_1c_2 \in \text{COCSR}$$

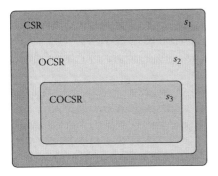

Figure 3.12 Relationship between classes CSR, OCSR, and COCSR.

3.9 **Commit Serializability**

Following the discussion in Section 3.8 it should be clear that conflict serializability is a reasonable starting point for a correctness criterion for histories even in practical applications. However, conflict serializability alone is certainly not enough since, for example, the dirty-read problem again remains undetected. In this section, we will present further observations of this kind, and will provide corresponding "corrections" for the deficiencies we will recognize on the serializability notions we have already established.

The choice of serializability as a correctness criterion for histories is partially based on the idealized assumption that transactions are processed in a failure-free environment so that each individual transaction always reaches a point of successful termination, and that additionally the system never crashes. In reality, however, this is not always the case, since transactions can abort and the system can be interrupted at any point. For these reasons, the following aspects are relevant to our discussion (and need consideration):

1. Since each transaction that is still active in a schedule can abort in the future (because it is not yet committed), and since a system crash can even force every active transaction to abort, a correctness criterion should actually take only the committed transactions into account.

2. Since a system crash can stop the processing of a schedule at any point, for a correct schedule each of its prefixes should also be correct.

We will now formalize these requirements as *closure properties of schedule properties*, an approach we have encountered already when discussing monotonicity. To this end, we will use schedule projections as introduced earlier in

Committed projection of a schedule

this chapter. Later we will often refer specifically to the projection of a schedule s onto the set commit(s) of its committed transactions, that is, to $\Pi_{\text{commit}(s)}(s)$; therefore, we will use the shorthand notation "CP(s)" (*committed projection* of s) for this particular projection.

DEFINITION 3.20 *Closure Properties of Schedule Properties*

Let E be a class of schedules.

1. E is *prefix closed* if
   for every schedule s in E each prefix of s is also in E.

2. E is *commit closed* if
   for every schedule s in E CP(s) is also in E.

Prefix commit closedness

Now requirements (1) and (2) above translate into the requirement that a correctness criterion for schedules that are processed in a not necessarily failure-free environment should exhibit *both* closure properties; in other words, it should be *prefix commit closed*. It follows that if a schedule class E is prefix commit closed, we have that if E holds for some schedule s, then E also holds for CP(s'), where s' is an arbitrary prefix of s.

The concrete schedule properties we will look at are membership in one of the classes FSR, VSR, and CSR; thus, we investigate whether membership in one of these classes is prefix commit closed. To start with, we have the negative result that membership in classes FSR and VSR is not prefix commit closed. For VSR, this follows immediately from the fact that membership in VSR is not monotone; hence it cannot be prefix closed. For FSR, the following schedule is a counterexample:

$$s = w_1(x)w_2(x)w_2(y)c_2w_1(y)c_1w_3(x)w_3(y)c_3$$

As is easily verified, $s \approx_v t_1t_2t_3$. Thus, $s \in$ VSR and hence $s \in$ FSR. Now consider the prefix $s' = w_1(x)w_2(x)w_2(y)c_2w_1(y)c_1$ of s. Clearly, CP(s') $= s'$; in addition, $s' \not\approx_f t_1t_2$ as well as $s' \not\approx_f t_2t_1$. Thus, $s' \notin$ FSR. In other words, we have identified a history $s \in$ FSR such that CP(s') ($= s'$) $\notin$ FSR for some of its prefixes s'. This proves the claim.

As we have already recognized FSR and VSR as unsuited for our purposes for reasons of complexity, this is not a "tragic" result. Fortunately, the following holds for CSR:

THEOREM 3.16

Membership in class CSR is prefix commit closed.

Proof

Let $s \in$ CSR. Then $G(s)$ is acyclic. For each restriction s' of s, $G(s')$ then is a subgraph of $G(s)$ and hence acyclic as well. In particular, for each prefix s' of s, the conflict graph of the projection onto those transactions already committed in s', i.e., the graph $G(CP(s'))$, is acyclic. Thus, $CP(s') \in$ CSR.

We next define *commit serializability* as a kind of "correction" for the situation discovered above for classes FSR and VSR, which intuitively requires that, in a correct execution, the already committed transactions have at any point in time been processed in a serializable way.

DEFINITION 3.21 *Commit Serializability*

Commit serializability

A schedule s is *commit serializable* if $CP(s')$ is serializable for every prefix s' of s.

In detail, we need to distinguish the following classes of commit-serializable schedules:

CMFSR: class of all commit final state serializable histories
CMVSR: class of all commit view serializable histories
CMCSR: class of all commit conflict serializable histories

From this definition, we can immediately deduce the following statements:

THEOREM 3.17

1. Membership in any of the classes CMFSR , CMVSR, and CMCSR is prefix commit closed.
2. CMCSR $\subset$ CMVSR $\subset$ CMFSR
3. CMFSR $\subset$ FSR
4. CMVSR $\subset$ VSR
5. CMCSR $=$ CSR

Proof

Statements (1) and (2) are straightforward from the definition of commit serializability as well as from the respective definitions of the underlying serializability notions and their relationships. The strictness of the inclusions mentioned in (2) is demonstrated by the following sample histories:

$$s = w_1(x)r_2(x)w_2(y)w_1(y)c_1c_2w_3(x)w_3(y)c_3 \in \text{CMFSR} - \text{CMVSR}$$
$$s' = w_1(x)w_2(x)w_2(y)c_2w_1(y)w_3(x)w_3(y)c_3w_1(z)c_1 \in \text{CMVSR} - \text{CMCSR}$$

(3) Let $s \in$ CMFSR. According to the definition of class CMFSR we then have $CP(s) \in$ FSR, since s is a prefix of itself. Let $trans(s) = \{t_1, \ldots, t_n\}$, and let without loss of generality $commit(s) = \{t_1, \ldots, t_k\}$, $abort(s) = \{t_{k+1}, \ldots, t_n\}$. Then $CP(s) \approx_f t_{\rho(1)} \ldots t_{\rho(k)}$ for a permutation ρ of $\{1, \ldots, k\}$, which implies

$$s \approx_f t_{\rho(1)} \ldots t_{\rho(k)} t_{k+1} \ldots t_n$$

Therefore, $s \in$ FSR, or CMFSR $\subseteq$ FSR. The sample history s used above to prove that membership in FSR is not prefix commit closed suffices to show that this inclusion is even strict.

(4) The proof is analogous to (3).

(5) The proof of CMCSR $\subseteq$ CSR is also analogous to (3). To show inclusion in the other direction, consider some history $s \in$ CSR. Since membership in CSR is prefix commit closed, $CP(s') \in$ CSR for every prefix s' of s. Since s is by definition complete, the claim follows.

The equality mentioned under (5) in the previous theorem has the following practical implication: since commit conflict serializable histories are always conflict serializable, and vice versa, conflict serializability is easily decided even for prefixes of a history by inspecting the projection onto committed transactions.

Summary of classes   Wrapping up, we now have identified the relationships between classes of serializable and of commit-serializable histories, as shown in Figure 3.13, where the histories mentioned are as follows:

$$s_1 = w_1(x)w_2(x)w_2(y)c_2w_1(y)c_1$$
$$s_2 = w_1(x)r_2(x)w_2(y)c_2r_1(y)w_1(y)c_1w_3(x)w_3(y)c_3$$
$$s_3 = w_1(x)r_2(x)w_2(y)w_1(y)c_1c_2$$
$$s_4 = w_1(x)w_2(x)w_2(y)c_2w_1(y)c_1w_3(x)w_3(y)c_3$$
$$s_5 = w_1(x)r_2(x)w_2(y)w_1(y)c_1c_2w_3(x)w_3(y)c_3$$
$$s_6 = w_1(x)w_2(x)w_2(y)c_2w_1(y)w_3(x)w_3(y)c_3w_1(z)c_1$$
$$s_7 = w_1(x)w_2(x)w_2(y)c_2w_1(z)c_1$$
$$s_8 = w_3(y)c_3w_1(x)r_2(x)c_2w_1(y)c_1$$
$$s_9 = w_3(y)c_3w_1(x)r_2(x)w_1(y)c_1c_2$$
$$s_{10} = w_1(x)w_1(y)c_1w_2(x)w_2(y)c_2$$

3.10 **An Alternative Correctness Criterion: Interleaving Specifications**

We conclude this chapter by presenting another notion of correctness for transactions in the read/write model, which on one hand is less restrictive than

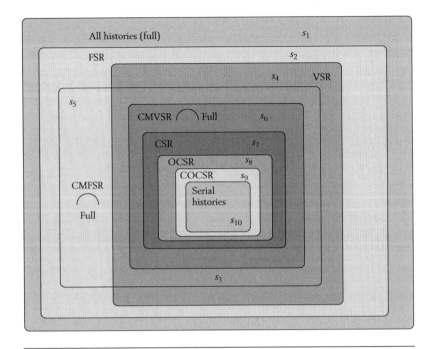

Figure 3.13 The landscape of serializable histories.

conflict-based serializability and, on the other, represents an attempt to take semantic information about transactions into account. Clearly, the possibilities to incorporate or exploit semantic information in the context of the read/write model are limited, but the considerations that follow can be, and have been, used in more general contexts as well.

Serializability is essentially based on the premise that a transaction has the ACID properties and in particular is a unit of isolation. In a correct schedule *all* steps of a transaction appear to be executed indivisibly to *all* other transactions in that schedule. There are two immediate generalizations to this: (1) consider units of isolation that do not necessarily consist of *all* the steps of a transaction, but of certain portions of the steps, and (2) consider *varying* units of isolation with respect to other transactions; that is, some steps may constitute an indivisible unit to some transactions, but not to others.

To motivate the discussion by way of a concrete application scenario, consider a bank where checking accounts belong to individuals, but savings accounts are shared by all members of a family. For simplicity, assume that the bank has only one couple as customers; so we need to manage two individual checking accounts, say, a and b, and a common savings account, say, c. Now consider three types of transactions on such accounts:

Motivation

- A *transfer* transaction moves money from one of the checking accounts to the savings account. So, we obtain the following two transaction instances:

$$t_1 = r_1(a)w_1(a)r_1(c)w_1(c) \quad \text{and}$$

$$t_2 = r_2(b)w_2(b)r_2(c)w_2(c)$$

- A *balance* transaction retrieves the balance of all accounts of the family, in our example:

$$t_3 = r_3(a)r_3(b)r_3(c)$$

- An *audit* transaction is initiated by the bank itself; it retrieves the balance of all accounts and writes the total into a special record, denoted z, for auditing purposes:

$$t_4 = r_4(a)r_4(b)r_4(c)w_4(z)$$

Now the question is whether this specific application bears some exploitable semantics that can be used when scheduling bank transactions. To this end, first notice that a bank audit should have strong interleaving constraints; it should indeed be executed as an indivisible unit with respect to transfer transactions, and vice versa. However, the interleaving constraints for transfer and balance transactions may be less stringent, since family members are assumed to trust each other. For example, it could be tolerated that a balance transaction "misses" some money because of a concurrently ongoing transfer transaction. After all, a customer should be used to taking into account the possibility of money transfers by her or his spouse. With this intuition in mind, two sample schedules that the application could consider as acceptable are

1. $r_1(a)w_1(a)r_2(b)w_2(b)r_2(c)w_2(c)r_1(c)w_1(c)$
2. $r_1(a)w_1(a)r_3(a)r_3(b)r_3(c)r_1(c)w_1(c)$

The first schedule is characteristic for the allowed interleavings of different transfer transactions. Note that this schedule is still conflict serializable. The second schedule, on the other hand, shows that a balance transaction can be interleaved with a transfer transaction in a relaxed manner such that the resulting execution is no longer conflict serializable, yet tolerable by the application. Of course, this shall not mean that all possible interleavings of these transactions are acceptable. For example, the following two example schedules should be disallowed:

1. $r_1(a)w_1(a)r_2(b)w_2(b)r_1(c)r_2(c)w_2(c)w_1(c)$
2. $r_1(a)w_1(a)r_4(a)r_4(b)r_4(c)w_4(z)r_1(c)w_1(c)$

The first of these two schedules would result in a lost-update anomaly, and the second one would not meet the stringent consistency demands of the bank's audit transaction.

Disclaimer about immediate practicality

Note that in reality, the transactions would be specified as high-level programs, typically using the SQL language embedded in some host language (e.g., Java), and these programs would be parameterized. So the specific accounts that are involved in a transaction *instance* are merely the actual parameter values of a general pattern, and each of the above transaction *types* could spawn a large number of different transaction instances. In full generality, it could even be the case that the transactions that result from a single program differ not only in the arguments of their read and write actions but also in their length and overall read/write pattern if the program contains conditional branches or loops. Exploiting the application-specific interleaving semantics would actually have to consider all possible transaction instances that result from a high-level program. In the following, however, we will disregard this substantial complication and rather assume that all transaction instances are explicitly given in advance. Indeed, we do not claim that the approach that we are going to develop in this section can be *directly* applied in practice. Nevertheless, the discussion will provide valuable insight into alternative correctness criteria.

Formalization

In the definitions that follow, we will formalize the approach by specifying for each pair of given transactions the indivisible units of one *relative to the other*. We can think of the borderline between two consecutive indivisible units of the same transaction as a "breakpoint" at which a transaction may be interleaved with another, and we can moreover think of such breakpoints as being specified *in advance*. In other words, if an application programmer who has to specify a transaction has sufficient knowledge of the semantics of the application for which the transaction is written, he or she may be able to state which interleavings with other transactions are acceptable and which are not.

For ease of exposition, we consider a static situation in what follows, in which a fixed set of transactions is given or known in advance. In addition, we restrict the attention to sequences of steps (i.e., total orders) when considering transactions, although the theory could also be generalized to partial orders.

DEFINITION 3.22   *Indivisible Units*

Indivisible units

Let $T = \{t_1, \ldots, t_n\}$ be a set of transactions. For $t_i, t_j \in T$, $i \neq j$, an *indivisible unit of t_i relative to t_j* is a sequence of consecutive steps of t_i such that no operations of t_j are allowed to be executed within this sequence.

Let $IU(t_i, t_j)$ denote the ordered sequence of indivisible units of t_i relative to t_j, and let $IU_k(t_i, t_j)$ denote the k-th element of $IU(t_i, t_j)$.

EXAMPLE 3.14

Consider the following three transactions:

$$t_1 = r_1(x)w_1(x)w_1(z)r_1(y)$$
$$t_2 = r_2(y)w_2(y)r_2(x)$$
$$t_3 = w_3(x)w_3(y)w_3(z)$$

The following specification may be given for these transactions relative to each other:

$$IU(t_1, t_2) = \langle\, [r_1(x)w_1(x)],\ [w_1(z)r_1(y)] \,\rangle$$
$$IU(t_1, t_3) = \langle\, [r_1(x)w_1(x)],\ [w_1(z)],\ [r_1(y)] \,\rangle$$

$$IU(t_2, t_1) = \langle\, [r_2(y)],\ [w_2(y)r_2(x)] \,\rangle$$
$$IU(t_2, t_3) = \langle\, [r_2(y)w_2(y)],\ [r_2(x)] \,\rangle$$

$$IU(t_3, t_1) = \langle\, [w_3(x)w_3(y)],\ [w_3(z)] \,\rangle$$
$$IU(t_3, t_2) = \langle\, [w_3(x)w_3(y)],\ [w_3(z)] \,\rangle$$

For example, $IU(t_1, t_2)$ is meant to say that if operations from t_2 have to be executed within t_1, then they may only be executed between $w_1(x)$ and $w_1(z)$, i.e., between $IU_1(t_1, t_2) = [r_1(x)w_1(x)]$ and $IU_2(t_1, t_2) = [w_1(z)r_1(y)]$.

We will say that an operation $q \in t_j$ is *interleaved with* the element $IU_k(t_i, t_j)$ of $IU(t_i, t_j)$ in the context of a schedule s if there exist operations p and p' from $IU_k(t_i, t_j)$ such that $p <_s q$ and $q <_s p'$.

Clearly, the meaning of a given indivisible unit $IU_k(t_i, t_j)$ will be that, for a schedule s to qualify for being "correct," no operations from t_j are interleaved in s with that unit.

EXAMPLE 3.15

Consider $IU(t_1, t_2)$ in Example 3.14: in a correct schedule, no operation from t_2 may occur inside any of the two units $IU_1(t_1, t_2)$ and $IU_2(t_1, t_2)$, but only before, after, or in between. Indeed, consider the schedule

$$s_1 = r_2(y)r_1(x)w_1(x)w_2(y)r_2(x)w_1(z)w_3(x)w_3(y)r_1(y)w_3(z)$$

Apparently, s_1 is not a serial schedule and not even a serializable one; however, it is correct with respect to the relative isolation specification given in the previous example: operations of t_1 are executed between $r_2(y)$ and $w_2(y)r_2(x)$, i.e., the isolation of t_2 relative to t_1 follows the specification and is hence preserved. As is easily seen, the same holds for the other interleavings in this schedule.

As a second example, consider the schedule

$$s_2 = r_1(x)r_2(y)w_2(y)w_1(x)r_2(x)w_1(z)r_1(y)$$

that interleaves the two transactions t_1 and t_2 in a way that would not be compliant with the allowed interleavings according to $IU(t_1, t_2)$. Note, however, that this schedule could be easily transformed into another schedule s_2' by exchanging $w_1(x)$ with all actions of t_2 such that $w_1(x)$ would precede t_2. This transformation seems perfectly legal, as all actions of t_2 are conflict free (i.e., commutative) with regard to $w_1(x)$, and the resulting schedule s_2' would be acceptable according to $IU(t_1, t_2)$.

The example of schedule s_2 above shows that it is desirable to combine the "traditional" reasoning about conflicts with the specification of indivisible units in order to allow more concurrent executions. In the following, we are aiming at a notion of serializability based on an equivalence relation to serial executions that reconciles interleaving specifications with conflict equivalence.

DEFINITION 3.23   *Dependence of Steps*

Let s be a schedule.

1. A step q *directly depends on* a step p in s, denoted $p \rightsquigarrow q$, if $p <_s q$ and either $p, q \in t$ for some transaction $t \in trans(s)$ and $p <_t q$, or p and q are from distinct transactions and p is in conflict with q.
2. Let $\overset{*}{\rightsquigarrow}$ ("*depends on*") denote the reflexive and transitive closure of $\rightsquigarrow$.

Depends-on relation on steps

Thus, the *depends-on* relation of a schedule is derived from conflicts and the internal structure of transactions.

The depends relation between steps now allows us to define the analog of serial schedules for the setting considered here. In a "relatively serial" schedule, an operation q from a transaction t_j may be interleaved with an indivisible unit of a transaction t_i relative to t_j if neither q is depending on an operation in that unit nor does an operation from that unit depend on q.

DEFINITION 3.24   *Relatively Serial Schedule*

A schedule s such that $trans(s) = T$ is *relatively serial* if for all transactions $t_i, t_j \in T$, $i \neq j$, the following holds: if an operation $q \in t_j$ is interleaved with $IU_k(t_i, t_j)$ for some k, then there is no operation $p \in IU_k(t_i, t_j)$ ($p \in t_i$) such that $p \overset{*}{\rightsquigarrow} q$ or $q \overset{*}{\rightsquigarrow} p$.

Relatively serial schedule

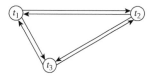

Figure 3.14 Conflict graph of schedule s_3 from Example 3.16.

EXAMPLE 3.16

Consider the specification from Example 3.14 again as well as the following schedule:

$$s_3 = r_1(x)r_2(y)w_1(x)w_2(y)w_3(x)w_1(z)w_3(y)r_2(x)r_1(y)w_3(z)$$

Here operation $r_2(y)$ is interleaved with $IU_1(t_1, t_2) = [r_1(x)w_1(x)]$, but notice that neither $r_1(x) \overset{*}{\leadsto} r_2(y)$ nor $r_2(y) \overset{*}{\leadsto} w_1(x)$ holds. Similarly, $w_1(z)$ is interleaved with $IU_2(t_2, t_1) = [w_2(y)r_2(x)]$ and $IU_1(t_3, t_1) = [w_3(x)w_3(y)]$, but there are no dependencies between the operations involved. Finally, $r_2(x)$ is interleaved with $IU_2(t_1, t_2) = [w_1(z)r_1(y)]$, but again neither $w_1(z) \overset{*}{\leadsto} r_2(x)$ nor $r_2(x) \overset{*}{\leadsto} r_1(y)$ holds. Thus, schedule s_3 is relatively serial according to Definition 3.24. On the other hand, the conflict graph of s_3 is shown in Figure 3.14. The conflict graph is obviously cyclic, so that $s_3 \notin CSR$.

We should think of a relatively serial schedule as the analog of a serial schedule in the theory we have developed earlier in this chapter. Thus, schedules that are relatively serial should always be acceptable, and schedules that are not relatively serial should be acceptable as long as they are conflict equivalent to a relatively serial schedule:

Relative serializability

DEFINITION 3.25 *Relative Serializability*

A schedule s is *relatively serializable* if it is conflict equivalent to some relatively serial schedule.

EXAMPLE 3.17

Consider the following schedule over the specification from Example 3.14:

$$s_4 = r_1(x)r_2(y)w_2(y)w_1(x)w_3(x)r_2(x)w_1(z)w_3(y)r_1(y)w_3(z)$$

Notice that s_4 is no longer relatively serial, since now $w_1(x)$ is interleaved with $IU_2(t_2, t_1) = [w_2(y)r_2(x)]$, and $w_1(x) \overset{*}{\leadsto} r_2(x)$. However, s_4 is conflict equivalent to schedule s_3 from Example 3.16, since steps $w_2(y)$ and $r_2(x)$ have only been moved beyond other steps with which they commute. Thus, s_4 is relatively serializable.

We mention that the classical theory of conflict-serializable schedules as developed in Section 3.8 is a special case of what we have decribed in this section. Indeed, traditionally, entire transactions are the only units of isolation, so that every serial schedule is also relatively serial since each operation of a serial schedule is not interleaved with the single indivisible unit of any transaction. However, it is easy to see that not every relatively serial schedule is serial under traditional isolation, basically because relatively serial schedules still allow interleavings of operations with the indivisible unit of other transactions that do not have any dependencies between them.

If a given schedule is not relatively serial, it may still be relatively serializable and hence acceptable from a semantic point of view. The latter may be the case if there are interleavings of operations with indivisible units of other transactions that should be forbidden (or at least avoided) due to dependencies between the operations involved. In particular, an operation that is interleaved with an indivisible unit can sometimes be "moved out" of the indivisible unit by allowed commutations.

EXAMPLE 3.18

Consider an indivisible unit $[w_1(x)r_1(z)]$ of a transaction t_1 with respect to a transaction t_2, and let

$$w_1(x) <_s r_2(x) <_s r_1(z)$$

occur in a schedule s. Clearly, that schedule cannot be relatively serial since $w_1(x) \overset{*}{\leadsto} r_2(x)$, but if the context of the schedule does not require otherwise, we can commute $r_2(x)$ and $r_1(z)$ in order to obtain

$$[w_1(x)r_1(z)] <_s r_2(x)$$

So, in a sense, we have pushed $r_2(x)$ forward in a conflict-preserving way and thereby (locally) restored relative seriality. *Push forward*

Next, suppose the same schedule s also contains a situation

$$r_3(z) <_s w_2(y) <_s r_3(y)$$

but the specification requires that $[r_3(z)r_3(y)]$ be an indivisible unit with respect to t_2. By a similar argument, we can correct this situation by pulling $w_2(y)$ backward in front of the indivisible unit, again by an allowed *Pull backward* commutation. We obtain

$$w_2(y) <_s [r_3(z)r_3(y)]$$

which again contributes to making this particular schedule acceptable.

We now formalize these observations by introducing the notions of pushing *forward* or pulling *backward* an operation. We will then be able to introduce a graph that contains edges representing these actions and that can be used to characterize relative serializability.

DEFINITION 3.26 *Push Forward and Pull Backward*

Let t_i and t_j be distinct transactions, and let $IU_k(t_i, t_j)$ be an indivisible unit of t_i relative to t_j. For an operation $p_i \in IU_k(t_i, t_j)(p_i \in t_i)$ let

1. $F(p_i, t_j)$ be the last operation in $IU_k(t_i, t_j)$,

2. $B(p_i, t_j)$ be the first operation of $IU_k(t_i, t_j)$.

Intuitively, $F(p_i, t_j)$ denotes the earliest operation from t_i beyond which an operation from t_j interleaved with $IU_k(t_i, t_j)$ can be pushed forward in order to restore relative isolation, and correspondingly $B(p_i, t_j)$ denotes the latest operation from t_i before which an operation from t_j interleaved with $IU_k(t_i, t_j)$ can be pulled backward. In Example 3.14 we have for $IU(t_1, t_2)$

$$F(r_1(x), t_2) = w_1(x) \quad \text{and}$$
$$B(r_1(y), t_2) = w_1(z)$$

We will now use these notions for graphically capturing ways to reorganize a given schedule so as to make it relatively serial, or to test a schedule for relative serializability:

Relative serialization graph

DEFINITION 3.27 *Relative Serialization Graph*

Let s be a schedule. The *relative serialization graph* $RSG(s) = (V, E)$ of s is defined by $V := op(s)$ and $E \subseteq V \times V$ containing four types of edges as follows:

1. if p and q are consecutive operations of the same transaction in s, then $(p, q) \in E$ (internal or I edge);

2. if $p \overset{*}{\leadsto} q$ for $p \in t_i$, $q \in t_j$, $i \neq j$, then $(p, q) \in E$ (dependency or D edge);

3. if (p, q) is a D edge such that $p \in t_i$ and $q \in t_j$, then $(F(p, t_j), q) \in E$ (push forward or F edge);

4. if (p, q) is a D edge such that $p \in t_i$ and $q \in t_j$, then $(p, B(q, t_i)) \in E$ (pull backward or B edge).

EXAMPLE 3.19

Consider the following three transactions:

$$t_1 = w_1(x)r_1(z)$$
$$t_2 = r_2(x)w_2(y)$$
$$t_3 = r_3(z)r_3(y)$$

Let the following interleaving specification be given for these transactions:

$$IU(t_1, t_2) = \langle\, [w_1(x), r_1(z)]\, \rangle$$
$$IU(t_1, t_3) = \langle\, [w_1(x)],\ [r_1(z)]\, \rangle$$

$$IU(t_2, t_1) = \langle\, [r_2(x)],\ [w_2(y)]\, \rangle$$
$$IU(t_2, t_3) = \langle\, [r_2(x)],\ [w_2(y)]\, \rangle$$

$$IU(t_3, t_1) = \langle\, [r_3(z)],\ [r_3(y)]\, \rangle$$
$$IU(t_3, t_2) = \langle\, [r_3(z)r_3(y)]\, \rangle$$

Now consider the following schedule:

$$s_5 = w_1(x)r_2(x)r_3(z)w_2(y)r_3(y)r_1(z)$$

Notice that we have analyzed the situation we see in this schedule in part in Example 3.18 already. The relative serialization graph of s_5 is shown in Figure 3.15.

LEMMA 3.3

If s is relatively serial, then $RSG(s)$ is acyclic.

Proof

We show for $RSG(s) = (V, E)$ that

$$(p, q) \in E \text{ implies } p <_s q$$

This is trivial for I as well as for D edges. Hence consider an F edge of the form (r, q), where $q \in t_j$, $r = F(p, t_j)$, r, $p \in t_i$, and (p, q) is a D edge. This situation implies that $p, r \in IU_k(t_i, t_j)$, $p <_s r$, and r is the last operation of

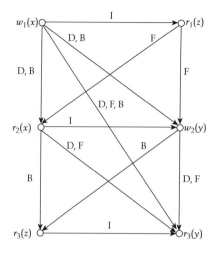

Figure 3.15 Relative serialization graph of schedule s_5 from Example 3.19.

this unit. Since $p \overset{*}{\leadsto} q$ and s is relatively serial, q appears after $IU_k(t_i, t_j)$ in s. Thus, $r <_s q$. The corresponding statement for B edges is shown similarly.

The following can now be proven:

THEOREM 3.18

A schedule s is relatively serializable iff $RSG(s)$ is acyclic.

Proof

(only if) If s is relatively serializable, then there exists an s' that is relatively serial such that s and s' are conflict equivalent. We first show $RSG(s) = RSG(s')$. To this end, both graphs have the same set of nodes, and both have the same I edges. Moreover, D edges are the same in both graphs due to equal I edges as well as to conflict equivalence of the two schedules. Since F and B edges depend on the D edges and on the indivisible units, the claim follows. Now since s' is relatively serial, $RSG(s')$ is acyclic by the previous lemma. Thus, $RSG(s)$ is acyclic as well.

(if) Let $RSG(s)$ be acyclic, and let s' be obtained by topologically sorting $RSG(s)$. Clearly, s and s' are conflict equivalent and hence $RSG(s) = RSG(s')$. It remains to be shown that s' is relatively serial. Assume, on the contrary, that it is not; that is, there exists a unit $IU_k(t_i, t_j)$ for some k, t_i, and t_j that has some $q \in t_j$ interleaved, but there is also some $p \in t_i$ in

$IU_k(t_i, t_j)$ such that $p \overset{*}{\leadsto} q$ or $q \overset{*}{\leadsto} p$ in s'. Let r be the last operation in $IU_k(t_i, t_j)$. If $p \overset{*}{\leadsto} q$, then there is an F edge (r, q) in $RSG(s)$; hence, in *any* topological sort of $RSG(s)$, we have $r < q$. However, in s', which is such a topological sort, we find $q < r$ due to the assumed interleaving, which gives a contradiction. A similar argument applies if $q \overset{*}{\leadsto} p$, since $RSG(s)$ in that case has a corresponding B edge. The theorem follows.

Since the relative serialization graph of a schedule can be constructed efficiently, the characterization given in Theorem 3.18 provides a test for relative serializability, which is polynomial in op(s). As an example, schedule s_4 above, which has an acyclic relative serialization graph, is relatively serializable.

3.11 **Lessons Learned**

We conclude this chapter by summarizing the discoveries we have made. First of all, the page-level transaction model, which may seem very simple and insufficient at first glance, turns out to give rise to a rich theory of serializability that allows for numerous concepts and approaches to schedule correctness. However, parts of this theory (in particular, those leading to classes FSR and VSR), although seemingly appropriate from a semantic point of view, are unrealistic for practical purposes, so that conflict serializability is the correctness notion of choice for the construction of schedulers. This is due to the high (and hence unacceptable) complexity of the decision problems related to final state as well as to view serializability.

Conflict serializability has a number of interesting properties that make it particularly amenable to real-world implementations: its decision problem is polynomial in the number of transactions considered, it enjoys desirable closure properties, and it allows establishing subclasses, or sufficient conditions, that capture additional and relevant properties. The ones we have seen here are order-preserving conflict serializability and commit order preservation.

In addition, the previous section has uncovered a first attempt to go beyond traditional conflict based serializability theory. Indeed, the idea of taking semantic information of the database or of the transactions (or maybe even of the application programs from which the transactions are issued) into account when considering the correctness of schedules is nearly as old as the notion of serializability itself, and relative serializability constitutes an interesting approach in this direction. Clearly, as the read/write model of transactions is of a highly syntactic nature, more can be expected in terms of semantic considerations when higher-level transaction models are employed.

We will reuse the notion of conflict serializability several times in subsequent chapters. In particular, we will demonstrate for completely different types of operations, such as update operations along the lines of SQL for relational databases, that a theory of serializability can mostly follow what we have described in this chapter, and that "serializability theorems" in the style of Theorem 3.10, which characterize (conflict) serializability in graph-theoretic terms, can be obtained for a variety of settings. In this sense, what we have done and seen in this chapter is on the one hand a major preparation for the practical aspects of concurrency control and of scheduler design that we will study next, but is on the other hand representative of a kind of method-ology that is available for deriving transaction models and their correctness criteria.

Exercises

3.1 Consider the following histories:

$$s = r_1(x)r_2(y)w_1(y)r_3(z)w_3(z)r_2(x)w_2(z)w_1(x)c_1c_2c_3$$
$$s' = r_3(z)w_3(z)r_2(y)r_2(x)w_2(z)r_1(x)w_1(y)w_1(x)c_3c_2c_1$$

Compute $H[s]$ and $H[s']$ as well as the respective RF and LRF relations. Show the step graphs of these histories.

3.2 Suppose the following schedule is given:

$$s = r_1(x)r_3(x)w_3(y)w_2(x)c_3r_4(y)w_4(x)c_2r_5(x)c_4w_5(z)w_1(z)c_1c_5$$

Now assume that it is known that for some transactions, the function computed by a write step is the *identity* function in one of its arguments, i.e., for $w_i(x)$ we have that $f_{ix}(v_1, \ldots, v_m) = v_j$ for some index j (such a function is a *copier* since it just copies information it has read into a data item). Compute the (Herbrand) semantics of s given the information that t_3 and t_4 are copiers. *Note:* Strictly speaking, this is no longer a Herbrand semantics, since some function symbols in $H[s]$ are now interpreted.

3.3 Suppose that in a given schedule the functions corresponding to the write steps represent increments of a counter, i.e., $f(x) = x + 1$. Compute the (Herbrand) semantics of the following schedules using this semantic information:

$$s = r_3(z)r_1(y)w_3(z)w_1(y)r_1(x)r_2(y)w_2(y)w_1(x)r_2(x)w_2(x)c_1c_2c_3$$
$$s' = r_3(z)w_3(z)r_2(y)w_2(y)r_1(y)w_1(y)r_2(x)w_2(x)r_1(x)w_1(x)c_3c_2c_1$$

3.4 Consider the following history:

$$s = r_1(x)r_3(x)w_3(y)w_2(x)r_4(y)c_2w_4(x)c_4r_5(x)c_3w_5(z)c_5w_1(z)c_1$$

Into which of the classes FSR, VSR, CSR does this schedule fall?

3.5 Complete the proof of Theorem 3.2, i.e., show that for any two schedules s and s', $s \approx_v s'$ iff $D(s) = D(s')$.

3.6 Consider $s = r_1(x)w_1(x)r_2(x)r_2(y)w_2(y)c_2w_1(y)c_1$. Show that $s \in$ FSR – VSR.

3.7 Prove Theorem 3.4, i.e., show that VSR and FSR coincide in the absence of dead steps.

3.8 Show that VSR = CSR in the absence of blind writes, i.e., if each write step on a data item x is preceded by a read step on x of the same transaction.

3.9 Let $s = r_1(z)r_3(x)r_2(z)w_1(z)w_1(y)c_1w_2(y)w_2(u)c_2w_3(y)c_3$. Show $s \in$ VSR – CSR.

3.10 Consider $s = r_1(x)w_1(z)r_2(z)w_1(y)c_1r_3(y)w_2(z)c_2w_3(x)w_3(y)c_3$. Using the conflict graph of s as an argument, show that $s \in$ CSR. Does $s \in$ OCSR also hold?

3.11 Show:

(a) Membership in class CSR is monotone.

(b) $s \in$ CSR $\Longleftrightarrow$ ($\forall\, T \subseteq$ trans(s)) $\Pi_T(s) \in$ VSR (i.e., CSR is the largest monotone subset of VSR).

3.12 Consider the traditional case where entire transactions are the only units of indivisibility with respect to other transactions. Show by way of an example that, in this setting, not every relatively serial schedule is also serial. Also show that under this kind of "absolute" isolation, every relatively serial schedule is conflict equivalent to some serial schedule.

Bibliographic Notes

Our exposition of the Herbrand semantics of schedules as well as that of the classes FSR, VSR, and CSR mostly follows Papadimitriou (1986) as well as Hadzilacos (1988). A major difference between the two is that the former ignores aborted transactions in the discussion of serializability, while the latter does not. The subtle difference between these viewpoints already comes up in the definition of reading a value from a write step, which has to be written as follows when aborted transactions are taken into account:

> A step $r_i(x) \in s$ of a transaction $t_i \in$ trans(s) reads the value written by the *last* $w_j(x) \in s$, $j \neq i$, that occurs before $r_i(x)$, such that $a_j \notin s$.

The seemingly innocent addition at the end that t_j should not be aborted in schedule s has interesting consequences. Indeed, consider the following (fragment of a) schedule:

$$s_1 = w_i(x)w_j(x)r_k(x)$$

According to what was said above, step $r_k(x)$ reads the value of x written by $w_j(x)$, since (1) there is no other step in between the two, and (2) a_j is not around. Next, suppose a scheduler appends a_j to s_1 to obtain

$$s_2 = w_i(x)c_i w_j(x)r_k(x)a_j$$

Now since t_j is aborted, step $r_k(x)$ no longer reads from $w_j(x)$, but from (the committed) step $w_i(x)$. If a_j would have been there just a little earlier, as in

$$s_3 = w_i(x)c_i w_j(x)a_j r_k(x)$$

it would have been clear from the outset that $r_k(x)$ does not read from $w_j(x)$. The problem we encounter in this little discussion is that the "reads-from definition" above formally introduces a well-defined notion (since $s_1 \neq s_2$); however, in a dynamic situation s_2 could be produced from s_1, and then the value read by $r_k(x)$ changes! We take this as evidence that failures are difficult to model, at least in a setting (as discussed in this chapter) where correctness of transaction executions is the focus, and have therefore decided not to consider aborted transactions in this chapter. See Lechtenbörger and Vossen (2000) for a recent discussion of this topic.

Presumably, the first publication that used the Herbrand semantics to characterize the correctness of schedules was by Casanova and Bernstein (1980). The notion of (final state) serializability along with the relations RF and LRF has been introduced by Papadimitriou (1979) as well as Bernstein et al. (1979). The notion of view serializability has been made fully explicit by Yannakakis (1984). Vidyasankar (1987) has extended this work, as well as that of Ibaraki et al. (1983) and Katoh et al. (1985), by introducing a generalized notion of *S serializability* where the subset S of the set of transactions under consideration reads the same values in a given schedule as in some serial execution. S serializability is then characterized in terms of an acyclic *transaction precedence graph* that expresses useful reads as well as useless writes. Moreover, S serializability coincides with view serializability if S contains all transactions in question.

The step graph construction and the proof that equality of reduced step graphs is equivalent to the fact that the histories in question are final state serializable is from Papadimitriou (1986). The NP completeness result on view serializability is from Papadimitriou (1979); a complete proof appears in Papadimitriou (1986). The latter source has also proven that conflict equivalence can be characterized in terms of commutativity. The related notion of weak view serializability of degree k (introduced in the Exercises above) is from Tuzhilin and Spirakis (1985). The most relevant notion of conflict serializability for practical purposes and the characterization of membership in CSR by the acyclicity of the associated conflict graph goes back to the seminal paper by Eswaran et al. (1976).

Order-preserving serializability was already discussed by Papadimitriou (1979) as well as Bernstein et al. (1979), originally named "strict" serializability; we should mention that order preservation makes sense not only for conflict-serializable schedules but also for those in FSR or in VSR, which then gives rise to restricted classes OFSR and OVSR, respectively. While the complexity of testing membership in OFSR or OVSR remained open in Papadimitriou (1979), Sethi (1982) clarified this by showing that order-preserving serializability of a history s can be decided in polynomial time for transactions in the two-step model (see Exercises in Chapter 2), provided all write steps in s are alive; the problem is NP complete in general.

The property of commit order preservation, discussed in Section 3.8.4, was proposed under different names by Weihl (1989), Breitbart and Silberschatz (1992), as well as Raz (1992, 1994); Raz (1992, 1994) and Guerraoui (1995) have also investigated a number of implications of this notion.

Our discussion of commit serializability again follows Hadzilacos (1988). A proof of the fact that CSR is the largest monotone subset of VSR (see Exercise 3.11) can be found in Yannakakis (1984).

Our presentation in Section 3.10 mostly follows Agrawal et al. (1994), Krishnaswamy et al. (1997), as well as Vidyasankar (1998). The idea of letting the user specify which interleavings of transactions are acceptable or of deriving such knowledge from the underlying application was first discussed by Garcia-Molina (1983) and then studied in detail by Lynch (1983). Lynch (1983) in particular took the idea of relative serializability across multiple levels of abstraction and consequently established a notion of "multilevel atomicity." This theory, which we have here restricted to the (lowest) read/write level only, has also been discussed by Cellary et al. (1988). Relative serializability was first established by Farrag and Özsu (1989), who used the notion of "breakpoints" for separating atomic units of a transaction t_i relative to another transaction t_j. Agrawal et al. (1994) extended this by allowing nondependent operations to interleave anywhere, and by basing dependency between operations on precedence as well as on conflict. Vidyasankar (1998) defined breakpoints relative to individual operations, not entire transactions, which may result in multiple F and B edges between nodes in a relative serialization graph.

CHAPTER FOUR

Concurrency Control Algorithms

The optimist believes we live in the best of all
possible worlds. The pessimist fears this is true.

—*Robert Oppenheimer*

Next week there can't be any crisis.
My schedule is already full.

—*Henry Kissinger*

4.1 Goal and Overview

In this chapter we will present a number of algorithms—called *scheduling algorithms*, or *schedulers* for short—that a data server could use to produce serializable schedules for multiple concurrent transactions. Following our discussion from the previous chapter, we will concentrate on schedulers that produce *conflict*-serializable schedules. We will also follow the previous chapter in that we do not yet consider transaction aborts or system failures; as before, we assume that system components other than the scheduler are capable of handling them properly. Later, in Part III of the book, we will expand the notion of schedules to make the implementation of aborts explicit. (This will lead to notions such as prefix reducibility in Chapter 11.)

Scheduling algorithms (schedulers)

We will place some emphasis in this chapter on the question of how to design scheduling protocols in general, and on how to verify a given protocol and prove it correct. With respect to the latter, we will be interested in two criteria: First, each protocol that we present has to be *safe* in the sense that all histories it outputs have to be members of CSR, the class of conflict-serializable schedules. Second, we are interested in the *scheduling power* of a protocol, or in its ability to produce some class of serializable histories (e.g., class CSR) in its entirety or partially only. For example, if scheduler S_1 can produce *every* history in CSR, and scheduler S_2 can produce a strict subset of CSR only, then S_1 intuitively has more options than S_2 to choose a CSR schedule for a given set of transactions, and hence has more scheduling power. In other words, the scheduling power of a scheduler is a kind of measure for the amount of parallelism it can utilize.

Locking schedulers

After some general considerations on the design of schedulers in Section 4.2, we will first look, in Section 4.3, at the most prominent type of schedulers, which are schedulers based on locking. As will be seen, this amounts to a rich class of scheduling protocols that essentially exploits a variety of options in the use of locks. Locking protocols are also the most important ones in practice, since they mostly (but not always) outperform all other scheduling protocols, are easy to implement, incur little run-time overhead, and can be generalized to various transaction-related settings. In particular, we will see that locking protocols can be successfully employed for both major computational models of this book—the page model considered here and the object model considered later. A second major class of protocols, discussed in Section 4.4, does not use locking at all, but replaces this mechanism with other constructs, such as timestamps in the timestamp ordering protocol or validation in so-called optimistic protocols. Finally, Section 4.5 briefly presents hybrid protocols that combine elements from both locking and nonlocking methods.

Nonlocking schedulers

Hybrid schedulers

4.2 General Scheduler Design

Before we look at actual protocols, we briefly provide a conceptual view of the system environment in which transaction processing takes place in a data server. To this end, we recall Figure 1.4 from Chapter 1, which gave an overview of the layered components involved in a data server such as a database system. We now consider an extension and, at the same time, a convenient abstraction of such a layered architecture by putting the scheduler component in its appropriate place. Conceptually, we insert a *transaction manager* (TM) as an additional component between two layers, typically (but not necessarily) between the query execution layer and the access layer or between the access layer and the storage layer. This TM intercepts all calls from one layer to the next lower layer, takes the necessary steps for concurrency control (and also recovery), and then passes the calls on to the lower layer to execute the invoked operation. With this abstract architecture, the further processing of the operations by the lower layer and the other layers underneath is not really relevant for the TM, nor is it observable by the TM anyway. Therefore, we can conceptually collapse all layers beneath the TM into a single "virtual" system component that we refer to as the *data manager* (DM). This architectural model and the dynamic behavior of a scheduler are illustrated in Figure 4.1. The scheduler dynamically interleaves data operations that result from the requests of multiple clients.

Transaction manager (TM)

The TM's main task is bookkeeping and in particular managing the lists *trans*, *commit*, *abort*, and *active* that we introduced for our model of schedules and histories. In addition it keeps a list of ready-to-execute steps for all the active transactions. From this list it selects individual steps and sends them

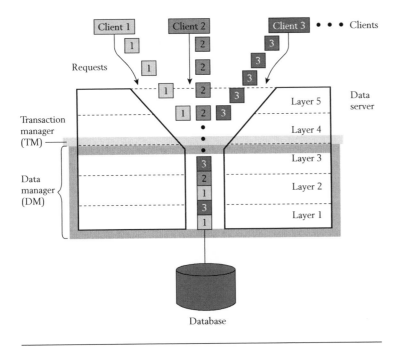

Figure 4.1 A transaction scheduler.

to the scheduler. In that way, the scheduler receives an arbitrary *input schedule* from the TM, and its task is to transform that into a serializable *output schedule*.

Since we have assumed in Chapter 3 that termination steps of transactions only become relevant in the context of a schedule or a history, we can assume now that the TM can recognize the beginning and the end of a transaction. Thus a transaction is delimited by its Begin transaction and Commit transaction (or, infrequently, Rollback transaction) calls. We furthermore assume that the TM:

- outputs a step c_i to the scheduler when it sees the Commit transaction request of t_i and no failures have occurred (from the TM's point of view) during the execution of t_i (normal termination),

- outputs a step a_i as soon as it recognizes an error situation for t_i (including the case that the transaction program explicitly requests a rollback).

Recall from Chapter 1 that this is in line with the way commercial data servers such as database systems operate when accessed through an application program; there are explicit commands such as Commit and Rollback for controlling transaction termination.

In addition, a scheduler can autonomously decide to abort a transaction, for example, if it discovers a situation that is no longer serializable. We remark

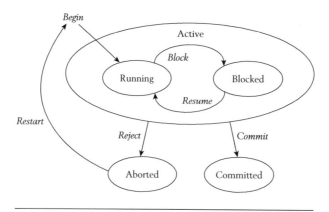

Figure 4.2 States of a transaction.

at this point that a transaction can be in various states during its lifetime, as shown in Figure 4.2.

Upon its Begin transaction call a transaction becomes *active*. An active transaction can execute a data operation or await the execution of the next such operation. In the former case it is in state Running; in the latter it is Blocked. The end of an active transaction can be either Aborted or Committed, where the latter state is the normal outcome.

Scheduler actions   Now the scheduler receives steps of the form r, w, a, and c in an input schedule and has to transform that into a serializable output schedule. To this end, it can perform one of the following actions:

1. *Output*: The step is output right away, that is, attached to the end of the present output schedule (which is initially empty) to form a new output schedule; in this case, the step can be an r, w, a, or c action.

2. *Reject*: The step is not output (e.g., since it is already clear that its execution would destroy the serializability of the output). In this case, it can only be an r or a w; the transaction in question is then aborted (terminated by an a).

3. *Block*: The step is neither output nor rejected, but considered as "currently not executable" and thus postponed. The execution of this step will then be retried later; again, the step in question can only be an r or a w. (Under special circumstances, the step could also be a c, e.g., if the scheduler is desired for COCSR.)

The data manager (DM) executes the steps of a (serializable) output schedule in the order that has been determined by the scheduler; in other words,

- for an r it reads a data item,
- for a w it writes a data item,

- for a *c* it initiates steps to make the results of the transaction persistent,
- for an *a* it initiates steps to undo the transaction.

In this chapter our main interest is in the scheduler, or in protocols on which such a device can be based. Regarding the design of a scheduling protocol, we already know that its output should at least fall into CSR. Once such a design goal has been fixed, a scheduler can conceptually be seen as a "filter," which lets exactly the members of that class pass unmodified. Thus, if the input schedule is from that class, it coincides with the output schedule; the serializable input schedules then form the scheduler's *fixpoint set*. Now a generic scheduler can be described roughly as follows:

```
scheduler ( ):
var newstep:  step;
{ state  :=initial_state;
  repeat
    on arrival(newstep) do
    { update(state);
      if test(state, newstep)
        then output(newstep)
        else block(newstep) or reject(newstep) }
    forever };
```

Generic scheduler

For a concrete scheduling algorithm we will now have to make precise:

1. what information characterizes a state and how the scheduler updates that information depending on a current step,
2. what makes up the test that decides upon the scheduler's next action (execute, block, or reject).

Depending on how the test result looks most of the time, schedulers can be classified as optimistic or pessimistic. A scheduler is

Scheduler classification

- *optimistic*, sometimes also referred to as "aggressive," if it mostly lets steps pass and rarely blocks; clearly, this bears the dangers of "getting stuck" eventually when the serializability of the output can no longer be guaranteed;

Optimistic schedulers

- *pessimistic*, sometimes also referred to as "conservative," if it mostly blocks (upon recognizing conflicts); in the extreme, albeit unlikely case, the output could become a serial schedule or history, namely, if all transactions but one were blocked.

Pessimistic schedulers

Locking schedulers, which we will consider in the next section, belong to the class of pessimistic schedulers. Nonlocking schedulers, on the other hand, to be considered in later sections, can be either optimistic or pessimistic.

Regarding the safety as well as the scheduling power of a protocol, we will use the following notions and notations:

DEFINITION 4.1 *CSR Safety*

A scheduler is called *CSR safe* if every output it produces is (conflict) serializable. If S denotes a scheduler, then $Gen(S)$ denotes the set of all schedules that S can generate as an output. Thus, a scheduler S is CSR safe if $Gen(S) \subseteq$ CSR.

4.3 Locking Schedulers

We now embark on a discussion of the first major class of scheduling protocols, the *locking schedulers*. We do this here from a purely conceptual point of view, in order to clarify the methodology as well as the options and implications behind it. For the time being, we entirely neglect implementation techniques such as *lock tables*, where each lock is represented as one entry with hash-based access on data item and transaction identifier, or *multiple granularity*, where transactions can choose an appropriate level of granularity depending on how many data items they intend to access and the contention for these items. Here we consider a uniform level of granularity like pages, which suffices for the discussion of this chapter. We will discuss such implementation issues in Chapter 10.

4.3.1 Introduction

Lock request, lock conflict, lock wait, and lock release

In a nutshell, the idea of a locking scheduler is to synchronize access to shared data by using *locks*, which can be set on and removed from data items on behalf of transactions. The intuitive meaning is that if a transaction holds a lock on a data item, the item is not available to other, concurrent transactions (i.e., those transactions are "locked out"). When a transaction *requests* a lock (or, actually, the scheduler requests the lock on behalf of a transaction), the scheduler checks whether the lock is already held by another transaction (in a conflicting mode, as we will explain shortly). If so, the lock request is considered to be a *lock conflict*, and the requesting transaction is suspended—it suffers a *lock wait* and becomes blocked. Otherwise, the requested lock can be granted, and we say that the transaction acquires the lock. Eventually, each transaction *releases* its locks that it holds at appropriate points in time. At this time the scheduler checks whether any waiting transaction can be resumed; if so, the scheduler will now grant the transaction's lock request that has formerly led to the lock wait, and the transaction can go ahead accessing the data item of interest.

Table 4.1 Lock mode compatibility.

		Lock requested	
		$rl_i(x)$	$wl_i(x)$
Lock	$rl_j(x)$	+	−
held	$wl_j(x)$	−	−

Lock modes: (shared) read lock, (exclusive) write lock

Since in our model, transactions can read or write data items, we will associate two types of locks, or *lock modes*, with every data item x: a *read lock* $rl(x)$, also known as *shared lock*, and a *write lock* $wl(x)$, also known as *exclusive lock*. As we do for other steps in a schedule, we use subscripts to distinguish the transactions that issue lock operations. We thus use rl and wl both to denote the lock status and mode of a data item and the operation that sets the lock. Even further, we neglect the distinction between requesting a lock on a data item and acquiring a (previously requested) lock; all of this should be subsumed by rl and wl.

Compatibility of locks

The following is now near at hand: two locks $pl_i(x)$ and $ql_j(y)$ are in conflict if $x = y$, $i \neq j$, and the data operations p and q are in conflict (i.e., $p = r \wedge q = w$ or $p = w \wedge q = r$ or $p = w \wedge q = w$). The immediate consequence of this is that our notion of conflict carries over to locks; we will encounter similar regulations in other transaction models later. It is common to describe the *compatibility* of locks (or lock modes) in tabular form, as shown in Table 4.1.

The table is to be read as follows: if a transaction t_i has already set a lock $pl_i(x)$ and a transaction t_j, $j \neq i$, requests a lock $ql_j(x)$, this latter lock can be granted (it is *compatible* or *not in conflict* with the former) if the corresponding table entry is a +; otherwise, it cannot be granted.

For unlocking data items—in other words, for releasing locks—we will use similar notations: $ru(x)$ will stand for "read unlock," $wu(x)$ for "write unlock" with respect to a data item x.

When using locks, a scheduler has to manage their usage by controlling the order in which transactions set and release locks. In light of the generic scheduling algorithm shown earlier, this proceeds as follows: Let a step $o_i(x)$ arrive as next input ($o \in \{r, w\}$). If $ol_i(x)$ is not set, the scheduler has to test whether some $pl_j(x)$, $j \neq i$, $p \in \{r, w\}$, has been set:

1. If this is not the case, $ol_i(x)$ will be set.

2. If it is the case, the scheduler has to test whether $ol_i(x)$ is in conflict with locks on x already set on behalf of other transactions:

   (a) If there is no conflict, then $ol_i(x)$ is set (actually, a lock on x is not set again, but the scheduler records in a *lock table* that now t_i also holds a lock on x).

   (b) If there exists a conflicting lock, transaction t_i is blocked.

Formally, a locking scheduler augments every transaction it processes by new actions of type rl, wl, ru, and wu, resulting in a "locked transaction." It now makes sense to restrict the use of locks by some near-at-hand rules; specifically, we will from now on require that for each transaction t_i that appears *completely* in a schedule s produced by the locking scheduler in question, the following *locking well-formedness rules* hold:

Rules for well-formed locking

LR1: If t_i contains a step of the form $r_i(x)$ $[w_i(x)]$, then schedule s also contains a step of the form $rl_i(x)$ $[wl_i(x)]$ *before* the data operation (i.e., a lock on x is held at the point of the operation on x). Moreover, s contains a step of the form $ru_i(x)$ $[wu_i(x)]$ somewhere *after* the operation.

LR2: For each x accessed by t_i, schedule s has at most one $rl_i(x)$ and at most one $wl_i(x)$ step; in other words, locks of the same type are set at most once per transaction and per data item.

LR3: No step of the form $ru_i(.)$ or $wu_i(.)$ is redundant (i.e., executed per transaction more than once).

These rules apply to schedules (i.e., incomplete histories) in an analogous fashion. For example, for an arbitrary schedule s, rule LR1 reads as follows:

If t_i contains a step of the form $r_i(x)$ $[w_i(x)]$, then s also contains a step of the form $rl_i(x)$ $[wl_i(x)]$ before the data operation. Moreover, s will eventually be augmented so that it also contains a step of the form $ru_i(x)$ $[wu_i(x)]$ somewhere after the operation.

In slight abuse of the terminology just introduced, we will also say that the rules above apply to a transaction, which then means that they apply to the transaction in the context of a schedule in which it occurs.

EXAMPLE 4.1

Consider transactions $t_1 = r_1(x)w_1(y)$ and $t_2 = w_2(x)w_2(y)$ as well as the following history:

$$s_1 = rl_1(x)r_1(x)ru_1(x)wl_2(x)w_2(x)wl_2(y)w_2(y)wu_2(x)wu_2(y)c_2$$
$$wl_1(y)w_1(y)wu_1(y)c_1$$

Clearly, s_1 satisfies rules LR1–LR3; the same applies to the following history:

$$s_2 = rl_1(x)r_1(x)wl_1(y)w_1(y)ru_1(x)wu_1(y)c_1wl_2(x)w_2(x)wl_2(y)$$
$$w_2(y)wu_2(x)wu_2(y)c_2$$

Notice that s_2 is even serial.

The schedules (and eventually the histories) produced by a locking scheduler contain data operations, termination operations, and lock and unlock steps.

Since it will sometimes be useful to distinguish schedules without lock and unlock operations from schedules in which these occur, we introduce the following notation: for some schedule s, let $DT(s)$ denote the projection of s onto the steps of type r, w, a, c (i.e., onto Data and Termination operations).

EXAMPLE 4.2

Let s_1 and s_2 be as in the previous example; then we have

$$DT(s_1) = r_1(x)w_2(x)w_2(y)c_2w_1(y)c_1$$
$$DT(s_2) = r_1(x)w_1(y)c_1w_2(x)w_2(y)c_2 \quad (= t_1 t_2)$$

Note that history s_1 of the above example cannot be an acceptable execution, since $DT(s_1) \notin CSR$. The reason is that between $ru_1(x)$ and $wl_1(y)$ both data items are written by t_2, so that a conflict-equivalent serial history would have to satisfy "$t_1 < t_2$" with respect to x, but "$t_2 < t_1$" with respect to y, which contradict each other. Clearly, a CSR safe scheduler has to avoid such situations.

Whenever there is no ambiguity, we will use the notation s rather than the above notation $DT(s)$ in order to refer to a schedule or history that is free of lock and unlock operations; however, keep in mind that there is a formal difference between the output produced by a locking protocol and the output needed to determine correctness.

We mention that our locking rules LR1–LR3 apply to *every* transaction in a schedule produced by a locking scheduler; in particular, they apply not only to active, but also to aborted transactions, where we assume for aborted transactions that the execution of the Abort operation also takes care of releasing all locks set on behalf of that transaction.

Transaction t_i *holds a lock* on data item x at all points in between t_i's lock acquisition (i.e., the $rl_i(x)$ or $wl_i(x)$ operation) and the corresponding lock release (i.e., the $ru_i(x)$ or $wu_i(x)$ operation). In general, we say that a scheduler operates according to a *locking protocol* if the following holds for each output s:

LR1–LR3: s satisfies the locking rules LR1–LR3,

LR4: if x is held locked by both t_i and t_j for $t_i, t_j \in \text{trans}(s)$, $i \neq j$, then these locks are not in conflict (i.e., they are *compatible*).

4.3.2 **The Two-Phase Locking Protocol**

We now present the first concrete scheduler based on locking, the *two-phase locking protocol (2PL)*. This protocol is the one used most in commercial database systems.

Within the family of locking protocols, two-phase locking is characterized by the following rule regarding the timepoints of lock releases:

DEFINITION 4.2   *Two-Phase Locking (2PL)*

A locking protocol is *two-phase* if for every output s and every transaction $t_i \in trans(s)$ it is true that no ql_i step follows the first ou_i step, $o, q \in \{r, w\}$. A two-phase locking protocol is abbreviated *2PL* or *2PL scheduler*.

In words, a locking protocol is two-phase if for every transaction a phase during which locks are set is distinguished from and strictly followed by a phase during which locks are released. (Later we will see deviations from this two-phase rule in which the two phases of a transaction are allowed to overlap; for the time being, this is not the case.)

EXAMPLE 4.3

Consider history s_1 from the previous example again: it obviously violates the two-phase rule since $ru_1(x) <_s wl_1(y)$. A possible correct execution order is history s_2 from the same example.

The next example, besides showing how a 2PL scheduler might process a given input, also shows how a transaction that first reads a data item and later writes it may start out by getting a read lock, and later upgrade this read lock to a write lock. Such an upgrade is also called *lock conversion*.

EXAMPLE 4.4

Consider the following input schedule:

$$s = w_1(x)r_2(x)w_1(y)w_1(z)r_3(z)c_1w_2(y)w_3(y)c_2w_3(z)c_3$$

A 2PL scheduler could transform s into the following output history (which, of course, is not uniquely determined):

$$wl_1(x)w_1(x)wl_1(y)w_1(y)wl_1(z)w_1(z)wu_1(x)rl_2(x)r_2(x)wu_1(y)$$

$$wu_1(z)c_1rl_3(z)r_3(z)wl_2(y)w_2(y)wu_2(y)ru_2(x)c_2wl_3(y)w_3(y)$$

$$wl_3(z)w_3(z)wu_3(z)wu_3(y)c_3$$

Here t_3 upgrades its read lock on z to a write lock, so that only the latter needs to be released at the end of t_3. Also note that locks need not be released in the same order in which they were set. The resulting execution

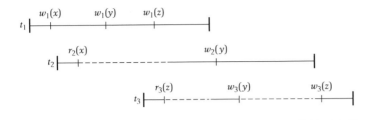

Figure 4.3 Example execution under the 2PL protocol.

is also illustrated in Figure 4.3, where time proceeds from left to right and
dashed lines correspond to lock waits.

We now discuss the (CSR) safety of the 2PL protocol. To this end, we need
to verify that $DT(s) \in CSR$ holds for each output s created by a 2PL scheduler.
The argument, which will deliver a positive result, goes along the following
lines:

LEMMA 4.1

Let s be the output of a 2PL scheduler. Then for each transaction $t_i \in$
$commit(DT(s))$ the following holds:

1. If $o_i(x)$ $(o \in \{r, w\})$ occurs in $CP(DT(s))$, then so do $ol_i(x)$ and $ou_i(x)$
   with the sequencing $ol_i(x) < o_i(x) < ou_i(x)$. (Here $CP(.)$ again denotes
   the committed projection of a schedule, introduced in Chapter 3.)

2. If $t_j \in commit(DT(s))$, $i \neq j$, is another transaction such that some
   steps $p_i(x)$ and $q_j(x)$ from $CP(DT(s))$ are in conflict, then either $pu_i(x) <$
   $ql_j(x)$ or $qu_j(x) < pl_i(x)$ holds. (If two steps are in conflict, then so are
   their lock operations; locks in conflict are not set simultaneously.)

3. If $p_i(x)$ and $q_i(y)$ are in $CP(DT(s))$, then $pl_i(x) < qu_i(y)$, i.e., every lock
   operation occurs before every unlock operation of the *same* transaction.

LEMMA 4.2

Let s be the output of a 2PL scheduler, and let $G := G(CP(DT(s)))$ be the
conflict graph of $CP(DT(s))$. Then the following holds:

1. If (t_i, t_j) is an edge in G, then $pu_i(x) < ql_j(x)$ for some data item x and
   two operations $p_i(x), q_j(x)$ in conflict.

2. If $(t_1, t_2, \ldots, t_n)$ is a path in G, $n \geq 1$, then $pu_1(x) < ql_n(y)$ for two data
   items x and y as well as operations $p_1(x)$ und $q_n(y)$.

3. G is acyclic.

Proof

(1) If (t_i, t_j) is an edge in G, then $CP(DT(s))$ comprises two steps $p_i(x)$ and $q_j(x)$ in conflict such that $p_i(x) < q_j(x)$. According to (1) in Lemma 4.1, this implies $pl_i(x) < p_i(x) < pu_i(x)$ and $ql_j(x) < q_j(x) < qu_j(x)$. According to (2) in Lemma 4.1, we moreover find (a) $pu_i(x) < ql_j(x)$ or (b) $qu_j(x) < pl_i(x)$. Case (b) means $ql_j(x) < q_j(x) < qu_j(x) < pl_i(x) < p_i(x) < pu_i(x)$ and hence $q_j(x) < p_i(x)$, a contradiction to $p_i(x) < q_j(x)$. Thus, $pu_i(x) < ql_j(x)$ (which is case (a)), which had to be shown.

(2) The proof goes by induction on n. The induction base $n = 2$ follows directly from part (1): If (t_1, t_2) is an edge in G, there is a conflict between t_1 and t_2. Thus, $pu_1(x) < ql_2(x)$, i.e., t_1 unlocks x before t_2 locks x. In other words, when t_2 sets a lock, t_1 has already released one.

Now assume our claim holds for n transactions on a path through G, and consider a path of length $n + 1$. The inductive assumption now tells us that there are data items x and z such that $pu_1(x) < ol_n(z)$ in s. Since (t_n, t_{n+1}) is an edge in G, it follows from (1) above that for operations $v_n(y)$ and $q_{n+1}(y)$ in conflict we have $vu_n(y) < ql_{n+1}(y)$. According to (3) of Lemma 4.1, this implies $ol_n(z) < vu_n(y)$ and hence $pu_1(x) < ql_{n+1}(y)$.

(3) Assume that G is cyclic. Then there exists a cycle, say, of the form $(t_1, t_2, \ldots, t_n, t_1)$, $n \geq 1$. By (2), $pu_1(x) < ql_1(y)$ for operations $p_1(x)$, $q_1(y)$, a contradiction to the two-phase rule (or to (3) of Lemma 4.1).

Since the conflict graph of an output produced by a 2PL scheduler is acyclic, and since by the serializability theorem (Theorem 3.10) we have proved in the previous chapter acyclicity of a conflict graph characterizes membership of the respective history in class CSR, we have thus shown:

THEOREM 4.1

A two-phase locking scheduler is CSR safe, i.e., $Gen(2PL) \subseteq CSR$.

Formally, the $Gen(S)$ of a locking scheduler S contains $DT(s)$ only for every output schedule s.

We note that the inclusion just proved is strict, that is, 2PL is unable to generate *all* of CSR:

EXAMPLE 4.5

Let $s = w_1(x)r_2(x)c_2r_3(y)c_3w_1(y)c_1$. As in a previous example we have $s \in$ CSR, since $s \approx_c t_3t_1t_2$. On the other hand, it is easily verified that s cannot be produced by a 2PL scheduler. The simple reason is that 2PL would start out by setting a write lock for t_1 on x; that would immediately block t_2. The next lock operation possible would then be to set a read lock for t_3 on y; once t_3 finishes, t_1 can set a lock on y and finish. Only thereafter t_2 would run, so if s was the input to 2PL, the following would be output: $s' = w_1(x)r_3(y)c_3w_1(y)c_1r_2(x)c_2$.

A fully formal proof of the infeasibility of s under 2PL proceeds as follows. First, by Lemma 4.2(2), we know that $wu_1(x) < rl_2(x)$ and $ru_3(y) < wl_1(y)$. Second, the well-formedness rules for locked schedules require $rl_2(x) < r_2(x)$ and $r_3(y) < ru_3(y)$. Third, the schedule itself includes the order $r_2(x) < r_3(y)$. Putting all these ordering constraints together and using transitivity, we infer that $wu_1(x) < wl_1(y)$, which contradicts the fundamental rule of the 2PL protocol. Therefore, the schedule is not feasible under 2PL, regardless of how lock and unlock operations may be inserted.

The example shows that the fact that a history has been created by 2PL is sufficient for membership in CSR, but not necessary. The latter can even be refined; to this end, recall the definition of OCSR from Definition 3.18: A history s is order preserving conflict serializable, if it is conflict serializable, that is, there exists a serial history s' such that $op(s) = op(s')$ and $s \approx_c s'$, and if the following holds for s' and all $t, t' \in \text{trans}(s)$: if t occurs completely before t' in s, then the same holds in s'. OCSR denotes the class of all order-preserving conflict-serializable histories. Now we have

$OCSR$

THEOREM 4.2

$\text{Gen}(2PL) \subset OCSR$

To see that the inclusion is proper, consider the schedule

$$w_1(x)r_2(x)r_3(y)r_2(z)w_1(y)c_3c_1c_2$$

This schedule, which is a slight variation of the sample schedule for showing that 2PL cannot generate all of CSR, is CSR and trivially falls into OCSR (as there is no pair of strictly sequential transactions), but is still not feasible under 2PL. In Section 4.3.5, we will discuss an alternative to 2PL that is capable of generating *every* schedule in OCSR.

In the output of a 2PL scheduler, for each transaction a *growing phase* (in which locks are set only) can be distinguished from a *shrinking phase* (in which locks are released only). This is illustrated in Figure 4.4. We will exploit this observation later for designing variants of 2PL.

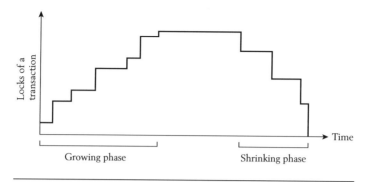

Figure 4.4 Growing and shrinking phase of a transaction under 2PL.

4.3.3 **Deadlock Handling**

Deadlocks   As locking protocols require transactions to wait when requested locks cannot be granted immediately, a set of transactions, each holding some locks and requesting an additional one, may end up being mutually blocked. For example, in the simplest case with only two transactions t_1 and t_2, t_1 may have requested a lock that t_2 is holding in a conflicting mode so that t_1 is waiting for t_2 to release this lock, while at the same time t_2 has requested a lock held by t_1 in a conflicting mode. Such cyclic wait situations are commonly known as *deadlocks*.

For an implementation of the 2PL protocol it is important to realize that it is not deadlock free. To see this, consider the above scenario, refined into the following input schedule:

$$r_1(x)w_2(y)w_2(x)c_2w_1(y)c_1$$

Let this schedule be submitted to a 2PL scheduler. The scheduler processes the input from left to right and hence creates

$$rl_1(x)r_1(x)wl_2(y)w_2(y)$$

At this point, it has to stop, since the next action would be $wl_2(x)$, which is incompatible with $rl_1(x)$, so that $w_2(x)$ has to be blocked. The only step left would then be $w_1(y)$, requiring lock operation $wl_1(y)$, which is incompatible with $wl_2(y)$. Notice that the scheduler cannot even execute $ru_1(x)$, since thereafter t_1 could no longer acquire new locks due to the two-phase rule. Hence the scheduler has encountered a deadlock. This situation is illustrated in Figure 4.5, with time proceeding from left to right and lock waits indicated by dashed lines.

Lock conversion   There is another situation that can cause deadlocks, namely, the already
leading to   mentioned lock conversion. Suppose a transaction t first reads and later writes
deadlock   a data item, and initially sets $rl(x)$; then it needs to upgrade this to $wl(x)$ at

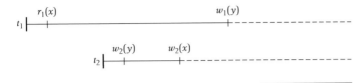

Figure 4.5 A deadlock.

some later point. If two transactions do this at the same time, the following can happen: let $t_1 = r_1(x)w_1(x)$ and $t_2 = r_2(x)w_2(x)c_2$, and let the scheduler execute

$$rl_1(x)r_1(x)rl_2(x)r_2(x)$$

Again, this prefix cannot be extended following the two-phase rule, since an upgrade of $rl_1(x)$ to $wl_1(x)$ would be in conflict with $rl_2(x)$, and analogously $wl_2(x)$ with $rl_1(x)$.

If a protocol allows deadlocks, such as 2PL does, it needs appropriate measures to detect and resolve them. There are various categories of approaches to handle deadlocks, which are discussed next. The first category, designed to allow deadlocks as in situations like the ones just described, comprises approaches for *deadlock detection*. Strategies for deadlock detection are generally based on the notion of a *waits-for graph* (WFG), which is a graph $G = (V, E)$ whose nodes are the active transactions, and in which an edge of the form (t_i, t_j) indicates that t_i waits-for t_j to release a lock that it needs. Clearly, a *cycle* in WFG exhibits a deadlock. *Deadlock detection*

For deadlock detection, a WFG needs to be built and maintained explicitly. In this approach the question arises, how often should a WFG be tested for cycles? There are essentially two options for this issue:

- Under *continuous detection*, the WFG is always kept cycle free by checking for cycles (and eventually breaking them) whenever a lock request is not granted immediately, that is, every time a transaction blocks.

- Under *periodic detection*, the WFG is tested only periodically for cycles, for example, once per second. Clearly, selecting an appropriate time interval for periodic detection is not an easy task and may even impact performance to some extent.

When the scheduler detects a cycle (or several cycles), it has to resolve the corresponding deadlock(s) by aborting at least one transaction from every cycle. Again, there are several *victim selection* criteria, including the following: *Deadlock resolution*

1. *Last blocked*: Pick the transaction that blocked most recently, that is, the one that just blocked in the case of continuous detection.

2. *Random*: From those involved in a deadlock cycle, pick one transaction randomly.

3. *Youngest*: Pick the transaction with the most recent start-up time, that is, the one that began running most recently.

4. *Minimum locks*: Pick the transaction that holds the fewest locks.

5. *Minimum work*: Pick the transaction that has consumed the least amount of resources (e.g., CPU time) so far.

6. *Most cycles*: Pick the transaction that breaks the largest number of cycles simultaneously.

7. *Most edges*: Pick the transaction that eliminates as many edges as possible.

Starvation (livelock)   The idea of the youngest, minimum locks and minimum work strategies is aimed at minimizing the amount of wasted work, for the victim's work so far is lost, the cost of the rollback itself is proportional to that work, and in most cases the transaction will be restarted some time after the rollback is completed. The three strategies are heuristics that approximate this goal to a certain extent, with the subsidiary goal of keeping the overhead extremely low. A problem with all victim selection strategies is that they are susceptible to *livelocks*— situations where a transaction (or, strictly speaking, different incarnations of the same transaction) is repeatedly chosen as deadlock victim, rolled back, and restarted, and thus appears to make progress from a microscopic perspective, but does not really come any closer to its commit from a global viewpoint. In essence, such a transaction would "starve," hence the other name, *starvation*, for this phenomenon. Heuristics for fixing this problem so that starvation freedom can be guaranteed are the subject of Exercise 4.3.

For the most cycles strategy, consider the example shown in Figure 4.6, where an insertion of the dashed edge in either graph closes several cycles simultaneously.

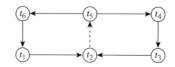

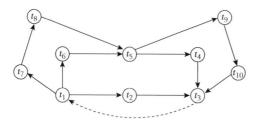

Figure 4.6 Waits-for graphs.

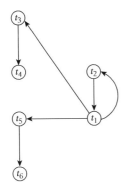

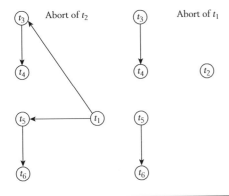

Figure 4.7 On choosing a deadlock victim.

For the most edges option, Figure 4.7 shows a WFG with a cycle and candidate victims t_1 and t_2. Depending on which of the two transactions is aborted, either two or four edges remain in the graph, and clearly the former is more desirable.

The second category of approaches to handle deadlocks is *deadlock prevention*, in which a WFG is not explicitly maintained. Since prevention amounts to never allowing blocked states that can lead to circular waiting, it is clear that conservative protocols are now needed. Possible restrictions include the following:

Deadlock prevention

1. *Wait-die*: If a lock request from transaction t_i leads to a conflict with t_j, resolve as follows: if t_i started before t_j, it is blocked (t_i "waits for" t_j); otherwise, it is restarted (t_i "dies"). In other words, a transaction can only be blocked by a younger transaction.

2. *Wound-wait*: If a lock request from transaction t_i leads to a conflict with another transaction t_j, resolve as follows: if t_i started before t_j, then t_j

is restarted (t_i "wounds" t_j); otherwise, t_i is blocked (t_i "waits for" t_j). Thus, a transaction can only be blocked by an older transaction, and a transaction can kill any younger one it conflicts with.

3. *Immediate restart*: If a lock request from t_i leads to a conflict with another transaction t_j, simply restart t_i. Thus, no transaction is ever blocked.

4. *Running priority*: If a lock request from t_i results in a conflict with t_j, resolve as follows: if t_j is currently waiting due to another conflict, then restart t_j and grant t_i's lock request; otherwise, block t_i. Thus, blocked transactions are not allowed to impede the progress of active ones.

Notice that in these approaches to deadlock prevention, a transaction that is restarted has not necessarily been involved in a deadlock, which indicates the conservativeness of the approaches.

Timeouts   Finally, the third category for dealing with deadlocks comprises just the *timeout* strategy: For each transaction t the scheduler maintains a timer that is activated as soon as a step of t is blocked. If the timer times out, t is aborted under the *assumption* that it has been involved in a deadlock. Clearly, this decision may be wrong, so the choice of the time period for which the timer runs is crucial. Again observe that an aborted transaction has not necessarily been involved in a deadlock.

4.3.4 **Variants of 2PL**

From Figure 4.4 above we can immediately derive the following two variants of 2PL:

DEFINITION 4.3   *Conservative 2PL*

Under *static* or *conservative* 2PL (C2PL) each transaction sets all locks that it needs in the beginning, i.e., before it executes its first r or w step. This is also known as *preclaiming* all necessary locks up front.

Conservative   The conservative 2PL variant is illustrated in Figure 4.8. An advantage of
2PL   C2PL over 2PL is that deadlocks are avoided, since a transaction can only ac-
(preclaiming)   quire all its locks prior to execution if these do not conflict with any others; thus, the scheduler never needs to abort transactions due to their involvement in a deadlock. On the other hand, each transaction has to declare its entire *read set* as well as its *write set* to the scheduler in advance, which is possible in restricted application scenarios only. When read and write sets of a transaction are known to the scheduler, it can try to obtain all necessary

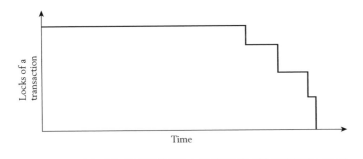

Figure 4.8 Conservative 2PL (preclaiming).

locks on behalf of that transaction; if that is impossible, the transaction has to wait. It follows that, under C2PL, a blocked transaction never holds a lock.

DEFINITION 4.4 *Strict 2PL*

Under *strict* 2PL (S2PL) all (exclusive) write locks that a transaction has acquired are held until the transaction terminates.

The strict 2PL variant is illustrated in Figure 4.9, assuming that all locks are exclusive. Strict 2PL is the protocol most often used in real-world implementations. The strict variant of 2PL is motivated by the observation that a scheduler—as long as the schedule it produces is incomplete—cannot be sure that a transaction t will not need any further locks and hence cannot release a lock held by t until the end of t. An S2PL scheduler has the interesting additional property of producing "strict" histories as output, which we will return to later in the context of transaction recovery.

Strict 2PL

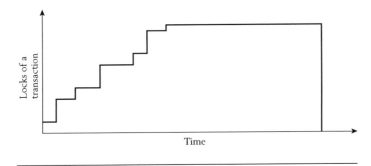

Figure 4.9 Strict 2PL (locking until end of transaction).

It can be shown that it can make a difference whether *all* locks of a transaction are held until its commmit, or this is true for write locks only. This leads to the following third variant of 2PL:

DEFINITION 4.5 *Strong 2PL*

Under *strong* 2PL (SS2PL), all locks (i.e., both (exclusive) write and (shared) read locks) that a transaction has acquired are held until the transaction terminates.

The difference between strict and strong 2PL, in terms of their scheduling power, becomes clear in the following theorem. Note that all inclusions in the theorem are proper.

THEOREM 4.3

$Gen(SS2PL) \subset Gen(S2PL) \subset Gen(2PL)$

Moreover, the following relationship holds, to be exploited in the context of distributed systems:

THEOREM 4.4

$Gen(SS2PL) \subset COCSR$

We will return to this issue in Chapter 11 when we discuss correctness notions for transaction recovery.

4.3.5 Ordered Sharing of Locks

In this subsection we introduce a generalization of 2PL that is less restrictive than 2PL, and which allows the generation of a larger subclass of CSR schedules. Recall the example from the end of Section 4.3.2 that showed that 2PL cannot generate all schedules in the class OCSR of order-preserving conflict-serializable schedules. This example, history

$$s = w_1(x)r_2(x)r_3(y)c_3r_2(z)c_2w_1(y)c_1$$

is not in $Gen(2PL)$, since an initial write lock of t_1 on x would block t_2. On the other hand, $s \in CSR$ and even $s \in OCSR$. The relaxation we are about to introduce will allow situations such as the one in s for the first two operations, and will allow the two conflicting locks to be held *simultaneously*.

The two lock modes we have used so far are *exclusive* (or *nonshared*) and *nonexclusive* (or *shared*), and one of the locking rules said that only two non-exclusive locks on the same data item may be set on behalf of distinct transactions at the same time, in order to share that data item. We now define a third lock mode as follows, thereby relaxing the compatibility of locks used so far:

> Two locks on the same data item, whether due to conflicting operations or not, can be held simultaneously by distinct transactions as long as the lock operations and the corresponding data operations are executed in the same order.

> Note that the corresponding scheduler thus needs to be more sophisticated than a "pure" lock manager, as it needs some bookkeeping about the ordering of operations in addition to the lock table.

We call this third mode *ordered sharing* and denote the corresponding relationship between lock operations by $pl_i(x) \rightarrow ql_j(x)$, $i \neq j$. Thus, given a schedule s, $pl_i(x) \rightarrow ql_j(x)$ implies $pl_i(x) <_s ql_j(x)$ and $p_i(x) <_s q_j(x)$. Ordered sharing from transaction t_i to transaction t_j hence indicates that t_j can acquire a lock on data item x, even though t_i holds a (possibly conflicting) lock on x, as long as the ordered sharing property will be guaranteed.

Ordered sharing

Ordered sharing is of course meant to replace the former exclusive mode, and in terms of Table 4.1, the lock compatibility table shown earlier, we can replace each "$-$" in this table by "$\rightarrow$," individually or in combination. We thus obtain eight compatibility or lock tables, as shown in Figure 4.10. As before, transaction t_i holds a lock in these tables, whereas transaction t_j is requesting one, and each table shows which types of locks can be shared, ordered shared, or not shared. Notice that lock table LT_1 is the one previously used in 2PL, in which *no* exclusive lock is replaced by ordered sharing.

EXAMPLE 4.6

Consider the following history:

$$s_1 = w_1(x)r_2(x)r_3(y)c_3w_1(y)c_1w_2(z)c_2$$

Suppose locks are set as requested by the operations as given, and imagine we replace the old lock compatibility table, i.e., table LT_1 in Figure 4.10, by lock table LT_2. A corresponding scheduler could then produce the following output:

$$wl_1(x)w_1(x)rl_2(x)r_2(x)rl_3(y)r_3(y)ru_3(y)c_3wl_1(y)$$
$$w_1(y)wu_1(x)wu_1(y)c_1wl_2(z)w_2(z)ru_2(x)wu_2(z)c_2$$

LT_1	$rl_i(x)$	$wl_i(x)$
$rl_j(x)$	+	−
$wl_j(x)$	−	−

LT_2	$rl_i(x)$	$wl_i(x)$
$rl_j(x)$	+	→
$wl_j(x)$	−	−

LT_3	$rl_i(x)$	$wl_i(x)$
$rl_j(x)$	+	−
$wl_j(x)$	→	−

LT_4	$rl_i(x)$	$wl_i(x)$
$rl_j(x)$	+	−
$wl_j(x)$	−	→

LT_5	$rl_i(x)$	$wl_i(x)$
$rl_j(x)$	+	→
$wl_j(x)$	→	−

LT_6	$rl_i(x)$	$wl_i(x)$
$rl_j(x)$	+	−
$wl_j(x)$	→	→

LT_7	$rl_i(x)$	$wl_i(x)$
$rl_j(x)$	+	→
$wl_j(x)$	−	→

LT_8	$rl_i(x)$	$wl_i(x)$
$rl_j(x)$	+	→
$wl_j(x)$	→	→

Figure 4.10 Selective use of ordered sharing in lock tables.

In particular, the write lock of t_1 on x and the read lock of t_2 on the same data item are now permitted simultaneously. Notice that lock tables LT_5, LT_7, and LT_8 would allow the same history.

Next consider the following history:

$$s_2 = r_1(x)w_2(x)r_3(y)c_3w_1(y)c_1w_2(z)c_2$$

By a similar argument, s_2 would be in the fixpoint set of a scheduler based on LT_3 (i.e., admitted by the scheduler without any blocks or reorderings of steps), and the same holds for schedulers based on LT_5, LT_6, or LT_8. Finally,

$$s_3 = w_1(x)w_2(x)r_3(y)c_3w_1(y)c_1w_2(z)c_2$$

would be allowed by a scheduler based on table LT_4, LT_6, LT_7, or LT_8.

Lock acquisition rule for ordered sharing

Although it should be intuitively clear how a locking protocol based on one of the tables from Figure 4.10 works, we now discuss this in more detail. Specifically, we need to extend our previous definitions by the following *lock acquisition rule*:

OS1: In a schedule s, for any two operations $p_i(x)$ and $q_i(x)$, $i \neq j$, such that $pl_i(x) \rightarrow ql_j(x)$ is permitted, if t_i acquires $pl_i(x)$ before t_j acquires $ql_j(x)$, then the execution of $p_i(x)$ must occur before the execution of $q_j(x)$.

The lock acquisition rule OS1 alone is not sufficient for guaranteeing conflict serializability. Consider the following counterexample:

$$wl_1(x)w_1(x)wl_2(x)w_2(x)wl_2(y)w_2(y)wu_2(x)wu_2(y)c_2wl_1(y)w_1(y)wu_1(x)$$
$$wu_1(y)c_1$$

This schedule would be allowed by the locking rules LR1–LR4 and OS1. The order of lock acquisitions on x entails a serialization order with t_1 before t_2. Once t_2 holds its write lock on y and has actually written y, t_1 would no longer be granted a write lock on y, as this would lead to the contradicting order with t_2 before t_1. In fact, rule OS1 disallows this lock acquisition. However, when t_2 commits and thus releases all its locks, there is no "marker" left that would prevent t_1 from acquiring the lock on y at some later point. This situation leads to a conflict cycle in the sample schedule above. The solution to this problem is also to enforce an ordering of unlock steps. If t_2 would be prevented from unlocking y until after t_1 starts its unlocking phase and thus would no longer be able to acquire new locks under a two-phase regime, then the second half of the above incorrect schedule would be disallowed but would still allow situations like the ordered sharing of the two write operations on x.

Lock release rule for ordered sharing

So for a correct protocol, we need a rule for unlocking. If we have a relationship $pl_i(x) \rightarrow ql_j(x)$ of ordered sharing between two transactions t_i and t_j, and t_i has not yet released any lock, t_j is called *order dependent* on t_i. If there exists any such t_i, transaction t_j is *on hold*. Now we have

OS2: While a transaction is on hold, it cannot release any of its locks.

In summary, we now obtain a family of locking protocols by using

1. locking rules LR1–LR4,
2. rules OS1 and OS2,
3. the two-phase property,
4. one of the eight compatibility tables shown in Figure 4.10.

O2PL

Notice that these protocols reduce to ordinary 2PL if ordered sharing is not used and locking is correspondingly based on table LT_1. If locking is based on LT_8, we will call the resulting protocol the O2PL *protocol* for a reason that will become clear shortly.

EXAMPLE 4.7

Consider an O2PL scheduler that receives the following input:

$$s = r_1(x)w_2(x)r_3(y)w_2(y)c_2w_3(z)c_3r_1(z)c_1$$

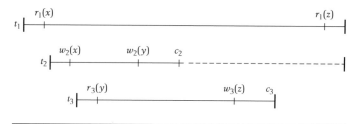

Figure 4.11 Example execution under the O2PL protocol.

It will produce the following output:

$$s' = rl_1(x)r_1(x)wl_2(x)w_2(x)rl_3(y)r_3(y)wl_2(y)w_2(y)wl_3(z)w_3(z)$$
$$ru_3(y)wu_3(z)c_3rl_1(z)r_1(z)ru_1(x)ru_1(z)wu_2(x)wu_2(y)c_2c_1$$

This resulting execution is also illustrated in Figure 4.11, where dashed lines correspond to waiting periods. Notice that t_2 is order dependent on t_1 and t_3, so it is on hold when c_2 arrives. According to lock rule OS2, t_2 cannot release any lock until the others have, which here means it has to unlock last.

The following can now be verified:

LEMMA 4.3

Let x be locked by pl_i and ql_j in ordered shared mode, i.e., $pl_i(x) \to ql_j(x)$, and let $pl_i(x) < ql_j(x)$, then $p_i(x) < q_j(x)$.

The above follows from the lock acquisition rule OS1, and the following is a consequence of the unlock rule OS2:

LEMMA 4.4

If $pl_i(x) \to ql_j(x)$ and $pl_i(x) < ql_j(x)$, then there exists an unlock operation of t_i preceding *all* unlock operations of t_j.

Finally, for truly incompatible locks, for which ordered sharing is disallowed according to the chosen lock compatibility table, the previous property can be strengthened as follows, corresponding to what can be said about standard 2PL:

LEMMA 4.5

If $pl_i(x)$ is incompatible with $ql_j(x)$ (i.e., without allowing order sharing) and $pl_i(x) < ql_j(x)$, then $pu_i(x) < ql_j(x)$. That is, if t_i locks x before t_j

and the two locks needed by these transactions are incompatible, then t_i has to release its lock on x before t_j can set one. (Note that this case does not occur in the O2PL protocol, as its lock compatibility table LT_8 allows ordered sharing for all conflict pairs.)

Now we can establish an argument similar to the one we had for the correctness of 2PL. Indeed, let s be a history produced by a two-phase protocol based on any of the new lock tables. Then an edge (t, t') in $G(s)$, the conflict graph of s, indicates that there exists an unlock operation of t preceding all unlock operations of t'. The same holds along a path in $G(S)$, so if $G(s)$ were cyclic, an unlock operation of some t along the path would precede all unlocks of t itself, a contradiction. Thus we have

---

THEOREM 4.5

Let $Gen(LT_i)$, $1 \leq i \leq 8$, denote the set of histories produced by a protocol defined as above and using lock table LT_i, then $Gen(LT_i) \subseteq CSR$.

Safety of ordered sharing

Theorem 4.5 in particular implies that O2PL (i.e., the protocol based on LT_8) generates histories in CSR. Let $s \in Gen(O2PL)$. Then there is a serial history s' conflict equivalent to s in which all conflicting operations occur in the same order as in s, due to the use of the ordered shared mode now for *every* pair of conflicting operations. Since s' is serial, this proves membership of s even in OCSR. In conclusion, we have

---

THEOREM 4.6

$Gen(O2PL) \subseteq OCSR$

An interesting point is that the converse of this latter statement is also true. To this end, consider some $s \in OCSR$. For each data operation in s the corresponding lock can be set immediately prior to the operation; note that even O2PL allows this. Let $t_1 \ldots t_n$ be the order-preserving conflict-equivalent serial order of the transactions in s; we may further assume that all unlock operations occur after all data operations in s, yet are in serialization order. Since O2PL permits that locks are released in exactly that order, it is possible to generate s using the O2PL protocol. Thus we have

Scheduling power of O2PL

THEOREM 4.7

$OCSR \subseteq Gen(O2PL)$

COROLLARY 4.1

Gen(O2PL) = OCSR

Despite these intriguing properties and its theoretical superiority over 2PL, ordered sharing is not necessarily the method of choice in practice. The reason is that it is not a truly "pure" locking protocol in that its implementation cannot be solely based on a lock table. Rather, ordered sharing needs to enforce the proper ordering of data accesses whenever it allows the sharing of write locks. Thus, an implementation requires additional data structures for bookkeeping and would incur additional run-time overhead. Depending on application and workload characteristics, the gain in concurrency may not be worth this additional overhead.

4.3.6 **Altruistic Locking**

Long transactions
We next present an extension to the 2PL protocol based on the following observation. Suppose we are given a transaction of long duration—a transaction that reads and writes many database items, performs extensive computations, pauses for user input, maybe all this in combination, and hence lives longer than most other transactions. Processing such a transaction with 2PL may result in serious performance problems, due to the fact that locks are held by this transaction for long periods of time, and hence other transactions wishing to access the same items have to face delays. In addition, long transactions are more likely than short ones to get involved in deadlocks. One conceivable way of handling long transactions could be to use the approach of interleaving specifications, which we have described in Chapter 3, and to specify how long transactions can interleave with others, thus relaxing serializability. However, as pointed out in Chapter 3, such techniques require additional considerations in the application design, as opposed to the automatically provided guarantee of serializability.

In this subsection, we look at another approach, which does preserve serializability and whose motivation derives from the following example.

EXAMPLE 4.8

Consider a database $D = \{a, b, c, d, e, f, g\}$, and suppose that transaction t_1 needs to access all seven items, say, in alphabetical order a through g. Further assume that while t_1 is accessing item d, three short transactions with the following data requirements attempt to run:

$$t_2 : \text{access to } a \text{ and } b$$
$$t_3 : \text{access to } c \text{ and } e$$
$$t_4 : \text{access to } f \text{ and } g$$

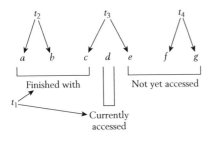

Figure 4.12 A long transaction delaying short ones.

If 2PL is used for scheduling these transactions, both t_2 and t_3 have to wait until t_1 finishes, since both want to access data items that are still locked by t_1. Note that, under 2PL, t_1 cannot unlock an item until it has obtained a lock on the last item g. On the other hand, t_4 can obtain locks on f and g and hence execute concurrently with t_1. The situation is illustrated in Figure 4.12.

With a little additional information, the scheduler could also allow t_2 to run concurrently with t_1. Suppose that, although t_1 still holds locks on a and b, it has finished accessing these items. As long as t_2 (and similarly, other transactions) accesses only such data items that t_1 is finished with, it can appear in a serialization of the schedule in question *after* t_1.

The key point of the above example is that the short transactions t_2 through t_4 access only *subsets* of the data items that are read or written by the long transaction t_1, and that such access profiles are often (but not always) known in advance. What is needed for such situations is a mechanism by which transactions like t_1 can inform the scheduler that they are finished with operating on a data item. This information could then be used to let other transactions access that item.

Such a mechanism is delivered by an extension of the 2PL protocol called *altruistic locking* (AL). As before, a transaction locks and unlocks items in a two-phase manner. However, unlike 2PL, and similar to ordered sharing discussed in the previous subsection, several transactions may hold conflicting locks on an item simultaneously under certain conditions. In terms of Example 4.8, AL will allow t_2 to acquire locks on items a and b, although t_1 holds locks on them. In order to make this work, AL uses a third access control operation, besides lock and unlock, which is called *donate*. The donate operation is used to inform the scheduler that access to a data item is no longer required by the transaction that has currently locked the item, so that the item can be "donated" for access to another transaction. The donating transaction is free to acquire other locks

Idea of altruistic locking (AL)

in the future, so that lock and donate operations do not need to follow a two-phase rule; but other than that, the transaction still has to be two-phase with respect to unlock operations.

The use of donate on item x by transaction t_i, subsequently denoted $d_i(x)$, has to follow certain rules, which are stated next:

AL rules

AL1: Items cannot be read or written by t_i once it has donated them; that is, if $d_i(x)$ and $o_i(x)$ occur in a schedule s, $o \in \{r, w\}$, then $o_i(x) <_s d_i(x)$.

AL2: Donated items are eventually unlocked; that is, if $d_i(x)$ occurs in a schedule s following an operation $o_i(x)$, then $ou_i(x)$ is also in s and $d_i(x) <_s ou_i(x)$.

AL3: Transactions cannot hold conflicting locks simultaneously, unless one has donated the data item in question; that is, if $o_i(x)$ and $p_j(x)$, $i \neq j$, are conflicting operations in a schedule s and $o_i(x) <_s p_j(x)$, then either $ou_i(x) <_s pl_j(x)$, or $d_i(x)$ is also in s and $d_i(x) <_s pl_j(x)$.

EXAMPLE 4.9

Consider again the situation from Example 4.8, and suppose that each access by one of the transactions is a write operation. Then the following schedule (in which t_1 and t_3 are unfinished) obeys the AL rules just stated:

$$s = wl_1(a)w_1(a)d_1(a)wl_2(a)wl_1(b)w_2(a)w_1(b)d_1(b)wl_2(b)w_2(b)$$
$$wl_1(c)ul_2(a)w_1(c)ul_2(b)c_2d_1(c)wl_3(c)w_3(c)wl_4(f)w_4(f)$$
$$wl_1(d)wl_4(g)w_4(g)w_1(d)ul_4(g)ul_4(f)c_4d_1(d)$$

Notice how t_2 can run concurrently with t_1, once t_1 starts donating items a and b. Transaction t_4 can even run independently of t_1, since t_1 has not yet reached items f and g. However, t_3 cannot yet finish, as only part of the items it wants to access are already donated by t_1.

Wake and indebtedness

Example 4.9 gives rise to some more terminology: intuitively, if transaction t_j locks a data item that has been donated and not yet unlocked by transaction t_i, $i \neq j$, we say that t_j is *in the wake* of t_i. More formally, we have the following:

1. An operation $p_j(x)$ from transaction t_j is in the wake of transaction t_i, $i \neq j$, in the context of a schedule s if $d_i(x) \in op(s)$ and $d_i(x) <_s p_j(x) <_s ou_i(x)$ for some operation $o_i(x)$ from t_i.

2. A transaction t_j is in the wake of transaction t_i if some operation from t_j is in the wake of t_i. Transaction t_j is *completely* in the wake of t_i if all of its operations are in the wake of t_i.

3. A transaction t_j is *indebted* to transaction t_i in a schedule s if $o_i(x)$, $d_i(x)$, $p_j(x) \in op(s)$ such that $p_j(x)$ is in the wake of t_i and either $o_i(x)$ and $p_j(x)$ are in conflict or some intervening operation $q_k(x)$ such that $d_i(x) <_s q_k(x) <_s p_j(x)$ is in conflict with both $o_i(x)$ and $p_j(x)$.

The notions wake and indebtedness are the basis for another AL rule, which is motivated by the following examples. First consider the following history:

$$s_1 = wl_1(a)w_1(a)d_1(a)rl_2(a)r_2(a)rl_2(b)r_2(b)ru_2(a)ru_2(b)c_2$$
$$rl_1(b)r_1(b)wu_1(a)ru_1(b)c_1$$

Clearly, s_1 is conflict serializable. Moreover, when $d_1(a)$ is dropped from s_1, the remaining history is in Gen(2PL). However, s_1 should not be admissible under altruistic locking, since transaction t_2 first enters the wake of t_1 by issuing $rl_2(a)$ and then leaves the wake again by issuing $rl_2(b)$, which should be prohibited. The intuitive reason is that, once a transaction has entered the wake of another transaction, it should get in there completely (and stay there) until that other transaction issues its first unlock operation, since otherwise it can no longer be guaranteed in general that the two get serialized in the appropriate order (determined by the wake relationship). For example, if in history s_1, above, $r_1(b)$ were replaced by $w_1(b)$, the resulting schedule would no longer be conflict serializable, but the locking protocol would not be able to prevent this conflict cycle, as t_2 has already released its lock on b by the time t_1 acquires its lock on b.

The solution to avoid this problem is to require t_2 to stay in the wake of t_1 once it has made use of t_1's donation and issued an operation that conflicts with t_1. Obviously, this makes sense only if it is known at this point that t_2 needs to access only a subset of the data items that have been or are going to be read by t_1. Most typically, this is the case when t_1 performs a table scan and t_2 is confined to accessing a few records of this table. If this kind of opportunity cannot be inferred at the time of the first conflict between t_1 and t_2, t_2 may choose to ignore the donation up front and wait for t_1 to unlock the requested data item.

Now consider the following history:

$$s_2 = rl_1(a)r_1(a)d_1(a)wl_3(a)w_3(a)wu_3(a)c_3rl_2(a)r_2(a)wl_2(b)$$
$$ru_2(a)w_2(b)wu_2(b)c_2rl_1(b)r_1(b)ru_1(a)ru_1(b)c_1$$

History s_2 shows that if a transaction is forced into another transaction's wake only when one of its locks conflicts with a donated lock, this can still result in incorrect behavior. Indeed, in s_2, transaction t_2 is now assumed not to enter the wake of t_1 when it reads data item a since t_1 also just reads this item. However, $s_2 \notin$ CSR. This tells us that even *indirect conflicts* between t_1 and t_2 (i.e., the order $r_1(a)w_3(a)r_2(a)$, with a third transaction's intermediate operation being in conflict with both t_1 and t_2) matter for the requirements on when a transaction must stay in the wake of another transaction.

The notion of indebtedness is intended to establish a condition under which a transaction should enter the wake of another transaction. We state this condition as another AL rule:

Another AL rule

AL4: When a transaction t_j is indebted to another transaction t_i, t_j must remain completely in the wake of t_i until t_i begins to unlock items. That is, for *every* operation $p_j(x)$ occurring in a schedule s, either $p_j(x)$ is in the wake of t_i or there exists an unlock operation $ou_i(y)$ in s such that $ou_i(y) <_s o_j(x)$.

AL protocol

With these preparations, it is now easy to establish the *altruistic locking protocol*, which we again abbreviate AL: a scheduler operates according to the AL protocol (or is an *AL scheduler*) if it is a 2PL scheduler and obeys the AL rules AL1–AL4. In the following theorems, let Gen(AL) denote the set of histories that the AL protocol can generate as output. Now the following is straightforward:

THEOREM 4.8

Gen(2PL) $\subset$ Gen(AL)

The reason why the AL protocol can generate at least all histories that are admissible under 2PL is because the 2PL rules are contained in the AL protocol; indeed, if no donations are performed, AL reduces to 2PL. The following history shows that the inclusion is strict:

$$s = r_1(x)w_2(x)c_2w_3(y)c_3r_1(y)c_1$$

Under 2PL, a read lock on x set by t_1 would conflict with a write lock on x from t_2, so t_2 (or t_3, because of y) would not be allowed to run concurrently with t_1, so $s \notin$ Gen(2PL). Under the AL protocol, however, transaction t_1 can donate x to t_2, thereby allowing t_2 to become indebted to t_1 and to run in its wake.

Thus, AL provides more concurrency than 2PL. On the other hand, not all conflict-serializable histories can be generated by the AL protocol.

THEOREM 4.9

Correctness of the AL protocol

Gen(AL) $\subset$ CSR

The full proof that Gen(AL) is contained in CSR is left to be worked out in Exercise 4.10). It essentially follows a standard argument, namely, that any AL-generated history s has an acyclic conflict graph $G(s)$ (from which containment then follows by the serializability theorem from the previous chapter). It can be shown that each edge of the form $t_i \rightarrow t_j$ in such a graph $G(s)$ is either a "wake edge," indicating that t_j is completely in the wake of t_i, or a "crest edge," indicating that t_i unlocks some item before t_j locks some item. In addition, for every path $t_1 \rightarrow \ldots \rightarrow t_n$ in $G(s)$, there is either a wake edge from t_1 or t_n, or there exists some t_k on the path such that there is a crest edge from t_1 to t_k. These properties suffice to prove the claim. To see that the containment is strict, consider history

$$s^* = r_1(x)r_2(z)r_3(z)w_2(x)c_2w_3(y)c_3r_1(y)r_1(z)c_1$$

Clearly, $s^* \approx_c t_3t_1t_2$, so $s^* \in$ CSR. On the other hand, either x or y (or both) must be locked by t_1 between operations $r_1(x)$ and $r_1(y)$. By rule AL1, either x or y (or both) must be donated by t_1 for $w_2(x)$ and $w_3(y)$ to occur, so either t_2 or t_3 (or both) must be indebted to t_1. However, neither $r_2(z)$ nor $r_3(z)$ are allowed to be in the wake of t_1 if the latter is well formed, since t_1 later reads z. Hence either t_2 or t_3 violate rule AL4.

We mention (without proof) that the set Gen(AL) has other interesting properties. For example, it has a nonempty intersection with the class COCSR of commit order-preserving histories (as any serial history is in both classes), but is otherwise incomparable with respect to set inclusion with COCSR. Indeed, a slight modification of history s^* above in which c_2 is moved to the very end makes s^* commit order preserving, but still not acceptable under AL. Conversely, history

$$r_1(x)w_2(x)c_2c_1$$

is in Gen(AL), but not in COCSR. We finally mention that a similar observation can be made for class OCSR discussed in the previous subsection and in Chapter 3; again it has a nonempty intersection with Gen(AL), but is otherwise incomparable to it. To this end, recall from the previous subsection that in a schedule s, $pl_i(x) \rightarrow ql_j(x)$ ($i \neq j$) implies $pl_i(x) <_s ql_j(x)$ and $p_i(x) <_s q_j(x)$, and operations p_i and q_j (or, more precisely, transactions t_i and t_j) must not finish in arbitrary order. In particular, t_j has to wait before releasing its locks until t_i is finished, which is no longer the case under AL.

4.3.7 **Non-Two-Phase Locking Protocols**

A crucial point for most of the schedulers discussed so far has been a guarantee of the two-phase property of transactions. We now present protocols that can do without this property, and that are even deadlock free. We should note up front, however, that these protocols are geared for very specific access patterns.

Thus, although they are developed as general-purpose protocols, they perform well only under such specific conditions and may be susceptible to degradation in settings for which they are not suited.

As we will show, the two-phase property is essentially replaced by ordering the accesses performed on the data; in other words, transactions have to follow certain access patterns. To this end, we will first assume that the access patterns follow a hierarchical organization of the data items; that is, the data items are viewed as the nodes of a tree, and accesses have to follow a path down the tree. If all accesses performed are write operations only, it is easily seen that the two-phase property can be relaxed. However, when transactions are allowed to perform read and write operations as before, we will show that additional measures are needed to ensure serializability, since one transaction could now bypass another while moving down the tree. The extra condition that avoids such races in the tree carries over to database organizations that are arbitrary directed acyclic graphs (DAGs).

Write-Only Tree Locking

In this subsection, we consider a restricted transaction model in which read operations are missing. Thus, a transaction can write a data item (or you may think of read and write applied to the same item as collapsed into one operation). Now consider a data item tree shown in Figure 4.13. Note that this tree is a "virtual" data organization only, in that the actual relationships (e.g., references) among data items may be quite different from such a hierarchy. The important point is that transactions exhibit treelike access patterns and are essentially top-down traversals of the tree. So we will require that write accesses to data items have to follow the order given by the tree. For example, if an access to item *d* is

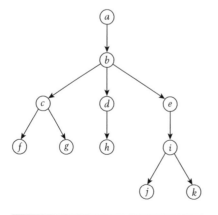

Figure 4.13 Tree organization of data items.

requested in the tree of Figure 4.13, a and then b must be accessed first. Note that the view that data accesses have to follow some order is frequently given in reality, for example, through the existence of index structures such as B^+ trees, which are accessed before actual data is touched. Specific protocols for B^+ tree indexes will be presented in Chapter 9, where we will show that the generic tree-oriented protocols that we are going to derive now form valuable building blocks for concurrency control on search structures.

It turns out that the enforcement of a certain access order for data items can serve as a replacement for the two-phase property. Under the *write-only tree locking* (WTL) protocol, lock requests and releases must obey the locking rules LR1–LR4 and the following additional rules for each transaction:

Write-only tree locking (WTL)

WTL1: If x is any node in the tree other than the root, $wl_i(x)$ can be set only if t_i currently holds a write lock on y, where y is the parent of x.

WTL2: After a $wu_i(x)$, no further $wl_i(x)$ is allowed (on the same data item x).

Rules WTL1 and WTL2 of the protocol imply that the scheduler can unlock an item x only after it has obtained locks on the relevant children of x.

EXAMPLE 4.10

Consider the tree from Figure 4.13 as well as transaction $t = w(d)w(i)w(k)$. Under the WTL protocol, t will be transformed into the following locked transaction (where accesses are underlined):

$$wl(a)wl(b)wu(a)wl(d)wl(e)wu(b)\underline{w(d)}wu(d)wl(i)wu(e)\underline{w(i)}$$
$$wl(k)wu(i)\underline{w(k)}wu(k)$$

As a verification of the WTL protocol, let $(x, z_1, \ldots, z_n, v)$ be a path in a given database tree from x to v, and assume (1) that t_i locks x *before* t_j does, and (2) that both t_i and t_j lock v. Then we can conclude that, due to the existence of $wl_i(x)$, lock $wl_j(x)$ cannot be set, and $wl_i(z_1) < wu_i(x)$ (rule WTL1). Thus, $wl_i(z_1) < wl_j(z_1)$, and the same holds along the entire path, which proves the following:

Safety of WTL

LEMMA 4.6

If transaction t_i locks x before t_j does, then each successor v of x in the data tree that is locked by both t_i and t_j is also locked by t_i before it is locked by t_j.

Now this implies:

THEOREM 4.10

Gen(WTL) $\subseteq$ CSR

Proof

Let (t_i, t_j) be an edge in the conflict graph G of an output of the WTL protocol. Then there are operations $w_i(x)$ and $w_j(x)$ in conflict such that $w_i(x)$ occurs before $w_j(x)$ in the output. According to the WTL rules, t_i unlocks x before t_j locks x. By Lemma 4.6, t_i locks the root of the data tree before t_j does, since x is a successor of the root and every transaction locks the root, and otherwise a contradiction to the lemma would result. But then t_i unlocks the root before t_j locks it. By induction it is then easily seen that the same applies to transactions t_i and t_j, which are connected via a path in G. Now if G were cyclic, say, with cycle $(t_1, t_2, \ldots, t_n, t_1)$, it would follow that t_1 unlocks the root before t_1 locks it, an obvious contradiction to rule WTL2.

A similar consideration reveals that the WTL protocol has the nice property of being immune to deadlocks.

THEOREM 4.11

The WTL protocol is deadlock free.

Proof

If t_i waits for a lock on the root, it cannot have set any other lock yet. If t_i waits-for a lock held by t_j (on a node that is not the root), then t_j unlocks the root before t_i locks it. Again by induction we may then conclude that if the waits-for graph has a cycle involving t_i, then t_i unlocks the root before t_i locks it, a contradiction.

We mention that the WTL protocol can be generalized in various directions, which may, however, require additional rules. For example, it could be allowed to lock *any* node in the data tree first and thereafter only data items in the subtree rooted at this node; in other words, locking the root initially is no longer required.

Finally, note that, although the protocol is specifically geared for treelike access patterns, it is a general-purpose protocol in the sense that it can be applied to arbitrary data access patterns, too. However, being forced to obey the protocol's four tree-oriented locking rules could then easily result in too many locks or unacceptable lock duration. For example, if a transaction were to access the nodes f, i, and b of the tree in Figure 4.13 in this order, these three accesses would have to be embedded in a virtual top-down tree traversal, requiring locks as if the transaction accessed all paths to these nodes. In particular, we would need to acquire a lock on the root a first, and this lock would have to be retained until we learn about the transaction's last access to b and acquire a lock on b; only then can we release the lock on the root a. So the lock on the critical root would be held for almost the entire duration of the transaction. Obviously, performance is likely to degrade in such situations. The bottom line is that tree locking is beneficial only for truly treelike access patterns, but it can cope with occasional nontreelike transactions.

Read/Write Tree Locking

We now generalize the WTL protocol introduced in the previous subsection "back" to read and write operations. To see what could cause a problem and why we looked at write operations only in the first place, consider once more the tree from Figure 4.13. Let t_1 and t_2 be two transactions, both accessing items a, b, e, i, and k in that order. Then the following could be a prefix of an acceptable schedule:

$$wl_1(a)w_1(a)wl_1(b)ul_1(a)wl_2(a)w_1(b)wl_1(e)w_2(a)\ldots$$

As we said in the previous subsection, the crucial points are that transactions need to move along the tree by at least keeping neighboring nodes locked (as in $wl_1(b)ul_1(a)$), and that two transactions doing the same thing must strictly follow each other. The important implication of this is that no transaction can pass another transaction; in the example, both t_1 and t_2 have to follow the a–b–e–i–k pattern.

Now consider the case where reads and writes are again allowed, and assume we still follow the WTL rules from above. Since a transaction might not want to read *and* write each data item it encounters, it may just read some items, in order to get to those it wants to write. As an example, consider the following two transactions operating on the tree of Figure 4.13:

$$t_1 = r_1(a)r_1(b)w_1(a)w_1(b)r_1(e)r_1(i)c_1$$
$$t_2 = r_2(a)r_2(b)r_2(e)r_2(i)w_2(i)c_2$$

Using the WTL rules but allowing read locks to be shared, the two transactions could result in a schedule like the following:

$$rl_1(a)rl_1(b)r_1(a)r_1(b)wl_1(a)w_1(a)wl_1(b)ul_1(a)rl_2(a)r_2(a)w_1(b)rl_1(e)ul_1(b)$$
$$rl_2(b)r_2(b)ul_2(a)rl_2(e)rl_2(i)ul_2(b)r_2(e)r_1(e)r_2(i)wl_2(i)w_2(i)wl_2(k)ul_2(e)$$
$$ul_2(i)rl_1(i)ul_1(e)r_1(i)\ldots$$

This example, albeit along the lines of tree locking, is no longer serializable, since there are conflicts between $w_1(a)$ and $r_2(a)$ as well as between $w_2(i)$ and $r_1(i)$; so the conflict graph is cyclic. The point is that we see here how the shared locks allow t_2 to pass t_1 in the schedule, since item i is the first item that t_2 writes; so it can read to this point faster than t_1 can, which starts writing items at the top and hence needs to spend more time on obtaining the appropriate locks.

Pitfalls   We now introduce the *read/write tree locking* (RWTL) protocol as a way to overcome the problem shown above. The trick is to require the two-phase property on certain subtrees, which are given as a "neighborhood" of read operations called a *pitfall*. Here, having the two-phase property on a set of data items means that the projection of the schedule onto these data items satisfies the rules of the two-phase locking protocol. Let t be a transaction accessing a database tree by read and write operations. The *read set* $RS(t)$ of t is the set of items read by t, and the *write set* $WS(t)$ of t is the set of items written by t. In the presence of a tree, $RS(t)$ spawns a subtree that will generally split into a number of connected components, say, $C_1, \ldots, C_m$. A pitfall of t is a set of the form

$$C_i \cup \{x \in WS(t) \mid x \text{ is a child or parent of some } y \in C_i\}, 1 \le i \le m$$

As an example, consider the database tree shown in Figure 4.14. We assume that transaction t is given by $RS(t) = \{f, i, g\}$ and $WS(t) = \{c, l, j, k, o\}$. Then $RS(t)$ has two connected components $\{f, i\}$ and $\{g\}$, and t has two pitfalls $pf_1 = \{c, f, i, l, j\}$ and $pf_2 = \{g, c, k\}$, which are the shaded areas in Figure 4.14. Notice that pitfalls do not need to be disjoint.

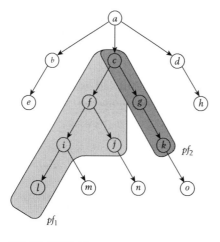

Figure 4.14 Another tree organization of data items.

We are now ready to state the RWTL protocol. The rules for each transaction t_i are those of the WTL protocol with the addition of one extra rule:

RWTL1: The transaction has the two-phase property on each of its pitfalls; that is, for each pitfall the transaction follows a two-phase rule with respect to setting and releasing locks on elements of that pitfall.

As is easily seen, our last schedule above on the tree from Figure 4.13 exhibits for transaction t_1 a read set $RS(t_1) = \{a, b, e, i\}$, which equals a pitfall of t_1; however, t_1 is *not* two-phase on that pitfall. The argument here is that this is a reason why WTL, if naively extended to reads and writes, fails to produce CSR schedules.

In order to show the safety of the RWTL protocol, the following observations need to be proven:

LEMMA 4.7

Let T be a given database tree, and let t be a transaction on T that obeys the rules of the RWTL protocol. Let $V \subseteq RS(t) \cup WS(t)$ span a connected subtree of T. Then the restriction $\Pi_V(t)$ of t to V also follows the rules of RWTL.

This is simply because for doing all the accesses to items in V, t just needs to act as before, that is, according to the RWTL rules.

LEMMA 4.8

Assume that transaction t has the two-phase property on $V \subseteq RS(t) \cup WS(t)$, and let $W \subseteq RS(t) \cup WS(t)$. Then $\Pi_W(t)$ has the two-phase property on $V \cap W$.

These lemmata can be used to show the safety of RWTL:

THEOREM 4.12

$Gen(RWTL) \subseteq CSR$

Once again, the proof assumes that the conflict graph of a schedule $s \in Gen(RWTL)$ has a cycle and derives a contradiction; it proceeds by induction on the length of a cycle.

DAG locking   We conclude this section by mentioning that the RWTL protocol can be generalized further, in particular to DAGs leading to the *DAG locking* protocol, essentially by allowing a transaction to lock any node in the given database graph first (the "entry point" of the transaction), and by replacing rule WTL1, which makes sure the access pattern of a transaction obeys the node ordering of the given tree, by the following rule:

> DAG1: A transaction may lock an item x (which is not the entry point into the graph) if it currently holds locks on the majority of predecessors of x.

4.3.8 On the Geometry of Locking

We conclude our discussion of locking schedulers by briefly mentioning a *geometric* interpretation of locking. To this end, we first give such an interpretation for the notion of conflict serializability and then extend that to transactions with lock and unlock operations.

Schedules   We restrict our attention to the case of two transactions for reasons of
as curves   simplicity; however, what we present in this subsection can be generalized to more than two transactions. We assume that our two transactions are completely known. For each transaction its sequence of steps is represented as a sequence of equidistant integer points on one of the axes spanning the Euclidean plane. The two transactions then define a rectangular grid in that plane, and a schedule becomes a monotone curve starting in the origin of the coordinates. A grid point is a *conflict point* if the two steps corresponding to its coordinates (one on the x axis, the other on the y axis) are in conflict.

EXAMPLE 4.11

Consider the two transactions $t_1 = r_1(x)w_1(y)$ and $t_2 = w_2(x)r_2(y)$. The schedule $s = r_1(x)w_2(x)r_2(y)w_1(y)$ can be represented geometrically, as shown in Figure 4.15. Conflict points are $(r_1(x), w_2(x))$ and $(w_1(y), r_2(y))$.

A schedule for two transactions *separates* given conflict points if, informally, these points occur on both sides of the curve; for example, such a situation is given in Figure 4.15. We note that the schedule shown in that figure has a cyclic conflict and hence does not belong to CSR. That this is not a coincidence is shown by:

THEOREM 4.13

A schedule s for two transactions t_1 and t_2 is in CSR iff the curve representing s does not separate any two conflict points.

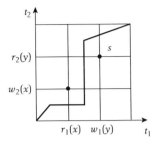

Figure 4.15 Geometrical representation
of a schedule.

The geometric interpretation can be directly generalized to transactions *Locked* comprising lock and unlock operations: All steps of both transactions are now *transactions* interpreted as points along the axes of a coordinate system spanning a plane, where only the data operations have integer coordinates. A schedule is a curve as before. Conflict points turn into *conflict regions*, which are delimited by pairs of conflicting locks of the two transactions together with their respective unlock operations. Blurring the distinction between read and write locks for a moment, let us for the sake of simplicity use a single type "$l(x)$" of lock operations and a single type "$u(x)$" of unlock operation; then any two lock operations of the two transactions referring to the same data item are in conflict. Moreover, the conflict region ("of x") is the square defined by the following pairs of coordinates:

$$(l_1(x),\ l_2(x))$$
$$(u_1(x),\ l_2(x))$$
$$(l_1(x),\ u_2(x))$$
$$(u_1(x),\ u_2(x))$$

EXAMPLE 4.12

Consider the following schedule consisting of two transactions:

$$s = l_2(z)w_2(z)l_1(x)w_1(x)l_1(y)w_1(y)u_1(y)l_2(y)u_2(z)l_1(z)w_1(x)$$
$$u_1(x)l_2(x)w_2(y)w_2(x)u_2(x)w_2(y)w_1(z)u_1(z)c_1u_2(y)c_2$$

(The fact that write operations may occur multiple times is allowed and of course determines the duration for which a lock needs to be held.) The geometrical interpretation of s in terms of conflict regions is shown in Figure 4.16.

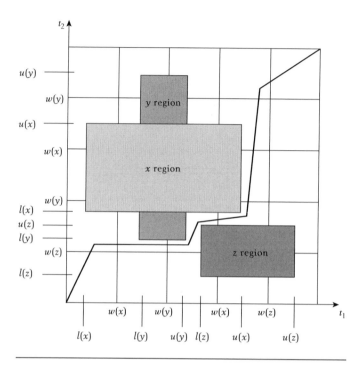

Figure 4.16 Schedule separating conflict regions.

> Notice that each region corresponds to exactly one data item, and that each point within a conflict region represents a state in which both transactions hold conflicting locks on the same data item.

Now it is clear that a schedule should avoid conflict regions, since, as we noticed, every point inside such a region means that two conflicting locks are set simultaneously. In other words, a schedule has to "bypass" conflict regions; however, it cannot do so in an arbitrary fashion due to the following generalization of the previous theorem:

THEOREM 4.14

Let s be a schedule for two transactions t_1 and t_2 containing lock and unlock operations for the transactions. Then $DT(s) \in CSR$ iff the curve representing s does not separate conflict regions.

Safety of lockings   These results have interesting applications from a theoretical point of view, since they allow us to reason about the "safety" of a system of locked transactions as well as on the scheduling power of locking protocols. Call a *locked transaction* a transaction in which lock and unlock operations have been placed in a syntactically correct manner (i.e., following the locking well-formedness rules LR1 through LR3 of Section 4.3.1). For a given set T of transactions, let $L(T)$ denote a set of locked transactions such that there is a transaction in T for each element of $L(T)$, and vice versa. Note that $L(T)$, which is called a *locking* of T, is not uniquely determined.

A schedule $s \in \text{shuffle}(L(T))$ is *legal* if a step of the form $u(x)$ occurs between any two steps of the form $l(x)$ (i.e., a data item must be unlocked before it can be locked again). For example, the schedule shown in Example 4.12 is legal. Next, a schedule $s \in \text{shuffle}(T)$ is *legal* with respect to $L(T)$ if there exists a legal schedule $s' \in \text{shuffle}(L(T))$ such that $DT(s') = s$. A locking $L(T)$ of T is *safe* if *all* legal schedules of T with respect to $L(T)$ are (conflict) serializable. As an illustration, since the schedule from Example 4.12 is not in CSR, the locking it is based on, that is,

$$l_1(x)w_1(x)l_1(y)w_1(y)u_1(y)l_1(z)w_1(x)u_1(x)w_1(z)u_1(z)$$

$$l_2(z)w_2(z)l_2(y)u_2(z)l_2(x)w_2(y)w_2(x)u_2(x)w_2(y)u_2(y)$$

is not safe.

The interest in efficient algorithms for deciding whether a given locking $L(T)$ is safe can be motivated as follows. Suppose a scheduler S is given a set T of transactions; from T, scheduler S produces a locking $L(T)$. If $L(T)$ were known to be safe, S could output *any* schedule satisfying the simple syntactic condition of legality, since the safety of $L(T)$ guarantees the CSR membership of any legal schedule. Thus, if all transactions were completely given in advance (in the form of partially ordered read and write actions on data items), the scheduler could be based on generating appropriate locks for conflict regions among transaction pairs, without requiring explicit locks on data items at run time. In terms of the allowed concurrency, this method could possibly outperform the more traditional data-oriented locking protocols. However, the method would require a potentially expensive preanalysis of the transactions and a "compile time" test for safety along with the appropriate lock generation. The latter could be based on exploiting the geometric interpretation as follows:

Preanalysis locking (PAL)

> A legal schedule avoids conflict regions. However, not every legal schedule is serializable, since it could avoid, yet separate such regions. On the other hand, the previous theorem says that a legal schedule is in CSR iff its curve does not separate conflict regions. Moreover, it can be shown that a locking is safe iff the geometrical "closure" of the conflict regions is connected. This opens a door for the use of computational geometry in the context of database transactions, further details of which can be found in the references cited at the end of the chapter.

4.4 **Nonlocking Schedulers**

In this section we present various alternatives to locking schedulers; the protocols discussed next can all guarantee the safety of their output *without* using locks. Their use in commercial database systems is limited, but they may be suited for distributed systems and can also be used in hybrid protocols (see Section 4.5).

4.4.1 **Timestamp Ordering**

Timestamp ordering rule (TO rule)

A first approach to getting rid of locks is to use *timestamps*. Generally, these are values from a totally ordered domain; for simplicity, we will use natural numbers. The transaction manager assigns to each transaction t_i a unique timestamp $ts(t_i)$, for example, by retrieving a clock value at the beginning of t_i or by maintaining a counter that is incremented every time a new timestamp is needed. The timestamp of a transaction is inherited by every operation of that transaction. A scheduler based on the use of timestamps now has to order conflicting operations based on their timestamps; therefore, it is said to operate according to a *timestamp ordering* (TO) protocol. The central TO rule is as follows:

If $p_i(x)$ and $q_j(x)$, $i \neq j$, are operations in conflict, the following has to hold:

$$p_i(x) \text{ is executed } before \ q_j(x) \text{ iff } ts(t_i) < ts(t_j)$$

THEOREM 4.15

Gen(TO) $\subseteq$ CSR

Proof

Let s be a history generated by the TO protocol, and let (t_i, t_j) be an edge in the conflict graph G of s. Then there are operations $p_i(x)$ and $q_j(x)$ in conflict such that $p_i(x) <_s q_j(x)$. By the TO rule, this implies $ts(t_i) < ts(t_j)$.

Now if a transaction t_k is involved in a cycle of G, by induction we find that $ts(t_k) < ts(t_k)$, a contradiction. Thus, G is acyclic, which means that $s \in$ CSR.

We next briefly discuss an approach for implementing the TO rule. A simple, optimistic implementation is to transfer each operation submitted by the TM to the data manager for execution right away, with the only exception of those that arrive "too late": operation $p_i(x)$ is *too late* if it arrives *after* the scheduler has already output a conflicting operation $q_j(x)$ such that $i \neq j$ and $ts(t_j) > ts(t_i)$.

If p_i is too late, it can no longer be output without violating the TO rule. Thus, $p_i(x)$ must be rejected, which implies that t_i has to be aborted. It can then be restarted later, at which point it will receive a timestamp with a larger value so that some, or ideally all, of the previous conflicts will now appear in the proper order.

In order to determine whether an operation has arrived too late, a *basic TO* (BTO) scheduler has to record the following timestamps for every data item x:

Basic timestamp ordering (BTO)

1. max-r-scheduled(x): the value of the largest timestamp of a read operation on x already sent to the data manager;

2. max-w-scheduled(x): the value of the largest timestamp of a write operation on x already sent to the data manager.

When some operation $p_i(x)$ arrives, then $ts(t_i)$ is compared to max-q-scheduled(x) for each operation q that is in conflict with p. If $ts(t_i) <$ max-q-scheduled(x) holds, $p_i(x)$ is rejected, since it has arrived too late. Otherwise it is sent to the data manager, and max-p-scheduled(x) is updated to $ts(t_i)$ if $ts(t_i) >$ max-p-scheduled(x).

The behavior of the BTO protocol is illustrated in Figure 4.17, where transactions t_2 and t_1 are eventually aborted because they issue operations "too late" relative to their timestamps (i.e., the begin of these transactions).

An important point here is that the scheduler has to make sure that the data manager executes all operations in the order the scheduler sends them. Note that 2PL enforces this automatically, since an operation is not output as long as conflicting operations already scheduled still hold their locks. A BTO scheduler can send an operation $p_i(x)$, ready for being scheduled, to the data manager only if every conflicting and previously sent $q_j(x)$ has been executed.

The data manager hence has to acknowledge the execution of every operation, and the scheduler has to await that acknowledgment for operations in conflict that are to be scheduled in timestamp order; such an alternating way of operation is commonly called a *handshake*.

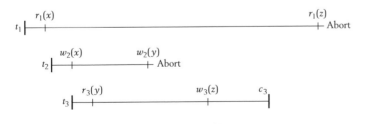

Figure 4.17 Example execution under the BTO protocol.

If a BTO scheduler receives new operations in an order that largely deviates from the timestamp order, it is likely to reject many of them and to abort the respective transactions. This suggests the use of more conservative variants, such as one in which operations could be blocked artificially: when $o_i(x)$ is received, a conflicting operation with a smaller timestamp could be received later. Thus, if $o_i(x)$ is retained, such conflicting operations hopefully arrive "on time." Clearly, the choice of the time slice for which an operation gets blocked artificially can be a critical performance factor.

4.4.2 Serialization Graph Testing

Serialization graph testing (SGT) scheduler

The next class of scheduling protocols we are going to present follows immediately from the serializability theorem from Chapter 3, which characterizes conflict serializability via the absence of cycles in the conflict graph. A *serialization graph tester* (*SGT protocol* for short) maintains a conflict graph in which nodes and edges are added or removed dynamically depending on the operations that arrive at the scheduler. The CSR property of the output is preserved by making sure that this graph remains acyclic at any time.

In more detail, an SGT protocol works as follows. Whenever a new operation $p_i(x)$ arrives from the transaction manager, the scheduler

1. creates a new node for transaction t_i in the current graph G if $p_i(x)$ is the first operation it sees from t_i;

2. inserts edges of the form (t_j, t_i) into G for each operation $q_j(x)$ that is in conflict with $p_i(x)$, $i \neq j$, and that has been output previously; now two cases can arise:

   (a) The resulting graph G is cyclic. If $p_i(x)$ were executed, the resulting schedule would no longer be serializable. Thus, $p_i(x)$ is rejected and t_i aborted, and the node for t_i and all its incident edges are removed from G.

   (b) G is (still) acyclic. Then $p_i(x)$ can be output—that is, added to the schedule already output—and the tentatively updated graph is kept as the new current one.

In an implementation, it would, in analogy to the BTO protocol, be essential to output a $p_i(x)$ (case (2b)) only if all conflicting operations previously output have been acknowledged by the data manager. Otherwise, $p_i(x)$ needs to be blocked until these acknowledgments have arrived.

THEOREM 4.16

$Gen(SGT) = CSR$

For the proof, note that "$\subseteq$" is trivial. The inverse inclusion can be proven by induction on the length of a schedule $s \in \text{CSR}$.

The description of SGT given above suggests that the conflict graph maintained by the scheduler grows indefinitely. However, from time to time information can also be removed from that graph. Unfortunately, the most obvious idea, that a transaction can be removed from the graph when it commits, does not work correctly. To see why, consider the following example:

$$s = w_1(x)w_2(x)w_2(y)c_2 \ldots w_1(y)$$

This schedule is clearly not in CSR. If we remove the node for t_2 upon the transaction's commit, c_2, then it would later be impossible to recognize the serialization graph cycle when transaction t_1 issues its $w_1(y)$ action. Note that the latter could possibly be a very long time after the commit of t_2. So this very simple idea is not feasible. To obtain more insight about when nodes can safely be removed from the graph, let us look at another example.

EXAMPLE 4.13

Consider

$$s = r_{k+1}(x) \underbrace{w_1(x)w_1(y_1)c_1}_{\text{all of } t_1} \underbrace{w_2(x)w_2(y_2)c_2}_{\text{all of } t_2} \ldots \underbrace{w_k(x)w_k(y_k)c_k}_{\text{all of } t_k} \ldots$$

The serialization graph of s is shown in Figure 4.18. Now suppose the next operation the scheduler receives is $w_{k+1}(z)$. According to what we stated above, $w_{k+1}(z)$ can be output if $z \notin \{x, y_1, \ldots, y_k\}$ holds. In order to test whether this is the case, the information on the t_i, $1 \le i \le k$, must still be available, although these transactions are already committed.

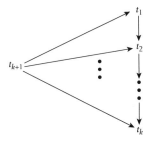

Figure 4.18 Serialization graph for Example 4.13.

As the example suggests, an SGT scheduler can remove a transaction t_i from its conflict graph, provided t_i will not get involved in a cycle anymore—not even at an arbitrary point in the future. Now, a node on a cycle has at least one incoming and one outgoing edge, and as the example shows, it may happen that *outgoing* edges are added to a node even after the respective transaction has already terminated. On the other hand, for a finished transaction there will be no more *incoming* edges added to its node; if t_i does not have incoming edges, it cannot be involved in a cycle. So the rule for eliminating a transaction from the conflict graph of an SGT scheduler is simply the following: *If t_i is finished and is a source (a node with outgoing edges only) in G, then it can be removed from G.*

Finally, note that an SGT scheduler, although attractive from a theoretical point of view since it is a simple approach to generating *all* of CSR, is not practical to implement. For example, the (worst case) *space* required to maintain the serialization graph grows with the square of the number of relevant transactions, some of which are not even active anymore. We even need to keep around the information about the read sets and write sets of such already committed transactions. In addition, and even more importantly, the testing of cycles in the graph, albeit only linear in the number of edges (i.e., quadratic in the number of nodes in the worst case), may be unacceptable at run time simply because such a test would be invoked very frequently. After all, concurrency control measures are part of a data server's innermost loops, and their run-time overhead is thus an extremely critical issue.

4.4.3 **Optimistic Protocols**

So far we have tacitly assumed that schedulers run in a transactional environment where conflicts are frequent events, so that measures must always be available for coping with them. Indeed, we have assumed that a scheduler needs to decide, on the spot, for each newly arriving step whether to execute, to reject, or to block it. Schedulers based on this assumption are called pessimistic schedulers. A different class of schedulers results from the opposite assumption that conflicts are rare events.

Consider, for example, a product catalog application where 99% of the transactions just read price information and descriptions of products. From time to time, prices are updated or new products are added, but this occurs with a very low frequency compared to their read events. If our application scenario were like that, a 2PL scheduler that keeps acquiring locks would be too restrictive, since it would waste a considerable amount of time managing locks instead of reading data items.

Validation protocols   Under the assumption that conflicts between transactions and their operations are rare, we can design optimistic schedulers that essentially let newly

Read	Validation	Write

Figure 4.19 The three phases of a transaction under an optimistic scheduler.

arriving operations simply pass, but test from time to time whether the schedule produced so far is still a serializable one. In other words, they have to *validate* their output occasionally, which is why they are also known as *validation protocols* (sometimes also called *certifiers*). Clearly, we do not interrupt the production of a schedule in order to validate what and how the scheduler has been doing so far, but we build this validation into the transactions themselves. To this end, it makes sense to perceive a transaction's execution as taking place in three phases (see Figure 4.19):

1. *Read phase*: The transaction is executed, but with all writes applied to a workspace that is private to the transaction only (not to the database). So the private "versions" of data items written by a transaction are not visible to other transactions (yet).

    Notice that at the end of the read phase of a transaction t, its *read set* $RS(t)$ as well as its *write set* $WS(t)$ are known.

2. *Validation phase*: A transaction that is ready to commit is validated; that is, the scheduler tests whether its execution has been "correct" in the sense of conflict serializability, and whether the transaction's result can be copied into the database. If this is not the case, the transaction is aborted; otherwise, the next phase is entered.

3. *Write phase*: The workspace contents are transferred into the database to conclude the transaction's commit.

We here assume as a simplification that phases (2) and (3) are executed indivisibly as a noninterruptible "critical section," meaning that all other transactions are suspended during such a critical section. We correspondingly call this combined phase the *val-write* phase. Note that the indivisibility of this phase may be quite problematic in a real implementation. If the write phase merely needs to modify a few entries in a page allocation table, for example, then the critical section is not really harmful. However, if the write phase needs to copy records from a working space into disk pages, suspending all concurrent transactions for such an extended time period would inevitably result in significant performance losses. If, on the other hand, the indivisibility condition were to be relaxed, the write phase of one transaction would be concurrent with the read phases of others. With the validation preceding the write phase, it is clear that additional measures would now be needed to ensure that these writes do not lead to conflict cycles. One possibility would be to introduce some limited form of exclusive locking during the write phase, but this would require read locks during the read phases as well and would obviously render the whole family of optimistic protocols much less attractive. To keep things simple, we thus assume indivisible val-write phases and leave the further discussion of relaxations as an exercise (see Exercise 4.18).

Since we are still interested in conflict-serializable schedules or, equivalently, schedules with an acyclic conflict graph, we can reduce the goal of transaction validation to keeping an acyclic graph acyclic after the insertion of a new node. The following lemma will turn out to be a key observation for what follows.

LEMMA 4.9

Let G be a DAG. If a new node is added to G in such a way that no edges start from the new node, then the resulting graph is still a DAG.

The simple reason why the lemma is true is that if a new node is added to an acyclic graph and the graph thereby becomes cyclic, then the new node must be involved in the cycle. But in order to be on a cycle, there would have to be at least one edge going into the node and at least one coming out.

We will use Lemma 4.9 as a guideline for the validation of transactions under an optimistic protocol. Indeed, we will establish "validation rules" by which acyclic serialization graphs will be kept acyclic if newly validated transactions are added.

We will essentially use two different types of validation approaches, based on the available options:

Backward-oriented and forward-oriented validation (BOCC and FOCC)

- Under *backward-oriented optimistic concurrency control* (BOCC), a transaction under validation executes a conflict test against all those transactions that are already committed.

- Under *forward-oriented optimistic concurrency control* (FOCC), a transaction is validated against all transactions that run in parallel, but that are still in their read phase.

Let us look at the two options in turn. Under BOCC validation, a transaction t_j is positively validated (or "accepted") if one of the following holds for each transaction t_i that is already committed (and hence has previously been accepted):

- t_i has ended before t_j has started (which implies that all of t_i has been executed before all of t_j); in this case, if there is a conflict between operations from t_j and t_i, the corresponding conflict edge will be of the form (t_i, t_j), and not vice versa.

- Otherwise, $RS(t_j) \cap WS(t_i) = \emptyset$, and the val-write phase of t_i has ended prior to the val-write phase of t_j (assuming a "critical section" as discussed earlier). Thus, t_j has not had a chance to read from t_i, and again if there are conflicts at all, they give rise to an edge from t_i to t_j, but one in the opposite direction is impossible.

So we may conclude, using Lemma 4.9, the following:

THEOREM 4.17

BOCC validation produces acyclic conflict graphs only, i.e., Gen(BOCC) $\subseteq$ CSR.

If the second case above fails (i.e., if $RS(t_j) \cap WS(t_i) \neq \emptyset$), it may be the case that t_j still did not read from t_i, since the schedule could look like this:

$$\ldots r_j(x) \ldots w_i(x) \ldots \ldots \text{validate}(t_j)$$

Following BOCC, we would abort t_j during its validation, although it has been clear much earlier (at the time t_i wrote x) that it would eventually fail. To accommodate such situations, the alternative to BOCC is FOCC, which validates a transaction t_j against all concurrent transactions t_i that are still reading. Let $RS^n(t_i)$ denote the read set of t_i at some time n. Then t_j is accepted under FOCC at that time n if the following holds for all transactions t_i that are still reading at time n:

$$WS(t_j) \cap RS^n(t_i) = \emptyset$$

Notice that this condition is immediately satisfied if t_j is read-only, a particularly nice property. The following can now be verified:

THEOREM 4.18

FOCC validation produces acyclic conflict graphs only, i.e., Gen(FOCC) $\subseteq$ CSR.

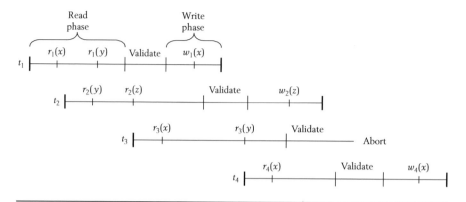

Figure 4.20 Example execution under the BOCC protocol.

FOCC ensures COCSR   In order to prove this theorem, the idea is again to use Lemma 4.9 for showing that under the given prerequisites, an insertion of t_j into a conflict graph that has so far been acyclic does not destroy this property. Details are left to be worked out in Exercise 4.13. Note that FOCC even guarantees that all output schedules are commit order preserving conflict serializable (COCSR). This is an immediate consequence of the fact that transactions validate against ongoing transactions, and the validation order corresponds to the commit order, with a critical section encompassing both the validation and the write phase.

As example executions under the BOCC and FOCC protocols, consider Figures 4.20 and 4.21. Both figures show the read, validation, and write phases of several concurrent transactions, with time proceeding from left to right.

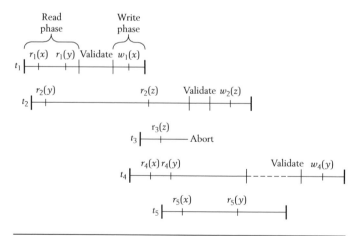

Figure 4.21 Example execution under the FOCC protocol.

In the BOCC scenario of Figure 4.20, transaction t_1 is trivially validated, as there is no concurrent, previously committed transaction. t_2 then is successfully validated against t_1, as its read set, $RS(t_2) = \{y, z\}$, does not overlap with the write set of t_1, $WS(t_1) = \{x\}$. Next, t_3 must validate against both t_1 and t_2; its read set, $RS(t_3) = \{x, y\}$, is disjoint with the write set of t_2 but has data item x in common with the write set of t_1, hence t_3 must be aborted. Finally, t_4 has started after the commit of t_1, so it must validate only against the committed, concurrent transaction t_2. Its read set, $RS(t_4) = \{x\}$, does not overlap with the write set of t_2; thus, t_4 is successfully validated.

In the (different) FOCC scenario of Figure 4.21, transaction t_1 must validate against the concurrent transaction t_2 by comparing its write set, $WS(t_1) = \{x\}$, with the *current* read set of t_2, $RS(t_2) = \{y\}$, as of the time of t_1's validation phase. Later, when t_2 initiates its validation, it detects that its write set, $WS(t_2) = \{z\}$, is disjoint with the *current* read sets $RS(t_4) = \{x, y\}$ and $RS(t_5) = \{x\}$, but does overlap with the current read set of t_3, which is $RS(t_3) = \{z\}$. Now, unlike under a BOCC protocol, FOCC allows t_2 to choose among several options. In the specific situation, either t_2 could abort itself, or it could enforce the abort of the "troublesome" concurrent transaction t_3. Since t_2 has been running for quite a while, whereas t_3 has just begun, we assume that t_3 will be aborted to minimize the amount of wasted work. A third option turns out to be profitable for the validation of transaction t_4, as that transaction detects that its write set, $WS(t_4) = \{y\}$, overlaps with the current read set of the concurrent transaction t_5, $RS(t_5) = \{x, y\}$. In addition to aborting either t_4 or t_5, the third option for t_4 is to wait (indicated by the dashed line in Figure 4.21) and let the conflicting transaction t_5 validate first, in the optimistic anticipation that t_5 would not lead to a (potential) conflict cycle and could thus successfully validate. Indeed, t_5 turns out to be a read-only transaction (i.e., its write set is empty) and therefore trivially validates. Subsequently, the validation of t_4 is resumed and now succeeds, as there are no more concurrent transactions. As the example shows, a significant practical advantage of FOCC over BOCC lies in the flexibility of choosing abort victims or even avoiding some aborts by forcing transactions to wait in their validation phase.

4.5 **Hybrid Protocols**

Figure 4.22 summarizes the protocols we have presented so far. The key distinction between the two major classes, pessimistic and optimistic protocols, is that the pessimistic methods conservatively perform tests that guarantee an acyclic conflict graph as early as possible (e.g., lock conflict tests, or searching for cycles in the conflict graph whenever a new edge is added); whereas optimistic methods postpone this testing until a transaction is ready to commit.

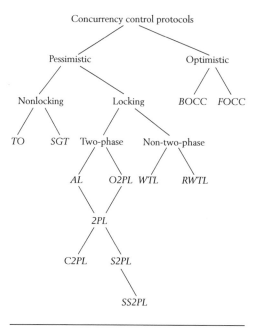

Figure 4.22 Summary of concurrency control
protocols.

Idea of
hybrid
protocols
The number of protocols shown in this figure could even be squared by decomposing the concurrency control problem into the following two subproblems, which could then be solved individually by possibly distinct protocols:

1. *rw* (and *wr*) synchronization: read operations are synchronized against write operations, or vice versa;

2. *ww* synchronization: write operations are synchronized against other write operations, but not against reads.

If these synchronization tasks are distinguished, a scheduler can be thought of as consisting of two components, one for each of the respective synchronization tasks. Since the two components need proper integration (as demonstrated by way of examples shortly), such a scheduler is called a *hybrid* scheduler.

For correctly integrating possibly distinct protocols for the two subtasks, the definition of conflicts from the previous chapter needs to be modified in order to account for the intended synchronization.

■ **For *rw* (and *wr*) synchronization:** two operations are in conflict if they access the same data item, and one is an *r* step, the other a *w* step.

■ **For *ww* synchronization:** two operations are in conflict if they access the same data item, and *both* are write operations.

EXAMPLE 4.14

Consider a hybrid scheduler that uses 2PL for *rw* synchronization and SGT for *ww* synchronization. The 2PL scheduler will now block an operation $w_i(x)$ only if some t_j, $j \neq i$, has a read lock on x. Thus, if several transactions hold write locks on the same data item, the 2PL scheduler does not care, since this is now the task of the other scheduler. Conversely, for the SGT scheduler an edge (t_i, t_j) in the conflict graph only indicates that there is a *ww* conflict between t_i and t_j.

To prove a hybrid scheduler correct, an obvious approach is to consider the two conflict graphs $G_{rw}(s)$ and $G_{ww}(s)$ of an output s that we now have and that represent *distinct* conflicts; whereas the single conflict graph we have so far been considering abstracted from the particular nature of conflicts. Since all protocols that we have discussed are CSR safe, we only need to make sure that the two graphs we now have represent *compatible* serialization orders; that is, if t_i occurs "before" t_j in one of the graphs, then the same holds for the other. In other words, the *union* of the two graphs now has to be acyclic. This may require additional preparations, as we now show.

Consider a hybrid scheduler that uses SS2PL for *rw* (and *wr*) synchronization, and that wants to use TO for *ww* synchronization. Observe that if a TO scheduler receives a step $w_i(x)$ *after* a step $w_j(x)$, where $ts(t_i) < ts(t_j)$, then $w_i(x)$ should be rejected, since the two are out of timestamp order. However, since the scheduler is interested in *ww* synchronization *only*, a rejection is not necessary. Indeed, if $w_i(x)$ is simply ignored, the effect will be the same, namely, that $w_j(x)$ writes x last. Thus, executing a sequence of write operations in timestamp order produces the same result as executing exclusively the write operation that carries the largest timestamp. This observation leads to a *ww* synchronization approach known as *Thomas' Write Rule* (TWR): Let t_j be the transaction that has written x and that has the largest timestamp prior to the arrival of $w_i(x)$. If $ts(t_i) > ts(t_j)$, then $w_i(x)$ is processed as usual; otherwise, it is ignored, and the execution of t_i continues. Notice that TWR applies to pairs of write steps only.

SS2PL + TO

Thomas' Write Rule (TWR)

EXAMPLE 4.15

Consider $w_1(x)r_2(y)w_2(x)w_2(y)c_2w_1(y)c_1$, where $ts(t_1) < ts(t_2)$. $w_1(y)$ is ignored (i.e., not executed at all) by TWR. The resulting output schedule (with $w_1(y)$ omitted) is conflict serializable.

On the other hand, consider the following variation of the example:

$$w_1(x)r_2(y)w_2(x)w_2(y)c_2r_1(y)w_1(y)c_1$$

The hybrid SS2PL/TWR protocol would still allow this schedule, and again TWR would suppress the $w_1(y)$ step of t_1. However, the $r_1(y)$ step would be executed, leading to a conflict cycle between t_1 and t_2. So although each of the two protocols works correctly as far as its limited perspective is concerned, the combination does not properly guarantee conflict serializability.

As the second example indicates, an integration of SS2PL and TO or TWR has to be done cautiously. If the protocols are used as described above, the following holds for every output s: (1) $G_{rw}(s)$ is acyclic (due to the use of SS2PL), and (2) $G_{ww}(s)$ is acyclic (due to TWR). To guarantee that $G(s) = G_{rw}(s) \cup G_{ww}(s)$ is acyclic as well, it apparently suffices to state the following:

$$(1) \ (t_i, t_j) \in G_{rw}(s) \Rightarrow ts(t_i) < ts(t_j)$$

Since $G_{ww}(s)$ already satisfies the corresponding condition, we conclude that $G(s)$ is acyclic, provided (1) holds. In order to guarantee (1) we note that if $(t_i, t_j) \in G_{rw}(s)$, then t_j cannot terminate before t_i releases a lock that t_j needs. Under SS2PL, every transaction holds its locks until commit, so $(t_i, t_j) \in G_{rw}(s)$ implies that t_i ends successfully before t_j ends. Thus, condition (1) can be met by

$$(2) \text{ if } t_i \text{ commits before } t_j \text{ does, then } ts(t_i) < ts(t_j).$$

For assuring (2), the scheduler needs to block the assignment of a timestamp to t_i until it reaches its commit point. Such commit order-preserving timestamping also entails deferring the setting of timestamps in the written data items. This can be accomplished with a workspace concept, in analogy to the deferred write approach of optimistic protocols. All writes are performed in a transaction's private workspace and transferred into the database only upon the transaction's commit.

Hybrid protocols for partitioned data　　Another, practically intriguing form of hybrid protocols is based on partitioning the set of data items, D, into disjoint subsets $D_1, D_2, \ldots, D_n$ (with $n \geq 2$, $D_i \cap D_j = \emptyset$ for $i \neq j$, and $\bigcup_{i=1}^{n} D_i = D$). Then, different concurrency control protocols could be used for each of the n partitions, provided, and this may be the crux, that the union of the conflict graphs over all partitions remains acyclic at each point. Such a setting naturally arises in a distributed federation of heterogeneous data servers. We will discuss this case in detail in Part IV.

Another application case for hybrid protocols within a centralized data server is to intentionally classify data items into disjoint classes according to their specific access characteristics. For example, a data server may manage a small set of very frequently modified data items—so-called *hot spots*—that constitute subset D_1, a large set of less frequently modified data items that form subset D_2, and a remaining subset D_3 of data items that are never updated online. Such a setting suggests using the protocol with the highest possible concurrency for D_1 regardless of its overhead (as D_1 is small), a low-overhead concurrency control protocol for the bulk of data items D_2, and no concurrency control at all for D_3. For example, we could combine SGT for D_1 with FOCC for D_2. However, we need to ensure that this combination preserves the acyclicity of the global conflict graph that is formed by the union of the two conflict graphs for D_1 and D_2. This is all but trivial for the two considered protocols, and may in fact require some additional cycle testing across both partitions. Such global overhead may, however, render the use of the "lightweight" FOCC protocol pointless, as the overhead of cycle testing would eventually be incurred for all of $D_1 \cup D_2$. A less adventurous combination would thus be using SS2PL for D_1 and FOCC for D_2. In this case, the fact that both protocols are commit order preserving conflict serializable (COCSR) eliminates the need for global checks. More considerations along these lines will be presented in Part IV in the context of distributed systems.

4.6 **Lessons Learned**

In this chapter, we have seen a variety of concurrency control protocols for the page model of transactions. There are two broad categories: locking schedulers, which require the explicit locking and unlocking of data items for the purpose of read or write access, and nonlocking schedulers that can do without locks. Moreover, locking schedulers can be two-phase, meaning that, on a per-transaction basis, locks precede unlocks; or they can be non-two-phase, provided access ordering is controlled in some other way.

We will show in subsequent chapters that as far as concurrency control is concerned, these are the fundamental ideas around. Indeed, we will apply the ideas underlying the protocols discussed in this chapter to various other (often more general) contexts as well. For example, an SGT protocol is immediately available, once a serializability theorem has been proven that relates conflict based serializability to the acyclicity of a suitably defined graph.

We will also show that, although there are a variety of algorithmic approaches to concurrency control, the strict variant of 2PL, S2PL, is actually *the* protocol around and hence the one most commonly found in commercial transactional servers for its versatility as well as robustness and the observation that it outperforms the other protocols in most practical situations.

Exercises

4.1 For each of the following (input) schedules, show the output produced by 2PL, S2PL, SS2PL, O2PL, BTO, and SGT:

$$s_1 = w_1(x)r_2(y)r_1(x)c_1r_2(x)w_2(y)c_2$$
$$s_2 = r_1(x)r_2(x)w_3(x)w_4(x)w_1(x)c_1w_2(x)c_2c_3c_4$$

4.2 A *lock point* of a transaction t denotes a point in time at which t has obtained all locks it needs, but has not yet released any. Show that for each history s produced by a 2PL scheduler there exists a conflict-equivalent serial history s' in which all transactions occur in the same order of lock points as in s.

4.3 Under the 2PL protocol it is possible for transactions to "starve" in the following sense: A transaction gets involved in a deadlock, is chosen as the victim and aborted. After a restart, it again gets involved in a deadlock, is chosen as the victim and aborted, and so on. Provide a concrete example for such a situation, and describe how 2PL could be extended in order to avoid starvation of transactions.

4.4 Describe the waits-for graphs resulting from the use of 2PL for each of the histories in Exercise 4.1.

4.5 Show that the wait-die and wound-wait approaches to deadlock prevention both guarantee an acyclic WFG at any point in time.

4.6 Consider $s = w_1(x)w_1(y)r_2(u)w_2(x)r_2(y)w_2(y)c_2w_1(z)c_1$. Extend this history by syntactically valid lock and unlock operations, and represent the result as a curve in the plane. Then determine the conflict regions and decide whether $DT(s)$ is in CSR.

4.7 Consider the schedule whose geometrical interpretation is shown in Figure 4.16. Exhibit a point in the plane of that figure that represents a deadlock.

4.8 Consider the following input schedules to the O2PL protocol (i.e., the ordered sharing generalization of 2PL, based on the lock compatibility table LT_8):

(a) $s_1 = w_1(x)r_2(x)c_2r_3(y)c_3w_1(y)c_1$
(b) $s_2 = w_1(x)r_2(x)r_3(y)c_3r_2(z)c_2w_1(y)c_1$

Which are the corresponding output schedules produced by O2PL? For each of the two schedules, give the details about when locks are requested, granted, attempted to be released, and eventually released.

4.9 Show that O2PL is susceptible to deadlocks (i.e., it is not deadlock free).

4.10 Show that Gen(AL) $\subseteq$ CSR—i.e., complete the proof of Theorem 4.9.

4.11 Investigate the relationship between Gen(BTO) and Gen(2PL). Is one more powerful than the other?

4.12 Consider the following condition for removing nodes (and edges) from the serialization graph in the SGT protocol: remove t_i when it is finished and none of the transactions that were active at the commit or abort of t_i are active anymore. Show that this condition, albeit seemingly natural, would lead to incorrect behavior of the SGT protocol.

4.13 Prove Theorem 4.18, thereby showing that FOCC is a CSR safe protocol.

4.14 Consider the following alternative variant of a BOCC protocol. Transaction t_j is successfully validated if one of the two following conditions holds for all other transactions t_i that are already successfully validated:

  (a) t_i terminates before t_j starts its read phase,
  (b) $RS(t_j) \cap WS(t_i) = \emptyset$ and t_i finishes its read phase before t_j enters its write phase (i.e., relaxing the original BOCC condition that t_i must finish its write phase before t_j initiates its validation).

Construct an example of a nonserializable schedule that would be allowed under this BOCC variant. On the other hand, prove that this variant guarantees conflict serializability under the additional constraint that $WS(t_k) \subseteq RS(t_k)$ holds for all transactions t_k.

4.15 Consider an alternative variant of BOCC where a transaction validates by comparing its write set against the read sets of concurrent, previously validated transactions. Would such a variant work correctly, i.e., ensure that all output schedules are CSR?

4.16 Consider the following input schedule of three concurrent transactions:

$$r_1(x)r_2(x)r_1(y)r_3(x)w_1(x)w_1(y)c_1r_2(y)r_3(z)w_3(z)c_3r_2(z)c_2$$

Which are the resulting output schedules under the BOCC and FOCC protocols? Remember that write steps are actually performed on private workspaces, the commit requests initiate the validation, and the write steps are performed on the shared database only after a successful validation.

4.17 Construct an example execution that demonstrates that FOCC may produce nonserializable schedules if the critical section condition for the val-write phases were dropped.

4.18 Develop variants of the BOCC and FOCC protocols that no longer need the critical section for the val-write phases of transactions. Discuss the pros and cons of such a relaxation, in comparison to locking protocols.

Bibliographic Notes

The first major comprehensive presentation of concurrency control protocols, which has also influenced the presentation in this chapter, was given by Bernstein et al. (1987). Theoretical questions, such as the scheduling power of protocols or the geometry of locking, were further discussed by Papadimitriou (1986). Implementation issues are covered in the textbooks by Bernstein and Newcomer (1997), Claybrook (1992), and in particular by Gray and Reuter (1993).

The 2PL protocol goes back to Eswaran et al. (1976). Its generalization O2PL, which can generate exactly OCSR, as well as the idea of using ordered sharing as a third locking mode, are from Agrawal and El Abbadi (1990, 1995); a performance study of locking based on ordered sharing appears in Agrawal et al. (1994). Agrawal, Carey, and McVoy (1987) provided a survey of techniques for handling deadlocks; the specific wound-wait and wait-die techniques are from Rosenkrantz et al. (1978), and the running priority technique is from Franaszek and Robinson (1985). Implementation issues of deadlock detection can be found in Beeri and Obermarck (1981) and Jiang (1988). Altruistic locking is from Salem et al. (1994). Early studies of giving up on the two-phase property and of replacing it by tree or DAG structures were done by Kedem and Silberschatz (1980, 1983), Silberschatz and Kedem (1980, 1982), Buckley and Silberschatz (1984, 1985), Dasgupta and Kedem (1983, 1990), and Mohan et al. (1984, 1985). Croker and Maier (1986) presented a dynamic tree-locking protocol.

Further details on the geometrical interpretation of locking can be found in Lausen et al. (1984, 1990) or in Papadimitriou (1982, 1983, 1986); proofs of Theorems 4.13 and 4.14 can be found in Papadimitriou (1986). Lausen et al. (1986) studied the exploitation of the geometrical interpretation for a form of preanalysis locking. Kung and Papadimitriou (1983) showed that a two-phase locking scheduler is "optimal" among schedulers that only use syntactic information. Wolfson (1986, 1987) used the geometric techniques for studying algorithms that allow early unlocking of database items. Yannakakis (1982, 1984) studied the safety of locking policies along these lines.

The TO procotol is from Thomas (1979); see also Bernstein and Shipman (1980) as well as Bernstein et al. (1980), or Leu and Bhargava (1987). Serialization graph testing is from Casanova (1981); the basic idea appeared in Schlageter (1978) as well. The rule for deleting completed transactions from a serialization graph is from Hadzilacos and Yannakakis (1989). The concepts of optimistic concurrency control algorithms were developed by Kung and Robinson (1981) as well as Härder (1984). The concept of private workspaces and deferred writes has also been studied with regard to other concurrency control protocols by Gold et al. (1985, 1986). Mohan (1992) provided a rather critical account of implementation and performance issues for optimistic concurrency control.

The idea of integrating multiple protocols by taking the various forms of synchronization problems apart is from Bernstein et al. (1987). Various approaches along these lines have been proposed, for example, by Lausen (1982), Boral and Gold (1984), and Yu and Dias (1992). Dynamically switching from one type of protocol to another for adaptation to evolving workloads has been proposed by Bhargava and Riedl (1989). Thomas' Write Rule is from Thomas (1979).

A comprehensive experimental study on the performance benefits and drawbacks of the various concurrency control protocols under different workload settings has been provided by Agrawal, Carey, and Livny (1987), focusing mostly on optimistic protocols versus two-phase locking. An excellent survey of analytic models for performance assessment has been given by Thomasian (1996b, 1998a).

CHAPTER FIVE

Multiversion Concurrency Control

A book is a version of the world. If you do not like it, ignore it;
or offer your own version in return.
—*Salman Rushdie*

What's the use of a good quotation if you can't change it?
—*Anonymous*

5.1 Goal and Overview

In this chapter we will consider an aspect of transaction processing that is both theoretically attractive and practically relevant. So far the underlying assumption has been that data items exist in exactly one copy each. As a result, write operations overwrite existing data items, and reads-from relationships between distinct transactions may fail to observe the transactional isolation requirement. Now imagine that more than one copy of each data item were allowed! This would, for example, render it possible to keep the "old" version of a data item that is subject to overwriting, at least until the transaction that writes a "new" version commits. More generally, distinct transactions could be given distinct versions of the same data item to read, or to overwrite.

In this chapter we will discuss the impact of allowing multiple versions on the various components of the framework we have developed so far: schedules, serializability, and concurrency control protocols. It will turn out that versioning demands some reasonable extensions of serializability theory, and, as will be shown in Part III, versioning is connected to recovery, as versions of modified data (*before images* or *after images*, or both) are sometimes maintained in some form by a recovery manager anyway. We will also look at the storage space needed to hold multiple versions. While theoretical considerations tend to assume space to be an unlimited resource, it turns out that the picture changes significantly should this not be valid anymore. In particular, we will show how multiversion serializability is affected by limiting the (total) number of versions around.

An important assumption we will make in this chapter is that versioning is *transparent* to the outside world. In other words, users or applications will not be aware of the fact that data items can appear in multiple versions. Note that such an assumption is different from versioning in design environments such as CAD (computer-aided design) or CASE (computer-aided software engineering), where database users need to play around with versions of data items in order to develop, change, alternate, or experiment with their designs. This type of versioning that users are aware of is also of increasing importance in the context of *repositories* for change and configuration management.

In this book we restrict ourselves to transparent versioning of data items. We will first derive, in Section 5.2, a suitable abstraction for such a setting from the read/write model. Intuitively, the idea is that because of the transparency requirement, correctness of histories and schedules "looks and feels" as if versioning were not applied, at least from a user's perspective. In Section 5.3 we will generalize our serializability notions to the augmented setting. After that, in Section 5.4 we take an in-depth look at the assumption, made in the very beginning, that the number of versions a system is capable of keeping around is unbounded; we will indicate how the picture changes if the total number of versions stored is limited. Finally, in Section 5.5 we look at concurrency control protocols and generalize some of those presented in the previous chapter to the management of versions.

The discussion in this chapter continues to consider unaborted transactions only.

5.2 **Multiversion Schedules**

In order to motivate the studies of this chapter more concretely, we start with an example to show that the presence of multiple versions of data items can indeed affect the correctness of histories or schedules.

EXAMPLE 5.1

Consider the following history:

$$s = r_1(x)w_1(x)r_2(x)w_2(y)r_1(y)w_1(z)c_1c_2$$

Obviously, $s \notin \text{CSR}$, since there is a cyclic conflict between t_1 and t_2. Informally, the reason for this is the fact that y has already been overwritten by t_2 when step $r_1(y)$ arrives at the scheduler; in other words, $r_1(y)$ is "too late" for making the schedule that already has a conflict (on x) between t_1 and t_2 an acceptable one.

Now suppose that the old value of y (in this case the initial value of y) were still available when $r_1(y)$ arrived. Then it would be possible to create a history equivalent to

$$s' = r_1(x)w_1(x)r_1(y)r_2(x)w_2(y)w_1(z)c_1c_2$$

which would be correct since $s' \in CSR$.

The existence of multiple versions of data items is based on the assumption that write operations are no longer executed "in place." Instead, the result of each and every write operation is individually kept as a new version of the data item in question. In Example 5.1 this would imply that old values would still be accessible for read operations that arrive "too late." Clearly, a scheduler would still have to decide which version of a data item is read by a particular read operation. We will look at this and other questions in what follows.

Our first goal will be an appropriate formalization of histories and schedules in the presence of multiple versions of data items. Since we are concerned with transparent versioning only, the transaction model can remain unchanged; only the interpretation of a transaction changes. Basically, a read step of the form $r(x)$ reads an (existing) version of x, and a write step of the form $w(x)$ (always) creates a new version of x (or overwrites an existing one). For simplicity of notation, we assume that each transaction writes every data item at most once; thus, if t_j contains operation $w_j(x)$, we can denote the version of x created by this write by x_j. Now we can define:

DEFINITION 5.1   *Version Function*

Let s be a history with initialization transaction t_0 and final transaction t_∞. A *version function* for s is a function h, which associates with each read step of s a previous write step on the same data item, and which is the identity on write steps.

Version function

Since we have already assumed that a step $w_j(x)$ creates version x_j of x, we may write the following when using a version function h in the context of a schedule s:

1. $h(r_i(x)) = w_j(x)$ for some $w_j(x) <_s r_i(x)$, and $r_i(x)$ reads x_j,
2. $h(w_i(x)) = w_i(x)$, and $w_i(x)$ writes x_i.

Thus, $h(r_i(x))$ essentially denotes the version of x that has been assigned to be read by $r_i(x)$. In slight abuse of the notation, we also write $w_j(x_j)$ for the write step that creates x_j, and we write $r_i(x_j)$ for the read step that has been associated with $w_j(x_j)$ by version function h. So following, the result of applying a version function to a read operation could be any of (1) the associated write operation, (2) the version assigned for reading, or (3) the "versioned" read operation.

Since all three possibilities are basically equivalent, this should not cause any confusion.

A version function translates each write step into a version creation step and each read step into a version read step. We are now ready to introduce the formal notion of a multiversion schedule, which is essentially a schedule (in the sense used so far) together with a version function:

Multiversion schedule

DEFINITION 5.2 *Multiversion Schedule*

Let $T = \{t_1, \ldots, t_n\}$ be a (finite) set of transactions.

1. A *multiversion history* (or complete multiversion schedule) for T is a pair $m = (\text{op}(m), <_m)$, where $<_m$ is an order on $\text{op}(m)$ and

    (a) $\text{op}(m) = h(\bigcup_{i=1}^{n} \text{op}(t_i))$ for some version function h (here we assume that h has been canonically extended from single operations to sets of operations)

    (b) for all $t \in T$ and all operations $p, q \in \text{op}(t)$ the following holds:

$$p <_t q \Rightarrow h(p) <_m h(q)$$

    (c) if $h(r_j(x)) = r_j(x_i)$, $i \neq j$, and c_j is in m, then c_i is in m and $c_i <_m c_j$.

2. A *multiversion schedule* is a prefix of a multiversion history.

In words, a multiversion history contains versioned read and write operations for its transactions whose ordering respects the individual transaction orderings. We mention that condition (1c) is needed here since otherwise $CP(m)$, the committed projection of a schedule m, is not necessarily complete (i.e., not a history).

EXAMPLE 5.2

The following is a totally ordered multiversion schedule for the history from Example 5.1 with a version function h that assigns, for example, version y_0 to the read step $r_1(y)$, i.e., $h(r_1(y)) = w_0(y)$ where t_0 is the initialization transaction (which is not mentioned explicitly in the schedule).

$$m = r_1(x_0)w_1(x_1)r_2(x_1)w_2(y_2)r_1(y_0)w_1(z_1)c_1c_2$$

Conventional schedules, as we have discussed them in the previous chapters, can be viewed as a special case of multiversion schedules. Such a *monoversion* schedule is obtained by restricting the version function of a multiversion schedule so that each read step reads the version produced by the *last* preceding write step. In other words, the effect of a monoversion schedule is the same as if only a single version of each data item is kept.

DEFINITION 5.3   *Monoversion Schedule*

A multiversion schedule is called a *monoversion schedule* if its version function maps each read step to the last preceding write step on the same data item.

An example of a monoversion schedule is

$$m = r_1(x_0)w_1(x_1)r_2(x_1)w_2(y_2)r_1(y_2)w_1(z_1)c_1c_2$$

Notice that the example differs from the previous multiversion example only in that now we have $h(r_1(y)) = w_2(y)$. Because the version function of a monoversion schedule is uniquely determined by the order of steps, we can also write m as if it were a conventional schedule, omitting version subscripts:

$$s = r_1(x)w_1(x)r_2(x)w_2(y)r_1(y)w_1(z)c_1c_2$$

In the discussions that follow we will often use monoversion schedules as in previous chapters, as well as multiversion schedules in the sense just introduced; in order to distinguish them, we will continue to use s, s', and so on, for the former, and we will use m, m', and so on, for the latter.

5.3 Multiversion Serializability

We next study various types of multiversion serializability. To this end, we will begin by following our previous practice, namely, devising a notion of view serializability and investigating whether it is feasible. Not surprisingly, it will again exhibit an NP complete decision problem, which motivates to look for a notion of conflict serializability. In addition, another important aspect will be to limit the number of versions that can be stored, and hence kept around, at the same time. As we will see in Section 5.4, such a limit drives home an entire hierarchy of classes of serializable schedules.

5.3.1 Multiversion View Serializability

As we have mentioned already, when making serializability precise for multiversion schedules, we have to keep in mind that we are here talking about *transparent* versioning, that is, versioning that is not visible to the outside world, in particular to application programs or even the user. Thus, from a user's point of view a "correct" multiversion schedule should be equivalent to an ordinary serial schedule without versions. To make equivalence precise, conflict equivalence of the usual style (i.e., according to Chapter 3) is not an appropriate candidate, as the following example indicates.

EXAMPLE 5.3

Consider the serial (monoversion) schedule $s = w_0(x)c_0w_1(x)c_1r_2(x)w_2(y)c_2$. A multiversion schedule exhibiting the same "step syntax" is

$$m = w_0(x_0)c_0w_1(x_1)c_1r_2(x_0)w_2(y_2)c_2$$

Notice that while s shows three different conflicts (between $w_0(x)$ and $w_1(x)$, between $w_0(x)$ and $r_2(x)$, and between $w_1(x)$ and $r_2(x)$), m exhibits only one conflict, the one between $w_0(x_0)$ and $r_2(x_0)$, since t_1 now writes a new version of x. Although we could define that a multiversion schedule m is conflict equivalent to a serial monoversion schedule s if all pairs of conflicting operations occur in m in the same order as in s (so that the two schedules shown above are indeed equivalent), the problem remains that the respective reads-from relations may be different, which is intuitively undesirable.

Already in this example we find that in s, transaction t_2 reads data item x from t_1, while in m, transaction t_2 reads the version of x produced by t_0; in other words, under the no-interpretation schedule semantics adopted so far (i.e., the Herbrand semantics, see Chapter 3), we should assume that both schedules yield distinct values of item y.

Considerations like the one just shown motivate the use of view equivalence for defining serializability in this context, suitably adapted to the presence of versions.

Reads-from relation

DEFINITION 5.4   *Reads-From Relation*

Let m be a multiversion schedule, $t_i, t_j \in \text{trans}(m)$.

The *reads-from relation* of m is defined by

$$\text{RF}(m) := \{(t_i, x, t_j) \mid r_j(x_i) \in \text{op}(m)\}$$

Now, following our general methodology from Chapter 3 in developing correctness criteria, we can directly obtain an appropriate notion of equivalence based on the reads-from relations of schedules.

DEFINITION 5.5   *View Equivalence*

Let m and m' be two multiversion schedules such that $\text{trans}(m') = \text{trans}(m)$. m and m' are *view equivalent*, abbreviated $m \approx_v m'$, if $\text{RF}(m) = \text{RF}(m')$.

View equivalence of multiversion schedules

A difference between this notion of view equivalence and the one introduced in Chapter 3 for monoversion schedules is that a consideration of final write operations is now irrelevant, for the simple reason that two multiversion schedules with identical sets of transactions *always* have the same final writes (since writes produce versions that are not erased anymore). As we will show shortly, this statement no longer holds, however, if the number of versions that can be stored is limited.

EXAMPLE 5.4

Let $m = w_0(x_0)w_0(y_0)c_0r_3(x_0)w_3(x_3)c_3w_1(x_1)c_1r_2(x_1)w_2(y_2)c_2$ and
$m' = w_0(x_0)w_0(y_0)c_0w_1(x_1)c_1r_2(x_1)r_3(x_0)w_2(y_2)w_3(x_3)c_3c_2$.
Then $m \approx_v m'$.

For defining (view) serializability, it is not sufficient to require that a given multiversion schedule m is view equivalent to a *serial* multiversion schedule m'. As the following example demonstrates, the reason is that even a serial m' does not necessarily have a reads-from relation that is compatible with a serial monoversion schedule.

EXAMPLE 5.5

Let $m = w_0(x_0)w_0(y_0)c_0r_1(x_0)r_1(y_0)w_1(x_1)w_1(y_1)c_1r_2(x_0)r_2(y_1)c_2$.

If each $r_i(x_j)$ occurring in m is replaced by an $r_i(x)$, and correspondingly each $w_i(x_i)$ by a $w_i(x)$, the following monoversion schedule results:

$$s = w_0(x)w_0(y)c_0r_1(x)r_1(y)w_1(x)w_1(y)c_1r_2(x)r_2(y)c_2.$$

Both schedules are serial; however, in s, transaction t_2 reads data item x from t_1, while in m, it reads x from t_0.

To address this problem, we need to be careful when defining view serializability for multiversion schedules. We actually need to compare multiversion schedules to monoversion schedules in terms of their reads-from relations. In fact, this insight should not be a big surprise given that versioning should be completely transparent to all application programs.

The schedule *m* from the previous example has a reads-from relation that differs from the reads-from relation of the corresponding monoversion schedule (as derived according to Definition 3.7 given in Chapter 3 for conventional schedules), since t_2 reads x_0, but not the version x_1 that was written last. Moreover, we can show that *m*'s reads-from relation differs from the reads-from relation of every possible serial monoversion schedule for the same transactions. This means that *m* cannot be view equivalent to a serial execution without versions, and should thus not be accepted as a correct multiversion schedule.

This example-driven discussion leads directly to the following correctness criterion:

Multiversion view serializability

DEFINITION 5.6   *Multiversion View Serializability*

Let *m* be a multiversion history. Then *m* is called *multiversion view serializable* if there exists a serial monoversion history *m'* for the same set of transactions such that $m \approx_v m'$.

Let MVSR denote the class of all multiversion view-serializable histories.

Thus, for a history $m \in$ MVSR there is always a serial monoversion history *s* for the same set of transactions such that $m \approx_v s$, where "$\approx_v$" is now well defined. The following example illustrates the relationships just described.

EXAMPLE 5.6

Let $m = w_0(x_0)w_0(y_0)c_0w_1(x_1)c_1r_2(x_1)r_3(x_0)w_3(x_3)c_3w_2(y_2)c_2$ and
$m' = w_0(x_0)w_0(y_0)c_0r_3(x_0)w_3(x_3)c_3w_1(x_1)c_1r_2(x_1)w_2(y_2)c_2$.

Then we have $m \approx_v m'$. Moreover, *m'* is view equivalent to history
$s = w_0(x)w_0(y)c_0r_3(x)w_3(x)c_3w_1(x)c_1r_2(x)w_2(y)c_2$.

Casting conventional schedules into multiversion schedules

The previous definition can be generalized to arbitrary schedules in a straightforward way: a multiversion schedule *m* is *multiversion view serializable* if there exists a serial monoversion history *m'* such that $CP(m) \approx_v m'$. Furthermore, we can now define multiversion view serializability even for conventional (input) schedules: a schedule is multiversion view serializable if there is a version function such that casting the schedule into a multiversion schedule with this version function yields a multiversion schedule whose committed projection is in MVSR.

5.3.2 **Testing Membership in MVSR**

A natural question now is what the complexity of recognizing members of MVSR is. To this end, it may not be expected that this problem is simpler than the corresponding one for VSR, since we have:

THEOREM 5.1

VSR $\subset$ MVSR

Inclusion of VSR in MVSR holds since every view-serializable history can be perceived as a monoversion history and hence as a specific multiversion history (in MVSR). The fact that the inclusion is strict can be seen from the following example; consider

$$m = w_0(x_0)w_0(y_0)c_0r_1(x_0)w_2(x_2)w_2(y_2)c_2r_1(y_0)c_1$$

Interpreted as a monoversion schedule by omitting the version subscripts, this schedule is the canonical example of an inconsistent read and clearly does not fall into class VSR. By having t_1 read an older version y_0, the multiversion schedule is, however, acceptable under the MVSR criterion, and is indeed view equivalent to the serial monoversion schedule with the order $t_0 < t_1 < t_2$. This once again demonstrates the significant performance improvements achievable by transparent versioning.

The previous theorem implies that the membership test for MVSR can intuitively not be easier than the one for VSR, since MVSR is a *relaxation* of conditions over VSR; in other words, with additional restrictions (in VSR) over MVSR, we obtain an NP complete decision problem. Indeed we can show the following:

THEOREM 5.2

The problem of deciding whether a given multiversion history is in MVSR is NP complete.

Proof

In order to show that the problem is in NP, we just "guess" a serial mono-version history m' for a given multiversion history m and test $m \approx_v m'$. Based on Theorem 5.1, this can be done in polynomial time simply by comparing the two sets of operations.

In order to show that the problem is NP complete, we reduce the corresponding decision problem for VSR to it: Let s be a monoversion history.

Transform s into a multiversion history m by replacing each operation $w_i(x)$ with $w_i(x_i)$, and each operation $r_j(x)$ with $r_j(x_i)$, provided t_j reads item x in s from t_i. By the definition of view serializability, it follows that $m \in$ MVSR iff there exists a serial monoversion schedule s' such that $m \approx_v s'$. Now s' exists iff $s \in$ VSR. Thus, we have $m \in$ MVSR iff $s \in$ VSR, and our claim follows.

Conflict graph   Different from the situation for monoversion histories, for multiversion histories there is a graph-theoretic characterization of membership in MVSR with a graph that has transactions as nodes (as opposed to the step graph constructions in Chapter 3, where a graph has the steps of a schedule as its nodes). This will become relevant later in this chapter when we discuss concurrency control protocols, since they will all guarantee this graph property. Thus, the characterization developed next will be used as a sufficient condition for membership in MVSR in the verification of protocols. We first recall the definition of a conflict graph given in Chapter 3, which can be simplified for multiversion schedules due to the fact that only conflicts of the form $(w_i(x_i), r_j(x_i))$, $i \neq j$, can still occur. Thus, the conflict graph $G(m)$ of a multiversion schedule m has an edge between (committed) transactions t_i and t_j (of the form $t_i \rightarrow t_j$, $i \neq j$) simply if $r_j(x_i)$ is in m. The following is then obvious:

THEOREM 5.3

For any two multiversion schedules m and m', $m \approx_v m'$ implies $G(m) = G(m')$.

The converse of this theorem is not true. Consider the multiversion schedules $m = w_1(x1_1)r_2(x_0)w_1(y_1)r_2(y_1)$ and $m' = w_1(x1_1)r_2(x_1)w_1(y_1)r_2(y_0)$ that have the same conflict graph but differ significantly in their version functions and their reads-from relations. So conflicts alone, in the limited sense that we consider version writes and reads on exactly these versions, are insufficient to reason about multiversion serializability.

We now extend the conflict graph of a multiversion schedule m as follows:

Version order   ---

DEFINITION 5.7   *Version Order*

If x is a data item, a *version order* for x is any nonreflexive and total ordering of all versions of x that are written by operations in m. A *version order* $\ll$ for m is the union of all version orders of data items written by operations in m.

Note that the version order is independent of the execution order in which the versions of a data item were created. So it is possible that for versions x_i

and x_j, such that $w_i(x_i)$ preceded $w_j(x_j)$ in the schedule, the version order is $x_j \ll x_i$. The version order rather serves to help determine the serialization order of transactions, that is, the order in which versions appear in an equivalent serial monoversion schedule.

EXAMPLE 5.7

Let m be the following schedule:

$$m = w_0(x_0)w_0(y_0)w_0(z_0)c_0r_1(x_0)r_2(x_0)r_2(z_0)r_3(z_0)w_1(y_1)w_2(x_2)w_3(y_3)$$
$$w_3(z_3)c_1c_2c_3r_4(x_2)r_4(y_3)r_4(z_3)c_4$$

A version order for m could be

$$x_0 \ll x_2, y_0 \ll y_1 \ll y_3, z_0 \ll z_3$$

DEFINITION 5.8 *Multiversion Serialization Graph (MVSG)*

For a given schedule m and a version order $\ll$, the *multiversion serialization graph* MVSG$(m, \ll)$ of m then is the conflict graph $G(m) = (V, E)$ with the following edges added for each $r_k(x_j)$ and $w_i(x_i)$ in CP(m), where k, i, and j are pairwise distinct: if $x_i \ll x_j$, then $(t_i, t_j) \in E$, otherwise $(t_k, t_i) \in E$.

Multiversion serialization graph (MVSG)

So for each triple of operations $w_j(x_j)$, $r_k(x_j)$, and $w_i(x_i)$ on the same data item x, the MVSG contains two out of the three potential edges:

- An edge from t_j to t_k is always present.
- In addition, there is either an edge from t_i to t_j, namely, if the version order is $x_i \ll x_j$, meaning that in an equivalent monoversion schedule $w_i(x_i)$ would precede $w_j(x_j)$, or
- an edge from t_k to t_i, namely, if the version order is $x_j \ll x_i$ so that $w_i(x_i)$ would follow $w_j(x_j)$ in an equivalent monoversion schedule and consequently has to follow also $r_k(x_j)$, as t_k needs to read the most recent version in a monoversion schedule.

EXAMPLE 5.8

Let m and $\ll$ be as in Example 5.7. The graph MVSG$(m, \ll)$ is shown in Figure 5.1. In this example the only edges that do not occur in $G(m)$ are

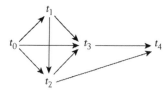

Figure 5.1 Multiversion serialization graph.

the following:

(t_1, t_2): $r_1(x_0)$, $w_2(x_2) \in \mathrm{op}(m)$, and $x_0 \ll x_2$
(t_1, t_3): $w_1(y_1)$, $r_4(y_3) \in \mathrm{op}(m)$, and $y_1 \ll y_3$
(t_2, t_3): $r_2(z_0)$, $w_3(z_3) \in \mathrm{op}(m)$, and $z_0 \ll z_3$

If a multiversion history happens to have an acyclic conflict graph, we can apply topological sorting to obtain a total order or, equivalently, a serial multiversion history; however, this schedule obtained does not need to be view equivalent to a serial monoversion history, since reads-from relationships may change during the transition from a multiversion to a monoversion history. Version order edges can be used to detect such situations: if $r_k(x_j)$ and $w_i(x_i)$ are in $\mathrm{CP}(m)$, a version order enforces that either $w_i(x_i)$ occurs before $w_j(x_j)$ or after $r_k(x_j)$; in both cases, the reads-from relation remains invariant from a transition to a monoversion history. A topological sorting of a multiversion serialization graph is possible only if the conflict graph is still acyclic after the addition of the version order edges. With these considerations, the following can be verified:

THEOREM 5.4

$m \in \mathrm{MVSR}$ iff there exists a version order $\ll$ such that $\mathrm{MVSG}(m, \ll)$ is acyclic.

Proof

(if) Since $\mathrm{MVSG}(m, \ll)$ is acyclic, it can be sorted topologically into a serial history m' such that $\mathrm{RF}(m) = \mathrm{RF}(m')$, i.e., $m \approx_v m'$. It remains to be shown that m' can be perceived as a monoversion history. To this end, suppose that m' contains operations $r_k(x_j)$, $k \neq j$, as well as $w_i(x_i)$, $i \neq j$ and $i \neq k$. If $x_i \ll x_j$, the graph contains version order edge $t_i \rightarrow t_j$, which enforces $t_i <_{m'} t_j$. Conversely, if $x_j \ll x_i$, then by definition the graph contains edge $t_k \rightarrow t_i$ enforcing $t_k <_{m'} t_i$ in m'. Thus, no transaction writes x between t_j and t_k in m', so that version numbers can essentially be dropped from m' without changing the reads-from relation.

(only if) For a given history m and version order $\ll$, let $MV(m, \ll)$ denote the graph that contains version order edges *only*. Since version order edges depend only on the operations in m and the version order, but not on the *sequencing* of the operations in m, we can conclude that if m and m' are multiversion histories such that $trans(m) = trans(m')$, then $MV(m, \ll) = MV(m', \ll)$ for every version order $\ll$.

Now let $m \in MVSR$, and let m' be a serial monoversion history for the same transactions such that $m \approx_v m'$. By the remark just stated, $MV(m, \ll) = MV(m', \ll)$ for every version order $\ll$. By Theorem 5.3, $G(m) = G(m')$. Clearly, $G(m')$ is acyclic (since m' is serial), hence so is $G(m)$. Now define a specific version order

$$x_i \ll_0 x_j :\Longleftrightarrow t_i <_{m'} t_j$$

(i.e., if $t_i \rightarrow t_j$ is in $G(m')$). Thus, if $MV(m', \ll_0)$ is added to $G(m')$, the resulting graph $MVSG(m', \ll_0)$ remains acyclic, and the same holds if $MV(m', \ll_0) = MV(m, \ll_0)$ is added to $G(m)$ [$= G(m')$].

Notice that the decision problem for MVSR is not made easier by this result, since for a given schedule m it cannot necessarily be tested in polynomial time whether a version order of the desired form exists. On the other hand, multiversion schedulers always produce such an order, so that their correctness can be verified on the basis of this theorem.

5.3.3 **Multiversion Conflict Serializability**

We next describe a subclass of MVSR that has a polynomial-time membership problem, which immediately results from a specific notion of *multiversion conflicts*:

DEFINITION 5.9 *Multiversion Conflict*

A *multiversion conflict* in a multiversion schedule m is a pair of steps $r_i(x_j)$ and $w_k(x_k)$ such that $r_i(x_j) <_m w_k(x_k)$.

Multiversion conflict

We emphasize that this notion of multiversion conflicts is fundamentally different from our earlier definition of conflicts where we had simply carried over the conventional notion of conflicts to a versioned setting in a syntactic manner so that only *wr* operation pairs on the same version counted as conflicts. In contrast, the above definition essentially says that in a multiversion schedule (including the special case of monoversion histories) the only relevant kind of conflicts are *rw* operation pairs on the same data item, not necessarily on the same version. It is easy to see that *ww* pairs on the same data item no longer count as conflicts, as they create different versions and it is up to the read steps to choose the proper version. To realize that *wr* pairs are not really conflicts is a bit more involved. The essence of a conflict pair *pq* is that we are not allowed to commute *p* with *q*. For *wr* pairs, however, commuting the pair so that the read would precede the write is admissible because it restricts the version selection choices for the read that can still render the schedule correct (i.e., MVSR). So if the resulting schedule, with the read before the write, is MVSR, the original schedule with the *wr* pair would definitely be MVSR as well. This is the rationale for considering *wr* pairs (on the same data item) as conflict free. The third remaining type of operation pairs, *rw* pairs, has the opposite effect: by commuting an *rw* pair so that the read would follow the write, we end up with a schedule that has one more choice in selecting an appropriate version for the read step. So, if we succeed in verifying that the resulting schedule is MVSR, this would still not say anything about the correctness of the original schedule. Thus, *rw* pairs on the same data item constitute conflicts in a multiversion setting.

Because of the above asymmetry in the treatment of *wr* and *rw* pairs, the notion of a multiversion conflict cannot be easily used for defining an equivalence relation on multiversion schedules. Rather it leads to an asymmetric notion of transforming one schedule into another by means of repeatedly commuting conflict-free operations. This obviously resembles the notion of commutativity based reducibility introduced in Chapter 3, with the decisive difference, however, that we do not have a symmetric commutativity relation in our current setting. If we can eventually produce a serial monoversion history by commuting operations such that we always (i.e., after each transformation step) respect the ordering of *rw* conflict pairs, then we know that a multiversion schedule is guaranteed to be MVSR. From this argument we can already suspect that this is only a sufficient but not necessary condition for membership in MVSR; this conjecture will soon be confirmed.

The above consideration leads to the following correctness criteria (which, for simplicity, is stated only for totally ordered multiversion histories, and would have to be extended, in a straightforward manner, by an ordering rule in the sense of Chapter 3, Section 3.8.3, to cover partial orders as well):

Multiversion reducibility

DEFINITION 5.10 *Multiversion Reducibility*

A (totally ordered) multiversion history *m* is *multiversion reducible* if it can be transformed into a serial monoversion history by a finite sequence of transformation steps, each of which exchanges the order of two adjacent steps, (i.e., steps p, q with $p < q$ such that $o < p$ or $q < o$ for all other steps o) but without reversing the ordering of a multiversion conflict (i.e., *rw*) pair.

DEFINITION 5.11   *Multiversion Conflict Serializability*

A multiversion history m is *multiversion conflict serializable* if there is a serial monoversion history for the same set of transactions in which all pairs of operations in multiversion conflict occur in the same order as in m. Let MCSR denote the class of all multiversion conflict-serializable histories.

Multiversion conflict serializability (MCSR)

From what we have discussed above, the following theorems can be derived.

THEOREM 5.5

A multiversion history is multiversion reducible iff it is multiversion conflict serializable.

THEOREM 5.6

MCSR $\subset$ MVSR.

In order to see that this inclusion is strict, consider the following multiversion history, which is effectively a monoversion history:

$$m = w_0(x_0)w_0(y_0)w_0(z_0)c_0r_2(y_0)r_3(z_0)w_3(x_3)c_3r_1(x_3)w_1(y_1)c_1w_2(x_2)c_2$$
$$r_\infty(x_2)r_\infty(y_1)r_\infty(z_0)c_\infty$$

The pairs $r_1(x_3)$ and $w_2(x_2)$ as well as $r_2(y_0)$ and $w_1(y_1)$ of operations can apparently not be exchanged without m losing its monoversion property; hence $m \notin$ MCSR. On the other hand, $m \approx_v t_0t_3t_2t_1t_\infty$, which implies $m \in$ MVSR.

It can be shown that membership of a history in class MCSR can be characterized in graph-theoretic terms using the following notion of a multiversion conflict graph.

DEFINITION 5.12   *Multiversion Conflict Graph*

Let m be a multiversion schedule. The multiversion conflict graph of m is a graph that has the transactions of m as its nodes and an edge from t_i to t_k if there are steps $r_i(x_j)$ and $w_k(x_k)$ for the same data item x in m such that $r_i(x_j) <_m w_k(x_k)$.

Multiversion conflict graph

Not surprisingly, we obtain:

THEOREM 5.7

A multiversion history is MCSR iff its multiversion conflict graph is acyclic.

So MCSR has a polynomial membership test, and all practical multiversion concurrency control protocols fall into this class. Note, however, that the equivalent serial monoversion history for an acyclic multiversion conflict graph cannot simply be derived by topologically sorting the graph. Rather the above theorem only states that acyclicity of the graph is a sufficient and necessary condition for the existence of a sequence of transformation steps (in the sense of the definition of multiversion reducibility) that yields a serial monoversion history. For proving the correctness of protocols, the graph characterization of the larger class MVSR along with an appropriately chosen version order turns out to be an elegant and more practical tool, as we will show in the next section.

Figure 5.2 summarizes the relationships between the various classes of histories studied in this chapter so far. In the histories of this figure, transaction t_0 is not explicitly shown, and neither is t_∞. Moreover, all histories are shown as monoversion histories, but it should by now be clear how versioning comes

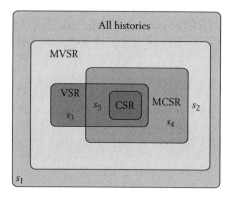

$s_1 = r_1(x)r_2(x)w_1(x)w_2(x)c_1c_2$
$s_2 = w_1(x)c_1r_2(x)r_3(y)w_3(x)w_2(y)c_2c_3$
$s_3 = w_1(x)c_1r_2(x)r_3(y)w_3(x)w_2(y)c_2c_3w_4(x)c_4$
$s_4 = r_1(x)w_1(x)r_2(x)r_2(y)w_2(y)r_1(y)w_1(y)c_1c_2$
$s_5 = r_1(x)w_1(x)r_2(x)w_2(y)c_2w_1(y)w_3(y)c_1c_3$

Figure 5.2 Classes of multiversion serializable histories.

into the picture. For example, s_2 is a representative for history

$$w_1(x_1)c_1r_2(x_1)r_3(y_0)w_3(x_3)w_2(y_2)c_2c_3$$

5.4 **Limiting the Number of Versions**

In our discussion so far we have always assumed that enough storage space is available for holding any number of versions. Thus, we have never put a limit on the number of versions of a particular data item, or on the number of versions of all data items taken together. While this is reasonable from a theoretical point of view, in that it has allowed us to develop a serializability theory for multiversion histories that indeed generalizes the monoversion case, it is rarely practical, since the number of versions will never be allowed to grow indefinitely. Even though disk space is relatively inexpensive, we cannot assume that a data server will be given unlimited space to manage its versions, nor can we assume that managing extremely large numbers of versions can be done efficiently. Therefore, it appears reasonable to impose an upper limit on the number of versions that the system can distinguish or keep around simultaneously. The important point we want to make in this section is that limiting the number of versions can make a difference, in the sense that schedules that are multiversion serializable if no upper bound on the number of versions exists may lose this property in the presence of a limit on the total number of versions.

As an example, we consider the following monoversion history:

$$m = w_0(x_0)c_0r_1(x_0)w_3(x_3)c_3w_1(x_1)c_1r_2(x_1)w_2(x_2)c_2$$

This history is obviously in MVSR, with the version order $x_0 \ll x_1 \ll x_2 \ll x_3$. However, it is not equivalent to any serial schedule that maintains at most two versions of x simultaneously. As is easily verified, there are six different serial monoversion histories for the three transactions t_1, t_2, and t_3 in m; they are as follows:

$$m_1 = w_0(x_0)c_0r_1(x_0)w_1(x_1)c_1r_2(x_1)w_2(x_2)c_2w_3(x_3)c_3$$
$$m_2 = w_0(x_0)c_0r_1(x_0)w_1(x_1)c_1w_3(x_3)c_3r_2(x_3)w_2(x_2)c_2$$
$$m_3 = w_0(x_0)c_0r_2(x_0)w_2(x_2)c_2r_1(x_2)w_1(x_1)c_1w_3(x_3)c_3$$
$$m_4 = w_0(x_0)c_0r_2(x_0)w_2(x_2)c_2w_3(x_3)c_3r_1(x_3)w_1(x_1)c_1$$
$$m_5 = w_0(x_0)c_0w_3(x_3)c_3r_1(x_3)w_1(x_1)c_1r_2(x_1)w_2(x_2)c_2$$
$$m_6 = w_0(x_0)c_0w_3(x_3)c_3r_2(x_3)w_2(x_2)c_2r_1(x_2)w_1(x_1)c_1$$

Since $m \approx_v m_1$, we first observe that $m \in$ MVSR. Now let us assume that the total number of versions that can exist at the same time is, for whatever reasons, limited to $k = 2$; since m and the serial histories for m's transactions only write x, this means only the last two versions of x that are written in a schedule will be stored.

For m_1 this means the following: First t_0 and t_1 produce x-versions x_0 and x_1, respectively. Next t_2 will overwrite version x_0, which is older, and t_3 will overwrite x_1. So when m_1 terminates, the database will comprise versions x_2 and x_3. Notice that history m will produce versions x_1 and x_2 as those that are written last; thus m can no longer be considered equivalent to m_1.

It can be verified by similar arguments that m is also not equivalent to *any* of the other serial monoversion schedules shown above, since the following holds:

1. m_2 (like m_1) produces versions x_2 and x_3,

2. m_3 and m_4 both produce versions x_1 and x_3,

3. m_5 and m_6 produce x_1 and x_2 (as does m), but m_5 comprises operation $r_1(x_3)$, while m_6 comprises $r_2(x_3)$, both of which do not occur in m.

Since m is not equivalent to any of the monoversion histories possible in this example, we may conclude that, different from the general case, history m is *not* a member of class MVSR if only two versions are allowed.

The above observations can be formalized. In the presence of an upper bound for the total number of data item versions, view equivalence of histories is again defined as in Chapter 3, namely, by asking for identical reads-from relations *and* equal final write operations. To be even more precise, we can furthermore incorporate a given bound k for the number of versions into the definition and hence speak of *k-version view serializability*; the corresponding classes of histories will be denoted by kVSR, $k > 0$.

For the sample schedule m discussed above, it then follows immediately that

$$m \in \text{MVSR} - 2\text{VSR}$$

In addition, it is easily verified that

$$\text{VSR} = 1\text{VSR}$$

and that

$$\text{MVSR} = \bigcup_{k>0} k\text{VSR}$$

Since we have stated above that MVSR has an NP complete decision problem, it moreover follows that the problem of deciding whether a given multiversion

schedule is in class kVSR is NP complete for every $k > 0$. Finally, it can be   *A hierarchy of*
shown that the various classes of k-version view-serializable histories form a   *classes*
strict hierarchy, that is,

$$\text{VSR} = 1\text{VSR} \subset 2\text{VSR} \subset 3\text{VSR} \subset \ldots \subset \text{MVSR}$$

5.5 **Multiversion Concurrency Control Protocols**

We now develop concurrency control protocols for multiversion databases, or
enhancements of known protocols for a multiversion environment. For all of
them, the important point is that they produce total version orders, so that their
correctness follows from the characterization of membership in class MVSR
stated in Theorem 5.4. In the discussion that follows we will assume (unless
stated otherwise) that all versions written can be stored (so that limiting the
number of available versions is not an issue). We will discuss enhancements of
the TO, 2PL, and SGT protocols (in this order).

5.5.1 **The MVTO Protocol**

A *multiversion timestamp ordering* (MVTO) scheduler essentially processes op-   *MVTO*
erations in first-in-first-out (FIFO) fashion. In particular, it transforms data op-   *scheduler*
erations into operations on versions of data items, and processes them in such
a way that the result appears as if it had been produced by a serial monoversion schedule with transactions in the order of timestamps that are assigned at
the beginning of a transaction. Each version carries the timestamp $ts(t_i)$ of the
transaction t_i by which it has been created. In detail, an MVTO scheduler acts
as follows:

1. A step $r_i(x)$ is transformed into a step $r_i(x_k)$, where x_k is the version of x
   that carries the largest timestamp $\leq ts(t_i)$ and was written by t_k, $k \neq i$.

2. A step $w_i(x)$ is processed as follows:
   (a) If a step of the form $r_j(x_k)$ such that $ts(t_k) < ts(t_i) < ts(t_j)$ has al-
       ready been scheduled, then $w_i(x)$ is rejected and t_i is aborted,
   (b) otherwise, $w_i(x)$ is transformed into $w_i(x_i)$ and executed.

3. A commit c_i is delayed until the commit c_j of all transactions t_j that
   have written new versions of data items read by t_i have been processed.
   (This part of the protocol is optional and included in order to ensure
   correct transaction recovery, e.g., avoiding anomalies such as dirty reads.
   This will be considered in depth in Chapter 11.)

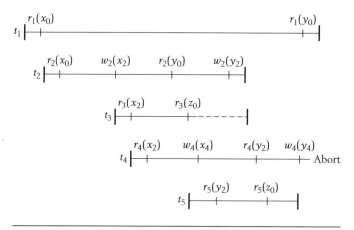

Figure 5.3 Sample execution under the MVTO protocol.

Note that we do not consider the case where a transaction can read an item after having written it; if this were allowed, a transaction would have to be able to see a version it has itself produced (see step 1).

Correctness of The important observation for proving the MVTO protocol correct, that
MVTO is, for showing that

$$\text{Gen(MVTO)} \subseteq \text{MVSR}$$

holds, is that a version order can be defined as follows:

$$x_i \ll x_j \iff ts(t_i) < ts(t_j)$$

Figure 5.3 shows a sample execution under the MVTO protocol. The interleaved execution of transactions t_1 and t_2 once more illustrates the great performance enhancement of multiversion concurrency control: as a monoversion schedule, the execution would have been a classical case of inconsistent reading; with versioning, however, the situation is perfectly acceptable, as t_1 simply reads the old version y_0, thus ensuring consistency with its previous reading of x_0. With MVTO in particular, this is the result of t_1's timestamp being smaller than that of the concurrent transaction t_2. Transaction t_3 needs to wait (as indicated by the dashed line in the figure) right before its commit, because it has read the uncommitted version x_2 (and indeed had to read this version because its timestamp is larger than that of t_2); once t_2 is committed, t_3 can commit as well. Transaction t_4 is an example for a "late" writer: it creates the new version y_4; however, transaction t_5 has already read the version y_2. As the timestamp ordering prescribes the serialization order $t_2 < t_4 < t_5$, t_5 should actually have read y_4 (which, of course, was impossible, as that version did not yet exist at the time of t_5's read). Thus, t_4's write occurs "too late," and t_4 must be aborted according to the MVTO rules.

5.5.2 **The MV2PL Protocol**

We next describe a scheduler that uses locks and a strong two-phase discipline (i.e., the SS2PL rules as far as unlocking is concerned). We first assume as a simplification that *all* versions of data items ever written are kept around; this will be relaxed later by considering a special case in which at most two versions of a data item exist simultaneously. We generally distinguish

- *committed versions*, which have been written by transactions that are already committed,
- the *current version* of a data item, which is the committed version of that data item written by the transaction that was committed last,
- *uncommitted versions*, which are all remaining versions (created by transactions that are still active).

The scheduler makes sure that at each point in time there is *at most one* uncommitted version of any data item. Depending on whether read steps are allowed to read only the current version or also uncommitted versions, several variants of this protocol can be distinguished. Moreover, the scheduler treats the final step of a transaction differently from the other steps, where "final" refers to the last data operation before the transaction's commit or to the commit itself. (Both interpretations are feasible under this protocol.) An individual step is handled as follows.

MV2PL scheduler

1. If the step is not final within a transaction:
   (a) an $r(x)$ is executed right away, by assigning to it the current version of the requested data item, i.e., the most recently committed version (but not any other, previously committed one), or by assigning to it an uncommitted version of x;
   (b) a $w(x)$ is executed only when the transaction that has written x last is finished, so that there are no other uncommitted versions of x.
2. If the step is final within transaction t_i, it is delayed until the following types of transactions are committed:
   (a) all those transactions t_j that have read the current version of a data item written by t_i,
   (b) all those t_j from which t_i has read some version.

The following example indicates how such a scheduler works.

EXAMPLE 5.9

Assume the MV2PL scheduler is supplied with the following sequence of steps:

$$s = r_1(x)w_1(x)r_2(x)w_2(y)r_1(y)w_2(x)c_2w_1(y)c_1$$

Then it proceeds as follows:

1. $r_1(x)$ is assigned to x_0 and is executed: $\qquad\qquad\qquad$ $r_1(x_0)$

2. $w_1(x)$ is executed since no other transaction is still active: $\quad$ $w_1(x_1)$

3. let $r_2(x)$ be assigned to x_1 and executed: $\qquad\qquad\qquad$ $r_2(x_1)$

4. $w_2(y)$ is executed: $\qquad\qquad\qquad\qquad\qquad\qquad\qquad$ $w_2(y_2)$

5. let $r_1(y)$ be assigned to y_0 and executed: $\qquad\qquad\qquad$ $r_1(y_0)$

6. if $w_2(x)$ were *not* the final step of t_2, it would be delayed since t_1 is still active and has written x_1. However, as it *is* the final step of t_2, the final-step rules need to be applied. It turns out that t_2 nonetheless has to wait for the following reason:

    (a) t_1 has read the current version of data item y (y_0), and t_2 overwrites this version,

    (b) t_2 has read x_1 from t_1.

7. $w_1(y)$, the final step of t_1, is executed since

    (a) t_2 has *not* read a current version of a data item written by t_1 (current versions are x_0, y_0),

    (b) t_1 has not read a version written by t_2. $\qquad\qquad\qquad$ $w_1(y_1)$

8. finally, $w_2(x)$ can be executed: $\qquad\qquad\qquad\qquad\qquad$ $w_2(x_2)$

2V2PL protocol   In the following further elaboration of the protocol, we restrict ourselves to a special case of MV2PL that is particularly relevant in applications, namely, the *2V2PL protocol* (two-version 2PL), which keeps at most two versions of any data item at each point in time. These two versions are those that a data server may need to keep around (in some form) for recovery purposes (see Part III). Suppose that t_i writes data item x, but is not yet committed, the two versions of x are its *before image* and its *after image*. As soon as t_i commits, the before image can be dropped since the new version of x is now stable, and old versions are no longer needed nor maintained. In other words, a 2V2PL scheduler always maintains a current version for a data item as well as, in the presence of transactions that write, candidates for successor versions. It is a characteristic property of the 2V2PL variant that at most one such uncommitted candidate is allowed at every point of time. So it is mostly read operations that benefit from versioning, and in 2V2PL read operations

Table 5.1 Lock mode compatibility for 2V2PL.

	$rl(x)$	$wl(x)$	$cl(x)$
$rl(x)$	$+$	$+$	$-$
$wl(x)$	$+$	$-$	$-$
$cl(x)$	$-$	$-$	$-$

are restricted to reading current versions only (i.e., the last committed version).

2V2PL uses three kinds of locks on data items (i.e., not on individual versions), all of which are kept until the termination of a transaction:

1. rl (read lock): An $rl(x)$ is set immediately prior to an operation $r(x)$ with respect to the current version of x.

2. wl (write lock): A $wl(x)$ is set (immediately) prior to an operation $w(x)$ for writing a new uncommitted version of x.

3. cl (certify (or commit) lock): A $cl(x)$ is set prior to the execution of the final step of a transaction (i.e., usually upon the transaction's commit request) on every data item x that this transaction has written.

The lock compatibilities for these three types of locks are given in Table 5.1 (as usual, $+$ denotes compatibility and $-$ incompatibility). Notice that unlock operations need to obey the 2PL rule.

The role of the write locks is to ensure that at most one uncommitted version can exist for each data item at each point in time. The key point to ensure that the resulting output schedules are multiversion serializable is the acquisition of the certify locks. The tests regarding the admissible orderings of reading current versions and creating new ones is encoded in the compatibility checking of read locks and certify locks. In this sense, certify locks play the role that write locks have in conventional, nonversioned locking. However, the fact that certify locks are acquired only at the end of the transaction and are thus usually held for a much shorter time is a great performance advantage over conventional, monoversion 2PL.

EXAMPLE 5.10

Consider the input schedule

$$r_1(x)w_2(y)r_1(y)w_1(x)c_1r_3(y)r_3(z)w_3(z)w_2(x)c_2w_4(z)c_4c_3$$

and let x_0, y_0, z_0 denote the current versions that exist before this input schedule starts. The 2V2PL protocol produces the following output

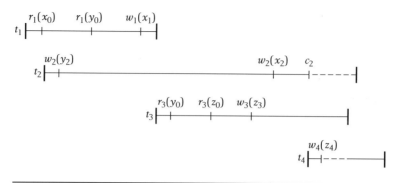

Figure 5.4 Sample execution under the 2V2PL protocol.

schedule, where ul denotes unlock operations that remove all locks of a transaction:

$$rl_1(x)r_1(x_0)wl_2(y)w_2(y_2)rl_1(y)r_1(y_0)wl_1(x)w_1(x_1)cl_1(x)ul_1c_1$$
$$rl_3(y)r_3(y_0)rl_3(z)r_3(z_0)wl_2(x)cl_2(x)wl_3(y)w_3(z_3)cl_3(z)ul_3c_3$$
$$cl_2(y)ul_2c_2wl_4(z)w_4(z_4)cl_4(z)ul_4c_4$$

The output schedule is also illustrated in Figure 5.4. Note that $cl_2(y)$ would be requested right before the begin of t_4, but cannot be granted until the commit of t_3 because of the conflicting read lock held by t_3. Further note that $wl_4(z)$ causes a lock wait, too, because of its incompatibility with the still held $wl_3(z)$; so t_4 is blocked until after the commit of t_3.

Correctness of
2V2PL

The correctness of the 2V2PL protocol follows from three facts. First, the order of the transactions' final steps (usually their commit requests) provides us with a total ordering from which we can derive a suitable version order. Second, because write locks on the same data item are incompatible, at most one uncommitted version can exist at a given time, so that the following choice of the version order is unambiguous: $x_i \ll x_j \iff f_i < f_j$, with f_i, f_j denoting the final steps of two transactions t_i and t_j that have both written (new versions of) x. Third, read operations are always directed to the current version, and certify locks of concurrent writers, which are incompatible with read locks, serve to determine situations when a new committed version is produced while a reader is still in progress. In the latter case the commit of the writer is blocked until the reader is terminated. Putting these three observations together allows us to construct the multiversion serialization graph for the specific version order, and to show that this graph is guaranteed to be acyclic.

The following example shows that, just like 2PL, 2V2PL (and hence MV2PL) is not deadlock free. Consider the following scheduler input:

$$r_1(x)r_2(y)w_1(y)w_2(x)c_1c_2$$

From this input, the scheduler produces

$$rl_1(x)r_1(x_0)rl_2(y)r_2(y_0)wl_1(y)w_1(y_1)wl_2(x)w_2(x_2)$$

where x_0 and y_0 denote the current versions as of the begin of the example schedule. Next t_1 needs a certify lock $cl_1(y)$, which is incompatible with $rl_2(y)$, and t_2 needs another certify lock $cl_2(x)$, which is incompatible with $rl_1(x)$. Thus, the scheduler is stuck in a deadlock. There are various techniques to cope with such a situation, as we already discussed in Chapter 4 for the ordinary 2PL protocol.

5.5.3 The MVSGT Protocol

A final multiversion scheduler we look at is another SGT protocol, now enhanced for managing multiple versions. We note that it is no longer possible, as in the monoversion case, to provide a protocol capable of generating *exactly* MCSR. Instead there now exists an unlimited number of schedulers, each of which generates a distinct subset of MCSR such that the union of all of them equals MCSR. We sketch a general framework for such schedulers here, which comprises certain nondeterministic steps; if these steps are made more precise, the various schedulers result.

The general scheduler maintains a multiversion conflict graph G whose nodes are the various transactions including t_0. In the beginning, G has edges from t_0 to all other nodes; in the end, when the input has been processed completely, G will contain all edges from the conflict graph plus a few additional ones, depending on the result of the nondeterministic steps.

MVSGT scheduler

Let us first consider the assignment of a new version to some read step: Assume that $r_i(x)$ arrives at the scheduler; *candidates* from which t_i can read are t_0 as well as all $w_j(x)$, which have already been scheduled. However, the following have to be excluded:

1. those t_j on a path that originates from t_i, since these are supposed to follow t_i in an equivalent serial schedule; let us call them *late*;

2. those t_j for which a path exists from t_j to another candidate t_k that writes x *and* from t_k to t_i, since in an equivalent serial schedule, t_k writes x after t_j; let us call them *early*.

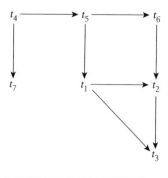

Figure 5.5 A conflict graph.

Now a first nondeterministic step consists of choosing a version for $r_i(x)$ among those written by transactions that are neither late nor early.

EXAMPLE 5.11

Let us consider the situation shown in Figure 5.5, where t_0 as well as the edges from t_0 to any other transaction t_i, $i \in \{1, \ldots, 7\}$, are not shown.

Suppose that $r_1(x)$ arrives at the scheduler, and that t_2 through t_7 have already written x; hence they are "candidates" in the sense just discussed. Late transactions are t_2 and t_3, while early ones are t_0 and t_4. Thus, there is a choice between candidates t_5, t_6, and t_7.

Now if the conflict graph G is acyclic, then for each read step there is at least one candidate that is neither late nor early. The simple reason is that not all transactions in a schedule are late; among those that are not late, choose one without pathwise connection to other nonlate candidates. The latter one is not early. The multiversion conflict graph G is now maintained as follows:

1. If $w_i(x)$ is executed, an edge of the form (t_j, t_i) is added to the graph for each t_j for which an $r_j(x)$ has already been scheduled; in this way, G remains a supergraph of the MVSG. If G becomes cyclic, then $w_i(x)$ is *not* executed; otherwise the version newly written is kept.

2. If $r_i(x)$ is scheduled and receives the version written by $w_j(x)$, an edge of the form (t_j, t_i) is added to G; since t_j is not late, this does not close a cycle. In addition, an edge of the form either (t_k, t_j) or (t_i, t_k) is added to G for each step $w_k(x)$ already scheduled, where t_k is neither late nor early.

Consider the previous example again: If t_7 is chosen from the set of candidates, the new edges (t_7, t_1), (t_5, t_7) (edge (t_1, t_5) would close a cycle), and (t_1, t_6) (alternatively (t_6, t_7)) result. More precisely, a choice is made such that (t_k, t_i) if there exists a path from t_k to t_i in G, and (t_i, t_k) otherwise. It can be shown that in this way G remains acyclic; in addition, each schedule produced is in MCSR.

5.5.4 A Multiversion Protocol for Read-Only Transactions

Many modern data-intensive applications exhibit workloads with a dominant fraction of read-only transactions that read and analyze large amounts of data. In the presence of (at least a nontrivial fraction of) concurrent update transactions, concurrency control is crucial to ensure that the read-only transactions "see" consistent data. In fact, such situations pose a stress test for the concurrency control component, because of the long duration of the read-only transactions. Under a conventional monoversion scheduler, say, a 2PL protocol, such long transactions would often lead to a high probability of blocking the update transactions and eventually to disastrous performance (e.g., unacceptably high response times).

Multiversion concurrency control protocols, on the other hand, can avoid many of these blocking situations by assigning "old" versions to readers. However, as we have seen in the previous subsections, such protocols can become fairly complex, are all but easy to implement, and are likely to incur noticeable run-time overhead. In this subsection we consider a simple hybrid protocol that aims to reconcile the simplicity of conventional (S)2PL or simple timestamping with the performance benefits of versioning. It does so by exploiting versioning only for read-only transactions, thus "picking the low-hanging fruit" in the sense that, say, 10 percent of the complexity of multiversion protocols is sufficient to achieve, say, 90 percent of the benefit. To this end, read-only transactions must be explicitly marked as such upon their beginning.

In practice, this is often feasible; if in doubt, a transaction would simply have to be marked as a (potential) updater. This dichotomy of transactions is the basis for the following combined protocol:

1. *Update transactions* are subject to the conventional S2PL protocol. They acquire conventional locks for both read and write steps, which are released according to the two-phase rule, with write locks held until commit (and possibly even read locks held until commit if the strong variant SS2PL is used). In contrast to the conventional monoversion setting, however, each write step creates a new version rather than overwriting the data item; each version is timestamped with the timestamp of its transaction that corresponds to the commit time of the transaction. So update transactions do not benefit from versioning at all, but provide

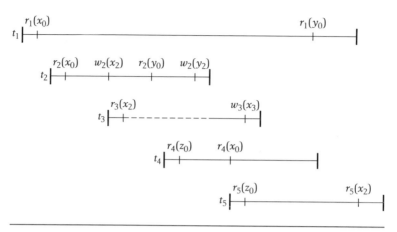

Figure 5.6 Sample execution under the ROMV protocol.

the potential to benefit the read-only transactions while keeping the overhead of the protocol as low as possible.

2. *Read-only transactions* are handled by a multiversion timestamp protocol, similar to the MVTO rules but with a twist on committed versus uncommitted versions. Each such transaction is assigned a timestamp that, unlike the update transactions, corresponds to the begin of the transaction (rather than its commit). Now the key point of the protocol is that a read operation by a read-only transaction is assigned to the most recent version that has been committed at the time of the reader's begin. In other words: the read-only transactions always access the version with the largest timestamp that is smaller than the transaction's timestamp (assuming that timestamps of different transactions are never equal).

Read-only multiversion protocol (ROMV)

Figure 5.6 shows a self-explanatory scenario of how the protocol works, with update transactions t_2, t_3, and read-only transactions t_1, t_4, and t_5. The lock wait of t_3 because of the (conventional) *wr* lock conflict on x is indicated by a dashed line.

Correctness of ROMV

A correctness proof for this protocol, let us call it *read-only multiversion protocol* (ROMV), is relatively straightforward: the version order for a data item is given by the commit order (and thus timestamp order) of the update transactions, and read-only transactions are placed in the serialization order according to their timestamps (i.e., between the update transactions). This argument could be further formalized by explicitly showing that the multiversion serialization graph is acyclic for the given version order. In fact, the ROMV protocol generates only schedules in the MCSR subclass, and another simple proof of its correctness would thus amount to showing the following: a serial monoversion history can be derived from a given ROMV-generated history by commuting conflict-free operations of update transactions and commuting the steps of read-only transactions with preceding writes such that each read-only transaction eventually follows right after the transaction with the most recent commit as of the transaction's begin.

Although the ROMV protocol is very simple, it does raise a number of nontrivial implementation issues. In particular, as versions are transient and merely serve concurrency control purposes, it is desirable to have some form of garbage collection for old versions that are definitely no longer beneficial for any read-only transaction. A simple sufficient condition for a version being eligible for garbage collection would be that it is (1) not the most recent committed version (which, of course, must not be garbage collected), and (2) its timestamp is older than the timestamp of the oldest active read-only transaction. This approach assumes that there is no explicit limit for the number of simultaneously kept versions of a data item. If there is such a limit, an additional complication is that some read-only transactions may have to be aborted because the version that they would have to read according to the timestamping rule is no longer available. Another nontrivial implementation issue is how to manage the timestamps for the versions themselves; this may be somewhat tricky because timestamps are assigned only upon the commit of a transaction. A straightforward solution could be to place timestamps in the versions themselves (e.g., in page headers, assuming that data items are pages), but this would require revisiting all accessed pages at commit time. Alternative approaches include additional data structures that temporarily maintain write sets and timestamps of committed update transactions.

Garbage collection of old versions

5.6 **Lessons Learned**

Keeping multiple versions of data items around is an attractive idea, and at the same time it is a practical one, as we will show when we discuss recovery. From a theoretical point of view, an adaptation of serializability theory to a multiversion setting is straightforward, as soon as the appropriate versioning restrictions have been identified. A tricky situation, considerably different from the general case, arises for a limited number of versions, as an entire hierarchy of classes of serializable histories enters the picture.

From a more practical point of view, adapting the various scheduling protocols to a multiversion setting is not too difficult, once the appropriate locks (or alternative synchronization mechanisms) have been found. Intuitively, multiversion protocols allow various degrees of freedom for assigning, or choosing, versions to process within a schedule. The special case of providing consistent views of the data to read-only transactions, discussed in Section 5.5.4, is of very high practical relevance and greatly benefits from versioning; protocols like the one described there are used in several commercial database systems.

Exercises

5.1 For the following three histories, test whether they are monoversion histories or members of MVSR or MCSR; in case a schedule is a member of MVSR, additionally find out for which values of $k > 0$ the history is in class kVSR.

$$m_1 = w_0(x_0)w_0(y_0)w_0(z_0)c_0r_3(x_0)w_3(x_3)c_3w_1(x_1)c_1r_2(x_1)w_2(y_2)w_2(z_2)c_2$$
$$m_2 = w_0(x_0)w_0(y_0)c_0w_1(x_1)c_1r_3(x_1)w_3(x_3)r_2(x_1)c_3w_2(y_2)c_2$$
$$m_3 = w_0(x_0)w_0(y_0)c_0w_1(x_1)c_1r_2(x_1)w_2(y_2)c_2r_3(y_0)w_3(x_3)c_3$$

For schedules in MVSR, also give an appropriate version function for a final transaction t_∞.

5.2 For the multiversion schedule

$$m = w_0(x_0)w_0(y_0)c_0r_1(x_0)w_1(x_1)r_2(x_1)w_2(y_2)w_1(y_1)w_3(x_3)$$

test whether there exists a version order $\ll$ such that $MVSG(m, \ll)$ is acyclic. If there is an acyclic graph, find an appropriate version function for a final transaction t_∞ such that the graph remains acyclic.

5.3 Prove: In the "no blind writes" model, where each data item written by a transaction must have been read before in the same transaction, MCSR = MVSR.

5.4 Prove: In the "action" model, where each step is a combination of a read operation immediately followed by a write operation on the same data item, MVSR = VSR.

5.5 Consider the following schedule, given in "conventional" form without a specific version function:

$$r_1(x)r_2(x)r_3(y)w_2(x)w_1(y)c_1w_2(z)w_3(z)r_3(x)c_3r_2(y)c_2$$

Show that this schedule is multiversion serializable, i.e., could be allowed by a multiversion concurrency control. Give a feasible version function and also a feasible version order. What do the resulting executions (i.e., output schedules) under the MVTO and the 2V2PL protocols look like?

5.6 Consider the input schedule:

$$w_1(x)c_1r_2(x)r_3(x)c_2r_4(x)w_3(x)c_4c_3$$

Give the resulting output schedule under the MVTO protocol.

5.7 Consider the input schedule of the MV2PL Example 5.9:

$$s = r_1(x)w_1(x)r_2(x)w_2(y)r_1(y)w_2(x)c_2w_1(y)c_1$$

Apply the specialized 2V2PL protocol to this input and give the resulting output.

5.8 Complete the proof sketches for the correctness of the MVTO, 2V2PL, and ROMV protocols.

5.9 Reconsider the ROMV protocol that has been specifically geared for read-only transactions. What happens if the protocol is relaxed in such a way that update transactions use the timestamp-based version selection for their read steps? That is, update transactions would still use conventional exclusive locks for writes but would exploit versioning for reads by selecting the most recent version that was committed at the time of the update transaction's begin. Is this protocol still correct in that it guarantees MVSR schedules?

Bibliographic Notes

The idea of using several versions of data items in concurrency control goes back to Reed (1978, 1983) and Bayer et al. (1980), which are also the origins of the MVTO and 2V2PL protocols, respectively. Further seminal papers on this topic have been written by Stearns and Rosenkrantz (1981) as well as Bernstein and Goodman (1983).

Our discussion in this chapter is along the lines of Bernstein and Goodman (1983) as well as Bernstein et al. (1987) and Claybrook (1992). The notion of a version function as used in the beginning of the chapter (see Definition 5.1) is essentially from Papadimitriou (1986); serial monoversion schedules are termed *1-serial* multiversion schedules in Bernstein et al. (1987), and members of MVSR are called *one-copy serializable*. The NP completeness results mentioned are from Bernstein and Goodman (1983), Lausen (1983), and Papadimitriou and Kanellakis (1984). The latter source also proved the hierarchy result mentioned in Section 5.2.4. A systematic investigation of multiversion serializability in the presence of a limited number of versions was done by Papadimitriou and Kanellakis (1984) as well as Morzy (1993). Hadzilacos and Papadimitriou (1986) investigated MCSR in more depth. Vidyasankar (1991) proved an alternative characterization of membership in MVSR.

Raz (1993) extended the notion of commit order preservation (COCSR) that we introduced in Chapter 3 to a multiversion setting. Commit order-preserving MVSR, or COMVSR for short, requires view equivalence to a serial monoversion history in which the transaction ordering corresponds to the commit order of the given multiversion history. To this end, Raz restricted the version order and introduced additional constraints between reads and writes.

The scheduling protocols we have discussed in this chapter are also described in Bernstein et al. (1987) or Papadimitriou (1986); for more material on protocols, see also Cellary et al. (1988) or Claybrook (1992). Agrawal and Sengupta (1993) described an approach for unbundling the aspects of scheduling and version management when implementing a protocol. Other approaches have been reported by Ahuja and Browne (1987), Bober and Carey (1992a, b), Buckley and Silberschatz (1983), T. Hadzilacos (1988), Ibaraki et al. (1990), and Yu and Rosenkrantz (1988).

The practically most relevant, hybrid protocol for read-only transactions has been first proposed by DuBourdieu (1982) and Chan et al. (1982, 1985). Mohan, Pirahesh, and Lorie (1992) is a good source for implementation issues of these protocols. A highly enjoyable, semitechnical paper on the general idea of versioning has been written by Schueler (1977).

We have called the concepts discussed in this chapter *transparent* versioning since versions are invisible from a user's point of view. There is another form of versioning, *nontransparent* versioning, which is relevant in application domains such as computer-aided design (CAD) or computer-aided software engineering (CASE), where a user needs to be able to handle versions explicitly. More on this form of versioning can be found, for example, in Cellary and Jomier (1990), Katz (1990), Bernstein (1998), and Härder et al. (2000).

CHAPTER SIX

Concurrency Control on Objects: Notions of Correctness

No matter how complicated a problem is, it usually can be reduced to a simple comprehensible form which is often the best solution.
—*An Wang*

Every problem has a simple, easy-to-understand, wrong answer.
—*Anonymous*

6.1 Goal and Overview

After the previous chapters' detailed exploration of page model concurrency control methods, we will now make a major step to enrich our underlying computational model by turning to the object model. This means, as you may recall from Chapter 2, that transactions are now modeled as trees of operation invocations rather than "flat" sequences (or partial orders) of simple read or write steps. The major incentive for studying the richer but also more complex object model lies in its potential for higher concurrency by exploiting specific semantic properties of the operations, in particular commutativity of higher-level operations such as Deposit or Withdraw on Bank account objects.

The goal of this chapter is to develop correctness criteria for concurrent executions of object model transactions. Analogously to the flow of arguments for the page model, these criteria will then serve as the basis for practical concurrency control algorithms, to be developed in the subsequent chapters. In our quest for appropriate correctness criteria we have to address two major differences from the page model: (1) the operations of a transaction are more general than merely read and write, and (2) operations can themselves invoke other operations, thus leading to a transaction tree. After introducing the syntactical notions of object model histories and schedules in Section 6.2, we will address these two issues in two steps: in Section 6.3 we will consider flat schedules with semantically rich operations; then we will look into the general case of transaction trees in Section 6.4.

It will turn out that allowing general operations but sticking to the flat structure of transactions is a relatively straightforward extension of what we have discussed within the framework of the page model. In particular, we will be able to generalize the notion of conflict serializability in an appropriate manner. Coping with transaction trees poses more fundamental difficulties. Here we will see that neither view serializability nor conflict serializability can be generalized directly, and we will thus need to develop a more elaborate correctness criterion, in the style of (commutativity based) reducibility, as briefly discussed in Chapter 3. This fundamental criterion, to be coined *tree reducibility*, will be the subject of Section 6.4. The need for algorithmic tractability will then motivate our exploration of sufficient, more "constructive" conditions for correctness in Section 6.5. These considerations will emphasize a particularly interesting special case of the object model, namely, the case of *layered transactions*, where the nodes of the transaction trees correspond to operations of a strictly layered system architecture (such as the five-layer database server sketched in Chapter 1). In the final Section 6.6, we will give an outlook on exploiting further semantic properties of operations, beyond the property of general (state-independent) commutativity.

6.2 **Histories and Schedules**

Let us first briefly recall from Chapter 2 how transactions are characterized in the object model. The dynamic invocations of operations by a transaction spawn a tree of labeled nodes, where each node corresponds to an invoked operation together with its input and possibly also output parameters. The parent of a node is the operation from which the node's operation was called, and the children of a node are the operations called by the node. Ultimately, each invoked operation results in calls of read and write operations, which thus form the leaves of the tree. As we again want to allow concurrent or parallel threads, even within a transaction, the execution order is modeled as a partial order of the leaves; the ordering (or nonordering, i.e., concurrent execution) of higher-level operations is derived from the leaf order: we say that p precedes q if p terminates before q begins, or more technically, the last leaf-level descendant of p precedes the first leaf-level descendant of q.

The next step is to consider interleavings of such transaction trees. Not surprisingly, this leads to a notion of partially ordered forests:

Object model history

DEFINITION 6.1 *Object Model History*

Let $T = \{t_1, \ldots, t_n\}$ be a (finite) set of transaction trees, where each $t_i \in T$ is a pair (op$_i$, $<_i$) of labeled tree nodes along with a partial order of the leaves. A *history s* (or complete schedule) for T is a partially ordered forest

$(op(s), <_s)$ with node set $op(s)$ and partial order $<_s$ such that:

1. $op(s) \subseteq \bigcup_{i=1}^{n} op_i \cup \bigcup_{i=1}^{n} \{a_i, c_i\}$, and $\bigcup_{i=1}^{n} op_i \subseteq op(s)$, i.e., s contains the operations of the given transaction trees and a termination operation c_i (commit) or a_i (abort) for each transaction $t_i \in T$;

2. $(\forall i, 1 \leq i \leq n)$ $c_i \in op(s) \Leftrightarrow a_i \notin op(s)$;

3. a_i or c_i is a leaf node with the transaction t_i as its parent;

4. $\bigcup_{i=1}^{n} <_i \subseteq <_s$, i.e., all transaction orders are contained in the partial order given by s;

5. $(\forall i, 1 \leq i \leq n)$ $(\forall p \in op_i) p <_s a_i$ or $p <_s c_i$;

6. any pair of leaf operations $p, q \in op(s)$ from distinct transactions accessing the same data item such that at least one is a write operation must be ordered in s, i.e., either $p <_s q$ or $q <_s p$.

Like the individual transaction trees, the partial order of a history refers to the leaves of the forest, and we can derive a partial order among all nodes by the following convention:

DEFINITION 6.2   *Tree-Consistent Node Ordering*

In an object model history $s = (op(s), <_s)$ the ordering $<_s$ of leaf nodes is extended to arbitrary nodes as follows: two nodes p and q are considered as ordered, i.e., $p <_s q$ if for all leaf-level descendants p' and q' of p and q, respectively, the order $p' <_s q'$ holds according to the original (i.e., nonextended) $<_s$. Such an ordering is called *tree consistent*.

Tree-consistent node ordering

Now the notion of a *prefix* of a history, which we introduced in Chapter 3 for the flat histories of the page model, can be applied to transaction forests: a prefix of a history $s = (op(s), <_s)$ is a forest $s' = (op(s'), <_s')$ with $op(s') \subseteq op(s)$ and $<_s' \subseteq <_s$ such that for each $p \in op(s')$ all ancestors of p and all nodes $q \in op(s)$ with $q <_s p$ must be in $op(s')$, too, and $<_s'$ equals $<_s$ when restricted to $op(s')$. Now the definition of an object model schedule is obvious:

DEFINITION 6.3   *Object Model Schedule*

An object model schedule is a prefix of an object model history.

Object model schedule

As an example consider a simplified version of the funds transfer transaction from Chapter 2, consisting of a Withdraw and a Deposit operation on two bank accounts. In contrast to the more elaborate example in Chapter 2, we assume

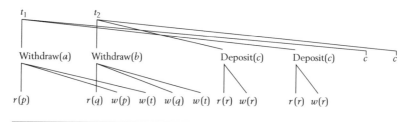

Figure 6.1 Example of an object model history.

that both of these operations are directly "translated" into page operations, that is, reads and writes. Figure 6.1 shows a history (i.e., concurrent execution) of two instances of such an object model transaction: t_1 transfers money from account a to c, and t_2 transfers money from b to c. We assume that the relevant records for accounts a, b, and c reside on pages p, q, and r, respectively, and that all Withdraw operations also need to access page t to obtain and track an (automatically generated) approval code; for simplicity, we disregard steps for locating these pages (e.g., index traversals). We also simplify the notation in that we only list those parameters of the invoked operations that are relevant for the discussion; for example, the Withdraw operation actually has two input parameters and one result parameter, namely, the ID of the bank account on which it operates, the amount of money to be withdrawn, and a returncode that states whether the withdrawal was successful or not. Figure 6.1 shows only the first argument, but in other examples we may need to make more parameters explicit as well.

In examples such as Figure 6.1 we will indicate the ordering of operations by drawing the leaf nodes in their execution order from left to right. As the caller-callee relationship in transaction trees is captured by vertical or diagonal arcs, the crossing of such arcs indicates that two (nonleaf) operations are concurrent. In Figure 6.1, for example, the two Withdraw operations that originate from t_1 and t_2, respectively, are concurrent. Of course, for nontotal leaf orders, we need a more explicit specification such as drawing directed arcs between ordered pairs of operations, as mentioned already in Chapter 3 for flat schedules.

Notation for caller-callee relationship

Sometimes it may also be necessary to indicate the caller-callee relationship more explicitly rather than drawing the arcs of the trees; we will then use subscripts for tree nodes as follows: (1) the subscript of a root t_i is i, and (2) the subscript of the j-th child of a node with subscript ω is ωj (i.e., the parent's subscript with j appended). So, in Figure 6.1, for example, the $w(t)$ operation belonging to t_1 would be denoted as $w_{113}(t)$, thus bearing the identification of its entire ancestor chain.

Now that we have both a formal definition and an intuitive understanding of object model schedules, the notion of a serial schedule can be defined in a straightforward way:

DEFINITION 6.4   *Serial Object Model Schedule*

An object model schedule is *serial* if its roots are totally ordered and for each root and each $i > 0$ the descendants with distance i from the root are totally ordered.

Serial schedule

The first condition in this definition states that transactions (i.e., the roots) are executed sequentially, and the second condition additionally requires that all steps within a transaction are also sequential. Note that it is not enough to require that all leaves of a root are ordered, as this would still allow interleaved executions of some inner-node operations.

A concept that is related to the notion of serial executions is the following:

DEFINITION 6.5   *Isolated Subtree*

A node p and the corresponding subtree in an object model schedule s are called *isolated* if

1. for all nodes q other than ancestors or descendants of p the property holds that for all leaves w of q either $w <_s p$ or $p <_s w$,

2. for each $i > 0$ the descendants of p with distance i from p are totally ordered.

Isolated subtree

The second condition is identical to one of the two requirements in Definition 6.4, simply stating that the subtree corresponds to a strictly sequential execution. The first condition requires that no other subtree can have any leaf operation between one of the leaves of subtree p (with the trivial exception of p's ancestors or descendants, including p itself). So the subtree rooted at p forms an indivisible unit. Note, however, that it is allowed for another subtree to have some leaves both preceding and following p. In the sense of the theory of relative serializability developed in Section 3.10, our notion of an isolated subtree p makes a statement only about the indivisible units of p relative to other subtrees, namely, forcing all of p to be a single indivisible unit; but we do not say anything about the interleavings of other subtrees (i.e., their indivisible units relative to p). A very strong special case is when *all roots* of a schedule are isolated: such a schedule must be serial.

The example in Figure 6.1 is special in that the two interleaved transaction trees are both perfectly balanced trees, meaning that all leaves, with the exception of the Commit operations, have the same distance from their roots. This is not by accident in the example; rather it captures a common case that the invoked operations correspond to fixed levels of a strictly layered system

Layered histories and schedules

architecture. We accounted for this specific structure already by drawing the tree nodes of Figure 6.1 in three levels: page accesses at the bottom level, method invocations on account objects at the middle level, and transactions at the top level. We refer to such highly structured object model schedules as *layered schedules*.

DEFINITION 6.6   *Layered History and Schedule*

An object model history is a *layered history* if all leaves other than Commit or Abort operations have identical distance from their roots. A layered history with a leaf-to-root distance of n is called an n-level history. In an n-level history, operations with distance i to the leaf level are called *level-i operations* (L_i operations) (i.e., leaves are at level L_0 and roots at level L_n).

A *layered schedule* is a prefix of a layered history.

So, according to this definition, the example of Figure 6.1 is a two-level history, with levels numbered from 0 to 2 in a bottom-up manner. Other examples, to be studied later, would include two-level histories with transactions at level L_2 that consist of record accesses at level L_1 that are translated into page accesses at level L_0. It is worth mentioning that page model schedules are a special case of n-level schedules with $n = 1$.

Two examples of nonlayered histories are shown in Figure 6.2. Both are similar to the previous funds transfer scenario, with the following differences: In the upper example, Withdraw operations do not include the step for obtaining and tracking an approval code, so that the transactions must invoke the

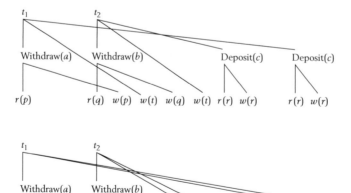

Figure 6.2 Two examples of nonlayered object model schedules.

data server operations that correspond to this specific step directly (resulting in the $w(t)$ operations). In the lower example, the deposit steps are no longer explicitly represented, and the corresponding page operations are invoked directly by the transactions. The latter scenario may appear a bit odd: why would the withdrawals be explicit, whereas the Deposit operations no longer show up? This may have (at least) two different explanations: First, it could happen that the transactions do, for efficiency or other reasons, "bypass" the object interface, avoiding the call of the Deposit method, although they do observe the encapsulation of account objects as far as withdrawals are concerned. The second possible explanation simply is that the histories on which we reason about correctness are merely *models* of the actual executions in that they track particularly relevant actions but do not necessarily need to be complete pictures of everything that happened in the underlying server. So it could well be that the read and write operations on page r were invoked on behalf of explicitly invoked Deposit operations, but these Deposit operations are not observed, and we only know the transactions to which these page operations belong. Of course, it is usually up to ourselves how completely and accurately we devise our modeling of some specific system, but the above should be taken as a word of caution that such "nonstandard" scenarios may arise and should be tractable within our framework.

6.3 Conflict Serializability for Flat Object Transactions

Within the class of layered schedules, a special subclass of particular interest is what we call *flat object schedules*. These are two-level schedules with object method invocations at the higher level L_1 and ordinary read/write operations at the lower level L_0. The decisive particularity, however, is that we essentially disallow concurrent L_1 operations in this subclass. In other words, transactions may be interleaved, but for each pair of object method executions we require an ordering.

DEFINITION 6.7 *Flat Object Schedule*

A two-level schedule s is called a *flat object schedule* if for each pair p, q of L_1 operations the following two conditions hold:

1. $(\forall p' \in child\,(p), q' \in child\,(q))\ \ p' <_s q'$ or
   $(\forall p' \in child\,(p), q' \in child\,(q))\ \ q' <_s p'$
2. $(\forall p', p'' \in child\,(p))\ \ p' <_s p''$ or $p'' <_s p'$

where $child\,(p)$ denotes the set of children of operation p.

Flat object schedule

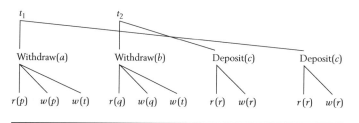

Figure 6.3   Example of a flat object schedule.

The first condition requires a total order among L_1 operations; the second condition demands that each L_1 operation is itself a serial execution of page accesses.

Figure 6.3 shows an example of a flat object schedule. Note that the total ordering of L_1 operations and their sequentiality are easily recognized by the observation that none of the caller-callee arcs from the L_1 operations to their L_0 children cross each other.

Our specific interest in flat object schedules lies in the fact that their structure is as close as possible to conventional, one-level schedules. As object-level operations are executed sequentially, the resulting page-level accesses are actually not of specific interest as far as concurrency control is concerned. So an intriguing abstraction step now is to disregard the page-level operations completely, effectively constructing a one-level schedule that consists of abstract, yet *indivisible* operations. It is in this sense that we now have a situation comparable to that for conventional page model schedules, with the key property of operations being their indivisibility.

The natural next step is to reconsider the technical approaches that we explored toward correctness criteria for the page model as to whether they are potentially applicable to our current setting as well. It is fairly obvious that the notions of view serializability and the underlying reads-from relation cannot be generalized to flat object schedules without "degrading" all operations into read and write actions and losing their richer semantics. The simpler notion of conflict serializability and its related notion of commutativity based reducibility, on the other hand, are indeed promising candidates for this purpose. In fact, a conflict between operations is nothing but the observation that the operations do not commute, and this is obviously something that can also be applied to semantically richer operations.

Commutative
operations

DEFINITION 6.8   *Commutative Operations*

Two operations p and q (on some objects) are *commutative* (or they *commute*) if for all possible sequences of operations α and ω, the return parameters in the concatenated sequence $\alpha p q \omega$ are identical to those in the sequence $\alpha q p \omega$.

So, for example, two operations deposit$(a, 10)$ and deposit$(a, 20)$ that deposit \$10 and \$20 into account a can be tested by various numbers of successive Withdraw operations to see that both possible orderings of the two Deposit operations achieve the same effects.

The above definition emphasizes the encapsulated nature of objects; the state of an object is observable only through explicitly invoked methods rather than being exposed to arbitrary reads. In this sense, commutativity demands that the ordering of two operations is irrelevant: different orderings cannot be distinguished as far as other explicit method invocations are concerned. So if two operations p and q are not commutative, the difference between the two possible orderings should be observable in the result parameters of p or q or some subsequently invoked operation. In the latter case, the operation to observe the noncommutativity of p and q is not necessarily the next one after p and q; the difference may become visible only after a finite number of additional operations (i.e., the sequence ω in the definition). Finally, note that we want commutativity to hold in every possible state of the object(s) on which p and q operate. As states are not directly visible, this means that we must take into account that p and q are executed after some (finite) history of operations that result in a certain state (i.e., the sequence α in the definition). We will refer to this most general notion of commutativity also as *state-independent* or *general-commutativity*, and will discuss possible relaxations later in Section 6.6.

State-independent commutativity

Commutativity can be a delicate property, which is all but trivial to specify. As soon as the programming language in which object methods are written is sufficiently expressive, the commutativity of two methods is, like most other interesting metaproperties of programs, undecidable. Our escape from this dilemma is that rather than automatically inferring such properties, we expect an application expert to *assert* the commutativity of operations. In doing this, the expert may be conservative in that operations are assumed as noncommutative if she is in doubt about a positive statement. After all, operations that may superficially appear commutative may have side effects on other objects that ultimately render them noncommutative. For example, two customer orders for different items (or even for the same item if the item is guaranteed to be in stock) are commutative as long as we consider only operations like PlaceOrder, Shipment, and Payment, but they turn out to be noncommutative if we add the twist that the customer who places the hundred-thousandth order wins a car. It is for exactly such reasons that we have avoided establishing a one-to-one correspondence between methods and objects in our above definition. Rather, we do allow methods to operate on more than one object, possibly in a transitive manner. Likewise, we do not infer from the disjointness of two operations' parameter lists that they are necessarily commutative.

Despite these potential pitfalls, we will, in many practical situations, positively assume that noncommutative operations arise only on the same object type, thus declaring operations on different object types as pairwise conflict

Table 6.1 Commutativity table for bank account operations.

	$Withdraw(x, \Delta_2)$	$Deposit(x, \Delta_2)$	$GetBalance(x)$
$Withdraw(x, \Delta_1)$	−	−	−
$Deposit(x, \Delta_1)$	−	+	−
$GetBalance(x)$	−	−	+

free. For the object type Bank account, for example, we may consider three methods Withdraw, Deposit, and GetBalance, all of which have an object ID as a primary input parameter. Withdraw and Deposit operations have an amount of money as a second parameter and merely return a binary status about the success or failure of the operation, and Get_Balance operations return the current balance of a bank account.

For this setting, two Deposit operations are commutative because of the fact that both merely increment the account's balance, without caring about the prior or resulting value of the balance. In contrast, a Withdraw operation does not commute with a Deposit operation, as withdrawals usually enforce an overdraft protection, so that money can no longer be withdrawn once the balance drops below a certain threshold. Thus, if an account's balance had a value equal to this threshold and a Deposit operation first incremented the balance, a Withdraw operation would succeed if the requested amount is at most as high as the deposited amount, whereas the withdrawal would fail to withdraw money if the Deposit operation were second in the ordering.

A complete commutativity specification for these three operation types is given in Table 6.1, with + standing for commutativity and − for noncommutativity. x denotes the account parameter of the operations and Δ the amount of money that is withdrawn or deposited. Strictly speaking, the table should also consider the case of two operations on different account objects x and y, but this is generally assumed as a + and therefore omitted. Also, we would typically assume that each of the three operations commutes with all operations on other object types such as customer objects.

Now that we have established a (symmetric) commutativity relation among the invoked operations, we can directly apply the notion of commutativity based reducibility to flat object schedules, essentially repeating the arguments from Chapter 3.

Commutativity based reducibility

DEFINITION 6.9 *Commutativity Based Reducibility*

A flat object schedule s is *commutativity based reducible* if it can be transformed into a serial schedule by applying the following rules finitely many times:

1. *Commutativity rule:* The order of two ordered operations p and q with, say, the order $p <_s q$ can be reversed if

   (a) both are isolated, adjacent in that there is no other operation r with $p <_s r <_s q$, and commutative, and

   (b) the operations belong to different transactions, or if they belong to the same transaction t_i, the reversal does not contradict the specified order $<_i$ within t_i.

2. *Ordering rule:* Two unordered leaf operations p and q can (arbitrarily) be ordered, i.e., assuming either $p < q$ or $q < p$ if they are commutative (i.e., both are reads, or they operate on different data items).

Note that the ordering rule is merely an auxiliary rule to cope with partial orders at the leaf level. Further note that the isolation condition is actually redundant for flat object schedules with a total ordering of the L_1 (i.e., object-level) operations. We nevertheless state this explicitly as it will play a crucial role when we turn back to the general case of object model schedules.

Consider the example of Figure 6.3. All we need to do to transform this schedule into a serial one is to exchange the order of t_1's Deposit operation with the deposit of t_2 and then, in a second transformation step, with the withdrawal of t_2. These steps pull t_1's Deposit operation back, out of the interleaving with t_2. Note once again that the transformations are feasible only because the affected L_1 operations are already isolated in that their page-level executions are strictly sequential.

A dual way of reasoning would be to consider the conflicts (i.e., noncommutative pairs of operations) and test for conflict equivalence with a serial schedule. This leads to the following criterion:

DEFINITION 6.10   *Conflict Equivalence and Conflict Serializability*

Two flat object schedules s and s' are *conflict equivalent* if they consist of the same operations and both have the same ordering for all noncommutative pairs of L_1 operations.

A flat object schedule is *conflict serializable* if it is conflict equivalent to a serial schedule.

Conflict equivalence, conflict serializability

Obviously, the conflict graph construction of Chapter 3 can be carried over to flat object schedules as well. Indeed, for a flat object schedule s, the corresponding conflict graph is a graph with the transactions of s as nodes and an edge from t_i to t_j if there are noncommutative L_1 operations p_i and q_j belonging to t_i and t_j, respectively. Now the following theorem is obvious:

THEOREM 6.1

Let s be a flat object schedule. Then s is conflict serializable iff its conflict graph is acyclic. Furthermore, s is conflict serializable iff it is commutativity based reducible.

The conflict graph for the example of Figure 6.3 does not have any edges because all L_1 operations commute, and thus it is trivially acyclic. Note, however, that a conventional conflict graph derived from the L_0 operations (i.e., page accesses of the two transactions) would have a cycle caused by the conflicts on pages t (with t_1 preceding t_2) and r (with t_2 preceding t_1). This shows exactly the benefit of exploiting the "semantic knowledge" about the object-level operations for withdrawals and deposits. We can now allow schedules that would be disallowed under the purely read/write based viewpoint of the page model.

6.4 **Tree Reducibility**

To generalize the notions of reducibility or serializability to nonflat and, ultimately, even nonlayered schedules, recall the example of Figure 6.1 from Section 6.2. The decisive difference between this schedule and a flat object schedule is that its object-level operations are again interleaved at the page level. So if we could reason that the page-level execution was equivalent to a schedule with isolated L_1 operations, then we would be in a position to abstract from the details of the page accesses and simply ignore the page level. This is essentially what we have done with flat object schedules anyway, with the only difference that we knew in advance about the isolation of the L_1 operations and thus found it easy to justify the abstraction step.

At this point it should be no surprise that the arguments for showing equivalence to operations being isolated are again commutativity arguments. In Figure 6.1, for example, the second and third page access of operation withdraw$_{11}(a)$, namely, $w_{112}(p)$ and $w_{113}(t)$, both commute with the preceding $r_{211}(q)$ operation belonging to t_2; hence the two write accesses of t_1 can be pulled back so that t_1's Withdraw operation would completely precede the Withdraw operation of t_2. Then, once we have "disentangled" the two interleaved Withdraw operations, the argument from the previous section is applicable: all object-level operations are isolated and commute with each other, so that the entire schedule is equivalent to either of the two possible serial orders of t_1 and t_2.

The key abstraction in the entire reasoning, disregarding the operations inside isolated subtrees, boils down to reducing such a subtree to its root. By adding an appropriate *tree pruning rule* to the notion of commutativity based reducibility, we finally arrive at the desired generalized type of reducibility, which we coin *tree reducibility*, as it is indeed applicable to the entire class of object model schedules.

DEFINITION 6.11   *Tree-Reducible History*

An object model history $s = (op(s), <_s)$ is *tree reducible* if it can be transformed into a total order of its roots by applying the following rules finitely many times:

1. *Commutativity rule:* The order of two ordered leaf operations p and q with, say, the order $p <_s q$, can be reversed provided that

   (a) both are isolated, adjacent in that there is no other operation r with $p <_s r <_s q$, and commutative; and

   (b) the operations belong to different transactions, or if they belong to the same transaction t_i, the reversal does not contradict the specified order $<_i$ within the transaction t_i; and

   (c) the operations p and q do not have ancestors, say, p' and q', respectively, which are noncommutative and totally ordered (in the order $p' <_s q'$).

2. *Ordering rule:* Two unordered leaf operations p and q can (arbitrarily) be ordered, i.e., assuming either $p < q$ or $q < p$ if they are commutative (i.e., both are reads, or they operate on different data items).

3. *Tree pruning rule:* An isolated subtree can be pruned in that it is replaced by its root.

An object model schedule is *tree reducible* if its committed projection is tree reducible.

Tree reducibility

Applying the tree pruning rule results in trees that are, strictly speaking, no longer object model schedules according to the definition of an object model transaction given in Chapter 2. The reason for this subtlety is that our original definition has required the leaves of such transactions to be page model read or write operations. Once we prune a tree, this condition is obviously no longer satisfied. To resolve this syntactic mismatch, we now relax the definition of object model schedules so that they are allowed to contain transactions whose leaves are high-level operations (i.e., have pruned the original page model leaves), provided that these high-level operations are guaranteed to appear as if they were indivisible operations. Indeed this is the whole point of pruning the tree: when we know that some lower-level interleaving has the same effect as if each of the corresponding high-level operations were an indivisible unit, then and only then can we safely prune the descendants of such high-level operations.

Abstractions of object model schedules

This is the key abstraction that we exploit in our reasoning about object model schedules; so object model schedules are now also allowed to contain *abstractions of object model transactions* in the above sense. Note, however, that the abstraction cannot be reversed: it does not make sense to expand again leaves of pruned trees, which correspond to high-level operations, into "full" trees with page model operations as leaves.

Compared to the earlier definitions of commutativity based reducibility for page model and flat object model schedules, the commutativity rule in Definition 6.11 has become more sophisticated by adding the third condition regarding ancestors. The reason for this addition is a subtle, yet important one. Whenever two higher-level operations are totally ordered and do not commute, this ordering is a hard constraint for their descendants. Reversing the ordering of two leaves that belong to such higher-level operations and, in the end, possibly reversing even the order of higher-level operations is not legitimate, as this could lead to different effects of the higher-level operations themselves. As the higher-level operations are in conflict, a reversal of their order would in general not preserve the original return values. As an example consider two serial Withdraw operations on the same bank account such that the first one is successful in withdrawing money, whereas the second one is unable to do so because of the account's overdraft protection. If we could rearrange the leaves of these two operations such that, ultimately, the second withdrawal preceded the first one, it would be impossible for the operations to have their original return values. So the fundamental problem is that reordering commutative leaf operations without carefully taking into account their ancestors would open a "back door" for implicitly (almost "unconsciously," so to speak) reordering these ancestors, even if such reordering were unacceptable.

Such subtleties never arise in the commutativity based reasoning for the page model and for flat object schedules, as the only possibly affected ancestors are the transaction roots. Different transactions, however, are usually assumed to be "independent" in the sense of being commutative; this is exactly the reason why the page model serializability theory considers *each possible* serial transaction order as acceptable.

As a second example for applying our new fundamental concept of tree reducibility, consider Figure 6.4 with record-level operations Store, Fetch, and Modify inside a database server, which are dynamically translated into page accesses. The example assumes that records w, x, and y initially are all located on page p, and that all operations first look up some address translation table on page t, say, for translating record identifiers into page numbers. During the execution of a store(z) operation for a new record z, record x is moved from p to q, say, for lack of space on page p, and the address translation table on page t is updated accordingly. Recall from our overview of database system internals in Chapter 1 that such situations are commonplace inside a data server.

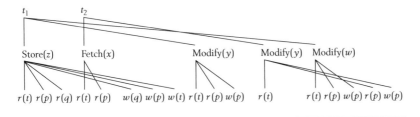

Figure 6.4 Example of a correct object model schedule with record-level operations.

In this example, the interleavings of the Store and Fetch pair and of the last two Modify operations can both be eliminated by pulling back the two page reads of fetch(x) so that they are placed in front of store(z), and pushing forward the $r(t)$ operation issued by t_2's modify(y) operation. The resulting schedule has all object-level operations isolated, so that the page-level subtrees can be pruned, with the following outcome:

$$\text{fetch}_{21}(x) \ \text{store}_{11}(z) \ \text{modify}_{12}(y) \ \text{modify}_{13}(w) \ \text{modify}_{21}(y)$$

Now the only noncommutative pair of operations consists of the two Modify operations on record y; so we rearrange the commutative operations (e.g., by pushing forward t_2's fetch(x) operation) to produce a serial order with all operations of t_1 preceding all of t_2. Now the transactions themselves (i.e., the roots in the forest) are isolated, and we can prune their record-level operations as well. In this way we have finally proven that the execution in Figure 6.4 can be reduced and thus is equivalent to a serial order of the transaction roots with $t_1 < t_2$.

Note that the serialization order with t_1 preceding t_2 is the only feasible one in the example of Figure 6.4. This may appear somewhat strange, as this order would imply that the fetch(x) operation of t_2 followed t_1's store(z) and thus the movement of record x from page p to page q. So it seems that the fetch$_{21}(x)$ operation should have a read access to q among its children; however, this was not the case in the original schedule where x has still been read from p. The explanation for this seemingly confusing observation simply is that we do not claim to have an equivalent serial execution with every detail of the necessary page accesses. Rather, the abstraction step of pruning these details once we have isolated subtrees cannot be reversed by later expanding the transactions with their original descendants. In the serial execution with $t_1 < t_2$, the fetch(x) operation of t_2 would again issue its descendants dynamically depending on the current internal state of the underlying data pages. However, this in no way affects the validity of our overall argumentation that the actual execution, as given by Figure 6.4, is equivalent to a serial execution

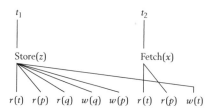

Figure 6.5 Example of a disallowed object model
schedule with record-level operations.

from the perspective of the transactions. The point is that the low-level details
such as the specific pages on which the various records reside do not matter
at a higher level of abstraction, provided that no internal (i.e., storage-level)
inconsistency can arise.

   To demonstrate that subtree isolation is all but trivial, consider another
example with record-level operations, shown in Figure 6.5. Here, because of
the page-level conflicts between $w_{115}(p)$ and $r_{212}(p)$ on one hand and $r_{211}(t)$
and $w_{116}(t)$ on the other, it is impossible to rearrange the page-level operations
toward isolating the store(z) and fetch(x) operations. Hence the schedule is
not tree reducible. Note that it does not help in this situation that the subtree
rooted at the fetch(x) operation is already isolated right away (but not the
other subtree rooted at store(z)). We could thus prune the Fetch subtree first
rather than trying to commute leaves, but then it would be impossible to apply
commutativity arguments to the fetch(x) operation with regard to the r and w
leaves of the Store subtree; so we could still not isolate the Store subtree. In fact,
the shown interleaving of page accesses would result in an inconsistent view
of the underlying storage structures: $fetch_{21}(x)$ would see the "old" contents of
the address translation table, as of before the relocation of record x, and then
erroneously access page p, although the record has meanwhile been moved
to q. It is of crucial importance to prevent such anomalies, and this is well
reflected in the tree reducibility criterion.

   As a final example in this section, consider the nonlayered schedule in
Figure 6.6. As mentioned before, tree reducibility can be applied to this most
general class of schedules as well. The example shows two transactions that issue operations for electronic purchases; these operations are then dynamically
transformed into steps for checking the availability of the desired items, initiating their shipping, and handling the customer's payment. For simplicity, all
parameters are omitted in the figure. The CheckItem operations are assumed
to initate stock refillings by means of appending appropriate entries to a list of
items with low quantity-on-hand. The two invocations of the Payment operation result in two different subtrees reflecting different types of payment; so this
again illustrates the dynamic nature of the transaction trees that are spanned

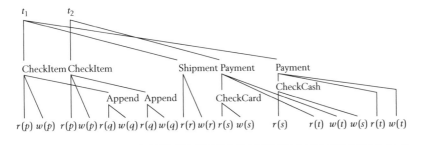

Figure 6.6 Example of a correct object model schedule from an e-Commerce scenario.

during the execution, depending on actual parameters and the current states of objects. The Payment operations also put entries into some kind of audit trail, stored on page t, for tracking purposes. It is for the importance of tracking and reproducing the exact timing of financial aspects that we consider Payment operations to be noncommutative among themselves. In contrast, the Shipment and CheckItem operations are assumed to be commutative with each other and also with Payment. Finally, CheckCard and CheckCash, the operations for verifying a credit card (or some form of cybercash), are assumed to be commutative; whereas Append operations on a list obviously do not commute. Under all these (admittedly arbitrary, but reasonably natural) assumptions, it is now left to you to verify that the schedule shown is indeed tree reducible, arriving at the serial order $t_2 < t_1$.

6.5 **Sufficient Conditions for Tree Reducibility**

The fundamental notion of tree reducibility is very intuitive, and it is easy to use for checking the correctness of a given schedule. However, it is not constructive in the sense that we can immediately derive from it a concurrency control algorithm that reconciles the higher concurrency that object model schedules give us over page model schedules with an efficient, low-overhead implementation. The purpose of this section is to introduce a number of sufficient conditions for tree reducibility that are more suitable for efficient scheduling algorithms. We will again focus on the special, but very important case of layered schedules first.

An obvious idea for layered schedules is to conceive concurrency control in the form of layers of conventional, conflict-driven schedulers, where each scheduler is modular in that it sees only operations of a particular level and knows about the parents of these operations but nothing else. For further elaborating this idea, the following notion of a level-to-level schedule is a convenient construct:

DEFINITION 6.12 *Level-to-Level Schedule*

Let $s = (\text{op}(s), <_s)$ be an n-level schedule with layers $L_0, \ldots, L_n$ (in bottom-up order). The *level-to-level schedule* from L_i to L_{i-1} with $i > 0$, or L_i-to-L_{i-1} *schedule* for short, is a one-level schedule $s' = (\text{op}(s'), <_{s'}$ with

1. $\text{op}(s')$ consisting of the L_{i-1} operations of s,
2. $<_{s'}$ being the restriction of the extended order $<_s$ to the L_{i-1} operations,
3. the L_i operations of s as the roots,
4. the parent-child relationship identical to that of s.

So a level-to-level schedule narrows down our view of the entire object model schedule to a pair of adjacent layers, with all ordering relationships of the original schedule being fully preserved. In terms of operation semantics, such as commutativity, we focus on the leaves of the resulting one-level schedule, that is, on L_{i-1}. The roots of the one-level schedule (i.e., the L_i operations) serve as transactions of the one-level schedule in that they denote the contexts for the L_{i-1} operations. In other words, the new roots tell us which new leaf operations belong together. Note that we implicitly generalize our initial definition of an object model schedule, as the latter would actually require all leaves to be read/write operations in the page model sense. This syntactic restriction will be dropped when we consider level-to-level schedules that are derived from a full-fledged object model schedule.

As an example, Figure 6.7 shows the two level-to-level schedules that can be constructed from our initial example in Figure 6.1. The operation subscripts are given explicitly to highlight the connection to the original schedule; the new roots of the L_1-to-L_0 schedule are cast into mere placeholders of the form t_{ij}, as we will not consider their semantics in this specific one-level schedule.

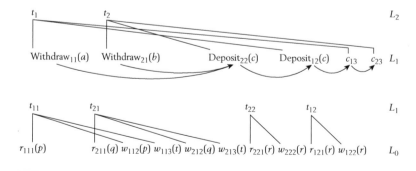

Figure 6.7 Level-to-level schedules constructed from the layered object model schedule of Figure 6.1.

Note that the L_2-to-L_1 schedule has partially ordered leaves, and the order is explicitly indicated by the directed arcs in the figure. This partial order is exactly the original schedule's partial order of the L_1 operations as derived from the ordering of their leaves (i.e., the original L_0 operations). For simplicity, we do not draw these arcs for the L_1-to-L_0 schedule, as this one still has totally ordered leaves.

Now the idea is to view each of the resulting level-to-level schedules as a flat object schedule and apply conflict serializability to each of them separately. To this end we need a conflict specification or, equivalently, its positive counterpart, a commutativity relation, for all operation types that belong to the same layer. As mentioned before, this cannot be derived automatically, say, from the code of the methods that belong to an encapsulated object, but intellectually defining a (possibly conservative) conflict/commutativity table does usually not pose any (insurmountable) difficulties.

What many of you may now intuitively expect is that a layered schedule is tree reducible if (or possibly even if and only if) all its level-to-level schedules are conflict serializable when viewed as flat object schedules. This modular decomposition principle is formally captured in the following conjecture; as we will see in a short while, this conjecture is not true, but with some appropriate amendments it will point us toward the correct theorems.

CONJECTURE 6.1

Let s be an n-level object model schedule. If for each i, $0 < i \leq n$, the L_i-to-L_{i-1} schedule derived from s is conflict serializable (CSR, see Chapter 3), then s is tree reducible.

In checking this criterion, a minor technical difficulty is that we may encounter conflicting but unordered operations in one of the level-to-level schedules, for example, two Withdraw operations on the same bank account. This is not the case in our example, but when such situations arise they are rather straightforward to rectify: as serial schedules have all operations ordered, an unordered conflict pair prevents a schedule from being equivalent to any serial schedule. In other words, unordered conflict pairs render a schedule nonserializable. In the example of Figure 6.7, however, both level-to-level schedules are conflict serializable: the L_1-to-L_0 schedule is equivalent to the serial order $t_{11} < t_{21} < t_{22} < t_{12}$, and the L_2-to-L_1 schedule is equivalent to $t_1 < t_2$ as well as $t_2 < t_1$. Intuitively, the serializability of the L_1-to-L_0 schedule is an argument for being able to prune the L_0 level, that is, apply the tree pruning rule to the subtrees rooted at the L_1 operations of the original two-level schedule. Then the ordering and the commutativity rules can be applied to the L_1 operations to arrive at either of the two possible serialization orders for t_1 and t_2.

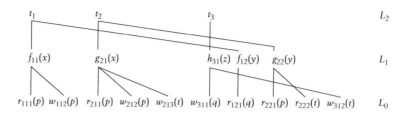

Figure 6.8 Non-tree-reducible layered object model schedule with conflict-serializable level-to-level schedules.

The above argumentation works perfectly for our example. However, it is treacherous, and it turns out that there are cases where the conflict serializability of all level-to-level schedules does not imply tree reducibility. The problem is that reordering commutative leaves regardless of what their ancestors look like could have undesirable or even unacceptable "side effects" on these ancestors. Figure 6.8 shows such an example. In the example, we consider object methods f, g, and h, where f and g are assumed to be in conflict when applied to the same object and h is assumed to commute with both f, g, and itself. The level-to-level schedule from L_2 to L_1 is conflict serializable, as each of t_1's two operations strictly precede, in terms of a total order, t_2's corresponding operations that lie in conflict with t_1; so the L_2-to-L_1 schedule is equivalent to $t_1 < t_2 < t_3$. In fact, t_3 can be arbitrarily ordered with regard to t_1 and t_2, as its operation h does not conflict with f or g. Between levels L_1 and L_0, on the other hand, we also observe a conflict-serializable level-to-level schedule, equivalent to the serial order $t_{11} < t_{21} < t_{22} < t_{31} < t_{12}$. However, it is impossible to isolate all three subtrees, t_{31}, t_{12}, and t_{22}, by means of the commutativity rule; hence the schedule is not tree reducible due to part 1(c) of Definition 6.11.

The decisive problem with the schedule of Figure 6.8 is that the serialization order for the L_1-to-L_0 schedule reverses the actual execution order of the two conflicting L_1 operations $f_{12}(y)$ and $g_{22}(y)$: $f_{12}(y)$ is completely executed before $g_{22}(y)$, but serialized the other way around as far as the underlying page accesses are concerned. This signals that there may be a major problem. If we know that these two L_1 operations are serialized in the order with $g_{22}(y)$ preceding $f_{12}(y)$, we would no longer consider the L_2-to-L_1 schedule serializable, as this observation contradicts the conflict order on object x. The fundamental reason for this troublesome situation is that the serialization order for the L_1-to-L_0 schedule does *not* preserve the execution order at level L_1; that is, the level-to-level schedule from L_1 to L_0, albeit conflict serializable, is not order preserving conflict serializable.

So we cannot completely modularize the concurrency control for layered schedules in that we consider level-to-level schedules in an absolutely separated, essentially "myopic" manner. But once we insist on order-preserving conflict serializability for each level-to-level schedule, we essentially add a "handshake" between successive level-to-level schedules by ensuring that the serialization order for the "lower" schedule is compatible with the execution order observed for the "higher" schedule. Indeed the following theorem holds:

THEOREM 6.2

Let s be an n-level object model schedule. If for each i, $0 < i \leq n$, the L_i-to-L_{i-1} schedule derived from s is order preserving conflict serializable (OCSR, see Chapter 3), then s is tree reducible.

Proof

Order-preserving conflict serializability from level 1 to level 0 allows us to apply the ordering and commutativity rules to isolate the subtrees rooted at level L_1 such that the execution order of L_1 is preserved. Then we can prune all operations of L_0 by the tree pruning rule. Now consider the new leaves of the pruned transaction forest (i.e., the operations at level 1). Any non-commutative operations among these new leaves must have been executed in total order, and because of the order-preserving serialization, this original execution order is retained. So the outcome of pruning all operations of level 0 is a transaction forest whose new leaf ordering is compatible with the original ordering of the operations at level 1 in the sense that all "critical" orderings between noncommutative operations are included, some previously unordered but commutative operations may have become ordered, and the original ordering of some commutative operations may have been switched. Thus, since the original level-to-level schedule from level 1 to level 0 is assumed to be OCSR, this property also holds for the result of the first pruning round. Then the same argument can be iterated, and by induction on the number of levels, we see that we arrive at a total order of the transaction roots.

OCSR level-to-level schedules imply tree reducibility

The converse of the implication in the above theorem does not hold: there are schedules that are tree reducible without all their level-to-level schedules belonging to OCSR. Figure 6.9 shows an example. The L_1-to-L_0 schedule is

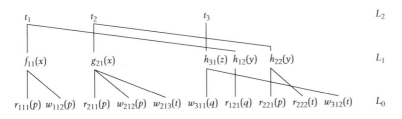

Figure 6.9 Tree-reducible layered object model schedule with non-OCSR level-to-level schedule.

not order preserving conflict serializable. The only possible serialization would reverse the order of $h_{12}(y)$ and $h_{22}(y)$, contradicting their actual execution order. In this case, however, this does not cause any harm, as the two h operations are commutative so that any arbitrary serial order is acceptable.

As the example in Figure 6.9 shows, the order preservation condition for all level-to-level schedules may sometimes be overly restrictive. What really matters is not order preservation in general but to prevent the serialization at one level from reversing the actual execution order of conflicting operations of the next higher level. This unacceptable effect would be impossible if the noncommutative higher-level operations would also lead to conflicting operation pairs at all lower levels. The reason why this situation fixes our problem is that even non-order-preserving conflict serializability can never reverse the order of a conflict pair. We refer to this setting as *conflict faithful* and define it formally as follows:

Conflict faithfulness

DEFINITION 6.13 *Conflict Faithfulness*

A layered object model schedule $s = (op(s), <_s)$ is *conflict faithful* if for each pair $p, q \in op(s)$ that are noncommutative and each $i > 0$ the corresponding sets of descendants with distance i to p and q contain at least one operation pair p', q' where p' and q' are descendants of p and q, respectively, and are in conflict.

Conflict faithfulness is a fairly natural property. What it boils down to is that some noncommutative operations at a semantically high level of abstraction must have conflicts on all lower levels of abstraction, where details such as storage representations are taken into account. For example, two Withdraw operations on the same bank account must touch and, in fact, write common records and ultimately common pages. It is natural for low-level conflicts to become irrelevant at higher abstraction levels, but not the other way around. Proving that schedules are conflict faithful is often fairly easy by studying properties of the underlying system layers rather than inspecting individual schedules. For example, all schedules that properly capture executions at the record and the page level of a database system must be conflict faithful.

An alternative way of ensuring conflict faithfulness is to consider operations as conflicting only if they have at least one conflict at a lower level *and* are semantically noncommutative in that their return values and side effects are dependent on the order. So if operations are specified as generally noncommutative, but do not exhibit a single lower-level conflict during their execution (as their behavior is dependent on the current states of the underlying objects), they would be considered as conflict free. Obviously, this condition would need to be checked for each schedule individually; from a system perspective, this would mean that the various subsystems across which a schedule extends (e.g., in a federated environment, see Chapter 1) need to report conflicts to their callers.

The nice property of conflict faithfulness is that it renders conflict serializability of all level-to-level schedules a sufficient condition for tree reducibility:

THEOREM 6.3

A layered object model schedule $s = (op(s), <_s)$ is tree reducible if it is conflict faithful and all its level-to-level schedules are conflict serializable.

Proof

The proof is by induction on the number n of nonroot levels. For $n = 1$, we consider a conventional single-layer flat object model or page model schedule, and the claim trivially holds. Now assume that our claim holds for $n - 1$ ($n > 1$) nonroot levels, and consider a schedule with n nonroot levels. By the induction hypothesis, we can prune all subtrees rooted at level $n - 1$ such that the resulting transaction forest preserves the original execution order of all noncommutative operations at level $n - 1$. Because of this property and since the level-to-level schedule from level n to level $n - 1$ is conflict serializable, we can isolate the operations at level n and once again prune subtrees (i.e., their children). What remains to be shown is that this pruning step must also preserve the execution order of any noncommutative operations at level n. So suppose that two such noncommutative level n operations, f and g with the original execution order $f < g$, are rearranged by the transformation steps for isolating the level n operations such that g precedes f in the resulting transaction forest. Now the property of conflict faithfulness tells us that f and g have children, say, f' and g', that are noncommutative at level $n - 1$. Since the original execution order is $f < g$, f' must have preceded g' originally. Therefore, the (conflict-serializable) serialization of the level-to-level schedule from level n to level $n - 1$ must have preserved this ordering. So it is impossible to violate the original execution order of noncommutative operations at level n.

As examples for this sufficient condition for tree reducibility, consider again the two scenarios of Figures 6.8 and 6.9. In both examples, all level-to-level schedules are conflict serializable. The schedule in Figure 6.9 is conflict faithful because the only L_1 conflict pair, $f_{11}(x)$ and $g_{21}(x)$, also exhibits page access conflicts on page p. The argumentation for the schedule in Figure 6.8 is more subtle: here we would additionally have to consider the two L_1 operations $f_{12}(y)$ and $g_{22}(y)$ as nonconflicting simply *because* their execution did not produce any page-level conflicts. So, although these operations may not commute

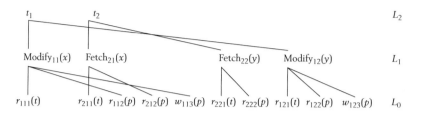

Figure 6.10 Tree-reducible schedule with concurrent, conflicting L_1 operations.

in general, the executions in the particular context of the given schedule turn out to be commutative.

A final observation is that the conjunction of level-to-level serializability and conflict faithfulness is not a necessary condition for tree reducibility. The point is that conflicting higher-level operations may be allowed to run concurrently (i.e., unordered) as long as they are properly serialized at the underlying implementation levels. Such concurrency would not be allowed by a conflict-serializable level-to-level schedule. Figure 6.10 shows a concrete example with conflicting, unordered record operations fetch(x) and modify(x). The schedule is tree reducible to the transaction order $t_2 < t_1$.

6.6 Exploiting State Based Commutativity

In this section we will discuss possible relaxations of general commutativity to further enhance concurrency. As this issue solely involves operations on the same object type, all previous considerations on the underlying operation invocation trees can be carried over without modification. Thus, for ease of presentation, we will assume that operations on ADT (abstract data type) objects are already isolated and restrict the discussion to flat object schedules, sometimes not even bothering to show the isolated page-level subtrees underneath.

General commutativity is a powerful means for enhancing concurrency beyond what a pure page-level perspective would allow; however, it also has its limits. For example, the following totally ordered object-level schedule would be considered inadmissible because the first two operations are in conflict with the ordering $t_1 < t_2$, whereas the second pair of Deposit and Withdraw operations conflicts with the order $t_2 < t_1$ (based on Table 6.1 from Section 6.3):

withdraw$_1(x, 30)$ deposit$_2(x, 50)$ deposit$_2(y, 50)$ withdraw$_1(y, 30)$

In this example, we have stated the amounts of money withdrawn or deposited as explicit parameters (e.g., \$30 for the first operation). Knowing these additional parameters alone does not help much. However, in conjunction with knowledge about the original balance of the account (i.e., before t_1's first Withdraw operation is invoked), we may be in a position to approve the above schedule as one that is equivalent to a serial execution. For example, if the original balance was known to be \$40 and the threshold for the overdraft protection was zero, then the first Withdraw operation could be viewed as commutative with the two deposits, thus eliminating the conflict cycle and rendering the schedule equivalent to the transaction order $t_2 < t_1$. The key point is that this equivalence is given only in a specific state of the bank account against which the entire schedule is run. For example, if the initial balance of the account was \$20 only, the first Withdraw operation would have signaled the overdraft protection and failed to obtain money, whereas it would be successful if it followed the first Deposit operation. We refer to the first mentioned, positive case with the initial balance of \$40 as a *state-dependent commutativity* argument.

DEFINITION 6.14   *State-Dependent Commutativity*

Two operations p and q on the same object are *commutative in object state* σ if for all possible sequences of operations ω, the return parameters in the concatenated sequence $pq\omega$ applied to state σ are identical to those in the sequence $qp\omega$ applied to σ.

State-dependent commutativity

So from a state-dependent commutativity viewpoint, the sample schedule above is acceptable, whereas it cannot be allowed under general, state-independent commutativity. Unfortunately, exploiting state knowledge poses severe difficulties in a real system environment. First, the notion of a state is not easy to define, given that operations may have side effects on more than one object, some of which may be observed much later. Second, even if we had a clean definition of object states, we would still need an algorithm for inspecting states. With encapsulated objects these methods may not be available, and even if they could, in principle, be added, they could be highly inefficient or even considered as a breach of the encapsulation and modularity (ultimately violating the information-hiding principle of good software engineering practice). With Bank account objects, for example, we may internally use the GetBalance method for testing the object state upon each Withdraw method, but this could result in inefficiencies and may no longer be sufficient if the internal state of objects also included an audit trail of cash flows, say, in the form of a list of balance modifications. In fact, the latter situation may render Withdraw and Deposit operations again noncommutative in every possible state.

So rather than actually inspecting states, we restrict ourselves to observing only operation parameters, but we can extend this approach to observing result parameters as well. In the case of Withdraw operations, the two possible outcomes—successful withdrawal or overdraft protection—would yield two different return values OK or No. Obviously, these return values are related to the object state against which an operation runs; so this provides a means for making particular facets of the object state visible without any additional steps. Commutativity arguments should then refer not only to operation types and their input parameters but also to the return values of the invoked operations.

This idea leads to the following definition of what we call *return value commutativity* and what can be considered as an indirect kind of state-dependent commutativity that respects the object encapsulation. To this end, we will now denote operation executions in the form $f(\downarrow x_1, \ldots, \downarrow x_m, \uparrow y_1, \ldots, \uparrow y_n)$, where the x_i are input parameters and the y_j output parameters, or in the simpler form $f(x_1, \ldots, x_m) \uparrow y$ when there is only a single output parameter, the *return value*.

Return value commutativity

DEFINITION 6.15   *Return Value Commutativity*

An operation execution

$$p(\downarrow x_1, \ldots, \downarrow x_m, \uparrow y_1, \ldots, \uparrow y_n)$$

is *return value commutative* with an immediately following operation execution

$$q(\downarrow x'_1, \ldots, \downarrow x'_{m'}, \uparrow y'_1, \ldots, \uparrow y'_{n'})$$

if for every possible sequence of operation executions α and ω such that p and q have indeed yielded the above return parameters in the sequence $\alpha p q \omega$, all operations in the sequence $\alpha q p \omega$ yield identical return parameters.

Note that the restriction of the considered sequences α is essential for enhanced concurrency: we consider only sequences α, and thus implicitly the resulting states, such that p and q yield the given return values when executed in the order $p < q$ right after α. This is a subset of all possible α sequences. For example, when p is a withdraw$(x, 30) \uparrow$ OK operation execution, only α sequences are relevant that resulted in an account balance of at least \$30, since otherwise the withdrawal would have returned No rather than OK. Further note that this subtle but important restriction of the implicitly observed initial states makes the notion of return value commutativity asymmetric. The set of relevant α sequences for the ordered pair pq may differ from that for the ordered pair qp. As an example assume $p = $ withdraw$(x, 30) \uparrow$ OK as above and $q = $ deposit$(x, 50) \uparrow$ OK. For the execution order pq the set of α has the above restriction, whereas for qp we implicitly remove this restriction, and Definition 6.15 thus refers to all possible α sequences because deposits return "OK" in every possible state.

Table 6.2 Return value commutativity table for bank account operations.

	Withdraw $(x, \Delta_2) \uparrow$ OK	Withdraw $(x, \Delta_2) \uparrow$ No	Deposit $(x, \Delta_2) \uparrow$ OK
Withdraw $(x, \Delta_1) \uparrow$ OK	+	−	+
Withdraw $(x, \Delta_1) \uparrow$ No	+	+	−
Deposit $(x, \Delta_1) \uparrow$ OK	−	+	+

Return value commutativity for a given object type can be stated in the form of a table, similar to general commutativity tables but with the difference that the entries refer to operation executions including return values rather than operation invocations with input parameters only. An example for the Bank account object is given in Table 6.2 (ignoring the GetBalance operations for simplicity), where Withdraw has two different possible return values and Deposit always returns "OK." The rows of the table are the p operations of Definition 6.15, and the columns are the q operations. Note the asymmetry that we discussed above.

The entry for the two successful withdrawals, for example, has the following intuitive explanation: since both operations returned "OK" in the considered α sequences, there must have been enough money in the account to cover the sum of Δ_1 and Δ_2; hence reversing the order of the withdrawals would lead to the same result. The entry for the unsuccessful withdrawal and a subsequent deposit, on the other hand, must state noncommutativity, as the withdrawal could have become successful if the deposit preceded it (without changing anything in the prior history α).

The table for return value commutativity could be further refined by adding conditions on the actual values of the input parameters. For example,

$$\text{withdraw}(x, \Delta_1) \uparrow \text{OK}$$

could be considered commutative with a subsequent withdraw$(x, \Delta_2) \uparrow$ No if $\Delta_2 > n\Delta_1$ and $\Delta_1 \geq x^{(0)}/m$, with n and m being constants such that $m \leq n$, where $x^{(0)}$ denotes the initial account balance (before the schedule begins), and we assume an overdraft protection threshold of zero. Namely, in this case we can infer that in the original schedule the value $x^{(0)}$ of the account balance before the first withdrawal must have been at least as high as Δ_1, but the resulting balance, $x^{(0)} - \Delta_1$, must have been smaller than Δ_2. All these inequalities together yield $x^{(0)} \leq m\Delta_1 < \frac{m}{n}\Delta_2$, and we can infer $x^{(0)} < \Delta_2$ because of $m \leq n$. So the second withdrawal operation would have been unsuccessful even if it were executed first. Such a kind of reasoning is, however, fairly involved. Therefore, we will not consider explicit constraints in a commutativity table any further, and will rather restrict ourselves to entries with plain + or − statements.

Return value commutativity for counters

The manipulation of account balances by Withdraw and Deposit operations is merely an example of the general concept of incrementing and decrementing *counters*. Counters arise in many highly relevant applications such as stock inventory where the quantity-on-hand of sales items is tracked, or reservation systems for airlines, hotels, rental cars, and so on, where the number of available seats, rooms, and cars needs to be maintained. So general considerations for highly concurrent counters surely pay off over a wide variety of applications. The approach is quite simple: counters are viewed as ADT objects with $incr(x, \Delta)$ and $decr(x, \Delta)$ as operations typically used in the operational transactions (e.g., for reserving seats on a flight) and an additional $getvalue(x)$ that will infrequently be used to read the actual counter value. If counters were absolutely unconstrained, then incr and decr would generally commute. However, in almost all applications, counters have lower bounds (e.g., zero in reservation systems), or upper bounds (e.g., the stock capacity in inventory management), or both. Since we lose general commutativity in such a setting but observe "uncritical" situations such as "plenty of seats still available" most of the time, state-dependent or return value commutativity is the intriguing resort. In fact, both incr and decr can be designed and implemented in such a way that they either return "OK" or "No" depending on whether they were successful in modifying the counter or hit a lower or upper bound and then did not modify the counter at all.

Working out the corresponding return value commutativity table is left as an (easy) exercise (see Exercise 6.6). Here we merely give an example of a highly concurrent schedule on objects x and y of type Counter, both with a lower bound of 0 and an upper bound of 50. Figure 6.11 shows this example schedule. The actual, encapsulated, and thus usually nonobservable intermediate states of the counters are shown for clearer illustration. This layered schedule is tree reducible when return value commutativity is allowed at the ADT level, namely, equivalent to the serial execution with t_1 preceding t_2, but it would not be feasible under general state-independent commutativity.

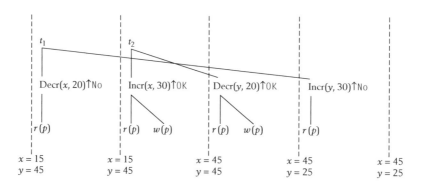

Figure 6.11 Example schedule on counter objects.

Another practically important standard ADT for which exploiting return value commutativity is feasible and may be worthwhile is the FIFO (first-in-first-out) *queue*. Such queues are of great benefit in implementing message handling systems such as mail servers or even distributed workflow management systems, as mentioned in Chapter 1. Queues provide operations for enqueueing entries (e.g., messages) at the tail of the queue and for dequeueing entries from its front. Transactional concurrency control is not necessarily required for messaging applications, but it can be of great benefit in order to ensure certain consistency guarantees such as preserving the order of a multiple-messages multicast to a number of recipients and other things along these lines. It should be emphasized at this point that messaging systems often need to serve a very large number of clients concurrently and that the underlying queue objects may well become hot spots in terms of their update frequency. Therefore, a liberal, yet consistency-preserving concurrency control for queues may be crucial.

Return value commutativity for queues

The two most important queue operations, Dequeue (or Deq for short) and Enqueue (or Enq), obviously do not commute in general. However, when the queue already contains at least one entry, then the order of an Enqueue and a subsequent Dequeue operation does not matter in that the two different orders cannot be distinguished by the application. As it would again be problematic to directly inspect the actually encapsulated queue state for the purpose of higher concurrency, we rather enrich the two operations by appropriate return values: Dequeue returns "OK" if it finds the queue nonempty and removes the front entry, otherwise it returns "empty." Enqueue returns "OK" when it adds an entry to an already nonempty queue, otherwise it reports the special case of an initially empty queue by returning "one" (for a new queue length of one). With these modifications we can construct the return value commutativity Table 6.3 (where the trivial input parameters are omitted).

The table contains some combinations that cannot occur, and they are marked as such. Note that without the exploitation of return value commutativity, all queue operations would be in conflict with each other, as both operations update the queue state. Thus, now allowing dequeueing and enqueueing on a nonempty queue to proceed without raising a conflict is already a great win in terms of the achievable concurrency of transactions.

Note that two Enqueue operations are still noncommutative regardless of whether we attempt to exploit return value information or not. The simple

Table 6.3 Return value commutativity table for queue operations.

	Enqueue ↑ OK	Enqueue ↑ one	Dequeue ↑ OK	Dequeue ↑ empty
Enqueue ↑ OK	−	impossible	+	impossible
Enqueue ↑ one	−	impossible	−	impossible
Dequeue ↑ OK	+	−	−	−
Dequeue ↑ empty	−	−	impossible	+

reason is that two entries enqueued in a specific queue will be dequeued in exactly this order; so a different order would later be observable. Here we simply touch on the essence of a FIFO queue. Further improving the concurrency among Enqueue operations can only be achieved by relaxing the FIFO semantics.

Semi-queues   Such a relaxation is indeed possible by redefining the Dequeue operation such that it nondeterministically selects and removes an arbitrary entry from the queue. A relaxed queue ADT is sometimes called a *semi-queue* or *weak queue* in the literature. In fact, it could as well be regarded simply as a set (or bag) of entries since the ordering of entries is now irrelevant; in conjunction with messaging applications, using a special name may be desirable. We leave a discussion of the return value commutativity of semi-queues as an exercise (see Exercise 6.8).

6.7 **Lessons Learned**

This chapter has made a major step in going beyond and generalizing the classical page model of transaction theory. We have introduced the technical details of a very powerful model for reasoning about transactions in semantically richer object-style settings, where an object may itself invoke operations on other objects to implement an operation provided at the object's interface. The resulting caller-callee relationships have been modeled as transaction trees, and the concurrent execution of several such trees has led us to a notion of transaction forests, the most general form of object model histories.

Transaction trees can be specialized in various ways, the practically most relevant one being a layered form where objects correspond to the implementation layers of a system. An even more specialized case is the restriction to a single layer, with the underlying assumption that the operations of this layer are executed one at a time, so that it is indeed justified to disregard the implementation of an individual operation. This argument has guided us to the general principle of reasoning about a transaction forest being equivalent to a sequential execution of the transactions: we first need to show that concurrently executed operations can be isolated in the sense of being transformable into a sequential execution, and only then can we abstract from these operations' implementation details and prune their corresponding subtrees. The technical correctness criterion that captures this kind of reasoning is the notion of tree reducibility. In addition, we have introduced a couple of simpler criteria that provide us with sufficient conditions for a layered object model schedule to be correct. These criteria will be the main tool for showing the correctness of several practically relevant protocols that we are going to present in the next chapter.

We have shown in this chapter that the classical notion of conflict, or noncommutative pairs of operations, is still the key to our correctness reasoning, but it now captures more semantics of operations and needs to be applied at different levels of object model transaction forests. We have also shown that the traditional state-independent form of commutativity can be further generalized for appropriate operations, bearing potential enhancements of the allowable concurrency.

Exercises

6.1 Consider the two-level schedule shown in Figure 6.12, which consists of two funds transfer transactions and a balance lookup transaction. Assume that the GetBalance operations do not commute with Withdraw operations nor with Deposit operations. Is this schedule tree reducible? If so, which is the equivalent serial execution? If not, how would the schedule have to be changed (as little as possible) so as to render it tree reducible?

6.2 Consider a data server with an SQL-style interface (see Chapter 1) and a database with a Person table whose rows contain a unique Name attribute and a City attribute. The server executes operations like

- `Select * From Person Where City = c`, where c is a parameter for looking up all persons living in a given city, and
- `Update Person Set City = c Where Name = n`, for recording that a given person has moved to a new city.

Let us abbreviate these two operation types as select(c) and update (n, c), respectively. The server executes these operations by decomposing them into index lookups (search(key)), record fetches (fetch(rid)), record modifications (modify(rid)), and index maintenance steps (insert (key, rid) and delete(key, rid)). Assume that B$^+$ tree index structures exist for each of the two relevant attributes, and that both of these trees have depth two, i.e., consist of a root node and a leaf level. All of the mentioned record and index operations are finally transformed into page reads and writes.

Now consider a transaction that finds all persons from two different cities, say, Los Angeles and New York, and a second transaction that

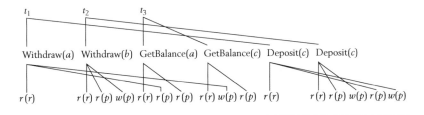

Figure 6.12 Two-level schedule of banking transactions.

records the moving of a couple, say, Liz and Jerry Smith, from Los Angeles to New York. Model the executions of both transactions as three-level transactions, and discuss possible schedules for them. Give (nontrivial, e.g., nonserial) examples for three-level schedules that are (a) tree reducible and (b) not tree reducible and thus not admissible.

6.3 Consider the two nonlayered schedules of Figure 6.2. Are these tree reducible?

6.4 Consider again the example of Figure 6.6. Give the necessary transformation steps, using the commutativity and the tree pruning rules, for proving that the schedule is tree reducible.

6.5 Consider the layered schedule in Figure 6.13, where i means (record) insert, d stands for (record) delete, s means store, m stands for modify, and e is for erase. Which of its level-to-level schedules are CSR, which ones are OCSR, and which ones satisfy the conflict faithfulness property? Is the schedule tree reducible?

6.6 Consider a counter object with operations with lower and upper bounds as constraints. The counter interface supports three operations: *Increment* adds a specified value Δ to the counter and returns "OK" if the upper bound is not exceeded; otherwise it returns "No" and leaves the counter unchanged. Analogously, *decrement* subtracts a given value from the counter or returns "No" if the lower bound was violated. Finally, *getvalue* returns the counter value. Give a return value commutativity table for these three operations. Discuss possible improvements of concurrency by taking into account explicit constraints among operation parameters.

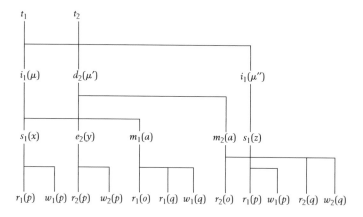

Figure 6.13 Layered schedule tree.

6.7 Construct a sample schedule with operations on FIFO queues that demonstrate the higher concurrency that return value commutativity can achieve over general commutativity.

6.8 Construct the return value commutativity table for a semi-queue. Show, by means of sample schedules, that semi-queues allow higher concurrency than FIFO queues.

6.9 Consider the following execution of operations on an initially empty queue q where a, b, and c are entries added to the queue:

$$\text{enq}_1(q, a) \ \text{enq}_2(q, b) \ \text{deq}_3(q) \ \text{enq}_1(q, c) \ \text{deq}_3(q)$$

Discuss whether this schedule is serializable assuming (a) general commutativity, (b) return value commutativity for queues, and (c) return value commutativity for semi-queues with nondeterministic selection of entries by Dequeue operations. In the last setting, which entries should be selected by the two Dequeue operations of t_3 to produce an intuitively correct execution?

6.10 Design an abstract data type "mailbox" with operations like Send (i.e., add a message to the mailbox), Receive (i.e., extract a message from the mailbox), and so on. Discuss the operations' commutativity relation for (a) general (i.e., state-independent) commutativity and (b) return value commutativity. Devise an implementation of mailbox objects in terms of queues, records, and ultimately, pages. Sketch the resulting transaction trees. Give an example of a concurrent execution, with as much concurrency as possible, for two transactions, where one sends two messages to two different mailboxes and the other receives all messages from one of the two mailboxes.

6.11 Even if two operations do not commute in the strict sense, the different effects that result from the two possible orderings may be considered as "effectively equal" from an application viewpoint. We could then simply declare the two operations as *compatible* and treat them as if they were commutative. An example would be a Deposit operation together with a new style of Withdraw operation that allows overdrafting but claims a penalty of, say, $10 each time the account balance is below the specified threshold and money is withdrawn. So the code for this relaxed variant of Withdraw would be

```
relaxed withdraw (x, Δ):
  x.balance := x.balance - Δ;
  if x.balance < 0 then
    x.balance := x.balance - 10 fi;
```

Give a sample schedule with these operations that is conflict serializable relative to the compatibility of the operations, but is not conflict serializable under a strict interpretation of commutativity. Discuss the acceptability of the resulting (worst-case) situations from an application viewpoint, of both the bank and the customer.

Bibliographic Notes

The formal notion of an object model schedule and the fundamental concept of tree reducibility are from Beeri et al. (1983, 1989), originally introduced under the name of "serializability for nested transactions." This seminal work also contains a detailed proof of Theorem 6.2. Informal ideas along these lines can be traced back to the highly inspiring, albeit rather semitechnical papers by Bjork (1973) and Davies (1973, 1978), Gray (1981), and Traiger (1983), who used the names "spheres of control" and "open nested transactions."

The practically most relevant special case of layered schedules, also known as "multilevel transaction schedules," has been intensively investigated by Weikum and Schek (1984) and Weikum (1986a, 1986b, 1991), Moss et al. (1986), as well as Beeri et al. (1988). The conceptual separation of logical and physical operations in a two-level concurrent system has also been studied by Bernstein, Goodman, and Lai (1981, 1983) and Minoura (1984). The general case of nonlayered schedules has been addressed by Muth et al. (1993) and Alonso et al. (1997, 1999a, 1999b).

The simpler case of flat object schedules with semantically rich operations beyond read/write operations has first been studied by Weihl (1983, 1988, 1989) as well as by Schwarz and Spector (1984). The subject is also treated in great detail in the textbook by Lynch et al. (1994). Interesting extensions can be found in Badrinath and Ramamritham (1992). The advanced form of exploiting even state based or return value commutativity dates back to Weihl's work as well, where our notion of return value commutativity has been called "backward commutativity" (see Weihl (1989)), and has also been further studied by Herlihy and Weihl (1991). The specific, but practically highly relevant example of increment and decrement operations on counters has been addressed especially in the work of Reuter (1982) and O'Neil (1986). An even more far-reaching approach to exploit both state based commutativity and logical pre- and postconditions of operations has been proposed by Agrawal et al. (1993) and further refined into a form of "assertional concurrency control" by Bernstein et al. (1998).

CHAPTER SEVEN

Concurrency Control Algorithms on Objects

A journey of a thousand miles must begin with a single step.

—*Lao-tzu*

The roots of education are bitter, but the fruit is sweet.

—*Aristotle*

7.1 Goal and Overview

In this chapter we will introduce practical concurrency control algorithms for systems based on the object model, with particular focus again on the important special case of layered systems. We will show that the presented protocols are correct in that they produce tree-reducible schedules only, or even the more restricted class of schedules where all level-to-level schedules are OCSR or CSR and conflict faithful. As the latter kind of decomposition already suggests, we will show that the conventional page model protocols can be used as building blocks in the construction of object model protocols. For the most part, we will even concentrate on locking protocols and particularly 2PL.

Throughout this chapter we will assume that commutativity is specified as a simple table on a per-object type or on a per-layer basis. Thus, operations on different object types can safely be assumed to be commutative, unless—as will be seen—one object type serves to implement the other, which will cause some complications. We will mostly focus on exploiting state-independent commutativity, and consider return value commutativity only in the final section of this chapter.

7.2 Locking for Flat Object Transactions

The commutativity table for an object can be directly interpreted as a lock mode compatibility table. For each operation $f(x_1, \ldots, x_n)$ with input parameters $x_1, \ldots, x_n$ a lock is acquired in lock mode f on items $x_{i_1}, \ldots, x_{i_m}$ $(m \leq n)$,

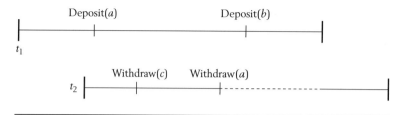

Figure 7.1 2PL applied to a flat object schedule.

where the $x_{i_1}, \ldots, x_{i_m}$ form a subset of the parameters relevant for deciding on conflicts. Most often, m will be 1. This case can be interpreted as follows: there is a "primary" object to which the operation refers; operations on different primary objects imply commutativity, whereas commutativity on the same object depends only on the operation type, not on the other input parameters.

As for the actual locking protocol—that is, the discipline according to which locks are acquired and released—we can apply 2PL, S2PL, or SS2PL to the enhanced setting of object model operations in a straightfoward way, and all correctness arguments also carry over in an almost trivial way. Note, however, that the object-level operations themselves need to be executed strictly sequentially (i.e., concurrency is limited to interleavings at the highest level below the transaction roots). The reason is that flat object schedules always assume that their object-level operations are indivisible (see Chapter 6).

Figure 7.1 shows an example of two concurrent transactions, consisting of Deposit and Withdraw operations, under the S2PL protocol driven by a commutativity based lock mode conflict table. As in previous illustrations of this style, dashed lines denote lock waits. Transaction t_2, which requests a withdraw lock on account a, has to wait until t_1, which holds an incompatible deposit lock on a, commits and releases its locks.

7.3 **Layered Locking**

When higher-level operations can be executed concurrently on lower levels, one way to ensure tree reducibility is to enforce the order-preserving conflict serializability (OCSR) of the level-to-level schedules. This can in turn be guaranteed by applying an appropriate flat concurrency control protocol between each pair of adjacent levels. One suitable protocol is 2PL or its derivatives S2PL and SS2PL; in fact, this family provides the most versatile and robust protocols that are known for flat schedules and are therefore our methods of choice.

Inner node operations as subtransactions When 2PL is applied to layered schedules, we arrive at a nicely modular architecture: the scheduler between level L_{i+1} and L_i needs to know only the operations at level L_i and the identifiers of their L_{i+1} parents. From the viewpoint of this scheduler, the L_{i+1} operations are transactions and the L_i

operations are the steps of these transactions. To better distinguish this role of L_{i+1} operations in a level-to-level schedule from the actual transaction roots, we will refer to them in the current context as *subtransactions*.

After these considerations, we are ready to give the rules for what we call *layered 2PL* for *n*-level schedules: *Layered 2PL*

1. *Lock acquisition rule:* When an L_i operation $f(x)$ with parent p is issued, an f-mode lock on x needs to be acquired before the operation can start its execution. This lock is called an L_i lock.

2. *Lock release rule:* Once an L_i lock, originally acquired by an operation $f(x)$ with parent p, is released, no other child of p is allowed to acquire any L_i locks.

3. *Subtransaction rule:* Upon the termination of an L_i operation $f(x)$, all locks at level L_{i-1} that have been acquired for the children of $f(x)$ are released.

So the key principle of layered 2PL is that locks at a certain level, say, L_i, are held on behalf of the corresponding subtransactions, the L_{i+1} operations. With SS2PL, this amounts to holding locks for the duration of a subtransaction, but no longer. It is exactly this "early release" of low-level locks such as page locks that makes layered 2PL such a powerful protocol. In terms of the possible concurrency, it is, by a large margin, superior to the conventional page model 2PL and other page model concurrency control methods.

As for the correctness of layered 2PL, we can now leverage the theory developed in Chapter 6 and obtain the following correctness proof with little effort:

THEOREM 7.1

Layered 2PL generates tree-reducible schedules only.

Proof

All level-to-level schedules are OCSR, hence the schedule is tree reducible according to Theorem 6.2.

To illustrate the layered 2PL protocol, reconsider the example from Figure 6.4 with operations on the record and page levels. Figure 7.2 shows a possible execution of this schedule under layered 2PL. This is an example for employing record-level locking in combination with short-term page locking for the duration of subtransactions, an extremely important case in practice. The subtransactions that define the scope of the page locks are highlighted by the gray triangles. As usual, lock waits are indicated by dashed lines, and we show that such a protocol may incur both record-level and page-level lock

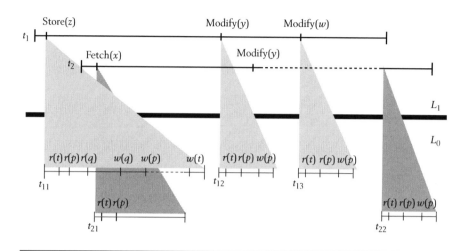

Figure 7.2 Layered 2PL applied to the record and page levels of a two-level schedule.

waits. Moreover, we also show that page lock waits are much shorter than they would be under pure page-level locking, where page locks would be held for the duration of the entire transactions.

Special case: page latches for single-page record operations

A special case of the above setting would be a system where all record-level operations access only a single page, like the fetch(x) operation in Figure 7.2. If we knew that all operations on a given set of records have such a structure, the necessary subtransaction-duration 2PL can be further streamlined. It would be sufficient to "latch" the affected page during the record operation, by atomically setting or resetting a bit in the page header, rather than acquiring a "full-fledged" page lock. The functionality of latching is similar to that of semaphores provided by an operating system, but latching avoids expensive operating system calls as much as possible. In comparison to explicit locking, latching does not provide higher concurrency, but its overhead is much lower than that of a lock manager. For example, latching does not keep a queue of waiting requestors, nor does it need to check for deadlocks. For this reason, commercial database systems use such latching techniques whenever they are applicable. However, as the example shows, storage structures can be fairly complex and may require multipage record-level operations, especially when dealing with hierarchically structured records as storage representations of composite objects or XML documents in object relational database systems.

Opportunities for index locking

So latching surely has its limits. In particular, latching is not easily applicable to index operations such as searching a key in a B^+ tree, which involves multiple pages in the tree traversal. Obviously, the situation becomes even more complicated for insertions and deletions of (key, RID) pairs, as this may trigger node splits in the B^+ tree. Nevertheless, this case is still special in that it leads to a limited class of page access patterns only, so that specialized concurrency control protocols could be attractive for such subtransactions (e.g., the tree locking protocol from Chapter 4). As index management is among the most important issues in data management with regard to performance, we postpone the details of this discussion and will look into this issue in a separate chapter, Chapter 9.

Another special case would be the situation where all object-level operations are a priori known to commute. Then no object-level locks would be necessary at all, and transactions are effectively decomposed into sequences of *chained subtransactions*. Locking would be strictly confined to the duration of subtransactions so that very high concurrency is possible. The caveat with regard to this approach is that the application must be designed very carefully to ensure an all-commutative object layer. Typically, this is feasible only for very specialized, functionally restricted applications. An example would be the interbank funds transfer application known as SWIFT, where all Withdraw and Deposit operations are declared to be commutative or, actually, "compatible," tolerating the application-wise "negligible" differences in the effect of differently ordered withdrawals. Note, of course, that this system would typically be used only for relatively small amounts of money, and it also relies on the legal rules and mutual guarantees for interbank business.

Special case: all-commutative chained subtransactions

Layered 2PL is, of course, applicable to more than two levels as well. As an example, consider the three-level schedule shown in Figure 7.3. It shows SQL-style query-level operations at level L_2, which are translated into record and index operations at level L_1, which finally result in page-level read and write operations. Recall from Chapter 1 that L_2 Insert operations need to maintain all indexes at level L_1, namely, indexes on the Age and City attributes of the Persons table in the example. Queries, on the other hand, may exploit multiple

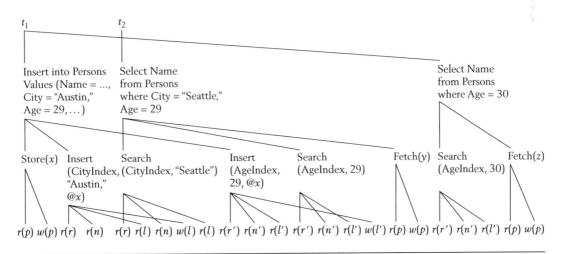

Figure 7.3 Example of a three-level schedule with query, record, and page level.

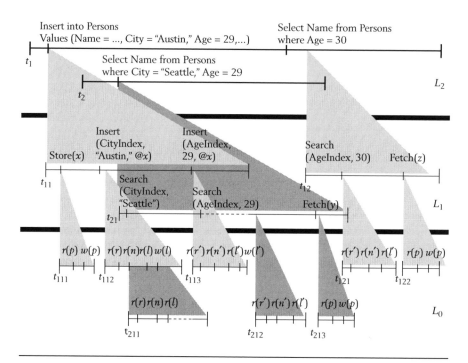

Figure 7.4 Layered 2PL applied to the query, record, and page levels of the three-level schedule of Figure 7.3.

indexes by looking up RID lists for the specified values of different attributes, intersecting the RID lists, and finally fetching only the records that satisfy the conjunction of the specified conditions.

The execution that results from this schedule under a three-level layered 2PL is shown in Figure 7.4. Subtransactions are again highlighted as shaded triangles, with different shading patterns used for the two transactions of the example. Here we assume that the locks at the query level L_2 are some form of *predicate locks*. The lock for the Select operation of t_2 essentially locks the conjunctive condition City = "Seattle" and Age = 29, whereas t_1's Select operation locks the condition Age = 30, and t_1's Insert operation essentially locks the conjunction of the inserted record's attribute values, namely, Name = ... and City = "Austin" and Age = 29 and .... A lock conflict exists whenever the predicates of two lock requests intersect. More precisely, this means that the conjunction of the two predicates is satisfiable in that it could possibly be satisfied by some record regardless of whether this record actually exists in the database. Conversely, when the predicates of two lock requests are disjoint in that their conjunction evaluates to false and is thus unsatisfiable, we can safely assume that no conflict exists at the query level L_2. We will further elaborate on the concept of predicate locking in Chapter 8. In the example, no predicate lock conflict exists at L_2, whereas conflicts arise for the index search keys at L_1 and incur lock waits. Note the lock wait of t_{21} in Figure 7.4 when it requests a lock for the operation search(AgeIndex, 29) at level $L1$. t_{21} has to wait until the conflicting lock for operation insert(AgeIndex, 29, @x) is released at the end of t_{11}. For this reason, t_{212} is forced to sequentially follow t_{113}, which explains the difference in the interleavings between these two subtransactions compared to the (input) schedule shown in Figure 7.3.

Layered 2PL can hence be applied to an arbitrary number of levels. However, although this may, in principle, be beneficial for concurrency, the inevitable overhead for the lock management suggests keeping the number of levels rather small, typically two or three. When given an n-level schedule with large n, the question is whether we can apply layered 2PL to a limited subset of the levels and still guarantee that the schedule will be tree reducible. It turns out that locks do not need to be acquired at all layers of such an n-level schedule. Rather, we can skip certain layers, say, layer L_i, by extending the scope of the subtransactions above L_i, which effectively leads to longer lock durations of the locks below L_i. So, for example, L_{i-1} locks could be held for the duration of the corresponding operations' grandparents, that is, the L_{i+1} subtransactions. In essence, this removes an entire layer from the schedule itself, as far as concurrency control is concerned, and extends the caller-callee relationship by connecting the L_{i-1} nodes in the transaction tree directly to their grandparents. Once this is accomplished, we have again a layered schedule with one level less, and we can apply our standard reasoning for layered schedules.

This consideration leads to a *selective layered 2PL* with the following rules, where out of the $n+1$ layers $L_n, \ldots, L_0$ of an n-level schedule a subset $L_{i_0}, \ldots L_{i_k}$, with $1 \le k \le n$, $i_v > i_{v+1}$, and $i_0 = n$, $i_k = 0$, can be selected with the following locking rules (which are merely slight modifications of the original layered 2PL rules):

1. *Lock acquisition rule:* When an L_{i_v} ($v > 0$) operation $f(x)$ with $L_{i_{v-1}}$ ancestor p is issued, an f-mode lock on x needs to be acquired before the operation can start its execution. This lock is called an L_{i_v} lock.

2. *Lock release rule:* Once an L_{i_v} lock, originally acquired by an operation $f(x)$ with $L_{i_{v-1}}$ ancestor p, is released, no other L_{i_v} descendant of p is allowed to acquire any L_i locks.

3. *Subtransaction rule:* At the termination of an L_{i_v} operation $f(x)$, all locks at level $L_{i_{v+1}}$ that have been acquired for the $L_{i_{v+1}}$ descendants of $f(x)$ are released.

Reconsider the example of Figure 7.3, whose resulting three-level layered 2PL execution was shown in Figure 7.4. With selective layered 2PL, applied to

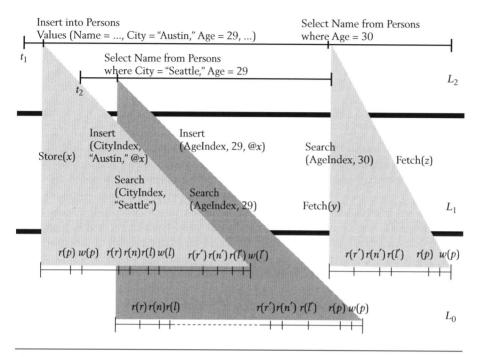

Figure 7.5 Selective layered 2PL applied to the query and page levels of the schedule of Figure 7.3.

the query level L_2 and the page level L_0, the resulting execution keeps page-level locks longer and leads to a longer lock wait for the L_0 operation $r_{211}(l)$, as shown in Figure 7.5.

Layered 2PL with intra-transaction parallelism

We have shown that a given layer manages the locks on behalf of the subtransactions that it sees, regardless of the further ancestors of these subtransactions. So a page-level lock manager that handles subtransactions, each of which corresponds to a record-level operation, does not even need to know to which transactions the various subtransactions belong. Thus, a nice observation is that the same lock manager could handle parallel subtransactions that originate from the same transaction without any additional means. This form of *intra-transaction parallelism* is, of course, only possible if the higher-level operations are conflict free and the transaction program or the server's query processing engine does not require any execution precedence among such high-level operations. When subtransactions are issued in parallel, the underlying layer will guarantee equivalence to some serial order, and this works even for parallelized update statements. As an example, consider the scenario shown in Figure 7.6.

In this scenario, transaction t_1 issues two subtransactions, t_{14} and t_{15}, in parallel, to reflect the modification of record x in the index on the City attribute.

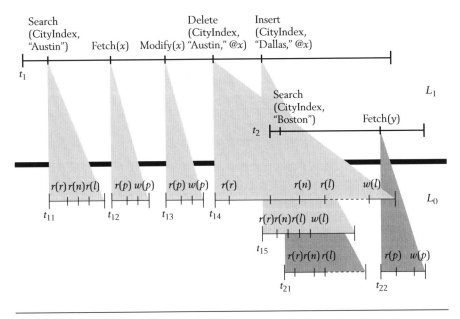

Figure 7.6 Layered 2PL with intra-transaction parallelism.

The RID for x is removed from the RID list associated with key "Austin" and added to the RID list for "Dallas." These two operations do not conflict conceptually, but they do have a page-level conflict on page l (i.e., the two keys happen to reside on the same leaf page of the index). The protocol takes care of this conflict by blocking one of the two subtransactions for a short while. In addition, a third subtransaction, t_{21}, issued by another transaction, t_2, has a similar conflict and exhibits a short lock wait, too. Note that without page locks (or some equivalent, carefully designed, latching protocol) intra-transaction parallelism for update statements would not be feasible despite the fact that there is no conflict at level L_1, as t_{14} and t_{15} could then interleave in an arbitrary way and render the index inconsistent.

7.4 **Locking on General Transaction Forests**

When trying to generalize the layered 2PL to nonlayered schedules, the main problem is exactly the missing layering and the resulting difficulty in identifying the appropriate scopes of locking. As an example, consider the schedule in Figure 7.7, where account objects are assumed to be implemented by a counter for the account balance and a list for recording all cash flows on the account.

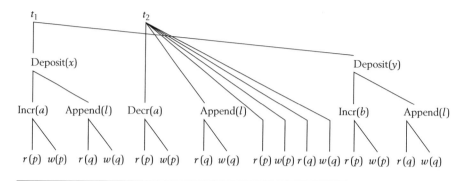

Figure 7.7 Example of a schedule for which layered locking does not work.

The decisive point is that t_2 "bypasses" the account abstraction and chooses to manipulate the counter and the list directly. (See Chapter 6 for a discussion of why and how such bypassing may occur.) At the time when the second transaction t_2 starts, we would expect t_1 to hold a deposit lock on account x and no other locks. The increment and append locks on the counter a and the list l would have been released already at the end of subtransaction t_{11} (i.e., the deposit(x) operation). The page locks for the underlying page reads and writes would have been released even much earlier, at the end of t_{111} and t_{112}, respectively. Now, when t_2 requests a decrement lock on counter a, it would not find any existing locks on a, and the lock request could be granted. The same situation holds for the subsequently needed append lock on list l.

The net result is that the schedule shown would be allowed under such a locking protocol. However, this concurrent execution is admissible only under specific assumptions on the semantics of t_2's operations. If we knew that the Decrement and Append operations of t_2 together implement an abstract operation that commutes with t_1's deposit, then the situation is acceptable. For example, if t_2 decrements the counter by a constant amount to charge a monthly fee for maintaining the account, this would be considered commutative with a deposit. On the other hand, if the Decrement and the Append together implement a withdrawal, the noncommutativity of Withdraw and Deposit operations should actually tell the lock manager that t_2 must not be allowed to run at this point. Analogous arguments could be made about the subsequent read/write children of t_2. Without any clue on the abstract semantics of t_2's operation sequence, we would conservatively have to assume a conflict with t_1's high-level Deposit operation.

The question now is when we can allow a low-level operation to proceed in a situation where incomparable high-level operations of concurrent transactions still hold locks. The answer lies in inspecting the ancestors of both the requesting transaction and the potentially conflicting high-level operations of the other transactions. If operation r of the requestor (e.g., t_2's Decrement) has an ancestor for which we know that it commutes with a previous operation h (e.g., t_1's Deposit) and such a condition holds for every transaction that holds an incompatible lock, then operation r can be allowed to proceed; otherwise it should be blocked. Since lock conflicts are actually detected only among operations on the same objects, the negative one of the two cases requires additional information for the previous operations on the object to which the requestor r refers. Essentially, we need to know that a lock on that object was held on behalf of a higher-level operation h but has meanwhile been released. For example, t_2's Decrement operation should be alerted by remembering the previous lock of t_1's Increment on a. Realizing that this is a potentially problematic situation should then lead to a more elaborate conflict test involving the ancestors of the operations.

A technical means for accomplishing the above ancestor conscious conflict testing is to retain the original locks of completed subtransactions for the purpose of alerting subsequent operations that access a lower-level object directly, bypassing the higher-level abstraction. In an implementation, regular locks would be converted into a special kind of *retained locks* upon the completion of the corresponding subtransaction. Retained locks merely serve the alerting bypassing operations; operations that are invoked on behalf of higher-level operations that have properly passed all conflict tests in a complete top-down descent along an object implementation hierarchy should never be blocked by a retained lock.

Putting all these considerations together, we arrive at the following principle: An operation r, the requestor, can ignore a retained lock, originally held by operation h, if and only if both operations have ancestors r' and h' such that h' is already completed and r' and h' commute. Otherwise, the retained lock of h is still considered "active" as far as r is concerned. In the worst case, the ancestor of h by which r could become blocked would be the transaction root of h. This would be the case in our example of Figure 7.7: $\text{decr}_{21}(a)$ would conflict with the retained lock, originally held by $\text{incr}_{11}(a)$, but the only "commutative" ancestors of the two operations are the transactions themselves. So $\text{decr}_{21}(a)$ would have to wait until the completion of t_1. Note that it is important that the ancestor of the retained lock holder h is completed; otherwise, we could end up with subtrees for commutative high-level operations for which we cannot guarantee isolation of the subtrees themselves.

We coin this protocol the (general) *object model 2PL*. It is completely described by the following rules:

Object model 2PL

1. *Lock acquisition rule:* When an operation $f(x)$ with parent p is issued, an f mode lock on x needs to be acquired before the operation can start its execution.

2. *Lock conflict rule:* A lock requested for operation $r(x)$ (called the requestor) is granted only if

(a) either no conflicting lock on x is held,

(b) or when for every transaction that holds a conflicting lock on behalf of an operation $h(x)$ (called the holder) the following condition is satisfied: the lock of $h(x)$ is a retained lock and r and h have ancestors r' and h', respectively, such that h' is already terminated and commutes with r'.

In the second case, if no such ancestors exist, $r(x)$ needs to wait until the completion of the lowest ancestor h' of h such that r has an ancestor r' that commutes with h'. In the "worst case," this lowest ancestor h' would be the transaction root to which h belongs.

3. *Lock release rule:* Once a lock, originally acquired by an operation $f(x)$ with parent p, is released, no other child of p is allowed to acquire any locks.

4. *Subtransaction rule:* At the termination of an operation $f(x)$, all locks that have been acquired for the children of $f(x)$ are converted into retained locks.

5. *Transaction rule:* At the termination of a transaction, all locks of its descendants are released.

The correctness arguments for this protocol are quite a bit more involved than those for the layered variant. By proper case analyses and application of the tree reducibility transformation rules, we arrive at the following result:

THEOREM 7.2

The object model 2PL generates tree-reducible schedules only.

Proof

First assume that all operations in a transaction tree retain all their locks until the commit of the transaction root. In this case each object model schedule would follow a flattened SS2PL protocol that gradually acquires locks for all nodes of an entire transaction tree and releases them in one stroke at the very end of the transaction. So in reasoning about the correctness of the actual protocol that allows certain operations to ignore retained locks, we can focus on the operations that are in conflict with a retained lock but have an ancestor that commutes with a completed ancestor of the retained lock's holder. So the canonical situation to be inspected more closely is the following: there is a retained lock holder f_1 (somewhere within a transaction tree) that is already completed, has a completed ancestor h_1, and belongs to active transaction t_1, and there is a lock requestor f_2 that would conflict with f_1, belongs to active transaction t_2, and has at least one active ancestor h_2 that commutes with h_1. This situation is depicted in

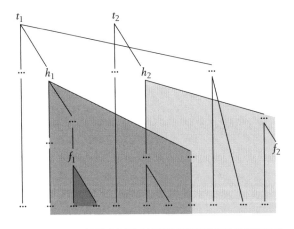

Figure 7.8 Canonical situation for conflict testing against a retained lock under the object model 2PL protocol.

Figure 7.8. All other cases are uncritical because of the locking nature of the protocol. For example, if t_1 was already completed when the lock for f_2 is requested, f_2 could immediately proceed; in this case it is guaranteed that t_1 and t_2 can be isolated from each other by commutativity and tree pruning arguments such that t_2 follows t_1. Another uncritical situation would be when no ancestor h_2 of f_2 exists that commutes with h_1; in that case, t_2 would have to wait until the completion of t_1.

For the canonical type of critical situation we now show that the subtrees rooted at h_1 and h_2 can always be isolated, with both of the two possible serialization orders among them being acceptable. We do so by induction on the longest path from a leaf to h_1 or h_2, whichever yields the maximum.

For the base case with maximum path length 1, both f_1 and f_2 must be leaves, and h_1 and h_2 are their immediate parents. In this case, the flat 2PL protocol for the tree leaves ensures that h_1 and h_2 can be disentangled (if they are concurrent), with h_2 following h_1.

Now suppose that the claim holds for all paths up to length i, and consider h_1 and h_2 such that the longest path from the leaves to one of these operations has length $i + 1$. By the induction hypothesis, we can isolate and then prune all subtrees rooted at the children of h_1 and h_2. Now consider two children g_1 and g_2 of h_1 and h_2. If g_1 and g_2 commute, then we can rearrange their order to whatever is needed for isolating h_1 and h_2. So assume that there is a conflict between g_1 and g_2. Since under the object model 2PL all conflicts are lock conflicts, one of the two operations must hold a lock that the other operation requests in a conflicting mode. We need to distinguish two cases with respect to the ordering: g_1 precedes g_2, or vice versa. In the first case, if h_1 is still active at the point when g_2 is invoked, g_2 needs to wait until the completion of h_1; then the 2PL rule would ensure that g_2 can be pushed after the entire subtree of h_1. If h_1 is already terminated at the point when g_2 is invoked, the lock for g_1 must be a retained lock; so g_2 follows the entire subtree of h_1 anyway and does not present any problems in isolating the subtrees of h_1 and h_2. At the next stage, when the subtrees rooted at h_1 and h_2 are pruned, it is perfectly acceptable to forget this serialization ordering between g_1 and g_2, for h_1 and h_2 are known to be commutative. In the second case, where g_2 precedes g_1, the same arguments can be applied analogously. The fact that the g_2 has a descendant f_2 that follows a conflicting descendant f_1 of g_1 does not matter anymore, since, by the induction hypothesis, it is possible to isolate and prune g_1 and g_2, with both possible serialization orders among them being equally acceptable. This completes the induction.

The result about h_1 and h_2 holds for all possible pairs of this kind and all possible path lengths from the leaves. Thus, we can now simply specialize h_1 and h_2 to become t_1 and t_2, the transaction roots. So, as a corollary, we obtain that the conflict between f_1 and f_2 does not interfere with the isolation of t_1 and t_2. Note that this does not yet say that t_1 and t_2 can be isolated with either serialization order, as there may be other operations that dictate such an order or may even prevent the isolation. However, those other operations are either of the same kind as f_1 and f_2, or are taken care of by the 2PL rule for nonretained locks.

A selective form of the protocol, where certain objects in the invocation trees are skipped, is also conceivable, and is analogous to the selective layered 2PL. However, as we do not need to explicitly model each and every invoked object method in the schedule in the first place, the same effect can be achieved by a less comprehensive form of schedule. So the concurrency control would not "see" the less important operations anyway. For this reason and because the selective version of the object model 2PL becomes notationally complex, we do not further elaborate on it here.

In summary, although the developed general object model 2PL is a fairly complex protocol, it is worth employing in situations where the discussed kind of bypassing object abstraction is possible. The alternative would be to resort to standard locking at the common lower-level objects, but this could severely limit the allowable concurrency. As we mentioned earlier, it is unlikely that the concurrency control is presented with very deep method invocation trees. So, in a practical application situation, it may also be possible to simplify and streamline the object model 2PL to a more restricted setting such as generalized two-level schedules where the object level L_1 can be bypassed by some transactions.

7.5 **Hybrid Algorithms**

Different protocols may be used at distinct levels of a layered system. For example, we could use an optimistic protocol or timestamping at the page level and 2PL at the record level. This can be advantageous, as the L_i operation patterns of subtransactions may have more specific characteristics than the patterns of the entire transactions, so that protocols that are specifically geared toward particular patterns could be favored. For example, with record-level and page-level concurrency control in a two-level system, the fraction of read-only subtransactions at the page level would typically be much higher than the fraction of read-only transactions (i.e., roots).

Thus, particularly attractive hybrid protocols for two-level schedules are the following:

- a combination of 2PL at the (object or record) level L_1 and the forward-oriented optimistic concurrency control, FOCC, at the page level L_0;
- a combination of 2PL at L_1 and the multiversion concurrency control protocol that uses timestamping for read-only (sub-)transactions and 2PL for update (sub-)transactions, coined ROMV in Chapter 5, at level L_0.

In both of these combinations, read-only subtransactions are treated particularly favorably and with extremely low overhead. Further note that both FOCC and ROMV can be implemented very easily and efficiently for very short (sub-)transactions on pages, whereas their implementation is much more problematic for longer transactions at the record level.

The correctness of the 2PL/FOCC combination follows more or less directly from the fact that both protocols generate OCSR schedules, thus leading us to the following result:

THEOREM 7.3

For two-level schedules, the combination of 2PL at L_1 and FOCC at L_0 generates tree-reducible schedules only.

Tree reducibility is also guaranteed by the 2PL/ROMV combination, but as ROMV does not generate CSR L_1-to-L_0 schedules, we need to use the tree reducibility transformation rules to show equivalence to a serial order of the roots. The transformation rules can be applied in a strictly layered manner, first isolating record-level operations, then pruning their subtrees, and finally, applying CSR-style commutativity arguments at the record layer to isolate transactions. The commutativity based reordering of the page-level children to isolate the record-level operations is a bit more sophisticated than with 2PL or similar protocols at the page layer. In addition to the usual commutativity relationship, a page read operation issued by a read-only record-level operation commutes with all page writes whose parents are concurrent with the read operation's parent. The read does not commute, however, with a write step whose parent terminated before the read's parent began. This notion of commutativity reflects the version function of the ROMV protocol. Then it is straightforward to see that record-level operations can be isolated without reversing any orderings among nonconcurrent record-level operations, and this yields the following result:

THEOREM 7.4

For two-level schedules, the combination of 2PL at L_1 and ROMV at L_0 generates tree-reducible schedules only.

The dual version of this combination with ROMV at the record layer L_1 and 2PL at the page layer L_0 is an intriguing protocol, too. As long as we restrict ourselves to simple Fetch and Modify operations at the record level, the above arguments are sufficient to prove the correctness of this protocol as well. To incorporate insertions and deletions of records, we can assume that deletions actually leave some form of marker in the underlying storage structures rather than removing the record (and its prior versions). With semantically richer operations like predicate-oriented SQL-style search commands, however, we would need to reconsider and extend the notions of a version function and a conflict relation. Thus we have

---

THEOREM 7.5

For two-level schedules, the combination of ROMV at L_1, applied to record-oriented Fetch, Modify, Store, and Erase operations, and 2PL at L_0 generates tree-reducible schedules only.

In commercial database systems, 2PL at the page layer would often be replaced by a carefully designed latching protocol for reduced overhead.

7.6 **Locking for Return Value Commutativity and Escrow Locking**

Locking protocols can also be fed by return value commutativity for defining the compatibility between different lock modes. In this case, each operation type in combination with its return value forms a separate lock mode. For example, in the bank account example, we would introduce lock modes like Withdraw ↑ OK, Withdraw ↑ NO, Deposit ↑ OK, and GetBalance ↑ OK. The lock mode compatibility would be derived from the table for return value commutativity in a straightforward way. As before, a lock can only be granted if no other transaction already holds a lock on the same object in an incompatible mode, and, of course, the rules of (layered or object model) 2PL also need to be in effect.

A problem with this approach is that return values and hence the necessary lock modes are known only at the end of an operation execution; so we cannot know in which mode to acquire the lock for the operation before it starts. The solution is to allow the execution without the appropriate lock; once we know the return value, a lock is requested in the corresponding mode. If there is no lock conflict at this point, the lock is granted and we do not need anything special. On the other hand, if we detect a lock conflict, this means that, in retrospect, we should not have been allowed to execute the operation at all. In this case, the escape is to roll back the operation, request the lock as if the operation were about to start just now, and—because the conflicting lock is already held—force the requesting transaction to wait until the current lock holder releases its lock. Note that it is only the operation that is rolled back, not the entire transaction. The approach can be viewed as an optimistic execution of the subtransaction that corresponds to the operation. Note that it is crucial for this subtransaction to acquire locks for its children in order to ensure that all of the semantically rich operations for which we want to exploit return value commutativity are indeed isolated. With this prerequisite, we can show that the sketched protocol guarantees that all resulting schedules are tree reducible.

Deferred lock conflict test at end of subtransaction

A special case of locking based on return value commutativity has been studied intensively for objects of the abstract data type Counter, a practically important case for reservation systems, inventory control, and other applications along these lines. In these applications, counters are typically constrained from both below and/or above. Recall that for counters without any constraints, Increment and Decrement operations generally commute, and return value commutativity would not be needed. So each counter object x is associated with a lower bound, $low(x)$, and an upper bound, $high(x)$, within which the value must be guaranteed to stay.

When transactions request to increment or decrement a counter, the locking protocol needs to ensure that the requested operation commutes with all previously executed Increment and Decrement operations issued by ongoing

Escrow locking on counter objects

transactions. As these transactions are still active and as we cannot take for granted that their effects will always be eventually committed, we need to consider a value interval within which the "true" value of a counter is guaranteed to stay, even if some of the active transactions abort. So for each such object x, the concurrency control maintains two values $\inf(x)$ and $\sup(x)$, the infimum and supremum of the possible value range for x. Return value commutativity is then tested against the infimum and supremum of a counter, which can be done very efficiently. This approach is called *escrow locking*, and the Increment and Decrement operations are referred to as escrow operations in this context, as they can be viewed as requesting some quantity of a resource into escrow, under the supervision of a notary. A concrete application example for this metaphor could be selling or buying stocks for a (constrained) portfolio or maintaining the quantity-on-hand of some item in a warehouse.

Following these considerations, the concurrency control code for the two escrow operations Incr and Decr is as follows:

```
incr (x, Δ):
 if x.sup + Δ ≤ x.high then
  x.sup := x.sup + Δ; return ok
 else if x.inf + Δ > x.high then
  return no
 else wait fi fi;

decr (x, Δ):
 if x.low ≤ x.inf - Δ then
  x.inf := x.inf - Δ; return ok
 else if x.low > x.sup - Δ then
  return no
 else wait fi fi;
```

In this pseudocode wait means waiting until the end of one of the active transactions that has operated on the corresponding counter. Upon the Commit or Abort of a transaction t the uncertainty interval of a counter value is reduced by increasing the infimum of a counter for each Increment operation and decreasing the supremum in the case of a Commit, or vice versa when the transaction aborts. To this end, the concurrency control also needs to maintain a list of all Increment and Decrement operations that have been issued by each active transaction. With this data structure at hand, the code to be executed upon Commit or Abort looks as follows:

```
Commit of transaction t:
 for each operation incr(x,Δ) executed by t do
  x.inf := x.inf + Δ od;
 for each operation decr(x,Δ) executed by t do
  x.sup := x.sup - Δ od;
```

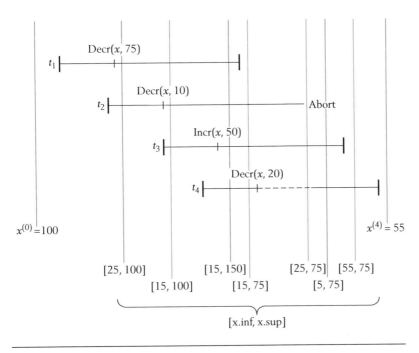

Figure 7.9 Example execution under escrow locking.

```
Abort of transaction t:
  for each operation incr(x,Δ) executed by t do
    x.sup := x.sup - Δ od;
  for each operation decr(x,Δ) executed by t do
    x.inf := x.inf + Δ od;
```

When no transaction is active, x.inf and x.sup for a counter x coincide again, yielding the actual value of the counter. An example scenario under the escrow locking protocol is shown in Figure 7.9, assuming that x.low is zero and x.high unbounded. In this figure, the vertical dotted lines show the actual value of x at the begin and end of the schedule as well as the infimum and supremum of x at the intermediate points. t_4 is forced to wait until t_2 terminates (by abort), for at the time when t_4 issues its decr$(x, 20)$ operation request x.inf is 15 (and x.sup equals 75). With the abort of t_2, x.inf becomes 25 so that t_4's decrement can safely proceed.

Like most locking protocols, escrow locking is susceptible to deadlocks. Such a situation is shown in Figure 7.10, where transaction t_4 waits for an

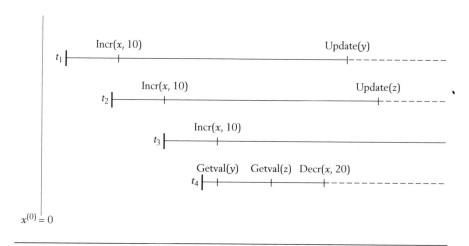

Figure 7.10 Example of a deadlock with escrow locking.

escrow lock but already holds "conventional" locks, and thus causes t_1 and t_2 to become blocked when they request conflicting locks. The resulting lock waits are illustrated by dashed lines. A particularity that arises here is that the lock waits are not simply blocking situations between pairs of transactions. Rather, transaction t_4 actually waits for a quantity of 20 of the resource managed by counter x. Once we know that the infimum of x is at least 20, t_4 could be resumed. With the three still-active transactions t_1, t_2, t_3, the infimum is still 0, but it would be sufficient that any two of these three transactions commit to increase the infimum to 20. So, in essence, t_4 is waiting for any two of the three transactions t_1, t_2, t_3; and t_1 and t_2 each wait for t_4. This form of deadlock would require some kind of "or edges" in a waiting graph and is more general than the kind of deadlocks that we are used to with conventional locking. In fact, it turns out that detecting that a deadlock exists is computationally more expensive than using simple waits-for graphs. However, given that escrow locking only serves to reduce lock waits, and deadlocks should be rare anyway, this additional complexity in deadlock handling is not a severe caveat.

Tolerating bounded inconsistency   An interesting twist on exploiting state based commutativity on counters is to relax the correctness requirements and tolerate some bounded inconsistency. More precisely, rather than guaranteeing that all reads of counter objects yield consistent values that are in line with a serializable history, an approximate value that falls into some form of "confidence interval" may be sufficient for the application. In contrast to a confidence interval used in statistics, however, the retrieved value should be guaranteed to be within the interval's bounds rather than having this property merely with very high probability.

In certain situations this behavior could be achieved without any concurrency control at all (other than short-term locks for the duration of a high-level operation), namely, when the Δ by which the counter value can be changed by a single transaction is very small and thus negligible relative to the absolute counter value. In such a situation (e.g., when the counter is the total of a large number of individual counters and updates manipulate only the individual counters), the number of concurrently active transactions times the maximum Δ per individual transaction yields the maximum deviation from the actual value that could be observed when all transactions run in a serializable manner.

However, in other situations, this kind of confidence interval may be unacceptably large, and we would wish to have explicit control over the observable deviation from the actual value. A criterion along these lines is the notion of ϵ *serializability*, which assures that each read operation sees a value that deviates by at most ϵ from the value that it would see in a serial schedule. Obviously, the approach of tracking the infimum and supremum of a counter's value that we discussed for escrow locking points us to possible implementation techniques for ϵ serializability: basically, a read operation needs to be blocked when the difference between the supremum and the infimum is larger than the acceptable ϵ.

The ϵ serializability approach can even be generalized to incorporate updates that are not necessarily commutative: as long as the value of the counter remains within a distance of ϵ from the value that would be produced in a serial schedule, the situation may be considered acceptable (depending on the application). This generalization requires additional mechanisms known as "divergence control" in the literature. An elegant property of the entire approach is that standard serializability is included as a special case, namely, for $\epsilon = 0$. In practice, a difficulty that could easily be underestimated is to understand the application well enough to derive a truly acceptable setting for ϵ. These are exactly the difficulties that are avoided by serializability (i.e., the case $\epsilon = 0$), which frees application architects and developers from thinking about the pitfalls of concurrency.

ε serializability

7.7 **Lessons Learned**

Based on the previous chapter's results on transaction forests with semantically rich operations, we have developed a couple of 2PL-based concurrency control protocols for the object model. In the simpler form, layered 2PL, we assume a layered structure of the transaction trees and simply apply 2PL at each layer. This is the fundamental concept in record granularity locking that industrial-strength data servers support: record locks are held for transaction duration, and short-term page locks are held for the scope of record operations to ensure that the corresponding subtransactions can be isolated. In practice, the restricted nature of record operations may even allow us to further relax the subtransaction 2PL to the extreme point where pages merely need to be latched while being accessed. The latter technique can be viewed as a very lightweight form of subtransaction locking.

The same principles carry over to other protocols, where 2PL is replaced by another conventional protocol at selected levels, as long as this protocol guarantees order-preserving conflict serializability. This way, optimistic or multiversion protocols can be integrated in a layered architecture, and even hybrid protocols are feasible with different concurrency control techniques at different levels.

For arbitrary transaction forests that do not conform to a layered structure, the protocol becomes more complex, as it needs to deal with situations where some transactions access certain data only through some ADT object interface, whereas others access that data directly. The notion of retained locks allows us to generalize the key properties of the layered 2PL to such an architecture, but the need to remember low-level locks past the completion of subtransactions and the additional complexity of the lock conflict testing may incur noticeable overhead. So although the general object model 2PL can cope with arbitrary collections of business objects, a performance-conscious system design will probably strive to limit the depth of the transaction forests or may even choose to embed the transaction forests into a layered structure.

Throughout most of this chapter, we have assumed a state-independent notion of commutativity. As a special case, when all direct children of all transaction roots are *a priori* known to be commutative (or more generally, some slice of operations across all transaction trees has this property), it is sufficient to provide concurrency control measures for the subtransactions that correspond to the roots' children. In such a setting, which is known as *decomposed transactions with chained subtransactions*, the subtransactions can be treated as if they were independent transactions as far as concurrency control is concerned. Exploiting this special case is, however, highly dependent on the application design. In a similar vein, special-purpose application objects may even want to exploit state-dependent commutativity. To this end, we have presented the efficient escrow locking protocol that is specifically geared for objects of type Counter with possible constraints on the counter value. This protocol can be integrated into the general object model 2PL or the layered variant on a per-object basis.

Exercises

7.1 Investigate what kind of deadlocks can arise in a layered system with layered 2PL, and how they can be detected and eliminated. Under what conditions is it sufficient that each layer tests only for "local" deadlocks caused by lock waits of one layer only? Under what conditions is it necessary to consider lock waits of all layers "globally" to detect all deadlocks?

7.2 Discuss the pros and cons of the selective layered 2PL. As an example, consider query-, record-, and page-level operations along the lines of Figure 7.4. Does having all three levels involved in locking rather than only two result in performance advantages? If locking should be limited to two levels, are there arguments for choosing certain levels over others?

7.3 Trace the lock requests, conflict tests, lock acquisitions, and lock releases for the execution of the schedule in Figure 7.7 under the general object model 2PL with an SS2PL variant. How would the sample execution change if the Append operations were dropped and t_2's Decrement operation was replaced by an incr(a) operation that commutes with other increments? How would the execution change if t_2 started first and t_1 was spawned after all of t_2's operations but before the commit of t_2?

7.4 Develop pseudocode for a restricted version of the object model 2PL, where a generalized form of two-level schedules is considered, with some transactions bypassing the object level L_1 and invoking L_0 operations directly. This setting is, for example, of interest in the context of federated information systems, where global transactions access a variety of databases through a federation layer, using commutativity based 2PL for high-level operations exported by the underlying databases, but local transactions are still allowed to access a database directly. Such an architecture is sometimes called a federation of "autonomous" databases.

7.5 Apply the following hybrid protocols to the schedule of Figure 7.3 in a selective way so that only two levels are involved in concurrency control:

(a) the forward-oriented optimistic concurrency control (FOCC, see Chapter 4) at the page level and strong 2PL at the record level,

(b) the forward-oriented optimistic concurrency control at the page level and strong 2PL at the query level,

(c) the hybrid multiversion protocol ROMV (see Chapter 5) at the page level and strong 2PL at the record level,

(d) the hybrid multiversion protocol ROMV at the page level and strong 2PL at the query level.

Sketch the resulting executions.

7.6 Prove the correctness of the 2PL protocol for two-level schedules with deferred lock conflict testing based on return value commutativity sketched in Section 7.6.

7.7 Trace the intermediate states of the escrow data structure (i.e., the infimum and supremum values) for the counter object x in the example execution of Figure 7.9.

7.8 Consider two counter objects x and y, with initial values $x = 100$ and $y = 50$. Both counters have zero as a lower bound and no upper bound. Apply the escrow locking method to the following schedule of three transactions, one of which aborts:

$$decr_1(x, 60)incr_2(x, 20)incr_1(x, 10)decr_3(x, 50)decr_2(y, 60)incr_2(x, 20)a_2$$
$$decr_1(y, 10)c_1c_3$$

7.9 Escrow operations can be further generalized into *conditional* Increment and Decrement operations, where the conditions may be stronger than the actual resource quantity needed, taking the form:

```
conditional_decr (x, ε, Δ):
    if x ≥ ε then x := x - Δ fi;
```

and an analogous Conditional_Incr operation. For the Conditional_Decr, the value of the ϵ parameter would be larger than or equal to the operation's Δ value, and the situation would be the other way around for the Conditional_Incr operation. In addition to such operation-specific conditions, the global invariants for x.low and x.high must be satisfied at all times. Discuss the notions of general and return value commutativity for these generalized escrow operations.

Bibliographic Notes

Layered 2PL has probably been around implicitly for record-level locking in commercial database systems for a long time. However, it has not been made explicit, identifying its principles rather than viewing it as an implementation trick, before the work of Weikum and Schek (1984) (see also Weikum (1991)) and Moss et al. (1986). The technique of selectively layered locking has been discussed in the work of Weikum and Schek as well. The use of layered 2PL in the context of intra-transaction parallelism has been discussed by Weikum and Hasse (1993) as well as by Hasse and Weikum (1997). Since some commercial database systems can parallelize update statements, these systems must use similar protocols, probably with clever latching instead of short-term page locks.

The special case of chained subtransactions (i.e., two-level schedules where all L_1 operations generally commute) was coined "Sagas" by Garcia-Molina and Salem (1987) and "S-transactions" by Veijalainen (1990) and Veijalainen et al. (1992). The decomposition of application processes into chains of "unbundled" steps that can be treated as independent transactions as far as concurrency control is concerned has been used in high-performance application design (e.g., for reservation systems) for a long time, but it has not been systematically rationalized before the above publications.

The general (i.e., nonlayered) case of object model locking has first been studied by Muth et al. (1993). Similar approaches have been discussed by

Deacon et al. (1994) and Schek et al. (1991) for the more restricted setting of federated database systems with a global federation layer and a layer of local databases underneath, which can also be accessed directly, bypassing the federation layer.

Layered concurrency control protocols that combine locking on one level with an optimistic or multiversion protocol on another layer have already been discussed by Weikum (1991). An interesting hybrid protocol that exploits commutativity for update operations and versioning for read operations has been introduced by Jagadish et al. (1997), with the special restriction that all update operations are assumed to be commutative among themselves (but do not commute with read operations). Herlihy (1990) discusses optimistic versus pessimistic protocols for exploiting state-dependent commutativity on abstract data type objects. Escrow locking for counter objects has been developed by O'Neil (1986); the complexity of escrow deadlocks has been studied in O'Neil (1991), and generalizations of escrow locking have been proposed by Härder (1988) as well as Soparkar and Silberschatz (1990). Preliminary forms of escrow-style concurrency control can be traced back to Gawlick and Kinkade (1985) and Reuter (1982) and were already used in the database and transaction processing product IMS/VS Fast Path in the 1970s. The notion of ϵ serializability for bounding inconsistent reads has been developed by Wu et al. (1997) and fully formalized by Ramamritham and Pu (1995). Related approaches have been studied by Garcia-Molina and Wiederhold (1982) as well as Barbara and Garcia-Molina (1992).

CHAPTER EIGHT

Concurrency Control on Relational Databases

Knowledge without wisdom is a load of books on the back of an ass.
—*Japanese proverb*

Do not fear to be eccentric in opinion, for every opinion now accepted was once eccentric.
—*Bertrand Russell*

8.1 Goal and Overview

In this chapter we take a closer look at semantic approaches to concurrency control. While there are many ways to do so, we restrict the attention to a particular data model, the relational model, as this is the most widely used and, as will be seen, allows for a variety of interesting observations and developments related to transactional concurrency control. In terms of what has been discussed in the previous chapters, we here consider a specific object model, in which the objects are relations that are manipulated as a whole by (query or update) operations. This is in line with layered object models, where, for example, operations on relations or sets of tuples are implemented through record-level operations, which in turn give rise to page operations. The important observation we have already made is that semantic knowledge available at a higher abstraction level can often be exploited in such a way that histories or schedules that are unacceptable from a read/write point of view become acceptable when considered from that higher level, as syntactic conflicts essentially disappear when the semantics of operations is taken into account. This is the kind of observation we will elaborate here for relational databases.

Exploiting semantic knowledge

In the terminology of Chapter 6, we restrict ourselves to studying flat object schedules and histories—that is, two-level schedules with higher-level operations at level L_1 and read/write operations at level L_0 such that all L_1 operations are isolated *a priori*. The generalization to nonflat or even nonlayered schedules is straightforward, using the results of Chapters 6 and 7, and not specific to the subject of the current chapter. The higher-level operations we are particularly interested in are the SQL query and update operations. We will essentially look at three approaches that indicate the variety of studies that can be conducted in the context of a particular object model.

The first is predicate-oriented concurrency control. Here the idea is to derive granules that are subject to locking from the relational query or update expressions that trigger the data accesses. For example, the WHERE condition in a SELECT expression determines a set of tuples (in a descriptive manner by means of a logical formula) that can serve as a unit of locking. Predicate-oriented concurrency control has already been mentioned in Section 7.3 in connection with layered locking.

The second approach is based on a model for update transactions in relational databases that takes SQL commands as the basic building blocks for database operations. A theory of concurrency control can be established for transactions formed from such updates that exploits semantic equivalence in a variety of ways. For example, while there are classes of serializable histories that resemble the classes FSR and CSR we have seen in the read/write model, there is also a rich hierarchy of history classes in between, all of which can be recognized in polynomial time. Moreover, functional dependencies, as special calls of database consistency constraints, allow for a state-dependent notion of correctness, and goal orientation marks a radical departure from serializability that emphasizes a user's view on transaction cooperation.

Finally, we will look at a way of exploiting transaction program semantic information as it can be derived from SQL operations, by chopping transactions into semantically equivalent smaller pieces that can be scheduled independently.

Note that these three approaches may be understood as samples of what can be done to utilize semantic knowledge; a host of additional ways and options can be found in the literature. However, we also point out right away that, although such semantic approaches to concurrency control appear attractive and elegant from a theoretical point of view, up to now they are hardly of practical relevance. The reason is that an efficient implementation is difficult to achieve, which is not surprising, as it is generally recognized in computer science that semantics is more complex than syntax.

Also, to avoid misunderstandings, we emphasize once again that the state of the art for concurrency control in relational database systems is record-level locking, as discussed in Chapter 7 (in combination with index locking, to be discussed in Chapter 9). So the advanced approaches covered in the current chapter should be understood as additional, potential enhancements that provide specific options.

8.2 Predicate-Oriented Concurrency Control

In Section 7.3 we discussed layered locking and in particular layered 2PL as a way of applying locking-based concurrency control to layered schedules.

An important point there was the fact that lock modes can be attached to operations (such that locks are in conflict if the corresponding operations do not commute), and scheduling can be done in a level-by-level fashion. The semantically rich, high-level operations of the previous chapter, such as "Select Name from Persons where Age=30," already suggest that *predicates* that are employed to determine a certain set of objects can be associated with locks. We will look into this view in more detail next.

We are using the relational data model as our platform of explanation. We assume you are familiar with the relational data model and its standard query language SQL at an elementary level. For our purposes, it suffices to view a relational database as a set of relations. Each relation, also known as a *table*, has a schema (also known as *table header*), which consists of a name R and a set of attributes (also known as *columns*) $A_1, A_2, \ldots, A_n$ and which is written in the form $R = (A_1, \ldots, A_n)$. Associated with each attribute A_i, $1 \le i \le n$ is a finite domain dom(A_i), so that a concrete relation (or an *instance* of a relation schema) can be considered as a set $r \subseteq$ dom$(A_1) \times \ldots \times$ dom(A_n) whose elements are called *tuples*. Additionally, a relation schema may comprise a set of *integrity constraints* such as *functional* or *key dependencies*; in the presence of dependencies, a relation that is to be considered *valid* or *consistent* has to observe the constraints.

Relational databases

When database relations are subject to transactional access, there are at least two extremes with respect to locking: entire relations and individual tuples. When a transaction locks an entire relation, it prevents other transactions from simultaneously accessing any subset of tuples from that relation; hence there will in general be unnecessary delays. Conversely, if a transaction locks each tuple that it touches individually, a large number of locks may result, which can create a lock administration problem. We postpone a discussion of this trade-off to Chapter 10, where we will introduce a pragmatic solution known as *multiple granularity locking*. Unfortunately, locks on individual tuples are also problematic from a correctness viewpoint, as the following example shows.

Transactions on relations

EXAMPLE 8.1

Consider a relation schema Emp holding employee information, with attributes Name, Department, Position, and Salary. The following is a sample relation over this schema:

Emp	Name	Department	Position	Salary
	Jones	Service	Clerk	20000
	Meier	Service	Clerk	22000
	Paulus	Service	Manager	42000
	Smyth	Toys	Cashier	25000
	Brown	Sales	Clerk	28000
	Albert	Sales	Manager	38000

Now consider a transaction for reorganizing a department that consists of the following steps: (a) fire the manager of the service department, (b) hire a new manager for this department, (c) move all employees of the service department (other than the new manager) to the sales department, (d) hire someone new for the service department to do the work under the supervision of the new manager. These steps translate into the following SQL statements:

(a) Delete the former manager (strictly speaking, all former managers) of the service department:

```
DELETE FROM Emp
WHERE Department = 'Service'
AND Position = 'Manager'
```

This removes the employee named Paulus from the database.

(b) Insert a new manager of the service department named Smith with a salary of $40,000:

```
INSERT INTO Emp
VALUES ('Smith', 'Service', 'Manager', 40000)
```

(c) Move all employees who are not managers from the service to the sales department:

```
UPDATE Emp
SET Department = 'Sales'
WHERE Department = 'Service'
AND Position <> 'Manager'
```

(d) Insert a new employee named Stone into the service department with a salary of $13,000:

```
INSERT INTO Emp
VALUES ('Stone', 'Service', 'Clerk', 13000)
```

Now consider a second transaction that consists of a query asking for name, position, and salary of all employees of the sales department. In SQL this is expressed as follows:

```
SELECT Name, Position, Salary
FROM Emp
WHERE Department = 'Service'
```

The issue that arises with this retrieval transaction is whether it can be interleaved with the four-step update transaction and if so, at which points the interleaving can be admitted. If the retrieval transaction ran right after step (a), the deletion of the old manager, it would see a department without a manager.

If it ran between steps (b) and (c), it would see the department with a new manager and the old staff. Finally, if it ran between (c) and (d), it would see a department with the new manager and no clerks for doing the actual work. So all conceivable interleavings are illegal in that they lead to an inconsistent view of the data.

The next question is whether standard locking protocols are good enough to prevent these illegal interleavings. Assume that both transactions lock exactly the tuples (or underlying stored records) of the Emp table that they are actually manipulating. So step (a), the deletion of the old manager Paulus, locks the tuple with name Paulus, and nothing else. If the retrieval transaction ran at this point, there would be no tuple left for the query to "trip" on a lock conflict. The query could not lock the tuple for the new manager Smith either, for this tuple does not yet exist in the database. Such tuples that have been deleted or are not yet existing but will be inserted in the future appear as "phantoms" to the query: they have latent relevance for the query's outcome but cannot be seen by the query, hence are not locked. For this analogy the problem situation discussed here is generally referred to as a *phantom problem*. A similar effect would occur if the retrieval transaction ran between steps (c) and (d), as the query could no longer lock the now "invisible" former clerks of the service department.

Phantom problem

This discussion seems to suggest that in the presence of INSERT or DELETE statements transactions need to lock entire tables (i.e., the Emp in the example), and such very coarse-grained locking would seem to be necessary even for UPDATE statements as they implicitly insert or delete tuples from the set of tuples that satisfy a given search predicate. Table locking would indeed be a feasible solution to the above problem, but it would come at the very high price of restricting concurrency to at most one active transaction on the same table at every point of time. Fortunately, there is a much better alternative to table locking that eliminates the phantom problem, too. It is based on the observation that relation accesses are commonly expressed through predicates such as those occurring in the WHERE clause of an SQL SELECT, UPDATE, or DELETE statement. So rather than locking individual tuples in a relation, a lock request can refer to a predicate that specifies, in a descriptive way and independently of the current contents of tables, a subset of the database to be locked. In logic, such predicates that capture the time-invariant meaning of a specification are also called *intensional*, as opposed to *extensional*, which refers to the current extension of a database.

Predicate locking

To be more precise, we consider predicates like those used in the above example, which are either *simple* conditions of the form

attribute_name comparison_operator value

for example,

Department = 'Sales'

or *conjunctions* of simple conditions, such as

$$\text{Department} = \text{'Service'} \land \text{Position} = \text{'Manager'}$$

Clearly, SQL allows more complex conditions to be expressed, but conjunctions of simple conditions will be sufficient for our purposes.

Conditions   In general, let $R = (A_1, \ldots, A_n)$ be a relation schema, and let C be a set of conditions over the attributes of R such that each condition in C is of the form "$A_i = a$" or "$A_i \neq a$," where $1 \leq i \leq n$ and a is a value from $\text{dom}(A_i)$. It is obvious what it means for a tuple over R to *satisfy* a condition or a set of conditions. For simplicity, we will only consider sets of conditions that are satisfiable (i.e., do not contain conditions that are mutually exclusive).

A set C of conditions over a given attribute set specifies a set $H(C)$ of tuples in a straightforward manner:

$$H(C) = \{\mu \in \text{dom}(A_1) \times \ldots \times \text{dom}(A_n) \mid \mu \text{ satisfies C}\}$$

We use the notation $H(C)$ since such a set is sometimes called a *hyperplane* (in a multidimensional "vector space" generated by the n attributes) in the literature.

Note that, given a relation r over $R = (A_1, \ldots, A_n)$ and a condition C over the attributes of R, it may happen that

- $r \subseteq H(C)$, or
- $H(C) \subseteq r$, or
- $R \cap H(C) = \emptyset$, or just
- $R \cap H(C) \neq \emptyset$.

Thus, a hyperplane may specify a superset or a subset of the tuples in a given relation, it may have a nonempty intersection with the relation, or it may be disjoint from the relation. Notice that this resembles the situation we have encountered in the previous example, where we were tempted to lock tuples that either moved out of the database (through a DELETE or an UPDATE) or were newly introduced into the database (through an INSERT or an UPDATE).

Compatibility   We can now imagine that an update or retrieval operation of transaction t
of predicate   comes with (1) a predicate or condition C_t specifying the tuples to be locked,
locks   and (2) a lock mode m_t stating whether the elements of $H(C_t)$ are to be locked in shared or exclusive mode (i.e., whether they are to be read or written). Next, two lock requests on behalf of transactions t and t' with associated predicates C_t and $C_{t'}$ as well as lock modes m_t and $m_{t'}$ are *compatible* if

- $t = t'$, or
- both m_t and $m_{t'}$ are read (shared) mode, or
- $H(C_t) \cap H(C_{t'}) = \emptyset$ (i.e., no tuple satisfies both conditions).

EXAMPLE 8.2

Returning to Example 8.1, consider the following predicates for the update transaction:

C_a: Department = 'Service' $\wedge$ Position = 'Manager'

C_b: Name = 'Smith' $\wedge$ Department = 'Service' $\wedge$ Position = 'Manager' $\wedge$ Salary = 40000

C_c: Department = 'Service' $\wedge$ Position $\neq$ 'Manager'

C_c': Department = 'Sales' $\wedge$ Position $\neq$ 'Manager'

C_d: Name = 'Stone' $\wedge$ Department = 'Service' $\wedge$ Position = 'Clerk' $\wedge$ Salary = 13000

Note that the UPDATE statement for step (c) has two conditions associated with it, one referring to the tuples that are to be modified and one that characterizes the result of the modification. These two conditions need to be locked separately; so each of them sets a predicate lock. This is necessary because such an UPDATE statement affects queries for both the service department and the sales department. The retrieval transaction, on the other hand, needs to acquire a lock on the condition

C_q: Department = 'Service'

In addition, consider another retrieval transaction that reads all employees of the sales department and thus needs a lock on

C_p: Department = 'Sales'

It is straightforward to verify that the following holds:

1. $H(C_a) \cap H(C_q) \neq \emptyset, H(C_b) \cap H(C_q) \neq \emptyset, H(C_c) \cap H(C_q) \neq \emptyset, H(C_d) \cap H(C_q) \neq \emptyset$
2. $H(C_c') \cap H(C_q) = \emptyset$
3. $H(C_a) \cap H(C_q) = H(C_b) \cap H(C_p) == H(C_c) \cap H(C_p) = H(C_d) \cap H(C_p) = \emptyset$
4. $H(C_c') \cap H(C_p) \neq \emptyset$

Thus, the SELECT operation for the sales department, which is based on C_p and which uses a lock in shared mode, would be compatible with the UPDATE statements of steps (a), (b), and (d), and also with the first one of the two predicate locks for step (c), but it would conflict with the second lock for step (c). The SELECT operation for the service department, based on C_q, on the other hand, is in conflict with all of the locks set by the four update steps except the lock for C_c' set by step (c).

A scheduler based on predicate locking has to keep track of the predicates *Scheduling* for which locks have already been granted. When a new lock request arrives, the scheduler performs a compatibility test and grants the lock only if the test shows no conflict (i.e., only disjoint predicates are locked in conflicting mode). Assuming SS2PL, when a transaction commits, its predicate locks are released, and the scheduler should now wake up blocked transactions that may be able to continue. Note, however, that with predicate locks, a transaction that has requested a lock for condition C may be blocked by two different predicates, say, P and Q, which could themselves be disjoint. Thus, when one of these two predicate locks, say, the one for P, is released, all the scheduler can do is to retry the lock request for C, but this transaction would still have to wait until the lock Q is released, too. This brief consideration already indicates that the implementation of lock waiting queues and the management of transaction threads in a data server are more complex with predicate locking than for locks on *discrete* (individually named) data items.

Although conceptually elegant, predicate locking is not exactly the method of choice in practical systems. This is mostly for the reason that testing whether two predicates are compatible, such as whether $H(C_t) \cap H(C_{t'}) = \emptyset$ holds for given C_t and $C_{t'}$, amounts to testing a Boolean formula for satisfiability, which is known to be an NP complete problem. In other words, predicate locking is prohibitively expensive in general. However, very limited special cases are of practical interest, and we will reconsider a very simple form of predicate-oriented locks in Chapter 9 on concurrency control for index structures.

Precision locking   A variant of predicate locking called *precision locking* avoids the satisfiability test, but still is not a lightweight protocol. The scheduler grants all lock requests right away, without testing predicates for compatibility. However, when a transaction reads or writes a tuple, this tuple is tested for compatibility with all other outstanding predicates of other transactions. A tuple read or write is rejected if the tuple in question intersects the hyperplane of another transaction's predicate and the corresponding lock modes conflict.

So precision locking tests discrete (or, in logic terminology, extensional) writes against predicate-oriented (intensional) reads; there are no predicates associated with write operations. Therefore, to detect conflicts between predicate-oriented UPDATE statements, such a statement needs to be handled as a predicate-oriented read (for the statement's retrieval part) followed by a discrete write of the qualifying tuples. For example, the predicate conflict between the two operations

```
DELETE FROM Emp
WHERE Department = 'Toys' And Position = 'Clerk'
```

and

```
INSERT INTO Emp VALUES
('Johnson', 'Toys', 'Clerk', 19000)
```

would be detected by conceptually splitting the DELETE statement into a query with the search condition Department = 'Toys' $\wedge$ Position = 'Clerk' and a sequence of simple, record-oriented deletions for the tuples in the query result. The inserted tuple for the new employee "Johnson" would satisfy the query's predicate, and a conflict would be signaled.

8.3 **Relational Update Transactions**

In this section we take a different look at relational concurrency control, where Insert, Update, and Delete operations are taken as the constituents of flat object model transactions. The theory presented here has been investigated for Update operations only; we leave it as an exercise to extend it in such a way that queries are covered as well (see Exercise 8.6). So the transactions to be considered next will consist of Update operations of the form shown earlier in Example 8.1; that is, they will be sequences of Insert, Delete, and Modify (formerly called Update) operations, hence the name *IDM transaction model*.

8.3.1 **Syntax and Semantics**

We continue to use the conditions that were introduced in the previous section for describing Update operations and introduce a simple language for expressing updates next. Let R be a relation schema:

Relational Update operations

1. An *insertion* is an expression of the form $i_R(C)$, where the conditions in C specify a complete tuple over R. This corresponds to the SQL statement

    INSERT INTO R VALUES C

2. A *deletion* is an expression of the form $d_R(C)$, where C is a set of conditions over R. In SQL we would write

    DELETE FROM R WHERE C

3. A *modification* is an expression of the form $m_R(C_1; C_2)$, where C_1 and C_2 are sets of conditions over R, and for each attribute A of R either $C_1|_A = C_2|_A$ or "$A = a$" $\in C_2$ holds; the equalities occurring in C_2 but not in C_1 state how the tuples in $H(C_1)$ are modified. In SQL, we would write

    UPDATE R SET C2 WHERE C1

In the following, an *Update operation* is an insertion, a deletion, or a modification.

The semantics of the Update operations, called their *effect*, should intuitively be the following. Let r be a relation (set of tuples) over schema R:

1. The *effect* of $i_R(C)$ is

$$\text{eff}[i_R(C)](r) := r \cup \{C\}$$

2. The *effect* of $d_R(C)$ is

$$\text{eff}[d_R(C)](r) := r - H(C)$$

3. The *effect* of $m_R(C_1; C_2)$ is

$$\text{eff}[m_R(C_1; C_2)](r) := (r - H(C_1)) \cup \{m_R(C_1; C_2)(\mu) \mid \mu \in H(C_1) \cap r\}$$

Here, the modified version $m_R(C_1; C_2)(\mu_1)$ of a tuple $\mu_1 \in H(C_1)$ under $m_R(C_1; C_2)$ is the tuple $\mu_2 \in H(C_2)$ such that

$$\mu_2(A) = \begin{cases} \mu_1(A) & \text{if } C_1|_A = C_2|_A \\ a & \text{if } "A = a" \in C_2 \end{cases}$$

for each $A \in X$, where $\mu_i(A)$, $i = 1, 2$, stands for the A component of tuple μ_i.

Thus, as mentioned above, an Insert operation inserts a completely specified new tuple. A Delete operation deletes all tuples satisfying a given condition, and a Modify operation takes out tuples to be modified and reinserts their modified versions.

With these preparations, we can now formally define the IDM relational transaction model:

IDM transactions

DEFINITION 8.1   *IDM Transaction*

An *IDM transaction* over a database schema D is a finite sequence of Update operations over D.

If $t = u_1 \ldots u_m$ is an IDM transaction over a given database, the *effect* of t, written $\text{eff}(t)$, is defined as

$$\text{eff}(t) := \text{eff}[u_1] \circ \text{eff}[u_2] \circ \ldots \circ \text{eff}[u_m]$$

where $\circ$ denotes function composition.

This definition of (the semantics of) a transaction immediately leads to a notion of transaction equivalence:

DEFINITION 8.2 *Transaction Equivalence*

Two IDM transactions t and t' over the same database schema are *equivalent*, written $t \approx t'$, if $\text{eff}(t) = \text{eff}(t')$, i.e., if t and t' have the same effect.

Equivalence of IDM transactions

It has been shown in the literature (see the Bibliographic Notes for this chapter) that equivalence of IDM transactions is "easy" to test, that is, for given IDM transactions t and t' it can be decided in polynomial time whether $t \approx t'$. There are two ways to exhibit a constructive proof of this statement: one is through the specification of a sound and complete axiomatization of equivalence; the other is through a graphical illustration of transaction effects. We will not look into details of any of these, but concentrate on a subset of the set of axioms that cover update commutativity.

For the exposition that follows, we mention that the effects of Update operations over distinct relations can be shown to be independent of each other, so that it suffices to consider transactions over a single relation in what follows. Most of the time, we even look at the simplest schema possible, which has a single attribute only. Thus, when we write $i(3)$, $d(2)$, or $m(1; 4)$, we mean that value 3 is inserted into, 2 is deleted from, and 1 is modified to 4 in the single-attribute relation at hand.

8.3.2 **Commutativity and Simplification Rules**

When performing Update operations on a relational database, it may or may not matter in which order a certain sequence of operations is applied. For example, two Insert operations commute if they refer to distinct tuples. In general, the following *commutativity rules* for IDM transactions hold, with C_1, C_2, C_3, and C_4 being sets of conditions that describe pairwise disjoint hyperplanes:

Commutativity rules

1. $i(C_1)i(C_2) \approx i(C_2)i(C_1)$
2. $d(C_1)d(C_2) \approx d(C_2)d(C_1)$
3. $d(C_1)i(C_2) \approx i(C_2)d(C_1)$ if $C_1 \neq C_2$
4. $m(C_1; C_2)m(C_3; C_4) \approx m(C_3; C_4)m(C_1; C_2)$ if $C_3 \neq C_1, C_2$ and $C_1 \neq C_4$
5. $m(C_1; C_2)i(C_3) \approx i(C_3)m(C_1; C_2)$ if $C_1 \neq C_3$
6. $m(C_1; C_2)d(C_3) \approx d(C_3)m(C_1; C_2)$ if $C_3 \neq C_1, C_2$

Formally, these rules generate a relation "$\leftrightarrow$" on the set of all transactions (for a fixed database), whose reflexive and transitive hull we denote by $\stackrel{*}{\leftrightarrow}$; thus,

$t_1 \overset{*}{\leftrightarrow} t_2$ means that the equivalence of t_1 and t_2 can be proved using only the commutativity rules. Notice that $t_1 \overset{*}{\leftrightarrow} t_2$ is sufficient for $t_1 \approx t_2$, but not necessary.

Simplification rules   Another group of axioms needed for a complete characterization of equivalence consists of *simplification rules*, which are to be applied from left to right; as before, let C_1, C_2, and C_3 be sets of conditions describing pairwise disjoint hyperplanes:

1. $i(C_1)i(C_1) \Longrightarrow i(C_1)$
2. $d(C_1)d(C_1) \Longrightarrow d(C_1)$
3. $i(C_1)d(C_1) \Longrightarrow d(C_1)$
4. $d(C_1)i(C_1) \Longrightarrow i(C_1)$
5. $m(C_1; C_1) \Longrightarrow \epsilon$
6. $m(C_1; C_2)i(C_2) \Longrightarrow d(C_1)i(C_2)$
7. $i(C_1)m(C_1; C_2) \Longrightarrow m(C_1; C_2)i(C_2)$
8. $m(C_1; C_2)d(C_1) \Longrightarrow m(C_1; C_2)$
9. $m(C_1; C_2)d(C_2) \Longrightarrow d(C_1)d(C_2)$
10. $d(C_1)m(C_1; C_2) \Longrightarrow d(C_1)$
11. $m(C_1; C_2)m(C_1; C_3) \Longrightarrow m(C_1; C_2)$ $(C_1 \neq C_2)$
12. $m(C_1; C_2)m(C_2; C_3) \Longrightarrow m(C_1; C_3)m(C_2; C_3)$

We emphasize again that the commutativity rules as well as the simplification rules alone are not enough for a complete axiomatization of transaction equivalence; however, for our purposes in this chapter these will suffice.

8.3.3 Histories and Final State Serializability

IDM histories   We are now ready to define a straightforward notion of histories for IDM transactions. Let $T = \{t_1, \ldots, t_n\}$ be a given set of IDM transactions. Then a history s for T contains all operations from each $t \in T$ in a way that preserves their original order. A history is *serial* if all transactions appear strictly one after the other. We could also consider termination operations here, but for simplicity just assume that all transactions eventually commit.

EXAMPLE 8.3

Let $T = \{t_1, t_2\}$ with $t_1 = d(3)m(1; 2)m(3; 4)$ and $t_2 = d(3)m(2; 3)$. Then

$$s = d_2(3)d_1(3)m_1(1; 2)m_2(2; 3)m_1(3; 4)$$

is a history for T.

Notice that, in a static situation, we could even imagine that a history is optimized before it gets processed. For example, we could obviously apply some simplification rules to s in order to obtain the following history:

$$s' = d(3)m(1;4)m(2;4)m(3;4)$$

We have $\text{eff}(s) = \text{eff}(s')$; however, from the latter history we can no longer tell from which transaction an update stems.

We can define a notion of serializability for IDM transactions that is analogous to final state serializability, which we defined earlier for read/write page model transactions. Because of the similarity between the two notions, we can even keep the same name:

DEFINITION 8.3 *Final State Serializability*

IDM final state serializability

A history s for a set $T = \{t_1, \ldots, t_n\}$ of IDM transactions is *final state serializable* if $s \approx s'$ for some serial history s' for T.

Let FSR_{IDM} (or $\text{FSR}_{IDM}(T)$) denote the class of all final state serializable histories (for T).

Notice that this notion is now defined via the semantics of a history considered as an IDM transaction, where the semantics is captured in the effects of the updates that are present.

EXAMPLE 8.4

Consider again $t_1 = d(3)m(1;2)m(3;4)$, $t_2 = d(3)m(2;3)$, and

$$s = d_2(3)d_1(3)m_1(1;2)m_2(2;3)m_1(3;4)$$

as in the previous example. The final effect of s is that value 3 is deleted, and 1 and 2 get modified to 4 (provided these values are present). We now find that $s \not\approx t_1 t_2$, since the latter serial history would first delete 3, then modify 1 and 2 to 3, and leave everything else unchanged. Next, we also find $s \not\approx t_2 t_1$, since now the serial history would delete 2 and 3, then modify 1 to 2. Thus, $s \notin \text{FSR}_{IDM}$.

According to common understanding, s would hence not be considered acceptable. However, the IDM model can allow for a more relaxed approach if transaction simplification is applied. Indeed, we can optimize the first transaction to omit the last update, which is redundant since value 3 is already deleted by the first update (provided it occurs in the current state). In other words, $t_1 \approx t_1' = d(3)m(1;2)$. If the same update is removed from *s*, we find for the resulting history *s'*:

$$s' = d_2(3)d_1(3)m_1(1;2)m_2(2;3) \approx t_1 t_2$$

Thus, *s'* is acceptable as an execution sequence for *T*. However, *s'* is no longer a history in the strict sense, since not all updates from the given transactions are still there; *s'* is only *equivalent* to some serial history for *T* and can therefore be considered a member of FSR*IDM*.

In general, we can eventually improve histories by removing redundant updates or by simplifying individual transactions and hence the history itself; as Example 8.4 indicates, this can make the difference between serializability and nonserializability.

A second generalization of the notion of history derives from another form of optimization, now applied to the updates of several *distinct* transactions occurring in a history. If we consider history *s'* from the previous example as an individual transaction, we find that

$$s' \approx s'' = d(3)m(1;3)m(2;3)$$

s'' is another simplification of *s'* in terms of the tuple operations to be executed, although the updates remaining in *s''* can no longer be directly associated with t_1 and t_2. We will not consider this form of generalization further here, but we mention that it can easily be exploited in the context of a concurrency control device that does some preprocessing on the (prefix of a) history that it is about to schedule.

We now briefly look into the question of how to test a given history for membership in class FSR*IDM*. As for read/write transactions, we can obviously do this for given *s* and $T = \{t_1, \ldots, t_n\}$ by checking for each permutation ρ of $\{1, \ldots, n\}$ whether $s \approx t_{\rho(1)} \ldots t_{\rho(n)}$. Again, it can be verified that most likely there is no significantly simpler test:

THEOREM 8.1

The problem of testing whether a given history is in FSR*IDM* is NP complete.

We are not giving the proof of this theorem in full detail here, but just mention two things about it. First, testing whether a given history *s* is in NP is as straightforward as it was for read/write transactions: just guess a permutation of the transactions and test whether *s* is equivalent to it. The latter can be done in polynomial time by looking at the corresponding transition specifications. Second, to show that the problem is indeed NP complete, the problem of testing whether a directed graph contains a Hamiltonian cycle can be reduced to it. To this end, with a given directed graph *G* with *n* nodes, a set of $n + 1$ IDM transactions and a history s can be associated in such a way that G has a cycle containing each node exactly once iff $s \in \text{FSR}_{IDM}$. Details of this reduction can be found in the literature.

This result is not surprising, since it is unreasonable to expect that testing membership in FSR_{IDM} becomes any easier when semantic information on transactions is available. On the other hand, it does not become any harder than in the read/write setting either, and as before it motivates looking for restrictions of the correctness notion that are decidable in polynomial time.

8.3.4 Conflict Serializability

A near-at-hand restriction of final state serializability results from establishing a suitable notion of conflict for IDM transactions; this is now easy (and fully in line with what we have done in the page model) using the commutativity rules shown earlier:

DEFINITION 8.4   *Conflict Serializability*

A history s for a set T of n transactions is *conflict serializable* if

$$s \stackrel{*}{\leftrightarrow} t_{\rho(1)} \ldots t_{\rho(n)}$$

for some permutation ρ of T, i.e., if the equivalence of s to a serial history can be proven using the commutativity rules alone.

Let CSR_{IDM} denote the class of all conflict-serializable histories.

IDM conflict serializability

Thus, for conflict serializability, we only take commutativity rules into account (in a similar way that we did for page model transactions in Chapter 3), and nothing else. In particular, the simplification rules listed earlier (or other rules that would contribute to an axiomatization of equivalence) are not considered for the moment.

As we could do for read/write transactions, we can test membership of a given history in class CSR_{IDM} by testing a suitably defined *conflict graph* that shows violations of commutativity rules through cycles:

DEFINITION 8.5   *Conflict Graph*

Let T be a set of IDM transactions and s a history for T. The *conflict graph* $G(s) = (T, E)$ of s is defined by

$$(t_i, t_j) \in E :\Longleftrightarrow (\exists\, t_i, t_j \in V, j \neq i)(\exists\, u \in t_i)(\exists\, u' \in t_j)$$
$$(u <_s u' \text{ and } uu' \not\approx u'u).$$

IDM conflict graph

In words, the conflict graph of a given history has the transactions as nodes and contains an edge of the form (t, t') between two transactions t and t' if an update from t does not commute with a subsequent update from t'.

EXAMPLE 8.5

Consider $s = d_1(0)m_1(0; 1)m_2(1; 2)m_1(2; 3)$. Then $G(s) = (V, E)$, where $V = \{t_1, t_2\}$ has exactly one cycle that results from the fact that $m_2(1; 2)$ commutes neither with its left nor with its right neighbor.

Now we have

THEOREM 8.2

Let s be a history for a set T of transactions. Then $s \in \mathrm{CSR}_{IDM}$ iff $G(s)$ is acyclic.

Proof

Let $G(s)$ be acyclic. We show by induction on $|T|$ that $s \overset{*}{\leftrightarrow} s'$ holds for a serial history s' for T. Clearly, the claim is trivial for $|T| = 1$. Let it be valid for all sets of less than n transactions, and consider a set T such that $|T| = n$; let s be a history for T such that $G(s)$ is acyclic. Then there exists a node $t \in V$ with out-degree 0 (i.e., that has no outgoing edge). For each pair (u, v) of updates such that $u \in t$, $v \notin t$, and $u <_s v$ it follows that u and v commute. Therefore, $s \overset{*}{\leftrightarrow} s_0 t$, where $s_0 = \pi_{T-\{t\}}(s)$. Since $G(s_0)$ is a subgraph of $G(s)$, $G(s_0)$ is again acyclic. Using the induction hypothesis, we may thus conclude that $s_0 \overset{*}{\leftrightarrow} s_1$, where s_1 is a serial history for $T - \{t\}$. Hence $s \overset{*}{\leftrightarrow} s_1 t$, that is, $s \in \mathrm{CSR}_{IDM}$.

Conversely, let s be a history for T such that $G(s) = (V, E)$ has a cycle, and suppose that $s \in \mathrm{CSR}_{IDM}$. The latter implies that there is a serial history s' for T such that $s \overset{*}{\leftrightarrow} s'$. Since $G(s)$ is cyclic, s' cannot contain the transactions from T in topological order. Thus, there exist transactions $t_i, t_j \in V$ for which $s = \ldots t_i \ldots t_j \ldots$, but $(t_j, t_i) \in E$. In addition, there exist Update operations $u_j \in t_j$ and $u_i \in t_i$ such that $s = \ldots u_j \ldots u_i \ldots$ and $u_j u_i \not\approx u_i u_j$. This implies that the equivalence of s' and s cannot be shown by using only the commutativity rules, a contradiction.

We conclude this subsection by mentioning that, not surprisingly,

$$\mathrm{CSR}_{IDM} \subset \mathrm{FSR}_{IDM}$$

By definition, each conflict-serializable history is final state serializable. Moreover, the inclusion is strict due to the fact that sometimes conflicts between pairs of updates from distinct transactions are compensated by their context.

EXAMPLE 8.6

Let $s = m_2(1; 2)m_1(2; 3)m_2(3; 2)$. Here $G(s)$ is cyclic, so $s \notin \text{CSR}_{IDM}$. On the other hand, $s \approx m_1(2; 3)m_2(1; 2)m_2(3; 2)$, and hence $s \in \text{FSR}_{IDM}$.

We also mention that a straightforward scheduling protocol for dynamically generating the class CSR_{IDM} of conflict-serializable IDM histories is obtained by adapting the protocol of serialization graph testing (SGT) appropriately.

8.3.5 Extended Conflict Serializability

So far we have established a direct analogy to the page model of transactions, namely, "global" (final state) serializability with an NP complete decision problem, and "local" (conflict based) serializability, where the latter is (again) a strong restriction of the former. A natural question to ask now is whether there is something in between. As will be seen next, it is here where the full power of IDM concurrency control arises.

Recall that conflict serializability only takes local conflicts into account, whereas final state serializability looks at the entire context at once. An intermediate approach would therefore be to look at some portion of the context only, and we will show next that in the IDM model of transactions this can be done in various ways.

We will first look at an approach that seems particularly amenable to dynamic scheduling, as the idea is to look at conflicts between single updates u from one transaction and prefixes of other transactions occurring in a given history prior to u. As for ordinary conflicts, a notion of serializability can be defined by means of an appropriately chosen graph:

DEFINITION 8.6 *Extended Conflict Graph and Serializability*

Let s be a history for a set $T = \{t_1, \dots, t_n\}$ of transactions.

1. The *extended conflict graph* $EG(s) = (T, E)$ of s is defined as follows:

$$(t_i, t_j) \in E :\Longleftrightarrow (\exists\, u \in t_j)\, s = s'us'' \text{ and } \pi_{\{t_i\}}(s')u \not\approx u\pi_{\{t_i\}}(s')$$

(Here $\pi_{\{t_i\}}(s')$ denotes the projection of s' onto $\{t_i\}$.)

2. s is *extended conflict serializable* if $EG(s)$ is acyclic.

Let ECSR_{IDM} denote the class of all extended conflict-serializable histories.

Extended IDM conflict graph

Thus, while ordinary conflict serializability looks at pairs of updates from distinct transactions only and whether they commute, extended conflict serializability looks at a transaction prefix as well as an update from another transaction and tests whether they commute. Now the effect of the entire prefix is taken into account, no longer just that of an arbitrary update within that prefix. As can be seen, this is a relaxation of conflict serializability, since inside a prefix there may exist updates that compensate or even completely reset the effect of others.

EXAMPLE 8.7

Let s be as in Example 8.5. Then $s \in \text{ECSR}_{IDM}$, since

$$s \approx m_2(1; 2)d_1(0)m_1(0; 1)m_1(2; 3) = t_2 t_1$$

EXAMPLE 8.8

Consider $s = m_1(0; 1)m_2(1; 2)m_1(2; 3)d_1(1)d_1(3)$. Then $s \notin \text{ECSR}_{IDM}$, but $s \in \text{FSR}_{IDM}$.

Notice that an application of the commutativity rules alone to pairs of updates is not sufficient for testing whether a prefix projection of a history s of the form $\pi_{\{t_i\}}(s')$ commutes with a subsequent update $u \in t_j$, since this projection and update u might commute even if u does *not* commute with each individual update in the projection. Thus, we exploit the transaction's semantics, and we can easily test whether given $\pi_{\{t_i\}}(s')$ and u commute by looking at the corresponding transition specifications.

Since the extended conflict graph of a given history can also be constructed and tested for acyclicity in polynomial time, membership in class ECSR_{IDM} is again efficiently decidable.

THEOREM 8.3

For every database schema, $\text{CSR}_{IDM} \subset \text{ECSR}_{IDM} \subset \text{FSR}_{IDM}$.

Proof

Clearly, $\text{CSR}_{IDM} \subseteq \text{ECSR}_{IDM}$, since the extended conflict graph of a given history s is acyclic if the same holds for the ordinary conflict graph of s. We next show by induction on $|T|$ that $\text{ECSR}_{IDM} \subseteq \text{FSR}_{IDM}$ for every T: the claim trivially holds for $|T| = 1$. Now suppose it holds for every T such that $|T| < n$. Let T be a set of transactions such that $|T| = n$, and let s be a history for T such that $s \in \text{ECSR}_{IDM}$. Since, by assumption, $EG(s)$ is acyclic, there exists a node t in EG with out-degree 0. Then s can be modified in such a way that all updates from t occur at the end: Let u be the first update from t occurring in s. Since t has no outgoing edge, u can be moved to the right in s by using the commutativity rules, until it hits the second update, say, u' from t. If u' is followed by an update v from another transaction, the pair uu' and v can be exchanged (since t has out-degree 0 and is hence not in conflict with a subsequent transaction). In this way, we can "collect" all updates from t and move them to the end of s. As a result, we obtain a history

$$s' = \pi_{T-\{t\}}(s)t$$

for which $s' \approx s$ holds. Since $\pi_{T-\{t\}}(s)$ has less than n transactions and $EG(\pi_{T-\{t\}}(s))$ is acyclic, our induction hypothesis applies; hence $s \in \text{FSR}_{IDM}$.

We have already seen in examples that the two inclusions are strict.

As for class CSR_{IDM}, a protocol that can generate histories in class ECSR_{IDM} can be based on SGT scheduling, since a decision on conflicts is made based on the knowledge that a scheduler already has about prefixes of transactions as well as on individual operations.

8.3.6 Serializability in the Presence of Functional Dependencies

We next present a further possibility for exploiting semantic information to enrich existing notions of serializability. The major difference from what we have done so far in this chapter will be that we are now going to take state information into account. In particular, we will assume that for each relational database on which we run transactions, there will not only be relations and attributes, but also *functional dependencies* (FDs) as semantic integrity constraints. For a relation R with attributes $A_1, \ldots, A_n$ a functional dependency is a logical invariant of the form

$$A_{i_1} \ldots A_{i_k} \to A_j \ (k \leq n)$$

with the meaning that for all tuples t, t' in relation R, either present or conceivable, the logical condition

$$t.A_{i_1} = t'.A_{i_1} \wedge \ldots \wedge t.A_{i_k} = t'.A_{i_k} \Rightarrow t.A_j = t'.A_j$$

must be true. In words, if two tuples have the same value for the attributes on the left side of an FD, they must have the same value for the attribute on the right as well. Primary key constraints are obviously a special case, but FDs can capture a wider class of integrity constraints.

Intuitively, when testing a given history for serializability, we can then restrict our attention to the effect of the history on states that satisfy the FDs. In other words, a history s is no longer required to have the same effect as a serial one for the same transactions on *every* state, but only on those respecting the FDs.

Serializability with regard to FDs

This intuition could suggest the following definition: Let R be a relation schema with attributes X and a set F of FDs over X. A history s for a set T of transactions over R is *serializable with regard to F* if there exists a serial history s' for T such that $\text{eff}(s)(r) = \text{eff}(s')(r)$ holds for every relation r over schema R that satisfies F. Here, $\text{eff}(s)(r)$ denotes the effect of s on r, analogously for s'.

Unfortunately, it can be shown that the class of histories that is serializable with respect to a given set F of FDs coincides with FSR_{IDM} (for each F), so that an alternative definition of serializability is required for appropriately exploiting the additional semantic information provided by FDs. The following example motivates how such a definition can be obtained:

EXAMPLE 8.9

Motivating example

Consider a relation schema R with two attributes A and B as well as an FD $A \to B$, and let the following history s be given (for two transactions t_1 and t_2 over R):

$$s = m_1(A=0, B=0; A=0, B=2)m_2(A=0, B=0; A=0, B=3)$$
$$m_2(A=0, B=1; A=0, B=3)m_1(A=0, B=1; A=0, B=2)$$

It is easily verified that $s \notin \text{CSR}_{IDM}$, $s \notin \text{ECSR}_{IDM}$, and even $s \notin \text{FSR}_{IDM}$. However, a detailed analysis of the conflicts occurring in s reveals the following: the first two modifications that imply a conflict between t_1 and t_2 apparently affect tuple $(0, 0)$; similarly, the last two modifications affect tuple $(0, 1)$. Therefore, the first conflict is relevant only to a relation containing $(0, 0)$, while the second is relevant only to a relation containing $(0, 1)$. The point now is that these two tuples cannot occur *simultaneously* in a relation satisfying $A \to B$! Thus, in any valid relation, at most one of the two conflicts will be relevant, so that depending on the current state, s is always equivalent either to $t_1 t_2$ or to $t_2 t_1$.

The above observation motivates a novel notion of serializability for which equivalence to seriality is state dependent:

IDM state serializability

DEFINITION 8.7 *State Serializability*

Let R be a relation schema with attributes X and FDs F. A history s for a set $T = \{t_1, \ldots, t_n\}$ of transactions is *state serializable with respect to F*

if for each relation r satisfying F there exists a serial history s_r for T that depends on r such that $\text{eff}(s)(r) = \text{eff}(s_r)(r)$.

Let SSR^F (or more precisely $\text{SSR}^F(T)$) denote the class of all histories that are state serializable with respect to F.

Notice that the particular permutation whose effect on r equals that of s is thus dependent on r itself. Now Example 8.9 demonstrates that there exist histories $s \notin \text{FSR}_{IDM}$ that are state serializable with respect to a given set F of FDs. More generally, it can be shown that FSR_{IDM} is a strict subset of SSR^F for each F containing at least one nontrivial FD. In addition, the tests for membership in CSR_{IDM} and in FSR_{IDM} described earlier in this chapter can be generalized in such a way that state information is taken into account.

We are not presenting the latter in full detail here, but just sketch how it can be accomplished for the case of class CSR_{IDM}. The basic idea follows directly from Example 8.9. For a given history s and a set F of FDs, a conflict graph $G(s)$ is constructed to represent the auxiliary information of which hyperplane is relevant to what conflict edge. Next, if a given database state d has an empty intersection with *every* hyperplane that is relevant to an edge (t_i, t_j), then the conflict between t_i and t_j (represented by this edge) can be ignored when history s is executed on state d. If $G(s)$ contains a cycle, it can be tested (using a particular form of the well-known chase procedure for enforcing FDs) whether there exists a state d satisfying the FDs that has a nonempty intersection with at least one relevant hyperplane of each edge on the cycle. If no such state can be found for any cycle of $G(s)$, history s is apparently state serializable with respect to F—in other words $s \in \text{SSR}^F$.

We mention that the test just sketched is a *sufficient* condition for membership in class SSR^F only; that is, not every state serializable history can be recognized in this way. Correspondingly, the class of histories recognized is denoted CSSR^F (for "conflict state serializable histories"). Moreover, the algorithm for testing membership in CSSR^F has exponential time complexity (due to the fact that there are exponentially many choices for sets of hyperplanes to which the chase procedure is applied). Instead of going further into details, we present another example showing the essence of what has been discussed in this subsection.

EXAMPLE 8.10

Consider a relation schema R with attributes ABC and FDs $A \rightarrow C$, $C \rightarrow B$. Let the following history be given:

$$
\begin{aligned}
s = \; & d_1(A = 3)m_1(A = 0, B = 0, C \neq 0; A = 3, B = 0, C \neq 0) \\
& d_2(A = 2)m_2(A = 0, B = 0, C \neq 0; A = 2, B = 0, C \neq 0) \\
& d_2(A = 0, B \neq 0, C = 1)d_2(A = 1, C = 0)d_1(A = 5) \\
& m_1(A = 0, B \neq 0, C = 1; A = 5, B \neq 0, C = 1) \\
& d_1(A = 1, C = 0)m_1(A = 0, C = 0; A = 1, C = 0)
\end{aligned}
$$

Note that both t_1 and t_2 are consistency preserving when considered in isolation. Obviously, $s \notin \text{CSR}_{IDM}$, since its conflict graph has edges (t_1, t_2) and (t_2, t_1) and is hence cyclic. However, we can associate labels with these edges as follows:

$$l((t_1, t_2)) = \{C_1\}$$
$$l((t_2, t_1)) = \{C_2, C_3\}$$

where

$$C_1 = \{A = 0, B = 0, C \neq 0\}$$
$$C_2 = \{A = 0, B \neq 0, C = 1\}$$
$$C_3 = \{A = 0, C = 0\}$$

Thus, there are two choices for sets of hyperplanes, $\{C_1, C_2\}$ as well as $\{C_1, C_3\}$. For both, the chase procedure will not be successful, meaning that no state will intersect a hyperplane from each edge simultaneously. It follows that s is conflict state serializable with respect to F, i.e., $s \in \text{CSSR}^F - \text{CSR}_{IDM}$.

The following theorem summarizes what can be shown for the scenario incorporating integrity constraints and hence state information outlined above:

THEOREM 8.4

For each set F of FDs with at least one nontrivial element, the following holds:

$$\text{CSR}_{IDM} \subset \text{CSSR}^F \subset \text{SSR}^F$$

8.3.7 Summary

The IDM transaction model as described in this section is a model of transactions that is essentially "located" at the conceptual level of a database, where a user is not concerned with pages or other internal objects of the system, but only looks at relations, their attributes, their values, and maybe their integrity constraints. As has been indicated, this view, as a particular case of flat object schedules as treated in Chapter 6, renders a number of investigations possible, of which we have presented only a few: commutativity based serializability, conflict serializability that takes an entire history prefix into account, or state based serializability. There are various other issues to investigate. For example, it can be shown that there is an infinite hierarchy of classes of serializable histories between CSR_{IDM} and FSR_{IDM}, which, in a sense, approximates the class FSR_{IDM}; the more time a scheduler is willing to invest, the closer it can get to unrestricted serializability. Yet there is still room for further study, in particular when it comes to scheduler design. Indeed, efficient, low-overhead management of the semantic information available in a model like this is a nontrivial problem, as we have also shown in previous chapters. For this particular transaction model, efficient implementations are yet to be seen.

8.4 **Exploiting Transaction Program Knowledge**

The third approach to exploiting semantic information is not particularly tied to the relational model, but again fits well with it. The ideas described in this section can be combined with predicate-oriented concurrency control, as discussed earlier in this chapter. They are also closely related to the approach of interleaving specifications, as introduced in Section 3.10. The key difference, however, is that we will now preserve serializability despite a more sophisticated interpretation of isolation, whereas the approach in Section 3.10 deliberately allowed deviating from serializability. The approach developed here can be viewed as a way of automatically deriving, by means of complete knowledge of transaction programs, those interleaving specifications that are compatible with serializability.

8.4.1 **Motivating Example**

The approach described in this section aims to reflect the basic tuning principle of "making transactions short" in order to reduce the probability of many conflicts and long delays. It is motivated by application scenarios along the following lines.

EXAMPLE 8.11

Suppose that a bank allows customers to withdraw a certain amount in cash per day from their accounts. At night, an update transaction inspects each account that has been accessed during the day, updates its balance, and then updates the corresponding branch total. The update transaction will typically be of long duration, and due to account accessibility through the Internet, the bank wants to move away from running the update transaction only at night. In order to improve service, solutions along the following lines are conceivable:

Bank example

1. The single large update transaction is replaced by many small ones, each of which updates one customer's account and the corresponding branch total. Clearly, the small transactions can now execute in parallel, and the effects on the individual accounts will be the same. Also, if additional transactions read a single customer's account balance, these will not see any difference compared to the original setting either.

2. As the small update transactions may now interfere with each other when updating the branch total, each of the small transactions could be decomposed further into two transactions, one that updates the customer's account and one that updates the corresponding branch total.

Note that the short transactions that result from this kind of "chopping" are not only perfectly tolerable from an application viewpoint, but they do in fact behave as if the original, long transactions were executed in a serializable manner. So it is conceivable that the chopping is automatically inferred from the transaction programs themselves, without any need for an application expert to provide additional semantic hints. However, the correctness of the above decomposition crucially builds on the fact that there are no other transaction programs that could, for example, access the accounts of all customers and compare their total to the sum of the bank's branch totals. Such a transaction would have an inconsistent view of the data, but if we knew that this type of access pattern does not occur, the chopping would be acceptable.

The sample scenario just described makes a point for *short* transactions, since long ones acquire more locks and therefore cause potentially more lock contention. However, as indicated by the example, whether or not a transaction can be broken into smaller pieces depends on which other transactions may possibly be running concurrently.

To cast the above considerations into a precise model, let us make the assumption that we know exactly which transactions may be running concurrently during some time period. To this end, let us continue the previous example and describe the transactions in terms of a straight-line sequence of parameter-less SQL calls. For simpler notation, we will abbreviate the SQL calls, which are very simple SELECT and UPDATE statements anyway, as if they were read and write steps on the account and branch objects. Later we will reconsider the approach and its practicality in the light of real application programs that have rich control flow and contain parameterized SQL calls.

EXAMPLE 8.12

Let us return to the bank example we considered in the previous example and assume from now on that the three types of transactions we discussed above exist as an alternative decomposition:

1. a transaction updating a single customer's account as well as the corresponding branch balance,

2. a transaction reading a customer's account balance,

3. a transaction comparing the grand total of all account balances with the sum of the branch balances.

Assume further that accounts A_1, A_2, and A_3 belong to branch B_1, and that A_4 and A_5 belong to B_2. Let the transactions be as follows:

$$t_1 = r_1(A_1)w_1(A_1)r_1(B_1)w_1(B_1)$$
$$t_2 = r_2(A_3)w_2(A_3)r_2(B_1)w_2(B_1)$$
$$t_3 = r_3(A_4)w_3(A_4)r_3(B_2)w_3(B_2)$$
$$t_4 = r_4(A_2)$$
$$t_5 = r_5(A_4)$$
$$t_6 = r_6(A_1)r_6(A_2)r_6(A_3)r_6(B_1)r_6(A_4)r_6(A_5)r_6(B_2)$$

Transactions t_1–t_3 update a customer's account balance as well as the corresponding branch balance; transactions t_4 and t_5 read a customer's balance; and transaction t_6 compares the grand totals of customer accounts to the sum of the branch totals.

Note once again that the transaction programs actually consist of SQL statements rather than read and write steps. So t_1, for example, would in reality be as follows:

```
SELECT Balance INTO :oldbalance FROM Accounts
   WHERE AccountNo = A1;
UPDATE Accounts SET Balance = :newbalance
   WHERE AccountNo = A1;
SELECT Total INTO :oldtotal FROM Branches
   WHERE BranchNo = B1;
UPDATE Branches SET Total = :newtotal
   WHERE BranchNo = B1;
```

It is only for more concise notation that we have denoted these statements as r and w steps.

8.4.2 Transaction Chopping

Assume that there are n transaction programs that can execute within some given interval, leading to n possibly concurrent transaction executions. If a program can be invoked multiple times within the considered interval, we treat it as if these were two different programs. We further assume that each program consists of a straight-line sequence of SQL statements with parameterless WHERE clauses. Decomposing, or *chopping*, a transaction program amounts to changing the program as follows:

Transaction chopping

DEFINITION 8.8   *Transaction Chopping*

Let t_i be a transaction program. A *chopping* of t_i is a decomposition of t_i into ordered pieces $t_{i_1}, \ldots, t_{i_k}$ ($k \geq 1$, most often $k \geq 2$) such that every database operation invoked by t_i is contained in exactly one piece, and the order of operation invocations is preserved.

In practice this transformation could be done simply by inserting additional COMMIT WORK statements into the original programs at all points where one piece ends and the next one begins. This is straightforward as long as the programs are indeed straight-line sequences of SQL statements, without any branching or loops. Also, the assumption that the pieces that result from the chopping of a transaction program obey the execution order of the original program is virtually self-guaranteed in our simplified setting.

If a piece that results from the chopping of a transaction program is aborted due to a deadlock, it needs to be restarted repeatedly until it commits. If a piece is aborted due to a program-initiated rollback (e.g., as a result of an explicitly coded consistency check), no other pieces of the same transaction should execute, and only the first piece is allowed to contain such program-initiated rollback statements. These assumptions need to be guaranteed by the programs themselves in combination with the underlying run-time system. In particular, the property that once the first piece is successfully committed, all subsequent pieces must be executed to completion exactly once, so that the atomicity of the original transaction is preserved, requires elaborate considerations on recovery. We will come back to this issue in Chapter 17, where a straightforward solution based on transactional message queues will be presented.

Our next goal is to test whether a given chopping for a set of transaction programs is correct in that it preserves serializability of the transactions that would be spawned by the original programs. This can be done by a simple form of *static program analysis*. For simplicity, we will again use the convenient read/write notation rather than SQL, and we will henceforth no longer explicitly distinguish between a straight-line transaction program and the totally ordered transaction or sequence of pieces that originate from the program. For the analysis, we introduce a particular kind of *chopping graph* defined as follows:

Chopping graph

DEFINITION 8.9   *Chopping Graph*

Let T be a given set of transactions, and let a chopping of the transactions in T be given. A *chopping graph* $C(T)$ is an undirected graph such that:

1. The nodes of $C(T)$ are the transaction pieces occurring in the chopping.

2. Let p, q be pieces from two different transactions. If p and q contain

operations that are in conflict, $C(T)$ contains an undirected edge between p and q labeled with a c (for "conflict").

3. If p and p' are pieces from the same transaction, $C(T)$ contains an undirected edge between p and p' labeled with an s (for "sibling").

Note that no edge in a chopping graph can have both an s and a c label. We say that a chopping graph contains an *sc cycle* if it contains a cycle with at least one s and at least one c edge.

EXAMPLE 8.13

Consider the following three transactions:

$$t_1 = r_1(x)w_1(x)r_1(y)w_1(y)$$
$$t_2 = r_2(x)w_2(x)$$
$$t_3 = r_3(y)w_3(y)$$

Let t_1 be chopped into two pieces as follows:

$$t_{11} = r_{11}(x)w_{11}(x)$$
$$t_{12} = r_{12}(y)w_{12}(y)$$

The corresponding chopping graph is shown in Figure 8.1. Obviously, there is no *sc* cycle.

Our goal is to deal only with choppings that are "correct" in the following sense:

Figure 8.1 A chopping graph.

Correct chopping

DEFINITION 8.10   *Correct Chopping*

A chopping of $T = \{t_1, \ldots, t_n\}$ is *correct* if every execution of the transaction pieces according to the following execution rules is conflict equivalent to some serial history for the original transactions T.

Rule 1:   When transaction pieces execute, they obey the precedence relationship defined by the original transaction program.

Rule 2:   Each piece will be executed according to some concurrency control protocol that ensures conflict serializability and will commit its changes when it ends.

The following can now be proven:

THEOREM 8.5

A chopping is correct if the associated chopping graph does not contain an *sc* cycle.

The proof assumes that transaction pieces are executed—for example, according to the two-phase locking protocol—and then exploits the fact that this protocol guarantees an acyclic conflict graph for the committed transactions.

EXAMPLE 8.14

Let us return to the bank example we considered in the previous two examples, where we already established the following transactions:

$$t_1 = r_1(A_1)w_1(A_1)r_1(B_1)w_1(B_1)$$
$$t_2 = r_2(A_3)w_2(A_3)r_2(B_1)w_2(B_1)$$
$$t_3 = r_3(A_4)w_3(A_4)r_3(B_2)w_3(B_2)$$
$$t_4 = r_4(A_2)$$
$$t_5 = r_5(A_4)$$
$$t_6 = r_6(A_1)r_6(A_2)r_6(A_3)r_6(B_1)r_6(A_4)r_6(A_5)r_6(B_2)$$

We first chop t_6 into two pieces as follows:

$$t_{61} = r_{61}(A_1)r_{61}(A_2)r_{61}(A_3)r_{61}(B_1)$$
$$t_{62} = r_{62}(A_4)r_{62}(A_5)r_{62}(B_2)$$

A look at the corresponding chopping graph, which is shown in Figure 8.2, indicates that the obtained chopping is correct.

Figure 8.2 Chopping graph without sc cycle.

We next try to chop transaction t_1 into the following pieces:

$$t_{11} = r_{11}(A_1)w_{11}(A_1)$$
$$t_{12} = r_{12}(B_1)w_{12}(B_1)$$

Now we obtain the chopping graph shown in Figure 8.3, which contains an sc cycle; hence, this chopping is not correct.

Example 8.14 indicates the fact that making a chopping finer can introduce sc cycles, and it is clear that once such a cycle has occurred, it cannot be broken again by chopping further (since a cycle has at least one c edge, and further choppings always introduce additional s edges). On the other hand, an algorithm can be devised for finding the "finest" chopping possible among a given set of transactions. This algorithm, which can be found in the references cited in the Bibliographic Notes, is based on the following observation:

From a given set $T = \{t_1, \ldots, t_n\}$, take any transaction t_i and chop it into $t_{i_1}, \ldots, t_{i_k}$. If the graph with nodes $\{t_1, \ldots, t_{i-1}, t_{i_1}, \ldots, t_{i_k}, t_{i+1}, \ldots, t_n\}$ does not contain an sc cycle, this chopping is a *private* chopping of t_i. If for each $t \in T$, a private chopping can be found, a chopping of T is simply obtained by taking the union of the n private choppings.

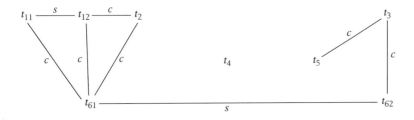

Figure 8.3 Chopping graph with sc cycle.

8.4.3 **Applicability of Chopping**

Chopping is a compile-time technique that transforms programs by inserting additional COMMIT WORK statements such that upon execution, the program issues a sequence of short transactions (coined *pieces*) rather than a single, longer transaction. The semantic knowledge that is necessary for applying the chopping algorithm can in a real-world situation, such as SQL application programs, be derived from the predicates in queries and UPDATE statements (i.e., the WHERE clauses). This information allows us to reason about high-level conflicts between statements, as discussed in the previous sections of this chapter. For example, if a database contains a relation Accounts with attributes such as Balance, AccountType, City, and a key AccountNo, then statements such as

```
SELECT AccountNo, Balance FROM Accounts
WHERE City = 'Austin'
```

and

```
UPDATE Accounts SET Balance = Balance * 1.05
WHERE City = 'San Francisco'
```

are not in conflict from a conceptual point of view, since disjoint records will be read (or, in the terminology used earlier, since the hyperplanes associated with the two conditions are disjoint). However, if the underlying relational database system actually employs page locking and accounts from the two different cities may possibly reside on the same page, or if the system uses record locking but there is a non-zero probability for a conflict on some auxiliary storage structures such as addressing or free space management tables; then the two SQL statements shown above would conservatively have to be assumed to be conflicting. Obviously this would lead to more c edges in a chopping graph, and may significantly limit chopping opportunities. So chopping would perform best if the underlying database system employed predicate-oriented concurrency control (which no commercial system does at this point).

Another form of conservativism is in order when we consider parameterized SQL statements, which contain program variables (see Chapter 1), denoted by prefixing the variable name with a colon. For example, consider the two statements

```
SELECT AccountNo, Balance FROM Accounts
WHERE AccountType = 'savings' AND City = :x
```

and

```
UPDATE Accounts SET Balance = Balance * 1.05
WHERE AccountType = 'checking' AND City = :y
```

We could safely infer that these two statements do not have a conflict at the level of the SQL predicates. However, for two instantiations of the second statement (the UPDATE statement), nothing could be concluded anymore, as the two instances of the program variable :y could possibly be bound to the same city value.

In this way, chopping relevant information can be extracted even from parameterized SQL programs, and this observation can be extended to entire application programs with embedded SQL statements, provided that these are "straight-line" programs without any control-flow branching. So in this limited setting the chopping method would be ready for practical use. For general application programs, however, where the statements are often part of loops or if-then-else constructs, the simple chopping algorithm does not work anymore. In this realistic setting the idea would be to conservatively construct a parameter-less straight-line program that *covers* all possible executions of the actual program. A chopping graph would then be established for this synthesized program, and the chopping algorithm could be applied.

For example, the program fragment

```
SELECT AccountNo, Balance FROM Accounts
WHERE AccountType = 'savings' AND City = :x;

if not found then
SELECT AccountNo, Balance FROM Accounts
WHERE AccountType = 'checking' AND City = :x;
fi;
```

would lead to the following straight-line, parameter-less fragment that *covers* the actual program:

```
SELECT AccountNo, Balance FROM Accounts
WHERE AccountType = 'savings';
SELECT AccountNo, Balance FROM Accounts
WHERE AccountType = 'checking';
```

Whether this conservative method is practically viable is an open issue. Skeptics may suspect that the covering straight-line, parameter-less program would often have to be so conservative that no real chopping is feasible anymore, but the true answer to such conjectures lies in more experimental research.

In Chapter 3 we discussed interleaving specifications as a way of generalizing the assumption underlying serializability that *all* steps of a transaction should appear to be executed indivisibly to *all* other transactions in a correct schedule. In particular, we discussed the following options: (1) to consider units of isolation that do not necessarily consist of *all* the steps of a transaction, but of certain subsets of the steps, and (2) to consider *varying* units of isolation with respect to other transactions—that is, some steps may constitute an indivisible unit to some transactions, but not to others. We formalized this by specifying for each pair of given transactions the indivisible units of one transaction *relative to the other*. The intuition was to think of the borderline between two consecutive indivisible units of the same transaction as a "breakpoint" at which a transaction may be interleaved with another transaction, and these breakpoints needed to be specified in advance. A similar intuition underlies transaction chopping. Indeed, if an application programmer specifying transactions has sufficient knowledge of the semantics of the application for which the transactions are written, she may be able to state which mutual interleavings or individual choppings are acceptable and which ones are not. In this sense, chopping can be considered as an approach to automate the derivation of an interleaving specification, which can basically be "read off" a chopping graph. Thus, when it comes to scheduling, it is not even necessary to develop a separate scheduler for handling interleaving specifications, but any scheduler yielding histories (for transaction pieces) in CSR will do.

8.5 **Lessons Learned**

The exposition in the chapter can be seen as a case study revealing the opportunities that arise with respect to concurrency control from the semantics of a particular object model. As we have shown, there are multiple options for the important case of relational databases, ranging from exploiting predicates as they arise in query expressions or integrity constraints like functional dependencies, to the systematic chopping of transactions into shorter pieces. The basic abstraction underlying all three approaches is the predicate or set of conditions that determines a set of tuples (those satisfying the predicate). These tuples may or may not be in the current database state, which could give rise to the phantom problem, but which is now elegantly covered by the uniform handling of predicates.

There is an obvious catch, however, to such case studies, which lies in the fact that the results obtained, though elegant and interesting, are hardly of immediate practical relevance. For example, testing the satisfiability of predicates is an NP complete problem, as is testing of final state serializability in the IDM transaction model. Nevertheless, there are "approximations" derived from the general scenarios discussed in this chapter that *are* practically relevant. For example, the ideas underlying predicate-oriented concurrency control are used in index key locking, as will be described in the following chapter, and they are also relevant to federated database systems, which will be covered in Chapter 18.

Exercises

8.1 Discuss how predicate locking can be extended to disjunctive conditions such as queries of the form

```
SELECT Name FROM Emp
WHERE Position = 'Manager' OR Department = 'Research'
```

Also discuss how join queries such as

```
SELECT Emp.Name, Emp.Department FROM Emp, Dept
WHERE Emp.Position = 'Manager' AND Dept.City = 'Toronto'
AND Emp.Department = Dept.Department
```

could be (conservatively) handled by predicate locking.

8.2 The sample histories we studied for IDM transactions in this chapter mostly referred to a database with one relation and one attribute. Show the following: if the database has more than one relation, the serializability of each projection of a given history onto an individual relation does *not* imply serializability of that history in general. Use the following scenario as a counterexample: let database schema D contain relation schemata R and S, where R has attributes A and B, and where S has attributes B and C, and consider the following transactions and history:

$$t_1 = m^R(A = 1; A = 2)m^S(C = 5; C = 6)$$
$$t_2 = m^R(A = 2; A = 3)m^S(C = 4; C = 5)$$
$$s = m_1^R(A = 1; A = 2)m_2^R(A = 2; A = 3)m_2^S(C = 4; C = 5)$$
$$m_1^S(C = 5; C = 6)$$

8.3 Consider a restricted IDM transaction model without Modify operations (i.e., a model of "ID transactions"). Show the following:

(a) Not every modification can be simulated by deletions followed by insertions; more precisely, such that $t_1 = m(0; 1) \not\approx t_2 = d(0)i(1)$ (by exhibiting a counterexample state).

(b) Show that $s = i_1(1)d_2(1)i_2(2)d_1(2)i_3(1)i_3(2) \in \text{FSR}_{IDM} - \text{CSR}_{IDM}$.

(c) Show that testing membership in FSR_{IDM} can be tested in polynomial time for histories of ID transactions.

8.4 The following approach is intended to "approximate" exact testing of membership in FSR_{IDM} by combining local and global testing in various degrees. Consider the following family of algorithms, which is based on an "exactness parameter" k determining the amount of exact testing a concrete algorithm will perform. The higher k, the more precisely FSR_{IDM} is approximated and the higher the particular algorithm's complexity. In the following description, let "coalesce(T_k, $G(s)$)" denote the graph obtained from the conflict graph $G(s)$ of a history s by collapsing all nodes whose transactions belong to $T_k \subseteq T$ into one node and by correcting the edge relation correspondingly (a node outside T_k is connected to T_k if it is connected to any node in T_k in $G(s)$).

Algorithm SR(k)

Input: A strict history s for a set T of n transactions;
Output: "yes" or "no"
Method:

```
{ for each Tₖ ⊆ T, |Tₖ| = k do
  if  coalesce(Tₖ, G(s)) acyclic then
   if  π_Tₖ(s) ∈ FSR then
    write("yes"); stop fi fi od;
  write("no")
}.
```

Notice that $s \overset{*}{\leftrightarrow} s'\pi_{T_k}(s)s''$ holds if coalesce(T_k, $G(s)$) is acyclic, where $s's''$ is a serial history for $T - T_k$ and s' only contains complete transactions. Thus, s is serializable if $\pi_{T_k}(s)$ is; therefore, the algorithm performs an exact test in step 3 for $\pi_{T_k}(s)$.

(a) Show that the SR(k) algorithms are of polynomial time complexity for any given k.

(b) Let SR_k denote the set of histories for which algorithm SR(k) returns "yes." Show the following:

  (i) $SR_0 = SR_1 = CSR_{IDM}$,
  (ii) $SR_k \subset SR_{k+1} \subset FSR_{IDM}$ for each $k \geq 1$,
  (iii) for each strict and final state serializable history s there exists an integer $k > 0$ such that $s \in SR_k$.

Thus, the classes SR(k) of "degree-k serializable" histories form an infinite hierarchy of classes of serializable histories and "converge" toward FSR_{IDM}.

8.5 Show for the IDM model of transactions:

(a) Final state serializability is not monotone.
(b) Final state serializability is not prefix commit closed.
(c) Conflict serializability is monotone.
(d) Extended conflict serializability is monotone.
(e) Both conflict and extended conflict serializability are prefix commit closed.

8.6 Extend the IDM transaction model by a suitably chosen SELECT operation and adapt the formalism, in particular the equivalence of schedules, appropriately. SELECT operations read values from a relational database, and two SELECT operations over the same relation must yield identical values in equivalent histories. Which of the theorems on IDM transactions can be generalized to such an extended model of "IDMS" transactions?

8.7 Consider the transactions from Example 8.13 again. Determine whether decomposing t_{11} any further still results in a correct chopping.

8.8 Consider the following transactions:

$$t_1 = r_1(x)w_1(x)r_1(y)w_1(y)$$
$$t_2 = r_2(x)$$
$$t_3 = r_3(y)w_3(y)$$

Try to decompose t_1 into three pieces such that the result is a correct chopping.

8.9 Prove Theorem 8.5.

8.10 Show that if a set of chopped transactions contains an *sc* cycle, any further chopping of any of the transactions will not render the graph acyclic.

8.11 Suppose that a *purchase* program processes the purchases made by a company by adding the value of an item purchased to the *inventory* and by subtracting the money paid for it from *cash*. The application specification requires that the value of *cash* never becomes negative, so that a transaction recording a purchase has to abort if subtracting the money from *cash* would make that value negative. The structure of such a program is given by a parameterized procedure purchase(i, p) recording the purchase of item i for price p, whose body can be written as follows:

```
if (p > cash )      then rollback
                    else inventory[i] := inventory [i] + p;
    cash := cash − p;
```

Discuss under which conditions and to what extent chopping can be applied to this scenario.

Bibliographic Notes

Predicate locking is a relatively old idea in concurrency control that goes back to Eswaran et al. (1976). Complexity arguments showing that testing satisfiability of predicates is NP complete even for simple predicates (i.e., Boolean combinations of atomic comparisons) where pointed out by Hunt and Rosenkrantz (1979). The phantom problem, which was already brought up by Eswaran et al. (1976), was systematically investigated by Bernstein et al. (1981). Predicate-oriented concurrency control techniques, both locking and optimistic variants, were later studied by many others, including Dadam et al. (1983), Reimer (1983), and Böttcher et al. (1986). Precision locking is from Jordan et al. (1981). A prototype implementation of predicate locking, based on techniques from

Dadam et al. (1983), has been described by Schaad et al. (1995). Reuter et al. (1992, 1997) have discussed the use of predicate-oriented concurrency control for synchronizing long-lived workflows with activity-specific entry and exit predicates as workflow invariants.

The IDM transaction model for relational databases goes back to the work of Abiteboul and Vianu (1988), who define the basic notions and give a host of results. Karabeg and Vianu (1991) have provided a sound and complete axiomatization for IDM transactions. Concurrency control for IDM transactions was studied in depth by Vianu and Vossen (1992); in particular, they studied the various notions and classes of histories for IDM transactions as well as the complexity results for recognizing FSR_{IDM} (for IDM as well as for ID transactions) and its restrictions. Moreover, the exploitation of FDs in this context is from that paper, and proofs for Theorems 8.1, 8.2, 8.3, 8.4, and others can be found there. Vossen (1992b) showed that dynamic aspects such as considering prefixes and taking closures of history properties can also be respected in the IDM transaction model.

Vianu and Vossen (1993) have investigated another foundation for concurrency control in the context of IDM transactions by describing an alternative notion of history correctness for histories that turns out to be orthogonal to serializability. While serializability is based on the assumption that *every* serial execution of given transactions is acceptable to all users, *goal correctness* tries to reflect the intended changes of a transaction to a database and whether these are compatible among the transactions that are ready for execution. Goal correctness is shown to be orthogonal to (final state) serializability, but is easier to test. On the other hand, it has its drawbacks when it comes to dynamic scheduling, essentially because it requires complete knowledge about transactions, since otherwise nothing can be said about their goals. Laurent et al. (1995) have investigated a different transaction model for relational databases in which goal correctness turns out to be subsumed by serializability.

Transaction chopping is from Shasha (1992) as well as Shasha et al. (1992, 1995); a proof of Theorem 8.5 can be found in these references. Recently, Bernstein et al. (1998, 1999) as well as Ammann et al. (1997) have continued the research that studies transaction interleavings as well as choppings and proposed a technique called *assertional concurrency control*.

CHAPTER NINE

Concurrency Control on Search Structures

Here grows the tree, the tree, whose roots are full of life.
—*Pablo Neruda*

When you come to a fork in the road, take it.
—*Yogi Berra*

9.1 Goal and Overview

Search structures such as B^+ tree indexes are among the most fundamental concepts for ensuring efficient data accesses. Therefore, we devote a separate chapter to the concurrency control issues for search structures. We will focus on B^+ tree indexes, but many of our considerations can potentially be generalized, or carried over, to other search structures.

The framework for our discussion is layered schedules with the access layer and the page layer of a data server. (See Chapter 1 for a brief overview of the layered architecture of database systems and similar data servers.) At first glance, this suggests considering record operations and the resulting page accesses. As for the access layer, paying attention to record operations alone falls short of ensuring serializability in the presence of "intensional," predicate-oriented record searches. In particular, merely locking the records that are fetched, updated, inserted, or deleted cannot prevent the so-called phantom problem. Recall from Chapter 1 that such problems arise when newly inserted, deleted, or updated records satisfy the search predicates of queries by concurrent transactions, although these records are not returned (and, in fact, possibly not even touched) by those queries themselves.

As an example, consider transaction t_1 that moves all 50-year-old and older people who live in Dallas, Texas, to Phoenix, Arizona, by issuing an SQL-style Update Persons Set City = "Phoenix" Where Age $\geq$ 50 And City ="Dallas." Concurrently, a second transaction t_2 first asks for all people who live in Phoenix and later submits a query to retrieve all people from Dallas; the update by t_1

is assumed to take place between these two queries. Now suppose that the update affects only a single record x representing the person who moves from Dallas to Phoenix. Further suppose that t_2's first query returns records p and q, and its second query returns d and e. So, record x is not found by either of the two queries, although the two together are supposed to find everybody from Dallas or Phoenix. If locking at the access layer is restricted to the actually accessed records, x for t_1 and p, q, d, and e for t_2, this phantom anomaly cannot be prevented. So instead we also need to lock either the predicates of the queries and the update themselves or the appropriate information in the underlying access paths that are used to execute these query-level operations. In the example, the above SQL operations could use a B^+ tree index on the City attribute of the Persons table. Recall from Chapter 1 that the leaf pages of such an index contain searchable (key, RID) pairs, where the key is one of the City values and RID is a pointer or a list of pointers to the records with this City value. So locking the keys "Dallas" and "Phoenix" (which appear in the above SQL operations) in this index, on behalf of both transactions, would render an explicit lock conflict and thus ensure a proper serialization.

Thus, concurrency control needs to consider index search keys in addition to the stored records. Furthermore, as with layered schedules, additional page locks are needed to ensure that the underlying search structures are properly traversed and manipulated, so as to ensure that the search and other operations of the access layer appear isolated. The default solution for this purpose would be to apply a protocol like 2PL (or even S2PL or SS2PL) to the subtransactions that correspond to index searches as well as insertions and deletions of (key, RID) pairs. Because of the special structure of index trees and the resulting highly specialized page access patterns, it is, however, possible to devise tailored protocols that allow more concurrency on the index pages than standard 2PL would. As concurrency control on search structures is a potential bottleneck in many high-performance applications, we should definitely strive for the best possible protocol.

This chapter provides solutions to the above issues that are structured according to our two-layer setting. Section 9.3 addresses the necessary locking of index keys for the operations at the access layer, postulating isolation of the operations themselves, for example, by assuming 2PL for the duration of the corresponding subtransactions. Section 9.4 then improves the underlying page layer protocol by introducing advanced techniques that are specifically geared for B^+ trees and similar structures. Finally, Section 9.5 looks into additional optimization techniques that mostly aim to reduce the overhead of the entire two-level protocol. To provide the necessary background on how search structures are typically implemented in data servers, we begin with a short review of B^+ trees in Section 9.2.

9.2 **Implementation of Search Structures by B⁺ Trees**

In this section we briefly review implementation techniques for search struc-   *B⁺ trees*
tures to the extent that this background is relevant for the discussion of concurrency control. The prevalent data structure for the implementation of the ADT
"search structure" is the B⁺ tree. This is a page-structured search tree whose
nodes correspond to pages and where all leaf nodes are at the same tree level
(i.e., have the same distance from the root node). An example B⁺ tree for an
index on the Name field of a Person table is shown in Figure 9.1. This tree has
height 2; it consists of a root node and three leaf nodes at the next lower level.
The leaf nodes contain all values of the indexed field that exist in the database.
Each value is followed by a list of RIDs to the corresponding records. Such a
combination of a key value and a RID list is called a *leaf node index entry*. A
leaf node consists of one or more of those entries, typically between ten and a
few hundred. The nonleaf nodes of the index consist of *inner-node index entries*,
each of which contains a value and a pointer to an index node of the next lower
level. The semantics of such an entry is that the value is the largest key value
that exists in the subtree to which the pointer refers. For example, the entry
in the root that points to the leftmost leaf has the value "Carl," as this is the
(lexicographically) largest key value in that subtree.

An index entry that points to the rightmost child of a nonleaf node does not
have a key value but merely consists of a pointer. In the example of Figure 9.1,
the third entry of the root simply points to the rightmost leaf, meaning that all
key values in this rightmost subtree are higher than the key value "Eve" in the
preceding entry of the root. Note that this technique not only is applicable to
the root, but avoids an explicit key value in the index entry for the rightmost
subtree among the children of the same node at all levels. The highest possible
key value within such a rightmost subtree is then determined by the index
entry for all subtrees with the same parent, which can be found in that parent's

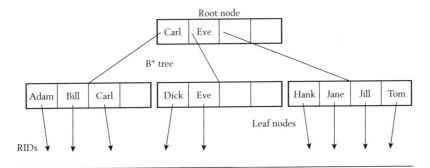

Figure 9.1 Example of a B⁺ tree.

parent. As a consequence, each nonleaf node has one more pointer to the next index level than it has key values.

Search algorithm

Because of this invariant between index entries and subtrees, inner-node index entries can serve as *routing entries* for a root-to-leaf key search in the tree. A search for a given key value starts at the root node. It determines within the currently inspected node the routing entry whose value is the smallest value that is larger than or equal to the given search key, and then follows the pointer of this routing entry. If the search key is larger than the highest value among the routing entries of the index node, then the search follows the pointer to the rightmost child. Within an index page, a simple binary search is performed, assuming that the index entries are kept sorted. This step per node is recursively applied until the leaf level is reached. There, either the given search key is found, and then we directly obtain the desired RID list for the qualifying records, or we realize that the search key is not present at all in the database. In the example tree, a search for the key "Dick" would follow the "Eve" router in the root and find the key in the middle leaf. In contrast, a search for the key "Joe" would follow the router to the rightmost leaf, where it would detect that this key does not exist in the database.

A range lookup is implemented in a similar manner: it searches for the lower-bound key, which would lead to the smallest existing key that is larger than or equal to the lower bound. From there the range lookup can scan all leaf nodes to the right of this starting entry until it reaches a key that is larger than the upper bound of the range. To this end, a typical implementation of a B^+ tree embeds both forward and backward pointers in the leaf nodes, so that all leaf nodes are linked in the sorting order of the indexed field's domain. (These pointers are not shown in Figure 9.1.)

I/O cost of index lookups

As long as it is guaranteed that the tree is balanced in the sense that all leaf nodes occur at the same level, the I/O costs of an index lookup are logarithmic in the size of the underlying data, namely, one disk I/O per index level (disregarding caching effects and the follow-up leaf accesses in a range lookup). In fact, the base of this logarithm is usually fairly high, as it coincides with the fan-out of the tree. Given that the inner nodes contain only short routing entries, fan-outs on the order of several hundred are typical in practice. You may even further increase the fan-out by compressing the routing entries' values. As these merely serve routing purposes, they do not necessarily have to be equal to the largest key in the corresponding subtree. Rather, any value that separates the key-value sets of two adjacent subtrees is eligible. For example, the routing value "Eve" in the root of Figure 9.1 could be compressed into a separator "Ex" or even "F," as both are lexicographically larger than "Eve" but still smaller than the smallest key value in the adjacent subtree to the right and thus satisfying (a slightly relaxed form of) the tree invariant that facilitates the logarithmic search. The resulting effect is a typical tree height of at most 3 in most database applications or at most 4 in some extremely large databases, and this is equal to the number of page accesses for an exact match lookup

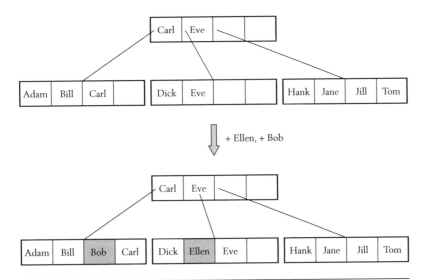

Figure 9.2 Insertion into a B$^+$ tree.

(disregarding the case of very long RID lists per key value that would span multiple pages).

A B$^+$ tree is an extremely efficient index structure for large collections of data records, provided it is guaranteed that it always remains balanced in the presence of insertions and deletions. There are simple cases of insertions that do not pose any problem at all. Consider the cases illustrated in Figure 9.2. Two new keys, "Ellen" and "Bob," along with RIDs of two new data records, are to be inserted into our example tree. In both cases, the key is first searched to check if it already exists. If it exists, then the new RID would simply be added to the RID list of the key. Otherwise the (unsuccessful) search stops in the leaf node where the key should reside if it existed. Hence this is exactly the leaf into which the key should be inserted. If this leaf still has sufficient free space available, the insertion is straightforward. This is exactly what happens in the cases of "Ellen" and "Bob."

Next consider the case when the leaf node into which a key is to be inserted *Node split* does not have enough free space. This case is illustrated in Figure 9.3. The new key value "Sue" is to be inserted into the rightmost leaf of the example tree, illustrated by the gray-filled box, but this causes what is known as a *page overflow*. A simple-minded remedy could now start building up a chain of linked pages that are anchored at the overflowed leaf, but this would obviously be susceptible to degeneration in that arbitrarily long overflow chains and thus poor search performance could not be ruled out. The actual solution, which is efficient as well as elegant, is based instead on an incremental reorganization of the tree that is known as a *node split* and grows the tree in a way that it remains

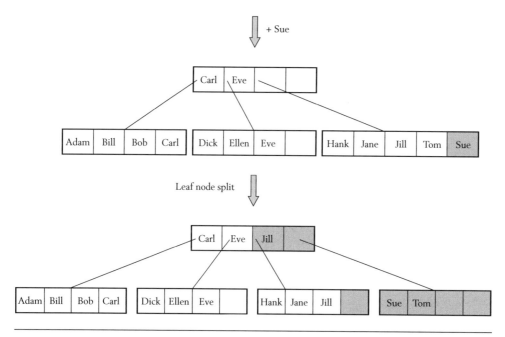

Figure 9.3 Insertion into a B$^+$ tree with a leaf node split.

balanced. This incremental reorganization proceeds in three steps:

Grow   1. A new, initially empty page is allocated as a new leaf node. This page will become the right sibling of the overflowed page.

Split   2. The index entries of the overflowed page, including the new entry, are partitioned across the overflowed and the newly allocated page. This is the actual split operation. A typical constraint here is that both pages end up with approximately the same number of entries or the same percentage of used space. This serves to ensure that the filling of all tree nodes is above a certain threshold of 50%; otherwise the tree would stay nominally balanced, but its height could become larger than necessary.

Post   3. The partitioning of the index entries ensures that the largest key value that remains in the original page is smaller than the smallest key value in the new page. Then, the last step consists of "posting" the largest key values of the two pages, along with the corresponding page pointers, as new index entries in the parent of the original node. So both pages will have the same parent node. The original index entry that pointed to the overflowed page is removed from the parent (or, equivalently, substituted by one of the two new index entries).

In the example, the keys "Hank," "Jane," and "Jill" remain in the split leaf node, and "Tom" and the new key "Sue" are placed in the newly allocated sibling. Consequently, the largest key that remains in the split page, along with pointers to the two sibling nodes that are separated by this router value, are posted in the parent node. As in the simple insertion case, all modified pages and entries are marked as shaded boxes in Figure 9.3.

The final case that we need to consider for insertions is now rather obvious: what if the parent node of a split page does not have sufficient space for the two new routing entries (after the removal of the original router to the split page) and becomes itself overflowed? The solution is to apply the above split operation recursively, going upward in the tree. In fact, we already described the three steps of a split operation in a generic way in that they can be applied not only to leaf pages but to all node levels in the tree. The recursive split propagation stops when the root level is reached. When the root node overflows, its split operation creates a sibling node.

Since we cannot have two root nodes in a tree, we now have to create a new root node that points to the old root and its new sibling. In other words, the tree grows by adding another root level on top of the old root level. This case is illustrated in Figure 9.4, where the insertion of the new key "Betty" leads to a split of the leftmost leaf, as shown in the top of the figure. The posting of "Bill" as a new router in the root node then causes the root to split. The resulting situation with a tree of height 3 is shown in the lower part of the figure.

The split operations ensure that a B$^+$ tree always remains perfectly balanced, while the operations themselves are very efficient, namely, with I/O costs that are logarithmic in the size of the tree. A dual solution can be devised for handling the deletions of keys in a tree. The counterpart to a split operation would be the merging of two adjacent siblings and the subsequent removal of a router from the parent node. One of the two merged pages can then be deallocated from the tree and returned to the free space management. So altogether, a B$^+$ tree can grow and shrink, both in width and height, dynamically in an incremental manner while guaranteeing that the filling of the allocated pages does not fall below a specified threshold of 50%. In practice, since insertions are so much more frequent than deletions, rather than implementing the merging-based algorithms for deletions, pages are often allowed to become underfull (i.e., filled less than 50%) due to deletions. Only when a tree node becomes completely empty would both the page and its routing entry in the parent be removed from the tree. Finally, updates of data records that cause the value of an indexed field in an existing data record to change are usually treated as a pair of key deletion and key insertion as far as the index structure is concerned.

The dynamic *grow-and-post* reorganization principle can be generalized to a much wider class of tree-based index structures, including indexes for multi-dimensional, spatial, or temporal search operations. Modern database systems therefore offer a broad repertoire of index choices and other physical design options to the database administration and tuning staff. For B$^+$ tree indexes alone, this spectrum includes the choice of fields or field combinations that

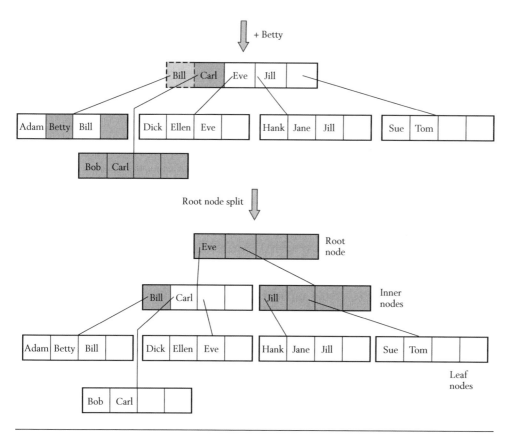

Figure 9.4 Insertion into a B$^+$ tree with a root node split.

are to be indexed—a choice between storing only keys and RIDs versus entire data records in the index leaves, the latter often called a *cluster* or *clustered index*—and many other fine-tuning options. Database systems make these options available to the database administrator in the form of parameters to the CreateIndex command of SQL.

9.3 Key Range Locking at the Access Layer

We assume an ADT interface for a search structure that provides the following operations:

> insert(key, RID)
> delete(key, RID)
> search(key)
> range_search(lowkey, highkey)

The Insert operation adds a (key, RID) pair to an index entry (stored in a leaf node of a search tree in the most common implementation of the index ADT). If the index is a unique one (i.e., allows at most one occurrence of each key), or if the new key is not yet present, then the Insert operation creates a new index entry. Analogously, the Delete operation removes a (key, RID) pair, possibly removing the entire index entry if no other RID exists for that key. The Search operation returns all RIDs for a given key, by looking up the appropriate index entry (by means of top-down descent from the root to the appropriate leaf node if in the search tree implementation). Finally, the Range_Search operation returns all RIDs of records that contain a value in a specified range between "lowkey" and "highkey" (including both of these bounds). Its implementation (on a search tree) would initially search for the smallest index entry whose key is equal to or larger than "lowkey," and would then scan all following index entries' leaf nodes of the index tree until it reaches an index entry with a key that is larger than "highkey." Recall from Chapter 1 that this procedure is known as an *index scan* or *range scan*.

Search structures as an ADT

Simple commutativity arguments tell us that Insert and Delete operations commute between each other, unless we consider a unique index. In the latter case, a delete followed by an insert for the same key would result in the key being present, whereas the other way around, the insert would fail as an attempt at adding a duplicate, and the subsequent delete would remove the key from the index. For simplicity, we will mostly assume that the index under consideration is not unique. The analogous derivations for the case of a unique index are left as an exercise (see Exercise 9.1). We can further infer that Search operations do not commute with inserts or deletes if they refer to the same key; otherwise they are conflict free from the viewpoint of the access layer. Finally, the Range_Search operation is in conflict with an Insert or Delete operation if the inserted or deleted key falls into the range from the "lowkey" to the "highkey" value of the range search.

With these considerations, we can immediately derive a possible locking protocol for the above search structure operations. Insert, Delete, and Search operations acquire locks on the specified keys, and Range_Search operations lock their corresponding key ranges. The lock conflict test must consider the equality of keys and the containment of a key in a key range. As for lock releases, the usual 2PL (or a stronger) discipline is used. This protocol, which we will refer to as the *simple key range locking* method, can be viewed as a very restricted form of predicate locking: it considers only the predicates of the form indexed attribute = key value or "lowkey" ≤ indexed attribute ≤ "highkey." These simple conditions are the result of decomposing the actual query's predicates into the operations at the access layer. This form of locking at the access layer is indeed sufficient to prevent anomalies and guarantee full serializability.

Simple key range locking

At this point, you may wonder how phantoms can be avoided when no index is used for executing predicate-oriented queries. In this case, a table scan must be used for finding qualifying records, and that table scan needs to look up a list of pages on which the records of the corresponding table reside. This list, which is part of the data server's storage layer metadata (for addressing and free space management, see Section 1.5), can be viewed as a key range from minus infinity to plus infinity (assuming numerical attributes) that is effectively read-locked by the lookup. Any concurrent insertion or deletion would have to inspect and actually modify this list, too, and would therefore need a write lock, thus revealing a lock conflict. So key range locking is a method that is not necessarily tied to the existence or usage of an index. An actual implementation may choose a different approach in the scenario sketched, but, in principle, all possible execution plans are correctly covered by the key range locking protocol. For the following, we simplify the presentation by assuming that an index is used for all queries.

Simple key range locking entails two major problems:

- First, it requires a lock manager that can manage value ranges, not just individual values, and has an efficient method for testing the containment of a value in an interval. Although this is surely not a dramatically challenging problem, the solution would inevitably incur more overhead than that of a standard lock manager for individual values only. As locking is part of a data server's innermost loops, such increased overhead is a concern.

- Second, a range search specifies the key range to be locked upon its start. At this point, the entire range is locked, although values close to the interval's upper bound (i.e., the "highkey" value) will be reached only in a while. The effect is similar to preclaiming: we lock out Update operations that refer to keys close to the upper bound for at least the entire duration of the range search. It would suffice, however, to start blocking updates once the range scan arrives at a certain key.

Incremental key range locking (previous key locking)

So we would like to improve key range locking with respect to its overhead and its concurrency by gradually building up the lock on a key range in an *incremental* manner; and, if possible, all locks should be implemented as if they were *individual key locks*. This will lead us to an *incremental and implicit key range locking* protocol, also known as *previous key locking* in the literature, for reasons that become clear in a short while. To this end, we first modify the interface of the index ADT by breaking up a range scan into multiple short steps that correspond to the actual implementation: a range search is viewed as a single key search followed by a sequence of Next operations that return the next index entry unless the specified "highkey" value was exceeded. So the "highkey" value of a range search serves as a stopping condition for the index scan. The Next operation is obviously a context-sensitive operation; it always takes up from where the scan was left by the previous Next or an initial Search operation. A sequence of Next calls must always be preceded by a Search call. Each Next call expects a current "cursor" position as an input parameter, in the form of the last visited key and the page number of the leaf node on which that

Index scans as sequences of Next operations

key resided. So the detailed form of Next operations and the preceding initial search is

search(searchkey) ↑ key ↑ page

next(currentkey, currentpage, highkey) ↑ key ↑ page

with input parameters searchkey, currentkey, currentpage, and highkey and return parameters key and page, where key is the found key and page is the page on which the returned key resides (which will become the currentkey and currentpage parameters for the subsequent Next call). A Range_Search("lowkey," "highkey") operation is mapped onto the following call sequence:

search(lowkey) ↑ currentkey ↑ currentpage

next(currentkey, currentpage, highkey) ↑ currentkey ↑ currentpage

next(currentkey, currentpage, highkey) ↑ currentkey ↑ currentpage

etc.

which terminates when a called operation finds that the next key in the scan is higher than the specified "highkey" and then yields nil for its return parameters. In the following discussion we will often use these operations without all parameters explicitly listed; the missing parameters are either irrelevant or can be easily derived from the context.

The second consideration toward a more efficient variant of key range locking is to restrict the lockable intervals to those that are actually present in the index. For example, if the index contains index entries with keys 22, 25, 29, and 30 but not the other values between 22 and 30, then the intervals [22, 25), [25, 29), and [29, 30) are among the lockable ranges. In general, a lockable interval is a one-sided open interval that starts from a key present in the index, including this key itself, and extends to the next higher key that occurs in the index, excluding this one. The fact that these intervals are one-sided open serves to make different intervals disjoint and allows us to uniquely name the intervals as follows. By identifying an interval with its left end (i.e., lower bound), we can lock an interval by acquiring a lock on its left-end value. So this simplifies the actual lock management, but we nevertheless use the convention that such a lock covers the entire interval.

The choice of exactly these intervals is, of course, not arbitrary. Rather, these are the intervals that are touched by the sequences of Next operations in a range scan. So now we are also close to the desired kind of incremental lock acquisition for range searches: each of the initial search and the subsequent next steps acquires a lock on the interval whose left-end value it returns to the caller. Using the above "encoding" convention of mapping intervals to their left-end value, this kind of locking eliminates both of our concerns about simple key range locking: locks are no longer acquired prematurely, and they can be managed with very little overhead.

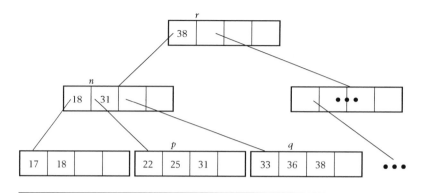

Figure 9.5 Sample B⁺ tree index.

As an example, consider the B⁺ tree index shown in Figure 9.5. A range search of the form range_search (23, 34) would lead to the sequence of operations and lock requests shown in Table 9.1.

Note that, in the end, the range search will have locked the entire interval [22, 36], thus properly covering the specified query range [23, 34]. The difference between this and the simple key range locking is that this interval comprises the smaller intervals that represent the actually present keys, and the entire interval is incrementally locked by gradually acquiring the locks on the constituent intervals.

Previous key locks Now we need to consider the necessary locking for Insert and Delete operations that would conflict with a range search (i.e., whose keys fall into the Search operation's specified range). An Insert operation for a key x would naturally lock x itself, representing the interval from x to the next present key. This holds regardless of whether x was already present or is newly inserted. For example, inserting the new key 27 into the index of Figure 9.5 should definitely acquire a lock for the interval [27, 31]. If the insert preceded the Next operation of the range scan that proceeded forward from 25 (i.e., with 25 as the last value returned by the previous Next call), the conflict between the two operations would be detected, as that Next operation would then have to acquire a lock on key 27, too. However, if the Insert operation followed the entire range search, no conflict would be signaled, as the formerly absent key 27

Table 9.1 Sample operations and lock requests on B⁺ tree index.

Operation	Lock request
Search(23) ↑ 25 ↑ p	Lock (22), representing the interval [22, 25)
Next(25, p, 34) ↑ 31 ↑ p	Lock (25), representing the interval [25, 31)
Next(31, p, 34) ↑ 33 ↑ q	Lock (31), representing the interval [31, 33)
Next(33, q, 34) ↑ nil ↑ nil	Lock (33), representing the interval [33, 36)

has, of course, not been locked by any of the Next operations. So the problem is to detect that key 27 falls into the interval [25, 31) by merely inspecting the left-end points of intervals.

The solution is to have an Insert operation also lock the interval that precedes its primarily locked interval. In our example, insert(27) needs to lock the interval [25, 27), too; and the technical means would be to write-lock the previous key 25, hence the name *previous key locking* for this protocol. Note that it is, in fact, fairly natural for the Insert operation to acquire this lock, too, as its effect is to split the former interval [25, 31) into two intervals. The literature also considers a dual variant of previous key locking that is known as *next key locking*. That protocol essentially requires operations to lock the key on which they operate and the next higher key (with some relaxations of this base scheme). We leave a discussion of the "isomorphism" between previous key and next key locking as an exercise (see Exercise 9.5.)

Dual variant: next key locking

Analogous considerations for Delete operations suggest that a delete(x) operation should lock both x and the largest preceding key that is present in the index, as its removal of key x potentially merges the interval starting at x with the preceding interval, thus connecting the original interval's right-end point with a different, smaller left-end point. Although this intuitive explanation would strictly hold only if the index entry for x contained only a single RID, we apply the same locking rule to the general case when x is still present after the delete of one (key, RID) pair. We will come back to possible relaxations of this rule for the latter case in Section 9.5.

Finally, an exact match search(x) operation can proceed in the most natural way, by merely acquiring a read lock on the key x that it searches for. However, if this key does not exist yet, but is later added by an Insert operation, it must still be possible to detect this conflict between the Search and the Insert operations. This is done by having the "unsuccessful" Search operation lock the interval starting at the next lower, currently present key, as this one would be the previous key lock to be acquired by a subsequent Insert operation. Again, this is, in fact, fairly intuitive. Not having found a key is a specific result that must be reflected in a proper serialization order, and one way of capturing the missing key is by remembering what next key was found in the place where the missing key would have had to be. For example, for the index in Figure 9.5, a search(25) operation would lock key 25 (i.e., the interval [25, 31)), and a search(24) operation would lock key 22 (i.e., the interval [22, 25)).

Putting all of the above considerations together, we arrive at the following set of lock acquisition rules for the operations of the index ADT:

Incremental key range (previous key) locking rules

- An operation search(x) requests a read lock on x if key x is present in the index; otherwise a lock on the largest key smaller than x is requested.

- An operation next(currentkey, currentpage, highkey) requests a read lock on currentkey.

- An operation insert(y, RID) requests write locks on y and the largest key smaller than y that is present in the index.

- An operation delete(y, RID) requests write locks on y and the largest key smaller than y that is present in the index.

In addition, the 2PL rules on lock releases and the usual well-formedness rules for all locking protocols must be in effect. Somewhat more liberal rules are conceivable, but we postpone a discussion of such additional optimizations to Section 9.5. All rules together ensure the correctness of the protocol, as captured by the following theorem:

THEOREM 9.1

Previous key locking generates only conflict-serializable schedules as far as index operations are concerned.

Proof

The proof shows that all potential conflicts between Search, Range_Search, Insert, and Delete operations are correctly recognized by acquiring key range locks. Since all locks are held according to the 2PL discipline, this is sufficient to prove serializability.

First, a conceptual conflict between a search(x) operation and insert(y, RID) or delete(y, RID) exists only for $x = y$. Since all three operations acquire a lock on the primarily affected key, this conflict is surely detected. For an unsuccessful search(x) operation, it is important for serializability to prevent a subsequent insertion of x as long as the search transaction has not committed (e.g., if the search transaction repeated its search after the insertion or accessed some other data that is logically related to the presence or absence of x). Since both an unsuccessful Search and Insert operation need to acquire a lock on the largest key smaller than x, this conflict situation is detected.

Second, there is a conceptual conflict between a range_search(lowkey, highkey) operation and insert(y, RID) or delete(y, RID) if the key y falls into the range from "lowkey" to "highkey" (including both bounds). This case is the decisive one that necessitates previous key locks. To see that such conflicts are properly detected, we only need to observe that a range search gradually acquires locks, through its initial search and the subsequent Next calls, on all existing keys starting from the largest existing key that is smaller than or equal to "lowkey" and ending with the largest existing key that is no larger than "highkey." Since both insert(y, RID) and delete(y, RID) operations request a lock on the previous key of y, they must have at least one lock conflict with the sequence of Search and Next operations of a conceptually conflicting range search.

Third, two Insert operations potentially conflict only if they refer to the same key, and even this is only a real conflict if the index is a unique one, disallowing duplicates. The remaining cases of two Delete operations or an Insert and Delete pair are analogous.

A further difficulty that arises once implementation considerations come into play is that the keys on which the various operations need to acquire locks are only partly known when the operation starts. The "previous keys" that need to be locked on behalf of inserts and deletes become known only during the execution of the operations. However, as the index operations themselves are performed as subtransactions, with an isolation guarantee by the underlying page layer, there is also no problem with acquiring access layer (i.e., higher-level) locks in the course of an operation's execution. This means that the lock requests of the two relevant layers, the access and the page layer, are interleaved rather than being timewise separated, as in the layered 2PL presented in Chapter 7. Recall, however, from Chapter 7 that the exploitation of return value commutativity also involved high-level lock acquisitions *after* the begin (and, in fact, not before the completion) of the corresponding high-level operations. So locks of both layers are dynamically acquired at the latest possible point, right when the "resources" to be locked become known. For example, an insert(27) index operation on the index structure of Figure 9.5 would go through the sequence of lock requests and execution steps, shown in Table 9.2, assuming a subtransaction scope 2PL discipline on the page layer.

We will come back to the interplay of index key and page locks when discussing more relaxed, B^+ tree–specific page lock release policies and other similarly "liberal" concurrency control methods in the next section.

9.4 **Techniques for the Page Layer**

Before we embark on the presentation of various algorithms for the page layer concurrency control of search structure operations, let us first illustrate once again the kinds of problems that arise. Throughout this section we focus on

Table 9.2 Operations and lock requests for sample insert into B^+ tree index.

Operation	Lock request
Read(r)	Lock page r
Read(n)	Lock page n
Read(p)	Lock page p
Find the previous key 25	Lock key 25, representing the interval [25, 31)
Add the new key 27	Lock key 27, representing the interval [27, 31)
	Release page locks on r, n, and p

B$^+$ trees as the most important case and also a paradigmatic example of search structures for disk-resident data. Consider the B$^+$ tree index shown in the top third, labeled "stage 0," of Figure 9.6, and assume that an insert(30) operation takes place on this index. After the operation has located the leaf p into which the new key would have to be inserted, but finds that page p is already completely full, it initiates a leaf node split of p, creating a new sibling p' ("stage 1" in Figure 9.6). The final stage, labeled "stage 2" in the figure, consists of posting this split in the parent of p and p', by adjusting the routing keys and pointers in node n (see Section 9.2).

Now suppose that a concurrent search(31) operation takes place. As a worst possible scenario, this Search operation could perform its top-down descent of the tree between the leaf node split but before the split is posted in the parent node n. So this operation would see the intermediate state shown in stage 1 of the insert. The routing keys in nodes r and n would direct the Search operation to the leaf node p, but would no longer find the key 31 there; so this search would erroneously return a "key not found" result. As an even worse scenario, suppose that an insert(31) operation rather than a search is interleaved in the above way with the split operation, and that the index is a unique index so that duplicate insertions should be disallowed. As the insert(31) would likewise be erroneously directed to the already split node p, nothing would prevent it from inserting another instance of the key 31 (together with some RID). As a result, the uniqueness condition would become violated, and the database would be inconsistent.

The most obvious way to prevent these problems and ensure serializability of the subtransactions that correspond to index operations is to employ 2PL (or S2PL, or even SS2PL) for such subtransactions. The purpose of this section, however, is to develop even better solutions in terms of the possible concurrency, taking specific advantage of the tree traversal access patterns and the special structure of B$^+$ tree indexes. The various approaches are classified into three types:

- lock coupling, which is essentially a refinement of the tree locking protocol that we introduced in Chapter 4,
- the link technique, which exploits a specific implementation aspect of B$^+$ tree–like search structures,
- the giveup technique, which is an optimistic variant.

9.4.1 **Lock Coupling**

The first method to be presented, coined *lock coupling*, follows the approach of the tree locking protocol introduced in Chapter 4. For simplicity, first consider only Search and Insert operations (i.e., no range searches or Next operations, and also no deletions). These operations basically perform a top-down descent into the tree, following exactly one path of the tree, and the Search operations even have the nice property that they never revisit a node again. This very specific page access pattern immediately suggests the use of the tree locking protocol. Recall that the basic principle of this protocol is to lock a node only after holding a lock on its parent, but to release the parent lock as early as possible, once we know that the operation will not go up in the tree again.

Unfortunately, the latter is exactly what Insert operations may occasionally do, namely, when they have to split a leaf node and need to post the split along the ancestor chain. So, although Search operations could release nonleaf node locks early, Inserts would have to hold all locks until they know that no split occurs. This consideration can be made stronger by exploiting the fact that most splits propagate only one tree level upward; only very infrequently, inner nodes need to be split, too, which would then necessitate adjustments (or even further splits) in additional ancestors. Now, when the Insert operation performs its top-down descent, it can observe information about the space utilization of the various nodes and whether a node can spacewise accommodate the posting of an additional routing key and child pointer. When the free space in a node suffices to hold an additional key and pointer from a node split at some level farther below, then we know for sure that the split will not propagate farther upward in the tree. So the parent of the node under consideration will definitely not have to be updated at all, which means that it will for sure not be revisited again by the Insert operation. We call such a parent node of a node with sufficient free space a *split safe node*. In the example of Figure 9.6, assuming a node capacity of four keys and pointers, node *r* can be recognized as split safe once the insert(30) operation has proceeded to node *n* and finds that node *n* can accommodate the posting of a split farther below without itself having to be split. In the implementation, the test for "sufficient free space" is complicated by the fact that keys can be of variable length. However, by assuming conservative upper bounds for the length of a routing key in an inner node, a proper decision can always be made.

Split safe tree nodes

These considerations immediately lead to a locking protocol for Search and Insert operations that is known as *lock coupling* and is driven by the following rules:

1. Search operations need to request a read lock on a node before the node can be accessed; Insert operations need to request a write lock.

2. A lock on a node can be granted only if no conflicting lock is currently held and the requesting operation holds a lock on the node's parent.

3. Search operations can release the lock on a node once they have acquired a lock on a child of that node.

4. Insert operations can release the lock on a node if (a) the node is split safe and (b) they have acquired a lock on a child of that node.

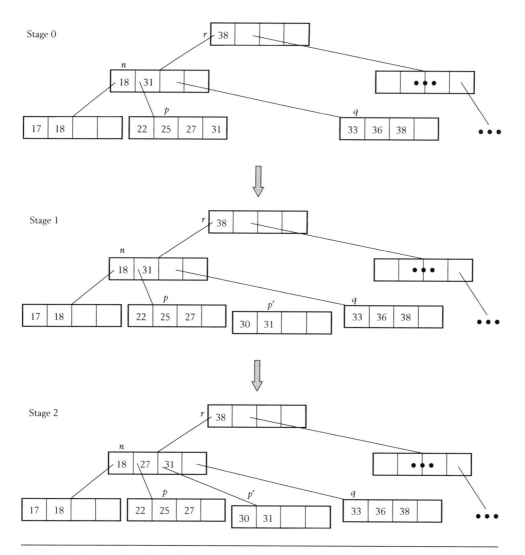

Figure 9.6 Stages of a B$^+$ tree leaf node split.

For the above example scenario with concurrent operations insert(30) and search(31) on the index of Figure 9.6, a possible execution under the lock coupling protocol is given in Table 9.3.

The correctness of this protocol is reflected in the following theorem:

THEOREM 9.2

The lock coupling protocol for Search and Insert operations generates only schedules that are OCSR.

Table 9.3 Sample execution of Insert and Search under lock coupling.

Insert(30)	Search(31)
Write lock r	
Write lock n	
Unlock r	
	Read lock r
	Request read lock on n
Write lock p	
Allocate new page p'	
Write lock p'	
Split contents of p onto p and p'	
Adjust contents of n	
Unlock n, p, and p'	
	Acquire read lock on n
	Unlock r
	Read lock p'
	Unlock n
	Return RID for key 31
	Unlock p'

The easy proof can be based on the fact that the protocol is a special case of the general tree locking protocol. Note that, although we allow both read and write locks, we do not encounter any problems with "pitfalls" in the sense of the read/write tree locking protocol of Chapter 4, as Insert operations acquire only write locks from the beginning. An alternative that requires a bit more thought for ensuring correctness would be to have Insert operations also start with acquiring only read locks on nonleaf nodes (but still a write lock on the leaf, of course); and only upon realizing the need for a split would read locks be converted to write locks. This is indeed a feasible option, but it entails the danger of deadlocks among Insert operations. Yet another alternative that has turned out to perform fairly well would be to start out with read locks and roll back an Insert operation once it realizes the need for a split. Note that only the operation should be rolled back, not the entire transaction, and this is more or less for free anyway since no updates have been made yet. Then, the Insert operation would be repeated, but now acquiring the necessary locks in write mode.

Now let us add range searches, or equivalently, Next operations to our considerations. A range search follows the forward linked chain among leaf nodes (see Chapter 1). So we are actually dealing with a DAG structure here, no longer a pure tree. Fortunately, as you may recall from Chapter 4, tree locking can be generalized to DAGs by requiring that a lock on a node can be granted only if the requestor holds locks on the majority of the node's predecessors. Strictly speaking, the leaf linked B^+ tree considered here is a dynamically evolving DAG, not a static one as originally assumed by the DAG locking protocol, but we will ignore this potential complication. As each leaf node has two predecessors—its parent in the tree and the preceding leaf—range searches would also have to visit and lock all inner nodes that point to the accessed leaves, and operations like Search and Insert that perform a top-down descent also need to acquire a lock on the leaf that precedes their actual target leaf. So, although we can in principle construct a working protocol from these considerations, chances are that it would not be very efficient.

On the other hand, we have a special situation that we can exploit to simplify the rule about having to lock the majority of predecessors. First, we have a clear separation between operations that need write locks and those that need read locks: searches need only read locks, and Insert operations could be implemented by acquiring only write locks. This suggests the following modification of the "majority rule": a read lock can be granted if a lock on at least one predecessor is held, and the prerequisite for granting a write lock on a node would then be holding write locks on all predecessors. This way, searches would have to acquire locks only along a single path to the leaf level, and range searches would only need locks for the leaf chain. There would still be a severe penalty on Insert operations, having to acquire locks on two leaves rather than one (in the no-split case). Fortunately, however, there is another particularity that we can exploit: splits create only new successors of a node, never a new predecessor (i.e., we always split "to the right"). With this restriction we can safely relax the lock-all-predecessors condition for insertions. It suffices that inserts lock the path to their target leaf and possibly a newly created leaf node.

Lock coupling with range searches   These considerations bring us to the following extended version of lock coupling, now including range searches:

1. Search and Range_Search operations need to request a read lock on a node before the node can be accessed; Insert operations need to request a write lock.

2. For Search and Insert operations as well as the initial descent of Range_Search operations, a lock on a node can be granted only if no conflicting lock is currently held and the requesting operation holds a lock on the node's parent.

3. Search operations can release the lock on a node once they have acquired a lock on a child of that node.

4. Insert operations can release the lock on a node if (a) the node is split safe and (b) they have acquired a lock on a child of that node.

5. Range_Search operations can acquire a lock on a leaf node only if they hold a lock on the leaf's parent in the tree or on the preceding leaf. The first case is relevant during the initial descent of the tree, locating the first relevant leaf; the second case covers the progress along the linked chain of leaf nodes.

Now recall from the previous section that a range search is effectively broken down into a regular Search operation and a sequence of Next operations. In the protocol described above, all these operations would still be considered as a single subtransaction as far as their page locks are concerned. There is nothing wrong with this interpretation; after all, Next operations are context dependent. The question, however, is whether this could be further relaxed. In particular, would it even be possible to release all page locks on behalf of a range search between two successive Next operations? The answer is positive. Because of the special structure of a B$^+$ tree and, particularly, the fact that splits are performed always "to the right," we can indeed treat each Next operation as a separate subtransaction. This actually relaxes the lock coupling rule assumed so far: a Next operation first reacquires a lock on the leaf that the previous Next or the initial Search operation had last locked, and it does so without holding a lock on the parent or preceding leaf. Once the Next operation then finds that it has to access the next leaf to retrieve the following key, it needs to acquire a lock on that leaf, now under the "protection" of already holding a lock on the preceding leaf. In essence, this prevents the preceding leaf from being split right in the moment of traversing the link to the next leaf.

These specific considerations for Next operations are captured by the following additional rule for lock coupling:

Lock coupling with Next operations

6. A next(currentkey, currentpage, highkey) operation needs to acquire a read lock on currentpage, and it can acquire a read lock on any other leaf page only if it holds a read lock on that page's preceding leaf.

THEOREM 9.3

Lock coupling with Next operations generates only OCSR schedules.

Proof

First note that without Next operations we would simply apply the tree locking protocol of Chapter 4. The special twist of not releasing locks on nodes that are not split safe is fully in line with standard tree locking. So the only complication is Next operations.

Assume that there is a conflict cycle among index operations, i.e., subtransactions, that involves a Next operation reading the two adjacent leaves p and q. The only way of forming such a cycle is to have at least one Insert or Delete operation between the $r(p)$ and $r(q)$ steps of the Next operation. However, that Insert or Delete operation would not be able to acquire a lock on p once p has been read by the Next operation. So the "worst case" is that the insert or delete takes place on q. If there is a split, it would affect only leaves to the right of q, never the left neighbor p. Therefore, such an insert or delete must follow the Next operation in the serialization ordering.

The order preservation of the protocol is easy to verify, as tree locking by itself ensures order-preserving conflict serializability, and the above consideration on Next operations already shows that their addition does not undermine this property.

Note that the equivalent serialization order for a schedule of Search, Next, and Insert operations may have a range search interleaved with inserts, as the above theorem only ensures that the individual next steps can be isolated from the inserts, but this does not consider the broader context of an entire range search. In combination with the incremental key range locks that an entire range search acquires and in fact holds for the duration of the entire transaction, we can guarantee that inserts that run concurrently with a range search can be "disentangled" by means of commutativity based transformations and tree pruning. An important observation toward the proof of this claim is that an insert can never take place behind the current "cursor" position of an ongoing range search, unless the insert key is smaller than the the range search's "lowkey." The reason for this property is that both the range search and the insert need key range locks at the access layer. So inserts can only occur after the current cursor position, and in this case one of the subsequent next steps of the range search would become blocked by the insert's key range lock (unless the inserted key is even higher than the "highkey" of the range search). This effectively means that such inserts should precede the range search in the resulting serialization order, but as all access layer locks would be held until the end of the entire transaction, no incompatible ordering of other operations is possible. This yields the following theorem:

THEOREM 9.4

Lock coupling at the page layer together with incremental key range locking at the access layer ensure the tree reducibility of all two-level schedules with these two layers.

Proof

Note that Theorems 9.1 and 9.3 together already show that schedules with Search, Insert, and Delete operations alone are tree reducible. This follows from the result of Chapter 6 that conflict serializability at the higher level of a two-layered system and order-preserving conflict serializability for the subtransactions of the lower level together guarantee tree reducibility. So again the complication is caused by Next operations on behalf of Range_Searches.

We already know from Theorem 9.3 that Insert, Delete, Search, and Next operations, if viewed as individual subtransactions, can be isolated by means of commutativity arguments. This argument is, however, not yet sufficient for isolating entire Range_Searches that consist of an initial search and a sequence of Next calls. So the case to be considered is of the following form:

... $search_i$(lowkey)
... $insert_k$(x, RID1)
... $next_i$(currentkey1, highkey)
... $insert_l$(y, RID2)
... $next_i$(currentkey2, highkey) ...

where a Range_Search of transaction t_i is interleaved with Insert operations of two concurrent transactions t_k and t_l. The situation with interleaved Deletes would be analogous and is not discussed here further (and an interleaved Search or Range_Search of another transaction could trivially be pushed outside t_i's Range_Search to form an isolated subtree).

Because of Theorem 9.3, such a pattern can be transformed into one with no interleaving of page accesses for the Search, Insert, and Next operations. Furthermore, the same arguments that we used in the proof of Theorem 9.1 show that the first Insert operation's key x cannot fall into the range [lowkey, currentkey1], as this would have provoked a lock conflict. So this Insert operation can be pushed to the left to precede t_i's initial search and thus becomes an isolated subtree. By the same token, the second Insert operation's key y cannot fall into the range [lowkey, currentkey2]; so it can again be commuted with the preceding steps of t_i's Range_Search. The general observation thus is that an Insert operation that is interleaved with a Range_Search cannot refer to any key in the range that the Range_Search has seen so far. On the other hand, if it refers to a key that will be visited by later Next steps of the Range_Search, then the Insert can always be pushed to the front of the Range_Search, thus preceding it in the equivalent serialization order.

This consideration shows that Inserts, Deletes, Searches, and entire Range_Searches can always be isolated, and in conjunction with Theorem 9.1 concludes the proof of tree reducibility.

As an illustrative example of the complete lock coupling protocol and its combination with incremental key range locking at the access layer, Table 9.4 shows the necessary lock requests, acquisitions, and releases for a range_search(24, 35) operation that runs concurrently with an insert(30) operation on the B$^+$ tree shown as stage 0 of Figure 9.6.

Finally, let us add Delete operations to make the protocol truly comprehensive. If deletes were also to initiate complex minireorganizations of the tree, we might need to revise our previous findings quite substantially. For example, if a leaf node whose space utilization falls below a certain threshold were to be merged with its left sibling, the correctness of the lock coupling for

Table 9.4 Sample execution of range search and insert under lock coupling with key range locking.

Range_search(24, 35)	Insert(30)
Search(24)	
Read lock r	
Read lock n	
Unlock r	
Read lock p	
Unlock n	
Read lock key 22	
Unlock p	
Return 25, p	
	Insert(30)
	Write lock r
	Write lock n
	Unlock r
Next(25, p, 35)	
Read lock p	
Read lock key 25	
Unlock p	
Return 27, p	
	Write lock p
Next(27, p, 35)	
Request read lock on p	
	Write lock key 30
	Write lock key 27
	Write lock p'
	$\vdots$
	Unlock p, p', n
Acquire lock on p	
Request read lock on key 27	
	$\vdots$
	Commit transaction
Acquire lock on key 27	
Read lock p'	
Unlock p, p'	
Return 30, p'	
Next(30, p', 35)	
Read lock p'	
Read lock key 30	
Unlock p'	
Return 31, p'	
Next(31, p', 35)	
Read lock p'	
Read lock key 31	
Read lock q	
Unlock p', q	
Return 33, q	
Next(33, q, 35)	
Read lock q	
Read lock key 33	
Unlock q	
Return nil, nil	

Next operations would become questionable, as reorganizations would no longer be confined "to the right" of the primarily affected node. Fortunately, these complications can be easily avoided. It is common practice (see also Chapter 1) that deletes do not trigger any such local reorganizations. Rather we would simply wait until a node becomes completely empty, leaving it connected within the B$^+$ tree structure, and only then would it be detached from both its parent and the linked chain of leaf nodes. But once we adopt such a lazy free space reclamation policy, we can wait even a bit longer to ensure that no concurrent operation has already seen a pointer to the empty page from one of its predecessors and henceforth attempts to follow this pointer after the empty node has been deallocated. A simple sufficient condition to ensure the avoidance of such problems is to deallocate an empty node only when no transaction that was active at the time when the node became empty is active anymore. Because of this delayed deallocation, this simple trick has been called the *drain technique*. Note that until its deallocation, an empty node would still have its forward link to the next leaf; so if a concurrent Next operation steps on such a node, it would simply continue traversing the linked chain until it finds the next existing key.

Drain technique for empty nodes

9.4.2 **Link Technique**

In the lock coupling technique with Next operations, an important point was that range searches with a cursor on a page to be split do not need to prevent the split, but rather have their next Next operation be prepared to follow the leaf link to the newly created sibling node. For example, assume that a leaf node contains keys 11, 12, 14, 15, 16, 17, 18, and 19, and that the last Next call of a range search for the interval [15, 18] was positioned on key 16, and a concurrent insert(13) operation splits the page, moving keys 16, 17, 18, and 19 to a new leaf. When the range search continues with another Next call, it would reacquire a lock on the split page but then immediately follow the link to the new sibling to proceed with key 17. Note that in this case there is no access layer conflict between the range search and the insert.

This forward stepping behavior built into Next operations can be generalized and adopted by single-key Search operations as well. The principle is that whenever the key being looked for is not found on the page where it is presumed to reside, the operation simply follows the forward-link chain of the leaves until it either finds the key or realizes that the key is definitely not present, regardless of whatever concurrent reorganizations may blur the picture. This behavior is called the *link technique*, and it allows us to avoid holding multiple node locks simultaneously for both range searches and exact match searches. So unlike lock coupling, during the descent in the tree, only the currently processed page needs to be kept locked, and no parent lock is needed to acquire a lock on a node. Likewise, range scans do not need to hold a predecessor lock before they can acquire a lock on the next leaf. The reasons why this seemingly spectacular relaxation still works correctly is that all tree reorganizations work by pushing existing keys to the right, so that they will inevitably be found by every sufficiently persistent Search operation. Furthermore, the ordering of keys along the leaves is guaranteed at all times, even during splits. Even if a range search is initially directed to a page, say, p, which is split multiple times into p', p'', and so on, before the range search actually accesses p, the worst thing that could happen is that the "lowkey" that the range search is looking for has been moved to some node p'' or p''' more than one "hop" away from where the search expected it to be. But even in this case, all the search needs to do is to follow the leaf chain to the first key that is equal to or smaller than its "lowkey" parameter.

Deletes do not present any problems if we again simply use the drain technique (and avoid getting into the hairy business of merging adjacent nodes). Insert operations, however, would still need to follow the lock coupling protocol, so that they are properly synchronized among each other. Putting the resulting protocol together into a set of locking rules is left as an exercise (see Exercise 9.8). Here we restrict ourselves to illustrating the lock requests and releases for our initial problem scenario with search(31) being executed concurrently to insert(30) in Table 9.5.

As a final word of caution, notice that although the link technique may superficially appear strictly superior to lock coupling, there are cases where it reveals limitations, whereas lock coupling is more robust with regard to possible

Table 9.5 Sample execution of insert and search using the link technique.

Insert(30)	Search(31)
	Read lock r
	Unlock r
	Read lock n
	Unlock n
Write lock r	
Write lock n	
Unlock r	
Write lock p	
	Request read lock on p
Allocate new page p'	
Write lock p'	
Split contents of p onto p and p'	
Adjust contents of n	
Unlock n, p, and p'	
	Acquire read lock on p
	Unlock p
	Read lock p'
	Return RID for key 31
	Unlock p'

generalizations. One such generalization of practical relevance concerns range searches that deliver their result in descending order. Such a search would most naturally locate its "highkey" first and then traverse the linked list of leaf nodes in backward order. Obviously this would require a bidirectionally linked chain among the leaves, which is indeed what many commercial implementations of B$^+$ trees have. Now the fact that splits always reorganize to the right is no longer that helpful, as "backward scans" proceed from right to left (assuming that left to right means ascending key order). In this setting, the link technique in the presented form no longer works correctly. Lock coupling, on the other hand, can be made to work again with moderate effort.

9.4.3 **Giveup Technique**

Another interesting technique for synchronizing index tree traversals with local reorganizations like node splits is the *giveup technique*. This is essentially an optimistic variant based on the premise that conflicts are rare. So tree traversals on behalf of both searches and inserts or deletes proceed in their top-down descent without any locks, or merely holding a short-duration lock or latch on the currently processed node (but none of the operations ever holds locks on two different nodes simultaneously).

For detecting conflicts with a possibly ongoing reorganization like a node split, a special *range field* is maintained in the page header of each node (both leaves and inner nodes). This range field contains a lower bound and upper bound for the keys that could potentially reside in the subtree rooted at the given node. So when no reorganization is in progress, then for a node n with left sibling l and right sibling r such that the parent of n, l, and r has routing entries that form the ordered sequence $(\ldots, @l, x, @n, y, @r, \ldots)$ (with $@l$ denoting a pointer to node l), the range field should be the interval $[x, y]$. For example, for the stage 0 tree of Figure 9.6, the range of nodes r, n, p, and q are $(-\infty, +\infty)$, $(-\infty, 38]$, $(18, 31]$, and $(31, 38]$, respectively. These range fields are redundant information, but their point is that they can be maintained (namely, shrunk) by splits on a per-node basis. So in stage 1 of the split shown in Figure 9.6, the range field of node p has been modified to $(18, 27]$, and the range field of the new sibling p' has been set to $(27, 31]$. Note that these modifications are done, and can indeed be done, before the new routing key 27 is posted to p's parent n. Note also that in this particular example, the range field of the inner node n stays the same, but when splits propagate across multiple tree levels, range fields have to be adjusted at all affected levels, one node at a time.

The range fields of nodes enable a Search operation to detect when a split (or, more generally, some tree reorganization) is in progress in the part of the tree that the search is traversing. When a top-down descent searching for key k is directed to a certain subtree and then finds that the range field of the subtree's root node n does not contain the search key k, this indicates that node *n* has been split but the necessary posting farther up in the tree has not been completed. In this case the descent is simply rolled back and retried a short while later. We say that the tree traversal operation "gives up" at this point, and repeats the entire descent, giving the ongoing split some time to be posted in the parent (or ancestors in general). Since such reorganizations should not involve disk I/O in the "critical phase," the retrial of the given-up traversal would typically have to wait for only a few milliseconds.

The giveup technique has extremely low overhead, and it is fairly attractive in terms of its performance, as long as tree reorganizations are infrequent. For example, when the workload mostly consists of searches with occasional inserts that may trigger splits only once in a while, then the giveup technique would perform very well. For workloads with many concurrent inserts and a higher rate of node splits, however, the two other techniques presented above are likely to perform better.

9.5 **Further Optimizations**

After having covered the principles of both layers of index concurrency control and their interrelationships, we introduce additional performance optimizations. In the following four sections, we will address improvements in terms of lock management overhead as well as special considerations on enhancing concurrency in certain situations.

9.5.1 **Deadlock-Free Page Latching**

Lock coupling at the page layer is still sufficiently close to the basic tree locking protocol of Chapter 4 that it can be implemented in a deadlock-free manner. Recall from Chapter 4 that deadlock freedom can be guaranteed when all lock request patterns follow the node ordering of a tree or DAG. If, during the upward propagation of leaf splits, additional locks are acquired, this guarantee can no longer be given. So for deadlock freedom, either the version of lock coupling with lock releases only for split safe nodes must be used, or splits have to be performed in a second tree traversal with more stringent locking up front (as briefly discussed in Section 9.4).

Latch coupling Once deadlock freedom is ensured, it is no longer necessary to manage the short-term locks on index pages in an explicit lock table. Rather, a common trick to reduce the overhead of such special page locks is to use so-called *latches* instead of locks. Latches are lightweight semaphores for mutual exclusion of concurrent processes or threads within a process. Latches are usually implemented in the form of flags in page headers that are manipulated through special, indivisible machine instructions of the test-and-set style. Both shared and exclusive access can be provided this way. So in contrast to full-fledged semaphores as provided by the operating system or a thread package, latches do not necessarily support fair queueing or deadlock detection (although some variations in this regard are conceivable). Within the context of index concurrency control, using latches instead of page locks effectively turns the lock coupling protocol into a latch coupling protocol.

9.5.2 **Enhanced Key Range Concurrency**

The incremental key range locking protocol demands Insert operations to acquire exclusive locks on both the inserted key (or key to which a new (key, RID) entry is added) and the previous key. These two locks serve to alert concurrent readers (i.e., Search and Next operations). However, they also prevent concurrent inserts in the locked key range, even if these insertions refer to different keys. Obviously this is unnecessarily restrictive. An initial solution is relatively straightforward: we simply make the specific semantics of Insert operations more explicit by introducing an insert lock mode and requiring inserts to request the two key range locks in insert mode rather than exclusively. Insert locks on the same key ranges are compatible with each other, but incompatible with read locks. This allows concurrent key insertions without any blocking among each other. Note that this is perfectly legal even if two Insert operations add entries to the same key. (Some subtleties may arise if the key to which the two inserts refer was not present at all in the index before the two operations were executed, but we do not delve into all these details here.)

Fewer and less restrictive locks for inserts

Once we conceptually view the locking requirements for Insert operations under the two facets of synchronizing inserts with other inserts and deletes and synchronizing inserts against concurrent readers, we should reconsider whether we may also relax the second type of synchronization to some extent. It is important for Insert operations to realize when they would insert a new key in a key range that has already been visited by a concurrent but not yet committed reader; this is what requires the previous key lock. However, when an Insert operation precedes a reader, it is sufficient that the reader will eventually be blocked at the inserted key. In other words, reading the previous key should still be admissible. This asymmetry in the execution ordering of readers and inserts can be exploited as follows. The Insert operation merely needs to check if a read lock is held on the previous key. If this is the case, then the insert must wait until the read lock is released, to guarantee serializability. If no read lock is currently held, however, the insert can proceed without really having to acquire a lock on the previous key. Technically, this protocol can be implemented by having Insert operations acquire an *instant duration* lock in insert mode: once the lock is granted, it is immediately released again. Note that this relaxation holds only for the previous key; the insert lock on the newly inserted key must be held until commit.

Instant duration lock on previous key for inserts

Although it may seem intriguing to introduce an analogous relaxation for Delete operations, there is an inherent asymmetry between inserts and deletes that would lead to correctness problems if we applied the corresponding optimization to deletes. The asymmetry lies in the fact that a deleted key disappears from the index and thus will no longer cause concurrent inserts or readers to realize the conflict at the point of the deleted key itself. Therefore, locking the previous key until commit is crucial for deletes (at least in certain situations).

Fewer locks for "deferred" deletes The situation becomes different, however, if we could distinguish when a Delete operation merely removes one RID from a key's RID list without becoming empty so that the key continues to exist in the index. This would indeed reestablish the symmetry with Insert operations. From this observation we can derive a technique that we will refer to as "deferred" deletes, where Delete operations never remove a key from the index, even if they delete the last RID from the corresponding RID list. In such a situation, the key would be kept with an empty RID list, essentially serving as a marker for concurrent inserts and readers to realize conflicts. Some systems refer to such a marker as a *ghost key*, which will be garbage-collected in the background at some appropriate later time, namely, when all transactions that may have ever seen the ghost key (or, for more efficient testing of this situation, the page on which the ghost key resides) are terminated. With this technique of deferred deletes it turns out that it is not even necessary to acquire an instant duration lock on the previous key; rather, the lock on the key to which the delete refers is fully sufficient to synchronize deletes versus inserts and readers.

Note that the write lock on a deleted key is not compatible with insert locks. Of course, we could introduce an operation-specific delete lock mode, but its compatibility with other lock modes would have to be as restrictive as an exclusive lock. Otherwise, allowing the insert of a new, seemingly nonexisting key right after the deletion of that key and before the commit of the deleting transaction would incur correctness problems if the index has a uniqueness constraint and the deleting transaction aborts and thus needs to reinsert the deleted key.

In summary, the outlined optimizations relax the incremental key range locking rules for insert and "deferred" delete operations as follows:

- An operation insert(y, RID) requests an insert lock on y, to be held until transaction commit, and an instant duration insert lock on the largest key smaller than y that is present in the index.

- An operation delete(y, RID) requests a write lock on y, to be held until transaction commit.

A final opportunity for further optimization lies in distinguishing unique versus non-unique indexes, that is, indexed attributes that either disallow or allow duplicate key values. It is fairly obvious that unique indexes may require more stringent concurrency control measures to preserve the uniqueness of keys in the presence of concurrent Insert and Delete operations. Conversely, non-unique indexes can be more liberal in terms of concurrency. A case analysis along these lines is left as an exercise (see Exercise 9.1).

9.5.3 Reduced Locking Overhead

Key range locking at the access layer of an index is complementary to the locking of the actual data records, and it applies to all indexes affected by an operation. Thus, every index lookup for an exact match query on a single indexed attribute incurs two object-level locks to be held for transaction duration—the index key lock and the record lock. For an Insert or Delete operation on a table with n indexes, $n + 1$ locks need to be maintained in total (not counting additional short-term locks on pages). Under certain circumstances the time and especially the space overhead of managing this number of locks may be critical. The alternative then is to combine the index key and data record locks for an operation into a single lock, possibly trading a potential loss of concurrency for reduced bookkeeping overhead.

A concrete protocol along these lines would treat the (key, RID) pairs of an index as the actual locking granules rather than locking keys or key ranges and RIDs separately, or would even lock only RIDs. In both variations, all index operations still need to follow the rules of the incremental key range locking (or its optimized versions). For example, a Delete operation for RID 1133 with key value 25 has to acquire an appropriate previous key lock in addition to the lock on the entry (25, 1133) itself. If this key has duplicates, say, RIDs 1117, 1129, and 1137, the previous key to be locked would be the entry (25, 1129); if there are no duplicates, the last RID of the preceding key, for example, (22, 1135), would need to be locked. These locks could be managed in a lock table by the corresponding RIDs alone, effectively locking simply the RIDs 1133 and 1129 in the above scenario with duplicates or 1133 and 1135 in the scenario without duplicates.

RID locks can be interpreted either in conjunction with a specific index or globally with regard to all indexes. In the first case, the RID lock for an index lookup is relevant only for other operations on the same index, thus allowing concurrent updates on other attributes of the same record. However, this still requires n locks for an Insert or Delete operation on a table with n indexes. This overhead is further reduced by the second option, at the expense of disallowing concurrent updates on the same record regardless of which attributes are affected. So in this second case, only a single RID lock is required for inserting or deleting a record.

The main incentive for combining index key and record locks into RID locks is to reduce overhead, possibly at the expense of less concurrency. However, in specific cases this technique can even improve concurrency, because

RID locks only

RIDs for keys with long RID lists are locked in a more incremental manner compared to the baseline version of incremental key range locking.

9.5.4 **Exploiting Transient Versioning**

Yet another enhancement of index concurrency control at the access layer is to extend the presented incremental key range locking protocol by keeping transient versions of index entries and exploiting them for read-only transactions along the lines of the ROMV protocol described in Chapter 5. Here the unit of versioning is a (key, RID list) pair. So each Insert or Delete operation leads to a new version of the index entry, and now it is mandatory that a Delete operation that removes the last RID for a given key leaves a "ghost" entry as a special marker. For each index entry, the most recent version should reside directly in the appropriate index leaf page; whereas older versions may reside somewhere else and could, for example, be connected to their "successor" version in a doubly linked chain. More details about the implementation of transient versioning in general can be found in Chapter 10.

9.6 **Lessons Learned**

Concurrency control for search structures like B^+ tree indexes may appear highly intricate upon first glance, because of the interplay between steps at the access layer and the page layer. By making these two layers explicit and separating their concerns, the state-of-the-art protocols become more comprehensible and easier to verify.

At the access layer, a limited form of predicate locks is needed to ensure the serializability of transactions. These locks refer to keys or key ranges, and can be cleverly encoded into what appears to be single keys by interpreting a key as a semi-open interval from one key in the index to the next higher existing key. Range queries should acquire such key range locks incrementally for higher concurrency, hence the name incremental key range locking. Further analysis shows that Insert and Delete operations then each have to acquire two of these key range locks as they change the existing key ranges in the index. The presented version of such protocols required inserts and deletes to lock also the largest key smaller than the one inserted or deleted, that is, the "previous key." In Section 9.5 we then discussed how this principal locking pattern at the access layer can be relaxed again by exploiting specific properties of Insert and Delete operations.

At the page layer, short-term locks or merely page latches are needed to isolate the individual index operations (i.e., to ensure order-preserving serializability of the corresponding subtransactions). In particular, tree traversals must be guaranteed to arrive at the correct leaf in the presence of concurrent node splits. The main technique for this purpose, coined lock or latch coupling, builds on the tree locking protocol, presented earlier in Chapter 4, to avoid 2PL for subtransaction duration. The basic principle is to allow acquiring a lock on a tree node only if the lock requestor holds a lock on the node's parent (or leaf-level predecessor in the case of index leaf scans); other than that, locks can be released as early as possible and do not have to follow the 2PL discipline. For Insert operations, the possibility of leaf splits that propagate upward in the tree requires additional care in that locks on "unsafe" nodes that may possibly be affected by a split must be held farther on. Alternatively, inserts that trigger splits could release all page locks or latches and simply initiate a second tree traversal with more stringent locking up front. This approach can be implemented in a deadlock-free manner, so that lightweight latches may be used instead of explicit page locks. Other concurrency control techniques for the page layer of B^+ tree–like indexes include the link and giveup approaches, and also various combinations of these techniques are feasible. Although we focused our presentation on B^+ trees as the prevalent form of search structures in data servers, many of our considerations can be carried over to a broader class of search structures, including indexes for multidimensional range queries or similarity search (with additional adjustments, however).

Exercises

9.1 Discuss how the incremental key range locking protocol on index keys has to be changed for a unique index. Discuss also how unique and non-unique indexes may be treated differently by the various optimizations sketched in Section 9.5.

9.2 Discuss which lock(s) need to be acquired by an unsuccessful exact match query for a key that is smaller than the smallest key that exists in the index. How can you ensure that a subsequent insertion of this particular key "steps" on a lock conflict?

9.3 Incremental key range locking based on read and write locks on index keys, as explained in Section 9.3, does not allow two Insert operations in the same, previously unoccupied key interval to proceed concurrently. For example, in the index of Figure 9.5, an insert(27) would block a later insert(28) operation, although none of these keys is initially present and the two operations should be considered as commutative. Discuss whether the resulting blocking of one of the two operations can be safely avoided and how this could be accomplished. Also discuss the analogous situation for Delete operations and the combination of Insert and Delete operations.

9.4 Discuss the locking requirements for an unsuccessful Insert operation on a unique index, i.e., when the key to be inserted already exists in the index.

9.5 In the presented form of the incremental key range locking protocol of Section 9.3, Insert and Delete operations are required to lock previous keys (hence the protocol's alias "previous key locking"). There is a dual variant that requires an operation of these two types to request a next-key lock, i.e., a lock on the interval immediately following the interval that is primarily affected by the operation. Elaborate on the detailed locking rules of this dual variant, which is known as "next key locking" in the literature.

9.6 Consider the following B$^+$ tree index on the attribute AccountNumber of an Accounts table. Assume that all tree nodes have a space capacity for holding up to four entries.

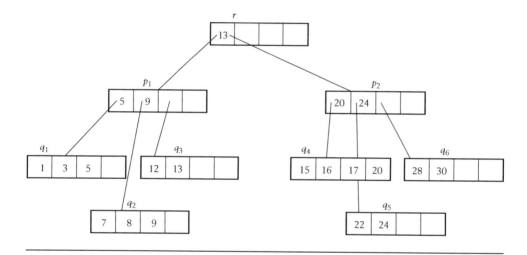

Which locks need to be requested for the execution of the following transaction, assuming incremental key range locking at the access layer and lock coupling at the page layer?

```
begin transaction;
 Select Count(*) From Accounts
  Where AccountNumber Between 11 And 25;
  Insert Into Accounts (AccountNumber,...) Values (27,...);
commit transaction;
```

9.7 Consider a situation where a node p in a B$^+$ tree is not split safe, but has a split safe descendant q, with both p and q on the traversal path of an Insert operation. Discuss how the lock coupling technique should handle this situation to minimize lock contention.

9.8 State explicit rules for lock requests and lock releases for the link technique (in a form similar to our presentation of locking rules for the lock coupling technique).

9.9 Assume that the leaf nodes of a B^+ tree index are linked bidirectionally (rather than only in forward direction). This may be useful to support range scans in descending key order, which in turn is of interest for returning qualifying records in descending sort order (as requested, for example, by a decision support query). Discuss the consequences of this bidirectional linkage with regard to the lock coupling and the link techniques for the page-level concurrency control. If possible, generalize these techniques to accommodate the new feature.

Bibliographic Notes

Historically, page-level concurrency control for single B^+ tree index operations was studied first, with Bayer and Schkolnick (1977) and Kung and Lehman (1980) as well as Lehman and Yao (1981) being the first papers on the lock coupling and link techniques, respectively. Kwong and Wood (1982) as well as Mond and Raz (1985) contributed to the improvement of lock coupling, and Manber and Ladner (1982) as well as Sagiv (1986) further enhanced the link technique. The textbook by Gray and Reuter (1993) describes a more elaborated version of lock coupling, named "lock crabbing." Shasha and Goodman (1988) finally came up with a taxonomy for the various techniques and proposed a formal framework for thorough reasoning on the correctness of these subtle algorithms.

Shasha (1985) also realized that the page-level measures for a single index operation were only one aspect of index concurrency control, and already suggested a layered approach in the direction of what we have presented in this chapter. The current state-of-the-art solution based on incremental key range locking for the access layer concurrency control has mostly been developed by Mohan (1990, 1996); the fundamentals of this work are described also in the textbook by Gray and Reuter (1993) who further credit additional independent work of other architects of commercial database systems that employ similar methods. Gray and Reuter describe the variant that we have referred to as previous key locking, whereas Mohan prefers the next key locking dual variant. Mohan presents full-fledged algorithms, coined ARIES/KVL and ARIES/IM, in great detail, based on highly optimized versions of incremental key range locking at the access layer and a combination of latch coupling (on index pages) and the giveup technique (using a "structure modification" bit in each page and a global tree latch) at the page layer. The ARIES/IM variant uses the RID-only locking optimization for reduced overhead. Mohan (1996) also provides solutions for several of the exercises.

Optimizations that strive for reduced locking overhead while retaining the high concurrency of incremental key range locking have been developed by Mohan (1992, 1996) and Lomet (1993). The latter has also discussed additional concurrency enhancements that can be achieved by treating key ranges and individual keys as separate resources for locking purposes. Generalizations toward applying such high-performance methods to multidimensional and other search structures beyond B^+ trees have recently been proposed by Lomet and Salzberg (1997) and Kornacker et al. (1997). Experimental and analytical performance studies of B^+ tree concurrency control methods have been conducted by Srinivasan and Carey (1991) and Johnson and Shasha (1993). Special considerations on text indexes for document management can be found in the work of Dadam et al. (1983, 1985), Barbara et al. (1996), Kaufmann and Schek (1995, 1996), Knaus and Schäuble (1996), Kamath and Ramamritham (1996), Grabs et al. (1999, 2001), as well as Weikum and Schek (1992).

CHAPTER TEN

Implementation and Pragmatic Issues

All theory, my friend, is grey; but the precious tree of life is green.
—*Johann Wolfgang von Goethe*

Between theory and practice, some talk as they were two.
Between theory and practice, both can be gained.
—*Bhagavad Gita 5:4*

10.1 Goal and Overview

So far we have emphasized a conceptual view of algorithms and techniques so as to separate the fundamental principles from the implementation issues in a specific system environment. In this chapter we provide an overview of the most important among such additional implementation and other pragmatic techniques that systems builders need to cope with.

We begin with implementation techniques for locking and transient versioning in Sections 10.2, 10.3, and 10.4. Next we consider the special aspect of lock management for multi-threaded transactions (i.e., with parallel threads within a single transaction) in Section 10.5. We discuss a variety of tuning techniques for concurrency control, both at the system and application level, in Section 10.6, and finally dedicate Section 10.7 to the specific issue of overload control.

10.2 Data Structures of a Lock Manager

As pointed out several times already, locking is the concurrency control method of choice for a wide spectrum of workloads and system settings. To implement an industrial-strength lock manager requires careful considerations on the underlying data structures, which are driven by the following three key requirements:

- When a lock is requested, we need an efficient way of checking whether a conflicting lock is already held by another transaction.

- When a lock is released, transactions that requested conflicting locks earlier and have therefore been suspended should now be considered for being resumed.

- When a transaction terminates, all locks (still) held on behalf of the transaction are released at once.

Resource control blocks   The first requirement dictates that we need an in-memory search structure for locks with associative access on the identifiers of the resources that are locked or requested to be locked. The most efficient choice for this purpose is a hash table. Recall that almost all locking protocols that we have covered in this book and that are used in practice are designed to map whatever abstract resources they need to lock (e.g., key ranges in an index) to concrete resources with unique identifiers (e.g., individual keys that occur in the index). Thus, it is indeed sufficient to use a single key hash table that merely supports exact match search on identifiers. The entries in the hash table then are pointers to some form of *resource control blocks* (RCBs), which are either dynamically allocated or, even better with respect to performance, taken from a preallocated pool of such control blocks. Hash conflicts are most often resolved by linking all RCBs with the same value of the hash function into a chain anchored at the corresponding entry of the hash table. With this kind of data structure, checking for a lock conflict merely requires a hash table lookup.

Lock control blocks   With shared locks, multiple locks can be simultaneously held for the same resource, and multiple lock requests may be waiting to be granted for that resource. The bookkeeping for this kind of situation amounts to managing a *queue* of *lock control blocks* (LCBs), which are attached to the same RCB. This queue can in turn be easily implemented as a linked list anchored at the RCB, with the ordering in the list determining the order in which waiting lock requests should be considered for being resumed. So the linked list of LCBs would typically have zero, one, or more LCBs with shared locks at its front, followed by at least one request for an exclusive lock, which could then be followed by an arbitrary number of both shared or exclusive lock requests. Note that, for fairness reasons (i.e., to avoid starvation), a shared lock request, in most situations, should not be allowed to pass a previously issued exclusive request that is already waiting for one or more shared locks to be released.

Transaction control blocks   Finally, the third requirement stated above makes it necessary to quickly identify all LCBs that belong to the same transaction. This can be implemented in a straightforward manner by maintaining a *transaction control block* (TCB) for each active transaction and including in the TCB the anchor of a linked list of the transaction's LCBs. Then, upon the commit or abort of the transaction, the

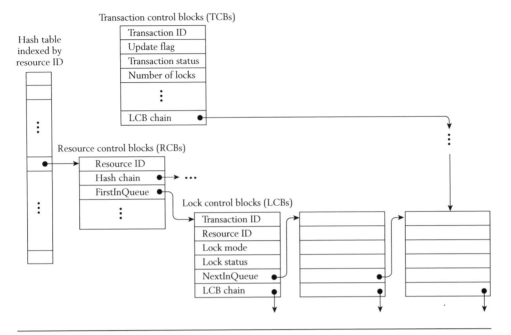

Figure 10.1 Data structures of a lock manager.

list of LCBs is traversed, and the LCBs should be removed from the queues of the corresponding RCBs. The successor LCBs in these resource-specific queues are the candidates for being resumed (in queue order).

This entire set of fairly simple data structures is illustrated in Figure 10.1. Whenever these structures are manipulated by the lock manager on behalf of a transaction, either upon a lock request or a lock release, some form of semaphore or "latch" (i.e., a flag that can be tested and set by an indivisible instruction) is needed to ensure the lock manager's internal consistency in a multi-threaded data server. To prevent this critical section from becoming a performance bottleneck, typically each entry in the hash table has its own latch, often implemented as a bit in the hash table entry itself.

To conclude this section, we point out that the outlined implementation is extremely versatile in the sense that it can be used for whatever locking units are considered appropriate. So RCBs can equally represent pages, records, index entries, or whatever "semantic locks" are needed for advanced object model locking, as long as the conflict test itself merely requires checking the equality of identifiers (as opposed to checking, for example, the disjointness of predicates or the inclusion of a value in a value interval). In the context of layered (or general object model) locking, either all locks of all layers could be managed in the same lock table, or multiple layer-specific lock tables could be instantiated.

10.3 **Multiple Granularity Locking and Dynamic Escalation**

From the previous section, it follows that a lock manager may create some non-negligible overhead in terms of memory consumption. Although the overhead for the various data structures is modest, a heavily loaded data server may end up with hundreds of TCBs and many thousands of RCBs and LCBs simultaneously, thus possibly occupying up to several megabytes of memory. Although this would still be a small amount relative to the large memory sizes of today's amply equipped servers, the point arises as to whether this memory fraction could and should be better used for other purposes, especially for caching data, rather than mere bookkeeping. To this end, it would be convenient to allow the lock manager to choose dynamically between fine-grained and coarse-grained locking, depending on the characteristics of the active transactions. Particularly for long transactions that would acquire many fine-grained locks such as record and index key locks, it may be worthwhile to reduce the space overhead of the lock manager at the expense of diminishing the possible concurrency. When concurrency is most critical, however, fine-grained locking would still be the method of choice.

Reconciling coarse-grained and fine-grained locking

The tension between fine-grained and coarse-grained locking granularities can be reconciled by supporting both kinds of locks, or possibly an entire hierarchy of locking granularities, in a form of *multiple granularity locking*. The practically most important case of this approach is to support the coexistence of record or page locks on the one hand, and locks on entire tables or tablespaces on the other. A *tablespace* is a logical unit of storage that can hold several database tables or indexes, and that may be subdivided into smaller units such as *containers*, which in turn may be a file system directory, a physical file, or a device such as a hard disk.

Intention locks

The problem that now arises is to test conflicts among such disparate granularities. For example, when a transaction requests a lock on an entire tablespace, how can we quickly find out if this request conflicts with some page locks that are already held? While this is not exactly a deep issue, system architects have developed a specific solution with the benefit of a particularly low overhead, which is always a concern, as locking is part of a server's innermost processing loops. The solution is based on *intention locks* to be set on the coarser granularities of the hierarchy by those transactions that prefer fine-grained locking. These locks serve to mark a path in the granularity hierarchy that leads to the items that are actually locked in shared or exclusive mode. This way, other transactions that prefer coarse-grained locking can easily detect conflicts by testing their shared or exclusive locks against the intention locks on the coarser granularities. This consideration leads to the lock mode compatibility matrix between shared and exclusive locks, on one hand, and the two corresponding intention lock modes, called IS and IX, on the other hand, shown in Table 10.1.

Table 10.1 Lock mode compatibility.

	S	X	IS	IX	SIX
S	+	−	+	−	−
X	−	−	−	−	−
IS	+	−	+	+	+
IX	−	−	+	+	−
SIX	−	−	+	−	−

A common special case that has been added to Table 10.1 in the form of another lock mode, coined SIX, is table scans that read a large number of pages and may update a very small fraction of these pages. For such transactions, page locking should be ruled out for the sake of lower overhead, but locking the entire tablespace would require an exclusive lock and thus prevent all other transactions from reading any page of that tablespace. The escape from this dilemma is to have such a transaction acquire both a shared lock and an IX lock on the entire tablespace, so that individual pages can still be locked in the exclusive mode when they turn out to have updates. These two locks can be conveniently combined into a single new lock mode, coined SIX in Table 10.1. Its compatibility properties are derived from the conjunction of an S lock and an IX lock.

Driven by such a lock compatibility table, the protocol for multiple granularity locking simply boils down to the following two rules (in addition to the usual rules for 2PL or whatever lock protocol is employed):

1. A transaction can lock any granule in S or X mode, depending on whether only reads or writes are intended.

2. Before a granule can be locked in S or X mode, the transaction has to hold an IS or IX lock, respectively, on all coarser granules that contain the one to be locked.

Lock escalation

Sometimes it is hard to choose between fine-grained or coarse-grained locking when a transaction starts. It may turn out only in the course of the transaction execution that it acquires a large number of locks and may create too much overhead in the lock manager. In such a situation, we would wish to dynamically convert the fine-grained locks already held into a single (or a few) coarse-grained lock(s). Such a conversion is known as *lock escalation* in the literature. It consists of first requesting a coarser-grained lock that implicitly comprises all currently held fine-grained locks, and only then the fine-grained locks can be released in a second step. So, although locking is then no longer two-phase in a narrow technical sense, the resulting behavior is as if the transaction would still hold its prior fine-grained locks and thus is equivalent to two-phase locking. In commercial systems, lock escalation is typically triggered by exceptions that are raised when the total amount of memory for RCBs and LCBs or the number of locks of an individual transaction exceed certain thresholds.

10.4 **Transient Versioning**

As explained in great detail in Chapter 5, transiently keeping around versions of modified pages, records, or index entries provides opportunities for enhanced concurrency by means of a multiversion concurrency control protocol. The most practical among the protocols presented in Chapter 5 is the read-only multiversion protocol (ROMV) that applies standard two-phase locking to update transactions and assigns versions to the retrieval operations of read-only transactions based on timestamps. More specifically, as you may recall from Chapter 5, new versions are timestamped with the commit time of the transaction that creates them, and read-only transactions read the most recent committed versions as of the transaction's begin.

In this section we sketch some implementation details for this kind of protocol. One of its salient properties is that it can be efficiently implemented at both the access layer, with versions of records and index entries, and the page layer. Here we focus on transient versioning of records, as this is the technique that is actually implemented in several commercial database systems. Other multiversion concurrency control protocols, such as the 2V2PL protocol of Chapter 5, would use similar implementation techniques and are not explicitly covered here.

Version pool   The key concept for transient record versioning is to keep the most recent version of a record (with a given RID) always in the place where the record would reside if there were no versioning, and to store all older versions in a separate area called the *version pool*, which may reside in memory or on disk. This way the most recent data stays organized as compact as possible so that transactions that access only current versions do not lose efficiency because of versioning. In particular, if the current data is organized by some specific clustering scheme, say, with records physically placed into pages in ascending order of a specific sorting key, this organization is in no way affected by the existence of old versions. Another advantage of a separate version pool is that it is much easier to perform garbage collection. In some systems, the version pool is even combined with the organization of recovery-related, temporary information (so-called logging entries, as we will see in Part III of the book) and therefore referred to as *rollback segments*.

Each version carries, as two extra fields, its creation timestamp and a pointer to the previous version of the same RID (or the same index key when versioning is applied to index entries). An Update operation on a record (or index entry)

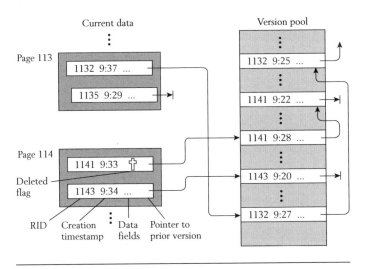

Figure 10.2 Storage organization for transient versioning.

copies the pre-update version of the record as a new version into the version pool, overwrites the current record, and maintains the linked chain among the record's versions. At commit time of the corresponding update transaction, all modified records are timestamped. This deferred timestamping is feasible, as readers would never be directed to an uncommitted version anyway. When a record is deleted, its last state is copied to the version pool, and a specially flagged "marker version" is kept in the place where the record used to reside. Figure 10.2 depicts this organization of the version pool. Here the record with RID 1141 was deleted at time 9:33; so its current version simply is a marker with a deleted flag. Versions with no predecessor, such as the current version of the record with RID 1135 or the version of RID 1143 that was created at time 9:20, were created by the insertion of a new record.

A read-only transaction, with a timestamp that reflects its begin, simply accesses the current versions of records and index entries that it requests to read, and then follows the corresponding linked chain until it finds a version whose timestamp is smaller than the transaction's timestamp. For example, with the data shown in Figure 10.2, a read-only transaction with timestamp 9:26 that requests to access RID 1141 would follow the version chain of the record's current version back to the version with creation timestamp 9:22 and return that version as the result of the read operation.

Instead of a linked chain for the versions of a given record, an alternative organization would be to store within the current version a small *version selection table* that contains the timestamps of and pointers to the older versions. The noncurrent versions themselves would again be kept in a separate version pool. This organization is particularly attractive when the number of versions for the same record is typically very small, say, two or three, or the underlying multiversion concurrency control protocol even enforces such a limit for the number of simultaneously existing versions. In this case it may even be considered to keep the noncurrent versions of a record or index entry in the same page as the current version, the justification being that this storage overhead is low for a strictly limited number of versions. A typical scenario could then be that out of, say, 100 records in a page, 90 records have only a current version and 10 have one or at most two additional noncurrent versions.

Garbage   Garbage collection is needed to identify and discard old versions that are
collection no longer needed, and to reclaim the storage space used by those versions. With the ROMV protocol, the identification of obsolete versions is straightforward: all noncurrent versions that have a successor (i.e., more recent version) whose timestamp is smaller than the timestamp of the oldest active read-only transaction can be safely discarded.

When versions are kept in the version pool in ascending order of their successor's creation timestamp, garbage collection can be implemented by keeping a roving pointer that marks the logical begin of the version pool as follows. Assume that the oldest active read-only transaction has timestamp TS. Then a noncurrent version with a timestamp less than TS is of interest and must not yet be garbage-collected only if its successor version has a timestamp greater than TS (i.e., if it is the youngest version with a timestamp less than TS for the given record). Phrased positively, all noncurrent versions whose successor in the corresponding record's chain has a timestamp less than TS can be safely discarded. Thus, by organizing the noncurrent versions *in ascending order of successor timestamps* and assuming that timestamp TS is itself not assigned to any version (as timestamps are unique among all transactions), the version whose successor has the smallest timestamp larger than TS divides the version pool into the garbage part and the "live" part that must be kept. Note that this ordering of versions in the version pool is, in fact, the most natural order, as versions are moved into the version pool at the time their successor is created.

In the example of Figure 10.2, the five versions shown in the version pool have ascending successor timestamps, namely, 9:27, 9:28, 9:33, 9:34, and 9:37. Thus, assuming that the timestamp of the oldest active read-only transaction is 9:30, the oldest two versions among the five shown versions can be garbage-collected (i.e., the ones for RID 1132 with timestamp 9:25 and RID 1141 with timestamp 9:22). The actual storage reclamation is easily implemented by simply moving the logical begin pointer of the version pool to the first version that must be kept (i.e., the one for RID 1141 with timestamp 9:28 if only the five shown versions were present).

If storage space is not a bottleneck, the garbage collection should discard only versions that are definitely obsolete in the sense that no transaction would ever have to access them. When storage is scarce, which could especially be the case when the version pool resides in memory or some specifically reserved, limited-size disk area, garbage collection may be forced to drop old versions more readily. Then it may happen that a long read-only transaction with a fairly old timestamp would have to access, for consistency, an old version that has been garbage-collected already. In such cases the data server would simply generate an error message to the application program and abort the transaction. In some commercial database systems this event is known as a "snapshot too old" message.

10.5 **Nested Transactions for Intra-transaction Parallelism**

When a transaction consists of multiple, parallel threads, locking protocols need to be refined a little in order to ensure that different threads of the same transaction are serialized as well. Otherwise, although different transactions could still be isolated, the execution within a transaction might no longer correspond to a serial computation. Note that this was no problem at all from the abstract viewpoint of the correctness criteria for concurrency control, as these simply treated such cases of intra-transaction parallelism by partial orders. The purpose of this section is to add the necessary protocol elements so that two-phase locking can cope with parallel threads inside a transaction.

In the literature, *multi-threaded transactions* are often referred to as *nested transactions* in that parallel threads form subtrees of a common parent that asynchronously spawned the threads. This consideration naturally leads to a tree whose leaves are the actual read and write data operations; siblings in the tree correspond to parallel threads. This computational model obviously resembles our notion of object model transactions, and can indeed be cast into the object model. The difference, however, is that with nested transactions, we cannot usually associate a semantically richer operation with an inner node of a transaction tree. So as far as concurrency control is concerned, the leaves of a nested transaction tree are all we need to consider; the inner nodes merely reflect parallel execution of threads.

Multi-threaded transactions or nested transactions

The additional issue that arises in a nested transaction is that two parallel threads need to be synchronized in order to make sure that their combined execution is equivalent to a serial one. Since we assume a locking protocol anyway, the solution is rather straightforward: each thread, also called a "sub-transaction" in this context, acquires locks according to the 2PL protocol. This automatically serializes parallel threads of the same transaction. When a thread terminates, it could allow a sibling (i.e., parallel thread of the same transaction) to proceed even if that sibling needs locks that were held by the terminated thread. After all, all these threads belong to the same transaction; so there is no need for isolating threads beyond their termination. Rather, threads can be viewed as cooperative lightweight processes. However, the locks of the terminated thread cannot simply be released; they are still needed to prevent other transactions from potentially creating conflict cycles. The technical solution is to keep these locks by having the parent of a thread *inherit* them upon the thread's termination. Then, of course, we need to reconsider the rules for lock conflicts: within a transaction, a thread's lock request can be in conflict only with a parallel thread, not with an already terminated one. So if a conflicting lock is held by an ancestor of the requesting thread, the lock can be safely granted.

These considerations lead to the following set of protocol rules:

2PL for nested transactions

- The leaves of a transaction tree acquire locks as needed by the corresponding data operations. These locks are held according to the 2PL for the duration of the transaction.

- Upon terminating a thread, all locks held by the thread are inherited by its parent.

- A lock request by a thread is granted if no conflicting lock on the same data item is currently held or the only conflicting locks are held by ancestors of the thread.

This protocol again resembles the concept of retained locks used in the general object model 2PL. Note, however, that the retained locks there serve an entirely different purpose, namely, to synchronize different transactions that operate on different abstraction levels. In contrast, inherited locks, as we prefer to call them, serve the intra-transaction synchronization among parallel threads of the same transaction. The specific objective of the nested transaction 2PL is to serialize the threads of a transaction tree, as stated more precisely in the following theorem:

THEOREM 10.1

The 2PL protocol for nested transactions generates only schedules that are equivalent to a serial execution of transactions where each transaction executes all its sibling sets serially.

Finally, we mention that parallel threads in a transaction can, of course, be combined with object model operation invocation trees. The protocol for this setting would then need both higher-level, operation-type specific "semantic" locks on objects, possibly even in the form of retained locks, and lock inheritance of leaf-level, typically page-level, locks. Although this combination sounds complicated, it is fairly straightforward to reconcile the rules of both protocols to implement the combined case.

10.6 **Tuning Options**

Two-phase locking is widely used for the concurrency control of commercial data servers. Its popularity primarily draws on the simplicity, versatility, and robustness of the protocol. So, unless we have specific information about an application's workload characteristics, 2PL is indeed the method of choice in most cases. In a given application setting, however, it may be desirable to tune the use of 2PL toward specific access patterns and application needs for enhanced concurrency and/or reduced overhead. To this end, most commercial data servers provide the administration staff and sometimes even application developers with a number of "tuning knobs" that refer to the locking protocol. This section serves to point out the most important of these tuning options. It should be stressed, however, that appropriate use of these options may be a delicate matter. When used inappropriately, tuning options may even lead to inconsistent data. So the techniques presented below are for true application and system experts only, and even the experts should use extreme caution when they exert options that deviate from standard protocols like 2PL.

10.6.1 **Manual Locking**

Many commercial data servers allow application developers to choose among different settings for locking granularity, mode, and duration dynamically when a transaction starts or even upon each client-server interaction (e.g., an SQL command) that initiates locking steps.

Locking granularity can be influenced by choosing one of the granularities supported under a multigranularity locking protocol, for example, table *Locking* locks versus page or record locks. Typically, a system administrator can spec- *granularity* ify a preferred locking granularity for each transaction program individually. In addition, the application programmer may sometimes specify the locking granularity dynamically on a per-program-invocation basis. In this case, the command that opens a new transaction would be parameterized to choose either coarse-grained or fine-grained locking. The application developer can, for example, program this decision based on user-provided input parameters to the program invocation, as these may affect the estimated number of locks the transaction would have to acquire.

Lock conversions—that is, "upgrading" a shared lock into an exclusive *Lock* lock on the same object—are a frequent cause of deadlocks. It may be more *modes* desirable to block one transaction earlier rather than risking a deadlock. To this end, some servers provide commands by which a transaction program can advise the server to acquire a stronger exclusive lock earlier. For example, when transactions iterate over query result sets via an SQL command like "open cursor" (and subsequent Fetch calls), they may have to update a fraction of the retrieved data records. Usually, the server would first acquire only shared locks on these records and would convert these into exclusive locks only on those records that need to be updated and only when the update command is issued. To alleviate the deadlock probability for multiple concurrent instances of this transaction type, the server may consider acquiring exclusive locks on the retrieved records up front (and possibly "downgrading" them to shared locks as soon as it is clear that a record is not updated). It is, however, very hard for the server to determine when this form of preclaiming (i.e., acquiring stronger locks ahead of time) is beneficial and when it would be better to tolerate the lock conversions. Therefore, programs can provide guidance to the server via special commands or additional parameters to the usual commands. These parameters may be implicit; for example, the SQL command "open cursor" has a variant of the form "open cursor for update," which is interpreted by some servers as a hint to acquire exclusive locks in the first place.

Lock durations　The dynamic tuning of lock modes sketched above already influences the duration for which exclusive locks are held. Some servers are even more liberal in this regard in that they allow programs to "manually" acquire locks at specific times and possibly also release locks when the program(mer) considers the situation "safe" enough. So rather than having the server acquiring and releasing all locks automatically on behalf of the transaction program's usual calls (e.g., SQL commands), programs can direct the server to manage locks via explicit Lock and Unlock calls. An example for this kind of extremely flexible, but also potentially dangerous tuning capability can be found in the concurrency services of CORBA-style object request brokers. Because it is then the program(mer) that determines the actual locking protocol, consistency preservation would be completely dependent on the overview and care of the application architect or developers. Thus, as far as the comfort and ease of use of transactions is concerned, such tuning options are actually a step backward, but they may occasionally be convenient for performance improvements of special applications.

10.6.2 **SQL Isolation Levels**

The idea of manually controlling the lock duration on a per-application or even a per-transaction basis, discussed in the previous section, can be made safer by allowing only a limited number of "locking style" options that the application architect or developer can choose from. These options are known as *isolation levels*, one of them being the usual notion of conflict serializability, and they have even been incorporated into the SQL standard. A specific isolation level is chosen by issuing a corresponding SQL command "set isolation level . . ."

The isolation levels supported by the SQL standard are defined in terms of controlled deviations from (strongly) strict two-phase locking. They should be understood, however, as schedule classes that, albeit generated by specific locking protocols, can be enforced by whatever appropriate concurrency control algorithm a server chooses to employ. The practically most important isolation levels are defined as follows:

DEFINITION 10.1 *Isolation Levels*

A schedule *s* is said to run under isolation level *read uncommitted* (also known as *dirty-read* or *browse* level) if write locks are acquired and released according to S2PL, i.e., all write locks are held until the end of a transaction.

A schedule *s* is said to run under isolation level *read committed* (also known as *cursor stability* level) if write locks are acquired and released according to S2PL, and read locks are held (at least) for the duration of each data server operation issued by a client.

A schedule *s* is said to run under isolation level *(conflict) serializability* if it can be generated by the S2PL protocol.

The three isolation levels differ in their lock durations for shared and exclusive locks. Essentially, read uncommitted does not require any read locks, and is useful for mere browsing or statistical evaluations where a consistent view of the data is not required (e.g., computing the average price of several thousand books, where the few books whose price is changed during the statistical analysis do not matter much). The long-duration write locks superficially appear to prevent the persistent data from becoming inconsistent, but this, in fact, cannot be guaranteed, since the data values that are written may now depend on arbitrarily inconsistent, even "dirty" (i.e., uncommitted and later aborted), reads.

Isolation level read uncommitted

The read committed level alleviates such problems to some extent; in particular, it eliminates dirty-read anomalies. It is characterized by short read locks and long write locks. Thus, it reduces the possible data contention, especially between long readers and short update transactions. This is a particularly useful and widely used option in practice, but it must be used with extreme caution as it can actually render the persistent data inconsistent. In fact, the read committed isolation level is still susceptible to lost-update anomalies, as the following example shows:

Isolation level read committed

$$r_1(x)r_2(x)w_2(x)c_2w_1(x)c_1$$

Some commercial data servers and even the SQL standard further distinguish between the level of full (conflict) serializability and a relaxed, ad hoc form of serializability that would tolerate phantom problems but "no other" types of inconsistencies. The latter is often referred to as the "repeatable read" level, although this is sometimes also used as a synonym for serializability. This ad hoc notion is not precisely defined, as the category of "other" inconsistencies is left somewhat vague.

Isolation levels serializability vs. repeatable read

As mentioned earlier, the above isolation levels are defined in terms of locking rules, but we can surely design other kinds of concurrency control algorithms that enforce a specific isolation level. If we wanted to employ even multiversion concurrency control protocols, the notion of a conflict that underlies the locking rules does not carry over directly. To this end, some commercial systems have introduced additional isolation levels that assume a multiversion concurrency control algorithm and specify a controlled relaxation from multiversion serializability.

Multiversion read committed, snapshot isolation

DEFINITION 10.2   *Multiversion Read Committed and Snapshot Isolation Levels*

A transaction run under the *multiversion read committed* isolation level reads the most recent versions of the requested data items that were committed at the time the read operation is issued. All writes that the transaction may invoke are subject to (nonversioned) exclusive locking with locks held until the transaction's termination.

For a transaction run under the *snapshot isolation* level, all operations read the most recent versions as of the time the transaction began. In addition, the write sets of each pair of concurrent transactions must be disjoint.

Of these two levels, snapshot isolation is the stronger one. While multiversion read committed is still susceptible to lost updates (despite the fact that it has consistent reads), snapshot isolation is fairly close to full serializability. In fact, if it were applied only to read-only transactions, all transactions would have a consistent view of the data, and the persistent data itself could be guaranteed to remain consistent. This can be easily seen by observing that the read-only multiversion (ROMV) protocol introduced in Chapter 5 generates histories that exactly match the above definition of snapshot isolation. However, the following history (with data item subscripts denoting versions) shows that snapshot isolation for update transactions can lead to situations that are not multiversion serializable:

$$r_1(x_0)r_1(y_0)r_2(x_0)r_2(y_0)w_1(x_1)c_1 w_2(y_2)c_2$$

As a concrete interpretation, assume that x and y are two numerical data items, both of which have the initial value 5 and are interrelated by a consistency constraint dictating $x + y \geq 0$. Now imagine two concurrent transactions, both of which read x and y and subtract 10 from one of the two data items. Under the read uncommitted level, this could result in the above history, which is not serializable and would result in both data items having a value of -5, thus violating the consistency constraint.

A nice property of snapshot isolation, on the other hand, is that it can be formalized and studied in a rigorous manner. Our above definition can be cast into the theory of multiversion concurrency control (see Chapter 5) as follows:

DEFINITION 10.3 *Formal Definition of Snapshot Isolation*

A multiversion schedule of transactions $T = \{t_1, \ldots, t_n\}$ satisfies the criterion of *snapshot isolation* if the following two conditions hold:

1. The version function maps each read action $r_i(x)$ to the most recent committed write action $w_j(x)$ as of the time of the begin of t_i; that is: $r_i(x)$ is mapped to $w_j(x)$ such that $w_j(x) < c_j < b_i < r_i(x)$ and there are no other actions $w_h(x)$ and c_h ($h \neq j$) with $w_h(x) < b_i$ and $c_j < c_h < b_i$, where b_i denotes the beginning of t_i.

2. The write sets of two concurrent transactions are disjoint; that is, if for two transactions t_i and t_j, either $b_i < b_j < c_i$ or $b_j < b_i < c_j$, then t_i and t_j must not write a common object.

Formal definition of snapshot isolation

The class of snapshot isolated schedules and the class MVSR are incomparable. On the one hand, snapshot isolation is a special case of MVSR in that it uses a particular version function, and it is more restrictive because of the write set disjointness condition. On the other hand, snapshot isolation does not require a reads-from relation that is compatible with that of a serial monoversion schedule; it is more liberal than MVSR in this respect.

The criterion of snapshot isolation can be easily characterized by a graph construction:

DEFINITION 10.4 *Snapshot Isolation Serialization Graph*

The snapshot isolation serialization graph of a multiversion history s is a directed graph with the transactions as nodes and the following edges: For each operation $r_j(x_i)$ in the schedule there is an edge $t_i \rightarrow t_j$ labeled x. For each pair of operations $r_k(x_j)$ and $w_i(x_i)$ there is an edge

1. $t_i \rightarrow t_j$ if $c_i < c_j$ and
2. $t_k \rightarrow t_i$ if $c_j < c_i$

labeled x in both cases.

THEOREM 10.2

Let s be a multiversion schedule that has a version function according to the snapshot isolation criterion and in which each write step on object x

is preceded by a read step on x within the same transaction. Then the following holds:

1. s is MVSR iff its corresponding snapshot isolation serialization graph is acyclic, and

2. s is snapshot isolated iff there is no object x such that the corresponding snapshot isolation graph has a cycle consisting only of edges labeled x.

Snapshot isolation can be implemented using the ROMV protocol introduced in Chapter 5, for all read operations (i.e., even those of update transactions) with an additional mechanism for ensuring the disjointness of the write sets of concurrent transactions. A straightforward approach for the latter would be to remember write sets and perform an explicit disjointness test upon the commit request of a transaction. If the test indicates overlap, the transaction is aborted. A better way, which can detect nondisjointness earlier and thus avoid wasting work in transactions that would eventually be aborted anyway, is to acquire locks for writes as usual and check these locks against the write sets of concurrent transactions that committed earlier. Note that this requires more than just the usual lock conflict test, as the already terminated transactions no longer hold their locks; rather, we need to consider the write locks that they held at their commit time.

10.6.3 **Short Transactions**

A well-known tuning principle is to strive for short transactions. The extent to which this is feasible depends, of course, on the application. Ideally, knowledge about the application semantics and structure of programs should be fed into automated methods, like "transaction chopping" discussed in Chapter 8, that decompose long transactions into shorter ones. In practice, however, such reasoning is more typically an intellectual task of the application designers. Not infrequently, the considerations along these lines are fairly pragmatic and exploit the fact that humans are, to a large extent, indulgent creatures and users can tolerate and cope with certain "pathological" situations.

One particularly popular rule of thumb is that a transaction should never span beyond dialog steps with the human user (also known as "user I/O"). This is to prevent locks from being held during (or the scope of other concurrency control measures extending over) the user's think time between receiving some output from the computer application and providing the next input. Instead, a "well-behaved" transaction program should accept an input message, begin and execute a database transaction, commit this transaction, and deliver a single output message. So applications such as flight reservations are broken down into a sequence of independent transactions. Finding out whether a particular flight has seats available and reporting the result to the user (i.e., the airline customer or the airline agent who speaks to the customer) would be a first transaction; then, once the customer has made up her mind, the actual booking of the flight would be a second transaction. Thus, it is possible that the customer sees available seats, but the attempt to book them a few minutes or even seconds later could possibly fail with a notification that the flight is fully booked. (Of course, it is common practice to overbook flights, but there should be some reasonable limit (say, 110% of the flight capacity), even with this relaxation.) Twenty years ago, such experiences were considered acceptable by the airlines, as they would happen infrequently enough and annoy only a tiny fraction of unlucky customers. Meanwhile most airlines seem to have fixed such inconveniences by taking care of the problem at the level of the application programs, while still employing the principle of short transactions. One solution could be to make a tentative reservation when the availability is checked, by explicit UPDATE statements on the underlying database. This reservation would be associated with an expiration period, and if the customer does not finalize the booking within this period, the tentative reservation is automatically dropped by a background program.

This example shows that striving for short transactions is not a panacea, and often comes at the expense of additional complexity at the application level, if feasible at all. A related pragmatic approach is to structure application programs such that the more critical write locks are held for the shortest possible time period, by moving UPDATE statements toward the end of the transaction and thus acquiring these exclusive locks as late as possible. So in this regard, a "good" transaction would have a read phase for querying information first, defer updates to permanent data by "making notes" about what needs to be done in the program's temporary, private variables and data structures, and finally, submit the corresponding UPDATE statements to the data server in a short write phase right before the transaction commit. This approach closely resembles the optimistic concurrency control method discussed in Chapter 4, where writes were deferred by means of a private workspace.

In contrast to this method where the workspace resides on the server and the deferral of writes is completely masked to the application programs, the outlined pragmatic approach requires additional programming discipline and efforts by application developers. On the other hand, such an application-level approach would work for all kinds of data servers regardless of whether the server uses locking, or optimistic methods, or whatever. Recall also that the workspace concept of optimistic concurrency control can be efficiently implemented for page-oriented methods, but may be impractical for record-oriented and index concurrency control. The deferral of Update calls in the application program can be seen as a way of simulating optimistic concurrency control for finer granularities.

The technique of postponing updates toward the end of a transaction, for the sake of short lock duration, is, in practice, often combined with choosing

Optimistic locking

relaxed isolation levels for the read phase. Many application developers have adopted the habit of choosing merely read committed as the isolation level. This, of course, neither ensures consistent reads nor prevents lost updates. A widely used practice that eliminates at least lost updates and thus eliminates the worst possible inconsistencies (but still cannot guarantee truly consistent data under all circumstances) is known as *optimistic locking*. So transactions read data without transaction duration locks (hence the name of the technique) but acquire locks for the updates in the application program's write phase. To rule out the possibility of lost updates, the UPDATE statements should be modified such that they include a test of whether the objects to be updated have been changed since they were initially read within the same transaction.

This test usually requires specific programming conventions and additional efforts. One popular way of implementing it for embedded SQL programs is to extend each database object with an additional counter field that serves as a timestamp or version number. During the read phase, all queries need to retrieve the corresponding counter value, and the program must remember these values in local variables. In the write phase, all SQL UPDATE statements are extended by an extra condition in the WHERE clause that tests the counter field's current value for equality with the previously read and remembered value. If the test fails, the UPDATE statement will not modify any data; the application program would be notified by an appropriate SQL returncode and would thus know that another transaction has concurrently modified the database object in question. Then, the application program would abort the transaction, initiating its rollback. So, for example, the code for retrieving and later modifying an account balance, say, after computing interest and fees, would have to be modified as follows:

```
SELECT Balance, Counter INTO :b, :c
FROM Accounts
WHERE AccountNo = :x;
...
compute interest and fees
set b to appropriate value
...
UPDATE Accounts
SET Balance = :b, Counter = Counter + 1
WHERE AccountNo = :x
AND Counter = :c;
```

Note that the Counter field is not part of the application's original database design, but needs to be added to the schema to enable this kind of optimistic locking technique. This approach resembles the notion of snapshot isolation, but it is implemented at the application level rather than inside the server, and it is strictly weaker as it does not even guarantee consistent reads. Needless to say, despite the popularity of this technique, we would not at all encourage application builders to use it, and we are skeptical that such tricks are practically viable in the long term. The popularity of the approach mostly comes from the fact that it allows smart application builders to develop multiuser applications with decent performance even if the underlying data server uses only page locking and would otherwise be a major bottleneck. The real solution, however, would be to use a better data server that employs high-performance, state-of-the-art techniques as presented in the previous chapters of this book.

10.6.4 Limiting the Level of Multiprogramming

Locks or, with respect to more general scheduling algorithms, data items are an abstract resource that concurrent transactions are competing for, in order to ensure consistent views of the data. This competition is known as *data contention*. Like many other forms of resource contention (e.g., memory contention), data contention is susceptible to "performance disasters," also known as *thrashing* phenomena. The reason for *data contention thrashing* is that with increasing concurrency, the probability of a lock request not being granted and the duration for which a transaction needs to wait upon a lock conflict increase superlinearly. In fact, when too many transactions run concurrently, we may end up with a situation where most transactions are blocked because of lock conflicts and only a few transactions are still running. It can be shown, both mathematically and experimentally, that this problem arises even if no deadlocks occur (e.g., if lock requests were ordered in accordance with data item numbers). Frequent deadlocks are an additive danger, possibly leading to CPU and disk I/O contention as well when many transactions need to be aborted and restarted for another trial.

Data contention thrashing

To avoid performance disasters of the above kind, virtually all data servers allow administrators to limit the *multiprogramming level* (MPL) (also known as the *degree of multiprogramming*), which is the maximum number of transactions that are allowed to run concurrently. When this limit is reached, newly arriving transactions are held in a *transaction admission queue*. In this case, one of these transactions is admitted for execution only upon the completion of a running transaction; the admission order typically is FIFO (also known as first-come-first-served, or FCFS for short) for fairness. Since the waiting time that a transaction spends in the transaction admission queue also adds to the response time that is perceived by the client, the MPL should be set as high as possible, but also sufficiently low to prevent data contention thrashing (for the usual workload characteristics of the server). When the MPL is set too high and thrashing occurs, the transaction throughput drops sharply and response times increase drastically, ultimately approaching infinity.

This behavior is illustrated in Figure 10.3, which shows typical curves for transaction throughput and mean response time as functions of the number of

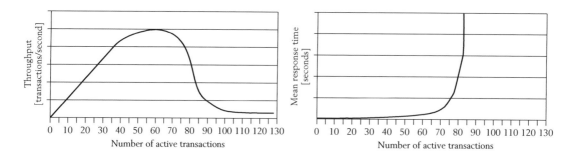

Figure 10.3 Data contention thrashing.

concurrently active transactions. So without limitation of the MPL, the server would operate in the catastrophic region on the right side of the charts, at least during load peaks. Figure 10.4 illustrates the impact of the MPL limit on a high server load, say, with 100 users who continuously submit transactions (with virtually no think time, or equivalently on the order of 1000 users with several seconds' think time). For overly conservative MPL, at the left end of the chart, many transactions spend a long time in the transaction admission queue, whereas for an unduely high MPL limit, at the right end of the chart, thrashing sets in.

Determining an appropriate MPL setting for a given workload is a delicate tuning problem. For workloads with short, frequently arriving transactions that acquire only a few locks, most of which are read locks only, the MPL can and should be set quite high—up to a few hundred, for example. On the other hand, when some of the transactions in the workload are fairly long, holding locks for an extended duration, or when their access patterns are highly skewed in that some very frequently updated data items form so-called hot spots, a much lower MPL is needed—often less than 10. Even worse, the variability of transaction lengths in a mixed workload is an important factor to consider as well.

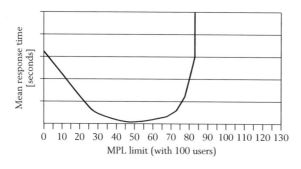

Figure 10.4 Impact of MPL limit.

Among two workloads that have the same mean duration of transactions, one of which has constant transaction length whereas the other has a high variance, the one with the high variance of the lock duration is much more susceptible to data contention and the danger of thrashing. For this reason, some data servers or TP monitor–style application servers even support MPL limitations on a per-transaction-class basis. For example, in an electronic commerce application, you could specify that up to 10 concurrent order entry transactions are acceptable, up to 20 concurrent payment transactions, but only up to 3 market analysis transactions. In addition, you would potentially have to consider subsets of these transaction types as well, for example, by allowing only up to 8 concurrent transactions that are either order entry or market analysis transactions, and so on. These kinds of tuning decisions are extremely difficult. In practice they are often based on a mix of guesswork by experienced administrators and extensive trial-and-error experimentation before an application system is deployed for real-world service. This makes tuning very expensive in terms of human time and cost, but it does correspond to the current state of the art as far as industry practice is concerned. In Section 10.7, we will present approaches toward automating this specific kind of tuning decision, which we hope will penetrate into commercial products soon.

10.7 Overload Control

Tuning the multiprogramming level, as discussed in the previous section, has the inherent disadvantage of relying on human intervention. It requires a highly skilled and expensive administration staff, and reaches manageability limits with increasingly complex workloads. In addition, a fundamental drawback of manual tuning methods is that they do not allow the system to react to the dynamics of workloads. It may be necessary to limit the MPL only during particular peak load periods with a particular mix of transactions, while the same limitation would be counterproductive during other periods. As these time periods are *a priori* unknown, a system administrator would need to monitor the system continuously, sitting in a pilot seat with a control stick for real-time adjustments to the MPL limit. Such a scenario is clearly infeasible, and therefore automatic methods for preventing overload are called for. Appropriate methods, driven by feedback from the server's performance, are presented in this section.

10.7.1 Feedback-Driven Method

The basic approach that we are going to present is an overload control method driven by feedback from the observed system performance, more specifically, a metric, coined the *conflict ratio*, that reflects the current degree of data

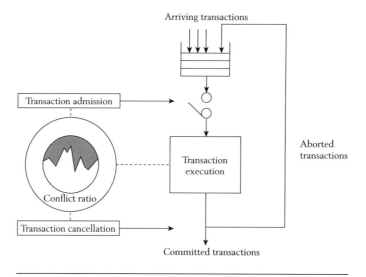

Arriving transactions

Transaction admission

Conflict ratio

Transaction cancellation

Transaction execution

Aborted transactions

Committed transactions

Figure 10.5 Overview of the conflict-ratio driven load control method.

contention in the server. This method resembles the "system pilot" analogy given above, except that the administrator is replaced by a piece of software. The basic principle, illustrated in Figure 10.5, is a feedback loop consisting of observation, prediction, and reaction steps. The method continuously monitors the conflict ratio or another appropriate metric. Based on these observations and possibly statistical knowledge about future transaction behavior (e.g., the expected number of locks yet to be acquired by the currently active transactions of specific types), the method predicts how the degree of data contention will evolve in the near future. When the data contention indicator is about to exceed a critical threshold, the overload control considers two kinds of appropriate reactions:

Admission control and cancellation control

1. *Admission control:* Newly arriving transactions are no longer admitted for execution; rather, they are held in a transaction admission queue. This measure effectively limits the multiprogramming level to its current value.

2. *Cancellation control:* In addition, it may be necessary to reduce the current multiprogramming level. This can be achieved by selecting a transaction as a cancellation victim, forcing it to abort and putting it back into the transaction admission queue. This step is repeated until the data contention indicator drops below the critical threshold.

Restart control

Transactions that have become cancellation victims should not be allowed to restart immediately, as this could easily lead to unstable, oscillating behavior with a high probability of immediately reentering the zone of critical data contention or even thrashing. It has been shown to be beneficial that an aborted transaction, either a deadlock or a cancellation victim, should be restarted only after all transactions by which the victim was blocked are successfully terminated. This restart policy is sometimes referred to as *restart waiting*.

A related issue is the problem of how to select a cancellation victim. Following similar considerations on deadlock resolution (see Chapter 4), a heuristically good choice is the transaction that holds the fewest locks, but only such transactions should be eligible that are blocked and do themselves block other transactions. Transactions that are not blocked are making progress and should be exempt from cancellation; likewise, transactions that do not block any other transaction do not cause much harm toward data contention thrashing. As with deadlock victims, this kind of selection bears the danger of starvation, where the same transaction is chosen for cancellation over and over again (strictly speaking, different "incarnations" of the same transaction). To prevent starvation and ensure a certain fairness, the victim selection policy needs to be rectified: one practically viable possibility is to choose as a cancellation victim the transaction with the smallest product of the *number of locks currently held × number of previous restarts*.

The key decision in such a feedback-driven approach is the choice of an appropriate metric as a data contention indicator and robust value for the critical threshold. For a homogeneous workload, where all transactions are of the same type and acquire approximately the same number of locks, it has been shown, both analytically and experimentally, that the *fraction of blocked transactions* is a good indicator for the degree of data contention. As long as the fraction of blocked transactions is below a critical value around 0.25, the server can maintain a high throughput. When this fraction exceeds the critical value, however, the risk of thrashing becomes unbearably high, and with more than 30% of the transactions being blocked, the system is usually thrashing.

Unfortunately, this metric is too simple to capture heterogeneous workloads with transactions of highly variable length. Depending on the number of locks that the various transactions hold, different values of the blocked transaction metric can be tolerated, so that it is impossible to derive a critical threshold that is meaningful across a wide spectrum of workloads. Therefore, a more appropriate metric is the conflict ratio, defined as the following quotient:

Conflict ratio

$$\frac{\text{total number of locks currently held by all transactions}}{\text{total number of locks currently held by all nonblocked transactions}}$$

Note that this metric implicitly attaches weights to the various currently active transactions: transactions that hold many locks have a higher weight. When all transactions have the same number of locks, which is the expected steady state situation under a homogeneous workload, the conflict ratio directly reflects the fraction of blocked transactions. With widely varying transaction lengths, however, it becomes crucial to factor the variability into the data contention metric. Analytic modeling as well as experimental studies have shown that there exists a value for the conflict ratio, coined the *critical conflict ratio*, that can serve as a reliable indicator for the onset of thrashing, and that value is approximately the same, namely, about 1.3, for a wide range of workload characteristics. So the critical conflict ratio can be viewed as a constant, and this renders the conflict ratio an appropriate metric for a robust, feedback-driven load control method.

Pseudocode for the conflict-ratio driven load control method

The complete feedback-driven load control method, with the conflict ratio as a data contention indicator, is described by the following pseudocode.

```
upon the begin request of transaction t:
  if conflict ratio < critical conflict ratio
  then admit t
  else put t in the transaction admission queue
  fi


upon a lock wait of transaction t:
  update conflict ratio
  while not (conflict ratio < critical conflict ratio)
    among the transactions that are blocked and block
    other transactions
      determine the transaction v with the smallest product
      number of locks held * number of previous restarts
      (with the transaction with the highest product
      being exempt)
    abort v and put in the transaction admission queue
    if no eligible transaction found then exit loop fi
  od


upon the termination of transaction t:
  if conflict ratio < critical conflict ratio then
    for each transaction q in the transaction admission
    queue do
      if (q will be started the first time) or
      (q has been a deadlock victim or cancellation victim
      before and all transactions that q was waiting for in its
      previous execution have been successfully terminated)
      then admit q
      fi
    od
  fi
```

10.7.2 **Wait-Depth Limitation**

An alternative approach to overload prevention that is a bit more aggressive in causing more transaction cancellations than the conflict-ratio driven method is known as *wait-depth limitation*. The wait depth of a transaction is recursively defined as follows:

- a running (i.e., nonblocked) transaction has wait depth 0, and
- a transaction that is blocked by a transaction with wait depth i (and no transaction with higher wait depth) has wait depth $i + 1$.

The wait depth of the currently active transactions can be viewed as an indicator of data contention. In particular, a wait depth of 2 or higher indicates that one or more blocked transactions do in turn block other transactions. Consequently, it has been suggested that transactions should be canceled whenever a wait depth of 1 is exceeded. A case analysis of these situations is illustrated in Figure 10.6, with existing lock waits indicated by solid edges and a newly arising lock wait by a dashed edge. In Case 1 of the figure, transaction t_k should be canceled (and put into the transaction admission queue as in the conflict-ratio driven method). In Case 2, we can cancel either t_k or t_{i1} to bring the maximum wait depth down to 1. In that case, a subsidiary victim selection policy should be used by canceling, for example, the "troublemaker" t_k unless it is the transaction with the largest number of currently held locks, in which case it appears more favorable to prioritize t_k and cancel t_{i1}.

Compared to the conflict-ratio driven load control, wait-depth limitation is a bit simpler to implement. When CPU and I/O resources are ample, its performance is about as good as that of the conflict-ratio driven method.

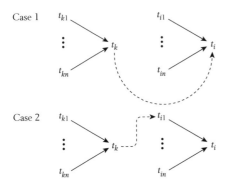

Figure 10.6 Case analysis for the wait-depth limitation method.

However, it tends to cancel more transactions under high data contention, and the resulting restarts may lead to a higher utilization of the CPU and the disks so that these resources could become bottlenecks in extreme situations.

10.8 **Lessons Learned**

Locking, as the concurrency control method used in most commercial systems, can be efficiently implemented with hash-based organization of lock control blocks. To control the overhead, especially the memory consumption, of the lock manager, locking protocols have been extended to cope with multiple granularities so that some loss in concurrency may be dynamically traded for reduced memory usage.

Locking controls can be enhanced by transient versioning and by exploiting versions for read-only transactions. We have shown that the storage management for versioning can be implemented with affordable overhead, and that effective and efficient garbage collection is feasible.

Parallel threads within a transaction can be elegantly supported by the model of nested transactions, but there are also other ways of supporting intra-transaction parallelism within a lock manager. Nested transactions should not be confused with object model transactions. The latter are sometimes referred to as *open nested transactions* because of the early release of low-level locks; nested transactions, which could then consequently be referred to as *closed nested transactions*, do not have this salient property of increased concurrency among independent transactions.

For system administrators and, to some extent, application developers, a suite of tuning knobs is available in the form of system-provided options or appropriate structuring of application programs. In particular, the various choices for SQL isolation levels are widely used, especially the read committed and the snapshot isolation levels. However, we would like to warn once again that these options should be used with extreme caution: if in doubt, do not use them. It is only in conjunction with specific properties of applications that they lead to acceptable behavior; if carelessly employed, they may lead to inconsistent data. So serializability (or multiversion serializability when transparent versioning is supported) remains by far the most appropriate choice for the safe and most productive development of multiuser applications.

Finally, we have shown that all concurrency control methods are susceptible to a performance catastrophe known as data contention thrashing, during load peaks. To avoid thrashing and ensure that performance deteriorates gracefully even under sudden load bursts, an explicit form of load control is needed. This is typically implemented by allowing system administrators to limit the server's multiprogramming level, but better "self-tuning" methods have been developed in the literature.

Exercises

10.1 Discuss to what extent lock escalation may incur deadlocks or livelocks.

10.2 Discuss if and under which conditions a form of lock de-escalation could make sense. De-escalation would essentially be the opposite of lock escalation—converting one (or a few) coarse-grained lock(s) into several fine-grained locks while a transaction is executing.

10.3 Give examples of schedules that fall into the following five isolation-level classes (but not into the next larger, surrounding class): not even read uncommitted, read uncommitted, read committed, repeatable read, serializability.

10.4 Give an example for a snapshot isolated history violating the consistency of the persistent data. Explain what kinds of inconsistencies may arise.

10.5 Design a concurrency control protocol that can guarantee snapshot isolation (and can indeed generate all snapshot isolated histories).

10.6 Give examples for showing that MVSR and snapshot isolation are incomparable classes of histories, i.e., neither one is included in the other.

Bibliographic Notes

The book by Gray and Reuter (1993) is an excellent source for the kind of pragmatic issues that we discussed in this chapter. Many of these issues, including multiple granularity locking and isolation levels, can be traced back to the seminal papers by Gray et al. (1975) and Gray (1978). The analog of multigranularity locks for optimistic and other nonlocking protocols has been studied by Carey (1983). Generalizations of multigranularity locking to low-overhead lock management for complex objects in CAD or CASE applications have been investigated by Herrmann et al. (1990), Cart and Ferrié (1990), and Rezende and Härder (1997).

Implementation techniques for transient versioning have first appeared in the work of Svobodova (1981) as well as Chan et al. (1982). More recent work that refines the various techniques and includes comparative performance studies has been done by Bober and Carey (1992a, 1992b, 1997). Mohan, Pirahesh, and Lorie (1992) have given a very detailed account of versioning for record- and index-entry based concurrency control.

Nested transactions have been invented by Moss (1985) and later studied by many other researchers, including Liskov et al. (1987), Härder and Rothermel (1993), and Lynch et al. (1994).

Tuning considerations related to locking have been surveyed by Shasha (1992). Good sources on application-level tuning for specific systems are the books by Corrigan and Gurry (1996), Schneider (1999), and Mullins (2000).

Isolation levels, as adopted by the SQL standard, have been critically reviewed by Berenson et al. (1995), who have also pointed out the practical importance of snapshot isolation. Recent studies of snapshot isolation that include precise characterizations have been carried out by Schenkel et al. (2000) as well as Adya et al. (2000); the latter has also cast other isolation levels into a formal framework.

Tay et al. (1985) were the first to analytically study and understand the fundamental phenomenon of data contention thrashing. The specific issue of feedback-driven overload control has been studied by Carey et al. (1990), Heiss and Wagner (1991), and Moenkeberg and Weikum (1991, 1992). Our presentation is adopted from Weikum et al. (1994). Important analytic foundations for the conflict-ratio based method have been laid by Thomasian (1993, 1996a). The wait-depth limitation method has been invented by Franaszek et al. (1992); related work on "cautious waiting" has been carried out by Balter et al. (1982) and Hsu and Zhang (1992). An excellent survey of the performance analysis of a wide variety of concurrency control and load control methods has been given by Thomasian (1996b, 1998a).

PART THREE

Recovery

CHAPTER ELEVEN

Transaction Recovery

And if you find a new way, you can do it today.
You can make it all true. And you can make it undo.
—*Cat Stevens*

Take heart, I said to myself: don't think of Wisdom now;
ask the help of Science.
—*Umberto Eco*

11.1 Goal and Overview

With this chapter we begin Part III of the book, in which we consider recovery methods to ensure the atomicity and persistence of transactions. This chapter focuses on the issue of transaction recovery, which is needed to implement transaction rollbacks while the server continues to process other transactions. A rollback is necessary when a transaction is aborted either because of an unacceptable exception in the application program currently executing at the client site (e.g., a pointer error) or upon detecting inconsistencies in the server's data that would arise from the current transaction's further execution. In addition, the server may choose to abort a transaction for internal reasons such as deadlock or overload (see Chapters 4 and 10). In all these cases, which are commonly subsumed under the term "transaction failures," the server continues to operate and is expected to restrict its recovery measures to the actually affected transaction while processing other transactions as usual.

Thus, the issue in transaction recovery is not so much to provide fault-tolerant service, which is something we will discuss in subsequent chapters when we consider server failures. Rather, this chapter focuses on the problem of how to *undo* the effects of an aborted transaction in the presence of concurrent transactions. This problem is all but trivial; in particular, it is not avoided by serializability-enforcing measures alone, nor is it avoided by simply suspending all currently active transactions while an aborted transaction is being rolled back. As a canonical example for illustrating the problem, reconsider the dirty-read anomaly from Chapter 2:

Undo of aborted transaction

Dirty-read anomaly

$$w_1(x)r_2(x)c_2a_1$$

This history should be considered unacceptable, since t_2's effects depend on having read a "dirty" (i.e., not yet committed) update that t_1 has made earlier. Later on, when t_1 aborts, we would expect some form of "cascading abort" that includes the dependent transaction t_2 as well, but at this point it is too late to abort the already committed transaction t_2. On the other hand, a scheduler based on serializability would surely accept this history, since it is perfectly conflict serializable. (Notice in this little discussion that an exchange of the two termination operations would immediately solve the problem, as the outcome of t_1 would be known at the end of t_2.)

Log of inverse operations   In order to establish a class of acceptable schedules that takes both serializability and transaction recovery issues into account appropriately, we will first make the necessary actions for rolling back a transaction explicit in that we expand a transaction abort into actual data operations that undo the transaction's prior updates. These actions can be determined from a *log* of each transaction's updates that is kept at the server. As the server itself is not affected by a single transaction failure, this log can be maintained in the server's volatile memory. For the same reason, the exact implementation of the log does not really matter; we will later pay more attention to the design of its underlying data structure once we start considering server failures in Chapter 12. For the time being, we can think of logs as lists of page values prior to the corresponding page write operations, organized on a per-transaction basis. More generally, a log can be perceived as a list of *inverse data operations*.

Once the previously implicit undo steps for an abort action are made explicit in what we will call an *expanded* schedule, we can again use serializability based arguments along the lines of commutative operations for reasoning about the correctness of transaction aborts and their interdependencies with concurrent transactions. We will present the theory that builds upon this idea for the page model of transactions first: we will introduce a notion of reducibility that takes Undo operations into account; then we will study a number of easy-to-implement, and syntactical, yet sufficient conditions for ensuring correctness, and we will finally look into the question of how to augment already known scheduling protocols in such a way that transaction aborts are correctly handled and anomalies like dirty reads are eliminated. Once the simpler case of page model transactions is completely covered, we will consider the more advanced case of object model transactions, and we will see that again some fundamental principles from the page model can be carried over, but need appropriate generalizations.

The chapter is organized as follows. Section 11.2 formalizes the concept of an expanded schedule. On this basis Sections 11.3 and 11.4 discuss fundamental correctness criteria, sufficient conditions that are more easily implementable, and further relationships among the various schedule classes that are of theoretical interest. Section 11.5 then exploits the conceptual underpinnings by showing how page model concurrency control methods can be easily extended to cope with transaction aborts. As the fundamental reasoning behind expanded schedules can be carried over to transaction executions with semantically rich operations and operation invocation trees, correctness criteria and algorithms for the object model can be discussed in a concise manner in Sections 11.6 and 11.7.

11.2 **Expanded Schedules with Explicit Undo Operations**

A major goal in this chapter is to derive a general correctness criterion for recovery that will be called *prefix reducibility,* and to characterize the corresponding class of schedules in a way that indicates how to augment known scheduling protocols in this direction. To begin with, we give an overview of the approach and summarize the underlying ideas.

11.2.1 **Intuition and Overview of Concepts**

The essence behind our approach to treating recovery from a conceptual point of view is to make the actions that are associated with an Abort operation occurring in a schedule or history explicit, and to treat them in the same way as ordinary operations. After a transaction failure, the goal is to restore the database to the state it was in before that transaction started; since this is not always possible in the presence of multiple transactions that are executing concurrently, let us consider it sufficient to undo the *write* operations that the transaction to be aborted has executed. If we include corresponding operations in the transaction that is to be terminated abnormally, Abort operations become obsolete, since what they need to accomplish is now explicit in the schedule or history in question.

As an example, consider the following history:

A history...

$$s = r_1(x)w_1(x)r_2(x)a_1w_2(x)c_2$$

Obviously, we show a dirty-read situation here, since the second transaction reads a value of x produced by the first, but since transaction t_1 aborts, that value should not have been made available to transaction t_2. We choose to "implement" operation a_1 by writing back the original value of x preceding $w_1(x)$ (assuming that this value can be obtained from the log); after that, we simply commit the transaction as if it had been successful. So now we are looking at the following history:

...and its expansion

$$s' = r_1(x)w_1(x)r_2(x)w_1^{-1}(x)c_1w_2(x)c_2$$

We assume that the two writes of t_1 on x are inverse to each other, so that the second compensates for the first. Thus, t_1 has no effect on the database, and now the problem is a different one: since s' has a cyclic conflict, it is an ordinary scheduling problem to avoid nonserializability, which can be accomplished by any of the known protocols. Notice that a 2PL scheduler, for example, would allow the original history s, as it is perfectly conflict serializable, but would detect the unacceptable behavior in the expanded history s'. Thus, if we make sure that s is replaced by s' prior to execution, we are guaranteed that no unacceptable history will result.

11.2.2 The Formal Model

We now make the idea of expanding schedules in response to a request to abort a transaction precise, and we will show that expanded schedules give rise to a uniform correctness criterion. As was briefly mentioned already, expanding schedules is essentially based on the following concepts:

Idea of expansions

1. All actions related to failures are made explicit in a schedule, that is, they are added to a given schedule as additional steps, and any Abort operation is replaced by a Commit operation.

2. A schedule so expanded is treated by ordinary serializability arguments, where special attention is paid to the interaction between steps on behalf of transaction aborts and regular steps.

Since we assume log-based recovery, we may assume that a transaction that will be aborted and hence needs its effects undone can simply be compensated for by "inverse" write operations: if s is a history such that $t_i \in \text{abort}(s)$ and $w_i(x) \in \text{op}(s)$, then the Undo operation corresponding to $w_i(x)$ is yet another write operation on x that restores the original value of x; such an operation is denoted by $w_i^{-1}(x)$ in what follows.

Read operations, on the other hand, will not need special treatment when aborting a transaction; we can assume that the results of a read are simply "forgotten," so that the steps themselves can be considered as "null steps."

Now each Undo operation of the form $w_i^{-1}(x)$ undoes a previously executed operation of the form $w_i(x)$ of transaction t_i, so that it makes sense to put Undo operations in *reverse order* of the corresponding Do operations in a history. If an aborted transaction has been expanded in this way, it can be treated like a committed one from that point on, so that we arrive at the following basic expansion strategy: if $t_i \in \text{abort}(s)$ holds in a given history s (i.e., $a_i \in \text{op}(s)$), then a_i is replaced by the Undo operations of all write steps of t_i (in reverse order), followed by c_i.

EXAMPLE 11.1

Consider history

Replacing aborts by inverse writes

$$s = r_1(x)w_1(x)r_2(y)w_1(y)w_2(y)a_1r_2(z)w_2(z)c_2$$

According to what was just said, s is rewritten into the following history (which will be called the *expansion* of s or the *expanded history* for s):

$$s' = r_1(x)w_1(x)r_2(y)w_1(y)w_2(y)w_1^{-1}(y)w_1^{-1}(x)c_1r_2(z)w_2(z)c_2$$

So far we have considered histories, and of course, we will need an extension of our approach to prefixes of histories (i.e., to schedules). Indeed, in a running scheduling situation, a scheduler commonly sees prefixes of histories only; if there is no explicit Abort operation yet, it is not immediately clear how to place abort actions in a schedule for a transaction that is still active.

To this end, we now make the following assumption: if s is a schedule and not a history—that is, for some transactions in s it is still open how they will end (i.e., active(s) $\neq \emptyset$)—s will be treated as if a system failure had occurred after the last operation in s so far. In other words, all transactions $t_i \in$ active(s) will be (implicitly) aborted and then of course be treated in the way described above. The only aspect that is different is the fact that now the reverse ordering of operations is no longer local to a single transaction, but global with respect to all aborted transactions.

EXAMPLE 11.2

Consider schedule

Terminating active transactions

$$s = w_1(x)w_2(x)w_2(y)w_1(y)$$

Since $t_1, t_2 \in$ active(s), s still appears acceptable, although there is already a cyclic conflict between t_1 and t_2. If both transactions are aborted according to the assumption above, we must be careful in sequencing the corresponding abort operations. Indeed, neither the ordering a_1a_2, resulting in

$$s' = w_1(x)w_2(x)w_2(y)w_1(y)w_1^{-1}(y)w_1^{-1}(x)c_1w_2^{-1}(y)w_2^{-1}(x)c_2$$

nor the ordering a_2a_1, resulting in

$$s'' = w_1(x)w_2(x)w_2(y)w_1(y)w_2^{-1}(y)w_2^{-1}(x)c_2w_1^{-1}(y)w_1^{-1}(x)c_1$$

represents a correct execution. Instead, a correct undo can in this case only be guaranteed if the undos corresponding to different aborts are executed in an overlapping fashion. Thus, the appropriate expansion of s must look as follows:

$$s''' = w_1(x)w_2(x)w_2(y)w_1(y)w_1^{-1}(y)w_2^{-1}(y)w_2^{-1}(x)w_1^{-1}(x)c_2c_1$$

We could formally capture situations like the one just seen through the notion of a *group abort*, representing the collective abort actions of all active transactions. However, we can do without explicit group aborts as long as we keep in mind that active transactions need a slightly different treatment than aborted ones.

We are now ready to make the above considerations precise as follows:

Expansion of a schedule

DEFINITION 11.1 *Expansion of a Schedule*

Let s be a schedule. The *expansion* of s, denoted $\exp(s)$, is defined as follows:

1. Steps of $\exp(s)$:
   (a) $t_i \in \text{commit}(s) \Rightarrow \text{op}(t_i) \subseteq \text{op}(\exp(s))$
   (b) $t_i \in \text{abort}(s) \Rightarrow (\text{op}(t_i) - \{a_i\}) \cup \{c_i\} \cup \{w_i^{-1}(x) \mid w_i(x) \in t_i\} \subseteq \text{op}(\exp(s))$
   (c) $t_i \in \text{active}(s) \Rightarrow \text{op}(t_i) \cup \{c_i\} \cup \{w_i^{-1}(x) \mid w_i(x) \in t_i\} \subseteq \text{op}(\exp(s))$

2. Step ordering in $\exp(s)$:
   (a) all steps from $\text{op}(s) \cap \text{op}(\exp(s))$ occur in $\exp(s)$ in the same order as in s;
   (b) all inverse steps of an aborted transaction occur in $\exp(s)$ after their original steps and before the respective Commit operation;
   (c) all inverse steps of transactions in $\text{active}(s)$ occur in $\exp(s)$ after the original steps of s and before their corresponding commits;
   (d) the ordering of inverse steps is the reverse of the ordering of the corresponding original steps.

EXAMPLE 11.3

Consider schedule

$$s = r_1(x)w_1(x)r_2(y)w_2(y)r_3(z)w_3(z)r_4(y)w_4(y)a_1c_3r_2(z)w_2(z)$$

Then we have

$$\exp(s) = r_1(x)w_1(x)r_2(y)w_2(y)r_3(z)w_3(z)r_4(y)w_4(y)$$
$$w_1^{-1}(x)c_1c_3r_2(z)w_2(z)w_2^{-1}(z)w_4^{-1}(y)w_2^{-1}(y)c_2c_4$$

11.3 **Correctness Criteria for the Page Model**

Now that we have fixed a way to treat aborted transactions such that serializability based schedulers could be enabled to discover undesirable situations that stem from transaction failures, we need to cast this approach into a formally precise correctness criterion. To this end, we will present a series of correctness criteria that, as will be seen, are in a sense orthogonal to each other. For practical purposes, we will later choose the one that exhibits the most attractive properties.

11.3.1 **Expanded Conflict Serializability**

As indicated above, the notion of serializability can be extended to expanded histories and schedules without further restrictions or constraints. In particular, our well-known notion of conflict remains the same as before: two steps from distinct transactions are *in conflict* if they access the same data item and at least one of them is a (direct or inverse) write operation.

DEFINITION 11.2   *Expanded Conflict Serializability*

Let s be a schedule s is *expanded conflict serializable* if its expansion $\exp(s)$ is conflict serializable.

Let XCSR denote the class of all expanded conflict-serializable schedules.

Expanded conflict serializability

EXAMPLE 11.4

Consider

$$s = r_1(x)w_1(x)r_2(x)a_1c_2$$

Then we have

$$\exp(s) = r_1(x)w_1(x)r_2(x)w_1^{-1}(x)c_1c_2$$

Since $\exp(s)$ exhibits a cyclic conflict between its two transactions, it follows that $s \notin$ XCSR. Next consider

$$s' = r_1(x)w_1(x)a_1r_2(x)c_2$$

Now we find

$$\exp(s') = r_1(x)w_1(x)w_1^{-1}(x)c_1r_2(x)c_2$$

Since $\exp(s')$ is equivalent to the serial execution t_1t_2, it follows that $s' \in$ XCSR.

Since the inverse write operations occurring in an expanded schedule can at most add to the conflict relation of a given schedule, it should be clear that if we omit them, we obtain a subhistory of the expanded schedule; if the expansion is conflict serializable, so is its subhistory. Thus, we find that class XCSR is a subclass of class CSR, and the first schedule in the previous example shows that this inclusion is strict:

LEMMA 11.1

XCSR $\subset$ CSR

Although expanded conflict serializability is already a reasonable step toward a formal treatment of transaction failures, it is too restrictive in certain situations. The reason is that some intuitively correct histories do not belong to XCSR, as shown in the following example:

EXAMPLE 11.5

Problems with XCSR

Suppose all transactions in a given history are aborted, as in

$$s = w_1(x)w_2(x)a_2a_1$$

For this history, we find

$$\exp(s) = w_1(x)w_2(x)w_2^{-1}(x)c_2w_1^{-1}(x)c_1$$

which apparently has a cyclic conflict; thus, s is not in XCSR. On the other hand, the cycle is technically irrelevant, as both transactions are aborted. In that sense, s is acceptable.

In Example 11.5, the acceptability of s crucially depends on the fact that the Undo operation of t_2 immediately follows its corresponding Do operation, so that in principle we can remove this pair of operations from s without changing its effect. Note that this would no longer be the case if the two abort steps of s were in reverse order.

If we perform the removal, we obtain

$$w_1(x)c_2w_1^{-1}(x)c_1$$

Since no operation from t_2 is left, we can drop c_2. Now $w_1(x)$ and its inverse operation have become adjacent, and by the same argument we just applied to t_2, we can now eliminate t_1 from s. So we are left with an empty schedule that does not perform any actions at all, which is exactly the desired effect, as both transactions were aborted.

We will now pursue this observation further and establish another correctness criterion that will ultimately serve as the goal of scheduling in what follows.

11.3.2 Reducibility and Prefix Reducibility

If a write operation and its inverse happen to be *adjacent*—that is, they occur right after one another—it is guaranteed that no operation can be between the two that is in conflict with either of them. If a write operation and its inverse are not adjacent, it may be possible to make them adjacent by performing allowed commutations in the given schedule, that is, by moving them together through pairwise exchanges with other operations. We will next cast this intuition into *transformation rules* that allow us to reorder and modify a given schedule in certain ways. Note that the notion of expanded serializability as introduced above does not exploit information about the presence of inverse operations or about their adjacency.

Transformation rules

DEFINITION 11.3   *Reducibility*

Reducibility

A schedule s is *reducible* if its expansion $\exp(s)$ can be transformed into a serial history by finitely many applications of the following rules (in any order):

1. Commutativity rule (CR): If $p, q \in \text{op}(\exp(s))$ such that $p < q$ and $(p, q) \notin \text{conf}(\exp(s))$, and if there exists no step $o \in \text{op}(\exp(s))$ such that $p < o < q$, then the order of p and q can be reversed.

2. Undo rule (UR): If $p, q \in \text{op}(\exp(s))$ are inverses of each other (i.e., of the form $p = w_i(x)$, $q = w_i^{-1}(x)$) with $p < q$) and if there is no step $o \in \text{op}(\exp(s))$ in between, i.e., $p < o < q$, then the pair p, q of steps can be removed from $\exp(s)$.

3. Null rule (NR): If $p \in \text{op}(\exp(s))$ has the form $p = r_i(x)$ such that $t_i \in \text{active}(s) \cup \text{abort}(s)$, then p can be removed from $\exp(s)$.

4. Ordering rule (OR): Two commutative, unordered operations can be arbitrarily ordered.

Let RED denote the class of all reducible schedules.

Notice that the presence of UR, the undo rule, will in most cases have the effect that the original schedule is not just transformed into a serial history (if possible), but that it will indeed be reduced to something equivalent (and serial, if possible). Ultimately, a given reducible schedule may be reduced to a sequence of Commit operations only, which is trivially serial (and also considered to be an "empty" schedule).

EXAMPLE 11.6

Consider

$$s = r_1(x)w_1(x)r_2(x)w_2(x)a_2a_1$$

Then we have

$$\exp(s) = r_1(x)w_1(x)r_2(x)w_2(x)w_2^{-1}(x)c_2w_1^{-1}(x)c_1$$

By using rules CR, UR, and NR, $\exp(s)$ can be reduced as follows:

by UR:	$r_1(x)w_1(x)r_2(x)c_2w_1^{-1}(x)c_1$
by NR:	$r_1(x)w_1(x)c_2w_1^{-1}(x)c_1$
by NR:	$w_1(x)c_2w_1^{-1}(x)c_1$
by CR:	$w_1(x)w_1^{-1}(x)c_2c_1$
by UR:	c_2c_1

As a result, $s \in \text{RED}$.

Notice that conflicts are defined for data operations only, so Commit operations can freely be commuted with reads or writes as long as the ordering of steps given by a transaction is not modified.

EXAMPLE 11.7

Consider

$$s = w_1(x)r_2(x)c_1c_2$$

Here, by CR , the only relevant transformation is into

$$w_1(x)c_1r_2(x)c_2$$

which is serial, so $s \in \text{RED}$. Notice, however, that in this case the reduction of s has not really removed any operation.

The notion of reducibility thus respects not only the commutativity of operations that are not in conflict in a given history or schedule, but also the elimination of adjacent Do and Undo operations.

As we have done for ordinary histories when we defined conflict serializability, we need to be able to decide about the reducibility of a given history by looking at a prefix only. As before, the reason for this is that a scheduler must be able to decide on the executability of a given operation without having seen the entire transaction or even the history under construction. In particular, the scheduler must take into account the fact that a transaction can be aborted at any moment.

EXAMPLE 11.8

Consider

$$s = w_1(x)w_2(x)c_2c_1$$

Suppose a scheduler has already executed the two write operations, and then commits t_2. If at that point t_1 would abort, the resulting schedule (i.e., prefix of s) would be expanded into

$$s' = w_1(x)w_2(x)c_2w_1^{-1}(x)c_1$$

which is neither in XCSR nor in RED. The latter holds since none of the reduction rules applies (except for ones involving the Commit operations, which does not help here), so reduction leaves the schedule essentially unchanged. Thus, s should not be acceptable, since it has an "unsafe" prefix.

We are therefore interested in the closedness of expandability as well as of reducibility under taking prefixes; since the latter is the more important notion, this is defined next. (For the other, see Exercise 11.6.)

DEFINITION 11.4   *Prefix Reducibility*

A schedule s is *prefix reducible* if each of its prefixes is reducible.

Let PRED denote the class of all prefix-reducible schedules.

Prefix reducibility

LEMMA 11.2

$\mathrm{PRED} \subset \mathrm{RED}$

Proof

Since every schedule is trivially a prefix of itself, the inclusion is straightforward. Next consider $s = w_1(x)w_2(x)c_2c_1$ from Example 11.8 once more. Obviously, $s \in \mathrm{RED} - \mathrm{PRED}$; in particular, prefix $w_1(x)w_2(x)c_2$ of s is not reducible.

EXAMPLE 11.9

Consider

$$s = w_1(x)w_2(x)a_2a_1$$

As we have discussed in Example 11.5 already, $s \notin$ XCSR. On the other hand, $s \in$ RED, since our discussion following Example 11.5 has already revealed that s can be reduced into a serial schedule. Moreover, it is easily verified that every prefix of s is also reducible. Thus, $s \in$ PRED.

To conclude this section, we establish the following relationships between the classes of schedules introduced so far:

THEOREM 11.1

1. XCSR $\subset$ RED

2. XCSR and PRED are incomparable with respect to set inclusion.

Proof

1. Consider some $s \in$ XCSR. By definition, $\exp(s)$ is thus conflict serializable, so there exists a serial history s' that is conflict equivalent to $\exp(s)$. Clearly, $\exp(s)$ can be transformed into s' using the rules from Definition 11.3 (except for UR and NR), performing allowed commutations, or ordering previously unordered steps only. Thus, $s \in$ RED. History s from Example 11.5 shows that the inclusion is strict.

2. In order to show that XCSR and PRED are incomparable with respect to set inclusion, it suffices to consider the following histories:

$$w_1(x)w_2(x)c_2c_1 \in \text{XCSR} - \text{PRED (Example 11.8)}$$
$$w_1(x)w_2(x)a_2a_1 \in \text{PRED} - \text{XCSR (Example 11.5)}$$

Part (2) of the previous theorem states that reducibility is independent from the considerations on prefixes we have done above. We will later prove another theorem, which states that PRED contains all intuitively correct schedules.

11.4 **Sufficient Syntactic Conditions**

Dirty-read anomaly   Consider again the history we looked at in the beginning of this chapter:

$$w_1(x)r_2(x)c_2a_1$$

We have already discussed why this history is not acceptable, and that a serializability based scheduler would nevertheless consider it valid. In this section we discuss correctness criteria for transaction recovery that are exclusively based on simple syntactical restrictions on the allowed schedules. Essentially, these restrictions state in what relative order the termination operations from various transactions that have interdependencies (such as read-from situations) are allowed to occur. And as you will see, putting more and more restrictions on the allowed placement of termination operations or on the relative ordering of reads, writes, aborts, and commits increasingly simplifies transaction recovery, but also limits the amount of parallelism that can be achieved. Compared to the criteria we have introduced earlier in this chapter, which emphasize a way of *processing* aborts, the syntactic notions presented next can be seen as sufficient conditions for correct recovery, as will become clear when we examine the relationships that exist between the various notions.

11.4.1 **Recoverability**

Our first syntactic notion is intended to avoid dirty-read situations that may arise when one transaction has read a data object from another and then commits "too early."

DEFINITION 11.5 *Recoverability*

A schedule s is *recoverable* if the following holds for all transactions $t_i, t_j \in$ trans(s), $i \neq j$: if t_i reads from t_j in s and $c_i \in op(s)$, then $c_j <_s c_i$.

Let RC denote the class of all recoverable schedules.

Recoverability

Thus, in a recoverable schedule, each transaction can only be committed after all transactions from which it has read have been committed.

EXAMPLE 11.10

Consider

$$s_1 = w_1(x)w_1(y)r_2(u)w_2(x)r_2(y)w_2(y)w_3(u)c_3c_2w_1(z)c_1$$

Then t_2 reads y from t_1 and $c_2 \in s$, but $c_1 \not<_s c_2$. It follows that $s_1 \notin$ RC. Next consider

$$s_2 = w_1(x)w_1(y)r_2(u)w_2(x)r_2(y)w_2(y)w_3(u)c_3w_1(z)c_1c_2$$

Then $s_2 \in$ RC, since the Commit operation of t_2 follows after that of t_1.

11.4.2 **Avoiding Cascading Aborts**

In history s_2 in the previous example we can identify another problem: if t_1 is aborted right after operation $r_2(y)$, we would again encounter a dirty-read situation, and the abort of t_1 would imply the abort of transaction t_2. In other words, sometimes aborts "cascade," and we can avoid this by a suitable restriction of class RC:

DEFINITION 11.6 *Avoiding Cascading Aborts*

A schedule *s avoids cascading aborts* if the following holds for all transactions $t_i, t_j \in$ trans(s), $i \neq j$: if t_i reads x from t_j in s, then $c_j <_s r_i(x)$.

Let ACA denote the class of all schedules that avoid cascading aborts.

Note that the cascading abort in Example 11.10 (s_2) is an inconvenience, but unlike the canonical dirty-read anomaly considered before, it does not incur any correctness problems, as the dirty reader transaction now is not yet committed at the time the other transaction would abort.

Thus, while recoverability of a schedule means that each transaction reaches its commit point *after* all transactions from which it has read are committed, the ACA property means that a transaction can only read values written by transactions that are already committed, that is, whose presence in the database is, in a sense, "guaranteed."

EXAMPLE 11.11

For s_2 from Example 11.10 we thus have $s_2 \notin$ ACA. However, for

$$s_3 = w_1(x)w_1(y)r_2(u)w_2(x)w_1(z)c_1r_2(y)w_2(y)w_3(u)c_3c_2$$

we can verify that $s_2 \in$ ACA.

History s_3 is still not entirely free of problems: suppose that t_1 aborts right after $w_2(x)$; then there is no need to abort t_2 as well, but the database is brought back into the state that it was in prior to the beginning of t_1, although t_2 has already written a new value of data item x. As we mentioned earlier, by far the most practical approach to implement transaction rollbacks is to undo operations of aborted transactions. In contrast, some schedules allowed under RC or ACA are intuitively recoverable only by first going back to a potentially very old state and then redoing a potentially long sequence of committed transactions. Obviously, such an approach is inordinately expensive for merely rolling back a single transaction while the server is continuing to process other transactions.

EXAMPLE 11.12

Consider a numeric data item x with an initial value of $x = 1$, and let schedule $s = w_1(x, 2)w_2(x, 3)c_2a_1$ be given, where $w_i(x, n)$ means that w_i writes value n for x. Thus, the undo of $w_1(x, 2)$ would restore the value as it was immediately before the operation was executed, setting x to 1; however, after a_1 the current value of x should be 3. So in this example, the only correct form of transaction recovery for t_1 would be to restore the value as of the beginning of the entire schedule and then redo the write of the already committed transaction t_2.

The general problem here is that the values that have to be restored after a transaction abort can differ from those that immediately preceded the write operations of the aborted transaction. Such differences generally result from mutual overwrites performed by active transactions whose outcome is open at the time they write.

11.4.3 Strictness

To avoid being forced to perform a more expensive transaction recovery different from the simple undo approach, we impose yet another syntactical restriction on schedules.

DEFINITION 11.7 *Strictness*   *Strictness*

A schedule s is *strict* if the following holds for all transactions $t_i \in \text{trans}(s)$ and for all $p_i(x) \in \text{op}(t_i)$, $p \in \{r, w\}$: if $w_j(x) <_s p_i(x)$, $i \neq j$, then $a_j <_s p_i(x) \vee c_j <_s p_i(x)$.

Let ST denote the class of all strict schedules.

In words, a schedule is strict if no data item is read or overwritten until the transaction that wrote it last has ended (either by commit or by abort).

EXAMPLE 11.13

For s_3 from Example 11.11 we find $s_3 \notin$ ST. Next, for

$$s_4 = w_1(x)w_1(y)r_2(u)w_1(z)c_1w_2(x)r_2(y)w_2(y)w_3(u)c_3c_2$$

we can verify that $s_3 \in$ ST.

11.4.4 Rigorousness

Our next class of recoverable schedules is a restriction of ST that is based on the following intuition: a schedule that is in class ST informally avoids write/read as well as write/write conflicts between uncommitted transactions; a schedule in the class RG defined next completes that picture by additionally avoiding read/write conflicts between uncommitted transactions. As will be seen shortly, this extra provision makes a remarkable difference in the relationship to serializability.

Rigorousness

DEFINITION 11.8 *Rigorousness*

A schedule s is *rigorous* if it is strict and additionally satisfies the following condition: for all transactions $t_i, t_j \in \text{trans}(s)$, if $r_j(x) <_s w_i(x), i \neq j$, then $a_j <_s w_i(x) \vee c_j <_s w_i(x)$.

Let RG denote the class of all rigorous schedules.

In words, a schedule is rigorous if it is strict and no object x is overwritten until all transactions that read x last are finished.

EXAMPLE 11.14

For s_4 from Example 11.13 we find $s_4 \notin \text{RG}$. Next, for

$$s_5 = w_1(x)w_1(y)r_2(u)w_1(z)c_1w_2(x)r_2(y)w_2(y)c_2w_3(u)c_3$$

we can verify that $s_5 \in \text{RG}$.

The relationship between the syntactical classes of schedules is intuitively such that they continuously put further restrictions on the set of admissible schedules, as suggested by our samples s_1–s_5. More formally, we can show the following theorem:

THEOREM 11.2

$$\text{RG} \subset \text{ST} \subset \text{ACA} \subset \text{RC}$$

Proof

The fact that $\text{RG} \subseteq \text{ST}$ immediately follows from the definition of RG. That the inclusion is strict is verified by s_4 from Example 11.14 ($s_4 \in \text{ST} \backslash \text{RG}$).

Next let $s \in \text{ST}$, and let t_i read x from t_j in s, $i \neq j$. By the definition of the reads-from relation, $w_j(x) <_s r_i(x)$ and $a_j \not<_s r_i(x)$ then hold. By the definition of class ST, this implies $c_j <_s r_i(x)$, i.e., $s \in \text{ACA}$. Thus, $\text{ST} \subseteq \text{ACA}$; s_3 from Example 11.11 proves that the inclusion is strict ($s_3 \in \text{ACA} \backslash \text{ST}$).

Next consider some schedule $s \in$ ACA, and suppose that t_i reads x from t_j in s, $i \neq j$, and that $c_i \in s$. Since $s \in$ ACA, it follows that $c_j <_s r_i(x)$. Clearly, we also have $w_j(x) <_s c_j$ and $r_i(x) <_s c_i$. This implies $c_j <_s c_i$, i.e., $s \in$ RC. Thus, ACA $\subseteq$ RC; s_2 from Example 11.10 moreover shows that this inclusion is also strict ($s_2 \in$ RC\ACA).

Another property that is easily verified by the definitions of RG, ST, ACA, and RC is that membership in any of the four classes is prefix commit closed; that is, if a schedule is, say, in ACA, the same holds for the committed projection of each of its prefixes (see Exercise 11.4).

We next look at the relationship between our syntactic classes of schedules and the serializable ones, where we restrict the attention to the most important class of conflict-serializable schedules: schedules whose committed projections are histories in CSR. Surprisingly, this relationship essentially is such that ST, ACA, and RC are incomparable to CSR with respect to set inclusion, while RG is not. This is illustrated in Figure 11.1, where the various histories mentioned are those from Examples 11.10, 11.11, 11.13, and 11.14, respectively. Moreover, history

$$w_1(x)w_2(x)w_2(y)c_2w_1(y)c_1$$

is an example of a history that is in RC, but not in CSR. Note that Figure 11.1 can be extended so that it also includes the classes of commit view serializable (CMVSR) and commit final state serializable (CMFSR) histories (see Chapter 3 for these classes).

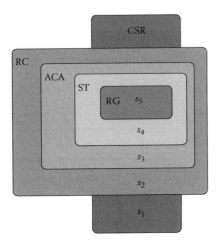

Figure 11.1 Relationship between schedule classes RC, ACA, ST, RG, and CSR.

While the incomparability between CSR and classes ST, ACA, and RC with respect to set inclusion is easily established through examples, containment of RG in CSR is implied by the following observation regarding RG and COCSR, the subclass of CSR containing all schedules whose committed projection is a commit-ordered conflict-serializable history: membership of a schedule s in class RG actually means that for any two operations $p \in \mathrm{op}(t_i)$ and $q \in \mathrm{op}(t_j)$, $i \neq j$, that are in conflict in s such that $p <_s q$, commit operation c_i also comes before q in s (provided that c_i indeed occurs in s). On the other hand, since q precedes c_j (if c_j occurs in s), we may conclude that c_i precedes c_j. Thus, we have shown that RG $\subseteq$ COCSR. History $s = r_1(x)w_2(x)c_1c_2 \in$ COCSR\RG additionally shows that this inclusion is strict, so we have

---

THEOREM 11.3

RG $\subset$ COCSR

Figure 11.2 summarizes the relationships just described. Thus, RG is the only class of schedules among the "syntactic" ones that is comparable to CSR with respect to set inclusion. In other words, recoverability, avoidance of cascading aborts, and strictness are properties of schedules that are *orthogonal* to serializability; thus, a history may be, say, strict without being conflict serializable. As a consequence, two criteria are required in order to make history and schedule "correctness" precise, as long as serializability and anything strictly "above" RG are preferable. This is no longer true for RG, clearly at the expense of disallowing some histories.

As the next theorem will show, RG is, in a sense, in line with the class of prefix-reducible schedules, as these also fall into the intersection of the classes of

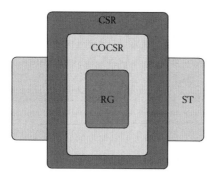

Figure 11.2 Relationship between schedule classes CSR, COCSR, RG, and ST.

conflict-serializable and of recoverable schedules, so that rigorousness or prefix reducibility *alone* suffices as a correctness criterion for schedules. However, class PRED is somewhat "better off" than RG, since the intersection of CSR and ST is *contained* in PRED, not vice versa. In detail, we can state the following theorem, a result that underlines the general importance of prefix reducibility in the context of database transactions:

THEOREM 11.4

$$\text{CSR} \cap \text{ST} \subset \text{PRED} \subset \text{CSR} \cap \text{RC}$$

PRED vs. ST and RC

Proof

Let us look at the left inclusion first and suppose that schedule s is both in CSR and ST. Let s' be an arbitrary prefix of s; since CSR and ST are both prefix closed, it follows that $s' \in \text{CSR} \cap \text{ST}$. Now assume that $s' \notin \text{RED}$. Then $\exp(s')$ cannot be transformed into a serial history using rules CR, NR, UR, and OR alone. However, since s' itself *is* serializable, this can only be caused by do/undo pairs of the form $(w_i(x), w_i^{-1}(x))$ that cannot be brought together by the transformation rules. Thus, there must exist an action p_j, $p \in \{r, w\}$, $j \neq i$ that is in conflict with $w_i(x)$ and with $w_i^{-1}(x)$, and which must be ordered as follows:

$$w_i(x) < p_j < w_i^{-1}(x)$$

We now consider both possible cases individually:

1. $w_i(x) < r_j(x) < w_i^{-1}(x)$: In this case, t_j must terminate with a commit operation, since the read operation would otherwise have been eliminated from the expanded schedule by rule NR. However, this contradicts the fact that $s' \in \text{ST}$, since t_j can read item x only after t_i is finished.

2. $w_i(x) < w_j(x) < w_i^{-1}(x)$: This immediately contradicts the fact that s' is strict.

As both cases lead to a contradiction, our assumption that $s' \notin \text{RED}$ was false, which concludes the first portion of the proof.

For the second inclusion stated by the theorem, consider a schedule $s \in \text{PRED}$. If s was not in CSR, the conflict graph of s would contain a cycle of the form $t_1 \to t_2 \to \ldots \to t_n \to t_1$ involving a committed transaction. But then s cannot be transformed into a serial history by the reduction rules, which contradicts our assumption that $s \in \text{PRED}$.

Next assume that $s \notin \text{RC}$. This can only happen in one of the following situations:

1. $w_i(x) < r_j(x) < c_j < c_i$: In this case, the prefix comprising the first three operations only is not reducible, a contradiction.

2. $w_i(x) < r_j(x) < c_j < a_i$: Here, the argument is the same as in case (1).

3. $w_i(x) < r_j(x) < a_i < c_j$: In this case, the expanded schedule cannot be prefix reducible, again a contradiction to the assumption $s \in \text{PRED}$.

11.4.5 Log Recoverability

Our next goal is to define a correctness criterion that is based on recoverability and in addition places an order on the termination operations of transactions that are involved in a write/write conflict. As it will turn out, this new criterion, if combined with serializability, can serve as a characterization of class PRED.

DEFINITION 11.9   *Log Recoverability*

A schedule s is *log recoverable* if the following two properties hold:

1. s is recoverable; i.e., for all transactions $t_i, t_j \in \text{trans}(s)$ $(i \neq j)$ we have: if t_i reads from t_j in s and $c_i \in s$, then $c_j <_s c_i$.

2. For all transactions $t_i, t_j \in \text{trans}(s)$ $(i \neq j)$ we additionally have: if there is a write/write conflict of the form $w_i(x) < w_j(x)$ in s, then $a_i < w_j(x)$ or $c_i < c_j$ if t_j commits, and $a_j < a_i$ if t_i aborts.

Let LRC denote the class of all log-recoverable schedules.

In essence, the definition of LRC is about the correct placement of termination operations in such a way that an isolated undoing of transactions in conflict can be guaranteed. We illustrate the basic effect on two prototypical schedules next. Let us first look at

$$s = w_1(x)r_2(x)$$

Here, the first part of the definition of class LRC applies, and as Table 11.1 shows, the cases that are not log recoverable are also not in PRED.

Next, we look at schedule

$$s = w_1(x)w_2(x)$$

to which the second part of the definition of class LRC applies. Interestingly, the unacceptable termination possibilities are again exactly those that are not in PRED, as shown in Table 11.2.

The following theorem shows that the above observations are not just a coincidence:

Table 11.1 Distinguishing *wr* cases for membership in PRED.

Case	History	Property
1	$w_1(x)r_2(x)a_1a_2$	$\in$ PRED
2	$w_1(x)r_2(x)a_1c_2$	$\notin$ PRED
3	$w_1(x)r_2(x)c_2c_1$	$\notin$ PRED
4	$w_1(x)r_2(x)c_2a_1$	$\notin$ PRED
5	$w_1(x)r_2(x)a_2a_1$	$\in$ PRED
6	$w_1(x)r_2(x)a_2c_1$	$\in$ PRED
7	$w_1(x)r_2(x)c_1c_2$	$\in$ PRED
8	$w_1(x)r_2(x)c_1a_2$	$\in$ PRED

Table 11.2 Distinguishing *ww* cases for membership in PRED.

Case	History	Property
1	$w_1(x)w_2(x)a_1a_2$	$\notin$ PRED
2	$w_1(x)w_2(x)a_1c_2$	$\notin$ PRED
3	$w_1(x)w_2(x)c_2c_1$	$\notin$ PRED
4	$w_1(x)w_2(x)c_2a_1$	$\notin$ PRED
5	$w_1(x)w_2(x)a_2a_1$	$\in$ PRED
6	$w_1(x)w_2(x)a_2c_1$	$\in$ PRED
7	$w_1(x)w_2(x)c_1c_2$	$\in$ PRED
8	$w_1(x)w_2(x)c_1a_2$	$\in$ PRED

THEOREM 11.5

A schedule s is prefix reducible iff it is log recoverable and (its committed projection is) conflict serializable, that is, PRED = LRC $\cap$ CSR.

Characterization of class PRED

To prove this theorem we need the following lemma:

LEMMA 11.3

If $s \in$ LRC, then all operations of uncommitted transactions can be eliminated from $\exp(s)$ using rules CR, UR, NR, and OR.

Proof

The claim is trivially satisfied for read operations, since read operations of uncommitted transactions can always be dropped from $\exp(s)$ for any s.

Therefore, we only need to prove the lemma for write operations of un-committed transactions in s. Let transaction t_i be uncommitted in s such that $w_i(x) \in op(s)$. Assume that n operations are performed on x and pre-ceding $w_i^{-1}(x)$ in $exp(s)$. We will show by induction on n that $w_i(x)$ can be eliminated from some modification of $exp(s)$.

First observe that for case $n = 0$, a direct application of rule UR eliminates $w_i(x)$ from $exp(s)$. Next, if $w_i(x)$ and $w_j(x)$ are such that $w_i(x) <_s w_j(x)$ and $a_i \not<_s w_j(x)$, we will say that $w_i(x)$ and $w_j(x)$ are in *active* conflict. Observe that if $w_i(x)$ and $w_j(x)$ are not in active conflict, but $w_i(x) <_s w_j(x)$, then in $exp(s)$ we have $w_i^{-1}(x) < w_j(x)$.

Now for the induction step, let $n > 0$, and assume the lemma holds for all $k < n$. Assume that $o_j(x)$ is the last operation with respect to the ordering in $exp(s)$ among the n operations satisfying $w_i(x) < o_j(x) < w_i^{-1}(x)$ in $exp(s)$. If $i = j$, then $o_j(x) = r_i(x)$, since each transaction contains at most one write operation per data object. But then $r_i(x)$ can be dropped from $exp(s)$, leaving us with $n - 1$ operations between $w_i(x)$ and its inverse, and by the induction hypothesis we conclude that $w_i(x)$ can be eliminated from $exp(s)$. If $i \neq j$, we consider three cases:

1. $o_j = r_j$: If transaction t_j is committed in s, then $s \notin \text{LRC}$, a contradic-tion to our general assumption. If t_j is not committed, then r_j can be eliminated from $exp(s)$ using rule NR, and by the induction hypothesis our claim holds.

2. $o_j = w_j$: If $w_i(x)$ and $w_j(x)$ are in active conflict, transaction t_j cannot be committed in s, since otherwise s would not be in LRC. Thus, t_j is either active or aborted in s, and in both cases $exp(s)$ must have $w_i(x) < w_j(x) < w_j^{-1}(x) < w_i^{-1}(x)$. Thus, $w_j(x)$ is not the last operation on x with respect to the ordering in $exp(s)$. Now if $w_i(x)$ and $w_j(x)$ are not in active conflict, then in $exp(s)$ we have $w_i(x) < w_i^{-1}(x) < w_j(x)$, which contradicts our assumption.

3. $o_j = w_j^{-1}$: If $w_i(x)$ and $w_j(x)$ are in active conflict in s, we have $w_j^{-1}(x) < w_i^{-1}(x)$ in $exp(s)$, and hence $w_i(x) < w_j(x)$. Operation $w_j(x)$ together with its inverse $w_j^{-1}(x)$ can be eliminated from $exp(s)$ using the inductive assumption, as can be operation $w_i(x)$. If $w_i(x)$ and $w_j(x)$ are not in active conflict, i.e., t_i aborts before operation $w_j(x)$ in s, then we have $w_i^{-1}(x) < w_j(x)$ in $exp(s)$. This again contradicts our assumption that $w_j^{-1}(x)$ is the last operation on x before $w_i^{-1}(x)$.

Proof of Theorem 11.5

"$\supseteq$:" Let $s \in \text{LRC} \cap \text{CSR}$, and assume that $s \notin \text{PRED}$. Then there exists a prefix s' of s that is not reducible. From the definition of LRC it follows that

s' is also in LRC; since membership in CSR is prefix closed, s' is also in CSR. By Lemma 11.3, all operations of uncommitted transactions can be eliminated from $\exp(s')$; call the result of this elimination s''. Thus s'' contains the committed transactions of s' only. Since $s' \in$ CSR, s'' can be transformed into a serial history by a finite number of applications of commutativity rule CR. Thus, s' is reducible, a contradiction. Consequently, our assumption was false, and $s \in$ PRED.

"$\subseteq$:" Conversely, let $s \in$ PRED, and assume that $s \notin$ LRC $\cap$ CSR. If $s \notin$ CSR, s cannot be in PRED by definition, so it suffices to assume that $s \in$ CSR$-$LRC. Suppose s contains a conflict of the form $w_i(x)w_j(x)$. Since $s \notin$ LRC, either

(a) t_j commits and either t_i does not commit or commits after t_j, or

(b) t_i aborts and either t_j does not abort or aborts after t_i.

Consider (a): If t_j commits and t_i does not commit, then we have $w_i(x) <_s w_j(x) <_s c_j$. Therefore, in $\exp(s)$ we have $w_i(x) < w_j(x) < w_i^{-1}(x)$, which is not reducible, a contradiction. If both t_j and t_i commit and $c_j <_s c_i$, then the prefix of s containing c_j but not c_i is not reducible, by the same reason as in the previous case, which again yields a contradiction.

Next consider (b): Assume that t_i aborts and t_j does not abort. Since t_i and t_j are in active conflict, we have that $w_i(x) <_s w_j(x) <_s a_i$. If t_j commits, it follows that $w_i(x) < w_j(x) < w_i^{-1}(x)$ in $\exp(s)$, which is not reducible. If t_j does not terminate in s, we find $w_i(x) < w_j(x) < w_i^{-1}(x) < w_j^{-1}(x)$ in $\exp(s)$, which is also not reducible. So we are again faced with a contradiction. Finally, if both t_i and t_j abort such that $a_i <_s a_j$, then the prefix of s containing a_i but not a_j is not reducible by the same reason as in the previous case, which again yields a contradiction to s being prefix reducible.

Similarly it can be shown that s must also be recoverable; in particular, note that a prefix of the form $w_i(x) <_s r_j(x) <_s c_j$ is not prefix reducible. This concludes the proof of Theorem 11.5.

The important point about Theorem 11.5 lies in the fact that there is now a syntactically testable condition available that, together with CSR, can characterize all of PRED. In particular, this condition places two rules on termination actions, which, as will be shown below, can easily be incorporated into scheduling protocols. Thus, the characterization of PRED provided by Theorem 11.5 is indeed a constructive one.

Figure 11.3 gives a more complete picture of the landscape of correctness criteria that refer to expanded schedules. Clearly, the "uniformity" exhibited by prefix reducibility is desirable, as a scheduler no longer needs to observe two distinct properties during operation; instead, it can now be sure that its output is correct as long as a single property is guaranteed. Note that Figure 11.3 also

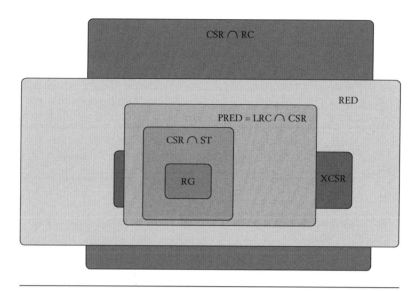

Figure 11.3 Relationship between reducible schedules and strict ones.

mentions the relationship between rigorousness and membership in XCSR (see also Exercise 11.6).

11.5 Page Model Protocols for Schedules with Transaction Aborts

In this section we present extensions of traditional concurrency control protocols we have examined in Chapter 4, suited to recognize schedules in the classes we have introduced in this chapter. We mainly concentrate on three of them, ST, RG, and PRED, as these have turned out to be most desirable.

11.5.1 Extending Two-Phase Locking for Strictness and Rigorousness

Recall the 2PL protocol from Chapter 4—a simple, yet effective protocol for generating histories in CSR. In Section 4.3.4., we briefly mentioned several variants of the basic 2PL protocol, among them *strict* 2PL (S2PL), which holds write locks of a transaction until that transaction terminates, and *strong* 2PL (SS2PL), which holds *all* locks of a transaction until that transaction terminates. Moreover, we have already shown that

- $Gen(SS2PL) \subset Gen(S2PL) \subset Gen(2PL)$, and
- $Gen(SS2PL) \subset COCSR$.

Earlier in this chapter we additionally found out that

- $RG \subset COCSR$.

We next complete this picture with the following result:

THEOREM 11.6

Strong two-phase locking (SS2PL) generates exactly the class of rigorous schedules, i.e., Gen(SS2PL) = RG.

SS2PL produces exactly RG

The proof is left as an exercise (see Exercise 11.7).

If we relax SS2PL to S2PL, we arrive at the following result (which can serve as a justification for the name "strict 2PL"):

THEOREM 11.7

Strict two-phase locking (S2PL) generates only schedules that are both CSR and strict, i.e., Gen(S2PL) $\subseteq$ CSR $\cap$ ST.

Proof

Consider a schedule s produced by an S2PL scheduler. Then for $w_i(x) <_s o_j(x)$, $i \neq j$, $o \in \{r, w\}$ we first find

1. $wl_i(x) < w_i(x) < wu_i(x)$, and
2. $ol_i(x) < o_j(x) < ou_i(x)$

due to the fact that an S2PL scheduler is in particular a 2PL scheduler. Since $wl_i(x)$ and $ol_i(x)$ conflict, it follows that either (a) $wu_i(x) < ol_j(x)$, or (b) $ou_j(x) < wl_i(x)$. However, (b) together with (1) or (2) leads to a contradiction ($o_j(x) < w_i(x)$). Hence (a) applies. Now if the scheduler keeps write locks until transaction termination, it follows that either $a_i < wu_i(x)$ or $c_i < wu_i(x)$, which means that either $a_i < o_j(x)$ or $c_i < o_j(x)$. The claim of the theorem follows.

11.5.2 Extending Serialization Graph Testing for Log Recoverability

We next look at concurrency control protocols, or extensions thereof, capable of generating schedules in class PRED. The general basis of these extensions is the characterization seen in Theorem 11.5, which states that PRED equals the intersection of CSR and LRC, the class of all log-recoverable schedules.

We study an extension of the SGT protocol first and then briefly look at other protocols for which the extensions are similar.

Basic idea: deferred commits and cascading aborts

The basic idea is to add sufficient bookkeeping to recognize essential orderings of commit and abort events that need to be enforced. The enforcement itself is based on *deferring commits* and enforcing *cascading aborts* whenever necessary. In essence, a write/read or write/write conflict from transaction t_i to t_j creates a commit ordering dependency, so that t_j must commit only after t_i. If t_j requests its commit before t_i is committed, t_j's commit request must wait. Conversely, if t_i aborts (in which case t_j must not yet be committed), it requires aborting t_j as well, and that abort must be performed first.

Annotated conflict graph

To develop the details of this approach, consider a schedule s. We use a refinement of the ordinary conflict graph $G(s)$ that (1) considers conflicts between any two transactions, not only committed ones, and in which (2) the edges are annotated with the respective type of conflict (*rw*, *wr*, or *ww*). Let us call this refinement the *fully annotated* conflict graph. What we are aiming at is a protocol that, according to the definition of LRC, produces schedules in RC (i.e., watches *wr* conflicts) and in addition takes appropriate care of *ww* conflicts. So what we actually want to look at is a *partially annotated* conflict graph that is obtained from the fully annotated one by dropping all edges that do *not* correspond to *wr* or *ww* edges (and also dropping all nodes that do not have any incoming or outgoing edges).

LRC revisited

We can now restate the LRC property as follows: A schedule s is in class LRC if for every edge of the form (t_i, t_j) in the partially annotated conflict graph the following holds: if t_i commits, then it commits before t_j does so, and if t_i aborts, then either t_i and t_j abort jointly in a group abort or t_i aborts after t_j aborts. As a schedule in PRED must be in LRC and CSR, we additionally need that, for a given schedule s, the ordinary conflict graph of the committed projection of s is acyclic.

We next define two sets of transactions related to an arbitrary transaction taken from a partially annotated conflict graph $G(s) = (V, E)$:

1. For $t_j \in V$, let $\text{precede}(t_j) := \{t_i \in V \mid (t_i, t_j) \in E\}$; in other words, $\text{precede}(t_j)$ contains the immediate predecessors of transaction t_j.

2. For $t_j \in V$, let $\text{follow}(t_j) := \{t_k \in V \mid t_k$ can be reached from $t_j\}$; thus, $\text{follow}(t_j)$ contains the transactions that are direct or transitive successors of t_j.

With these preparations, we are ready to outline a (pessimistic) serialization graph tester as follows:

1. When an operation o_i that is neither an Abort nor a Commit operation arrives, the scheduler creates a node for t_i in the serialization graph, if

it is not already there; in addition, the scheduler adds all relevant ww, wr, and rw edges. If a cycle occurs, transaction t_i is aborted; that is, a_i is executed.

2. When a commit c_i arrives, the scheduler checks whether precede$(t_i) = \emptyset$. If this is the case, c_i is executed; afterward all Commit operations of all successors of t_i that are waiting to commit are scheduled for execution. Then t_i is removed from all immediate predecessor lists as well as from all successor lists. If t_i is a source in the serialization graph, it can also be removed from the graph. If precede$(t_i) \neq \emptyset$, t_i is placed in a queue of transactions waiting to commit.

3. When an abort a_i arrives, the scheduler checks whether follow$(t_i) = \emptyset$; if so, a_i can be executed. Otherwise, a_j is submitted for execution for every transaction $t_j \in$ follow(t_i); thereafter, all aborted transactions are removed from a queue of transactions waiting to commit, from the serialization graph, and from all immediate predecessor and successor lists.

Let us call the above protocol *extended SGT* or ESGT for short. Note that   *Extended SGT*
it is possible that an Abort operation is issued when the transaction in question has already been aborted as a result of cascading aborts. It is also assumed in this protocol that the scheduler has some mechanism for ensuring that no two conflicting operations are processed at the same time.

The correctness of ESGT is established by the following theorem:

THEOREM 11.8

Gen(ESGT) $\subseteq$ PRED

Proof

We use the characterization of membership in class PRED given in Theorem 11.5: by rule 1 of the ESGT protocol presented above, each schedule generated by ESGT is conflict serializable. With respect to the LRC properties, we observe the following: in case of a direct conflict of the form

$$w_i(x)r_j(x)$$

$c_i < c_j$ is ensured by rule 2. This is because t_j cannot commit until precede(t_j) is empty. By definition, $t_i \in$ precede(t_j), so t_i must have been committed or aborted (in the latter case, t_j will also be aborted). Thus, ESGT produces schedules in RC.

In case of a direct conflict of the form

$$w_i(x)w_j(x)$$

we have that

(a) either $c_i < c_j$ (by rule 2, similar to the previous case),

(b) or $c_i < a_j$ (once t_i commits, it does not impose any further restrictions on t_j),

(c) or $a_j < c_i$ (as rule 3 does not depend on the precede set),

(d) or $a_j < a_i$ (an abort of t_j does not affect t_i at all, so t_i can still be committed or aborted once t_j aborts).

No other combination is possible, since rule 2 does not allow t_j to commit until t_i terminates, and rule 3 forces the abort of t_j before t_i can be aborted.

EXAMPLE 11.15

Suppose that $w_1(x)w_2(x)w_2(y)$ has already been executed, and that $w_1(y)$ arrives at the scheduler. Clearly, the scheduler finds a cycle in the conflict graph, so $w_1(y)$ is rejected, and by rule 1 a_1 is executed instead. Moreover, the scheduler finds follow$(t_1) = \{t_1, t_2\}$, so by rule 3 a_2 is executed as well.

EXAMPLE 11.16

Suppose that $w_1(x)r_2(x)$ has been executed, and that c_2 is submitted. The scheduler now finds precede$(t_2) = \{t_1\}$. Therefore, t_2 is put on the queue of transactions waiting to be committed (rule 2). After that, c_1 is submitted for execution. Since precede$(t_1) = \emptyset$, c_1 is executed right away. Thereafter, t_2 is removed from the waiting queue, and c_2 is submitted for execution.

The above protocol is "pessimistic" in that a cycle test on the conflict graph is executed frequently, that is, whenever a new edge has been added. An optimistic variant of the protocol would perform such a test less frequently, for example, only upon processing a transaction's commit request; this can be accomplished at the expense that processing a commit gets slightly more complex.

11.5.3 Extending Other Protocols for Log Recoverability

A protocol along the lines of ESGT presented in the previous subsection can be implemented to recognize all LRC (and hence all PRED) schedules. However, every SGT-style protocol incurs significant overhead related to the proper maintenance of the conflict graph. So an alternative would be to extend the two-phase locking (2PL) protocol for PRED, again on the basis of its characterization through LRC.

In order to guarantee that the basic 2PL protocol generates schedules in class LRC, the protocol must be extended with additional rules that constrain the ordering of commits and aborts of all transactions. To this end, we again assume the maintenance of sets $precede(t_i)$ and $follow(t_i)$ for each transaction t_i as for the ESGT protocol. The extension of 2PL is then obtained by combining standard 2PL with rules 2 and 3 of the ESGT protocol.

Extended 2PL (E2PL)

It can be shown that not every LRC schedule can be generated in this way. For example, history $w_1(x)w_2(x)w_3(y)w_1(y)c_3c_1c_2$ is in LRC, but not in Gen(E2PL), since t_1 would have to release the write lock on x before acquiring the write lock on y.

Another protocol that can be considered for extension is the timestamp ordering (TO) protocol. Once again, the idea is to combine the standard TO rule with rules 2 and 3 from the ESGT protocol presented above, and again the result is such that some schedules from LRC are missed. For example, $w_2(x)w_1(x)c_2c_1$ is in LRC, but not in Gen(ETO), if we assume that t_1 has a smaller timestamp than t_2.

Extended TO (ETO)

11.6 Correctness Criteria for the Object Model

In this section we extend our considerations regarding transaction recovery by looking at correctness criteria for the object model of transactions. We no longer do this in the general way that we have examined correctness for the page model, but restrict our attention to practically relevant cases.

Essentially and as before, there are two types of object schedules to look at: flat ones and general ones. We will look at flat ones first and indicate that the theory developed earlier in this chapter mostly carries over to this model. In particular, the notions of expanded serializability and prefix reducibility can readily be adapted to this model. Thus, we can again establish rules (such as an "undo rule") for testing whether operations and their inverses can safely be eliminated from a given history or schedule, and we can design scheduling protocols based on appropriate characterizations. For general object schedules, it may be possible to apply such rules in a level-by-level fashion, but we can also refer back to the syntactic conditions we have established earlier for page-level schedules.

11.6.1 Aborts in Flat Object Schedules

To generalize expanded serializability as well as prefix reducibility to flat object schedules, all we need to do is to make sure that undo rule UR can be applied to semantically richer operations as well. Undoing an operation such as Withdraw simply amounts to invoking an *inverse operation*; such inverses

Inverse operations (compensating steps)

have also been coined *compensating steps* in the literature. The inverse of an operation depends on the type of the original operation, its input parameters, and often its output parameters as well. Thus, inverses are derived dynamically when the "forward" operation to which an inverse refers executes, as opposed to a static definition of operation pairs. For example, the inverse of a successful withdrawal consists of depositing the same amount of money back into the account, and the inverse of an unsuccessful withdrawal (i.e., a Withdraw operation with return value "no") is empty and can be viewed as a special "null operation" without any effects. It is important to note that inverses refer to the same abstract view that underlies the commutativity considerations of the corresponding forward operations. For example, if an unsuccessful withdrawal leaves an entry in an audit trail, depositing the money back could be viewed as an appropriate inverse, even if it does not remove that entry. It is for this reason that some people prefer the term compensating step, as we do not necessarily need "exact inverses" that undo each and every detail of the forward operations' effects.

Inverse operation

DEFINITION 11.10   *Inverse Operation*

An operation $f'(x'_1, \ldots, x'_{m'}, \uparrow y'_1, \ldots, \uparrow y'_{k'})$ with input parameters x'_1 through $x'_{m'}$ and output parameters y'_1 through $y'_{k'}$ is the *inverse operation* of operation $f(x_1, \ldots, x_m, \uparrow y_1, \ldots, \uparrow y_k)$ if for all possible sequences α and ω of operations on a given interface (e.g., an object type), the return parameters in the concatenated sequence

$$\alpha f(\ldots) f'(\ldots) \omega$$

are identical to those in the sequence $\alpha \omega$.

We will also write $f^{-1}(\ldots)$ rather than $f'(\ldots)$ in this case and will omit the parameters whenever the context is clear.

Once a method for deriving the inverse operation from the input and output parameters of an executed forward operation is defined, all our prior considerations on expanded schedules and prefix reducibility carry over in a straightforward way.

EXAMPLE 11.17

Prefix reducibility

Consider the following schedule of two funds transfer transactions:

$$s = \text{withdraw}_1(a)\text{withdraw}_2(b)\text{deposit}_2(c)\text{deposit}_1(c)c_1 a_2$$

The expanded schedule that makes the undo steps for the abort of transaction t_2 explicit looks as follows:

$$\exp(s) = \text{withdraw}_1(a)\text{withdraw}_2(b)\text{deposit}_2(c)\text{deposit}_1(c)$$
$$c_1\text{reclaim}_2(c)\text{deposit}_2(b)c_2$$

where the Reclaim operation is an unconditional withdrawal without overdraft protection, thus commuting with deposits. This expanded schedule can be reduced to a serial order of t_1 and the empty transaction t_2, or equivalently to t_1 alone. As a consequence, s is reducible in a sense generalized to flat object schedules.

The complete transaction trees for the expansion of Example 11.17, including the underlying page-level actions for the isolated object-level operations, are depicted in Figure 11.4. Note that the high-level inverse operations do not have page-level children in the expansion. In the actual implementation, the inverse operations will, of course, again spawn lower-level page operations, but these are created dynamically during their execution and are not precisely known in advance. For example, the $\text{reclaim}_2(c)$ operation issued on behalf of t_2's abort may actually access a page q different from the page p that its corresponding forward operation accessed. This may occur if the record that represents the account object c has been moved to a different page by a low-level storage reorganization in between the forward and the inverse operation. (See Chapter 1 for a brief outline of such storage management issues.)

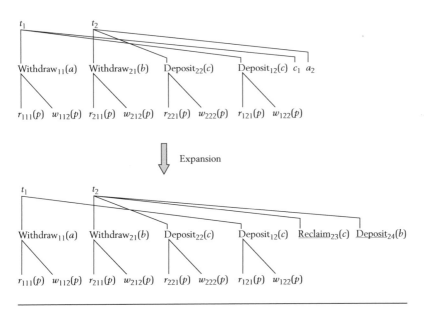

Figure 11.4 Example of an expanded schedule for the flat object model.

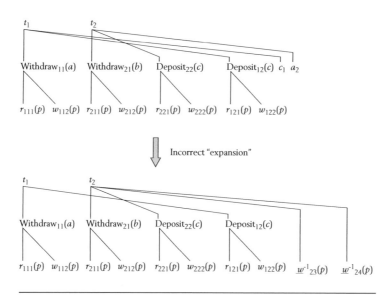

Figure 11.5 Incorrect "expansion" of the example of Figure 11.4.

Page-level undo is incorrect for object model transactions

Figure 11.5 illustrates why, in Example 11.17, the abort of t_2 cannot simply be implemented by issuing inverse page-level writes to undo t_2's effects. The resulting incorrectly "expanded" schedule is not tree reducible, and there is no way of commuting the page-level writes such that the inverse writes of t_2 and its forward write steps become adjacent operations.

As the previous example indicates, object-level operations and their inverses or their compensations need to be considered at the same level of abstraction, and compensation cannot simply be achieved by looking at the "technical" level of page writes.

EXAMPLE 11.18

For another example, consider

$$s = \text{insert}_1(x)\text{delete}_2(x)\text{insert}_3(y)a_1a_2a_3$$

We can expand s as before to obtain the following

$$\exp(s) = \text{insert}_1(x)\text{delete}_2(x)\text{insert}_3(y)\text{insert}_1^{-1}(x)c_1$$
$$\text{delete}_2^{-1}(x)c_2\text{insert}_3^{-1}(y)c_3$$

Since $\text{delete}_2(x)$ and $\text{insert}_1^{-1}(x)$ do not commute, we cannot eliminate t_1 from $\exp(s)$, so s is not reducible. Note that s is also not expanded serializable, as there is a conflict from t_1 to t_2 on x as well as one from t_2 to t_1, also on x.

Table 11.3 Ordinary commutativity relation.

	$r_j(x)$	$w_j(x)$
$r_i(x)$	$+$	$-$
$w_i(x)$	$-$	$-$

Thus, we may find flat object schedules reducible or nonreducible according to the same rules as before, and the same applies to the notion of conflict serializability when that is based on commutativity or noncommutativity of operations. Thus, scheduling protocols can again be designed as generalizations of the protocols we have previously introduced, such as 2PL and its variants; especially the strict 2PL (S2PL) protocol turns out to be relevant in this context.

Locking protocols generally base their notion of conflicting locks on the corresponding notion of conflicting operations. For example, in the page model with its read and write operations, we have seen earlier that the ordinary commutativity relation is that shown in Table 11.3, where $+$ indicates commutativity and $-$ indicates the contrary.

We can extend Table 11.3 for inverse operations in a straightforward way, as in Table 11.4. Here it is assumed that an inverse read is actually an all-commutative "null operation" and can thus be omitted.

The latter commutativity relation has an interesting property: if two operations p and q commute, then all other combinations of these operations or their inverses—that is, p with q^{-1}, p^{-1} with q, and p^{-1} with q^{-1}—commute as well, provided that none of these operations is a null operation (which trivially commutes with every other operation). Moreover, if p and q do not commute, the same holds for all their other combinations. A commutativity relation exhibiting this property is called *perfect*. In the general setting of object-level schedules, we formally have the following definition:

DEFINITION 11.11   *Perfect Commutativity*

Given a set of operations for an object type, such that for each operation $f(x, p_1, \ldots, p_m)$ an appropriate inverse operation $f^{-1}(x, p'_1, \ldots, p'_{m'})$ is included. A commutativity table for these operations is called *perfect* if the following holds:

$$f(x, p_1, \ldots, p_m) \text{ and } g(x, q_1, \ldots, q_n) \text{ commute}$$
$$\Leftrightarrow f(x, p_1, \ldots, p_m) \text{ and } g^{-1}(x, q'_1, \ldots, q'_{n'}) \text{ commute}$$
$$\Leftrightarrow f^{-1}(x, p'_1, \ldots, p'_{m'}) \text{ and } g(x, q_1, \ldots, q_n) \text{ commute}$$
$$\Leftrightarrow f^{-1}(x, p'_1, \ldots, p'_{m'}) \text{ and } g^{-1}(x, q'_1, \ldots, q'_{n'}) \text{ commute}$$

Perfect commutativity

Table 11.4 Commutativity relation including inverse writes.

	$r_j(x)$	$w_j(x)$	$w_j^{-1}(x)$
$r_i(x)$	+	−	−
$w_i(x)$	−	−	−
$w_i^{-1}(x)$	−	−	−

Deadlock freedom during rollback   For object types with perfect commutativity, the S2PL protocol is directly applicable. A particularly nice property of perfect commutativity becomes obvious in the context of deadlock resolution. When we choose a transaction as a deadlock victim and initiate its rollback by means of appropriate inverse operations, these inverse operations could, in principle, request additional locks. Consequently, a transaction that is being rolled back could again become involved in a deadlock. It is not that this situation could not be handled, but to ensure freedom of starvation for deadlock victims, it is most desirable to avoid acquiring additional locks during rollback. With perfect commutativity, such additional locks are unnecessary, since the locks that have been acquired on behalf of the transaction's regular "forward" operations are sufficient for the inverse operations as well. Of course, this consideration does not hold for lower-level locks that are needed within a subtransaction (e.g., short-term page locks for the duration of a high-level inverse operation). Such short-term locks will still have to be acquired during rollback, but usually do not present a problem regarding starvation.

We next show that for semantically rich operations, perfect commutativity may not always be achievable:

EXAMPLE 11.19

Consider the following operations on an object of type Set:

1. insert(x) inserts element x into a given set and returns 1 if x was actually inserted, and 0 otherwise (x was already contained in the set),

2. delete(x) deletes element x from a given set, and returns 1 if x was actually deleted, and 0 otherwise (x was not present in the set),

3. test(x) returns 1 if x is a member of a given set, and 0 otherwise.

Let inverses for these "forward" operations be defined as follows:

1. insert$^{-1}(x)$, where x is either the value that was inserted by the corresponding forward operation or 0 if the value was present already, deletes x from the given set if $x \neq 0$, and does nothing otherwise; it always returns 0.

2. delete$^{-1}(x)$, where x is either the value that was deleted by the corresponding forward operation or 0 if the value was not present, inserts x if $x \neq 0$, and does nothing otherwise; it also returns 0.

3. test$^{-1}(x)$ is a null operation that will not be further considered.

The commutativity relation for these operations is shown in the following table:

	Insert(x)	Delete(x)	Test(x)	Insert$^{-1}(x)$	Delete$^{-1}(x)$
Insert(x)	–	–	–	–	–
Delete(x)	–	–	–	–	–
Test(x)	–	–	+	–	–
Insert$^{-1}(x)$	–	–	–	+	–
Delete$^{-1}(x)$	–	–	–	–	+

Notice that, for example, insert(x) does not commute with itself due to the different return values resulting from an attempt to insert the same element twice. On the other hand, insert$^{-1}(x)$ *does* commute with itself, and similar comments apply to delete. Thus, the commutativity table shown is not perfect.

From a lock-based scheduler's point of view, for non-perfect commutativity an inverse operation may need an additional, stronger lock that has not already been obtained with the lock for its corresponding forward operation. This problem can be rectified by forcing the lock manager to preclaim the necessary stronger lock already with the forward operation, effectively using a somewhat coarser version of the lock compatibility table derived as follows:

DEFINITION 11.12 *Perfect Closure*

The *perfect closure* of a commutativity table for the operations of a given object type is the largest perfect subset of the original commutativity table's commutative operation pairs.

Analogously, the perfect closure of the corresponding lock compatibility table contains the smallest number of – entries such that all – entries of the original lock compatibility table are included and for each operation pair $f(\ldots)$ and $g(\ldots)$, either all four combinations among $f(\ldots)$, $f^{-1}(\ldots)$, $g(\ldots)$, and $g^{-1}(\ldots)$ have + entries or all four have – entries.

Perfect closure of a lock compatibility table

Thus, considering the perfect closure of a commutativity table that is not perfect is a convenient workaround for a scheduler. It does not need additional

Table 11.5 Perfect closure of commutativity relation for set operations.

	Insert(x)	Delete(x)	Test(x)	Insert^{-1}(x)	Delete^{-1}(x)
Insert(x)	–	–	–	–	–
Delete(x)	–	–	–	–	–
Test(x)	–	–	+	–	–
Insert^{-1}(x)	–	–	–	–	–
Delete^{-1}(x)	–	–	–	–	–

locks for inverse operations, as these are already covered by the locks acquired for the corresponding forward operations, and the potential loss in concurrency compared to using the original, non-perfect commutativity table is marginal in practice. Also, as mentioned earlier, this way there is no danger that rolling back a transaction as a deadlock victim can again lead to deadlocks.

For the operations of Example 11.19, we obtain the perfect closure shown in Table 11.5. Although it may appear that by having replaced two + entries with − entries, resorting to the perfect closure could result in significantly more lock conflicts, we should note that this is rarely the case, as only inverse operations are affected and transaction aborts should be infrequent anyway.

Another restriction on commutativity relations that is closely related to the notion of perfectness is the following:

Normal commutativity

DEFINITION 11.13   *Normal Commutativity Table*

A commutativity table for a given object type is *normal* if for all operations $f(\ldots)$ and $g(\ldots)$ the following holds: if $f(\ldots)$ does not commute with $g(\ldots)$, then $f^{-1}(\ldots)$ does not commute with $g(\ldots)$ and $f(\ldots)$ does not commute with $g^{-1}(\ldots)$ (provided that these inverse operations are not null operations, in which case commutativity is self-guaranteed).

Obviously, every perfect commutativity table is also normal, but in general the converse does not hold. The property is of theoretical interest because it can be shown (see the literature cited in the Bibliographic Notes) that classes PRED and LRC ∩ CSR coincide for normal commutativity tables, which generalizes Theorem 11.5 to the flat object model. The same holds for perfect commutativity; yet normal commutativity is a weaker prerequisite for the equality of the two classes PRED and LRC ∩ CSR.

At this point, we have all the ingredients to apply prefix reducibility to flat object schedules, but we know well that this is not a constructive method to build practical schedulers. So, in perfect analogy to our considerations in the page model, we should now look out for syntactic, easily implementable conditions that imply prefix reducibility. In doing this, we are willing to sacrifice generality by assuming that commutativity tables are perfect. From the above mentioned generalization of Theorem 11.5 we know that conflict serializability in combination with log recoverability would be such a syntactic condition, and that this one would even be sufficient and necessary (under the assumptions about commutativity tables). However, notwithstanding our sketch of LRC-based extended concurrency control algorithms for the page model in Section 11.5, practical systems often require simpler methods with very low overhead. For this reason, the most intriguing syntactic criterion toward such practically viable protocols is the notion of strictness. In the flat object model, strictness needs to be redefined as follows:

DEFINITION 11.14 *Strictness*

Strictness

A flat object model schedule s (with a perfect commutativity table) is *strict* if for all L_1 actions $p_i(\ldots)$ and $q_j(\ldots)$ of transactions t_i and t_j, $i \neq j$, such that p_i is an update operation (i.e., not a read-only operation) and $p_i(\ldots)$ and $q_j(\ldots)$ do not commute, the ordering $p_i <_s q_j$ implies that either $c_i <_s q_j$ or $a_i <_s q_j$.

As in the page model, the class of strict schedules is denoted as ST.

This notion of strictness is the intuitive analog of the notion of strictness we have introduced earlier in this chapter for the page model, as there the operation that came first was a write, and strictness meant that no data item is read or overwritten until the last writer has terminated. At a higher level, a writer is more generally an update operation that *yields* a write operation at the page level, so we essentially require the same condition here.

Now recall Theorem 11.4, which for the page model showed that prefix reducibility contains the intersection of CSR and ST. It does not come as a surprise that a corresponding result can be proved for flat object schedules and the generalized notion of strictness just introduced:

THEOREM 11.9

A flat object schedule s (with a perfect commutativity table) that is conflict serializable and strict is also prefix reducible.

This theorem implies that the relationships between the various classes of schedules in the flat object model are essentially those that were shown earlier in Figure 11.3 for the page model. For example, an obvious corollary from the preceding theorem is that rigorousness implies prefix reducibility as in the page model. In a similar way, other results carry over to the model in question here.

11.6.2 Complete and Partial Aborts in General Object Model Schedules

In the general object model, a complication is that not only entire transactions may abort and have their inverse operations interleaved with other transactions, but also subtransactions may abort without rolling back the entire transaction. This option, sometimes called a *partial rollback* (as far as the transaction root is concerned), is available for every nonleaf operation in a transaction tree. From a performance viewpoint, partial rollbacks are an attractive option, as they can be used, for example, to resolve a deadlock between two subtransactions and later automatically restart the deadlock victim without resorting to an abort of the entire transaction. As far as our formal model and correctness reasoning is concerned, the first preparation to cope with this additional complication of complete versus partial aborts is to attach a termination operation, Commit or Abort, to each subtransaction as follows:

DEFINITION 11.15 *Terminated Subtransactions*

An object model history has *terminated subtransactions* if each nonleaf node p_ω has either a child $a_{\omega\nu}$ or a child $c_{\omega\nu}$ that follows all other children of p_ω (assuming that there are $\nu - 1$ such children). So each inner node operation has a termination operation, Abort or Commit, for the corresponding subtransaction.

An object model schedule has terminated subtransactions if it is a prefix of an object model history with terminated subtransactions. (See Chapter 6 for the proper notion of prefix in the context of transaction forests.)

Thus, an object model history with terminated subtransactions has termination operations at all levels (except the highest). In the following we consider only histories and schedules that have terminated subtransactions.

An example of an object model schedule in which both a subtransaction and an entire transaction are aborted is shown in Figure 11.6.

Now the next step will be to define the expansion of a history or schedule in the general object model. Basically, the approach is as before: aborts are replaced by inverse operations and a commit, while active transactions get artificially terminated. However, for various reasons the situation is now far more complex: First of all, Abort operations can occur at any level, and any L_i $(i > 0)$ operation can already have been undone at the next lower level, so that it does not have any effect at all (and hence does not even need a compensation in

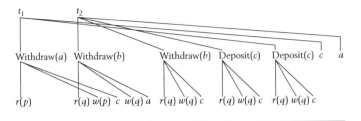

Figure 11.6 Example of an object model schedule with both partial
and complete aborts.

response to an abort). Next, compensating operations at higher levels $L_i, i > 0$
yield subtransactions at their lower levels, where the implementation—that is,
the sequence of operations that actually *does* the compensation—is generally
state dependent and hence can be determined dynamically at run time only.
The following definition reflects these complications.

DEFINITION 11.16 *Expanded Object Model Schedule*

Let s be an object model schedule with terminated subtransactions. The
expansion of s, denoted $\exp(s)$, is an object model history that is derived
from s in the following way:

1. All operations whose parent has a commit child are included in $\exp(s)$.

2. For each operation whose parent p_ω has an abort child $a_{\omega v}$, an inverse
   operation for each of p's $v - 1$ forward operations is added, provided the
   forward operations themselves have a commit child, the abort child of
   p is removed, and a child $c_{\omega(2v-1)}$ is added to p. The inverse operations
   have the reverse order of the corresponding forward operations and
   follow all forward operations; the Commit operation follows all other
   children of p. All new children of p precede an operation q in $\exp(s)$ if
   the abort child of p preceded q in s.

3. For each transaction in active(s), inverse operations and a final commit child are added as children of the corresponding transaction root,
   with their ordering defined analogously to the above case of an aborted
   subtransaction.

---

*Expanded
schedule with
partial aborts*

With this generalized kind of expansion, the resulting schedules look as
if they were normal object model schedules. As a consequence, the natural
correctness criterion to be applied simply needs to adopt both notions of tree
reducibility and (prefix) reducibility simultaneously by allowing *all* the underlying transformation rules, as summarized in the following definition (which
we no longer state explicitly for *prefixes* of object model schedules):

Extended tree reducibility (ETRED)

DEFINITION 11.17 *Extended Tree Reducibility*

An object model schedule s is called *extended tree reducible* if its expansion, $\exp(s)$, can be transformed into a serial order of s's committed transaction roots by applying the following transformation rules finitely many times:

1. the commutativity rule applied to adjacent leaves, i.e., two adjacent leaves that are not in conflict can be commuted;

2. the tree pruning rule for isolated subtrees, i.e., if all L_i operations of a transaction are isolated, then its L_{i-1} operations can be eliminated;

3. the undo rule applied to adjacent leaves, i.e., two adjacent leaf operations p and p^{-1} that are inverses of each other can be replaced by a null operation;

4. the null rule for read-only operations;

5. the ordering rule applied to unordered leaves.

Let ETRED denote the class of all extended tree-reducible object model schedules.

Notice that extended tree reducibility extends tree reducibility as introduced in Chapter 6 (see Definition 6.11) by the undo and null rules.

The expanded schedule that results from the schedule of Figure 11.6 is given in Figure 11.7. The figure has inverse operations underlined to highlight them. As before, reclaim is an unconditional Withdraw operation to compensate the effect of a deposit. For simplicity, we have omitted all commit steps of subtransactions and transactions in the figure, as the expansion has only commits and no aborts anyway. It is rather straightforward to reduce the expanded schedule to a serial order of t_1 and t_2. Removing empty subtransactions and transactions further reduces the schedule to the committed transaction t_1 alone.

Notice that the schedules we have been looking at so far are indeed *layered* object model schedules as we have defined them in Chapter 6. Recall that in a layered schedule all leaves other than commits or aborts have the same distance

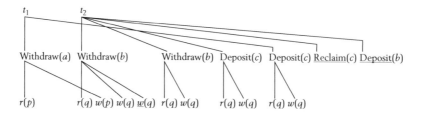

Figure 11.7 Expanded schedule for the example of Figure 11.6.

from their roots, a condition that (a) makes a transaction tree a regular and balanced structure and (b) allows levelwise testing of the tree for correctness. Indeed, we have seen in Chapter 6 that a sufficient condition for a layered object model schedule to be *tree reducible* is that it is conflict faithful and all its level-to-level schedules are conflict serializable. Keeping this in mind, and considering the results we have obtained earlier in this chapter, the following generalization does not come as a surprise:

THEOREM 11.10

A layered object model schedule s (with perfect commutativity tables at all levels) is extended tree reducible, i.e., in class ETRED, if all its level-to-level schedules are conflict serializable and strict and s is conflict faithful.

Moreover, it turns out that conflict faithfulness—that is, the situation that a pair of noncommutative operations at a higher level of a transaction tree must have conflicts among their descendants at all lower levels of the tree—can be replaced by requiring that the level-to-level schedules are *order preserving* conflict serializable.

THEOREM 11.11

A layered object model schedule s (with perfect commutativity tables at all levels) is in ETRED if all its level-to-level schedules are order preserving conflict serializable and strict.

Intuitively, if a level-to-level schedule is both in OCSR and ST, we can apply the undo and commutativity rules to the respective layer as in a flat object schedule, then prune the layer in question and proceed farther up. Repeating this for every layer, we finally obtain extended tree reducibility. From a scheduler's point of view, we thus need to make sure that a corresponding protocol yields OCSR and ST level-to-level schedules only. We look at such a protocol, again derived from the well-studied S2PL, in the next section.

11.7 Object Model Protocols for Schedules with Transaction Aborts

With respect to concurrency control protocols for object model schedules that exhibit complete as well as partial aborts, we again restrict ourselves to *layered* schedules and mostly focus on the practically most important class of

2PL protocols. Recall from Chapter 7 that layered 2PL is a reasonable way to generate tree-reducible schedules, since it can make sure that level-to-level schedules are OCSR; moreover, its strict variant (S2PL) assures that these level-to-level schedules are strict. Together with the conditions we just saw at the end of the previous subsection, we thus have

---

THEOREM 11.12

The layered S2PL protocol generates only schedules in ETRED.

Recall from Theorem 6.2 that if all level-to-level schedules derivable from a given schedule s are OCSR, then s itself is tree reducible; moreover, recall from Chapter 7 that the layered 2PL protocol assures this prerequisite and hence produces tree-reducible schedules only. Next, layered strict 2PL additionally guarantees that every level-to-level schedule is in ST; this implies extended tree reducibility because we can simply apply undo and commutativity rules to one layer, exactly like on a flat object schedule, then prune that layer and proceed farther up the transaction tree.

As a concrete scenario for applying the layered S2PL protocol to a two-level schedule, consider the sample schedule from Figure 11.6 once more, in which both a complete rollback (transaction abort) occurs at level L_1 and a partial one (subtransaction abort) occurs at level L_0. At the page level, the schedule shown could be executed by the protocol as given, since the subtransactions spawned by operations $withdraw_1(a)$ and the first $withdraw_2(b)$ do not require conflicting locks. Likewise, there is no lock conflict at the object level, for the Deposit operations on c commute with each other, and $deposit_1(c)$ also commutes with the inverse operation of $deposit_2(c)$, the unconditional $reclaim_2(c)$. Note that the mode of the lock that t_2 acquires for the Deposit operation must implicitly cover the potentially necessary inverse operation as well (under strict 2PL with perfect commutativity table), but this does not cause a lock conflict with the given operations.

We conclude this section by mentioning that other extensions to layered concurrency control protocols are also feasible in this context, for example, extensions of optimistic protocols that assure properties of level-to-level schedules like ST, RG, or LRC; however, locking remains the most important technique for practical applications.

11.8 Lessons Learned

In this chapter we have introduced and studied the theoretical foundations of transaction recovery. As we have shown, there are essentially two approaches: a "syntactic" one that merely pays attention to a proper sequencing of Commit or Abort operations, and a more "semantic" one that tries to make the actions that have to be performed in response to an Abort operation as explicit as possible. The latter leads to interesting classes of schedules, due to the fact that some fall into the intersection of the classes of conflict-serializable and of recoverable schedules, while CSR and RC are otherwise incomparable with respect to set inclusion. Moreover, the class PRED of prefix-reducible schedules, which is the most important one of the semantic categories, can be characterized in a way that gives rise to fairly straightforward extensions of standard concurrency control protocols. Thus, we have seen in this chapter that it is indeed possible to obtain an appropriate conceptual framework for transaction recovery that can be easily built into known protocols.

Besides the "uniform" criterion that is rendered possible through prefix reducibility, additional beauty lies in the fact that PRED can also be adapted to the object model. Indeed, the framework we have set up here for transactions in the page model carries over to the object model of transactions. To this end, the major issue is to properly define the "undo" operations for the object-level operations considered, and to determine what properties the corresponding commutativity relations have. As a result, this approach to transaction recovery is also suitable for flat object schedules as well as for layered transaction systems. The sufficient conditions known from the page model can be generalized, as can protocols such as S2PL.

The combination of tree reducibility introduced in Chapter 6 with rules that take care of undoing operations into the notion of extended tree reducibility (ETRED) shows that even in the object model, a modular approach to transaction recovery is possible that uses the individual criteria as its building blocks. Moreover, the resulting combinations can be easily implemented, for example, by the strict two-phase protocol, first adapted to object model schedules (as done in Chapter 7) and implicitly geared for transaction recovery conditions.

Exercises

11.1 Let $s_1 = w_1(x)w_1(y)r_2(u)w_2(x)r_2(y)w_2(y)a_2w_1(z)c_1$ and
$s_2 = w_1(x)w_1(y)r_2(u)w_2(x)r_2(y)w_2(y)w_1(z)a_1c_2$
Determine $\exp(s_1)$ and $\exp(s_2)$ as well as the corresponding reductions.

11.2 Which of the properties RC, ST, RG, PRED, and LRC are satisfied by the following schedules:

$$s_1 = r_1(a)r_2(a)w_1(a)c_1c_2$$
$$s_2 = r_1(a)w_1(a)r_2(b)w_2(b)w_2(a)c_2c_1$$
$$s_3 = r_1(a)\text{incr}_2(a)\text{incr}_2(b)\text{incr}_3(b)c_3a_2c_1$$

Some of the above properties cannot be applied to a schedule with operations other than read and write, such as schedule s_3 above. Try to define generalizations of these properties to flat object schedules with arbitrary operations.

11.3 For each of the following schedules, determine to which of the classes RC, ACA, or ST it belongs:

$$s_1 = w_1(x)r_2(y)r_1(x)c_1r_2(x)w_2(y)c_2$$
$$s_2 = w_1(x)r_2(y)r_1(x)r_2(x)c_1w_2(y)c_2$$
$$s_3 = w_1(x)r_2(y)r_2(x)r_1(x)c_2w_1(y)c_1$$

11.4 Show that membership in each of the classes RC, ACA, ST, RG, and PRED is a prefix commit closed property.

11.5 Consider COCSR, the class of all histories that are commit order preserving conflict serializable, and show the following:

(a) COCSR $\cap$ RC $\neq \emptyset$, COCSR $\not\subseteq$ RC, RC $\not\subseteq$ COCSR

(Thus, COCSR $\cap$ RC $\subset$ COCSR and COCSR $\cap$ RC $\subset$ RC.)

(b) COCSR $\cap$ ACA $\subset$ ACA

(c) COCSR $\cap$ ACA $\subset$ COCSR $\cap$ RC

(d) COCSR $\cap$ ST $\subset$ ST

(e) COCSR $\cap$ ST $\subset$ COCSR $\cap$ ACA

11.6 A schedule s is *prefix expanded conflict serializable* if each of its prefixes is expanded conflict serializable. Let PXCSR denote the class of all prefix-expanded conflict-serializable schedules. Show the following:

(a) PXCSR $\subset$ XCSR

(b) PXCSR $\subset$ PRED

(c) RG $\subset$ PXCSR

(d) PXCSR = ST $\cap$ XCSR

(e) Based on results (a)–(d), complete Figure 11.3.

11.7 Prove Theorem 11.6 stating that Gen(SS2PL) = RG.

11.8 Consider a database consisting of positive integers with the following operations defined on them:

- incr(x): increments x if $x > 0$ and returns 1; otherwise does nothing and returns 0.
- incr$^{-1}(x, y)$: decrements x if y is the return value of the corresponding forward operation and $y \neq 0$; otherwise does nothing, always returns 0.
- reset(x): resets x to 1 and returns the old value of x.

- reset$^{-1}(x)$: sets x to value y, where y is the return value of the corresponding forward operation; always returns 0.
- retrieve(x): returns the current value of x.
- retrieve$^{-1}(x)$: is a null operation and returns an empty sequence.
- decr(x): decrements x and returns 0.
- decr$^{-1}(x)$: increments x and returns 0.

Determine the commutativity relation for these operations, and find out whether it is perfect or normal. If one of the latter properties does not hold, try to restrict the relation in such a way that this respective property is achieved.

11.9 Prove Theorem 11.5 for an object model in which the relevant operations have a normal commutativity relation.

11.10 Consider an implementation of transaction recovery that makes use of transaction-private workspaces in that all updates are initially executed on such workspaces and thus deferred until the transaction's commit as far as the shared, persistent data is concerned. Upon the commit of a transaction, the workspace updates would be reexecuted against the shared data; upon a transaction abort, the workspace would be discarded.

Is it possible to apply the notions of ST, PRED, and LRC to such a workspace-based deferred update implementation? Is it meaningful? If appropriate, try to redefine these properties for a deferred update setting.

Bibliographic Notes

Historically, the purely syntactic criteria known as RC, ACA, and ST preceded the more general model based on expanded schedules and an explicit undo rule as part of a transformation-based correctness criterion. The formalization of the syntactic criteria goes back to Hadzilacos (1988), where they are discussed in detail. Our presentation of these criteria is based on Bernstein et al. (1987). Algorithmic and performance implications of these classes have been studied by Graham et al. (1984). The class of rigorous histories was introduced by Breitbart et al. (1991). A solution to Exercise 11.5 can be found in Raz (1992).

The concept of an expanded schedule that has led to a "unifying approach" to serializability and transaction recovery, on the other hand, has been introduced by Schek et al. (1993), building on earlier ideas from Moss et al. (1986) and Weikum (1986a). Schek et al. (1993) also introduced the important notions of reducibility and prefix reducibility. The syntactically oriented and thus more "constructive" criterion of log recoverability has been presented by Alonso, Vingralek, Agrawal et al. (1994); in conjunction with conflict serializability it was originally named "serializability with ordered termination" and shown to be equivalent to prefix reducibility in the page model and flat object model with perfect commutativity. Alonso, Vingralek, Agrawal et al. (1994) have also discussed the extensions that are needed for the various classes of concurrency control algorithms in order to integrate transaction recovery.

Schek et al. (1993) considered a flat object model. This approach was later generalized by Vingralek et al. (1998) to non-perfect commutativity relations and by Hasse-Ye (1996) to the general object model. Solutions to Exercises 11.8 and 11.9 can be found in the former reference. Other work along the lines of the unifying model includes Moss et al. (1986), who discussed a subset of prefix-reducible schedules with the "revocability" property; Weihl (1993), who has studied both a log-based model for transaction recovery and a workspace-based model where updates to persistent data are deferred until the commit point of a transaction; Rastogi et al. (1993), who have introduced the notion of strictness for schedules with semantically rich operations; Korth et al. (1990); Levy (1991) and Levy et al. (1991); as well as Krychniak et al. (1996).

Papadimitriou (1986) as well as Papadimitriou and Yannakakis (1987) have described an approach to transaction recovery that is based on the idea that even after a transaction has been aborted, a "reliable" schedule can be continued in such a way that ultimately a (view) serializable history results. It has been shown, however, that the problem of deciding whether a given schedule is "reliable" is PSPACE complete and hence of little practical relevance. The idea of leaving the semantics of an operation unchanged in every continuation of a given schedule has also been pursued by Lechtenbörger and Vossen (2000), who have shown that with minor adaptations of the traditional Herbrand semantics, classes of correct histories that strictly *contain* PRED can be established.

Soisalon-Soininen and Ylönen (1995) have studied a way to relax the RC and ACA requirements for histories through a slight variation of the transaction model. The idea is to allow reading and writing from a transaction that has not yet committed, but that has performed all its operations *and* has issued a "request" to commit. Under normal circumstances, such a transaction will thereafter commit, and the "partial strictness" obtained in this way is then roughly sufficient for membership in RC or ACA. They add a new operation c^r, called *commit request*, to the set of possible operations of a transaction. In a transaction t_i, c_i^r may only occur as the second but last operation; i.e., the only operations that can still follow from t_i are a commit c_i or an abort a_i. Conversely, if a transaction commits—i.e., ends with operation c_i—this c_i must be preceded by c_i^r. Next, a history s is *partially strict* if the following conditions hold for all transactions $t_i, t_j \in \text{trans}(s)$, $i \neq j$:

1. if $w_j(x) <_s r_i(x)$, then $c_j^r <_s r_i(x)$,

2. if $w_j(x) <_s w_i(x)$, then $a_j <_s w_i(x)$ or $c_j^r <_s w_i(x)$,

3. if $c_j^r <_s c_i^r$ and $c_j \in s$, then $c_j <_s c_i$.

It can then be shown that if s is partially strict and for no transaction $t_i \in$ trans(s) we have $c_i^r <_s a_i$, then $s \in$ RC.

CHAPTER TWELVE

Crash Recovery: Notion of Correctness

Hansel and Gretel left behind a trail of crumbs which would allow them to retrace their steps (by following the trail backwards) and would allow their parents to find them by following the trail forwards. This was the first undo and redo log. Unfortunately, a bird ate the crumbs and caused the first log failure.

—Jim Gray

We will meet again if your memory serves you well.

—Bob Dylan

12.1 Goal and Overview

This chapter and the next three discuss a notion of correctness and algorithms for the crash recovery of a data(base) server. We denote as a *crash* all kinds of failures that bring down the server and cause all data in volatile memory to be lost, but leave all data on stable secondary storage intact. Then, in a nutshell, the goal of a crash recovery algorithm is to restart the server and bring its permanent data back to its most recent, consistent state. More precisely, this amounts to ensuring the atomicity and durability of transactions. Thus, the most recent, consistent state is defined as including all updates of committed (and hence durable) and no update of uncommitted or previously aborted (and hence to be "eliminated") transactions, in the serialization order of the original pre-crash execution. Being able to maintain or reconstruct a consistent state in the presence of failures is often referred to as *failure resilience, fault tolerance,* or, in most general terms, *reliability* of the data server. (In some fraction of the literature, subtle differences are made between these terms, but these are negligible for our purposes.)

Crash recovery goal: failure resilience, fault tolerance, reliability

The main challenge of crash recovery beyond the scope of the transaction recovery of Chapter 11, lies in efficiently implementing transactional durability. Since a crash may lose updates that have not yet been reflected in stable secondary storage, crash recovery will have to consider the *redo recovery* of affected data updates that were made by committed transactions. For uncommitted transactions, on the other hand, the atomicity property of the

Redo and undo recovery

ACID paradigm dictates the *undo recovery* of updates. Algorithms for the latter are conceptually identical to those that we presented for transaction recovery in Chapter 11. However, a crash recovery algorithm has to take into account the potentially delicate interplay between redo and undo steps as well. As we will show in this chapter and the next, an important idea to keep crash recovery relatively simple and manageable is to minimize this interplay by separating redo versus undo considerations as much as possible.

Failure model: soft, fail-stop crash

The failure model that we assume in this chapter is sometimes referred to as the *soft crash* case, since it leaves all data on secondary storage intact, unlike a *hard crash* that corrupts secondary storage media. We will consider hard crashes later in Chapter 16. The soft crash model is fairly general and comprises most of the failures that cause outages of data servers in real applications, most notably, software errors in the operating system or database system code, and also errors made by system administrators. Traditionally, power outage is often mentioned as the most typical cause of a soft crash, but with battery-backed uninterruptible power supplies, this failure type has become more of an anecdote than a practically pressing concern. The real culprits are errors in the system software. Empirical studies have shown that those errors that lead to system crashes typically have some mean properties: they occur in a "nondeterministic" manner, often related to concurrent execution threads, under high load or otherwise uncommon situations, and they are difficult if not impossible to track down and reproduce. For these reasons, such errors cannot be easily eliminated by more extensive software testing. Jim Gray has coined the term "Heisenbugs" for this class of errors, after Heisenberg's uncertainty relation.

All practical experience with large applications has shown that the best way of dealing with Heisenbugs is to bring down the server as quickly as possible, recover the server's permanent data to a consistent state based on redo and undo according to the ACID paradigm, and restart the server. Because this recovery procedure reinitializes the server, it turns out that Heisenbugs are extremely unlikely to occur again after the restart. In contrast, approaches that aim at continuing the server's "forward processing" based on a fault-tolerant hardware and OS platform have turned out to be less effective in coping with Heisenbugs. The most successful of these approaches (e.g., tandem computer systems) have eventually limited their nonstop processing capabilities to the underlying hardware resources (e.g., by "failing over" to another processor in a cluster) and adopted transactional crash recovery algorithms at a higher software layer. An important ingredient in this currently prevalent solution is that failures should have the *fail-stop* property, in the sense that the server is indeed brought down immediately after detecting an error. Strictly speaking, this is only an idealized behavior, as error detection will not be perfect, but it can be sufficiently well approximated in real systems by intensive self-checking.

While performing crash recovery after a system failure, a server and its data are unavailable to clients. Therefore, minimizing the recovery or restart time is our most important performance goal. Assume that, on average, a server *Recovery* fails once every MTTF time units, where MTTF stands for *mean time to failure.* *performance* Upon a failure, the recovery takes on average MTTR time units, where MTTR *and system* stands for *mean time to repair.* Then, the *availability* of the system, which is the *availability* probability that a randomly probing client finds the server ready to serve data requests, is given by

$$\frac{MTTF}{MTTF + MTTR} \tag{12.1}$$

For example, a server that fails once a month and takes 2 hours to recover has an availability of approximately 99.7%, which translates into an expected downtime of 26 hours per year. This would be insufficient for many mission-critical applications. If, on the other hand, the server fails once every 48 hours but can be recovered and restarted in 30 seconds on average, then the availability would be increased to 99.98% or, equivalently, to an expected downtime of 105 minutes per year. This consideration shows that fast recovery is the key to high availability (given that, in practice, Heisenbugs pose limits to the improvement of the MTTF).

A second performance metric that is of great importance for a crash recovery algorithm is the additional resource consumption that is required during normal operation of the system to make crash recovery work when the system fails. For example, logging data updates on a log file requires additional disk I/O. If this extra work becomes too high, then it could adversely affect the performance of regular data requests during normal operation.

A requirement that may appear trivial at first glance is that crash recovery *Correctness of* should work correctly under all possible circumstances. However, it cannot *recovery* be overemphasized that recovery algorithms need to cope with a tremendous *algorithms* state space and that it is all but trivial to make sure that the state space is exhaustively covered by the algorithm. Crashes are rare events, relative to the normal processing speed of a server, but even crashes during the recovery from a crash are possible and do actually occur, and not that infrequently, in real applications. As the often cited Murphy's Law puts it: "whatever can go wrong, will go wrong." And developers who have implemented a full-fledged crash recovery algorithm may add that Murphy was an optimist!

The large state space that crash recovery has to deal with also makes the *Simplicity and* testing and debugging of a recovery algorithm very hard, much harder than *testability* testing, for example, a cache manager. At the same time, the recovery code is much more critical than all other components of a data server. Errors in the query processor, for example, cause only transient damage and are likely to be limited to specific queries. An erroneous recovery algorithm, on the other hand, amounts to risking permanent, irreversible damage to mission-critical data. It is for these reasons that we heavily emphasize correctness reasoning.

An important step toward correct crash recovery is to keep the algorithms as simple as possible (but no simpler, to paraphrase Einstein). Simplicity eases correctness reasoning, and it also supports software testing. The latter aspect particularly suggests reusing code for the recovery algorithm that has been written and is executed for the system's normal operation, as this code can be and typically has been much more stress tested. We will point out examples of this pragmatic consideration later.

Correctness reasoning   Simplicity is highly desirable, but it should not come at the expense of overly degrading the recovery algorithm's performance, especially the restart time. Unfortunately, there is a trade-off in this regard: simplicity versus performance. Therefore, we will discuss various recovery algorithms in the subsequent chapters, in increasing order of complexity. Some of them are actually too simple to be practically viable, but they serve as starting points and will subsequently be extended and refined. In this way, we greatly simplify the correctness reasoning. We will first show certain invariants to hold for the simpler algorithms, and will then verify that subsequent extensions and optimizations leave the invariants valid.

The chapter is organized as follows: Section 12.2 discusses the architectural issues that are relevant for crash recovery, and Section 12.3 introduces an abstract model as the basis for correctness reasoning. Section 12.4 then develops the criterion that correctly working crash recovery must satisfy. Finally, Section 12.5 gives a brief survey and taxonomy of recovery algorithms that have been proposed in the literature. Detailed algorithms for crash recovery along with correctness arguments will then be presented in the next chapters.

12.2 System Architecture and Interfaces

The components of the system architecture that are relevant for crash recovery and are thus considered throughout this and the subsequent chapter are the following:

Stable database   1. The *stable database* is organized as a set of pages that reside in stable storage. Here *stable storage* is an abstraction comprising all storage media that are resilient to the soft crash failures that we aim to recover from. Most typically, this abstraction is implemented by secondary storage on magnetic disks, but it could also be nonvolatile RAM along with additional protection steps to guard its contents from software errors such as runaway pointers.

Database cache   2. The *database cache* consists of a (dynamically evolving) subset of the stable database pages that is copied into volatile memory. All database modifications are performed on the cache and are later copied back into the stable database by an explicit "flush" action. Therefore, the cached version of a page may be more recent than the page's stable version in that its contents captures more updates. At each point in time, the database cache and the noncached fraction of the stable database together constitute the *cached database* (or *current database*) on which all regular data requests operate.

3. The *stable log* consists of a set of *log entries* that describe the history of updates on the cached database, and possibly additional bookkeeping records on the system history. In its most general form, the log entry for an update contains sufficient information that allows the recovery either to undo or redo the update depending on the outcome of the corresponding transaction. However, more specialized formats of log entries are conceivable as well. The stable log resides on stable storage, typically implemented as one or more disk-resident files.

Stable log

4. The *log buffer* is a data structure in volatile memory that serves as a buffer in writing log entries to the stable log. Log entries are first created in the log buffer, and are explicitly copied to the stable log by means of a "force" action.

Log buffer

As far as crash recovery is concerned, the contents of these four components entirely determine the system state. Since database cache and log buffer reside in volatile memory, which is lost in a crash, the recovery algorithm itself relies on the stable database and the stable log as its input. The stable log is most often implemented as a sequential append-only file. However, our architectural model is general enough to allow alternative implementations such as organizing versions of database pages in a random access file (sometimes referred to as a *shadow database*).

Stable log and log buffer taken together also provide the undo information for rolling back aborted transactions during normal operation. Thus, log entries serve both transaction recovery and crash recovery. A transaction recovery algorithm may, however, choose to keep an additional copy of log entries in a separate data structure in memory for faster access. This holds especially for entries in the stable log, where a transaction abort would require random disk access and could interfere with the otherwise sequential write patterns of the stable log.

Transaction recovery reconsidered

During normal operation, the system performs various types of actions that modify the system state in a way that affects the recovery algorithms. The following list contains these actions, grouped into different categories. Each action performed by the system is assigned a unique *sequence number*, so that actions can be referred to by the various system components and also by other actions. The sequence numbers are guaranteed to be monotonically increasing among all actions that refer to the same page and among all actions that refer to the same transaction.

Actions during normal operation

Sequence numbers

1. Transaction actions:

   (a) begin(*t*): marks the beginning of a transaction identified by *t*.

   (b) commit(*t*): marks the successful completion of the transaction identified by *t*. Its effect is that all updates of the transaction become committed and will be guaranteed to persist even in the presence of a soft crash.

   (c) rollback(*t*): marks the unsuccessful completion of the transaction identified by *t*. Its requested effect is that all updates of the transaction be undone, so that none of the updates remain in the cached database.

   (d) save(*t*): marks a *savepoint* inside a transaction. The transaction can request to roll back to a savepoint, preserving all updates that were made before the savepoint, rather than having to roll back the entire transaction.

   (e) restore(*t*, *s*): rolls back the transaction identified by *t* to the savepoint identified by the sequence number *s*.

   Thus, we now need more detailed operations for the development of recovery algorithms than we needed for devising the page model of transactions from a conceptual point of view; the same holds for the action categories described below.

   We will ignore the action types *save* and *restore* in Chapters 13 and 14; they will be reconsidered and incorporated into the algorithms developed in Section 15.3 of Chapter 15.

2. Data actions:

   (a) read(*pageno*, *t*): reads the page identified by *pageno* on behalf of the transaction identified by *t*. In particular, this involves pinning the page to a fixed virtual-memory address in the database cache, so that it can neither be dropped from the cache nor moved in memory; reading the page contents; and finally, unpinning the page.

   (b) write(*pageno*, *t*): reads and writes the page identified by *pageno* on behalf of the transaction identified by *t*. As with reads, this involves pinning and later unpinning the page in the database cache, with the difference that the page is explicitly declared as modified or "dirty" when it is unpinned. Since this notion of a write action includes a previous read, it also captures page modifications that refer to byte-level operations inside a page, such as moving a byte sequence (e.g., a data record) within a page. This type of write action has been referred to as a "physiological action" by Gray and Reuter (1993).

   (c) full-write(*pageno*, *t*): writes the page identified by *pageno* on behalf of the transaction identified by *t*. In contrast to the previous, general write action type, a full-write does not read the page before modifying it. Rather, full-writes assign a (new) value to all bytes of a page. This type of action has often been referred to as a "physical action."

(d) exec(*op, obj, t*): executes the database operation *op* on the database object identified by *obj* on behalf of the transaction identified by *t*. This execution in turn triggers other actions, in particular, read and write actions on database pages, but it may also invoke the execution of other database operations. These database operations can be "native" operations of the system interface, such as storing a data record or retrieving a set of data records based on a search key, or they can be a user-defined operation on an instance of an imported abstract data type.

3. Caching actions:
   (a) fetch(*pageno*): copies the previously noncached page identified by *pageno* from the stable database into the database cache.
   (b) flush(*pageno*): copies the cached page identified by *pageno* to the stable database, but also leaves the page in the cache. A flush action is only invoked on a dirty page whose cached version is more recent than its stable version. The purpose of this action thus is to bring the stable version up-to-date and to reset the cached page's status from "dirty" to "clean" (i.e., identical to the stable version).

4. Log actions:
   (a) force( ): forces all log entries in the log buffer to be copied to the stable log.

The four major system components and the actions that operate on them are illustrated in Figure 12.1.

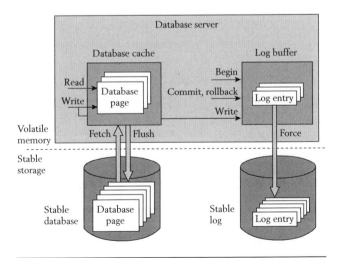

Figure 12.1 Overview of the system architecture components relevant to crash recovery.

When the system is started, the recovery algorithm is the first step invoked. So the system always assumes that it is started immediately following a crash, and we will refer to the entire recovery procedure as the restart(.) action. Only if the restart finds evidence on stable storage that the last event in the system history was a normal shutdown, as opposed to a failure terminating the system, can it skip all further recovery steps. As will be seen in the next chapter, the details on how the necessity of recovery work is recognized depend on the recovery algorithm itself.

12.3 System Model

This section casts the system architecture we have introduced in the previous section into more rigorous definitions, which will then be used as the basis for the correctness reasoning throughout Chapter 13. Since our goal is to show that the recovered database preserves the effects of exactly all committed updates in the serialization order of the executed transactions, the system history is an important reference point for the correctness of the recovery. Compared to earlier chapters, we need some extensions in defining the system history. In particular, caching actions are of interest for the recovery and therefore are included in the history.

Extended history

DEFINITION 12.1 *Extended History*

The *extended system history* of a transactional data server is a partially ordered forest of actions, with the set of actions denoted by A, where

- the roots are transaction identifiers or caching actions (fetch or flush);
- the leaves are read, write, or full-write actions or transaction actions (begin, commit, rollback, . . .);
- only *exec* actions can appear as intermediate nodes;
- the ordering of actions, denoted by $<$, is tree consistent (i.e., for a nonleaf node i and an arbitrary node j, the relationship $i < j$ $(j < i)$ holds if $p < j$ $(j < p)$ holds for all leaves p that are descendants of i).

A specialization that we will consider first is the one for the page model, which is characterized by the absence of *exec* nodes. Then, an extended history specializes to a forest where all trees have depth 2. In the rest of the chapter we always consider extended histories rather than "plain" histories. Therefore, there is no need to distinguish the two notions explicitly, and we will henceforth refer to extended histories simply as histories.

Since the stable log keeps bookkeeping records about the system history, it can be defined by its relationship to the extended history as follows:

DEFINITION 12.2   *Stable Log*   *Stable log*

For a given system history, the *stable log* is a totally ordered subset of the history's action set such that the log ordering is compatible with the history order (i.e., does not contradict $<$). These logged actions are referred to as *log entries*.   *Log entries*

As mentioned earlier, a log entry may contain information for both the undoing and the redoing of an update action, as an outcome of the corresponding transaction is usually still unknown at the time the log entry is created. In the abstract model, however, we do not explicitly distinguish the undo and redo parts of a log entry. Rather we treat the logged action itself as the redo information and assume that we can always infer from the log entry an inverse action, in the sense of Chapter 11, which serves as the original action's undo information. We have to keep in mind, however, that the implementation of log entries needs to incorporate additional details; for example, input parameters of an inverse action may depend on result parameters of the original action and have to be remembered explicitly in the log entry.

Thus, the log is essentially a linearization of the system history. We assume that all logged actions carry sufficient information to identify their ancestors in the history. In particular, all log entries carry a transaction identifier. Most recovery algorithms restrict the log entries to certain action types, as we will see in detail later. In particular, almost all algorithms avoid logging reads.

Now the log buffer can be defined simply as the "tail" of the history (or, actually, the logged part of the history) that captures the most recent actions that are not yet recorded on the stable log.

DEFINITION 12.3   *Log Buffer*   *Log buffer*

For a given system history, the *log buffer* is a totally ordered subset of the history's action set such that the log ordering is compatible with the history order and all entries in the log buffer follow (with respect to the total order) all entries in the stable log for that history.

Finally, as for the stable database and for the cached database, an impor-   *Database state*
tant consideration is that we do not need to formalize all aspects of the data organization itself. Rather, our focus is on tracking which updates are present or absent in the database, how these updates relate to the logged actions, and how the recovery advances the database state. To this end, it is appropriate to

view the state of a database also as a set of update actions, namely, those actions that have led to the state.

Page sequence numbers as state identifiers

Obviously, the resulting state depends on the order in which the actions were performed on the database; so we need to include some knowledge about action ordering in our formal definition. To remain consistent with practical considerations, we have to consider that the exact order in which updates were performed cannot be inferred from a given database alone. However, by including additional information in the database itself, we can obtain some partial knowledge of the order. To this end, we assume that each database page is tagged with a sequence number, by which we can keep track of the most recent action of certain types that were executed on that page. This *page sequence number*, or *page state identifier*, is assumed to be embedded in the page itself. Therefore, it is always carried along when a page is fetched into the database cache or flushed back from the cache to the stable database. The existence of such a page sequence number is a special assumption that we are making, but note that it is perfectly in line with all implemented systems that we are aware of. Indeed, page sequence numbers can be easily implemented with very little overhead as a field in the page header. Contrast this with conceivable assumptions on tagging all data records with a sequence number or transaction identifier, whose implementation would not be at all clear and would be likely to incur high overhead.

The key point of a page sequence number is that it can give us some partial knowledge about the order of the write actions (including full-write actions) that have been performed on it. Namely, for a page with sequence number s, we know that all write actions on that page with a sequence number less than s must precede the write action with sequence number s in the history order $<$. We still do not have any knowledge about the ordering among those earlier actions, but we will see that this knowledge is not necessary for a recovery algorithm anyway.

These considerations lead to the following definitions of cached and stable databases, respectively. The only difference between the two is that the page sequence numbers of the cached database correspond to the most recent write actions in the history; whereas in the stable database the sequence number of a page corresponds to the most recent write action before the most recent flush action for that page.

Cached database

DEFINITION 12.4 *Cached Database*

For a given system history, the *cached database* is a partially ordered set of all write actions in the history, including full-write actions, such that the ordering is a subset of the history order, and for each page number p, the maximum element among the write actions on p in the history is also the maximum element among all write actions on p in the cached database.

DEFINITION 12.5   *Stable Database*

For a given system history, the *stable database* is a partially ordered subset of the history's write actions, including full-write actions, such that the ordering is a subset of the history order, and for each page number p,

- all write actions on p that precede the most recent flush(p) action in the history are included in the stable database,
- the maximum element among all those included write actions in the history is also the maximum element among all write actions on p in the stable database.

By casting all system components into partially ordered sets of actions, these definitions allow us to relate and directly compare the stable database to the stable log and the stable log in turn to the system history. These cross-relationships lead us to the correctness criterion developed in the following section.

12.4 **Correctness Criterion**

Now that we have defined the building blocks of a formal model, we can precisely state the correctness criterion that every algorithm for crash recovery has to satisfy. In doing so, we assume that the database history is order preserving serializable and log recoverable; in other words, it must be reducible to the roots of the committed transactions (see Chapter 11). From our earlier discussion of concurrency control and transaction recovery, it is clear that this assumption is not a severe restriction. Correct crash recovery then simply means that the equivalence to the roots of the committed transactions is preserved despite possible system failures.

DEFINITION 12.6   *Correct Crash Recovery*

A crash recovery algorithm is *correct* if it guarantees that after a system failure, the cached database will eventually—that is, possibly after repeated failures and restarts—be equivalent to a serial order of the committed transactions that coincides with the serialization order of the history.

Note that this definition intentionally refers "merely" to the cached database rather than the stable database. It is our goal to complete the recovery as quickly as possible to maximize the system availability. Once the cached database is brought into the desired state, we wish to allow new transactions to access the data as soon as possible and therefore consider the recovery as already complete at this point. The stable database, on the other hand, can be brought to its desired state subsequently, by simply performing a sufficient number of flush actions to write back all dirty pages of the cache. If no new transactions were executed and no further crashes occurred, the stable database would be guaranteed to reach the same state as the cached database. But note that this is an implication of the cache manager rather than a result of the recovery algorithm, and therefore we do not consider the final state of the stable database as a goal in our correctness criterion.

A potential fallacy in our above definition is that we do not guarantee termination of the algorithm; we use the adverb "eventually" with good reason. Indeed, we can conceive of an infinite series of crashes where the recovery algorithm is invoked after each crash but the system crashes again before the recovery achieves any "crash surviving" progress. However, this scenario is extremely unlikely and would indicate a fundamental problem with the entire system rather than the recovery algorithm. Therefore, we will not further consider the theoretically possible problem of nontermination. Rather we "axiomatically" assume that only a finite number of crashes can occur before the recovery eventually completes without being interrupted.

At this point, without already narrowing the scope of possible algorithms, no more specific correctness criteria can be stated. However, without referring to the steps during restart, we can already consider necessary conditions for ensuring that the stable log does indeed contain all necessary information for recovery. These conditions, which refer to the relationship between the stable database and the stable log during normal operation, constitute a sanity check for a recovery algorithm: without the proper information on the log, no recovery algorithm can achieve its goal.

Logging rules

DEFINITION 12.7   *Logging Rules: Redo Rule, Undo Rule, Garbage Collection Rule*

A recovery algorithm (or, actually, its logging component during normal operation) satisfies

- the *redo logging rule* if for every transaction t in the history such that the history contains a commit(t) action, all data actions of t that occur in the history are contained in the stable log or in the stable database;

- the *undo logging rule* if for every data action p of transaction t in the history such that the history does not contain a commit(t) or rollback(t) action, the presence of p in the stable database implies that p is contained in the stable log;

- the *garbage collection rule* if for every data action p of transaction t in the history, the absence of p from the stable log implies that p is in the stable database if and only if the history contains a commit(t) action.

These rules capture invariants that must hold in the relationship between the stable database and the stable log in order to facilitate recovery. From an implementation viewpoint, the rules initiate the forcing of the log buffer upon certain events:

- The redo logging rule requires forcing all redo information of a transaction to the stable log when a transaction becomes committed. In fact, a transaction is usually only viewed as committed (and includes the commit in the history) if and only if a commit log entry has been written to the stable log.

- The undo logging rule requires forcing the undo information for a page to the stable log before that page is flushed to the stable database. This rule is historically referred to as the *write ahead logging* rule, or WAL rule for short, but this name may bear misleading connotations with specific implementations.

- The garbage collection rule disallows removing a log entry from the stable log unless it is guaranteed that this log entry will no longer be needed for recovery. Note that, although this rule may appear to be an optional element, the option of removing obsolete log entries and effectively truncating the stable log is a crucial optimization in order to speed up recovery and achieve high availability.

We will later verify these rules for a complete family of recovery algorithms as a fundamental first step in the correctness reasoning and a simplification of the reasoning about the actual recovery during a restart.

12.5 **Road Map of Algorithms**

The three logging rules of the previous section are fundamental invariants upon which every correct recovery algorithm relies. Some algorithms are, however, even more restrictive in terms of the relationships allowed between the cached database, the stable database, and the stable log. These additional invariants can be used to categorize a wide spectrum of crash recovery algorithms; in fact, all algorithms that have ever been proposed in the literature naturally fit into this categorization. The main idea is to distinguish algorithms by their need to perform undo and/or redo steps during restart. This leads to a taxonomy with four cases, as discussed next.

1. *No-undo/no-redo algorithms*: This class of algorithms maintains the invariant that the stable database contains exactly the actions of all committed transactions. Thus, during restart, neither undo nor redo recovery

No-undo/ no-redo algorithms

is needed; the "magic" of crash recovery is completely embedded in the additional work during normal operation. More formally, the invariant reads as follows: if an action p of transaction t in the history is in the stable database, then there must be a commit(t) action in the stable log, and if the stable log contains a commit(t) action of transaction t, then all data actions of transaction t must be present in the stable database.

To ensure the first condition of the invariant, a recovery algorithm has to guarantee that no page is ever flushed to the stable database if it contains any dirty updates made by uncommitted transactions. This property has been coined the "no-steal property" by Härder and Reuter (1983) because its most straightforward implementation is to build into the database cache manager that no such page can be "stolen" out of the cache as a replacement victim. For the second condition of the invariant, all pages that contain updates of a committed transaction must obviously be flushed at the commit point. Because of these "forced" disk I/Os on the stable database, this property has been coined the "force property" by Härder and Reuter.

No-undo/
with-redo
algorithms

2. *No-undo/with-redo algorithms*: This class of algorithms maintains the invariant that the stable database contains no actions of an uncommitted transaction. More formally, this reads as follows: if an action a of transaction t in the history is in the stable database, then there must be a commit(t) action in the stable log. This is the first condition of the no-undo/no-redo invariant. Correspondingly, algorithms in this class are also known as *no-steal algorithms*. Restart after a crash potentially requires redo steps, but no undo recovery.

With-undo/
no-redo
algorithms

3. *With-undo/no-redo algorithms*: This class of algorithms maintains the invariant that the stable database contains all actions of committed transactions. More formally, this reads as follows: if there is a commit(t) action for a transaction t in the stable log, then all data actions of transaction t must be present in the stable database. This is the second condition of the no-undo/no-redo invariant. Correspondingly, algorithms in this class are also known as *force algorithms*. Restart after a crash potentially requires undo steps, but no redo recovery.

With-undo/
with-redo
algorithms

4. *With-undo/with-redo algorithms*: This class of algorithms does not maintain any special invariants other than the general logging rules of the previous section. Therefore, it is also known as the class of *no-steal no-force algorithms*. Restart after a crash potentially requires both undo and redo steps.

Deferred-
update
algorithms

Algorithms of the two no-undo categories are also referred to as *deferred-update algorithms*, since they have to postpone updates to the stable database until after the updates become committed. Such algorithms can be implemented in a variety of ways, based on different organizations of the stable log:

- With a *no-steal database cache*, the stable log can be implemented in its "standard form" as a sequential append-only file of log entries, where log entries need to capture only redo information, and various formats of log entries are possible.

- In a *shadowing* approach, the stable log organizes updates of uncommitted transactions in pages such that these pages can be assigned to the (cached) database in an atomic manner. A simple and reasonably efficient implementation is to keep two versions of the database page addressing table, which is the table that translates page numbers into on-disk addresses such as extent or file numbers along with an offset. When performing (not yet committed) updates, new versions of the affected pages are created and registered in one version of the addressing table, while the other version of the addressing table is left unchanged. At commit time, the system switches from the unchanged, old version of the addressing table to the new version by atomically changing a stable "master pointer." At this time, old page versions that are no longer needed are released by giving them back to the free space management. The old page versions that temporarily coexist with the new ones are often referred to as *shadow pages* and the entire unchanged database as a *shadow database*. In addition to the new page versions, the stable log still needs to keep redo information in this approach, usually in a separate file, unless shadowing is coupled with a policy that forces the new page versions to disk before commit.

- In a general *versioning* approach, the stable log file maintains versions of database objects, not necessarily in a page-oriented organization. These versions serve as a *differential file* to the database; the cached database and hence also the stable database are left unchanged until reaching a commit point. Updates of uncommitted transactions create new versions, and the commit of a transaction moves all versions that were created by the transaction into the cached database. Similar to shadowing, pointer switching techniques may be employed on a per-object basis for "installing" the new versions, or physical copying of versions if necessary. When commutativity properties of semantically rich database operations are exploited for higher concurrency, such operations may even have to be reexecuted to install their effects into the (cached) database. In this case, the differential file is more appropriately called an *intention list*. As with shadowing, the redo part of the stable log is still necessary in a versioning approach, unless new versions are forced to disk before commit.

Algorithms of the two with-undo categories, on the other hand, are commonly known as *update-in-place algorithms*, as updates are performed directly on the original database pages. The entire taxonomy of crash recovery algorithms discussed above is summarized in Figure 12.2.

Update-in-place algorithms

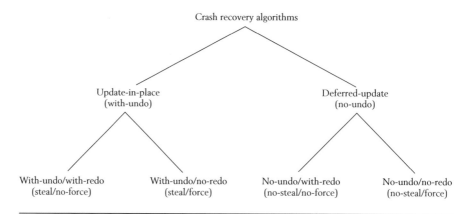

Figure 12.2 Taxonomy of crash recovery algorithms.

The case for with-undo/ with-redo algorithms

Our overriding performance goal of minimizing recovery time after a crash seems to make a strong case for the no-undo/no-redo algorithms as the method of choice. These algorithms achieve virtually instantaneous recovery by guaranteeing that the stable database is always in its correct state. However, focusing on recovery time alone would be too shortsighted. We also need to consider the extra work that the recovery algorithm incurs during normal operation. This is exactly the catch with the class of no-undo/no-redo algorithms. By and large, they come at the expense of a substantial overhead during normal operation that may increase the execution cost per transaction by a factor of two or even higher. In other words, it reduces the achievable transaction throughput of a given server configuration by a factor of two or more.

Cost of no-undo

The bad news on performance degradation needs to be explained in more detail. First consider the no-undo or deferred-update aspect of an algorithm. Its implementation is relatively inexpensive with a page-oriented shadowing approach. However, since such an algorithm is inherently restricted to installing complete pages at commit time, it works correctly only in combination with page-granularity concurrency control. The detailed arguments for this important observation are essentially the same as in Chapter 11 on transaction recovery. Thus, this approach would rule out fine-grained concurrency control. We could resort to a general versioning approach, but there the commit of a transaction incurs substantial additional work, in the worst case, the copying of all new versions or even the reexecution of the transaction's update actions. This causes the factor-of-two degradation in terms of disk I/O.

Cost of no-redo

Now consider the no-redo aspect, which is even worse. The only way to avoid redo recovery is by flushing all modified pages at the commit of a transaction—the force property. However, this would typically cause as many random disk I/Os on the stable database as the number of pages that were modified by the committing transaction. Compared to the sequential disk I/Os for appending the corresponding log entries to a stable log file, the extra cost for the no-redo guarantee may exceed a factor of 10. Therefore, the force policy of a no-redo algorithm is absolutely unacceptable in terms of performance.

The above discussion has brought up compelling arguments against both no-undo and no-redo algorithms, leaving us with the class of with-undo/with-redo algorithms. This latter class is indeed the most general one in that it does not make any assumptions on the relationships between cached database, stable database, and stable log during normal operation (other than the three logging rules) and provides means for both undo and redo steps if these are necessary after a crash. As we will see in the course of the next chapter, there are effective ways to limit the amount of undo and redo work during a restart and hence bound the recovery time at an acceptable level (on the order of one minute). In addition, the with-undo/with-redo algorithms provide high flexibility with regard to trading off an increased overhead during normal operation for faster restart. This can be achieved simply by intensifying the cache manager's activity of flushing dirty pages, without changing anything in the crash recovery algorithm.

For these reasons, the class of with-undo/with-redo algorithms is the only one that has found its way into commercial systems, and we have seen strong arguments that this choice is not incidental: the other classes are inherently inferior in significant aspects. Finally, a salient property of the with-undo/with-redo algorithms is that they require relatively little (but subtle and carefully designed) changes when we want to move from the page model with page-granularity concurrency control to the more general object model. For all these reasons, we restrict ourselves in the following chapters to the class of with-undo/with-redo algorithms.

Throughout this chapter, and the subsequent chapters, an inherent assumption is that transactions are executed concurrently during normal operation. This has consequences on crash recovery in that it rules out very simple solutions. Under certain conditions, however, it can make sense to completely abandon concurrency and execute transactions strictly sequentially. Such a radical solution is attractive for servers where all data fits into main memory and the throughput requirement for transactions can be met by a uniprocessor computer. In such a setting, concurrency is no longer needed to fully exploit the underlying hardware resources (disks and processors). Concurrent transaction scheduling may still be needed to cope with highly variable transaction lengths, for example, to prevent long transactions from monopolizing resources. However, there are certain applications, for example, in financial trading, where virtually all transactions are short. Then, under these premises, sequential transaction execution is perfectly acceptable, and crash recovery can be greatly simplified. In particular, a no-undo algorithm that atomically writes redo information to the stable log upon transaction commit could be implemented very easily and efficiently in such a setting. For the remainder of the book, however, we will not make such radical assumptions about excluding

Simplifications for sequential execution

concurrency, but we will briefly come back to the issue of main-memory data servers in Chapter 15.

12.6 **Lessons Learned**

In this chapter we have laid the foundations for crash recovery algorithms, which include three major preparations for the detailed discussion of algorithms in subsequent chapters:

1. We have more precisely identified the kinds of failures that crash recovery should cope with.

2. We have introduced a concise model for the system components that are relevant to crash recovery algorithms—namely, stable log, log buffer, stable database, and cached database—and we have identified the relevant operations on these components. This model abstracts from details of concrete implementations such as commercial database systems while allowing us to describe crash recovery algorithms in a compact manner and reason about their correctness.

3. Based on this abstract system model we have defined a notion of correctness that requires the cached database to be restored after a crash such that its contents, viewed as system history, are equivalent to a serial execution of the committed transactions in the serialization order of the original history. Logging rules that describe invariants between the log and the stable database are necessary, but not sufficient conditions for the ability to perform correct recovery after a crash.

Finally, an important point already visible here is a *trade-off* between the simplicity of a recovery algorithm and its performance, and, with regard to the latter, also a trade-off between the algorithm's overhead during normal operation and its efficiency during restart. These aspects will also guide the discussion of concrete algorithms in the subsequent chapters.

Exercises

12.1 Assume that both the database cache and the log buffer are, to a large extent, crash resilient (i.e., they survive a system failure and are thus accessible with their pre-crash contents during restart) by using battery-backed, nonvolatile RAM (also known as *RAM disk* or *flash memory*). Discuss which types of failures still need recovery measures. How safe is such a safe-RAM approach?

12.2 Assume again that both the database and the log buffer reside in safe RAM. In addition, assume that virtual-memory page protection bits are used to carefully control the software access to these data structures during normal operation. Discuss again which types of failures still need explicit recovery measures. For the class of system failures (i.e., soft crashes), which of the following statements are true, which ones are false?

(a) Undo recovery is no longer needed at all.

(b) Redo recovery is no longer needed at all.

(c) When a page is flushed from the database cache during normal operation, the log buffer must be forced beforehand.

(d) When a page is flushed from the database cache during restart, the log buffer must be forced beforehand.

(e) When a transaction commits (during normal operation), the log buffer must be forced beforehand.

Bibliographic Notes

In the entire area of crash recovery, the knowledge, tricks, and pragmatic techniques of commercial system builders have largely preceded the published literature and the systematic understanding of the underlying principles. Gray (1978), Härder and Reuter (1983), and Bernstein, Goodman, and Hadzilacos (1983) wrote the first, seminal articles that shed systematic light onto the "black art" of crash recovery; the latter two articles are also the original sources of the taxonomy that we presented in Section 12.5. Among the more recent literature, Mohan, Haderle, et al. (1992) have provided the most comprehensive treatment of advanced recovery techniques.

Empirical studies on the causes and circumstances of system failures were reported by Gray (1986), where the terms Bohrbugs and Heisenbugs were coined. Surveys of fundamental fault-tolerance techniques and fault-tolerant system architectures in general have been given by Randell (1978), Kim (1984), Cristian (1991), as well as Gray and Siewiorek (1991). Gray (1986) has provided an excellent discussion of the rationale for the transition from solely relying on fault-tolerant hardware and operating system mechanisms to failure-resilient, highly available systems based on the transaction paradigm in conjunction with lower-level fault-tolerance techniques.

The use of "safe RAM" within the context of crash recovery, as mentioned in Exercise 12.1, has been discussed by Copeland et al. (1989) and Sullivan and Stonebraker (1991). Specialized recovery techniques for sequential transaction execution in a main-memory data server, with great simplifications, have been discussed by Whitney et al. (1997).

CHAPTER THIRTEEN

Page Model Crash Recovery Algorithms

History is written by the winners.
—*Alex Haley*

History is a people's memory, and without a memory,
man is demoted to the lower animals.
—*Malcolm X*

13.1 **Goal and Overview**

This chapter discusses with-undo/with-redo crash recovery algorithms for the page model. So according to our correctness considerations from the previous chapter, we essentially restrict the database history to the roots and leaves of the executed transaction trees. In particular, the only data actions that are of interest to recovery algorithms are (partial) write actions that modify certain bytes in a single page as well as full-write actions that overwrite all bytes of a page. A major difficulty that we will encounter with partial writes and need to address in detail is that such operations are not necessarily idempotent: when an operation is described as a "function" that, for example, shifts certain bytes in a page by a specified offset, invoking the function twice yields an effect that is different from performing it (exactly) once. Note that such functions could always be logged as full-writes, by simply recording the complete state of the page that results from the operation's execution. However, as pages are rather large and typically only a few bytes are modified, treating all writes as full-writes would not exploit a potential for performance improvement. By keeping the amount of logged data as small as possible, the data server's throughput during normal operation may be enhanced (or at least logging does not become a bottleneck); furthermore, the time for processing the log during recovery can often be reduced, thereby increasing the server's availability.

Partial writes vs. full-writes

As discussed in the previous chapter, we assume that disk-based stable storage is resilient to (transient) system failures, so that both the stable database and the stable log are not affected by crashes. Single write (or full-write) actions are assumed to be atomic, and the same assumption is made for single flush

Crash-resilient stable storage and page action atomicity

447

actions that write a page from the cache back into the stable database on disk. Low-level techniques for detecting interrupted actions on a single page and ensuring action atomicity involve maintaining special checksums at the beginning and at the end of a page and keeping a temporary, volatile page copy for backup. (These implementation techniques are described in great detail in the 1993 book by Gray and Reuter.)

Throughout this chapter we assume that histories during normal operation are prefix reducible in the sense of Chapter 11. So execution histories are constrained to be conflict serializable in terms of their page read/write conflicts and log recoverable in terms of the allowed orderings of commit and abort actions (see Chapter 11).

Page model algorithms are limited to work only in combination with page-granularity concurrency control. Nevertheless, these algorithms are interesting for two reasons. First, since they are simpler than the object model algorithms, they are perfectly suited for applications that exhibit very little data contention even with page-granularity concurrency control (e.g., read-mostly applications). Second and most importantly from a pedagogical viewpoint, page model algorithms already contain many concepts and techniques that form the building blocks of more sophisticated object model algorithms. In general, the presentation in this chapter will develop simpler algorithms first, which may be inefficient or even incomplete in certain ways, and will then gradually refine and extend the algorithms until we obtain state-of-the-art and industrial-strength solutions. The key advantage of this approach is that it allows us to provide correctness arguments in an incremental and concise manner.

Redo-winners vs. redo-history paradigm   In our discussion of the recovery steps performed during restart, we distinguish two approaches that differ fundamentally, each with its own virtues. The first approach, coined the *redo-winners paradigm*, limits redo steps to the updates of committed, so-called winner transactions. The second approach, coined the *redo-history paradigm*, extends redo steps to all updates that occurred before a given crash, thus essentially reestablishing the database state as of the crash, from which undo recovery then proceeds further. We postpone a discussion of the pros and cons of the two paradigms until we have seen the algorithms in more detail.

Both paradigms have a number of fundamental points in common:

- Redo steps are performed for logged operations in chronological order, and essentially repeat the serialization order of the transactions before the crash. This requires a forward pass over the log, and may involve a number of important optimizations, for example, so-called checkpoints, to minimize the work during this pass.

- Undo steps for so-called loser transactions that have not yet been committed at the time of the crash are performed in reverse chronological order. This requires a backward pass over the log.

- With partial writes that are not necessarily idempotent, the recovery needs to be careful to avoid performing a certain redo or undo step twice. Without special care, this could happen, for example, when the server crashes again during the recovery and a second restart is initiated. The solution involves testing the state of a page, using timestamp-like sequence numbers, before it is decided to perform a given redo or undo step.

- Transactions that have been aborted and completely rolled back during normal operation (or, even worse, whose rollback is interrupted by a crash) require special care as well. The reason is that unless we tightly control the cache manager's page flushing activity and thus compromise the server's disk I/O performance, an arbitrary subset of such a transaction's regular "forward" operations and rollback-induced inverse operations may become lost by the crash, and other transactions, both winners and losers, may have subsequently modified some of the affected pages. The best solution to address the resulting problems involves logging inverse operations as well, and treating these so-called compensation log entries appropriately during restart.

The remainder of this chapter is organized as follows: Section 13.2 introduces the basic data structures upon which virtually all industrial-strength recovery algorithms are built. Sections 13.3 and 13.4 develop, in a step-by-step manner, the two major types of algorithms, referred to as the redo-winners and the redo-history algorithms. Finally, Section 13.5 puts the various pieces together by summarizing the method of choice for page-level crash recovery. Note that the goal of the chapter is not only to learn the best recovery algorithm, but also to understand why the algorithm is good, which entails learning about trade-offs, design alternatives, and so on.

13.2 **Basic Data Structures**

Throughout this section we build on the abstract model for the various components of the system architecture that we have described in Section 12.3 of Chapter 12. However, for concrete notation, we also introduce specific data structures that correspond to the components of the model. The data structures give an implementation-oriented view, whereas the abstract model captures the system state in a more formal and concise manner. We will state the exact relationship between the concrete data structures and the abstract model.

We assume that the stable log is implemented as a sequential append-only file, or a set of such files that are used in round-robin manner (see also Chapter 16). We further assume that log entries are tagged with chronologically increasing sequence numbers, referred to as *log sequence numbers* (also abbreviated as LSNs), and that each page in the stable database and the database cache carries a page sequence number that is coupled with the log sequence numbers of the log entries for this page in a specific manner so that we can test the presence of a logged update in the page's state. As we will later discuss in more detail, a straightforward method to facilitate this kind of state testing is to define the page sequence number of a page as the maximum log sequence number of the log entries for this page. Sequence numbers are also used to "locate" log entries in the stable log, and page numbers are used to "locate" pages in the stable database and the database cache. We use arraylike subscript notation for such indexed sets. For example, StableLog[s] denotes the log entry with sequence number *s* on the stable log. Other than that, our notation is Pascal-like, and should be self-explanatory.

Basic data structures

```
/* Basic data structures of page model recovery algorithms: */
type Page: record of
  PageNo: identifier;
  PageSeqNo: identifier;
  Status: (clean, dirty); /* only for cached pages */
  Contents: array [PageSize] of char;
  end;
persistent var StableDatabase:
  set of Page indexed by PageNo;
var DatabaseCache:
  set of Page indexed by PageNo;
type LogEntry: record of
  LogSeqNo: identifier;
  TransId: identifier;
  PageNo: identifier;
  ActionType: (write, full-write, begin, commit, rollback);
  UndoInfo: array of char;
  RedoInfo: array of char;
  PreviousSeqNo: identifier;
  end;
persistent var StableLog:
  ordered set of LogEntry indexed by LogSeqNo;
var LogBuffer:
  ordered set of LogEntry indexed by LogSeqNo;
type TransInfo: record of
  TransId: identifier;
  LastSeqNo: identifier;
  end;
var ActiveTrans:
  set of TransInfo indexed by TransId;
```

In comparison to the architectural model of Section 12.3, the major changes are that the structure of pages and, especially, log entries are refined and made more explicit. In addition to its actual byte contents of fixed length (PageSize) and the page sequence number (PageSeqNo) in its header, a page has a status associated with it. This status is not part of the page itself, and it is relevant (and maintained) only for pages that currently reside in the database cache. Its value is either "dirty," meaning that the cached version of the page contains more recent updates than the one in the stable database, or "clean," meaning that the cached version is identical to the stable one. In terms of page sequence numbers, a cached page is dirty if and only if its page sequence number is greater than the page sequence number of the page's version in the stable database. Note that this use of the term dirty is different from our use in Chapter 11 on transaction recovery, where dirty meant modified by an uncommitted transaction. As the term is commonly used both ways and the context always renders it unambiguous, there is no harm in sticking with this overloaded term.

Page structure

Status of cached pages: dirty or clean

The structure of a log entry includes the entry's LSN and, furthermore, the action type, the page number, and the transaction identifier of the logged action. Furthermore, each log entry for a transaction t contains the LSN of the transaction's previous log entry. So log entries are effectively backward chained on a per-transaction basis. We will use nil to denote an undefined value for such log entry pointers. The anchors for these chains are maintained in the volatile ActiveTrans structure. The backward chaining of log entries is also beneficial for transaction recovery during normal operation, to retrieve all log entries of an aborting transaction in reverse chronological order. However, transaction recovery algorithms could also choose to use their own separate data structures for this purpose.

Structure and backward chaining of log entries

Figure 13.1 illustrates the use of sequence numbers in log entries and page headers. In this figure, pages q and z in the cache are dirty, which can be seen from their page sequence numbers being strictly larger than those of the corresponding page versions in the stable database; pages b and p, on the other hand, are clean. The last update on page q, with sequence number 4219, is not yet recorded on the stable log, but this is compatible with the logging rules because this log entry belongs to an uncommitted transaction, t_{17}, and the update is not yet contained in the stable database either.

The information in a log entry to undo or redo the action can be encoded in different ways; so we simply define it as a variable-length byte string. For full-write actions, the redo information is the full contents of the page after the modification, often referred to as the *after image*, and the undo information is the full page contents before the modification, known as the *before image* of the page. Note that the data server mostly reads a page before overwriting it, but if the read action is "strictly local" in that the read data does not affect any of the further actions other than the immediately following write, then we do not bother mentioning the read in the history at all and denote the write as a full-write.

Physical log entries: before images, after images

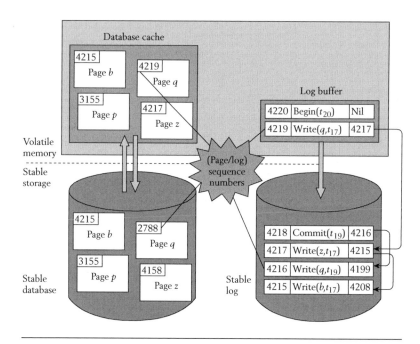

Figure 13.1 Sequence numbers in log entries and page headers.

Physiological
log entries   For arbitrary write actions, before images and after images are feasible encodings of the undo and redo information, too, and in this case we simply treat the write as a full-write as far as the recovery is concerned. In general, there are other options for write actions as well. For example, you can merely log the old and new values of the byte range that was actually modified in the page. In some cases, you can describe the update by an operation such as shifting a certain number of bytes by a certain offset, or the undo and redo information may even refer to the storage layout of the data records (at least as long as data records do not span pages). In any case, however, such write operations must be confined to depend on and affect only a single page; no other database pages must be read, and all input values that the page modification depends on must be part of the log entry's UndoInfo or RedoInfo fields (or retrievable from the page itself). This class of log entries has been coined physiological log entries, as they describe logical operations on physical units (namely, pages). A frequent property of such physiological operations is that they are *not necessarily idempotent*; so performing such an operation twice has a different effect on the page than performing it once.

Correspondence
of data
structures and
abstract model   The state of the above data structures can be translated into the state of our abstract system model in the following straightforward manner. The key point is that the page sequence number of a page, say, s, tells us that all data actions on that page that have sequence numbers less than or equal to s are reflected in

the page contents. Conversely, none of the data actions with sequence numbers higher than s have made any effect on that page (version).

- An action with sequence number s is contained in the *stable log* if and only if LSN s is in StableLog.
- A write or full-write action with sequence number s on page p (i.e., the page with page number p) is contained in the *stable database* if and only if

$$StableDatabase[p].PageSeqNo \geq s$$

- A write or full-write action with sequence number s on page p is contained in the *cached database* if and only if p is in DatabaseCache and

$$DatabaseCache[p].PageSeqNo \geq s$$

or

$$StableDatabase[p].PageSeqNo \geq s$$

These relationships are "axiomatic" in the sense that they state the intrinsic (and unprovable) connection between the data structures of the system and our abstract model. It becomes very clear at this point that the abstract model disregards some details but, other than that, essentially captures the same information as the concrete data structures.

The most straightforward and most widely employed way of ensuring the above relationships is by defining for all pages p:

$$DatabaseCache[p].PageSeqNo := max\{s.LogSeqNo | s \text{ is a log entry},$$
$$\text{in the log buffer or in the stable log, with } s.PageNo = p\}$$

So the page sequence number of a page is set to be the maximum log sequence number of the log entries that refer to this page, which is very easy to implement. In particular, it is sufficient to maintain the page sequence numbers of the pages in the database cache; when such a page is written back to the stable database, it automatically carries the correct page sequence number.

13.3 Redo-Winners Paradigm

In this section we present crash recovery algorithms that are based on the redo-winners paradigm. Thus, during restart, redo steps are performed only for updates of committed transactions. We begin our presentation with a precise description of the actions during normal operation in Section 13.3.1, and

Transaction aborts disregarded then consider a simple three-pass recovery algorithm in Section 13.3.2. For pedagogical reasons, *we first disregard transactions that have been aborted and rolled back during normal operation*; so undo steps are limited to transactions that are still in progress at the time of the crash. The following Sections 13.3.3 and 13.3.4 then remove this simplification and gradually add more sophisticated steps to the simple algorithm to make it complete and improve its efficiency.

13.3.1 **Actions during Normal Operation**

Actions during normal operation Based on the concrete data structures introduced in Section 13.2, we can precisely describe the various actions that occur during normal operation. We use a Pascal-like pseudocode notation for this purpose, which is sufficiently formal to allow rigorous arguments on invariants. For sets or arrays, respectively, we use the notation += and -= to denote the insertion and deletion of one or more elements.

```
write or full-write (pageno, transid, s):
 DatabaseCache[pageno].Contents := modified contents;
 DatabaseCache[pageno].PageSeqNo := s;
 DatabaseCache[pageno].Status := dirty;
 newlogentry.LogSeqNo := s;
 newlogentry.ActionType := write or full-write;
 newlogentry.TransId := transid;
 newlogentry.PageNo := pageno;
 newlogentry.UndoInfo := information to undo update
  (before image for full-write);
 newlogentry.RedoInfo := information to redo update
  (after image for full-write);
 newlogentry.PreviousSeqNo :=
  ActiveTrans[transid].LastSeqNo;
 ActiveTrans[transid].LastSeqNo := s;
 LogBuffer += newlogentry;


fetch (pageno):
 DatabaseCache += pageno;
 DatabaseCache[pageno].Contents :=
  StableDatabase[pageno].Contents;
 DatabaseCache[pageno].PageSeqNo :=
  StableDatabase[pageno].PageSeqNo;
 DatabaseCache[pageno].Status := clean;
```

```
flush (pageno):
 if there is logentry in LogBuffer with logentry.PageNo = pageno
 then
  force ( );
 end /*if*/;
 StableDatabase[pageno].Contents :=
  DatabaseCache[pageno].Contents;
 StableDatabase[pageno].PageSeqNo :=
  DatabaseCache[pageno].PageSeqNo;
 DatabaseCache[pageno].Status := clean;

force ( ):
 StableLog += LogBuffer;
 LogBuffer := empty;

begin (transid, s):
 ActiveTrans += transid;
 ActiveTrans[transid].LastSeqNo := s;
 newlogentry.LogSeqNo := s;
 newlogentry.ActionType := begin;
 newlogentry.TransId := transid;
 newlogentry.PreviousSeqNo := nil;
 LogBuffer += newlogentry;

commit (transid, s):
 newlogentry.LogSeqNo := s;
 newlogentry.ActionType := commit;
 newlogentry.TransId := transid;
 newlogentry.PreviousSeqNo :=
  ActiveTrans[transid].LastSeqNo;
 LogBuffer += newlogentry;
 ActiveTrans -= transid;
 force ( );
```

Note that the force action can be invoked by the system itself rather than being invokable only on behalf of a transaction. Typically, the system will force the log buffer whenever it is filled up, but it can also do so anytime at its discretion. While the disk I/O for writing the log buffer contents to the stable log is in progress, the server cannot append new log entries to the log buffer, or it needs appropriate low-level synchronization (i.e., using latches or semaphores) for the management of memory space. To prevent such synchronization from becoming a potential performance bottleneck, most systems simply have two log buffers and use them in an alternating way. So while one log buffer is being written to disk, the other one is used for new log entries, and these roles are switched at the next force action.

Correctness reasoning

Also note that replacement of cached pages (based on a policy such as LRU or its variations and generalizations) is assumed to be under the control of the cache manager and thus not shown in the pseudocode. When the cache manager decides to drop a dirty page from the cache, it must initiate a flush action for this page and wait for its completion before reusing the corresponding memory space that held the page. Clean pages, on the other hand, can simply be overwritten when the cache manager decides that they should be dropped from the cache.

Other than that, the above pseudocode is straightforward. In terms of its correctness, we can show that the code satisfies the three invariants that we coined as logging rules in Section 12.4 of Chapter 12. Recall that these rules—the redo logging rule, the undo logging rule, and the garbage collection rule—dictate the following invariants: log entries of committed transactions must be kept in a stable place, log entries for pages modified by uncommitted transactions must be in a stable place once such a page is written into the stable database, and log entries of committed transactions must be kept until all their modified pages are written back into the stable database. The following theorem certifies that during normal operation, the three invariants always hold, and, therefore, all necessary information for correct recovery is available during restart.

THEOREM 13.1

Validity of logging rules

During normal operation, the redo logging rule, the undo logging rule, and the garbage collection rule are satisfied.

Proof

First let us make a subtle point about when exactly an action is part of the history. This matters because we require certain actions of the history to be in the stable database or stable log. The only reasonable answer is to consider an action to be in the history if either the pseudocode of the action is completely executed or at least one of the stable components of the system, stable database or stable log, contains some evidence of the action. So an action that is in progress when the system fails and has so far not affected the stable components—neither flushed a modified page to disk nor written any log entry to the stable log—is not considered part of the history because its partial execution leaves no traces at all and no return-code has been given to the action's caller.

Next we can observe from the pseudocode that every action in the history immediately creates a log entry in the log buffer (i.e., before the action's pseudocode completes). Now consider the three rules.

- *Redo logging rule:* A commit(t) action causes the log buffer to be forced to the stable log. Therefore, all data actions of transaction t are contained in the stable log, which is a sufficient condition for the redo logging rule.

- *Undo logging rule:* The only way of inserting a data action into the stable database is by flushing the corresponding page. However, a flush action first forces the log buffer to the stable log and thereby inserts the data action into the stable log.

- *Garbage collection rule:* This invariant can be inferred from the other two rules because the stable log is monotonically increasing: the pseudocode (as specified so far) never removes any entries from the stable log. This monotonicity will be relaxed later, and we will then reconsider the validity of the garbage collection rule.

In terms of its performance impact during normal operation, the major overhead of logging arises from forced and thus synchronous I/O on the stable log. Such force actions are triggered by flush actions by the cache manager, due to the undo logging rule, and by commit actions, due to the redo logging rule. The first class of trigger events should be relatively infrequent with a sufficiently large database cache and an intelligent cache replacement policy that avoids replacing dirty pages that have been modified by active transactions whenever possible. The second class, however, occurs at a rate that equals the transactions' completion rate. The latter in turn equals the transactions' arrival rate, because almost all transactions should terminate with a commit action. Therefore, the commit-induced forced log I/Os are a potential bottleneck that may limit the server's transaction throughput: the maximum log I/O rate that can be sustained with the disk(s) on which the stable log resides is an upper bound for the transaction throughput.

Cost of forced log I/O during normal operation

A technique that overcomes this potential throughput bottleneck is the *batching* of log I/Os. This requires postponing a log I/O for a while so that it can be combined into a single longer I/O together with other log entries that are created in the meantime. Trading multiple short I/Os for a single long I/O yields a high benefit because it avoids rotational delays and can therefore utilize the disk bandwidth much better. In the specific context of the forced log I/O upon a commit event, this batching technique is known as *group commit*. When a transaction issues a commit request, the corresponding log entry is created in the log buffer, but the force action for writing the log buffer to the stable log is postponed until a "group commit timer" expires or the log buffer is full and must be written to disk anyway. The timer ensures that the group commit technique does not incur unduly long deferrals under light load when commit actions are infrequent. The timer's initial value is a fine-tuning parameter whose optimization presents fairly difficult mathematical problems. Fortunately, however, it is not that hard to find a reasonably robust, albeit suboptimal, setting in practice, usually on the order of 100 milliseconds.

Group commit for log I/O batching

13.3.2 **Simple Three-Pass Algorithm**

The simplest recovery algorithm for the redo-winners paradigm proceeds in three phases, each of which performs a pass over the stable log:

Analysis pass

1. The *analysis pass* starts at the beginning of the stable log and reads all log entries in ascending order of LSNs until it reaches the end of the log. During this pass, the transaction identifiers in the log entries are inspected, and two lists of transactions are collected:

Winner and loser transactions

- *winner transactions* (or "winners" for short) are those transactions for which a commit log entry is encountered,
- *loser transactions* (or "losers" for short) are those for which no commit log entry exists in the stable log.

The entries in the loser list also track the LSN of the most recent data action for each transaction; these are referred to as the *last LSNs*.

Start and end of the stable log

Note that it may be nontrivial to locate the beginning and the end of the stable log, depending on how the log is actually implemented. State-of-the-art implementations use a set of preallocated fixed-size files, with dynamic truncation of the actually used part and cyclic reuse (which is not yet incorporated in our simple algorithm). Then the beginning of the

Master record

log is usually located by looking up a *master record* on stable storage that is maintained as truncations are performed. In the pseudocode given below, we refer to the beginning of the stable log by the oldest LSN, with the understanding that this is determined from the master record. The end of the log cannot be determined this way without a severe performance penalty, the reason being that a master record pointing to the end would have to be updated on stable storage with every force action, which we expect to be much more frequent than log truncations. Rather, the end of the log is determined as the log scan progresses by checking the monotonicity of timestamps that are embedded in the blocks of the stable log file(s): we realize that we have reached an older, previously truncated part of the log when we see a decreasing timestamp. In the pseudocode given below we do not capture such low-level implementation techniques, and rather refer to the end of the log by the highest occurring LSN, with the understanding that this log sequence number is a priori unknown to the recovery algorithm and merely indicates the point where all forward-scanning passes over the stable log stop.

Note also that we expect the list of loser transactions to be small, as it contains only the transactions that were running at the time of the crash. Thus, it is no problem to build this list in memory during the analysis pass. In contrast, the list of winner transactions may become fairly large depending on the time period that is covered by the stable log and the load intensity of the system during this period. However, if the size of the winner list is a concern, we can easily avoid maintaining it explicitly. In fact, every transaction that does not eventually show up in the loser list must be a winner. So it suffices to maintain the loser list.

2. The *redo pass* starts again at the beginning of the log and reads the entire stable log in ascending order of LSNs. Whenever it encounters a log entry that describes a data action on a page p that was performed by a transaction that is not in the loser list, the page is fetched from the stable database, and the data action is repeated based on the redo information in the log entry. *Redo pass*

3. The *undo pass* looks up all log entries for data actions of loser transactions in descending order of their LSNs, fetches the corresponding page, and performs an inverse write action based on the undo information in the log entry. Note that the ordering of log sequence numbers is a global one across all loser transactions. This traversal of several backward chains of log entries is implemented by performing a backward pass over the stable log starting from its current end (which is now known from the analysis pass) and locating the highest LSN among all "last LSNs" in the loser list. Then, whenever an undo step for a loser transaction t has been performed, the last LSN of t in the loser list is replaced by the LSN of the transaction's preceding log entry. The latter is given by the PreviousSeqNo field in the log entry itself (i.e., the backward chaining of log entries on a per-transaction basis). Thus, the overall effect of this procedure can be viewed as if all log entries of all loser transactions are dynamically merged into a globally descending sorted list. Note that although the undo pass locates a set of log entries in a random-access manner, it is advantageous to embed this access sequence into sequential disk I/Os because of the ordering and the expectation that the requested log entries are relatively close to each other in the stable log (as they belong to the same small set of fairly recent transactions). *Undo pass*

After these three passes, the restart is completed by flushing all dirty pages from the cache back to the database and then reinitializing the stable log (i.e., conceptually discarding all log entries). According to the general objective of crash recovery, this global flushing would not be necessary, as we merely need to establish a correct state of the cached database, and the resulting amount of random disk I/O is indeed a major shortcoming in terms of restart duration and thus availability. We will discuss in Section 13.3.4, under Undo Completion, why this relatively drastic measure is necessary unless we add other techniques for restart completion, and we will then present much more efficient alternatives.

For reasons that will become clear in a short while, we restrict the data actions for this algorithm to be full-writes. The complete pseudocode for the algorithm looks as follows.

```
/* Simple three-pass crash recovery algorithm: */
restart ( ):
 analysis pass ( ) returns losers;
 redo pass ( );
 undo pass ( );
 for each page p in DatabaseCache do
  if DatabaseCache[p].Status = dirty then flush (p); end /*if*/;
 end /*for*/;
 reinitialize StableLog;

analysis pass ( ) returns losers:
var losers: set of record
  TransId: identifier;
  LastSeqNo: identifier;
 end indexed by TransId;
 losers := empty;
 min := LogSeqNo of oldest log entry in StableLog;
 max := LogSeqNo of most recent log entry in StableLog;
 for i := min to max do
  case StableLog[i].ActionType:
   begin:
    losers += StableLog[i].TransId;
    losers[StableLog[i].TransId].LastSeqNo := nil;
   commit:
    losers -= StableLog[i].TransId;
   full-write:
    losers[StableLog[i].TransId].LastSeqNo := i;
  end /*case*/;
 end /*for*/;

redo pass ( ):
 min := LogSeqNo of oldest log entry in StableLog;
 max := LogSeqNo of most recent log entry in StableLog;
 for i := min to max do
  if StableLog[i].ActionType = full-write and
  StableLog[i].TransId not in losers
  then
   pageno = StableLog[i].PageNo;
   fetch (pageno);
   full-write (pageno)
    with contents from StableLog[i].RedoInfo;
  end /*if*/;
 end /*for*/;
```

```
undo pass ( ):
 while there exists t in losers
  such that losers[t].LastSeqNo <> nil
 do
  nexttrans = TransNo in losers
    such that losers[nexttrans].LastSeqNo =
    max {losers[x].LastSeqNo|x in losers};
  nextentry = losers[nexttrans].LastSeqNo;
  if StableLog[nextentry].ActionType = full-write
  then
   pageno = StableLog[nextentry].PageNo;
   fetch (pageno);
   full-write (pageno)
    with contents from StableLog[nextentry].UndoInfo;
   losers[nexttrans].LastSeqNo :=
    StableLog[nextentry].PreviousSeqNo;
  end /*if*/;
 end /*while*/;
```

An observation that can be made about the simple three-pass algorithm is that it is "perfectly idempotent" in the following sense: when the system crashes again during a restart (i.e., before the point when new transactions are admitted), the recovery algorithm performs exactly the same steps as it did during the previous restart, regardless of whether the system flushes pages during restart. Note that this idempotence property is all but trivial, as full-write actions, and also their redoing or undoing, take place only in the cache, and the cache manager can arbitrarily flush pages during restart. Further note that no additional log entries are created by the recovery algorithm. The reason why this behavior is valid lies in our restriction to full-writes as data actions. For each page that is affected by recovery, it is only the very last full-write that matters. This observation is a key point in the proof of the following theorem.

Correctness reasoning

THEOREM 13.2

When restricted to full-writes as data actions, the simple three-pass recovery algorithm performs correct recovery.

Correctness of simple algorithm with full-writes

Proof

First recall our basic assumption that the original history before the crash (before the first crash following the last fully completed restart, to be precise) is conflict serializable and log recoverable. This implies that for each page, the order of writes from different transactions coincides with the order in which the transactions terminated. We need to show that after the completion of the recovery algorithm, the cached database contains exactly all updates of committed transactions in the serialization order of the original history. The reasoning why this is true proceeds in three steps, corresponding to one of the three phases of the algorithm.

1. *Analysis pass:* It is clear from the pseudocode that at the end of the analysis pass, set losers consists of all transactions with at least one log entry, but no commit entry in the stable log. What remains to be shown is that these are exactly the uncommitted transactions of the history that require undo recovery. This can be verified in two steps:

   (a) First, we know from the redo logging rule that the committed transactions of the history must have a commit entry in the stable log. Conversely, we obtain that the transactions in losers are indeed uncommitted in the history.

   (b) Second, the undo logging rule tells us that any transaction that has made an update to the stable database must have an entry in the stable log. Therefore, the uncommitted transactions of the history that are missing in losers must be irrelevant in that their updates have been restricted to the database cache and the log buffer.

   Analogous arguments show that the LastSeqNo field of the elements in losers does indeed point to the most recent stable log entry of the corresponding transaction. Again, any log entries that were merely in the log buffer and have become lost in the crash do not matter since their effects on the database must have been lost by the crash, too.

   Finally, a side effect of determining the set losers is that we can test if a transaction is a winner by checking that it is not in losers. All transactions with at least one log entry in the stable log that do not appear in losers must have a commit log entry and are therefore winners.

2. *Redo pass for winners:* First note that the redo pass redoes all full-write actions of all committed transactions, because these writes are guaranteed to be on the stable log by the redo logging rule (and the fact that the stable log is never truncated in this simple algorithm), and the log scan does not skip any log entries other than those of losers. Further note that the full-writes are redone in the original order of the history, because log entries are created immediately and their order is preserved by force actions. So for each page p

that was modified by at least one winner transaction, we obtain a sequence of full-write actions with the following structure:

$$s_{i_1} : w(p, T_{n_1}) \ldots s_{i_2} : w(p, T_{n_2}) \ldots s_{i_k} : w(p, T_{n_k})$$
$$\text{crash}_1 \ s_{i_1} : w(p) \ldots \text{crash}_2 \ldots$$
$$\ldots$$
$$\text{crash}_m \ s_{i_1} : w(p) \ldots s_{i_k} : w(p)$$

This entire sequence is equivalent to the very last full-write with sequence number s_{i_k}, and this full-write does in turn contain all the committed full-writes, with sequence numbers s_{i_1} through s_{i_k}, that occurred before the original, first crash. By the basic assumption that the original history was conflict serializable and log recoverable, the final full-write reflects the original serialization order of all committed transactions.

If there were no loser transactions at all, then the proof would already be complete. As for the interrelationship of winner and loser log entries, we know that the history is log recoverable and can therefore infer that for every page p, all loser updates must follow all winner updates on p. (Recall that we have excluded transactions that have been completely rolled back before the crash.) Further note that a full-write of page p with sequence number s includes all actions on p with sequence numbers up to s and removes all actions on p with higher sequence numbers. Therefore, all pages with at least one winner update are in their correct state at the end of the redo pass: the cached database, restricted to those pages, contains exactly all write actions of the committed transactions in their serialization order. Furthermore, the idempotence of a full-write action ensures that this property holds even after repeated crashes and restarts, once the redo pass is completed.

For all remaining pages, which have been modified only by loser transactions, the database (still) contains all writes that precede the most recent flush action of the corresponding page.

So in more formal terms, what we have shown is that throughout the redo pass the following invariant holds:

∀ log sequence numbers $s \in$ stable log such that
  the log has been processed for redo up to and including s :
  ∀ pages p : ∀ transactions t : ∀ operations $o \in$ stable log :
    (o belongs to t and refers to $p \wedge t$ is a winner $\wedge o \leq s$)
    $\Rightarrow o \in$ cached database

where $o \leq s$ refers to the order of log entries in the stable log, which in turn corresponds to the order of the extended history. So as the log sequence number s is advanced to the end of the stable log, all winner writes are eventually contained in the cached database.

3. *Undo pass for losers:* From the observation that uncommitted writes must follow all committed writes on a page, we know that none of the undo steps will undo any of the committed and possibly redone winner updates. Thus, we need to show that the undo pass does indeed cover all loser updates that have affected the stable database. The argument on the analysis pass has already shown that for each page, the most recent uncommitted write that was followed by a flush action before the crash is covered: this must be one of the LastSeqNo values in the losers set. Then, by following the backward chains of all loser transactions, we see that all those writes are included. Further, by conceptually merging all log entries of all backward chains into a single descending order, we see that the loser writes are undone in the reverse order of the history. Therefore, if the original loser write is actually present in the stable database after the crash, the undo step performs its corresponding inverse action. At the end of the undo pass, all loser writes are undone by inverse actions.

The only case that needs further analysis is when an undo step is performed although the original loser write has become lost by the crash and is not contained in the stable database (and thus not in the post-crash cached database either). In this case, by performing a full-write based on the page before image, the undo step actually inserts into the cached database the original full-write action that preceded the "undone" action within the loser transaction. From this point on, all subsequent undo steps for the affected page find all prior updates to be included in the cached database. This process terminates with inverting all updates from a page that followed the page's most recent committed write (or the page's initial state if no committed write exists).

Finally, we need to consider the possibility of repeated crashes. However, this does not introduce any new types of situations: if a page is flushed during the restart after having performed an undo step on it, the effect is simply as if the page were certain not to be flushed after the corresponding original write action before the crash. This case is handled correctly by the undo pass.

In formal terms, the undo pass satisfies the following invariant:

$\forall$ log sequence numbers $s \in$ stable log such that all more recent
     log entries of losers, including s, have been processed for undo :
     $\forall$ pages p : $\forall$ transactions t : $\forall$ operations $o \in$ stable log :
         (o belongs to t and refers to $p \wedge t$ is a loser $\wedge o \geq s$)
         $\Rightarrow o \notin$ cached database

So when the log sequence number s finally reaches the oldest loser update during the backward pass over the log, none of the loser updates is contained in the cached database anymore. Furthermore, because of the assumption that the original history is conflict serializable and log recoverable, all loser writes for a given page must follow all winner actions on the same page in the history. Therefore, the logical invariant that resulted from the redo pass (see above) remains unaffected by the undo pass and continues to hold. Together the two formulas imply that the cached database contains exactly all winner writes at the end of the entire restart.

It may be worthwhile to point out that the same result would have been achieved by switching the order of the redo and undo passes; that is, first performing the undo pass and then the redo-winners pass would be equally correct. Note, however, that a crucial prerequisite in this result is that all loser writes for a page follow all winner writes for the same page in the history. Once this is relaxed (and we will do so later), the order with redo first and undo second will become essential.

The simple three-pass algorithm for full-writes is illustrated by the example in Figure 13.2. A pictorial overview is given in Figure 13.3. The example shows the actions and resulting effects for four transactions (t_1 through t_4) on six different pages (a through f); flush actions are introduced at arbitrarily chosen points to illustrate their effects. The example assumes a repeated crash during the redo pass of the recovery. Thus, the actions are grouped into three parts: normal operation, first incomplete recovery attempt, second and completed recovery.

It may be worthwhile to point out a few special situations that occur in the example, all of which are correctly handled by the algorithm without special code:

- The log entry with sequence number 21 is lost in the crash, since it was only in the log buffer at the time of the failure. This is harmless, as the corresponding transaction, t_5, must be a loser transaction.

- For page d, the actions with sequence numbers 8 and 11 are redone in the first recovery attempt, although the stable database already contained these actions. This is feasible because the actions are full-writes whose effects include all prior writes on the same page.

- Because of the flush action for page d after the redo step for sequence number 8, the first recovery attempt leaves page d in a state that is actually older than the state after the original crash where the page sequence number in the stable database was 11. So the first recovery leads to even more "losses" of committed updates. However, this situation is by no means abnormal. It is guaranteed that once the redo pass

Sequence number: action	Change of cached database [PageNo: SeqNo]	Change of stable database [PageNo: SeqNo]	Log entry added to log buffer [LogSeqNo: action]	Log entries added to stable log [LogSeqNo's]
1: begin(t_1)			1: begin(t_1)	
2: begin(t_2)			2: begin(t_2)	
3: write(a, t_1)	a: 3		3: write(a, t_1)	
4: begin(t_3)			4: begin(t_3)	
5: begin(t_4)			5: begin(t_4)	
6: write(b, t_3)	b: 6		6: write(b, t_3)	
7: write(c, t_2)	c: 7		7: write(c, t_2)	
8: write(d, t_1)	d: 8		8: write(d, t_1)	
9: commit(t_1)			9: commit(t_1)	1, 2, 3, 4, 5, 6, 7, 8, 9
10: flush(d)		d: 8		
11: write(d, t_3)	d: 11		11: write(d, t_3)	
12: begin(t_5)			12: begin(t_5)	
13: write(a, t_5)	a: 13		13: write(a, t_5)	
14: commit(t_3)			14: commit(t_3)	11, 12, 13, 14
15: flush(d)		d: 11		
16: write(d, t_4)	d: 16		16: write(d, t_4)	
17: write(e, t_2)	e: 17		17: write(e, t_2)	
18: write(b, t_5)	b: 18		18: write(b, t_5)	
19: flush(b)		b: 18		16,17,18
20: commit(t_4)			20: commit(t_4)	20
21: write(f, t_5)	f: 21		21: write(f, t_5)	
System crash				
Restart				
Analysis pass: losers = {t_2, t_5}				
redo(3)	a: 3			
redo(6)	b: 6			
flush(a)		a: 3		
redo(8)	d: 8			
flush(d)		d: 8		
redo(11)	d: 11			
Second system crash				
Second restart				
Analysis pass: losers = {t_2, t_5}				
redo(3)	a: 3			
redo(6)	b: 6			
redo(8)	d: 8			
redo(11)	d: 11			
redo(16)	d: 16			
undo(18)	b: 6			
undo(17)	e: 0			
undo(13)	a: 3			
undo(7)	c: 0			
Second restart complete: resume normal operation				

Figure 13.2 Example scenario for the simple three-pass recovery algorithm with full-writes.

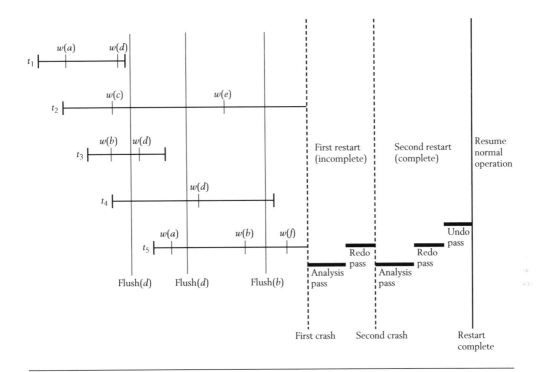

Figure 13.3 Overview of the example scenario.

completes, all committed writes are contained in the cached database. In the example, we can easily verify that this is indeed the case after the second restart is completed.

Incorporating General Write Actions as Physiological Log Entries

In the simple three-pass algorithm described so far we have exploited the property that a full-write on a page contains all prior write actions on that page and also the resulting idempotence of full-writes. Because of these properties, we did not need any special care with regard to repeated crashes. In the scenario of Figure 13.2, for example, the fact that the redoing of the action with sequence number 8 on page d takes place twice, in both of the two restarts, does not lead to any incorrect results. Likewise, redoing that action at all, despite the fact that it is already included in the stable database at the time of the first crash, is correct because of the nature of full-writes. In contrast, if these write actions and their corresponding redo steps were general, nonidempotent writes, then the steps in the example of Figure 13.2 would lead to an incorrect database. The action with sequence number 8 would be executed three times in total. When this action corresponds to a physiological action such as shifting a byte range within a page, the result clearly differs from executing the action only once. More precisely, the second and third executions should not be regarded as repetitions of the original action but rather as additional, "new" actions that are erroneously "invented" by the recovery algorithm.

State testing during the redo pass

The solution to this problem is to ensure that every winner action is executed only once, regardless of the number of repeated crashes and restarts. Thus, the recovery algorithm must guarantee that it does not redo an action that has already been contained in the stable database before the original crash or has been redone and flushed to the stable database in an earlier, incomplete restart. The key to this guarantee is to exploit the page sequence number that is embedded in a database page. By comparing an action with a given sequence number against the page sequence number of the affected page, we can tell if that action is already included in the current state of the page. This test needs to be performed for each possible redo step, and the corresponding action is redone only if the test indicates that the action is not yet present in the page state. Furthermore, if the action needs to be redone, we need to protect ourselves from erroneously redoing it again during a later restart. Again, page sequence numbers come in handy for this purpose. All we need to do is to set the page sequence number to the sequence number of the redone action, and once the page gets flushed to the stable database, we can later (i.e., after one or more further crashes) easily test that that action is already present.

State testing during the undo pass

The complication with general, not necessarily idempotent writes arises not only for the redo recovery but also during the undo pass. Here the situation to be avoided is that an action is "undone" although the original action has been lost by the crash or has already been undone in an earlier restart that subsequently flushed the affected page back to the stable database. In both cases, the undo pass is confronted with the problem that the action under consideration is not (or no longer) present in the page state. "Undoing" the action would then erroneously add another, "new" inverse action.

Not surprisingly, testing the page sequence number again provides the solution. If the page sequence number is smaller than the sequence number of the considered action, then we must not invoke an undo step for that action. This is the dual solution to the one for the redo pass. And similarly, when we perform an undo step, we must make the resulting state modification testable by adjusting the page sequence number.

In the undo case, the appropriate new value of the page sequence number would be the sequence number of the page's most recent action that preceded the undone action. Determining this predecessor sequence number would, however, require introducing another pagewise backward chaining of log entries. Although the necessary additional storage space is surely not a tremendous overhead, it can be avoided by the following trick: rather than identifying a page's predecessor of an undone action, it is sufficient to set the page sequence number to any value that lies between the sequence number of the undone action and its predecessor. This value may actually correspond to the sequence number of an action on a different page, but this does not matter at any point in the algorithm; there is no danger of misinterpretation. Rather, the new value of the page sequence number perfectly serves its purpose in that it tells us, upon a state test, that the undone action is no longer present, whereas all preceding actions are still present. In practice, the concrete value of the new page sequence number is usually chosen by decrementing the original value by one.

The solution to incorporate arbitrary physiological actions into the redo and undo pass of the simple algorithm can be summarized as follows:

- When a log entry for page p with sequence number i is encountered during the *redo pass*, the logged action is redone only if i is larger than the page sequence number of p. In this case, the page sequence number of p is then set to i.

- When a log entry for page p with sequence number i is encountered during the *undo pass*, the logged action is undone only if i is smaller than or equal to the page sequence number of p. In this case, the page sequence number of p is then set to $i - 1$.

The necessary changes to the pseudocode of the simple three-pass recovery algorithm are given below.

```
redo pass ( ):
  ⋮
  fetch (pageno);
  if DatabaseCache[pageno].PageSeqNo < i
  then
    read and write (pageno)
     according to StableLog[i].RedoInfo;
    DatabaseCache[pageno].PageSeqNo := i;
  end /*if*/;
  ⋮
```

Redo pass with general writes

```
undo pass ( ):
  ⋮
  fetch (pageno);
  if DatabaseCache[pageno].PageSeqNo >= nextentry.LogSeqNo
  then
    read and write (pageno)
     according to StableLog[nextentry].UndoInfo;
    DatabaseCache[pageno].PageSeqNo := nextentry.LogSeqNo − 1;
  end /*if*/;
  ⋮
```

Undo pass with general writes

Note that state testing based on merely a page sequence number is feasible only because flush actions have the effect of including all write actions up to a certain sequence number, and both the redo pass and the undo pass proceed in chronological order and inverse chronological order, respectively. If this were not the case, then allowing physiological log entries would require a more general state testing capability for arbitrary, not necessarily chronologically consecutive sets of actions. Such generality would surely incur much higher implementation overhead. The simplification that results from chronological processing is also exploited in the correctness reasoning for the following theorem.

THEOREM 13.3

Correctness of simple algorithm with general writes

The simple three-pass recovery algorithm with sequence number testing performs correct recovery for general writes.

Proof

The proof needs to show that

1. all write actions of winner transactions are executed exactly once in chronological order of the original history, and

2. all write actions of loser transactions are inverted exactly once in reverse chronological order.

Once we have established these properties, the rest of the correctness reasoning is identical to the arguments given in the proof of Theorem 13.2 and therefore omitted here.

(1) The redo pass still considers all winner actions in their original history order. It suppresses only actions that are already included in the cached database according to the page-state test. These actions must have been in the stable database already after the most recent crash, or they must have been redone earlier in the current restart. In the first case, we know that no further redo step or flush action for that page can remove the action under consideration. Therefore, the action will never be redone (again). In the second case, if the page is flushed later in the same restart, then the page sequence number in the stable database is automatically increased and indicates that the considered action is now included. Otherwise, that is, if the system crashes again before the restart completes or the page is flushed, the subsequent restart will correctly redo the action again. In more formal terms, the redo pass satisfies the following invariant in every step:

$\forall$ log sequence numbers s such that
the log has been processed for redo up to but excluding s :
  $\forall$ pages p : $\forall$ transactions t :
    (s belongs to t and refers to $p \wedge t$ is a winner)
    $\Rightarrow$ (s is redone $\Leftrightarrow$ $s \notin$ stable database)

After s is redone, it is contained in the cached database. Since the cached database is (re-) initialized from the stable database right after each crash and the redo pass processes each winner log entry at most once in between two crashes, we can formally infer the same invariant that we observed for the algorithm with full-writes only:

> ∀   log sequence numbers $s \in$ stable log such that
>   the log has been processed for redo up to and including s :
>   ∀   pages p : ∀ transactions t : ∀ operations $o \in$ stable log :
>   (o belongs to t and refers to $p \wedge t$ is a winner $\wedge o \leq s$)
> $\Rightarrow o \in$ cached database

(2) The undo pass considers all loser actions in reverse chronological order. When it actually performs an undo step, reducing the affected page's sequence number by one guarantees that no loser action is skipped, and the reverse ordering in which these actions are considered is not affected either. When an undo action is suppressed because of the page-state test, the cached database must already contain the inverse action for the considered action (so that this pair has been reduced to "null"). If this holds for the stable database as well (because of a previous flush action), it is guaranteed that the undo is never repeated again. Otherwise, if the system crashes again before the restart completes or the page is flushed, the subsequent restart will correctly undo the action again.

These correctness arguments can be further formalized analogously to our above elaboration for the redo pass. Since the state testing during the undo pass is perfectly dual to that of the redo pass, we omit this additional formalization.

To illustrate the algorithm and especially its use of page-state testing with a concrete example, we reconsider the scenario of Figure 13.2. Figure 13.4 shows again all actions during normal operation and during the first and second restart; this time, however, we assume that all writes are physiological actions rather than physical full-writes. The actions during normal operation are, of course, identical to the earlier example (Figure 13.2) but listed again for self-containedness. In the restart part, we also list and explicitly mark redo and undo steps that are considered but not performed because the state testing indicates so.

The necessity and correcting effect of the page-state testing becomes obvious at several points. For example, both the first and the second restart consider redoing actions on page d, but those redo steps with sequence numbers less than or equal to the (stable) page sequence number 11 are suppressed. In Figure 13.4, the suppressed steps are denoted as "consider-redo" steps (as opposed to the actually performed "redo" steps). During the undo pass of the second restart, none of the considered undo steps except the one on page b is actually performed because the page sequence numbers indicate that the

Sequence number: action	Change of cached database [PageNo: SeqNo]	Change of stable database [PageNo: SeqNo]	Log entry added to log buffer [LogSeqNo: action]	Log entries added to stable log [LogSeqNo's]
1: begin(t_1)			1: begin(t_1)	
2: begin(t_2)			2: begin(t_2)	
3: write(a, t_1)	a: 3		3: write(a, t_1)	
4: begin(t_3)			4: begin(t_3)	
5: begin(t_4)			5: begin(t_4)	
6: write(b, t_3)	b: 6		6: write(b, t_3)	
7: write(c, t_2)	c: 7		7: write(c, t_2)	
8: write(d, t_1)	d: 8		8: write(d, t_1)	
9: commit(t_1)			9: commit(t_1)	1, 2, 3, 4, 5, 6, 7, 8, 9
10: flush(d)		d: 8		
11: write(d, t_3)	d: 11		11: write(d, t_3)	
12: begin(t_5)			12: begin(t_5)	
13: write(a, t_5)	a: 13		13: write(a, t_5)	
14: commit(t_3)			14: commit(t_3)	11, 12, 13, 14
15: flush(d)		d: 11		
16: write(d, t_4)	d: 16		16: write(d, t_4)	
17: write(e, t_2)	e: 17		17: write(e, t_2)	
18: write(b, t_5)	b: 18		18: write(b, t_5)	
19: flush(b)		b: 18		16, 17, 18
20: commit(t_4)			20: commit(t_4)	20
21: write(f, t_5)	f: 21		21: write(f, t_5)	
System crash				
Restart				
Analysis pass: losers = {t_2, t_5}				
redo(3)	a: 3			
consider-redo(6)	b: 18			
flush(a)		a: 3		
consider-redo(8)	d: 11			
consider-redo(11)	d: 11			
Second system crash				
Second restart				
Analysis pass: losers = {t_2, t_5}				
consider-redo(3)	a: 3			
consider-redo(6)	b: 18			
consider-redo(8)	d: 11			
consider-redo(11)	d: 11			
redo(16)	d: 16			
undo(18)	b: 17			
consider-undo(17)	e: 0			
consider-undo(13)	a: 3			
consider-undo(7)	c: 0			
Second restart complete: resume normal operation				

Figure 13.4 Example scenario for the simple three-pass recovery algorithm with physiological write actions.

corresponding original actions with sequence numbers 17, 13, and 7 were lost in the first crash. The only action that requires undo is the one with sequence number 18 on page b. After having performed the undo step, the page sequence number of b is set to $18 - 1 = 17$. Although there has never been an action with sequence number 17 on page b, the new page sequence number perfectly serves its purpose in that it indicates that action 18 is no longer present, whereas all actions on b up to 17 are included in the current page state.

13.3.3 Enhanced Algorithm: Log Truncation, Checkpoints, Redo Optimization

The simple three-pass recovery algorithm presented in the previous subsection has a number of fundamental drawbacks that give rise to severe performance bottlenecks: *Performance bottlenecks*

1. The analysis pass has to scan the entire stable log. This may be fairly long, equivalent to hours of server operation, and often only a short tail fraction, say, the last five minutes, contains loser transactions at all.

2. The redo pass has to scan the entire stable log. Again, if the log captures hours of operation, we would expect that most of the logged winner actions are already in the stable database because of flush actions.

3. The redo pass incurs many random I/Os to fetch pages from the stable database. Note that this cost arises even if the subsequent page-state test indicates that no redo step is necessary.

These bottlenecks affect the restart time after a crash and therefore reduce the system availability in a possibly dramatic manner. Recall from Section 12.1 that this compromises our most important design objective. In the following, we will further elaborate on the three-pass recovery algorithm to eliminate these bottlenecks. To this end we will introduce effective ways of *log truncation* to shorten the scan time for the stable log. Furthermore and most importantly, we will introduce periodic *checkpoints* that establish additional invariants between the cached database and the stable database so as to limit the fraction of the stable log that needs to be scanned at all. Finally, we will consider the *logging of flush actions* for further optimization of the redo pass with the goal of minimizing the number of random database I/Os during restart.

Log Truncation

Over time, the stable log collects a large number of log entries, some of which, we can infer, are no longer relevant regardless of when and how exactly the system crashes (as long as the stable database remains intact, which is our basic premise in this chapter). More specifically, we know that

- a log entry for page p with sequence number s is no longer needed for redo recovery if the page sequence number of p in the stable database is equal to s or higher,

- a log entry is needed for undo recovery only as long as the corresponding transaction is not yet completed.

Advancing the start of the stable log

All log entries that are no longer needed, neither for redo nor for undo, can be removed from the stable log as a form of garbage collection. However, it is not at all easy to implement this garbage collection on a log file without interfering too much with the concurrent sequential I/Os for appending new log entries. Therefore, we restrict the scope of the garbage collection to remove only entire prefixes of the stable log. The implementation then simply requires advancing the pointer to the start of the stable log, which is kept in a separate master record on stable storage. The new start pointer is chosen to be the maximum LSN such that all log entries with smaller sequence numbers are obsolete. This point is computed by taking the minimum value over the following "lower bounds" for the still essential log entries:

SystemRedoLSN

- For each cache resident and dirty page p, the sequence number of the oldest write action on p that was performed after the last flush action for p. This sequence number is called the *redo (log) sequence number* or *RedoLSN* of p. The minimum among the redo sequence numbers of the dirty cache pages is called the *system redo sequence number* or *SystemRedoLSN*.

OldestUndoLSN

- The sequence number of the oldest write action that belongs to an active transaction. This sequence number is called the *oldest undo (log) sequence number* or *OldestUndoLSN*.

The oldest undo sequence number can be computed easily by remembering, in memory, the sequence numbers of the "begin" log entries for all currently active and, therefore, potential loser transactions. Determining the redo sequence number of a page requires a small and extremely low-overhead extension of the cache manager: it remembers, in its bookkeeping data structures in memory, the sequence number of the first write action on a page after that page has been fetched into the cache. When a page is flushed but remains in the cache, this remembered sequence number is reset to "undefined," just as the page becomes "clean" again by the flush action. So this extension requires merely an additional sequence number field for each page frame of the cache.

Log truncation can occur at any arbitrary point, but in practice it is good enough to invoke it only periodically, say, every five or ten minutes. A log truncation is in effect once the master record has been updated on stable storage.

Subsequently, both the analysis pass and the redo pass are accelerated by scanning a shorter log. An inconvenient situation that can arise when a log truncation is attempted is the following. If the very first, that is, the very oldest, log entry in the stable log is still needed, then no truncation is possible, even if this first entry is immediately followed by a large number of obsolete entries. Such a "blocking" of the log truncation is unlikely to occur because of the oldest undo sequence number; this would only be possible if a transaction can remain active for the time frame of the entire stable log, typically hours. This is an unlikely situation, because truly long running activities such as workflows are not based on a single transaction. So the real troublemaker would be the oldest redo sequence number among the dirty pages in the cache. It is not very likely that it would be hours before a dirty page was flushed back to the stable database, but if the situation were so, there is a fairly simple remedy to enable the log truncation. At this point, a flush action should be enforced for the corresponding page, removing the page from the list of dirty pages. As a consequence, the minimum of the redo sequence numbers would then be advanced to the lowest redo sequence number among the remaining pages.

The overall procedure for log truncation is given by the pseudocode below.

```
log truncation ( ):
 OldestUndoLSN :=
  min {i|StableLog[i].TransId is in ActiveTrans};
 SystemRedoLSN := min {DatabaseCache[p].RedoLSN};
 OldestRedoPage := page p such that
  DatabaseCache[p].RedoLSN = SystemRedoLSN;
 NewStartPointer := min{OldestUndoLSN, SystemRedoLSN};
 OldStartPointer := MasterRecord.StartPointer;
 while OldStartPointer - NewStartPointer
   is not sufficiently large
 and SystemRedoLSN < OldestUndoLSN
 do
  flush (OldestRedoPage);
  SystemRedoLSN := min{DatabaseCache[p].RedoLSN};
  OldestRedoPage := page p such that
   DatabaseCache[p].RedoLSN = SystemRedoLSN;
  NewStartPointer := min{OldestUndoLSN, SystemRedoLSN};
 end /*while*/;
 MasterRecord.StartPointer := NewStartPointer;
```

Log truncation during normal operation

The correctness of the log truncation procedure follows directly from the garbage collection rule introduced in Section 12.4. A log truncation removes a subset of the log entries that can be eliminated according to the garbage collection rule. We do not consider a more formal statement or proof to be necessary here.

Log truncation for full-writes   If the stable log contains full-write log entries, then log truncation can be even more aggressive. As a full-write contains all prior write actions on the same page, such a log entry renders all preceding log entries obsolete as far as the redo steps for that page are concerned. It is sufficient to keep only the most recent after image for each page that has been updated by a winner transaction. Furthermore, our previous consideration on flush actions is still valid: no after image needs to be kept when the page has been flushed to the stable database after its most recent winner update.

Database safe   Both considerations together yield the result that, as far as redo recovery is concerned, the stable log can be minimized to contain at most one after image for each currently cache resident dirty page. Such a stable log can be implemented in an extremely compact manner: the name *database safe* has been proposed for it in the literature. Its size is on the same order as the server's database cache size, and if we keep the log entries for undo separately, the redo pass boils down to merely loading the database safe into the cache. Thus, we can obtain an extremely efficient restart with such an implementation.

The database safe approach is a special case of our general three-pass recovery algorithm, with redo logging being restricted to complete page after images. Managing the safe still requires continuous or periodic log truncation, based on tracking redo sequence numbers, as discussed above. The major drawback of the approach is that it seems to require a second stable log that holds before images for undo recovery. An alternative, where before images are held in the cache only (under the assumption of a no-steal cache replacement policy, see Chapter 12), has been worked out in the literature, and it is also possible to extend the method such that before images are appended to the safe as well so that a single stable log holds all physical log entries. In any case, however, using before images for undo recovery is inherently restricted to the page model where page-granularity concurrency control is required. Therefore, we do not further consider the special database safe approach in the rest of this chapter.

Combining physiological and physical log entries   Note that it is perfectly feasible for a log manager with physiological log entries to occasionally create full page after images and append them to the stable log, thus mixing physiological and physical log entries in the same log. This way the log manager can advance the RedoLSN of a critical page without depending on the cache manager to flush the page. This combined approach reconciles the advantages of physiological logging (lower log space consumption) with those of physical logging (more aggressive log truncation and faster redo) in a dynamically controllable manner. In the following, we will simply consider page after images as a special case of log entries, and will continue to focus on the more general notion of physiological log entries.

Periodic Checkpoints

Heavyweight checkpoint   We already mentioned that log truncation can be initiated continuously or periodically. We also explained that the cache manager can facilitate more effective log truncation by enforcing flush actions for dirty pages. A periodically invoked log truncation along with *flushing all dirty pages* to the stable database is known as a *checkpoint*. Because flushing all dirty pages incurs a substantial amount of additional work during normal operation, we refer to this specific variant as a *heavyweight checkpoint*. (As you can easily guess, we will later consider a lightweight variant.)

The effect of flushing all dirty cache pages back to the stable database is that all previous log entries are rendered obsolete at once, as far as redo recovery is concerned. Technically, the redo sequence numbers of all dirty cache pages are reset after the flushing is complete. Consequently, the oldest undo sequence number is the limiting factor in the log truncation; all log entries up to that point are discarded. If it happens that no transaction is active at the time the checkpoint is taken, then the stable log can even be completely reinitialized as the empty set. But this special situation would be rather exceptional.

Acceleration of the redo pass

Once a checkpoint is taken, the redo pass after a subsequent crash can safely ignore all log entries that are older than the checkpoint. In fact, it does not need to scan the part of the stable log that precedes the most recent checkpoint. To take this additional advantage, however, we need to be able to determine the position in the stable log when the checkpoint occurred. This can be achieved easily by creating a special *checkpoint log entry* as a marker in the log and forcing this entry to the stable log when the checkpointing activity, especially the flushing of dirty pages, is complete. Then the sequence number of the checkpoint can be stored in the master record on stable storage, so that after a crash, the most recent checkpoint log entry can be located in the stable log and forms the starting point of the redo pass.

Checkpoint log entries

So far a checkpoint benefits only the redo pass of the recovery algorithm. The undo pass is rather uncritical with regard to restart performance in that it is typically based on the most recent tail of the stable log, and it may even skip major parts of the log file in its backward reading scan when loser log entries are sufficiently sparse. The analysis pass, however, would then form the major bottleneck, as it still has to scan the entire stable log. To overcome this bottleneck, additional bookkeeping efforts can be included in the checkpoint activity so that the analysis pass does not need to consider the part of the log that precedes the most recent checkpoint. The required information for this purpose is simply a list of transactions that are active at the time of the checkpoint. This list serves to initialize a potential loser list, which is then brought up-to-date in the analysis pass by scanning the part of the log that follows the checkpoint.

Acceleration of the analysis pass

At the end of the analysis pass, we have an accurate list of loser transactions. We should note, however, that the undo pass later also needs a pointer to the last log entry for each of these loser transactions. If a loser transaction has at least one log entry between the most recent checkpoint and the end of the log, then the correct value for the LastSeqNo field in the "losers" list is found by the analysis pass's log scan. If, however, the last log entry of a loser

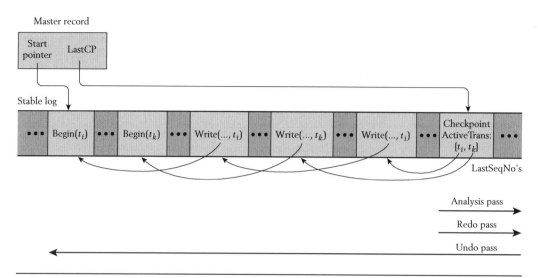

Figure 13.5 Heavyweight checkpoints.

transaction lies in the part of the log that precedes the checkpoint, then we need another way of deriving this information. The solution is to include in our additional bookkeeping at the time of the checkpoint the last log entry of each potential loser transaction as of that time. These values initialize the LastSeqNo fields and are brought up-to-date by the analysis pass at no extra cost. A final issue to be resolved is where to store this additional bookkeeping information. Since its size is bounded by the maximum number of concurrently active transactions, we are dealing with a relatively small, compact structure. It is therefore easy to include it in the checkpoint log entry that is written to the stable log anyway. (Alternatively, we could also use the master record for this purpose.)

The major aspects of this notion of heavyweight checkpoints are illustrated in Figure 13.5. The figure shows especially the portions of the stable log that are now relevant for the three passes during restart. Detailed pseudocode for the activities during a checkpoint and the resulting modifications of the analysis pass and redo pass are given below. Note that the undo pass is in no way affected by the presence of checkpoints.

Pseudocode for heavyweight checkpoint

```
checkpoint ( ):
  for each p in DatabaseCache do
    if DatabaseCache[p].Status = dirty
    then flush (p);
    end /*if*/;
  end /*for*/;
  logentry.ActionType := checkpoint;
```

```
logentry.ActiveTrans :=
 ActiveTrans (as maintained in memory);
logentry.LogSeqNo := new sequence number;
LogBuffer += logentry;
force ( );
MasterRecord.LastCP := logentry.LogSeqNo;

analysis pass ( ) returns losers:
 cp := MasterRecord.LastCP;
 losers := StableLog[cp].ActiveTrans;
 max := LogSeqNo of most recent log entry in StableLog;
 for i := cp to max do
  case StableLog[i].ActionType:

    ⋮
   maintenance of losers
     as in the algorithm without checkpoints

    ⋮
  end /*case*/;
 end /*for*/;

redo pass ( ):
 cp := MasterRecord.LastCP;
 max := LogSeqNo of most recent log entry in StableLog;
 for i := cp to max do

   ⋮
  page-state testing and redo steps
    as in the algorithm without checkpoints

   ⋮
 end /*for*/;
```

Analysis pass with heavyweight checkpoint

Redo pass with heavyweight checkpoint

We illustrate the algorithm with our previous scenario (first introduced in Figure 13.2). The table in Figure 13.6 shows the differences that result from the existence of a checkpoint (at an arbitrarily chosen point) in boldface type. For self-containedness the full scenario before the crash is given again, but we now assume that the first restart completes successfully.

Note that the flush action for page *d* with sequence number 16 is stated only as a "leftover" from the original scenario. It is meaningless and would no longer be initiated by the cache manager at this point, because the page has already been flushed by the preceding checkpoint and is still "clean" at the point of sequence number 16.

Sequence number: action	Change of cached database [PageNo: SeqNo]	Change of stable database [PageNo: SeqNo]	Log entry added to log buffer [LogSeqNo: action]	Log entries added to stable log [LogSeqNo's]
1: begin(t_1)			1: begin(t_1)	
2: begin(t_2)			2: begin(t_2)	
3: write(a, t_1)	a: 3		3: write(a, t_1)	
4: begin(t_3)			4: begin(t_3)	
5: begin(t_4)			5: begin(t_4)	
6: write(b, t_3)	b: 6		6: write(b, t_3)	
7: write(c, t_2)	c: 7		7: write(c, t_2)	
8: write(d, t_1)	d: 8		8: write(d, t_1)	
9: commit(t_1)			9: commit(t_1)	1, 2, 3, 4, 5, 6, 7, 8, 9
10: flush(d)		d: 8		
11: write(d, t_3)	d: 11		11: write(d, t_3)	
12: begin(t_5)			12: begin(t_5)	
13: write(a, t_5)	a: 13		13: write(a, t_5)	
14: checkpoint		a: 13, b: 6, c: 7, d: 11	14: CP ActiveTrans: {t_2, t_3, t_4, t_5}	11, 12, 13 14
15: commit(t_3)			15: commit(t_3)	15
16: [flush(d)]		d: 11		
17: write(d, t_4)	d: 17		17: write(d, t_4)	
18: write(e, t_2)	e: 18		18: write(e, t_2)	
19: write(b, t_5)	b: 19		19: write(b, t_5)	
20: flush(b)		b: 19		17, 18, 19
21: commit(t_4)			21: commit(t_4)	21
22: write(f, t_5)	f: 22		22: write(f, t_5)	
System crash				
Restart				
Analysis pass: losers = {t_2, t_5}				
redo(17)	d: 17			
undo(19)	b: 18			
consider-undo(18)	e: 0			
undo(13)	a: 12			
undo(7)	c: 6			
Restart complete: resume normal operation				

Figure 13.6 Example scenario for the simple three-pass recovery algorithm with physiological write actions and heavyweight checkpoints.

Some particularly noteworthy points about the example scenario are

- the ordering of the individual steps at the checkpoint: first force the log buffer if dictated by the undo rule, then flush the dirty pages, and finally, force the checkpoint log entry and update the master record (not shown in the example);

- the resulting effect that the redo pass is shortened drastically;
- the side effect that the undo pass has to perform more work because the stable database contains more loser actions.

The latter point may sound more spectacular than it really is. In typical situations, the increase in the number of undo steps that need to be performed should be rather negligible. In fact, we would not expect many loser actions preceding the most recent checkpoint.

The frequency at which checkpoints should be taken is usually a tuning parameter of the data server. Frequent checkpoints typically yield shorter upper bounds for the restart time, whereas less frequent checkpoints reduce the overhead during normal operation. This tuning problem can be expressed as an optimization issue, where the goal could be to maximize the transaction throughput over multiple periods of normal operation and restart. Mathematical approaches along these lines can be found in the literature (see the Bibliographic Notes at the end of this chapter). In practice, however, the checkpoint frequency is chosen based on rules of thumb, like initiating a checkpoint at least once every five minutes but not more often than once a minute. Fine-tuning within this range is usually a matter of trial and error. We will soon show, however, that the tuning problem is less of an issue with a different, more lightweight notion of checkpoints.

As a final remark, we point out that checkpoints are "merely" an optimization feature to shorten the restart time. They should not be confused with the different notion of checkpoints that is sometimes used for storing the state of long-running computations to limit the amount of lost work upon a failure. In this case, checkpoints are obviously a fundamental prerequisite for achieving the desired effect. We will see the difference more clearly when we next "relax" the activity of a checkpoint to a mere bookkeeping event without direct impact on the stable database.

Lightweight Checkpoints

The major drawback of a heavyweight checkpoint lies in its flushing of all dirty cache pages. With the general trend of increasing cache sizes, the number of affected pages may be fairly large so that such a checkpoint incurs a significant burst of disk I/O load. Because of contention for disk I/O time, regular page fetches may then end up being delayed in the disk I/O queue, so that the response time of transactions is degraded whenever a checkpoint is in progress.

Lightweight checkpoint

A better approach that minimizes the impact of flush actions on the performance of page fetches is to invoke flush actions continuously by a low-priority background process rather than creating periodic load bursts. Such a background process is referred to as a *write-behind daemon* by various products. In addition to smoothing out the disk I/O load over an extended time period and

Write-behind daemon

exploiting disk idle periods, it also offers a better potential for I/O batching and seek-time optimizations, for example, by combining flush actions with fetch actions for pages on the same disk track or cylinder.

Flushing dirty pages is the decisive step in reducing the amount of work during the redo pass. However, to fully exploit this opportunity, the redo pass must have some information that tells which pages require redo steps and from which LSN(s) the redo should start. Otherwise, the redo pass would still have to fetch every page for which it encounters a winner log entry, often only to find that no redo is necessary. Not having to perform some redo steps is an important cost savings, but the savings would be substantially higher if we could avoid fetching such pages from the database in the first place. The solution is to include certain bookkeeping information about dirty pages and their redo sequence numbers in the stable log, and the best way of doing this is to put this information into a checkpoint log entry. This leads us directly to the notion of a *lightweight checkpoint*: without enforced flush actions, but with additional bookkeeping information. In the literature, this type of checkpoint is also referred to by the historical name *fuzzy checkpoint*, in contrast to a "sharp" heavyweight checkpoint, but these terms can easily be misinterpreted. We will see that there is nothing fuzzy about the concept of a lightweight checkpoint, and we will avoid the historical terminology.

Dirty page list   The information about dirty pages that is needed to drive the redo pass is similar to what we considered for log truncation in general. Our goal is to limit the portion of the stable log that precedes the most recent checkpoint and needs to be considered for redo. This can be determined by recording in the checkpoint log entry

- the set of cached pages that are dirty at that time and
- for each such page, the sequence number of the oldest write action that followed the page's most recent flush action (or its last fetch action if no flush action took place in the meantime).

The set of dirty pages is commonly referred to as the *dirty page list*, and the relevant LSNs that we need to record are exactly what we coined the redo sequence number of these pages when we discussed log truncation.

The minimum among the redo sequence numbers in the dirty page list gives us the starting point of the redo pass. Furthermore, when we encounter a winner log entry for a page of the dirty page list in the part of the stable log that precedes the most recent checkpoint, we can check if the action to be redone is already in the stable database so that the page does not have to be fetched at all at this point. We may still fetch some pages unnecessarily, namely, if a page has been flushed after the most recent checkpoint. With the information available to us so far, it is impossible to determine this situation without fetching the page. However, once we have fetched a page for the first time during the redo pass, we know its page sequence number and can then use that number as the page's redo sequence number. A more far-reaching extension based on additional log entries is discussed further below.

Thus, lightweight checkpoints accelerate the redo pass without the disadvantage of having to flush all dirty pages upon a checkpoint. They do not incur much overhead that could affect the performance of ongoing transactions. Therefore, there is no longer a need for careful tuning of the checkpoint frequency. Lightweight checkpoints can be initiated in almost arbitrarily short intervals; in practice, taking a checkpoint once every minute is usually sufficiently frequent. As for the analysis pass and undo pass, a lightweight checkpoint is no different from a heavyweight checkpoint. In fact these two passes are usually not critical with regard to restart time. Note, however, that the fact that lightweight checkpoints can be taken more frequently without any disadvantages also shortens the analysis pass.

Analysis pass reconsidered

In addition, the analysis pass can contribute to another efficiency gain for the redo pass by enhancing the information about dirty pages. Namely, it can complete the dirty page list, starting with the list as of the most recent checkpoint and then adding pages that potentially require redo steps during its forward scanning of the log tail. Then, at the end of the analysis pass, we know the full set, or possibly a superset, of the pages that need to be accessed during the redo pass. Thus, we are in a position to asynchronously prefetch pages from the stable database shortly before they are needed by a redo step.

I/O optimization for fetching dirty pages

But even better optimizations are possible. Since the order in which redo steps are performed matters only if the same page is affected, we can sort the dirty page list and process pages in an order that minimizes the disk seek time. This savings can be substantial, given that we would otherwise perform random disk I/Os on the database. A prerequisite for this optimization, however, is that the relevant log entries can be kept in memory for the time period between reading them from the stable log and fetching the corresponding page to apply the redo steps. Otherwise, we would have to scan the stable log more than once during the redo pass. If memory is too small to keep all relevant log entries for the required period, this I/O optimization can still be performed for groups of pages that occur in a certain fraction of the stable log. As far as that memory demand is concerned, physiological log entries have a clear advantage over complete page after images because of their smaller size. On the other hand, if a database administrator is particularly concerned about restart time, giving extra memory to the system during the restart would be very beneficial. For example, the administrator could suspend other operating system and application processes, or defer their start upon rebooting. This temporarily obtains additional memory for the database cache, which will be returned to the operating system when the redo pass is complete.

As for the undo pass, the amount of work there depends mostly on the length of transactions (i.e., their number of actions) and the multiprogramming level (i.e., the maximum number of concurrent transactions), as the latter is an upper bound for the number of loser transactions. None of these factors can be influenced by whatever notion of checkpoint is employed.

Undo pass reconsidered

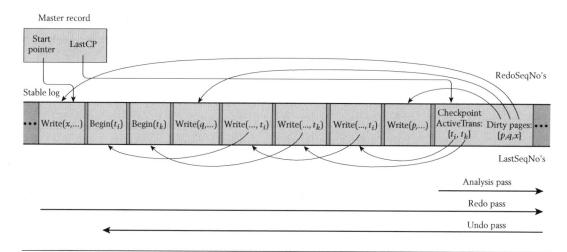

Figure 13.7 Lightweight checkpoints.

The major aspects of lightweight checkpoints are illustrated in Figure 13.7. As in the illustration of heavyweight checkpoints, we again highlight the portions of the stable log that are relevant for the three passes during restart. Detailed pseudocode for the activities during a checkpoint and the resulting modifications of the analysis pass and redo pass (without the additional I/O optimization) are given below.

Pseudocode for a lightweight checkpoint

```
checkpoint ( ):
  DirtyPages := empty;
  for each p in DatabaseCache do
    if DatabaseCache[p].Status = dirty
    then
      DirtyPages += p;
      DirtyPages[p].RedoSeqNo :=
        DatabaseCache[p].RedoLSN;
    end /*if*/;
  end /*for*/;
  logentry.ActionType := checkpoint;
  logentry.ActiveTrans :=
    ActiveTrans (as maintained in memory);
  logentry.DirtyPages := DirtyPages;
  logentry.LogSeqNo := new sequence number;
  LogBuffer += logentry;
  force ( );
  MasterRecord.LastCP := logentry.LogSeqNo;
```

Analysis pass with lightweight checkpoint

```
analysis pass ( ) returns losers, DirtyPages:
  cp := MasterRecord.LastCP;
```

```
losers := StableLog[cp].ActiveTrans;
DirtyPages := StableLog[cp].DirtyPages;
max := LogSeqNo of most recent log entry in StableLog;
for i := cp to max do
 case StableLog[i].ActionType:

   ⋮
 maintenance of losers
   as in the algorithm without checkpoints

   ⋮
 end /*case*/;
 if StableLog[i].ActionType = write or full-write
  and StableLog[i].PageNo not in DirtyPages
 then
  DirtyPages += StableLog[i].PageNo;
  DirtyPages[StableLog[i].PageNo].RedoSeqNo := i;
 end /*if*/;
end /*for*/;
```

```
redo pass ( ):
 cp := MasterRecord.LastCP;
 SystemRedoLSN := min{cp.DirtyPages[p].RedoSeqNo};
 max := LogSeqNo of most recent log entry in StableLog;
 for i := SystemRedoLSN to max do
  if StableLog[i].ActionType = write or full-write
   and StableLog[i].TransId not in losers
  then
   pageno := StableLog[i].PageNo;
   if pageno in DirtyPages
    and i >= DirtyPages[pageno].RedoSeqNo
   then
    fetch (pageno);
    if DatabaseCache[pageno].PageSeqNo < i
    then
     read and write (pageno)
      according to StableLog[i].RedoInfo;
     DatabaseCache[pageno].PageSeqNo := i;
    else
     DirtyPages[pageno].RedoSeqNo :=
      DatabaseCache[pageno].PageSeqNo + 1;
    end /*if*/;
   end /*if*/;
  end /*if*/;
 end /*for*/;
```

*Redo pass with
lightweight
checkpoint*

We treat the checkpoint log entry as a single entry for simplicity, but an implementation could actually split the entry into separate begin-checkpoint and end-checkpoint log entries with the possibly long DirtyPageList and the ActiveTransactionList written in multiple pieces between the two boundary-marking log entries. Then, the checkpoint would be considered complete when the "end-checkpoint" entry is written to the stable log, but the start pointer in the master record should point to the begin-checkpoint entry. Such details of how checkpoints are taken are, however, more a matter of implementation convenience, with virtually no impact on the overall recovery algorithm.

We illustrate the recovery algorithm once more with our example scenario. As in the previous example with heavyweight checkpoints, we again assume that the first restart completes successfully. The table in Figure 13.8 shows the differences that result from taking a lightweight checkpoint (at the same point as the heavyweight checkpoint in the previous Figure 13.6) in boldface type.

The most important point to be noted in this scenario is that the redo pass can skip the redo log entry with sequence number 8 without fetching the affected page d from the database at all.

Flush Log Entries

As already mentioned, the dirty page list that is recorded in a lightweight check-point still does not perfectly prevent us from unnecessarily fetching database pages during the redo pass. The case where this can arise is when a page is flushed after the most recent checkpoint. If the page also occurs in the check-point's dirty page list, then the page's redo sequence number must have been encountered before the redo pass crosses the checkpoint log entry, and the page must have been fetched at this point. Once the page has been fetched, its page sequence number tells us the actual point from which redo steps must be performed. So there is nothing to optimize further in this case.

The interesting case, on the other hand, is when a page is not included in the checkpoint's dirty page list but is updated and later flushed at one or more points after the checkpoint. To avoid having to fetch such a page at least once to determine its page sequence number, additional information can be placed into the stable log. If we know the sequence numbers of the page's flush actions or, more specifically, the page's last flush action before the crash, we can skip all log entries for that page with sequence numbers smaller than the one of its last flush action. The straightforward implementation of this idea is also to create log entries for flush actions and append them to the log (buffer) just like the other log entries. Since these log entries are very small and do not require any forced log I/Os, this additional logging is indeed a viable, low-overhead solution. It has been adopted by at least one commercial database system.

During restart, flush log entries are exploited in the analysis pass to improve the quality of the information in the dirty page list. The pseudocode for this

Sequence number: action	Change of cached database [PageNo: SeqNo]	Change of stable database [PageNo: SeqNo]	Log entry added to log buffer [LogSeqNo: action]	Log entries added to stable log [LogSeqNo's]
1: begin(t_1)			1: begin(t_1)	
2: begin(t_2)			2: begin(t_2)	
3: write(a, t_1)	a: 3		3: write(a, t_1)	
4: begin(t_3)			4: begin(t_3)	
5: begin(t_4)			5: begin(t_4)	
6: write(b, t_3)	b: 6		6: write(b, t_3)	
7: write(c, t_2)	c: 7		7: write(c, t_2)	
8: write(d, t_1)	d: 8		8: write(d, t_1)	
9: commit(t_1)			9: commit(t_1)	1, 2, 3, 4, 5, 6, 7, 8, 9
10: flush(d)		d: 8		
11: write(d, t_3)	d: 11		11: write(d, t_3)	
12: begin(t_5)			12: begin(t_5)	
13: write(a, t_5)	a: 13		13: write(a, t_5)	
14: checkpoint			14: CP DirtyPages: {a, b, c, d} RedoLSNs: a: 3, b: 6, c: 7, d: 11 ActiveTrans: {t_2, t_3, t_4, t_5}	11, 12, 13, 14
15: commit(t_3)			15: commit(t_3)	15
16: flush(d)		d: 11		
17: write(d, t_4)	d: 17		17: write(d, t_4)	
18: write(e, t_2)	e: 18		18: write(e, t_2)	
19: write(b, t_5)	b: 19		19: write(b, t_5)	
20: flush(b)		b: 19		17, 18, 19
21: commit(t_4)			21: commit(t_4)	21
22: write(f, t_5)	f: 22		22: write(f, t_5)	
System crash				
Restart				
Analysis pass: losers = {t_2, t_5} **DirtyPages = {a, b, c, d, e}** **RedoLSNs: a: 3, b: 6, c: 7, d: 11, e: 18**				
redo(3)	a: 3			
consider-redo(6)	b: 19			
skip-redo(8)				
consider-redo(11)	d: 11			
redo(17)	d: 17			
undo(19)	b: 18			
consider-undo(18)	e: 0			
consider-undo(13)	a: 3			
consider-undo(7)	c: 0			
Restart complete: resume normal operation				

Figure 13.8 Example scenario for the simple three-pass recovery algorithm with physiological write actions and lightweight checkpoints.

additional optimization is given below. The redo pass does not require any modification to benefit from the improved dirty page list.

Analysis pass with lightweight checkpoint and flush log entries

```
analysis pass ( ) returns losers, DirtyPages:
 cp := MasterRecord.LastCP;
 losers := StableLog[cp].ActiveTrans;
 DirtyPages := StableLog[cp].DirtyPages;
 max := LogSeqNo of most recent log entry in StableLog;
 for i := cp to max do
  case StableLog[i].ActionType:
    ⋮
   maintenance of "losers"
     as in the algorithm without checkpoints
    ⋮
   end /*case*/;
   if StableLog[i].ActionType = write or full-write
    and StableLog[i].PageNo not in DirtyPages
   then
    DirtyPages += StableLog[i].PageNo;
    DirtyPages[StableLog[i].PageNo].RedoSeqNo := i;
   end /*if*/;
   if StableLog[i].ActionType = flush
   then
    DirtyPages -= StableLog[i].PageNo;
   end /*if*/;
  end /*for*/;
```

The additional benefit of flush action logging is illustrated by our example scenario in Figure 13.9, in which boldface type highlights the differences in merely using lightweight checkpoints.

The point to be noted here is that the updated dirty page list after the analysis pass now contains a higher redo sequence number for page *d*, so that another log entry, the one with sequence number 11, can be skipped during the redo pass. Also, page *b* is removed from the dirty page list so that it does not have to be considered at all during the redo pass. In general, this kind of situation pays off most. In the particular example, however, the last update on page *b* is a loser update so that the page must be fetched during the undo pass anyway. Note, however, that this is indeed a particularity of the example and not necessarily a frequent case.

We complete this subsection by considering again the correctness of the recovery algorithm. At this point we benefit from our approach of incrementally introducing additional features. It suffices to show that the extensions of the enhanced three-pass algorithm do not affect the behavior of the simple three-pass algorithm in an essential way.

Sequence number: action	Change of cached database [PageNo: SeqNo]	Change of stable database [PageNo: SeqNo]	Log entry added to log buffer [LogSeqNo: action]	Log entries added to stable log [LogSeqNo's]
1: begin(t_1)			1: begin(t_1)	
2: begin(t_2)			2: begin(t_2)	
3: write(a, t_1)	a: 3		3: write(a, t_1)	
4: begin(t_3)			4: begin(t_3)	
5: begin(t_4)			5: begin(t_4)	
6: write(b, t_3)	b: 6		6: write(b, t_3)	
7: write(c, t_2)	c: 7		7: write(c, t_2)	
8: write(d, t_1)	d: 8		8: write(d, t_1)	
9: commit(t_1)			9: commit(t_1)	1, 2, 3, 4, 5, 6, 7, 8, 9
10: flush(d)		d: 8	**10: flush(d)**	
11: write(d, t_3)	d: 11		11: write(d, t_3)	
12: begin(t_5)			12: begin(t_5)	
13: write(a, t_5)	a: 13		13: write(a, t_5)	
14: checkpoint			14: CP DirtyPages: $\{a, b, c, d\}$ RedoLSNs: a: 3, b: 6, c: 7, d: 11 ActiveTrans: $\{t_2, t_3, t_4, t_5\}$	10, 11, 12, 13, 14
15: commit(t_3)			15: commit(t_3)	15
16: flush(d)		d: 11	**16: flush(d)**	
17: write(d, t_4)	d: 17		17: write(d, t_4)	
18: write(e, t_2)	e: 18		18: write(e, t_2)	
19: write(b, t_5)	b: 19		19: write(b, t_5)	
20: flush(b)		b: 19	**20: flush(b)**	16, 17, 18, 19
21: commit(t_4)			21: commit(t_4)	20, 21
22: write(f, t_5)	f: 22		22: write(f, t_5)	
System crash				
Restart				
Analysis pass: losers = $\{t_2, t_5\}$ **DirtyPages = {a, c, d, e}** **RedoLSNs: a: 3, c: 7, d: 17, e: 18**				
redo(3)	a: 3			
consider-redo(6)	b: 19			
skip-redo(8)				
skip-redo(11)				
redo(17)	d: 17			
undo(19)	b: 18			
consider-undo(18)	e: 0			
consider-undo(13)	a: 3			
consider-undo(7)	c: 0			
Restart complete: resume normal operation				

Figure 13.9 Example scenario for the simple three-pass recovery algorithm with physiological write actions, lightweight checkpoints, and flush action logging.

THEOREM 13.4

Correctness of the enhanced three-pass algorithm

Extending the simple three-pass recovery algorithm with log truncation, heavyweight or lightweight checkpoints, and flush action logging (or any subset of these features) preserves the correctness of the crash recovery.

Proof

First we verify that the log truncation observes the garbage collection rule; so we do not discard any essential log entries prematurely. It is straightforward to realize that the log truncation retains all log entries of losers and also all winner log entries that correspond to writes that are not yet in the stable database. The latter is ensured as the redo sequence numbers of the cached pages reflect the oldest corresponding write that is not yet in the stable database at the time of the truncation.

The optimizations from checkpointing and flush log entries affect the analysis pass and the redo pass. Since the analysis pass determines losers (and then infers winners implicitly) and starts with the active transactions as of the checkpoint time, it is sufficient for correct analysis to consider only the transaction begins and terminations that follow the checkpoint.

Finally, the correctness of the redo pass follows immediately from the observation that only such log entries are skipped for which we know that the corresponding writes are already in the stable database. This argument holds for all log entries that precede a page's redo sequence number (or the last checkpoint itself if heavyweight checkpointing is in effect); and this information can be inferred either from the checkpoint log entry, from the page's sequence number after reading it from the stable database during recovery, or from a flush log entry. Any one of these three possibilities provides correct information. In formal terms, the invariant during the redo pass that makes the redo optimizations feasible is

$$\forall \quad \text{pages } p : \forall \text{ operations } o \in \text{stable log} :$$
$$(o \text{ refers to } p \ \wedge \ (p \notin \text{DirtyPages} \ \vee \ o < \text{DirtyPages}[p].\text{RedoSeqNo}))$$
$$\Rightarrow o \in \text{stable database}$$

provided that flush log entries have been created and analyzed before the redo pass starts. Without flush log entries, the invariant is a bit weaker in that the term $p \notin \text{DirtyPages}$ is missing, so that we may have more uncertainty about whether an operation is already in the stable database. In this case, we can still view reading the page from the stable database and looking up its sequence number as if the DirtyPages information were brought more up-to-date during recovery. So conceptually the above formula holds for all the discussed variants of redo optimizations.

13.3.4 **The Complete Algorithm: Handling Transaction Aborts and Undo Completion**

So far we have considered only two classes of transactions: committed ones and those that were left incomplete by the crash. However, a third class that a complete algorithm must be able to handle is that of transactions aborted and rolled back during normal operation. In this subsection we discuss how to incorporate such transactions. In addition, we reconsider and solve the related problem, pointed out in the discussion of log truncation, that loser transactions can prevent log truncation even after the restart is complete.

Handling Transaction Aborts

The seemingly most straightforward, but as it turns out rather naive, approach would be to treat aborted transactions as loser transactions. Superficially, it seems that this would allow us to apply the three-pass recovery algorithm without any changes at all. However, such an approach would have drastic implications:

Aborted transactions treated as losers

- First, to determine all "loser" transactions in this extended sense would now require that the analysis pass has to read the entire log rather than restricting itself to the log tail following the most recent checkpoint. Even worse, there is no longer an easy way of truncating the log at all, once we view all aborted transactions as relevant for the undo pass.

- Second, performing undo steps for aborted transactions leads to severe problems, as it is quite different from the undo of incomplete transactions. The reason is that it is now possible that a "loser" transaction precedes a committed transaction in the history (and the serialization order), whereas we could so far build on the invariant that all incomplete transactions follow all committed ones.

Whereas the first problem is "only" a matter of inefficiency, the second one endangers the correctness of the recovery algorithm. To see this problem more clearly, consider the scenario given in Figure 13.10, which is also shown in pictorial form in Figure 13.11. To keep the example simple, we assume that no checkpoints occur and flush action logging is not in effect.

The problematic point is when the undo pass encounters the log entry with sequence number 5 that belongs to the aborted transaction t_2. Executing an undo step for this action at this point is incorrect because we would then have the action sequence

Incorrect handling of aborted transactions

$$\dots 5 : \text{write}(a, t_2) \dots 8 : \text{write}(a, t_3) \dots \text{write}^{-1}(a, t_2)$$

where a winner action for page a lies between the loser action and the

Sequence number: action	Change of cached database [PageNo: SeqNo]	Change of stable database [PageNo: SeqNo]	Log entry added to log buffer [LogSeqNo: action]	Log entries added to stable log [LogSeqNo's]
1: begin(t_1)			1: begin(t_1)	
2: write(a, t_1)	a: 2		2: write(a, t_1)	
3: commit(t_1)			3: commit(t_1)	1, 2, 3
4: begin(t_2)			4: begin(t_2)	
5: write(a, t_2)	a: 5		5: write(a, t_2)	
6: abort(t_2)			6: abort(t_2)	4, 5, 6
7: begin(t_3)			7: begin(t_3)	
8: write(a, t_3)	a: 8		8: write(a, t_3)	
9: commit(t_3)			9: commit(t_3)	7, 8, 9
10: begin(t_4)			10: begin(t_4)	
11: write(b, t_4)	b: 11		11: write(b, t_4)	
12: write(a, t_4)	a: 12		12: write(a, t_4)	
13: flush(a)		a: 12		10, 11, 12
System crash				
Restart				
Analysis pass: losers = {t_2, t_4}				
consider-redo(2)	a: 12			
consider-redo(8)	a: 12			
undo(12)	a: 11			
consider-undo(11)	b: 0			
undo(5)	a: 4			

Figure 13.10 Example scenario for the problem caused by aborted transactions.

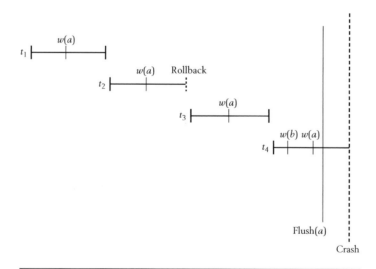

Figure 13.11 Pictorial overview of the "abort problem" scenario.

corresponding inverse action. As these actions are in general not commutative, this sequence cannot be reduced to the winner action alone. In other words, we would violate the equivalence to a history that contains only the winner transactions in their original serialization order. This problem is fundamental. Note that it cannot be eliminated by performing the undo pass before the redo pass, which may be superficially viewed as a last resort. In the example, this would not change anything about the nonreducible action sequence shown above, since page a has been flushed right before the crash. But it would create additional, even more bizarre problems with regard to the page-state testing. As the undo step for the "loser" action 5 should decrease the page sequence number, setting it to 4, a redo pass after the undo pass would be misguided to erroneously redo again the winner action 8. If this winner action is not idempotent, then the resulting state of the page is clearly incorrect.

A similar, yet more subtle problem with nonidempotence also arises with the undo step for the aborted transaction itself. Since the transaction was aborted and rolled back during normal operation, its action with sequence number 5 has already been undone by means of an inverse action before the crash and, most importantly, even before the subsequent winner transaction t_3 started. Since the page was flushed later on, the effect of inverting action 5 is already present in the page state after the crash. Then undoing action 5 again by invoking the inverse action a second time results in an incorrect page state unless we make very restrictive assumptions on idempotence.

The latter observation points the way to solving our problem with transaction aborts. Whenever a rollback is completed during normal operation, we can actually view an aborted transaction as a winner, as its total effect is equivalent to a null action or an empty transaction at this point. All we have to do is to ensure that this effect is not modified in retrospect by the steps of the crash recovery.

Aborted transactions are winners

By far the simplest approach to guarantee that the recovery algorithm does not introduce additional, unwanted effects is to *expand* the aborted transaction by making its inverse actions explicit. This is the same approach that we introduced in Chapter 11 for correctness reasoning on transaction recovery; now we use it to revise our crash recovery algorithm. Once the inverse actions during a rollback are explicit "first-class citizens," it is perfectly logical that they should be logged as well. So we assume that each inverse action creates a log entry in the log buffer. Then, when the rollback is completed, the log buffer is forced just as if the transaction were committed.

Note that there is no real need to distinguish the log entries for inverse actions from those for regular write actions. For better illustration, however, we will refer to them as *compensation log entries*, abbreviated as CLEs, and we will indicate them as a new action type compensation in the log entry. This distinction will also turn out to be useful later when we consider the redo-history paradigm, and especially for object model recovery.

Compensation log entries

The elegance of this solution is underlined by the fact that the only change in our algorithm affects the steps during normal operation, more specifically, only the algorithm for transaction rollbacks that we have not given so far anyway. Pseudocode for transaction rollbacks is given below. Note that it requires a forced log I/O upon completing a rollback. However, given that transaction aborts should be infrequent if not exceptional, these I/Os should not present any significant performance problem. In addition, the group commit technique is applicable here, so that log entries for an aborted transaction can be effectively piggybacked on the forced log I/O for a batch of committed transactions.

```
abort (transid):
 logentry :=
  ActiveTrans[transid].LastSeqNo;
 while logentry is not nil and
  logentry.ActionType = write or full-write
 do
  newlogentry.LogSeqNo := new sequence number;
  newlogentry.ActionType := compensation;
  newlogentry.PreviousSeqNo :=
   ActiveTrans[transid].LastSeqNo;
  newlogentry.RedoInfo :=
   inverse action of the action in logentry;
  newlogentry.UndoInfo :=
   inverse action of the inverse action
   of the action in logentry;
  ActiveTrans[transid].LastSeqNo :=
   newlogentry.LogSeqNo;
  LogBuffer += newlogentry;
  write (logentry.PageNo)
   according to logentry.UndoInfo;
  logentry := logentry.PreviousSeqNo;
 end /*while*/
 newlogentry.LogSeqNo := new sequence number;
 newlogentry.ActionType := rollback;
 newlogentry.TransId := transid;
 newlogentry.PreviousSeqNo :=
  ActiveTrans[transid].LastSeqNo;
 LogBuffer += newlogentry;
 ActiveTrans -= transid;
 force ( );
```

Handling of a crash during transaction rollback

A situation that may require additional thought is when a transaction has started to roll back during normal operation and this rollback is interrupted and left incomplete by a crash. However, by our approach of treating the rollback itself as an expansion of the transaction, we can consider the transaction as if it were a to-be-committed transaction that is interrupted and turned into a loser. Thus, this case is in no way different from our general handling of loser transactions.

The uniformity and resulting simplicity of handling transaction aborts more or less like transaction commits is illustrated by applying the complete algorithm to our previous example scenario of Figure 13.10. To make it more interesting, we now assume that transaction t_4 has initiated but not yet completed its rollback before the crash. The table in Figure 13.12 illustrates the

Sequence number: action	Change of cached database [PageNo: SeqNo]	Change of stable database [PageNo: SeqNo]	Log entry added to log buffer [LogSeqNo: action]	Log entries added to stable log [LogSeqNo's]
1: begin(t_1)			1: begin(t_1)	
2: write(a, t_1)	a: 2		2: write(a, t_1)	
3: commit(t_1)			3: commit(t_1)	1, 2, 3
4: begin(t_2)			4: begin(t_2)	
5: write(a, t_2)	a: 5		5: write(a, t_2)	
6: abort(t_2)				
7: compensate (5: write(a, t_2))	a: 7		7: compensate(a, t_2)	
8: rollback(t_2)			8: rollback(t_2)	4, 5, 7, 8
9: begin(t_3)			9: begin(t_3)	
10: write(a, t_3)	a: 10		10: write(a, t_3)	
11: commit(t_3)			11: commit(t_3)	9, 10, 11
12: begin(t_4)			12: begin(t_4)	
13: write(b, t_4)	b: 13		13: write(b, t_4)	
14: write(a, t_4)	a: 14		14: write(a, t_4)	
15: abort(t_4)				
16: compensate (14: write(a, t_4))	a: 16		16: compensate(a, t_4)	
17: flush(a)		a: 16		12, 13, 14, 16
System crash				
Restart				
Analysis pass: losers = {t_4}				
consider-redo(2)	a: 16			
consider-redo(5)	a: 16			
consider-redo(7)	a: 16			
consider-redo(10)	a: 16			
undo(16)	a: 15			
undo(14)	a: 13			
consider-undo(13)	b: 0			
Restart complete: resume normal operation				

Figure 13.12 Example scenario for the correct handling of aborted transactions.

expansion of transaction aborts and the creation of compensation log entries as well as the straightforward treatment of these log entries during restart.

A particularly important point about the example is that the undo pass undoes both the inverse action 16 and the original action 14 that was inverted by 16 before the crash occurred. So our solution involves the possibility of "doubly" inverse actions to undo inverse actions. This may look like a complication upon first glance, but it actually is a great simplification to handle such cases in a uniform manner. Also, from a performance viewpoint, the overhead of occasionally performing such doubly inverse actions is negligible given that it arises only for rollbacks that are interrupted by a crash, which is clearly a rare case. We will nevertheless reconsider this approach to inverse actions later (in Section 13.4) as we encounter new aspects, and we will then introduce a way of avoiding the doubly inverse actions.

We conclude this subsection, as we did the previous one, with a statement on the correctness of our extension for handling transaction rollbacks.

THEOREM 13.5

Correctness of the complete three-pass recovery algorithm

The extension for handling transaction rollbacks during normal operation preserves the correctness of the three-pass crash recovery algorithm.

Proof

Transactions that are aborted are treated as winners if their rollback is completed before the crash, and as losers otherwise.

In the first case, forcing the log buffer upon completing the rollback (which is the same as what we do upon a transaction commit) ensures that all log entries for both the transaction's regular forward operations and the rollback-induced inverse operations are on the stable log. By the assumption that the original history is conflict serializable and log recoverable, redoing all these operations by means of regular and compensation log entries repeats the effect of the original transaction without affecting any other transaction. Because the original history was prefix reducible (in the sense of Chapter 11 on transaction recovery), the effect is that of an empty transaction that is isolated from all concurrent transactions. So the redo pass correctly repeats, if necessary (i.e., using page-state testing), the rollback that was carried out before the crash.

In the second case, if the transaction's rollback was interrupted by the crash, then the stable log will contain all writes, both original ones and inverse operations, that have already affected the stable database. These will be undone, by treating the transaction as a loser and employing the usual page-state testing, in reverse chronological order. So the undo pass essentially performs standard transaction recovery as if the transaction were still alive, the only difference being that some of the newly generated inverse operations could actually be doubly inverse operations. If the server crashes repeatedly, the transaction remains a loser. When its rollback eventually completes, the resulting effect will be that of an empty transaction. Because of the assumption that the original history was conflict serializable and log recoverable, this resulting effect appears isolated from all other transactions.

Undo Completion

In the simple algorithm we have assumed that the entire restart procedure is completed by flushing all dirty pages from the cache back to the database and reinitializing the stable log. This is a drastic measure that incurs a potentially large amount of random disk I/O, significantly increases the restart duration, and thus adversely affects availability, as the admission of new transactions has to be postponed until all pages are flushed. We will now discuss the nature of the underlying problem, and will devise a more efficient solution.

Assume that we would not flush dirty pages at the end of the restart procedure. Then the problem would arise that only the cached database is brought to a correct state by the restart itself; in particular, the stable database could still contain loser updates. So we would also depend on subsequent page flushes, during normal operation, to gradually bring the stable database to a correct state. This does not seem to be a fundamental issue, as crash recovery is generally idempotent and it is therefore sufficient to recover the cached database, but the consequences are drastic and even lead to a subtle correctness problem. First note that we need to continue keeping loser log entries on the stable log even after normal operation is resumed. So the oldest loser log entry (i.e., the one with the "oldest undo sequence number") remains relevant beyond the restart and would severely hamper or even prevent log truncation. Flushing all dirty pages as a final step of the simple recovery algorithm is merely a brute force solution to avoid this problem, but it facilitates log truncation upon restart completion. In addition, however, once we accept this global flushing, it is mandatory that the stable log be reinitialized at this point. Otherwise, we may later, upon the next crash after a period of normal operation, be mistakenly led to consider log entries of losers from previous crashes for undo if these log entries are still on the (nongarbage part of the) stable log. This would present a correctness problem, for the redo pass that precedes the undo pass could increase the sequence number of a page such that we would later erroneously reexecute undo steps for an old loser of the *previous* crash.

The handling of aborted transactions as if they were winners, discussed earlier in Section 13.3.4, under Handling Transaction Aborts, suggests a better solution. Namely, we can record the fact that the undo of a loser transaction is complete by an additional log entry, say, an "undo-complete" marker, whose further handling should be equivalent to a commit log entry. In particular, a transaction with an "undo-complete" log entry should not need any further undo recovery when the system crashes once again. This is the key idea to allow discarding the transaction's log entries and ultimately truncating the log.

Unfortunately, this approach still has a catch. When the undo-complete log entry is created, the undo is really completed only in the cached database,

Sequence number: action	Change of cached database [PageNo: SeqNo]	Change of stable database [PageNo: SeqNo]	Log entry added to log buffer [LogSeqNo: action]	Log entries added to stable log [LogSeqNo's]
1: begin(t_1)			1: begin(t_1)	
2: write(a, t_1)	a: 2		2: write(a, t_1)	
3: commit(t_1)			3: commit(t_1)	1, 2, 3
4: begin(t_2)			4: begin(t_2)	
5: write(a, t_2)	a: 5		5: write(a, t_2)	
6: abort(t_2)				
7: compensate (5: write(a, t_2))	a: 7		7: compensate(a, t_2)	
8: rollback(t_2)			8: rollback(t_2)	4, 5, 7, 8
9: begin(t_3)			9: begin(t_3)	
10: write(b, t_3)	b: 10		10: write(b, t_3)	
11: commit(t_3)			11: commit(t_3)	9, 10, 11
12: begin(t_4)			12: begin(t_4)	
13: write(b, t_4)	b: 13		13: write(b, t_4)	
14: write(a, t_4)	a: 14		14: write(a, t_4)	
15: abort(t_4)				
16: compensate (14: write(a, t_4))	a: 16		16: compensate(a, t_4)	
17: flush(a)		a: 16		12, 13, 14, 16
18: begin(t_5)			18: begin(t_5)	
19: write(c, t_5)	c: 19		19: write(c, t_5)	
20: begin(t_6)			20: begin(t_6)	
21: write(d, t_6)	d: 21		21: write(d, t_6)	
22: flush(c)		c: 19		18, 19, 20, 21
System crash				
Restart				
Analysis pass: losers = {t_4, t_5, t_6}				
consider-redo(2)	a: 16			
consider-redo(5)	a: 16			
consider-redo(7)	a: 16			
redo(10)	b: 10			
consider-undo(21)	d: 0			
undo(19)	c: 18			
undo(16)	a: 15			
undo(14)	a: 13			
consider-undo(13)	b: 10			
flush(a)		a: 13		
flush(c)		c: 18		
23: undo-complete(t_4)			23: undo-complete(t_4)	
24: undo-complete(t_5)			24: undo-complete(t_5)	
25: undo-complete(t_6)			25: undo-complete(t_6)	
force				23, 24, 25
Restart complete: resume normal operation				

Figure 13.13 Example scenario for the undo completion method.

whereas the stable database may still contain loser updates. Only flushing the relevant pages adds the transaction's inverse actions to the stable database. So the solution is to enforce the flushing of those pages at the end of the undo—not exactly a low price but a lot better than flushing the entire cache. Once this flushing is complete, the undo-complete log entries of the now completely and permanently undone loser transactions are created and forced to the stable log. From now on, these transactions are handled as if they no longer exist. If the system crashes again, the log entries of these transactions are ignored. The undo-complete markers essentially render those log entries obsolete, and this enables further log truncation.

Note that it would not be correct to treat the completely undone transactions as winners in a subsequent restart after another crash. This would erroneously redo their original updates without also redoing the inverse actions. In this respect, the handling of loser transactions differs from that of aborted transactions that have been completely rolled back during normal operation. This does not sound like an elegant method, and we will indeed see later in Section 13.4 that there is a simpler solution that treats aborted and undone transactions in a uniform manner. However, this more elegant solution is based on the redo-history paradigm, whereas we are still focusing on the redo-winners paradigm in the current subsection.

The algorithm for undo completion during restart is illustrated by the scenario in Figure 13.13, with the newly introduced flush and undo-complete actions typed in boldface.

The pseudocode for the complete undo pass now looks as follows.

```
undo pass ( ):
 FlushList := empty;
 while there exists t in losers
  such that losers[t].LastSeqNo <> nil
 do
  nexttrans := TransNo in losers
   such that losers[TransNo].LastSeqNo =
   max {losers[x].LastSeqNo|x in losers};
  nextentry = losers[nexttrans].LastSeqNo;
  if StableLog[nextentry].ActionType = write
  then
   pageno := StableLog[nextentry].PageNo;
   fetch (pageno);
   if DatabaseCache[pageno].PageSeqNo >= nextentry.LogSeqNo;
   then
    read and write (StableLog[nextentry].PageNo)
     according to StableLog[nextentry].UndoInfo;
    DatabaseCache[pageno].PageSeqNo := nextentry.LogSeqNo - 1;
    FlushList += pageno;
```

Complete
undo pass

```
          end /*if*/;
          losers[nexttrans].LastSeqNo :=
            StableLog[nextentry].PreviousSeqNo;
        end /*if*/;
      end /*while*/;
      for each p in FlushList do
        flush (p);
      end /*for*/;
      for each t in losers do
        newlogentry.LogSeqNo := new sequence number;
        newlogentry.ActionType := undo-complete;
        newlogentry.TransId := losers[t].TransId;
       LogBuffer += newlogentry;
      end /*for*/;
      force ( );
```

The correctness arguments for the undo completion method are summarized in the following theorem.

THEOREM 13.6

Correctness of undo completion

The method for undo completion preserves the correctness of the three-pass crash recovery algorithm.

Proof

When a loser transaction is completely rolled back during the undo phase of a restart, flushing all pages that have been modified on behalf of undoing the transaction includes all operations of the transaction into the stable database. This holds regardless of whether the transaction was a regular, active transaction or was in the course of being rolled back when the crash hit. It is possible that during restart only a subset of the transaction's originally modified pages is updated by inverse operations. However, this can happen only if the missing pages were already modified by inverse operations during a prior incarnation of the undo phase (i.e., a previous restart in the case of repeated crashes) or a rollback during normal operation, and these pages were already written into the stable database earlier. So by the end of the undo phase, all pages that are affected by loser transactions are in the stable database. Therefore, it is valid to "forget" all their log entries by truncating the log. If, on the other hand, some of these log entries are not immediately discarded, there is no harm either: the analysis pass of the next restart will recognize the nature of these transactions from their undo-complete log entries, and all their log entries will then simply be disregarded by both the redo and the undo pass.

13.4 **Redo-History Paradigm**

The intriguing property of the redo-winners paradigm is the fact that its redo pass considers only winners and thus aims to minimize the recovery work in that phase. However, as seen in the previous section, this property entails certain complications in the handling of transaction aborts and the effective log truncation after the undo phase. In this section, we consider the alternative paradigm of redoing the entire history, that is, all actions of both winners and losers in chronological order and also including aborted transactions. Thus, the redo-history family of algorithms first reconstructs the state of the (cached) database as of the time of the crash, and then undoes loser transactions from there.

An immediate consequence of this approach is that the restart may end up first redoing certain loser actions that are subsequently undone in the undo phase, thus increasing the overall amount of work. Given that the number of loser transactions is bounded and fairly small, this "double work" is not a critical concern in terms of restart performance. On the other hand, we will see in this section that the redo-history paradigm simplifies the overall recovery algorithm substantially in that it allows us to treat winners, losers, and aborted transactions more uniformly. This uniformity will also result in some efficiency gains during restart; namely, we will show that the redo-history algorithm never has to flush any pages during restart. (Recall that the redo-winners algorithm has to flush pages that were modified in the undo phase in order to complete the undo phase and facilitate log truncation.) Another characteristic property of the redo-history paradigm is that its undo phase requires creating new log records. But similarly to the double-work issue mentioned above, switching on the logging activity during the restart simplifies the overall algorithm and has only marginal overhead.

13.4.1 **Actions during Normal Operation**

The redo-history paradigm differs from the redo-winners algorithms only in its actions during restart. During normal operation, it proceeds exactly like the algorithms presented in Section 13.3.1. Also, the redo-history algorithm makes use of page sequence numbers (introduced in Section 13.3.2) in the same way as the redo-winners paradigm, in order to cope with general, nonidempotent write actions. In what follows, we will always assume general write actions, implicitly covering the special case of full-writes.

13.4.2 **Simple Three-Pass and Two-Pass Algorithms**

Like the redo-winners paradigm, the restart of a redo-history algorithm proceeds in three phases:

Three-pass redo-history algorithm

Analysis pass   1. The *analysis pass* locates the relevant start point of the log (which is usually the most recent checkpoint log entry when checkpointing is in effect) from the master record, and scans the log in forward direction to identify all loser transactions, that is, all transactions for which neither a commit nor rollback log entry is found on the stable log.

Redo pass   2. The *redo pass* starts from the oldest log entry that has not "survived" the crash in the sense that it is not reflected in the stable database. This point is either the beginning of the log (when no checkpoint is available) or the SystemRedoLSN that is recorded in or derived from the information of the most recent checkpoint log entry. All updates that follow the SystemRedoLSN are then considered for redo, and those that are not yet reflected in the stable database, as indicated by testing page sequence numbers or looking up the DirtyPages information if available, are actually redone. Note that this redo pass does not discriminate *Reconstructing* winner versus loser transactions; it redoes all updates regardless of the *the "crash state"* transaction status. The net effect of the redo pass and fundamental invariant of the entire redo-history paradigm is that it reconstructs the exact state of the cached database as of the time of the crash.

Undo pass   3. Once the crash state has been reconstructed, the *undo pass* can now proceed as if the system were already operational, or in other words, as if the crash had never happened. In particular, it can treat loser transactions as if they were still active or reincarnated again and simply initiate abort *Treating loser* actions for them. Thus, the undo of loser transactions more or less uses *transactions* the algorithm for rolling back a transaction that is aborted during normal *as rollbacks* operation. However, since locking information (or whatever information the concurrency control is based on) usually becomes lost in a crash, the system cannot really admit new transactions until the entire undo phase is completed. Otherwise, the reads and writes of new transactions could become interleaved with the undo steps in a way that would no longer be equivalent to a serializable schedule of exactly all committed transactions. (An advanced technique for relaxing this constraint will be presented in Chapter 15.)

Treating the loser transactions as rollbacks of aborted transactions in the undo phase is the decisive difference from the redo-winners paradigm and the key to the (relative) simplicity of the redo-history approach. It is made possible by starting from the database state as of the crash. So this is where the (marginally) larger amount of work of the redo-history phase pays off. An important implication is that the undoing of a loser transaction does in turn create log entries during restart, namely, compensation log entries, as described in Section 13.3.4. These inverse actions would later be redone in the next restart if the system should fail once more during the undo phase. This may appear somewhat complicated at first glance, but incurs absolutely no extra complexity, as this procedure is necessary for transaction rollbacks anyway. In fact, this approach achieves the desirable property that the code for crash recovery reuses code that is used during normal operation. As we already pointed out in the introduction to this chapter (Section 13.1), this leads to simpler, much better stress-tested, and ultimately more robust recovery procedures.

Pseudocode for the redo phase and the undo phase of the redo-history algorithm is given below. The code for the analysis phase remains identical to that of Section(s) 13.3.2 (and 13.3.3 when checkpointing is added).

```
redo pass ( ):
 min := LogSeqNo of oldest log entry in StableLog;
 max := LogSeqNo of most recent log entry in StableLog;
 for i := min to max do
  pageno = StableLog[i].PageNo;
  fetch (pageno);
  if DatabaseCache[pageno].PageSeqNo < i
  then
   read and write (pageno)
    according to StableLog[i].RedoInfo;
   DatabaseCache[pageno].PageSeqNo := i;
  end /*if*/;
 end /*for*/;
```

Redo pass of the simple three-pass redo-history algorithm

```
undo pass ( ):
 ActiveTrans := empty;
 for each t in losers do
   ActiveTrans += t;
   ActiveTrans[t].LastSeqNo := losers[t].LastSeqNo;
 end /*for*/;
 while there exists t in losers
   such that losers[t].LastSeqNo <> nil do
 nexttrans := TransNo in losers
   such that losers[nexttrans].LastSeqNo =
   max {losers[x].LastSeqNo|x in losers};
  nextentry := losers[nexttrans].LastSeqNo;
  if StableLog[nextentry].ActionType in {write, compensation}
  then
   pageno := StableLog[nextentry].PageNo;
   fetch (pageno);
   if DatabaseCache[pageno].PageSeqNo >= nextentry.LogSeqNo;
   then
    newlogentry.LogSeqNo := new sequence number;
    newlogentry.ActionType := compensation;
    newlogentry.PreviousSeqNo := ActiveTrans[transid].LastSeqNo;
```

Undo pass of the redo-history algorithm

```
         newlogentry.RedoInfo :=
          inverse action of the action in nextentry;
         newlogentry.UndoInfo :=
          inverse action of the inverse action
          of the action in nextentry;
         ActiveTrans[transid].LastSeqNo := newlogentry.LogSeqNo;
         LogBuffer += newlogentry;
         read and write (StableLog[nextentry].PageNo)
          according to StableLog[nextentry].UndoInfo;
         DatabaseCache[pageno].PageSeqNo := newlogentry.LogSeqNo;
       end /*if*/;
        losers[nexttrans].LastSeqNo :=
          StableLog[nextentry].PreviousSeqNo;
       end /*if*/;
       if StableLog[nextentry].ActionType = begin
       then
        newlogentry.LogSeqNo := new sequence number;
        newlogentry.ActionType := rollback;
        newlogentry.TransId := StableLog[nextentry].TransId;
        newlogentry.PreviousSeqNo := ActiveTrans[transid].LastSeqNo;
        LogBuffer += newlogentry;
        ActiveTrans -= transid;
        losers -= transid;
       end /*if*/;
      end /*while*/;
      force ( );
```

To illustrate the behavior of the algorithm, consider the example in Figures 13.14 and 13.15, the two parts of which are based on the scenario of Figure 13.4 that we initially considered in Section 13.3.2. The actions during normal operation are identical to those of the earlier example. To make the scenario more illustrative in the context of the redo-history paradigm, we now assume that the second crash occurs during the undo phase of the first restart.

A number of entries in the tables of Figures 13.14 and 13.15 should be singled out to illustrate the intrinsic features of the algorithm:

- The undo phase never performs any page-state testing. This is unnecessary as the redo-history paradigm ensures that the undo phase always starts with the state as of the crash and thus "sees" all log entries that survived the crash reflected in the cached database.

- The undo phase creates a new compensation log entry for each of its undo steps. These need not be forced to the stable log, unless flushing a page triggers a forced log I/O. Thus, compensation log entries may get

Sequence number: action	Change of cached database [PageNo: SeqNo]	Change of stable database [PageNo: SeqNo]	Log entry added to log buffer [LogSeqNo: action]	Log entries added to stable log [LogSeqNo's]
1: begin(t_1)			1: begin(t_1)	
2: begin(t_2)			2: begin(t_2)	
3: write(a, t_1)	a: 3		3: write(a, t_1)	
4: begin(t_3)			4: begin(t_3)	
5: begin(t_4)			5: begin(t_4)	
6: write(b, t_3)	b: 6		6: write(b, t_3)	
7: write(c, t_2)	c: 7		7: write(c, t_2)	
8: write(d, t_1)	d: 8		8: write(d, t_1)	
9: commit(t_1)			9: commit(t_1)	1, 2, 3, 4, 5, 6, 7, 8, 9
10: flush(d)		d: 8		
11: write(d, t_3)	d: 11		11: write(d, t_3)	
12: begin(t_5)			12: begin(t_5)	
13: write(a, t_5)	a: 13		13: write(a, t_5)	
14: commit(t_3)			14: commit(t_3)	11, 12, 13, 14
15: flush(d)		d: 11		
16: write(d, t_4)	d: 16		16: write(d, t_4)	
17: write(e, t_2)	e: 17		17: write(e, t_2)	
18: write(b, t_5)	b: 18		18: write(b, t_5)	
19: flush(b)		b: 18		16, 17, 18
20: commit(t_4)			20: commit(t_4)	20
21: write(f, t_5)	f: 21		21: write(f, t_5)	
System crash and restart				

Figure 13.14 Example scenario for the simple three-pass redo-history recovery algorithm, part 1.

lost in another crash. In the example, among the four log entries that are created during the first restart, only the entries with log sequence numbers 22 and 23 survive the second crash.

- The redo pass may explicitly redo an action that later needs to be undone in the undo pass. For example, during the first restart of the scenario, this is the case for log entries 13 and 17, whereas log entry 18 was already reflected in the stable database before the original crash and thus would have needed explicit undo in the redo-winners approach, too. The situation appears "even worse" in that the redone action 13 becomes reflected in the stable database during the first restart by flushing page a, although the action 13 is already known to belong to a loser transaction. These are examples of the additional work that the redo-history algorithm may end up doing. But note that these specific situations are included in the scenario on purpose, almost in a contrived manner. The fact that they appear so prominently and almost dominate the scenario should, however, not misguide us. In a realistic setting we would perform a lot more redo work on behalf of winner transactions, so that the possible double work on behalf of loser transactions would most likely constitute a negligible fraction of the overall recovery work.

- Unlike the redo-winners algorithms, the undo pass no longer decreases the page sequence number when an undo step is performed on a page.

Sequence number: action	Change of cached database [PageNo: SeqNo]	Change of stable database [PageNo: SeqNo]	Log entry added to log buffer [LogSeqNo: action]	Log entries added to stable log [LogSeqNo's]
Analysis pass: losers = $\{t_2, t_5\}$				
redo(3)	a: 3			
consider-redo(6)	b: 18			
flush(a)		a: 3		
redo(7)	c: 7			
consider-redo(8)	d: 11			
consider-redo(11)	d: 11			
redo(13)	a: 13			
redo(16)	d: 16			
redo(17)	e: 17			
consider-redo(18)	b: 18			
flush(a)		a: 13		
22: compensate(18)	b: 22		22: compensate(18: b, t_5)	
23: compensate(17)	e: 23		23: compensate(17: e, t_2)	
flush(b)		b: 22		22, 23
24: compensate(13)	a: 24		24: compensate(13: a, t_5)	
25: rollback(t_5)			25: rollback(t_5)	
Second system crash and second restart				
Analysis pass: losers = $\{t_2, t_5\}$				
consider-redo(3)	a: 13			
consider-redo(6)	b: 22			
redo(7)	c: 7			
consider-redo(8)	d: 11			
consider-redo(11)	d: 11			
consider-redo(13)	a: 13			
redo(16)	d: 16			
redo(17)	e: 17			
consider-redo(18)	b: 22			
consider-redo(22)	b: 22			
redo(23)	e: 23			
26: compensate(23)	e: 26		26: compensate(23: e, t_2)	
27: compensate(22)	b: 27		27: compensate(22: b, t_5)	
28: compensate(18)	b: 28		28: compensate(18: b, t_5)	
29: compensate(17)	e: 29		29: compensate(17: e, t_2)	
30: compensate(13)	a: 30		30: compensate(13: a, t_5)	
31: rollback(t_5)			31: rollback(t_5)	
32: compensate(7)	c: 32		32: compensate(7: c, t_2)	
33: rollback(t_2)			33: rollback(t_2)	
force				26, 27, 28, 29, 30, 31, 32, 33
Second restart complete: resume normal operation				

Figure 13.15 Example scenario for the simple three-pass redo-history recovery algorithm, part 2.

Rather, the page sequence number is increased to capture the fact that the compensation action was performed. This way of tracking the state of a page is perfectly in line with the fact that compensation actions are themselves logged.

- During the second restart, compensation log entries that have survived the second crash are themselves redone. In the example, this holds for log entries 22 and 23, for which the undo then creates again compensation log entries describing the inverse actions for the inverse actions of the original actions. Note that this seemingly complicated behavior is perfectly in line with the redo-history paradigm: in the given scenario, the redo pass of the second restart reconstructs the database state as of the time of the second crash. Also note that creating compensation log entries for possibly undoing undo steps is actually a very natural thing to do, once we think of the loser transactions as reincarnated active transactions that are to be rolled back (possibly after having already performed some undo steps in their prior incarnation). We will nevertheless come back to this issue in Section 13.4.4 for efficiency reasons.

- When a loser transaction is eventually rolled back completely, this is marked in the log by creating a rollback log entry, exactly like we handled transaction aborts in Section 13.3.4. Finally, when the undo pass, and thus the entire restart, is completed, it is desirable to force the log entries of the undone transactions to the stable log. In this way we avoid another reincarnation of these transactions if the system were to fail again shortly afterward. However, this forced log I/O is optional; the algorithm would work correctly without it.

The relative simplicity of the redo-history paradigm, in comparison to the redo-winners approach, also leads to fairly straightforward correctness reasoning. In particular, it nicely separates the issue of redo recovery from the arguments about undo recovery. Here only the latter needs to consider the interleaving of transactions, whereas the redo phase merely repeats the chronology of logged events and thus simply reinstatiates the pre-crash serialization order, including all incomplete transactions. The correctness arguments about the transaction interleaving for undo recovery, however, are more or less the same that we have used for reasoning about transaction recovery during normal operation in Chapter 11. The modularity and simplicity of these correctness arguments are reflected in the fairly straightforward proof of the following theorem.

THEOREM 13.7

The simple three-pass redo-history recovery algorithm performs correct recovery.

Correctness of simple three-pass redo-history algorithm

Proof

The analysis pass is identical to that of the redo-winners algorithm. The redo pass reconstructs the state as of the crash time, including all regular "forward" operations of winners as well as losers and inverse operations of transactions that were being rolled back when the crash hit. Thus, by the end of the redo phase, the following invariant holds:

$$\forall \text{ pages } p : \forall \text{ transactions } t : \forall \text{ operations } o \in \text{stable log} :$$
$$(o \text{ belongs to } t \text{ and refers to } p) \Rightarrow o \in \text{cached database}$$

The undo pass simply performs transaction recovery following Chapter 11, as if the server had to perform aborts for a group of transactions during normal operation. Note that the undo pass does not even need to perform any page-state testing, as it knows that the preceding redo pass has redone all writes. Specifically, the undo pass generates inverse operations for all logged operations of loser transactions, covering regular forward operations as well as inverse operations from transactions whose rollback during normal operation was interrupted by the crash. From the assumption that the original history was conflict serializable and log recoverable, it follows that for each page, all writes of loser transactions must follow the writes of winners. Therefore, by applying the transformation rules of Chapter 11 on transaction recovery, the inverse operations generated during the undo pass can be commuted back and pairwise combined with their corresponding forward operations, and finally reduced to null steps without any effect. For the entire loser transactions, this means that they are reduced to empty transactions. Thus, by the end of the undo phase, the following invariant holds:

$$\forall \text{ pages } p : \forall \text{ transactions } t : \forall \text{ operations } o \in \text{stable log} :$$
$$(o \text{ belongs to } t \text{ and refers to } p \wedge t \in \text{losers}) \Rightarrow o \notin \text{cached database}$$

Since loser writes must follow winner writes in the history, the (redone) effects of winner transactions are untouched by the undo phase, so that the invariant after the redo pass is now tightened to:

$$\forall \text{ pages } p : \forall \text{ transactions } t : \forall \text{ operations } o \in \text{stable log} :$$
$$(o \text{ belongs to } t \text{ and refers to } p \wedge t \in \text{winners}) \Rightarrow o \in \text{cached database}$$

A final complication that we should explicitly consider is the fact that the server may crash again during either the redo pass or the undo pass. In the first case—another crash during the redo pass—the situation is no different from the redo-winners algorithm: the redo phase in its entirety is idempotent due to the page-state testing upon each redo step, so that we can simply reinitiate the redo pass.

In the second case, the situation differs from the redo-winners algorithm. Each inverse operation that has been generated during the prior undo pass has created a compensation log entry; so the history has become longer by these actions during the previous restart. Note that only such undo steps leave these traces whose compensation log entries have made it to the stable log before the crash; however, the ones whose log entries have become lost in the log buffer do not matter, as they cannot have made any impact on the stable database anyway (given that the undo logging rule is in effect during the restart as well). The prolongation of the history during the undo phase affects only loser transactions and is guaranteed to stay log recoverable, because the operations to be undone are considered in reverse chronological order. This is the same result that we would get from initiating a group abort, in the sense of Chapter 11, for the entire history of loser transactions. So the bottom line is that the situation after a crash during the undo pass is not really any different from what the previous undo pass had to clean up. In combination with the fact that the preceding redo pass will always redo whatever prolonged history it finds on the stable log (i.e., including doubly or multiple-times inverse operations), these considerations prove the idempotence of the undo pass.

Since the redo pass of the redo-history paradigm redoes all updates regardless of whether they belong to winner or loser transactions, it is clear that the redo pass itself does not depend on having an analysis pass preceding it. The undo pass still needs to know the set of loser transactions and thus requires some prior analysis of the log. However, the redo phases's traversal of the log typically includes the part of the log that would be inspected by the analysis pass. Therefore, the redo pass can perform the task of identifying loser transactions without any extra I/O cost. So we realize that we could easily change the three-pass redo-history algorithm into a two-pass algorithm by simply discarding the explicit analysis pass, thus saving one scan of (a fraction of) the log.

Two-pass redo-history algorithm

An analysis pass is indeed merely optional under the redo-history paradigm. However, it can still be beneficial, and a three-pass algorithm may still possibly outperform a two-pass algorithm in terms of the overall restart time. To see this point, we should first realize that the redo pass is guaranteed to include the fraction of the log that the analysis pass would scan only if no redo optimizations, in the sense of Section 13.3.3, are performed. Of course, without an analysis pass, these optimizations are no longer feasible, for the most part; in particular, the SystemRedoLSN is then really guaranteed to precede, in terms of LSNs, the point where the analyis pass would start (i.e., the most recent checkpoint, or the beginning of the stable log in the worst case). However, once we incorporate redo optimizations like the inclusion of DirtyPages information in checkpoint log entries and the logging of flush actions, the SystemRedoLSN that we determine in the analysis pass may well turn out to be higher than the LSN of the point where the analysis pass starts.

The bottom line from this discussion is that the redo pass can be optimized only if it is preceded by an explicit analysis pass that determines sufficiently recent DirtyPages information. The I/O savings from these redo optimizations may be worth an additional prior pass over the relevant fraction of the log. Whether this is indeed the case depends on many workload and system-tuning parameters such as page reference locality or checkpointing frequency, and these dependencies are inherently hard to analyze mathematically, if not intractable. Thus, we cannot give a definitive answer on whether a two-pass or three-pass algorithm is preferable. From a system builder's viewpoint, both options could easily be implemented, and a database administrator could choose the one that is more appropriate for a given application. However, this merely puts the burden on the administrator staff, making system tuning more complicated and ultimately more expensive. Therefore, we would like to offer at least a "first order" approximative answer, which advocates the three-pass algorithm. The argument for this preference is that the analysis pass can potentially reduce the amount of random I/O activity on the stable database in a possibly significant way, whereas reducing the number of log scans from three to two merely saves sequential I/Os on the log tail, which may be tightly bounded in size anyway.

13.4.3 Enhanced Algorithms: Log Truncation, Checkpoints, and Redo Optimization

All checkpointing and I/O reduction techniques that we introduced in Section 13.3.3 for the redo-winners paradigm apply equally to the redo-history approach without any modification. In particular, these techniques are applicable to both the three-pass and the two-pass redo-history algorithms. Note that the two-pass algorithm, despite not having an analysis phase, still benefits fundamentally from checkpointing in that it shortens the redo pass. It can also exploit DirtyPages information to avoid fetching pages unnecessarily from the stable database. None of these techniques requires any special adaptations of the redo algorithm that we gave for the redo-winners approach (other than the obvious difference that loser updates are now redone as well). Also, all correctness arguments presented in Section 13.3.3 can be carried over to the redo-history paradigm in a trivially straightforward manner.

13.4.4 Complete Algorithms: Handling Transaction Rollbacks and Undo Completion

Undo completion   In the redo-winners paradigm, we encountered problems with the completion of the undo phase, as a naive approach could prevent further log truncation indefinitely, which would be a serious problem (see Section 13.3.4). The reason was that when an undo-complete log entry is created for a loser transaction, the undo is really completed only in the cached database, whereas the stable database may still contain loser updates. Thus, we cannot discard any log entries of loser transactions until we definitely know that all undo-affected pages have been flushed from the database cache. Enforcing flush actions for those relevant pages at the end of the undo phase also adds the loser transactions' inverse actions to the stable database, and this was the solution that we adopted for the redo-winners paradigm.

Under the redo-history paradigm, a much better solution is obtained from the fact that undo steps will be logged again and will be redone if another crash occurs. Thus, the redo-history approach ensures that, by redoing the undo step if necessary, the effects of the undo step are guaranteed to survive further crashes. In terms of the durability of the undo steps, this is as good as if the undo-affected pages were flushed, but without the I/O cost of the flush actions. In addition, creating compensation log entries for all undo steps provides us with a way of exactly tracking the progress of the undo phase. If the system crashes again before the undo phase is completed, redoing the effects of the compensation actions will again reconstruct the state as of the most recent crash, from where we know exactly which steps still need to be undone. As already pointed out in Section 13.4.2, this whole approach can be viewed as if loser transactions were reincarnated and treated like active transactions that are to be rolled back during normal operation. An example for how this approach works was already given in Figures 13.14 and 13.15 in Section 13.4.2.

Log truncation, which was our original motivation for "completing" the undo phase, is now straightforward. We only have to take into accout the redo sequence numbers of the cached pages (as maintained in the DirtyPages information), and this is what we do for log truncation anyway. Moreover, we can directly leverage our repertoire for advancing the oldest redo sequence number (i.e., the SystemRedoLSN) that we introduced in Section 13.3.3. So the undo phase of the restart no longer complicates the important issue of log truncation at all.

Log truncation

The algorithm for the undo phase, as given in the pseudocode of Section 13.4.2, so far has the somewhat peculiar property that it may end up performing inverse actions of inverse actions if the system crashes during a restart. For example, assume a loser transaction t_i that has performed write actions on pages a, b, and c, all of which have been recorded on the stable log, before the system crashes the first time. Suppose that the system crashes a second time after having undone the update on pages c and b. When the system is restarted once more and the undo phase finally completes, we obtain the history shown in Figure 13.16 (as far as this transaction is concerned).

Inverse actions of inverse actions

In Figure 13.16, numbers 10, 20, and so on, are arbitrarily chosen LSNs. So the second restart first redoes the actions with LSNs 10 through 50, and then initiates, in its undo phase, the action with sequence number 60, which is the inverse action of the inverse action 50 of the original action 20, and so on. This effect, which we already encountered in the scenario of Figures 13.14 and 13.15 of Section 13.4.2, may appear somewhat confusing at first glance, but it is actually as straightforward as it could be and does not present any implementation difficulties at all. In fact, we have already proven in Theorem 13.7, using very

$10 : write(t_i, a)$ $20 : write(t_i, b)$ $30 : write(t_i, c)$
... first crash ...
$40 : write(t_i, c)^{-1}$ $50 : write(t_i, b)^{-1}$ ...
... second crash ...
$60 : (write(t_i, b)^{-1})^{-1}$ $70 : (write(t_i, c)^{-1})^{-1}$ $80 : write(t_i, c)^{-1}$
$90 : write(t_i, b)^{-1}$ $100 : write(t_i, a)^{-1}$
... second restart complete

Figure 13.16 Example transaction with multiple-times inverse actions.

simple reduction arguments in the style of Chapter 11, that such a sequence of original actions, inverse actions, and multiple-times inverse actions is guaranteed to be equivalent to a "null" action, not leaving any traces in the database.

Problem with multiple-times inverse actions

So, neither from a correctness nor from an implementation viewpoint do we see any problems with the possibility of multiple-times inverse actions. However, the approach may be considered moderately harmful in terms of the restart efficiency under certain circumstances. To see this point, notice that in Figure 13.16, the second restart needs to perform more work than the first restart. The reason is that the second restart (1) needs to redo not only the original actions of t_i but also the already executed inverse actions of the first restart's undo phase, and (2) then needs to perform doubly inverse actions of the first restart's inverse actions and inverse actions of the original actions. So if the system crashes repeatedly without completing any of its restarts, the duration of successive restarts increases. In general, we cannot even give any upper bounds on the nesting depth of multiple-times inverse actions and the resulting restart duration.

Avoidance of multiple-times inverse actions

Of course, such repeated crashes should be extremely rare and would be an indication of some other instability problem anyway; so we do not consider a typical, critically important case here. However, if this problem ever occurs, it could be potentially troublesome. Fortunately, there is a relatively simple way of fixing this problem. As it will turn out later in Chapters 15 and 16 in the contexts of intra-transaction savepoints and media recovery, this remedy proves very useful in much wider generality. The solution is to figure out, from the compensation log entries during the redo pass, which of the original actions of a loser transaction have already been undone in the previous restart. Those actions do not need to be considered anymore at all; in particular, neither the compensation actions nor the original, compensated actions require any further inverse actions. Given that the redo pass covers all compensation actions as well, we further know that all undo steps that have created compensation log entries on the stable log are indeed *successfully undone* in the sense that each pair of original action and inverse action together leaves a "null" effect on the database. Finally, by having the compensation log entries on the stable log, we also have at hand the information about which of the original actions have not yet been compensated and still need undo steps.

Technically, an elegant solution for identifying those loser actions that still require inverse actions is based on introducing a backward chain among the log entries of a transaction. Note that this chain is in addition to the usual PreviousSeqNo linking of log entries; we introduce a new *next undo (log) sequence number* field (NextUndoSeqNo for short) into the data structure of log entries. The linking in this additional backward chain is the following:

NextUndoSeqNo backward chaining

- For log entries of original actions, the NextUndoSeqNo field is identical to the PreviousSeqNo; that is, it points to the previous log entry of the same transaction that would indeed be the next one to be undone within this transaction.

- For a compensation log entry (CLE), the NextUndoSeqNo field points to the predecessor (within the same transaction) of the log entry whose update is undone by the inverse action described in the CLE. That is, the NextUndoSeqNo of the CLE is set to the PreviousSeqNo of the original action that is compensated.

Thus, for the above simple example of Figure 13.16 with transaction t_i updating pages a, b, and c, we would obtain the sequence of actions and log entries shown in Figure 13.17. A graphical illustration of the log for this scenario is given in Figure 13.18, with compensation log entries shown as white boxes.

Note that the second restart in the example identifies the first log entry that requires an undo step—the entry with LSN 10 in this case—by looking up the NextUndoSeqNo field of the transaction's most recent log entry, which is the entry with LSN 50 in the example.

The pseudocode for the complete undo pass looks as follows. As usual, the code assumes that the preceding analysis pass has built up the "losers" data structure reflecting the state as of the most recent crash.

10 : write(t_i, a), NextUndoSeqNo = nil
20 : write(t_i, b), NextUndoSeqNo = 10
30 : write(t_i, c), NextUndoSeqNo = 20
... first crash ...
... redo 10, 20, 30 ...
40 : write(t_i, c)$^{-1}$, NextUndoSeqNo = 20
50 : write(t_i, b)$^{-1}$, NextUndoSeqNo = 10
... second crash ...
... redo 10, 20, 30, 40, 50 ...
60 : write(t_i, a)$^{-1}$, NextUndoSeqNo = nil
... second restart complete

Figure 13.17 Example transaction with NextUndoSeqNo backward chain.

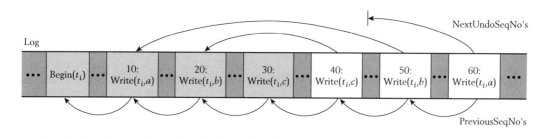

Figure 13.18 The NextUndoSeqNo backward chain for the example of Figure 13.17.

Undo pass with
compensation
log entries and
NextUndoSeqNo
backward
chaining

```
undo pass ( ):
ActiveTrans := empty;
for each t in losers do
  ActiveTrans += t;
  ActiveTrans[t].LastSeqNo := losers[t].LastSeqNo;
end /*for*/;
while there exists t in losers
  such that losers[t].LastSeqNo <> nil
do
  nexttrans := TransNo in losers
    such that losers[nexttrans].LastSeqNo =
    max {losers[x].LastSeqNo|x in losers};
  nextentry := losers[nexttrans].LastSeqNo;
  if StableLog[nextentry].ActionType = compensation then
    losers[nexttrans].LastSeqNo :=
    StableLog[nextentry].NextUndoSeqNo;
  end /*if*/;
  if StableLog[nextentry].ActionType = write then
    pageno = StableLog[nextentry].PageNo;
    fetch (pageno);
    if DatabaseCache[pageno].PageSeqNo >= nextentry.LogSeqNo
    then
      newlogentry.LogSeqNo := new sequence number;
      newlogentry.ActionType := compensation;
      newlogentry.PreviousSeqNo :=
       ActiveTrans[transid].LastSeqNo;
      newlogentry.NextUndoSeqNo :=
       nextentry.PreviousSeqNo;
      newlogentry.RedoInfo :=
       inverse action of the action in nextentry;
      ActiveTrans[transid].LastSeqNo :=
       newlogentry.LogSeqNo;
```

```
      LogBuffer += newlogentry;
      read and write (StableLog[nextentry].PageNo)
       according to StableLog[nextentry].UndoInfo;
      DatabaseCache[pageno].PageSeqNo := newlogentry.LogSeqNo;
    end /*if*/;
    losers[nexttrans].LastSeqNo :=
      StableLog[nextentry].PreviousSeqNo;
    end /*if*/;
    if StableLog[nextentry].ActionType = begin then
     newlogentry.LogSeqNo := new sequence number;
     newlogentry.ActionType := rollback;
     newlogentry.TransId := StableLog[nextentry].TransId;
     newlogentry.PreviousSeqNo :=
      ActiveTrans[transid].LastSeqNo;
     LogBuffer += newlogentry;
     ActiveTrans -= transid;
     losers -= transid;
    end /*if*/;
  end /*while*/;
  force ( );
```

A prerequisite of the above undo algorithm is that the NextUndoSeqNo   *Transaction*
chain is maintained during normal operation and in the undo phase itself. This   *rollbacks*
must include the processing of transactions that are to be aborted. So the algorithm for transaction rollback has to maintain the NextUndoSeqNo chain,
too, while it is creating compensation log entries. An additional benefit of this
uniform procedure is that the undo work after a crash is also bounded for
transactions that were in the process of rolling back when the system was hit
by the crash. Actions that have already been undone, on behalf of the transaction abort, before the crash do not require further undo steps during restart.
Let us emphasize once again (and for the last time in this chapter) that this is
feasible because the redo pass also redoes the compensating actions that were
performed and logged before the crash. The pseudocode for transaction rollbacks is given below. The differences to the pseudocode given in Section 13.3.4
are rather small: (1) we have to add the maintenance of the NextUndoSeqNo
chain, and (2) the compensation log entries no longer need to contain any undo
information (i.e., the inverse action of the inverse action of the original action),
as the complete recovery algorithm will only consider redoing compensation
log entries but never needs to undo a compensation action anymore.

```
    abort (transid):
     logentry :=
      ActiveTrans[transid].LastSeqNo;
```

Transaction rollback during normal operation using NextUndoSeqNo backward chaining

```
while logentry is not nil and
   logentry.ActionType = write or full-write
do
   newlogentry.LogSeqNo := new sequence number;
   newlogentry.ActionType := compensation;
   newlogentry.PreviousSeqNo :=
    ActiveTrans[transid].LastSeqNo;
   newlogentry.RedoInfo :=
    inverse action of the action in logentry;
   newlogentry.NextUndoSeqNo :=
    logentry.PreviousSeqNo;
   ActiveTrans[transid].LastSeqNo :=
    newlogentry.LogSeqNo;
   LogBuffer += newlogentry;
   write (logentry.PageNo)
    according to logentry.UndoInfo;
   logentry := logentry.PreviousSeqNo;
end /*while*/
newlogentry.LogSeqNo := new sequence number;
newlogentry.ActionType := rollback;
newlogentry.TransId := transid;
newlogentry.PreviousSeqNo :=
 ActiveTrans[transid].LastSeqNo;
newlogentry.NextUndoSeqNo := nil;
LogBuffer += newlogentry;
ActiveTrans -= transid;
force ( );
```

For completeness of the presentation, the algorithm for undo completion during restart is illustrated by the scenario in Figure 13.19. The example is based on the scenario in Figures 13.14 and 13.15 of Section 13.4.2; the differences are in the undo phase of the two restarts, where we now make use of the NextUndoSeqNo chaining technique. The log entries whose NextUndoSeqNo fields are important appear in boldface type.

We conclude this section by casting the already presented correctness arguments for the undo completion method in the rigorous form of a theorem.

Correctness of undo completion with NextUndoSeqNo backward chaining

---

THEOREM 13.8

The method for undo completion, based on executing compensation actions and creating compensation log entries that are backward chained to reflect the next undo log sequence numbers, preserves the correctness of the three-pass redo-history recovery algorithm.

Sequence number: action	Change of cached database [PageNo: SeqNo]	Change of stable database [PageNo: SeqNo]	Log entry added to log buffer [LogSeqNo: action]	Log entries added to stable log [LogSeqNo's]
1: begin(t_1)			1: begin(t_1)	
2: begin(t_2)			2: begin(t_2)	
3: write(a, t_1)	a: 3		3: write(a, t_1)	
4: begin(t_3)			4: begin(t_3)	
5: begin(t_4)			5: begin(t_4)	
6: write(b, t_3)	b: 6		6: write(b, t_3)	
7: write(c, t_2)	c: 7		7: write(c, t_2)	
8: write(d, t_1)	d: 8		8: write(d, t_1)	
9: commit(t_1)			9: commit(t_1)	1, 2, 3, 4, 5, 6, 7, 8, 9
10: flush(d)		d: 8		
11: write(d, t_3)	d: 11		11: write(d, t_3)	
12: begin(t_5)			12: begin(t_5)	
13: write(a, t_5)	a: 13		13: write(a, t_5)	
14: commit(t_3)			14: commit(t_3)	11, 12, 13, 14
15: flush(d)		d: 11		
16: write(d, t_4)	d: 16		16: write(d, t_4)	
17: write(e, t_2)	e: 17		17: write(e, t_2)	
18: write(b, t_5)	b: 18		18: write(b, t_5)	
19: flush(b)		b: 18		16, 17, 18
20: commit(t_4)			20: commit(t_4)	20
21: write(f, t_5)	f: 21		21: write(f, t_5)	
System crash and restart				
Analysis pass: losers = {t_2, t_5}				
redo(3)	a: 3			
consider-redo(6)	b: 18			
flush(a)		a: 3		
redo(7)	c: 7			
consider-redo(8)	d: 11			
consider-redo(11)	d: 11			
redo(13)	a: 13			
redo(16)	d: 16			
redo(17)	e: 17			
consider-redo(18)	b: 18			
flush(a)		a: 13		
22: compensate(18)	b: 22		22: compensate(18: b, t_5) NextUndoSeqNo: 13	
23: compensate(17)	e: 23		23: compensate(17: e, t_2) NextUndoSeqNo: 7	
flush(b)		b: 22		22, 23
24: compensate(13)	a: 24		24: compensate(13: a, t_5) NextUndoSeqNo: nil	
25: rollback(t_5)			25: rollback(t_5)	
Second system crash and second restart				
Analysis pass: losers = {t_2, t_5}				
consider-redo(3)	a: 13			
consider-redo(6)	b: 22			
redo(7)	c: 7			
consider-redo(8)	d: 11			
consider-redo(11)	d: 11			
consider-redo(13)	a: 13			
redo(16)	d: 16			
redo(17)	e: 17			
consider-redo(18)	b: 22			
consider-redo(22)	b: 22			
redo(23)	e: 23			
26: compensate(13)	a: 26		26: compensate(13: a, t_5) NextUndoSeqNo: nil	
27: rollback(t_5)			27: rollback(t_5)	
28: compensate(7)	c: 28		28: compensate(7: c, t_2) NextUndoSeqNo: nil	
29: rollback(t_2)			29: rollback(t_2)	
force				26, 27, 28, 29
Second restart complete: resume normal operation				

Figure 13.19 Example scenario for the undo completion of the three-pass redo-history recovery algorithm.

Proof

For operations of loser transactions that already have an inverse operation on the stable log (in the form of a compensation log entry), the redo pass will redo both the forward and the inverse operation; so this pair already reduces to a null step. By traversing the NextUndoSeqNo backward chain, the undo pass considers exactly those operations for which no inverse operation has been tracked on the stable log; so these operations to be undone must be regular forward operations. By creating a compensation log entry whose NextUndoSeqNo pointer bypasses the undone operation, this property keeps holding even if the server crashes again immediately after the undo step. In formal terms, the invariant that holds throughout the undo pass is

$\forall$ log sequence numbers $s \in$ stable log such that all more recent
       log entries of losers, including $s,$ have been processed for undo :
       $\forall$ operations $u \in$ stable log with u.LogSeqNo $\geq s$.LogSeqNo :
       $\forall$ operations $o \in$ stable log :
           $(u.\text{TransId} \in \text{losers} \wedge o.\text{TransId} = u.\text{TransId} \wedge o.\text{LogSeqNo}$
           $> u.\text{NextUndoSeqNo}) \Rightarrow o \notin$ cached database

13.5 **Lessons Learned**

This section summarizes the method of choice for page model crash recovery, putting together the various optimizations of the previous sections. Overall, we consider the redo-history algorithm as preferable over the redo-winners paradigm because of its uniform and thus simpler treatment of winner versus loser transactions and transaction rollbacks. This uniformity also results in a potentially significant performance advantage by not being forced to flush any pages during restart, unlike the undo phase of the redo-winners algorithm. It further pays off in that it makes the overall algorithm conceptually simpler, which usually results in a more robust implementation. However, the two recovery paradigms still have more commonalities than differences. The major building blocks common to both algorithms are

- a three-pass structure for log analysis, redo recovery, and undo recovery;
- lightweight checkpoints as an effective and low-cost way of log truncation, accelerating both the analysis pass and the redo pass;
- additional flush log entries for further cost savings during the redo pass;
- compensation log entries for transaction rollbacks during normal operation, and the completion of loser transactions during the undo phase of the restart to facilitate further log truncation.

In addition, the redo-history algorithm has its unique way of handling loser transactions:

- a redo pass that includes all actions of loser transactions,
- an undo pass that completes loser transactions as if they were winners (including the creation of new log entries for the necessary compensation actions), thus simplifying the undo algorithm and completely eliminating the need for having flush pages during restart.

The algorithms developed in this chapter allow both physiological and physical log entries. The only forced log I/Os are those due to the undo rule and upon commit actions, including the group commit option. Thus, the logging overhead during normal operation is no bottleneck.

For fast restart, the recovery algorithm should be complemented by a write-behind daemon that flushes dirty cache pages to support log truncation upon a checkpoint. The algorithm's ability to handle the coexistence of physiological and physical log entries is also beneficial with regard to restart time in that it allows further advancing the redo sequence number of a page when the analysis or redo pass encounters a full-write log entry. In addition, the recovery algorithm may even generate and log its own full-write actions during normal operation, in order to discard older log entries for a page without having to flush the page. So the recovery algorithm performs excellently in terms of restart time, and can thus achieve very high system availability.

13.5.1 **Putting Everything Together**

Pseudocode for the complete algorithm of choice, including the various optimizations, is given below. There is no need for another discussion of correctness, given the incremental arguments of the previous sections. The pseudocode is based on the following data structures; the difference from the basic data structures introduced in Section 13.2 is that we now include all details related to checkpoints and the I/O optimizations during the redo pass.

```
/* Data structures for the page model recovery algorithm
 of choice: */
type Page: record of
 PageNo: identifier;
 PageSeqNo: identifier;
 Status: (clean, dirty);
 Contents: array [PageSize] of char;
 end;
persistent var StableDatabase:
 set of Page indexed by PageNo;
```

Data structures for page model recovery algorithm

```
            var DatabaseCache:
             set of Page indexed by PageNo;
            type LogEntry: record of
              LogSeqNo: identifier;
              TransId: identifier;
              PageNo: identifier;
              ActionType: (write, full-write, begin, commit, rollback,
               compensate, checkpoint, flush);
              ActiveTrans: set of TransInfo;
               /* present only in log entries of type checkpoint */
              DirtyPages: set of DirtyPageInfo;
               /* present only in log entries of type checkpoint */
              UndoInfo: array of char;
              RedoInfo: array of char;
              PreviousSeqNo: identifier;
              NextUndoSeqNo: identifier;
             end;
            persistent var StableLog:
              ordered set of LogEntry indexed by LogSeqNo;
            var LogBuffer:
              ordered set of LogEntry indexed by LogSeqNo;
            persistent var MasterRecord: record of
              StartPointer: identifier;
              LastCP: identifier;
             end;
            type TransInfo: record of
              TransId: identifier;
              LastSeqNo: identifier;
             end;
            var ActiveTrans:
              set of TransInfo indexed by TransId;
            typeDirtyPageInfo: record of
              PageNo: identifier;
              RedoSeqNo: identifier;
             end;
            var DirtyPages:
              set of DirtyPageInfo indexed by PageNo;
```

The pseudocode for the actions during normal operation then looks as follows.

Actions during
normal
operation
```
write or full-write (pageno, transid, s):
  DatabaseCache[pageno].Contents := modified contents;
  DatabaseCache[pageno].PageSeqNo := s;
  DatabaseCache[pageno].Status := dirty;
```

```
newlogentry.LogSeqNo := s;
newlogentry.ActionType := write or full-write;
newlogentry.TransId := transid;
newlogentry.PageNo := pageno;
newlogentry.UndoInfo := information to undo update
  (before image for full-write);
newlogentry.RedoInfo := information to redo update
  (after image for full-write);
newlogentry.PreviousSeqNo :=
  ActiveTrans[transid].LastSeqNo;
ActiveTrans[transid].LastSeqNo := s;
LogBuffer += newlogentry;
if pageno not in DirtyPages then
 DirtyPages += pageno;
 DirtyPages[pageno].RedoSeqNo := s;
end /*if*/;

fetch (pageno):
 DatabaseCache += pageno;
 DatabaseCache[pageno].Contents :=
  StableDatabase[pageno].Contents;
 DatabaseCache[pageno].PageSeqNo :=
  StableDatabase[pageno].PageSeqNo;
 DatabaseCache[pageno].Status := clean;

flush (pageno):
 if there is logentry in LogBuffer with logentry.PageNo = pageno
 then
  force ( );
 end /*if*/;
 StableDatabase[pageno].Contents :=
  DatabaseCache[pageno].Contents;
 StableDatabase[pageno].PageSeqNo :=
  DatabaseCache[pageno].PageSeqNo;
 DatabaseCache[pageno].Status := clean;
 newlogentry.LogSeqNo := next sequence number to be generated;
 newlogentry.ActionType := flush;
 newlogentry.PageNo := pageno;
 LogBuffer += newlogentry;
 DirtyPages -= pageno;

force ( ):
 StableLog += LogBuffer;
 LogBuffer := empty;
```

```
begin (transid, s):
 ActiveTrans += transid;
 ActiveTrans[transid].LastSeqNo := s;
 newlogentry.LogSeqNo := s;
 newlogentry.ActionType := begin;
 newlogentry.TransId := transid;
 newlogentry.PreviousSeqNo := nil;
 LogBuffer += newlogentry;


commit (transid, s):
 newlogentry.LogSeqNo := s;
 newlogentry.ActionType := commit;
 newlogentry.TransId := transid;
 newlogentry.PreviousSeqNo :=
  ActiveTrans[transid].LastSeqNo;
 LogBuffer += newlogentry;
 ActiveTrans -= transid;
 force ( );


abort (transid):
 logentry :=
  ActiveTrans[transid].LastSeqNo;
 while logentry is not nil and
  logentry.ActionType = write or full-write
 do
  newlogentry.LogSeqNo := new sequence number;
  newlogentry.ActionType := compensation;
  newlogentry.PreviousSeqNo :=
   ActiveTrans[transid].LastSeqNo;
  newlogentry.RedoInfo :=
   inverse action of the action in logentry;
  newlogentry.NextUndoSeqNo :=
   logentry.PreviousSeqNo;
  ActiveTrans[transid].LastSeqNo :=
   newlogentry.LogSeqNo;
  LogBuffer += newlogentry;
  write (logentry.PageNo)
   according to logentry.UndoInfo;
  logentry := logentry.PreviousSeqNo;
 end /*while*/
 newlogentry.LogSeqNo := new sequence number;
 newlogentry.ActionType := rollback;
 newlogentry.TransId := transid;
```

```
newlogentry.PreviousSeqNo :=
 ActiveTrans[transid].LastSeqNo;
newlogentry.NextUndoSeqNo := nil;
LogBuffer += newlogentry;
ActiveTrans -= transid;
force ( );

log truncation ( ):
 OldestUndoLSN :=
  min {i|StableLog[i].TransId is in ActiveTrans};
 SystemRedoLSN := min {DirtyPages[p].RedoSeqNo};
 OldestRedoPage := page p such that
  DirtyPages[p].RedoSeqNo = SystemRedoLSN;
 NewStartPointer := min{OldestUndoLSN, SystemRedoLSN};
 OldStartPointer := MasterRecord.StartPointer;
 while OldStartPointer - NewStartPointer
   is not sufficiently large
 and SystemRedoLSN < OldestUndoLSN
 do
  flush (OldestRedoPage);
  SystemRedoLSN := min{DatabaseCache[p].RedoLSN};
  OldestRedoPage := page p such that
   DatabaseCache[p].RedoLSN = SystemRedoLSN;
  NewStartPointer := min{OldestUndoLSN, SystemRedoLSN};
 end /*while*/;
 MasterRecord.StartPointer := NewStartPointer;

checkpoint ( ):
 logentry.ActionType := checkpoint;
 logentry.ActiveTrans := ActiveTrans (as maintained in memory);
 logentry.DirtyPages := DirtyPages (as maintained in memory);
 logentry.LogSeqNo := next sequence number to be generated;
 LogBuffer += logentry;
 force ( );
 MasterRecord.LastCP := logentry.LogSeqNo;
```

Finally, the pseudocode for the three phases of the restart is given "in one piece" below. (All ingredients appeared earlier in this chapter, but were scattered throughout the discussion.)

```
restart ( ):                                           Recovery
 analysis pass ( ) returns losers, DirtyPages;         algorithms
 redo pass ( );
 undo pass ( );
```

```
analysis pass ( ) returns losers, DirtyPages:
 var losers: set of record
  TransId: identifier;
  LastSeqNo: identifier;
 end indexed by TransId;
 cp := MasterRecord.LastCP;
 losers := StableLog[cp].ActiveTrans;
 DirtyPages := StableLog[cp].DirtyPages;
 max := LogSeqNo of most recent log entry in StableLog;
 for i := cp to max do
  case StableLog[i].ActionType:
   begin:
   losers += StableLog[i].TransId;
   losers[StableLog[i].TransId].LastSeqNo := nil;
  commit:
   losers -= StableLog[i].TransId;
  full-write:
   losers[StableLog[i].TransId].LastSeqNo := i;
  end /*case*/;
  if StableLog[i].ActionType = write or full-write or compensate
   and StableLog[i].PageNo not in DirtyPages
  then
   DirtyPages += StableLog[i].PageNo;
   DirtyPages[StableLog[i].PageNo].RedoSeqNo := i;
  end /*if*/;
  if StableLog[i].ActionType = flush
  then
   DirtyPages -= StableLog[i].PageNo;
  end /*if*/;
 end /*for*/;


 redo pass ( ):
  SystemRedoLSN := min {DirtyPages[p].RedoSeqNo};
  max := LogSeqNo of most recent log entry in StableLog;
  for i := SystemRedoLSN to max do
   if StableLog[i].ActionType = write or full-write or compensate
   then
    pageno = StableLog[i].PageNo;
    fetch (pageno);
    if pageno in DirtyPages and
     DirtyPages[pageno].RedoSeqNo < i
    then
     fetch (pageno);
```

```
     if DatabaseCache[pageno].PageSeqNo < i
     then
      read and write (pageno)
       according to StableLog[i].RedoInfo;
      DatabaseCache[pageno].PageSeqNo := i;
     end /*if*/;
    end /*if*/;
   end /*if*/;
 end /*for*/;

undo pass ( ):
 ActiveTrans := empty;
 for each t in losers
 do
  ActiveTrans += t;
  ActiveTrans[t].LastSeqNo := losers[t].LastSeqNo;
 end /*for*/;
 while there exists t in losers
  such that losers[t].LastSeqNo <> nil
 do
  nexttrans := TransNo in losers
   such that losers[nexttrans].LastSeqNo =
   max {losers[x].LastSeqNo|x in losers};
  nextentry := losers[nexttrans].LastSeqNo;
  if StableLog[nextentry].ActionType = compensation
  then
   losers[nexttrans].LastSeqNo := StableLog[nextentry].NextUndoSeqNo;
  end /*if*/;
  if StableLog[nextentry].ActionType = write or full-write
  then
   pageno = StableLog[nextentry].PageNo;
   fetch (pageno);
   if DatabaseCache[pageno].PageSeqNo >= nextentry.LogSeqNo
   then
    newlogentry.LogSeqNo := new sequence number;
    newlogentry.ActionType := compensation;
    newlogentry.PreviousSeqNo := ActiveTrans[transid].LastSeqNo;
    newlogentry.NextUndoSeqNo := nextentry.PreviousSeqNo;
    newlogentry.RedoInfo :=
     inverse action of the action in nextentry;
    ActiveTrans[transid].LastSeqNo := newlogentry.LogSeqNo;
    LogBuffer += newlogentry;
    read and write (StableLog[nextentry].PageNo)
     according to StableLog[nextentry].UndoInfo;
```

```
        DatabaseCache[pageno].PageSeqNo := newlogentry.LogSeqNo;
        end /*if*/;
        losers[nexttrans].LastSeqNo =
        StableLog[nextentry].PreviousSeqNo;
      end /*if*/;
      if StableLog[nextentry].ActionType = begin
      then
        newlogentry.LogSeqNo := new sequence number;
        newlogentry.ActionType := rollback;
        newlogentry.TransId := StableLog[nextentry].TransId;
        newlogentry.PreviousSeqNo := ActiveTrans[transid].LastSeqNo;
        LogBuffer += newlogentry;
        ActiveTrans -= transid;
        losers -= transid;
      end /*if*/;
    end /*while*/;
    force ( );
```

Exercises

13.1 Consider the action history given in Figure 13.20, including checkpoints and flush actions. Assume that there is a system crash right after the last action. Determine the necessary logging actions during normal operation and the recovery actions during restart by completing the table. First consider the case where heavyweight checkpoints are used and flush actions are not logged; then consider lightweight checkpoints; and finally, discuss the additional effect of keeping log entries for flush actions. In all cases, assume that the redo-history paradigm is employed.

Now consider the extended scenario given in Figure 13.21. In contrast to the previous scenario, this action history contains two transaction rollbacks during normal operation, one of which is completed before the crash, whereas the second one is interrupted by the crash. Determine again the necessary logging and restart actions for this scenario by completing Figure 13.21.

13.2 Consider the redo-winners three-pass recovery algorithm for the page model. Reconsider the undo pass for the following variations: assume that the history, rather than being log recoverable, is only recoverable or strict. Especially, for the strict case, show that it is feasible to undo each loser transaction separately in arbitrary transaction order rather than having to merge all loser backward chains into a single ordering.

13.3 Consider the following specialization of the redo-winners algorithm. Assume that all updates are logged as full-writes, so that log entries have

Sequence number: action	Change of cached database [PageNo: SeqNo]	Change of stable database [PageNo: SeqNo]	Log entry added to log buffer [LogSeqNo: action]	Log entries added to stable log [LogSeqNo's]
1: begin(t_1)				
2: write(p, t_1)				
3: write(q, t_1)				
4: commit(t_1)				
5: flush(p)				
6: begin(t_2)				
7: write(p, t_2)				
8: write(r, t_2)				
9: checkpoint				
10: commit(t_2)				
11: begin(t_3)				
12: flush(p)				
13: write(p, t_3)				
14: write(q, t_3)				
15: flush(q)				
16: write(r, t_3)				

Figure 13.20 Sample history for Exercise 13.1.

the form of page before images or after images. Further assume that the database cache is large enough to have the no-steal property, which guarantees that a page that has been modified by an active (i.e., incomplete) transaction is never flushed. In addition, assume that the log buffer is also large enough to contain all before images of all active transactions. Design a special recovery algorithm under this premise that (a) should be simpler than the general-purpose redo-winners algorithm and (b) aims to shorten the restart duration as much as possible. In particular, address the following issues: Are checkpoints still needed at all (under the no-steal premise)? How can you handle transaction aborts? Is there a way of gracefully degrading the special algorithm if the no-steal property cannot be guaranteed but the database cache is almost always large enough to avoid flushing pages whose last modification belongs to an active transaction?

Hint: The DB Cache algorithm of Bayer and Elhardt (1984) is such an algorithm (see Bibliographic Notes).

13.4 Reconsider the redo pass of the redo-history algorithm. Show that writes for a page that originate from loser transactions and are not followed by any winner writes on the same page do not need to be redone during the redo pass. Design a variant of the redo-history algorithm, both the redo and the undo pass, that avoids redoing writes in the above category,

Sequence number: action	Change of cached database [PageNo: SeqNo]	Change of stable database [PageNo: SeqNo]	Log entry added to log buffer [LogSeqNo: action]	Log entries added to stable log [LogSeqNo's]
1: begin(t_1)				
2: write(p, t_1)				
3: write(q, t_1)				
4: commit(t_1)				
5: flush(p)				
6: begin(t_2)				
7: write(p, t_2)				
8: write(r, t_2)				
9: checkpoint				
10: abort(t_2)				
11: compensate(8:write(r, t_2))				
12: compensate(7:write(p, t_2))				
13: rollback(t_2) complete				
14: begin(t_3)				
15: flush(p)				
16: write(p, t_3)				
17: write(q, t_3)				
18: flush(q)				
19: write(r, t_3)				
20: abort(t_3)				
21: compensate(18:write(r, t_3))				
22: begin(t_4)				
23: compensate(17:write(q, t_3))				
24: write(s, t_4)				
25: flush(q)				
26: commit(t_4)				

Figure 13.21 Sample history with rollbacks for Exercise 13.1.

thus reducing the overall work of the redo pass. Note that this reduction is usually not a major gain, as it affects only a small fraction of log entries; this variant is interesting in that it consolidates and deepens the understanding of the relationships between the redo and the undo pass.

Hint: The ARIES/RRH algorithm by Mohan and Pirahesh (1991) is such a variant of the redo-history algorithm (see Bibliographic Notes).

Bibliographic Notes

The algorithmic state of the art for the page model is documented by Crus (1984), with the commercial database system DB2 from IBM as a reference implementation. This system already employed a redo-history algorithm, and it made use of compensation log entries, coined "compensation log records (CLRs)" there. Mohan, Haderle, et al. (1992) made the redo-history paradigm explicit, generalized it, and provided enhanced algorithmic techniques. Mohan coined the name "ARIES" (Algorithm for Recovery and Isolation Exploiting Semantics) for the redo-history algorithm. Mohan and Pirahesh (1991) studied certain variations of the ARIES algorithm. Lindsay et al. (1979) provided a detailed discussion of checkpointing techniques, and is also the original source of the redo optimization based on the logging of page flushes; detailed discussions of checkpointing can also be found in the seminal articles by Gray (1978) and Härder and Reuter (1983). Full implementation details, down to the level of C code, on many of the discussed aspects (such as implementing a sequential log file and the log file buffer) can be found in the book by Gray and Reuter (1993).

A specialized page model recovery method that is tailored to a no-steal database cache was elaborated by Elhardt and Bayer (1984) into a method called "DB Cache algorithm." This method was initially limited to physical log entries for full-writes, but has been generalized by Moss et al. (1987) to allow physiological log entries as well. Another approach along these lines, with more advanced techniques for garbage collection of unneeded log entries, has been proposed by Keen and Dally (1997). Rosenblum and Ousterhout (1992) have even developed an entire log-structured file system organization based on full-write logging with efficient garbage collection.

The group commit technique has been explicitly mentioned by Gawlick and Kinkade (1985); commercial implementations such as IMS Fast Path predated the published account of this technique. The optimization of group commit timers has been analyzed by Helland et al. (1987). Mathematical considerations for the optimization of (heavyweight) checkpoint intervals have been presented by Chandy et al. (1975), Gelenbe (1979), and Reuter (1984). Alternative algorithms that do not belong to the with-undo/with-redo family have been developed by Lorie (1977), who introduced the concept of shadow storage; Reuter (1980), who considered transaction-oriented variants of shadow storage; Severance and Lohman (1976); as well as Aghili and Severance (1982), who presented deferred-update techniques based on differential files.

Attempts to formalize the correctness reasoning on crash recovery algorithms have been made by Hadzilacos (1988), Kuo (1996), Wallace et al. (1995), Lomet and Tuttle (1995), and Martin and Ramamritham (1997). In particular, a variant of Theorem 13.1 has been presented by Hadzilacos (1988). Performance issues were studied by Reuter (1984), Kent et al. (1985), as well as Agrawal and DeWitt (1985a), with a focus on analyzing the normal operation overhead and its impact on system throughput, and by Jhingran and Khedkar (1992) as well as Goes and Sumita (1995), who also considered restart duration and system availability.

CHAPTER FOURTEEN

Object Model Crash Recovery

This we know. All things are connected.
—*Chief Seattle*

Already know you that which you need.
—*Yoda*

14.1 Goal and Overview

In this chapter we extend the discussion of crash recovery to the object model. We will mostly focus on layered executions, and our exposition will present the special case of two-level systems first and in great detail, and later generalize the presented algorithms to the general case of nonlayered object model executions. Note that the two-level case is of utmost practical importance, as it captures the transaction management at the access layer of modern, industrial-strength database systems with fine-grained record and index-key locking. In addition, a layer of object-style application services on top of a data server, such as e-Commerce services, is also appropriately described by the two-level architectural model.

Our approach in this chapter is to leverage insights from the previous chapters. In particular, we will focus on the redo-history paradigm for crash recovery and ignore any other conceivable algorithmic approaches. In fact, the arguments for a redo-history algorithm are even more compelling in the context of the object model; a redo-winners algorithm would encounter extreme difficulties in the generalization to higher-level operations. The basic principle of redoing history, as explained in Chapter 13, is to reconstruct a system state as of the time of the crash, and once this is established, the further recovery steps can essentially proceed as if the system were running normally and simply initiate transaction recovery steps as in Chapter 11. This is, of course, a simplified picture of what we need for object model crash recovery, but it underlines the simplicity and elegance of the approach, with simplicity and modularity being important assets for increasing our confidence in the correctness of algorithms. For the same reason, we will again develop the recovery method in an incremental manner, starting out with a simple, not necessarily very efficient algorithm, and gradually refining and enhancing it into a highly optimized, industrial-strength method.

Throughout this chapter we will assume that the history during normal operation is tree-prefix reducible. Recall from Chapter 11 what this means: the combined effect of higher-level operations—both "forward" and inverse operations on behalf of transaction aborts—and the underlying low-level operations is equivalent to a serial execution of the roots of committed transactions. Moreover, this equivalence can be proven by reducing the history to these roots using simple transformation rules. Furthermore we assume, for simpler explanation, that all nonleaf operations in a transaction are totally ordered. So we essentially rule out the option for parallel subtransactions within the same transaction. Generalizing the algorithms developed to cover this case is not particularly difficult; we thus leave this task for you to complete in Exercise 14.4.

The chapter is organized as follows. Section 14.2 presents the fundamental principles of object model crash recovery based on the redo-history paradigm. Section 14.3 then develops a simple, yet complete recovery algorithm for two-level executions. Section 14.4 enhances this algorithm by integrating various performance improvements, but is still restricted to the two-level framework. Finally, Section 14.5 generalizes the developed algorithm so that it is applicable to all object model executions, layered as well as nonlayered ones.

14.2 Conceptual Overview of Redo-History Algorithms

The additional difficulty that an object model crash recovery method has to address is the handling of semantically rich, high-level operations such as increment and decrement on counters or operations on index structures for searching, inserting, or deleting keys, to recall just two prominent examples. This problem entails two issues:

1. How to redo the effects of high-level operations if they belong to a winner transaction.

2. How to undo the effects of high-level operations if they belong to a loser transaction.

The necessity of high-level undo   With regard to the undo issue, we do not have much of a choice. The arguments that dictate using high-level inverse operations for undo steps given in Chapter 11 in the context of transaction recovery (i.e., transaction rollbacks during normal operation) apply to the crash recovery setting as well. Once we allow two commutative update operations on the same object to proceed concurrently and later face the need for undoing the effect of the first operation while wishing to retain the effect of the second operation, invoking a high-level inverse operation that commutes with the second operation is the only correct form of undo recovery.

As for the redo issue, however, we have more flexibility. We may choose to redo transactions, if necessary, by reinvoking their high-level operations and executing them again in full-fledged form; or alternatively, we may simply redo the page writes that were issued on behalf of the original high-level operations. Between these two alternatives, the page-oriented redo is much preferred for the following reason. The duration of the redo pass is the most critical factor in the restart time and thus in the server's availability. Reexecuting high-level operations would, however, duplicate most of the operation's original work, typically including many page reads from the underlying disk-resident database or files. Contrast this amount of work with merely having to read and write the pages that were actually written in the original execution, which is often more than an order of magnitude less work. So in view of this restart cost comparison, the choice in favor of the purely page-oriented redo method is obvious.

The case for page-level redo

This discussion leads us directly to the following three-phase recovery method:

1. The *analysis phase* works exactly like the page model algorithms to determine loser transactions; there is nothing special about high-level operations in this phase.

2. The *redo phase* performs redo steps for all logged page writes (regardless of whether they belong to winners or losers), based on physical or physiological page-oriented log entries. All optimizations introduced in Chapter 13 for the page model redo pass apply here as well.

3. The *undo phase* invokes inverse high-level operations for all logged high-level operations of loser transactions, based on scanning appropriate "logical" log entries in reverse chronological order.

So the "big picture" is quite simple and not that dissimilar from the page model recovery method. There are, however, two major complications that were not present in the page model:

First, high-level operations are not atomic by themselves, so that an invoked inverse operation may find the data in a state that contains *partial* results of high-level operations. Note that this can occur by the crash interrupting an ongoing high-level operation or because of having flushed some but not all of the pages that were written by an operation. In either case, the inverse operation is no longer well defined in the state reconstructed by a redo-history pass. For example, suppose that a server crashes right after having inserted a new index key that led to a split (or even crashes in the middle of this split), and the newly created index leaf survives the crash (i.e., has been flushed before the crash);

Problem: atomicity of high-level operations

whereas the update to the affected leaves' parent becomes lost due to the crash. The necessary inverse operation (deleting the key) cannot be executed on the resulting state, as it would perceive the index structure itself as corrupted.

Problem: idempotence of high-level operations

The second problem has to do with the fact that high-level operations such as incrementing or decrementing a counter are often not idempotent. In the page model, we used page sequence numbers (i.e., LSNs in page headers) to allow the recovery method to test a page's state with regard to which writes were present and which were absent. In particular, before we introduced compensation log entries (CLEs), our method for tracking the progress of undo steps was to decrease the page sequence number in the header of the affected page. In the object model, however, we need to generalize this kind of state testing to higher-level operations beyond the scope of individual pages. For example, suppose that the Delete operation for the above index example has been performed as part of the recovery's undo phase. We cannot simply reset the affected page sequence numbers to the LSNs of the original writes' immediate predecessors as we did in the (simple) redo-winners algorithm for the page model. Rather, we need to take into account that one or more of the affected pages may contain chronologically later winner updates as well that were redone before the undo pass. If such a page was flushed to disk after the undo step and the server failed again, the subsequent restart would erroneously redo the winner update a second time. So the fundamental problem that we encounter here is that the same page may contain both winner and loser updates such that the loser update preceded the winner update in the history. This situation is inherent in fine-grained, object model–style concurrency control. The bottom line is that state tracking and testing is no longer possible by page LSNs, at least not by page LSNs alone. We will see in a short while that appropriate use of CLEs and always increasing page sequence numbers provide a solution that is very similar to the complete redo-history algorithm for the page model.

As a more concrete illustration of the two problems, consider the sample execution in Figure 14.1, with time proceeding from left to right, and assume that the server crashes after the commit of t_2 but before t_1 is completed. Further assume that each of the Increment operations in the scenario needs to write two different pages, for example, to maintain some derived data as part of the operations' ADT semantics. The restart after the failure would first redo all page writes of the example and then needs to undo t_1 by issuing two appropriate Decrement operations on y and x, respectively. But then, no matter how we set the page LSN of page p, which was modified by both t_1 and t_2, we lose the ability to test for the presence of each of the two operations: resetting the page LSN to a value preceding t_{11} would no longer indicate the presence of t_{21}, even if the page was flushed after (the redo of) t_{21}; leaving the page LSN's value as it was set by t_{21}, on the other hand, can no longer detect whether the inverse operation of t_{11} has been successfully carried out. Even more obvious than this subtle pitfall with regard to idempotence is the atomicity problem. Suppose

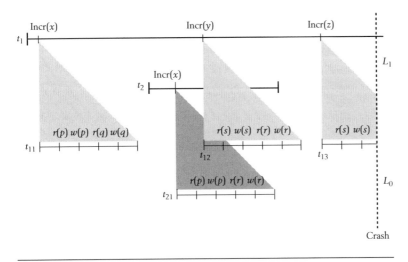

Figure 14.1 Example execution illustrating the problems of object model crash recovery.

that the server crashes right after t_{11}'s write operation on page p and that p has been flushed to disk before the crash. In this state, it may be impossible to execute the inverse decr(x) operation correctly, as this operation would see only one of the two relevant pages in the state after the original incr(x).

The solution to these problems is twofold:

1. We need to ensure the *atomicity of subtransactions* by keeping page-level undo log entries, in the physical or physiological form, in addition to the high-level undo log entries for inverse operations. Then, during restart, we need to augment the redo pass with page-level undo steps that eliminate all partial effects of subtransactions. So strictly speaking, we need an additional phase during recovery, but this does not create much overhead and may even be viewed as an implicit extension of the redo pass. Together these measures constitute the *page-level stage* of a two-level crash recovery scheme. The result of this page-level stage is to reconstruct the effects of exactly all subtransactions that were completed at the time of the crash and ensure that no other effects are present. The implementation of the page-level recovery stage can essentially adopt the best-known techniques from Chapter 13, simply replacing the word "transaction" with "subtransaction."

    Solution: subtransaction atomicity by page-level undo

2. Once the page-level recovery stage completes and leaves only the effects of completed subtransactions, the *object-level stage* of the two-level recovery scheme is in a position to initiate inverse operations for the

*Solution:
object-level
idempotence by
logging during
restart*

high-level operations of loser transactions, by looking up the "logical undo" entries in the log. Since page LSNs are no longer useful in this stage, tracking the progress of the undo must be based on re-creating log entries during restart. This is very similar to the creation of CLEs for aborted transactions and during the undo phase of the page model redo-history algorithm, as discussed in Chapter 13. Once each successfully complete inverse operation is logged on the stable log, we can later perform an analysis on these log entries to avoid erroneously invoking the inverse operation a second time. However, this holds only if the first execution of the inverse operation is guaranteed to survive the crash, and is guaranteed so in its entirety. This guarantee is obtained from the underlying page-level stage of the recovery, as we consider a completed subtransaction. So the page-level stage should redo page writes of the inverse operation, so that the existence of an object-level CLE-style log entry correctly reflects the absence of the original high-level operation (or, equivalently, the presence of the compensation) in the current state of the data.

14.3 A Simple Redo-History Algorithm for Two-Layered Systems

In this section we present a simple recovery algorithm for two-layered systems based on the redo-history paradigm. We emphasize conceptual clarity for the sake of confidence in the algorithm's correctness. In subsequent sections, we will derive more efficient enhanced algorithms from this simple baseline.

14.3.1 Actions during Normal Operation

The simple recovery algorithm uses separate logs for the two levels of operations:

- the L_0 *log* contains physical or physiological undo/redo log entries for page writes on behalf of *subtransactions*,
- the L_1 *log* contains logical undo log entries (i.e., sufficient information about the inverse of a high-level operation) on behalf of *transactions*.

L_0 log   Both logs can be viewed simply as different instantiations of the log structures described in Chapter 13 for the page model. The L_0 log is, in fact, absolutely identical to the page model log, with the only difference being that all its elements refer to subtransactions rather than transactions. In

particular, all algorithms for the page model's redo-history recovery can be carried over without any changes. This also holds for the full spectrum of optimizations such as checkpointing, flush log entries, and CLEs that we discussed in Chapter 13. All we need to do is to replace transaction identifiers by subtransaction identifiers, but as far as the actual management of the L_0 log is concerned, there is no difference. For clarity of the presentation, we will, however, use the terms "subbegin," "subcommit," and "subrollback" when referring to L_0 log entries. During restart, the L_0 recovery will redo all completed subtransactions—that is, those for which it finds a subcommit or subrollback log entry—and will undo all incomplete ones.

The L_1 log can also be viewed as an instantiation of the log structure of Chapter 13. The difference, however, is that we will never perform any redo steps using this log, and the undo steps inferred from the log correspond to the invocation of inverse operations rather than page-oriented undo. The latter was occasionally referred to as compensation in Chapter 13, too, for example, when we introduced CLEs; in fact, there is no real conceptual difference between page-oriented low-level compensation and the high-level compensation that we need now for the L_1 operations. Other than the specific content of log entries and their restriction to undo purposes, the L_1 log is identical to a page model log. In particular, the technique of creating CLEs for undo steps and completing the undo of a transaction with a rollback log entry should be adopted here, too. Note that the fact that the L_1 log merely serves the undo of transactions renders our repertoire of redo optimizations pointless; so there is no notion of checkpointing for the L_1 log, for example.

L_1 log

Each of the two logs consists of a log buffer and a stable log. So we need to analyze at what points one or both of the log buffers have to be forced for correctness:

Log force rules

- The L_0 log buffer needs to be forced whenever a dirty page is flushed to the stable database and the log buffer contains log entries for this page. This is the usual application of the undo log rule from Chapter 12, and not at all specific to the object model. Note that without this forcing we would not be able to guarantee that incomplete subtransactions can be undone and would lose the subtransaction atomicity guarantee.

- The L_1 logbuffer needs to be forced upon the commit of a transaction. This is the usual application of the redo log rule from Chapter 12. As in the page model, it is the existence of the commit log entry on the stable log that really makes a transaction committed, and the transaction commit log entries belong to the transaction-oriented L_1 level in the object model.

   However, the existence of the commit log entry on the L_1 log implies the promise that the transaction's effects can be redone. So at this point, we need to ensure that the log entries for the L_0 redo steps are on stable storage, too. This requires forcing the L_0 log, too, and this writing of the L_0 log buffer onto disk must precede the forcing of the L_1 log buffer. So each commit of a transaction requires forcing both log buffers.

- Once a subtransaction commits (or actually, subcommits) on the L_0 log, it will later be redone by the L_0 recovery if the server crashes. As long as it belongs to an incomplete transaction, however, we need to ensure that we have the necessary information to logically undo the transaction at the L_1 level. This consideration leads to the third and last log force rule: the L_1 log buffer needs to be forced each time the L_0 log buffer is written to the stable log, and the L_1 forcing must precede the forcing of the L_0 log. So we are guaranteed to have the proper inverse operation in our stable log for each subtransaction that survives the crash or will be redone at level L_0. Note, however, that we may find an inverse L_1 operation on the stable log even if the corresponding subtransaction does not survive the crash and will not be redone either. This case may arise if the server fails after having forced the L_1 log but before forcing the L_0 log. We will discuss how to handle this situation in Section 14.3.2.

Note that the two requirements of forcing the L_0 log before the L_1 log and forcing the L_1 log before the L_0 log, stated in the second and third items above, are not contradictory, as they refer to different events. The first of the two orderings applies to transaction commits, and the second one to situations where the L_0 log buffer is full or forced because of flushing a dirty page.

It is important to notice that the L_0 log buffer does not need to be forced upon a subcommit. In this respect, the behavior of the L_0 log differs from simply using a page model log for subtransactions as ACID units. Subtransactions need to be made atomic by the L_0 logging, but unlike transactions, they do not have to be made persistent upon each subcommit. This point is important because the number of forced log I/Os is the most influential factor as far as the server's overhead during normal operation and potential throughput limitations are concerned. The good news about our approach for object model recovery is that, compared to the page model, this overhead is only moderately increased: we have essentially the same number of events that trigger the forcing of a log buffer, but the undo logging rule requires forcing both the L_1 and the L_0 log buffers sequentially, and the commit logging rule requires forcing the L_0 and the L_1 log buffers, again sequentially. We will show in Section 14.4 how this extra burden can also be eliminated in an enhanced version of the algorithm, by merging the log entries for both levels into a single log.

Given that the algorithmics for almost all action types fall out from the page model algorithms and log force rules discussed above, we merely give pseudocode for the L_1 exec actions, which are the only actions during normal operation that are specific to the object model. Note that the log entry created for an L_1 operation may sometimes be generated only at the end of the corresponding subtransaction (i.e., after having performed all its underlying L_0 read/write steps), the reason being that the inverse of such an operation may depend on the forward operation's return values and sometimes even on specific observations on internal state during the execution. In the latter case, the creation of an undo log entry would have to be integrated into the implementation of the ADT to which the operation belongs. In most cases, observing input parameters and return values should suffice, however. Finally, note that the log entry for an L_1 exec action contains both a transaction identifier and a subtransaction identifier; the latter will be seen to be useful in the following subsection.

14.3.2 **Steps during Restart**

Given the two logs that are available after a crash, the overall algorithm for the restart is fairly straightforward:

- First, page-level recovery is carried out by means of the L_0 log. This essentially reconstructs the state as of the crash with all partial effects of incomplete subtransactions removed. Some of the very recently completed subtransactions may be lost, too, if their log entries were not yet forced to the stable log, but no subtransaction of a committed transaction can be lost. As in the page model, this stage of the recovery requires three passes over the log and is based on the redo-history paradigm.
- Second, the L_1 recovery performs an analysis pass over the L_1 log to determine loser transactions, and then performs an undo pass over the L_1 log to initiate the necessary inverse operations for all subtransactions whose (complete) effects are present in the cached database after the L_0 recovery.

The overall restart procedure is summarized in the pseudocode below. Note that the L_0 analysis pass needs to report not only losers but also an explicit list of winner (i.e., completed and possibly redone) subtransactions. This is necessary for the L_1 undo pass, as it may encounter a log entry for a subtransaction that has been undone by the L_0 recovery or did not leave any traces after the crash at all. Recall that this situation may occur because the L_1 log buffer is forced before the L_0 log buffer when the L_0 log buffer is full or a dirty page is about to be flushed. Now the L_1 undo pass has to have a means for testing whether or not a subtransaction is present in the reconstructed state. This is done by looking up the explicit winner list of the L_0 recovery.

Execution of high-level operation

```
exec (op, transid, inputparams, ↑returnvalues, s):
  subbegin ( ) ↑subtransid;
  execute operation;
  newlogentry.LogSeqNo := s;
  newlogentry.ActionType := exec;
  newlogentry.TransId := transid;
  newlogentry.SubtransId := subtransid;
  newlogentry.UndoInfo := information on the
    inverse operation and its parameters;
  newlogentry.PreviousSeqNo := ActiveTrans[transid].LastSeqNo;
  ActiveTrans[transid].LastSeqNo := s;
  L₁LogBuffer += newlogentry;
  subcommit (subtransid);
```

The list of winner subtransactions may be represented in a compact manner, so that it does not incur severe overhead during the L_0 recovery. For example, a specific implementation could use the same unique and monotonically increasing log sequence numbers for both logs together, and the L_0 log analysis could determine the maximum LSN of subbegin log entries in the L_0 log. When a subtransaction has a subbegin log entry on the stable log and is not a loser, then it must be a winner. This observation can be exploited by including the subbegin LSN in the L_1 log entry for the corresponding high-level operation (e.g., instead of, or in addition to, the subtransaction identifier). Then, when we inspect the L_1 log entry during the L_1 undo pass, we compare the entry's subbegin LSN with the maximum subbegin LSN found during the L_0 analysis pass to distinguish the following cases:

- If the L_1 entry's subbegin LSN is higher than the maximum subbegin LSN on the L_0 log, then the subtransaction is not a winner and its further L_1 log entries can be ignored.

- If the L_1 entry's subbegin LSN is smaller than or equal to the maximum subbegin LSN on the L_0 log and the subtransaction is not in the loser list produced by the L_0 log analysis, then it is an L_0 winner and must be undone at level L_1.

- In the remaining case—that is, when the L_1 entry's subbegin LSN is smaller than or equal to the maximum subbegin LSN on the L_0 log and the subtransaction is in the L_0 loser list—then the subtransaction must not be undone at level L_1.

So it suffices for the L_0 analysis pass to keep the much shorter list of winners and determine the maximum subbegin LSN. This information gives us a low-overhead state-testing mechanism for the L_1 undo pass.

```
restart ( ):
  L0 analysis pass ( ) returns losers, winners, DirtyPages;
  L0 redo pass ( );
  L0 undo pass ( );
  L1 analysis pass ( );
  L1 undo pass ( );
```
Simple two-level recovery algorithm

Since all passes of the L_0 recovery and the L_1 analysis pass follow the standard algorithms that we derived for the page model in Chapter 13 (including the various optimizations such as checkpointing or CLEs), we provide pseudocode only for the L_1 undo pass. Note that L_0 logging is again in effect during the execution of high-level inverse operations (which is not shown explicitly in the pseudocode, but can be inferred from the fact that the execution spawns a subtransaction) and that the L_1 undo pass also generates CLEs and links them into undo backward chains, just like the page model redo-history algorithm. Overall, the L_1 undo algorithm is not that different from the L_0 undo pass; the only fundamental difference is the testing of whether an L_1 log entry corresponds to a winner subtransaction.

```
L1 undo pass ( ):                                          L1 undo pass
  ActiveTrans := empty;
  for each t in L1 losers do
   ActiveTrans += t;
   ActiveTrans[t].LastSeqNo := losers[t].LastSeqNo;
  end /*for*/;
  while there exists t in losers
        such that losers[t].LastSeqNo < > nil
  do
    nexttrans := TransNo in losers
      such that losers[nexttrans].LastSeqNo =
      max {losers[x].LastSeqNo|x in losers};
    nextentry := losers[nexttrans].LastSeqNo;
    if StableLog[nextentry].ActionType = compensation then
       if StableLog[nextentry].CompensatingSubtransId is in L0 winners then
        losers[nexttrans].LastSeqNo := StableLog[nextentry].NextUndoSeqNo;
     else
        losers[nexttrans].LastSeqNo := StableLog[nextentry].PreviousSeqNo;
    end /*if*/;
  end /*if*/;
  if StableLog[nextentry].ActionType = exec then
   if StableLog[nextentry].SubtransId is in L0 winners then
   subbegin ( );
   newlogentry.LogSeqNo := new sequence number;
   newlogentry.ActionType := compensation;
```

```
     newlogentry.PreviousSeqNo := ActiveTrans[transid].LastSeqNo;
     newlogentry.NextUndoSeqNo := nextentry.PreviousSeqNo;
     ActiveTrans[transid].LastSeqNo := newlogentry.LogSeqNo;
     LogBuffer += newlogentry;
     execute inverse operation
      according to StableLog[nextentry].UndoInfo;
      subcommit ( );
     end /*if*/;
     losers[nexttrans].LastSeqNo := StableLog
     [nextentry].PreviousSeqNo;
    end /*if*/;
    if StableLog[nextentry].ActionType = begin then
     newlogentry.LogSeqNo := new sequence number;
     newlogentry.ActionType := rollback;
     newlogentry.TransId := StableLog[nextentry].TransId;
     newlogentry.PreviousSeqNo := ActiveTrans[transid].LastSeqNo;
    LogBuffer += newlogentry;
    ActiveTrans -= transid;
    losers -= transid;
   end /*if*/;
  end /*while*/;
  force ( );
```

A complete example of how the simple two-level recovery algorithm works is given in Figures 14.2 (actions during normal operation) and 14.3 (steps during restart), using the scenario given earlier in Figure 14.1. For ease of presentation, no checkpoints or other redo pass optimizations are included in the example. Also, we do not distinguish between log entries in log buffers versus those on stable logs; rather we assume that all log entries are appended to stable logs before the crash. Note that in the example scenario, the high-level inverse operations like $incr^{-1}(x, \, t_1)$ with the LSN 2 can already be created upon invoking the corresponding L_1 "forward" operation, as they do not depend on any result parameters of the forward operations. In general, however, it could be that the L_1 inverse operation is known only upon the subtransaction's subcommit; then the corresponding log entry would be generated and would carry a higher LSN.

Further note that in Figure 14.3 the notation "compensate(. . .) $\uparrow t_{ij}$" indicates that the invocation of an inverse operation itself spawns a new subtransaction t_{ij}. For example, "compensate(11, t_{12}) $\uparrow t_{14}$" means that an inverse operation has been initiated for the logged operation with LSN 11, which corresponded to subtransaction t_{12}, and that this inverse operation has in turn spawned a new subtransaction t_{14}.

As a final remark, note that it may be worthwhile to reconsider special derivatives of the redo-history algorithm as a building block in the specific

Sequence number: action	Cached changes [PageNo: SeqNo]	Stable changes [PageNo: SeqNo]	Log entry added to L_0 log [LogSeqNo: action]	Log entry added to L_1 log [LogSeqNo: action]
1:begin(t_1)				1: begin(t_1)
2: incr(x, t_1)				2: incr^{-1}(x, t_1)
3: subbegin(t_{11})			3: subbegin(t_{11})	
4: write(p, t_{11})	p: 4		4: write(p, t_{11})	
5: write(q, t_{11})	q: 5		5: write(q, t_{11})	
6: subcommit(t_{11})			6: subcommit(t_{11})	
7: begin(t_2)				7: begin(t_2)
8: incr(x, t_2)				8: incr^{-1}(x, t_2)
9: subbegin(t_{21})			9: subbegin(t_{21})	
10: write(p, t_{21})	p: 10		10: write(p, t_{21})	
11: incr(y, t_1)				11: incr^{-1}(y, t_1)
12: subbegin(t_{12})			12: subbegin(t_{12})	
13: write(s, t_{12})	s: 13		13: write(s, t_{12})	
14: flush(p)		p: 10		
15: write(r, t_{21})	r: 15		15: write(r, t_{21})	
16: flush(s)		s: 13		
17: subcommit(t_{21})			17: subcommit(t_{21})	
18: commit(t_2)				18: commit(t_2)
19: write(r, t_{12})	r: 19		19: write(r, t_{12})	
20: subcommit(t_{12})			20: subcommit(t_{12})	
21: incr(z, t_1)				21: incr^{-1}(z, t_1)
22: subbegin(t_{13})			22: subbegin(t_{13})	
23: write(s, t_{13})	s: 23		23: write(s, t_{13})	
System crash				

Figure 14.2 Example scenario for the simple two-level crash recovery algorithm.

context of two-level recovery. Particularly, the "database safe" approach mentioned in Section 13.3.3, under Log Truncation (also known as the DB Cache method in the literature, see the Bibliographic Notes in Chapter 13), which is based on physical logging of full-writes, could be attractive for the page level L_0, given that we now deal with subtransactions that are much shorter than full transactions. The database safe method keeps before images separately from after images, and is designed to hold before images in memory in most cases, which is feasible for short subtransactions. Then, the actual log, coined *safe* in this method, consists only of after images, and unlike physiological log entries, the log truncation can be implemented very effectively with very little overhead. As a result, the duration of the redo pass can essentially be bound to the time for reloading the cache. This attractive property is usually outweighed by the fact that this method works only in combination with page model concurrency control. But when applied to subtransactions, this is not

Sequence number: action	Cached changes [PageNo: SeqNo]	Stable changes [PageNo: SeqNo]	Log entry added to L_0 log [LogSeqNo: action]	Log entry added to L_1 log [LogSeqNo: action]
Restart				
L_0 analysis pass: L_0 losers = {t_{13}}, L_0 winners = {t_{11}, t_{21}, t_{12}}				
consider-redo(4)				
redo(5)	q: 5			
consider-redo(10)				
consider-redo(13)				
redo(15)	r: 15			
redo(19)	r: 19			
redo(23)	s: 23			
24: compensate(23)	s: 4		24: CLE(23), next = nil	
25: subrollback(t_{13})			25: subrollback(t_{13})	
L_1 analysis pass: L_1 losers = {t_1}				
consider-compensate(21, t_{13})				
26: compensate(11, t_{12}) ↑ t_{14}				26: CLE(11, t_{12}, t_{14}), next = 2
27: subbegin(t_{14})			27: subbegin(t_{14})	
28: write(s, t_{14})	s: 28		28: write(s, t_{14})	
29: write(r, t_{14})	r: 29		29: write(r, t_{14})	
30: flush(r)		r: 29		
31: subcommit(t_{14})			31: subcommit(t_{14})	
32: flush(q)		q: 5		
33: compensate(2, t_{11}) ↑ t_{15}				33: CLE(2, t_{11}, t_{15}), next = nil
Second system crash				
Second restart				
L_0 analysis pass: L_0 losers = {t_{15}}, L_0 winners = {t_{11}, t_{21}, t_{12}, t_{13}, t_{14}}				
consider-redo(4)				
consider-redo(5)				
consider-redo(10)				
consider-redo(13)				
consider-redo(15)				
consider-redo(19)				
redo(23)	s: 23			
redo(24)	s: 24			
redo(28)	s: 28			
consider-redo(29)				
34: subrollback(t_{15})			34: subrollback(t_{15})	
L_1 analysis pass: L_1 losers = {t_1}				
35: compensate(2, t_{11}) ↑ t_{16}				35: CLE(2, t_{11}, t_{16}), next = nil
36: subbegin(t_{16})			36: subbegin(t_{16})	
37: write(p, t_{16})	p: 37			
38: write(q, t_{16})	q: 38			
39: subcommit(t_{16})			39: subcommit(t_{16})	
40: rollback(t_1)				40: rollback(t_1)
Second restart complete: resume normal operation				

Figure 14.3 Example scenario for the simple two-level crash recovery algorithm, continued.

a limitation anymore. There are, however, some nontrivial problems with this approach to L_0 recovery; these problems and their solutions are the subject of Exercise 14.2.

14.4 An Enhanced Redo-History Algorithm for Two-Layered Systems

An obvious improvement to the previous section's simple algorithm is to combine the two logs into one. One advantage of this lies in the manageability of the stable log: stable logs exhibit sequential append-only access patterns during normal operation that should result in sequential I/Os on the underlying disk, and these are an order of magnitude more efficient than random I/Os. However, this holds only if we can more or less dedicate a disk to the log. With two separate logs, this condition is obviously harder to guarantee than with a single, combined log.

Single, combined log

There is another benefit from merging the two level-specific logs. Recall that the L_1 log buffer had to be forced immediately before the L_0 log buffer was written to disk. The reason was that we wanted to ensure that the L_1 undo log entry survives the crash if the corresponding subtransaction's subcommit log entry survives the crash. With a single, combined log, we can do even better than this: we can ensure that the L_1 undo log entry is present in the stable log *if and only if* the corresponding subtransaction completely survives the crash. The way to achieve this very nice effect is to combine the L_0 subcommit log entry and the L_1 undo log entry into a single log entry. In other words: we simply need to write the L_1 undo log entry as the very last log entry of the subtransaction and then reinterpret it as the subtransaction's subcommit entry.

Simplified log force rules

The reason why this interpretation of the L_1 undo log entry as a subcommit is a great simplification for the recovery procedure is that it renders the state testing during the L_1 undo pass unnecessary. Now we know for sure that each L_1 undo log entry that we encounter on the stable log is associated with a winner subtransaction. Of course, during the L_1 undo pass, the L_1 undo log entries still serve to provide the information about the appropriate inverse operations, in addition to the role as subcommit log entries.

No state testing needed during L_1 undo pass

So the merging of the two logs into a single one has significant advantages. On top of this, note that we do not have to change the algorithms for the restart procedure other than simplifying it. So we can still use the previous section's structure for the entire crash recovery—the usual three passes for L_0 and the analysis and undo passes for L_1—only all of these passes operate on the same combined log. Also, each of these passes remains essentially identical to what we presented in the previous section; the noticeable exceptions being that the L_0 analysis pass does not need to determine winner subtransactions and the L_1 undo pass no longer needs to test the status of subtransactions.

Reduced number of passes over the log

There is, however, an opportunity to reduce the number of passes over the combined log with the following enhancements:

- The two analysis passes can be easily combined, as they cover the same part of the log anyway (i.e., typically starting from the most recent checkpoint). So a single analysis pass is sufficient to determine the DirtyPages list, the list of loser subtransactions, and the list of loser transactions.

- The two undo passes can be combined as well. All we need to do is to identify the type of log entry—for example, by including appropriate tags in the log entries—and either perform page-oriented undo steps for loser subtransactions or invoke an inverse operation for a high-level L_1 operation. The latter case spawns a new subtransaction during restart, which will again generate L_0 log entries. Both types of log entries that require undo lead to the creation of CLEs to track the undo progress.

The reason why both types of undo steps can be combined into a single backward pass over the log is that incomplete subtransactions can never precede a completed subtransaction whose L_1 operation is in conflict with that of the incomplete subtransaction. This is a consequence of the fact that all histories must be conflict serializable and log recoverable. Furthermore, for each loser transaction, if there is an incomplete subtransaction, it must correspond to the transaction's very last L_1 operation before the server crashed. So if the undo were organized on a per-transaction basis, we would first encounter the relevant L_0 log entries in the backward scan, and once we find the first L_1 log entry, we no longer need to consider incomplete subtransactions. The conflict serializability and log recoverability of the history then allows us to cover all loser transactions in the usual single, "global" backward pass over the log.

These considerations provide us with the following result:

THEOREM 14.1

The enhanced two-level crash recovery method, with three passes over the combined log, provides correct recovery.

Proof

First note that by reconstructing the state as of the crash time, the redo pass establishes all winner updates in the cached database, plus all updates of loser transactions, where the latter may include effects of partially executed high-level operations. The undo pass gradually removes these loser effects, without affecting any of the winner updates, on the assumption that the original history was tree-prefix reducible and the undo steps are identical to what a group abort (in the sense of Chapter 11) would generate. So writes of incomplete subtransactions are undone by inverse write operations, and the effects of completed subtransactions are undone by inverse high-level operations.

The undo pass traverses the NextUndoSeqNo backward chains of the loser transactions. At each point, all log entries that are reachable by the Next-UndoSeqNo chains of the transactions in the ActiveTrans data structure are exactly those loser updates that are still present in the cached database. In formal terms, the following invariant holds throughout the undo pass:

$\forall$ log sequence numbers $s \in$ stable log such that
$\quad s =$ ActiveTrans[t].LastSeqNo for some loser transaction t :
$\quad\quad \forall$ operations $o \in$ stable log :
$\quad\quad\quad$ (o belongs to t) $\Rightarrow$
$\quad\quad\quad$ (o is reachable along ActiveTrans[t].NextUndoSeqNo $\Leftrightarrow$
$\quad\quad\quad\quad o \in$ cached database)

Note that these reachable loser operations include both L_0 writes of incomplete subtransactions and L_1 high-level operations. So by the end of the undo pass, all effects of loser transactions are removed from the cached database such that the history prolonged by these undo steps is reducible to the roots of the winner transactions.

The final thing to show is that the above invariant during the undo pass is not destroyed by a subsequent crash. Here the argument is simple: the redo pass of the restart following another crash will again redo history. This includes CLEs for all undo steps that have already been executed in the prior undo pass. These CLEs refer to both L_0 writes of incomplete subtransactions and L_1 high-level operations that correspond to subtransactions that were completed before the most recent crash. In addition, the log is also guaranteed to include regular log entries for all L_0 writes that were executed on behalf of high-level undo steps. By redoing history, the redo algorithm ensures that exactly those loser updates will be present in the cached database that were still present at the time of the crash. Furthermore, all these log entries created during restart will be appropriately linked in the NextUndo-SeqNo backward chain. So the undo pass of this second restart after the original crash starts out with the same invariant, given above, that the undo pass of the first restart was based on, and then proceeds, maintaining the invariant. At no point does the undo pass need to know whether the most recent crash occurred during normal operation or during a previous restart.

Eventually, the traversal of the NextUndoSeqNo backward chains of the loser transactions will reach the very first log entries of the involved transactions (i.e., the begin log entries or the first write log entry) and terminate. At this point, the above invariant states that no loser effect is present in the cached database anymore.

To streamline the implementation of the enhanced undo pass as much as possible, we extend our use of the transaction-oriented NextUndoSeqNo backward chaining (see Chapter 13) of log entries as follows:

- As usual, a log entry for an L_0 write action points to the transaction's preceding L_0 log entry, unless it is the first write of a subtransaction. The log entry for this first L_0 write points to the L_1 log entry for the preceding (and definitely completed) subtransaction.

- A log entry for an L_1 high-level operation points to the transaction's preceding L_1 log entry.

- Finally, as in the page model, a CLE points to the predecessor, with regard to the NextUndoSeqNo backward chain, of the log entry whose undo is represented by the CLE. This holds for both L_0 and L_1 log entries.

The relationships among log entries are schematically illustrated in Figure 14.4.

With these extensions to the NextUndoSeqNo backward chains, the undo pass can cover both L_0 and L_1 log entries in a uniform way, generating CLEs for both of them. When traversing the backward chains of the loser transactions, the undo pass simply needs to distinguish the three types of possible log entries: CLEs do not require any action in the undo pass and merely serve to follow their NextUndoSeqNo pointer to the first relevant log entry; regular L_0 log entries that describe page-level forward operations require a page-level undo step and the generation of a CLE; and regular L_1 log entries that describe high-level forward operations require the invocation of a high-level inverse operation

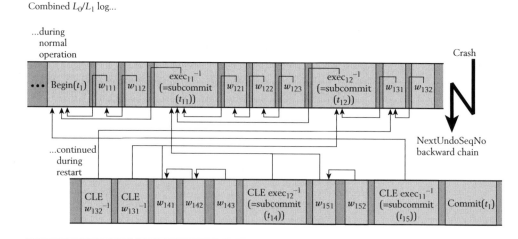

Figure 14.4 Schematic illustration of log entries and their NextUndoSeqNo chaining on the combined L_0/L_1 log.

and the generation of a CLE. The pseudocode for this undo procedure is given below.

```
undo pass ( ):                                          Combined
 ActiveTrans := empty;                                  L₀/L₁ undo
 for each t in losers do                                pass
  ActiveTrans += t;
    ActiveTrans[t].LastSeqNo := losers[t].LastSeqNo;
 end /*for*/;
 while there exists t in losers such that losers[t].LastSeqNo < > nil
 do
   nexttrans = TransNo in losers
    such that losers[nexttrans].LastSeqNo =
    max {losers[x].LastSeqNo|x in losers};
   nextentry := losers[nexttrans].LastSeqNo;
   if StableLog[nextentry].ActionType = compensation then
    losers[nexttrans].LastSeqNo := StableLog[nextentry].NextUndoSeqNo;
   end /*if*/;
   if StableLog[nextentry].ActionType = write or full-write then
    pageno := StableLog[nextentry].PageNo; fetch (pageno);
    if DatabaseCache[pageno].PageSeqNo > = nextentry.LogSeqNo then
     newlogentry.LogSeqNo := new sequence number;
     newlogentry.ActionType := compensation;
     newlogentry.PreviousSeqNo := ActiveTrans[transid].LastSeqNo;
     newlogentry.NextUndoSeqNo := nextentry.PreviousSeqNo;
     newlogentry.RedoInfo := inverse action of the action in nextentry;
     ActiveTrans[transid].LastSeqNo := newlogentry.LogSeqNo;
     LogBuffer += newlogentry;
     read and write (StableLog[nextentry].PageNo)
      according to StableLog[nextentry].UndoInfo;
     DatabaseCache[pageno].PageSeqNo := newlogentry.LogSeqNo;
    end /*if*/;
    losers[nexttrans].LastSeqNo := StableLog[nextentry].NextUndoSeqNo;
   end /*if*/;
   if StableLog[nextentry].ActionType = exec then
    subbegin ( );
    execute inverse operation according to StableLog[nextentry].UndoInfo;
    newlogentry.LogSeqNo := new sequence number;
    newlogentry.ActionType := compensation;
    newlogentry.PreviousSeqNo := ActiveTrans[transid].LastSeqNo;
    newlogentry.NextUndoSeqNo := nextentry.NextUndoSeqNo;
    ActiveTrans[transid].LastSeqNo := newlogentry.LogSeqNo;
    LogBuffer += newlogentry;
    subcommit ( );
   losers[nexttrans].LastSeqNo := StableLog[nextentry].NextUndoSeqNo;
  end /*if*/;
```

```
    if StableLog[nextentry].ActionType = begin then
    newlogentry.LogSeqNo := new sequence number;
    newlogentry.ActionType := rollback;
    newlogentry.TransId := StableLog[nextentry].TransId;
    newlogentry.PreviousSeqNo := ActiveTrans[transid].LastSeqNo;
    LogBuffer += newlogentry;
    ActiveTrans -= transid; losers -= transid;
    end /*if*/;
  end /*while*/;
  force ( );
```

As an example, we show again in Figures 14.5 and 14.6 the logging activity and the recovery steps for our earlier scenario (see Section 14.3), using the enhanced two-level crash recovery algorithm.

Sequence number: action	Cached changes [PageNo: SeqNo]	Stable changes [PageNo: SeqNo]	Log entry added [LogSeqNo: action] [NextUndoSeqNo]
1: begin(t_1)			1: begin(t_1), next = nil
2: incr(x, t_1)			
3: subbegin(t_{11})			
4: write(p, t_{11})	p: 4		4: write(p, t_{11}), next = nil
5: write(q, t_{11})	q: 5		5: write(q, t_{11}), next = 4
6: subcommit(t_{11})			6: incr^{-1}(x, t_1), next = nil
7: begin(t_2)			7: begin(t_2)
8: incr(x, t_2)			
9: subbegin(t_{21})			
10: write(p, t_{21})	p: 10		10: write(p, t_{21}), next = nil
11: incr(y, t_1)			
12: subbegin(t_{12})			
13: write(s, t_{12})	s: 13		13: write(s, t_{12}), next = 6
14: flush(p)		p: 10	
15: write(r, t_{21})	r: 15		15: write(r, t_{21}), next = 10
16: flush(s)		s: 13	
17: subcommit(t_{21})			17: incr^{-1}(x, t_2), next = nil
18: commit(t_2)			18: commit(t_2)
19: write(r, t_{12})	r: 19		19: write(r, t_{12}), next = 13
20: subcommit(t_{12})			20: incr^{-1}(y, t_1), next = 6
21: incr(z, t_1)			
22: subbegin(t_{13})			
23: write(s, t_{13})	s: 23		23: write(s, t_{13}), next = 20
System crash			

Figure 14.5 Example scenario for the enhanced two-level crash recovery algorithm.

Sequence number: action	Cached changes [PageNo: SeqNo]	Stable changes [PageNo: SeqNo]	Log entry added [LogSeqNo: action] [NextUndoSeqNo]
Restart			
Analysis pass: losers = {t_1}; LastSeqNo(t_1) = 23			
consider-redo(4)			
redo(5)	q: 5		
consider-redo(10)			
consider-redo(13)			
redo(15)	r: 15		
redo(19)	r: 19		
redo(23)	s: 23		
24: compensate(23)	s: 24		24: CLE(23), next = 20
25: compensate(20, t_{12}) ↑ t_{14}			
26: subbegin(t_{14})			
27: write(s, t_{14})	s: 27		27: write(s, t_{14}), next = 20
28: write(r, t_{14})	r: 28		28: write(r, t_{14}), next = 27
29: flush(r)		r: 28	
30: subcommit(t_{14})			30: CLE(20, t_{12}, t_{14}), next = 6
31: flush(q)		q: 5	
32: compensate(6, t_{11}) ↑ t_{15}			
Second system crash			
Second restart			
Analysis pass: losers = {t_1}; LastSeqNo(t_1) = 30			
consider-redo(4)			
consider-redo(5)			
consider-redo(10)			
consider-redo(13)			
consider-redo(15)			
consider-redo(19)			
redo(23)	s: 23		
redo(24)	s: 24		
redo(27)	s: 28		
consider-redo(28)			
33: compensate(6, t_{11}) ↑ t_{15}			
34: subbegin(t_{15})			
35: write(p, t_{15})	p: 35		35: write(p, t_{15}), next = 6
36: write(q, t_{15})	q: 36		36: write(q, t_{15}), next = 35
37: subcommit(t_{15})			37: CLE(6, t_{11}, t_{15}), next = nil
38: rollback(t_1)			38: rollback(t_1)
Second restart complete: resume normal operation			

Figure 14.6 Example scenario for the enhanced two-level crash recovery algorithm, continued.

During the first restart of Figure 14.6, the undo pass for the loser transaction t_1 starts with LSN 23, which was an L_0 write of an incomplete subtransaction, and then proceeds backward along the NextUndoSeqNo chain, abbreviated as "next" in the figure, to undo the operations with LSNs 20 and 6, both of which were completed L_1 high-level operations. As shown in Figure 14.6, these undo steps create new log entries. The CLEs among these new log entries point to the predecessor, with regard to the NextUndoSeqNo backward chain, of the undone operation. For example, the CLE with LSN 24 points to LSN 20 (after the undo of the L_0 operation with LSN 23), and the CLE with LSN 30 points to LSN 6 (after the undo of the L_1 operation with LSN 20). During the second restart of Figure 14.6, the undo pass for the loser transaction t_1 starts with LSN 30, but as the log entry with this LSN is a CLE, it immediately proceeds with the NextUndoSeqNo predecessor, which is the log entry with LSN 6.

Note that the compensation of the encountered L_1 high-level operations involves spawning new subtransactions denoted by the ↑ symbol in the figure. For example, compensate(20, t_{12}) ↑ t_{14} means that an inverse operation has been initiated for the logged operation with LSN 20, which corresponded to subtransaction t_{12}, and the newly spawned compensating subtransaction has the identifier t_{14}. Finally, note that regular log entries are created for the L_0 writes of these compensating subtransactions; in the example, these are log entries with LSNs 27 and 28 on behalf of t_{14} and log entries with LSNs 35 and 36 on behalf of t_{15}.

14.5 A Complete Redo-History Algorithm for General Object Model Executions

Let us now address the most general case of nonlayered object model transactions. It turns out that this is not that much more difficult than the two-level case that we have considered so far. We will see shortly that the enhanced two-level recovery algorithm with three passes over a combined log already provides a suitable framework and needs only relatively simple adaptations to the more general setting. But let us first reconsider an example of the general case, to analyze what kinds of additional problems we face. The example is shown in Figure 14.7. Its operations Shipment and Payment refer to a simplified e-Commerce scenario, where Payment includes Withdraw operations on the customers' bank accounts, a Discount operation that modifies one customer's discount rate because of sales volume or purchasing frequency, and also write steps whose semantics is not explicitly reflected. For simplicity, no read steps are shown in the figure.

Assume that the server fails right after the last operation shown in Figure 14.7 and that t_2 is committed. Further assume that all subtransactions of t_1

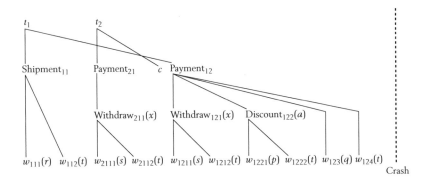

Figure 14.7 Example of a nonlayered object model history.

are completed (for simplicity, their commits are not shown in the figure), but t_1 itself is not yet committed.

As far as the analysis pass and the redo pass are concerned, the recovery algorithm of the previous section is applicable without any changes. So the redo pass takes care of the winner transaction t_2 and also redoes, if necessary, all updates of t_1 up to the point of the crash. The remaining issue is how we determine which actions need to be undone on behalf of the loser transaction t_1. The overall rationale for this undo phase is the same as for the transaction recovery discussed in Chapter 11 (i.e., transaction rollbacks during normal operation). We need to identify all incomplete subtransactions, including the transaction roots, and invoke inverse operations for each of these subtransactions' children (unless these children are themselves aborted subtransactions, a case that we disregard in this chapter for ease of explanation). As in transaction recovery, all the necessary inverse operations need to be executed in reverse chronological order, and they should ideally be organized into a single backward pass over the log. To be prepared for these undo steps, all we need to do during normal operation is to create a log entry, in the log buffer, with sufficient information about the inverse operation, whenever a subtransaction is about to commit. As in the previous section, this log entry also serves as a subcommit log entry, and this holds regardless of any layering and thus generalizes to our current setting without any modifications.

In the example, the inverse operations to be spawned for undoing t_1 are, in the given order (i.e., the reverse order of the corresponding forward operations):

$$\text{write}^{-1}(t)\,\text{write}^{-1}(q)\,\text{discount}^{-1}(a)\,\text{withdraw}^{-1}(x)\,\text{shipment}^{-1}$$

If the crash had interrupted the subtransaction t_{122} (i.e., t_1's Discount operation), say, after the write step on p, then we would need to undo this write step and then proceed with the inverse operation of the preceding and completed

Withdraw operation and finally compensating the Shipment. If, on the other hand, the crash had occurred after the completion of the subtransaction t_{12} but still before the transaction's commit (and no other actions in between), then the low- and intermediate-level undo steps would have to be replaced by a single inverse operation for the commit subtransaction payment$_{12}$.

Transaction undo stack   These example-driven considerations show that the necessary undo steps for an incomplete subtransaction vary as subtransactions commit or new subtransactions are spawned in the course of a transaction's execution. This naturally leads to a kind of *transaction undo stack* that contains all relevant inverse operations for a given transaction at a given point in time. Its maintenance, on a per-transaction basis, is driven by two rules:

- Upon each exec(*op, trans,* ...) action or write step, information about the appropriate inverse operation is pushed on the stack.

- Upon each subcommit, the stack is popped until the committing subtransaction's inverse operation becomes the top of the stack. So this removes all inverse operations for descendants of the committing subtransaction.

For the example of Figure 14.7, the undo stack of the transaction t_1 varies during the execution (with the stack top on the right end), as shown in Table 14.1.

Table 14.1 Undo stack for t_1 from Figure 14.7.

Action	Undo stack
shipment$_{11}$	shipment$_{11}^{-1}$
write$_{111}(r)$	shipment$_{11}^{-1}$ write$_{111}^{-1}(r)$
write$_{112}(t)$	shipment$_{11}^{-1}$ write$_{111}^{-1}(r)$ write$_{112}^{-1}(t)$
subcommit(t_{11})	shipment$_{11}^{-1}$
payment$_{12}$	shipment$_{11}^{-1}$ payment$_{12}^{-1}$
withdraw$_{121}(x)$	shipment$_{11}^{-1}$ payment$_{12}^{-1}$ withdraw$_{121}^{-1}(x)$
write$_{1211}(s)$	shipment$_{11}^{-1}$ payment$_{12}^{-1}$ withdraw$_{121}^{-1}(x)$ write$_{1211}^{-1}(s)$
write$_{1212}(t)$	shipment$_{11}^{-1}$ payment$_{12}^{-1}$ withdraw$_{121}^{-1}(x)$ write$_{1211}^{-1}(s)$ write$_{1212}^{-1}(t)$
subcommit(t_{121})	shipment$_{11}^{-1}$ payment$_{12}^{-1}$ withdraw$_{121}^{-1}(x)$
discount$_{122}(a)$	shipment$_{11}^{-1}$ payment$_{12}^{-1}$ withdraw$_{121}^{-1}(x)$ discount$_{122}^{-1}(a)$
write$_{1221}(p)$	shipment$_{11}^{-1}$ payment$_{12}^{-1}$ withdraw$_{121}^{-1}(x)$ discount$_{122}^{-1}(a)$ write$_{1221}^{-1}(p)$
write$_{1221}(t)$	shipment$_{11}^{-1}$ payment$_{12}^{-1}$ withdraw$_{121}^{-1}(x)$ discount$_{122}^{-1}(a)$ write$_{1221}^{-1}(p)$ write$_{1222}^{-1}(t)$
subcommit(t_{122})	shipment$_{11}^{-1}$ payment$_{12}^{-1}$ withdraw$_{121}^{-1}(x)$ discount$_{122}^{-1}(a)$
write$_{123}(q)$	shipment$_{11}^{-1}$ payment$_{12}^{-1}$ withdraw$_{121}^{-1}(x)$ discount$_{122}^{-1}(a)$ write$_{123}^{-1}(q)$
write$_{124}(t)$	shipment$_{11}^{-1}$ payment$_{12}^{-1}$ withdraw$_{121}^{-1}(x)$ discount$_{122}^{-1}(a)$ write$_{123}^{-1}(q)$ write$_{124}^{-1}(t)$

A similar undo stack needs to be maintained for the winner transaction t_2 as well, up to the point when it commits; at this point, the stack is popped as many times as the number of the transaction root's children and then becomes empty and is dropped. Now it could be intriguing to simply make these transaction-specific undo stacks recoverable as the basis for undo recovery, but then it would be unclear what kind of data structure is needed for holding all stacks of all active transactions to make the undo phase as efficient as possible. A better idea toward log-based undo with a single backward pass of the log during restart is to embed the information from these undo stacks into the log by appropriate log entries, and with appropriate UndoNextSeq backward chaining to "emulate" the stack pop operations. So push operations on a stack simply correspond to creating a log entry and appending it to the log buffer, and pop operations correspond to a new log entry whose NextUndoSeq pointer skips all preceding log entries whose corresponding stack entries are to be popped.

Embedding the undo stacks into the log

With this kind of log entry backward chaining it is indeed possible to perform the entire undo phase with all relevant inverse operations of all loser transactions in a single backward pass over the log. So the transaction-specific undo stacks exist only conceptually, and the implementation is solely log based as before. In fact, this approach also solves another difficulty that we swept under the rug in the discussion of the undo stack approach: the inverse operation for a nonleaf operation can often be determined only at the end of the subtransaction, that is, after its children and further descendants were pushed onto the stack. Then the inverse operation of the entire subtransaction would actually have to replace all its descendants *atomically*. It is not at all obvious how to implement a sequence of pop operations followed by a single push operation as an atomic stack operation. However, achieving this effect with the log-based approach is straightforward: writing the log entry for the subtransaction's inverse operation along with a NextUndoSeq backward pointer that skips all its children is a simple, atomic step. If this log entry survives the crash, then the subtransaction must have been committed, and its undo requires an inverse operation; otherwise, the undo can be performed by undoing the operation's children.

In summary, we apply the following rules for setting the NextUndoSeq pointer of a log entry:

- If the operation that corresponds to the log entry is not the first child of its parent, then its NextUndoSeq pointer points to its immediately preceding sibling.

- If the operation is the first child of its parent, its NextUndoSeq pointer points to its parent's immediately preceding sibling if there is one, and to the transaction root otherwise.

- For CLEs that are created during the undo pass or during a transaction rollback, the NextUndoSeq pointer points to the predecessor of the forward operation that is matched by the CLE. Here "predecessor" means the forward operation's immediately preceding sibling if there is one, or the immediately preceding sibling of its parent (or if this does not exist either, to the transaction root).

The way these rules are phrased seems to require that all operations within a transaction are totally ordered. They can, however, be rephrased to cover the case of partial orders as well; so parallel subtransactions within a transaction can also be supported with this approach. We leave the details for you to work out in Exercise 14.4. The log entries for our example scenario above are shown in Figure 14.8.

We conclude this section by pointing out that the pseudocode for the restart procedure is absolutely identical to that of the enhanced two-level algorithm. The analysis pass and the redo pass are identical to those of the page model redo-history algorithm anyway, and the undo pass simply follows the NextUndoSeqNo backward chains of the loser transactions. The generalization compared to the enhanced two-level algorithm simply lies in the fact that these chains contain log entries of action type exec that correspond to all committed subtransactions with uncommitted parents, regardless of any layering.

14.6 **Lessons Learned**

The redo-history paradigm for the redo phase of the crash recovery has been the key asset to cope with the complexity of object model transactions: the restart procedure first reconstructs the state of the data as of the time of the crash, and then initiates what is essentially transaction recovery for loser transactions as if these transactions were to be rolled back during normal operation. Furthermore, performing the redo pass solely by means of page-oriented physical or physiological writes makes this most critical phase of the overall recovery very efficient, and allows us to carry over the clever optimizations from the page model. As for the undo pass, once we merged the log entries for the operations of the various levels into a single log, the use of the Next-UndoSeqNo backward chaining to capture the undo stack of a loser transaction appeared fairly natural, and the avoidance of undoing already undone operations made possible by compensation log entries could be carried over from the page model and applied to higher-level operations as well without significant changes.

In summary, a state-of-the-art object model crash recovery algorithm includes the following techniques:

- applying page-oriented redo of both winner and loser updates by means of physical or physiological log entries;

Sequence number: action	Log entry added [LogSeqNo: action] [NextUndoSeqNo]
1: begin(t_1)	1: begin(t_1), next = nil
2: shipment$_{11}$	
3: subbegin(t_{11})	
4: write$_{111}$(r)	4: write$_{111}$, next = nil
5: write$_{112}$(t)	5: write$_{112}$, next = 4
6: subcommit(t_{11})	6: shipment$_{11}^{-1}$, next = nil
7: begin(t_2)	7: begin(t_2), next = nil
8: payment$_{21}$	
9: subbegin(t_{21})	
10: withdraw$_{211}$(x)	
11: subbegin(t_{211})	
12: write$_{2111}$(s)	12: write$_{2111}$(s), next = nil
13: write$_{2112}$(t)	13: write$_{2112}$(t), next = 12
14: subcommit(t_{211})	14: withdraw$_{211}^{-1}$(x), next = nil
15: subcommit(t_{21})	15: payment$_{21}^{-1}$, next = nil
16: commit(t_2)	16: commit(t_2)
17: payment$_{12}$	
18: subbegin(t_{12})	
19: withdraw$_{121}$(x)	
20: subbegin(t_{121})	
21: write$_{1211}$(s)	21: write$_{1211}$(s), next = 6
22: write$_{1212}$(t)	22: write$_{1212}$(t), next = 21
23: subcommit(t_{121})	23: withdraw$_{121}^{-1}$(x), next = 6
24: discount$_{122}$(a)	
25: subbegin(t_{122})	
26: write$_{1221}$(p)	26: write$_{1221}$(p), next = 23
27: write$_{1222}$(t)	27: write$_{1222}$(t), next = 26
28: subcommit(t_{122})	28: discount$_{122}^{-1}$(a), next = 23
29: write$_{123}$(q)	29: write$_{123}$(q), next = 28
30: write$_{124}$(t)	30: write$_{124}$(t), next = 29

Figure 14.8 Log entries for the general object model example of Figure 14.7.

- merging log entries for all levels into a single log, and performing crash recovery with a single undo pass (in addition to the usual analysis and redo passes);

- treating log entries for high-level operations as subcommit log entries for the corresponding subtransactions, thus making subtransactions atomic;

- encoding the undo stack of inverse operations of different levels that are necessary to undo a loser transaction into an appropriate linking of log entries in the NextUndoSeqNo backward chain;

- generating compensation log entries for inverse operations of all levels to track the undo progress and make the undo pass effectively idempotent;

- finally, treating high-level inverse operations that are invoked during the undo pass again as subtransactions that create low-level log entries for redo purposes and a concluding compensation log entry upon the subtransaction's subcommit, so that subtransaction atomicity is also maintained during restart.

Although the entire recovery algorithm is a fairly complex procedure that would be hard to understand all at once, each of its above constituents is relatively straightforward. Our general approach of starting out with a simple, albeit restricted algorithm and gradually adding extensions and optimizations, which we already used in several of the book's chapters, has again paid off in providing us with high confidence in the correct and efficient behavior of the final algorithm.

Exercises

14.1 Consider the algorithm for object model recovery. Assume that the undo information and the redo information for an action are recorded in separate log entries, rather than always being combined in one log entry. What is the impact on the algorithm? In particular, what are the implications for the order in which log entries must be created and the forcing of the log buffer? Sketch the modified algorithm.

14.2 Consider the DB Cache method (see Exercise 13.3), applied to subtransactions, for implementing the L_0 recovery of the simple two-level recovery algorithm. When adopted in a straightforward way, this method would force after images to the stable log, coined the *safe*, upon each subcommit. Discuss under which conditions these forced log I/Os can be avoided. As a hint, assume that a set of after images can be written to the safe atomically, and analyze what happens when the forcing of a subtransaction's after images is deferred until the transaction's commit. In particular, analyze how to deal with subtransactions, belonging to the same or different transactions, whose write sets have pages in common. How do such "dependencies" between subtransactions affect the deferral of forced log I/Os?

14.3 Consider the two-level action history given in Figure 14.9, with operations on records (store, modify) and index keys (insert, delete). For the latter operations, the first parameter denotes a key and the second parameter the RID (i.e., address) of a stored record. Assume that there is a system crash right after the last action. Determine the necessary logging

Sequence number: action	Cached changes [PageNo: SeqNo]	Stable changes [PageNo: SeqNo]	Log entry added [LogSeqNo: action] [NextUndoSeqNo]
1: begin(t_1)			
2: modify(x, t_1)			
3: subbegin(t_{11})			
4: write(p, t_{11})			
5: begin(t_2)			
6: store(y, t_2)			
7: subbegin(t_{21})			
8: write (q, t_{21})			
9: write(r, t_{21})			
10: subcommit(t_{21})			
11: write(r, t_{11})			
12: subcommit(t_{11})			
13: delete($a, @x, t_1$)			
14: subbegin(t_{12})			
15: write(l, t_{12})			
18: subcommit(t_{12})			
19: insert($f, @x, t_1$)			
20: subbegin(t_{13})			
21: write(l, t_{13})			
22: write(k, t_{13})			
23: write(n, t_{13})			
24: subcommit(t_{13})			
25: begin(t_3)			
26: store(z, t_3)			
27: subbegin(t_{31})			
28: write(q, t_{31})			
29: write(r, t_{31})			
30: subcommit(t_{31})			
31: insert($h, @z, t_3$)			
32: subbegin(t_{32})			
33: write(k, t_{32})			
34: subcommit(t_{32})			
35: commit(t_3)			
36: insert($b, @y, t_2$)			
37: subbegin(t_{22})			
38: write(l, t_{22})			

Figure 14.9 Two-level history for Exercise 14.3.

actions during normal operation and the recovery actions during restart, by completing the table. Use the enhanced two-level recovery algorithm with a single log from Section 14.4.

14.4 Discuss which (minor) adaptations are necessary for the general recovery algorithm to work with parallel subtransactions within a transaction (i.e., partially ordered operations in general object model transactions). In particular, explain how the NextUndoSeqNo backward chain of log entries must be organized so as to guarantee that the proper inverse operations will be invoked in the correct order during the undo phase, using a single backward pass over the log.

Hint: The ActiveTrans and losers data structures need to be extended so that they can maintain multiple LastSeqNo entries whenever more than one subtransaction of the same transaction is in progress or incomplete simultaneously.

Bibliographic Notes

Higher-level crash recovery, with a focus on database records, has first been addressed by Gray et al. (1981). This work, however, did not follow a redo-history paradigm, but rather required an expensive form of heavyweight checkpointing based on shadow storage in combination with both high-level undo and high-level redo. So this was a fairly expensive method, and has not been further pursued in commercial products. The fallacies of this approach have been discussed in Mohan et al. (1992), who also developed the state-of-the-art ARIES algorithm for record-level recovery. Since the focus of ARIES was to provide industrial-strength recovery for a relational database system, this line of work was not further advanced toward general object model architectures. However, it clearly contained all the necessary building blocks already; for example, it included, as so-called nested top-level actions, a limited form of organizing the undo-relevant inverse operations into the NextUndoSeqNo backward chain. The multilevel recovery work by Weikum et al. (1990), Weikum and Hasse (1993), and Lomet (1992), on the other hand, aimed at fundamental insights and generalizations rather than commercial product use, and independently arrived at results very similar to ARIES. Weikum and Hasse (1993) and Hasse (1995) also discussed the use of the DB Cache method as a page-level building block in multilevel recovery (see also Exercise 14.2), including the support of parallel subtransactions within a transaction (see also Exercise 14.4). The most general object-level execution stack algorithm has been described by Broessler (1994).

CHAPTER FIFTEEN

Special Issues of Recovery

Success is a lousy teacher.
—*Bill Gates*

It's not easy being green.
—*Kermit*

15.1 Goal and Overview

The crash recovery algorithms developed in the previous chapters, for the page and the object model, are as general as possible in that they can handle arbitrary kinds of data servers with arbitrary kinds of objects. For specific objects, however, special considerations may be worthwhile for further optimizations of the logging space and time overhead or efficiency during restart. Likewise, specific architectural settings—for example, multiprocessor computers with very large main memory or computer "clusters" as platforms for data servers—offer the potential for tailored adaptations and additional improvements to the general-purpose algorithms. In this chapter we discuss various extensions and adaptations of the previously developed recovery algorithms to accommodate and exploit such specific settings.

The chapter is organized as follows. Section 15.2 presents special logging considerations for the recovery of B^+ tree index structures and large data objects such as images or mail attachments that are typically manipulated in a specifically constrained manner. Section 15.3 adds a "convenience" feature to our repertoire of supported recovery cases, namely, the possibility of dynamically declaring savepoints within a transaction and initiating partial rollbacks to a previous savepoint rather than rolling back an entire transaction. Section 15.4 introduces advanced techniques for speeding up the restart after a crash by exploiting parallelism and making the server available for normal operation as quickly as possible. The last two sections, Sections 15.5 and 15.6, address the performance opportunities of specific hardware settings for data servers, namely, servers where all data fits into main memory and so-called data sharing clusters that combine a small number of computers into a shared disk, distributed memory system.

15.2 **Logging and Recovery for Indexes and Large Objects**

Special object types that are of great importance in various classes of server types and are manipulated in a highly specific manner are index structures, such as B$^+$ trees, and large objects, such as images and mail attachments. Applying standard logging to these object types may result in a fairly high amount of logging volume. This is not necessarily a dramatic problem, as the log I/O bandwidth can be easily scaled up by striping the log across multiple disks. However, there are methods that can reduce the logging costs for these structures, as discussed next.

15.2.1 **Logical Log Entries for the Redo of Index Page Splits**

Object model recovery applied to index structure

Index structures such as B$^+$ trees are handled by the enhanced variant of the general-purpose crash recovery algorithm for the object model (or, more specifically, the two-level case) as follows:

- For each index page that is modified by the insertion or deletion of a (key, RID) pair, a physical or physiological log entry is created. These log entries serve to ensure the atomicity of the subtransaction that corresponds to the Insert or Delete operation, and the persistence of the entire transaction to which the index operation belongs.

- At the end of the index operation, a higher-level, logical log entry is created that describes the inverse operation of the executed index operation, that is, deleting or reinserting the affected (key, RID) pair. The purpose of the log entry is to provide the ability to undo the surrounding transaction by means of compensation (if the transaction turns out to be a loser). This log entry follows all of the index page–oriented log entries mentioned above, and also serves as a subcommit log entry for the subtransaction.

Note that none of the above log entries requires forcing the log buffer. So the standard procedure is already fairly efficient as far as logging costs are concerned. As an example, consider an operation insert$_{ij}(k, @x)$ for key k and the RID of record x, executed as the j-th operation of transaction t_i. Assume that the operation traverses a B$^+$ tree of height 3, starting from the root page r, proceeding through an intermediate-level page n, and ending at leaf page l, which turns out to be split into l and the newly allocated leaf page m and requires posting a new routing entry in the parent node n. The log entries created for this operation are

$$\mathrm{write}_{ij1}(l)\; \mathrm{write}_{ij2}(m)\; \mathrm{write}_{ij3}(n)\; \mathrm{insert}_{ij}^{-1}(k, @x)$$

Recall that the last log entry has the additional implicit meaning of a subcommit$_{ij}$ log entry for the corresponding subtransaction t_{ij}.

During crash recovery, the write steps will be redone; subsequently, if t_i is a loser transaction and the log entry for the inverse Insert operation is found on the stable log, the inverse operation will be invoked during the undo pass. If, on the other hand, the server crashed with only some of the write log entries on the stable log and without remembering the inverse operation, these surviving write steps will be undone in a page-oriented manner. Recall that both cases can be handled uniformly within a single undo pass on a single log. The same principle also works fine for all other kinds of local reorganizations in B$^+$ trees (e.g., splits that propagate all the way up to the root node and may even split the node and increase the tree height) and also for most other kinds of index trees, including R trees on multidimensional data. For simplicity, the following discussion restricts itself to the above B$^+$ tree split scenario, which captures the most typical practical case.

The amount of logged data in our example above is actually larger than it may appear upon first glance. Even with physiological logging, a leaf page split eventually winds up putting the contents of the original and the newly created leaf node on the log. Even worse, the log entries include both undo and redo information, so that all (key, RID) pairs of the original leaf may even appear twice on the log. With the current trend toward larger index pages, driven by the increasing ratio of sequential versus random disk I/O times and page sizes currently on the order of 64KB, the space for these log entries is no longer a completely minor issue. *Problem with physical logging of index page splits*

The key observation toward further reducing this amount of logged data is that the split itself does not really modify any of the previously existing (key, RID) pairs; it merely redistributes them across two pages. We surely cannot avoid logging the split, as we need to ensure the atomicity of the current and also subsequent index operations, but we can choose to record the split event in a logical, higher-level form. During the redo pass after a crash, we may then end up having to reexecute such an operation, something we carefully avoided so far for the sake of restart speed. However, in this very specific case, we could indeed favor logical log entries over physiological ones, even for redo purposes. So the general idea is to trade off a small if not negligible increase of the restart duration for a significant reduction in logging costs; for the special case of index page splits, there is no additional restart cost at all (compared to the restart cost of physiological logging).

Deriving the logical log entry for the split itself is straightforward: we merely need to record the page numbers of the original and newly created leaf and the median of the affected keys, which will be the highest key to remain *Logical logging of detached split operations* on the originally existing leaf. The difficulty with this approach lies in the interdependencies between the Split operation and the Insert operation that triggered the split: first, we also need to log the Insert operation for possible undo or redo of the surrounding transaction, and second and above all, we still need to ensure the atomicity of the entire index operation.

For the first point, we detach the local reorganization of the index tree from the insertion of a new (key, RID) pair, turning it into a completely separate "system-induced" transaction. So whenever an Insert operation encounters a leaf page with insufficient space, the server first initiates a separate split transaction that consists solely of splitting the affected leaf page. Once this special transaction is committed, the Insert operation can proceed without causing any reorganization (as the probability for being passed by so many other concurrent Insert operations that the freshly split page becomes full again is very close to zero). Further note that from this point, the log entry for the split transaction is needed for redo purposes only; if the surrounding transaction should be undone later, the inserted (key, RID) pair will be removed, but the split will not be undone.

As for the second point—the atomicity of the detached split transaction—we can exploit the special page access pattern of this transaction (and we will later generalize these considerations). The split reads pages l (the original leaf to be split) and n (the parent of l on which the split must be posted), and it writes pages l, m (the new sibling of l), and n. A crash may "lose" any subset of the three modified pages, depending on which pages are flushed to the stable database before the crash. So redoing the split will be faced with some pages in their old state (i.e., as of a time before the split) and some in their new state (i.e., including the effects of the split). The redo step for the logged split operation must therefore distinguish the following eight cases:

1. All three pages are in their old state.
2. l is in the new state, and m and n are in the old state.
3. m is in the new state, and l and n are in the old state.
4. n is in the new state, and l and m are in the old state.
5. l and m are in the new state, and n is in the old state.
6. l and n are in the new state, and m is in the old state.
7. m and n are in the new state, and l is in the old state.
8. All three pages are in the new state.

Clearly, the easy cases are 1 and 8, as they preserve the atomicity of the original split operation; in case 1 the split is completely reexecuted, and in case 8 nothing needs to be done. These two cases are indeed detectable by inspecting the LSNs of the three involved pages during the redo pass and comparing them to the LSN of the logged split operation. This standard state-testing procedure can also discriminate the six remaining cases, assuming that the page numbers of the three pages are included in the split's log entry. But now the redo step must proceed carefully, as the prior execution of the split has left partial effects in the stable database. Among cases 2 through 7, the cases where the newly allocated leaf m is in its new state (i.e., cases 3, 5, and 7) are easy to handle: the redo step needs to remove the (key, RID) pairs that are above the split key from the originally existing leaf l and post the split to the parent n (in case 3), or merely post the split (in case 5), or it needs to remove the (key, RID) pairs that are now on l's sibling m from l (case 7). In case 4, where only the parent node n is in the new state, the split itself needs to be repeated, and if the newly allocated sibling of l turns out to be different from the one that was posted to n in the original execution, this can be fixed easily by changing the page number of the routing entry in n. (Note that such a situation could occur because of liberal page allocation policies that do not necessarily comply with the serialization order of transactions.) Finally, the remaining two cases, 2 and 6, are the only ones that are indeed troublesome: in both of these cases, the original leaf l is in its new state, but the intended sibling m is still in its old state. This means that we have only the lower half of the originally existing (key, RID) pairs available in l but have lost the upper half that has been moved to m. In these cases, having logged the Split operation merely in a logical manner is insufficient to perform the redo step.

The way out of this dilemma is to prevent the two troublesome cases, 2 and 6. This can be achieved by controlling the order in which pages are flushed from the cache during normal operation. All we need to do is to make sure that the originally existing leaf node l is not flushed earlier than the new leaf m. If we want to avoid possibly readjusting the page number in the newly posted routing entry of the parent node n (case 4 above), we can further constrain the *flush ordering* by making sure that n can be flushed only after flushing m. So altogether we arrive at a flush order $m \prec l \prec n$, where $\prec$ denotes the order in which flush actions must take place. This technique of enforcing a specific flush order for the pages in an operation's (or transaction's) write set is also known as *careful (cache) replacement* in the literature.

Careful flush ordering

Note that the cache manager can enforce such an ordering relatively easily by maintaining a flush graph according to the $\prec$ relation. In system environments where this would be considered too much overhead, a lightweight variation could further decompose the entire split transaction into a first part that affects only the leaf nodes l and m and a second part that treats the posting of the routing entry in the parent node m as a separate system-induced transaction. Since the latter affects only a single page, its atomicity is self-guaranteed and the posting can be logged in compact logical form. The first part, sometimes referred to as a *half-split* operation, now involves only two pages. By creating an additional physical or physiological log entry for the page that would have to be flushed first (i.e., the new leaf node m), the flush-order dependency becomes obsolete. This would still save the log space for one physical or physiological log entry (namely, for the *l*).

Note that the log entry for the posting would follow the log entries for the half split in the stable log; so when we redo the posting as a separate transaction, it is guaranteed that both leaves are in their new state. The only remaining problem arises when the server crashes between the half split and the posting transaction. In this case, however, we can resort to the link technique for B$^+$ tree–style index structures that we discussed for index concurrency control in Chapter 9. This technique assumes that each node in the index tree has a pointer to its right sibling and follows this pointer upon an unsuccessful search until it can definitely determine the absence or presence of the searched key. In Chapter 9, the link technique was intended for situations where a Search operation would end up on a leaf that was just split by a concurrent operation without having seen a routing entry for the new leaf in its descent through the tree. Here we can consolidate the analogous case where such a situation is the result of the half split surviving the crash and the posting being lost. Whenever a Search operation detects this situation during normal operation, it would simply initiate the posting, again as a separate system-induced transaction.

As a final remark on logical logging for index page splits, note that the approach in the form described above works only if there is at most one Split operation along a path through the tree. This is not a severe restriction, as it is rather unlikely that multiple splits with nodes in common are in progress simultaneously. For example, a case that we would disallow, by means of appropriate concurrency control techniques (see Chapter 9), would be a split of a leaf node *p* (say, into *p* and *q*) that has the same parent as *l*, namely, node *n*, and executes concurrently with the split of *l*. Concurrent splits in disjoint branches of the index tree are, however, feasible anytime. We will see in the next subsection that the restriction can nevertheless be relaxed by using a more general notion of flush-order dependencies.

15.2.2 Logical Log Entries and Flush Ordering for Large-Object Operations

The logging of operations on large objects such as images or mail attachments poses problems and gives rise to optimization opportunities similar to what we have discussed above for index structures. Consider a copy(a, b) operation that copies the contents of large object *a* onto object *b*. The usual kind of physical or physiological log entries would end up putting all pages of the modified object *b* on the log for redo purposes, possibly on the order of megabytes. If object *b* existed before, the undo information of the log entry may be of similar size. On the other hand, if we knew that object *a* would remain unchanged, we could simply create a logical log entry for the Copy operation, and read *a* from the stable database during recovery to redo the operation. We may still have to log a large amount of data for the undo information, but the savings for the redo part would be a significant gain. Note that reading the original contents of a from the database during recovery rather than reading the redo information for b from the log is almost equivalent from a performance viewpoint: since large objects typically comprise megabytes of data and reside on contiguous disk space, reading from the database leverages sequential disk I/O in this case, too. This is an important difference from the case of relatively short records, for which we would favor the sequential reading from the log over the random access to the database.

A major complication that we need to address lies in the fact that other operations may later modify the source object a of the considered copy(a, b) operation, and these modifications may be flushed to the stable database before the crash. Then, during recovery, the redo step for the copy(a, b) operation can no longer read the original value of a and thus cannot restore the proper value of b. The solution to avoid this kind of problem is again to constrain the order in which the involved objects a and b are flushed. As these objects may reside on a large number of pages, such flush-order dependencies actually refer to sets of pages. However, for simpler explanation, we first assume that each object occupies only a single page; for simplicity of notation, we refer to these two pages by the same names as the objects—a and b, respectively. Now the flush-order dependency requires that b be flushed before a. Once this is guaranteed, the case where the redo step for copy(a, b) finds the source page a already overwritten by a later operation is no longer disturbing: the redo step may read this page, but when trying to write into the target page b, it would realize, by testing the page's LSN, that b is already in a more recent state, and the write therefore must not be performed.

The fundamental reason for the above kind of flush-order dependency is that there is a *read/write dependency* (in the sense of the page model conflict serializability theory of Chapter 3) between the two involved operations for which we consider logical redo. This observation suggests the following general definition: there exists a *redo dependency* from the logged operation $f(\ldots)$ to the logged operation $g(\ldots)$ if f precedes g on the log and there exists a page x such that $x \in$ readset(f) and $x \in$ writeset(g). From this redo dependency relation among operations we can derive the relevant *flush-order dependencies* for modified pages: page y must be flushed before page z if there are operations f and g with $y \in$ write set(f), $z \in$ write set(g) and a redo dependency (due to some page x) from f to g. As an example consider Figure 15.1, which is a concrete instantiation of our above scenario for Copy operations on large objects.

Redo dependency

Flush-order dependency

The flush order can be enforced by the cache manager with little overhead, by maintaining a graph for the flush-order relation. A page can be flushed only if it has no predecessors in this graph; in other words, when the cache manager intends to flush a page it must first initiate the flushing of that page's (transitive) predecessors. A conceptual difficulty arises, however, when the flush-order relation turns out to be cyclic. Such a situation is depicted in Figure 15.2.

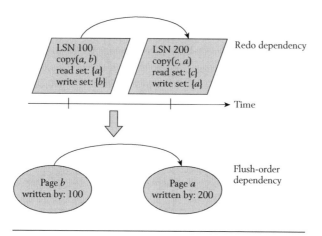

Figure 15.1 Example of a redo dependency and the derived flush-order dependency.

In this example, two additional operations merge(b, c, a), which merges the contents of two objects b and c (e.g., images) into object a, and merge(a, c, b) create another flush-order dependency that requires b to be flushed before a and thus produces a cycle in the flush-order graph.

Cyclic dependencies of this kind are obviously much harder to deal with by the cache manager. In full consequence, all pages that are related by a flush-order cycle would have to be flushed in a single atomic action. With random-access writes into the stable database, such a multipage action would again require some form of logging to ensure atomicity, which seems highly

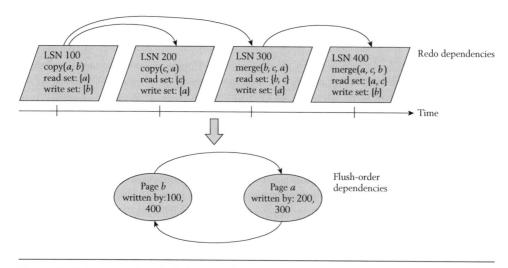

Figure 15.2 Example of cyclic flush-order dependencies.

unattractive given our goal of reducing the amount of logged data. Fortunately, there is a much less expensive method for coping with flush-order cycles. First observe that rather than really flushing all affected pages, it is actually sufficient to create physical log entries (i.e., full after images) for those pages in the log buffer as if there were a full-write action on each of the pages, and to make sure that the log buffer is appended to the stable log atomically. The latter is straightforward to implement with sequential I/O, by marking the last block to be written atomically.

Once all these full after images are on the stable log, the cache manager no longer needs to care about these pages as far as flush-order dependencies are concerned. The pages are still dirty in the sense that they need to be written back into the stable database before they can be dropped from the cache, but determining the appropriate time for this is now completely at the discretion of the cache manager and no longer dependent on redo dependencies. The reason for this removal of flush-order dependencies lies in the fact that during recovery, the redo pass will eventually restore all affected pages to a state as captured by the logged after images. This state includes all prior (partial) writes to those pages, so that the effect of logically redoing operations that appear earlier in the log will eventually be overwritten anyway. As a seemingly irritating consequence, the logical redo of an operation may result in a possibly inconsistent state that never existed in the chronological history, namely, if only some of the pages in its write set have been flushed between the time of the operation and the crash. However, it is guaranteed that all pages that are inconsistently modified by such redo steps will be overwritten by later redo steps with their correct state. Note that all logical redo steps still read all pages for which the state matters in the proper version, since flush-order dependencies for pages that were not involved in the dissolved cycle would still have been enforced by the cache manager.

Atomic groups of physical log entries dissolve cyclic dependencies

Upon a closer look at this problem, it becomes clear that it is not even necessary to create physical log entries for *all* pages in a flush-order cycle to dissolve the cycle. Creating a physical log entry for a page conceptually allows us to remove, in retrospect, the page from the write sets of the preceding operations, as this page no longer needs to be reconstructed by the logical redo of these operations. However, this optimization in the sketched simple form is feasible only if the page has not been read between a write and the physical logging, for otherwise these reads could possibly see an improper version of the page during redo recovery. In the presence of such intermediate reads, the remedy would be to make sure that the write sets of the intermediate readers are flushed or physically logged first, before the cycle-breaking page is flushed (i.e., the page that initially triggered this optimization).

Selective subsets of physical log entries dissolve cyclic dependencies

Note that flush-order dependencies may arise even within a single operation, whenever there is a read/write dependency among the operation's page accesses. To this end, we refine the notion of flush-order dependency as follows (with slightly fewer dependencies than in the earlier definition): for operations f and g such that page x is contained in f's read set and g's write set and

Cyclic flush-order dependencies within a single operation

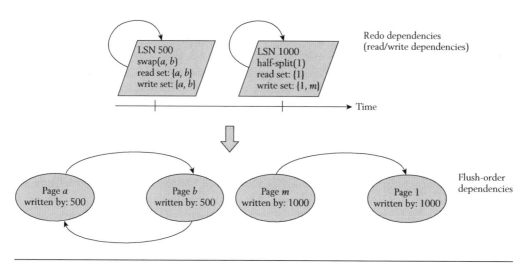

Figure 15.3 Flush-order dependencies within an operation.

f's read precedes g's write, there is a flush-order dependency from every page in write set$(f) - \{x\}$ to x. With this definition, f and g may be the same operation. Figure 15.3 shows two examples, one referring to an operation swap(a, b), which exchanges the contents of two large objects, and the other reconsidering the half-split operation on index leaf nodes discussed earlier. The index example leads to the requirement that the newly created sibling m be flushed before the originally existing leaf node l (assuming that m does not need to be read by the redo step for the operation). So we see here the general principle behind the technique of careful flush ordering introduced in the previous subsection. The presented method based on an explicit flush-order graph even allows concurrent split operations on nondisjoint paths in the index tree, a case that was disregarded in the previous subsection. The example with the swap operation even exhibits a flush-order cycle, as there are both read and write actions for each of the two involved pages. The cycle can be dissolved by creating a physical log entry for either of the two pages.

Logical logging of stored procedure execution state   A special kind of "large object" for which logical logging may be attractive is *recoverable stored procedures*. By this term we mean that a stored procedure that executes in the address space of the data server can be made failure resilient by logging its state modifications, where the state includes not only the contents of the procedure's variables but also cursor positions for fetching query result sets and temporary files. Once we view the procedure's state simply as a large object under the control of the data server, we realize that many of its operations are of the style whereby some possibly large contents is read from some data objects into the "procedure object," resembling the case of Copy operations on large objects. By logging these operations in logical form we can provide redo recovery for the state of executing procedures in a relatively cost-effective manner. So after a crash, the restart would reestablish the most recent state of the procedure, and the procedure could then be resumed from this point. This is an important step toward making applications recoverable, as opposed to merely providing data recovery. The sketched technique is, however, fairly limited in that it could cope only with "mini-applications" that are directly embedded in the data server. We will address the recovery problem for full-fledged client-server applications in Chapter 17.

In summary, the presented methods for coping with flush-order dependencies allow us to log operations in logical form (for redo purposes) with the guarantee that the redo steps for these operations "see" the underlying pages in an appropriate state and can thus be assumed atomic, or they will be overwritten by a later redo step anyway. Such redo steps must still perform the usual LSN-based state test on each of the pages that are considered to be modified and suppress modifications when a page's LSN is more recent than the LSN of the logged operation. The key advantage of the logical redo approach is the savings in logging costs, which is significant for specific operations on large objects or index structures. For conventional operations on short records, logical logging is still inferior to physiological logging because of the higher redo costs and the resulting increase of the restart time. Fortunately, it is easy to combine the different kinds of log entries and redo techniques on a per-operation basis. So the log and recovery manager can arbitrarily mix logical, physiological, and physical log entries even for the same object.

Mixing logical and physiological log entries

15.3 Intra-transaction Savepoints and Nested Transactions

Application programs may sometimes find it convenient to be able to roll back only a part of an ongoing transaction to some explicitly established point within the transaction. Such intra-transaction *savepoints* are dynamically created by explicit calls of the program, and the rollback to a previously established savepoint is initiated upon another explicit call. These types of calls extend our repertoire of actions to be supported by the recovery algorithm (as briefly mentioned already in Chapter 12):

The case for partial rollbacks

- save(t) creates a savepoint inside a transaction, returning a savepoint identifier s (which could be just a (log) sequence number).

- restore(t, s) rolls back the transaction to savepoint s, undoing all updates that were made after the savepoint.

An executing transaction program may create multiple savepoints and can later choose to which savepoint the rollback should be performed. We refer to such rollbacks that undo only a portion of the transaction's updates as *partial rollbacks*. Supporting this feature can be very convenient for application structuring. For example, a transaction may initiate certain logical consistency checks against the data (e.g., by means of firing an SQL trigger or as the effect of a declarative SQL assertion) at any point. When such a check reveals a logical inconsistency (e.g., promising the express shipment of an ordered product that is out of stock), the transaction can back out just a bit and try an alternative in its execution path (e.g., shipping another product that the customer would consider equivalent) while retaining most of its prior work (e.g., the processing of other products in the same customer order).

Partial rollbacks for deadlock resolution   Partial rollbacks may also be initiated by the data server itself to resolve deadlocks among concurrent transactions. The idea is to roll back one of the affected transactions to a point where the deadlock did not yet exist. In effect, this partial rollback releases the locks that were acquired after the corresponding savepoint and led to the deadlock. In this case savepoints are internal ones, invisible to the transaction program. Typically, the scope of these system-induced partial rollbacks is limited to an individual SQL statement (or data server call in general) issued by the application. After the rollback, the same SQL statement is reinvoked by the data server. Note that this can be done transparently to the application program, whereas rolling back to some point farther back would require the program to be resumed from this earlier point, which cannot be masked to the program and would therefore require explicit program-established savepoints. Nevertheless, system-induced partial rollbacks for deadlock resolution can provide significant performance gains, as they reduce the work to be undone and subsequently retried.

Supporting savepoints and partial rollbacks in the recovery algorithm is not that difficult. Whenever a savepoint is created, by an executing transaction program or internally by the data server, a "savepoint" log entry is created in the log buffer, along with a corresponding log sequence number (LSN). This LSN internally serves as the savepoint identifier. Later, in a rollback to a prior savepoint s by a restore(t, s) call, the recovery algorithm simply traverses the transaction's backward chain of log entries, through the PreviousSeqNo pointers of log entries and starting from the LastSeqNo pointer in the ActiveTrans data structure (see Chapter 13), until it encounters the savepoint log entry.

Problem: nested rollbacks   A complication arises, however, when a transaction that has been rolled back to a savepoint is later interrupted by a crash and becomes a loser transaction. Now we need to find out which updates were already undone by the partial rollback during normal operation. Fortunately, in Chapter 13 we have already shown and successfully solved very similar problems, such as a crash occurring in the middle of the rollback for an aborted transaction. The solution devised there was to create compensation log entries (CLEs) for undo steps and link these CLEs back to the predecessor of the undone action's log entry through the additional NextUndoSeqNo backward chain. The same technique solves the above problem of partial rollbacks as well. It also copes with even

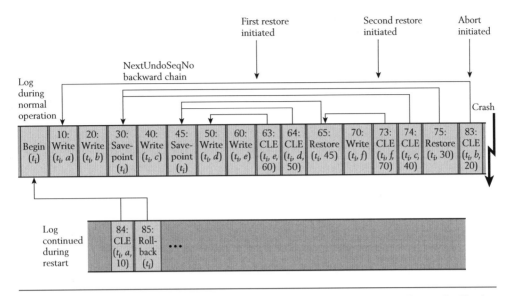

Figure 15.4 NextUndoSeqNo backward chain of log entries in the presence of nested rollbacks.

trickier situations, all of which fall into the category of some form of *nested rollbacks*. For example, a transaction that has been restored to a previous save-point may later initiate another partial rollback to an older savepoint, and may eventually become aborted entirely, but the complete rollback becomes interrupted by a server crash. Figure 15.4 illustrates the log entries and their proper NextUndoSeqNo backward chain for such a scenario. For simplicity, the figure shows only the nontrivial NextUndoSeqNo pointers, that is, those that do not point to the immediate PreviousSeqNo predecessor. It should be clear that the algorithms for the analysis, redo, and undo passes of the redo-history crash recovery can be used in exactly their previously developed form (see Chapters 13 and 14) to handle this case correctly as well.

Once the appropriate use of the NextUndoSeqNo backward chaining is clear, the algorithms for the `savepoint` and `restore` actions fall out in a straightforward manner and are given below in pseudocode form.

```
savepoint (transid):                                          Savepoint
  newlogentry.LogSeqNo := new sequence number;                algorithm
  newlogentry.ActionType := savepoint;
  newlogentry.PreviousSeqNo := ActiveTrans[transid].LastSeqNo;
  newlogentry.NextUndoSeqNo := ActiveTrans[transid].LastSeqNo;
  ActiveTrans[transid].LastSeqNo := newlogentry.LogSeqNo;
  LogBuffer += newlogentry;
```

Restore
algorithm
(partial
rollback)

```
restore (transid, s):
  logentry := ActiveTrans[transid].LastSeqNo;
  while logentry is not equal to s
  do
    if logentry.ActionType = write or full-write
    then
      newlogentry.LogSeqNo := new sequence number;
      newlogentry.ActionType := compensation;
      newlogentry.PreviousSeqNo := ActiveTrans[transid].LastSeqNo;
      newlogentry.RedoInfo :=
        inverse action of the action in logentry;
      newlogentry.NextUndoSeqNo := logentry.PreviousSeqNo;
      ActiveTrans[transid].LastSeqNo := newlogentry.LogSeqNo;
      LogBuffer += newlogentry;
      write (logentry.PageNo) according to logentry.UndoInfo;
      logentry := logentry.PreviousSeqNo;
    end /*if*/;
    if logentry.ActionType = restore
    then
      logentry := logentry.NextUndoSeqNo;
    end /*if*/
  end /*while*/
  newlogentry.LogSeqNo := new sequence number;
  newlogentry.ActionType := restore;
  newlogentry.TransId := transid;
  newlogentry.PreviousSeqNo := ActiveTrans[transid].LastSeqNo;
  newlogentry.NextUndoSeqNo := s.NextUndoSeqNo;
  LogBuffer += newlogentry;
```

The presented algorithm also handles system-induced partial rollbacks for deadlock resolution in a proper manner. Note that for this purpose, it is crucial that the locks that were acquired for the operations to be undone can be released. Therefore, it is important that a subsequent rollback, partial or complete, whose scope includes the previous one does not attempt to undo any of the undo steps for the previous rollback. This is not a critical issue for the undo steps during crash recovery where concurrency is strictly under the control of the recovery algorithm, but during normal operation where concurrent transactions could interfere with the transaction that is undergoing a nested rollback, anomalies could arise. By releasing the locks after the first partial rollback is complete, a concurrent transaction could perform noncommutative operations on the corresponding data, and a subsequent second rollback would have to reacquire locks, thus violating the two-phase locking protocol and leading to incorrect behavior. The following example illustrates this case:

$$l_1(x)w_1(x)l_1(y)w_1(y)w_1^{-1}(y)u_1(y)l_2(y)w_2(y)c_2l_1(y)\left(w_1^{-1}(y)\right)^{-1}w_1^{-1}(y)w_1^{-1}(x)$$

Here l stands for lock acquisitions, u for unlocking (i.e., lock releases), and c for commit with the release of all held locks; the first $w_1^{-1}(y)$ action is issued by a partial rollback, and the actions after c_2 are the undo steps initiated by the abort of the entire transaction t_1. The execution is not prefix reducible in the sense of Chapter 11; so it is incorrect when we take into account the interleaving of regular forward operations and the inverse operations executed on behalf of (partial) rollbacks. It could be made prefix reducible by requiring t_1 to continue holding its lock on y even after the partial rollback, thus preventing t_2 from accessing y in between the partial rollback and the eventual abort of t_1. However, this remedy would render partial rollbacks useless for the purpose of deadlock resolution, where the whole point is to release locks. In contrast, the presented algorithm for nested rollbacks does indeed allow releasing of locks for undone actions and handles the above situation correctly by guaranteeing that the traversal of the NextUndoSeqNo backward chain never results in invoking a doubly inverse operation. With this technique the above execution would look as follows, meeting the correctness criterion of prefix reducibility and being feasible under two-phase locking:

$$l_1(x)w_1(x)l_1(y)w_1(y)w_1^{-1}(y)u_1(y)l_2(y)w_2(y)c_2w_1^{-1}(x)$$

A specific form of specifying savepoints and initiating partial rollbacks is by embedding all data operations of a transaction program in a *nested transaction*. Recall from Chapter 10, where we introduced this kind of nesting for multi-threaded transactions, that a nested transaction corresponds to a tree whose leaves are read and write operations. In contrast to the transaction trees of the object model, the inner nodes of a nested transaction do not correspond to higher-level operations (at least not necessarily) and rather are of syntactic nature only. Figure 15.5 shows an example of a nested transaction. Assume for now that there is no concurrency among subtransactions (although this is a major feature of nested transactions, as you may recall from Chapter 10). So at each point, no two siblings in the tree can be active simultaneously, and the leaf nodes read from left to right denote the execution history.

Nested transactions denote intra-transaction savepoints

In a nested transaction, the begin of a subtransaction implicitly creates a new savepoint. When the transaction program requests the abort of a subtransaction, it essentially initiates to restore the corresponding savepoint. Because of the nesting of subtransactions, savepoints are nested, too. The savepoints for the example of Figure 15.5 are indicated by the black arrows in the figure. Since completed subtransactions can no longer be aborted other than by aborting an incomplete parent, only those savepoints that correspond to

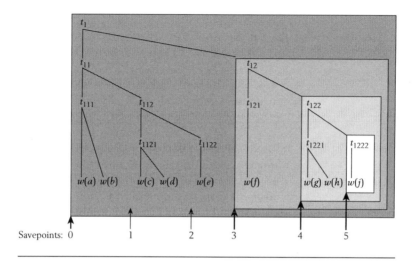

Figure 15.5 Example of a nested transaction and the corresponding save-points.

active subtransactions can be referred to by a partial rollback. In the figure, it is assumed that t_{12}, t_{122}, and t_{1222} are not yet terminated, and their savepoints and corresponding rollback scopes are highlighted by thick arrows and rectangles, respectively. In addition, the begin of the entire transaction t_1 is an implicit savepoint, too. So at each point, the "available" savepoints that can be used by a restore action correspond to the set of active subtransactions that form a single ancestor chain in the tree. This is obviously a restricted style of specifying savepoints, but the strict form of nesting offers an easy-to-use way of structuring the creation of savepoints in an application program. Once this relationship between intra-transaction savepoints and nested transactions has become clear, supporting subtransaction aborts is merely a special case of the partial rollback algorithm given above.

Coping with intra-transaction parallelism
    This matter becomes a bit more difficult when we allow concurrent subtransactions in more than one ancestor chain within a nested transaction. This means that two or more subtransactions, neither of which is an ancestor of the other (e.g., being siblings), can execute concurrently in multiple threads. For example, if transaction t_1 of Figure 15.5 would spawn both of its children asynchronously in separate threads without waiting for the completion of the previously initiated subtransaction, and the same would be done for the children and further descendants of t_{11} and t_{12}, then all 10 subtransactions of the example could be simultaneously active. Then all five savepoints shown in the example for the subtransactions t_{1222}, t_{122}, t_{12}, t_{1122}, and t_{112} (plus the implicit one for the entire transaction t_1) would be available to be used by a restore action. In addition, the other five active subtransactions would correspond to five further savepoints (not shown in the figure) for subtransactions t_{1221}, t_{121}, t_{1111},

t_{111}, and t_{11}. Aborting a subtransaction now means undoing all write actions that are descendants of the corresponding node in the tree. For example, aborting t_{112} requires a partial rollback that undoes the write actions on c, d, e and nothing else. When concurrent subtransactions access nondisjoint page sets, the concurrency control must, of course, constrain the allowable concurrency (see Chapter 10).

The solution for this case of multi-threaded nested transactions is to organize the log entries of each simultaneously active ancestor chain of subtransactions into separate NextUndoSeqNo backward chains. The oldest log entry of a given subtransaction would then point to the most recent log entry of the subtransaction's siblings that were already completed at the time when the subtransaction was spawned. If there is no such preceding sibling, the subtransaction's oldest log entry points to the parent's begin log entry, and this begin log entry in turn points to the most recent log entry of the lowest ancestor's descendants that were completed when the considered subtransaction began. Equivalently, the begin log entries may be skipped in these chains and could then be completely omitted. Aborting a subtransaction then involves a backward traversal of all chains of its active descendants. These backward chains will be "confluent" in the sense that they have common prefixes once they reach a common ancestor.

This technique may sound complicated, but it is relatively straightforward to implement. In fact, it is more or less identical to the logging and recovery algorithm for the general object model when we allow concurrent high-level operations, or subtransactions within the same transaction (see the last section of Chapter 14). Nested transactions are even simpler to handle, as we need undo/redo log entries only for the leaves of the transaction trees, and all other log entries are mere bookkeeping to remember the scopes of the subtransactions. As with intra-transaction parallelism for the general object model, the only more fundamental extension of the recovery algorithm is that the Active-Trans data structure needs to hold a LastSeqNo pointer for each active subtransaction. An abort request for a specific subtransaction can then be easily translated into rollbacks for all its descendants, whose ActiveTrans entries serve as starting points for the backward traversal on the log. Note in particular that subtransaction aborts during normal operation do not raise any complications: we simply create compensation log entries for undone actions (to be redone after a crash) and maintain the NextUndoSeqNo backward chains as usual.

15.4 **Exploiting Parallelism during Restart**

As emphasized already a number of times, fast restart is crucial for high availability of the data server. Thus, it is highly desirable to parallelize the recovery work to the greatest possible extent. One technique that we already mentioned

Parallelized redo

in Chapter 13 is to exploit asynchronous and possibly batched disk I/O for fetching pages from the stable database during the redo pass. The necessary information for such optimizations can be collected during the analysis pass by reconstructing the DirtyPages data structure as of the time of the crash (see Chapter 13). Since large databases reside on multiple disks, this technique provides a great performance improvement to reduce the restart duration.

Parallelized log scans

An even more far-reaching approach is to parallelize the log scan. To this end we need to partition the stable log into multiple fragments on different disks that can be processed in parallel. For example, the log entries could be assigned to fragments based on a hash function on page numbers. Of course, with such a log that is spread across multiple files, LSN-based pointers among log entries need to be global (i.e., valid across files), and specific log entries like checkpoint log entries could be (redundantly) present in all log files. This organization of the stable log allows parallelizing the analysis pass, with one log-scanning thread per file and a common data structure for determining losers and the DirtyPages data structure. Once the analysis pass is complete, the redo pass, which is usually the largest portion of work during restart, can process the log fragments in parallel without any further synchronization, as all log entries for the same page are guaranteed to be in the same log file. This parallelized redo phase, which achieves the major speedup, assumes that log entries for redo purposes are physiological or physical, so that each log entry refers to exactly one page—our standard assumption throughout the previous chapters. With logical redo, as discussed in Section 15.2, such an approach would become

Parallelized undo

much more involved. Finally, the undo pass can be parallelized as well by creating one parallel thread for each loser transaction. However, each of these threads may have to access multiple, possibly all log fragments, if the undo information in the log entries is not page oriented and rather refers to high-level inverse operations. So the undo threads should be coordinated with one or more additional log-scanning threads to avoid inefficient, random disk I/O on the log files.

Early admission of new transactions

In addition to speeding up the restart after a crash, another, orthogonal way of improving the server's availability is to allow new transactions to access "uncritical" portions of the data even before the restart is complete. Of course, such an approach needs to preserve the prefix reducibility (i.e., serializability and correct handling of undo steps) of the original history, and the difficulty lies in determining exactly what data objects are uncritical in this regard. The basic technique for supporting this optimization is to reacquire locks for loser transactions during the analysis or redo pass, and to admit new transactions once all locks that will possibly be needed for transaction undo are held again.

Reacquiring locks for loser transactions

In essence, this amounts to reincarnating all loser transactions and proceeding as if they were active again during normal operation. Reacquiring the locks held before the crash prevents new transactions from accessing data that still needs to undergo undo steps. So we continue a strict two-phase locking protocol (with perfect or perfectly closed commutativity, see Chapter 11) beyond the crash, and this is what ensures prefix reducibility according to the corresponding theorem of Chapter 11.

The exact nature of the locks that need to be reacquired before new transactions can be admitted depends on the locking method employed by the server. With page locking, the relevant locks can be seen directly from the log because each (redo) log entry includes a page number. Of course, only exclusive locks have to be reacquired, and in fact, only these can be inferred from the log. With high-level locks for object model transactions, it may be more difficult to derive the proper locks from the log information alone. In this case, we may have to know input and also result parameters in addition to the operation type of the original forward operation and not just the (minimum) information about the inverse operation that is kept on the log. If high server availability is of utmost importance for a given application, we can simply enhance the log entries written during normal operation so that they include all necessary information for lock reacquisition during restart.

So once again, a system or application architect needs to carefully trade off the server availability versus the logging overhead during normal operation. This is a highly delicate task, but such advanced optimization techniques do exhibit inherent trade-offs whose complexity is beyond the state of the art in autotuning capabilities. In fact, even the reacquisition of exclusive page locks during recovery may create an overhead that is not acceptable in every system environment. Fortunately, there are several techniques for conservatively approximating the necessary locks at much lower expense. A simple technique is to reacquire only coarse-grained locks, such as tablespace locks, rather than page locks or even object model–style locks. Of course, this would block more of the newly admitted transactions and thus reduce the advantage of resuming normal operation early, but it is still better than allowing new transactions only after the undo phase is completed.

Other low-overhead techniques along these lines exploit the information gathered during the usual analysis pass on the log. Specifically, the Oldest-UndoLSN is usually determined for future log truncation anyway. This LSN denotes the oldest log entry of a loser transaction, and is easily derived from the information in the most recent checkpoint log entry and the forward pass of the log analysis. With page locking or any other coarser locking, the undo pass will not need to access any page whose page LSN (i.e., the LSN stored in the page's header) after the redo pass is lower than the OldestUndoLSN. In other words, such a page has not been modified after the oldest loser began. Since advanced recovery algorithms already know the eventual page LSN of a page after the analysis pass by having reconstructed the DirtyPages data structure, we can derive immediately after the log analysis a set of pages that are definitely not involved in any of the following redo or undo steps: namely, all pages that are not in the DirtyPages list and whose page LSN must be older than the OldestUndoLSN. Those pages can be made accessible for newly admitted transactions during the redo pass. Once new transactions start acquiring locks,

Low-overhead testing of page accessibility during restart

the pages in this category can be identified either by keeping an explicit list (possibly using hash-based bit vector approximations for compact space) or by performing the above LSN test upon their first access and then setting a specific bit in their page headers.

Note that the comparison with the OldestUndoLSN is a conservative one: a page whose page LSN is more recent than the OldestUndoLSN may still be irrelevant for undo if the more recent updates are winner updates. One way of making this test more "precise" would be to determine an OldestUndoLSN for each page or some appropriate coarser granule (e.g., tablespaces) separately. Then a page is known to be uncritical for undo if its page LSN is older than the page-specific OldestUndoLSN. Of course, if new transactions are already admitted during the redo pass, the page must not be dirty in addition, in order to be accessible right away. Determining page-specific OldestUndoLSNs incurs more overhead, however, as it requires additional information in checkpoint log entries, and this is why this technique is more appropriate for tablespaces or similarly coarse granules than for individual pages.

15.5 Special Considerations for Main-Memory Data Servers

Modern data servers are often equipped with huge amounts of memory, and the technological and price trends will allow more and more databases to reside entirely in the server memory, thus eliminating all disk I/O on the data itself. Such databases are commonly called *main-memory databases*. For certain classes of performance-critical applications, avoiding disk I/O is indeed crucial in order to guarantee real-time response times. In particular, telecommunication applications require extremely fast lookups of switching and customer information for call routing and billing (e.g., for service call centers or cellular phone numbers and mobile clients in general).

The case for main-memory databases

Main-memory databases thus allow higher transaction throughput and stronger (but still stochastic) guarantees for real-time response times, such that, for example, 99% of all transactions are completed within 100 milliseconds. On the other hand, with all regular disk I/O eliminated, they also suggest a data organization that may radically differ from that of disk-resident databases. For example, index structures may no longer be page oriented, and the entire notion of a page, with its embedded header, slot array, and so on, may be substituted with substantially larger "segments" that serve as containers for loading a main-memory database.

Crash recovery needs to load the entire database

The usual methods for crash recovery may have to be reconsidered as well in such a drastically changed system environment. It turns out, however, that the overall log-based redo-history paradigm is still the method of choice, but certain details may have to be revised. Most importantly, crash recovery for a main-memory database amounts to loading the entire database. This is a particularity that we can optimize for. Within the framework used in this book, the most promising option is to move from physiological to physical log entries as far as redo is concerned. So entire after images of pages or an appropriately sized kind of segments (see above) are read from the stable log during the redo pass, and there is no longer a need for randomly fetching pages from the stable database, which is now merely a backup for the main-memory database. In the most radical approach, the stable log could be viewed as the stable database, or equivalently, the stable database itself could be organized more like a sequential log. In this case, log truncation should strive for discarding all after images of a page other than the most recent one. It is also feasible, however, to combine physical with physiological log entries in such an approach, so that small changes can still be logged as a byte-oriented operation rather than a full-fledged after image; but then the log manager should make sure that complete after images are created sufficiently frequently for an effective log truncation.

The above sketched approach essentially views the stable log as the backup database from which the main-memory database is reloaded after a crash. In a less radical approach, where at least the not so frequently modified data pages or segments reside in a conventionally organized disk-based stable database, the task of checkpointing and flushing dirty pages is the key issue. Recall from Chapter 13 that asynchronous checkpoints that write DirtyPages information on the stable log are preferable over synchronous checkpoints that really flush dirty pages at checkpoint time. This is still the case for a main-memory database, as synchronous flushing would incur delays for ongoing transactions. Rather, as discussed in Chapter 13, a background process should flush pages back into the stable database more or less continuously. In a main-memory database, where such flushing is the only disk I/O during normal operation, this background process can be specifically optimized toward strictly sequential, high-bandwidth I/O. In the literature on main-memory databases, this process is commonly referred to as a *fuzzy checkpoint*. In fact, it resembles the process of creating a database backup for media recovery, to be discussed in Chapter 16, and thus extends our standard meaning of the term "checkpoint."

For main-memory databases, the outage during crash recovery is an even more severe problem than usual, given their otherwise excellent responsiveness during normal operation and the fact that many target applications require extremely high availability, especially in the telecommunication industry. Thus, the techniques presented in the previous section for early admission of new transactions are of utmost importance for main-memory data servers. In addition, it can be worthwhile to devise the entire recovery in an incremental manner, where recovery steps for a certain data unit are performed only when the first new transaction requests that data. So the main-memory database would be accessible immediately after the analysis pass. Then, when certain data is requested by a regular transaction and thus needs to be brought into

Incremental redo on demand

memory anyway, the necessary redo steps and undo steps for this data unit are performed on the fly. Of course, the usual redo recovery should nevertheless be initiated right after the analysis pass, too, as a background process. The key difference from standard redo is that the order in which data units are recovered is no longer solely driven by the chronological ordering of log entries but rather takes the demands of new transactions into account. This technique requires an appropriate organization of the stable log, possibly with some auxiliary data structures built up in memory during the analysis pass (e.g., lists of all relevant LSNs for critical data units) and an appropriate choice of "data units," which may be much larger than a page.

All of the above considerations mostly refer to redo recovery, which constitutes the bulk of the work during restart. The undo pass does not differ from the conventional recovery algorithms of Chapters 13 and 14, but may also include certain optimizations in the underlying log organization. In particular, with very large memory, it should be feasible to avoid writing undo information to the stable log at all. The main-memory database can easily employ a no-steal caching policy (see Chapter 12), where pages or segments with uncommitted updates are never written back to the stable database. Since the database is all-cache anyway, all it takes to this end is to coordinate with the fuzzy checkpoint background process that flushes dirty pages, and possibly keep two versions of a page temporarily in memory—a before image and an after image. Upon transaction commit, all relevant after images or the redo portion of the corresponding physiological log entries are atomically appended to the stable log, and the before images or undo portion of the log entries can then be discarded. The deferral of writing log entries to the stable log may require a somewhat larger log buffer than usual, but in general, the slight increase in the memory requirements for logging and recovery should be negligible with a main-memory data server. Making log entries stable may even be based on safe-RAM technology (i.e., battery-backed, nonvolatile memory, see Chapter 12) for an extended notion of log buffer, removing the need for (synchronous) disk I/O even at commit time. But this issue is not really specific to main-memory data servers.

For object model transactions where undo necessitates high-level inverse operations, the atomic appending of a transaction's redo log entries needs to be extended. Recall from Chapter 14 that each high-level operation corresponds to a subtransaction. Upon the end of the subtransaction, both the physical or physiological redo log entries of the subtransaction and the undo information about the high-level inverse operation are appended to the stable log in a single atomic write. This guarantees the atomicity of subtransactions, which is necessary for the applicability of the high-level inverses and also the persistence of the subtransaction's low-level writes (unless compensating steps are later invoked for transaction undo). With low-level page locks held for the duration of a subtransaction, as in the layered or general object model two-phase locking protocols of Chapter 7, the written log entries contain only effects of committed subtransactions. Forcing the log buffer upon each subtransaction commit is inexpensive with safe RAM, but may be unacceptable if it requires disk I/O. In the latter case, the log writes for subtransactions can be deferred and batched to combine multiple committed subtransactions; the log is still forced at transaction commit at the latest. This batching is straightforward to implement as long as the chronological order of log entries is respected. With physical log entries, an obvious additional enhancement could be to write only the latest after image of a page to the stable log onto disk.

15.6 **Extensions for Data-Sharing Clusters**

Servers for data-intensive applications with very high throughput and very high availability guarantees are often built as *data-sharing systems*, also known as *clusters*. A cluster is a small number of computers, typically between two and eight, that share all their disks through a special high-speed interconnect. Each of these computers, which we will henceforth refer to as the individual servers of the cluster, runs its own copy of the operating system, database system, and so on, and could be a powerful shared memory multiprocessor. The key characteristic of a cluster is, however, that each server has its own "private" memory; there is no shared memory across servers. This architecture provides much better failure containment (i.e., no failure propagation across servers) than the tight coupling of processors with shared memory. So when a server fails, the other servers of the cluster continue operating and may take over the load of the failed server. The necessary actions for this kind of *failover* procedure can be performed significantly faster than a full-fledged restart for the failed server, hence the very high availability of a cluster. Note that it is crucial for this purpose that the "surviving" servers can access the failed server's disks; in fact, in such a shared disk setting, a data disk is not associated with any specific server.

Clusters can be configured for very high throughput by simply adding disks and servers (in addition to upgrading the number of processors and memory size per server, but this is less robust in terms of availability), and this approach provides reasonable scalability. The practical viability of cluster architectures has been demonstrated in many high-end database applications and also for high-end Web servers. Transactions are typically routed to one of the servers of a cluster complex in a round-robin manner or driven by tables on workload profiles and the "affinity" of transaction types to data units such as tablespaces, in order to coarsely balance the load across the servers. In most implementations, a transaction is then executed entirely on a single server. When a transaction accesses a page, this page is brought into the memory of the corresponding server, either from the shared disks on which the data resides permanently or from the memory of another server that happened to have that page in its cache.

Data-sharing clusters for very high availability and throughput

Data shipping This operational principle is known as *data shipping*. The flexibility of being able to make each page accessible on each server provides good load sharing and usually results in good load balance across servers, at least when certain tuning options (which have no relevance for the scope of this book) are exerted. In addition to data shipping, such a system could also dynamically distribute operations of a transaction to servers other than the transaction's origin for better data locality or parallelization, which is known as *function shipping*, but this is rarely used in practice and not considered here.

Coherency control for dynamic page transfers As far as crash recovery is concerned, the key characteristic of a cluster is that each server has its private page cache, and there are intensive, dynamic page transfers between these caches. A problem that arises in this setting, and is even present independently of the notion of transactions, is how to ensure that a server does not access a stale version of a page. This could happen if a page resides in more than one cache for an extended period and is modified in one of these caches without notifying the other servers. To prevent this incorrect behavior, a *coherency control* protocol must be used in these kinds of distributed memory systems. All servers of the cluster complex must have sufficient bookkeeping and agree on a message-based protocol, so that stale pages are invalidated and it is known where an up-to-date version of a page can be fetched if needed by a server. We do not delve into the details of such a protocol here, as this will be a subject of Chapter 18 in conjunction with how concurrency control responsibilities are distributed across servers. For the context of the current section, it is sufficient to realize the main invariants that each page-oriented coherency control protocol needs to ensure:

- Multiple caches can hold up-to-date versions of a page simultaneously as long as the page is only read.

- Once a page has been modified in one of the caches, this cache is the only one that is allowed to hold a copy of the page. (So we can assume that all other caches "immediately" discard their copies of the page upon this write access.)

As a consequence of these invariants, each page undergoes the following cycle in terms of the number of its simultaneously valid copies: Initially, there is only one copy in the stable database on disk. The first access to the page creates a copy in one of the caches. Then, as long as no write takes place, the page may be transferred to other caches, thus creating multiple copies. Upon the first write, all copies but one are discarded, so that only one cache holds a copy. This brings us back to the second stage in the cycle, from which the page can again be shipped to other caches. Finally, when the page is dropped from all the caches that happen to hold it at some point (by being chosen as a regular page replacement victim), we are back to the first stage of the cycle: the page only resides on disk.

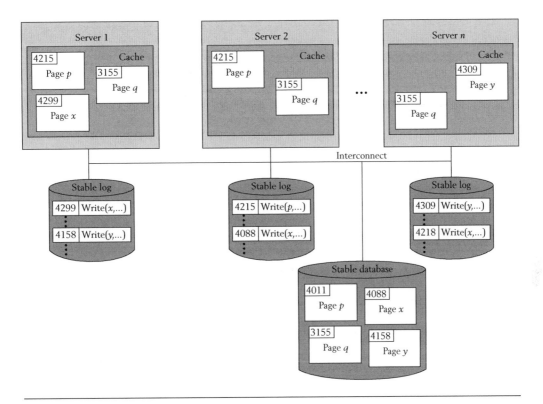

Figure 15.6 A data-sharing cluster.

Coherency control is usually performed on a per-page basis, although other granularities are conceivable. Note, however, that this by no means implies that concurrency control is page oriented. We can still employ object model concurrency control schemes such as record and index-key locking in conjunction with page-oriented coherency control. Consequently, a page may be transferred back and forth multiple times between two caches during two concurrently executing transactions.

The data-sharing cluster architecture is illustrated in Figure 15.6. The numbers in the headers of the various pages denote (log) sequence numbers to indicate when they were last modified. Note that pages p and q reside in two different caches, and the sequence numbers of the two copies must be identical by the above coherency invariant. Further note that the cached version of page p is more recent than the one in the stable database on disk, as indicated by their sequence numbers. This is possible, as we do not necessarily require flushing the page to the stable database before we transfer a modified page to another cache; rather it should be allowed to ship pages directly from the memory of one server into another server's memory.

"Private" log for each server

As for logging, life would obviously be simple if all servers of a cluster wrote to a single shared log; then the usual redo-history recovery algorithm could be applied without any changes. However, the log could possibly be a bottleneck in such an approach, requiring synchronization among servers and impeding scalability. So a cluster should instead have a private log, both log buffer and stable log file, for each of its servers, as shown in Figure 15.6. We will discuss details of the figure's log entries in a short while.

Ideally, each server should write only its own local log, and this is indeed easily achievable for all undo-related log entries, as these are transaction oriented, and each transaction is executed entirely on a single server. With redo-related log entries, however, such perfect locality is much harder to achieve. One approach could be to partition the logging responsibilities for the data pages across the servers, so that all (redo) log entries for the same page would be appended to the same log file. Analogously to the parallel logging scheme mentioned in Section 15.4, this could be implemented by using a hash function on the page number to determine the log file to which a log entry is assigned. However, depending on the details of the interconnect between the disks and the computers in the cluster, such "nonlocal" logging may lead to unduly high consumption of interconnect bandwidth, and the bandwidth should better be used for transferring data pages between disks and memory or directly between caches.

Local logging to private log

So for the sake of lower communication costs and better scalability, we assume that each server writes log entries *only locally* to its private log. Thus, we can encounter the situation depicted in Figure 15.6, where the log entries for a single page, x or y, for example, are dispersed across multiple logs. In this figure, the log sequence numbers in the log entries and the page versions on disk and in memory capture the chronology of page modifications. Note that it is possible for a page, such as x, to have log entries in multiple logs, all of which are more recent than the page's sequence number in the stable database. This can occur if pages can be transferred directly between caches rather than flushing a page to disk before it can be fetched again into another cache. If each page transfer is accompanied by flushing the page, then this situation is prevented, and we would know that all log entries of a page that are really relevant for redo (i.e., are more recent than the page sequence number in the stable database) must reside in a single cache, namely, one where the page is currently cached and was updated last. In Figure 15.6, this simpler situation is assumed for page y. For generality and because memory-to-memory transfer is significantly faster than transferring a page via two disk I/Os, we do not restrict ourselves to the case of a single relevant log, however.

Globally monotonic sequence numbers

The general case, where redo-relevant log entries for the same page may be dispersed across multiple private logs, still requires some form of handshake among the different log managers to ensure that log sequence numbers are properly coordinated. It would be easy to create globally unique log sequence numbers by simply padding a server identifier to the local sequence numbers. These numbers would even form a clusterwide total order, but the problem is that this order does not reflect the chronological order of modifications at different servers. If among two updates to the same page at different servers, the one that occurred later could end up having a lower sequence number, the tracking of page states via log sequence numbers in page headers and, in fact, the entire redo-history paradigm would become incorrect. Fortunately, it is not that difficult to construct appropriately coordinated log sequence numbers. To this end, note that it is sufficient to have globally monotonically increasing sequence numbers for each page separately, as these numbers are relevant only for redo steps (assuming a redo-history algorithm with compensation log entries for undo steps, see Chapter 13). So when a page is freshly transferred to a server and modified there, the local log manager must only ensure that the newly assigned log sequence number is larger than all of the page's prior log entries including the sequence number in the page header. This is achieved by setting the new sequence number as follows:

new sequence number for update to page p :=
  max { current sequence number in the page header of p,
    largest local log sequence number used so far } + 1

Similar techniques have been devised for synchronizing global clocks in distributed systems. Note that this kind of coordination does not require any extra messages; all the relevant information is implicitly piggybacked (in the page headers) on the regular page transfers between servers. A minor complication is that such globally pagewise monotonic sequence numbers can no longer be used for direct byte addressing in a log file, but appropriate solutions can be constructed easily (e.g., by storing both chronological sequence numbers and byte addresses where needed).

The careful design of how log entries are created in a data-sharing cluster, as outlined above, provides the basis for the actual recovery algorithm when a server fails. In this case, we do not have to wait for the failed server to come up again; instead one of the other, surviving servers can take over the role of the failed server and initiate the necessary recovery steps immediately. This is feasible because all data and log disks are still accessible. Even better, such a failover technique can shorten the recovery time substantially, as the surviving servers may still have up-to-date information about the dirty pages in the failed server's cache. Note that such bookkeeping information is maintained and disseminated according to particular rules by the coherency control protocol anyway.

Very fast recovery from single-server failure

The server in charge of the recovery for the failed server first needs to read and conceptually merge the private log files of all servers that could possibly hold redo-relevant log entries for dirty pages that were in the cache of the failed server. The merging would, of course, be pipelined with the actual redo steps, so that all affected log files can still be scanned with maximum-speed sequential I/O and need to be scanned only once. Once the redo pass is completed, the recovery initiates the usual undo pass to roll back the effects of transactions that were active on the failed server. This undo pass is based solely on the private log of the failed server.

Reading and merging multiple log files can be avoided if a dirty page is always flushed to the stable database when it is transferred to another server. The page transfer itself can still be of the memory-to-memory form and the disk I/O on the stable database may be asynchronous, thus alleviating this variant's costs during normal operation. In this case, the only redo-relevant log entries must reside in the private log of the failed server itself. On the other hand, having to access multiple logs is not as much of an overhead as it may appear upon first glance. If the information about the failed server's dirty pages is (still) known to the surviving servers, the fraction of the stable logs that needs to be scanned would typically be very short. Moreover, there is no need for an analysis pass, at least not for reconstructing the DirtyPages data structure. Only determining the set of loser transactions requires an analysis pass, but this involves only the private log of the failed server.

Recovery from failure of entire cluster

The above recovery procedure has very little overhead during normal operation and still allows very fast recovery after a single server failure. Another recovery case that is very unlikely but still possible arises when a software failure brings down an entire cluster. If all information on disk is still undamaged, the global restart then involves analysis passes, redo passes, and undo passes over all of the cluster's stable logs. Furthermore, the redo passes must be performed in a way that the logs are merged on the fly, so that all log entries for the same page are seen in chronological order.

Log shipping and recovery for client caching architectures

Despite the additional complexity of the recovery procedures outlined above, data-sharing clusters are a widely deployed architecture for scalable throughput and especially very high availability. The developed algorithms can also be carried over to a popular variation of client-server database systems where clients cache data pages within and also beyond long-running transactions. Such client caching architectures do not make much sense for conventional OLTP applications, but are intriguing for computer-aided design applications on top of object-oriented databases. The architecture bears many resemblances to data-sharing clusters in that caching is distributed, a page-oriented coherency control protocol is used, and log entries are created in a dispersed manner. In contrast to clusters, however, the overall work is not distributed among peers; rather there is still a notion of a central server that simplifies logging and recovery. The main design issue in logging is to decide when and in which form client-created log entries are shipped to the server, and how this can be optimized in conjunction with transferring dirty pages from a client back to the server. The more data management functionality we impose on the clients, for example, allowing them to write log entries to a stable log locally and defer their shipping to the server, the more the clients act as if they were servers in a data-sharing system. In the extreme, there is no longer a real difference from a full-fledged cluster.

15.7 **Lessons Learned**

In this chapter we have discussed various extensions of the crash recovery methods introduced in the previous chapters. These extensions yield benefits along several dimensions: (1) logging overhead may be reduced by creating logical log entries for redo purposes; (2) application convenience and the efficiency of deadlock resolution can be enhanced by supporting intra-transaction savepoints and partial rollbacks (with nested transactions being a specific case); (3) server availability is enhanced by parallelizing recovery and admitting new transactions after the analysis pass, with reacquired locks for loser transactions or some conservative low-overhead approximation of such locks; and (4) specific architectural settings of great practical importance like main-memory databases and data-sharing clusters are accommodated, with various optimizations customized to these architectures.

An important insight from having considered such a variety of extensions, adaptations, and optimizations is that the algorithmic framework for crash recovery that we developed in Chapters 13 and 14 is still the backbone of the extended methods. All extensions introduced in the current chapter can be integrated into the previous chapter's standard methods in a localized and incremental way. Furthermore, most of the extensions do not replace the prior techniques, but rather complement them in that they cover additional cases or can be combined with the prior techniques so as to choose the most appropriate option at run time on a per-operation basis. A good example for the latter is the reconciliation of logical, physiological, and physical redo log entries into a single algorithm.

Exercises

15.1 Reconsider the two-level action history in Figure 15.7, which was already discussed in Exercise 14.3. It contains operations on records (store, modify) and index keys (insert, delete); for the latter operations, the first parameter denotes a key and the second parameter the RID (i.e., address) of a stored record. Assume that the insert(f, @x, t_1) operation initiates a split of leaf page l, creating the new leaf page k and posting the split to the parent node n. Discuss to what extent logical log entries for the higher-level operations are feasible for redo purposes. (For undo, such

Sequence number: action	Cached changes [PageNo:] [SeqNo]	Stable changes [PageNo:] [SeqNo]	Log entry added [LogSeqNo: action] [NextUndoSeqNo]
1: begin(t_1)			
2: modify(x, t_1)			
3: subbegin(t_{11})			
4: write(p, t_{11})			
5: begin(t_2)			
6: store(y, t_2)			
7: subbegin(t_{21})			
8: write (q, t_{21})			
9: write(r, t_{21})			
10: subcommit(t_{21})			
11: write(r, t_{11})			
12: subcommit(t_{11})			
13: delete($a, @x, t_1$)			
14: subbegin(t_{12})			
15: write(l, t_{12})			
18: subcommit(t_{12})			
19: insert($f, @x, t_1$)			
20: subbegin(t_{13})			
21: write(l, t_{13})			
22: write(k, t_{13})			
23: write(n, t_{13})			
24: subcommit(t_{13})			
25: begin(t_3)			
26: store(z, t_3)			
27: subbegin(t_{31})			
28: write(q, t_{31})			
29: write(r, t_{31})			
30: subcommit(t_{31})			
31: insert($h, @z, t_3$)			
32: subbegin(t_{32})			
33: write(k, t_{32})			
34: subcommit(t_{32})			
35: commit(t_3)			
36: insert($b, @y, t_2$)			
37: subbegin(t_{22})			
38: write(l, t_{22})			

Figure 15.7 Two-level history for Exercise 15.1.

log entries are needed anyway.) Can we avoid creating physiological log entries altogether? Which flush-order dependencies need to be observed for the execution?

15.2 Give all log entries and their proper NextUndoSeqNo backward chains for the nested transaction scenario of Figure 15.5. Assume that all of t_{11} is executed sequentially in the sense that a new subtransaction begins only after its previously initiated siblings are terminated, and that t_{12} is spawned after the termination of t_{11}. Within t_{12} assume that all subtransactions are spawned asynchronously in separate threads; so at the end of the scenario all subtransactions of t_{12} are simultaneously active. Describe the necessary steps to abort subtransaction t_{12}.

15.3 Revise the pseudocode for the undo pass of the page model redo-history algorithm given at the end of Chapter 13 so that it processes different loser transactions in parallel. Use appropriate primitives for spawning new threads, suspending a thread to wait for an event, and raising an event to resume waiting threads.

15.4 Develop pseudocode for the lock conflict test of new transactions that are admitted during the redo pass of a restart, assuming that the Oldest-UndoLSN and the DirtyPages data structures have been determined by the analysis pass and serve as an approximate test for "uncritical" pages that require neither redo nor undo steps. Assume that page locking is used, but no explicit locks are reacquired during the restart, to keep the overhead low.

15.5 Reconsider and streamline the pseudocode for the analysis and redo pass of the page model redo-history algorithm given at the end of Chapter 13 so that it is particularly suitable for a main-memory database.

15.6 Design a scenario, with concrete page numbers, transaction identifiers, log sequence numbers, and so on, that shows the need for synchronizing the local log sequence numbers created at different servers of a data-sharing cluster. Construct anomalies that would arise if the global sequence numbers merely were local numbers padded with server identifiers.

15.7 Develop pseudocode for the crash recovery in a data-sharing cluster, based on the algorithms outlined in Section 15.6. Assume that all undo-related log entries for the same transaction are confined to a single private log, but redo log entries for the same page may be dispersed across multiple logs. Further assume that pages can be directly transferred between the caches of different servers, without having to be flushed to disk. Distinguish two cases:

(a) recovery from a single server crash, where one of the other servers takes over the failed server's role,

(b) recovery from a software failure that brings down the entire cluster (which is unlikely, but still possible), assuming that none of the disks is damaged.

Bibliographic Notes

Recovery for index structures has been described in great detail by Mohan and Levine (1992) as well as Mohan (1996), based on the object model recovery principles from Chapter 14. Generalizations to other kinds of index trees, including R trees, have been described by Kornacker et al. (1997). For the logging optimizations presented here we have mostly followed Lomet (1998a, b) as well as Lomet and Salzberg (1997). Lomet and Tuttle (1995, 1999) developed the method for logical redo with proper handling of flush dependencies; this work has been the basis for our presentation of how logging costs for large-object operations can be reduced. Other approaches to efficient logging and recovery for large objects, mostly based on shadowing (i.e., a page-oriented form of versioning, see Chapter 12), have been discussed by Lehman and Lindsay (1989) as well as Panagos and Biliris (1997). Low-level optimizations for storage-layer metadata, particularly free space management, have been described by Mohan and Haderle (1994).

Our discussion of intra-transaction savepoints and partial rollbacks has followed the seminal work by Mohan, Haderle, et al. (1992) on the ARIES recovery method. Rollback for explicitly structured nested transactions has been incorporated in the recovery algorithms by Moss (1987), Härder and Rothermel (1987), Rothermel and Mohan (1989), and Lomet (1992). Full-fledged implementations of nested transactions have been described by Eppinger et al. (1991) and Liskov et al. (1987).

The section on exploiting parallelism during restart and allowing new transactions before the restart is complete is based on Mohan, Haderle, et al. (1992) and Mohan (1993b). Early work on parallelizing logging and recovery can be traced back to R. Agrawal (1985) as well as R. Agrawal and DeWitt (1985b). DeWitt and Gray (1992) give an introduction to parallel database technology in general. Early work about recovery for main-memory databases goes back to DeWitt et al. (1984), Hagman (1986), and Lehmann and Carey (1987), and overviews about the subject have been given by Salem and Garcia-Molina (1990), Garcia-Molina and Salem (1992), and Dunham et al. (1998). State-of-the-art object model techniques for fast, incremental restart have been described in detail by Levy and Silberschatz (1992), Jagadish et al. (1993), and Rastogi et al. (1998). A specialized approach to main-memory data servers with sequential execution of (short) transactions has been described by Whitney et al. (1997).

Our presentation of recovery for data-sharing clusters has mostly followed Mohan and Narang (1991, 1992a, b). Other methods along these lines have been developed by Rahm (1991) and Lomet (1990). Molesky and Ramamritham (1995) have discussed extensions to and optimizations for cache-coherent shared memory multiprocessors. The scheme for coordinating sequence numbers across different servers is essentially a Lamport clock, named after Leslie Lamport (1978). A mathematical analysis of the expected restart time in a cluster has been carried out by Dan et al. (1997). A more general account of the benefits and problems of cluster architectures has been given by Vogels et al. (1998). Recovery issues for the highly related client caching architecture have been discussed by Franklin et al. (1992), Mohan and Narang (1994), as well as Panagos and Biliris (1997).

CHAPTER SIXTEEN

Media Recovery

More than any time in history mankind faces a crossroads. One path leads to despair and utter hopelessness, the other to total extinction. Let us pray that we have the wisdom to choose correctly.

—Woody Allen

Don't worry, be happy.

—Bobby McFerrin

16.1 Goal and Overview

The failure category of server crashes that we have considered in the previous chapters assumes that disk-resident data always survives failures without becoming corrupted. Now we extend our failure model to consider damage to disk-resident data. So that it also includes other storage technologies such as tapes or optical disks, this failure category is referred to as *media failures*, and the corresponding measures to recover data from such failures are summarized under the notion of *media recovery*. Our goal is to ensure that no data is ever lost in the presence of single media failures, that is, when a single disk or other storage unit becomes damaged. Multiple failures of this type within a short window of vulnerability may lead to data losses, however. The techniques that we are going to present in this chapter can be easily generalized to protect the data against simultaneous failures of two or more disks, but this comes at an additional cost that is not always warranted. Disk storage technology is highly reliable, so multiple failures have very low probability. Therefore, we will mostly focus on recovery from a single disk failure, and merely point out occasionally how to cope with multiple failures.

Media failures

Modern disks and their controllers are smart enough to detect failures themselves by means of appropriate error-detecting codes. Typically, this means that a particular set of disk blocks, such as a specific track, are no longer readable. To some extent, disk controllers provide recovery by automatically remapping such blocks to other areas on the disk platters. However, when the block contents is not available elsewhere and can no longer be read from the original disk address, the block is declared as corrupted. Of course, it is also possible, albeit unlikely, that an entire disk becomes damaged at once, for example, because of mechanical problems with the disk-arm assembly. In either case, media recovery needs to be initiated by the data server, to recover either a smaller set of affected blocks or all blocks of a disk.

In addition to the hardware failures discussed so far, a server's data blocks can also become corrupted because of software bugs, for example, in the code of the database system's index manager. In theory, this should never happen, but we all know that modern software is so complex that such bugs cannot be ruled out completely. For this reason, the software may itself maintain additional redundant information in page headers or storage-level metadata so that it can at least detect corrupted pages as soon as possible. Then, the server software would initiate media recovery, and we will show that the same kind of recovery steps also apply to this case.

Environmental failures
We can further broaden the class of failures that we aim to consider with respect to media recovery measures to what is best characterized as *environmental failures*. This would include cases such as finding out, in retrospect, that the server has been operating with a software release that contained serious bugs over some time period (e.g., one week), having run certain transactions with erroneous user input that was not captured by any consistency checks, and so on. Also and most importantly, damage by fire, broken water pipes, and so on, falls into the class of environmental failures. For the latter cases, media recovery can be generalized into what is known as *disaster recovery*, leveraging the techniques for dealing with simple disk failures. For the more bizarre problems, such as having used incorrect server software for a while, recovery can be provided only to a very limited extent and in a highly heuristic manner. In this chapter we will only point out how the techniques for conventional media recovery can also be helpful with regard to these more exotic, yet not unrealistic cases.

Taxonomy: log-based method vs. redundant storage
All approaches to media recovery must necessarily be based on some form of data redundancy. The traditional approach is to periodically create a backup of the data on tapes or additional disks, say, once a week. Upon a media failure, we can then restore the damaged data by replacing the failed disk with a new one (or simply remapping unreadable disk blocks) and copying the backup data. However, this would result in a possibly week-old database, and we would lose committed transactions. To preserve the transactional ACID contract, especially the durability guarantee, the notion of logging needs to be extended: the server keeps an extended log, the *archive log*, which can be applied to the backup data to redo lost effects of committed transactions and restore the data up to the point of the media failure. A salient property of this log-based method is that it can also be easily enhanced to provide some meaningful recovery steps with regard to environmental failures.

The other category of recovery methods is based on building redundancy into the storage system, without any knowledge about transactions. Often, appropriate measures are provided directly by the storage hardware, for example, in the controller of a *disk array* (but, strictly speaking, much of the controller intelligence is implemented in embedded software). Very popular storage architectures along these lines are *RAID systems* (with RAID standing for "redundant array of independent disks") or *mirrored disks*. The common feature among these architectures is that they provide very effective protection against media failures in the narrow sense, but are unsuitable for addressing server software bugs that lead to corrupted pages or other forms of environmental failures. Therefore, mission-critical servers frequently combine both kinds of redundancy—backups with archive logging as well as RAID storage technology.

The criteria for assessing the effectiveness of a media recovery method are threefold:

Assessment criteria: availability, survivability, mean time to data loss (MTTDL)

- The *availability* of the data is the probability that a client request issued at a random point in time can actually obtain the desired data (see also Chapter 12). Availability is dependent on the length of the outage after a media failure, the mean time to repair (MTTR), and the mean time to disk failure (MTTF). Some approaches even allow new transactions to be processed while the repair is being performed; then the availability would not be compromised at all. But these methods only cope with disk failures in the narrow sense.

- The *survivability level* of the data is the number of simultaneous media failures that can be sustained without permanently losing any data. Here, "simultaneous" actually refers to a certain time window of vulnerability, depending on the details of the recovery; typically, the duration of this window is on the order of the mean time to repair for a single media failure. The minimum and also typical survivability level that we consider in this chapter is one; that is, we should be able to survive a single failure without permanent data loss.

- The *mean time to data loss* (MTTDL) is the expected time until some data becomes permanently lost (i.e., cannot be recovered by the media recovery procedures that are in effect). This metric refines the survivability level along the time dimension. The MTTDL depends on the degree of redundancy, and the MTTR for a single failure is a second, very critical factor that influences the MTTDL. If we can repair a single failure fast enough before another failure occurs (or a third one, etc.), then chances are higher that we can operate the server for a very long time before we will eventually encounter the worst possible failure-cascade scenario that leads to data loss. Note that the MTTDL is always finite (i.e., eventual data losses are inevitable), but media recovery can provide the means for an extremely high MTTDL, on the order of geological time frames, so that by all practical standards, we can achieve the best possible protection against data losses.

The chapter is organized as follows. Section 16.2 discusses the most versatile recovery approach based on an archive log and periodic backups. Section 16.3 then presents the techniques for media recovery in the narrow sense, based on redundancy built into the storage system. Finally, Section 16.4 sketches how the various techniques can also be employed to provide some protection against disasters such as fire.

16.2 **Log-Based Method**

The log-based media recovery method relies on periodic backups of the data and an archive log in order to restore damaged data after a failure. The unit of backup and restore is typically a tablespace or some other storage-oriented unit that may comprise a number of semantically related tables or collections (e.g., mail folders in a mail server) and their indexes. In addition, however, it is possible to restore only a single page or small number of corrupted pages (e.g., all pages of the same disk track) by the same method.

In either case, the recovery is generally structured into two phases: in the first phase, after replacing the failed disk or remapping the damaged disk blocks, the relevant pages from the backup are copied to the stable database (i.e., onto the corresponding blocks of the new disk); in the second phase, the archive log is used to redo the updates since the backup was taken. This redo phase itself is essentially identical to the method for crash recovery; in particular, it is also based on the redo-history paradigm, observes compensation log entries (CLEs) for aborted or undone transactions, and so on. Also, it is usually preceded by an analysis phase for determining loser transactions that were active at the time of the disk failure, and it is followed by an undo phase for these losers.

Note that, as with crash recovery, the redo-history paradigm greatly simplifies the recovery procedure. With a redo-winners approach, the proper handling of transactions that were rolled back during normal operation or undone during the restart after a soft crash would be very complicated (see Chapter 13). Particularly note that it is not that unlikely to have server crashes and restarts between the time the backup was taken and the media recovery is initiated; so dealing with undone transactions is a common case in media recovery. Finally, note that the archive log is typically at least an order of magnitude longer than the stable log that is used for crash recovery redo. So, the simplicity and speed of the redo pass is practically the only thing that counts for media recovery.

Limited, pragmatic forms of environmental recovery

The log-based redo also opens up opportunities for coping with limited forms of environmental failures. For example, the media recovery may skip certain time periods or transactions that are known to be "polluted" by having used software versions with severe bugs, or may skip the redoing of individual transactions that were later found to be based on erroneous user input. This skipping of log entries is, however, feasible only if the subsequent log entries are self-contained, in that they do not depend on the ones that were skipped. Purely physiological log entries that describe mini-reorganizations within a page as an operation can be troublesome in this regard. Also, redo log entries for index operations may depend on earlier actions like page splits; so these page splits cannot simply be skipped. With log entries that are closer to physical log entries—to page after images in the extreme case—it is, however, often possible to employ such corrective measures for specific kinds of environmental failures. It should be stressed that such techniques are highly heuristic and can at best be seen as pragmatic efforts. So, when commercial database systems provide tools along these lines, administrators have to be extremely careful in using them.

In the following two subsections, we will first describe the procedures for taking data backups and maintaining an archive log during normal operation, and will then discuss details of the actual media recovery upon a failure.

16.2.1 Database Backup and Archive Logging during Normal Operation

A backup of a tablespace or a similar unit can be *complete* in that it copies all data pages of that unit, or *incremental* in that it copies only pages that have been modified since the previous backup. It is up to the server administrator staff to choose among these options and generally define the backup policies for the various tablespaces. Database systems typically provide flexible options along these lines (but only little support for optimized or even meaningful settings). For example, the administrator may specify a daily complete backup for certain critical tablespaces, and a complete backup for the other tablespaces only once a week with daily incremental backups. Furthermore, to spread the overhead of taking backups over the low-load periods of all weekdays, she may specify that certain tablespaces are backed up every Monday, another set of tablespaces every Tuesday, and so on.

Complete or incremental backup

A *naive backup method* would deactivate the server so that no transaction is active, and then start copying the tablespace(s) to be backed up onto separate disk(s) or tape(s). The advantage would be that the backup reflects only updates of committed transactions, and it reflects exactly those transactions that terminated before the backup. However, such an approach would effectively take the server offline for an extended period, and this is unacceptable from an availability viewpoint for many applications. So this method is usable only in limited settings that can tolerate long, preplanned outages.

Naive backup method

A much better and generally applicable method is to take backups during online operation as a background process without any noticeable interruption of the ongoing, regular transactions. This online backup method creates a "fuzzy" copy of the data that contains partial effects of in-flight transactions and possibly also effects of transactions that become aborted or undone later.

Online backup method

So the backup alone is an inconsistent image of the database, but this can and will be rectified during media recovery by the redo pass. All we need is for the redo pass to employ the usual LSN-based state testing and also to redo inverse operations documented by compensation log entries (CLEs) of aborted or undone transactions to arrive at an image that reflects the state as of the failure. Analogously to crash recovery, a subsequent undo pass is then needed to undo the effects of transactions that were active at the time of the failure. In principle, this undo pass can be based on the stable log that the system keeps for crash recovery anyway. It is essentially the redo pass that requires an additional archive log over an extended time frame, as discussed below.

A backup is taken by scanning the free space management tables (or some form of page-mapping table) of the affected tablespaces and then copying physically contiguous pages in larger groups (e.g., one or more adjacent tracks). This way, backup mostly performs large sequential I/Os, and we can also avoid copying empty (i.e., unallocated) pages. For incremental backup, flags in the free space management tables indicate whether a page has been modified since the last backup; these flags need to be set by regular transactions and are reset by the backup process. Note that pages that constitute the free space management tables are themselves subject to crash recovery if the server should fail when the update flags have been manipulated by incomplete transactions or the backup process. The copy procedure of the backup may bypass the server's page cache for code efficiency and to avoid "polluting" the page cache; so it may copy a stale version of a page, and this needs to be taken into account during recovery, as discussed below.

When the backup process itself becomes interrupted by a soft crash, it should ideally be able to resume the backup at its current scan position after the server has been restarted. Starting the backup all over again should be avoided. Note that backups take a long time; so server crashes while a backup is in progress are not that unlikely. One way of preserving the prior work of the backup process is by recording the current scan position of an ongoing backup in the checkpoint log entries of the stable log. After restart, the backup will then start its scan and copying procedure from this position, and will thus repeat only a very small portion of work in the worst case.

Archive logging   The archive log simply collects all regular log entries of the stable log (maintained for crash recovery) since the last backup. This includes page-level redo/undo log entries as well as high-level undo log entries for object model transactions, and also CLEs for aborted and undone transactions. The implementation could simply replicate the stable log on independent disk(s) or tape(s), or it could periodically copy the stable log into the separate archive log. For the latter approach it is convenient to organize the stable log into a set of files that are used in a round-robin fashion so that currently passive files can be copied without interfering with the I/Os on the stable log. The begin and end of when a backup is taken is recorded in the log by creating special "begin-backup" and "end-backup" log entries.

All this assumes that the system needs to recover only from a single disk failure, so that either the stable database or the stable log may be lost but not both at the same time; more far-reaching protection against double or triple disk failures can be achieved by replicating the stable log.

We noted above that the archive log comprises all log entries since the last complete backup. As the backup itself is a fuzzy one, we need to refine this rule to ensure the correctness of log truncation. Garbage collection for the archive log (or, equivalently, the portion of the stable log that has not yet been copied to the archive log) requires additional restrictions to avoid discarding log entries too early. We need to observe the following rules:

Archive log truncation, MediaRecovery-LSN

- All log entries that follow the begin-backup log entry must be kept until the *next* complete backup is completely taken. This is necessary because the pages that are scanned last may not be copied before the end of the backup.

- When the backup bypasses the database cache and may thus copy stale versions of pages (which have more recent versions in the cache), all log entries that follow the SystemRedoLSN for the crash recovery as of the time of the begin-backup point must be kept (including that log entry itself). This marker remains relevant even if the SystemRedoLSN is advanced later.

- As the backup may include updates of transactions that turn out to be losers soon afterward, all log entries that follow the OldestUndoLSN for the crash recovery must be kept (including that log entry itself). However, this only holds until the OldestUndoLSN is advanced. So, with extremely high probability, this rule is insignificant for the truncation of the archive log, but in principle, there could be very long transactions that live throughout the period between the begin and the end of a backup.

Putting the three rules together means that only log entries that precede the minimum of these positions can be garbage-collected. This minimum position is known as the *MediaRecoveryLSN*. It can actually be kept for each tablespace separately, and the administrator has to make sure that all tablespaces are backed up completely at a sufficient rate to avoid problems with truncating the archive log. Alternatively, the archive log could be partitioned by tablespaces, effectively maintaining it on a per-tablespace basis.

16.2.2 **Database Restore Algorithms**

The algorithm for restoring a lost tablespace or a set of corrupted pages is straightforward and given by the following pseudocode. Note that the analysis pass and the undo pass can be performed on either the archive log or the stable log; if the analysis is carried out on the archive log, it is only the relatively tiny portion between the most recent checkpoint and the end of the log that needs to be scanned for this purpose. Further note that it does not matter if this analysis precedes the redo-history pass or is performed subsequently. This is in contrast to the crash recovery algorithms, where the analysis pass also serves to determine the DirtyPages information to optimize the redo pass. In media recovery, such optimizations are not feasible.

```
restore (pageset):
 for each page in pageset do
  identify the most recent (incremental or complete) backup
   that contains a copy of the page;
  copy the page onto the replaced disk;
 end /*for*/;
 perform redo pass on the archive log using the redo-history algorithm,
  starting from MediaRecoveryLSN and
  ignoring all log entries that do not refer to pages in pageset;
 perform analysis pass on the log, starting from most recent checkpoint,
  to identify loser transactions;
 perform undo pass on the log for loser transactions;
```

The fact that media recovery simply performs a redo-history pass, which starts from the available backup and uses LSN-based page-state testing to avoid redoing writes that are already present in the backup itself, and subsequently initiates a crash recovery undo pass, immediately gives us the following correctness result, without any need for a detailed proof:

THEOREM 16.1

The backup/log-based media recovery algorithm provides correct recovery after media failures, i.e., the data is reconstructed such that it captures exactly all winner transactions in the original serialization order.

Advancing the backup (shadow database)

To speed up the redo pass, parallelism may be exploited along the lines of the log partitioning techniques introduced in Chapter 15. The redo pass can also be shortened by merging multiple incremental backups into a complete backup, so that very old portions of the archive log become obsolete. In a similar vein, portions of the archive log may be merged into a complete backup on a separate computer. Effectively, this redoes some of the history on the backup to produce a more recent backup. Such methods are sometimes referred to as maintaining a *shadow database* (or *backup database*, as opposed to a merely passive backup) on a separate, possibly dedicated computer. Because of the additional resources needed for this purpose, it may be worthwhile to maintain a shadow database only for very critical tablespaces. Upon a media failure of the actual data server, the shadow database is viewed as the most recent backup, and the media recovery can start by copying data from the shadow database. The archive log can be truncated accordingly, so that the redo pass is drastically shorter.

The same recovery methods are applicable to restore individual, corrupted pages (as opposed to restoring entire tablespaces). To this end, it is advisable to partition the archive log by page numbers (e.g., hashing log entries onto a moderate number of logs, using the log entries' page numbers as the arguments of the hash function), even if the incentive is not parallelism. This way, the amount of log data that simply needs to be scanned during the redo pass for a small number of corrupted pages can be substantially reduced. In contrast to crash recovery, where the random database I/Os for redoing updates on dirty pages are the main performance issue, the mere scanning of the archive log is a major factor for the duration of the media recovery.

As mentioned earlier, the availability of the data is determined by the MTTR. For the log-based method, this is the time to copy data from the backup and redo the relevant updates from the archive log. For large databases, the recovery time after a disk failure would be on the order of 10 minutes to an hour, assuming that the server has spare disks attached that are ready to use immediately. This is already a severe impact on the availability, and motivates additional measures at the level of the disk storage components, which we will discuss in the next section. Note, however, that the log-based method is much more versatile than the redundant storage methods in that it can also cope with software-induced page corruptions, and so on. For this reason, backups and archive logs are maintained even if the disk storage system provides protection against disk failures.

The survivability level of the log-based method depends on the degree of redundancy that is chosen for the backups and especially the archive log. With no replication of these components, the method can sustain only a single media failure at a time. If, on the other hand, you are willing to pay the price for replicating both backups and archive logs m times, then the approach can tolerate m simultaneous media failures.

The mean time to data loss for the backup/log-based media recovery, denoted $MTTDL_{backup/log\text{-}based\ recovery}$ below, can be analyzed using Markov chain or other stochastic state-transition models. For the baseline case of nonreplicated backups, and nonreplicated archive logs, the following can be derived (under certain simplifying assumptions):

$$MTTDL_{backup/log\text{-}based\ recovery} = \frac{MTTF}{3} * \frac{MTTF}{2\,(MTTR_{rec} + MTTR_{back})}$$

A simplified explanation of the formula considers the reciprocals of the two factors. First the server is in high danger of losing data if one of the three involved disks (or storage devices in general) becomes corrupted: the database disk, the backup disk, or the disk on which the archive log is kept. The probability of one of these three components failing is proportional to $\frac{1}{\text{MTTF}}$ times 3. Once we have lost one disk, the server enters a critical window of vulnerability. Here we need to distinguish two cases. First, if it is the database disk that was lost, then we cannot afford losing either the backup disk or the log disk during the MTTR_{rec} of the media recovery for the database disk. The probability of this type of second failure is proportional to $\frac{\text{MTTR}_{\text{rec}}}{\text{MTTF}}$ times 2, where the factor 2 accounts for the fact that a failure of either the backup disk or the log disk results in data loss. The second case of entering the window of vulnerability is when either the backup or the log disk fails, but the database disk is still in good shape. In this situation the server has to take a new backup, but if a second disk failure occurs before the backup is completed, which takes $\text{MTTR}_{\text{back}}$ time units on average, we end up losing data. The probability of this second failure thus is proportional to $\frac{\text{MTTR}_{\text{back}}}{\text{MTTF}}$ times 2, where again the factor 2 accounts for the fact that a failure of either of the two surviving disks (the database disk from which the backup is taken or the disk on which the archive log resides) means data loss. The above two cases refer to disjoint events; so the probabilities are additive, and this is why their reciprocal leads to the factor $\frac{\text{MTTF}}{2\,(\text{MTTR}_{\text{rec}} + \text{MTTR}_{\text{back}})}$ in the formula for the MTTDL. A more elaborate derivation of the above formula will be given shortly in Section 16.2.3.

Note that the mean time to repair is the most critical factor; so it is crucial also from the viewpoint of minimizing data losses (i.e., not just from the availability perspective) to perform the media recovery as fast as possible. Since typical disks have an MTTF of at least 500,000 hours (50 years), a short MTTR of at most 1 hour pays off in an MTTDL of approximately 12.5 million years. Of course, this astronomically large figure is hard to interpret; after all, it is merely an expected value derived from a probabilistic model—we could still have the bad luck of losing data after a week of operation, but only with very low probability. In practice, such figures are used to compare the quality of different options relative to each other and relative to empirical behavior. Under this perspective, an MTTDL of several million years is typically good enough for almost all data servers, except perhaps some extremely mission-critical applications such as online trading at stock exchanges or aircraft traffic control.

Figure 16.1 summarizes the overall architecture of backups, (replicated) logs, and the relevant markers in the archive log, in an illustrative manner.

16.2.3 Analysis of the Mean Time to Data Loss

Stochastic state-transition model for MTTDL

A full-fledged derivation of the MTTDL formula given above models the system as a stochastic state-transition model where a finite number of states reflects the possible combinations of the database, the backup, and the log disk (or more generally, device) being damaged or still available. Transitions between

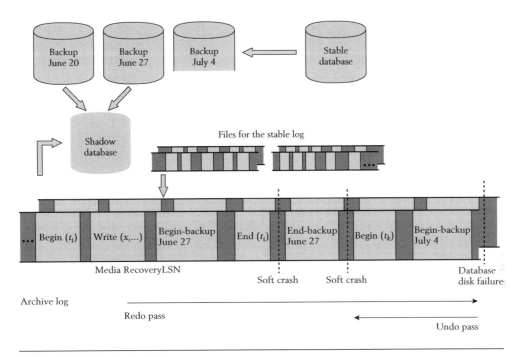

Figure 16.1 Components of log-based media recovery.

states reflect failures of disks or the successful repair of a failed component. For example, the database disk's state changes from "failed" to "ok" when the media recovery completes. Such a state-transition model for the backup/log-based method is given in Figure 16.2. In this model, the state with number 4, denoted "db failed; backup or log failed," is a so-called absorbing state from which we can no longer repair the data. So such absorbing states are exactly the ones that capture data loss. Note that our state space does not distinguish the two cases where either the backup or the log disk has failed. These two cases are equivalent in that they render the server susceptible to exactly the same data loss event, namely, when the database disk fails while either the backup or the log is still not completely repaired. Also, both cases require the same repair measures, namely, taking a new backup. Note that even if it is the archive log that has failed, the backup alone is insufficient to restore the database if the database disk should fail. Since we cannot repair the archive log but can only continue to collect new log entries in the archive log, the server must take a new backup in this situation. Recall that simply copying the backup to the database produces a stale image of the data, losing the effects of possibly many winner transactions; even worse, since the backup is itself merely a fuzzy image taken over an extended period during which many transactions arrive and complete, we would not be able to reconstruct a consistent database even if out-of-date data were acceptable.

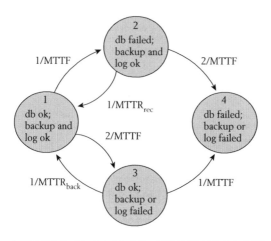

Figure 16.2 Stochastic state-transition model for deriving the MTTDL of the backup/log-based media recovery technique.

We associate with each transition between two states a *transition rate*, which can be interpreted as the mean number of occurrences per time unit that the system moves between the two states connected by the transition. (More precisely, a rate is the limit of the probability that a given state is left within time Δt divided by Δt for Δt approaching zero.) In our model, the rates are assumed to be constant and, especially, independent of the state-transition path on which the state has been reached. Such models are known as *Markov chains* and enjoy particularly nice mathematical properties. When a component fails, the transition into the resulting state has the failure rate of that component as its transition rate. Likewise, when a repair is completed and the system moves back into a better state, the corresponding transition rate is the repair rate of the affected component. These failure and repair rates are exactly the reciprocals of the component-specific MTTF and MTTR values. For simplicity we assume that all three components (i.e., the database, the backup, and the log disk) have the same MTTF values, although in practice the backup and the log may have a higher MTTF than the database, as they are less susceptible to software errors. As for the MTTR values, we distinguish the database and the backup disks, for repairing the latter requires taking a new backup. In the model of Figure 16.2 the rate from the initial state with all disks in good shape into state 3, denoted "db ok; backup or log failed," is $\frac{2}{\text{MTTF}}$ rather than $\frac{1}{\text{MTTF}}$ because this transition takes place when either the backup or the log disk fails. Analogously, the transition rate from state 2 into state 4 is also $\frac{2}{\text{MTTF}}$.

Generally, the reciprocal of the sum of the rates of a state's outgoing transitions can be shown to be the mean time that the system stays within a state between entering the state and leaving it. (More specifically, this mean state-residence time can be shown to be an exponentially distributed random variable for each state, with state-specific mean value.) From this information we can now infer the mean time that it takes the system to reach one of the absorbing states after having been started in the initial state where all components are "ok." To this end we define the following probabilistic measures for states i, j, k, where from now on we use state numbers rather than the mnemonic labels for convenient notation; "$P[\ldots]$" and "$E[\ldots]$" denote probabilities and expectation values, respectively, and r_{ij} is the transition rate from state i to state j:

$$E_{ij} = E \text{ [time from entering state } i \text{ until entering state } j]$$
$$H_i = E \text{ [time between entering and leaving state } i]$$
$$= 1/\sum_{j \neq i} r_{ij}$$
$$p_{ik} = P \text{ [transition from } i \text{ to } k \mid \text{state } i \text{ is left]}$$
$$= r_{ik}/\sum_{j \neq i} r_{ij}$$

Now we can construct a linear equation system that correlates the E_{ij} values with the expected state-residence times H_i and the state-transition probabilities p_{ik}. The following equation must hold for all states i, j:

$$E_{ij} = H_i + \sum_{k \neq i} p_{ik} E_{kj}$$

These equations should be read as follows: the mean time from entering state i until entering state j is the mean time spent in i plus the time from entering some other state k until entering j, where we consider all possibilities for the choice of k and "condition" the E_{kj} values by the probabilities that k is entered upon leaving i. Naturally, the values of E_{ij} for $i = j$ are zero, and the values of E_{ij} for state pairs such that j is not reachable at all from state i are set to zero, too. E_{ij} is also known as the "first passage time" of state j, provided the system starts in state i. For our model of Figure 16.2, we obtain the linear equation system, where the H_i and p_{ik} values are given (i.e., easily derived from the transition rates according to their definitions), and the E_{ij} values are the unknowns to be solved for

$$E_{12} = H_1 + p_{13} E_{32}$$
$$E_{13} = H_1 + p_{12} E_{23}$$

$$E_{14} = H_1 + p_{12}E_{24} + p_{13}E_{34}$$
$$E_{21} = H_2$$
$$E_{23} = H_2 + p_{21}E_{13}$$
$$E_{24} = H_2 + p_{21}E_{14}$$
$$E_{31} = H_3$$
$$E_{32} = H_3 + p_{31}E_{12}$$
$$E_{34} = H_3 + p_{31}E_{14}$$

Such a system of linear equations can be easily solved using standard mathematical methods. Then, with initial state 1 and absorbing state 4, the value of E_{14} yields the MTTDL for the backup/log-based recovery. Substituting all the H_i and r_{ij} values with the concrete values according to Figure 16.2, we arrive at

$$
\begin{aligned}
E_{14} &= \frac{H_1 + p_{12}H_2 + p_{13}H_3}{1 - p_{12}p_{21} - p_{13}p_{31}} \\
&= \frac{\frac{\text{MTTF}}{3} + \frac{1}{3}\left(1/\left(\frac{2}{\text{MTTF}} + \frac{1}{\text{MTTR}_{\text{rec}}}\right)\right) + \frac{2}{3}\left(1/\left(\frac{1}{\text{MTTF}} + \frac{1}{\text{MTTR}_{\text{back}}}\right)\right)}{1 - \frac{1}{3}\left(\frac{2}{\text{MTTR}_{\text{rec}}}/\left(\frac{2}{\text{MTTF}} + \frac{1}{\text{MTTR}_{\text{rec}}}\right)\right) - \frac{2}{3}\left(\frac{1}{\text{MTTR}_{\text{back}}}/\left(\frac{1}{\text{MTTF}} + \frac{1}{\text{MTTR}_{\text{back}}}\right)\right)} \\
&\approx \frac{\text{MTTF}^2}{6\,(\text{MTTR}_{\text{rec}} + \text{MTTR}_{\text{back}})}
\end{aligned}
$$

The final approximation, after some lengthy term manipulations, is by neglecting all terms other than those that are quadratic in MTTF. This way we arrive at the formula that we gave in the previous subsection. While the result is not surprising and the derivation may not be that exciting for mathematically uninitiated readers, we want to point out that the presented kind of stochastic model and the methodology can be used to analyze much more sophisticated reliability techniques. We will present results from such analyses in the following section, but will no longer delve into the actual derivations.

16.3 Storage Redundancy

The techniques that exploit storage redundancy for media recovery can be categorized into two classes: the first one mirrors (replicates) data on two or more disks, and the second one maintains error-correcting codes (ECCs) in addition to the otherwise nonreplicated data. Both can sustain a single disk failure in their baseline variants; and both can be enhanced to cope with multiple simultaneous disk failures, but this is rarely needed in practice. Another commonality is that these methods are typically implemented within storage system controllers, for example, in a disk array controller. However, host-based implementations in the server itself are feasible as well, for example, as part of the server's operating system or the storage layer of a database system.

A salient feature of the storage redundancy approaches is that they do not lead to any outages upon a media failure. So all data remains 100% available, although the performance of data accesses will typically be degraded after a failure until the repair completes. The general procedure for the recovery is to replace a failed disk with a *hot-standby* spare disk that is already attached to the storage controller and ready for use; then the recovery restores the data blocks of the failed disk on the spare, with details depending on the actual form of redundancy.

Continuous availability

In the next two sections we will discuss these details of the mirroring and the ECC-based techniques, respectively. Note once again that these techniques only address media failures in the more limited sense of disk failures or unreadable disk blocks, and are not amenable to software-induced page corruptions or even more extended forms of environmental failures. Therefore, database systems typically still employ backup and archive logging policies, in addition to using storage redundancy, and sometimes only the backup/log-based method is used alone (i.e., without any disk-level storage redundancy).

In the following, what we will consider as read and write requests for disk-resident data are actually fetch and flush actions on pages as far as the data server is concerned; so reads and writes that merely affect cached pages are not considered. To follow the standard storage system terminology but to avoid confusion with our earlier notion of reads and writes, we will call these disk operations *disk-reads* and *disk-writes*.

16.3.1 Techniques Based on Mirroring

Simple mirroring replicates all data blocks on a pair of disks (or conceivably a triplet of disks if this were required), with all disk-writes going to both disks simultaneously. Disk-read requests, on the other hand, are directed to one of the two disks only. A common option is to use the disk whose disk arm is closer to the track where the requested block(s) resides. Alternatively or in combination with this seek-time optimization, the disk scheduling can aim to balance the load across both disks and minimize queueing delays by giving each disk approximately the same number of disk-read requests.

Simple mirroring

The two disks that form the mirrored pair should have independent failure modes: they should be addressable through different, multiported disk controllers, they should have independent power supply, and so on. For these reasons, mirrored disks are provided by storage system vendors as complete, ready-to-use solutions, along with spare disks, online pluggability of disks to be replaced, and other robustness features along these lines. The server software

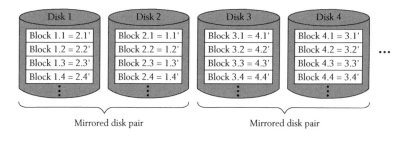

Figure 16.3 Mirrored disk pairs.

typically addresses a pair of mirrored disks as if it were a single device. The architecture of mirrored disks is illustrated in Figure 16.3.

Upon a disk failure, all subsequent disk-read and disk-write requests are directed only to the surviving disk of the affected mirror pair. So the failure can be completely masked to the server software, and all data remains continuously available as long as there is only a single failure. After replacing the failed disk with a spare disk, the data is reconstructed by copying the blocks from the surviving disk. This can be and is typically done in parallel to the regular work-load, without any offline time. The copying from the surviving disk onto the activated spare disk proceeds in large batches, on one or more contiguous tracks.

Regular disk-write requests that arrive during this repair period must therefore be sent to both disks. For regular disk-read requests that refer to blocks that have already been copied to the activated spare disk, the disk scheduling can choose among the two disks, but the optimization is now complicated by the fact that both disks need to sustain the reconstruction load, too. At the beginning of the reconstruction, the disk-read load of the surviving disk is doubled, whereas more and more disk-reads are eligible for being directed to the spare disk as the reconstruction makes progress. Now the optimization problem to be solved is what fraction of disk-reads should be sent to which disk at which point during the repair (i.e., for a given fraction of data already copied to the spare disk). References to solving this problem are given in the Bibliographic Notes at the end of this chapter.

The MTTDL of the simple mirroring technique can be derived as follows:

$$MTTDL_{simple\ mirroring} = \frac{MTTF}{2} * \frac{MTTF}{MTTR_{simple\ mirroring}}$$

An intuitive, albeit simplified, explanation would be similar to the one already given for the MTTDL of the backup/log-based recovery. The factor 2 accounts for the fact that we lose data upon another failure (within the critical time period of length MTTR) of one out of two disks. So this formula holds for a single pair of mirrored disks. With *N* such mirrored pairs—that is, a total of 2*N* disks—the overall, systemwide MTTDL would be only one *N*-th of the above value.

A major problem with simple mirroring is the drastic performance penalty *Declustered* in the "degraded mode" when the surviving disk essentially needs to take over *mirroring* the failed disk's load and also has to sustain the reconstruction load during the repair. So with most regular disk requests being reads, the load of the surviving disk is more than doubled temporarily. This in turn may create queueing delays that adversely affect the regular requests' response time and also make the MTTR longer. A possible remedy that has led to the enhanced concept of *declustered mirroring* is to spread the replicas of a disk's blocks across multiple disks in a disk group, rather than mirroring them one-to-one all on the same disk of a pair. For a group of size G disks, the replicas of the blocks of disk j $(1 \leq j \leq G)$ are simply placed round-robin style on disks $j + 1, \ldots, G, 1, \ldots, j - 1, \ldots$. So the replica of the block numbered k of disk j, denoted $j.k$, resides on disk $(j + 1 + (k \bmod (G - 1))) \bmod G + 1$ (with the numbering of both disks and blocks starting at 1). This placement of block replicas is illustrated in Figure 16.4 for $G = 4$. The picture assumes that each disk has two separate areas, each physically contiguous, for storing its "primary" blocks and the replicas of other disks. The local addresses of replicated blocks can then be computed easily; with more flexible layouts on each disk, the blocks' local addresses could be determined by appropriate mapping tables.

Upon the failure of one of the G disks of a declustered mirroring group, the disk-reads for blocks of the failed disk are evenly distributed across the $G - 1$ surviving disks. So the load of each disk is increased by one $(G - 1)$th of a single disk's load in the worst case. On top of this, each surviving disk is involved in the reconstruction of the failed disk's data on the activated spare disk, but again this extra load is spread evenly across all $G - 1$ survivor disks.

So the key advantage of declustered mirroring is that it eases the performance degradation after a failure and potentially shortens the MTTR compared to simple mirroring. The drawback is that we now lose data as soon as a second disk within a group of G disks fails, as opposed to a specific second disk with simple mirroring. For this reason, a good choice of G is all but trivial. In

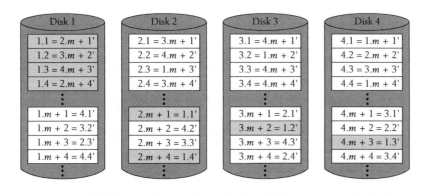

Figure 16.4 Declustered disk mirroring.

practice, a value on the order of 4 to 16 is a good compromise between the per-disk load reduction after a failure and the higher risk of a second failure in the same group. The MTTDL for declustered mirroring with group size G is given by

$$\text{MTTDL}_{\text{declustered mirroring}} = \frac{\text{MTTF}}{G} * \frac{\text{MTTF}}{(G-1) * \text{MTTR}_{\text{declustered mirroring}}}$$

and the MTTDL for an entire storage system with a total of N disks is

$$\frac{\text{MTTDL}_{\text{declustered mirroring}}}{N/G}$$

assuming for simplicity that N is a multiple of G.

16.3.2 Techniques Based on Error-Correcting Codes

A major cost factor in mirrored disk architectures is the duplication of the disk space. By keeping a block of error-correcting code (ECC) information for groups of blocks from different disks, this extra cost can be scaled down at the expense of a certain performance penalty during normal operation and during the reconstruction of a failed disk. The simplest but also practically prevalent case stores the parity of a number of blocks in a separate *parity block* on a separate disk. This approach is widely known as a RAID architecture. More precisely, the idea gives rise to a family of RAID architectures, with different options for the scope and placement of parity blocks. The simple mirroring of the previous section can even be viewed as a special case, known as RAID-1, as the parity block derived from a single block (i.e., a group of size one) is a replica of that block. In the following we will look at various alternatives for placing parity blocks onto disks, and will then discuss the consequences for the reconstruction of failed disks.

Storage Organizations

RAID architectures with parity groups   The simplest variant of a parity-based RAID architecture is the RAID-4 method illustrated in Figure 16.5. We assume $N+1$ disks, N of which hold data blocks and one of which is dedicated to hold parity blocks. The N data blocks that reside at the same block address of the N data disks form a *parity group*. The bitwise parities of the bits of these N blocks are kept in a separate parity block that is stored at the same block address on the parity disk. Sometimes, parity groups are also referred to as *stripes*, but this term primarily refers to the regular partitioning and allocation of application data across the N data disks, which is actually an orthogonal issue not related to media recovery. So instead

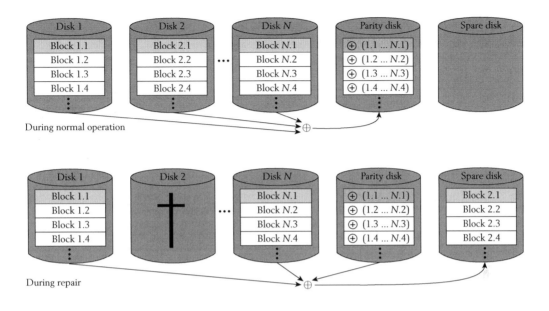

Figure 16.5 A parity-based RAID-4 storage architecture.

of lumping these aspects together, as it is often done in the storage systems community, we will avoid the term stripe.

During normal operation, a disk-write, say, of block k of disk j must be extended to maintain the parity block. One way of doing this is to fetch all blocks of the same parity group from the disks, compute the new parity from the blocks $1.k, \ldots (j-1).k, (j+1).k, \ldots, N.k$ and the new value of the block $j.k$ to be written, and initiate disk-writes for both the affected data block $j.k$ and the corresponding parity block. It is obvious that this method is expensive in terms of the additional I/O cost. A much better way, however, is to compute the new parity block incrementally, and this is feasible because of the fact that the parity can be obtained by a logical XOR (exclusive-or) operation, denoted $\oplus$, on the underlying bits, and by exploiting properties of the $\oplus$ function. Since only one data block of a parity group is modified, the new contents of the parity block can be computed by applying the $\oplus$ function to the old contents of the block to be written, that block's new contents, and the old contents of the parity block:

Parity maintenance: small-write penalty

$$\text{new parity}(1.k, \ldots, N.k) :=$$
$$\text{old parity}(1.k, \ldots, N.k) \oplus \text{old contents}(j.k) \oplus \text{new contents}(j.k)$$

In terms of extra I/O load, this method requires two additional disk-reads, to obtain the old contents of the data block and the parity block, and an additional disk-write for the new parity block. This overhead is known in the literature as the *small-write penalty* of RAID architectures. Since in transaction-oriented servers most data blocks are typically read before written, appropriate caching (e.g., in the disk array controller) can often avoid the additional read for the old contents of the data block, but the maintenance of the parity block is still a significant overhead for disk-writes: two additional disk I/Os versus one with mirroring. The overhead becomes smaller when applications mostly issue disk-writes for all data blocks of a parity group together; hence the name small-write penalty. This can be achieved for some application classes that mostly manage large uninterpreted byte containers such as images, by appropriate layout of the data blocks across disks. For transaction processing and other server applications that deal with fine-grained information (e.g., by making intensive use of indexes), such special write patterns are usually infeasible or unattractive. So within our setting, parity-based RAIDs have a penalty with regard to I/O throughput; so for the same application workload, they would require a larger number of disks to sustain the I/O load (but typically less than twice the number of disks, as most workloads are dominated by disk-reads).

The small-write penalty is especially troublesome in a RAID-4 architecture, as the extra I/O load for the parity blocks refers to a single disk, the parity disk. Once this disk becomes saturated, the overall throughput of the entire disk array cannot be increased further regardless of how many disks might be added. To avoid this kind of bottleneck created by the parity disk, the overall array could be partitioned into groups of G disks, each consisting of $G - 1$ data disks and one parity disk whose parity blocks are computed over the data blocks within the group. However, because small groups introduce larger storage costs as the ratio of parity blocks and data blocks becomes smaller, RAID-4 groups are not the best possible solution. Rather, it is advantageous to spread the parity blocks across all disks of a group and thus avoid the parity disk bottleneck regardless of the group size—a concept known as RAID-5 architecture.

RAID-5 architecture with parity block striping   The RAID-5 architecture, as illustrated in Figure 16.6, spreads all parity blocks in a round-robin manner across all disks of a group. Such regular round-robin placements of disk blocks in a disk array are often referred to as *striped placements* or *striping*; therefore we will use the term *parity block striping* for this simple but effective layout. So, with $N + 1$ disks, the parity block for the N data blocks with number k, which are located on disks $(k - 1) \bmod(N + 1) + 1$ through $(k + N - 2) \bmod(N + 1) + 1$, resides on disk $(k + N - 1) \bmod (N + 1) + 1$ (assuming that disks and block numbers start with one). This way, the I/O load for maintaining the parity information is nicely balanced across all disks.

The MTTDL of a RAID-5 group with $G + 1$ disks can be shown to be

$$\text{MTTDL}_{\text{RAID-5}} = \frac{\text{MTTF}}{G + 1} * \frac{\text{MTTF}}{G * \text{MTTR}_{\text{RAID-5}}}$$

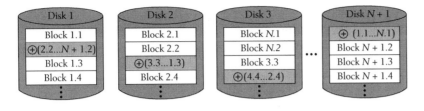

Figure 16.6 RAID-5 storage architecture with parity striping.

With a total number of N disks in the system and assuming that N is a multiple of $G + 1$, the systemwide MTTDL is a factor of $\frac{N}{G+1}$ smaller.

RAID-5 still exhibits the same small-write penalty as RAID-4. However, its less rigid placement is already a step in the right direction. To further alleviate the penalty of small-writes, we should place parity blocks such that they incur as little I/O costs as possible. For example, it would be most convenient if we could write them onto a dynamically chosen track of any disk that does not hold a data block of the affected parity group; then we could select locations in the vicinity of the current arm positions of eligible disks. This way, at least the cost of the parity block disk-writes is minimized. The price for such a flexible allocation of parity blocks, also known as *floating parity*, is that we need to maintain a more elaborated block-mapping table. Since modern disks can easily be equipped with a suitable amount of nonvolatile RAM (using battery backup for the power supply), this approach is indeed cost-beneficial. Yet another approach in a similar vein would be to defer the disk-writes of modified parity blocks, holding them in the nonvolatile RAM for a while and then writing them sequentially in large batches to dedicated log areas onto one of the disks. The log areas would be spread across all disks and should be used so as to balance this extra I/O load. This approach is known as *parity logging* and is probably the best in terms of reducing the small-write penalty.

Reducing the small-write penalty

Floating parity blocks, parity block logging

An improvement of the MTTR—and thus the duration of the time period with degraded performance and, indirectly, the MTTDL—is possible by spreading the reconstruction load for a failed disk across an even larger number of disks so that each individual disk receives a smaller amount of extra work. The key to achieving this goal is to relax the placement invariants for the RAID-5 architecture: we now consider groups of C disks for placing the parity blocks, each of which is still computed over $G + 1 < C$ data blocks, and we allow more flexible placements beyond the simple parity block striping scheme of RAID-5. This approach has been coined *parity block declustering*, but is also known by the name *clustered RAID*, as the group of C disks is referred to as a disk cluster. Note that the condition $G + 1 < C$ is essential; otherwise (i.e., with $G + 1 = C$), we would again arrive at a placement that is equivalent to RAID-5. An example of a declustered parity block placement is given in Figure 16.7, with $G = 3$ and $C = 5$.

Declustered parity blocks

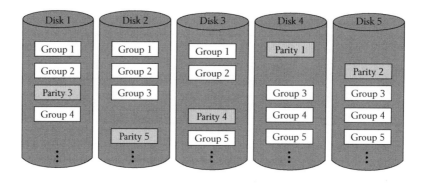

Figure 16.7 Parity block declustering scheme (with C = 5, G = 3).

Declustered parity block schemes should ideally satisfy a number of combinatorial properties. Consider C disks that hold a total of n parity groups each consisting of $G+1$ blocks (G data blocks and a parity block) with $G < C$. The $n^*(G+1)$ blocks should be placed on the C disks so that the following conditions hold:

- For each group, the $G+1$ blocks of the group must reside on different disks (the standard condition of all RAID architectures). Otherwise, we could not recover from a single disk failure.

- Each disk holds n/C parity blocks. So the parity maintenance load during normal operation is distributed evenly across all C disks.

- For the $m = n * (G+1)/C$ different groups that are represented by the blocks of a given disk, the $m * G$ blocks that belong to these groups but reside on other disks are distributed evenly across all other $C-1$ disks. This condition ensures that if the considered disk should fail, the reconstruction work for the disk's m blocks induces the same amount of work on each of the surviving disks.

Placement schemes that satisfy the above properties fall into the family of so-called combinatorial *block designs*. Finding such block designs for given values of G and C is a very difficult problem. Thus, implementations have been developed in an approximative manner, using specific kinds of random permutations and a mapping table for the actual block allocations.

The higher the difference between G and C, the better the load balancing of the reconstruction work after a failure and the lower the extra load on each of the surviving disks. However, a second failure on any of the $C-1$ surviving disks results in a data loss. For this reason, C cannot be chosen arbitrarily high.

The MTTDL of the declustered parity block architecture is

$$\text{MTTDL}_{\text{parity block declustering}} = \frac{\text{MTTF}}{C} * \frac{\text{MTTF}}{(C-1) * \text{MTTR}_{\text{parity block declustering}}}$$

With reasonably chosen values for G and C, this architecture achieves very high MTTDL and, most importantly, a much shorter MTTR than RAID-5 architectures as well as significantly less performance degradation during the repair. In the worst case (i.e., with all requests being disk-reads) RAID-5 would double the load per disk after a disk failure. This is so because a disk-read sent to the failed disk induces a disk-read on each of the surviving disks. In contrast, with declustered parity blocks the increase of the per-disk load in the degraded mode after a failure is only a fraction of $\frac{G}{C-1}$ of a single disk's regular load.

All the various RAID architectures discussed above have a survivability level of one; so they can sustain only a single disk failure, and a second failure before the reconstruction of the failed disk is completed leads to data loss. As this is sufficient for most applications with the very high reliability of modern disks, we do not further elaborate on the more advanced techniques that can be adopted within a RAID to achieve a higher survivability level. The key idea is to substitute the simple parity by advanced ECCs that contain sufficient redundancy to reconstruct the data of two (or even more) simultaneously failed disks. Such approaches have sometimes been referred to as RAID-6 architectures, with different choices used for the ECC (e.g., Reed-Solomon codes). All these approaches do, however, come at the expense of a significant reduction in the disks' sustainable I/O throughput during normal operation and a potentially increased MTTR after failures. *Coping with multiple failures (RAID-6)*

We conclude this subsection by giving pseudocode for all basic operations of a RAID architecture. The pseudocode holds for RAID-5 as well as its enhanced derivatives with parity logging, declustered parity blocks, and so on. For the ease of notation, we assume a basic RAID-5 system with $N + 1$ disks, and without loss of generality we assume that a disk that will be hit by a media failure has the number $N + 1$. Note that the pseudocode for disk-reads during normal operation is trivial and thus omitted. We use the terms `fetch` and `flush` for transferring a block from a single disk into the disk array controller or from the controller back onto disk.

```
disk-write (data block j.k) during normal operation:
  fetch (data block j.k) from disk j,
   unless the block's old contents are still available
   in RAM;
  fetch (parity block of the parity group to which
  j.k belongs);
```
Disk-writes during normal operation

```
compute new parity block :=
 old contents of parity block XOR
 old contents of data block j.k XOR
 new contents of data block j.k;
flush (data block j.k) onto disk j;
flush (new contents of parity block);
```

Disk-reads in degraded mode

```
disk-read (block (N+1).k):
 fetch (block 1.k);...; fetch (block N.k)
  using the algorithm as during normal operation;
 return 1.k XOR 2.k XOR ... XOR N.k
  as the contents of block (N+1).k;
```

Disk-writes in degraded mode

```
disk-write (block (N+1).k):
 fetch (block 1.k);...;fetch (block N.k);
 old contents of block (N+1).k := 1.k XOR
 2.k XOR ... XOR N.k;
 let j.k be the parity block of this parity group;
 flush (block (N+1).k) using the block's new contents;
 compute new parity block j.k :=
  old contents of block j.k XOR
  old contents of block (N+1).k XOR
  new contents of block (N+1).k
 flush (block j.k) using new parity as block contents;
```

Reconstruction of failed disk

```
reconstruct (disk N+1) on spare disk:
 for each block k of the failed disk N+1 do
  disk-write (block (N+1).k)
   using the algorithm for disk-writes in degraded mode;
 end /*for*/;
```

Rebuild Algorithms

The algorithm for rebuilding the failed disk after its replacement with a spare disk has already been given in the previous subsection. As this rebuilding takes place online under potential contention with regular disk requests, it is worthwhile to investigate additional optimizations. The first and most important enhancement is to avoid reading an entire parity group on behalf of a regular disk-read request once the requested block has already been reconstructed on the activated spare disk. Then, we save disk I/O work by *redirecting disk-reads* to the new disk. To be able to do so, we need to track the progress of the rebuilding process, using a simple table. Similarly, disk-writes to an already rebuilt block can be performed by reading and writing merely this block and the corresponding parity block, rather than reading the entire parity group.

A second possible optimization has to do with the scheduling of the disk I/Os for the rebuilding of the failed disk. As the entire rebuilding is a background process anyway, whose priority should be set lower than that of regular requests, it is intriguing to batch the rebuilding I/Os and dispatch them at particularly convenient points. One specific opportunity for rebuilding a block is when we need to serve a regular disk-read request for this block anyway. All we need to do is to keep the reconstructed block in a dedicated area in RAM (typically within the disk array controller), and when we have collected a sufficiently large number of such reconstructed blocks we can write them onto the new disk in a sequential sweep. So, in essence, the *rebuilding work is piggybacked on regular disk-reads*. An especially intriguing point of this approach is that it tends to rebuild frequently accessed blocks first, so that these blocks no longer suffer from the degraded performance of yet-to-be-reconstructed blocks. On the other hand, you have to make sure that all blocks are eventually rebuilt on the spare disk.

Both of these optimizations—redirecting disk-reads as soon as possible and piggybacking disk-reads for the rebuilding process on the regular requests—are included in the following pseudocode.

```
disk-read (block (N+1).k):
 if block (N+1).k has already been rebuilt then
  fetch (block (N+1).k);
 else
  fetch (block 1.k);...; fetch (block N.k)
   using the algorithm as during normal operation;
  contents of block (N+1).k := 1.k XOR
  2.k XOR ... XOR N.k;
  return the contents of block (N+1).k;
  flush (block (N+1).k)
   at the discretion of the disk scheduling for disk N+1;
  mark block (N+1).k as rebuilt;
 end /*if*/;
```
Optimized disk-reads in degraded mode

```
disk-write (block (N+1).k):
 if block (N+1).k has already been rebuilt then
  fetch (block (N+1).k)
   unless the block is still available in RAM;
  fetch (parity block j.k of the parity group to which
   (N+1).k belongs);
 else
  fetch (block 1.k);...; fetch (block N.k);
  old contents of block (N+1).k := 1.k XOR
  2.k XOR ... XOR N.k;
  let j.k be the parity block of this parity group;
```
Optimized disk-writes in degraded mode

```
end /*if*/;
compute new parity block j.k :=
 old contents of block j.k XOR
 old contents of block (N+1).k XOR
 new contents of block (N+1).k
flush (block (N+1).k) using the block's new contents;
flush (block j.k) using new parity as block contents;
mark block (N+1).k as rebuilt;
```

Optimized online rebuilding of failed disk

```
rebuild (disk N+1) on spare disk:
 for each block k of the failed disk N+1 do
  if the block has not yet been rebuilt
   disk-write (block (N+1).k)
    using the algorithm for disk-writes in degraded mode,
    with low priority for the resulting fetch and
    flush I/O requests;
  end /*if*/;
 end /*for*/;
```

16.4 **Disaster Recovery**

The log-based method for media recovery can be generalized to protect the data against environmental disasters such as fire by maintaining remote copies of both the backups and the archive log. This involves dedicated high-speed communication lines to a second computer center in sufficient distance. With the more frequent disasters such as fire or broken water pipes in mind, it suffices to have the second center about a mile away, so that the appropriate communication technology for this distance is available at reasonable costs. Obviously, such a setup would not provide much protection against earthquakes and other more global disasters, but such special concerns are beyond our scope.

Remote backup   Algorithmically, there is not much difference from what we do for media recovery: backups are taken remotely by copying pages to the second center, and the archive log can be continuously copied to the remote place, too. However, unless the primary center's stable log is duplicated at the second site as well, the remote archive log may lag a little behind the primary's log. This can be avoided by actually running all transactions as distributed transactions that would at least create log entries at both sites simultaneously or may even update replicated data at both sites. However, as we will show in Part IV of the book, such distributed transactions have to pay an extra price in terms of communication, forced logging, and some potential response-time delays. So this solution, which would otherwise be straightforward, is not always accepted in practice.

Distributed transactions vs. log shipping

Without the use of distributed transactions, the remote archive logging amounts to having to ship large portions of the primary's archive log to the remote site. Then, when the primary site is hit by a disaster, the remote site may still miss some of the most recent log entries. This may result in losing some updates of committed transactions. In any case, however, the log entries should be shipped such that only transactions at the tail of the log may be lost. In other words, the correctness criterion for this log shipping method is the following: if the remote site has received all log entries of a committed transaction t, then it must have received all log entries of all committed transactions that preceded t in the primary's *serialization* ordering.

Once we are willing to live with the possibility of losing some committed transactions and the log shipping is not done in firm real time, an intriguing performance enhancement is to ship redo log entries of winner transactions only (but note that these would include CLEs of transactions that were rolled back to facilitate redo-history recovery). This simplifies the recovery at the remote site, as it would merely have to perform the redo-history pass using the archive log entries that it has received. Furthermore, without the complications of the additional undo pass at the remote site, it is simpler to parallelize the recovery, for example, by partitioning log entries based on page numbers, so that the data becomes available again as early as possible.

For extremely mission-critical servers, the remote site may even serve as a hot-standby backup server in that it prepares for more or less immediate takeover once it is detected that the primary server has failed. Note that this may also be useful for failures that are not as drastic as a fire. To this end, the backup server essentially maintains a shadow database, as mentioned in Section 16.2. So log entries that are shipped from the primary server while it is still operational are continuously applied to the shadow database. The backup server, albeit designed for immediate failover, may serve its own regular workload. So after the failover, its load is increased until the primary server becomes available again.

Hot-standby backup server

This architecture can be viewed as a variation of a data-sharing cluster introduced in Chapter 15, with the following differences:

- Servers have larger physical distance: different buildings or even cities as opposed to the same room.

- The data sharing is conceptually implemented by "lazy" replication, as opposed to physically shared disks: all servers maintain a database copy with updates propagated lazily via log shipping (or within distributed transactions).

- Consequently, there is no perfect coherency control across servers (unless distributed transactions are used), so that a backup copy (shadow database) may be slightly out of date, which becomes relevant only upon failover.

Maintenance of the shadow database incurs continuous extra work on the backup server. So it is important to keep that extra work as small as possible. Optimizations along these lines entail batched processing of redo log entries on the shadow database. Once the failover takes place, however, it is crucial to process whatever log entries still need to be applied as fast as possible to minimize the unavailability of the data, and this may entail additional techniques for parallel processing of redo log entries.

16.5 **Lessons Learned**

The combination of taking archive backups during normal operation and redoing writes of corrupted pages or entire disks from the archive log is the baseline method of choice that every industrial-strength data server should support. Note that the actual recovery algorithm is very close to that for crash recovery: both follow the redo-history paradigm, both exploit LSN-based page-state testing for idempotence of redo steps, and both depend on the presence of compensation log entries to identify updates that were already rolled back or undone during the restart after a server crash. Furthermore, the redo pass of the media recovery is followed by a standard crash recovery undo pass as if there had been a soft server crash. The main difference from crash recovery is that the media recovery redo pass starts with a usually much older LSN, coined the MediaRecoveryLSN, which is the minimum of the begin-backup log entry's LSN for the most recently completed backup and the SystemRedoLSN as of the time when that backup was initiated. Other than that, media recovery greatly leverages the previous chapter's fundamental considerations on crash recovery.

Media recovery based on archive logging is the most versatile among the presented techniques in that it can cope with individual page corruptions, disk failures, and certain classes of software-induced environmental failures. Furthermore, it can be easily carried over to a setting where the backup and the archive log are shipped to a remote site so as to protect the server against disasters such as fire.

Nevertheless it is often desirable to complement backups and archive logging with additional techniques based on storage redundancy at the disk level. Such techniques, whose popularity has come along with the advent of so-called RAID or disk array storage systems, either mirror data blocks on two or more disks or place error-correcting codes for groups of disk blocks on appropriately chosen disks. All these techniques can mask a single disk failure without any interruption of the server, provided that a spare disk is already plugged in and available without human intervention. So the advantage compared to the backups and archive logging lies in maintaining 100% availability, as long as we consider only a single disk failure at a time and limit ourselves to "traditional" failures of the disk hardware. A second disk failure while the previously failed disk is rebuilt on the spare disk would lead to data loss. Therefore, a number of optimization techniques for minimizing the mean time to repair are of great importance for such approaches. Most notably, the technique of declustering mirrored blocks or parity blocks across a larger number of disks can be very beneficial, so as to balance the reconstruction load across the surviving disks and to keep the extra load that each disk has to sustain during repair below a certain threshold.

Exercises

16.1 Reconsider the MediaRecoveryLSN for the method based on backups and archive logging. Give concrete examples, with histories referring to concrete page numbers, etc., to show each of the following points:

(a) It is insufficient to start the redo pass of the media recovery at the most recent begin-backup log entry if this most recent backup was not completed before the media failure occurred.

(b) It is insufficient to start the redo pass of the media recovery at the begin-backup log entry of the most recently completed backup if the copying procedure for a backup bypasses the server's page cache.

(c) It may be necessary (albeit extremely unlikely) to start the redo pass of the media recovery at the OldestUndoLSN as of the time when the most recent complete backup was initiated.

16.2 Investigate the mean time to data loss (MTTDL) for mirrored disks as well as for "triple mirroring," where each block is replicated on three different disks. To this end, design a stochastic state-transition model and derive from it an exact formula for the MTTDL, in close analogy to the derivation that we carried out in Section 16.2.

16.3 Design an efficient procedure for shipping log entries to a remote site such that the remote server is able to redo winner transactions in serialization order and may lose only a few such transactions from the tail of the serialization order. In other words, if transaction tk is redone at the remote site and transaction ti precedes tk in the serialization order of the original history, then it must be ensured that the remote site redoes ti as well.

Bibliographic Notes

The media recovery method based on backups and archive logging was already sketched by Crus (1984) and has been in use in commercial database systems for a long time. Mohan, Haderle, et al. (1992) have also leveraged the redo-history paradigm in the context of media recovery explicitly, and presented the ARIES algorithm to cover both crash and media recovery in an integrated form. Mohan and Narang (1993) have presented detailed algorithms for creating database backups, including many low-level optimizations that are relevant in industrial-strength commercial systems. The duration of creating a backup and recovering corrupted data from the backup and archive log has been analyzed by Stoerl (1997). Mathematical underpinnings for our analysis of the MTTDL, based on a Markov chain model, can be found, for example, in the textbook by Tijms (1994).

An excellent overview of storage redundancy techniques, with emphasis on RAID architectures, has been given by Chen et al. (1994). The original RAID concept was proposed by Patterson et al. (1988); a mathematical analysis of the MTTDL for various RAID configurations can be found in Gibson (1992). Disk mirroring, on the other hand, has been in use in commercial systems long before it was scientifically studied in the paper by Bitton and Gray (1988). The same holds for declustered mirroring; its advantages in terms of MTTR and MTTDL have been analyzed by Copeland and Keller (1989). Additional generalizations of declustered replication in the context of highly available, multisite data servers have been investigated by Torbjornsen (1995).

Variations of parity-based RAID architectures have been an intensive subject of the last decade's research and development. Rebuild algorithms have first been studied systematically by Muntz and Lui (1990). Thomasian and Menon (1994) and Thomasian (1998b) have presented thorough performance evaluations for various rebuild algorithms. Flexible placement schemes for parity blocks have been investigated, for example, by Menon et al. (1993), Stodolsky et al. (1993), and Mogi and Kitsuregawa (1994). The concept of parity block declustering was first proposed by Muntz and Lui (1990) and later was further studied by Merchant and Yu (1992), Holland et al. (1994), and Alvarez et al. (1998). Foundational work on such advanced placement schemes and more general error-correcting codes that can mask multiple disk failures has been done by Rabin (1989) and Gibson et al. (1989).

Using remote backups and log shipping as a protection against site disasters has been studied in much detail by King et al. (1991), Mohan et al. (1993), and Humborstad et al. (1997). These sources also contain some information about and additional pointers to disaster recovery support in commercial systems. The log shipping methods that may lose a few winner transactions have been referred to as the case of "1-safe transactions" in the above literature, as opposed to "2-safe transactions," which are distributed transactions that are fully atomic across two sites (at the expense of a substantially higher overhead).

CHAPTER SEVENTEEN

Application Recovery

> The 9000 series is the most reliable computer ever made. No 9000 computer has ever made a mistake or distorted information. We are all, by any practical definition of the words, foolproof and incapable of error.
>
> . . .
>
> I've just picked up a fault in the AE35 unit. It's going to go 100% failure in 72 hours.
>
> . . .
>
> It can only be attributable to human error.
>
> *—HAL*
>
> Basic research is what I'm doing when I don't know what I'm doing.
>
> *—Wernher von Braun*

17.1 Goal and Overview

In this chapter we shift the focus from the server to the clients of a transactional information system. So we now take it for granted that the consistency of the server's data is ensured to the best possible extent, but we ask ourselves how clients may and should react to "bad" returncodes that signal transaction aborts, server failures, and other unusually long delays that the client may interpret as a server outage.

Exactly-once execution

The server ensures the all-or-nothing atomicity of each transaction, but the client is actually interested in executing a user request to completion and achieving this *exactly once*. So upon receiving a returncode that indicates the "nothing" outcome for a transaction, it is the client's responsibility to reinitiate the transaction until it eventually succeeds. This should happen transparently to the human user on behalf of which the client acts, and it involves reinitializing the application program and starting the transaction again as a new transaction. The difficulty in this procedure lies in the fact that the client cannot always determine the outcome of a previously initiated transaction with 100% certainty. So if the server crashed after committing the transaction but before sending the returncode to the client, the client would be tempted to initiate the transaction again. Then, as the transaction's behavior is usually

623

not idempotent and the server, after having been restarted, sees the transaction as a new one with no connection to its previous incarnation, such an approach would violate the desired exactly-once semantics of transactional client requests.

Process recovery, message recovery

This chapter presents techniques for guaranteeing the exactly-once semantics of client requests. The failure types that we consider in this chapter include client failures as well as server failures, in the sense of both soft process crashes and limited forms of communication failures, in that messages may be lost because of process failures. So in addition to the data recovery that we have addressed in the previous chapters, we will discuss how to provide process recovery and message recovery. In full generality, no industrial-strength solution is known yet, despite the fact that the fault-tolerant and distributed computing communities have been tackling the problem area for many years. We will restrict our setting to typical transaction-style applications. In particular, we will consider only request-reply communication patterns between clients and a server, as opposed to arbitrarily asynchronous message exchanges between peer processes.

We will first consider, in Section 17.2, the special case of transactions that consist of a single request-reply pair between the client and the server and relatively small and simple application programs. Albeit very special, this case is a common one in classical OLTP application programs: users provide input by completing a form, this triggers a transaction on the server, and the result is displayed to the user in that form. The solution will involve the management of request and reply messages in persistent and recoverable message queues. Transactions that utilize such queues are commonly referred to as *queued transactions*.

In Section 17.3 we will generalize our considerations to applications that involve conversations with the human user; so they consist of a sequence of request-reply pairs. Often each request-reply pair corresponds to one transaction on the server, a case that is known as *pseudo-conversational transactions*. In contrast to the first case above, an application program needs to maintain local state data in between interactions with the server: such an application is called *stateful*, as opposed to the *stateless* programs that consist of a single request-reply pair. It has turned out, however, that many traditional OLTP applications (e.g., in banking or reservation systems) need to hold only a small amount of local data, say, a few local variables, so that the *process state* of the executing process is very compact. We emphasize this fact because it can be exploited in the technical solution for process recovery. Section 17.3 is specifically devoted to this case, and we will show that recoverable queues can be nicely leveraged for pseudo-conversational transactions as well.

Section 17.4 takes these considerations one step further and addresses failure resilience in long-lived workflows that involve heterogeneous and largely autonomous servers. Recall from Chapter 1 that workflows such as travel planning or insurance claim processing consist of multiple activities, each of which may be a transaction. So a workflow usually does not have the ACID property in its entirety; more specifically, isolation is relaxed or even completely given up. However, we do desire a guarantee that a workflow is executed completely once it has been started (without prejudicing any one of multiple possible outcomes) and that it is executed exactly once. We will see that queued transactions are very convenient in achieving this goal.

Finally, we consider the most general case in Section 17.5, where applications may spawn long-running processes with large state data. This case becomes relevant if the application is itself a semantically rich generic service, for example, an office tool, a software repository, or a workflow engine. In this case, a full-fledged approach to process recovery is needed, which involves periodically saving the application process's state as well as logging interactions with the user and the data server.

For a large part of this chapter we restrict ourselves to two-tier system architectures with clients (i.e., home or office PCs) connected to data servers and application programs running on the clients. For ease of presentation, we will mostly focus on a single client and a single data server, but it is trivial to incorporate multiple clients with each running its own application. The generalization to multiple data servers in a federated system is also straightforward, provided we understand how to handle distributed transactions; we will cover this base technology in Part IV of the book and simply assume support for transactional updates across multiple data servers for the scope of the current chapter.

Embedding into system architecture

Extensions to three-tier architectures with an application server (e.g., a Web server) as "middle man" are feasible, too, and widely used in practice. Recall from Chapter 1 that in a three-tier system the client merely handles presentation issues (i.e., the interactions with the human user) and the actual application logic resides in a program that is run under the control of the application server (e.g., a Web servlet executed as a thread within the application server's address space). As long as the various application programs that simultaneously run on the application server do not have any shared-state data (e.g., shared data structures within a common address space or common events) at the application level, the application server's different threads can simply be perceived as if each of them were a single client. This way, application recovery for two-tier client-server systems carries over to three-tier systems in a fairly straightforward manner.

17.2 **Stateless Applications Based on Queues**

In this section we consider only applications that are stateless in the sense that the underlying application programs never have to remember anything beyond a user interaction. So the execution of an application program consists of the following steps:

Behavior of a stateless client

1. The user sends *input* to a computer, typically her PC but possibly also through a chipcard, a cellular phone, or other device. That computer, the client, spawns a program execution on behalf of this input. (Technically, the computer would have a program running already that polls for user input, but this can be viewed as part of the operating system.)

2. The executing application program constructs a *request* to a data server and sends it there.

3. The data server receives the request, processes it as a transaction, constructs a *reply* to the client, and sends it there.

4. The client receives the reply, derives a suitable *output* message to the user, and presents it to the user.

At the end of the last step, the stateless application can forget everything about the prior history; the next user input will initiate a new, independent invocation of the same or a different program. This is why this kind of application is called stateless; there is no notion of a user session. Despite this limitation, this application class is highly relevant in practice, and this is the reason for considering it in detail. The next subsection will extend this application model to capture richer behavior. Here, we will simplify the above model even further by disallowing any asynchronous requests of clients. So a client is not allowed to continue its program execution after having sent a request to a data server; rather the client needs to "pause" until it receives the reply. As a consequence, a client can have at most one outstanding request for the completion of which it is waiting. This restriction could be relaxed, but it simplifies the presentation and allows us to concentrate on the salient features of the techniques that we are going to develop.

Message recovery by persistent, recoverable message queues
The main difficulty in coping with such stateless applications lies in handling the message traffic between the user, the client, and the data server. The particular question within the framework of recovery is, of course, how we should deal with message losses induced by client or server crashes, and how we can ensure that the user's input is processed and the output is eventually delivered despite such failures. The solution for message recovery that we study in this section is based on *persistent, recoverable message queues*: all messages are delivered via such queues; the sender enqueues a message, and the receiver dequeues it.

Queue manager
A message queue itself is an ADT-style persistent object that is implemented on (page-structured) persistent storage and managed by a server with appropriate measures for crash recovery and concurrency control, as a queue may be accessed by many clients. Such a server is often referred to as a *queue manager*. For concurrency control it can and should exploit the semantics of the queue operations, Enqueue and Dequeue, often relaxing the queue behavior

to that of a non-FIFO queue (see Chapter 7), and for recovery it can employ the standard techniques for data recovery of the previous chapters.

The queue manager may be embedded in the data server, which is what we will assume for ease of presentation, or it may be provided by a middle-tier application server in a three-tier architecture (see Chapter 1). In practice, the latter case is prevalent and typically involves deploying a TP monitor or advanced ORB product (see Chapter 1) or the corresponding functionality of a business application framework such as SAP R/3. It is important that the operations on a message queue, Enqueue and Dequeue, can be included in transactions, and that the queue manager has the technical provisions for guaranteeing the ACID contract. When the queue manager is part of an explicit application server separated from the data server, we will actually need distributed transactions. This will involve standard techniques to be presented in Part IV of the book, but conceptually there is no difference from a centralized transaction, and we can therefore simplify the presentation by assuming that message queues are under the direct control of the data server.

Queued transactions

The key to ensuring that user input is not lost and will eventually be processed is to place the input in a recoverable place as soon as possible. This is what recoverable message queues are intended for. As a client program does not involve much computation before the request to the data server is derived from the user's input, the natural solution is to enqueue the request within a transaction and commit that transaction right away. Once this is done, the user input is guaranteed to survive crashes by the recovery measures of the queue manager. This step essentially amounts to force-logging the user input immediately after receiving it (namely, by committing the enqueueing transaction).

Exactly-once execution guarantee

The next issue then is to ensure that this request to the data server is processed exactly once, and the reply will definitely be delivered to the client. This is the part where we strive for a correctness criterion beyond the traditional ACID contract. The atomicity of a server transaction would merely require an all-or-nothing outcome; so rolling back an incomplete transaction and "forgetting" it would be legitimate. From the application viewpoint, however, the transaction would have to be retried until it eventually succeeds; this is sometimes called an *at-least-once* execution guarantee. The way to achieve this is to include the dequeueing of the request into the actual transaction that the data server runs against its data. So if the transaction is aborted before its completion, the dequeueing of the request will be undone, too, so that it is still available in the message queue to the server once the transaction or crash recovery has been carried out. Then the server simply needs to check its request queue again to automatically retry the transaction. To arrive at an exactly-once execution guarantee, the server needs to ensure that a request is never processed twice with the corresponding transaction committing. Again, this can be achieved by exploiting the transaction support of the queue manager: we simply include the enqueueing of the server's reply in the same transaction that initially dequeued the request. The effect is that a transaction abort or a server failure

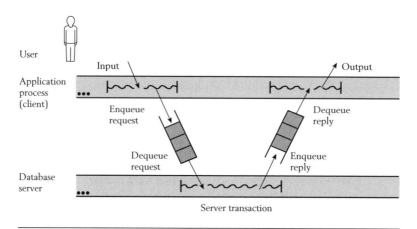

Figure 17.1 Queued transactions.

will undo all three steps if necessary: the reply is removed from the queue, the transaction's effects on the data are undone, and the request will be returned to the request queue. The reply message becomes visible to the client only upon the commit of the server transaction. To make sure that the client does not accidentally lose the reply message, the dequeueing of the message will again be enclosed in a transaction. This entire protocol is known as a queued transaction. Note, however, that it actually consists of three transactions—two client-initiated ones and the one by the server. An illustration of this simple, yet highly effective technique is shown in Figure 17.1.

As discussed above, the illustration of Figure 17.1 assumes a two-tier architecture in which the application runs on the client. The request received by the data server would, for example, spawn a stored procedure or some other form of ADT-style method invocation on encapsulated data, and the result of the procedure execution would be returned to the client. If the client issues a sequence of individual query and update commands using some form of embedded SQL API (e.g., ODBC) rather than invoking an entire stored procedure, then the server would open its transaction upon dequeueing the first call and close the transaction upon receiving the application program's commit request and enqueueing the reply message to the client. In between, all SQL commands and their results can be exchanged directly between the data server and the client without using the transactional queues since there is not yet any output to the user, but all the effects of these calls on the server's data must be part of the server transaction.

In a three-tier architecture with an explicit application server between the client and the data server, the picture changes a bit, but its fundamental characteristics remain the same. Now the client simply forwards the user input to the application server, which typically runs the queue manager and is in charge of enqueueing the request derived from the user input. The server transaction

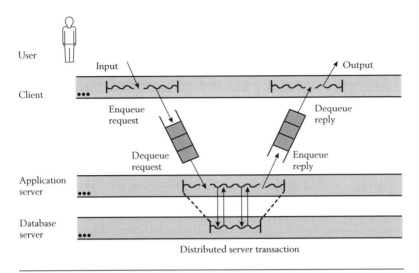

Figure 17.2 Queued transactions in a three-tier architecture.

that dequeues the request and initiates its processing on the data server side is now a distributed transaction that involves both the application server and the data server. All operations on queues take place on the application server, and all operations on persistent data take place on the data server. Again, the data server may either execute merely a stored procedure or a sequence of SQL commands issued by the application program on the application server. This use of queued transactions in a three-tier architecture is illustrated in Figure 17.2, assuming the case of an SQL command sequence. Conceptually and within our current context, the fact that the two servers together execute a distributed transaction does not make any essential difference to the case of a two-tier architecture. The important point is that the servers together fulfill the ACID contract for this transaction. In Part IV of the book we will discuss which additional handshakes between the two servers are involved in such a distributed transaction.

Queued transactions incur a significant overhead. On the other hand, they also constitute a major added value in that they enhance the all-or-nothing guarantee of ACID transactions into an exactly-once execution guarantee for each user-initiated request. As far as the user output is concerned, however, the guarantee is a bit weaker in that we can ensure only at-least-once delivery. The reason is that the client could fail in between sending the output to the user and committing the transaction that dequeues the server reply. Then, the recovery would put the reply back into the queue, so that the restarted client would see it again. Now the client has absolutely no way to determine whether it has already sent the output. So, unless it receives some form of acknowledgment from the user, it should try resending the output message. The acknowledgment may be an implicit one, like observing that the user already sends her next input message and thus must have seen the previous output (or is no longer interested in it). Note that this less-than-ideal behavior should be extremely infrequent because it happens only when a client failure occurs within a very small window of vulnerability.

Testable output   If nonidempotent output messages to users are so critical that sending them twice is absolutely unacceptable, we need an explicit way of testing the state of the output device to resolve the potential ambiguity. An important example is automatic teller machines that hand out cash to customers. These machines have special hardware counters that can be read by the software, and are automatically incremented each time cash is dispensed. Then, the client transaction that dequeues the server reply can read the counter before initiating the output and write it to a persistent, failure-resilient place. So the value of the counter is remembered across client failures, and the client is the only entity that can manipulate the counter. Therefore, after a restart, the client can simply read the current value of the hardware counter and compare it to the remembered value to suppress initiating the output a second time. Note that in this scenario, the client is the automatic teller machine itself (i.e., its software). Further note that it is not possible to embed this kind of user output in the client transaction itself, as the output is an inherently non-undoable, real-world effect. So dispensing cash is nontransactional, but it is testable. Overall, these considerations lead to the following correctness criterion that queued transactions can satisfy in a way that can be proven:

THEOREM 17.1

With the queued transaction protocol for stateless applications, the following guarantees hold:

1. Once the user-input transaction is committed, a request is executed by the server exactly once.

2. Once the user-input transaction is committed, the user output is delivered at least once.

3. If user output is testable, the user output is delivered exactly once, provided the user-input transaction has been committed.

Proof

The proof is essentially a case analysis that considers client and server failures at various stages in the processing.

First, assume that the client fails after the user input is successfully enqueued (which is our overall premise). The server is not affected by this failure and can dequeue the request independently of the client. If the client restarts, it no longer cares about the request queue; so it is irrelevant how far the server has progressed in executing the request. If the server has already enqueued the reply message before the client completes its restart, the client will find the reply there and will process it and deliver output to the user as if there were no failure at all. If the reply message is not yet (committed) in the reply queue, the client will wait until the message appears and can be dequeued. So again, this is the usual client behavior during normal operation. In either case, the client will eventually dequeue the reply and send it at least once to the user. If the user output is testable, the client can determine whether it had already delivered the same output once and would suppress it in this case.

The second case is that the server fails at some point in the processing. If it fails before it dequeues the request message, there is nothing to do upon the server restart: the request will still be available in the queue. If the server failure occurs after the dequeueing but before the commit of the server transaction, the server recovery will undo all effects on both the data and the queue. So the request message will be placed back into the queue by the standard procedure for crash recovery. Upon restart, the server will find it there as if it were a new message and will again process it. Since the prior incarnation's updates on the server's data have been undone as well, the fact that the request appears as a new message is perfectly acceptable. Further note that the request message can be assumed to be "self-describing" in that its contents tells the server which stored procedure or other method it should invoke to process the request; so the server does not need to remember anything across crash-restart cycles other than what is in the queue. Assuming that the server will eventually be operational long enough to completely execute the transaction and commit the reply message in the reply queue, the server's part of the overall execution has been performed exactly once. So the request has been executed exactly once, and it is up to the client to deliver the output message (see the first case above).

To conclude this section, the details for the client and server behavior during normal operation are given in the following pseudocode. For simplicity, we assume a two-tier architecture, with the application running on the client and the queue manager on the data server. Furthermore, the pseudocode does not capture the case of testable output devices; this is left as an exercise (see Exercise 17.1).

```
user-input processing by client:
  begin transaction;
  enqueue (request);
  commit transaction;
```

*Client during
normal
operation*

```
user-output processing by client:
 wait until reply queue is not empty;
 begin transaction;
 dequeue (reply);
 while user has not acknowledged the reply
  or sent the next request
 do
  present reply to user;
 end /*while*/;
 commit transaction;
```

Server during normal operation
```
request-reply processing by data server:
 begin transaction;
 dequeue (request);
 perform data operations and generate reply;
 enqueue (reply);
 commit transaction;
```

After failures, the client and the server perform the following restart procedures:

Client restart
```
check reply queue;
if not empty then
 process reply like during normal operation;
end /*if*/;
```

Server restart
```
check request queue;
if not empty then
 initiate processing of requests like during normal operation
end /*if*/;
```

17.3 Stateful Applications Based on Queues

The technique of using queued transactions that has been developed in the previous section has so far been geared and restricted to the special case of transactions with a single user input and a single user output. Now we will consider the natural generalizations of transactions that contain entire conversations with the user. Such a *conversational transaction* would still be initiated by the first input message from the user, but the subsequent output message should not close the server transaction. Rather it should be possible to combine an entire sequence of user inputs, request-processing steps, and output messages into a single transaction as far as the atomicity, persistence, and isolation of the updates to the server's data are concerned. And, of course, we would like to preserve the exactly-once execution guarantee and the at-least-once output delivery once the first user-input message has been successfully enqueued.

It turns out that it is not at all easy to include multiple user interaction steps (i.e., message exchanges between the application program and the user) into a single transaction, because that user output is not really undoable. When a transaction aborts after sending output messages to the human user, we cannot easily convince the user that these messages should be viewed as if they have never been sent. Such behavior may be acceptable under specific conditions, but we should strive for something better. The solution that has been established in many commercial OLTP applications over the last three decades is to break down the entire conversation into a sequence of transactions that are chained together. The link between the transactions is provided by the queue manager. Similar to the server not losing its request when the enqueueing of the reply fails because of a transaction undo, we can combine two message exchange steps between the client and the user into a transaction: when the client dequeues the server reply and presents the output to the user, the client does not immediately close the transaction, but waits for the subsequent user input in the conversation and enqueues the resulting request that is still within the same transaction.

This chaining of multiple queued transactions is illustrated in Figure 17.3. Its key point is that once the enqueueing of the initial user input has been committed, the chain will never be "broken" by a server or client crash. In positive terms, it is guaranteed, despite (temporary) computer and network failures, that there will be at least one request or reply message in one of the message queues; in fact, with our restriction to single-threaded application programs that do not spawn requests asynchronously, there will be exactly one message recovered from whatever client and server crashes will occur.

Queue-based message recovery for conversations

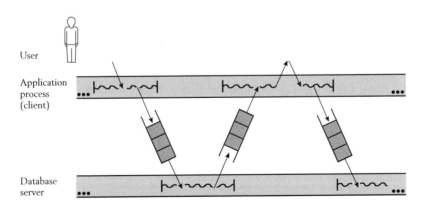

Figure 17.3 Pseudo-conversational queued transactions.

Then, after the restart of the failed component, the entire conversation can be resumed with this recovered message. So it is the queue-based message recovery that keeps the conversation alive. This argument can be cast into the following theorem:

THEOREM 17.2

With the queue-based message recovery for conversational multistep transaction chains, the following guarantees hold:

1. Once the initial user-input transaction that starts the entire conversation is committed, the entire transaction chain is executed by the server exactly once.

2. Once the initial user-input transaction is committed, each user-output message throughout the conversation is delivered at least once.

3. If user output is testable, each user-output message is delivered exactly once, provided the initial user-input transaction has been committed.

Proof

The proof can be viewed as an extension of the proof of Theorem 17.1, developed in the previous section. The decisive invariant that holds throughout the conversation is that either the last committed request or the last committed reply will be available after whatever failure might occur, assuming our basic premise that the initial user input has been successfully enqueued. To verify that this invariant holds, we need to consider all possible points of failure of the client and the server, analogously to our case analysis in the proof of Theorem 17.1.

As for client failures, the critical case is a failure in between dequeueing a reply and sending the resulting user output. In this case, however, the recovery will undo the client transaction and make the reply message available again. The same holds if the failure occurs after sending the user output or receiving the next user input, but before the next request is enqueued. In these cases, the client may send an output message more than once, and it may even have to prompt the user to repeat the last input message. The latter behavior is undesirable and fairly unlikely but cannot be completely ruled out; within the small window between receiving the user input and forcing it to the queue by committing the client transaction, the client is susceptible to losing user input. Note, however, that this undesirable behavior refers only to the last user input immediately preceding a client crash. In any case, it is only at the client transaction's commit that the previous reply message becomes definitely forgotten, but at this point the next request is safely recorded in the queue.

As for server failures, the situation does not really differ from that of Theorem 17.1. The server dequeues a request at the beginning and enqueues the corresponding reply at the end of the same atomic transaction.

So the invariant that the committed state of the queue always holds exactly one message (either a request or a reply) is proven. All our claims follow immediately from this invariant that the message chain never becomes broken. The exactly-once delivery of user-output messages requires a testable user-output device, but once this is available, the situation is identical to that of Theorem 17.1, as the problem of double output is independent of the conversational context.

At this point, we point out that there are also some caveats with this queue-based approach. First, the fact that the entire conversation is broken down into multiple server transactions compromises the isolation of the application's data updates on the server. So for this approach to be feasible, we need to ensure that this behavior is acceptable for the application. This corresponds to the special case of chained transactions that we mentioned in Chapter 7 for the object model concurrency control. Recall that this case builds on the fact that all higher-level operations that correspond to the individual server transactions are commutative or are at least viewed as compatible with each other. If this condition does not hold, we would need to acquire semantic locks or provide some other form of concurrency control for the high-level operations on the server. Also, if the entire conversation were to be stopped prematurely by the user, the server would have to initiate compensating transactions for the already committed transactions. Note, however, that many applications can be designed to provide such compensating transactions. Further note that server or client crashes do not necessitate such compensating steps; rather the restart of the server or the client would recover the last request or reply message and would always roll the entire conversation forward.

The second caveat affects the application programs themselves. Recovering the last message is not good enough to resume an interrupted program execution, as the process in which the program executes could rely on the proper and up-to-date state of its local variables. Here we apply a trick to support at least a limited but common case of stateful application programs. As long as the local state data that is needed to recover the process and resume the execution is sufficiently small, the client can store this state data into the recoverable queues by combining it with the request messages that it enqueues. When the server dequeues the request, it should extract and remember that state data and put it back into the queue when it enqueues the reply message at the end of the server transaction. This way, a failed client can always recover not only the last relevant message but also the corresponding local process state. Thus, client restart amounts to loading the corresponding program in an initial state, extracting the relevant state data from the queue, and setting its local variables

Using queues to recover "small" process state

to these most recent values. In commercial implementations of this approach, application programs have to be written in a stylized manner using special calls for saving and extracting process state data with the queue manager.

So, in essence, the entire user/application conversation and the stateful process that executes the application program are both transformed into a sequence of quasi-stateless single-interaction steps, each of which corresponds to a single transaction using the recoverable queues as intermediate store for messages and (a small amount of) process state data. To reflect the specific, essentially stateless and nonconversational nature of the resulting transactions, this approach is known by the name *pseudo-conversational transactions* in the commercial world. Despite its somewhat tricky nature and limitations, the approach has been widely successful in practice. For example, the widely popular type of business application frameworks whose best-known archetype is SAP R/3 have adopted this concept of queue-based conversations; in R/3 this is termed a "logical unit of work." In Section 17.4 we will show that the concept can also be leveraged in general-purpose workflow management. In Section 17.5 we will finally consider a truly general, unrestricted, and possibly also conceptually cleaner approach to message and process recovery for client-server applications, but we will also show that the generality has a higher price in terms of computational costs and especially complexity of the necessary protocols.

Typical application examples for queue-based pseudo-conversational transaction chains can be found in travel reservation systems. Suppose you wish to book a package consisting of a flight, hotel, and rental car from a travel agency or an automated, Internet-based travel agent. The client starts the conversation by entering data about the required transportation and accommodation such as traveling dates, origin and destination sites, hotel and rental car preferences, and so on. When the server dequeues this initial request, it could, for example, first make flight reservations on the chosen airline's data server and commit the transaction of this first step. Part of this first server transaction is enqueueing the reply message, which may include, for example, details about the reserved flights such as departure and arrival time. In addition, and this is the basic trick of pseudo-conversational transactions, it would also place all relevant information about the initial user request in the enqueued message, for example, the hotel preferences and the current state of the conversation, such as the money "spent" so far on the airfare. Thus, when the user confirms that the reserved flights are acceptable and requests to continue with the next step, the client applies the same trick. Therefore, the next request that the server dequeues will contain all the necessary information about the initial request and the current state of the entire conversation, such as the currently "spent" amount of money. This way, the server does not need to remember anything across user interactions, other than what is kept in the queue. In the last step of the conversation, the server finds all information about all the individual reservations in the queue and can construct the billing statement as part of its final reply. It is worthwhile to mention that in this application, the various steps that constitute the entire conversation are typically performed against different data servers, since airlines, hotel chains, and rental car companies are autonomous enterprises. But note that this does not require anything special as far as the transactional recovery is concerned, as each step refers to exactly one data server (plus the queue manager, which would reside on a separate application server in a three-tier architecture).

Another application class that would benefit from the presented concepts are electronic commerce services. When you shop electronically, say, in an Internet-based book- or CD store, your PC essentially opens a conversation with the store's data server. The individual steps of this conversation would consist, for example, of filling an electronic shopping cart, and the final step would present the cart's contents to the user for purchasing decisions. In terms of the underlying structure, this application is very close to the travel reservation scenario, with the inessential differences that all steps interact with the same server and that the number of these steps may be significantly higher, depending on how much time the user spends browsing the store. This application is stateful in that it has a conversation context that needs to be maintained across interactions, but this information is surely enough to be kept in a transactional queue. The interesting and somewhat ironic fact about such applications, which can be easily tried out on the Internet, is that most of them are currently built in exactly this way, with the sad difference that they use much less reliable, nontransactional concepts as intermediate store rather than building on highly reliable queues. The typically used Web-style concepts are *cookies*, which are local files on the client that are manipulated by the user's Internet browser to maintain context information, or—even worse—the URLs of the server's Web pages to which appropriate information is padded across browsing steps. These tricks have evolved on the Internet to build conversations on top of the otherwise stateless HTTP protocol. So in some sense, today's e-Commerce applications have reinvented the concept of queue-based conversations, but the sad point is that cookies or "padded URLs" do not provide much failure resilience against client or server crashes at "inconvenient" points. We are, therefore, convinced that the next generation of e-Commerce services will adopt some of the transactional techniques presented in this book.

17.4 **Workflows Based on Queues**

Workflow management for the enactment of computerized business processes can greatly leverage transaction technology and, especially, queued transactions as far as failure resilience and exactly-once execution are concerned. Recall from Chapter 1 that a workflow consists of a set of automated or interactive activities along with a formal specification of the control and data flow among the activities. Such specifications can be expressed in different ways, ranging

Workflows

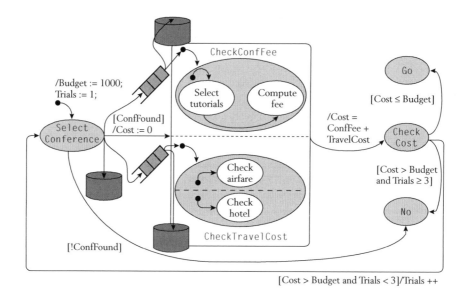

Figure 17.4 Use of queued transactions in travel planning workflow.

from various forms of logic-based and state-transition models to special script languages. One particularly intriguing specification technique is the statechart, which has been adopted by the UML industry standard for the modeling of system behavior. Figure 17.4 gives an example of such a statechart specification, repeating the example of a simplified travel planning scenario presented in Chapter 1. For now, ignore the little queue and disk symbols in the figure, whose meaning will be discussed shortly.

The workflow proceeds through different states (the ovals in the figure), each of which corresponds to an activity for planning a trip to attend a conference. States can be nested in the sense that a state again contains an entire statechart, to express hierarchical designs. The control flow between states, or actually the corresponding activities, is specified in terms of transition rules, which are shown as annotations of the arcs in the figure. A transition fires in a given state if a specified event occurs and a specified condition holds at this point (the part of the arc annotations shown in brackets); the result is that a specified action is executed (the part of the annotations following the slash), and a new state is entered. When a business process allows parallelism, the statechart of a workflow enters multiple states in parallel; these are referred to as orthogonal components and are graphically denoted by nested statecharts separated by a dashed line within a surrounding state. In the example of Figure 17.4, the states (and corresponding activities) CheckConfFee and CheckTravelCost are orthogonal components, both of which are further refined into nested statecharts.

When a client initiates a workflow execution (e.g., an instance of our travel planning example), a *workflow engine* is responsible for the execution, particularly, for *maintaining the state and context* of the workflow instance as it executes. By the "state" of a workflow we refer to the states of the statechart specification that are currently entered, and thus to the currently invoked activities. By its "context" we mean the values of the statechart variables that capture input and output parameters of activities and other data that drives the control flow among activities. The workflow engine runs on a special kind of generic application server, which we also refer to as a workflow server. This server essentially interprets the workflow specification, plugs in parameter values, fires activities according to the control flow, and invokes applications as required by the activities. The applications themselves may run on different application servers and typically access and manipulate various databases (and other information sources) that are in turn managed by separate database servers.

Workflow engine

Next, we briefly discuss how transactional technology and, especially, queued transactions are extremely helpful in coping with failures and keeping the state and context of ongoing workflows consistent throughout their long-lived and possibly decentralized execution. In Section 17.4.1 we first consider the case where a workflow executes entirely on a single workflow server. Then, in Section 17.4.2 we extend our scope by including decentralized workflows that involve activities on different workflow servers according to the organizational structure of the underlying enterprise(s).

17.4.1 Failure-Resilient Workflow State and Context

Consider a failure of the workflow server after the workflow execution has entered the state CheckCost for the first time. If, upon being restarted, the server had simply forgotten the state and context of the workflow, the client would have to manually reinitiate the entire workflow, possibly being forced to retype the same input, repeat dialogs, and so on. With realistic, long-lived workflows that would be much more complex than our simple example scenario, a substantial amount of work over an extended period may be lost, and nobody would ever be willing to rely on workflow technology for mission-critical processes.

The straightforward solution for the workflow server is to keep the state and context of a workflow in a persistent, reliably managed store, and record the necessary updates whenever the workflow performs a state transition or the value of a workflow variable changes. The most obvious implementation would use a database for this purpose; alternatively, the workflow server could maintain its own stable log file. However, it is not sufficient simply to record each change to the state or context separately. Rather it is crucial that all variable changes that are associated with the completion of an activity and the subsequently firing state transitions are embedded within a single atomic

Workflow execution on a single server

transaction. To see that this is indeed necessary, consider a situation where the workflow has reached the state CheckCost and the value of the Cost variable is 2000 with an allowed Budget of 1000. Now suppose the workflow server records the state transition itself on persistent store but does not do so with the updated value of the Cost variable. When the server fails at this point and is later restarted, it would resume the workflow in the CheckCost state but with an assumed value of 0 for the Cost variable (i.e., the variable's last value before the nonrecorded update). As a result, the workflow would then erroneously enter the Go state.

So we require that all actions on behalf of the current state's outgoing transition are combined into an atomic transaction. This transaction includes

- all updates to workflow variables that have been modified by the activity that is run in the current state (i.e., the returncode and other result parameters of the activity),

- the state modification that results from the firing of the current state's outgoing transition,

- all updates to workflow variables that are triggered by the transition itself.

With this kind of *transactional state and context tracking*, problems such as the one above are eliminated, and the server is guaranteed to recover from a failure to the most recent, workflow-consistent state and context. So once the initialization of a workflow execution has been successfully recorded on the server, the server guarantees the complete execution of the workflow, and more than that, an *exactly-once execution*.

17.4.2 Decentralized Workflows Based on Queued Transactions

Workflow execution on multiple servers

The issue of the previous subsection becomes more complicated when the workflow execution is spread across multiple, independent workflow servers. This will be the standard situation for workflows that span different enterprises, for example, to support so-called virtual enterprises in the context of business-to-business electronic commerce (e.g., outsourcing of service provisioning). In fact, even large enterprises often have largely autonomous organizational units where the decentralized responsibilities for certain activities or subworkflows typically entail a distributed workflow execution. In our example scenario, this could be the case for the two parallel activities CheckConfFee and CheckTravelCost (with the latter's subactivities possibly being again decentralized across an airline and a hotel reservation server). So the firing of the transition from state SelectConference to the superstate (left unnamed in Figure 17.4) that contains the two parallel subordinate statecharts should spawn two follow-up activities. In a distributed execution, however, the two corresponding servers need to be notified by the workflow server that was in charge of SelectConference activity and the firing transition. If only one of these two servers, say, the one for CheckTravelCost is successfully notified, and the corresponding message to the other server is lost by a network or server failure, the overall workflow system may end up with an inconsistent situation. The sending server would have to repeat its notification message to the second server, whereas the message to the first server must not be resent to ensure the exactly-once semantics.

The solution to this problem is to combine the notifications of both receiving servers in a single, distributed transaction. Even better, we can combine the update of the sending server's state and context information with the two notifications into a single, three-site transaction. The atomicity of this transaction guarantees that the state transition out of the SelectConference state is globally perceived as taking place exactly once.

There are, however, situations where the above solution incurs certain inconveniences in terms of the independence and ultimately performance of the involved servers. For example, if one of the receiving servers is temporarily unavailable, it may not be possible to commit the three-party transaction. Then even the activity of the available receiving server could not be started until the other server is restarted (or reconnected to the network) and commits the notification. As the processing times of activities may vary by orders of magnitude, this delay of one out of two parallel activities could possibly become a severe problem. So a better solution is to "decouple" the involved servers by using a middleman in the form of failure-resilient, transactional queues. The sender simply places the notification in two queues, one for each receiver, and can immediately commit the update of its own local state and context. The two receivers can now independently dequeue the notification. When doing this, each of them must, however, still combine the dequeueing and its own persistent recording into a single transaction. The benefit of this method is that the dequeued message would automatically be placed back in the receiver's queue (by the undoing of the transaction) if the update to the receiver's local state and context fails. So the overall three-party protocol is broken down into three transactions. Each of these three is still a distributed transaction, between a workflow server and a queue manager. The net result is that the workflow can progress across largely autonomous servers in a loosely coupled manner while ensuring the exactly-once execution of the workflow.

The atomic update to the queues and a server's persistent recording of the local state and context data are illustrated by the queue and disk symbols in Figure 17.4. Upon completing the SelectConference activity, the corresponding server's enqueueing and local recording steps are denoted by the three arrows connecting the two queues and the server's disk icon. For each of the two receiving servers, the dequeueing and local recording are denoted by the arrows that go out of the queues.

17.5 **General Stateful Applications**

The applications that were allowed under the queue-based approaches of the previous sections were limited in that they had to be stateless or quasi-stateless in the sense that all necessary state information for an entire conversation could be stored in the message queue. The current section presents a general approach to client-server application recovery that can cope with arbitrarily "rich," stateful applications. Such applications may include office automation or cooperative work tools, software and other kinds of engineering design repositories, and also workflow management, including arbitrarily invoked applications (which were disregarded in the previous section). Throughout the section we restrict ourselves to two-tier architectures, however, where such applications run on the client side and interact directly with a data server.

Our goal is to provide recovery measures that can mask system failures to human users in almost all cases, rare exceptions being duplicating an output message or having to prompt the user for a previously entered input a second time. The exactly-once execution guarantee for queue-based applications encompasses user-transparent recovery. A key observation from the previous sections that provides a conceptual starting point for generalization is that failure-interrupted applications can be restarted if we can recover the last decisive message(s). The *decisive* message is the initial user request in the case of simple queued transactions, the last request or reply message in the case of pseudo-conversational transactions, or a set of parallel request messages in the case of queue-based workflows. Restarting the entire application then boils down to reloading the application program and feeding the recovered decisive message(s) into the program. With more general applications, we may have to recover an entire history of messages, and we may have to feed all these messages into the reloaded program as it is executed a second time. We refer to this kind of message-based reexecution of an application program as *replaying* the application. We will see in a short while that the message recovery itself does not necessarily have to be based on queues, but may directly utilize some form of message logging with possible improvements in performance.

Message logging for message recovery and deterministic program replay

Message-based replay makes one fundamental assumption, without which we would face tremendous complications: applications are assumed to be *piecewise deterministic* in that potentially nonreproducible behavior is caused only by exchanging messages with the server or the human user. This is usually not a real limitation for business-oriented applications, but it would be prohibitive in certain real-time applications that deal with interrupts and other forms of asynchronous events. For a piecewise deterministic application, if we can reconstruct all the original messages of a failed application process, we can recover the process by reinitializing it and replaying its prior execution, feeding the process with the original messages and possibly suppressing messages that were already sent earlier. Obviously, the reconstruction of the original messages needs some form of *message logging*, which is what the queue manager effectively did in the previous sections. In this section we no longer refer to a queue manager but rather analyze the minimum logging requirements for messages, thus aiming to minimize the overhead of the entire protocol. It will turn out that a solution can be developed whose forced logging costs are actually lower than that of a queue-based approach.

Ideally this approach should be able to mask all failures to the user, so that neither server nor client failures should be noticeable. However, this failure masking can be truly effective only if the outages after a failure are short enough; long outages will be perceived as service disruptions by the user, even if no message is lost or duplicated and the functional behavior is as smooth as during normal operation. With general applications that maintain rich state data, such as office tools or workflow engines, reexecuting the program from scratch may take too long. Therefore, the process state should be periodically saved to stable storage, and the execution after a failure and the client's restart should be resumed from the most recently saved state. We call this way of saving a process's state an *installation point*. The existing literature often refers to this technique as program or process "checkpointing," but we deliberately do not adopt this terminology to avoid confusion with the different notion of checkpointing in data recovery (see Chapter 13).

Installation points for process recovery and reduced program replay

In the following, we will first, in Section 17.5.1, discuss design considerations and alternatives from a conceptual viewpoint, thus stepwise developing the design rationale for a specific algorithm coined *server reply logging method*. Section 17.5.2 then provides an overview of this algorithm. The subsequent Sections 17.5.3 through 17.5.8 present details of the algorithm in terms of data structures, logging procedures during normal operation on the server and the client side, log truncation, and the restart procedures for the server and the client. We prove the algorithm's correctness in Section 17.5.9, and we conclude this entire section with a short discussion in Section 17.5.10 of the presented algorithm's applicability to three-tier and general multi-tier system architectures.

17.5.1 **Design Considerations**

Message logging could be done on the server, on the client, or on both. However, it can be shown that it is sufficient to *force*-log specific messages on only one of the two parties. Upon a failure of the party that cannot reconstruct the last relevant message, that party has to communicate with the other party to obtain the message. Further analysis shows that it is advantageous if the responsibility for force-logging messages is with the server, for the following reasons:

- The server communicates with many clients concurrently. Hence, it can exploit batching to improve the disk I/O efficiency of logging.

- The server usually processes multiple requests of different clients concurrently. Since it does not have to commit itself to an ordering of these requests until it sends replies, it can perform optimizations that are impossible in a general message-passing framework. However, this means that the server will not be piecewise deterministic between message events unless it does sufficient logging to be able to reconstruct the exact interleaving of database reads and writes. Such extensive logging can be expensive. Not interleaving request executions is unacceptable, as it leads to poor server throughput.

- The server is much more reliable, because it is carefully administered, than the clients are. Therefore, client applications may be willing to rely on the server's availability, but the server should never depend on the clients—quite an asymmetric situation.

Client-server problem scenario

To illustrate the complications that arise from the fact that the server executes requests concurrently and is thus *a priori* not piecewise deterministic, consider the example in Figure 17.5. When the first client fails and is restarted, it would try to replay its original execution by extracting the original user-input

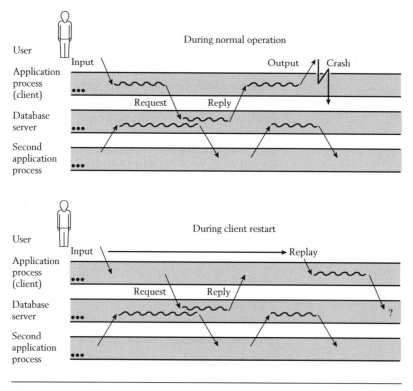

Figure 17.5 Problem scenario with replaying general client-server applications.

message from a log and reexecuting the program with this input until it reaches the point where the client would again send the request to the server. Note that it is guaranteed that the same request message will be constructed in the replayed execution because the original user input is used (as opposed to asking the user for entering some input again). But then, when the server receives the request again, it does not know whether it has previously processed the request or received a new request. Once it starts executing the request, however, the server can no longer guarantee that it will produce the same reply as the previous incarnation of the request, simply because the reply (and also the exact effects on the data) depends on the nondeterministic interleaving with other request-processing threads. In the example, because of the request processing on behalf of the second client, the server may well produce a different reply message this time. Once the client receives a different reply, however, the application program could possibly produce a different output to the user. Sending this output would definitely confuse the user, so that the failure is no longer masked. Suppressing the output, on the other hand, may make things even worse, because from now on the entire execution trajectory of the client program differs from that of the previous incarnation. So from this point on, application recovery in a way that is transparent to the human user becomes infeasible.

We could view the server's concurrent request executions as a set of message-passing threads, whose "messages" correspond to the interleaved accesses to the shared database, and each would have to be force-logged. Fortunately, the fact that the execution of interleaved requests is not exactly reproducible does not matter until the resulting effects propagate outside of the server, that is, when a reply is sent to a client. Thus, sending a reply *commits the state of the server*. From this point on, the server promises that it will *deterministically replay* a previously executed request if a failed and restarted client should resubmit the request. This commitment has three aspects: *Server considerations*

- *Re-create reply*: The reply for a resubmitted request must be identical to the original reply.

- *Redo database updates*: Effects of the original request on the server's database are redone if necessary, and the reexecution of a request is idempotent.

- *Isolate other requests*: The redo of database updates does not alter the data values previously read by concurrently executed requests.

Client applications, unlike the server, are piecewise deterministic between requests. Hence, to recover the state of a client application, we need merely log the external input that it has seen and initiate replay from a saved installation point. The client exploits the recoverable request-reply mechanism when a request-reply needs to be replayed to recover one of its applications. The replay of the application up to the point of the request guarantees that the request is *Client considerations* regenerated, the fundamental requirement placed on clients. A repeat of the request causes the redelivery of the reply to the client application.

Application installation points are generated at the client, where the application is executing. The client may choose to store its installation points on a server for reliable storage, but the server then treats the installation point information as regular data that it stores and retrieves upon the client's demand.

The client must also deal with input and output messages from and to the external world (e.g., the human user). It must log input messages and force them to stable storage promptly to minimize the frequency with which the user may have to resubmit input, so there is not much room for optimizations. Responsibility for logging these messages lies naturally with the client as the client receives them. For the rest of the discussion, we assume that the client logs such external input messages. Note, however, that the input message log entries should reside in the same stable log file that holds other client log entries.

There is no need to log output messages to the external world, as they can be deterministically re-created if the application fails and restarts. During the restart, previously sent output is suppressed, except when an output message is immediately followed by a failure. Then, it is impossible to tell if the user has already received the output, whatever logging might be done. Therefore, such a message is resent and may thus be seen twice by the user.

17.5.2 **Overview of the Server Reply Logging Algorithm**

The above considerations strongly suggest that the server should be responsible for the stable logging of reply messages. This enables fully independent server recovery after a failure; that is, the server becomes available again without exchanging information with clients (that may be unavailable at this time). Server independence is a major design goal. Once we decide on server reply logging, most other aspects of the solution are natural consequences of our analysis. If replies are recoverable, requests are recoverable as well. Client applications are piecewise deterministic, and hence their replay re-creates the request. So the server reply logging method need not perform any forced request logging on client or server. This leaves us with only one forced log I/O for each request-reply pair.

Server reply logging minimizes the server's forced logging frequency while providing the best solution in terms of recovery independence and fast server restart. The only aspect where it may be inferior to more client-centric approaches is a possibly increased restart time for client applications and that client recovery becomes dependent on the server. Given our design goals, especially server independence, and the fact that the client depends on the server in any event, these disadvantages are surely acceptable. Therefore, our method of choice is server reply logging. In this section we give a detailed description of the server reply logging method. We elaborate on the optimizations to minimize forcing the log and on the subtle details of log truncation, on both server and clients, to speed up restart and, ultimately, guarantee very high availability.

The server forces reply log entries to the log before sending a reply. It does this by flushing the database log buffer, including the write log entries of the corresponding request-reply pair, the reply log entry being the last log entry that must be written. In addition, the server may perform an optimization similar to group-commit (see Chapter 13); that is, it postpones sending a reply until either a timeout occurs or a sufficiently large batch of log entries has accumulated. It then writes the batch to the stable log in a single disk I/O.

The server can choose among a number of options for replaying requests. It knows when a request execution is incomplete so that an undo scheme is applicable given appropriate isolation. Equally, it can choose to replay a request to completion. Replay would now be necessary only for incomplete requests (i.e., when the reply is not yet stable). While these options require that the request and all database reads be logged in addition to the normally logged database writes, no additional forced log I/O is needed. Forcing the reply log entry ensures that all preceding log entries are written to the stable log as well. In fact, we will later show that there is an opportunity for further optimizations in this regard.

A failed and restarting client may resubmit requests, hence asking the server for some earlier replies. Because the server logs replies, the server is always able to look up the corresponding reply and send it back to the client without replaying its request. However, this may randomly access the server's stable log, a potential disk I/O efficiency problem. Therefore, the server keeps the reply log entries in a separate randomly accessible data structure—ideally in main memory—called the *message lookup table*. During recovery after a server failure, the server rebuilds this table from its stable log to avoid random I/Os to the log for resubmitted requests.

Message lookup table

From the client's viewpoint, a drawback of this method is that client restart time can be significantly longer than with client logging. Communication latency with a potentially highly loaded server to obtain the reply log entries is a serious issue. To ease this problem, the client can perform some *lazy logging*— writing reply log entries to stable storage in a nonforced manner whenever there is available disk bandwidth.

Lazy client logging

Client recovery dependency on log entries kept by the server causes subtle difficulties for log truncation at the server. Without an additional mechanism, the server would never be able to truncate its stable log, and the log scan time during a restart would grow without bound. To avoid this, clients inform the server when log entries are no longer needed by sending *stability notifications* to the server whenever the client

Log truncation based on stability notifications

- generates an installation point (log entries preceding an installation point are not needed for client recovery),

- makes reply log entries stable by additional lazy logging of replies at low priority.

The client can piggyback stability notifications on its regular messages to the server. Application recovery is not compromised when the server garbage-collects reply log entries that will never be used by a client.

17.5.3 **Data Structures**

In addition to the usual recovery data structures, the server reply logging method uses the following two data structures, instantiated at both the server and the client:

- an *active application table* (AT) that contains status information about ongoing (possibly failed or restarting) applications that the server or the client is responsible for

- a *message lookup table* (MT) that contains (log entries about) messages of active applications, most importantly, reply messages.

These data structures, illustrated in Figure 17.6 and described in detail in pseudocode notation below, reside in volatile storage with entries made stable by forcing them to the log.

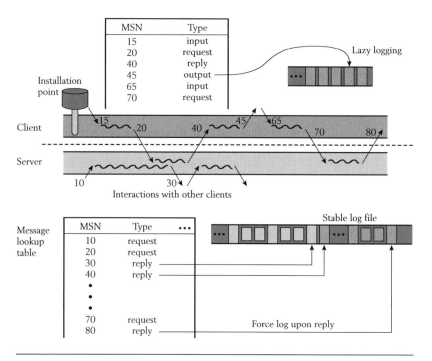

Figure 17.6 Data structures for the server reply logging method.

We explain the various fields as we discuss the algorithm. A message is tagged with

- an application identifier (AppID) that includes an encoding of the host client and is unique across all applications of all clients,
- a message sequence number (MSN) that is unique and monotonically increasing within each client application.

Messages include the input and output messages documenting client interactions with the external world.

Data structures of server reply logging method

```
AT: array[AppID] of record /* Active Application Table */
 LastMSN: integer;
 /* MSN of application's last message event (only relevant on client) */
 StableMSN: integer;
 /* MSN such that all prior message events of the application,
 including this one, are known to be on stable storage locally
 (only relevant on client) */
 RedoMSN: integer;
 /* MSN of the oldest non-obsolete message event
 (for the client, this is always the most recent installation point
 or the oldest MSN that follows it) */
 RedoLSN: integer;
 /* LSN of log entry that corresponds to the RedoMSN */
 end;
MT: array[AppID,MSN] of record /* Message Lookup Table */
   MsgType: (request, reply, input, output);
    /* input and output are only needed for client-to-user messages */
   MsgContents: array of char;
 end;
LF: persistent array[LSN] of record /* Stable Log File */
   LogRecType:
    (write, read, undo, request, reply, input, IP, start-IP, term-IP, CP);
   LogRecContents: array of char;
   AppID: integer;
   MSN: integer;
 end;
```

For convenience, we consider an application installation point (IP) as a message with an MSN, and we distinguish start and termination installation points (start-IP and term-IP) from the regular ones.

The client tracks the last used MSN for each application, by recording it as the LastMSN in the active application table. The client keeps two additional

MSN fields. The RedoMSN is the oldest MSN that follows the most recent installation point of the application or the installation point MSN itself if no more recent message exists. The StableMSN is the most recent MSN for which it and all smaller MSNs of the client have stable log entries. The client's StableMSN is the server's RedoMSN for the given application. All server message log entries on its stable log with an MSN smaller than the server RedoMSN of the corresponding application are obsolete and can be garbage-collected.

During the recovery analysis pass, relevant entries for the active application table and the message lookup table are recovered in volatile storage with information from the stable log. Thus, server recovery has the usual two scans over the stable log (analysis pass and redo pass), yet all relevant information on applications and reply messages is readily accessible for restarting clients.

17.5.4 **Server Logging during Normal Operation**

The server generates log entries for each of its database write operations and each request and reply message, as well as some additional temporary log entries to cope with incomplete requests, discussed below. These log entries are posted in a conventional log buffer, which is forced to disk whenever it is full or according to write-ahead-logging or force-at-commit rules. In addition, the log entries for messages are kept in the message lookup table described in the previous section. A reply log entry is forced to stable storage, by flushing the database log buffer, before the reply message is sent to the client. Making the reply log entry stable does not imply that we discard it from the message lookup table. Because a restarting client may re-request a log entry, keeping the reply in main memory can save random disk I/O on the stable log file.

To force a reply message, the server flushes its log buffer in a single atomic write to the log. If the message lookup table still contains the corresponding request message (which must have the largest preceding MSN of the application), then this message can be discarded once the atomic write to the stable log is completed.

Logging for incomplete requests   We need to take special care when the server fails in the middle of a request execution. Note that this problem arises with at most one request per active application, namely, the last, outstanding request of an application. The server has two principal options to achieve this goal:

1. *Roll back request and execute again:* The server knows when the original reply has not yet been sent to the client. Then it has no obligation to deterministically replay as long as all database writes of concurrently executed requests are kept isolated. Thus, the server can undo incomplete requests and reexecute them all as new requests with different

interleaving and effects. This requires that the effects of incomplete requests be kept isolated. Isolation typically holds if a request-reply interaction is inside one ACID transaction that uses, for example, strict two-phase locking. When a client request initiates a sequence of transactions on the server (e.g., a request that starts a mini-batch stored procedure on the server), undo requires compensating transactions. The effects of the original transactions would have to be kept quasi-isolated at a higher level of abstraction, taking into account application semantics.

2. *Redo/continue request execution:* To make the server's nondeterministic behavior deterministically replayable, the server logs all database reads as well as writes. To ensure deterministic replay after the reply message is sent, the server must flush the log buffer before sending the reply. This makes stable all read and write log entries generated for the completed request execution. During server restart, a missing reply for an unfinished request is reconstructed by redoing and completing the request. During replay, database reads and writes are intercepted. Writes are applied to the database using LSN testing for idempotence. There are two ways in which to handle reads:

(a) Log physical read operations that record the values read by database reads. During recovery, read values are extracted from the logged values. The danger is that logging read values can greatly increase the amount of data logged.

(b) Log logical read operations that record the occurrence of a database read and its source. During recovery, read values are reread from the database. Thus, recovery must read the same versions as originally read. However, current cache managers write pages back to the stable database in any order, and hence may overwrite the version required by a read. Thus, the cache manager must not overwrite a page whose prior version is still needed to replay a read, by tracking and enforcing flush-order dependencies (see Chapter 15). A danger is that flush-order dependencies may prevent the flushing of a dirty page (containing a version needed for recovery) for a very long time. Forced logging of the reply ends this flush-order dependency.

None of the options incurs additional forced log I/O for incomplete requests. Also, request log entries and either undo log entries or read log entries are irrelevant once the reply log entry is forced. Therefore, if any of these log entries are still in the log buffer, they can be safely discarded without being written. However, should these log entries be written to the stable log, they must appear in the log in their chronological order for correct recovery.

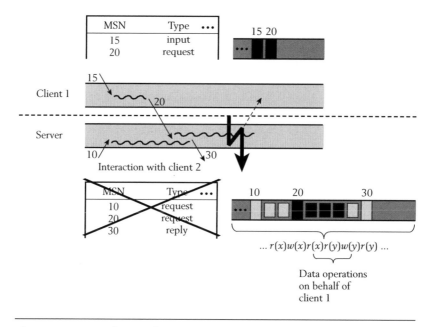

Figure 17.7 Server logging for replaying incomplete requests.

There is no clear choice among the above options. For concreteness, the pseudocode below is based on logging read values and redoing/continuing request executions (option 2a). This method based on read logging is illustrated in Figure 17.7. In this example, the server interleaves the execution of request 20 by client 1 with the execution of request 10 by client 2. The resulting data operations on behalf of client 1 are shown in black and labeled; all other data operations, shown in light gray, are performed on behalf of client 2. Note that this specific interleaving, which appears to be nonserializable, is feasible and correct when a client request spawns a sequence of ACID transactions (e.g., from the execution of stored procedures) with intermediate commits or transactions run under relaxed isolation levels (see Chapter 10). In this situation, the server's logging of data reads for request 20 (i.e., the additional logging of the $r(x)$ and $r(y)$ actions that precede the $w(y)$ update) allows the server to replay the request's execution up to its point of failure and continue from there without interfering with the already externalized effects of the concurrent request 10 shown in light gray.

Checkpoint log entries   As in standard database recovery, the server creates checkpoint (CP) log entries that contain certain bookkeeping information to shorten the analysis and redo pass of recovery. The CP log entries identify which parts of the log are irrelevant and effectively truncate the log. However, since we need to take into account both server and client needs, log truncation is more complicated

than with database recovery alone. We postpone the detailed discussion of this
until we have presented the client logging algorithm.

Server during
normal
operation

- after receiving a request message with MSN m from client application a:
  create log entry r in MT with r.MSN=m, r.AppID=a, r.MsgType=request,...
- upon read or write operations in the execution of a request with MSN m
  from client application a:
  if operation type is write then
   create a redo log entry r with r.MSN=m, r.AppID=a, r.LogRecType=write,...
  else /* read operation */
   create a read log entry r with r.MSN=m, r.AppID=a, r.LogRecType=read,...
  end /*if*/;
- before sending a reply message with MSN m to the client application a:
  create log entry r in MT with r.MSN=m, r.MsgType=reply,...
  append MT[a,m] to the database log buffer
  remove from the database log buffer
   all read and request log entries with MSN m - 1
  atomically write the database log buffer to the stable log
  if there exists MT[a,m-1] with MT[a,m-1].MsgType=request then
   discard MT[a,m-1] from MT
  end /*if*/;
- upon detecting a stability notification <a,m> or <term-IP,a,m>:
  if AT[a] does not yet exist then AT += a end /*if*/;
  AT[a].RedoMSN = m + 1
  Discard from MT all entries MT[a,k] with k ≤ m
  Create log entry r in the database log buffer with r.LogRecType=IP,
   r.MSN=m,...
  if type of IP is term-IP then
   force log entry r to the stable log
   AT -= a
   send acknowledgment to client
  end /*if*/;
- upon creating a checkpoint log entry r:
  r.LogRecType = CP
  r.LogRecContents = copy of AT
   (plus standard bookkeeping info, e.g., a copy of the DirtyPageTable)
  When r is written to the stable log,...
   write its LSN in the master record

17.5.5 Client Logging during Normal Operation

A client creates log entries for each request and reply exchange with the server.
In addition, it creates log entries for each input message from the external world
(human user or sensor/actor, e.g., in an embedded control system). These log

entries are kept in a message lookup table with the same layout as on the server. The client forces log entries for external input to the stable log immediately. The other messages are not forced to the stable log. Rather, the client writes them "lazily."

The client maintains a StableMSN for each application, which tracks by how much the client lags behind the server in terms of its stable message logging. The StableMSN is increased when the client writes a set of (chronologically) consecutive request and reply messages to the stable log. One concrete policy is to ensure that this "backlog" (relative to the server) is limited, by initiating a write to the stable log whenever LastMSN − StableMSN reaches some threshold.

Each application periodically generates an installation point, saving the entire process state of an application onto stable storage on a per-application basis, using a shadowing technique to provide atomicity of installation points. Each installation point is tagged with the MSN assigned to it and is thus self-describing. Once an installation point is completed, all earlier log entries of the corresponding application can be discarded. They are now lower than the RedoMSN for the application, which is advanced to the MSN of the IP log entry.

Client during normal operation   Like the server, the client can also occasionally write checkpoint log entries to allow truncation of its log. Only the "discarded" log entries above are truncated. The issue of log truncation is discussed in detail in the next subsection.

```
/* processing in response to messages received or sent */
CurrentMSN = AT[AppID].LastMSN ++;
```
- After completing an installation point of application a:
  ```
  AT[a].RedoMSN = CurrentMSN;
  Discard all entries r from MT with r.MSN < CurrentMSN;
  if type is application start-IP or regular IP then
   Create log entry r in MT
    with r.MSN=CurrentMSN, r.AppID=a, r.MsgType=IP or start-IP
   Piggyback stability notification <a,CurrentMSN> on next message to server
  else /* type is application term-IP */
   send stability notification message <term-IP,a,CurrentMSN> to server
   wait until message is acknowledged
   ActiveAppTable -= a
   Create log entry r with r.MSN=CurrentMSN,r.AppID=a, r.MsgType=term-IP
  end /*if*/;
  ```
- Before sending a request message to the server:
  ```
  Create log entry r in M with r.MSN=CurrentMSN, r.MsgType=request,...
  ```
- After receiving a reply message from the server:
  ```
  Create log entry r in M with r.MSN=CurrentMSN, r.MsgType=reply,...
  ```
- After receiving an input message from the external world:
  ```
  Create log entry r in M with r.MSN=CurrentMSN, r.MsgType=input,...
  Force log entry r to the stable log
  ```

```
/* processing independent of a specific message */
■ After writing a set R of message log entries from MT to the stable log:
  for each application a with a message in R do
  m = max r.MSN | r in R and r.AppID=a
  AT[a].StableMSN = m
  Piggyback stability notification <a,m> on next message to server
■ Upon creating a checkpoint log entry r:
  r.LogRecType = CP
  r.LogRecContents = copy of AT
  When r is written to the stable log,...
    write its returned LSN in the master record
```

17.5.6 **Log Truncation**

Both server and client continuously truncate obsolete parts of both the stable log file and the message lookup table. This is important to free disk and memory space and shorten the log tail scanned during the restart-redo pass. Log truncation, a form of garbage collection, is especially important for the server. If the server cannot delete log entries after some time, then its log processing upon restart becomes excessively long, and the server's availability is compromised by its role in application recovery. Below, we first consider when clients can discard log entries, which is the simpler of the two cases, and then discuss server log truncation.

A client discards all log entries and message lookup table entries of an active application at each new installation point for that application. However, when the client runs multiple applications simultaneously, this does not yet allow truncating the stable log, as other applications may still need old parts of the log. The client marks the progress for the installed application in the active application table by setting its RedoMSN entry to the MSN of the installation point. (For convenience, installation points are viewed as messages here, so that they can be identified by an MSN. We also tag installation points with the MSN of their associated log entry.) The minimum RedoMSN among all active applications then determines the part of the stable log that the client needs to keep. To reconstruct the minimum RedoMSN after a failure without having to scan the entire log, the client periodically generates a checkpoint log entry that contains the active application table. This is a standard technique of database-style logging and recovery, applied here to application message logging. The applications play the role of dirty database pages.

Client log truncation

As the server does not itself install applications, it has no direct information about when it can safely discard log entries and thus truncate its stable log. The server relies on the clients notifying it about their steps that allow it to discard log entries. These stability notifications need not incur extra messages, as the relevant information is piggybacked on the next request message. The

Server log truncation based on client stability notifications

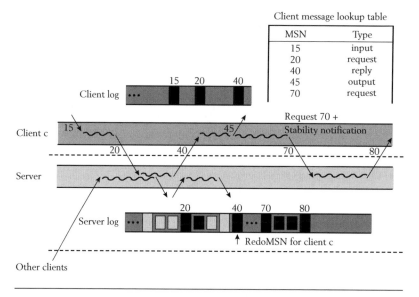

Figure 17.8 Server log truncation based on stability notifications.

client steps that trigger a stability notification are an application installation or the writing of reply log entries to the client stable log. In both cases, the client increases its StableMSN, and it is this that is sent to the server. Upon receiving a stability notification with StableMSN m, the server discards all entries of its message lookup table with MSNs smaller than or equal to m. The server also sets the application's RedoMSN in the active application table to the smallest MSN higher than m and adjusts the corresponding system RedoLSN accordingly.

This technique is illustrated in Figure 17.8. In this scenario the client in the figure's upper half has recorded the events with MSNs 15, 20, 40, 45, and 70 (which correspond to the depicted client-server interactions) in its message lookup table, but only the events up to MSN 40 have been written to the client's stable log. The request with MSN 70 then contains a stability notification with StableMSN 40, which allows the server to advance its RedoMSN for this particular client to 40 (or actually the smallest MSN of this client that is larger than 40). This in turn may facilitate garbage collection on the server log provided that no earlier log entries for other clients, depicted as light gray boxes on the server log, are needed anymore.

The server does not need to make the changes to its message lookup table and active application table stable. It should, however, generate a log entry to mark this event in the log, but this (very short) log entry need not be forced. Consequently, when the server fails, it may not remember that it effectively truncated its stable log, and it may scan the log starting from overly old RedoMSNs. This does not affect correctness, and the stale RedoMSN information will usually be updated soon by the next stability notification from the client.

The only case where a stale RedoMSN could result in a permanent and critical problem is the server loss of a stability notification from a terminating application that will not send more notifications. Log entries for this application would become permanently unreclaimed garbage, forever preventing the server from truncating its log. Thus, we require that stability notifications for application termination be specially tagged. The server must force a term-IP log entry to the log or generate a checkpoint log entry with an updated copy of the entire active application table. The client must await an acknowledgment from the server before it can remove the application from its own active application table and thus commit the termination.

17.5.7 **Server Restart**

After a server failure, the server restarts by performing an analysis pass and a redo pass over the stable log. The analysis pass starts from the most recent checkpoint log entry (found by looking up the master record, see Chapter 13) and scans all log entries until the end of the log. For application recovery, this pass rebuilds the active application table. This table is reinitialized from the checkpoint log entry, and is then updated whenever the log scan encounters an installation point log entry for an application. At the end of the analysis pass, the server knows for which applications it may have to re-create replies. It also knows a RedoMSN and a corresponding RedoLSN for each application, bounding the part of the log that contains the required reply log entries.

The redo pass then starts from the minimum of RedoMSNs among active applications or the minimum RedoLSN among dirty database pages, whichever is older. For client application recovery, we focus on the redo of the message log entries, understanding that request execution can write to pages of the database, and hence that we must, in this redo scan, do normal database redo as well. The server redo pass rebuilds the message lookup table, restoring it to its state as of the crash. The server can then deliver logged replies to resubmitted requests in case a client application has failed and is itself restarting.

A case that needs special consideration is the handling of incomplete request executions where the server has logged redo steps for database writes of a request. Then the request log entry itself and corresponding undo or read log entries are guaranteed to be on the stable log at their original points in the interleaved request execution history. We consider two cases:

- Undo log entries permit the server to undo the database writes of all incomplete requests, subsequently reexecuting these requests as if they were new requests and regenerating the corresponding replies (option

1 in the earlier discussion of logging for incomplete requests, valid for isolated request-reply interactions only).

- Read log entries permit the server to deterministically replay the partial execution of the incomplete requests and then continue executing the requests to completion (options 2a and 2b in the discussion of logging for incomplete requests).

The replies are then handled like replies during normal operation: they are inserted into the message lookup table, forced to the stable log, and finally, sent to the client. From this point on, the server is in its normal operation mode. Client requests that are lost because the request log entry is not forced are

Server restart   reexecuted when the client resubmits the request.

```
initialization:
 locate most recent checkpoint log entry cp (from master record)
 initialize AT = cp.AT /* and initialize DirtyPageTable, etc. */
 initialize ReplayList = empty set
 /* incomplete requests to be replayed and completed */
analysis pass:
 for each log entry r between most recent checkpoint log entry and end of log
 do
  if AT[r.AppID] does not yet exist then AT += r.AppID end /*if*/;
  case r.LogRecType of
   term-IP: AT -= r.AppID
   Other IP: AT[r.AppID].RedoMSN = r.MSN + 1
   write: maintain DirtyPageTable (as in standard data recovery)
   request: ReplayList += <r.AppID,r.MSN>
   reply: ReplayList -= <r.AppID,r.MSN-1>
   otherwise: skip log entry
 end /*for*/;
 restartMSN = min{a.RedoMSN such that a in AT}
 restartLSN = min{min{a.RedoLSN | a in AT},
                  min{x.RedoLSN | x in DirtyPageTable}}
redo pass:
 for each log entry r between restartLSN and end of log do
  case r.LogRecType of
   write: redo database update, using LSN testing for idempotence
   read: if <r.AppID,r.MSN> in ReplayList then
            pass r.LogRecContents (the read value)
            to request execution thread end /*if*/;
   reply: if AT[r.AppID] exists and r.MSN >= AT[r.AppID].RedoMSN then
            insert r into MT end /*if*/;
          if MT[a,r.MSN-1] exists with MT[a,r.MSN-1].MsgType=request then
            discard MT[a,r.MSN-1] end /*if*/;
```

```
request: if AT[r.AppID] exists and r.MSN >= AT[r.AppID].RedoMSN then
            insert r into MT end /*if*/;
if <r.AppID,r.MSN> in ReplayList then
    activate request execution thread end /*if*/;
otherwise: skip log entry
for each activated request execution thread <a,m> in ReplayList do
complete request execution and generate reply
```

17.5.8 Client Restart

Client restart also consists of analysis and redo passes over its stable log. The analysis pass is identical to the server's and rebuilds the active application table. The redo pass, however, differs from the server's. The server merely rebuilds bookkeeping data that may be needed by failed clients. Client recovery actually restarts the applications active at the client failure, resuming their execution in a way that is transparent to the human user. This leads to the following differences.

The RedoMSN of an application identifies the oldest log entry needed for recovery, the installation point log entry, or the application log entry following it. Note that the RedoMSN determined by the analysis pass is a lower bound on the real RedoMSN. It is possible for an installation point to occur just before the system fails and for the log entry describing it not to reach the stable log. In this case, a better RedoMSN can be determined from reading the application installation point and examining its tag MSN.

The redo pass scans the log from the oldest RedoMSN of all applications in the reconstructed active application table. We process the log entries of all applications at this client in a single pass over the log as opposed to making a separate pass per application. This is an important optimization for clients running middle-tier application services with a large number of concurrently active applications. Each application is reincarnated upon encountering its analysis-determined RedoMSN log entry (i.e., the lower bound for the RedoMSN) during the redo pass. The MSN that tags the application installation point is then used to determine the true RedoMSN, which may be later because the system may have failed before the stable writing of the log entry for this installation point. All log entries for the application are ignored until the true RedoMSN is encountered. This is the application analog to the way that updates to data pages are bypassed when the log entry LSN for the update is less than the LSN stored on the page.

An application then reexecutes asynchronously to the further redo processing of the log (i.e., in a separate process or thread). As in normal operation, application requests are intercepted. At these points, either client recovery has already encountered the corresponding reply log entry or the application process pauses until it is encountered. If the reply has been encountered, then it is replayed. Otherwise the application waits and replays the reply when it shows up on the log. Application replay proceeds after the reply has been redone. Note that with asynchronous application reexecution, restart is substantially faster, which is especially important if applications perform long computations between server interactions.

The redo pass over the log proceeds in parallel with application reexecution. It re-creates the message lookup table to the state as of the last stable log entry. During the application reexecution, user-input messages are consumed from the message lookup table, and output messages to the user can be re-created as part of the application reexecution. All output messages that are known to be followed by a log entry of that application are suppressed (i.e., not sent to the user), as they would be duplicated.

There is a chance of repeating the final output message or of missing the final input message. Regardless of how quickly we force the log, a system failure can occur between the time of the input and the time when the input is logged. The best that we can do is to reduce the probability that this will occur. Similarly, on output, it is possible for the output to be lost before the user sees it, even if it were sent. Regardless of logging, it is impossible to tell whether the user has seen the output or not until the user acknowledges the message in some way. Thus, the last (unacknowledged) output must be re-presented.

For requests and replies, the client's analysis pass also reconstructs the StableMSN for each active application. So the redo pass knows which log entries it will eventually encounter on its stable log. All other, more recent reply log entries have to be retrieved from the server. However, the client does not know its exact point of failure; so it does not know if there are additional log entries on the server. When application reexecution reaches the last locally logged reply, application execution simply continues beyond this point and reenters normal operation. The client executes the application until the next interception point and sends the request to the server. The client cannot (and does not have to) tell whether this request is a resend or if it is the original send. On a resend, the server sends back a previously logged reply. For a new request, the server does its normal request execution. An obvious optimization is to ask the server, right after the client's analysis pass, to asynchronously ship the reply log entries that are more recent than the client's StableMSN. This *Client restart* approach is more complicated and therefore not pursued here.

```
initialization:
 locate most recent checkpoint log entry cp (from master record)
 initialize AT = cp.AT
analysis pass:
 for each log entry r between most recent checkpoint log entry and end of log
 do
  AT[r.AppID].StableMSN=r.MSN;
  case r.LogRecType of
```

```
    start-IP: AT += r.AppID
    term-IP: AT -= r.AppID
    Other IP: AT[r.AppID].RedoMSN = r.MSN
    otherwise: skip log entry
 end /*for*/;
 for each a in AT do
  inspect tag MSN of most recent IP file
  if tag MSN > AT[a].RedoMSN then AT[a].RedoMSN = tag MSN
  restartMSN = mina.RedoMSN | a in AT end /*if*/;
 end /*for*/;
redo pass:
 for each log entry r between restartMSN and end of log do
  if r.AppID in AT then
   if r.MSN = AT[r.AppID].RedoMSN
   /* r is the application's most recent installation point */
   then
    spawn execution thread and asynchronously execute application a
   else
    if r.MSN > AT[r.AppID].RedoMSN and r.LogRecType = reply or input
    then insert r into MT else skip r end /*if*/;
   end /*if*/;
  else skip r
  end /*if*/;
asynchronous execution of application a:
 intercept application upon reaching a message event with MSN m
 case MsgType of
 request: if MT[a,m+1] exists /* corresponding reply is (already) in MT */
          then generate reply from MT[a,m+1] and
           resume application past event m + 1
          else if m + 1 <= AT[a].StableMSN
          then wait until message log entry m + 1 in the local redo pass
          else send request to server (resume normal client operation)
          end /*if*/;
          end /*if*/;
 input: if MT[a,m] exists then
          generate input message from MT[a,m]
          consume input into application state
          and resume application past event m
        else wait until message log entry m in the local redo pass
        end /*if*/;
 output: if analysis pass has seen a log entry with MSN higher than m then
           suppress output                    .
         else send output to user
         end /*if*/;
```

17.5.9 **Correctness Reasoning**

In this section we present a correctness proof for the server reply logging algorithm, with emphasis on the structure of the correctness reasoning rather than on mathematically detailed proof steps. To this end, we first develop a formal correctness criterion for the message exchanges between client and server and the recovery of messages. Once this criterion is proven for the presented algorithm, we can then easily derive the result that applications appear to the human user as if they are executed exactly once.

Correctness criterion　　Consider a set of processes $P_1, \ldots, P_m$ that exchange messages. Other than being influenced by received messages, they perform deterministic state transitions. The state of a process is volatile and may be lost upon a process failure. The state can be saved to disk by creating occasional installation points. We reason about dependencies among the states of the different processes and the interaction events between them. A state of a process is defined as the sequence of interaction events that the process is aware of in this state. Process execution builds an expanding sequence of events. Note that this notion of state is local to a process; there is no global state so far.

The relevant types of events are the following:

- $install_i$: Process P_i generates an installation point for its state.

- $send_i(j, m)$: Process P_i sends message m to process P_j (this is an event in process P_i only).

- $receive_i(j, m)$: Process P_i receives message m from process P_j (this is an event in process P_i only).

For each process we distinguish three different states:

- The volatile state of process P_i, $VS(P_i)$, is the state that contains all events of P_i up to now.

- The installed state of process P_i, $IS(P_i)$, is the state that contains all events of P_i up to and including the most recent installation point of P_i. (Note that "most recent" is well defined by referring to a sequence of events.)

- The recovered state of process P_i, $RS(P_i)$, is the state reconstructed during restart after a failure, before new steps are executed. Reconstruction is based on stable (i.e., failure-resilient) information that the process can access, locally or remotely.

The installed state is always a subsequence (i.e., order-preserving subset) of the recovered state, which in turn is a subsequence of the volatile state. (We restrict ourselves to redo recovery and do not consider possible undo steps.)

The human user or external world is modeled as a separate process whose volatile state always coincides with its installed state.

Based on the presented computational model, we can now express the following fundamental correctness criterion, which essentially states that each message exchange is atomic for both the sender and the receiver and is re-creatable once the message has been received:

If P_i is in volatile state s_{ik} and it has previously sent a message to P_j, which has received the message and is now in volatile state s_{jl} (i.e., send$_i(j, m) \in s_{ik}$ and receive$_j(i, m) \in s_{jl}$), then the following conditions must hold for all such messages:

1. *Enforce causal consistency:*
   receive$_j(i, m) \in RS(P_j)$ /* the receive is guaranteed to persist */
   $\Rightarrow$ send$_i(j, m) \in RS(P_i)$ /* if the sender fails, the send can be replayed */

   Causal consistency

2. *Ensure re-creatability of received messages:*
   send$_i(j, m) \in RS(P_i)$ /* the send is guaranteed to persist */
   $\Rightarrow$ receive$_j(i, m) \in RS(P_j)$ /* if the receiver fails, the message can be re-created */

   Message re-creatability

The first condition is the well-known causal consistency often encountered in reasoning about distributed states. It is required to ensure deterministic replay, which is our goal. The second condition copes with a process failing shortly after having received a message. If the send persists, the receiver must recover the receive, too. However, that the send is guaranteed to be recovered does not imply that the message can be re-created, since the recovery of the sender may be based on an installation point rather than replaying message events. So the receive must itself be made part of the receiver's recovered state.

The major argument for the correctness of the server reply logging algorithm is the following theorem:

THEOREM 17.3

The server reply logging algorithm ensures causal consistency and the re-creatability of sent messages.

Correctness theorem

Proof

The argument is a case analysis on the various message types. We need to consider three process classes: server, client, and user. For each case, we can use induction on the length of a process state (recall that states are sequences of events) to construct the proof. We consider only one application per client; the arguments trivially carry over to multiple applications.

Case 1: Messages between client and server

We show that both request and reply messages are in *RS*(client) if and only if they are in *RS*(server).

Case 1a: Reply messages

In the absence of failure, the server sends each reply. Either the client will eventually log it or the client application will perform an installation point. The reply then becomes part of *RS*(client). Hence, we consider server failure and its restart, and the server's efforts to preserve the reply messages upon which the client relies.

Because the client relies on the server regenerating the reply, those replies successfully preserved at the server will also be in *RS*(client). A reply message becomes part of *RS*(server) once the server forces the reply to the log. Before the server's forced log I/O, the reply is obviously not in *RS*(client) either. After this point, the reply is in both *RS*(server) and *RS*(client), in the absence of log truncation at the server, which we consider next.

That the server does not discard log entries too early follows from the log truncation protocol. The server keeps all reply log entries with an MSN higher than the highest MSN declared to it in a client's stability notification. The stability notifications in turn have the client's StableMSN as an upper bound. Therefore, we obtain the invariant:

$$Server.RedoMSN \leq \{m \mid client\ has\ sent\ stability\ notification\ with\ MSN\ m\} + 1$$
$$\leq Client.StableMSN + 1$$

Furthermore, the client garbage-collects only message log entries older than its RedoMSN. The client RedoMSN is the oldest log entry needed to recover the client. That is, either it is the MSN of the most recent application installation point or it is the first application log entry following that installation point. Thus, all messages older than and including the client's RedoMSN are in *RS*(client). So we have the invariant:

$$Client.RedoMSN \leq Client.MSN\ (most\ recent\ IP) + 1$$

Both invariants together show that server and client together cover the entire interval of reply MSNs from the most recent installation point through the last sent reply. The client is guaranteed to cover all MSNs until and including its StableMSN, and the server is guaranteed to cover all MSNs from the client's StableMSN until the last sent reply.

Case 1b: Request messages

First, we claim that all request messages in the client's volatile state, *VS*(client), are also in its recovered state, *RS*(client). The reason for this is that a client is piecewise deterministic. The client's specific interaction pattern, apart from input and output messages, always alternates requests and replies, with the client application suspended in between the two events.

- First, we show that all output messages of *VS*(client) are in *RS*(client). To verify this claim, consider the last message event of a client preceding an output message. Because of the client's passiveness when it waits for a reply, the last preceding event cannot be a request. Input messages, reply messages, and installation points are known to be in *RS*(client); so if the last preceding event falls into one of these classes, the output message is in *RS*(client) because the client can deterministically replay it. Therefore, we need consider only the case when the last preceding event is also an output message. For this case, we can now show by induction that all output messages are in *RS*(client).

- Now consider request messages. Analogously to the argument for output messages, we consider the last message event of a client preceding the request. This can be either an installation point, an input or output message, or a reply message (but it can never be another request). Since we know that all of these are in *RS*(client), the piecewise deterministic execution of the client ensures that the request can be re-created and hence is in *RS*(client).

Now assume that a request in *RS*(client) is not in *RS*(server), which is the only case that could violate the correctness criterion. There are two cases to consider:

- When the server has already force-logged the reply for this request, then the reply is in *RS*(server). Hence, the request is in *RS*(server), too, because the server will simply deliver again the logged reply when the request is re-presented.

- When the server has not yet logged the reply, the client is guaranteed to resubmit the request either upon a restart of a client failure or because of a timeout if the server has failed. Therefore, in both cases the request is also in *RS*(server).

Case 2: Messages between client and user

We must show that all input and output messages (except the last such message, for which we do not provide complete recovery) are in *RS*(client) if and only if they are in *RS*(user).

The *RS*(user) state, by definition of transparent recovery, has all input and output messages that the user sends or receives, except perhaps the last output message. So, it surely contains all but the last message. We need to show that these messages are also in *RS*(client).

- The client force-logs every input message promptly, i.e., before the next input message arrives. Hence, all input messages, except perhaps the last, are on the client's log. Hence, only the last input message might be lost. All others are in *RS*(client) because they are on the client's log.

■ For output messages, recall that the client application is piecewise deterministic. Hence, by having all input and reply messages in *RS*(client), and by the argument presented in case 1 above, the client application is deterministic and can reconstruct the output messages. Hence, all output messages (including the last) are in *RS*(client) without their needing to be explicitly logged.

This concludes the proof.

The atomicity and re-creatability of all message exchanges between client and server in conjunction with the fact that user-input messages are immediately force-logged leads us to the following corollary:

COROLLARY 17.1

Once a client application has started (i.e., its start-IP has been taken), it is guaranteed to appear to the human user as if it is executed exactly once.

This final corollary states that both client and application failures can be recovered in a way that the failures are masked to the human user, to the best possible extent. Only under rare circumstances, the last output message before a client crash may be sent twice, or some entered user input that could not be force-logged quickly enough before a client crash interrupted the application process may have to be reentered.

17.5.10 **Applicability to Multi-tier Architectures**

Our detailed presentation of the server reply logging method in the preceding subsections has been based on a two-tier client-server system architecture. However, the algorithm is applicable in three-tier, and even more general multi-tier, federated systems given that certain prerequisites are satisfied. The key property on which we have built is that a client runs a single application process and that this application is piecewise deterministic. So the application should be single threaded, should use only synchronous messages where a process is suspended after sending a message and waits until the reply message is received, and should not depend on real-time events such as timers and other external signals.

Although the above property appears to be fairly restrictive at first glance, many Internet applications, including three-tier applications, easily meet these conditions. The trick is that we can view a more complex, multi-threaded application as if it were a set of virtual clients, each running its own single-threaded application. This approach works fine as long as there is no application-relevant shared state among threads. So the only deeper problem would be asynchronous events such as interrupting an application upon an external signal, but these mechanisms are used very infrequently in mainstream business applications.

Once we have conceptually decomposed a complex application, we realize that it also does not matter whether the application runs on a dedicated client machine or on a middle-tier application server (e.g., a Web server). The application server even runs multiple applications, but they can be handled as if they were multiple clients unless there was shared state among the applications of application-noticeable relevance (i.e., discounting low-level state data such as request queues, buffers, etc.). The application server would run the server part of the general algorithm developed in this section with regard to each of its clients, and it would run the client part with regard to the data servers that it interacts with. This way the algorithm can be cascaded along a hierarchy of servers, so that even multi-tier federated applications fall into the scope of applicability. This does not mean, however, that the algorithm is ready for all possible e-Service applications on the Internet. There are, of course, complex applications such as decentralized auctions or collaborative authoring that require even more far-reaching forms of application recovery. Such applications call for future research on recovery guarantees for arbitrary multi-tier systems.

17.6 **Lessons Learned**

Application recovery involves recovery measures for data, messages, and processes, the latter two being novel issues relative to the previous chapters' focus on data server recovery. A limited kind of message and process recovery that has gained extreme importance in OLTP applications is based on transactional, recoverable message queues. For simple applications that consist of a single user interaction with a single data-oriented transaction in between the user input and the delivery of the output, queued transactions are a simple paradigm for ensuring an exactly-once execution. This solution consists of three transactions: the first one, executed by the client, enqueues the user's request; the second transaction, executed by the server, dequeues the request, processes it against the data, and enqueues the reply; the third one, again executed by the client, finally dequeues the reply and delivers the user output. With testable user-output devices, this approach can even guarantee that user output is delivered exactly once.

The fact that such simple, stateless applications do not "live" across user interactions implies that there is no need for explicit recovery of the application process. When we move on to conversational applications that repeat the above input-processing-output cycle, some amount of process state information needs to be maintained in a recoverable way. By keeping this state data in the recoverable messages and continuing the transactional dequeueing and enqueueing of request and reply messages along the entire conversation, queued transactions are generalized to provide exactly-once execution and at-least-once output delivery for some classes of stateful and conversational applications, including long-lived workflows. In addition to the server transactions that combine operations on their data and the message queue, this solution requires the client to dequeue a reply, present output to the user, receive the next input, and enqueue the next request all in one transaction. This way the chain of successive transactions never becomes broken. Because of the limitation to a small amount of process state data and the fact that the approach provides isolation only for a single step rather than the entire chain, this technique has become known as pseudo-conversational transactions.

Despite their fairly wide practical applicability, the above techniques that combine message and process recovery based on queues are inherently limited. Modern applications with "rich" state, such as office automation or cooperative work tools, require more general methods of application recovery with explicit provision for process recovery in addition to message recovery. One such method is the server reply logging algorithm, which we have presented in much detail in this chapter. This algorithm makes the data server responsible for recovering all reply messages. Under the assumption that client applications are piecewise deterministic and force-log all user-input messages, applications can thus be deterministically replayed, including their effects on the server in the presence of concurrent request executions. This holds regardless of whether the requests consist of multiple transactions on the server data or are embedded in a single transaction across multiple request-reply pairs, and it also holds for relaxed isolation levels that do not enforce transactional serializability.

For efficiency the server reply logging method maintains a message lookup table at the server to aid the application recovery of its clients; if the server crashes, its recovery reconstructs this table during the usual redo pass over the stable log with very little extra cost for the server recovery. To speed up the application restart at the client side, a client may periodically take an installation point, saving the application process state on disk, and may also lazily write its own log entries for server replies in a nonforced manner. In summary, this method provides transparent application recovery that masks almost all failures to the human user for a very general class of client-server applications, and it is even considerably more efficient, in terms of forced log I/O, than the techniques based on queued transactions.

Exercises

17.1 Extend the pseudocode for stateless queued transactions in a two-tier architecture, given in Section 17.2, to include the case of testable output devices such as automatic teller machines. The extended pseudocode should have the value-added property that, once a user input is successfully enqueued, the corresponding output message is delivered exactly once.

17.2 State an explicit correctness theorem, similar to the ones given in Sections 17.2 and 17.3, for workflows whose state transitions are "protected" by queued transactions as explained in Section 17.4.

17.3 Consider a conversational client application such as the travel reservation scenario of Section 17.3. Compare the number and data volume of forced log I/Os for running this application as a pseudo-conversational queued transaction chain versus using the general server reply logging method of Section 17.5, to provide application recovery. Assume that the queue manager resides on the data server, and forced logging is required only upon the commit of a transaction.

17.4 Construct a concrete example, with concrete transaction identifiers, page numbers, and so on, that shows the necessity for the data server to log data read operations on behalf of client requests for the general client-server application recovery, based on the server reply logging method of Section 17.5.

Hint: Consider, for example, a client request that invokes a stored procedure on the data server whose execution consists of a sequence of transactions.

17.5 Discuss possible generalizations of the server reply logging method for general client-server applications in the following settings:

(a) client applications that interact with more than one data server;

(b) a data server that itself invokes requests on another data server, for example, to resolve a higher-level data view or wrapped ADT-style object interface by collecting some of the underlying data from a remote site, or to propagate high-level updates onto the underlying base data (e.g., by firing remote triggers), including the important case of maintaining replicated data at multiple sites;

(c) a three-tier architecture where the applications run on the middle-tier application server.

Hint: Lomet and Weikum (1998) provide some high-level ideas about possible generalizations and also point out difficulties in specific kinds of extensions.

Bibliographic Notes

Queued transactions, including the variant of pseudo-conversational transactions, have been implemented in TP monitors and used in OLTP applications for about three decades. These developments are documented in great detail in the textbooks by Gray and Reuter (1993) and Bernstein and Newcomer (1997). Probably the first scientific paper that explains transactional queues in a systematic, product-independent manner was by Bernstein et al. (1990). The use of transactional guarantees and, particularly, queued transactions for work-flow management has been proposed and investigated by Reuter et al. (1992), Alonso et al. (1995), Salzberg and Tombroff (1996), Muth et al. (1998), and Weikum (1999).

Application recovery based on recoverable processes and messages was pioneered around 1980 for fault-tolerant computer architectures, as documented in the papers by Bartlett (1981), Borr (1981, 1984), and Borg et al. (1983, 1989). Kim (1984) gave a survey on this generation of fault-tolerant systems, which were typically used for extremely mission-critical high-end OLTP-style applications only. Freytag et al. (1987) made an early proposal on how to generalize such approaches. Gray (1986) and Härder (1987) have provided insightful discussions on how fault-tolerant computer architectures can be combined with the transaction paradigm. Application recovery as a "commodity" option for modern applications has been revived by Lomet (1998a). Our exposition on general-purpose client-server application recovery has followed Lomet and Weikum (1998). Message logging and recovery for message-passing computations has been intensively investigated in the distributed computing research community for many years, with major results contributed or reviewed in papers by Strom and Yemini (1985) as well as Strom et al. (1988), Johnson and Zwaenepoel (1987, 1990), and Alvisi and Marzullo (1995). This work has had little impact on deployed systems, however, for reasons related to impractical assumptions as further explained by Huang and Wang (1995).

PART FOUR

Coordination of Distributed Transactions

CHAPTER EIGHTEEN

Distributed Concurrency Control

No culture can live if it attempts to be exclusive.
—*Mahatma Gandhi*

People of the world together join to serve the common cause.
—*Bertolt Brecht*

18.1 **Goal and Overview**

Up to now we have continuously assumed that the data server under consideration is *centralized*, meaning that all the data (at least conceptually) resides in one place and that this place is under the control of one server that processes the requests sent by clients or by application servers. As we have pointed out in Chapter 1 already, for many present-day application scenarios this view is no longer appropriate; it is often unreasonable to assume that all the information processing needs of an application can be satisfied through a single data server. Instead, modern enterprises are typically based upon a *distributed* architecture comprising multiple application and data servers. These servers can be homogeneous or heterogeneous in terms of products, interfaces, and protocols, and they can either be largely autonomous or reliant on other servers. As a result, we are generally looking at a federated architecture as we have previously seen in Figure 1.3. For ease of reference, we show this architecture here again in Figure 18.1.

In this part of the book we look at concurrency control and recovery in federated architectures; this chapter will deal with the former topic and the next one with the latter. When data is distributed across multiple servers, essentially two cases can arise that have to be dealt with for both concurrency control and recovery. First, the servers participating in the federation can logically be part of a single system; we can then assume that they all run the same suite of protocols, and they may even be under the control of a "master site" that manages global information pertaining to the entire system (however, this master site

Homogeneous vs. heterogeneous federations

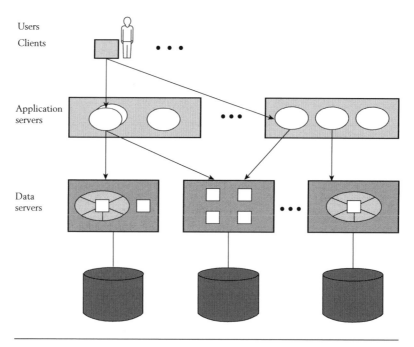

Figure 18.1 Federated system architecture.

will rarely be seen by applications). Second, the servers in the federation can be entirely autonomous and independent of each other; it is just that they are addressed together by some application server with a particular set of requests. In this case, we cannot assume uniformity across the federation with respect to protocols, and we will show that this makes the situation potentially harder to deal with. On the other hand, the second, heterogeneous, scenario is the more realistic one in applications; in the case of database servers, variations that occur in a federation may specifically refer to the data model used, the SQL version and options employed (e.g., isolation levels, see Chapter 10), and the programming language interfaces adopted, as well as to system implementation concepts. We mention that federated systems in which all servers are database servers are often called *multidatabase systems* in the literature.

From an application's or user's point of view, a homogeneous federation is characterized by *distribution transparency*—the federation is perceived by the outside world as if it were not distributed at all. Thus, for example, details of data placement and locality or request servicing are hidden and need not be taken into account when placing a request. Ideally, we can think of a homogeneous federation as providing identical functionality at all sites, so that it is immaterial to which site a particular service request is sent. On the other hand, in a heterogeneous federation the participating sites are autonomous, so that an application placing a request may well have to decide which server(s) to send the request to and how to handle results.

With respect to transactions and concurrency control in federated systems, we can use the same models as before: the page as well as the object model, schedules and histories, and suitable adaptations of the various protocols (details below). Conceptually, transactions in a homogeneous system are ordinary transactions, whereas in a heterogeneous system a transaction accessing several servers may interfere with transactions that a particular server is processing locally. Thus, we have local as well as global transactions in the latter case, and we only have to deal with global transactions in the former case. It will turn out that this distinction puts some burden on the concurrency control problem. In particular, this distinction carries over to schedules and histories; that is, there are local histories under execution at a single server, and there are global histories under execution by multiple servers, maybe even according to different conditions. The crucial point will be to make local correctness—that is, serializability at each site—sufficient for global correctness.

Local vs. global transactions and schedules

We start in Section 18.2 by reviewing correctness and looking at concurrency control in homogeneous federations, which are natural generalizations of centralized servers as we have discussed them up to now in this book. Since all transactions can essentially be assumed to be global, and since we can assume that all servers run the same concurrency control protocol, it is near at hand to study generalizations of protocols such as 2PL or TO, which are mostly straightforward, yet need to be equipped with some "global control" that makes sure the individual servers produce compatible serialization orders. For example, if one server serializes transaction t before transaction t', while another server serializes t' before t, we obtain a cycle, which is locally invisible and globally unacceptable. Another complication for homogeneous servers is the danger of deadlocks, which are not as easy to detect and deal with, since again, control as well as possibilities of observation are now distributed. We examine various algorithmic approaches to the deadlock detection problem, which are important in practice, in Section 18.3. The considerations in Sections 18.2 and 18.3 apply equally to page model and object model transactions. For ease of explanation, we will use page model terminology.

Applicability to page model and object model

We start discussing transaction processing and concurrency control for heterogeneous federations in Section 18.4. For correctness purposes, we adapt conflict serializability, which now has to account for the problems related to the presence of local transactions. A new situation is that global transactions that are not in conflict at all when considered by themselves may be involved in indirect conflicts through the presence of a local transaction. Having established a notion of global conflict serializability, we look in Section 18.5 into the question of how to enforce this property. It will turn out that seemingly "innocent" criteria such as rigorousness or commit ordering play an important role in this context; if local sites stick to one of these conditions, global correctness is guaranteed. Having laid the foundations for concurrency control protocols, we present several such protocols in Section 18.6. The important point here will be to make local conflicts between global transactions observable from a global perspective; typical techniques involve the use of so-called tickets for global transactions. Section 18.7 discusses the applicability of such techniques to the object model and generalizations for handling global transactions with semantically rich operations. Finally, we look at coherency and concurrency control for data-sharing clusters in Section 18.8.

18.2 Concurrency Control in Homogeneous Federations

In this section we look into the concurrency control problem for homogeneous federations. As we have said already, this type of system does not require any fundamental changes in our model of transactions, histories, and schedules. However, since most notions are useful for heterogeneous federations as well and as we later want to emphasize the differences, we collect a few preliminaries first. Then, we consider the question of how to adapt the protocols we have described in Chapter 4 for centralized systems to the situation where transactions are globally executed in a distributed, but still homogeneous environment. We will not look at each protocol we have described previously in the same detail as before. On the one hand, we have seen already that not all of them are practically relevant; on the other hand, some are easy to generalize to a distributed scenario, and some are not.

18.2.1 Preliminaries

(Global) transactions
We consider a fixed number of sites across which the data is distributed. The server at site i, $1 \leq i \leq n$, is responsible for a (finite) set D_i of data items; if there are n pairwise disjoint such sets, the (global) database under consideration is $D = \bigcup_{i=1}^{n} D_i$. For simplicity, we assume that no data item is replicated at any two sites. So if there is replication, the various replicas will be treated as if they were different data items, and transactions would have to explicitly access multiple replicas of the same data item. All transactions are global, that is, they potentially access multiple sites; importantly, we may assume that all relevant knowledge about data locations and participating sites is generally available to all servers. A client issuing a transaction sends the steps of this transaction to the servers holding the desired data in a way that is transparent to the underlying application. From a local perspective, the operations of one transaction can be treated as a transaction in its own right, and these operations can hence be incorporated in a schedule that is locally produced, or a *local schedule*. From the global perspective, the transparency requirement implies that all transactions have to be considered together when it comes to a decision on serializability. This leads to the following definition:

DEFINITION 18.1   *Global History*   *Global history*

Let the federation under consideration consist of n sites, and let $T = \{t_1, \ldots, t_m\}$ be a set of (global) transactions. Finally, let $s_1, \ldots, s_n$ be local histories.

A *global history* for T and $s_1, \ldots, s_n$ is a history s for T (in the sense defined in Chapter 3) such that its local projection equals the local history at each site, i.e., $\Pi_i(s) = s_i$ for all i, $1 \leq i \leq n$.

In the above definition, "$\Pi_i(s)$" denotes the projection of history   *Subtransactions*
s *onto site* i (not onto the i-th transaction); such a projection hence restricts
history s to the steps of global transactions that execute at a given site. In the
following, we call the projection *of a transaction* t onto site i a *subtransaction*
of t, which comprises all steps of t at site i.

EXAMPLE 18.1

Consider a federation of two sites, where $D_1 = \{x\}$ and $D_2 = \{y\}$. Then
$s_1 = r_1(x)w_2(x)$ and $s_2 = w_1(y)r_2(y)$ are local schedules, and

$$s = r_1(x)w_1(y)w_2(x)c_1r_2(y)c_2$$

is a global history. Note that $\Pi_1(s) = s_1$ and $\Pi_2(s) = s_2$ (up to the Commit operations in either case).

For better readability, we will often write global histories and schedules in the following form:

Server 1:	$r_1(x)$	$w_2(x)$	$\ldots$
Server 2:	$w_1(y)$	$r_2(y)\ldots$	

This way of writing schedules is intended to capture both where data is accessed and the ordering of operations, which is assumed to be from left to right.

Notice that global transactions formally have to have Commit operations
at all sites at which they are active, but we may omit these commits, as we
assume in this chapter that all transactions terminate successfully.

With respect to correctness of histories, the requirement pertaining to con-   *Global vs. local*
currency control continues to be *conflict serializability*, in particular that of   *serializability*
global histories under consideration. For global histories we call this property
global serializability; correspondingly, we speak of *local serializability* for local
histories. More formally, we have the following definition:

DEFINITION 18.2   *Conflict Serializability*

A global [local] history s is globally [locally] conflict serializable if there exists a serial history over the global [local] (sub-) transactions that is conflict equivalent to s.

This definition can be applied to local histories that result from projecting global histories onto specific sites; in this case the local transactions include subtransactions of global transactions.

In a homogeneous setting, we can assume that each participating server runs the same protocol for scheduling transactions, and this protocol can be assumed to produce conflict-serializable schedules. However, local serialization orders might not be compatible; indeed, one server may produce a history such that $t < t'$ for two transactions t and t', while another produces a history in which $t' < t$.

EXAMPLE 18.2

Consider a scenario as in the previous example, but with the following slightly different transactions:

$$\text{Server 1:}\quad r_1(x)\qquad\quad w_2(x)\quad\ldots$$
$$\text{Server 2:}\qquad\qquad r_2(y)\qquad\quad w_1(y)\ldots$$

Here, the scheduler at site 1 will produce a serialization in which $t_1 < t_2$, while the scheduler at site 2 will opt for the reverse ordering. Thus, the conflict graph of the corresponding global history will have a cycle and will hence not be acceptable.

Thus, the question is how the servers can process transactions or operation requests locally in such a way that global serializability is achieved. To this end, the following result is fundamental:

THEOREM 18.1

Let s be a global history with local histories $s_1, \ldots, s_n$ involving a set T of transactions such that each s_i, $1 \leq i \leq n$, is conflict serializable. Then the following holds:

s is *globally conflict serializable* iff there exists a total order "$<$" on T that is consistent with the local serialization orders of the transactions, i.e.,

$$(\forall\, t,\ t' \in T,\ t \neq t')\quad t < t' \Longrightarrow$$
$$(\forall\, s_i,\ 1 \leq i \leq n,\ t,\ t' \in \text{trans}(s_i))(\exists\, s_i',\ s_i'\ \text{serial},\ s_i \approx_c s_i')\ t <_{s_i'} t'$$

Proof

(if) Suppose "<" is a total order of the transactions of the desired form, and assume s is not globally conflict serializable, i.e., its conflict graph has a cycle. Since each local schedule is conflict serializable by assumption, there must exist transactions $t_1, \ldots, t_m \in T$, $m \geq 2$, such that $t_1 <_{s_{i_1}} t_2$, $t_2 <_{s_{i_2}} t_3, \ldots, t_{m-1} <_{s_{i_{m-1}}} t_m$, and $t_m <_{s_{i_m}} t_1$. This must imply $t_1 < t_2, t_2 < t_3$, $\ldots, t_m < t_1$, which is a contradiction since $<$ is a total order. Thus, s must be globally serializable.

(only if) Let s be globally serializable. Then there exists a total order $<_s$ such that for all transactions $t, t' \in T$ either $t <_s t'$ or $t' <_s t$. Suppose that $t <_s t'$ for two distinct transactions, then t must also be serialized before t' in s_j, $1 \leq j \leq n$. As a result, $<_s$ satisfies the requirements of the total order $<$ we are looking for.

According to this theorem, the crucial point in all protocol adaptations that follow will be to make sure that such a total order among the transactions can be established.

18.2.2 Distributed 2PL

To start the discussion of protocols, let us consider the well-known two-phase locking (2PL) protocol. For applying this to a homogeneous federation, the basic idea is the following: each server runs a scheduler that operates according to the 2PL protocol and locally maintains locks as needed for synchronizing access to the data items (set D_i, $1 \leq i \leq n$) that it controls. Thus, an $r(x)$ step or a $w(x)$ step is locally executed after the corresponding lock has been obtained, which in turn depends on the locks that might already be held on object x. As in the fully centralized case (see Chapter 4), the goal is to avoid conflicting locks being held simultaneously. Moreover, locks on data items can be released as soon as the object in question is no longer needed by the respective transaction; however, releasing locks is again subject to the two-phase rule for the scope of the entire global transaction.

The problem that has to be solved is to decide globally *when* a lock can be *Releasing locks* released, since this determines the global order requested by Theorem 18.1. Recall that a transaction may enter its unlock phase only if it will not request any further locks. This now has to occur in a globally consistent fashion; in other words, the situation must be avoided in which a transaction, having been active at multiple sites, is already unlocking at one site but still obtaining new locks at another. Thus, a local scheduler cannot release any locks held by a transaction t as long as it does not know whether t is ready to release its locks at all other sites where it has been active as well, or has reached its "lock point" (see Chapter 4). So as long as a transaction's entry into the unlock phase is synchronized, globally serializable schedules result.

Primary site 2PL   The various proposals for determining whether a transaction has reached its lock point all assume just a simple 2PL protocol at each site. One is the *primary site 2PL*, which assumes that lock management is done exclusively at a distinguished site. Clearly, this site then has global knowledge about the lock intentions of all transactions and can easily come to a consistent decision about whether or not a transaction can enter its unlock phase. On the other hand, in primary site 2PL, the central site can easily become a performance bottleneck, and the entire system crucially depends on the availability of that site.

Distributed 2PL (D2PL)   Another approach is to exploit the fact that the federation is a homogeneous one, and hence all knowledge about the sites is available globally. In a *distributed 2PL* (D2PL) protocol, this is exploited in one form or another. In one approach, the information on all local schedules is repeated at all sites; thus, each server always knows what the others are doing, which obviously requires a lot of communication since each operation or lock request must be transmitted to every member of the federation. In another approach, concurrency control is more strictly separated from communication in that the latter only occurs when necessary: when a server wants to start unlocking objects on behalf of a transaction, it communicates with all other servers regarding the lock point of that transaction. In either protocol, it is clear that additional overhead arises due to the communication needed between servers.

Strong 2PL   As a side remark, we mention that the above scenarios can straightforwardly be extended to account for recoverability as well. Indeed, if all locks acquired on behalf of a transaction are held until the transaction wants to commit, or, stated differently, if all servers run the strong 2PL (SS2PL) protocol, then the resulting global history is not only conflict serializable but also strict. In this case the global two-phase property is self-guaranteed without any explicit measures.

A problem pertaining to the use of 2PL in a homogeneous distributed setting as just described is the danger of deadlocks, as you may recall from the centralized case. When using 2PL in one way or another, every scheduler must be aware of deadlocks, and must be capable of detecting and resolving them. However, deadlock detection in distributed databases is considerably more difficult than in centralized ones and requires more advanced techniques; for this reason, we devote a separate section to this topic below.

18.2.3 Distributed TO

Next, we consider the timestamp ordering (TO) protocol, which is particularly easy to adapt to the distributed case. First recall the TO rule we described in Chapter 4:

If $p_i(x)$ and $q_j(x)$, $i \neq j$, are operations in conflict, the following has to hold with unique timestamps $ts(t_i)$, $ts(t_j)$ assigned to transactions t_i and t_j:

$$p_i(x) \text{ is executed } \textit{before } q_j(x) \text{ iff } ts(t_i) < ts(t_j)$$

Timestamp ordering (TO) rule revisited

We have noted earlier that this rule is easy to implement if a (centralized) scheduler makes sure that each newly arriving transaction gets a timestamp larger than that of the transaction that committed last. In a homogeneous federation, each local scheduler executes its private TO protocol for synchronizing data accesses in its portion of the database. The decision of whether a given operation should be executed, delayed, or rejected depends only on concurrent operations on the same data item, but not on anything outside the particular site. As all relevant information is available locally, a local scheduler can make its decisions independently of other schedulers. However, timestamp assignment is more complicated due to the fact that each scheduler will have a different view of which transaction committed last, even when the schedulers are processing subtransactions from the same global transaction.

Distributed TO

EXAMPLE 18.3

Consider again the scenario from the previous example:

Server 1: $r_1(x)$ $w_2(x)$ . . .
Server 2: $r_2(y)$ $w_1(y)$ . . .

If timestamps were assigned as in the centralized case, each of the two servers would assign a value of 1 to the first transaction that it sees locally, t_1 on server 1 and t_2 on server 2, which would obviously lead to globally incorrect results.

So we need to find a way to assign globally unique timestamps to transactions at all sites. There are essentially two ways to do so, a centralized one and a distributed one.

Generating timestamps

- In the centralized approach, a particular server is responsible for generating and distributing timestamps; this server can use a logical counter or its local clock to this end.

- In the distributed approach, each server generates a unique local timestamp using a counter or its clock. A globally unique timestamp is derived from these local ones by "scaling" them with a server's identifier at the server that executes the transaction's first step. Once the timestamp is assigned, it will be carried along by the transaction and seen by all servers that subsequently execute steps of the transaction. In particular, if $ts(t_i)$ is the value of the local timestamp for transaction t_i at some site whose identifier is, say, j, then a globally unique timestamp is obtained by adding j in the least significant position(s), that is, by composing the two into $(ts(t_i),\ j)$.

EXAMPLE 18.4

Continuing the previous example, where

> Server 1: $r_1(x)$ $w_2(x)$ ...
> Server 2: $r_2(y)$ $w_1(y)$...

we would now obtain a timestamp of (1, 1) for transaction 1 and of (1, 2) for transaction 2. According to lexicographical ordering,

$$(1,\ 1) < (1,\ 2),$$

so both servers would try to make sure that, in case of a conflict, transaction 1 is scheduled before transaction 2. Clearly, this would not be possible here, so t_2 would be aborted.

Lamport clock   The scheme sketched above for generating globally unique timestamps may get into trouble when some servers generate local timestamps at a faster rate than others, since the faster ones will always have larger timestamps. To avoid such anomalies, more refined techniques can be employed, such as Lamport clocks, which solve the more general problem of fixing a notion of *logical* time in an asynchronous network. A *Lamport clock* assumes that sites communicate through messages, which—in our setting—invoke read or write steps or deliver query results or returncodes for writes. As above, servers maintain local clocks that are advanced when messages are received in order to keep them synchronized appropriately. A logical time is a pair $(c,\ i)$ where c is a nonnegative integer and i is a transaction number; as before, pair ordering is lexicographic. Initially, $c = 0$ at each server, and the clock variable gets increased by 1 at every transaction operation (now including send and receive events) that occurs for some t_i. The logical time of an operation is defined as the value of the clock immediately after the operation, again paired with the transaction ID as a tiebreaker. Whenever transaction i performs a send, it first increments its clock variable to obtain the value v for the Send operation, and then attaches v as a timestamp to the operation being sent. When an operation is received by a server, the corresponding clock variable is increased to be not only strictly larger than its previous value but also strictly larger than the timestamp of the operation received.

Since each transaction increments its clock at every step, it is easy to see that a Lamport clock makes sure that no two operations are assigned the same logical time, and that the logical times of operations within each transaction are strictly increasing.

18.2.4 **Distributed SGT**

Another pessimistic concurrency control protocol we introduced in Chapter 4 is serialization graph testing (SGT), which we look at next. For this protocol a generalization to a distributed scenario is considerably more complicated than it was for the two protocols discussed before, due to the fact that the central serializability test is based on a dynamically maintained conflict graph, which is an inherently global structure that is difficult to distribute across sites. In particular, it is not sufficient that each local scheduler maintains its local conflict graph and tests that for cycles, as demonstrated by the following example.

Distributed SGT

EXAMPLE 18.5

Consider again the scenario from above, where the transactions are as follows:

$$\text{Server 1:} \quad r_1(x) \qquad w_2(x) \quad \dots$$
$$\text{Server 2:} \qquad\qquad r_2(y) \qquad\qquad w_1(y) \dots$$

If each server locally maintains a conflict graph, the one at server 1 would have the edge (t_1, t_2), while the one at server 2 would have the reverse edge. Thus, both local graphs are acyclic, whereas their *union* is not. The point is that neither of the servers has all the knowledge needed to detect the cycle.

The problem of testing a distributed conflict graph for cycles is closely related to the problem of testing a distributed waits-for graph for cycles, which also arises in distributed deadlock detection (see below).

We will next sketch a restricted possibility of building a distributed SGT scheduler. Let us for the moment assume that each transaction to be executed is fully known in advance, that is, all steps have been predeclared. For a set T of predeclared transactions, a centralized scheduler can construct a *conflict multigraph* $M(T)$, which has the transactions as nodes and which has an undirected edge for *each* individual conflict between two transactions; each edge is labeled with the data item on which the potential conflict arises. As there may be multiple conflicts between the same transactions (on distinct data items), this graph may have multiple edges between any pair of nodes. A sample graph is shown in Figure 18.2. The conflict multigraph of a set of transactions shows the potential conflicts between the various operations at a glance; when scheduling these transactions, multiple edges between nodes are (hopefully) shrunk

Conflict multigraphs

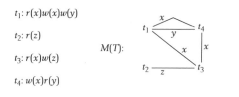

$t_1: r(x)w(x)w(y)$

$t_2: r(z)$

$t_3: r(x)w(z)$

$t_4: w(x)r(y)$

Figure 18.2 Conflict multigraph (centralized case).

into single ones, provided the various conflicts between the two transactions involved can all be resolved (directed) in the same way. Thus, if $G(s)$ is the conflict graph of a history s for the transactions in T, each edge of $G(s)$ corresponds to one or more edges in $M(T)$. If $G(s)$ is cyclic, then $M(T)$ has an undirected cycle involving the same transactions as the (directed) cycle in $G(s)$; in general, for each cycle in $G(s)$ there is a corresponding undirected one in $M(T)$. Conversely, if $M(T)$ is acyclic, then $G(s)$ is acyclic as well, and this holds *for each history s* for T.

Now let us consider the distributed case. We now incorporate site information into the conflict multigraph, for example, by distinguishing solid from dotted lines to represent data items from two different sites, as in Figure 18.3. $M(T)$ still represents conflicts that the scheduler needs to resolve successively. For example, if in Figure 18.3 $w_1(v)$ is placed by the local scheduler before $w_2(v)$ in server S_1, the conflict between t_1 and t_2 has been resolved such that t_1 from now on has to precede t_2 in *every* equivalent serial history. In other words, the edge between t_1 and t_2 in $M(T)$ has been directed from t_1 to t_2.

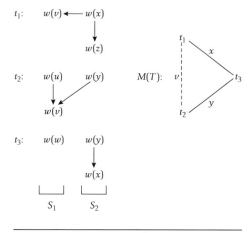

Figure 18.3 Conflict multigraph (distributed case).

Now we can imagine that an SGT scheduler resolves the conflicts given in $M(T)$ one after the other in such a way that the resulting conflict graph never becomes cyclic. However, as the example above already demonstrates, not every sequence of conflict resolution steps can occur: since $w(x) <_{t_1} w(v)$, the conflict between t_1 and t_3 on x must have been resolved before the conflict between t_1 and t_2 on v can be resolved by creating an edge of the form $t_1 \rightarrow t_2$.

This consideration indicates that there is a partial order $<_t$ among the *edges* of $M(T)$ that join in node t. This order states that an edge e cannot be directed before all edges e' such that $e' >_t e$ have been assigned an orientation. For the multigraph shown above this ordering is as follows:

$$\{t_1, t_2\} <_{t_1} \{t_1, t_3\}, \ \{t_1, t_2\} <_{t_2} \{t_2, t_3\}, \ \{t_1, t_3\} <_{t_3} \{t_2, t_3\}$$

Now a distributed SGT scheduler can roughly be realized as follows. Each site maintains a copy of the graph $M(T)$, in which some node may already have been assigned a direction. When a new step arrives at some server, the receiving scheduler requests the current state of the multigraph from every other server. When such a query arrives at a server, it responds with its current multigraph and interrupts its scheduling until the result of the attempt of integrating the new step into the schedule is known. As soon as the requestor has received all answers from the other servers, it can assign directions to all edges that have been directed in another site already; then the scheduler can test whether the new step would close a cycle. If the latter is not the case, the step can be executed; otherwise, it is rejected. In both cases all other servers are informed about the result so that they can resume their execution.

Distributed SGT with predeclaration

It should be clear right away that this approach, on the one hand, has polynomial complexity; on the other hand, it comes with *communication costs* that are intuitively very high and that—relative to an appropriate formalization—can even be shown to have a PSPACE-complete minimization problem. Thus, the core of the problem remains unchanged, namely, that it is difficult to make distributed SGT work efficiently.

18.2.5 Optimistic Protocols

Recall from Chapter 4 that there are application scenarios in which the *pessimistic* approach to concurrency control as supported by 2PL, TO, or SGT is too restrictive, and that an *optimistic* approach assuming that conflicts between transactions are rare is more appropriate in such a situation. Under optimistic concurrency control, every transaction is essentially processed in three phases:

1. *Read phase*: The transaction is executed, but with all writes applied to a workspace that is private to the transaction only (not to the database).

So the private "versions" of data items written by a transaction are not visible to other transactions (yet).

2. *Validation phase*: A transaction that is ready to commit is validated; that is, the scheduler tests whether its execution has been "correct" in the sense of conflict serializability, and whether the transaction's result can be copied into the database. If this is not the case, the transaction is aborted; otherwise, the next phase is entered.

3. *Write phase*: The workspace contents are transferred into the database to conclude the transaction's commit.

In a homogeneous federation, the same protocol, which comes in the variants of *backward-oriented* as well as *forward-oriented* optimistic concurrency control (see Chapter 4), can be applied by every participating server. Thus, subtransactions of global transactions execute in their various phases at the servers where they access data, and the only crucial point is that validation comes to the same result at every site where a global transaction has been active. Several proposals have been devised for how to accomplish this, most notably, by use of timestamps that are assigned to transactions. However, the resulting protocols are rarely used even in prototype systems, which is why we do not discuss them further here.

18.3 **Distributed Deadlock Detection**

Global deadlock In the previous section we have seen several situations where a cycle test had to be performed for a graph whose nodes and edges are distributed over the various sites, that is, for which no single server has complete information. In particular, this applies to the distributed 2PL protocol, which exhibits the danger of running into deadlocks as in the centralized case. The sample situation shown in Figure 18.4 indicates the core of the problem. Each server keeps a waits-for graph locally for tracking which transaction is waiting for which other transaction(s) to release a lock. The transaction waited for may itself wait for a message from another site regarding the completion of an operation that has to be performed before it can continue. In Figure 18.4, such a combination of *local lock waits* and *interserver communication waits* is shown for the case of three servers. Since the global deadlock cannot be detected by local means only, the entire system will eventually be blocked.

Centralized detection Clearly, there is a simple workaround for the situation just described: introduce some form of centralized monitor that collects local wait information from all servers, analyzes it, and notifies the participating sites as soon as a deadlock occurs. This approach may leave deadlocks undetected for some time, since a cycle test would be performed only when a new lock wait message arrives, and

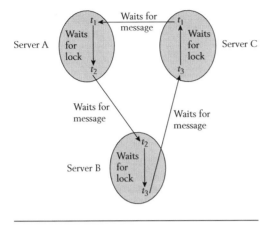

Figure 18.4 Example of a global deadlock.

these messages could come with a certain delay. Moreover, *detecting* a deadlock is not enough, but the centralized monitor would also have to make sure that a deadlock is *resolved* once it is found. To this end, the monitor would have to determine an appropriate victim (using selection criteria along the lines we discussed in Chapter 4), again by communicating (e.g., regarding rollback costs) with individual sites. A global monitor could also become a bottleneck, and when it is down, a new monitor has to be elected, or deadlocks could not be handled anymore. So this centralized approach is attractive only for federations with very fast and highly reliable communication connections between servers, but typically infeasible for widely distributed servers that communicate over the Internet.

Detection of false deadlocks

The time delay with which messages may arrive at the global monitor can have another undesired side effect. Consider the sample situation from Figure 18.4 once more, and assume that immediately after the last edge that closes a cycle has been recorded by the monitor, one of the transactions aborts. Before the monitor learns about this, it has already decided that a deadlock has occurred, and it may even have decided to abort *a second* transaction as the deadlock victim. In this case, the monitor has detected a *false deadlock*—a deadlock that no longer exists at the time it is detected (since at least one edge on the corresponding cycle in the waits-for graph has already disappeared, and the central monitor is not yet aware of this).

Although false deadlocks are a problem in general, and deadlock detection algorithms need to be designed carefully such that they do not run into situations like the one just described, it can be shown that there is a relationship between the occurrence of false deadlocks and the presence of "spontaneous" (i.e., application-induced as opposed to server-enforced) aborts (as in our sample scenario):

THEOREM 18.2

In the presence of a central monitor, false deadlocks do not occur if each scheduler runs a 2PL protocol and no transaction spontaneously aborts.

Proof

Suppose that the central monitor detects a cycle of the form $t_1 \rightarrow t_2 \rightarrow \ldots \rightarrow t_n \rightarrow t_1$, but there is actually no deadlock. Since no transaction has aborted, each will commit at some point, as none is stuck in a deadlock. Thus, the conflict graph must contain an edge (t_{i+1}, t_i) for each edge (t_i, t_{i+1}) in the global waits-for graph, since each waiting conflict has existed at some point, and the waiting transaction is executed later. Therefore, the conflict graph contains the same cycle as the waits-for graph, albeit in reverse direction, which contradicts the correctness of 2PL.

We mention that it can be shown, using an argument based on probability theory, that most cycles in a waits-for graph are of length 2, that is, involve only two transactions blocking each other. Intuitively, it would then be preferable if the two affected sites communicate directly, since the deadlock could then be detected faster. In the worst case, however, each site would be communicating with every other site, which may cause very high overhead.

Timeouts   So a centralized monitor is often replaced by a distributed one when the goal is to detect distributed deadlocks or, more generally, cycles in graphs whose nodes are distributed over various places. We mention that, as in a centralized system, it is again possible to use *timeouts*, where a server starts a timer as soon as a transaction gets blocked, and starts aborting that transaction when the timer expires. Since the transaction abort may be unnecessary, some overhead is produced by this approach. As already discussed in Chapter 4, setting the timeout to an appropriate value, neither too short nor too long, is a tricky problem, and it is even more difficult for a distributed system.

So the most intriguing approach is a truly decentralized form of deadlock detection. These approaches roughly fall into two categories: edge chasing and path pushing algorithms.

Edge chasing   In *edge chasing*, each transaction that becomes blocked in a wait relationship sends its identifier in a special message called a *probe* to the blocking transaction. If a transaction receives a probe, it forwards it to all transactions by which it is itself blocked, provided it is indeed waiting (otherwise, it just ignores the probe). Now if a probe in this way comes back to the transaction by which it was initiated—that is, if a transaction receives a probe with its own identifier—this transaction will know that it is participating in a *cyclic* waiting situation and is hence part of a deadlock. In order to resolve this deadlock, the transaction can, for example, then initiate its own abort.

Path pushing   In a *path pushing* algorithm, entire paths are circulated between transactions instead of single transaction identifiers, and individual sites can compose these in order to eventually obtain cyclic portions of a waits-for graph. In more detail, the basic algorithm is as follows:

1. Each server that has a waits-for path from transaction t_i to transaction t_j such that t_i has an incoming waits-for message edge and t_j has an outgoing waits-for message edge sends that path to the server along the outgoing edge, provided the identifier (or timestamp) of t_i is smaller than that of t_j.

2. Upon receiving a path, the server concatenates this with the local paths that already exist, and forwards the result along its outgoing edges again. If there exists a cycle among n servers, at least one of them will detect that cycle in at most n such rounds.

We illustrate this using the sample situation shown earlier in Figure 18.4. Here, $n = 3$, and we assume that first, server A encounters a waits-for situation of the form $t_1 \rightarrow t_2$ with t_2 waiting for a message from server B. It sends this partial graph to server B, which has meanwhile detected a waits-for situation $t_2 \rightarrow t_3$ with t_3 waiting for a message from server C. Thus, server B concatenates the two partial graphs into $t_1 \rightarrow t_2 \rightarrow t_3$ and forwards it to server C, which, we assume, has already discovered a local waits-for situation $t_3 \rightarrow t_1$. Server C is hence able to detect the global deadlock. This is shown in Figure 18.5.

Note the asymmetry of the communication pattern. Server C does *not* report its local waits-for edge $t_3 \rightarrow t_1$ to server A because (the identifier of) t_3 is larger than (that of) t_1. This is the point of the condition about transaction identifiers stated above; otherwise, path pushing would send unnecessary messages, and multiple servers would simultaneously and redundantly detect the same deadlock.

In general, the path pushing approach may detect false deadlocks, but this may only reduce its efficiency, not limit its correctness. A false deadlock results in transaction aborts that are actually unnecessary, but even this is easily corrected by adding another round of verification messages whenever a server believes to have determined a deadlock. Path pushing has the additional advantage over edge chasing that, as soon as a deadlock is detected, *all* transactions involved in this deadlock are known, so that a judicious choice of the victim can be made.

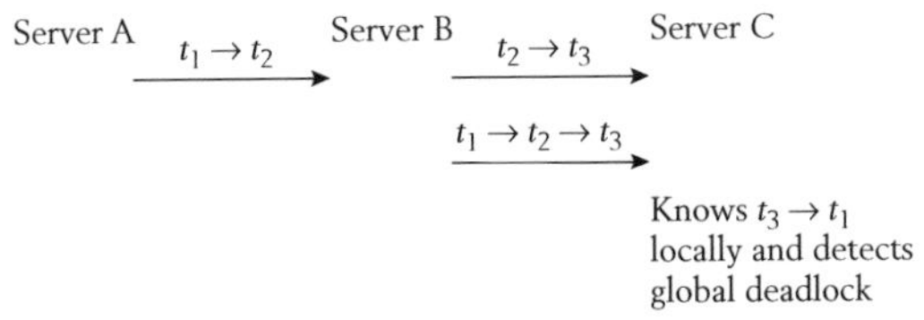

Server A $t_1 \rightarrow t_2$ Server B $t_2 \rightarrow t_3$ Server C

$t_1 \rightarrow t_2 \rightarrow t_3$

Knows $t_3 \rightarrow t_1$
locally and detects
global deadlock

Figure 18.5 The path pushing algorithm.

18.4 **Serializability in Heterogeneous Federations**

We now turn to the discussion of *heterogeneous* federations, which are federations of servers that, besides ordinary data servers, may involve legacy systems that have been developed independently of the federation, or highly specialized data servers that have been developed for a specific type of application, such as a text database system for office documents. Such federations are generally characterized by high autonomy requirements of the participants, so "global knowledge" or participation in a "global protocol" is usually not an option. For example, think of the servers of the various divisions of a multinational organization; here, it is unlikely that a distributed 2PL protocol can be employed, as no division will allow other divisions to hold onto its resources for potentially unbounded periods of time.

The distinction between homogeneous and heterogeneous federations boils down to two major differences. From a conceptual point of view, local autonomy is a hard requirement; so all protocols used in concurrency control and recovery have to be "localized" in one way or another and can no longer rely on the ability to communicate with other arbitrary sites. From a more technical point of view, we will have to take the presence of local transactions (in addition to global ones) into account. As will be seen, this alone creates new problems that do not exist in a homogeneous federation.

A heterogeneous federation is called a multidatabase system (MDBS) if all servers are database servers. As before, a (local) database at server i is a (finite) set D_i of data items; if there are n pairwise disjoint databases of this type, the global database under consideration is $D = \bigcup_{i=1}^{n} D_i$.

Local vs. global transactions
A transaction over D is *local* if the data items accessed by it belong to exactly one D_i, $1 \le i \le n$, only; otherwise it is again global. The basic scenario we now look at is as follows (see Figure 18.6 for illustration). Global transactions submit their operations to a *global transaction manager* (GTM), which controls their execution and their distribution to the local transaction managers (LTMs) of the individual servers, which now also process local transactions from local users. We will assume here that the GTM runs at a particular site, but can be addressed from each site in the system. Local transactions, on the other hand, submit their operations to local servers only and are unknown to the GTM. We assume that local transactions are even unknown to the LTMs, and that the latter handle subtransactions of global transactions only. These assumptions reflect the fact that many mission-critical data servers are operated mostly autonomously yet wish to support participation in server federations.

It is tempting to assume that the situation we are confronted with in a heterogeneous federation reduces to a homogeneous one if the participating servers use the same concurrency control protocol and if each server locally guarantees serializability. We will see shortly, however, that this is not the case, but that we can hope for sufficient conditions under which global serializability can be achieved.

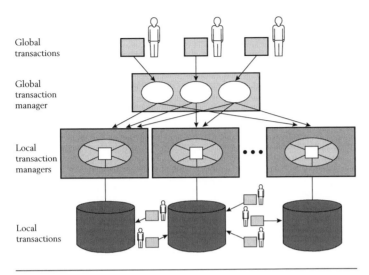

**Global
transactions**

**Global
transaction
manager**

**Local
transaction
managers**

**Local
transactions**

Figure 18.6 Multidatabase system model.

18.4.1 **Global Histories**

We continue to look at the page model of transactions, and for simplification we assume that all transactions eventually commit.

A local history of D_i, $1 \leq i \leq n$, comprises the local transactions of that particular site as well as the subtransactions of those global transactions that access data items from D_i.

Local history

EXAMPLE 18.6

Consider a federation of two servers with local databases $D_1 = \{a, b\}$ and $D_2 = \{c, d, e\}$, i.e., globally we have the set $D = \{a, b, c, d, e\}$ of data items. Then the following transactions are local, as they access data items in one of the two sites only:

$$t_1 = r(a)w(b)$$
$$t_2 = w(d)r(e)$$

On the other hand, the following transactions are global:

$$t_3 = w(a)r(d)$$
$$t_4 = w(b)r(c)w(e)$$

The following histories are local:

$$s_1 = r_1(a)w_3(a)c_3w_1(b)c_1w_4(b)c_4$$
$$s_2 = r_4(c)w_2(d)r_3(d)c_3r_2(e)c_2w_4(e)c_4$$

While a local history may contain both local transactions and subtransactions of global transactions, a *global history* is now made up of all operations from both local and global transactions. This way of looking at global histories, which does not contradict the autonomy assumption mentioned earlier, can be motivated by the fact that a GTM, although it is not capable of controlling local scheduling, at least needs information about the sequencing in which the global transactions it has to manage have been executed together with the local transactions. For this reason, we modify the notion of a global history as follows (and continue to call it global history as long as no confusion can arise):

Global history revisited

DEFINITION 18.3   *Global History*

Let the heterogeneous federation under consideration consist of n sites, and let $T_1, \ldots, T_n$ be sets of local transactions at sites $1, \ldots, n$, T be a set of global transactions. Finally, let $s_1, \ldots, s_n$ be local histories such that $T_i \subseteq$ trans(s_i) and $T \cap$ trans$(s_i) \neq \emptyset$ for $1 \leq i \leq n$.

A *(heterogeneous) global history* (for $s_1, \ldots, s_n$) is a history s for $\bigcup_{i=1}^{n} T_i \cup T$ (in the sense defined in Chapter 3) such that its local projection equals the local history in each site, i.e., $\Pi_i(s) = s_i$ for all i, $1 \leq i \leq n$.

Regarding the correctness of histories, we can continue to use conflict serializability; however, applying this criterion to global schedules is not as easy as it may seen, as the following examples illustrate.

EXAMPLE 18.7

Consider two servers with local databases $D_1 = \{a\}$ and $D_2 = \{b, c\}$, and let the global transactions $t_1 = r(a)w(b)$ and $t_2 = w(a)r(c)$ as well as the local transaction $t_3 = r(b)w(c)$ be given. Suppose now the GTM decides to execute t_1 first; thus, it will send all operations from t_1 to the servers before it starts processing t_2. The GTM is hence conservatively attempting to execute the global transactions in a *serial* fashion. This attempt may lead to the following local histories (local Commit operations omitted):

Server 1: $s_1 =$	$r_1(a)$			$w_2(a)$	
Server 2: $s_2 =$		$r_3(b)$	$w_1(b)$		$r_2(c)$	$w_3(c)$

Note that the two global transactions are executed strictly serially at both sites in the same order. The global history in the sense of Definition 18.3 looks as follows:

$$s = r_1(a)r_3(b)w_1(b)c_1 w_2(a)r_2(c)c_2 w_3(c)c_3$$

Apparently, we have s_1, $s_2 \in$ CSR, but $s_1 \approx_c t_1 t_2$, while $s_2 \approx_c t_2 t_3 t_1$. As a consequence, the conflict graph of s contains a cycle, which implies that the serial execution order $t_1 t_2$ chosen by the GTM is *not* acceptable.

The notation $t_2 t_3 t_1$ used in the previous example in connection with history s_2 is supposed to mean only the relevant local portion of a global transaction as it applies to the site in question, that is, in this example, the sequence $r_2(c) r_3(b) w_3(c) w_1(b)$ of operations. Although a bit informal, we will sometimes use this simplified notation without always pointing it out.

The previous example shows that in a heterogeneous federation not every serial execution order of transactions is acceptable for global histories. Moreover, we can observe in the previous example that history s_1 exhibits an ordinary conflict between the two global transactions. However, in history s_2 the global transactions are in an *indirect* conflict caused by the local transaction present in server 2. In particular, global transaction t_2 is in a (direct) conflict with local transaction t_3, and t_3 is in a (direct) conflict with global transaction t_1; therefore, t_2 is transitively or indirectly in conflict with transaction t_1. Thus, in order to guarantee conflict serializability of global histories, a heterogeneous federation has to take indirect conflicts into account as well. *Indirect conflicts*

The following example shows that indirect conflicts may even arise when there is no direct conflict between global transactions.

EXAMPLE 18.8

Consider two servers with local databases $D_1 = \{a, b\}$ and $D_2 = \{c, d\}$, respectively, as well as global transactions $t_1 = r(a) r(d)$ and $t_2 = r(b) r(c)$, which are both read-only. Additionally, let the local transactions $t_3 = r(a) r(b) w(a) w(b)$ and $t_4 = r(c) r(d) w(c) w(d)$ be given. Locally, the following histories may be produced (where s_2 can start only after s_1 has finished):

| Server 1: | $s_1 =$ | $r_1(a)$ | $r_3(a)$ | $r_3(b)$ | $w_3(a)$ | $w_3(b)$ | $r_2(b)$ |
| Server 2: | $s_2 =$ | $r_2(c)$ | $r_4(c)$ | $r_4(d)$ | $w_4(c)$ | $w_4(d)$ | $r_1(d)$ |

Again, both local histories are conflict serializable, since $s_1 \approx_c t_1 t_3 t_2$ and $s_2 \approx_c t_2 t_4 t_1$. However, as in the previous example, the global transactions have different serialization orders at the two sites, so that a global history whose local projections are s_1 and s_2 cannot be correct.

The previous examples have shown that indirect conflicts between global transactions can lead to different local serialization orders. A solution to this situation, to be formally presented in the next subsection, is reminiscent of Theorem 18.1: as in the homogeneous case, correctness intuitively requires that global transactions have to maintain the *same* relative serialization order at *each* site, even in the absence of (direct) conflicts between these transactions.

In general, we assume that the execution of a global transaction proceeds in such a way that the GTM transmits newly arriving operations to the relevant server individually, so that the sequence of operations received by a particular server forms the subtransaction. However, before the GTM can send another operation from some transaction to a server, it must wait for an acknowledgment of the previous operation's execution; in this way it can be guaranteed that a local scheduler, receiving more than one operation from the same global transaction, does not alter their ordering. In a dynamic situation, the global history produced by the GTM will then reflect the order in which the operations from global transactions have been acknowledged by local transaction managers (where acknowledgments arriving simultaneously at the GTM can be ordered arbitrarily). This assumption makes sure that the global history satisfies the conditions of Definition 18.3, even in a dynamic setting.

18.4.2 **Global Serializability**

In a heterogeneous federation, the global transaction manager (GTM) has no direct control over local schedules; the best it can do is to control the serialization order of global transactions by carefully controlling the order in which operations are sent to local systems for execution and in which these get acknowledged. We next define a notion of serializability intended to capture this, and will then look into ways of guaranteeing serializability in that sense. In particular, it will turn out that criteria known from Chapters 3 and 11 already can be used as sufficient conditions in the present context.

We first formalize the types of conflicts we have already described by way of examples for transactions operating in a heterogeneous federation:

Direct and indirect conflicts

DEFINITION 18.4 *Direct and Indirect Conflict*

Let s_i be a local history, and let t and t' be transactions from trans(s_i), $t \neq t'$.

1. t and t' are in a *direct* conflict in s_i if the following holds:

$$(\exists \, p \in t)(\exists \, q \in t') \, (p, q) \in \text{conf}(s_i)$$

(i.e., the ordinary notion of conflict from Chapter 3).

2. t and t' are in an *indirect conflict* in s_i if there exists a sequence $t_1, \ldots, t_r$ of transactions from trans(s_i) such that t is in s_i in a direct conflict with t_1, t_j is in s_i in a direct conflict with t_{j+1}, $1 \leq j \leq r - 1$, and t_r is in s_i in a direct conflict with t'.

3. t and t' are in *conflict* in s_i if they are in a direct or indirect conflict in s_i.

In what follows, a conflict can always be a direct or an indirect one. There- *Conflict* fore, *conflict equivalence* of two local or two global histories means that the *equivalence* histories in question contain the same operations and the same direct or indi- rect conflicts; for simplicity, we again use the notation "$\approx_c$" to indicate this.

We also point out that operations in an indirect conflict *do* commute, mean- *Commutativity* ing that they can be exchanged in a given history as long as the remainder of the history is unchanged (see the next example). The simple reason for this is the fact that an indirect conflict between two transactions t and t' requires the presence of a third transaction with which neither t nor t' commutes; but as t and t' are not in (direct) conflict, they can be exchanged in any schedule in which they both occur.

EXAMPLE 18.9

Let D_1 and D_2 be as in Example 18.7. In the local history

$$s_1' = w_2(a)r_1(a)$$

t_2 and t_1 are in a direct conflict, whereas in the local history

$$s_2 = r_3(b)w_1(b)r_2(c)w_3(c)$$

t_2 and t_1 are in an indirect conflict. Note that we can commute $w_1(b)$ and $r_2(c)$ in s_2 to obtain history

$$s_2' = r_3(b)r_2(c)w_1(b)w_3(c)$$

but this commutation obviously leaves their indirect conflict unchanged.

For global histories, it is easy to see that Theorem 18.1 still applies when we take into account both direct and indirect conflicts, a fact that can again be used to verify concurrency control protocols. Before we turn to this issue, we prove an analog to the serializability theorem from Chapter 3 (Theorem 3.10), which characterizes serializability in graph-theoretic terms. To this end, we first adapt the notion of a conflict graph to the modified setting:

DEFINITION 18.5   *Global Conflict Graph*   *Global conflict*
                                                                              graph
Let s be a global history for the local histories $s_1, \ldots, s_n$; let $G(s_i)$ denote the conflict graph of s_i, $1 \le i \le n$ derived from direct and indirect conflicts. The *global conflict graph* of s is defined as the union of all $G(s_i)$, $1 \le i \le n$, i.e.,

$$G(s) := \bigcup_{i=1}^{n} G(s_i)$$

It should be intuitively clear that an *acyclic* global serialization graph means that the (committed) global transactions can be put in a serialization order that is consistent with each ordering given by a local history. We will prove this next and show that the converse is also valid.

THEOREM 18.3

Multidatabase serializability theorem

Let the local histories $s_1, \ldots s_n$ be given, where each $G(s_i)$, $1 \leq i \leq n$, is acyclic (i.e., $s_i \in CSR$). In addition, let s be a global history for the s_i, $1 \leq i \leq n$. Then s is globally conflict serializable iff $G(s)$ is acyclic.

Proof

(if) Let $\bigcup_{i=1}^{n} G(s_i)$ be acyclic. Then there exists a total ordering "$<$" of all transactions (obtainable through topologically sorting the global conflict graph). The global transactions committed in s are then serialized in the same order in each local history s_i. For any two such transactions t and t' such that $t < t'$, there hence exists for each s_i in which subtransactions of these transactions occur a conflict-equivalent serial history s_i' such that $t <_{s_i'} t'$, i.e., s is globally conflict serializable.

(only if) Conversely, let s be globally conflict serializable, and suppose that $\bigcup_{i=1}^{n} G(s_i)$ has a cycle; without loss of generality, let the cycle be of length 2. Since by assumption all local graphs $G(s_i)$ are acyclic, there must exist transactions t and t' $(t \neq t')$ as well as local histories s_i and s_j $(i \neq j)$ such that $G(s_i)$ contains the edge (t, t'), while $G(s_j)$ contains the edge (t', t). This contradicts Theorem 18.1, which states that for the (committed) global transactions there exists a total ordering that is consistent with all s_k, $1 \leq k \leq n$.

In the next section, we look at various ways of obtaining global conflict serializability, or of generating the required total ordering of global transactions. Before we do so, we briefly discuss an alternative correctness criterion that has been proposed in the literature.

18.4.3 **Quasi Serializability**

The alternative correctness criterion we are about to discuss is motivated by the observation that guaranteeing global serializability could result in a low degree of parallelism between transactions, or in a high number of transaction aborts. To alleviate this problem, the alternative requires certain properties from the set of all local histories *only*. Its basic idea is that in order to preserve global database consistency, only global transactions need to be executed in a serializable way, but with proper consideration of the effects of local transactions.

The new notion in this context is that of a *quasi-serial* history, which differs   *Quasi seriality*
from an ordinary serial history in that only global transactions are required to
execute one after the other. As will be shown later, this together with the serializability of local histories suffices to guarantee global correctness. Formally,
we have: a set $\{s_1, s_2, \ldots, s_n\}$ of local histories is *quasi serial* if $s_i \in$ CSR for
$1 \leq i \leq n$ and there exists a total order "$<$" on the set T of global transactions
such that $t_i < t_j$ for $t_i, t_j \in T$, $i \neq j$, implies that in each local history s_k,
$1 \leq k \leq n$ the t_i subtransaction occurs completely before the t_j subtransaction (provided that both t_i and t_j occur in s_k). The second condition intuitively
requests that global transactions that are in an indirect conflict in a local history
are already ordered in such a way in the history that no further reordering is
needed from a global scheduler's point of view.

With this notion, we can say that a set $\{s_1, s_2, \ldots, s_n\}$ of local histories is   *Quasi*
quasi serializable if there exists a set $\{s'_1, s'_2, \ldots, s'_n\}$ of quasi-serial local histories   *serializability*
such that $s_i \approx_c s'_i$ holds for $1 \leq i \leq n$. The latter definition can immediately be
restated for global histories: a global history s (for $s_1, \ldots, s_n$) is *quasi serializable*
if the set $\{\Pi_1(s), \ldots, \Pi_n(s)\}$ of its local projections is quasi serializable. Again,
this can be characterized in graph-theoretic terms.

EXAMPLE 18.10

Consider a federation consisting of $D_1 = \{a, b\}$ and $D_2 = \{c, d, e\}$. Let
transactions $t_1 = w(a)r(d)$ and $t_2 = r(b)r(c)w(e)$ be global, and transactions $t_3 = r(a)w(b)$ and $t_4 = w(d)r(e)$ be local. Moreover, local histories
are given as follows:

$$s_1 = w_1(a)r_3(a)w_3(b)r_2(b)$$
$$s_2 = r_2(c)w_4(d)r_1(d)w_2(e)r_4(e)$$

Then the set $\{s_1, s_2\}$ is quasi serializable, as it is element-wise conflict equivalent to the quasi-serial set $\{s_1, s'_2\}$, where

$$s'_2 = w_4(d)r_1(d)r_2(c)w_2(e)r_4(e)$$

The global history

$$s = w_1(a)r_3(a)r_2(c)w_4(d)r_1(d)c_1w_3(b)c_3r_2(b)w_2(e)c_2r_4(e)c_4$$

is also quasi serializable, since we have $\Pi_1(s) = s_1$ as well as $\Pi_2(s) = s_2$;
on the other hand, s is not globally serializable.

Since the quasi-serialization order is always compatible with the orderings
of subtransactions in the various local histories, quasi serializability is relatively
easy to achieve for a GTM. In a quasi-serial schedule a global transaction is perceived by all other global transactions as an isolated, indivisible step, as these
transactions are executed serially. By the same token, global transactions are

perceived by local transactions as isolated steps, since the local histories are serializable. However, the crucial prerequisite is that the underlying global order is known—a requirement that is easily overlooked. So quasi serializability is an interesting alternative to explore further, but far from being an immediate, universal solution.

18.5 Achieving Global Serializability through Local Guarantees

The examples we have shown earlier have illustrated the central problem in constructing globally serializable schedules: local transactions may cause indirect conflicts between global transactions that may otherwise not be in conflict at all. In particular, it may thus happen that local conflict edges arise that cause a cycle in the global conflict graph. Essentially, this is a situation we have encountered in homogeneous federations as well, and have found difficult to handle there; what makes the problem easier to deal with now is the fact that the GTM establishes a form of global control, which is either not available or deemed unacceptable in a homogeneous system. In heterogeneous federations, on the other hand, some form of GTM is inherently unavoidable anyway.

In order to avoid cycles in a global conflict graph, the GTM has to take appropriate action; in the model considered here the GTM can assume that local histories are conflict serializable. In general, its actions can be pessimistic or optimistic, where the former means that the GTM will delay transactions in order to avoid cycles in the global serialization graph. In an optimistic approach, real or potential cycles will be detected and resolved by aborting global transactions.

In the following we will look at various scenarios for guaranteeing global serializability, depending on additional knowledge the GTM may have on local sites.

18.5.1 Rigorousness

Suppose the GTM can assume that local schedulers produce not only conflict-serializable histories but also rigorous ones. Recall from Chapter 11 that a history s is *rigorous* if it satisfies the following condition:

$$(\forall t_i, t_j \in \text{trans}(s))$$
$$p_j(x) <_s q_i(x), i \neq j, p, q \text{ in conflict} \Rightarrow a_j <_s q_i(x) \vee c_j <_s q_i(x)$$

As we have noted in Chapter 11, a fundamental property of the class RG of rigorous histories is that RG is contained in *both* CSR and ST, where the latter denotes the class of all strict histories. In particular, histories in RG avoid any type of *rw*, *wr*, or *ww* conflict between uncommitted transactions.

Our next goal is to show that rigorousness is also relevant in the context of multidatabase systems discussed here. However, as the following example indicates, the requirement that all local histories in a federation are rigorous is not sufficient for guaranteeing global serializability.

Use of rigorousness

EXAMPLE 18.11

Consider two servers where $D_1 = \{a, b\}$ and $D_2 = \{c, d\}$; moreover, let global transactions $t_1 = w(a)w(d)$ and $t_2 = w(c)w(b)$ as well as local transactions t_3 and t_4 be given such that the following local histories are formed:

$$s_1 = w_1(a)c_1r_3(a)r_3(b)c_3w_2(b)c_2$$
$$s_2 = w_2(c)c_2r_4(c)r_4(d)c_4w_1(d)c_1$$

Both s_1 and s_2 are rigorous, but they yield different serialization orders of the two global transactions.

The two local histories in the previous example could have been formed as follows. First, the GTM sends $w_1(a)c_1$ to server 1 as well as $w_1(d)c_1$ to server 2, then corresponding operation sequences for global transaction t_2. The local schedulers produce the local histories as given. The point is that the problem of different global serializations can be avoided by restricting the treatment of Commit operations of global transactions appropriately:

DEFINITION 18.6 *Commit-Deferred Transaction*

A global transaction t is *commit-deferred* if its Commit operation is sent by the GTM to the local sites in which the transaction was active only *after* the local executions of all data operations from t have been acknowledged at all sites.

Now we can show:

THEOREM 18.4

Let s be a global history for $s_1, \ldots, s_n$. If $s_i \in RG$ for $1 \le i \le n$ and all global transactions are commit-deferred, then s is globally serializable.

Proof

Let s be a global history for the given local ones. By Theorem 18.3, s is globally serializable iff $G(s)$ is acyclic. Now suppose this graph has a cycle of the form $(t_1, \ldots, t_k)$ such that $t_k = t_1$. Since $s_i \in RG$, $1 \le i \le n$, and since $RG \subset CSR$, each local conflict graph is acyclic. Hence the global cycle is "distributed" over several local graphs, and let us assume it does so in such a way that edge (t_j, t_{j+1}) is contained in $G(s_j)$ for $1 \leq j < k$. Again, since each local history is rigorous, we conclude that $c_j <_{s_j} c_{j+1}$ for $1 \leq j < k$. Thus, t_1 is committed in s_1 before t_2, and t_{k-1} is committed in s_{k-1} before t_1. In other words, t_1 is already committed in s_1, although it is still active in s_{k-1}, a contradiction to our assumption that all global transactions are commit-deferred.

18.5.2 Commitment Ordering

We next look at another criterion giving rise to a sufficient condition for global serializability—the notion of commit order-preserving conflict serializability (COCSR), also introduced in Chapter 3. Membership of a history s in COCSR is given if for any pair of transactions that are in conflict in s their Commit operations occur in conflict order. The following example indicates that, just like for rigorousness, the requirement that all local histories are commit order preserving conflict serializable alone is not enough for guaranteeing global serializability.

EXAMPLE 18.12

Let D_1 and D_2 be as in Example 18.11, and let the following local histories be given:

$$s_1 = r_1(a)w_3(a)w_3(b)r_2(b)c_1c_3c_2$$
$$s_2 = w_4(c)r_1(c)r_2(d)w_4(d)c_2c_4c_1$$

Clearly, $s_1, s_2 \in$ COCSR, but again the two histories have different serialization orders.

Use of commitment ordering

Fortunately, just as in the case of rigorousness, the addition of a condition that is easy to test in reality provides the solution:

THEOREM 18.5

Let s be a global history for $s_1, \ldots, s_n$. If $s_i \in$ COCSR for $1 \leq i \leq n$ and if all global transactions perform their commits strictly sequentially, then s is globally serializable.

The additional condition given in this theorem intuitively means the following. While the Commit operation of a global transaction is being distributed to the sites at which it has been active, the GTM does not issue a Commit operation for any other global transaction.

EXAMPLE 18.13

Let us illustrate the effect of the condition just introduced by way of the following two histories, which are slightly modified versions of those considered in Example 18.12 (in such a way that their Commit operations are ordered the same way in either history in order to meet the condition of the theorem):

$$s_1 = r_1(a)c_1w_3(a)w_3(b)c_3r_2(b)c_2$$
$$s_2 = w_4(c)r_1(c)r_2(d)r_4(e)c_1c_2 \ [w_4(d)c_4]$$

Assume that s_2 has been executed up to but excluding the portion shown in brackets. Notice that the two global transactions run interleaved at site 2 (t_2 reads data item d before t_1 is committed). Now if server 2 assures that each generated history is in COCSR, the continuation of s_2 shown above cannot occur, because the indirect conflict between t_2 and t_1 then caused by t_4 would require commitment of these transactions in the order of this conflict, which is no longer possible. A COCSR scheduler would therefore have to abort t_4.

For commit order-preserving conflict serializability, it can moreover be shown that (under additional prerequisites) the global history s is in COCSR if the same holds for the $s_i \in$, $1 \le i \le n$. On the other hand, the following is easily verified (see Exercise 18.6): if s is a global history, then

$$s \in COCSR \implies (\forall i, 1 \le i \le n)\Pi_i(s) = s_i \in COCSR$$

Finally, note that similar considerations apply to the case where membership in COCSR is required for global transactions only (i.e., not necessarily for local transactions). To this end, we have the following:

DEFINITION 18.7 *Extended Commitment Ordering*

A (local or global) history s is *extended commit order preserving conflict serializable* if for every pair of *global* transactions $t_i, t_j \in \text{commit}(s)$, $i \ne j$, that are in conflict in s such that an operation from t_i conflicts with a subsequent operation from t_j, then $c_i <_s c_j$ holds.

Let ECOCSR denote the corresponding class of histories.

Extended commitment ordering

Clearly, the following holds, as the COCSR condition is no longer applied to all transactions:

COROLLARY 18.1

$COCSR \subset ECOCSR$

Now the statement made above for class COCSR can be restated for class ECOCSR, subject to minor additional prerequisites.

18.6 **Ticket-Based Concurrency Control**

What the considerations at the end of the previous section suggest for practical concurrency control in a heterogeneous federation is that (1) the local systems are expected to produce CSR histories only (and the federation does not really care which method they use in this respect), and (2) additional properties like RG or COCSR have to be ensured locally to guarantee global correctness. Under these conditions no global mechanism for federated concurrency control is needed, and we do not really need an explicit GTM. Without such additional local properties, global correctness requires further measures at the global level of the federation. In this section we present the *ticket method* as a representative of explicit measures for ensuring global serializability on top of a variety of servers that are solely known to provide locally CSR schedules. The ticket method is a particularly lightweight mechanism; one of its salient features is its versatility in coping with a broad variety of server types and underlying local protocols.

18.6.1 **Explicit Tickets for Forcing Conflicts**

As motivation consider the following example:

EXAMPLE 18.14

Let two servers be given with local databases $D_1 = \{a, b\}$ and $D_2 = \{c, d\}$ (as previously in Example 18.8); let the global transactions be $t_1 = r(a)r(c)$ and $t_2 = r(b)r(d)$. Also, let the local transactions $t_3 = w(a)w(b)$ and $t_4 = w(c)w(d)$ be given. Similar to what we have seen in Example 18.8, the following local histories do not lead to global correctness:

$$s_1 = r_1(a)c_1 w_3(a)w_3(b)c_3 r_2(b)c_2$$
$$s_2 = w_4(c)r_1(c)c_1 r_2(d)c_2 w_4(d)c_4$$

The reason is that $s_1 \approx_c t_1 t_3 t_2$, whereas $s_2 \approx_c t_2 t_4 t_1$.

Now let us consider the case that the GTM has already executed t_1, but has not yet started t_2. Locally we then have the following schedules of which the steps shown in brackets are not yet executed:

$$s_1 = r_1(a)c_1 \; [w_3(a)w_3(b)c_3r_2(b)c_2]$$
$$s_2 = w_4(c)r_1(c)c_1 \; [r_2(d)c_2w_4(d)c_4]$$

The GTM wants to avoid the execution continuations shown in brackets in either case, since that would result in the local histories seen before. One way of achieving this is to delay the execution of t_2 until the GTM can be sure that a cycle involving t_2 is no longer possible. Since the GTM has no control over site 2, it cannot know when t_4 will end; on the other hand, it must make sure that t_2 is executed after t_4 at this site. The pessimistic approach mentioned earlier hence does not work in this case. Similarly, an optimistic approach does not work either.

A solution to the problem indicated in the previous example consists of locally *forcing* (direct) conflicts between global transactions, or to convert indirect conflicts (which may exist, but are not observable by the GTM) into direct (observable) conflicts. Suppose that in the previous example, transaction t_1 was forced to write a special data item at each site in which it is active, and that transaction t_2 was forced to read that object if it also becomes active in one of these sites. Then the serialization ordering "t_1t_2" would be automatically enforced, provided the GTM starts executing t_2 only after t_1 has ended. In this way, it would be assured that site 2 cannot produce a reverse serialization (i.e., one that reverses the actual execution order), since this would now result in a cycle in the corresponding *local* conflict graph.

Forced conflicts

In the more general case that global transactions are not executed serially, the following approach can be used. Each local database maintains a special data item called a *ticket*, which is accessed only by global transactions. We can think of the ticket as a logical timestamp whose value is stored as a regular data item on each server. Each subtransaction of a global transaction has to read the ticket or issue a *take-a-ticket* operation, then increment it and write it back, so that the value of the ticket at each point in time corresponds to the serialization order of the global transactions at the site under consideration. We assume that these ticket operations can be accomplished through ordinary reads and writes; in particular, incrementing a ticket I and writing it back results in an operation written as $w(I + 1)$.

Operations on tickets

EXAMPLE 18.15

Consider a situation with two servers and local databases $D_1 = \{a\}$ and $D_2 = \{b, c\}$, global transactions $t_1 = r(a)w(b)$ and $t_2 = w(a)r(c)$, as well as local transaction $t_3 = r(b)w(c)$. We have seen already in Example 18.7

that a decision of the GTM to execute t_1 first will result in the following local histories:

$$\text{Server 1: } s_1 = r_1(a)c_1w_2(a)c_2$$
$$\text{Server 2: } s_2 = r_3(b)w_1(b)c_1r_2(c)c_2w_3(c)c_3$$

As we noted earlier, $s_1, s_2 \in \text{CSR}$, but $s_1 \approx_c t_1t_2$, while $s_2 \approx_c t_2t_3t_1$.

Using tickets, the local histories would look as follows:

$$s_1 = r_1(I_1)w_1(I_1 + 1)r_1(a)c_1r_2(I_1)w_2(I_1 + 1)w_2(a)c_2$$
$$s_2 = r_3(b)r_1(I_2)w_1(I_2 + 1)w_1(b)c_1r_2(I_2)w_2(I_2 + 1)r_2(c)c_2w_3(c)c_3$$

Now the indirect conflict between the global transactions in history s_2 has been turned into an explicit one; as a result, $s_2 \notin \text{CSR}$, which implies that s_2 will no longer be allowed by the local scheduler (its conflict graph is now cyclic). Clearly, the following local history would be acceptable at site 2:

$$s_2 = r_1(I_2)w_1(I_2 + 1)w_1(b)c_1r_2(I_2)w_2(I_2 + 1)r_2(c)c_2r_3(b)w_3(c)c_3$$

In the previous example, we assumed that transactions take their tickets at the beginning of their local executions, which is not necessary. In fact, transactions may take their tickets at any time during their execution without affecting the correctness of the approach. The following theorem shows that the tickets obtained by the subtransactions at each server are guaranteed to reflect their relative serialization order.

THEOREM 18.6

If global transaction t_1 takes its ticket before global transaction t_2 in a server, then t_1 will be serialized before t_2 by that server.

Proof

Suppose that, at a particular site, t_1 takes its ticket before t_2, i.e., $r_1(I) < r_2(I)$ in the local history. Since a subtransaction takes its ticket first and then increments its value, only the following execution orders can occur:

$$s_1 = r_1(I)r_2(I)w_1(I + 1)w_2(I + 1)$$
$$s_2 = r_1(I)r_2(I)w_2(I + 1)w_1(I + 1)$$
$$s_3 = r_1(I)w_1(I + 1)r_2(I)w_2(I + 1)$$

However, among these schedules only s_3 is serializable and hence allowed by the local scheduler of the server under consideration. Therefore, t_1 increments the ticket value before t_2 reads it, and t_2 obtains a larger ticket than t_1.

In order to show that t_1 can now be serialized only before t_2, it suffices to note that the ticket operations of t_1 and t_2 create a direct conflict of the form $t_1 \rightarrow t_2$. But this conflict forces t_1 and t_2 to be serialized according to the order in which they take their tickets. Specifically, we have to consider two cases. For the first case assume that there are other conflicts between t_1 and t_2, which may be indirect ones caused by local transactions, such that $t_1 \rightarrow t_2$. In this case, the local history remains serializable, and both t_1 and t_2 are allowed to commit. In the second case, where other (direct or indirect) conflicts exist such that $t_2 \rightarrow t_1$, the ticket conflict creates a cycle in the *local* conflict graph, and the resulting history becomes nonserializable. In conclusion, indirect conflicts can be resolved through the use of tickets, even if the GTM cannot detect their existence.

So far we have seen that tickets make indirect conflicts visible to the GTM, but in order to guarantee global serializability, the *optimistic ticket method* (OTM) that we are discussing must ensure that the subtransactions of each global transaction have the *same* relative serialization order in their corresponding servers. To this end, the basic idea is to allow the subtransactions of each global transaction to proceed, but to commit them only if their ticket values have the same relative order in all participating sites.

Optimistic ticket method (OTM)

Ensuring global serializability this way can be implemented by a graph-based approach as follows. The GTM maintains a *ticket (order) graph* whose nodes correspond to active global transactions. An edge of the form $t_i \rightarrow t_j$ in this graph indicates that at least one subtransaction of global transaction t_i has read a ticket value that is smaller than the value read by t_j (at the same site). When a transaction t requests its Commit operation, the graph is tested for cycles involving t: if there is no such cycle, t can be committed, otherwise it is aborted.

Ticket graph

OTM does not affect the way a server handles the execution of a global transaction up to the point when the transaction requests its commit. However, since global transactions may take their tickets in any order, OTM may suffer from global aborts caused by ticket operations that occur out of order. Indeed, if global transaction t_1 obtains its ticket at one site before global transaction t_2, but is unable to do so at another site, the GTM will inevitably abort one of the two transactions. Even worse, incompatible orders in which global transactions take their tickets can lead to *global deadlocks* if the participating servers use locking.

Problems with OTM

For these reasons, an alternative to OTM is the *conservative ticket method* (CTM), which avoids transaction aborts to a large extent. Like OTM, CTM requires subtransactions of global transactions to take tickets at their corresponding sites. However, CTM controls the order in which this happens and ensures that the relative order of ticket taking is the same at all participating servers.

Conservative ticket method (CTM)

It is important to emphasize that in both presented variants of explicit ticket methods, tickets need to be taken only by subtransactions of global transactions. Local transactions do not need to take tickets; their correct execution is guaranteed by the local CSR property alone.

18.6.2 Implicit Tickets

Both ticket methods presented above, the optimistic and the conservative variant, merely require the underlying servers to guarantee local conflict serializability as a "lowest common denominator." Often, servers in a federation may have additional, slightly stronger properties that are, however, not as strong as local rigorousness or the COCSR property. The question then is to what extent the ticket method can leverage such additional properties for reducing overhead and gaining efficiency.

This question has a positive, elegant answer for servers whose local schedules are guaranteed to avoid cascading aborts (i.e., schedules with the ACA property introduced in Chapter 11). The combination of CSR and ACA is strong enough either to force a local conflict cycle at one of the servers or ensure that all servers produce compatible ticket orders and thus compatible serialization orders for the subtransactions of global transactions. In other words, there is no longer a need for maintaining a ticket order graph or controlling the ordering of the take-a-ticket operations at the GTM level. This result is captured in the following theorem:

THEOREM 18.7

If each server in a heterogeneous federation guarantees the CSR and ACA properties for its local schedules, and each subtransaction of a global transaction includes a take-a-ticket operation, then all resulting histories are globally conflict serializable.

Proof

From Theorem 18.6 we already know that the ticket order of subtransactions at the same site reflects the local serialization order. What remains to be shown is that every possible cycle at the global level that could result from incompatible local serialization orders at different sites must imply a local cycle at one of the sites. Assume that two global transactions t_i and t_j are involved in a global cycle that results from two different ticket (and thus local serialization) orders at sites A and B: t_i before t_j at A and t_j before t_i at B. Because of the local ACA properties, t_j cannot read and write the ticket at A before the commit of t_i, and t_i cannot read and write the ticket at B before the commit of t_j. So the global cycle would imply that the global commit of t_i precedes the global commit of t_j, and vice versa. This is impossible (assuming a total ordering of global commits under an appropriate distributed commit protocol that we will discuss in Chapter 19). Thus, one of the two transactions cannot commit. If there is a conflict cycle, it will arise locally at one of the two sites, caused by regular conflicts and the forced conflict on the local ticket.

The above result is of high practical importance, because most practical protocols for local schedulers satisfy the ACA property. Thus, the overhead of maintaining an explicit ticket order graph at the GTM level is rarely ever needed. Under such conditions we refer to the ticket-based approach as an *implicit ticket method*.

The most far-reaching form of implicit tickets is, of course, when all underlying servers even have the RG or COCSR property. In this case there is no need for the take-a-ticket operation. In fact, this extreme form of implicit tickets boils down to the solutions presented in Section 18.5 that rely solely on local properties without an explicit GTM.

18.6.3 **Mixing Explicit and Implicit Tickets**

Realistic federations comprise servers of different quality levels: some provide only CSR, some can guarantee CSR and ACA, and some even ensure local RG or COCSR properties. But it is unlikely that all servers are uniform in terms of these properties (in addition to their heterogeneity in terms of local protocols). So it seems that we must resort to the lowest common denominator, the explicit ticket method for servers with local schedules in CSR, if at least one underlying server does not provide anything stronger than CSR. Fortunately, this is not the case, and it is indeed a great strength of the ticket method family that it can leverage different quality levels within one federation. It suffices to maintain the ticket graph for the "weakest" servers only—those that guarantee only local CSR—and take-a-ticket operations are needed only for subtransactions at those sites that do not have the local RG or COCSR property. Thus, in addition to being very easy to implement, the ticket technique has the particularly appealing property of incurring as little overhead as possible on the underlying servers.

A somewhat critical issue in using ticket methods for federated concurrency control is the appropriate choice for when to issue the take-a-ticket operation on a specific server. For example, suppose that a server uses the TO protocol for ensuring local serializability. TO assigns a timestamp $ts(t)$ to the subtransaction t of a global transaction when it begins its execution. Let t' be another subtransaction such that $ts(t) < ts(t')$. If explicit tickets are used and the one obtained by t has a larger value than that of t', t will be aborted; therefore, *Using tickets with TO t* has to take its ticket first under this timestamp order. More generally, it is advisable that subtransactions do not take their tickets at arbitrary points in time in the presence of TO, but as close as possible to the point when they are assigned their timestamps, that is, at the beginning of their execution. Similar considerations for other protocols are the subject of Exercise 18.8.

With TO as the underlying local protocol, we can actually turn the above impediment into an opportunity, and eliminate explicit tickets. The GTM can ensure that a global transaction *t* obtains a local timestamp smaller than the timestamp of transaction *t'* by delaying the submission of *t'* until *t* has completed its first database operation. The submission order of the subtransactions will then determine their local serialization order. The approach can hence be applied to all servers that allow transactions to commit only if their respective local serialization order reflects their local submission order. The net effect is that such servers save the cost of explicit tickets and instead use the implicit ticket method.

18.7 Object Model Concurrency Control in Heterogeneous Federations

As mentioned in Section 18.1, most of the previous sections' theoretical and algorithmic considerations apply to both page model and object model transactions. Our presentation has been in terms of page model operations, but most results carry over to the semantically richer object model. Here we will briefly reconsider our main results on (1) homogeneous federations, (2) local properties for global serializability in heterogeneous federations, and (3) additional, explicit measures at the GTM level of a federation such as tickets. For the third line of reasoning, the object model is indeed much more appropriate, and we will explain why this is so.

Object model transactions in homogeneous federations   As for homogeneous federations, Theorem 18.1 carries over to distributed object model transactions in a straightforward manner. Each site produces a local serialization order, and the protocol used at all sites needs to ensure that the local serialization orders are compatible with each other so that their union remains acyclic. The standard protocols, most notably the 2PL family, ensure this property, and this holds regardless of the kind of data items, operations, and conflict relations that we consider. So the theorem and its implications also hold, for example, for transactions that invoke high-level operations on business objects such as Withdraw and Deposit on bank accounts. Recall from Chapters 6 and 7 that such transactions are broken down into lower-level subtransactions, each of which corresponds to one of the high-level operations. These subtransactions may themselves be distributed across sites (e.g., for an operation funds transfer that spans different enterprises), but in practice they would more typically be confined to steps at a single site. The bottom line is that we can simply combine the results derived from Theorem 18.1 with the rich theory of object model concurrency control developed in Chapters 6 and 7 in order to obtain a practically viable solution for distributed transactions with semantically rich operations.

In heterogeneous federations the approaches that build on local properties like RG or COCSR and do not need an explicit GTM mechanism can be used for object model transaction management without any additional considerations. The local properties need to be ensured in terms of the involved servers' interface operations, which are now semantically richer operations rather than page reads and writes. This generalization of properties like RG and COCSR is again straightforward, and has been discussed in Chapter 11. So we can easily compose a variety of object servers into a federated system as long as each server locally provides rigorousness or at least commit order-preserving conflict serializability with regard to the operations that the client invokes against the servers' interfaces. This is a fundamental result of great practical relevance for multi-tier Internet-based e-Service applications, which we simply harvest from the theoretical underpinnings of Section 18.5 as well as Chapters 6, 7, and 11.

Object model transactions in heterogeneous federations with strong local properties

In the most general case of heterogeneous federations with servers that merely provide local conflict serializability, the additional measures that are needed in an explicit GTM at the federation level must refer to data items and operations that are *observable* at the interfaces of the underlying servers. So, our previous abstraction that "taking a ticket" amounts to a read and write step on a single data item as in the page model is not quite accurate from an implementation viewpoint. Rather, tickets need to be tested and manipulated through the servers' interface operations such as SQL commands. On the other hand, this simple observation suffices to "lift" the presented page model ticket method to federations with object model servers. All theorems from Section 18.6 still hold, and the ticket method is immediately applicable to such richer and realistic systems. In implementation terms, a ticket then is actually a tuple in a relational table or an encapsulated object in an object-oriented or object relational database. For data servers other than database systems similar implementations are straightforward.

Object model transactions in heterogeneous federations with explicit GTM measures

The layered form of object model transaction management is particularly attractive for federated systems for two reasons. First, the GTM and LTM levels naturally correspond to a two-level concurrency control scheme. Second, the GTM can refer only to operations that are observable at the interfaces of the underlying servers; these are often specifically exported methods on encapsulated objects such as bank accounts, purchase orders, inventories, and so on. Local operations at the page level of a server, on the other hand, are usually not observable outside the server, which renders all GTM methods that explicitly refer to page-level conflicts more or less impractical.

With layered transactions, each high-level operation that is passed to a server is locally handled as if it were a separate, local, and short transaction. This ensures atomicity and isolation of individual object-level operations. On top of this, the GTM layer needs to keep additional long-duration locks (or take equivalent steps such as cycle testing on a serialization graph) in order to guarantee that the overall transactions appear atomic and semantically serializable to their clients. If the object-level operations are SQL commands that constitute the interface of a server, the federation layer needs to extract appropriate predicates from them as the basis for global predicate locking; here techniques from Chapter 8 can be leveraged. Of course, an inevitable consequence of committing each high-level operation as a separate transaction as early as possible is that undoing an entire transaction, for example, on behalf of a client-requested rollback, entails issuing *compensating* operations for those transactions that are already committed on the underlying servers. This situation is not really different from what we have discussed in Chapters 11 and 14 on object model recovery, and can be handled using methods developed in those chapters.

18.8 **Coherency and Concurrency Control for Data-Sharing Systems**

Data-sharing cluster In this section we consider concurrency control in a specific form of distributed system, the data-sharing system, which we have encountered already in Chapter 15. Recall that data servers for applications with very high throughput and availability requirements are often built as data-sharing systems in which independent computers or servers running the same software can access a common database, which in turn is kept on a collection of disks. Thus, the servers share the disks and the data, while each has its individual main memory and in particular its local page cache. This architecture is (once again) illustrated in Figure 18.7. A data-sharing system, also known as a shared disk system, is often realized in the form of a *cluster* in which the servers are locally close, for example, in the same room, with a high-bandwidth, low-latency interconnect.

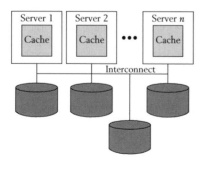

Figure 18.7 Data-sharing system.

Besides recovery from failures discussed in Chapter 15, the problems that have to be solved for data-sharing systems are the *concurrency control problem* and the *cache coherency problem*. Both stem from the fact that data pages can be dynamically replicated in more than one server cache to exploit access locality. Therefore, the synchronization of reads and writes requires some form of distributed lock management, and invalidations of stale copies of data items or propagations of updated data items must be communicated among the servers. Both problems are closely related, and solutions to them are typically such that they treat both aspects in an integrated manner. For reasons of clarity, however, we will first look at the two issues separately and later discuss an integrated solution known as callback locking.

A common assumption for data-sharing systems is that each individual transaction, once routed to a specific server within the cluster, is executed solely on this server (i.e., the transaction does not migrate across servers during its execution). For synchronizing concurrent transactions, data-sharing systems mostly use locking protocols. Each server has a global lock manager and a local lock manager. Data items are assigned to global lock managers in a static manner (e.g., based on a hash function), so that each lock manager is "responsible" for a fixed subset of the data items. We say that a specific global lock manager has the *global lock authority* for a data item. A special case would be that all data items are assigned to a single, centralized lock manager, but a much more scalable variant is, of course, an assignment that partitions the data items among the servers. The global lock manager for a data item knows at each point in time whether the item is locked and, if so, by which servers and in which mode. The local lock managers of the corresponding servers would then have detailed information about which transactions hold locks.

Concurrency control

When a transaction requests a lock or wants to release a lock, it first addresses its local lock manager, which can then contact the global lock manager. The simplest solution is to forward all lock and unlock requests to the global lock manager that has the global lock authority for the given data item. On the other hand, if a local lock manager is authorized to manage at least read locks locally, it can save message exchanges with the global lock manager. We say that a *local read authority* enables a local lock manager to grant local read locks for a data item, while a *local write authority* enables it to grant read or write locks locally. These local lock authorities need to be "borrowed" from the global lock manager that is responsible for a data item (i.e., has the global lock authority). Clearly, write authority can only be "lent" to exactly one local lock manager, and only if no other server currently holds a lock on the given data item. A write authority has to be returned to the corresponding global lock manager if another server wants to access the data item. A read authority, on the other hand, can be held by several servers simultaneously, and has to be revoked when some server wants to perform a write access to the data item.

Lock authorities

The outlined approach is geared for exploiting access locality. Typically, newly incoming transactions are routed to servers according to their transaction type (e.g., new order entry versus payment processing), or characteristic input parameters (e.g., customer ID), or a combination of both and possibly further factors. The aim is to establish a high degree of access locality at each of the servers: a high probability that subsequent transactions find "their" data already cached at the server and a low probability that data that is to be updated also resides in the cache of another server. Under such conditions, most lock requests could be handled solely locally once the necessary local lock authorities have been granted to the corresponding server. Of course, this kind of locality is not static and undergoes fluctuations as the profile of transaction arrivals and their access characteristics vary and evolve over time. For this reason it is crucial that local lock authorities are assigned in a dynamic manner (as opposed to the static assignment of global authorities).

Cache coherency   Access locality is also the overriding consideration for distributed caching in a data-sharing system. In order to reduce data transfers and hence communication overhead within a cluster, servers keep frequently and recently accessed pages in their local caches. Because the access profiles at different servers may overlap and evolve over time, multiple copies of the same page may reside in several caches across a cluster, and these copies need to be kept mutually consistent. As we mentioned in Chapter 15, a cache coherency protocol is employed to this end, and the main invariants such a (typically page-oriented) protocol needs to ensure is that

- multiple caches can hold up-to-date versions of a page simultaneously as long as the page is only read, and
- once a page has been modified in one of the caches, this cache is the only one that is allowed to hold a copy of the page.

Thus, each page undergoes the following cycle in terms of the number of its simultaneously valid copies. Initially, there is only one copy in the stable database on disk. The first access to the page creates a copy in one of the servers' caches. Then, as long as no write takes place, the page may be transferred to other caches, thus creating multiple copies. Upon the first write, all copies but one are discarded, so that only one cache holds a copy. This brings us back to the second stage in the cycle, from which we can again start shipping the page to other caches. Finally, when the page is dropped from all the caches that happen to hold it at some point (by being chosen as a regular cache replacement victim), we are back to the first stage of the cycle, that is, the page only resides on disk.

Owner-based coherency control   A protocol maintaining this invariant is *owner-based coherency control*, which works as follows. Initially, each page is statically assigned to one of the servers in the cluster; this server is called the *home* of the page. A server holding an up-to-date and ready-to-access copy of a page is an *owner* of that page. When a server requests a page for read access and is not yet an owner, it must obtain a recent copy from one of the owners and add itself to the list of owners, which is maintained at the page's home. When a server requests a page for write access, it has to identify all owners of the page (either by a lookup at the home or by broadcast to all servers in the cluster) and issue *callback* requests to all of them, by which their copies are invalidated (or "revoked"); the server thereby becomes the only owner of the page and can then perform the desired write access.

Note the high similarity to the dynamic assignment of lock authorities for distributed concurrency control. Indeed, the home and owner(s) of a page are, to a first approximation, equivalent to the global lock manager that is responsible for the page and the local lock manager(s) that hold(s) a local lock authority for the page. Another way of looking at this similarity is to view the lock table entries for which a global lock manager is responsible as data units that are dynamically cachable in the local lock managers; the dynamic management of local lock authorities essentially boils down to a coherency control protocol for the cached lock table entries.

A protocol that integrates concurrency and coherency control is known by the name *callback locking* and works as follows. For simplicity we first assume that both concurrency and coherency control are page oriented, and will later discuss how this assumption can be relaxed. Initially, the lock responsibility for a page rests with its home. Every owner of a page holds a read lock authority for the page and is therefore able to acquire and release read locks locally. An exclusive owner of a page holds a write lock authority. Finally, the callback of a page also revokes the local lock authority.

Callback locking

EXAMPLE 18.16

Consider the sequence diagram shown in Figure 18.8, with time proceeding from top to bottom. Here, server A wants to set a read lock on page x on behalf of transaction t_1 and is granted read lock authority by the home of x. Then server B wants to do the same on behalf of transaction t_2 and also becomes an owner of x with read lock authority. At a later stage, transaction t_1 commits at server A, and transaction t_3 reads x at server A, which still has read lock authority and can therefore grant the read lock without contacting the home of x again. Next, transaction t_4 wants to write x at server C, which now requests write authority from the home of x. The home, knowing that x has other owners, must send callback messages to servers A and B, and needs to await acknowledgments (shown as "OK" in Figure 18.8) from these two servers before server C can be granted write lock authority. Server B, which still has an ongoing transaction with x in its write set, lets this transaction finish its work and only then sends its acknowledgment to the callback request. Finally, the home of x can grant write lock authority to server C.

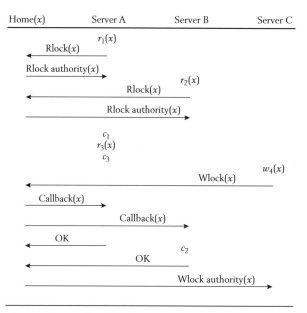

Figure 18.8 Callback locking example.

As mentioned above, lock entries do not necessarily refer to pages; rather they may be associated with finer granules such as records for higher concurrency. Also, at the level of global lock authorities, coarser granules such as tablespaces may be an attractive alternative to minimize the overhead of granting and revoking local lock authorities. And finally, both of these alternatives may be combined in a multigranularity approach (see Chapter 10): coarse items for global lock managers and fine items within local lock managers.

Callback locking with flexible granularities   The implementation of flexible granularities in a data-sharing system requires certain extensions to the basic callback locking protocol. We conclude this section by sketching three such extensions. Their key point is that pages are still the unit of data shipping between servers, but the granularity of lock authorities can be more fine grained or coarse grained depending on the relative importance of data contention versus bookkeeping overhead.

1. Servers can be extended with fine-grained locking and referring to records, index entries, or some form of objects as follows. First consider read operations. Records that reside in pages in a server's cache can be locally locked, read, and unlocked without interaction with other servers. When a page that holds a requested record is not in the local cache, the server queries the page's home about other owners of the page. If there is currently no owner, the server can fetch the page from disk and becomes the only owner. Otherwise, the home ensures that none of the current owners has a write lock on the requested *record*

and then asks one of the owners to ship the *page* to the newly added owner. When shipping the page, all records that are currently write-locked by other transactions (at one or more of the already existing owners) in an incompatible mode are marked as "unavailable." Then the receiving server can read all records in the page except those marked unavailable. In other words, the server has obtained a local read lock authority for all records except those that are already write-locked at other servers. When the server wishes to update an object, it requests a transaction-duration write lock for the record and, at the same time, a short-term write lock on the page from the page's home, which may trigger a page callback from all other current owners of the page. This callback does not revoke the local lock authorities held by the other owners for the unavailable records in the page, but the page itself needs to be re-obtained from the updating server in order to ensure that each owner has an up-to-date copy of the page.

2. The callback mechanism just described can be improved based on the observation that a page typically contains multiple records, which would so far be handled by individual callback requests when a server wants to update more than one record in the same page. In such cases the requesting server may request a write lock authority for the entire page from the page's home. The home will initiate a callback for all records that reside in the page, but this will be granted only when no other server holds any locks on any of the affected records.

3. Finally, locking and callbacks can be done in an adaptive fashion with regard to granularities. When a server wishes to read a record that is not in its cache or is currently marked unavailable in a cached page, it sends a read request to the page's home, which then checks for conflicts at both record and page granularity. If no other server holds a write lock on any record in the requested page, a write lock authority for the entire page can be granted. Otherwise, currently locked records are exempt from the lock authority and marked as unavailable in the page that will be shipped. Of course, if the requested record itself is currently locked at another server, the read request will be blocked. If the read request conflicts with a page-level write lock held by another server, that server is asked to *de-escalate* its lock authority. To do so, it obtains record-level write locks for all records that it has updated or is about to update; then the page lock is released. After de-escalation, the server checks for record-level conflicts and then proceeds along the lines of one of the two cases above.

Note that the above extensions apply equally well to records or index entries in a cluster of relational database servers (or other forms of data servers) and to "true" objects in an object-oriented or object relational database system.

Client caching in (object-oriented) client-server systems

A special case that is of particular interest for object-oriented client-server systems is the situation where clients can locally cache objects that they fetch from a common server. In this architecture, the server takes the role of the home for all data, and clients can become owners on a dynamic basis as in the general data-sharing architecture. Typical applications with this characteristic include CAD systems where clients extract complex objects (e.g., geometry descriptions of automobile or aircraft parts) from the server and run intensive computations on the data in their local caches.

Existing systems exhibit two basic approaches with regard to the granularity of the client-server interactions. In a *page server* architecture, clients request pages from their servers and assemble them into the objects an application requires. In an *object server* architecture, clients can talk to servers in terms of objects, and can henceforth request entire objects on behalf of an application; here it is the server that assembles the object from the pages on which it is physically stored. As mentioned before, both cases can be handled by variations of the callback locking protocol for general data-sharing systems outlined above.

18.9 **Lessons Learned**

In this chapter we have looked at serializability and concurrency control in homogeneous as well as heterogeneous federations. While the former type emphasizes transparency, the latter emphasizes autonomy. As we have seen, this distinction has a minor impact on the notion of transactions (manifested in the distinction between local and global transactions), but makes a big difference for concurrency control. We can mostly reuse the various protocols we have discussed for centralized systems at the local sites, but, in addition, we have to ensure that the local serialization orders are mutually compatible.

Heterogeneous federations occur frequently in present-day applications and are becoming more important than homogeneous ones. Technically, transactions in heterogeneous federations may be subject to indirect conflicts, and coping with these makes life harder. Fortunately, it turns out that global serializability in heterogeneous federations can be achieved by combining various degrees of local properties in combination with some form of global control. With sufficiently strong local guarantees that all servers of a federation uniformly provide, there is no need for an explicit global control. Most importantly, these local properties include rigorousness or commit order preservation in combination with local conflict serializability. In the most general case, where we can rely only on local serializability, additional measures are needed at the global federation level.

An important point from a practical perspective is that such explicit mechanisms at the global level should refer only to operations and their effects that are observable at the interfaces of the underlying, heterogeneous and autonomous, servers. In this regard the ticket method is the most practical approach among the various alternatives that have been devised in the scientific literature. The ticket method is easy to implement and lightweight in terms of the overhead for the take-a-ticket operations and the maintenance of the global ticket graph. Furthermore the ticket graph needs to capture ticket-order edges only for the "weaker" servers of a federation, whereas the "stronger" ones that have local properties such as rigorousness need only implicit tickets.

Both the approach that requires strong local properties and the ticket approach also work well in combination with object model transactions. In this context semantically rich operations are typically confined to a single site, and this case can be handled in a straightforward manner with object model concurrency control at local sites and one of the presented approaches for global serializability at the federation level. This way transaction management for component-based global information systems can be implemented in a reasonably simple manner.

Finally, we have looked at concurrency and coherency control in data-sharing systems, where data may be dynamically replicated in local caches, giving rise to the need for some form of coherency control. We have seen that callback locking is the method of choice here, which can be employed for a variety of granularities.

Exercises

18.1 Consider the (partially ordered) distributed history shown in Figure 18.9 with transactions t_1 through t_5. Assume that data items x, y, and z are managed by server 1, while data items u and v are under the control of server 2. Describe an execution under each of the distributed 2PL and TO protocols that results in s_1.

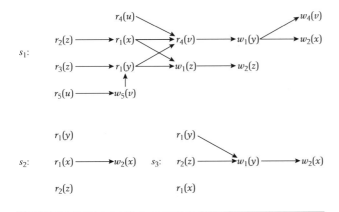

Figure 18.9 Distributed history for Exercise 18.1.

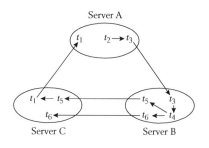

Figure 18.10 Distributed waits-for graph for Exercise 18.3.

18.2 Give a sample execution of a distributed history s such that (a) s itself is not conflict serializable, but (b) each local projection of the execution obeys the distributed 2PL protocol. In particular, state the exact order in which a scheduler acquires and releases locks and executes read and write steps.

18.3 Consider the distributed waits-for graph for transactions t_1 through t_6 running on servers A, B, and C shown in Figure 18.10. Assume that transaction t_1 now requests a lock on server A for which transaction t_2 already holds an incompatible lock. Simulate the path pushing algorithm for deadlock detection at this point, and give the resulting messages.

18.4 Apply the optimistic ticket method (OTM) to the local histories from Examples 18.8, 18.11, and 18.12 and show how global serializability can be obtained in each of these cases.

18.5 Prove Theorem 18.5.

18.6 Show the following for a global history s in a heterogeneous federation with servers 1 through n, where $\Pi_i(s)$ is the projection of s onto the steps at server i: if $s \in$ COCSR then $(\forall\, i,\, 1 \le i \le n)\ \Pi_i(s) = s_i \in$ COCSR. Furthermore, establish additional conditions under which the converse is also true.

18.7 Find a sample history proving that the containment COCSR $\subset$ ECOCSR is proper.

18.8 Discuss appropriate points for the take-a-ticket operation during the execution of a global transaction's subtransaction under the assumption that the underlying server uses (a) 2PL, (b) strict 2PL, (c) strong 2PL, (d) BOCC, (e) FOCC, (f) ROMV (see Chapters 4 and 5) for its local schedule. Consider the possibility that other servers on which the global transaction executes may use different protocols.

18.9 Discuss if and under which conditions the optimistic ticket method can be used with servers that provide multiversion serializability for their local schedules (as opposed to conflict serializability).

Hint: The key property that a server has to ensure is that the ticket order reflects the local serialization order.

18.10 Discuss the use of the optimistic ticket method for servers that merely guarantee local snapshot isolation, as opposed to local conflict serializability (see Chapter 10 for the notion of snapshot isolation). What global correctness criteria can be guaranteed this way? What are the performance implications?

18.11 Consider a data-sharing system with three servers A, B, and C. Suppose server C is the home of pages a, b, c, and d, and these pages are dynamically accessed during the execution of transactions on servers A and B. Give the necessary messages between these servers under a page-oriented callback locking protocol for the following distributed history:

A: $r_1(a)w_1(a)r_1(c)$ $c_1 r_3(a)w_3(a)c_3$ $r_6(b)r_6(d)c_6$

B: $r_2(c)c_2$ $r_4(a)r_4(b)r_4(d)c_4 r_5(b)w_5(b)r_5(d)c_5$

Bibliographic Notes

Distributed database systems in general are covered by the textbook of Özsu and Valduriez (1999). Distributed concurrency control algorithms have been discussed in detail by Bernstein et al. (1987), Papadimitriou (1986), or Cellary et al. (1988). Theorem 18.1 was originally stated by Breitbart and Silberschatz (1988), and a detailed proof has been given by Mehrotra et al. (2000). Distributed concurrency control, including deadlock handling, is also relevant for operating systems; see Silberschatz and Galvin (1998) or Tanenbaum (1995), for example.

The principles of distributed locking have been outlined already in the pioneering work of Gray (1978). Primary site 2PL originates from Alsberg and Day (1976); further discussion of distributed locking can be found in Menasce et al. (1980) and Traiger et al. (1982). Distributed serialization graph testing and timestamp ordering was introduced by Bernstein et al. (1980) as well as Bernstein and Goodman (1980); the former also exploited knowledge from analyzing potential conflicts among predeclared transactions. More sophisticated timestamp-based techniques for distributed systems have been studied by Boksenbaum et al. (1984). The technique for determining globally unique, monotonically increasing timestamps goes back to Lamport (1978) and has become known as a Lamport clock or Lamport time. The problem generally occurs in asynchronous networks, where there is no built-in notion of global time, yet events taking place at various sites of the network need to be globally ordered or at least related from a causal point of view. Techniques for determining global time have been surveyed by Lynch (1996); a generalization of Lamport clocks into "vector clocks" has been proposed by Mattern (1989). Optimistic concurrency control was extended to distributed systems by Schlageter (1981) as well as Ceri and Owicki (1982).

The path pushing algorithm for distributed deadlock detection is from Obermarck (1982). Edge chasing algorithms have originated from the work by Chandy et al. (1983). Surveys of deadlock handling techniques have been given by Elmagarmid (1986), Knapp (1987), Singhal (1989), or Zöbel (1983). Further algorithms have been described by Badal (1986), Bukhres (1992), Choudhary et al. (1989), Menasce and Muntz (1979), Roesler and Burkhard (1989), Sinha and Natarajan (1985), or Krivokapic et al. (1999). Deadlock detection under the specific constraints of multidatabase systems with autonomous servers has been investigated by Breitbart, Litwin, and Silberschatz (1991) as well as Scheuermann and Tung (1992).

Introductions to and surveys of the wide area of heterogenous federations and their autonomy aspects have been given by Litwin et al. (1990), Sheth and Larson (1990), Hurson et al. (1993), Bukhres and Elmagarmid (1996), and Elmagarmid et al. (1998). Seminal work on concurrency control for such systems has been done by Gligor and Popescu-Zeletin (1986), Breitbart and Silberschatz (1988), Pu (1988), and Barker and Özsu (1990). Our exposition of multidatabase concurrency control has partly followed the survey by Breitbart et al. (1992).

Theorem 18.3 is from Breitbart and Silberschatz (1988). Rigorousness as a property of histories has been studied by Breitbart et al. (1991). Commit order-preserving conflict serializability, as mentioned in Chapter 3, was proposed, using different terminology, by Weihl (1989), Breitbart et al. (1991), and Breitbart and Silberschatz (1992), as well as Raz (1992, 1993, 1994). The correctness criterion of quasi serializability as well as a study of consistency preservation by way of this condition was presented by Du and Elmagarmid (1989) as well as Du et al. (1991). Further discussion of correctness criteria for multidatabase histories can be found in Mehrotra et al. (1992, 1997, 1998, 2000) as well as Zhang and Elmagarmid (1993).

The ticket method with forced conflicts was proposed by Georgakopoulos et al. (1991, 1994); Theorem 18.6 is from the latter reference, and this paper also contains correctness arguments for mixing explicit and implicit tickets in the same federation. The ticket method has been extended by Schenkel et al. (2000) to federations in which some of the servers cannot guarantee full (conflict) serializability but only a weaker SQL isolation level such as snapshot isolation; this work has also addressed Exercise 18.10. Schenkel and Weikum (2000) have continued this line of investigation using graph-based global concurrency control. Veijalainen (1990), Veijalainen et al. (1992), Weikum et al.

(1993), and Deacon et al. (1994) have discussed object model transaction management in a multidatabase environment. Schaad et al. (1995) have presented implementation techniques for such a setting, and Muth (1997) has discussed application-specific adaptations of layered transactions in such a setting.

Owner-based coherency control for distributed memory systems in general has been presented by Li and Hudak (1989). Rahm (1986a, b) was among the first to study the concurrency control problem in data-sharing clusters. Later studies that looked at cache coherency and concurrency control in an integrated manner have been done by Dias et al. (1989), Mohan and Narang (1991, 1992a), as well as Rahm (1993). Callback-style protocols were introduced for distributed file systems by Howard et al. (1988) and Nelson et al. (1988), and further developed for object-oriented client-server systems by Lamb et al. (1991). Callback locking has been investigated in detail in the work of Franklin (1996) and the papers by Franklin et al. (1997), as well as Zaharioudakis et al. (1997). Other, closely related algorithms have been discussed by Wilkinson and Neimat (1990), Wang and Rowe (1991), Adya et al. (1995), and Panagos et al. (1996). Implementation and performance aspects of concurrency and coherency control for data-sharing clusters have been discussed by Joshi (1991), Lomet (1994), and Dan and Yu (1992). Distributed forms of escrow locking have been discussed by Härder (1988) as well as Barbara and Garcia-Molina (1994).

CHAPTER NINETEEN

Distributed Transaction Recovery

A distributed system is one where the failure of some
computer I've never heard of can keep me from getting my work done.

—Leslie Lamport

To marry is to halve your rights and to double your duties.

—Arthur Schopenhauer

19.1 **Goal and Overview**

Distributed system architectures with multiple servers present difficulties with regard to recovery similar to the issue of centralized versus distributed concurrency control. More specifically, the all-or-nothing semantics of atomicity must extend to a transaction's updates on multiple servers. So either all updates on all servers are committed, or all updates on all servers must be undone.

The fundamental reason for the extra complexity of distributed transactions is that a distributed system can *fail partially* in the sense that one server fails while others continue their normal operation. Furthermore, servers need to exchange messages to agree upon whether a distributed transaction that has accessed and manipulated data on multiple servers should be committed or aborted. If some of these messages get lost—for example, because of a router or gateway failure—it is all but trivial to guarantee a unanimous decision about the transaction's commit versus abort termination. When a server does not get a message that it expects to receive from another server, it is impossible for the receiving server to tell exactly whether the message got lost, whether the sending server is simply extremely slow and the message is delayed, or whether the sending server has failed. So the conservative assumption must be that the sending server has crashed. Unfortunately, it is also impossible to figure out the exact point of that crash. If one server has just started actions to commit its part of the transaction while the other server has had the bad luck of failing right before it could complete the decisive part of its side of the commit, we end up with the unacceptable situation that the transaction's updates on one server become committed, but the other, failed, server will have to undo its updates of the transaction during restart. Such a case would lead to potentially inconsistent data.

Two-phase commit (2PC)

The solution out of this dilemma is to set up a special handshake protocol between the involved servers from a family of distributed commit protocols, with the so-called two-phase commit (2PC) protocol being the most important instantiation. This protocol builds upon each server's local capabilities for logging and transactional crash recovery. What it adds is a couple of message rounds to establish a "contract" between the servers to ensure that either all servers commit the transaction or the transaction will be undone on all servers, and this contract must be fulfilled regardless of whether some servers fail (and later become restarted) or messages get lost (and need to be resent as part of the protocol).

In-doubt (uncertain) transactions

As we will see in this chapter, the protocol inevitably implies that there are certain circumstances under which a failed server must communicate to other servers during its restart to find out the systemwide decision about the termination status of one or more *in-doubt transactions*, also known as *uncertain transactions*. In other words, servers are no longer autonomous in that they can always independently recover "in splendid isolation." This complication is the inherent price for maintaining the consistency of distributed data. This may sound very expensive, and many application architects have traditionally been reluctant to use distributed transactions. However, the implementation techniques that we will look at in this chapter are very efficient, and the general progress on computer and network resources as well as server reliability makes distributed commit protocols a practically viable cornerstone of modern information systems.

Distributed commit protocols are mandatory for both homogeneous distributed database systems (i.e., one conceptual database partitioned or possibly replicated across multiple sites, all of which run the same database system software) and arbitrary federated systems that may involve a heterogeneous set of database systems, mail servers, document servers, queue managers or workflow servers, and so on. An elegant property of the protocol is that it makes very few assumptions about how the various servers implement their local recovery, as long as they understand the notion of winner versus loser transactions. Therefore, it is also relatively easy to implement a distributed commit protocol in a federated system. The requirement there is that the rules of the commit protocol itself are followed by all parties; to this end the two-phase commit protocol has been standardized and is generally accepted in the software industry. We will discuss the basic two-phase commit protocol in great detail in Section 19.2.

Federated systems are multi-tier systems in the sense that each server may outsource some work to another server or implement its business objects by means of other, more primitive objects provided by other servers (see Chapter 1 for terminology and examples). In this setting a transaction often implicitly manipulates data along entire hierarchies of servers and spans a tree of work units that are all subject to the distributed commit protocol. Such scenarios are appropriately handled by a hierarchical protocol that iterates the basic behavior of the two-phase commit protocol. We will discuss this generalization of the flat two-phase commit to trees in Section 19.3.

Both the flat and the hierarchical variants of two-phase commit open a number of opportunities for optimizations, especially the exploitation of special properties of transaction profiles, server-specific strengths, and the communication topology. Most optimizations aim to reduce the communication and/or logging overhead of the protocol, and some of them also consider the issue of maximizing the probability that servers can recover and resume normal operation independently. Section 19.4 discusses the practically most important optimizations from a large set of options.

19.2 The Basic Two-Phase Commit Algorithm

This section presents the basic two-phase commit algorithm in three subsections: we begin with the actual protocol that specifies the message exchange and logging actions during normal operation, we will then cover the necessary steps when failures occur, then finally discuss opportunities for and limitations of independently recovering individual servers after a failure.

19.2.1 2PC Protocol

The protocol known as (basic) two-phase commit, or 2PC, that we are going to present in this section serves to ensure the atomicity of a distributed transaction. The critical point within such a transaction that has made updates on more than one data server is when the application program requests the commit of these updates. Assume that this request initiates writing some kind of commit log entry to the stable logs of all involved servers. Each server will be responsible for the crash resilience of its local updates. In the following we will refer to the participating servers as *participants*; this also denotes the parts of the transactions on behalf of which the various servers act. The literature sometimes denotes these local parts of the transaction as "agents," but we will not explicitly distinguish the different notions for a local agent and the corresponding server, as no ambiguities arise. In the context of distributed commit, the servers on which the participants run are usually referred to as *resource managers* (especially in the standards and product literature) to emphasize that not only traditional data servers (e.g., database systems) can participate in a transaction but also more general servers, such as queue managers (see Chapter 17).

In the absence of shared storage among the participants, it is possible that a subset of the participants succeeds with their local commits, whereas other

Participants (agents) running on resource managers

participants fail and must later undo the transaction's local updates. Note that the latter may even have lost the log entries that would be necessary to redo their part of the transaction, which is feasible because log buffers do not need to be forced before commit. The committed participants, on the other hand, will release the transaction's local locks (or perform the analogous steps in a nonlocking type of concurrency control protocol) so that new transactions can see the updates and even modify the same data. This implies that, in full generality, there is no way to undo the updates of the successfully committed participants at some later point when it becomes known that one or more other participants failed. Even the invocation of high-level compensation steps would only be feasible if no subsequent transaction has performed a semantically conflicting operation; otherwise we could not ensure the reducibility (in the sense of Chapter 11) of the resulting schedule and would violate the isolation property of the transactional ACID contracts.

(Transaction)
coordinator

The solution out of this dilemma is to introduce a transaction *coordinator* that mediates between the application program's commit request and the various participants. In a certain sense, which will be made precise in the following, the coordinator emulates the missing shared storage, but the coordinator is the only one that can directly access this "storage," and participants need to communicate with the coordinator via messages. The coordinator is a process that can run on the client or any server; most often it is combined with one of the participants by simply running it on the same data server in the same process (possibly as an additional thread). The "shared storage" maintained by the coordinator is nothing more than a stable log that holds log entries about the commit status of a transaction (i.e., no log entries about data updates). When the coordinator is combined with a participant, the coordinator's log entries are simply embedded in the stable log file of the server. In the following we will nonetheless consider the coordinator as if it were a separate process with a separate log, for ease of explanation.

Global commit
needs
unanimous
local commits

The coordinator ensures a unanimous outcome of the transaction—either all participants perform local commits or all perform local rollbacks—by initiating two rounds of message exchanges with the participants (hence the name two-phase commit). In the first round, the *voting* or *preparation phase*, the coordinator conducts a form of voting, or poll, by asking every participant whether it is ready to commit the transaction. For reasons that will become clear soon, this message is usually called a *prepare* message or sometimes *request-to-vote* or *request-to-prepare*. A participant replies "yes" if it has all log entries on the stable log that would be necessary for redoing the local updates; to this end it may have to force its log buffer before sending the reply. If a participant has had a recent crash or some other reason for not being able or willing to commit the transaction's local updates, it replies "no." When the coordinator receives a yes vote from all participants, it knows that the transaction can be safely committed at all underlying servers and announces the result of the voting phase by sending a definitive "commit" message to every participant. This is the second

First phase:
voting (prepare)

of the two message rounds, the *decision phase*. Otherwise, when at least one participant replied "no," the coordinator announces "abort." In either case, the participants acknowledge the receipt of the coordinator's message about the transaction's fate in the form of a special "ack" message.

Second phase: decision (commit or abort)

This message exchange resembles the protocol in a wedding ceremony, with the priest or judge in the role of the coordinator. (Obviously, getting married is such a complicated endeavor that you need a third person to accomplish it.) To make the analogy even closer, we assume that the bride and the groom cannot talk to each other directly (i.e., neither of them hears what the other one says) but only communicate with the coordinator (via messages, so to speak); imagine, for example, that this is an Internet wedding. The priest asks the bride whether she is willing to take the groom as her husband, and the bride replies to the priest; then the groom is asked the same question and gives his reply. Only if both bride and groom reply "yes" will the priest announce that they are from now on a married couple; otherwise, the wedding party will be canceled.

The message exchange for the case of a positive transaction outcome is depicted in Figure 19.1 as a sequence diagram, where time proceeds from top

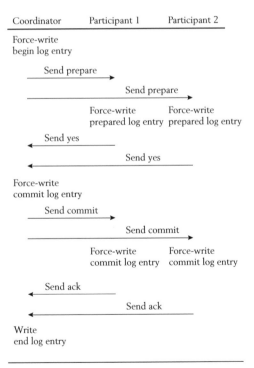

Figure 19.1 Sequence diagram for the two-phase commit protocol in the case of a global commit.

to bottom, each of the three columns represents a process, and arcs that connect two columns denote messages between the corresponding processes. The figure also shows some local actions of the three processes, namely, writing log entries, which we will discuss later.

Both protocols, distributed transaction commit and distributed marriage, are susceptible to failures: messages can get lost (e.g., if the bride speaks too low) or may be repeated (e.g., someone says "yes, yes, yes"), and any of the involved parties, including the coordinator, may fail at any point (e.g., if the priest faints or the groom runs away without saying a word). So the commit protocol needs to be made failure resilient with regard to certain failure classes. The failures that we consider here are as follows:

Failure model: message losses, message duplications, transient crashes

- *Message losses*: a message does not arrive at the destination process because of a network failure (e.g., router failure or software failure in a gateway).

- *Message duplications*: some network component may end up duplicating a message, for example, in an attempt to recover from a transient failure, so that the same message arrives multiple times at its destination (but possibly interleaved with other messages and therefore not trivial to detect).

- *Transient process failures*: one or more of the involved processes, participants or coordinators, exhibit a soft crash (in the sense of Chapter 12) and need to be restarted, but without any damage to data on secondary storage.

It seems intriguing to distribute the responsibilities for handling the various failure classes among the transactional federation and the underlying communication system. The latter could obviously be in charge of handling message losses and duplicate messages. Message losses could be detected by requiring system-generated acknowledgments for all messages as part of the network protocol. So the communication software on a computer (often as part of the operating system) would repeat sending a message until it receives an acknowledgment from the communication software of the recipient. Duplicate messages could be detected by establishing a session for every pair of communicating processes with a session-specific message counter that is incremented by one each time a new message is sent. This way the receiver can easily determine when it receives a message for the second time, and it can even detect gaps in a message sequence that can be used to guarantee order-preserving message delivery regardless of the actual message routing. The TCP/IP protocol could provide these guarantees if this was desired, and even more far-reaching communication services, such as atomic multicasting to multiple recipients of the same message, could be implemented as part of a powerful communication system. However, these services, especially session-oriented communication as opposed to so-called datagrams, come at a high price in terms of their overhead. Furthermore and most importantly, it turns out that two-phase commit cannot be truly simplified by handling two of the above three failure classes already in the communication system. Even with a perfectly reliable network there is no reduction in complexity, say, by reducing the number of messages for the commit of a distributed transaction, because of the need to cope with process failures among the participants and the coordinator. For these reasons, two-phase commit does not make any assumptions about the underlying communication system and works with datagrams as the simplest type of unacknowledged, sessionless messages between processes (or, actually, between pairs of IP number and port number in the prevalent Internet and LAN protocols).

All of the above failure types fall into the broad class of *omission failures*, as opposed to *commission failures*, which would include messages with maliciously manipulated contents (e.g., saying "yes" although the participant actually sent a "no"). We assume that none of the participants of a transactional federation has any interest in deceiving the other; therefore, we disregard commission failures. Taking manipulated messages into account would lead us into an even broader class of *distributed consensus protocols*, also known as *Byzantine agreement*. The latter name stems from the hypothetical scenario that two generals planned to jointly attack the ancient town of Byzantium (nowadays known as Istanbul in Turkey) and needed an agreement on the timing of the attack. The generals' armies were (assumed to be) on two hills so that they had to send messengers for communicating the plan of attack. Messengers could get lost or, and this is the point, could be caught by the enemy who could then deceive the generals by sending their own people disguised as messengers. Note that manipulated messages are critical here because unless both armies would attack at exactly the same time, they would not be able to conquer Byzantium.

Distributed consensus (Byzantine agreement)

To leave the various analogies aside, the two-phase commit protocol sketched above needs to be able to cope with message and process omission failures. In particular and most critically, it is possible that a participant replies "yes" to the coordinator's poll in the first message round and then crashes. Now the participant can no longer simply perform local crash recovery as if there were no distributed transactions at all. The fact that it is able to redo the transaction's local updates does not mean that this is the correct way of recovery. Rather, the coordinator may decide that the entire transaction needs to be rolled back because some other participant voted "no," and this fact may not even be known at the time the failed participant restarts (it is definitely not known to the restarted participant itself). The solution is that the restarted participant needs to check back with the coordinator first before it can decide to consider the transaction as a winner. This implies that the participant may now learn from the coordinator that the transaction needs to be globally rolled back. Therefore, every participant that votes "yes" must actually be *prepared* to go either way—redo the transaction's local updates or undo the updates. Furthermore, the participant needs to have a means of detecting, during restart,

Prepared log entry for in-doubt transaction

that it already replied to the coordinator's poll before the crash and now needs to contact the coordinator (or wait until the coordinator resends the decision once again). This problem is solved by writing a special log entry, called a *prepared log entry*, to the participant's stable log before sending a "yes" reply to the coordinator. This does not require extra log forcing; when the log buffer is written to disk it includes the prepared log entry and also all preceding undo/redo log entries for the pending transaction (unless these were written to the stable log even earlier). From this point on, the participant considers the transaction, or actually, its local part, as prepared or in doubt, as the participant does not yet know the decision about the transaction's fate (global commit or global abort). Note that before the participant sends its "yes" reply or if it replies "no," it can unilaterally abort the transaction and roll back its local part. Later on it would simply reply "no" when asked by the coordinator, and the coordinator would then have to announce global abort; so this option does not affect the consistency of the transaction's global outcome.

Susceptibility to blocking   The fact that a participant becomes dependent on the coordinator, in that it has to communicate with the coordinator, once it is in the Prepared state can be viewed as a certain loss of the participant's autonomy. As the coordinator may itself fail at the time a failed and restarted participant wants to contact the coordinator to resolve its Prepared state (or messages between the coordinator and this participant become lost), there is no guarantee that the transaction can be globally committed or rolled back within a bounded time period. The same holds even if the participant did not fail at all but simply does not receive any messages from the coordinator after having sent its "yes" vote. So the participant may become blocked for an indefinite period by waiting for the decision from the coordinator. Two-phase commit is therefore called a *blocking* protocol. This is a potentially critical aspect, as a blocked participant, without knowledge about the transaction's global fate, cannot release any locks that are held on behalf of the prepared transaction's local parts (and there may be multiple prepared transactions at the same time). Recall from Chapter 11 on transaction recovery (i.e., rollbacks during normal operation) that this is so because a rollback of the transaction, one of the two possible outcomes, performs additional inverse operations that need to be reflected in the concurrency control protocol. Two-phase commit has been criticized because of this potential blocking property, but as we will soon show, there is no way of ensuring global atomicity and global data consistency with absolutely no risk of blocking. So operating federations of servers with distributed transactions inherently implies that the participating data servers must accept some impact on their autonomy. In practice, however, this issue is not nearly as critical as it may sound, at least not with carefully operated, highly reliable servers and network connections, and distributed transactions that do not span more than a few (e.g., less than five) servers. There is impressive evidence for the practical viability of two-phase commit in many industrial-strength information systems, including Internet-based applications.

In addition to the participants' prepared log entries and the final commit or rollback log entries, the coordinator needs to write additional log entries to track the progress in the protocol. Specifically, the coordinator needs to write a *begin log entry* before it starts its polling message round. This log entry is usually forced to the stable log before the coordinator sends out messages. Furthermore, the coordinator needs to write an *end log entry* at the end of the second protocol phase once it has received ack messages from all participants, but this log entry does not need to be forced immediately. In order to create the end log entry at the appropriate time, the coordinator needs to have a list of participants from which it anticipates ack messages, and this list should be resilient to coordinator failures. To this end, the coordinator includes the list of participants in the begin log entry.

Begin log entry

These log writes are shown in Figure 19.1 for the case of a transaction commit. Analogous log entries are created when the transaction ends up as a loser. In the figure, "force-write" means that a log entry is created in the log buffer and the log buffer is then forced to disk. Note that the (nonforced) end log entry, written by the coordinator at the end of the protocol, is important for garbage collection on the coordinator log. At some point in the future, the coordinator would like to discard log entries about distributed transactions that have been terminated a while ago. Otherwise the coordinator log would grow indefinitely, and log truncation is crucial for fast restart, especially given the fact that the coordinator log is often embedded in a server's regular log file. So once the end log entry is on the stable log, the coordinator can forget the transaction and consider its coordinator-specific log entries as garbage. For this reason the end log entry is sometimes also referred to in the literature as a "forgotten" or "done" log entry.

End (forgotten, done) log entry for garbage collection

All these log entries serve to remember the last relevant state of a process, with regard to an ongoing instance of the two-phase commit protocol. When a process fails and is restarted, it resumes its part of the protocol in the last locally remembered state. For example, when a participant is restarted in the Prepared state, which is determined from the existence of a prepared log entry and the nonexistence of a commit or rollback log entry in the stable log, it sends out its yes reply and waits for the coordinator's decision. Note that there is no way for the participant to detect from its stable log whether it has already sent the reply before the crash or whether it crashed in between writing the prepared log entry and sending the reply. Also note that this uncertainty is inherent and cannot be eliminated by additional log entries, the reason being that it is not possible (with commodity hardware) to combine a disk write and message send into an atomic unit. Such atomicity would itself require a mechanism like distributed transactions; so assuming this kind of atomicity for implementing distributed commit would be a circular and thus infeasible argument. Likewise, when the coordinator fails and is restarted in the Begin state—that is, with the begin log entry as the most recent trace of the transaction in the coordinator log—it simply reinitiates the poll by sending prepare

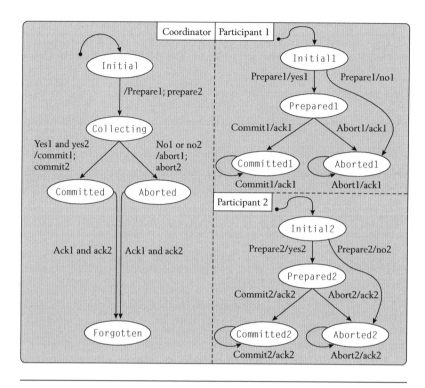

Figure 19.2 Statechart for two-phase commit protocol.

messages to all participants, possibly creating duplicate messages to some or even all participants.

Statechart representation of 2PC

These considerations can be systematically cast into a finite state automaton that specifies the behavior of a participant or coordinator. Figure 19.2 gives a full picture of the states through which the various processes proceed and the messages that are sent and/or expected to be received in a given state. More specifically, the figure shows a statechart specification—a formalism that we already used in Chapter 1 in a different context, namely, to describe long-lived business workflows. To briefly recapture this formalism, a statechart is essentially a finite state automaton (or, equivalently, a set of communicating automata whose cross-product forms the entire statechart) with logical conditions attached to state transitions.

The ovals in Figure 19.2 show the states of a process; each state corresponds to a specific log entry: the process is considered to be in this state if and only if the stable log contains the corresponding log entry. In this sense the coordinator's Forgotten state corresponds to the presence of the end log entry; the other states are self-explanatory. Initial states are indicated by incoming edges with a small point as origin; final states have no outgoing edges.

Transitions are labeled with event-condition-action rules (ECA rules for short) in the form "event [condition]/action," where each component of the triple is optional and omitted when insignificant (e.g., when no action is specified or the condition is the constant "true"). A transition fires if the specified event occurs and its condition is true; the state transition then executes the specified action, the current state is left, and the new state is entered.

In our setting, events are message receipts and actions are message sends. For example, the transition label Prepare1/yes1 from the first participant's Initial1 state to the Prepared1 state indicates that the transition is made upon the receipt of a prepare1 message and then sends the message yes1 as the transition's action. Note that the origin and destination of each message is uniquely determined by the protocol itself (e.g., the prepared1 message must originate from the coordinator). The entire statechart of Figure 19.2 consists of three orthogonal components, one for each process in the protocol, that can execute in parallel but are synchronized by the message exchanges according to their state transitions. Recall from Chapter 1 that orthogonal components are themselves full-fledged statecharts. The two participants have, of course, identical behavior. They may thus be viewed as two instantiations of the same statechart, but we distinguish their states and messages by the number suffix to avoid notational ambiguities.

19.2.2 **Restart and Termination Protocol**

The protocol of Figure 19.2 is robust with respect to failures in the sense that each failed and restarted process resumes its work in the last remembered state. However, this is not yet truly failure resilient in the sense that all processes guarantee active progress toward a global commit or rollback, even after a failure. For example, assume that the coordinator fails in the Collecting state where it has already received one yes vote but is still waiting for the other participant's vote. If this other vote was sent during the coordinator's outage, it may never be sent again, and the restarted coordinator may end up waiting in the Collecting state forever. Because messages can get lost without any of the three involved processes failing, such problems can arise even during normal operation. For example, we need to specify how the coordinator should behave when it does not receive a vote from a participant for an extended period. An obvious remedy could be to resend the prepare message once again and keep doing so until the participant replies. Such periodic repetition of message sends should be driven by timeouts.

Process behavior after failures and upon timeouts

Casting the above considerations into a systematic form leads us to two extensions of the basic two-phase commit protocol:

Restart and termination protocol

- A *restart protocol* specifies how a failed and restarted protocol should proceed.

- A *termination protocol* specifies how a process should behave upon a timeout while it is waiting for some message.

As all participants follow the same protocol, we have to specify four cases:

1. *The coordinator restart protocol*: the continuation of the coordinator's protocol after a coordinator failure.
2. *The coordinator termination protocol*: the coordinator's behavior upon timeout, for example, when it suspects a failure of some participant or a network problem.
3. *The participant restart protocol*: the continuation of a participant's protocol after a failure of the participant.
4. *The participant termination protocol*: the participant's behavior upon timeout, for example, when it suspects a coordinator failure and is unable to communicate with the coordinator.

Note that a process usually cannot distinguish whether a communication partner has failed or whether there is "merely" a network problem. The ability to distinguish these two cases would require additional networking services for error diagnosis, but as network components such as routers can fail, too, there is no foolproof way of accomplishing this kind of error analysis. Therefore, the termination protocols handle both cases uniformly.

For the precise specification of restart and termination behavior, we extend the statechart of Figure 19.2 by two kinds of additional transitions:

- *F transitions* are triggered during restart after a process failure. Once the process's last state is determined from the log entries on the process's stable log, the transition is made without any further preconditions.
- *T transitions* are triggered upon timeout and are also made without further preconditions.

Figure 19.3 shows the complete 2PC statechart with T and F transitions from all relevant states. Note that some states do not require any actions, such as the Forgotten state of the coordinator. For other states, the termination or restart behavior may require additional auxiliary states such as A-pending and C-pending; these do not require any additional log entries, though, and are thus not persistent across crashes.

The restart and termination transitions are crucial for progress toward a global commit or rollback, as discussed in the following case analysis.

1. *Coordinator restart*: When the coordinator fails in the Initial state, it automatically reinitiates the entire protocol (which does not require an

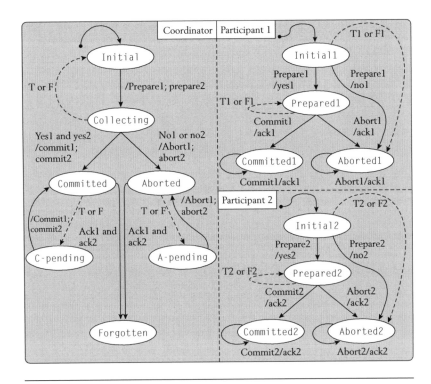

Figure 19.3 Statechart for two-phase commit protocol with termination and restart protocol.

additional F transition). Alternatively, the coordinator may simply forget the transaction after a failure in this state, the effect of which would be an implicit decision to abort the transaction. When the coordinator fails in the `Collecting` state, it cannot remember whether it already received some participant replies (at least not in this simple variant of 2PC) and needs to go back to the `Initial` state. Finally, and this is the most interesting case, when it fails in the `Committed` or `Aborted` state, it resends the commit or abort message, possibly duplicating some messages, and waits (again) for the participants' ack messages. So the coordinator actively drives the protocol toward termination.

2. *Coordinator termination*: When the coordinator observes a timeout, because one or more participants have not replied (in time), it resends messages according to its current state. The behavior is essentially the same as in the coordinator restart protocol, and again, the coordinator actively attempts to advance the states of the involved processes. In contrast to the restart protocol, the coordinator termination protocol could be more selective in terms of resending messages. For example, in a

situation where it has received the vote from one participant and a timeout occurs for another participant, the prepare message does not need to be resent to the first participant. For simpler presentation, this refinement is not shown in Figure 19.3.

3. *Participant restart*: When a participant fails in its Initial state, it has not yet given up its decision autonomy and can choose to unilaterally abort its part of the transaction. When it is later asked for its vote, it would simply reply no. This option for unilateral abort is important because long delays during a two-phase commit, with the pending transaction's locks being held for an extended period, could adversely affect the response time of other transactions that are waiting for locks. On the other hand, this option is available only in the Initial state. Once the participant has entered the Prepared state, it must wait for the coordinator decision. This is why the F transition from the Prepared state simply leads back into the same state. An alternative could be to make participants more eager (after a failure and also upon timeouts) and have them actively contact the coordinator, or even other participants that may have received the coordinator's decision, to resolve the transaction's in-doubt state as quickly as possible. This extension is not specified in Figure 19.3, but we will return to such considerations in Section 19.4.

4. *Participant termination*: The participant behavior upon timeout is essentially the same as during restart. However, it could make sense to be more patient in the Initial state, and rather than choosing the unilateral abort option, the participant could stay for one or two timeout periods in the Initial state. This is a reasonable alternative, as the timing in a server federation may have much higher variance than within a single server, even during normal operation and especially in a wide area network like the Internet.

Note that the statechart of Figure 19.3 provides complete algorithms for coordinator and participant, as there are generic interpreters for statecharts. In pseudocode form the algorithms look as follows:

2PC
coordinator
algorithm

```
2PC coordinator ( ):
ParticipantReplies: array[1..max] of Boolean;
/* initiate protocol */
n := number of participants;
for j:=1 to n do
 ParticipantReplies[j] := false;
 send prepare message to participant j;
od;
upon receiving a message from participant i:
case message type of
```

```
yes:        ParticipantReplies[i] := true;
            if and(ParticipantReplies[j], j=1..n) = true then
              write commit log entry; force ( );
              for j:=1 to n do
                ParticipantReplies[i] := false;
                send commit message to participant j;
              od;
            fi;
            wait for next message;
no:        if rollback log entry already written
            then ignore message else
                write rollback log entry; force ( );
                for j:=1 to n do
                  ParticipantReplies[j] := false;
                  send abort message to participant j;
                od;
            fi;
            wait for next message;
ack:        ParticipantReplies[i] := true;
            if and(ParticipantReplies[j], j=1..n) = true
            then write end log entry; fi;
/* termination protocol */
upon timeout when waiting for a message:
case last coordinator log entry of
 begin:    for j:=1 to n do
                if ParticipantReplies[j] = false then
                send prepare message to participant j fi;
            od;
 commit:   for j:=1 to n do
                if ParticipantReplies[j] = false then
                send commit message to participant j fi;
            od;
 rollback: for j:=1 to n do
                if ParticipantReplies[j] = false then
                send abort message to participant j fi;
            od;
wait for next message;
/* restart protocol */
analogous to termination protocol


2PC participant ( ):
upon receiving a message from coordinator:
case message type of
```

2PC participant algorithm

```
    prepare:    if transaction not yet aborted then
                    write prepared log entry; force ( );
                    send yes to coordinator;
                    wait for commit or abort message;
                else send no to coordinator;
                fi;
     commit:        write commit log entry; force ( );
                send ack to coordinator;
     abort:         if transaction not yet aborted then
                    roll back transaction:
                    write rollback log entry; force ( );
                fi;
                send ack to coordinator;
/* termination protocol */
upon timeout when waiting for a message:
if prepared log entry does not exist then
 roll back transaction;
else if no commit or rollback log entry exists then
 wait for commit or abort message from coordinator; fi; fi;
/* restart protocol */
analogous to termination protocol
```

From the formal specification of 2PC given in Figure 19.3 we can infer a number of key properties. Most importantly, we can prove the correctness of the 2PC protocol; for simplicity we disregard the coordinator's Forgotten state in the following and assume that Committed and Aborted are final states.

THEOREM 19.1

The 2PC protocol guarantees the atomicity of distributed transactions, in that it ensures that if one process reaches a final state (i.e., its local Committed or Aborted state), then either all processes (i.e., all participants and the coordinator) are in their Committed states or all of them are in their Aborted states.

Proof

The proof assumes that all processes start in their initial states and considers the possible state combinations as the protocol is executed. In the following, we refer to the state combination of $n + 1$ processes, n participants, and one coordinator, as the *global state* of the protocol. The set of global states is a subset of the cross-product of the state sets of the $n + 1$ individual processes. We refer to the latter as *local states*. Now we can consider the set of possible *computation paths*, where a computation path is a feasible sequence of global states starting with the $(n + 1)$-tuple (Initial, Initial, ..., Initial) and entering new states as transitions fire. The rules of the protocol, as specified by the statechart, eliminate certain combinations of local states as feasible global states. For example, it is impossible for the system of processes to be in the global state (Initial, Committed, ..., Committed) where the first component of the $(n + 1)$-tuple denotes the local state of the coordinator and the other components refer to the participants. Such a global state is impossible because the participants can leave their Initial states only after receiving a commit message from the coordinator, but this message is sent only from the coordinator's Committed state and there is no path from this state back to the Initial state in the coordinator's statechart. The set of feasible computation paths constrains the possible global states even further, as we require that a state must be reachable from the global Initial state by making state transitions according to the given statechart specification.

After these preliminaries, it is now clear what we have to show for the proof: no global state with at least one aborted and at least one committed component is reachable via a computational path from the global Initial state. To see that such a global state is infeasible, we first observe that a participant can enter its Committed (Aborted) state only after having received a commit (abort) message, and such a message is sent only by the coordinator and only when the coordinator is entering its Committed (Aborted) state. So to arrive at the unacceptable global state, the coordinator would have to be in the local state Committed at some point and in the local state Aborted at another point. However, once the coordinator is in either of these two states, it can never reach the other state, for the simple reason that there is no path of connecting transition arcs between the Committed and the Aborted state. Therefore, a global state in which some components are committed and others are aborted is not reachable.

Proofs like the one just given that are essentially case analyses over a finite, but possibly very large, state space can even be automated using *model checking* techniques. Model checking takes a (temporal) logical formula over computation paths as an input argument and checks whether the given finite state automaton is a model of this formula, using clever techniques for efficiency.

The above theorem guarantees a *safety property* in that a certain unacceptable outcome can be ruled out. Safety properties generally state that "nothing bad will ever happen." In addition, however, we are interested in a termination guarantee, which falls into the class of *liveness properties* stating that "something good will eventually happen." So we would like to prove that the system of processes will indeed reach either the global state (Committed, ..., Committed) or the global state (Aborted, ..., Aborted) after a *finite* number of state transitions (including T and F transitions from a state back to itself). This liveness property is captured in the following theorem under the assumption that there is no infinite number of failures so that all processes are running for a sufficiently long period of time.

THEOREM 19.2

For a finite number of failures (process failures with subsequent restarts or message losses), the 2PC protocol will reach a final global state (with either all participants committed or all participants aborted) with a finite number of state transitions.

Proof

With a finite number of failures and a bounded restart time for each process, the system of processes performs a finite number of transitions before it will eventually reach a sufficiently long stable period to complete the protocol. From this point a finite number of transitions will bring all processes to a final local state because no local state is ever entered more than once unless there is a failure or timeout.

So in the worst case none of the processes has made any progress during the period of failures, and all of them will start from their Initial states in the stable period. In reality, of course, the failure period and the stable period are not separated. So some processes make progress while others fail and restart, and this brings these processes even closer to a final state.

A general assumption throughout all our previous explanations has been that the commit protocol is initiated only when the actual transaction execution is finished. So none of the participants should perform any further data actions (i.e., reads or writes of data items) once the commit protocol has begun. In practice, this assumption, albeit extremely intuitive, does not always hold for the reason that some data servers may have deferred some special operations until commit time. This may apply, for example, to the checking of declaratively specified consistency constraints and the modification of derived data to rectify temporary inconsistencies. Such deferred operations can be implemented at the application level using SQL triggers, but servers may also adopt such an option for internal use (e.g., to check foreign key constraints in relational or object relational databases and initiate cascading updates at commit time). These options may be encapsulated by the involved servers, so that the transaction coordinator is not necessarily aware of them.

Reinfected participants   The problem with these kinds of application-level deferred updates is that a participant that had already prepared itself and voted yes may need to perform additional updates during the second phase of the 2PC protocol. Such a participant is called *reinfected*. The solution is for the coordinator to wait with its decision until it is definitely known that all of the potentially possible deferred updates have been done and all participants are truly prepared. At this point the coordinator may also have to update its list of participants, which is relevant for determining from which processes the coordinator anticipates ack messages. This can be done by simply including in the commit or rollback log entry the network addresses of all those additional participants that were not yet known at the time the begin log entry was written.

For a participant the reinfection problem implies that the participant may need multiple prepare steps, namely, when it prepared itself and voted yes the first time and subsequently when it becomes reinfected by the request for performing a deferred operation that could originate from another participant. So a participant that is already prepared and receives an additional data operation request from a participant that is about to prepare itself needs to perform the operation and prepare itself once again before it can reply that the requested data operation has been successfully executed. If the data operation fails, there is no harm, as the operation's requestor cannot be prepared yet and would then vote no.

19.2.3 **Independent Recovery**

From our earlier discussion we know that 2PC is a potentially blocking protocol, which is a disadvantage. Now the natural question is whether we could modify the protocol into a variant that would never block regardless of which failures occur. More precisely, what we would wish to construct is a protocol that ensures *independent recovery* for each process. This means that a failed and restarted process can always make local transitions into a local final state without communicating to any other process. We will soon see that such a protocol is, in full generality, impossible, but under special assumptions we may be able to guarantee independent process recovery. More specifically, we assume that at most one process failure occurs during the execution of the commit protocol, and no message losses occur other than the ones that result from the process failure. This assumption is called the *single-failure assumption*.

Independent process recovery

THEOREM 19.3

Under the single-failure assumption, independent recovery can be guaranteed by an appropriately designed distributed commit protocol.

Before we outline the proof of this theorem, we discuss why it is hard to guarantee independent recovery. For the purpose of this discussion we ignore the coordinator's Forgotten state (which is relevant only for garbage collection) and assume that Committed and Aborted are the actual final states. The critical problem is that a participant can be in its Prepared state while another participant is already in a final state that can be either Committed or Aborted. Such a situation rules out independent recovery, for the prepared participant cannot determine from its own local state whether the other participant is committed or aborted. This observation is stated in more general terms in the following lemma.

LEMMA 19.1

A distributed commit protocol that contains reachable global states with the property that one component is in a nonfinal local state while another component can be in multiple local final states cannot guarantee independent recovery even under the single-failure assumption.

The trick is to eliminate the troublesome situation that the lemma refers to. When a component is in a local nonfinal state as part of some global state, there should be only a single possibility for other components to be in a final state. So when one participant is merely prepared, all possible computation paths that lead to such a configuration must constrain the set of possible final states that other processes may have reached to a single choice, and this choice must be the same for all computation paths that continue from the given configuration. The protocol that ensures independent recovery is a variation of 2PC that modifies the meaning of the Prepared state of a participant and adds "Buffer state" to the coordinator's statechart in between the coordinator's Collecting and Committed states. When a participant fails in the Prepared state or observes a timeout in this state, it simply chooses to proceed into the Aborted state. To guarantee unanimous outcome among all processes, the coordinator's behavior needs to be adapted to this specific choice. To this end, it can no longer make a direct transition from its Collecting state into the Commit state (because of the above lemma). So when the coordinator decides to commit the transaction, it merely enters a Buffer state named Willing-to-commit and sends the commit message to all participants. At this point all participants must be in their Prepared state if no process failure has occurred. If a participant fails in this global state and later proceeds independently into the local state Aborted, the coordinator will notice a timeout for the acknowledgment from this participant. This is the signal for the coordinator that a process failure has occurred; note that under the single-failure assumption there is no other explanation. In this case the coordinator makes a transition from the Willing-to-commit state to the Aborted state. Otherwise, if the coordinator receives all acknowledgments, it does indeed proceed into the Committed state. This consideration completes the constructive proof of Theorem 19.3.

As the outlined proof shows, the constructed protocol is highly tailored to the single-failure assumption. The same construction would not work with multiple failures or a combination of a single process failure and message losses. In fact, the major impossibility result in the area of distributed transactions is the following theorem.

THEOREM 19.4

There exists no distributed commit protocol that can guarantee independent process recovery in the presence of multiple failures.

Proof

Consider a system with two processes (i.e., one coordinator and one participant) and assume that both can perform independent recovery from every local state. When there are no failures, the distributed commit protocol proceeds on a computation path with global states $G_0, G_1, \ldots, G_m$ with G_m having all components committed. When a process fails and is restarted in the initial state G_0 (or detects a timeout in this state and thus suspects that the other process has failed), it should independently proceed into its local aborted state, and this holds for both processes. So along the computation path from G_0 to G_m there must be a state G_k with minimum k such that one of the two processes, say, Process 1, would independently recover into the local committed state from G_k, but both processes would independently recover into their local aborted states from G_{k-1}. Since the two processes communicate via messages and do not have globally shared storage, the global state transitions in the considered computation path change only one component at a time. So we can assume that only the local state of Process 1 has changed in the step from G_{k-1} to G_k. Now, if the other process, Process 2, would fail in G_k, too, it must still independently recover into its local aborted state from the global state G_k. So G_k is a state that would lead to inconsistent results if independent recovery were possible. Therefore, distributed commit with all processes either committing or rolling back is impossible with independent recovery once more than one failure can occur during the protocol's execution.

The multiple-failure situation that we considered in the proof of Theorem 19.4 is not unrealistic: double failures within a short time window of vulnerability, albeit very infrequent, do occur. So we have to accept that distributed commit and independent process recovery cannot be reconciled for fundamental reasons. In other words, the potential for blocking under certain conditions is an inherent property of *every* conceivable commit protocol, and there is no point in searching for a protocol that would eliminate this weak point of 2PC. (As we will see in Section 19.4, there are other reasons for and ways of improving 2PC.)

Network partitioning perceived as double failure

Double failures are not the only cause for the impossibility of independent recovery. There are other situations in which two or more of the involved processes may perceive timeouts as if there were a double failure but all processes may still be running. *Network partitioning* is the most extensively studied failure class along these lines. This type of failure situation occurs when a router or gateway fails, all processes are still alive, but are now partitioned into two or more subsets such that the processes within a subset can still communicate, but the communication across subsets has broken down because of the router failure. Processes in one subset may interpret this as if the processes in another subset had failed, and vice versa; hence the indistinguishability from a double failure. The literature on communication networks has looked for ways to distinguish a network partitioning from process failures. One obvious approach is to reduce the probability of network partitioning by providing multiple communication paths for each pair of processes, so that messages can be dynamically rerouted. Indeed, modern network topologies like the Internet are unlikely to exhibit network partitioning with a single router failure, but security firewalls and the fact that many routers run the same highly complex and thus failure-prone software again introduces single points of vulnerability. The bottom line is that network partitioning is very infrequent, but cannot be completely ruled out.

19.3 The Transaction Tree Two-Phase Commit Algorithm

In the previous section we have left open which of the processes involved in a transaction takes the role of the coordinator. A judicious choice of the coordinator depends on many aspects:

- *Transaction initiator*: Who is the initiator of the transaction? That is, where does the program run that issues the commit or rollback request? Is it a client (e.g., a home PC hooked up to the Internet) or an application server (e.g., a Web server or an ORB)? Even a database server may itself spawn new transactions from executing stored procedures.

- *Reliability and speed of participants*: How many participants does the transaction involve? What are the characteristics of the various participants: how reliable is a participant, how fast is its network connection, how fast will it respond in the message rounds of the commit protocol (depending on the participant's current load, speed of its hardware, etc.)?

- *Communication topology and protocol*: What network protocol does the transaction initiator use to communicate to the participants while the transaction is executing, and to what extent and by what means do participants communicate to each other? For example, does the initiator establish sessions with each participant and participants do not communicate at all with each other, or is it possible that a participant that receives a request for an update operation from the initiator itself issues further requests to other data servers (e.g., because an SQL trigger fires or an email notification is initiated) using datagrams or newly opened sessions? In the latter case the newly involved servers dynamically join the distributed transaction as additional participants.

In the simplest and seemingly most natural case, the transaction initiator is chosen as the coordinator. This makes perfect sense if the initiator is a reliable, fast, and well-connected application server. If the initiator is a client, it often makes more sense to choose one of the participating data servers to fill the coordinator role in the commit protocol. This choice can be made dynamically when the initiator issues its commit request (via some local stub software that can make this choice or contact one of the servers to choose a coordinator). This approach is straightforward to implement when all participants can communicate with each other without extra costs.

For example, in a LAN the network addresses of all servers are known, and everybody can talk to everybody else using inexpensive datagrams or even newly established sessions without incurring unacceptable overhead. In a WAN environment like the Internet, on the other hand, when a participant "transitively" submits requests to dynamically added participants, it is not at all self-guaranteed that the initiator knows (the network addresses of) all participants at the time it issues the commit request and can communicate with all of them directly and efficiently. Even if direct communication were, in principle, possible, it might require opening new sessions, which could incur unacceptable delays.

These considerations reveal three important observations:

- During the execution of the transaction, the involved processes dynamically form a tree with the initiator as the root. Each edge in this *process tree* corresponds to a dynamically established communication link over which a process (i.e., the initiator or a participating server) submits a request (e.g., an SQL update command or a remote method invocation) to another participant and receives the corrresponding reply (e.g., a returncode). These edges are created whenever a new participant is added to the transaction. Once a link between two processes is established, it can be reused for subsequent requests. *Process trees rooted at transaction initiator*

- For the execution of the commit protocol (i.e., when the initiator has issued its commit request), the process tree could be *flattened* by choosing a coordinator, for example, the initiator itself, and having the coordinator talk to each process in the tree directly (i.e., without using other processes as intermediate nodes). Such flattening is feasible in most cases because all processes could piggyback their network addresses and those of their callees upon the reply message that they send to their caller anyway; so at commit time the initiator could have gathered all necessary network addresses.

Flattened or hierarchical commit

However, in a federation of servers, some servers may encapsulate the fact that they outsource some requests to other servers, hiding this fact from their own callers, and could thus be unwilling to pass the network addresses of their callees farther up in the tree. In this case, or if the flattening of the communication topology is too expensive because it may require establishing new sessions, the commit protocol needs to be organized in a *hierarchical* manner. The root of the process tree serves as a global coordinator, and all other nodes are both participants with regard to their caller (i.e., parent in the tree) and coordinator for their callees (i.e., children) and, more generally, their subtree (i.e., descendants). For leaf nodes, which do not have children, the coordinator part is, of course, unnecessary. For this kind of hierarchical commit protocol, the communication topology that has been used during transaction execution is reused for the commit protocol.

These two cases—flattened commit protocol and hierarchical commit for a tree of processes—are depicted in Figure 19.4.

■ Flattening can be seen as a special case of restructuring the communication tree that arose during transaction execution for the purpose of optimizing the execution of the commit protocol. For example, by picking some inner node of the tree as the coordinator based on this node's high reliability, it could become the root of a newly constructed commit communication tree. The commit communication tree could reuse all existing communication links and simply "rotate" the tree around the newly chosen coordinator. We will come back to such techniques in Section 19.4.

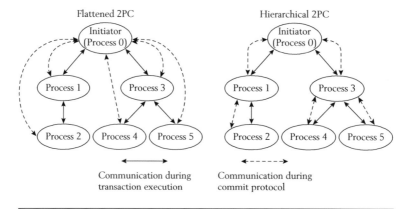

Figure 19.4 Flattened vs. hierarchical commit protocol for a tree of processes.

In the hierarchical commit protocol the message flow and writing of log entries follows from the two roles of an intermediate node, *participant with regard to its caller* and *coordinator for its subtree*, in a straightforward manner. For example, when a nonroot, nonleaf process receives a prepare message, it must not immediately write its prepared log entry and reply yes to the caller. Rather, because its reply will be interpreted as the unanimous vote of the entire subtree, it first needs to take care of its own callees. So the process first sends prepare messages to its children. This message flow cascades down the tree in a recursive manner until it reaches the leaf nodes, which are mere participants. Then a reply wave moves upward in the tree. When a nonroot, nonleaf process receives yes votes from all its children, it can finally force-write its prepared log entry and send a yes vote to its parent. If there is at least one no vote farther down in the tree, all ancestors of the process that gave this negative reply are guaranteed to reply no to their parent as well. In the second phase of the protocol, a commit message wave moves down the tree, and finally ack messages are collected.

The hierarchical message flow is depicted in Figure 19.5 for the case of a global commit with the processes and topology from Figure 19.4. In the figure, Processes 1 and 3 are participants of the protocol coordinated by the initiator, Process 0. At the same time, Process 1 is the coordinator for its child Process 2, and Process 3 coordinates the participants 4 and 5.

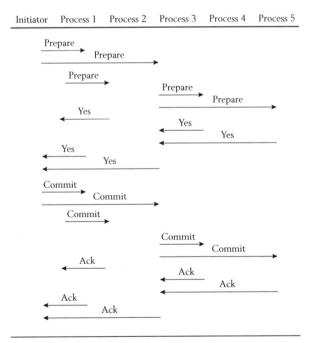

Figure 19.5 Message flow for hierarchical 2PC in the commit case.

The correctness of hierarchical 2PC follows directly from the fact that it is simply a finite number of instantiations of the basic 2PC protocol. All we need to additionally ensure is that all intermediate nodes behave consistently: if they decide, as a coordinator for their subtree, that the subtree should commit the transaction, they must vote yes to their parent, and the same must analogously hold for the abort case. This invariant is guaranteed. As for the restart and termination protocol, we can simply adopt the specification from Section 19.2.2. Each intermediate node needs to execute the statecharts for the coordinator role and the participant role simultaneously, and simply has to initiate the corresponding T and F transitions in both automata during restart or upon timeout.

19.4 **Optimized Algorithms for Distributed Commit**

Two-phase commit incurs different kinds of execution costs and potential bottlenecks that have led to a number of possible optimizations. The performance dimensions that are addressed by a suite of extensions are the following:

Fewer messages and (forced) log writes
1. Reducing the number of messages and the number of log writes, especially forced log writes, that are needed by the protocol, in order to minimize run-time overhead and maximize the transaction throughput that can be sustained with given computer and network resources.

Shorter critical path
2. Shortening the "critical path" from the begin of the commit protocol to the point when local locks can be released, in order to minimize local lock contention and response times.

Reduced potential of blocking
3. Reducing the probability of blocking, or equivalently, striving for independent recovery under as many cirumstances as possible.

The number of messages and forced log writes can be reduced by introducing specific conventions for the *presumed behavior* of a process (i.e., its default reaction) in the absence of more explicit information. For example, if a participant did not force a commit or abort log entry and could thus lose this information in a local crash, this participant could by default contact the coordinator to obtain the missing information. The difficulty in working out this idea is to ensure an appropriate, globally consistent behavior even if the coordinator has already truncated its log and forgotten the transaction. Protocols along these lines are presented in Section 19.4.1.

Fewer messages and log writes can generally speed up the commit protocol and thus contribute also to the second dimension of shorter time until lock releasing. Parallelizing the message waves down and up an entire process tree can have a similar effect, and so does the early elimination of subtrees from the protocol's message rounds when these subtrees can be inferred to be irrelevant. To this end, a *read-only subtree optimization* for the hierarchical commit protocol will be presented in Section 19.4.2.

In the presence of failures, another key for minimizing the critical path of participants is to make a judicious choice for the coordinator. It can be beneficial, for example, to choose the most reliable server as coordinator or the one that can communicate with all other participants most efficiently, within existing sessions, to minimize message turnaround times. Such considerations require a dynamic form of *coordinator transfer* that will be discussed in Section 19.4.3.

All of the above optimizations also implicitly help to reduce the blocking probability, as they aim to shorten the duration of the entire protocol and thus the time window of susceptibility to blocking, and to reduce the probability of a coordinator failure or nonreachability of the coordinator. In addition, the 2PC protocol itself can be extended, for example, by introducing additional message rounds, to completely eliminate blocking in restricted situations such as single failures and to minimize the blocking probability in the general case. Approaches along these lines have sometimes been called *nonblocking* commit protocols, although they can have this property only under very special assumptions (see Section 19.2.3). Section 19.4.4 will discuss these extended protocols.

19.4.1 Presumed-Abort and Presumed-Commit Protocols

The basic 2PC protocol as described in Section 19.2, when executed in its flat form with n participants and an additional coordinator, incurs a total execution cost of $4n$ messages and $2n + 2$ forced log writes. The number of forced log writes is derived from two log entries for each participant, namely, the prepared and the commit or rollback log entry, and two forced log entries for the coordinator, namely, the begin and the commit or rollback log entry.

The forcing of the coordinator's begin log entry is necessary so that the coordinator can remember the transaction and the need for driving its termination in the case that the coordinator fails before the commit or rollback log entry is written. Therefore, if the process that fills the coordinator role has already written some other evidence of the transaction's existence to its stable log during the transaction's execution, there is no need for the begin log entry. This is typically the case when the coordinator is an application server that most likely has stably tracked the transaction when it began anyway. Likewise, when the coordinator is one of the participants and does not separate the coordinator log from the process's regular stable log, it could first prepare itself, and then its prepared log entry would also serve as a stable reminder of the transaction's existence. So in many cases the number of forced log entries can be reduced to $2n + 1$ without explicit optimizations. Even if the coordinator did not have any

Begin log entry reconsidered

stable clue about the transaction, there is no absolute need for the begin log entry: if the coordinator forgets the transaction after a failure and does not resume the commit protocol, the transaction could simply be regarded as a loser, and the participants could implicitly learn this by not hearing from the coordinator for an extended (timeout) period or by receiving something like a "transaction unknown" message when "pinging" the coordinator. This outcome could unfortunately arise even if all participants were able to commit the transaction, and we initially introduced the forced begin log entry exactly to avoid this situation.

Basic 2PC = presumed-nothing (PN) protocol

The above discussion shows that there is a potential for reducing the message and forced logging cost of 2PC by making specific *presumptions* about a process's behavior when a certain piece of information is missing. This consideration leads to two different variations of the 2PC, known as the *presumed-abort (PA)* and *presumed-commit (PC) protocols:* one protocol whose default behavior is to roll back a transaction when there is no information about the global decision and also no way of reconstructing this information, and one protocol that presumes that the transaction should be committed in this kind of situation. Of course, these protocols need to be cautiously designed to rule out inconsistent behavior among the participating processes. Because the basic 2PC does not make any presumptions along these lines, it is also known as the *presumed-nothing (PN) protocol.*

We may miss certain pieces of information during the commit protocol, simply because we do not force certain log entries or do not send specific types of messages: this is exactly the optimization potential for the protocols based on presumptions. More specifically, the candidates for such relaxation are

- the coordinator's begin log entry (see the discussion above),
- the participants' commit or rollback log entries, whose forcing could be avoided, as this information can be obtained again from the coordinator (who must have a stable commit or abort log entry),
- the participants' ack messages in the second phase of the commit protocol.

Presumed-abort (PA) protocol

For loser transactions it is indeed possible to drop all three of the above pieces of information without risking globally inconsistent decisions. Assume that no begin log entry is written, the participants' rollback log entry is not forced, and that no acknowledgments are sent during the second phase. Without acknowledgments the coordinator would either have to keep its log entries about a transaction forever, adversely interfering with log truncation, or we would have to assume that it can discard its log entries about a transaction regardless of the presence or absence of ack messages. Let us assume the latter. When a participant fails after having received the coordinator's decision (the abort message) but before forcing its local rollback log entry, it would contact the coordinator to query the transaction's outcome. If the coordinator still has the rollback log entry on its stable log, it can tell the inquiring participant once again that the transaction is a loser. If the coordinator has already garbage-collected all log entries about this transaction, it could still resort to the presumption that, in the absence of any information, the transaction should be aborted. This default behavior guarantees a globally consistent transaction outcome for the following reason. After having forgotten the transaction (i.e., garbage-collecting its log entries) the coordinator can no longer discriminate the state of the transaction before the coordinator's commit or rollback log entry has been written (i.e., the first phase of the protocol) and the state after the entire protocol is considered finished by the coordinator. Presuming that the transaction should be aborted in both cases is perfectly fine and leads to a globally consistent decision, and therefore the coordinator does not really have to distinguish the two cases. Furthermore, this shows that even the coordinator itself does not have to force the rollback log entry to its stable log, as the presumed decision does not depend on the stability of this log entry. The protocol that we have just described is known as the presumed-abort (PA) protocol.

The described optimization works only for loser transactions; for winner transactions the presumed-abort protocol cannot afford missing all three of the above mentioned pieces of information. To see the problem, reconsider the scenario that we just discussed, with the decisive difference that the coordinator now sends a commit message. When the coordinator is pinged by a participant that has lost its nonforced commit log entry in a local failure, the coordinator is in trouble if it can no longer distinguish whether it is still in the protocol's first phase or already in a stage after the entire protocol is finished and log entries are discarded. In the first case, the presumption that no information about the transaction means that the transaction should be rolled back is still acceptable, but in the second case the same presumption would tell the inquiring participant to roll back the transaction, although it is possible that other participants have already committed the transaction. The solution to this problem is that for committed transactions (1) the participants must still force commit log entries to their local logs, and (2) they also must still send ack messages to the coordinator to notify the coordinator about the fact that their local commit log entries are stable, and garbage collection can now start legally discarding the coordinator's information about the transaction. If either of these two measures were missing, inconsistent decisions could arise.

The complete behavior of the presumed-abort protocol is depicted in Figure 19.6 for both the rollback and the commit case, in the form of sequence diagrams. The figure's scenario applies the protocol to a process tree consisting of the coordinator as the root, Processes 1 and 2 as direct children of the coordinator, and Process 3 as a child of Process 2. So Process 2 needs to execute both the participant role (with regard to its parent, the coordinator) and the (sub-) coordinator role (with regard to its child, Process 3). The figure shows that once the presumed-abort optimization is fully understood, applying it to the hierarchical form of 2PC is straightforward.

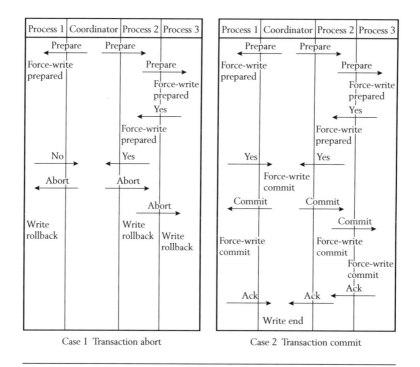

Case 1 Transaction abort   Case 2 Transaction commit

Figure 19.6 Messages and log entries for the presumed-abort protocol.

So the presumed-abort protocol saves messages and forced log writes for loser transactions, but is identical to the basic 2PC for winner transactions. It is therefore intriguing to construct a dual version of presumed abort, the presumed-commit protocol, whose basis is the presumption that a transaction with missing information should be considered committed. By analogy or superficial symmetry arguments the hope would be that presumed commit would not need to force commit log entries and could also eliminate ack messages for the much more frequent case of winner transactions. Unfortunately, this version of presumption is much more intricate than the presumed-abort case, the reason being that (unilateral) rollback is always feasible in the first phase of the commit protocol, but commit really requires a global decision. In colloquial terms, committing a transaction is a constructive endeavor that requires a true commitment of all involved parties with stable memory of the fact that specific promises were given. Rolling back a transaction, on the other hand, is like a destructive act, much easier to achieve than moving forward.

To see this fundamental asymmetry between commit and abort, assume that the presumed-commit protocol would indeed not force-write commit log entries and would not include ack messages. So when a participant is restarted in the prepared state and queues the coordinator about the transaction's outcome, the coordinator can be in one of three different stages: (1) in the first phase of the commit protocol before the coordinator's commit log entry is written, (2) in the second phase with a stable commit log entry still available, (3) after the entire protocol with all log entries for the transaction already garbage-collected. Again, the problem is that the coordinator cannot distinguish the first and the third stage, and its presumption should be consistent with the correct behavior in these two cases. Unfortunately, the appropriate decisions in the first stage, to initiate rollback, and the third stage, to consider the transaction as committed, are incompatible with each other. So the coordinator must definitely force-write its commit log entry to discriminate the two cases, and it must not discard this critical piece of information before receiving acknowledgments from all participants in the second phase of the protocol.

Alternatively, we can work out another solution with force-written commit but without ack messages. So once the coordinator's commit log entry is garbage-collected, later inquiries by participants should be answered according to the commit presumption. To make sure that this third stage of the coordinator is not confused with the first stage, the coordinator must have a stable log entry that captures its being in the first phase of the protocol. We can use the begin log entry of the basic 2PC for this purpose, but now forcing this entry to the stable log is a must for correctness. These considerations are the characteristic features of the actual presumed-commit (PC) protocol: forced begin and commit log entries at the coordinator, no ack messages for winner transactions, but explicit acknowledgments for losers. So the participants do not need to force the commit log entry to their local log, which is still a significant savings of logging costs.

Presumed-commit (PC) protocol

Figure 19.7 depicts the behavior of the presumed-commit protocol for both the abort and the commit case, in the form of sequence diagrams. The figure's scenario is identical to the one in Figure 19.6, and again we see that the generalization to hierarchical commit for a process tree is straightforward. Note that the intermediate node in this scenario, Process 2, would naturally force-write a commit log entry in its role as a subcoordinator in the case of transaction commit. However, this forcing is actually unnecessary for intermediate nodes, as they could reobtain this information from the top-level coordinator, that is, the root node. So the hierarchical presumed-commit protocol may contain additional, minor optimizations compared to the mere cascading of presumed-commit protocol instances.

In summary, the presumed-abort variant of the 2PC protocol for n participants saves n messages (the ack messages) and $n + 2$ forced log writes for aborted transactions (including the coordinator's begin log entry, see the discussion at the beginning of this subsection), and there are no savings for committed transactions. The presumed-commit protocol, on the other hand, saves n messages and n forced log writes (for the participants' commit log entries), and there are no savings for the case of aborted transactions. So the savings in network and disk resource consumption are slightly higher for the presumed-abort

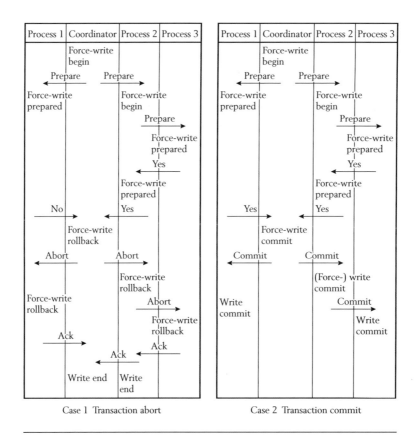

Case 1 Transaction abort   Case 2 Transaction commit

Figure 19.7 Messages and log entries for the presumed-commit protocol.

protocol, but it optimizes the much more infrequent case. However, as we will see in Section 19.4.2, both of these presumption-based protocols can be combined with other optimizations, most importantly, the read-only subtree optimization. It turns out that the combination with this other optimization gives a significant advantage to the presumed-abort protocol. We will see that intermediate nodes in a process tree need to force-write a begin log entry under the presumed commit protocol even if their entire subtree is read-only, and this cost does not arise with the presumed-abort protocol. For this reason, presumed abort has been considered as the method of choice and has been

XA standard   selected as the basis for the industry standard XA, the officially standardized version of the hierarchical presumed abort 2PC. However, for the flattened version of 2PC, presumed commit is certainly the more attractive approach.

Presumed-   An interesting variation of the presumed-commit protocol is to eliminate
commit with   the need for forcing the begin log entry at the expense of making garbage
nonforced begin collection more complicated and potentially incomplete. The idea is to infer
log entry   from the coordinator log approximative, but conservative, information about

the identifiers of transactions that *might have been active* at the time of a coordinator failure. A specific technique for this purpose could be based on maintaining lower and upper bounds for those transaction identifiers that would be periodically written to the log (i.e., in a lazy, usually nonforced manner). During restart after a crash the coordinator is able to refine this candidate set into a set of potential loser transactions about which pending participants may possibly still send inquiries, by removing all transactions with a commit log entry. This set of potential losers is approximative in that it may contain transaction identifiers of transactions that did not enter the commit protocol or even nonexisting transactions; however, it is conservative in the sense that it never contains a winner transaction. Now the trick is to keep this list of potential losers with possibly outstanding inquiries in compressed form and separately from the log itself. This way the stable log can be garbage-collected as usual, but the potential loser list may have to be kept forever. When a participant later queries the outcome of a transaction, the coordinator presumes commit only if the transaction is not in the potential loser list. So the list allows the coordinator to discriminate transactions that were in the first stage (i.e., were not yet decided) from those whose commit has already been forgotten. The size of the list has an upper bound on the order of the number of transactions that were active while failures occurred throughout the system lifetime. So under usual circumstances with sufficiently infrequent crashes, the list requires only a modest amount of space (say, a few megabytes at most).

Presumed-abort (PA) and presumed-commit (PC) 2PC (and also the presumed-nothing (PN) basic 2PC) can coexist within the same federation of servers. Usually, however, a consistent choice must be made for each transaction: either all participants and the coordinator of a transaction employ the presumed-commit protocol, or all of them employ the presumed-abort protocol. The choice needs to be made at the time the transaction initiator issues the commit (or rollback) request and the actual commit protocol begins. The choice can be made dependent on the number of participants, their estimated reliability, the probability of certain subtrees being read-only, and so on. *Coexistence of presumed abort and presumed commit*

In a heterogeneous federation of servers it may, however, be the case that a given server can handle only one out of the three protocols PA, PC, and PN, and these capabilities vary across servers. So when a distributed transaction involves servers with different capabilities, the problem arises how to reconcile PA, PC, and PN within a single transaction. The solution, recently published as the *presumed-any protocol*, is to ensure that the coordinator includes sufficient information in the form of forced log entries to cope with both PA and PC participants; no special steps are necessary for PN, as this option essentially boils down to either PA or PC depending on the given transaction's outcome. So a presumed-any coordinator force-writes begin, commit, and rollback log entries, and it expects acknowledgments from PA participants for committed transactions and from PC participants for aborted transactions. *Presumed-any protocol*

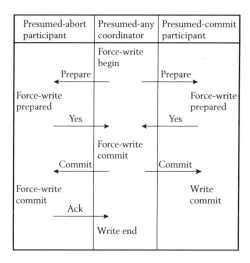

Presumed-abort participant	Presumed-any coordinator	Presumed-commit participant

Figure 19.8 Messages and log entries for the presumed-any protocol.

In a process tree the steps to cover both protocols must be made by each subcoordinator (i.e., intermediate node in the tree) as well. In addition, the coordinator (and again also subcoordinators) needs to know which of its children uses which protocol. This way the coordinator knows when it can expect acknowledgments and when it cannot. Note that this information is crucial for the coordinator to facilitate log truncation. The coordinator remembers this information even across failures by including the network addresses of its participants and their choice of PA, PC, or PN in the stable begin log entry.

Details of this unified presumed-any protocol can be found in the literature mentioned in the Bibliographic Notes for this chapter. For illustration, Figure 19.8 shows a possible scenario with a coordinator and a PA and a PC participant as direct children for a winner transaction.

19.4.2 **Read-Only Subtree Optimization**

In a process tree the coordinator does not know a priori all participants of the transaction. Some participants may not have performed any updates on their local data; these may include both intermediate nodes in the tree and leaf nodes. However, it is often impossible to know these read-only participants at the time the coordinator initiates the commit protocol. Therefore, an important optimization is to eliminate read-only participants from the commit protocol's message and logging efforts as early as possible. To this end, we can introduce a third kind of vote, called "read-only," in addition to the two options "yes" or "no" that we considered so far. A participant that has voted "read-only" in the first phase can be eliminated from the second message round: it does not need to receive the coordinator's decision. When it receives the prepare message and has sent its read-only vote, the participant can immediately go ahead with releasing its local locks without writing any log entries.

There are two complications with this highly intriguing and seemingly straightforward optimization. First, intermediate nodes in the process tree can vote read-only only if none of their descendants in the entire subtree has performed any updates. So these subcoordinators first need to collect votes from their subtrees, and respond to their parent with a read-only vote only if they have received no "yes" or "no" vote. Second, this optimization needs to be integrated with other optimizations, particularly the ones based on presumption. A closer analysis shows that the presumed-commit protocol still needs to have forced begin log entries for the top-level coordinator and all subcoordinators (i.e., intermediate nodes). (We have seen in the previous subsection that further optimizations are possible to eliminate the force-write of subcoordinators or even the forcing of the top-level begin log entry, but these additional optimizations have trade-offs with regard to other metrics that are nontrivial to quantify.) So there is a significant logging cost under the presumed-commit protocol even if the *entire* process tree is read-only. Under the presumed-abort protocol, on the other hand, read-only subtrees do not need any log entries at all, and transactions that are read-only on all involved servers have zero logging cost. It is for this reason that presumed abort is widely considered superior to presumed commit, at least for hierarchical commit.

A final complication arises when participants can perform deferred operations during the commit protocol, that is, after having received the prepare message. We have mentioned this problem of reinfection already in Section 19.2.2. In combination with the read-only optimization, such reinfection may create a serious correctness problem. Once a participant has voted read-only, it can release its local locks (or, equivalently, consider its local part of the transaction finished under a nonlocking concurrency control protocol). When another, reinfected participant later performs deferred operations, that other participant may have to acquire additional locks. So such a transaction violates the two-phase property of the 2PL concurrency control at the global level. We have seen in Chapter 18 that although each participant still obeys 2PL locally, we may end up with a globally nonserializable schedule under these conditions. The only solution is to exert the read-only optimization with caution: it should be used only when it is sure that a transaction does not trigger deferred operations in the voting phase. Another conceivable alternative would be that participants that vote read-only still keep their locks until the decision phase, but this would come at the expense of having to send commit or abort messages to read-only participants (but still without logging at read-only participants).

19.4.3 **Coordinator Transfer**

For reliability or communication efficiency reasons it may be desirable to choose a coordinator that differs from the transaction initiator. For a process tree this amounts to choosing a new root and "rotating" the tree around this new root node. This new tree has exactly the same edges as the old one, but the parent-child relationship is reversed for all edges along the path from the new root to the old one. Figure 19.9 shows an example for this simple transformation. Note that the resulting commit tree uses exactly the same bilateral communication links between processes that were already established during transaction execution. So the commit protocol does not have to open new sessions in the case that the communication is generally session oriented.

Linear 2PC with last-agent optimization   The choice of the coordinator and the corresponding conceptual rotation of the tree can be dynamically carried out when the initiator has issued the commit (or rollback) request. Once this is done, the commit protocol is executed as usual. So the full spectrum of optimizations (presumed abort, etc.) is available. For special but frequently occurring communication topologies, we can go one step further and tailor the actual commit protocol to the specific type of dynamic coordinator transfer. This is particularly attractive and has been proposed as one of the very earliest 2PC optimizations for linear communication where the process tree forms a single, nonbranching path. Even if the tree has more general shape, we could derive a linear communication structure, possibly at the expense of having to establish new bilateral sessions. However, the case that the tree is already a linear path with a small number of processes, often only two, is very frequent in practice. The optimization that we are going to describe for this case is therefore known as the *linear 2PC*. The major benefit of this 2PC variant is gained from choosing the last participant in the chain—the leaf of the linearized tree—as the coordinator. This choice is known as the *last-agent optimization*. (We do not call it "last-participant" optimization to be consistent with the majority of the literature.)

In linear 2PC with the last-agent optimization the dynamic coordinator transfer is part of the first phase of the commit protocol, and it is piggybacked on the prepare messages that are sent down the tree (i.e., along the linear chain

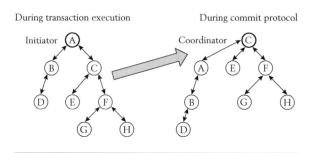

Figure 19.9 Example of coordinator transfer.

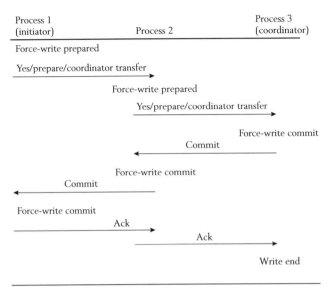

Figure 19.10 Linear 2PC with last-agent optimization.

in our special case). Each process, starting with the initiator and proceeding along the linear chain, prepares itself before sending the prepare message and delegates the choice of the coordinator to its successor process. So the prepare message here actually means: "I am prepared and you decide." When the last participant in the chain receives the prepare message, it has implicitly become the coordinator. As it knows that all its predecessors in the chain are prepared, it can go ahead and make the final decision about the transaction outcome. So when the last participant sends its reply up the tree, it is not simply a yes vote, but actually a definitive commit or abort message. The net effect of using these combined message types is that the entire process chain can be committed with fewer messages. In addition, the last participant being also the coordinator and force-writing only a single log entry reduces the logging cost. This protocol is illustrated in Figure 19.10 for the case of a committed transaction.

For the rollback case, when a process is unable to prepare itself and forward the prepare message, it can simply abort unilaterally and send an abort message to both its predecessor and successor in the chain. So in this case the first process with a no vote becomes the coordinator.

The improvement of the last-agent optimization is most significant for the frequently occurring case of transactions with exactly two participants, one of which is the initiator. Note that this is the case, for example, when a transaction is initiated by an application server that also serves as a transactional queue manager (see Chapter 17) and this transaction operates on exactly one data server. In this situation the commit protocol needs only three messages and three forced log writes for a winner transaction.

The last-agent optimization is not necessarily tied to linear 2PC but can also be applied to the basic 2PC or the various optimizations based on presumption. In this case, all processes but one carry out the first phase of the basic 2PC protocol. Once all but the last process are prepared, the last participant is notified and asked to be the coordinator. This option is attractive if there is one particularly critical server that insists on staying independent for recovery. By making this server the coordinator at the time all other processes are prepared, the server can always unilaterally abort the transaction and is never prone to blocking.

Dynamic 2PC   The idea of choosing as coordinator the process that is prepared and first knows that all other processes are prepared as well can be generalized to arbitrary tree topologies but requires more complex message flow. The resulting protocol has been coined *dynamic 2PC*. The goal of the protocol is to find a coordinator with the above property as soon as possible by initiating parallel waves of yes votes both downward and upward in the tree. In the first phase of the protocol, the transaction initiator (i.e., the root of the tree) initiates the wave of prepare messages down the tree. When leaf nodes receive the prepare message they prepare themselves and send a yes vote to their parent. Now, usually a nonleaf node would wait for the yes votes from all its children before it prepares itself and sends yes to its parent. In the dynamic 2PC protocol, however, a nonleaf node waits only until it has received votes from all but one of its neighbors (i.e., children and parent). At this point, the node prepares itself and sends a yes vote to this last neighbor, delegating the responsibility for the node's subtree to this neighbor. The last neighbor can be either the node's parent, which corresponds to the standard case in hierarchical 2PC, or one of the node's children. In the latter case the node essentially uses the last-agent optimization by telling this child that everybody else in its "proximity" is prepared, including the node itself. So to reemphasize the key point, the decisive rule for dynamic 2PC is the following:

> A node can consider itself prepared (in the sense of the last-agent optimization) and send a yes vote to its neighbor if it has received yes votes from all but one of its neighbors (now being sufficiently prepared as a subcoordinator) and has itself written a prepared log entry to its stable log (also being prepared as a participant).

Of course, when a node is not able to prepare itself it will send a no vote to its neighbors, and the entire procedure works analogously.

It can be shown for the dynamic 2PC protocol that exactly one node will receive yes votes from all its neighbors, and this distinct node will be the coordinator. Let us emphasize once again that this node will be determined dynamically, depending on the speed of the various messages and the nodes' local logging. In this sense the coordinator will be an arbitrary node, but the goal of the protocol has merely been to find a coordinator as quickly as possible. If additional considerations like node reliability are a concern, then dynamic 2PC should not be used or would have to be specifically adapted.

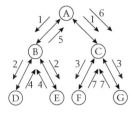

1. A →prepare B, A →prepare C
2. B →prepare D, B →prepare E
3. C →prepare F, C →prepare G
4. D→yes B, E →yes B
   B prepared
5. B→yes A
   A prepared
6. A→yes C
7. F→yes C, G →yes C
   C becomes coordinator

Figure 19.11 Example execution of the dynamic 2PC protocol.

Figure 19.11 shows a sample execution of the dynamic 2PC protocol for a tree with seven nodes labeled A through G. The time line of prepare and yes messages is given by the numbered arrows in the picture and the annotations in the right half of the figure. In this scenario the root A receives the yes votes from its left branch faster than from its right child C. Since only one neighbor's yes vote is missing, namely, that of process C, process A prepares itself and sends a yes vote down the right branch of the tree (i.e., to C). This is the key difference from the basic form of hierarchical 2PC where A would have to wait for the vote coming up the right branch of the tree (i.e., ultimately sent from C). By eagerly pushing its vote to its last neighbor C, it is eventually process C that has received votes from all neighbors (F, G, and A) and becomes the coordinator. The second phase of the protocol then follows the standard procedures using the presumed-nothing, presumed-abort, or presumed-commit rules.

Log sharing

To conclude this subsection, we briefly mention an interesting approach to the reduction of 2PC logging costs that follows a completely different route than the above optimizations. The idea is to allow *log sharing* among the participants and the coordinator of a transaction: all these processes write their log entries to the same stable log file, which is kept, for example, at the coordinator's site and accessed by the participants via remote procedure calls. Obviously, such an approach bears a great potential for reducing forced log writes and is attractive for LAN-based federations where a shared log file is easy to implement efficiently. So this approach somewhat redefines the problem of distributed commit into a centralized commit. But note that it is still a coordination problem that involves distributed servers that communicate via messages. So the details of such a log-sharing 2PC variant are not trivial.

19.4.4 **Reduced Blocking**

As we have seen in Section 19.2.3, 2PC is prone to blocking, and this holds for all of the above mentioned optimized variants, too. Theorem 19.4 has indeed shown us that the impossibility of independent recovery is an inherent property of the distributed commit problem. So the best we can do is to decrease the probability of running into blocking situations as much as possible. One way of doing this is to refine a commit protocol such that it eliminates blocking in certain relatively simple situations like single process failures and to make sure that it behaves correctly under all possible circumstances (but is then susceptible to blocking).

Three-phase commit (3PC)

Following the proof outline of Theorem 19.3 in Section 19.2.3, the basic idea for such a protocol is to avoid global states whose set of possible successor states contains both local commit and local rollback states. A full-fledged protocol based on this idea is the *three-phase commit* (3PC) protocol. In 3PC the coordinator first collects votes and causes participants to become prepared, then it disseminates the outcome of the voting phase to all participants, waiting until it is certain that all participants know the result. Only after this newly introduced message round does the coordinator finally ask the participants to commit or roll back (i.e., initiate the actual decision phase).

Voting, dissemination, and decision phases

So there are three message rounds in 3PC (hence the name), each accompanied by (forced) log entries: the voting phase, the dissemination phase, and the decision phase. Since the transaction outcome is known to each participant before the participants make the decisive move into the Committed or Aborted state, independent recovery is possible even if the coordinator fails. However, consistent and independent recovery can be guaranteed only if there is at most one process failure, the single-failure assumption that we already considered in Section 19.2.3. Multiple failures within a short time window could lead to incorrect behavior, or we would have to give up independent recovery. The latter is still all but trivial, as the protocol needs to infer that more than one failure has occurred. It is feasible to enhance the 3PC protocol so that it can cope with multiple failures correctly and becomes a full-fledged, general-purpose solution. For details see the literature mentioned in the Bibliographic Notes. The entire family of 3PC and other nonblocking commit protocols has not gained much practical relevance, however; the advantage of being able to avoid blocking in certain highly specific situations is outweighed by the significantly higher message and logging costs.

Cooperative termination

Another approach to avoid blocking when the coordinator fails or becomes unreachable because of communication failures is the following. When a participant is prepared and desires to learn the transaction fate to cease its uncertainty, it can actively contact other participants. If the coordinator has sent out some (but possibly not all) commit or rollback messages before the failure, there is a good chance that at least one other participant knows the decision. This approach is called *cooperative termination*. The key point for making it work is that all participants need to have a list of other participants. This information can be piggybacked on the prepare message in the first phase of the protocol.

Heuristic commit or abort

Finally, the literature has also suggested a brute force, extremely pragmatic way of getting out of blocking situations, known as *heuristic commit or abort*.

The approach is to define a default termination rule for a server when blocking situations persist too long. So that a server does not become "hostaged" in its control over lock releases and its local performance by being a blocked participant in a transactional federation, we could simply specify that such "in doubt" should be aborted after a sufficiently long "grace period." Likewise, we could specify local commit as the default measure in such extreme situations. Of course, this may lead to inconsistent results at the global level, with some participants being committed and others rolled back. But in practice, such drastic measures could still be better than leaving the transaction pending and not being able to release local locks indefinitely. After all, in some applications the coordinator could be a home PC that may have been switched off too early, and it could take days before the user starts the PC again and thereby resumes the transaction coordinator. Heuristic commit or abort makes sense, still from an extremely pragmatic viewpoint but as a matter of practicality in the real world, when associated with specific transaction types. For example, a bank might specify heuristic commit when its part of a distributed transaction is a deposit and heuristic abort when its part is a withdrawal.

19.5 **Lessons Learned**

Two-phase commit (2PC) is a fundamental asset of transactional technology for ensuring consistent effects of distributed transactions. Its two-phase structure consists of a voting and decision phase, both driven by a coordinator process. The first phase ensures that all participants of a transaction move into the prepared state, equally ready for either commit or rollback, and that they send their votes to the coordinator. The second phase disseminates the global decision to the participants and ensures that the coordinator can eventually garbage-collect its log entries about the transaction. Altogether, the basic 2PC protocol has execution costs of $2n + 2$ forced log entries and $4n$ messages for n participants plus the coordinator. For process trees that result from iterating remote method invocations on servers in a federated system, 2PC can either flatten the communication structure at commit time or employ a hierarchical form of 2PC, with intermediate nodes taking both the role of a participant with regard to their parent and the role of a subcoordinator with regard to their children.

To understand the correctness of the 2PC protocol, we have used the formal notation of a statechart, a variant of finite state automata. To cope with process failures and timeouts because of failures of message losses, we introduced additional failure and termination transitions into the protocol automaton. This way we were able to formally verify that 2PC guarantees consistent transaction outcome and achieves this goal in a finite number of steps. In addition, we obtained insight into the limitations of distributed commit from the formal statechart model. We have proven the impossibility of a commit protocol that can cope with arbitrary process and network failures but at the same time allows independent recovery so that a failed and restarted process could always terminate its part of the protocol without communicating to other processes. This negative result shows that the susceptibility to blocking is an inherent, unavoidable property of distributed transactions.

The message and logging costs of 2PC can be reduced by making presumptions about how a process should behave in the absence of information about the transaction. This idea has led us to the presumed-abort (PA) and presumed-commit (PC) protocols. In the first case, the coordinator and the participants can afford to be more relaxed about aborted transactions (no forced logging of rollback log entries and no ack messages); in the second case, similar savings apply to committed transactions. Although both superficially appear to be symmetric versions, presumed commit needs one additional forced log write (namely, for the begin log entry) to distinguish the situations of an early aborted transaction and a committed transaction whose information has been forgotten (i.e., garbage-collected). Both protocols also save messages in specific cases. Both can also be combined with an optimization for read-only participants or entire subtrees, which can be left out of the protocol's decision phase after having sent a read-only vote. The presumed-commit protocol still needs to force-write begin log entries even for entirely read-only transactions, and for this reason presumed abort is widely considered as the better protocol, although a detailed assessment depends on other issues as well, such as the communication topology and applicability of additional optimizations.

Two equally important aspects to optimize are the critical path until the participants can release their locks and the probability of a participant becoming blocked. To this end, we have discussed various options for flexible coordinator transfer, in order to choose a particularly reliable server as coordinator or to choose the coordinator such that the entire protocol terminates as quickly as possible. Along the latter lines, we have presented the last-agent optimization for linear 2PC and the dynamic 2PC for arbitrary process trees. Recall that speeding up the protocol's execution also implicitly reduces the danger of blocking by shortening the window of vulnerability. Other means for reduced blocking include three-phase commit that completely avoids blocking in single-failure situations at the expense of always requiring three rather than two message rounds, and the cooperative termination protocol that gives more flexibility to participants in the case that they have lost connectivity with the coordinator but can still communicate to other participants.

For a long time, 2PC has been considered with very mixed feelings in practice because of its susceptibility to blocking, and many applications have been designed to avoid distributed transactions. It is still true that 2PC does not exactly scale up to transactions that span hundreds of servers, but for a small number of participants on carefully administered and thus highly reliable servers, the benefit of achieving distributed data consistency in an easy-to-program way largely outweighs the small danger of creating performance problems. Even in heterogeneous federations with autonomously operated servers, the standardized form of distributed commit, known as XA and supported by all important commercial systems, is an excellent option to build applications with decentralized, interrelated data like e-Commerce and more advanced e-Services on the Internet.

As 2PC can incorporate general classes of resource managers including message queue servers, an important alternative to transactional updates on multiple data servers is to use queued transactions to preserve the atomicity of transaction chains with relaxed isolation. This option is attractive in situations when global serializability is not needed, and even as a compromise when the performance degradation caused by 2PC and especially the impact of potentially prolonged lock duration on the "native" local transaction workload of a critical server are considered as an unacceptable breach of the server's local autonomy.

Exercises

19.1 Give a complete statechart specification for the 2PC variant that guarantees independent recovery under the single-failure assumption (see the proof of Theorem 19.3).

19.2 Consider the following scenario. A transaction is initiated from a PC to make reservations for a vacation. The initiator communicates directly with a travel agency and a rental car company. The travel agency communicates with a travel wholesaler, which books two of the necessary flights (or flight legs) on the servers of the corresponding airlines, and also with two other airlines to book the rest of the necessary flights. All these steps belong to one distributed transaction, and all involved participants are able and willing to commit the transaction. The communication structure of this transaction is illustrated in Figure 19.12.

(a) Give the message flow and log entries for the hierarchical 2PC protocol for this scenario. Indicate which log entries need to be immediately forced to the stable log.

(b) Which of the various optimizations that we discussed in this chapter are applicable and promising for the given scenario? What are the implications for the protocol's message and logging costs?

(c) How does the protocol and its execution cost change if the coordinator role is transferred to the server of the travel agency (at the time the initiator issues its commit request)?

(d) Give the message flow and log entries for the case that the server of airline 3 is unable to commit and votes no in the hierarchical 2PC protocol.

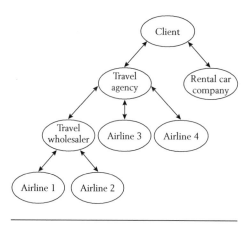

Figure 19.12 Process tree for travel booking.

(e) Apply the presumed-abort protocol to the case where the server of airline 3 votes no. Give the resulting message flow and log entries.

19.3 Consider a binary, perfectly balanced tree of processes of height n where all leaf nodes have the same distance from the root; so there is a total number of $m = 2^n - 1$ nodes in the tree. Assume that the root is the coordinator of the commit protocol. Determine the number of messages and forced log writes for the presumed-nothing (i.e., basic 2PC), presumed-abort, and presumed-commit protocols for the following situations:

(a) all processes have performed updates and the transaction commits,

(b) all processes have performed updates and the transaction aborts,

(c) all nonroot nodes are read-only and the transaction commits,

(d) all leaf nodes are read-only and the transaction commits.

19.4 Develop a protocol that combines the presumed-commit optimization with the last-agent optimization. Give sequence diagrams for the messages and logging for the commit and abort cases. Do the same exercise with the presumed-abort optimization.

Bibliographic Notes

The two-phase commit protocol has been independently described by Gray (1978), Lindsay et al. (1979), and Lampson and Sturgis (1976). The book by Gray and Reuter (1993) contains a brief historical account of the evolution of 2PC, including remarks about the use of 2PC-style protocols in industrial systems that predate the first scientific publications on this topic. A comprehensive and rigorous state-transition model has been presented by Skeen and Stone-braker (1983), who have also proven the impossibility of distributed commit with independent local recovery. The statechart formalism that we used in our presentation was developed by Harel (1987, 1997).

Extensive treatments of distributed commit protocols can also be found in the textbooks by Bernstein et al. (1987), Gray and Reuter (1993), Bernstein and Newcomer (1997), and Özsu and Valduriez (1999). Detailed descriptions of system implementations with distributed transactions have been given by Eppinger et al. (1991), Haskin et al. (1988), and Nett et al. (1985). Good sources on the broader context of distributed consensus algorithms, reliable messaging, and failure resilience of distributed systems in general are the books by Mullender (1993), Lynch (1996), and Coulouris et al. (1994). For even broader background on networks and communication protocols, see, for example, the excellent textbooks by Kurose and Ross (2000) or Walrand and Varaiya (2000).

Database-centric considerations on Byzantine agreement can be found in the work of Mohan et al. (1983), Garcia-Molina and Pittelli (1984), and Rothermel and Pappe (1993); the latter has presented a distributed commit protocol that can cope with commission failures by malicious participants. The most foundational publications on general forms of distributed consensus are by Lamport et al. (1982), who also coined the term "Byzantine agreement," and Fischer et al. (1985).

The first work that explicitly addressed distributed commit for transaction trees was by Mohan and Lindsay (1983); see also Mohan et al. (1986). These researchers also developed the presumed-abort and presumed-commit protocols and the read-only optimization for process trees described in Sections 19.4.1 and 19.4.2. More recent work on improved presumed-commit protocols has been done by Lampson and Lomet (1993) as well as Al-Houmaily et al. (1997). Centralized log sharing among participants and coordinator for reduced logging costs has been studied by Stamos and Cristian (1993).

Algorithms for coordinator transfer to minimize communication costs and to shorten the critical path until locks can be released have been developed by Segall and Wolfson (1987), Wolfson (1991), and Raz (1995); the latter has developed the full-fledged version of the dynamic 2PC protocol outlined in Section 19.4.3. The last-agent optimization has been introduced already in the pioneering work by Gray (1978).

Three-phase extensions for independent recovery in the limited setting of single failures have been developed by Skeen (1981). The textbook by Bernstein et al. (1987) contains an excellent treatment of 3PC. Babaoglu and Toueg (1983) have given a survey of the entire family of nonblocking commit protocols. Performance issues of cooperative termination have been discussed by Duchamp (1989).

Samaras et al. (1995) and Chrysanthis et al. (1998) have given excellent overviews of the plethora of optimizations for distributed commit protocols.

The latter has also provided quantitative results about the performance of different protocol variants; other performance studies include the work by Gupta et al. (1997) and Liu et al. (1998). The reconciliation of different 2PC variants, especially of the presumed-outcome family, in a federation of heterogeneous servers has been studied by Al-Houmaily and Chrysanthis (1999), who have coined the term "presumed any" for the protocol sketched at the end of Section 19.4.1. For a similar setting of heterogeneous servers, Wolski and Veijalainen (1991) as well as Muth and Rakow (1991) have investigated how to emulate 2PC on top of servers that do not by themselves support the participant protocol of 2PC.

PART FIVE

Applications
and Future
Perspectives

CHAPTER TWENTY

What Is Next?

This is the end, my only friend, the end.
—Jim Morrison

When shall we three meet again, in thunder, lightning, or in rain?
—William Shakespeare

20.1 **Goal and Overview**

To conclude the book's intensive tour of technical material, this chapter steps back again and sketches a "big picture" of the achievements and opportunities of transactional technology from both application and research perspectives. We summarize the most important highlights of transactional concurrency control and recovery in Section 20.2 and point out, once again and for the last time, their contributions to modern information systems. We will then briefly discuss selected subjects that are closely connected to transactional information systems but could not be covered in this book for obvious space reasons. Each of these subjects could easily fill a book by itself. We will sketch various issues of data replication in Section 20.3, advanced e-Services and workflow management in Section 20.4, and the elusive goal of performance and availability guarantees in Section 20.5.

20.2 **What Has Been Achieved?**

In this section we briefly review the most important algorithms and their underlying fundamentals. We consider three levels of sophistication:

- developers (and also undergraduate students) who need ready-to-use "recipes,"
- advanced system builders (and ambitious undergraduate students who would like to pursue a career as a system architect) who need in-depth knowledge of the very best practically viable solutions,

771

- researchers (including graduate students) who want to understand complex issues and are looking for further challenges to advance the state of the art.

20.2.1 **Ready-to-Use Solutions for Developers**

For the first level, the page model is a sufficient basis for building systems that provide transactional ACID contracts. For the isolation property, conflict serializability (CSR) is the adequate correctness criterion, and strict or even strong two-phase locking (S2PL or SS2PL) is the method of choice to guarantee CSR schedules. Under these protocols, all write locks (or even all locks under SS2PL) are held until transaction commit, and no locks can be acquired once the first lock has been released. Locking can be implemented with very low overhead, using lock control blocks in an appropriately designed hash table, which is crucial because lock requests take place in some of the innermost loops of the server code. Both S2PL and SS2PL have the additional advantage of ensuring the strictness property for correct and efficient handling of transaction aborts.

To guarantee atomicity and persistence in the presence of system failures (soft crashes) and media failures, logging on stable storage is mandatory. For the efficiency of this restart procedure and thus for overall system availability, it is crucial that the log is periodically truncated based on appropriate garbage collection rules. Recovery from such failures is most effectively performed by the redo-history algorithm in three passes over the stable log: an analysis pass to identify loser transactions that were active at the time of the crash and to collect information about dirty pages for more efficient redo; a redo pass that repeats all page writes based on physiological log entries using a page versus log sequence number (LSN) comparison for idempotence; and an undo pass that executes inverse page writes for loser transactions in reversed chronological order. The algorithm for media recovery, including the reconstruction of individual corrupted pages, is very similar, except that it starts from a backup version of the data and its redo pass covers an extended time span captured in the archive log.

"Recipes" for developers   These are the core assets for the implementation of concurrency control and recovery of a simple transactional data server. In addition, the proliferation of applications that interact with multiple servers in a federated manner, such as Internet-based e-Services and workflows, requires that a server supports the standardized two-phase commit (2PC) protocol. Finally, it is important to understand that global serializability is not a self-guaranteed property in a distributed system. For many applications this is not a real problem, but for those cases that do require stringent control over distributed executions in order to ensure data consistency, either all underlying servers need to guarantee commit order-preserving conflict serializability (COCSR) (or even rigorousness), or

additional conflict-testing measures must be taken at the federation or application layer.

The above assets are fundamental for developers of transactional servers (e.g., specialized e-Commerce servers), but also for application developers (e.g., of personalized e-Commerce agents), understanding the principles, limitations, and performance impact of transactional concurrency control and recovery is indispensable.

20.2.2 State-of-the-Art Techniques for Advanced System Builders

At the level of more sophisticated and more ambitious system architects and developers, we have covered techniques for high-performance, highly available servers suitable for advanced applications such as highly dependable e-Services (e.g., high-traffic e-Commerce or auction servers). In such settings, lock contention (or, in more general terms, data contention due to concurrency control) can be a bottleneck so that page-granularity locking (or page-granularity conflict testing) would be critical. Transient versioning can significantly reduce lock contention for workloads with a very large fraction of read accesses or even a large fraction of read-only transactions. The fundamental concept that underlies this option is the multiversion serializability (MVSR) criterion, and the most widely adopted protocol along these lines is the ROMV protocol that combines timestamping for read-only transactions with standard locking for update transactions. Other means to alleviate data contention include the use of relaxed isolation levels that no longer guarantee serializability and the use of optimistic conflict-testing techniques in application programs. However, these are very brittle options that should be employed with extreme caution, as the application correctness now depends on intellectual insights of the application architects and their detailed understanding of the application's consistency requirements and synchronization needs. In contrast, protocols that guarantee CSR or MVSR executions provide an automatic, foolproof solution to concurrency control, and thus lead to much higher productivity and lower cost of application development.

For the above techniques the page model is still sufficient for explanation and correctness reasoning. However, page-oriented concurrency control has inherent limitations (even with transient versioning and other enhancements) that can be overcome only with a finer granularity of locking or conflict testing. The best commercial database systems use record-granularity locking, and future generations of business object managers or federation mediators with persistent objects need to adopt (and possibly adapt) these solutions if they want to provide competitive performance. The most important concern in this context is index concurrency control, to minimize the lock duration on index pages while also ensuring full serializability for predicate-oriented data access.

State-of-the-art techniques for advanced system builders

To explain sophisticated solutions like the incremental key range locking with short-term page latching and to obtain insight into why it works, we have made intensive use of the object model and its fundamental correctness criterion of tree reducibility. The object model and its special case of layered systems also play an overriding role in concurrency control on ADT (abstract data type) objects, where commutativity properties of semantically rich operations can be exploited for higher concurrency at the ADT interface level, and subtransaction locks at the underlying implementation level(s)—ultimately the page level—ensure the isolation of individual ADT operations. Special techniques along these lines, such as escrow locking for (bounded) counters (e.g., quantity-on-hand in a warehouse), are extremely useful for high-end applications such as stock trading or auctions, and more general solutions will gain practical importance as Web application architectures move toward multi-tier systems with business object components.

Once we exploit the additional expressiveness of the object model for enhanced concurrency, recovery also becomes more complex, as we can no longer roll back a transaction in isolation by undoing its page writes. Rather, high-level semantic operations need to be invoked for compensating the effects of an aborted transaction. To reason about the correctness of interleaving transaction rollbacks with regular forward operations of (to-be-) committed transactions, the criterion of tree reducibility has been extended and applied to the expansion of a schedule where all undo steps of transaction rollbacks are made explicit, "first-class" operations. With this proper understanding of how rollbacks need to be implemented, extending the redo-history crash and media recovery algorithm to the object model is made relatively simple by viewing high-level operations as subtransactions. The undo pass needs to invoke high-level compensation steps for completed subtransactions and low-level undo steps for incomplete subtransactions in the appropriate order. The analysis pass and the redo pass remain the same as in the page model; in particular, page-oriented redo is usually preferred for fast restart. Recovery idempotence is ensured by keeping track of both forward and compensation steps using a clever backward chaining of compensation log entries. We have also seen that the redo-history recovery algorithm forms a framework into which a suite of other optimizations can be incorporated when the given workload makes them beneficial. Most importantly, the recovery algorithm can be adapted to the special architecture of a data-sharing cluster where multiple computers have shared access to the disk system and a server crash is handled by "failing over" to one of the surviving servers in the cluster. This setup avoids delays for software initialization (rebooting the OS, starting the database system, reestablishing sessions, etc.) and is thus the architecture of choice for applications with stringent availability requirements.

Media recovery based on backups and archive logging can be further optimized to minimize downtime, and combined with redundancy in the storage system, based on mirroring or error-correcting codes, to mask disk failures without service interruption. Recovery can also be extended to cope with disasters that hit an entire computer complex (e.g., a fire in the computer building) via log shipping to a remote backup server during normal operation and failing over to that server when a disaster occurs. To simplify the exception handling code of application programs and to improve the availability at the application level as perceived by the end users, we have also described techniques for application recovery with failure-resilient messages and processes, based on transactional message queues for simple, stateless or pseudo-conversational applications or specific logging and restart techniques for general stateful applications. All these techniques complement data recovery so that virtually all failures can be masked to the human users. Last but not least, we have also discussed transaction management in heterogeneous server federations, including concurrency control techniques that can cope with diverse local protocols and various optimizations to the standardized 2PC protocol for distributed atomicity with lower overhead and lower blocking probability.

20.2.3 Methodology and New Challenges for Researchers

Finally, for the most advanced readers and particularly those with ambitions to pursue their own research in the area of transactional information systems (e.g., graduate students), our aim has been not just to present the prevalent techniques but to discuss why they work and why they are more versatile, efficient, or robust than other conceivable alternatives. This is why we have emphasized the foundations of these algorithms and included a thorough discussion of alternative algorithms for the same problem setting and the various trade-offs, for example, the pros and cons of physical, physiological, and logical logging, or redo-history versus redo-winners algorithms for crash recovery. We have also included a good fraction of promising but somewhat immature (or incomplete) directions such as interleaving specifications and other very high-level forms of semantic concurrency control. After all, technology moves on and the workload characteristics and requirements of typical applications will change over time, so that researchers should continue to reassess and improve existing algorithms and devise new departures.

A particularly important point of our pedagogical concept has been reasoning about the correctness of the presented algorithms. More advanced algorithms are more complex, thus it is more difficult to gain confidence in their correctness. Consequently, we have added many correctness proofs, with emphasis on the structure of the proof arguments rather than trying to cover all cases in painstaking detail. This is why we have gradually relaxed the mathematical rigor in the presentation. For most of the presented material it should still be possible to refine the correctness arguments into whatever detail is desired by a skeptical reader or extremely careful system builder. However, for some of the most advanced material, working out all system-relevant details of

Research methodology and new challenges for graduate students

the algorithms and proving their correctness (e.g., for the most general form of comprehensive application recovery) still poses significant challenges and, we believe, rewarding research subjects for the next generation of graduate students.

20.3 **Data Replication for Ubiquitous Access**

Data replication deals with the maintenance of multiple *copies* of the same data items placed on different servers; these copies are also referred to as *replicas*. A *replication control* component serves to ensure the consistency among *the same data item's multiple copies*, which is in contrast and complementary to concurrency control considering the consistency across *different*, logically interrelated data items.

Relevance of replication   Replication is of great practical relevance for two reasons: (1) *data availability*, to mask outages of servers that would otherwise hold the only copy of a requested data item, and (2) *responsiveness*, to compensate for servers with poor performance by accessing a copy on a faster server. It is obvious that replication is beneficial for applications with a high fraction of read accesses, whereas having to maintain multiple copies is usually not worthwhile for update-intensive applications. As modern applications are typically dominated by read access, replication plays a key role in many Internet-based information systems. In particular, replication is an indispensable asset for mobile clients (e.g., notebooks, palmtops, or cellular phones) that do not have continuous server connectivity. Similarly, worldwide Internet applications with a very large number of clients all over the globe, such as e-Commerce services or business portals, often replicate data on a number of decentralized sites closer to the clients. Distributed Web caching can be viewed as a form of *dynamic replication* along these lines.

Eager (synchronous) replication   Ideally, replication would be transparent, analogously to versioning in multiversion concurrency control. So a client could access an arbitrary copy of a replicated data item, for example, the closest one in terms of access speed, and would be guaranteed to see the most up-to-date value of the data. Correspondingly, updates to a copy would be propagated immediately to all other copies of the same data item with negligible delays, to prevent concurrent readers of other copies from seeing out-of-date values. The correctness criterion for this kind of transparent replication is known as *one-copy serializability*: a history with read and write steps that refer to individual copies must be equivalent to a serial history with only one copy per data item. If both read and write steps always accessed *all* copies of a data item under the transactional isolation guarantee of the concurrency control component, one-copy serializability would be self-guaranteed. For example, this would amount to locking all copies of all data items in a transaction's read and write set within the transaction. The point of replication, however, is that read access should be much faster and much less expensive than reading all of a data item's copies. A replication control method is an algorithm that determines which copies need to be read and written, or tested, *eagerly (synchronously)* within the transaction boundaries to ensure one-copy serializability. For updates, copies that are not written within the transaction itself still need to be brought up-to-date, but this can be done "lazily" outside the transaction.

The simplest and probably earliest replication control protocol is the *primary copy method*. In this method, each data item has a designated copy that serves as an anchor point, the primary copy. All measures of the concurrency control, for example, requesting a lock on a data item, are directed to the primary copy of the corresponding data item. Once the concurrency control has approved the access, for example, when the lock is acquired, the replication control passes a timestamp (or sequence number or version number) to the transaction, reflecting the last update to the primary copy, and the transaction is then allowed to read *any* copy. It does not necessarily have to read the primary copy, but may choose to access a copy that is closer to the client. However, the transaction tests that copy's timestamp against the one obtained from the primary copy, and the transaction gives up on the closer copy if it turns out to be out of date. The point is that this test should be successful most of the time, and then the long message for reading a data item has low cost; whereas the short message for obtaining the primary copy's timestamp is unavoidable in this protocol. Writes are always directed to the primary copy, and it is sufficient to update the primary copy eagerly, that is, within the transaction boundaries. All other copies can be updated lazily in the background. So, in summary, the primary copy serves as a bookkeeping anchor to make sure that no transaction can access a stale copy.

Primary copy method

A critique of the primary copy method is the observation that a failure of the server where a given primary copy resides renders all other copies of the same data items useless. Even if other copies are available, no transaction is allowed to access them as long as they cannot check the primary copy. This situation is avoided with an alternative known as the *read-one write-all method* (ROWA). As the protocol's name suggests, a read request can access any arbitrary copy without any restrictions and without any prior testing. Write steps, on the other hand, now have to update all copies eagerly. This ensures that all copies of a data item are up-to-date when the transaction commits.

Read-one write-all method (ROWA)

In between the primary copy and the ROWA methods there is a spectrum of intermediate strategies to trade off read costs versus write costs. A method that penalizes reads and writes by equal terms is *majority voting*: both reads and writes have to eagerly access a majority of the copies that exist for a given data item. For example, with three copies, read steps need to test the recency of two out of the three copies (and read the actual value of the data item from one of them), and write steps need to update two copies eagerly within the ongoing transaction. If only two copies exist, the protocol degenerates into a read-all write-all variant.

Majority voting

Quorum consensus (weighted voting) The point of majority voting is to ensure that for every pair of conflicting operations on a data item, the sets of eagerly accessed copies of that data item are nondisjoint. In this way the replication control enables the concurrency control to detect the conflict, although the concurrency control is completely unaware of replication. This principle can be generalized by introducing a read quorum and a write quorum, which are numbers of copies that need to be accessed such that the sum of read and write quorums exceeds the total number of copies for the data item, and the same must hold for twice the write quorum. In this way the replication control can tune the costs of read versus write steps on a per-data-item basis. To further take into account the different failure rates (or expected downtimes) and response times of the various servers that hold copies, the various copies can be given different weights in the voting scheme. Then the sum of read and write quorums and also the sum of two write quorums need to exceed the total of the weights. This generalization is known as *quorum consensus* or *weighted voting*. Although this method is already very flexible and customizable to the target environment, yet another generalization is to allow dynamic adjustment of voting weights and quorums to consider longer outages of servers. Such *dynamic voting* schemes need careful considerations for detecting outages (as opposed to network partitioning, see Chapter 19) and for handling the reintegration of servers after some downtime period. A special case of the dynamic approach is the *read-one write-all-available* protocol that limits eager updates to the copies that reside on currently running servers (provided that this distinction can be safely made).

Lazy (asynchronous) replication The use of eager replication control methods as outlined above is limited to small degrees of replication (i.e., small numbers of copies per data item) for the simple reason that none of the protocols scales up to tens or hundreds of replicas. For larger degrees of replication, for example, in the World Wide Web, applications typically resort to completely *lazy* (*asynchronous*) replication. In these approaches transactions read and write any copy, and merely initiate the updates to other copies as a background task outside the transaction. It is up to the application to cope with access to stale copies, and in many Web applications, out-of-date information is even exposed to the human users (so the application does not really do anything on this matter).

Epidemic replication In a large-scale distributed system it is still all but trivial to ensure that the update to one copy will eventually reach all other copies and that all copies of the same data item will converge to the same value. Algorithms for this purpose are often referred to as *epidemic replication* and involve a fair amount of distributed bookkeeping.

With lazy replication it can happen that two different copies of the same data item are simultaneously updated by two different transactions. Later, when these two updates are propagated to all other copies, these other copies will be faced with the problem of having to decide which of the two updates they should apply. Under an epidemic replication protocol, acceptance of both updates will be avoided, for this would likely result in different update orderings at the various replicas. The goal instead is to ensure at least *eventual consistency* among copies, meaning that all copies converge to identical updates if all update activity was phasing out. The decision on which update a copy will accept can be based on real-time timestamps—the younger update wins—or more sophisticated distributed timestamping (e.g., so-called vector clocks), or on the origin of the updates—the more "important" server on which the original update occurred wins. Combinations are also possible, and the notion of an important, or primary, server may be a dynamically adjustable one. For example, updates that originate from the server in San Francisco win during daytime in the Pacific time zone, and updates from the server in Frankfurt, Germany, win during nighttime (i.e., daytime in Europe). Such flexible *conflict resolution policies* are supported by most commercial database systems.

Under specific conditions that restrict the access patterns of transactions, the communication topology and network properties, and/or the way data is replicated, enhanced forms of lazy replication can still ensure one-copy serializability. See the Bibliographic Notes for publications that have proposed protocols along these lines.

In summary, the proliferation of Web-based applications has made replication control a very important aspect for ubiquitous data access, and replication in this setting still poses many exciting research problems. In particular, we still need a much better understanding of the complex trade-off between consistency and scalability and how to make judicious design choices for specific applications with regard to this fundamental trade-off.

20.4 **E-Services and Workflows**

Recall from Chapter 1 that one of the most challenging application classes for transactional concepts is *workflows*, which are defined as long-lived collections of activities (or steps) that have to be executed together in order to achieve certain business goals. Workflows are also at the heart of advanced, business-to-consumer (B2C) or business-to-business (B2B) e-Services on the Internet, for example, electronic auctions (B2C) or supply chains (B2B). As an example, we have already considered (in Chapters 1 and 17) the activities that occur in planning a trip to a conference; the graphical representation is repeated here in Figure 20.1.

The overall workflow involves the following activities. First, a conference is selected; if nothing suitable is found, the process is terminated. Next, the cost of the trip to the selected conference is checked, typically by delegation to a travel agency. In parallel, the applicable registration fee for the conference is determined. Thereafter, the total cost of attending is compared to the budget allowance, and a decision is made whether or not the conference can be attended.

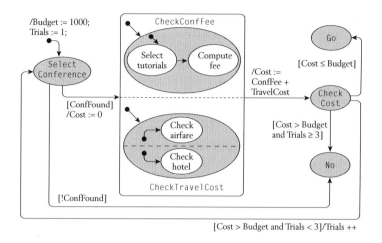

Figure 20.1 The travel planning workflow.

Workflow specification by statecharts

Writing down the activities of a workflow together with their data and control flows amounts to *specifying* a workflow as a collection of activities that may be nested within each other, that may involve human as well as software processing entities, and in which the executing participants can play various roles. For the specification of workflow, various models and methods have been proposed and various tools developed. As mentioned previously, the illustration shown in Figure 20.1 is based on statecharts, where each oval denotes a state in which the workflow can be during its execution. Each state in turn corresponds to one activity; the activity is spawned when the state is entered. When the workflow is started, an initial state (SelectConference) is entered, and the workflow terminates when a final state (Go or No) is reached.

Alternatives to statecharts include variants of *Petri nets* (e.g., condition-event nets or predicate-transition nets), *temporal logic*, *process algebras*, or *event-driven process chains*. In any of these formalisms, important workflow aspects to be specified may include, besides the various activities involved, pre- and postconditions for each activity; the control flow among activities; data items that are manipulated by an activity or passed from one activity to the next (i.e., the data flow among activities); requirements on the processing elements that execute an activity; deadlines or time intervals; and so on.

Local vs. global correctness

An important distinction to be made here is between *local conditions* that apply to individual activities or their nearby context, and *global conditions* that affect the workflow as a whole. Indeed, workflows are typically designed such that they represent enterprise operations and hence have goals or maintain constraints that are global in nature and largely independent of the resources used while the workflow is being executed. On the other hand, an individual activity within a workflow may just have to assure conditions that are local to the database on which it is run. Think, for example, of a credit approval workflow in a bank. The clerk in charge may issue data accesses on the customer's bank account and its income, which are executed as queries on an underlying database and eventually also updates when the credit request is approved and money is transferred into the customer's account. Such local activities need to maintain the consistency of the bank's database. From a global perspective, on the other hand, a bank must be careful in responding to credit requests in order to avoid undue risk because of too many approvals; thus, the overall workflow has to maintain the condition that the bank retains enough money for staying in healthy business after every such transfer. This observation can be modeled by associating distinct *invariants* with activities and with workflows, which express constraints to be preserved locally or globally. A local invariant has to be respected by individual activities of a workflow, whereas a global one must be maintained by workflow executions as a whole.

While the specification of a workflow often leads to a state-transition diagram such as the one shown in Figure 20.1 as well as to allowed states and their contexts, workflow *execution* must rely on a specific infrastructure, in particular a *workflow engine* that can read a specification, instantiate new workflow instances, and execute them according to the data and control flow that has been specified. In general, the control flow allows conditional execution as well as loops based on high-level predicates; in addition, it allows parallel execution (e.g., of the two states `CheckConfFee` and `CheckTravelCost`). The underlying workflow engine has to take care of these execution options. The engine can be a centralized one, or it can be distributed in the sense of a server federation; that is, portions of an executable workflow are handled by different workflow engines.

The activities within a particular workflow can be completely automated or based on interaction with a human user. This implies that workflows can be long-lived activities that last up to several days or weeks or even months and years. A typical characteristic of workflows is that the activities are distributed across different responsible persons and different, independent information systems, possibly across different enterprises. In particular, an activity can spawn requests to an arbitrary "invoked application" that is provided by some application server independently of the current workflow. From the point of view of transactions, various scenarios can now be envisioned.

First, the activities themselves can spawn requests to information systems that lead to transactional executions in these systems. For example, this can be assumed for the `CheckTravelCost` activity in the travel planning workflow, which most likely will figure out prices as well as make reservations in the underlying databases. Obviously, booking a flight to a certain city and a hotel room in that city makes sense only if both reservations are successful. If either of the two is unavailable, the whole trip no longer makes sense. So

Activities as ACID transactions

these two steps need to be tied together into a single transaction. Note that this transaction is a distributed one, but we can imagine that the servers that participate in its execution can guarantee transactional properties. In general, we can think of a workflow in execution as being composed of a number of ACID transactions. Each server involved in the execution of the activity would then have to guarantee an *exactly-once execution* as described in Chapter 17. Regarding the invariants expressing local or global conditions we mentioned above, the ideal situation becomes that (1) a schedule is serializable in the traditional sense (i.e., equivalent to some serial schedule and hence preserving the local invariant), and (2) the global invariant is implied by the schedule as well; in other words, local correctness implies global correctness.

Activities as layered object model transactions

If we consider the nested structure that a workflow specification might have, it makes sense to distinguish low-level activities such as database operations from higher-level activities such as reservation activities. Under this perception, a workflow execution boils down to an object model transaction that exhibits a layered structure. As we have seen in previous chapters, concurrency control for such executions can be done by using different levels.

Compensating activities

Taking into account the fact that workflows may be long-running activities, it may happen that a number of activities in a workflow end successfully, but the entire workflow (or some larger portion of it) may have to be unsuccessfully terminated at some point. From a layered transaction perspective, this means that some subtransactions are committed already when the root transaction ultimately aborts. The transactional concepts we have seen in Chapters 11 and 14 suggest solutions even in these cases, namely, by injecting into the root transaction *compensating* subtransactions that account for whatever state changes the already committed subtransactions have previously made. Such a rollback of an entire workflow spawning compensating activities is correct if the latter commutes with interleaving activities of concurrent workflows, for which such concepts like tree reducibility (see Chapter 6), layered locking and locking for return value commutativity (see Chapter 7), or transaction chopping (see Chapter 8) are applicable.

Returning to our trip reservation example, note that the outcome of the flight and hotel reservations affects the further processing of the workflow. The requests against the various information systems technically return status codes that should be stored in variables associated with the workflow and would be relevant for the future control flow. For example, not being able to make one of the two necessary reservations in the selected city should trigger going back to the initial `SelectConference` state for another trial. Thus, it is desirable (if not mandatory) that the modification of the workflow's variables be embedded in the same transaction that accesses the airline and hotel databases. In other words, the *state of the workflow application* should be under transactional control as well. We could model this into the workflow specification of Figure 20.1 by adding a new activity such as ContactCustomer, which makes sure that the travel agent informs the customer if the hotel or the flight reservation fails, so that a change in the itinerary can be worked out.

An alternative way of handling the situation described above is by defining appropriate *spheres of compensation* that combine the partial rollback of (composite) activities. A compensation sphere allows collections of activities to be grouped together at specification time. A compensation sphere with one or more "semantically failing" activities is aborted by running appropriate compensation activities, and the abort of such a sphere can be requested at any time, even if the control flow has already left the sphere. Note that transactional activities and nontransactional ones may be mixed in a compensation sphere. In particular, if one activity in the sphere does not execute successfully, all others that have already been executed must also be corrected via compensating activities. In our example, the activities whose failure may have resulted in customer contact are now put in a compensation sphere; more precisely, the flight and hotel reservation activities lead to corresponding cancellation actions as compensations.

Compensation spheres

Although the concept of spheres of compensation appears attractive, making it work is a nontrivial problem. Indeed, the workflow specification language must be extended appropriately so that a user or a workflow designer can define compensation spheres as needed by the application or the process in question. Typically, this requires rule-based languages for expressing which activities are combined into a compensation sphere under what conditions. Moreover, the underlying workflow execution engine must be equipped with mechanisms to coordinate a rollback that occurs inside a sphere.

In summary, transactional technology as presented in this book provides major building blocks and great leverage for dependable execution of long-lived workflows and e-Services. However, the seamless integration of semantically rich workflow specifications, the underlying full-fledged workflow engines, and the transactional capabilities of the involved activity servers still require further research. In particular, the full formalization and rigorous correctness reasoning for a comprehensive workflow system remains an important open issue.

20.5 **Performance and Availability Guarantees**

Throughout this book, our discussion of different algorithms has laid much emphasis on performance and, for recovery algorithms, on availability. However, all our comparisons have been qualitative, and we have not quantified how well a particular algorithm would perform in a particular system setting under a particular workload. In many cases a qualitative assessment was sufficient to obtain insight into the *relative performance potential*, for example, of different locking policies (by characterizing their admissible schedules) or different levels of optimizations for crash recovery. For a number of reasons, we should still aim at providing a quantitative assessment of the various algorithms and their interplay in a complex system:

- Often there are trade-offs among different algorithms. One algorithm is better with regard to a specific metric (e.g., performance during normal operation), whereas the other is better with regard to another metric (e.g., restart performance and thus availability). These trade-offs can be very subtle (e.g., admissible concurrency on one hand and overhead for concurrency control bookkeeping on the other hand).

- The pros and cons of the considered algorithms typically depend on the underlying hardware resource parameters (i.e., CPU speed, memory size, number and type of disks, and also very subtle parameters such as CPU cache effectiveness and the resulting rate of memory stalls). Additional influences are the workload characteristics of the application (e.g., length of transactions, fraction of update statements, etc.). In view of these trade-offs and environmental dependencies we are naturally interested in knowing by how much a certain algorithm outperforms an alternative in a given setting and whether the winner in this situation is still competitive in certain other settings.

- Because performance depends on the underlying hardware resources, system administrators are faced with the problem of determining an appropriate system configuration (e.g., memory size and also software tuning parameters such as data cache size). For this kind of capacity and configuration planning, considering the current or an anticipated workload (e.g., number of clients of a server and their rate of generating transactions), a quantitative assessment of the overall system for different, often hypothetical, configurations is crucial.

- Finally, predictability of the system behavior, including its performance under usual as well as stressful conditions (e.g., during the peak business hour) is of utmost importance in a world that critically depends on IT infrastructure. The 1998 report of the U.S. President's Advisory Committee on Information Technology has clearly stated that "our ability to analyze and predict the performance of the enormously complex software systems that lie at the core of our economy are painfully inadequate." Ultimately, information systems should be deployed together with performance and service quality guarantees for highly dependable services that users can truly rely on.

So quantitative analysis of the performance of transactional information systems and, as building blocks of the analysis, their underlying concurrency control and recovery algorithms is of extremely high importance. The metrics that we are most interested in include (but are not necessarily restricted to) the following:

- *Throughput*: the maximum number of transactions per second that a system can sustain over an extended period.

- *Response time*: the time span between initiating a transaction from a client or application server and receiving the response (e.g., a commit acknowledgment).

- *Reliability*: the probability that the system does not have a nonrepairable failure (i.e., one that leads to data loss, in our context of data servers) within a given lifetime or observation period. (The mean time to data loss that we have considered in Chapter 16 is closely related to reliability.)

- *Availability*: the probability that the system is running and can serve incoming requests at a randomly chosen point in time, within a given observation period. (The observation period is often assumed to be infinitely long, provided that the corresponding mathematical limit, the so-called stationary availability, exists.)

Response time can refer to the mean response time, averaged over all transactions, or to specific transaction classes formed by types of underlying programs (e.g., processing a new order versus preparing a daily sales report in an online sales application) or different user/customer categories (e.g., frequent flyers versus standard customers in an airline reservation system). An orthogonal issue is whether we consider merely the mean response time or also its variance or even percentiles of the response time distribution. The latter is often important for ensuring that the system's responsiveness is acceptable most of the time; for example, we could require that 95% or 99% of all transactions (of a specific class) should have a response time of two or five seconds at most. These requirements may be stated as explicit performance goals of the system, which in turn require appropriate, all but trivial, capacity and configuration planning and also specific transaction processing techniques that use priorities for different transaction classes. Such approaches are sometimes referred to as *goal-oriented transaction processing*.

Availability measures the system's capability to quickly recover from transient, repairable failures. As we discussed in Chapters 15 and 16, there are techniques to keep the system available even during the recovery from certain failures (e.g., disk failures if there is sufficient storage and data redundancy or server failures in a data-sharing cluster). However, during such degraded periods the performance will not be as good as if all resources (disks, processors, server processes, etc.) were up simultaneously and no recovery actions were in progress. Note that planned downtimes of components for software maintenance also lead to degraded states. For large system complexes with substantial degrees of (data and process) replication, the system will be in a

Performability

degraded mode relatively often, and the resulting effects on the overall, long-term response times should be taken into account. The *performability* metric combines the performance and availability dimensions by weighting the performance in degraded states in proportion to the expected duration of the degraded period.

Among the above metrics, response time is usually most difficult to analyze for two fundamental reasons:

- Response time depends on many factors and their complex interplay. With regard to concurrency control alone, lock conflict probabilities, lock waiting times, deadlock probabilities, and so on, all contribute to the overall transaction response time. Additional, equally important factors include the database cache hit ratio, the disk I/O rate and access patterns in the processing of queries and transactions, the CPU time consumption, and so on. Thus, predicting the overall performance at the system level requires a detailed analysis of all these underlying factors, each of which in turn already poses significant difficulties.

- Response time needs to be analyzed under the constraint that the system sustains a certain throughput that corresponds to the total user-induced load (e.g., an arrival rate of operations or a number of concurrently active users). This gives rise to the complication that response time involves queueing delays because of contention for system resources (e.g., memory, disk I/O, network bandwidth, locks on data), an effect that is largely underrated, yet can become disastrous during load peaks. Network and server queueing is exactly what makes many services on the World Wide Web so awfully slow.

Queueing is an inherently stochastic phenomenon, since it depends on the user activity as it evolves over time and the resulting workload characteristics, which can usually be characterized only statistically. For example, the variability in the load patterns, such as arrivals of new transactions or transaction lengths, can have a dramatic influence on performance. This is analogous to and indeed has the same fundamental causes as the well-known effect of automobile speed variability on traffic jams. Likewise, the complexity of the system internals suggests that the system behavior itself (e.g., patterns of lock conflicts) be best modeled in terms of random variables with specific probability distributions. Finally, similar considerations hold for the analysis of availability or performability as well: failures cannot be deterministically predicted and rather need to be characterized stochastically, which in turn renders recovery time a random variable (with *a priori* unknown distribution).

Real-time transaction scheduling   In certain applications, it is paramount that queueing delays, including lock waits, be bounded so that certain response times can be guaranteed for *all* transactions (of certain classes), not just for a very large percentile of them.

So at the time a transaction arrives it is assigned a *deadline* that its execution has to meet. Such applications are known as *real-time applications* and include, for example, the trading platforms of stock exchanges or air traffic control. Applications may also exhibit a mix of real-time and non-real-time transaction classes or may tolerate infrequent violations of deadlines under certain conditions. Regardless of these variations, a real-time application setting requires a deadline-conscious CPU scheduler, and this has drastic consequences for concurrency control and further aspects of a transactional data server. For example, a transaction that holds locks and blocks another transaction that has a pressing deadline should either be canceled (i.e., forced to be rolled back) or itself be expedited to release its locks as quickly as possible. It turns out that such considerations lead to a new set of trade-offs among optimistic and pessimistic concurrency control protocols, and generally need careful integration with CPU and disk scheduling of the underlying operating system. This area has been researched to some extent (see the Bibliographic Notes), but still poses challenges and opportunities for future research.

For all these reasons, stochastic models and especially so-called queueing models are of overriding importance for the performance analysis and predictability of information systems. The "only" reason for having excluded such material from this book is because it is a major subject of its own (see the Bibliographic Notes for textbooks) and would thus have required far too much additional space and also special mathematical prerequisites. The strategic importance of this area is best underlined by the observation that Web-based services especially become increasingly complex to configure, administer, and operate with acceptable performance and continuous availability while the cost of human system administrators and tuning experts increasingly dominates the overall cost of these information services.

Bibliographic Notes

Replication control is treated in the textbooks by Bernstein et al. (1987) and Özsu and Valduriez (1999) with emphasis on eager replication. A broader account of replication, including lazy replication methods, has been given in the book by Helal et al. (1996). The notion of one-copy serializability has been introduced by Bernstein and Goodman (1986). The original sources on the primary copy, ROWA, majority voting, and quorum consensus protocols are Alsberg and Day (1976), Stonebraker (1979), Thomas (1979), and Gifford (1979). Various improvements and generalizations have been proposed, for example, by Bernstein and Goodman (1984), Garcia-Molina and Barbara (1985), Barbara et al. (1989), and El Abbadi and Toueg (1989), as well as Jajodia and Mutchler (1990). An insightful discussion of the scalability problem for replication has been given by Gray et al. (1996). Epidemic replication goes back to Demers et al. (1987) and has been studied more recently, for example, by Rabinovich et al. (1996) and Agrawal et al. (1997). Recent algorithms on how to reconcile lazy and eager replication and on how to make replication scalable include the work by Breitbart and Korth (1999) as well as Kemme and Alonso (2001).

Much research over the past 10 years has investigated extensions (mostly relaxations) of the classical transaction domain to application domains such as workflow management; see, for example, Barghouti and Kaiser (1991), Elmagarmid (1992), Rusinkiewicz and Sheth (1995), Ramamritham and Chrysanthis (1996), or Jajodia and Kerschberg (1997). Results of these investigations include extensible transaction models (ETMs) (see Elmagarmid (1992) for an overview), customizable transaction management (CTM) (see Georgakopoulos et al. (1996)), and frameworks for the specification of transaction models and their properties (see Chrysanthis and Ramamritham (1994) and Barga and Pu (1997)). For example, the ACTA framework, developed by Chrysanthis and Ramamritham, is a tool for synthesizing ETMs and can be used for specification of and reasoning about transaction effects and interactions. Extended transaction models along these lines are intended to meet the requirements imposed by workflow management and other computer-supported collaborative work (CSCW) applications (e.g., concurrent CAD), since their characteristics concern issues such as transaction structure, intra-transaction parallelism, intertransaction execution dependencies, relaxed isolation requirements, restricted failure atomicity, or controlled termination; some among the many relevant references (in addition to the surveys mentioned above) are the papers by de By et al. (1997), Alonso et al. (1996), Attie et al. (1993), Breitbart et al. (1993), Chen and Dayal (1996a, b), Hsu (1993), Klein (1991), Mitschang et al. (1996), Reuter et al. (1992, 1997), Salzberg and Tombroff (1996), Worah and Sheth (1997), or Zhang et al. (1994). Recent work in this category with special attention to Internet-based e-Services includes Alonso et al. (1999), Casati et al. (2000), Geppert et al. (1999), Muth et al. (1999), and Schuldt et al. (2000). For expressing control and data flow between activities as well as organizational aspects, workflow specification methods have been described in the books by Dogac et al. (1998), Jablonski and Bussler (1996), and Leymann and Roller (2000).

Local versus global correctness was studied by Ebert and Vossen (1997). The notion of a compensation sphere is from Leymann (1995) and appears in more refined form in Leymann and Roller (2000). The idea of decoupling transactional properties (in particular atomicity and isolation) into appropriate spheres was originally suggested by Bjork (1973) and Davies (1973, 1978), and reappeared in various forms in the work by Wächter and Reuter (1992), Weikum and Schek (1992), Chrysanthis and Ramamritham (1994), and Barga and Pu (1997).

Excellent textbooks on stochastic models for performance and availability analyis have been written, for example, by Allen (1990), Tijms (1994),

Nelson (1995), and Bolch et al. (1998), with emphasis on the underlying mathematics, and Sahner et al. (1996), Haverkort (1998), and Menasce and Almeida (1998, 2000), with emphasis on applications. An up-to-date account of the state of the art and future trends in performance analysis has been given by Haring et al. (2000). The most comprehensive and authoritative source on the qualitative assessment of concurrency control algorithms are the surveys by Thomasian (1996b, 1998a), which also provide extensive references to the original literature. The notions of class-specific performance guarantees and goal-oriented transaction processing have been discussed by Ferguson et al. (1993), Brown et al. (1994), and Rahm (1997). Transaction scheduling policies for real-time applications have been presented, for example, by Abbott and Garcia-Molina (1992), Haritsa et al. (1993, 1995), O'Neil et al. (1995), Bestavros and Baraoudakis (1996), Soparkar et al. (1996), and Ulusoy and Buchmann (1998).

References

Abbott, R.K., and H. Garcia-Molina (1992): Scheduling Real-Time Transactions: A Performance Evaluation. *ACM Transactions on Database Systems* **17**, pp. 513–560.

Abiteboul, S., and V. Vianu (1988): Equivalence and Optimization of Relational Transactions. *Journal of the ACM* **35**, pp. 70–120.

Adam, N., O. Dogramaci, A. Gangopadhyay, and Y. Yesha (1998): *Electronic Commerce: Technical, Business, and Legal Issues.* Englewood Cliffs, NJ: Prentice Hall.

Adya, A., R. Gruber, B. Liskov, and U. Maheshwari (1995): Efficient Optimistic Concurrency Control Using Loosely Synchronized Clocks. In *Proc. ACM SIGMOD International Conference on Management of Data*, pp. 23–34.

Adya, A., B. Liskov, and P. O'Neil (2000): Generalized Isolation Level Definitions. In *Proc. 16th IEEE International Conference on Data Engineering*, pp. 67–78.

Aghili, H., and D.G. Severance (1982): A Practical Guide to the Design of Differential Files for Recovery of On-Line Databases. *ACM Transactions on Database Systems* **7**, pp. 540–565.

Agrawal, D., J.L. Bruno, A. El Abbadi, and V. Krishnaswamy (1994): Relative Serializability: An Approach for Relaxing the Atomicity of Transactions. In *Proc. 13th ACM SIGACT-SIGMOD-SIGART Symposium on Principles of Database Systems*, pp. 139–149.

Agrawal, D., and A. El Abbadi (1990): Locks with Constrained Sharing. In *Proc. 9th ACM SIGACT-SIGMOD-SIGART Symposium on Principles of Database Systems*, pp. 85–93.

Agrawal, D., and A. El Abbadi (1995): Constrained Shared Locks for Increasing Concurrency in Databases. *Journal of Computer and System Sciences* **51**, pp. 53–63.

Agrawal, D., A. El Abbadi, and A.E. Lang (1994): The Performance of Protocols Based on Locks with Ordered Sharing. *IEEE Transactions on Knowledge and Data Engineering* **6**, pp. 805–818.

Agrawal, D., A. El Abbadi, and A.K. Singh (1993): Consistency and Orderability: Semantics-Based Correctness Criteria for Databases. *ACM Transactions on Database Systems* **18**, pp. 460–486.

Agrawal, D., A. El Abbadi, and R.C. Steinke (1997): Epidemic Algorithms in Replicated Databases. In *Proc. 16th ACM SIGACT-SIGMOD-SIGART Symposium on Principles of Database Systems*, pp. 161–172.

Agrawal, D., and S. Sengupta (1993): Modular Synchronization in Distributed, Multiversion Databases: Version Control and Concurrency Control. *IEEE Transactions on Knowledge and Data Engineering 5*, pp. 126–137.

Agrawal, R. (1985): A Parallel Logging Algorithm for Multiprocessor Database Machine. In *Proc. 4th International Workshop on Database Machines*, pp. 256–276.

Agrawal, R., M.J. Carey, and M. Livny (1987): Concurrency Control Performance Modeling: Alternatives and Implications. *ACM Transactions on Database Systems 12*, pp. 609–654.

Agrawal, R., M.J. Carey, and L.W. McVoy (1987): The Performance of Alternative Strategies for Dealing with Deadlocks in Database Management Systems. *IEEE Transactions on Software Engineering 13*, pp. 1348–1363.

Agrawal, R., and D.J. DeWitt (1985a): Integrated Concurrency Control and Recovery Mechanisms: Design and Performance Evaluation. *ACM Transactions on Database Systems 10*, pp. 529–564.

Agrawal, R., and D.J. DeWitt (1985b): Recovery Architectures for Multiprocessor Database Machines. In *Proc. ACM SIGMOD International Conference on Management of Data*, pp. 131–145.

Ahuja, M.L., and J.C. Browne (1987): Concurrency Control by Preordering Entities in Databases with Multiversioned Entities. In *Proc. 3rd IEEE International Conference on Data Engineering*, pp. 312–321.

Al-Houmaily, Y.J., and P.K. Chrysanthis (1999): Atomicity with Incompatible Presumptions. In *Proc. 18th ACM SIGACT-SIGMOD-SIGART Symposium on Principles of Database Systems*, pp. 306–315.

Al-Houmaily, Y.J., P.K. Chrysanthis, and S.P. Levitan (1997): An Argument in Favor of the Presumed Commit Protocol. In *Proc. 13th IEEE International Conference on Data Engineering*, pp. 255–265.

Allen, A.O. (1990): *Probability, Statistics, and Queueing Theory with Computer Science Applications*. Boston: Academic Press.

Alonso, G., D. Agrawal, and A. El Abbadi (1994): Reducing Recovery Constraints on Locking-Based Protocols. In *Proc. 13th ACM SIGACT-SIGMOD-SIGART Symposium on Principles of Database Systems*, pp. 129–138.

Alonso, G., D. Agrawal, A. El Abbadi, M. Kamath, R. Günthör, and C. Mohan (1996): Advanced Transaction Models in Workflow Contexts. In *Proc. 12th IEEE International Conference on Data Engineering*, pp. 574–581.

Alonso, G., S. Blott, A. Fessler, and H.-J. Schek (1997): Correctness and Parallelism of Composite Systems. In *Proc. 16th ACM SIGACT-SIGMOD-SIGART Symposium on Principles of Database Systems*, pp. 197–208.

Alonso, G., A. Fessler, G. Pardon, and H.-J. Schek (1999a): Transactions in Stack, Fork, and Join Composite Systems. In *Proc. 7th International Conference on Database Theory*, Lecture Notes in Computer Science **1540**, Berlin: Springer-Verlag, pp. 150–168.

Alonso, G., A. Fessler, G. Pardon, and H.-J. Schek (1999b): Correctness in General Configurations of Transactional Components. In *Proc. 18th ACM SIGACT-SIGMOD-SIGART Symposium on Principles of Database Systems*, pp. 285–293.

Alonso, G., U. Fiedler, C. Hagen, A. Lazcano, H. Schuldt, and N. Weiler (1999): WISE: Business to Business E-Commerce. In *Proc. 9th IEEE International Workshop on Research Issues in Data Engineering*, pp. 132–139.

Alonso, G., C. Mohan, R. Günthör, D. Agrawal, A. El Abbadi, and M. Kamath (1995): Exotica/FMQM: A Persistent Message-Based Architecture for Distributed Workflow Management. In *Proc. IFIP WG 8.1 Working Conference on Information System Development for Decentralised Organizations*, also available as IBM Research Report RJ9912, IBM Almaden Research Center, San Jose, CA.

Alonso, G., R. Vingralek, D. Agrawal, Y. Breitbart, A. El Abbadi, H.-J. Schek, and G. Weikum (1994): Unifying Concurrency Control and Recovery of Transactions. *Information Systems* **19**, pp. 101–115.

Alsberg, P., and J.D. Day (1976): A Principle for Resilient Sharing of Distributed Resources. In *Proc. 2nd International Conference on Software Engineering*, pp. 562–570.

Alvarez, G.A., W.A. Burkhard, L.J. Stockmeyer, and F. Cristian (1998): Declustered Disk Array Architectures with Optimal and Near-Optimal Parallelism. In *Proc. 25th ACM/IEEE International Symposium on Computer Architecture*, pp. 109–120.

Alvisi, L., and K. Marzullo (1995): Message Logging: Pessimistic, Optimistic, and Causal. In *Proc. 15th IEEE International Conference on Distributed Computing Systems*, pp. 229–236.

Ammann, P., S. Jajodia, and I. Ray (1997): Semantic-Based Decomposition of Transactions. In Jajodia and Kerschberg (1997), pp. 153–180.

Attie, P.C., M.P. Singh, A.P. Sheth, and M. Rusinkiewicz (1993): Specifying and Enforcing Intertask Dependencies. In *Proc. 19th International Conference on Very Large Data Bases*, pp. 134–145.

Babaoglu, Ö., and K. Marzullo (1993): Consistent Global States of Distributed Systems: Fundamental Concepts and Mechanisms. In Mullender (1993), pp. 55–96.

Babaoglu, Ö., and S. Toueg (1993): Non-blocking Atomic Commitment. In Mullender (1993), pp. 147–168.

Badal, D.Z. (1986): The Distributed Deadlock Detection Algorithm. *ACM Transactions on Computer Systems* **4**, pp. 320–337.

Badrinath, B.R., and K. Ramamritham (1992): Semantics-Based Concurrency Control: Beyond Commutativity. *ACM Transactions on Database Systems* **17**, pp. 163–199.

Balter, R., P. Berard, and P. Decitre (1982): Why Control of the Concurrency Level in Distributed Systems Is More Fundamental Than Deadlock Management. In *Proc. 1st ACM Symposium on Principles of Distributed Computing*, pp. 183–193.

Barbara, D., and H. Garcia-Molina (1992): The Demarcation Protocol: A Technique for Maintaining Arithmetic Constraints in Distributed Database Systems. In *Proc. 3rd International Conference on Extending Database Technology*, Lecture Notes in Computer Science **580**, Berlin: Springer-Verlag, pp. 373–388.

Barbara, D., and H. Garcia-Molina (1994): The Demarcation Protocol: A Technique for Maintaining Constraints in Distributed Database Systems. *The VLDB Journal* **3**, pp. 325–353.

Barbara, D., H. Garcia-Molina, and A. Spauster (1989): Increasing Availability under Mutual Exclusion Constraints with Dynamic Vote Reassignment. *ACM Transactions on Computer Systems* **7**, pp. 394–426.

Barbara, D., S. Mehrotra, and P. Vallabhaneni (1996): The Gold Text Indexing Engine. In *Proc. 12th IEEE International Conference on Data Engineering*, pp. 172–179.

Barga, R.S., and C. Pu (1997): The Reflective Transaction Framework. In Jajodia and Kerschberg (1997), pp. 63–89.

Barghouti, N.S., and G.E. Kaiser (1991): Concurrency Control in Advanced Database Applications. *ACM Computing Surveys* **23**, pp. 269–317.

Barker, K., and M.T. Özsu (1990): Concurrent Transaction Execution in Multidatabase Systems. In *Proc. IEEE COMPSAC Conference*, pp. 224–233.

Bartlett, J.F. (1981): A NonStop Kernel. In *Proc. 8th ACM Symposium on Operating Systems Principles*, pp. 19–22.

Bayer, R., H. Heller, and A. Reiser (1980): Parallelism and Recovery in Database Systems. *ACM Transactions on Database Systems* **5**, pp. 139–156.

Bayer, R., and M. Schkolnick (1977): Concurrency of Operations on B-Trees. *Acta Informatica* **9**, pp. 1–21.

Beeri, C., P.A. Bernstein, and N. Goodman (1989): A Model for Concurrency in Nested Transaction Systems. *Journal of the ACM* **36**, pp. 230–269.

Beeri, C., P.A. Bernstein, N. Goodman, M.-Y. Lai, and D. Shasha (1983): A Concurrency Control Theory for Nested Transactions. In *Proc. 2nd ACM Symposium on Principles of Distributed Computing*, pp. 45–62.

Beeri, C., and R. Obermarck (1981): A Resource Class Independent Deadlock Detection Algorithm. In *Proc. 7th International Conference on Very Large Data Bases*, pp. 166–178.

Beeri, C., H.-J. Schek, and G. Weikum (1988): Multi-level Transaction Management, Theoretical Art or Practical Need? In *Proc. 1st International Conference on Extending Database Technology*, Lecture Notes in Computer Science **303**, Berlin: Springer-Verlag, pp. 134–154.

Berenson, H., P. Bernstein, J. Gray, J. Melton, E. O'Neil, and P. O'Neil (1995): A Critique of ANSI SQL Isolation Levels. In *Proc. ACM SIGMOD International Conference on Management of Data*, pp. 1–10.

Bernstein, A.J., D.S. Gerstl, W.-H. Leung, and P.M. Lewis (1998): Design and Performance of an Assertional Concurrency Control System. In *Proc. 14th International Conference on Data Engineering*, pp. 436–445.

Bernstein, A.J., D.S. Gerstl, and P.M. Lewis (1999): Concurrency Control for Step-Decomposed Transactions. *Information Systems* **24**, pp. 673–698.

Bernstein, P.A. (1998): Repositories and Object Oriented Databases. *ACM SIGMOD Record* **27(1)**, pp. 88–96.

Bernstein, P.A., and N. Goodman (1980): Timestamp-Based Algorithms for Concurrency Control in Distributed Database Systems. In *Proc. 6th International Conference on Very Large Data Bases*, pp. 285–300.

Bernstein, P.A., and N. Goodman (1982): Concurrency Control Algorithms for Multiversion Database Systems. In *Proc. 1st ACM Symposium on Principles of Distributed Computing*, pp. 209–215.

Bernstein, P.A., and N. Goodman (1983): Multiversion Concurrency Control—Theory and Algorithms. *ACM Transactions on Database Systems* **8**, pp. 465–483.

Bernstein, P.A., and N. Goodman (1984): An Algorithm for Concurrency Control and Recovery in Replicated Distributed Databases. *ACM Transactions on Database Systems* **9**, pp. 596–615.

Bernstein, P.A., and N. Goodman (1986): Serializability Theory for Replicated Databases. *Journal of Computer and System Sciences* **31**, pp. 355–374.

Bernstein, P.A., N. Goodman, and V. Hadzilacos (1983): Recovery Algorithms for Database Systems. In *Proc. 9th IFIP World Computer Congress on Information Processing*, pp. 799–807.

Bernstein, P.A., N. Goodman, and M.Y. Lai (1981): Laying Phantoms to Rest. In *Proc. 5th IEEE International Computer Software and Application Conference*, pp. 1–11.

Bernstein, P.A., N. Goodman, and M.Y. Lai (1983): Analyzing Concurrency Control Algorithms When User and System Operations Differ. *IEEE Transactions on Software Engineering* **9**, pp. 233–239.

Bernstein, P.A., V. Hadzilacos, and N. Goodman (1987): *Concurrency Control and Recovery in Database Systems*. Reading, MA: Addison-Wesley.

Bernstein, P.A., M. Hsu, and B. Mann (1990): Implementing Recoverable Requests Using Queues. In *Proc. ACM SIGMOD International Conference on Management of Data*, pp. 112–122

Bernstein, P.A., and E. Newcomer (1997): *Principles of Transaction Processing for the Systems Professional*. San Francisco: Morgan Kaufmann.

Bernstein, P.A., and D.W. Shipman (1980): The Correctness of Concurrency Mechanisms in a System for Distributed Databases (SDD-1). *ACM Transactions on Database Systems* 5, pp. 52–68.

Bernstein, P.A., D.W. Shipman, and J.B. Rothnie, Jr. (1980): Concurrency Control in a System for Distributed Databases (SDD-1). *ACM Transactions on Database Systems* 5, pp. 18–51.

Bernstein, P.A., D.W. Shipman, and W.S. Wong (1979): Formal Aspects of Serializability in Database Concurrency Control. *IEEE Transactions on Software Engineering* SE-5, pp. 203–216.

Bestavros, A., and S. Braoudakis (1996): Value-Cognizant Speculative Concurrency Control for Real-Time Databases. *Information Systems* 21, pp. 75–101.

Bhargava, B., and J. Riedl (1989): A Model for Adaptable Systems for Transaction Processing. *IEEE Transactions on Knowledge and Data Engineering* 1, pp. 433–449.

Bitton, D., and J. Gray (1988): Disk Shadowing. In *Proc. 14th International Conference on Very Large Data Bases*, pp. 331–338.

Bjork, L.A. (1973): Recovery Scenario for a DB/DC System. In *Proc. 1st ACM Annual Conference*.

Bober, P.M., and M.J. Carey (1992a): On Mixing Queries and Transactions via Multiversion Locking. In *Proc. 8th IEEE International Conference on Data Engineering*, pp. 535–545.

Bober, P.M., and M.J. Carey (1992b): Multiversion Query Locking. In *Proc. 18th International Conference on Very Large Data Bases*, pp. 497–510.

Bober, P.M., and M.J. Carey (1997): Indexing for Multiversion Locking: Alternatives and Performance Evaluation. *IEEE Transactions on Knowledge and Data Engineering* 9, pp. 68–84.

Boksenbaum, C., M. Cart, J. Ferrie, and J.-F. Pons (1984): Certification by Intervals of Timestamps in Distributed Database Systems. In *Proc. 10th International Conference on Very Large Data Bases*, pp. 377–387.

Bolch, G., S. Greiner, H. De Meer, and K.S. Trivedi (1998): *Queueing Networks and Markov Chains: Modeling and Performance Evaluation with Computer Science Applications*. New York: John Wiley & Sons.

Boral, H., and I. Gold (1984): Towards a Self-Adapting Centralized Concurrency Control Algorithm. In *Proc. ACM SIGMOD International Conference on Management of Data*, pp. 18–32.

Borg, A., J. Baumbach, and S. Glazer (1983): A Message System Supporting Fault Tolerance. In *Proc. 9th ACM Symposium on Operating System Principles*, pp. 90–99.

Borg, A., W. Blau, W. Graetsch, F. Herrmann, and W. Oberle (1989): Fault Tolerance under UNIX. *ACM Transactions on Computer Systems* 7, pp. 1–24.

Borr, A. (1981): Transaction Monitoring in Encompass: Reliable Distributed Transaction Processing. In *Proc. 7th International Conference on Very Large Data Bases*, pp. 155–165.

Borr, A. (1984): Robustness to Crash in a Distributed Database: A Non Shared-Memory Multi-processor Approach. In *Proc. 10th International Conference on Very Large Data Bases*, pp. 445–453.

Böttcher, S., M. Jarke, and J.W. Schmidt (1986): Adaptive Predicate Managers in Database Systems. In *Proc. 12th International Conference on Very Large Data Bases*, pp. 21–29.

Boucher, K., and F. Katz (1999): *Essential Guide to Object Monitors*. New York: John Wiley & Sons.

Breitbart, Y., A. Deacon, H.-J. Schek, A. Sheth, and G. Weikum (1993): Merging Application-Centric and Data-Centric Approaches to Support Transaction-Oriented Multi-system Workflows. *ACM SIGMOD Record* **22(3)**, pp. 23–30.

Breitbart, Y., H. Garcia-Molina, and A. Silberschatz (1992): Overview of Multidatabase Transaction Management. *The VLDB Journal* 1, pp. 181–239.

Breitbart, Y., D. Georgakopoulos, M. Rusinkiewicz, and A. Silberschatz (1991): On Rigorous Transaction Scheduling. *IEEE Transactions on Software Engineering* 17, pp. 954–960.

Breitbart, Y., and H.F. Korth (1999): Replication and Consistency in a Distributed Environment. *Journal of Computer and System Sciences* 59, pp. 26–69.

Breitbart, Y., W. Litwin, and A. Silberschatz (1991): Deadlock Problems in a Multidatabase Environment. In *Proceedings of IEEE COMPCON Conference*, pp. 145–151.

Breitbart, Y., and A. Silberschatz (1988): Multidatabase Update Issues; In *Proc. ACM SIGMOD International Conference on Management of Data*, pp. 135–142.

Breitbart, Y., and A. Silberschatz (1992): Strong Recoverability in Multidatabase Systems. In *Proc. 2nd International Workshop on Research Issues in Data Engineering—Transaction and Query Processing*, pp. 170–175.

Broessler, P. (1994): *Flexible and Efficient Support of Transactions on Persistent Objects* (in German). Ph.D. Dissertation, University of Bremen, Germany.

Brown, K.P., M. Mehta, M.J. Carey, and M. Livny (1994): Towards Automated Performance Tuning for Complex Workloads. In *Proc. 20th International Conference on Very Large Data Bases*, pp. 72–84.

Buckley, G.N., and A. Silberschatz (1983): Obtaining Progessive Protocols for a Simple Multiversion Database Model. In *Proc. 9th International Conference on Very Large Data Bases*, pp. 74–80.

Buckley, G.N., and A. Silberschatz (1984): Concurrency Control in Graph Protocols by Using Edge Locks. In *Proc. 3rd ACM SIGACT-SIGMOD Symposium on Principles of Database Systems*, pp. 45–50.

Buckley, G.N., and A. Silberschatz (1985): Beyond Two-Phase Locking. *Journal of the ACM* **32**, pp. 314–326.

Bukhres, O. (1992): Performance Comparison of Distributed Deadlock Detection Algorithms. In *Proc. 8th IEEE International Conference on Data Engineering*, pp. 210–217.

Bukhres, O.A., and A.K. Elmagarmid (eds.) (1996): *Object Oriented Multi-database Systems: A Solution for Advanced Applications*. Englewood Cliffs, NJ: Prentice Hall.

Carey, M.J. (1983): Granularity Hierarchies in Concurrency Control. In *Proc. 2nd ACM SIGACT-SIGMOD Symposium on Principles of Database Systems*, pp. 156–165.

Carey, M.J., S. Krishnamurthi, and M. Livny (1990): Load Control for Locking: The "Half-and-Half" Approach. In *Proc. 9th ACM SIGACT-SIGMOD-SIGART Symposium on Principles of Database Systems*, pp. 72–84.

Cart, M., and J. Ferrié (1990): Integrating Concurrency Control into an Object-Oriented Database System. In *Proc. 2nd International Conference on Extending Database Technology*, Lecture Notes in Computer Science **416**, Berlin: Springer-Verlag, pp. 363–377.

Casanova, M.A. (1981): *The Concurrency Control Problem for Database Systems*. Lecture Notes in Computer Science **116**, Berlin: Springer-Verlag.

Casanova, M.A., and P.A. Bernstein (1980): General Purpose Schedulers for Database Systems. *Acta Informatica* **14**, pp. 195–220.

Casati, F., S. Ilnicki, L. Jin, V. Krishnamoorthy, and M.-C. Shan (2000): Adaptive and Dynamic Service Composition in eFlow. In *Proc. 12th International Conference on Advanced Information Systems Engineering*, pp. 13–31.

Cattell, R.G.G. (1994): *Object Data Management—Object-Oriented and Extended Relational Database Systems*, revised edition. Reading, MA: Addison-Wesley.

Cellary, W., E. Gelenbe, and T. Morzy (1988): *Concurrency Control in Distributed Database Systems*. Amsterdam: North-Holland.

Cellary, W., and G. Jomier (1990): Consistency of Versions in Object-Oriented Databases. In *Proc. 16th International Conference on Very Large Data Bases*, pp. 432–441.

Ceri, S., and S.S. Owicki (1982): On the Use of Optimistic Methods for Concurrency Control in Distributed Databases. In *Proc. 6th Berkeley Workshop on Distributed Data Management and Computer Networks*, pp. 117–129.

Chan, A., S. Fox, W.K. Lin, A. Nori, and D.R. Ries (1982): The Implementation of an Integrated Concurrency Control and Recovery Scheme. In *Proc. ACM SIGMOD International Conference on Management of Data*, pp. 184–191.

Chan, A., and R. Gray (1985): Implementing Distributed Read-Only Transactions. *IEEE Transactions on Software Engineering* **11**, pp. 205–212.

Chandy, K.M., J.C. Browne, C.W. Dissly, and W.R. Uhrig (1975): Analytic Models for Rollback and Recovery Strategies in Data Base Systems. *IEEE Transactions on Software Engineering* **1**, pp. 100–110.

Chandy, K.M., and J. Misra (1982): A Distributed Algorithm for Detecting Resource Deadlocks in Distributed Systems. In *Proc. 1st ACM Symposium on Principles of Distributed Computing*, pp. 157–164.

Chandy, K.M., J. Misra, and L.M. Haas (1983): Distributed Deadlock Detection. *ACM Transactions on Computer Systems* **1**, pp. 144–156.

Chen, P.M., E.K. Lee, G.A. Gibson, R.H. Katz, and D.A. Patterson (1994): RAID: High-Performance, Reliable Secondary Storage. *ACM Computing Surveys* **26**, pp. 145–185.

Chen, Q., and U. Dayal (1996a): Contracting Transaction Hierarchies. In *Proc. 6th International Workshop on Research Issues in Data Engineering*, pp. 70–75.

Chen, Q., and U. Dayal (1996b): A Transactional Nested Process Management System. In *Proc. 12th IEEE International Conference on Data Engineering*, pp. 566–573.

Choudhary, A.N., W.H. Kohler, J.A. Stankovic, and D. Towsley (1989): A Modified Priority Based Algorithm for Distributed Deadlock Detection and Resolution. *IEEE Transactions on Software Engineering* **15**, pp. 10–17; correction in *IEEE Transactions on Software Engineering* **15**, 1644.

Chrysanthis, P.K., and K. Ramamritham (1994): Synthesis of Extended Transaction Models Using ACTA. *ACM Transactions on Database Systems* **19**, pp. 450–491.

Chrysanthis, P.K., G. Samaras, and Y.J. Al-Houmaily (1998): Recovery and Performance of Atomic Commit Processing in Distributed Database Systems. In Kumar and Hsu (1998), pp. 370–416.

Claybrook, B. (1992): *OLTP—Online Transaction Processing Systems*. New York: J. Wiley & Sons.

Copeland, G., T. Keller, R. Krishnamurthy, and M. Smith (1989): The Case for Safe RAM. In *Proc. 15th International Conference on Very Large Data Bases*, pp. 327–335.

Copeland, G.P., and T. Keller (1989): A Comparison of High-Availability Media Recovery Techniques. In *Proc. ACM SIGMOD International Conference on Management of Data*, pp. 98–109.

Corrigan, P., and M. Gurry (1996): *Oracle Performance Tuning.* Sebastopol, CA: O'Reilly & Associates.

Coulouris, G., J. Dollimore, and T. Kindberg (1994): *Distributed Systems: Concepts and Design.* Reading, MA: Addison-Wesley.

Cristian, F. (1991): Understanding Fault-Tolerant Distributed Systems. *Communications of the ACM* **34(2)**, pp. 56–78.

Croker, A., and D. Maier (1986): A Dynamic Tree-Locking Protocol. In *Proc. 2nd IEEE International Conference on Data Engineering*, pp. 49–56.

Crus, R.A. (1984): Data Recovery in IBM Database 2. *IBM Systems Journal* **23**, pp. 178–188.

Dadam, P., V. Lum, U. Praedel, and G. Schlageter (1985): Selective Deferred Index Maintenance & Concurrency Control in Integrated Information Systems. In *Proc. 11th International Conference on Very Large Data Bases*, pp. 142–150.

Dadam, P., P. Pistor, and H.-J. Schek (1983): A Predicate Oriented Locking Approach for Integrated Information Systems. In *Proc. 9th IFIP World Computer Congress on Information Processing*, pp. 763–768.

Dan, A., and P.S. Yu (1992): Performance Analysis of Coherency Control Policies through Lock Retention. In *Proc. ACM SIGMOD International Conference on Management of Data*, pp. 114–123.

Dan, A., P.S. Yu, and A. Jhingran (1997): Recovery Analysis of Data Sharing Systems under Deferred Dirty Page Propagation Policies. *IEEE Transactions on Parallel and Distributed Systems* **8**, pp. 695–711.

Dasgupta, P., and Z.M. Kedem (1983): A Non-Two-Phase Locking Protocol for Concurrency Control in General Databases. In *Proc. 9th International Conference on Very Large Data Bases*, pp. 92–94.

Dasgupta, P., and Z.M. Kedem (1990): The Five-Color Concurrency Control Protocol: Non-Two-Phase Locking in General Databases. *ACM Transactions on Database Systems* **15**, pp. 281–307.

Davies, C.T. (1973): Recovery Semantics for a DB/DC System. In *Proc. 1st ACM Annual Conference*.

Davies, C.T. (1978): Data Processing Spheres of Control. *IBM Systems Journal* **17**, pp. 179–198.

Deacon, A., H.-J. Schek, and G. Weikum (1994): Semantics-Based Multilevel Transaction Management in Federated Systems. In *Proc. 10th IEEE International Conference on Data Engineering*, pp. 452–461.

de By, R.A., W. Klas, and J. Veijalainen (eds.) (1997): *Transaction Management Support for Cooperative Applications.* Hingham, MA: Kluwer Academic Publishers.

Demers, A., D. Greene, C. Hauser, W. Irish, J. Larson, S. Shenker, H. Sturgis, D. Swinehart, and D. Terry (1987): Epidemic Algorithms for Replicated Database Maintenance. In *Proc. 6th ACM Symposium on Principles of Distributed Computing*, pp. 1–12.

DeWitt, D.J., and J. Gray (1992): Parallel Database Systems: The Future of High Performance Database Systems. *Communications of the ACM* **35(6)**, pp. 85–98.

DeWitt, D.J., R. Katz, F. Olken, D. Shapiro, M. Stonebraker, and D. Wood (1984): Implementation Techniques for Main Memory Database Systems. In *Proc. ACM SIGMOD International Conference on Management of Data*, pp. 1–8.

Dias, D.M., B.R. Iyer, J.T. Robinson, and P.S. Yu (1989): Integrated Concurrency-Coherency Controls for Multisystem Data Sharing. *IEEE Transactions on Software Engineering* **15**, pp. 437–448.

Dogac, A., L. Kalinichenko, M.T. Özsu, and A. Sheth (eds.) (1998): *Workflow Management Systems and Interoperability*. NATO ASI Series F: Computer and System Sciences, Vol. **164**, Berlin: Springer-Verlag.

Du, W., and A.K. Elmagarmid (1989): Quasi Serializability: A Correctness Criterion for Global Concurrency Control in InterBase. In *Proc. 15th International Conference on Very Large Data Bases*, pp. 347–355.

Du, W., A.K. Elmagarmid, and W. Kim (1991): Maintaining Quasi Serializability in Multidatabase Systems. In *Proc. 7th IEEE International Conference on Data Engineering*, pp. 360–367.

DuBourdieu, D. (1982): Implementation of Distributed Transactions. In *Proc. 6th Berkeley Workshop on Distributed Data Management and Computer Networks*, pp. 81–93.

Duchamp, D. (1989): Analysis of Transaction Management Performance. In *Proc. 12th ACM Symposium on Operating Systems Principles*, pp. 177–190.

Dunham, M.H., J.L. Lin, and X. Li (1998): Fuzzy Checkpointing Alternatives for Main Memory Databases. In Kumar and Hsu (1998), pp. 574–616.

Ebert, J., and G. Vossen (1997): I-Serializability: Generalized Correctness for Transaction-Based Environments. *Information Processing Letters* **63**, pp. 221–227.

El Abbadi, A., and S. Toueg (1989): Maintaining Availability in Partitioned Replicated Databases. *ACM Transactions on Database Systems* **14**, pp. 264–290.

Elhardt, K., and R. Bayer (1984): A Database Cache for High Performance and Fast Restart in Database Systems. *ACM Transactions on Database Systems* **9**, pp. 503–525.

Elmagarmid, A.K. (1986): A Survey of Distributed Deadlock Detection Algorithms. *ACM SIGMOD Record* **15(3)**, pp. 37–45.

Elmagarmid, A.K. (ed.) (1992): *Database Transaction Models for Advanced Applications*. San Francisco: Morgan Kaufmann.

Elmagarmid, A.K., M. Rusinkiewicz, and A.P. Sheth (eds.) (1998): *Management of Heterogeneous and Autonomous Database Systems*. San Francisco: Morgan Kaufmann.

Elmasri, R., and S.B. Navathe (2000): *Fundamentals of Database Systems*, 3rd edition. Redwood City, CA: Benjamin/Cummings.

Eppinger, J.L., L.B. Mummert, and A.Z. Spector (eds.) (1991): *Camelot and Avalon: A Distributed Transaction Facility*. San Francisco: Morgan Kaufmann.

Eswaran, K.P., J. Gray, R.A. Lorie, and I.L. Traiger (1976): The Notions of Consistency and Predicate Locks in a Database System. *Communications of the ACM* **19**, pp. 624–633.

Farrag, A.A., and M.T. Özsu (1989): Using Semantic Knowledge of Transactions to Increase Concurrency. *ACM Transactions on Database Systems* **14**, pp. 503–525.

Ferguson, D.F., L. Georgiadis, C. Nikolaou, and K. Davies (1993): Goal Oriented, Adaptive Transaction Routing for High Performance Transaction Systems. In *Proc. 2nd International Conference on Parallel and Distributed Information Systems*, pp. 138–147.

Fischer, M., N. Lynch, and M. Paterson (1985): Impossibility of Distributed Consensus with One Faulty Process. *Journal of the ACM* **32**, pp. 374–382.

Franaszek, P.A., and J.T. Robinson (1985): Limitations of Concurrency in Transaction Processing. *ACM Transactions on Database Systems* **10**, pp. 1–28.

Franaszek, P.A., J.T. Robinson, and A. Thomasian (1992): Concurrency Control for High Contention Environments. *ACM Transactions on Database Systems* **17**, pp. 304–345.

Franklin, M.J. (1996): *Client Data Caching: A Foundation for High Performance Object Database Systems*. Hingham, MA: Kluwer Academic Publishers.

Franklin, M.J., M.J. Carey, and M. Livny (1997): Transactional Client-Server Cache Consistency: Alternatives and Performance. *ACM Transactions on Database Systems* **22**, pp. 315–363.

Franklin, M.J., M.J. Zwilling, C.K. Tan, M.J. Carey, and D.J. DeWitt (1992): Crash Recovery in Client-Server EXODUS. In *Proc. ACM SIGMOD International Conference on Management of Data*, pp. 165–174.

Freytag, J.C., F. Cristian, and B. Kähler (1987): Masking System Crashes in Database Application Programs. In *Proc. 13th International Conference on Very Large Data Bases*, pp. 407–416.

Garcia–Molina, H. (1983): Using Semantic Knowledge for Transaction Processing in a Distributed Database. *ACM Transactions on Database Systems* **8**, pp. 186–213.

Garcia-Molina, H., and D. Barbara (1985): How to Assign Votes in a Distributed System. *Journal of the ACM* **32**, pp. 841–860.

Garcia-Molina, H., and F. Pittelli (1984): Is Byzantine Agreement Useful in a Distributed Database? In *Proc. 3rd ACM SIGACT-SIGMOD Symposium on Principles of Database Systems*, pp. 61–69.

Garcia-Molina, H., and K. Salem (1987): Sagas. In *Proc. ACM SIGMOD International Conference on Management of Data*, pp. 249–259.

Garcia-Molina, H., and K. Salem (1992): Main Memory Database Systems: An Overview. *IEEE Transactions on Knowledge and Data Engineering* **4**, pp. 509–516.

Garcia-Molina, H., J.D. Ullman, and J. Widom (2000): *Database System Implementation*. Upper Saddle River, NJ: Prentice Hall.

Garcia-Molina, H., and G. Wiederhold (1982): Read-Only Transactions in a Distributed Database. *ACM Transactions on Database Systems* **7**, pp. 209–234.

Gawlick, D., and D. Kinkade (1985): Varieties of Concurrency Control in IMS/VS Fast Path. *IEEE Data Engineering Bulletin* **8(2)**, pp. 3–10.

Gelenbe, E. (1979): On the Optimum Checkpoint Interval. *Journal of the ACM* **26**, pp. 259–270.

Georgakopoulos, D., M. Hornick, and F. Manola (1996): Customizing Transaction Models and Mechanisms in a Programmable Environment Supporting Reliable Workflow Automation. *IEEE Transactions on Knowledge and Data Engineering* **8**, pp. 630–649.

Georgakopoulos, D., M. Rusinkiewicz, and A.P. Sheth (1994): Using Tickets to Enforce the Serializability of Multidatabase Transactions. *IEEE Transactions on Knowledge and Data Engineering* **6**, pp. 166–180.

Georgakopoulos, D., M. Rusinkiewicz, and G. Thomas (1991): On Serializability of Multidatabase Transactions through Forced Local Conflicts. In *Proc. 7th IEEE International Conference on Data Engineering*, pp. 314–323.

Geppert, A., M. Kradolfer, and D. Tombros (1999): Trading Workflows on Electronic Markets. In A. Dogac, M.T. Özsu, O. Ulusoy (eds.), *Current Trends in Data Management Technology*, Hershey, PA: Idea Group Publishing, pp. 15–38.

Gibson, G.A. (1992): Redundant Disk Arrays—Reliable, Parallel Secondary Storage. *ACM Distinguished Dissertation*. Cambridge, MA: The MIT Press.

Gibson, G.A., L. Hellerstein, R.M. Karp, R.H. Katz, and D.A. Patterson (1989): Failure Correction Techniques for Large Disk Arrays. In *Proc. 3rd ACM International Conference on Architectural Support for Programming Languages and Operating Systems*, pp. 123–132.

Gifford, D.K. (1979): Weighted Voting for Replicated Data. In *Proc. 7th ACM SIGOPS Symposium on Operating Systems Principles*, pp. 150–162.

Gligor, V.D., and R. Popescu-Zeletin (1986): Transaction Management in Distributed Heterogeneous Database Management Systems. *Information Systems* **11**, pp. 287–297.

Goes, P.B., and U. Sumita (1995): Stochastic Models for Performance Analysis of Database Recovery Control. *IEEE Transactions on Computers* **44**, pp. 561–576.

Gold, I., and H. Boral (1986): The Power of the Private Workspace Model. *Information Systems* **11**, pp. 1–7.

Gold, I., O. Shmueli, and M. Hofri (1985): The Private Workspace Model Feasibility and Application to 2PL Performance Improvements. In *Proc. 11th International Conference on Very Large Data Bases*, pp. 192–208.

Grabs, T., K. Böhm, and H.-J. Schek (1999): A Document Engine on a DB Cluster. In *Proc. International Workshop on High Performance Transaction Processing Systems*.

Grabs, T., K. Böhm, and H.-J. Schek (2001): High-Level Parallelism in a Database Cluster: A Feasibility Study Using Document Services. In *Proc. 17th IEEE International Conference on Data Engineering*, April 2001, pp. 121–130.

Graham, M.H., N. Griffeth, and B. Smith-Thomas (1984): Reliable Scheduling of Database Transactions for Unreliable Systems. In *Proc. 3rd ACM SIGACT-SIGMOD Symposium on Principles of Database Systems*, pp. 300–310.

Gray, J. (1978): Notes on Database Operating Systems. In R. Bayer, M.R. Graham, G. Seegmüller (eds.), *Operating Systems: An Advanced Course*, Lecture Notes in Computer Science **60**, Berlin: Springer-Verlag, pp. 393–481.

Gray, J. (1981): The Transaction Concept: Virtues and Limitations. In *Proc. 7th International Conference on Very Large Data Bases*, pp. 144–154.

Gray, J. (1986): Why Do Computers Stop and What Can Be Done about It? In *Proc. 5th Symposium on Reliability in Distributed Software and Database Systems*, pp. 3–12.

Gray, J., P. Helland, P. O'Neil, and D. Shasha (1996): The Dangers of Replication and a Solution. In *Proc. ACM SIGMOD International Conference on Management of Data*, pp. 173–182.

Gray, J., R.A. Lorie, G.R. Putzolu, and I.L. Traiger (1975): Granularity of Locks in a Large Shared Data Base. In *Proc. 1st International Conference on Very Large Data Bases*, pp. 428–451.

Gray, J., P.R. McJones, M.W. Blasgen, B.G. Lindsay, R.A. Lorie, T.G. Price, G.R. Putzolu, and I.L. Traiger (1981): The Recovery Manager of the System/R Database Manager. *ACM Computing Surveys* **13**, pp. 223–243.

Gray, J., and A. Reuter (1993): *Transaction Processing: Concepts and Techniques*. San Francisco: Morgan Kaufmann.

Gray, J., and D.P. Siewiorek (1991): High-Availability Computer Systems. *IEEE Computer* **24**, pp. 39–48.

Guerraoui, R. (1995): Modular Atomic Objects. *Theory and Practice of Object Systems* **1**, pp. 89–99.

Gupta, R., J.R. Haritsa, and K. Ramamritham (1997): Revisiting Commit Processing in Distributed Database Systems. In *Proc. ACM SIGMOD International Conference on Management of Data*, pp. 486–497.

Hadzilacos, T. (1988): Serialization Graph Algorithms for Multiversion Concurrency Control. In *Proc. 7th ACM SIGACT-SIGMOD Symposium on Principles of Database Systems*, pp. 135–141.

Hadzilacos, T., and C.H. Papadimitriou (1986): Algorithmic Aspects of Multiversion Concurrency Control. *Journal of Computer and System Sciences* **33**, pp. 297–310.

Hadzilacos, T., and M. Yannakakis (1989): Deleting Completed Transactions. *Journal of Computer and System Sciences* **38**, pp. 360–379.

Hadzilacos, V. (1988): A Theory of Reliability in Database Systems. *Journal of the ACM* **35**, pp. 121–145.

Hagman, R.B. (1986): A Crash Recovery Scheme for a Memory-Resident Database System. *IEEE Transactions on Computers* **C-35**, pp. 839–847.

Härder, T. (1984): Observations on Optimistic Concurrency Control. *Information Systems* **9**, pp. 111–120.

Härder, T. (1987): Fault-Tolerance Issues in Transaction Processing Systems (in German). In *Proc. 3rd GI/ITG/GMA Conference on Fault-Tolerant Computing Systems*, pp. 324–335.

Härder, T. (1988): Handling Hot Spot Data in DB-Sharing Systems. *Information Systems* **13**, pp. 155–166.

Härder, T., W. Mahnke, N. Ritter, and H.-P. Steiert (2000): Generating Versioning Facilities for a Design-Data Repository Supporting Cooperative Applications. *International Journal of Cooperative Information Systems* **9**, pp. 117–146.

Härder, T., and A. Reuter (1983): Principles of Transaction-Oriented Database Recovery. *ACM Computing Surveys* **15**, pp. 287–317.

Härder, T., and K. Rothermel (1987): Concepts for Transaction Recovery in Nested Transactions. In *Proc. ACM SIGMOD International Conference on Management of Data*, pp. 239–248.

Härder, T., and K. Rothermel (1993): Concurrency Control Issues in Nested Transactions. *The VLDB Journal* **2**, pp. 39–74.

Harel, D. (1987): Statecharts: A Visual Formulation for Complex Systems. *Science of Computer Programming* **8**, pp. 231–274.

Harel, D., and E. Gery (1997): Executable Object Modeling with Statecharts. *IEEE Computer* **30(7)**, pp. 31–42.

Haring, G., C. Lindemann, and M. Reiser (2000): *Performance Evaluation: Origins and Directions*. Lecture Notes in Computer Science **1769**, Berlin: Springer-Verlag.

Haritsa, J.R., M.C. Carey, and M. Livny (1993): Value-Based Scheduling in Real-Time Database Systems. *The VLDB Journal* **2**, pp. 117–152.

Haritsa, J.R., M.C. Carey, and M. Livny (1995): Firm Real-Time Concurrency Control. In Kumar (1995), pp. 461–493.

Haskin, R.L., Y. Malachi, W. Sawdon, and G. Chan (1988): Recovery Management in QuickSilver. *ACM Transactions on Computer Systems* **6**, pp. 82–108.

Hasse, C. (1995): *Inter- and Intra-transaction Parallelism in Database Systems* (in German). Ph.D. Dissertation, ETH Zurich, Switzerland.

Hasse, C., and G. Weikum (1997): Inter- and Intra-transaction Parallelism for Combined OLTP/OLAP Workloads. In Jajodia and Kerschberg (1997), pp. 279–299.

Hasse-Ye, H. (1996): *Unified Theory of Correctness Criteria for Concurrent and Recoverable Executions of Database Transactions* (in German). Ph.D. Dissertation, ETH Zurich, Switzerland; appeared as DISDBIS **13**, St. Augustin, Germany: infix-Verlag.

Haverkort, B.R. (1998): *Performance of Computer Communication Systems: A Model-Based Approach*. New York: John Wiley & Sons.

Heiss, H.-U., and R. Wagner (1991): Adaptive Load Control in Transaction Processing Systems. In *Proc. 17th International Conference on Very Large Data Bases*, pp. 47–54.

Helal, A.A., A.A. Heddaya, and B.B. Bhargava (1996): *Replication Techniques in Distributed Systems*. Boston: Kluwer Academic Publishers.

Helland, P., H. Sammer, J. Lyon, R. Carr, P. Garrett, and A. Reuter (1987): Group Commit Timers and High Volume Transaction Systems. In *Proc. 2nd International Workshop on High-Performance Transaction Systems*, pp. 301–329.

Herlihy, M. (1990): Apologizing Versus Asking Permission: Optimistic Concurrency Control for Abstract Data Types. *ACM Transactions on Database Systems* **15**, pp. 96–124.

Herlihy, M., and W. Weihl (1991): Hybrid Concurrency Control for Abstract Data Types. *Journal of Computer and System Sciences* **43**, pp. 25–61.

Herrmann, U., P. Dadam, K. Küspert, E.A. Roman, and G. Schlageter (1990): A Lock Technique for Disjoint and Non-disjoint Complex Objects. In *Proc. 2nd International Conference on Extending Database Technology*, Lecture Notes in Computer Science **416**, Berlin: Springer-Verlag, pp. 219–237.

Holland, M., G.A. Gibson, and D.P. Siewiorek (1994): Architectures and Algorithms for On-Line Failure Recovery in Redundant Disk Arrays. *Distributed and Parallel Databases* **2**, pp. 295–335.

Howard, J., M. Kazar, S. Menees, D. Nichols, M. Satyanarayanan, R. Sidebotham, and M. West (1988): Scale and Performance in a Distributed File System. *ACM Transactions on Computer Systems* **6**, pp. 51–81.

Hsu, M. (ed.) (1993): Special Issue on Workflow and Extended Transaction Systems. *IEEE Data Engineering Bulletin* **16(2)**.

Hsu, M., and B. Zhang (1992): Performance Evaluation of Cautious Waiting. *ACM Transactions on Database Systems* **17**, pp. 477–512.

Huang, Y., and Y.-M. Wang (1995): Why Optimistic Message Logging Has Not Been Used in Telecommunications Systems. In *Proc. 25th International Symposium on Fault-Tolerant Computing Systems*, pp. 459–463.

Humborstad, R., M. Sabaratnam, S.-O. Hvasshovd, and O. Torbjornsen (1997): 1-Safe Algorithms for Symmetric Site Configurations. In *Proc. 23rd International Conference on Very Large Data Bases*, pp. 316–325.

Hunt, H.B., and D.J. Rosenkrantz (1979): The Complexity of Testing Predicate Locks. In *Proc. ACM SIGMOD International Conference on Management of Data*, pp. 127–133.

Hurson, A.R., M.W. Bright, and S.H. Pakzad (eds.) (1993): *Multidatabase Systems—An Advanced Solution for Global Information Sharing*. Los Alamitos, CA: IEEE Computer Society Press.

Ibaraki, T., T. Kameda, and N. Katoh (1990): Multiversion Cautious Schedulers for Database Concurrency Control. *IEEE Transactions on Software Engineering* **16**, pp. 302–315.

Ibaraki, T., T. Kameda, and T. Minoura (1983): Disjoint-Interval Topological Sort: A Useful Concept in Serializability Theory. In *Proc. 9th International Conference on Very Large Data Bases*, pp. 89–91.

Jablonski, S., and C. Bussler (1999): *Workflow Management—Modeling Concepts, Architecture, and Implementation*. Bonn, Germany: International Thomson Computer Press.

Jagadish, H.V., I.S. Mumick, and M. Rabinovich (1997): Scalable Versioning in Distributed Databases with Commuting Updates. In *Proc. 13th IEEE International Conference on Data Engineering*, pp. 520–531.

Jagadish, H.V., A. Silberschatz, and S. Sudarshan (1993): Recovering from Main-Memory Lapses. In *Proc. 19th International Conference on Very Large Data Bases*, pp. 391–404.

Jajodia, S., and L. Kerschberg (eds.) (1997): *Advanced Transaction Models and Architectures*. Hingham, MA: Kluwer Academic Publishers.

Jajodia, S., and D. Mutchler (1990): Dynamic Voting Algorithms for Maintaining the Consistency of Replicated Databases. *ACM Transactions on Database Systems* **15**, pp. 230–280.

Jhingran, A., and P. Khedkar (1992): Analysis of Recovery in a Database System Using a Write-Ahead Log Protocol. In *Proc. ACM SIGMOD International Conference on Management of Data*, pp. 175–184.

Jiang, B. (1988): Deadlock Detection Is Really Cheap. *ACM SIGMOD Record* **17(2)**, pp. 2–13.

Johnson, D.B., and W. Zwaenepoel (1987): Sender-Based Message Logging. In *Proc. 17th International Symposium on Fault-Tolerant Computing Systems*, pp. 14–19.

Johnson, D.B., and W. Zwaenepoel (1990): Recovery in Distributed Systems Using Optimistic Message Logging and Checkpointing. *Journal of Algorithms* **11**, pp. 462–491.

Johnson, T., and D. Shasha (1993): B-Trees with Inserts and Deletes: Why Free-at-Empty Is Better Than Merge-at-Half. *Journal of Computer and System Sciences* **47**, pp. 45–76.

Jordan, J.R., J. Banerjee, and R.B. Batman (1981): Precision Locks. In *Proc. ACM SIGMOD International Conference on Management of Data*, pp. 143–147.

Joshi, A.M. (1991): Adaptive Locking Strategies in a Multi-node Data Sharing Environment. In *Proc. 17th International Conference on Very Large Data Bases*, pp. 181–191.

Kamath, M., and K. Ramamritham (1996): Efficient Transaction Support for Dynamic Information Retrieval Systems. In *Proc. 19th Annual International ACM SIGIR Conference on Research and Development in Information Retrieval*, pp. 147–155.

Karabeg, D., and V. Vianu (1991): Simplification Rules and Complete Axiomatization for Relational Update Transactions. *ACM Transactions on Database Systems* **16**, pp. 439–475.

Katoh, N., T. Ibaraki, and T. Kameda (1985): Cautious Transaction Schedulers with Admission Control. *ACM Transactions on Database Systems* **10**, pp. 205–229.

Katz, R.H. (1990): Toward a Unified Framework for Version Modeling in Engineering Databases. *ACM Computing Surveys* **22**, pp. 375–408.

Kaufmann, H., and H.-J. Schek (1995): Text Search Using Database Systems Revisited—Some Experiments. In *Proc. 13th British National Conference on Databases*, pp. 204–225.

Kaufmann, H., and H.-J. Schek (1996): Extending TP Monitors for Intra-transaction Parallelism. In *Proc. 4th IEEE International Conference on Parallel and Distributed Information Systems*, pp. 250–261.

Kedem, Z., and A. Silberschatz (1980): Non-Two-Phase Locking Protocols with Shared and Exclusive Locks. In *Proc. 6th International Conference of Very Large Data Bases*, pp. 309–317.

Kedem, Z., and A. Silberschatz (1983): Locking Protocols: From Exclusive to Shared Locks. *Journal of the ACM* **30**, pp. 787–804.

Keen, J.S., and W.J. Dally (1997): Extended Ephemeral Logging: Log Storage Management for Applications with Long-Lived Transactions. *ACM Transactions on Database Systems* **22**, pp. 1–42.

Kemme, B., and G. Alonso (2001): A New Approach to Developing and Implementing Eager Database Replication Protocols. *ACM Transactions on Database Systems*, to appear.

Kemper, A., and G. Moerkotte (1994): *Object-Oriented Database Management—Applications in Engineering and Computer Science*. Englewood Cliffs, NJ: Prentice Hall.

Kent, J., H. Garcia-Molina, and J. Chung (1985): An Experimental Evaluation of Crash Recovery Mechanisms. In *Proc. 4th ACM SIGACT-SIGMOD Symposium on Principles of Database Systems*, pp. 113–122.

Kim, W. (1984): Highly Available Systems for Database Applications. *ACM Computing Surveys* **16**, pp. 71–98.

King, R.P., N. Halim, H. Garcia-Molina, and C.A. Polyzois (1991): Management of a Remote Backup Copy for Disaster Recovery. *ACM Transactions on Database Systems* **16**, pp. 338–368.

Klein, J. (1991): Advanced Rule Driven Transaction Management. In *Proc. 36th IEEE International Computer Conference*, pp. 562–567.

Knapp, E. (1987): Deadlock Detection in Distributed Databases. *ACM Computing Surveys* **19**, pp. 303–328.

Knaus, D., and P. Schäuble (1996): The System Architecture and the Transaction Concept of the SPIDER Information Retrieval System. *IEEE Data Engineering Bulletin* **19(1)**, pp. 43–52.

Kornacker, M., C. Mohan, and J.M. Hellerstein (1997): Concurrency and Recovery in Generalized Search Trees. In *Proc. ACM SIGMOD International Conference on Management of Data*, pp. 62–72.

Korth, H.F., E. Levy, and A. Silberschatz (1990): A Formal Approach to Recovery by Compensating Transactions. In *Proc. 16th International Conference on Very Large Data Bases*, pp. 95–106.

Krishnaswamy, V., D. Agrawal, J.L. Bruno, and A. El Abbadi (1997): Relative Serializability: An Approach for Relaxing the Atomicity of Transactions. *Journal of Computer and System Sciences* **55**, pp. 344–354.

Krivokapic, N., A. Kemper, and E. Gudes (1999): Deadlock Detection in Distributed Database Systems: A New Algorithm and a Comparative Performance Analysis. *The VLDB Journal* **8**, pp. 79–100.

Krychniak, P., M. Rusinkiewicz, A. Cichocki, A. Sheth, and G. Thomas (1996): Bounding the Effects of Compensation under Relaxed Multi-level Serializability. *Distributed and Parallel Databases* **4**, pp. 355–374.

Kumar, V. (ed.) (1996): *Performance of Concurrency Control Mechanisms in Centralized Database Systems*. Englewood Cliffs, NJ: Prentice Hall.

Kumar, V., and M. Hsu (eds.) (1998): *Recovery Mechanisms in Database Systems*. Upper Saddle River, NJ: Prentice Hall.

Kung, H.T., and P.L. Lehman (1980): Concurrent Manipulation of Binary Search Trees. *ACM Transactions on Database Systems* **5**, pp. 339–353.

Kung, H.T., and C.H. Papadimitriou (1983): An Optimality Theory of Concurrency Control for Databases. *Acta Informatica* **19**, pp. 1–11.

Kung, H.T., and J.T. Robinson (1981): On Optimistic Methods for Concurrency Control. *ACM Transactions on Database Systems* **6**, pp. 213–226.

Kuo, D. (1996): Model and Verification of a Data Manager Based on ARIES. *ACM Transactions on Database Systems* **21**, pp. 427–479.

Kurose, J.F., and K.W. Ross (2000): *Computer Networking: A Top-Down Approach Featuring the Internet*. Reading, MA: Addison-Wesley.

Kwong, Y.S., and D. Wood (1982): Method for Concurrency in B-Trees. *IEEE Transactions on Software Engineering* **SE-8**, pp. 211–223.

Lamb, C., G. Landis, J.A. Orenstein, and D. Weinbreb (1991): The ObjectStore Database System. *Communications of the ACM* **34(10)**, pp. 50–63.

Lamport, L. (1978): Time, Clocks, and the Ordering of Events in a Distributed System. *Communications of the ACM* **21**, pp. 558–565.

Lamport, L., R. Shostak, and M. Pease (1982): The Byzantine Generals Problem. *ACM Transactions on Programming Languages and Systems* **4**, pp. 382–401.

Lampson, B., and D. Lomet (1993): A New Presumed Commit Optimization for Two Phase Commit. In *Proc. 19th International Conference on Very Large Data Bases*, pp. 630–640.

Lampson, B.W. (1981): Atomic Transactions. In B.W. Lampson, M. Paul, H.J. Siegert (eds.), *Distributed Systems—Architecture and Implementation: An Advanced Course*, Lecture Notes in Computer Science **105**, Berlin: Springer-Verlag.

Lampson, B.W., and H. Sturgis (1976): *Crash Recovery in a Distributed Data Storage System*. Technical Report, Xerox Palo Alto Research Center, Palo Alto, CA.

Laurent, D., N. Spyratos, and G. Vossen (1995): *Optimization and Serializability of Update Transactions in Marked Databases*. Rapport de Recherche **No. 95-10**, Laboratoire d'Informatique Fondamentale d'Orléans, Université d'Orléans, France.

Lausen, G. (1982): Concurrency Control in Database Systems: A Step towards the Integration of Optimistic Methods and Locking. In *Proc. 10th ACM Annual Conference*, pp. 64–68.

Lausen, G. (1983): Formal Aspects of Optimistic Concurrency Control in a Multiple Version Database System. *Information Systems* **8**, pp. 291–301.

Lausen, G., E. Soisalon-Soininen, and P. Widmayer (1984): Maximal Concurrency by Locking. In *Proc. 3rd ACM SIGACT-SIGMOD Symposium on Principles of Database Systems*, pp. 38–44.

Lausen, G., E. Soisalon-Soininen, and P. Widmayer (1986): Pre-analysis Locking. *Information and Control* **70**, pp. 193–215.

Lausen, G., E. Soisalon-Soininen, and P. Widmayer (1990): On the Power of Safe Locking. *Journal of Computer and System Sciences* **40**, pp. 269–288.

Lausen, G., and G. Vossen (1998): *Models and Languages of Object-Oriented Databases*. Harlow, UK: Addison-Wesley.

Lechtenbörger, J., and G. Vossen (2000): On Herbrand Semantics and Conflict Serializability of Read-Write Transactions. In *Proc. 19th ACM SIGACT-SIGMOD-SIGART Symposium on Principles of Database Systems*, pp. 187–194.

Lehman, P.L., and S.B. Yao (1981): Efficient Locking for Concurrent Operations on B-Trees. *ACM Transactions on Database Systems* **6**, pp. 650–670.

Lehman, T.J., and M.J. Carey (1987): A Recovery Algorithm for a High-Performance Memory-Resident Database System. In *Proc. ACM SIGMOD International Conference on Management of Data*, pp. 104–117.

Lehman, T.J., and B.G. Lindsay (1989): The Starburst Long Field Manager. In *Proc. 15th International Conference on Very Large Data Bases*, pp. 375–383.

Leu, P.J., and B. Bhargava (1987): Multidimensional Timestamp Protocols for Concurrency Control. *IEEE Transactions on Software Engineering* **13**, pp. 1238–1253.

Levy, E. (1991): *Semantics-Based Recovery in Transaction Management Systems*. Ph.D. Dissertation, University of Texas at Austin.

Levy, E., H.F. Korth, and A. Silberschatz (1991): A Theory of Relaxed Atomicity. In *Proc. 10th ACM Symposium on Principles of Distributed Computing*, pp. 95–109.

Levy, E., and A. Silberschatz (1992): Incremental Recovery in Main Memory Database Systems. *IEEE Transactions on Knowledge and Data Engineering* **4**, pp. 529–540.

Leymann, F. (1995): Supporting Business Transactions via Partial Backward Recovery in Workflow Management Systems. In *Proc. 6th German Conference on Database Systems in Office, Engineering and Scientific Applications*, pp. 51–70.

Leymann, F., and D. Roller (2000): *Production Workflow—Concepts and Techniques*. Upper Saddle River, NJ: Prentice Hall.

Li, K., and P. Hudak (1989): Memory Coherence in Shared Virtual Memory Systems. *ACM Transactions on Computer Systems* **7**, pp. 321–359.

Lindsay, B.G., P.G. Selinger, C. Galtieri, J.N. Gray, R.A. Lorie, T.G. Price, F. Putzolu, and B.W. Wade (1979): *Notes on Distributed Databases*. IBM Research Report RJ2571, San Jose, CA.

Liskov, B., D. Curtis, P. Johnson, and R. Scheifler (1987): Implementation of Argus. In *Proc. 11th ACM Symposium on Operating System Principles*, pp. 111–122.

Litwin, W., L. Mark, and N. Roussopoulos (1990): Interoperability of Multiple Autonomous Databases. *ACM Computing Surveys* **22**, pp. 267–293.

Liu, M.L., D. Agrawal, and A. El Abbadi (1998): The Performance of Two Phase Commit Protocols in the Presence of Site Failures. *Distributed and Parallel Databases* **6**, pp. 157–182.

Lomet, D.B. (1977): Process Structuring, Synchronization, and Recovery Using Atomic Actions. *ACM SIGPLAN Notices* **12(3)**, pp. 128–137.

Lomet, D.B. (1990): *Recovery for Shared Disk Systems Using Multiple Redo Logs*. Technical Report CRL **90/4**, Cambridge Research Lab, Digital Equipment Corp.

Lomet, D.B. (1992): MLR: A Recovery Method for Multi-level Systems. In *Proc. ACM SIGMOD International Conference on Management of Data*, pp. 185–194.

Lomet, D.B. (1993): Key Range Locking Strategies for Improved Concurrency. In *Proc. 19th International Conference on Very Large Data Bases*, pp. 655–664.

Lomet, D.B. (1994): Private Locking and Distributed Cache Management. In *Proc. 3rd International Conference on Parallel and Distributed Information Systems*, pp. 151–159.

Lomet, D.B. (1998a): Persistent Applications Using Generalized Redo Recovery. In *Proc. 14th IEEE International Conference on Data Engineering*, pp. 154–163.

Lomet, D.B. (1998b): Advanced Recovery Techniques in Practice. In Kumar and Hsu (1998), pp. 697–710.

Lomet, D.B., and B. Salzberg (1997): Concurrency and Recovery for Index Trees. *The VLDB Journal* **6**, pp. 224–240.

Lomet, D.B., and M. Tuttle (1999): Logical Logging to Extend Recovery to New Domains. In *Proc. ACM SIGMOD International Conference on Management of Data*, pp. 73–84.

Lomet, D.B., and M.R. Tuttle (1995): Redo Recovery after System Crashes. In *Proc. 21st International Conference on Very Large Data Bases*, pp. 457–468.

Lomet, D.B., and G. Weikum (1998): Efficient Transparent Application Recovery in Client-Server Information Systems. In *Proc. ACM SIGMOD International Conference on Management of Data*, pp. 460–471.

Lorie, R.A. (1977): Physical Integrity in a Large Segmented Database. *ACM Transactions on Database Systems* **2**, pp. 91–104.

Lynch, N. (1983): Multilevel Atomicity—A New Correctness Criterion for Database Concurrency Control. *ACM Transactions on Database Systems* **8**, pp. 484–502.

Lynch, N. (1996): *Distributed Algorithms*. San Francisco: Morgan Kaufmann.

Lynch, N., M. Merritt, W. Weihl, and A. Fekete (1994): *Atomic Transactions*. San Francisco: Morgan Kaufmann.

Manber, U., and R.E. Ladner (1982): Concurrency Control in a Dynamic Search Structure. In *Proc. 1st ACM Symposium on Principles of Database Systems*, pp. 268–282.

Martin, C.P., and K. Ramamritham (1997): Toward Formalizing Recovery of (Advanced) Transactions. In Jajodia and Kerschberg (1997), pp. 213–234.

Mattern, F. (1989): Virtual Time and Global States of Distributed Systems. In M. Cosnard (ed.), *Parallel and Distributed Algorithms* (Proc. International Workshop on Parallel and Distributed Algorithms, France, 1988), Amsterdam: North-Holland, pp. 215–226.

Mehrotra, S., H.F. Korth, and A. Silberschatz (1997): Concurrency Control in Hierarchical Multidatabase Systems. *The VLDB Journal* **6**, pp. 152–172.

Mehrotra, S., R. Rastogi, Y. Breitbart, H.F. Korth, and A. Silberschatz (1992): The Concurrency Control Problem in Multidatabases: Characteristics and Solutions. In *Proc. ACM SIGMOD International Conference on Management of Data*, pp. 288–297.

Mehrotra, S., R. Rastogi, Y. Breitbart, H.F. Korth, and A. Silberschatz (2000): Overcoming Heterogeneity and Autonomy in Multidatabase Systems. *Information and Control*, to appear.

Mehrotra, S., R. Rastogi, H.F. Korth, and A. Silberschatz (1998): Ensuring Consistency in Multidatabases by Preserving Two-Level Serializability *ACM Transactions on Database Systems* **23**, pp. 199–230.

Menasce, D.A., and V.A.F. Almeida (1998): *Capacity Planning for Web Performance: Metrics, Models, and Methods*. Upper Saddle River, NJ: Prentice Hall.

Menasce, D.A., and V.A.F. Almeida (2000): *Scaling for E-Business: Technologies, Models, Performance, and Capacity Planning*. Upper Saddle River, NJ: Prentice Hall.

Menasce, D., and R. Muntz (1979): Locking and Deadlock Detection in Distributed Data Bases. *IEEE Transactions on Software Engineering* **5**, pp. 195–202.

Menasce, D.A., G.J. Popek, and R.R. Muntz (1980): A Locking Protocol for Resource Coordination in Distributed Databases. *ACM Transactions on Database Systems* **5**, pp. 103–138.

Menon, J., J. Roche, and J. Kasson (1993): Floating Parity and Data Disk Arrays. *Journal of Parallel and Distributed Computing* **17**, pp. 129–139.

Merchant, A., and P.S. Yu (1992): Design and Modeling of Clustered RAID. In *Proc. 22nd International Symposium on Fault-Tolerant Computing*, pp. 140–149.

Minoura, T. (1984): Multi-level Concurrency Control of a Database System. In *Proc. 4th IEEE Symposium on Reliability in Distributed Software and Database Systems*, pp. 156–168.

Mitschang, B., T. Härder, and N. Ritter (1996): Design Management in CONCORD: Combining Transaction Management, Workflow Management and Cooperative Control. In *Proc. 6th IEEE International Workshop on Research Issues in Data Engineering*, pp. 160–168.

Moenkeberg, A., and G. Weikum (1991): Conflict-Driven Load Control for the Avoidance of Data-Contention Thrashing. In *Proc. 7th IEEE International Conference on Data Engineering*, pp. 632–639.

Moenkeberg, A., and G. Weikum (1992): Performance Evaluation of an Adaptive and Robust Load Control Method for the Avoidance of Data-Contention Thrashing. In *Proc. 18th International Conference on Very Large Data Bases*, pp. 432–443.

Mogi, K., and M. Kitsuregawa (1994): Dynamic Parity Stripe Reorganizations for RAID5 Disk Arrays. In *Proc. 3rd International Conference on Parallel and Distributed Information Systems*, pp. 17–26.

Mohan, C. (1990): ARIES/KVL: A Key-Value Locking Method for Concurrency Control of Multiaction Transactions Operating on B-Tree Indexes. In *Proc. 16th International Conference on Very Large Data Bases*, pp. 392–405.

Mohan, C. (1992): Less Optimism about Optimistic Concurrency Control. In *Proc. 2nd International Workshop on Research Issues in Data Engineering*, pp. 199–204.

Mohan, C. (1993a): ARIES/LHS: A Concurrency Control and Recovery Method Using Write-Ahead Logging for Linear Hashing with Separators. In *Proc. 8th IEEE International Conference on Data Engineering*, pp. 243–252.

Mohan, C. (1993b): A Cost-Effective Method for Providing Improved Data Availability during DBMS Restart Recovery after a Failure. In *Proc. 19th International Conference on Very Large Data Bases*, pp. 368–379.

Mohan, C. (1996): Concurrency Control and Recovery Methods for B^+-Tree Indexes: ARIES/KVL and ARIES/IM. In Kumar (1996), pp. 248–306.

Mohan, C., D. Fussell, Z.M. Kedem, and A. Silberschatz (1985): Lock Conversion in Non-Two-Phase Locking Protocols. *IEEE Transactions on Software Engineering* **11**, pp. 15–22.

Mohan, C., D. Fussell, and A. Silberschatz (1984): Compatibility and Commutativity of Lock Modes. *Information and Control* **61**, pp. 38–64.

Mohan, C., and D. Haderle (1994): Algorithms for Flexible Space Management in Transaction Systems Supporting Fine-Granularity Locking. In *Proc. 4th International Conference on Extending Database Technology*, Lecture Notes in Computer Science **779**, Berlin: Springer-Verlag, pp. 131–144.

Mohan, C., D. Haderle, B. Lindsay, H. Pirahesh, and P. Schwarz (1992): ARIES: A Transaction Recovery Method Supporting Fine-Granularity Locking and Partial Rollbacks Using Write-Ahead Logging. *ACM Transactions on Database Systems* **17**, pp. 94–162.

Mohan, C., and F. Levine (1992): ARIES/IM: An Efficient and High Concurrency Index Management Method Using Write-Ahead Logging. In *Proc. ACM SIGMOD International Conference on Management of Data,* pp. 371–380.

Mohan, C., and B. Lindsay (1983): Efficient Commit Protocols for the Tree of Processes Model of Distributed Transactions. In *Proc. 2nd ACM Symposium on Principles of Distributed Computing,* pp. 76–88.

Mohan, C., B. Lindsay, and R. Obermarck (1986): Transaction Management in the R* Distributed Data Base Management System. *ACM Transactions on Database Systems* **11**, pp. 378–396.

Mohan, C., and I. Narang (1991): Recovery and Coherency-Control Protocols for Fast Intersystem Page Transfer and Fine-Granularity Locking in a Shared Disk Transaction Environment. In *Proc. 17th International Conference on Very Large Data Bases,* pp. 193–207.

Mohan, C., and I. Narang (1992a): Efficient Locking and Caching of Data in the Multisystem Shared Disk Transaction Environment. In *Proc. 3rd International Conference on Extending Database Technology,* Lecture Notes in Computer Science **580**, Berlin: Springer-Verlag, pp. 453–468.

Mohan, C., and I. Narang (1992b): Data Base Recovery in Shared Disks and Client-Server Architectures. In *Proc. 12th International Conference on Distributed Computing Systems,* pp. 310–317.

Mohan, C., and I. Narang (1993): An Efficient and Flexible Method for Archiving a Data Base. In *Proc. ACM SIGMOD International Conference on Management of Data,* pp. 139–146.

Mohan, C., and I. Narang (1994): ARIES/CSA: A Method for Database Recovery in Client-Server Architectures. In *Proc. ACM SIGMOD International Conference on Management of Data,* pp. 55–66.

Mohan, C., and H. Pirahesh (1991): ARIES-RRH: Restricted Repeating of History in the ARIES Transaction Recovery Method. In *Proc. 7th International Conference on Data Engineering,* pp. 718–727.

Mohan, C., H. Pirahesh, and R. Lorie (1992): Efficient and Flexible Methods for Transient Versioning of Records to Avoid Locking by Read-Only Transactions. In *Proc. ACM SIGMOD International Conference on Management of Data,* pp. 124–133.

Mohan, C., H.R. Strong, and S. Finkelstein (1983): Method for Distributed Transaction Commit and Recovery Using Byzantine Agreement within Clusters of Processors. In *Proc. 2nd ACM Symposium on Principles of Distributed Computing,* pp. 89–103.

Mohan, C., K. Treiber, and R. Obermarck (1993): Algorithms for the Management of Remote Backup Data Bases for Disaster Recovery. In *Proc. 8th International Conference on Data Engineering*, pp. 511–518.

Molesky, L.D., and K. Ramamritham (1995): Recovery Protocols for Shared Memory Database Systems. In *Proc. ACM SIGMOD International Conference on Management of Data*, pp. 11–22.

Mond, Y., and Y. Raz (1985): Concurrency Control in B^+-Trees Using Preparatory Operations. In *Proc. 11th International Conference on Very Large Data Bases*, pp. 331–334.

Morzy, T. (1993): The Correctness of Concurrency Control for Multiversion Database Systems with Limited Number of Versions. In *Proc. 9th IEEE International Conference on Data Engineering*, pp. 595–604.

Moss, J.E.B. (1985): *Nested Transactions: An Approach to Reliable Distributed Computing*. Ph.D. Dissertation, Cambridge, MA: The MIT Press.

Moss, J.E.B. (1987): Log-Based Recovery for Nested Transactions. In *Proc. 13th International Conference on Very Large Data Bases*, pp. 427–432.

Moss, J.E.B., N.D. Griffeth, and M.H. Graham (1986): Abstraction in Recovery Management. In *Proc. ACM SIGMOD International Conference on Management of Data*, pp. 72–83.

Moss, J.E.B., B. Leban, and P.K. Chrysanthis (1987): Finer Grained Concurrency for the Database Cache. In *Proc. 3rd IEEE International Conference on Data Engineering*, pp. 96–103.

Mullender, S. (1993): *Distributed Systems*, 2nd edition. Reading, MA: Addison-Wesley.

Mullins, C. (2000): *DB2 Developer's Guide*. Indianapolis, IN: Macmillan Computer Publishing.

Muntz, R., and J. Lui (1990): Performance Analysis of Disk Arrays under Failure. In *Proc. 16th International Conference on Very Large Data Bases*, pp. 162–173.

Muth, P. (1997): Application Specific Transaction Management in Multidatabase Systems. *Distributed and Parallel Databases* 5, pp. 357–403.

Muth, P., T.C. Rakow, G. Weikum, P. Brössler, and C. Hasse (1993): Semantic Concurrency Control in Object-Oriented Database Systems. In *Proc. 9th IEEE International Conference on Data Engineering*, pp. 233–241.

Muth, P., J. Weissenfels, and G. Weikum (1999): What Workflow Technology Can Do for Electronic Commerce. In A. Dogac, M.T. Özsu, O. Ulusoy (eds.), *Current Trends in Data Management Technology*, Hershey, PA: Idea Group Publishing, pp. 1–13.

Muth, P., D. Wodtke, J. Weissenfels, G. Weikum, and A. Kotz-Dittrich (1998): Enterprise-wide Workflow Management Based on State and Activity Charts. In Dogac et al. (1998), pp. 281–303.

Nelson, M., B. Welch, and J. Ousterhout (1988): Caching in the Sprite Network File System. *ACM Transactions on Computer Systems* **6**, pp. 134–154.

Nelson, R. (1995): *Probability, Stochastic Processes, and Queueing Theory—The Mathematics of Computer Performance Modeling.* New York: Springer-Verlag.

Nett, E., K.E. Grosspietsch, A. Jungblut, J. Kaiser, R. Kröger, W. Lux, M. Speicher, and H.-W. Winnebeck (1985): *PROFEMO—Design and Implementation of a Fault Tolerant Distributed System Architecture.* Technical Report, GMD (German National Research Center for Information Technology), Birlinghoven, Germany.

Obermarck, R. (1982): Distributed Deadlock Detection Algorithm. *ACM Transactions on Database Systems* **7**, pp. 187–208.

O'Neil, P.E. (1986): The Escrow Transactional Method. *ACM Transactions on Database Systems* **11**, pp. 405–430.

O'Neil, P.E. (1991): Deadlock Prediction for Escrow Transactions. *Information Systems* **16**, pp. 13–20.

O'Neil, P.E., and E. O'Neil (2001): *Database: Principles, Programming, and Performance,* 2nd edition. San Francisco: Morgan Kaufmann.

O'Neil, P.E., K. Ramamritham, and C. Pu (1995): A Two-Phase Approach to Predictably Scheduling Real-Time Transactions. In Kumar (1995), pp. 494–522.

Orfali, R., D. Harkey, and J. Edwards (1999): *The Essential Client/Server Survival Guide,* 3rd edition. New York: John Wiley & Sons.

Özsu M.T., and P. Valduriez (1999): *Principles of Distributed Database Systems,* 2nd edition. Upper Saddle River, NJ: Prentice Hall.

Panagos, E., and A. Biliris (1997): Synchronization and Recovery in a Client-Server Storage System. *The VLDB Journal* **6**, pp. 209–223.

Panagos, E., A. Biliris, H. Jagadish, and R. Rastogi (1996): Fine-Granularity Locking and Client-Based Logging for Distributed Architectures. In *Proc. 5th International Conference on Extending Database Technology,* Lecture Notes in Computer Science **1057**, Berlin: Springer-Verlag, pp. 388–402.

Papadimitriou, C.H. (1979): The Serializability of Concurrent Database Updates. *Journal of the ACM* **26**, pp. 631–653.

Papadimitriou, C.H. (1982): A Theorem in Database Concurrency Control. *Journal of the ACM* **29**, pp. 998–1006.

Papadimitriou, C.H. (1983): Concurrency Control by Locking. *SIAM Journal on Computing* **12**, pp. 215–226.

Papadimitriou, C.H. (1986): *The Theory of Database Concurrency Control.* Rockville, MD: Computer Science Press.

Papadimitriou, C.H., and P. Kanellakis (1984): On Concurrency Control by Multiple Versions. *ACM Transactions on Database Systems* **9**, pp. 89–99.

Papadimitriou, C.H., and M. Yannakakis (1987): The Complexity of Reliable Concurrency Control. *SIAM Journal on Computing* **16**, pp. 538–553.

Patterson, D.A., G.A. Gibson, and R.H. Katz (1988): A Case for Redundant Arrays of Inexpensive Disks (RAID). In *Proc. ACM SIGMOD International Conference on Management of Data*, pp. 109–116.

Pu, C. (1988): Superdatabases for Composition of Heterogeneous Databases. In *Proc. 4th IEEE International Conference on Data Engineering*, pp. 548–555.

Rabin, M. (1989): Efficient Dispersal of Information for Security, Load Balancing, Fault Tolerance. *Journal of the ACM* **36**, pp. 335–348.

Rabinovich, M., N. Gehani, and A. Kononov (1996): Scalable Update Propagation in Epidemic Replicated Databases. In *Proc. 5th International Conference on Extending Database Technology*, Lecture Notes in Computer Science **1057**, Berlin: Springer-Verlag, pp. 207–222.

Rahm, E. (1986a): Concurrency Control in DB Sharing Systems. In *Proc. 16th GI Annual Conference*, pp. 617–632.

Rahm, E. (1986b): Primary Copy Synchronization for DB-Sharing. *Information Systems* **11**, pp. 275–286.

Rahm, E. (1991): Recovery Concepts for Data Sharing Systems. In *Proc. 21st International Conference on Fault-Tolerant Computing*, pp. 368–377.

Rahm, E. (1993): Empirical Performance Evaluation of Concurrency and Coherency Control Protocols for Database Sharing Systens. *ACM Transactions on Database Systems* **18**, pp. 333–377.

Rahm, E. (1997): Goal-Oriented Performance Control for Transaction Processing. In *Proc. 9th German Conference on Performance Measurement, Modeling, and Assessment of Computer and Communication Systems*, Freiberg, Germany, pp. 285–300.

Ramakrishnan, R., and J. Gehrke (2000): *Database Management Systems*, 2nd edition. New York: WCB/McGraw-Hill.

Ramamritham, K., and P.K. Chrysanthis (1996): *Advances in Concurrency Control and Transaction Processing*. Los Alamitos, CA: IEEE Computer Society Press.

Ramamritham, K., and C. Pu (1995): A Formal Characterization of Epsilon Serializability. *IEEE Transactions on Knowledge and Data Engineering* **7**, pp. 997–1007.

Randell, B. (1978): Reliable Computing Systems. In R. Bayer, M.R. Graham, G. Seegmüller (eds.), *Operating Systems: An Advanced Course*, Lecture Notes in Computer Science **60**, Berlin: Springer-Verlag, pp. 282–391.

Rastogi, R., P. Bohannon, J. Parker, A. Silberschatz, S. Seshadri, and S. Sudarshan (1998): Distributed Multi-level Recovery in Main-Memory Databases, *International Journal on Distributed and Parallel Databases* **6**, pp. 41–71.

Rastogi, R., H.F. Korth, and A. Silberschatz (1993): Strict Histories in Object-Based Database Systems. In *Proc. 12th ACM SIGACT-SIGMOD-SIGART Symposium on Principles of Database Systems*, pp. 288–299.

Raz, Y. (1992): The Principle of Commitment Ordering, or Guaranteeing Serializability in a Heterogeneous Environment of Multiple Autonomous Resource Managers Using Atomic Commitment. In *Proc. 18th International Conference on Very Large Data Bases*, pp. 292–312.

Raz, Y. (1993): Commitment Ordering Based Distributed Concurrency Control for Bridging Single and Multi Version Resources. In *Proc. 3rd International Workshop on Research Issues in Data Engineering: Interoperability in Multidatabase Systems*, Vienna, Austria, pp. 189–199.

Raz, Y. (1994): Serializability by Commitment Ordering. *Information Processing Letters* **51**, pp. 257–264.

Raz, Y. (1995): The Dynamic Two Phase Commitment (D2PC) Protocol. In *Proc. 5th International Conference on Database Theory*, Lecture Notes in Computer Science **893**, Berlin: Springer-Verlag, pp. 162–76.

Reed, D.P. (1978): *Naming and Synchronization in a Decentralized Computer System*. Ph.D. Dissertation, MIT, Cambridge, MA.

Reed, D.P. (1983): Implementing Atomic Actions on Decentralized Data. *ACM Transactions on Computer Systems* **1**, pp. 3–23.

Reimer, M. (1983): Solving the Phantom Problem by Predicative Optimistic Concurrency Control. In *Proc. 9th International Conference on Very Large Data Bases*, pp. 81–88.

Reuter, A. (1980): A Fast Transaction-Oriented Logging Scheme for Undo Recovery. *IEEE Transactions on Software Engineering* **6**, pp 348–356.

Reuter, A. (1982): Concurrency on High-Traffic Data Elements. In *Proc. 1st ACM SIGACT-SIGMOD Symposium on Principles of Database Systems*, pp. 83–92.

Reuter, A. (1984): Performance Analysis of Recovery Techniques. *ACM Transactions on Database Systems* **9**, pp. 526–559.

Reuter, A., K. Schneider, and F. Schwenkreis (1997): ConTracts Revisited. In Jajodia and Kerschberg (1997), pp. 127–151.

Reuter, A., F. Schwenkreis, and H. Wächter (1992): Reliable Execution of Large-Scale Distributed Applications with ConTracts—Architecture of a Prototype Implementation (in German). In R. Bayer, T. Härder, P. Lockemann (eds.), *Object Bases for Experts*, Berlin: Springer-Verlag, pp. 197–219.

Rezende, F.F., and T. Härder (1997): Exploiting Abstraction Relationships' Semantics for Transaction Synchronization in KBMSs. *Data & Knowledge Engineering* **22**, pp. 233–259.

Roesler, M., and W.A. Burkhard (1989): Resolution of Deadlocks in Object-Oriented Distributed Systems. *IEEE Transactions on Computers* **38**, pp. 1212–1224.

Rosenblum, M., and J.K. Ousterhout (1992): The Design and Implementation of a Log-Structured File System. *ACM Transactions on Computer Systems* **10**, pp. 26–52.

Rosenkrantz, D.J., R.E. Stearns, and P.M. Lewis II (1978): System Level Concurrency Control for Distributed Database Systems. *ACM Transactions on Database Systems* **3**, pp. 178–198.

Rothermel, K., and C. Mohan (1989): ARIES/NT: A Recovery Method Based on Write-Ahead Logging for Nested Transactions. In *Proc. 15th International Conference on Very Large Data Bases*, pp. 337–346.

Rothermel, K., and S. Pappe (1993): Open Commit Protocols Tolerating Commission Failures. *ACM Transactions on Database Systems* **18**, pp. 289–332.

Rusinkiewicz, M., and A. Sheth (1995): Specification and Execution of Transactional Workflows. In W. Kim (ed.), *Modern Database Systems*. Reading, MA: Addison-Wesley, pp. 592–620.

Sagiv, Y. (1986): Concurrent Operations on B*-Trees with Overtaking. *Journal of Computer and Systems Sciences* **33**, pp. 275–296.

Sahner, R., K.S. Trivedi, and A. Puliafito (1996): *Performance and Reliability Analysis of Computer Systems*. Hingham, MA: Kluwer Academic Publishers.

Salem, K., and H. Garcia-Molina (1990): System M: A Transaction Processing Testbed for Memory Resident Data. *IEEE Transactions on Knowledge and Data Engineering* **2**, pp. 161–172.

Salem, K., H. Garcia-Molina, and J. Shands (1994): Altruistic Locking. *ACM Transactions on Database Systems* **19**, pp. 117–165.

Salzberg, B., and D. Tombroff (1996): DSDT: Durable Scripts Containing Database Transactions. In *Proc. 12th IEEE International Conference on Data Engineering*, pp. 624–633.

Samaras, G., K. Britton, A. Citron, and C. Mohan (1995): Two-Phase Commit Optimizations in a Commercial Distributed Environment. *Distributed and Parallel Databases* **3**, pp. 325–360.

Schaad, W., H.-J. Schek, and G. Weikum (1995): Implementation and Performance of Multi-level Transaction Management in a Multidatabase Environment. In *Proc. 5th International Workshop on Research Issues in Data Engineering—Distributed Object Management*, pp. 108–115.

Schek, H.-J., G. Weikum, and W. Schaad (1991): A Multi-level Transaction Approach to Federated DBMS Transaction Management. In *Proc. 1st International Workshop on Research Issues in Data Engineering—Interoperability in Multidatabase Systems*, pp. 280–297.

Schek, H.-J., G. Weikum, and H. Ye (1993): Towards a Unified Theory of Concurrency Control and Recovery. In *Proc. 12th ACM SIGACT-SIGMOD-SIGART Symposium on Principles of Database Systems*, pp. 300–311.

Schenkel, R., and G. Weikum (2000): Integrating Snapshot Isolation into Transactional Federations. In *Proc. 7th International Conference on Cooperative Information Systems*, Lecture Notes in Computer Science **1901**, Berlin: Springer-Verlag, pp. 90–101.

Schenkel, R., G. Weikum, N. Weissenberg, and X. Wu (2000): Federated Transaction Management with Snapshot Isolation. In G. Saake, K. Schwarz, C. Türker (eds.), *Transactions and Database Dynamics*, Lecture Notes in Computer Science **1773**, Berlin: Springer-Verlag, pp. 1–25.

Scheuermann, P., and H.-L. Tung (1992): A Deadlock Checkpointing Scheme for Multidatabase Systems. In *Proc. 2nd International Workshop on Research Issues in Data Engineering—Transaction and Query Processing*, pp. 184–191.

Schlageter, G. (1978): Process Synchronization in Database Systems. *ACM Transactions on Database Systems* **3**, pp. 248–271.

Schlageter, G. (1981): Optimistic Methods for Concurrency Control in Distributed Database Systems. In *Proc. 7th International Conference on Very Large Data Bases*, pp. 125–130.

Schneider, T. (1999): *SAP R/3 Performance Optimization*. San Francisco: Sybex.

Schueler, B.-M. (1977): Update Reconsidered. In *Proc. IFIP Working Conference on Architecture and Models in DBMS*, Amsterdam: North-Holland, pp. 149–164.

Schuldt, H., A. Popovici, and H.-J. Schek (2000): Automatic Generation of Reliable E-Commerce Payment Processes. In *Proc. 1st International Conference on Web Information Systems Engineering*, Hong Kong.

Schwarz, P.M., and A.Z. Spector (1984): Synchronizing Shared Abstract Types. *ACM Transactions on Computer Systems* **2**, pp. 223–250.

Segall, A., and O. Wolfson (1987): Transaction Commitment at Minimal Communication Cost. In *Proc. 6th ACM SIGACT-SIGMOD Symposium on Principles of Database Systems*, pp. 112–118.

Sethi, R. (1982): Useless Actions Make a Difference: Strict Serializability of Database Updates. *Journal of the ACM* **29**, pp. 394–403

Severance, D.G., and G.M. Lohman (1976): Differential Files: Their Application to the Maintenance of Large Databases. *ACM Transactions on Database Systems* **1**, pp. 256–267.

Shasha, D. (1985): What Good Are Concurrent Search Structure Algorithms for Databases Anyway? *IEEE Data Engineering Bulletin* **8(2)**, pp. 84–90.

Shasha D. (1992): *Database Tuning—A Principled Approach*. Englewood Cliffs, NJ: Prentice Hall.

Shasha, D., and N. Goodman (1988): Concurrent Search Structure Algorithms. *ACM Transactions on Database Systems* **13**, pp. 53–90.

Shasha, D., F. Llirbat, E. Simon, and P. Valduriez (1995): Transaction Chopping: Algorithms and Performance Studies. *ACM Transactions on Database Systems* **20**, pp. 325–363.

Shasha, D., E. Simon, and P. Valduriez (1992): Simple Rational Guidance for Chopping Up Transactions. In *Proc. ACM SIGMOD International Conference on Management of Data*, pp. 298–307.

Sheth, A.P., and J.A. Larson (1990): Federated Database Systems for Managing Distributed, Heterogeneous, and Autonomous Databases. *ACM Computing Surveys* **22**, pp. 183–236.

Silberschatz A., and P.B. Galvin (1998): *Operating System Concepts*, 5th edition. New York: John Wiley & Sons.

Silberschatz, A., and Z. Kedem (1980): Consistency in Hierarchical Database Systems. *Journal of the ACM* **27**, pp. 72–80.

Silberschatz, A., and Z. Kedem (1982): A Family of Locking Protocols for Database Systems That Are Modeled by Directed Graphs. *IEEE Transactions on Software Engineering* **8**, pp. 558–562.

Silberschatz, A., H.F. Korth, and S. Sudarshan (1997): *Database System Concepts*, 3rd edition. New York: McGraw-Hill.

Singhal, M. (1989): Deadlock Detection in Distributed Systems. *IEEE Computer* **22(11)**, pp. 37–48.

Sinha, M.K., and N. Natarajan (1985): A Priority Based Distributed Deadlock Detection Algorithm. *IEEE Transactions on Software Engineering* **11**, pp. 67–80.

Skeen, D. (1981): Nonblocking Commit Protocols. In *Proc. ACM SIGMOD International Conference on Management of Data*, pp. 133–142.

Skeen, D., and M. Stonebraker (1983): A Formal Model of Crash Recovery in a Distributed System. *IEEE Transactions on Software Engineering* **9**, pp. 219–228.

Soisalon-Soininen, E., and T. Ylönen (1995): Partial Strictness in Two-Phase Locking. In *Proc. 5th International Conference on Database Theory*, Lecture Notes in Computer Science **893**, Berlin: Springer-Verlag, pp. 139–147.

Soparkar, N., H.F. Korth, and A. Silberschatz (1996): *Time-Constrained Transaction Management—Real-Time Constraints in Database Transaction Systems*. Hingham, MA: Kluwer Academic Publishers.

Soparkar, N., and A. Silberschatz (1990): Data-Value Partitioning and Virtual Messages. In *Proc. 9th ACM Symposium on Principles of Database Systems*, pp. 357–367.

Srinivasan, V., and M. Carey (1991): Performance of B-Tree Concurrency Control Algorithms. In *Proc. ACM SIGMOD International Conference on Management of Data*, pp. 416–425.

Stamos, J.W., and F. Cristian (1993): Coordinator Log Transaction Execution Protocol. *Distributed and Parallel Databases* **1**, pp. 383–408.

Stearns, R.E., and D.J. Rosenkrantz (1981): Distributed Database Concurrency Controls Using Before-Values. In *Proc. ACM SIGMOD International Conference on Management of Data*, pp. 74–83.

Stodolsky, D., G. Gibson, and M. Holland (1993): Parity Logging: Overcoming the Small-Write Problem in Redundant Disk Arrays. In *Proc. 20th International Symposium on Computer Architecture*, pp. 64–75.

Stoerl, U. (1997): Analytic Models for Backup and Recovery Techniques in Database Systems (in German). In *Proc. 9th German Conference on Performance Assessment of Computer and Communication Systems (ITG/GI-Fachtagung Messung, Modellierung und Bewertung von Rechen- und Kommunikationssystemen)*, Freiberg, Germany, pp. 267–283.

Stonebraker, M. (1979): Concurrency Control and Consistency of Multiple Copies of Data in Distributed Ingres. *IEEE Transactions on Software Engineering* **3**, pp. 188–194.

Strom, R.E., D.F. Bacon, and S.A. Yemini (1988): Volatile Logging in n-Fault-Tolerant Distributed Systems. In *Proc. 18th International Symposium on Fault-Tolerant Computing*, pp. 44–49.

Strom, R.E., and S. Yemini (1985): Optimistic Recovery in Distributed Systems. *ACM Transactions on Computer Systems* **3**, pp. 204–226.

Sullivan, M., and M. Stonebraker (1991): Using Write Protected Data Structures to Improve Software Fault Tolerance in Highly Available Database Management Systems. In *Proc. 17th International Conference on Very Large Data Bases*, pp. 171–180.

Svobodova, L. (1981): A Reliable Object-Oriented Data Repository for a Distributed Computer System. In *Proc. 8th ACM Symposium on Operating Systems Principles*, pp. 47–58.

Tanenbaum, A.S. (1995): *Distributed Operating Systems*. Englewood Cliffs, NJ: Prentice Hall.

Tay, Y.C., N. Goodman, and R. Suri (1985): Locking Performance in Centralized Databases. *ACM Transactions on Database Systems* **10**, pp. 415–462.

Thomas, R.H. (1979): A Majority Consensus Approach to Concurrency Control for Multiple Copy Databases. *ACM Transactions on Database Systems* **4**, pp. 180–209.

Thomasian, A. (1993): Two-Phase Locking Performance and Its Thrashing Behavior. *ACM Transactions on Database Systems* **18**, pp. 579–625.

Thomasian, A. (1996a): A More Realistic Locking Model and Its Analysis. *Information Systems* **21**, pp. 409–430.

Thomasian, A. (1996b): *Database Concurrency Control: Methods, Performance, and Analysis*. Hingham, MA: Kluwer Academic Publishers.

Thomasian, A. (1998a): Concurrency Control: Methods, Performance, and Analysis. *ACM Computing Surveys* **30**, pp. 70–119.

Thomasian, A. (1998b): RAID5 Disk Arrays and Their Performance Evaluation. In Kumar and Hsu (1998), pp. 807–846.

Thomasian, A., and J. Menon (1994): Performance Analysis of RAID5 Disk Arrays with a Vacationing Server Model for Rebuild Operation Mode. In *Proc. 10th IEEE International Conference on Data Engineering*, pp. 111–119.

Tijms, H.C. (1994): *Stochastic Models—An Algorithmic Approach*. New York: John Wiley & Sons.

Torbjornsen, O. (1995): *Multi-site Declustering Strategies for Very High Database Service Availability*. Ph.D. Dissertation, University of Trondheim, Norway.

Traiger, I.L. (1983): Trends in System Aspects of Database Management. In *Proc. 2nd International Conference on Databases*, pp. 1–21.

Traiger, I.L., J. Gray, C.A. Galtieri, and B.G. Lindsay (1982): Transactions and Consistency in Distributed Database Systems. *ACM Transactions on Database Systems* 7, pp. 323–342.

Tuzhilin, A., and P. Spirakis (1985): A Semantic Approach to Correctness of Concurrent Transaction Executions. In *Proc. 4th ACM SIGACT–SIGMOD Symposium on Principles of Database Systems*, pp. 85–95.

Ulusoy, Ö., and A.P. Buchmann (1998): A Real-Time Concurrency Control Protocol for Main-Memory Database Systems. *Information Systems* **23**, pp. 109–125.

Veijalainen, J. (1990): *Transaction Concepts in Autonomous Database Environments*. Munich, Germany: Oldenbourg Verlag.

Veijalainen, J., F. Eliassen, and B. Holtkamp (1992): The S-Transaction Model. In Elmagarmid (1992), pp. 467–513.

Vianu, V., and G. Vossen (1992): Conceptual Level Concurrency Control of Relational Update Transactions. *Theoretical Computer Science* **95**, pp. 1–42.

Vianu, V., and G. Vossen (1993): Static and Dynamic Aspects of Goal-Oriented Concurrency Control. *Annals of Mathematics and Artificial Intelligence* **7**, pp. 257–287.

Vidyasankar, K. (1987): Generalized Theory of Serializability. *Acta Informatica* **24**, pp. 105–119.

Vidyasankar, K. (1991): Unified Theory of Database Serializability. *Fundamenta Informaticae* **XIV**, pp. 147–183.

Vidyasankar, K. (1998): Generalized Relative Serializability. In *Databases for the Millenium 2000, Proc. 9th International Conference on Management of Data*, pp. 313–327.

Vingralek, R., H. Hasse-Ye, Y. Breitbart, and H.-J. Schek (1998): Unifying Concurrency Control and Recovery of Transactions with Semantically Rich Operations. *Theoretical Computer Science* **190**, pp. 363–396.

Vogels, W., D. Dumitriu, K. Birman, R. Gamache, M. Massa, R. Short, J. Vert, J. Barrera, and J. Gray (1998): The Design and Architecture of the Microsoft Cluster Service. In *Proc. 28th International Conference on Fault-Tolerant Computing Systems*, pp. 422–431.

Vossen, G. (1991): *Data Models, Database Languages and Database Management Systems*. Wokingham, England: Addison-Wesley.

Vossen, G. (1992a): Databases and database management. In E.G. Coffman, J.K. Lenstra, A.H.G. Rinnooy Kan (eds.), *Handbooks in Operations Research and Management Science*, Vol. **3**: *Computing*, Amsterdam: North-Holland, pp. 133–193.

Vossen, G. (1992b): Commit-Serializability of Schedules for Relational Update Transactions. *Foundations of Computing, and Decision Sciences* **17**, pp. 153–169.

Vossen, G. (1995): Database Transaction Models. In J. van Leeuwen (ed.), *Computer Science Today—Recent Trends and Developments*, Lecture Notes in Computer Science **1000**, Berlin: Springer-Verlag, pp. 560–574.

Vossen, G. (1996): Database Theory: An Introduction. In A. Kent, J.G. Williams (eds.), *Encyclopedia of Computer Science and Technology*, Vol. **34**, Supplement **19**. New York: Marcel Dekker, Inc., pp. 85–127.

Wächter, H., and A. Reuter (1992): The ConTract Model. In Elmagarmid (1992), pp. 219–263.

Wallace, C., Y. Gurevich, and N. Soparkar (1995): Formalizing Recovery in Transaction-Oriented Database Systems. In *Proc. 7th International Conference on Management of Data*, Pune, India, pp. 166–185.

Walrand, J., and P. Varaiya (2000): *High-Performance Communication Networks*, 2nd edition. San Francisco: Morgan Kaufmann.

Wang, Y., and L. Rowe (1991): Cache Consistency and Concurrency Control in a Client/Server DBMS Architecture. In *Proc. ACM SIGMOD International Conference on Management of Data*, pp. 367–376.

Weihl, W. (1983): Data-Dependent Concurrency Control and Recovery. In *Proc. 2nd ACM Symposium on Principles of Distributed Computing*, pp. 63–75.

Weihl, W. (1988): Commutativity-Based Concurrency Control for Abstract Data Types. *IEEE Transactions on Computers* **37**, pp. 1488–1505.

Weihl, W. (1989): Local Atomicity Properties: Modular Concurrency Control for Abstract Data Types. *ACM Transactions on Programming Languages and Systems* **11**, pp. 249–282.

Weihl, W.E. (1993): The Impact of Recovery on Concurrency Control. *Journal of Computer and System Sciences* **47**, pp. 157–184.

Weikum, G. (1986a): *Transaction Management in Database Systems with Layered Architecture* (in German). Ph.D. Dissertation, Technical University of Darmstadt, Germany.

Weikum, G. (1986b): A Theoretical Foundation of Multi-level Concurrency Control. In *Proc. 5th ACM SIGACT-SIGMOD-SIGART Symposium on Principles of Database Systems*, pp. 31–42.

Weikum, G. (1991): Principles and Realization Strategies of Multi-level Transaction Management. *ACM Transactions on Database Systems* **16**, pp. 132–180.

Weikum, G. (1999): Towards Guaranteed Quality and Dependability of Information Services. In *Proc. 8th German Conference on Database Systems in Office, Engineering, and Scientific Applications*, Freiburg, Germany, pp. 379–409.

Weikum, G., A. Deacon, W. Schaad, and H.-J. Schek (1993): Open Nested Transactions in Federated Database Systems. *IEEE Data Engineering Bulletin* **16(2)**, pp. 4–7.

Weikum, G., and C. Hasse (1993): Multi-level Transaction Management for Complex Objects: Implementation, Performance, Parallelism. *The VLDB Journal* **2**, pp. 407–453.

Weikum, G., C. Hasse, P. Brössler, and P. Muth (1990): Multi-level Recovery. In *Proc. 9th ACM SIGACT-SIGMOD-SIGART Symposium on Principles of Database Systems*, pp. 109–123.

Weikum, G., C. Hasse, A. Moenkeberg, and P. Zabback (1994): The COMFORT Automatic Tuning Project. *Information Systems* **19**, pp. 381–432.

Weikum, G., and H.-J. Schek (1984): Architectural Issues of Transaction Management in Layered Systems. In *Proc. 10th International Conference on Very Large Data Bases*, pp. 454–465.

Weikum, G., and H.-J. Schek (1992): Concepts and Applications of Multilevel Transactions and Open Nested Transactions. In Elmagarmid (1992), pp. 515–553.

Whitney, A., D. Shasha, and S. Apter (1997): High Volume Transaction Processing without Concurrency Control, Two Phase Commit, SQL or C++. In *Proc. 7th International Workshop on High Performance Transaction Systems*.

Wilkinson, W., and M. Neimat (1990): Maintaining Consistency of Client Cached Data. In *Proc. 16th International Conference on Very Large Data Bases*, pp. 122–133.

Wolfson, O. (1986): An Algorithm for Early Unlocking of Entities in Database Transactions. *Journal of Algorithms* **7**, pp. 146–156.

Wolfson, O. (1987): The Virtues of Locking by Symbolic Names. *Journal of Algorithms* **8**, pp. 536–556.

Wolfson, O. (1991): The Communication Complexity of Atomic Commitment and of Gossiping. *SIAM Journal of Computing* **20**, pp. 423–450.

Wolski, A., and J. Veijalainen (1991): 2PC Agent Method: Achieving Serializability in Presence of Failures in a Heterogeneous Multidatabase.

In N. Rishe, S. Navathe, D. Tal (eds.), *Databases: Theory, Design, and Applications*, Los Alamitos, CA: IEEE Computer Society Press.

Worah, D., and A.P. Sheth (1997): Transactions in Transactional Workflows. In Jajodia and Kerschberg (1997), pp. 3–34.

Wu, K.-L., P.S. Yu, and C. Pu (1997): Divergence Control Algorithms for Epsilon Serializability. *IEEE Transactions on Knowledge and Data Engineering* **9**, pp. 262–274.

Yannakakis, M. (1982): A Theory of Safe Locking Policies in Database Systems. *Journal of the ACM* **29**, pp. 718–740.

Yannakakis, M. (1984): Serializability by Locking. *Journal of the ACM* **31**, pp. 227–244.

Yu, C.T., and W. Meng (1998): *Principles of Database Query Processing for Advanced Applications*. San Francisco: Morgan Kaufmann.

Yu, L., and D.J. Rosenkrantz (1988): Minimizing Time-Space Cost for Database Version Control. In *Proc. 7th ACM SIGACT-SIGMOD Symposium on Principles of Database Systems*, pp. 294–301.

Yu, P.S., and D.M. Dias (1992): Analysis of Hybrid Concurrency Control Schemes for a High Data Contention Environment. *IEEE Transactions on Software Engineering* **18**, pp. 118–129.

Zaharioudakis, M., M.J. Carey, and M.J. Franklin (1997): Adaptive, Fine-Grained Sharing in a Client-Server OODBMS: A Callback-Based Approach. *ACM Transactions on Database Systems* **22**, pp. 570–627.

Zhang, A., and A.K. Elmagarmid (1993): A Theory of Global Concurrency Control in Multidatabase Systems. *The VLDB Journal* **2**, pp. 331–360.

Zhang, A., M.H. Nodine, B.K. Bhargava, and O.A. Bukhres (1994): Ensuring Relaxed Atomicity for Flexible Transactions in Multidatabase Systems. In *Proc. ACM SIGMOD International Conference on Management of Data*, pp. 67–78.

Zöbel, D. (1983): The Deadlock Problem: A Classifying Bibliography. *ACM Operating Systems Review* **17**, pp. 6–16.

Index

About the Authors

Gottfried Vossen received his M.Sc., Ph.D. and German Habilitation from the Technical University of Aachen, Germany. He is professor of computer science and director of the Institut für Wirtschaftsinformatik (Department of Information Systems) at the University of Münster, Germany. He has held visiting positions at the University of California, San Diego, Karlstad Universitet in Sweden, and the German universities of Kiel, Düsseldorf, and Koblenz as well as an associate professorship at the University of Giessen in Germany. His research interests include conceptual and practical issues as well as applications of object-based database systems, in particular models for data and objects, database languages, transaction processing in database systems, integration of databases into scientific applications, XML and its applications, and workflow management. Dr. Vossen is on the editorial boards of *Information Systems* and the *International Journal of Computational and Numerical Analysis and Applications*, and has served on numerous program committees of international conferences and workshops. He has authored or coauthored over 70 papers on databases and many books on databases, business process modeling, e-Commerce, and computer architecture.

Gerhard Weikum received both the diploma and doctoral degrees in computer science from the University of Darmstadt, Germany. He is a full professor in the department of computer science at the University of the Saarland at Saarbrücken, Germany, where he is leading a research group on database and information systems. His former affiliations include MCC in Austin, Texas, and ETH Zurich in Switzerland. During his sabbatical in 1997, he was a visiting senior researcher in the database research group of Microsoft. His research interests include parallel and distributed information systems, transaction processing and workflow management, database optimization and performance evaluation, multimedia data management, and intelligent search on Web data. Dr. Weikum serves on the editorial boards of *ACM Transactions on Database Systems*, *IEEE CS Data Engineering Bulletin*, the *VLDB Journal*, and the *Distributed and Parallel Databases Journal*, and has served on numerous program committees of leading international conferences. He has been elected onto the board of trustees of the VLDB Endowment.

Printed and bound by CPI Group (UK) Ltd, Croydon, CR0 4YY

12/10/2024

01773439-0001